Third Edition

TRANSFORMING THE SCHOOL COUNSELING PROFESSION

Bradley T. Erford
Loyola University Maryland

Boston   Columbus   Indianapolis   New York   San Francisco   Upper Saddle River
Amsterdam   Cape Town   Dubai   London   Madrid   Milan   Munich   Paris   Montreal   Toronto
Delhi   Mexico City   Sao Paulo   Sydney   Hong Kong   Seoul   Singapore   Taipei   Tokyo

Vice President and Editor in Chief: Jeffery W. Johnston
Acquisitions Editor: Meredith D. Fossel
Editorial Assistant: Nancy Holstein
Vice President, Director of Marketing: Quinn Perkson
Marketing Manager: Christopher Barry
Senior Managing Editor: Pamela D. Bennett
Project Manager: Renata Butera
Creative Art Diretor: Jayne Conte
Senior Art Director: Diane Lorenzo
Cover Designer: Karen Salzbach
Cover Art: © Radius / SuperStock
Full-Service Project Management: GGS Higher Education Resources, PMG
Composition: GGS Higher Education Resources, PMG
Printer/Binder: Hamilton Printing Co.
Cover Printer: Lehigh/Phoenix Color Corp.
Text Font: Minion

Credits and acknowledgments borrowed from other sources and reproduced, with permission, in this textbook appear on the appropriate pages within text.

Every effort has been made to provide accurate and current Internet information in this book. However, the Internet and information posted on it are constantly changing, so it is inevitable that some of the Internet addresses listed in this textbook will change.

Library of Congress Cataloging-in-Publication Data
Transforming the school counseling profession / [edited by] Bradley T. Erford. — 3rd ed.
    p. cm.
Includes bibliographical references and index.
ISBN-13: 978-0-13-246295-2
ISBN-10: 0-13-246295-8
    1. Educational counseling—United States—Handbooks, manuals, etc.   I. Erford, Bradley T.
LB1027.5.T65 2011
371.4—dc22

    2009050190

10   9   8   7   6   5   4   3   2   1

www.pearsonhighered.com

ISBN 10:   0-13-246295-8
ISBN 13: 978-0-13-246295-2

This effort is dedicated to The One: the Giver of energy, passion, and understanding; Who makes life worth living and endeavors worth pursuing and accomplishing; the Teacher of love and forgiveness.

PREFACE

Myriad societal changes have created significant academic, career, and personal/social developmental challenges for today's students. A short list of these challenges includes high academic standards; suicide; substance abuse; technological changes recasting future labor-force needs; violence in schools, homes, and communities; and high-stakes testing. The prominence of these and many other challenges that confront the children and youth of today makes professional school counselors more essential than ever to the missions of schools.

In the past, many educators have viewed school counseling as an ancillary service. More recently, due to national school reform and accountability initiatives, school counselor leaders have encouraged professional school counselors in the field to dedicate their programs to the schools' mission objectives, which typically focus on academic performance and the achievement of high academic standards by all students. Without question, school counseling programs with curricula emphasizing affective skills associated with academic performance help students become motivated to perform, "learn how to learn," and cope with the challenges of our diverse and changing world. Historically, professional school counselors have focused on career and personal/social needs as ends in themselves.

This new focus on academic performance in support of a school's educational mission is necessary to win the respect of school reform advocates and achievement-focused educators. Thus, professional school counselors must ensure that comprehensive, developmental school counseling programs address career and personal/social issues with the end goal of removing barriers to, and improving, educational performance. To accomplish this goal, however, professional school counselors must develop programs offering a broad range of services aimed at the increasingly diverse needs of systems, educators, families, and students. *Transforming the School Counseling Profession*, Third Edition, was written to help to accomplish this goal.

Designed as an introduction to the school counseling profession, this book may also serve as a school counseling program development resource. Its goal is to inform the reader about how the seemingly diverse roles of the professional school counselor fit together in a comprehensive manner. Some topics are treated more thoroughly than others. Whereas most school counselor educational programs offer entire courses on some of these topics, others are barely touched on before students encounter them in the field. This book will help school counselors in training to prepare for their entry into a career as a professional

school counselor and to avoid mistakes. Experienced professional school counselors and counselor supervisors interested in new ideas may also find the book stimulating in its offering of new perspectives and detailed descriptions aiding program development. At times both idealistic and futuristic, the authors attempt to be realistic and practical as well, while pointing out more effective methods. Although our goal is primarily to educate the reader, we also seek to provoke discussion among professional school counselors, school counselors in training, school counselor educators and supervisors, and the broader educational community.

ORGANIZATION OF THE TEXT

Transforming the School Counseling Profession, Third Edition, begins with a glimpse of current barriers to effective implementation of a comprehensive, developmental school counseling program and presents a vision for the 21st century. Patricia J. Martin of the College Board and Stephanie G. Robinson of the Education Trust's Transforming School Counseling Initiative present some interesting perspectives on how to remove barriers to academic performance.

In Chapter 2, Dr. Edwin L. Herr of Penn State University and I provide a concise, yet comprehensive, synopsis of the history of the profession and then highlight issues that will determine its future course. Chapter 2 concludes with an explanation of 10 roles emerging from the current school counseling literature that must be considered in order to effectively implement a comprehensive school counseling program. In Chapter 3, I summarize the *ASCA National Model* (2005a), its various components, and its application to school counseling.

Dr. Susan C. Whiston and Robert F. Quinby of Indiana University provide a concise summary of school counseling outcomes research in Chapter 4, concluding that, although little research is available, existing research is generally supportive of school counseling services. In Chapter 5, Dr. Lynn Linde of Loyola University Maryland focuses on the importance of ethical, legal, and professional issues related to the practice of school counseling.

In Chapter 6, Dr. Cheryl Holcomb-McCoy of the University of Maryland and Dr. Stuart F. Chen-Hayes of CUNY–Lehman bring their unique scholarly perspectives to bear on answering the question "What does a multiculturally competent school counselor look like?" The vignettes and questionnaire provided are certain to provoke interesting classroom discussions!

In Chapter 7, Dr. Stuart F. Chen-Hayes of CUNY–Lehman, Dr. Deryl F. Bailey and Dr. Yvette Q. Getch of the University of Georgia, Emily M. Miller, and I provide practical, down-to-earth advice on leadership in the schools and how to advocate, and teach others to advocate, for academic success and social equity. This chapter focuses on the professional school counselor as leader and as academic and social advocate and is an exciting addition to school counseling literature and practice.

Beginning with Chapter 8, the "how to" of comprehensive and data-driven school counseling programs begins to take shape. Dr. Vivian V. Lee of the College Board and Dr. Gary E. Goodnough of Plymouth State University summarize the planning and implementation of a systemic data-driven school counseling program. Dr. Gary E. Goodnough, Dr. Rachelle Pérusse, and I expand on the curriculum development and implementation processes in Chapter 9 and extend into the classroom guidance component of a developmental program. Chapter 10, authored by Dr. Debbie W. Newsome and Elisabeth S. Harper of Wake Forest University, provides a basic introduction to the individual and group counseling components of a comprehensive program. In Chapter 11, Dr. Patrick Akos of UNC–Chapel Hill, Dr. Spencer (Skip) G. Niles of Penn State University, Emily M. Miller, and I expand on the educational- and career-planning component of a comprehensive program that, although historically a focus in high school, has received greater emphasis recently in K–8 curricula. Chapter 12 reviews the importance of consultation and collaboration, setting the stage for systemic collaboration and parent/community outreach. Chapter 13 explores the many facets of school counseling accountability, including needs assessment, program evaluation, service assessment, outcomes evaluation, and performance appraisal. School reform movements around the country have made accountability a critical element in all educational components, and professional school counselors are wise to become knowledgeable leaders in this area.

No discussion of school counseling would be complete without some attention to violence in the school and community and to students with complex problems. Chapter 14 focuses on systemic solutions, as well as assessing and counseling youth with complex problems through just such systemic solutions. Chapter 14 also addresses the development of conflict resolution and peer mediation programs in schools to combat violence and enhance interpersonal communication and problem solving.

Dr. Elana Rock of Loyola University Maryland and Erin H. Leff, a lawyer who specializes in education law, provide an exceptionally comprehensive look in Chapter 15 at the professional school counselor's role in meeting the needs of students with disabilities, providing sufficient justification to protect the counselor from being overused in the special education process, while providing enough information to allow professional school counselors to advocate for the needs of these students.

Finally, an excellent introduction to mental and emotional disorders is provided by Dr. Carol J. Kaffenberger of George Mason University in Chapter 16. Although professional school counselors may not diagnose these conditions in their workplace, knowledge of the medical model and characteristics of mental and emotional disorders will surely facilitate appropriate referrals, liaising with mental health practitioners, and integration of students with mental and emotional disorders into the school environment.

Transforming the School Counseling Profession seeks to be more than just an introductory text. Its purpose is to strike a chord with professional school counselors and school counselors in training all around the world and to lead the professional practice of school counseling in new and exciting directions that will benefit students, educators, parents, and the entire community. Professional school counselors can and must provide advocacy, leadership, and support in the school reform and accountability movements, helping to ensure that no student falls through the cracks.

WHAT'S NEW IN THIS EDITION

The school counseling profession is changing rapidly, and the purpose of this revision is to accurately reflect these changes in practice and the extant literature, as well as providing direction and leadership for future practice and scholarship. In this Third Edition of *Transforming the School Counseling Profession*, readers and instructors will note the following changes:

- The addition of Chapter 3: The ASCA National Model: Developing a Comprehensive, Developmental School Counseling Program, which provides an overview of the *ASCA National Model* (ASCA, 2005a) and how it can be applied to practice in the schools.
- Major revisions to Chapter 1: Transforming the School Counseling Profession and Chapter 8: Systemic, Data-Driven School Counseling Practice and Programming for Equity to reflect evolutionary changes in systemic school counseling program and practice philosophy.
- Nearly every chapter has incorporated a new feature called "Voices from the Field," which provides brief passages written by professional school counselors or interns that express their perspectives on, challenges of, and successes in implementing the transformed role.

- Nearly every chapter has incorporated a new feature called "Theory into Practice," which provides brief passages written by professional school counselors that demonstrate real-life examples of practitioners applying the theory and concepts covered in the chapter to actual practice venues, thus providing students with concrete applications.
- Chapter 14: Systemic Approaches to Counseling Students Experiencing Complex and Specialized Problems demonstrates a major change in tone. In past editions, the term *at-risk* was used. But, as is pointed out regularly in the literature and media, everyone is probably at risk for something. Chapter 14 recognizes that the problems experienced by many children are complex and require a systemic approach, either to treatment or to the student's environmental context. If the problems of "at-risk" youth were simple or linear, solutions would be straightforward and simple; recognition of the complexity of issues presented by youth naturally leads to use of systemic approaches to removing barriers to access, attainment, and achievement.
- Revisions have been made to the PowerPoint® slides available to instructors and the test questions provided in the Instructor's Manual.
- As a result of updating the literature, more than 70% of the Third Edition's references are as recent as 2000 and about one-third are as recent as 2005.

SUPPLEMENTAL INSTRUCTIONAL FEATURES

Supplemental to this book are pedagogical tools helpful to school counselor educators choosing to use this book as a course textbook. The companion Instructor's Manual contains at least 30 multiple-choice questions, 20 essay questions, and 15 classroom or individual activities per chapter. In addition, a comprehensive Microsoft PowerPoint® presentation is available from the publisher for counselor educators to use or modify for classroom presentations. Case studies and vignettes included in the text can stimulate lively classroom discussions.

ACKNOWLEDGMENTS

This book is dedicated to the thousands of professional school counselors and school counselors in training who struggle daily to meet the seemingly ever-expanding needs of the students, families, educational colleagues, and communities they serve. This dedication extends to the thousands of counselor educators and supervisors who have devoted their lives to their profession, colleagues, and students. Thank you for making this a profession to be proud of! I especially want to thank the authors who contributed their perspectives and words of wisdom. They are all true experts in their specialty areas and are truly dedicated to the betterment of the profession. It is an honor to work closely with such an august group of scholars. I especially want to thank my graduate assistant extraordinaire, Emily Miller, for her expertise and focus throughout the production of this book. Emily kept me from drowning in the myriad details and minutia that must be attended to when constructing a text, Instructor's Manual, PowerPoint® slides, and other ancillary products. Meredith Fossel and Nancy Holstein of Pearson deserve special mention for their stewardship during the editing of this book. Additional mention goes out to Renata Butera, my project director at Pearson and Suganya Karuppasamy, my production editor at GGS Higher Education Resources, for their outstanding service. I am also grateful to the reviewers—Timothy Goothaus, Old Dominion University; Michael Moyer, University of Texas, San Antonio; Susan Norris Huss, Bowling Green State University—for their helpful and supportive comments. Finally, I am forever grateful to my family, whose tolerance for my periodic quest of solitude makes projects such as this possible.

ABOUT THE AUTHORS

EDITOR

Dr. Bradley T. Erford, Ph.D., LCPC, LPC, NCC, LP, LSP, is professor of educational specialties in the school counseling program at Loyola University Maryland. He is an American Counseling Association (ACA) Fellow and recipient of the ACA Research Award, ACA Arthur A. Hitchcock Distinguished Professional Service Award, ACA Professional Development Award, ACA Carl D. Perkins Government Relations Award, Association for Assessment in Counseling and Education (AACE) Exemplary Practices Award, Association for Counselor Education and Supervision's Robert O. Stripling Award for Excellence in Standards, Maryland Counselor of the Year, Maryland Association for Counseling and Development (MACD) Counselor Advocacy Award, MACD Professional Development Award, and MACD Counselor Visibility Award. He is the editor or author of 15 books, including *Transforming the School Counseling Profession* (3rd ed., 2011); *Professional School Counseling: A Handbook of Principles, Programs, and Practices* (2nd ed., 2009); *Orientation to the Counseling Profession* (2010); *Group Work in the Schools* (2010); *Systemic Process and Theory of Group Work* (2011); *35 Techniques Every Counselor Should Know* (2010); *Developing Multicultural Counseling Competency* (2010); *The Counselor's Guide to Clinical, Personality, and Behavioral Assessment* (2006); *Assessment for Counselors* (2007); *Educational Applications of the WISC-IV* (2006); *Group Activities: Firing Up for Performance* (2007); and *Research and Evaluation in Counseling* (2008). His research specialization falls primarily in development and technical analysis of psychoeducational tests and has resulted in the publication of numerous refereed journal articles, book chapters, and published tests. He is past president of the AACE; past chair of the ACA–Southern (US) Region; past chair of the ACA's Task Force on High Stakes Testing; past chair of the ACA's Interprofessional Committee; past chair of the ACA's Public Awareness and Support Committee (and cochair of the National Awards Subcommittee); past president of the MACD; past president of the Maryland Association for Counselor Education and Supervision; and past president of the Maryland Association for Measurement and Evaluation. Dr. Erford is a Licensed Clinical Professional Counselor, Licensed Professional Counselor, Nationally Certified Counselor, Licensed Psychologist, and Licensed School Psychologist. Prior to arriving at Loyola, Dr. Erford was a school psychologist/counselor in the Chesterfield County (VA) Public Schools. He maintains a private practice specializing in assessment and treatment of children and adolescents. A graduate of the University of Virginia (Ph.D. in counselor education), Bucknell University (M.A. in school psychology), and Grove City College (B.S. in biology and psychology), he teaches courses in Testing and Measurement, Lifespan Development, School Counseling, Research and Evaluation in Counseling, and Stress Management.

CONTRIBUTING AUTHORS

Dr. Patrick Akos is an associate professor of school counseling in the School of Education at the University of North Carolina at Chapel Hill. He is a former middle school counselor and was recognized as the American School Counselor Association's 2004 Counselor Educator of the Year. Dr. Akos's research focuses on school transitions, middle school counseling, and strengths-based school counseling. Currently, his research continues on how school personnel can promote successful transitions into and out of middle school (and the assorted configurations found in school districts) and how professional school counselors can intervene and advocate for optimal development of early adolescents.

Dr. Deryl F. Bailey is an associate professor and program coordinator of the school counseling master's program at the University of Georgia. He earned a master's degree in guidance and counseling from Campbell University, in North Carolina, and Ed.S. and Ph.D. degrees in counselor education from the University of Virginia. His primary research areas are adolescent development, psychosocial development among adolescent African-American males, school counseling, and issues related to multiculturalism and diversity. He is the developer of Empowered Youth Programs, an enrichment program that develops and nurtures academic and social excellence in children and adolescents, with a special emphasis on African-American males.

Dr. Stuart F. Chen-Hayes is an associate professor of counselor education at Lehman College of the City University of New York. Dr. Chen-Hayes has coordinated Lehman College's companion institution status with the Education Trust's National Center for Transforming School Counseling (NCTSC) Initiative since 1999. Dr. Chen-Hayes helped to write a $1.2 million Elementary and Secondary

School Counseling Demonstration Act Grant for the New York City Department of Education to transform all elementary school counseling programs (with intensive staff development for all elementary school counselors, principals, and academic intervention team leaders in the *American School Counselor Association National Model* and the NCTSC principles) in New York City during the 2004–2007 school years, and he works as a lead trainer/consultant on the project with the Education Trust's NCTSC. Dr. Chen-Hayes has published many refereed journal articles and book chapters in school, family, and sexuality counseling. He is on the editorial boards of *Professional School Counseling* and *The Journal of LBGT Issues in Counseling* and has given more than 150 professional presentations and workshops in counselor education and advocacy related to transforming school counseling, family counseling, and sexuality counseling.

Dr. Yvette Q. Getch is an associate professor at the University of Georgia. She earned a B.S. in social work at Florida State University, an M.Ed. in rehabilitation counseling from the University of Arkansas, and a Ph.D. in rehabilitation education and research from the University of Arkansas. Her primary areas of research include advocacy skills training for students who have disabilities or chronic illnesses, the impact of a child's chronic illness on the family, and advocacy for accommodations for children with chronic illness and disabilities in schools.

Dr. Gary E. Goodnough, NCC, coordinates the school counseling program at Plymouth State University, New Hampshire. He received a Ph.D. in counselor education from the University of Virginia in 1995 and is a National Certified Counselor and state-licensed clinical mental health counselor. A former high school director of guidance, Dr. Goodnough has authored several articles and book chapters and has made numerous regional and national professional presentations on school counseling.

Elisabeth S. Harper, MATS, is an M.A. student at Wake Forest University in the Department of Counseling. Her research interests include GLBT concerns and incorporating spirituality and counseling, and she works with undergraduate counseling students at Wake Forest's University Counseling Center.

Dr. Edwin L. Herr, NCC, NCCC, is distinguished professor emeritus of education (counselor education and counseling psychology) and associate dean emeritus, College of Education, Pennsylvania State University. Dr. Herr served as a school counselor, a local director of guidance, the first state director of guidance and testing, and, subsequently,

the first director of the Bureau of Pupil Personnel Services in the Pennsylvania Department of Education. From 1968 until 1992, Dr. Herr served as head of the Department of Counselor Education, Counseling Psychology, and Rehabilitation Services Education or other department iterations at Pennsylvania State University. During this time, he also served as university director of Vocational Teacher Education and director of the Center for Professional Personnel Development in Vocational Education and as interim dean in 1972–1973 and 1998–1999. Dr. Herr received a B.S. in business education from Shippensburg State Teachers College in 1955 and an M.A. in psychological foundations, a Professional Diploma in coordination of guidance services, and an Ed.D. in counseling and student personnel administration from Teachers College, Columbia University, where he was an Alumni Fellow. Dr. Herr is past president of the American Association for Counseling and Development (now the American Counseling Association), the National Vocational Guidance Association, the Association for Counselor Education and Supervision, and Chi Sigma Iota, the Counseling Academic and Professional Honor Society International. Dr. Herr was a member of the Executive Committee of the International Round Table for the Advancement of Counseling from 1976 to 1984 and of the Board of Directors of the International Association of Educational and Vocational Guidance from 1991 to 1999. He is the author or coauthor of over 300 articles and book chapters and 33 books and monographs, a former editor of the *Journal of Counseling and Supervision* (1993–1996) and *Counselor Education and Supervision* (1971–1974), and a member of several other editorial boards.

Dr. Cheryl Holcomb-McCoy received her Ph.D. in counseling and educational development from the University of North Carolina at Greensboro in 1996. Prior to her appointment as professor in the Department of Counseling and Human Services at Johns Hopkins University, Dr. Holcomb-McCoy was an associate professor in the Department of Counseling and Personnel Services at the University of Maryland, College Park. She also served as the director of the school counseling program at Brooklyn College of the City University of New York (1996–1998). Her areas of research specialization include the measurement of multicultural self-efficacy in school counseling, the measurement of school college-going culture, and best practices in urban school counselor preparation. Dr. Holcomb-McCoy is currently the principal investigator of a three-year research project funded by the College Board that examines school counselors' impact on the college-going rates of urban high school students.

Dr. Carol J. Kaffenberger's research interests include the transformation of school counseling, help for children with chronic illness, and the effectiveness of school counseling preparation programs. She has recently coauthored a book on the use of data to address educational issues and also completed a study of the impact of cancer on academic achievement and school reentry. She has written professional articles and chapters on school reentry issues, coping with cancer, and the transformation of school counseling. She developed a model and training handbook for school reintegration that provides training to school counselors, social workers, and school nurses. She is a consultant for the Education Trust's National Center for the Transformation of School Counseling. Dr. Kaffenberger is an editor for *Professional School Counseling* and is serving a three-year term on the American School Counselor Association Board as Counselor Educator Vice President.

Dr. Vivian V. Lee is the higher education school counselor specialist at the National Office for School Counselor Advocacy of the College Board. Dr. Lee is a former teacher, secondary school counselor, director of school counseling, and counselor educator. She continues to teach school counseling courses as an adjunct at the University of Maryland at College Park. Her work includes research in the area of school counselor professional development, she has served as trainer with the Education Trust's National Center for Transforming School Counseling Initiative, and she has published articles and book chapters on developing school counseling programs, conflict resolution and violence, and group counseling. Dr. Lee worked in public education for 24 years before joining the College Board. She received her master's and doctoral degrees from the University of Virginia.

Erin H. Leff is an attorney, retired school psychologist, and mediator who has worked in special education for over 30 years. She earned an M.S. in educational psychology from the University of Wisconsin–Madison and a J.D. from Rutgers–Camden. Ms. Leff has worked as a school psychologist as well as a program administrator in multiple states. She has been a special education due process hearing officer, appeals officer, and mediator. Ms. Leff has provided training on various topics in special education and mediation.

Dr. Lynn Linde is an assistant professor of education and the director of clinical programs in the school counseling program at Loyola University Maryland. She received her master's degree in school counseling and her doctorate in counseling from George Washington University. She was previously the chief of the Student Services and Alternative Programs Branch at the Maryland State Department of Education, the state specialist for school counseling, a local school system counseling supervisor, a middle and high school counselor, and a special education teacher. She has made numerous presentations, particularly in the areas of ethics and legal issues for counselors and public policy and legislation, over the course of her career. Dr. Linde is an American Counseling Association (ACA) Fellow and the recipient of the ACA Carl Perkins Award, the Association for Counselor Education and Supervision's Program Supervisor Award, and the Southern Association for Counselor Education and Supervision's Program Supervisor Award, as well as numerous awards from the state association and from the state of Maryland for her work in student services and youth suicide prevention. She has held a number of leadership positions in the ACA and its entities and is the 2009–2010 president of the ACA.

Patricia J. Martin is a nationally recognized leader in the reform of school counseling and efforts to design training opportunities to help practicing counselors become an integral part of the primary mission for schools. Pat holds a B.A. in mathematics and an M.A. in school counseling from Our Lady of the Lake College in San Antonio, Texas. Pat has more than 30 years of experience as a public school educator, having worked as a teacher, professional school counselor, district supervisor of counselors, high school principal, chief educational administrator, and assistant superintendent of schools in Prince George's County, Maryland. In her work as the senior program manager at the Education Trust, she provided the leadership and technical expertise that solidly launched the National Transforming School Counseling Initiative, which was underwritten by the DeWitt Wallace Foundation. She is currently an assistant vice president at the College Board, leading the National Office for School Counselor Advocacy in Washington, D.C. In this capacity, she continues working to establish a national presence in education reform for school counselors as they seek to advance the academic agenda for all students.

Emily M. Miller, M.Ed., is a professional school counselor and a graduate of the school counseling program at Loyola University Maryland, where she served as Dr. Brad Erford's graduate assistant for almost two years. She has authored several articles and book chapters.

Dr. Debbie W. Newsome, LPC, NCC, is an associate professor of counseling at Wake Forest University, North Carolina, where she teaches courses in career counseling, appraisal procedures, and statistics and supervises master's students in their field experiences. In addition to teaching and supervising, Dr. Newsome counsels children, adolescents, and families at a nonprofit mental health organization in Winston-Salem, North Carolina.

Dr. Spencer G. Niles is a professor and head of the Department for Counselor Education, Counseling Psychology, and Rehabilitation Services at Pennsylvania State University. He is a National Career Development Association (NCDA) Fellow (2002) and a recipient of the NCDA Eminent Career Award (2007). He is also an American Counseling Association (ACA) Fellow (2007) and a recipient of the ACA's David Brooks Distinguished Mentor Award (2003), the ACA Extended Research Award (2004), and the University of British Columbia Noted Scholar Award (2001). Within the NCDA, Dr. Niles has served in such roles as president (2004) and Governing Council representative (2008–2011). Currently, he is the editor of the *Journal of Counseling and Development* and has authored or coauthored approximately 95 publications and delivered over 90 presentations on career development theory and practice. He is an Honorary Member of the Japanese Career Development Association (2003), an Honorary Member of the Italian Association for Educational and Vocational Guidance (2005), and a Lifetime Honorary Member of the Ohio Career Development Association (2003).

Dr. Rachelle Pérusse, NCC, NCSC, has been an associate professor in the counseling program at the University of Connecticut since the fall of 2004. Prior to this appointment, she was a tenured associate professor and the school counseling coordinator at Plattsburgh State University in Plattsburgh, New York, from 1997 to 2004. She received a Ph.D. in counselor education from Virginia Polytechnic Institute in 1997. Before becoming a school counselor educator, Dr. Pérusse worked with poor and minority youth as a high school counselor in a rural school district in Georgia. She is a National Certified Counselor and a National Certified School Counselor. Professionally, she has served as secretary for the North Atlantic Regional Association for Counselor Education and Supervision (2000–2002), secretary for the Association of Counselor Education and Supervision (2005–2006), and president of the North Atlantic Regional Association for Counselor Education and Supervision (2007–2008). Since 2002, she has been a consultant with the Education Trust's National Transforming School Counseling Initiative. Dr. Pérusse has published numerous articles about national trends in school counselor education and has coedited two books: *Critical Incidents in Group Counseling* and *Leadership, Advocacy, and Direct Service Strategies for Professional School Counselors.*

Robert F. Quinby, M.S., is a doctoral student in counseling psychology at Indiana University in the Department of Counseling and Educational Psychology. He received his M.S. degree in school counseling at Indiana University and has interests in both school counseling and career counseling research.

Stephanie G. Robinson, Ph.D., is a founding partner of Ed Trust in 1993, Stephanie worked with school boards, administrators, principals, teachers, and communities to implement policies and practices aimed at improving teaching and learning. She helped create the Standards-in-Practice professional development initiative that encouraged standards-based education in districts across the nation as well as Ed Trust's National Center for Transforming School Counseling. Stephanie was a teacher and administrator in the Montclair, N.J., schools, education director for the National Urban League, and deputy superintendent of the Kansas City, Mo., schools. A graduate of Douglass College, she received a master's in social work from Rutgers University and a doctorate in human growth and development/school administration from the Union Institute.

Dr. Elana Rock is an associate professor and director of the special education programs at Loyola College Maryland. Her responsibilities include teaching undergraduate and graduate special education courses, developing and revising curriculum, and assessing the personnel preparation needs of local schools. Dr. Rock earned a B.A. from the University of Pennsylvania, an M.A. in teaching children with emotional disturbance from New York University, and an Ed.D. in special education from Johns Hopkins University. Prior to earning her doctorate, Dr. Rock taught elementary and secondary students with learning disabilities and emotional/behavioral disorders. For the past six years, Dr. Rock has served as expert research consultant to the U.S. District Court's Special Master overseeing special education service delivery in the Baltimore City Public Schools. Her research publications and presentations focus on children with concomitant high-prevalence disorders, the evaluation of service delivery in special education, and special education teacher education.

Dr. Susan C. Whiston is a professor at Indiana University in the Department of Counseling and Educational Psychology. She has been teaching school counseling courses since 1986 and has published many articles concerning empirical support for school counseling. She has been on the editorial boards of *Career Development Quarterly* and the *Journal of Career Assessment* and was associate editor for research for the *Journal of Counseling and Development.* She also serves on the National Evidence Based School Counseling Practices Panel. Prior to receiving her doctorate from the University of Wyoming, she worked in secondary schools as a counselor for low-income students.

BRIEF CONTENTS

CONTENTS

Chapter 4   **Outcomes Research on School Counseling Interventions and Programs   58**
Susan C. Whiston and Robert F. Quinby

Chapter 5   **Ethical, Legal, and Professional Issues in School Counseling   70**
Lynn Linde

Chapter 6 Culturally Competent School Counselors: Affirming Diversity by Challenging Oppression 90

Cheryl Holcomb-McCoy and Stuart F. Chen-Hayes

Chapter 10   Counseling Individuals and Groups in School   178

Debbie W. Newsome and Elisabeth S. Harper

Chapter 11   Promoting Educational and Career Planning in Schools   202

Patrick Akos, Spencer G. Niles, Emily M. Miller, and Bradley T. Erford

Chapter 16   Helping Students with Mental and Emotional Disorders   342

Carol J. Kaffenberger

Transforming the School Counseling Profession

Patricia J. Martin and Stephanie G. Robinson*

E ditor's Introduction: Welcome to an exciting career—and adventure. Transforming school counseling involves changing its substance and appearance. The changes encouraged in this book are not cosmetic but deep, meaningful changes that encourage professional school counselors to become agents of education reform and social change. The effective professional school counselor seeks to remove barriers to educational, career, and personal/social development, whether for a single student or an entire society. Although professional school counselors are usually pursuing a common purpose, each one must understand and integrate the school's mission and goals, the needs of the school community, and his or her own strengths into a comprehensive, developmental school counseling program. Such an approach adds uniqueness to each program, while ensuring that needs are addressed in a comprehensive manner.

THE SCHOOL: THE PRIMARY WORKPLACE FOR SCHOOL COUNSELORS

The 21st century brings a new age in the profession of school counseling, one in which traditional methods must be transformed to meet current and future challenges. Professional school counseling must evolve into a model that will both fit the needs of the students in this rapidly changing society and conform to the demands of school reform and accountability mandates, while working as leaders and advocates in schools to remove barriers to student success.

The Context of Professional School Counseling

> *A system is an interconnected complex of functionally related components that work together to try to accomplish the aim of the system.*
>
> —W. Edwards Deming

Professional school counselors work in schools and therefore must be knowledgeable about the venue in which they must effectively practice. School counseling is one component of a complex system that is being held accountable for educating today's students to a higher level of academic proficiency than ever before. School counselors must therefore exit from pre-service training programs with the knowledge and skills that will prepare them to function effectively in systems with policies and practices that affect all participants. As a result, school counselor education must provide an understanding of the new mission of schools, how schools function, and the school counselor's accountability for

---

*The first and second editions of this chapter were coauthored by Dr. Reese M. House, may he rest in peace.

helping schools achieve the mission—to educate all students to high levels to enable them to lead a productive life in a democratic society.

Schools are systems undergoing reform. This reform effort is requiring an assessment of the inputs, processes, and outcomes of the schools' systemic components. Much attention has been given to the components of curriculum, teaching and learning, and assessment. There has been considerable emphasis on making sure that the inputs and processes of the systemic components are aligned with the new mission of schools to deliver the desired academic outcomes for students in these schools. Likewise, the transformed school counseling profession must align the inputs, processes, and outcomes of its programs for students with the new mission of schools. Pre-service training for school counselors must prepare them with the knowledge and skills needed to align the goals of their comprehensive school counseling programs with the academic achievement goals of the school.

Schools are multifaceted, institutional systems that operate according to a set of norms that govern the behavior of people within those systems. Each system—in this case, the school—is governed by both written and unwritten policies and practices that are implemented, maintained, and institutionalized by people who, for the most part, believe that these actions are necessary to achieve the results they seek for the students, families, and communities they serve.

> *When placed in the same system, people, however different, tend to produce similar results.*
> —Peter Senge

Professional school counselors are part of an educational system that has historically produced disparate results for different populations of students and has thus ensured unequal future life opportunities and choices for many young people. Changing the outcomes for underachieving student populations will require that the inputs and processes accepted and traditionally implemented by all professionals in the school system be examined, altered, and/or reconstructed.

Most important, the transforming school counseling movement must be an effort that adds value to school reforms designed to change the educational outcomes for students in schools today. School counseling is a critically important professional component among the many components that make schools work. The transformed school counselor must function in schools in an interdependent, interconnected fashion to meet the 21st-century goal of educating all students to higher levels of literacy, numeracy, and analytic functioning than ever before achieved. Consequently, the word *school* in the title *professional school*

counselor has incredible significance for what is expected of the professionals who occupy this role in K–12 public schools today.

In this chapter, we discuss the forces driving change in schools and the implications of those changes for professional school counselors. The resulting changes in education policy and the implications for school counselors are discussed at length, as are the changes in practice that will be required for school counseling to remain a viable component of the educational system. Finally, we posit some changes that school counselor educators must make to ensure the viability of the profession.

FOUR FORCES DRIVING CHANGE IN SCHOOLS

Public schools have been "reforming" almost constantly since their inception. However, the impetus for change in the early 1990s was occasioned by several factors, including but not limited to the following: (1) inequities in the educational system, (2) changes in the nation's demographics and school populations, (3) changes in the economy and the workplace, and (4) major changes in education public policy. Each of these will be explored below.

Inequities in the Educational System

In the 1980s, the nation's attention was directed to the inequities in the educational system by the seminal report *A Nation at Risk* (National Commission on Excellence in Education, 1983), which concluded that the educational system in the United States lagged behind those of other industrialized nations in meeting world-class educational standards. The report identified the decline in student performance in the United States as a function of curriculum content, expectations, time spent on academics, and teaching. The report decried the watered-down "cafeteria"-style high school curriculum and the migration of students from more rigorous courses to the "general" course track.

One of the significant observations in the report was that the United States' educational system lacked a set of coherent academic content standards to define what all students should know and be able to do as a result of their 12 years of public education. The report went on to recommend that the high school core curriculum be strengthened, along with stiffer graduation requirements. The *Nation at Risk* report also issued recommendations for strengthening science instruction and teacher education. The report, however, did not identify education inequities relative to race, gender, or disabiity in relation to differences in student performance.

Subsequent to this report, the Commission on Chapter 1 (1992)—a group of policy makers, education practitioners, researchers, and grantmakers—issued a seminal report, which identified structural inequities in the educational system that contributed to the problems cited in the *Nation at Risk* report. This commission's report highlighted the systemic barriers that contribute to (1) the poor achievement/underachievement of students of color and students from low-income families and (2) the achievement gap that exists between these students and their more affluent peers. According to the commission (1992) and the Education Trust (2005a), the achievement gap among students exists primarily because schools that serve poor students and large numbers of students of color consistently

- Expect and demand less in the way of academic performance of children of color and those from low-income families;
- Provide these same students with watered-down, weak curriculum that lacks academic content rigor;
- Assign inexperienced and the least qualified teachers to students who have the most serious academic need; and
- Provide fewer material resources to students who have the greatest needs. In fact, studies show that school-funding formulas too often shortchange the schools that serve the most educationally needy students.

In short, the educational system systematically and consistently provides less to students who have the greatest educational needs (Haycock, 2009). These deep, structural inequities went mostly unnoticed by the general public and many policy makers. Additionally, these inequities were ignored by too many educators and school support personnel, including school counselors. Like the educators in the system, many professional school counselors acceded to the policies often without realizing the implications for their students. On the other hand, other school counselors, through herculean efforts, labored valiantly to save, push, and encourage individual students to achieve success, often by circumventing policy barriers. Even so, currently there remain too many schools across the nation where some groups of students (those who have been historically underserved) remain systematically excluded from the quality of curriculum and instruction that would prepare them to be successful in the workplace and in postsecondary settings. The educational system that operates in this manner represents an inherently inequitable state of affairs that professional school counselors are obliged to address. As a profession, school counseling has prided itself on being in the forefront of issues related to social justice and competency in multicultural knowledge and practice. As education reform shifts its emphasis from implementing programmatic interventions for some students to patch up a broken system to making changes in the policies and practices that inhibit student and educator success, so, too, must the school counseling profession shift to systemic interventions. The school counseling profession must connect its actions to changing the systemic problems that contribute to student failure (Education Trust, 2005a).

Changes in the Nation's Demographics and School Populations

This passage from the *Prospectus* (2001) of Teachers for a New Era captures some of the titanic changes occurring in the U.S. demography:

> There are today in the United States more adherents of Islam than there are Episcopalians. More than 70% of the pupils in the Los Angeles unified school district are immigrants from Latin America, as are more than 50% of the pupils in Dodge City, Kansas. In many of the nation's largest cities, some districts are composed by majorities of more than 90% of pupils whose parents are Americans with family histories hundreds of years old on this continent and of African descent. In many communities Asian families form an imposing majority, and everywhere a current tide of immigration from throughout the world is affecting the makeup of the nation's classrooms.

The implications of these changes for school counselor practice and school counselor education are discussed in a later section of this chapter.

The demographic changes occurring in the United States constitute another catalyst for change in the educational system, as Figure 1.1 indicates. Communities and schools are changing as a result of immigration, declining birth rates among some populations, and the general aging of the population. To maintain the nation's status as a world power and to protect and maintain the democratic way of life, it is imperative that the educational system educate all of its citizens. We need an educated population in order for the United States to maintain its position as a world leader and an economic and social power and to maintain its thriving democratic society. Being "educated" in this society entails more than acquiring the basic skills of reading (decoding) and writing. We need a population that is literate, able to think analytically, and scientifically and mathematically literate. We need citizens who are knowledgeable about world cultures, can make informed decisions based on data, and can think critically about the data they use. Given the

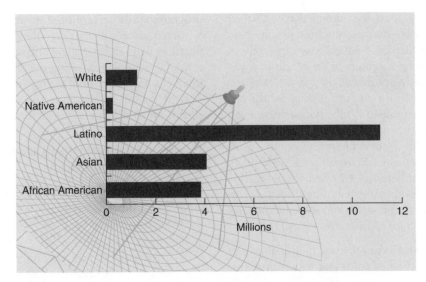

FIGURE 1.1 The demographics of the United States are changing rapidly: Projected increase in the population of 25- to 64-year-olds, 2000 to 2020.

Source: U.S. Census Bureau (2009). Retrieved April 21, 2009, from http://www.census.gov/population/www/projections/usinterimproj

demographic changes indicated in Figure 1.1, we must have an educational system where "all" means "all." Resources must be distributed equitably, based on student need (i.e., those who need more should get more) if we are to meet the mandate to educate all students to higher levels of academic proficiency.

Changes in the Economy and the Workplace

The global economy, technological advances, and the explosion of knowledge in science and related fields have resulted in major changes in the workplace, the way we work, and the requirements for success in the workplace. In the past, professional school counselors could support the placement of students into less demanding courses, possibly without considering this action a severe detriment to the students' future life options. This is no longer the case because all students need to be provided with the opportunity to master challenging academic content in order to participate successfully in the local and global economy.

There have been significant increases in the skills and knowledge required for success at all levels in the 21st-century workplace—from entry-level to professional jobs. According to Achieve, Inc. (2004), an organization that has studied requirements for success in the workplace and college, the skills and knowledge needed for success in the 21st-century workplace are essentially the same as those needed for success in a postsecondary education setting. For example, building engineers (formerly known as building custodians) must master mathematics and technology because many functions required for building maintenance

are computerized. Doctors must understand the latest scientific discoveries that affect medical advances. Twenty-first-century entry-level jobs require analytic and literacy skills and problem-solving competencies, as well as the ability to work successfully in teams.

As Figure 1.2 indicates, just when a more highly skilled workforce and more highly educated citizens are needed, the educational system is producing an overabundance of high school graduates and a dearth of two- and four-year college graduates. This mismatch of talent to the needs in the workplace is potentially disastrous to our country. This trend is a threat to our democracy and our economy and must be staunched by an educational system that teaches all students to achieve high levels of academic proficiency.

In the United States and in the global workplace, the economic demand for a more knowledgeable workforce equipped to work in an ever-expanding technological world is growing. Concurrent with these demands, school reform is being driven by the data that indicate that the student population is increasingly more diverse and now includes higher numbers of students of color, students from low-income families, and students who are English Language Learners living in urban and rural communities. These students need additional academic and social supports to succeed. Educational institutions have not served these populations well in the past and are faced with dire consequences if the job is not done better (V. V. Lee, 2005).

Concurrent with the need for more highly skilled workers, especially in the fields of science, engineering, and technology, the academic performance of U.S. students is being surpassed by the students in industrialized

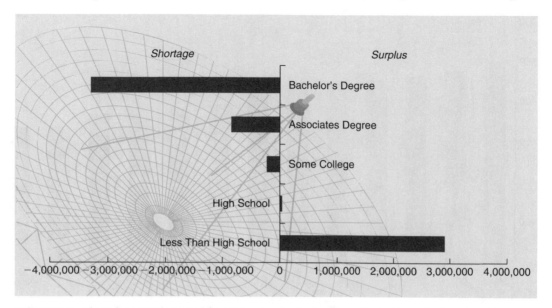

FIGURE 1.2 There is a growing need for higher levels of education: Projections of education shortages and surpluses in 2012.

Source: Analysis by Anthony Carnevale (2006) of Current Population Surveys (1992–2004) and U.S. Census population projection estimates.

competitor countries (American Institutes for Research, 2005). Not only are these countries graduating higher percentages of students from high schools and college, but also the students typically have mastered rigorous science and mathematics curricula. Many more of these students are graduating with the technical, mathematical, and scientific knowledge demanded by the 21st-century world job market than in the United States. Students in the United States consistently score lower on international assessments of mathematics and science than do students in other industrialized and even some nonindustrialized nations. Most distressing is that U.S. students' performance levels decrease as they move through the system, as indicated by Figures 1.3 and 1.4.

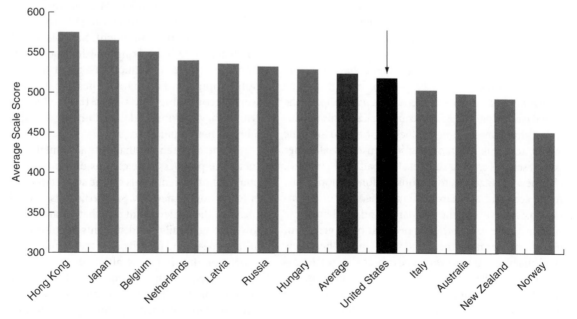

FIGURE 1.3 TIMSS grade 4 mathematics, 2003.
Source: American Institutes for Research (2005, November).

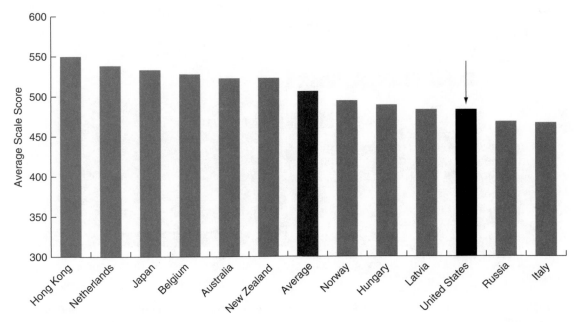

FIGURE 1.4   PISA mathematics, 15-year-olds, 2003.
Source: American Institutes for Research (2005, November).

Major Changes in Education Public Policy

Changes in demographics and workplace skill requirements, as well as recognition of the inequities in the educational system, spurred significant education policy changes in the current school reform movement. In the early 1990s, American education began its not-yet-completed shift to a standards-based system of education. An agreed-upon set of content standards in the major academic subject areas would guide instruction for all students. Reforms in assessment and accountability were designed to produce a more equitable educational system.

The 1994 reauthorization of the *Elementary and Secondary Education Act* (ESEA)—also known as the *Improving America's Schools Act*—brought a sea change to the educational landscape. The ESEA required all schools to educate students from low-income families according to the same challenging academic content standards used by all other schools (i.e., schools serving students from affluent families). Under the new law, states were responsible for developing the challenging academic standards, aligning rigorous criterion-referenced assessments to the standards, and implementing accountability systems to measure progress of all groups of students toward meeting the standards. Under these new policies, virtually all students would be expected to reach proficient levels on the challenging state academic standards.

The ESEA instituted another deep policy change, a change from a focus on measuring inputs to one on measuring success. For example, the previous focus may have assessed "*How many computers were purchased* with Title 1 funds?" while the current focus now measures results such as "*What have students learned* when they used the computers that were bought with Title 1 funds?" This change from using inputs" to using the students' academic learning as the measure of success constituted an enormous change for educators. For the first time, public policy put the accountability for student learning (not just teaching) squarely on the shoulders of educators. Those accountable for student learning ranged from the classroom teacher to the superintendent. Schools and districts that consistently failed to raise student achievement had to improve or face consequences—all of this in the glare of public opinion. For many educators, the idea that they were accountable for successfully educating students whom they previously deemed unable to learn constituted a brand new experience.

The requirement that state accountability plans document the progress that groups of students made toward attaining proficient levels on the state standards was another feature of the new law. States, districts, and schools had to measure the achievement gap that separated students from low-income families and students of color from their more affluent peers and identify how they would close that gap. In short, for the first time all states, districts, and schools receiving federal support from Title 1 of the ESEA would be accountable for the academic results of all students—both what students learned and their progress toward meeting proficiency levels on state standards.

The new accountability system was supported by a mandate to report disaggregated achievement data not only to educators, but also to parents and the public in an understandable format. Public reporting is still being worked on in many states. This mandate for public reporting of educational data was instituted so that states, districts, schools, and communities (and especially parents) could monitor the progress that groups of students made toward attaining proficiency on state academic standards. In other words, school systems must now expect all groups of students to achieve proficient levels of academic work, measure each group's progress toward proficiency, and provide public monitoring of the process. This sweeping policy change altered the landscape for educators, professional school counselors, and other support personnel in schools. For example, school counselors, working as ancillary professionals in schools and not directly connected to the new mandates for accountability for the school success of all students, sometimes found themselves being viewed as "would be nice to have, but not essential to the mission of schools."

With data more available to them than ever before, parents, community advocates, policy makers, and professional school counselors are equipped with the tools to measure student success and to develop and implement policies and practices that will promote academic success for all students. For the first time, professionals and parents had disaggregated data they can use to monitor more closely the progress of groups of students traditionally underserved by the system. These data revealed just how inequitable the system was in some cases.

As required by law, the ESEA was reauthorized in 2000 and came to be known as the *No Child Left Behind Act* (NCLB). NCLB is a contiuation the 1994 reauthorization. It stregthened the accountability provisions of the orginal law because these requirements were being ignored for the most part by states and districts. NCLB, among other changes, requires states to set time lines for closing acheivement gaps and to set a 12-year time frame for getting all students to proficiency. Accountability was strengthened by adding a formula to track student progress. Schools had to make enough progress toward meeting standards, called adequate yearly progress (AYP), that all groups would meet proficient levels by a time certain—at most 12 years into the future. The outcry from educators was deafening, and as of this writing, the law is due for reauthorization, and changes are expected in the time frame. However, the basic concepts of high standards for all students, accountability of educators and educational systems for results, and public reporting of data will still hold.

All of these forces for change in schools have profound implications for school counselor training and practice. The accountability policies affect all of the professionals in the educational system.

FROM THE PRESIDENT

In a global economy where the most valuable skill you can sell is your knowledge, a good education is no longer just a pathway to opportunity—it is a prerequisite. . . . I ask every American to commit to at least one year or more of higher education or career training. This can be community college or a four-year school, vocational training or an apprenticeship. But whatever the training may be, every American will need to get more than a high school diploma.

—President Barack Obama

EDUCATION REFORM

The College/Work–Ready Policy and School Reform

The policy to promote college-level learning for all students is a response to changes in the demographic and economic landscape. Over the last 15 years, educators, policy makers, community groups, and business leaders across the nation have worked in venues as diverse as boardrooms, legislative arenas, school districts, and universities, and even at kitchen tables, to reform K–16 education (National Center for Public Policy & Higher Education, 2000). Recently, these efforts received a very public boost when the National Governors Association (NGA) proclaimed high school reform in America a highest priority and declared that students must graduate from high school ready for college, work, and citizenship (Gates, 2005). Partly as a result of this attention, most states have increased their graduation requirements and are requiring students to complete a rigorous curriculum in the core courses of mathematics, science, English/language arts, and foreign language. States have eliminated their "seat time" diploma in favor of a diploma that represents successful completion of such courses.

Later, this chapter will explore the significant implications these changes in policies have for the practice of school counseling and what school counselors need to know and do to be successful. To work effectively in today's schools, professional school counselors must be knowledgeable about the academic side of the education house and collaborate with other professionals in the school to ensure that policies are equitably implemented. Not only must all students be able to access challenging rigorous content, but also schools must have the support systems in place for those students who need them.

CHANGING TIMES, CHANGING DEMANDS

Maintenance workers in modern buildings, such as the newly constructed mega conference centers and office buildings, must be computer literate. Upon summoning a "janitor" to change the room temperature in one of these centers, we learned that he was the building engineer and that the room temperature was controlled by a central computer system, which he had to access to change the room temperature.

Teachers, students, and school administrators visited a car manufacturing plant owned by a foreign car company and built in a southern rural county of the United States. The visitors were stunned to learn that entry-level jobs (no postsecondary training) required mastery of trigonometry.

Policies That Promote College-Level Rigor for All Students Drive Changes in School Counselor Practice

As is so often the case in the initiation of sweeping education reforms, there is a lag between policy adoption and successful implementation. As noted earlier, systems and the people in them tend to perpetuate behavior even when the behavior is no longer appropriate. In other words, old habits die hard. For example, the practice of sorting students into those who are college bound and those who are not is proving very resistant to change. "Guiding" students into college-bound and non-college-bound education "tracks" seemed like the correct action to take as long as education policies supported the differentiated content in the two tracks. The sorting practice helped to perpetuate the multitiered curricular tracking system—the college-bound curriculum for some, the "general" curriculum for others, and the technical and "business" tracks for still others. The movement toward college-level content for all students makes these tracking practices unnecessary. These changes requiring college-level rigorous coursework does not negate additional opportunities for students to take content courses in business, technology, and other technical fields. However, because of the mandated levels of academic proficiency, students pursuing these interest areas must not be tracked out of the rigorous courses. It is this rigorous course work that will enable students to reach required proficiency and keep their options open for postsecondary education and academic training beyond high school. Sadly, meeting the mandate for rigorous course work for all students in some schools across the nation ends up being a pretense,

giving a course a "rigorous" label such as Algebra 1, but providing content that is actually advanced basic arithmetic and bears little resemblance to the real algebra content needed for both college and work readiness.

Expecting all students to achieve at proficient levels makes obsolete the long-standing practice of school sytems and counselors of sorting students into college-bound and non-college-bound categories. All students are now to be educated to academic levels that will allow them to make the choice to enter postsecondary training without the need for remediation—and succeed. Professional school counselors must turn their attention to helping all students succeed in a challenging curriculum and working to change policies and practices that are impediments. Professional school counselors also need to help develop and implement institutional policies to ensure that all students have access to the challenging curriculum required by NCLB.

The lines between college preparatory courses and other courses have blurred as far as content is concerned. All students must have the opportunity to learn challenging core academic subjects. The delivery of the content can vary greatly from "vocational" settings to community classrooms and laboratories, but under the new policy, the goal is for all students to receive the same rigorous academic experiences. If some students are not getting challenging work, professional school counselors must develop comprehensive plans to eliminate this type of barrier to school success. They can use academic standards to gauge whether or not all students are actually receiving the rigorous curriculum to which they are entitled and which school districts are obligated to provide. Academic content standards, when translated into documents that the public can understand, provide powerful tools to support advocacy efforts to provide high-quality education to all students.

The transformed school counselor, while addressing the needs of individual students, will have an eye on the institutional policies and practices that impede student progress. For example, the professional school counselor may gather data on the achievement patterns of groups of students in different levels of academic classes to highlight differences in acheivement that may be the result of variations in the intensity of the curriculum to which the students are exposed rather than their lack of ability. This difference in exposure to challeging content is a major contributor to the achievement gap.

Studies (Achieve, Inc., 2005; Johnson, Arumi, & Ott, 2006; Johnson, Farkas, & Bers, 1997) have indicated that most students want to be challenged, and indeed, many feel their high school experiences are not challenging at all. Professional school counselors deal with the behavioral results of student malaise and boredom every day by applying programs to help these students change their behavior. In some instances, the behavior may be a reaction to an "unhealthy" school situation. School counselors have the skills to determine the reasons for student behavior and to develop comprehensive interventions to address the root causes of student failure.

An earlier discussion focused on how changes in the economy and changing demands in the workplace add to the notion that all students need to be prepared for success at the postsecondary level or in the workplace. It is important for professional school counselors to know that more states are joining the American Diploma Project (Achieve, Inc., 2004) in its efforts to raise high school exit requirements and demand that the high school curriculum be made more rigorous. This policy is in place now in 34 states. Transformed school counselors must focus on practices to ensure that this policy creates a stepping stone, rather than a barrier, to better opportunities in life for all students by ensuring that they get the academic, social, and emotional support they need to meet the new requirements.

TRANSFORMING THE SCHOOL COUNSELING PROFESSION

School Reforms Prompt the Transforming School Counseling Movement

Because of the many changes in schools and the world (e.g., demograhics of students enrolled in schools; public policies, including state and federal mandates for increases in student achievement; workplace demands for more educated workers and a better educated citizenry), all educational professionals must be involved in educating children for a new global economy. School counseling, along with all other components of the educational system, was subject to review, change, and/or reorganization. The stage was set for changes in school counseling that brought the profession from a position of ancillary support to one of leadership and advocacy, supporting school success for all students. The Education Trust and the American School Counselor Association (ASCA) stepped forward with actions that were far reaching and are still pivotal in guiding the transformation of the profession.

> *Vision is the capacity to create and communicate a view of a desired state of affairs that induces commitment among those working in an organization.*
> —Thomas Sergiovanni

The Transforming School Counseling Initiative

The forces pushing for change in education and the resulting revisions in education policies cited above provided the impetus for the Transforming School Counseling Initiative (TSCI), which was developed at the Education Trust beginning in 1994 and is continuing its work to transform policies and practices in the field. Supported by a grant from the DeWitt Wallace Foundation, the TSCI was built on the premise that school counseling, as a profession, had to move from a focus primarily on fixing individual students to one on removing the systemic barriers to student success for whole groups of students. While still serving some individual students, to achieve equitable results for all students, the systemic barriers that hinder all students had to be addressed by the profession. Initially, TSCI worked to change pre-service training of school counselors so that newly trained practitioners would enter the profession with the knowledge and skills needed to perform effectively in 21st century schools, where accountability for students' acacemic success had become the focus of the nation.

The new vision for school counseling that was developed and distributed by the Education Trust (1996) through the TSCI emphasized changes that would align the school counselors' role with new educational changes and mandates for educators in schools (House & Martin, 1998). This new vision highlighted movement of the professional school counselor from engaging in traditional practice to being a proactive change agent and advocate who focuses on supporting and creating pathways that allow all students to have school success (see Table 1.1). This new vision created considerable upheaval, as well as a great deal of discussion, in the counseling field. Change in school counseling being posited by an organization that was virtually unknown by leaders in the counseling field was difficult to accept, even though in subsequent years many of the conceptual changes put forth by the Education Trust have been embraced by the ASCA, school leaders, and counselor educators.

Teaming, collaboration, advocacy, and leadership are the lynchpins for the TSCI's structured changes in the way professional school counselors should be trained. The universities involved in the TSCI addressed changes in their pre-service training programs to align with the new vision. They also revised practices in the areas of candidate selection; curriculum content and structure and sequence of courses; methods of instruction, including field experiences and practice; practicum experiences; induction into the profession; and working relationships with community partnerships. In 1998, using a grant from the Met Life

TABLE 1.1   Transformation of the Role of Professional School Counselor

Present Focus	New Vision
Mental health issues	Academic and student achievement
Individual student concerns and issues	Whole school and system concerns and issues
Clinical model focused on student deficits	Academic focus, building on student strengths
Providing service, one-to-one and small groups	Leading, planning, and developing programs
Primary focus on personal/social	Focus on academic counseling, learning and achievement, supporting student success
Ancillary support personnel	Integral members of educational team
Loosely defined role and responsibility	Focusing on mission and role identification
Record keeping	Using data to effect change
Sorting, selecting course placement process	Advocating inclusion in rigorous preparation for all, especially students from low-income and minority families
Work in isolation or with other counselors	Teaming and collaboration with all educators in school in resolving issues involving the whole school and community
Guarding the status quo	Acting as change agent, especially for educational equity for all students
Involvement primarily with students	Involvement with students, parents, education professionals, community, and community agencies
Little or no accountability	Full accountability for student success, use of data, planning and preparation for access to wide range of postsecondary options
Dependence on use of system's resources for helping students and families	Brokering services for parents and students from community resources/agencies, as well as school system's resources
Postsecondary planning with interested students	Creating pathways for all students to achieve high aspirations

Foundation, the TSCI turned its attention to changing the way practicing counselors work and continued pushing for a focus on academic counseling, advocacy, and collaboration with colleagues in the educational system. Leadership, advocacy, teaming and collaboration, counseling and coordination, and assessments and use of data with accountability for results became the foundation for reforming practice and pre-service training (see Table 1.2).

National Standards for School Counseling Programs

In 1997, the ASCA published *The National Standards for School Counseling Programs* (C. Campbell & Dahir, 1997), consisting of nine standards, three each in the domains of academic, career, and personal/social development. The *National Standards* provided a standardized basis for the creation of comprehensive, developmental guidance programs. The competencies (i.e., the knowledge and skills to be acquired) that accompanied the *National Standards* led the way to development of comprehensive school counseling curricula in school districts. The *National Standards* gave

direction to a profession searching for ways to solidify an identity and role in standards-based school reform. They provided professional school counselors in districts across the nation with a common set of expectations for each of the three ASCA domains: academic, career, and personal/social development. Metrics for students' achievement of proficiency in accomplishing the *National Standards*, however, were not addressed, as the standards were not written in the format of course content standards with student outcomes. Nonetheless, the *National Standards* became unifying elements that helped professional school counselors find ways to respond affirmatively that school counseling was a discipline in schools with standards that resembled those of other content disciplines (e.g., math, science, social studies).

The ASCA National Model: A Framework for School Counseling Programs

Subsequent to publishing the *National Standards*, the ASCA developed and published *The ASCA National Model: A Framework for School Counseling Programs* (2005a),

TABLE 1.2 **New Vision for Professional School Counselors**

Leadership	Advocacy and Systemic Change	Teaming and Collaboration	Counseling and Coordination	Assessment and Use of Data
Promoting, planning, and implementing prevention programs, career and college activities, course selection and placement activities, social/personal management, and decision-making activities	Making available and using data to help the whole school look at student outcomes	Participating in or consulting with teams for problem solving; ensuring responsiveness to equity and cultural diversity issues, as well as learning styles	Providing brief counseling of individual students, groups, and families	Assessing and interpreting student needs and recognizing differences in culture, languages, values, and backgrounds
Providing data snapshots of student outcomes, showing implications and achievement gaps, and providing leadership for school to view through equity lens	Using data to effect change; calling on resources from school and community	Collaborating with other helping agents (peer helpers, teachers, principal, community agencies, business)	Coordinating resources, human and other, for students, families, and staff to improve student achievement (community, school, home)	Establishing and assessing measurable goals for student outcomes from counseling programs, activities, interventions, and experiences
Arranging one-to-one relationships for students with adults in school setting for additional support and assistance in reaching academic success	Advocating student experiences and exposures that will broaden students' career awareness and knowledge	Collaborating with school and community teams to focus on rewards, incentives, and supports for student achievement	Working as key liaison with students and school staff to set high aspirations for all students and develop plans and supports for achieving these aspirations	Assessing building barriers that impede learning, inclusion, and/or academic success for students
Playing a leadership role in defining and carrying out the guidance and counseling function	Advocating student placement and school support for rigorous preparation for all students	Collaborating with school staff members in developing staff training on team responses to students' academic, social, emotional, and developmental needs	Coordinating staff training initiatives that address student needs on a schoolwide basis	Interpreting student data for use in whole school planning for change

which represented a more comprehensive approach for integration of the *National Standards* into a school counseling program. The model addressed elements of program foundation, delivery, management, and accountability. The ASCA incorporated into the framework of its model the themes of leadership, advocacy, collaboration, and systemic change, themes that were foundational to the work of the TSCI at the Education Trust (House & Martin, 1998). The *National Model* is widely used by counselors across the nation and has provided coherence to districtwide and individual school counseling programs. More detailed information on the *National Model* and its impact on the work of professional school counselors will be provided in Chapter 3 and in later chapters of this book.

A WORD FROM MAYA ANGELOU

Each one of us has the right and responsibility to assess the roads that lie ahead and those roads we have traveled.

And if the future road looms ominous and unpromising and the roads back uninviting, then we need to gather our resolve and carrying only the necessary baggage, step off that road to a new direction.

(From *Wouldn't Take Nothing for My Journey Now*, by Maya Angelou)

IMPACT OF CHANGE ON SCHOOL COUNSELOR PRACTICE

Accountability in School Counselor Practice

Accountability, measurable evidence of positive impact on student academic success, is a critical driver for school reform with far-reaching implications for school counseling practice. Practitioners' use of school data for identifying problems; developing programs and strategies for ameliorating disparities in students' educational access, achievement, and attainment outcomes; and ensuring and documenting equity in access and success for all students requires systemic approaches for solutions (College Board, 2008b). The fundamental work of professional school counselors in the development of school counseling program goals and the implementation of focused, data-driven strategies must align with the schools' goals. With significant emphasis in school reform being put on outcomes for students, as opposed to inputs, professional school counselors must transform and/or reframe the work they do in order to create concrete, measurable outcomes for students. Doing "good work" is now deemed less important than "doing work that produces student results." School counselors' work that supports the three ASCA domains (i.e., academic, career, and personal/social) is still applicable, but not essential to school reform if not aligned with or contributing to the schools' goals and driven by relevant school data, school culture/climate circumstances, and educational equity (Elam, McCloud, & Robinson, 2007).

Accountability for student achievement is everybody's business, but traditionally it has been seen as the turf of teachers, administrators, and central office personnel in charge of curriculum and instructional programs. In reality, accountability is the responsibility of everyone in the school setting, including professional school counselors, students, parents, and the community at large. Until recently, professional school counselors have been left out of discussions regarding school reform, student achievement, and accountability. This omission is deleterious to the accomplishment of the goals for 21st-century K–12 school reform. School reform that constitutes systemic change for all students will not occur without the involvement of all the critical players.

Professional school counselors need to integrate themselves into school reform by collaborating with all school staff instead of working as ancillary personnel removed from the instructional side of schools. For professional school counselors to work effectively in schools, they must design data-driven school counseling programs that fit into the mission of today's schools to provide rigorous standards and accountability for all students. Consider the typical challenges raised in Case Study 1.1.

When professional school counselors operate under an ancillary model with programs that are peripheral to the major mission of the school, they focus on services addressing individual issues and concerns. Most often, those services have to do with social and emotional development. This role is often seen by decision makers as nonessential to teaching and learning. Indeed, when professional school counselors operate in this manner, it is often labeled as an ineffective use of resources, as well as fiscal irresponsibility, by policy makers, school boards, and school system leaders who are being held accountable for increasing student achievement. This knowledge and state of affairs in school buildings do not mean that school counselors must relinquish their programs, goals, and activities that address the personal/social needs of their students. Nor does this mean that one-on-one counseling is removed from their repertoire of counseling strategies. It does mean, however, that if these activities subsume the bulk of school counselors' time without producing measurable student results that align with the system's primary goal of educating all students to high levels, then the value of having school counselors and counseling programs will be irreparably diminished. Quoting the title of a recent minister's sermon, "Without a presence, there is no absence" in today's schools. Value in schools is now being defined in terms of student academic achievement and is driven and supported by federal law, the economy (i.e., lowered funding levels in constricted budgetary time periods), and business and industry roundtables seeking a better prepared workforce and hence the ability to continue to compete in a global marketplace. The confluence of these extremely powerful influencers is moving the educational agenda in schools across the nation. As one counselor educator stated, "The train has left the station and we find ourselves running to jump onboard."

Advocacy in School Counseling Practice

Traditionally, professional school counselors have described themselves as advocates for their students and agents of change (ASCA, 2005; Education Trust, 1996). And, indeed, many counselors have performed in ways that help their students negotiate their way in an inherently inequitable system. Professional school counselors have provided services to individual students, changed the students' course schedules, responded to teacher and parent referrals regarding adjustments and behavior issues, worked with and made outside referrals for

CASE STUDY 1.1

Typical Academic Challenges Professional School Counselors Face in the World of Education Reform: High Standards and Accountability

Consider strategies for addressing each of the following challenges.

Challenge 1.

Only a very small number of students of color are enrolled in rigorous academic classes. When pressed, the other students of color do not want to be placed in rigorous academic subjects. However, they still think they are going to college, and their parents want them to go and, in fact, think they are going. Both the students and the parents are clueless about what it takes to get into college and succeed.

Challenge 2.

Over 50% of the students in your school are English Language Learners and/or students of color. Over 80% of the student body participates in the free and reduced lunch program. Their state basic test scores are low—less than 10% of the students are proficient in English/language arts and mathematics, according to the state tests, and the SAT/ACT scores are extremely low. Faced with the threat of state takeover for not meeting adequate yearly progress for the last three years, your school must show improved results immediately.

Challenge 3.

Your school has been mandated to raise the average daily attendance rate. The school staff has not been able to do so in years past. However, it is now part of the school report card and one of the elements by which the principal will be evaluated at the end of the year. He is putting pressure on the whole staff to make it happen—constantly monitoring and documenting all departments' contributions to this goal.

Challenge 4.

The building strategic plan calls for all educators to be part of the school plan to improve attendance, create a safe and orderly environment, increase test scores, get more students into Advanced Placement classes, and raise SAT/ACT scores. The principal is requiring each department to submit a plan for its work that will support these system goals.

Challenge 5.

Of the students taking Algebra I in your school, 75% are earning D's & F's. Your math teachers have a reputation for being tough and openly state that this is a weeding-out class or that those students who fail should never have been in the classes in the first place. They see high failure rates as a sign of rigor. However, one teacher—one with low influence with other department members—seems to have success with her students. The parents in the community all want their children in this teacher's classes. The other math teachers think this teacher is too easy on the students. You can show that she is not by using data on continued success of her students in higher-level classes. The successful teacher appears to have a handle on how to engage students in the learning with hands-on activities and creativity.

Challenge 6.

At Whitaker Elementary School over the last three years, there has been a rise in the number of students being referred for evaluation and placed in special dducation classes. The school counselor has become alarmed at the number of children who are put on the child study list for testing and placement. She suspects that most of the students being referred and placed are not really in need of this drastic change in school programming. She has no method of proving what she thinks, but is aware that the referrals are mostly African-American males.

individual students with complex social and mental health needs that required extensive therapeutic interventions, and initiated group activities to help students improve organization, study, and test-taking skills—all laudable activities. Nonetheless, these supports have not been broad-based enough to support the bulk of the students in need of help, and professional school counselors have not been able to show they had measurable systemic impact in the school. Seemingly intractable school data continue to show that identifiable populations of students enter school with advantages that grow as they progress through the educational system, while other populations suffer, fail to thrive, and even drop out. When schools' disaggregated data are reviewed, this latter group will most often represent disproportional numbers of students of color, students from low-income families, and students for whom English is a second language.

Thus, successful school counselors in 21st-century schools will shift from focusing on fixing individual students to fixing the policies and practices in the educational system that contribute to academic failure of students. This shift is predicated on the assumption that a major source of academic failure for some students is the way the educational system is organized to deliver services to different groups of students (Commission on Chapter 1, 1992).

As we move further into the 21st century, it is critical for professional school counselors to move beyond their current role as "helper-responder" and become proactive leaders and advocates for the success of all students. To do this, professional school counselors must move out of the traditional mode of operation and begin collaborating with other school professionals to influence systemwide changes and become an integral part of their schools and school reform (House & Hayes, 2002). This approach requires counselors to examine and question inequitable practices that do not serve the interests of all students.

> *I have recently returned to high school counseling after spending the past year and a half in the district office. As I returned to a school I realized more than ever how important it is for counselors to act as leaders. Counselors serving on committees such as Faculty Advisory or School Advisory Council is important because we need to be a part of the "big picture."*
>
> —School Counselor from Georgia

> *I have been closely involved in bringing professional learning communities to our school as well as analyzing data to decide the direction of both professional development and curriculum/instruction for our school. I have always been actively involved in writing the School Improvement Plan as well as presenting it to the district for approval. I find that working at a systemic level gives me the "big picture" and better enables me to communicate academic expectations to our parents and students. Collaborating weekly with the 8th grade teacher team as well as meeting weekly with the leadership team enables me to help lead the school toward fulfilling the most important goal we have, student learning. This involvement gives me a framework for underscoring my role of student support and advocacy. When I am working with students to remove the barriers that often prevent students from focusing on their education, I can begin to link their future education and career goals with the need for them to take advantage of their education now.*
>
> —Texas school counselor

In order for professional school counselors to work as leaders and advocates to effect systems change, it is of paramount importance that their role undergo a transformative change. To "transform" means to alter, to shift, or to change the way one works. For professional school counselors, it means moving away from a primary focus on mental health and individual changes to a focus on whole-school and systemic concerns that fit the schools' mission—academic achievement (see Table 1.1).

Through data-driven advocacy that purposefully highlights and focuses on marginalized populations, the scope of the professional school counselor's work will be expanded and transformed. The use of data allows professional school counselors to be accountable for their actions and to show they can make a difference in the academic success of all students. The results of these deliberate actions can be documented by "hard data" that move school counseling from the periphery of school business to a position front and center in constructing and supporting student success.

Professional school counselors are ideally positioned in schools to serve as conductors and transmitters of information to promote schoolwide success for all students. When professional school counselors aggressively support quality education for all students, they create a school climate where access and support for rigorous preparation is expected. In so doing, they give students who have not been served well in the past a chance at acquiring the skills necessary to unconditionally participate in the 21st-century economy.

A CALL FOR CHANGE IN SCHOOL COUNSELOR PREPARATION PROGRAMS

For the professional school counselor to assume the role of leader and advocate working to make systemic change to benefit all students, professional school counselor preparation programs will need to change practices. The Transforming School Counseling Initiative (Education Trust, 2005b) suggested eight essential elements of change that would transform counselor education programs and, thus, the school counseling profession, including changes in admission and induction practices, the practicum experience, certification requirements, and changes in the curriculum to include advocacy.

Since the 1960s, most professional school counselors have been taught the three "Cs"—counseling, consultation, and coordination—as a way of defining their role in schools. This role served the profession well over the years, but it is now too limiting and no longer provides enough breadth and depth of scope for professional school counselors to be effective. In addition, the older model does not provide a basis for serving all students. Instead of limiting professional school counselor training and practice to this role, counselor educators and practitioners must broaden their role to include leadership, advocacy and systemic change, teaming and collaboration, counseling and coordination, and assessment and use of data (see Table 1.2).

Teaching professional school counselors these new approaches broadens the scope of the work so that it is systemically more inclusive and thus helpful to more students. The model allows competent professional school counselors to work as leaders and team members with parents and members of the educational community to create supportive pathways that allow all students to succeed. Examples of school counselor preparation programs preparing students in this transformed model can be found at the Education Trust website (www.edtrust.org) under the Transforming School Counseling tab.

ACCOUNTABILITY: MAKING SCHOOL COUNSELING COUNT

School counseling programs that are accountable are built around specific strategies using student data to create vision and targeted change. These strategies include clear indicators that the school counseling program is producing results. In this accountability model, professional school counselors are

key to removing barriers to learning and achievement and promoting success for all students. Removal of these barriers is critical to the future success of students and their families. Holding low expectations and believing that students cannot achieve due to life circumstances cause irrevocable damage to their future life options. To act as agents of school and community change, professional school counselors must

1. Articulate and provide a well-defined developmental counseling program with attention to equity, access, and support services.
2. Routinely use data to analyze and improve access to, and success in, rigorous academic courses for all students, and especially underrepresented students.
3. Actively monitor the progress of underrepresented students in rigorous courses and provide assistance or interventions when needed.
4. Actively target and enroll underrepresented students into rigorous courses.
5. Develop, coordinate, and initiate support systems designed to improve the learning success of students experiencing difficulty with rigorous academic programs.

Leadership and Transformed School Counselor Practice

Advocating for high achievement for all students by serving as a leader and team member (see Table 1.1) in schools becomes the key role for counselors in this new approach to school counseling. It places professional school counselors at the center of the mission of school and school reform. In addition to having counseling skills, professional school counselors will need to

- Expect all students to achieve at a high level.
- Actively work to remove barriers to learning.
- Teach students how to help themselves (e.g., organization, study and test-taking skills).
- Teach students and their families how to successfully manage the bureaucracy of the school system (e.g., teach parents how to enroll their children in academic courses that will lead to college, make formal requests to school officials on various matters, and monitor the academic progress of their children).
- Teach students and their families how to access support systems that encourage academic success (e.g., inform students and parents about tutoring and academic enrichment opportunities and teach students and parents how to find resources on preparation for standardized tests).
- Use local, regional, and national data on disparities in resources and academic achievement to promote system change.
- Work collaboratively with all school personnel.

- Offer staff development training for school personnel that promotes high expectations and high standards for all students.
- Use data as a tool to challenge the deleterious effects of low-level and unchallenging courses.
- Highlight accurate information that negates myths about who can and cannot achieve success in rigorous courses.
- Organize community activities to promote supportive structures for high standards for all students (e.g., after-school tutoring programs at neighborhood religious centers).
- Help parents and the community organize efforts to work with schools to institute and support high standards for all children.
- Work as resource brokers within the community to identify all available resources to help students succeed.

What Prevents Professional School Counselors from Changing?

The call for change in the role of the professional school counselor is not new. Although professional school counselors are identified in educational literature as being important to the success of students in schools (Hayes, Dagley, & Horne, 1996), it seems that the profession has changed very slowly until recently. The following obstacles, or barriers, to changing the way professional school counselors practice may help explain why.

- There is sometimes an unwillingness to change that results in maintaining the status quo.
- Administrative practices can dictate the role of professional school counselors, even if the dictated role is different from counselor training.
- Professional school counselors can be pliable, often accepting responsibilities that are not part of their counseling role and function (e.g., bus duty and cafeteria duty).
- Pressure from special-interest groups may dictate the role of professional school counselors.
- Many counselor educators have little or no ongoing involvement with K–12 institutions, including little or no follow-up with recent graduates.
- Special education mandates for assessment, documentation, and ongoing services take too much of the counselor's time.
- Large numbers of practicing professional school counselors are functioning as highly paid clerical staff and/or quasi-administrators.
- Professional school counselors sometimes function as inadequately trained therapeutic mental health providers with unmanageable client loads.

- The role of professional school counselors is frequently determined by others, rather than by the counselors' developing their own purposeful, comprehensive programs.
- Little or no professional development is provided for professional school counselors.
- Crisis management on a day-to-day basis usurps too much of the professional school counselor's time.
- Professional school counselors may choose not to be involved in school reform efforts in school buildings.
- Professional school counselors may not see academic achievement as their goal or mission.
- Professional school counselors generally work to change the student, not the system in which the student functions. Thus, the student, not the system, is assumed to be the "problem."

Professional school counselors who continue to use these "excuses" to avoid change often serve as maintainers of the status quo, advocating for the school system, rather than for students and marginalized groups. They become "sorters and selectors," perpetuating the accepted placements and systemic barriers that cause an inequitable distribution between achievers and nonachievers based on race and socioeconomic status (Hart & Jacobi, 1992).

A Sense of Urgency Is Propelling Change

The sense of urgency to help all students be successful in school is propelling professional school counselors to change. Indeed, many professional school counselors are seizing the opportunity to be leaders in schools and work as advocates for students. The *ASCA National Model* (2005a) provided the structure to implement a comprehensive approach to program foundation, delivery, management, and accountability. The ASCA (2005) *National Model* provides the mechanism with which professional school counselors and school counseling teams design, coordinate, implement, manage, and evaluate their programs for students' success. It provides a framework for the program components; the professional school counselor's role in implementation; and the underlying philosophies of leadership, advocacy, teaming and collaboration, and systemic change.

In many states, professional school counselors are working as a part of school reform efforts to increase access and opportunity for students. For example,

- Project 720 in Pennsylvania is a high school reform effort that identifies key components that schools must address to improve student achievement. School counseling and advocacy is one component under review, and professional school counselors are actively involved in the planning and implementation of this school reform effort. More information about this project can be found at the following website: www.pde.state.pa.us.

- The College Board's EXCELerator Schools across the country and schools in The Florida Partnership for Minority Student Achievement both have made school counselors part of the leadership teams schoolwide and/or systemwide where they are analyzing data, developing and implementing goals for their school counseling programs to support the systems' goals for increasing college-going rates, increasing equitable participation and success in the Advanced Placement programs and decreasing dropout rates (see http://professionals.collegeboard.com/k-12/readiness-system/models/excelerator and http:// professionals.collegeboard.com/policyadvocacy/policy/flp/schools/conferences#2007).

These are a few examples where professional school counselors are at the table and integrating themselves into school reform by collaborating with all school staff. They are integrally involved in planning systemic changes in schools and school systems that have the goal of closing the achievement gap and increasing proficiency of all students.

CASE STUDY 1.2

Application of New Vision: Transformed Practice Knowledge: Individual Students or Systemic Issues?

Many school counselors have felt that addressing systemic issues was beyond their purview—and at one point, it may have been. However, the transformed school counselor is now working in school districts that are held accountable for making sure that all students have an opportunity to achieve academic success in challenging curricula. Professional school counselors must maximize their capacity to impact the greatest number of students in need of their help. The "transformed" school counselor must develop the capacity to determine when the intervention should be focused on helping individual students and when the intervention should be focused on changing the policies and practices being implemented by the system that are the source of student failure and/or student social distress.

Professional school counselors can make such a determination only by using data to understand patterns in student success and failure, analyzing the policies and practices for their impact on student success, and working with the adults in the system who are responsible for student success to maximize their capacity to work successfully together to fulfill the academic mission of the schools.

Professional school counselors must ask themselves if it is ethical to counsel a student to "adjust" to conditions in school that may actually contribute to the antisocial behavior exhibited by the student. Should a school counselor continue to change classes for individual students from a particular teacher's class when the data reveal that the teacher has disproportionately high failure rate with the group of students that have asked to change classes? Consider this scenario:

Mr. E is in his second year as a professional school counselor in a middle school in a first-ring suburb in a midwestern state. The community has undergone significant demographic changes, going from a predominately White, lower-middle-income town to a multiethnic community with a large influx of non-native-English-speaking families, including a sizable population of students from South East Asia. In the last 10 years, the school demographics have changed from predominately White students to over 50% students of color who are from both low- and middle-income families. A small percentage of the families of color have resided in the community for years, but have not been notably visible. Now, these families of color, primarily African American, have become more visible in the community, and their children seem to have become more visible in the school community.

The school has a past reputation for being one of the "better" middle schools in the community. Their students feed into two high schools, one an "academic" high school and the other a "general" high school. High school placement is determined by grades and teacher recommendations. There is no written policy, and no data are consistently collected.

Over the past few years, the number of students attending the academic high school has declined. There are discussions among some parents that the students who attend the general high school are predominately students of color. They are concerned that their children are not being well prepared for postsecondary success, but have no organized effort to address the issues.

The principal has been at the school for the past six years and has come under increasing pressure to raise test scores. The teaching staff has remained stable, but is aging, and a significant percentage is or will be eligible for retirement in the next couple of years. The teaching staff is predominately White, while custodial and helping staff are persons of color. The staff increasingly feels that they are "under the gun" and being pressured to narrow their curriculum to get all students to pass the state tests.

(Continued)

Teachers complain that it is difficult to teach because of the increasing need to address the discipline problems caused (they say) mostly by the minority students or the "new" students. They argue that students are not prepared academically to do the level of work they expect and decry the lack of parental involvement.

Recently, the district's test scores have been published in the local paper. Current state policy requires that the scores to be disaggregated by race, socioeconomic status, and disability. The data show an achievement gap between the students of color and low-income students and their White and Asian peers.

In the past, professional school counselors have concentrated on getting students into the academic high school, helping students chart their high school courses, and keeping a lid on the discipline problems by providing group counseling programs, community mentoring, and after-school activities, which were voluntary and poorly attended. Staff are demoralized, and morale in the school is low.

Discussion Questions

This scenario is designed to prompt a discussion about school counselor intervention strategies.

- How would the professional school counselor go about formulating an intervention plan to assist the school in closing the achievement gap?
- What issues should the professional school counselor address and why?
- What data would the professional school counselor collect to construct an intervention plan?
- What are the major change dynamics operating in the scenario?

Summary/Conclusion

The work of school counselors in schools today has been profoundly impacted by forces that have driven all professionals in schools to change and/or ratchet up their contributions to raising student achievement, especially for students who have not had school success in the past. Schools as systems undergoing reformation have historically produced disparate results for different populations of students. School counseling, a critical working component of the system, has undergone, and is still undergoing, a transformation in which traditional inputs and processes are changing to support raising student achievement.

The vision for professional school counselors presented in this book is cutting edge, compelling, and essential to maintaining the profession in the 21st century and beyond. This vision puts professional school counselors in the middle of school reform and gives them an opportunity to demonstrate that they do make a difference in the success of students. Professional school counselors will be valued when they demonstrate effectiveness in making systemic changes that allow all students access to rigorous academic programs and support for success. Education is a substantial quality-of-life issue that determines the life options of students, their immediate and future families, and the economic viability of our nation, as well as our nation's position as a global leader. Professional school counselors who transform their practice as described in this book can be indispensable to schools in accomplishing the new mission of educating all students to high levels.

Activities

1. Research the schools in your local community. Find test scores, percentages of students who graduate, percentages of low-income students, and racial and ethnic breakdowns. How would the specifics of the schools in your area affect your focus as a professional school counselor in one of those schools?

2. Brainstorm ways that a professional school counselor could conduct and transmit information to an entire school to promote success of all students. Design several activities or lessons a guidance department could implement to support student achievement for all.

3. Read *The ASCA National Model: A Framework for School Counseling Programs* (2005a). What are some of the significant themes effecting change in the profession? How could you incorporate this model in a new program that you have been assigned to begin?

2

Historical Roots and Future Issues

Edwin L. Herr and Bradley T. Erford

ditor's Introduction: It has been said that to know who you are, you must understand where you came from. When attempting to discern the future, historical events provide intriguing perspectives. Likewise, when beginning a journey of professional transformation, it is essential to understand the profession's roots and key developmental events. This chapter offers both a synopsis of the historical roots of the school counseling profession and, from this perspective, a peek at some of the profession's current and future challenges.

THE RISE OF PROFESSIONAL SCHOOL COUNSELING IN THE UNITED STATES

It can be argued that school counseling is the earliest form of intentional or systematic counseling in the United States or, perhaps, in the world. It also can be argued that many of the philosophical ideas and process methods incorporated into what professional school counselors now do could be traced in a fragmented way into ancient history (Dumont & Carson, 1995; C. H. Miller, 1961; G. Murphy, 1955; Williamson, 1965) as elders, teachers, or mentors engaged in dialogues intended to provide guidance to young people. Throughout history, every society has found methods beyond the family by which to provide selected young people direction and support as they grapple with questions of who they might become and how to achieve such goals. In some instances, the persons who delivered such guidance were philosophers, physicians, priests or other clerics, medicine men or shamans, teachers, or masters of apprentices. But such "guidance" or "counseling" was neither equally available to all young people, nor was it planned and systematic.

Given this context, it is fair to suggest that the pervasive, formal, and systematic provision of guidance and counseling in schools is an American invention. Although notions that arose in European research laboratories about individual differences, assessment techniques, and psychological classifications and explanations for behavior were conceptually important in shaping some of the content and methods of school counseling, they were not the stimuli that caused school counseling to come into being.

Like other major social institutions, guidance and counseling in schools did not arise spontaneously, nor did they occur in a vacuum. Although there were visionaries, scholars, and early practitioners of guidance and counseling who were critical to the implementation of school counseling, the historical moment had to be right for the ingredients of change to take root and begin to flourish. In the last quarter of the 19th century in the United States, political and social conditions converged to prod the nation to initiate education reform and to sensitize it to emerging issues of human dignity and the exploitation of children in the workplace, to the dynamics of massive immigration, and to the demands for human resources by the burgeoning Industrial Revolution.

Various authors during the 20th century have identified the different conditions that gave rise to guidance and counseling in U.S. schools. Brewer (1942) contended that four of the most important conditions were the division of labor, the growth of technology, the extension of vocational education, and the spread of modern forms of democracy. Traxler and North (1966) contended that the guidance movement in schools could be traced to five divergent sources: "philanthropy or humanitarianism, religion, mental hygiene, social change, and the movement to know pupils as individuals" (p. 6).

Clearly, there were many background or contextual variables that influenced the rise of school counseling at the end of the 19th and the beginning of the 20th century. But there is general consensus that the beginnings of school counseling in the 20th century lay in vocational guidance. It also is clear that many of the concerns that gave rise to school counseling were focused on the quality and utility of existing educational processes. Embedded in the emerging concepts of both vocational guidance and education reform were issues of individual freedom of choice and dignity. These three factors, interacted and intertwined as philosophies and models of school guidance or counseling, were introduced by various pioneers in the field.

There are different persons who can be described as early visionaries or practitioners of school guidance and counseling. History has failed to record the names of many of them. But among those about whom we know, several persons have been worthy of special note: George Merrill, who in 1895 developed the first systematic vocational guidance program in San Francisco; Jesse B. Davis, who in 1898 began working as a counselor in Central High School in Detroit and in 1908 organized a program of vocational and moral guidance in the schools of Grand Rapids, Michigan; and Eli W. Weaver, principal of a high school in Brooklyn, who authored *Choosing a Career* in1908. Although each made important contributions to the founding of vocational guidance, the person generally regarded as the primary architect of vocational guidance in the United States, the man who has come to be known as the "father of vocational guidance," is Frank Parsons.

Parsons was a man with multiple interests and a social conscience. Trained as a civil engineer and as a lawyer, throughout much of his adult life Parsons was heavily involved in the activities of settlement houses in central Boston and in other cities along the eastern seaboard. It was there that he learned firsthand about the plight of immigrants and others trying to survive physically and find appropriate access to the rapidly growing occupational structure of the cities to which they had come. Such experiences fueled Parsons's concerns about the need to deal with what he viewed as the excesses of the free enterprise system and the management of industrial organizations that led, in his view, to the debasement of individual dignity.

As these experiences grew, Parsons turned his attention to strengthening industrial education and creating the process of vocational guidance. His perception was that too many people, especially the immigrants from Europe, were not able to effectively use their abilities and to prosper economically and socially because of the haphazard way they found work and made the transition to the specialized world of the factory. Parsons created not only a counseling approach, which will be described later, but also what to him was a moral and social imperative to value and facilitate the effective use of human resources. In this sense, Parsons's initiatives in vocational guidance were congruent with the growing emphasis of the time on vocational guidance as the "conservation of human resources" (Spaulding, 1915), the effort to avoid the waste of human talent by identifying and maximizing its use.

After several years of experience in providing vocational guidance and counseling, Parsons founded the Vocations Bureau of the Civic Services in Boston in January 1908, serving as the director and vocational counselor. The setting was not a school, but rather the Civic Service House (C. H. Miller, 1961), with branch offices in the Young Men's Christian Association (YMCA), the Economic Club, and the Women's Educational and Industrial Union in Boston. Unfortunately, Parsons died only a few months after founding the Vocations Bureau. His legacy to the field of vocational guidance was captured in his major work, *Choosing a Vocation*, which was published posthumously in 1909. This extraordinary book laid out the principles and methods of implementing vocational guidance, collecting and publishing occupational information, conducting a group study of occupations, carrying on individual counseling, and processing individual assessment. Perhaps Parsons's most famous contribution was what became known as a trait and factor approach: his articulation of the three broad factors or steps of the vocational guidance process. The trait and factor approach called for the following:

> First, a clear understanding of yourself, aptitudes, abilities, interests, resources, limitations, and other qualities. Second, a knowledge of the requirements and conditions of success, advantages and disadvantages, compensation, opportunities and prospects in different lines of work. Third, true reasoning on the relations of these two groups of facts. (Parsons, 1909, p. 5)

Following Parsons's death, the work of the Vocations Bureau was extended to the Boston schools, and training of vocational counselors was undertaken. In 1917, the Vocations Bureau became part of the Division of Education at Harvard University. During the years following the publication of *Choosing a Vocation*, many leaders in American education began to recognize the social significance of and adapt to Parsons's paradigm of vocational guidance (Bloomfield, 1915). This process was compatible with the growing calls for educational reform in the nation's schools. Parsons himself, among many observers of the time, attacked the public schools for their specialization in book learning and advocated that "book work should be balanced with industrial education; and working children should spend part time in culture classes and industrial science" (Stephens, 1970, p. 39).

Such views, targeted on the public schools, and particularly those in the cities, reflected both the rising issues of child labor—children aged 8, 10, or 12 years working in coal mines and factories and not receiving the opportunity to go to school—and the dynamics of the Industrial Revolution that served as the backdrop for concerns about social and education reform. In the late 1800s and early 1900s, the United States was in the midst of making the transition from a national economy that was, in general, agriculturally based to one that was increasingly based in manufacturing and industrial processes. As this transition ensued, urbanization and occupational diversity increased, as did national concerns about strengthening industrial education as a way to prepare young people to take advantage of the growing opportunities in the workforce. To play out such goals effectively required information about how persons could identify and get access to emerging jobs. By the turn of the 20th century, particularly in urban areas, such information was so differentiated and comprehensive that families or local neighborhoods could no longer be the primary sources of occupational information or of the allocation of jobs, This set the stage for more formal mechanisms, including vocational guidance in the schools.

The issues of vocational guidance in the schools and elsewhere in society became confounded by the changing demographics of the potential workforce. At the beginning of the 20th century, large numbers of immigrants from nations with poor economic opportunities were coming to the United States seeking new lives and options for themselves and for their children. Likewise, people within the United States were migrating from rural to urban areas, spurred by the concentration of large plants producing steel, furniture, automobiles, and other capital goods.

Such social and economic phenomena as industrialization, urbanization, and immigration stimulated concerns about whether existing forms of education were appropriate in a rapidly growing industrial society, how to meet the need for less bookish and more focused industrial education, how to bridge the gap between schooling and the realities of the adult world, how to make the school-to-work transition, and how to adapt the new educational theories being advanced (e.g., Progressive Education, the concepts of John Dewey) for use in the schools.

Stephens (1970), a historian, spoke about the relationship between industrial or vocational education and vocational guidance, indicating that, in this context, vocational education and vocational guidance were seen as a partnership. Certainly, as one of the major roots of the professional school counselor's role, engaging in vocational guidance was seen as a significant emphasis. However, other forces were also at work shaping the role of the professional school counselor at the beginning of the 20th century. For example, Cremin (1964), also a historian, suggested that the clearest reminder in the schools of the impact of the Progressive Education movement, spanning the latter quarter of the 19th century and the first 50 years of the 20th century, is the guidance counselor.

THE ROLE OF THE PROFESSIONAL SCHOOL COUNSELOR IN THE 1920s, 1930s, AND 1940s

As the layers of expertise expected of the vocational counselor began to be defined in the 1880s and 1890s and in the first decades of the 1900s, debates about approaches to the philosophy and the role of counselors continued to occur in the 1920s, 1930s, and 1940s. These issues tended to be affected by other forces coming to prominence in schools and in educational philosophy at the same time. Some of these forces directly affected the extant perspectives about school counseling; others were more indirect. Hutson (1958) suggested that, in addition to the importance of vocational guidance as a powerful force shaping the guidance counselor's role, there were five others: student personnel administration; psychologists, working as researchers and clinicians; personnel work in industry; social work; and mental health and psychiatry. Each deserves further comment.

Student Personnel Administration

This concept originated in higher education, where it essentially related to the identification of a specific official, often called the Dean of Students, whose responsibility was dealing with the personal and disciplinary problems of students. In time, this person would be expected to administer or provide leadership to all of the nonacademic services that facilitate the progress of the students through the institution. Included were such services as admissions, counseling, student orientation, financial aid, and placement. This concept was seen in the 1920s as having relevance to the secondary schools, and perhaps the elementary schools, as the functions of the vocational counselor took on an increasingly large array of responsibilities. Some high schools in the United States continued to use titles such as Dean of Students or Dean of Boys or Girls into the latter decades of the 20th century. Perhaps more important, this concept foreshadowed the creation of positions now commonly titled Director of Guidance Services or Director of Pupil Personnel Services or, in some larger school districts, Assistant Superintendent of Pupil Personnel Services.

Psychologists, Working as Researchers and Clinicians

The content and methodology of school counseling owe much to psychology as the major discipline providing insights into student development, cognition, behavior classification and analysis, and effective interventions. In his observations, Hutson (1958) referred to two particular contributions of psychologists. The first had to do with psychologists' research into the development of objective instruments for measuring human behavior (e.g., interest inventories, aptitude and achievement tests, diagnostic tests), without which many would see the role of the vocational counselor as nothing more than "organized common sense." But the availability of these tools and their use gave vocational counselors areas of expertise and information that enriched their ability to engage in vocational guidance and increased their professional credibility.

The second contribution of psychologists in a clinical sense was to provide specialized services to specific groups of students experiencing particular learning or behavioral problems. To the degree that psychologists were available in school districts or child guidance clinics to deal with these students, vocational counselors could focus their energies on other segments of the student population.

Personnel Work in Industry

As personnel work in industry grew during the first 50 years of the 20th century, it provided job requirement specifications, motivation studies, and tests for job application and vocational guidance purposes. Personnel work in industry also broadened the application of counseling to specific job-related problems such as meeting job requirements, getting along with fellow workers, and other factors that could interfere with a worker's job efficiency. Such information helped to broaden the content and processes of vocational guidance in schools.

Social Work

Starting with the visiting teacher movement that originated in 1906 and 1907 in settlement houses or civic associations and involved working with problem pupils and their parents, school social work was taking on its own identity in the 1930s and 1940s. School social workers represented an official liaison among the school, the home, and community social agencies. The introduction of social workers to school staffs replaced the former concepts of law and punishment

of problem or delinquent children by truant officers with such emphases as diagnosis, understanding, and adjustment. As school social workers became available to deal with specific problem children—those who were habitually truant and whose behavior was being monitored by legal or family services—the role of the school social worker also affected the role of the vocational counselor. Where social workers were available, counselors tended to be less directly involved with home visits or with community social agencies. The social worker tended to be the community liaison; the counselor was more school bound. In addition, as the school social worker and community agencies provided interventions for specific problem children, the professional school counselor could focus more fully on the children who needed primarily educational and vocational guidance.

Mental Health and Psychiatry

With the rise in psychiatric attention to schools, beginning in the early decades of the 20th century, the National Association for Mental Hygiene and related organizations disseminated the principles of mental health and information about various types of personality maladjustment and advocated that the development of wholesome personalities "is the most important purpose of education" (Hutson, 1958, p. 13). In the 1920s and subsequent decades, psychiatry focused on combating juvenile delinquency and sought to establish "child guidance clinics" for the psychiatric study and treatment of problem children in the schools. While the direct impact of guidance clinics on problem children was small, the insights about maladaptive behavior and the principles of treatment subtly affected how professional school counselors were prepared, whom they referred to community agencies for treatment, and how they viewed the fostering of mental health as part of their role.

Each of these influences or forces shaped perspectives on why counselors were important in schools; how they needed to differ from, but be collaborators with, psychologists, social workers, and psychiatric specialists; and what functions they could serve in schools and with what groups of students. Such perspectives extended the analysis of the relationship of counselors to schools per se to why schools should appoint counselors. Cowley (1937) reported three areas of emphasis that were evolving in the public schools: (1) guidance as the personalization of education, (2) guidance as the integration of education, and (3) guidance as the coordination of student personnel services. Like so many other issues and possibilities for action that occurred as guidance and counseling were taking root in the schools, these three areas continue to influence contemporary issues.

Guidance as the Personalization of Education

Cowley (1937) suggested that of most importance, "counselors have been appointed to counteract the deadening mechanical limitations of mass education" (p. 220). He decried the depersonalization of both higher and secondary education, the growing lack of close relationships between teachers and students, the lack of a personal touch in education, and the decreased concern on the part of administrators about student problems. All of these factors led Cowley to argue as follows:

> No matter how expert personnel people may be as technically trained psychological testers or diagnosticians, the real test of a personnel program is the extent to which it makes the student feel that he individually is important—that he is not being educated in a social vacuum (1937, p. 221).

In more contemporary terms, guidance as personalization of education continues, with different language, to be embedded in statements about the professional school counselor's role as one in which the student is helped to achieve academic development (ASCA, 2005a).

Guidance as the Integration of Education

Cowley (1937) was particularly concerned with the explosion of knowledge and the rapid growth of curricular offerings: the movement away from a fixed curriculum, which all students took advantage of in elective courses, and toward the compartmentalization of knowledge and the specialization of instruction. Cowley saw the professional school counselor as the person who would help each student facing such challenges to effectively sort through the educational options and create for himself or herself a unified course of instruction—that is, as the person who would discover each student's talents and motivations and bring the resources of the institution to bear on developing these talents and motivations.

Guidance as the Coordination of Student Personnel Services

While Cowley saw educational counseling as the most important function that professional school counselors undertook, he felt it was necessary to coordinate the counseling function with the other functions professional school counselors engaged in, in relation to the roles of other mental health workers (e.g., psychologists, social workers, and psychiatrists). He was concerned that a student could be "chopped up," seen as a person with a specific problem rather than as a whole person. Thus, Cowley argued that the guidance counselor should be responsible for coordinating all of the specialist services available to students and for integrating those findings into a coordinated set of directions and support.

Arthur J. Jones provided additional perspectives on the needs of students and schools for counselors. In the two editions of his classic work, *Principles of Guidance* (A. J. Jones, 1930, 1934), he summarized both the need for providing guidance and the significance of the schools offering the guidance. He advocated for the need for guidance from the standpoint of the individual and the significance of providing guidance to enhance the school climate and support the school mission.

By the mid-1930s, when Jones was discussing the status of school guidance and counseling in the nation (A. J. Jones, 1934), the approach to school counseling often, but not always, followed a trait and factor, or directive, approach. Tests had increasingly become available, although the range of behavior they assessed was still limited primarily to "intelligence," aptitude, achievement, and interests. There were not yet any major theories of school counseling per se. Philosophies and principles of school counseling were being shaped by the Progressive Education movement, by psychiatry, and by other emerging theories. Jones also described "methods of guiding students," which in his view included counseling; homeroom guidance and group guidance; educational guidance with regard to choices of courses, schools, and colleges; "stay in school" campaigns; vocational guidance (beginning in the elementary school), including instruction, tryout, exploration, choice, placement, and follow-up relative to occupations; leadership guidance; and leisure-time guidance. Jones also explicitly stated that it is necessary to distinguish between counseling and the other activities that the counselor does:

> This distinction is not a trivial one . . . Counselors are now so burdened with other work as to make it impossible to do counseling well. If we can focus the attention upon counseling as the center and core of the work, we shall do much to relieve the situation. (A. J. Jones, 1934, p. 273)

Today, professional school counselors sometimes struggle with similar role diffusion and overload. Focusing on the comprehensive and important work of Jones illustrates that many contemporary issues related to counseling versus guidance and the role of the professional school counselor have antecedents that have not yet been brought to closure. Support for and refinement of the techniques, the tools, and the philosophies of school counseling continued throughout the 1920s, 1930s, and 1940s. Space is not available here to analyze the continuing support for school counseling or the additional techniques made available to the counselor through these three decades. Suffice it to say that during the 1920s, concerns about the dignity and rights of children flourished, as did concerns for greater emphasis on mental hygiene in the schools in which professional school counselors would be important players. In 1926, New York became the first state to require certification for guidance workers and, in 1929, the first state to have full-time guidance personnel in the State Department of Education, providing leadership to school systems for the integration of professional school counselors in schools.

Given the growing deterioration of the national economy, the need to certify and train people in school counseling was overshadowed by the need for the techniques and processes associated with vocational guidance counseling. These included the creation, during the Great Depression of the 1930s, of a national occupational classification system, which resulted in the 1939 publication of the first edition of the *Dictionary of Occupational Titles* by the U.S. Department of Labor, and establishment, in 1940, of the U.S. Bureau of Labor Statistics. In 1933, the Wagner-Peyser Act established the U.S. Employment Service, and several laws enacted during the 1930s provided fiscal support for vocational guidance activities. In 1938, a Guidance and Personnel Branch was created in the Division of Vocational Education in the U.S. Office of Education. This unit continued until 1952 as the only federal office dealing with guidance in the schools, but restricting the federal emphasis to vocational guidance. The major issues of technological unemployment during the Great Depression tended to focus on vocational guidance as a placement activity, causing some debate about whether school counselors or vocational educators should undertake the vocational guidance activities funded by the federal government.

The 1940s were a period in which the utilization of testing grew dramatically in response to the armed forces' need for worker classification as World War II ensued and, later, as veterans returned to society and were provided guidance services through schools, colleges, and community agencies. The *Occupational Outlook Handbook* was first published by the U.S. Bureau of Labor Statistics in 1948 (U.S. Department of Labor, 1949). During this period, federal support continued for vocational guidance and counseling in schools in support of vocational education.

In 1942, Carl Rogers published *Counseling and Psychotherapy*, which defined the counseling process as that concerned with other than traditional medical models, disease entities, and psychoanalytic approaches in which the counselor was a directive authority. Rogers's book heralded the beginning of client-centered counseling in which the counselor and client were seen as collaborators. Such perspectives were incorporated into the expansion of guidance techniques and increasing eclectic models of what school counseling might be.

SCHOOL COUNSELING COMES INTO ITS OWN: THE 1950s AND 1960s

In a sense, all of the important strides made in support of counseling and guidance in schools during the first 50 years of the 20th century were a prelude to the major events of the 1950s and 1960s. These were the watershed years of legislation and professional development that essentially defined the importance of school counseling for the remaining decades of the 20th century.

Until the 1950s, there were relatively few school counselors across the United States; the opportunities for the professional preparation of school counselors were relatively limited; the advocacy for professional school counselors by professional organizations was not systematic; and the legislative support for school counseling, other than for vocational guidance, was largely nonexistent. All of these conditions changed in the 1950s and 1960s.

Among the extraordinarily important indicators of support for school counseling in the 1950s was the founding of the American School Counselor Association (ASCA) in 1952 and its becoming, in 1953, a division of the American Personnel and Guidance Association (APGA), formed in 1952 from the merger of the National Vocational Guidance Association, the American College Personnel Association, the National Association of Guidance Supervisors and Counselor Trainers, and the Student Personnel Association for Teacher Education.

It is important to note that the perspectives that the founding organizations brought to the creation of the APGA shaped for the ensuing several decades the language and the emphases within which professional school counselors were evolving. For example, the term *guidance*, not *counseling*, was the accepted term for all that counselors did (Sweeney, 2001)—school counselors were often called guidance counselors in the decades immediately before and after the founding of APGA. Frequently, what professional school counselors did was called personnel work. The term *guidance* was widely viewed as conveying the notion that the professional school counselor was primarily involved in a directive form of advice giving to the students. Personnel work suggested that the professional school counselor was engaged primarily in administrative tasks related to maintaining student records about their schedules and progress. While these terms lost favor by the early 1980s, their residual effects were to distort the images of professional school counselors. Indeed, one could argue that many, if not most, of the members of the four founding organizations were themselves administrators, not counselors. For example, to this day, the American College Personnel Association is composed primarily of deans of students and related administrative personnel. The same was true of the Student Personnel Association for Teacher Education before it was renamed and significantly changed in purpose in 1974, when it became the Association for Humanistic Education and Development, and again in 1999, when it changed its name to the Counseling Association for Humanistic Education and Development (C-AHEAD).

Nevertheless, this federation of professional organizations speaking for counseling in K–12 schools, in institutions of higher education, and in workplaces gave credibility to and advocated for standards, ethical guidelines, and training for professional counselors working with various populations and in various settings. In 1953, *School Counselor* was created as the professional journal of the ASCA. Also in 1953, the Pupil Personnel Services Organization of the Division of State and Local School Systems was created in the U.S. Office of Education, a move that significantly broadened the view of school counseling as more than vocational guidance.

In 1957, the APGA created the American Board for Professional Standards in Vocational Guidance. In 1959, the National Association of Guidance Supervisors and Counselor Trainers undertook a five-year project designed to build a set of standards for education in the preparation of secondary school counselors.

In 1959, James B. Conant, the former president of Harvard, wrote *The American High School Today*, an influential analysis of the need for strengthened secondary school education. In the book, Conant argued for 1 full-time counselor (or guidance officer) for every 250 to 300 pupils in each American high school, a criterion that has been used frequently, even though such a ratio of school counselors to students has rarely been met at the elementary or middle school level.

The National Defense Education Act, 1958–1968

By the 1930s, nearly every city of 50,000 or more inhabitants had some formal guidance work in the schools and professional school counselors employed to carry it out. Courses to train professional school counselors had been developed and were being offered in several universities (e.g., Harvard University; Teachers College, Columbia University; the University of Pennsylvania; Stanford University), and textbooks were being written to identify the techniques by and assumptions on which such work could be undertaken (A. J. Jones, 1930). Guidance work in the schools continued to grow, and the number of professional school counselors multiplied through the 1940s and 1950s. But the major stimulus to the education and implementation of school counseling clearly was the National Defense Education Act (NDEA) of 1958 (Herr, 1979).

Although not often considered in this vein, the NDEA, like the legislation on vocational education and vocational guidance that preceded it, identified professional school counselors as sociopolitical instruments to achieve national goals. In the case of the NDEA, professional school counselors became indirect participants in the Cold War between the United States and the Soviet Union. To be more specific, in 1957, the Soviet Union launched *Sputnik I*, the first human-made object to orbit the earth. As a result, although the United States was close to launching its own space vehicle, the Soviet launch precipitated a major national outpouring of news articles suggesting that the United States had lost the space race; that our science and engineering capabilities were inferior to those of the Russians; and that, once again, American schools had failed to produce students whose scientific and mathematical skills were competitive with those of students in the Soviet Union. The NDEA was the result. Passed by the U.S. Congress in 1958, the NDEA required states to submit plans of how they would test secondary school students so that academically talented students could be identified and encouraged to study the "hard sciences" in high school and go on to higher education, emphasizing courses of study in the sciences, engineering, and mathematics. These legislative goals were not altruistic or concerned with the self-actualization of students. They were designed to increase the scientific capacity of the United States as it competed in the Cold War.

Central to the provisions of the NDEA were the training of large numbers of secondary professional school counselors and their placement in schools primarily to test students, to identify those capable of entering higher education in the sciences, and to encourage them to do so. Title V of the NDEA provided funds for school systems to hire and provide resources (e.g., tests, occupational and educational materials) to secondary professional school counselors and to reeducate existing secondary school counselors, as well as funds for universities to prepare professional school counselors in full-time, year-long guidance and counseling institutes or to offer more specialized programs (e.g., precollege guidance) in summer guidance and counseling institutes. The 1964 amendments to the NDEA emphasized guidance and counseling for all students, giving impetus to elementary professional school counseling and to counseling in technical institutes and other nonbaccalaureate postsecondary educational institutions.

It is not possible to discuss all of the effects of the NDEA, but there are several obvious results. With the full force of federal legislation behind the preparation and employment of secondary professional school counselors, the number of these counselors and the high schools employing them exploded. So did the number of colleges and universities providing preparation programs. Literature on professional school counseling became more comprehensive, as did the state certification requirements for counselors. The programs were transformed from simply taking courses on a piecemeal basis until one had completed what was needed for certification to full-time, more systematic and integrated curricula, usually leading to a master's degree. Certainly, many more students in the United States were being served by professional school counselors in the 1960s and beyond than ever before; some state departments of education mandated that schools maintain specific counselor-to-student ratios to receive state funding. As the large amounts of federal support ended in the late 1960s, professional school counselors had become embedded in schools and were engaged in initiatives that went beyond the expectations of the NDEA. Even though the responsibility for funding school guidance and counseling programs shifted from the federal government to local school districts, by the end of the 1960s professional school counselors were vital participants in achieving the multiple missions of schools (e.g., dropout prevention, academic scheduling, educational and career guidance, crisis intervention).

The Great Society Legislation of the 1960s

As the impact of the NDEA legislation unfolded during the late 1950s and throughout the 1960s, other major legislation was developed to address the Civil Rights Movement, the beginnings of technological impact on the occupational structure, rising unemployment, poverty, and other social ills. In many of these legislative acts, education was viewed as the instrument to restructure society, and again, professional school counselors were supported. For example, the Elementary and Secondary Education Act (ESEA) of 1965 designated funds for guidance and counseling. The 1969 amendments to the ESEA combined funds from the NDEA's Title V-B with funds from the ESEA's Title III into one appropriation for guidance. The Vocational Education Act Amendments of 1968 advocated for career guidance programs; responses to people who were disadvantaged and people with disabilities; and the expansion of a broadened concept of guidance and counseling, including its extension into the elementary schools. These pieces of legislation stimulated a large number of national and state conferences on guidance and counseling and innovative projects in career guidance, counseling, and placement.

THE YEARS OF CONSOLIDATION AND REFINEMENT: THE 1970s AND BEYOND

The outpouring of federal legislation that specifically focused on guidance and counseling in the schools essentially reached its zenith in the 1960s. However, there were important legislative initiatives in the 1970s, 1980s, and 1990s and into the first decade of the third millennium. Much of the legislation in the 1970s focused on vocational education and career education. For example, career education was seen as a school reform initiative as it developed in the early 1970s and as it was reflected in the Career Education Incentive Act of 1976. Career education indirectly institutionalized career guidance in schools and infused its concepts and experiences as part of the teaching and learning process. The educational amendments—the ESEA—of 1976 included major support for guidance and counseling in schools, a major emphasis on vocational guidance in schools, and the implementation of an administrative unit in the U.S. Office of Education. The purpose of this administrative unit was to coordinate legislative efforts in the Congress on behalf of guidance and counseling and to serve in a consultative capacity with the U.S. Commissioner of Education about the status and needs of guidance and counseling in the nation's schools.

During this period, a large amount of theory building took place, leading to the development of materials on decision making, career education, drug abuse prevention, and self-development, which became available for specialists in guidance and counseling. Fears of economic crisis and concerns about widespread unemployment among youth continued to spur development of career guidance initiatives. The impact of the Civil Rights and Women's Liberation Movements, as well as legislation effectively mainstreaming all special education students, refocused the attention of professional school counselors to diversity in schools and the needs of special populations for guidance and counseling.

Multicultural Diversity

It is important to note that beginning in the 1960s, federal legislation and state and local educational initiatives began to incorporate responses to multicultural diversity in the schools. The civil rights legislation had essentially banned segregated schools and caused municipalities throughout much of the United States to embark on policies and tactics by which to integrate African-American children into schools with White children. Such policies struck down notions of "separate but equal schools" and expected that children of all ethnic and racial backgrounds would be in the same classrooms and courses, on the same athletic teams, in the same musical groups, and at the same social events. Children of different racial backgrounds and genders and those having other special characteristics could no longer be the target of discrimination or segregation.

Schools and communities used many methods to integrate schools. The busing of children from one part of town to another or from one town to another to change the demographic mix of students in a particular school was a frequently used method. In many schools, professional school counselors were given responsibility to develop plans of action and to work with culturally diverse groups of students in classrooms, in group counseling, and in other settings to help them to learn more about each other, to air their fears and concerns about integration, and to learn to respect each other and reduce conflict.

Part of the problem at the time was a lack of attention to issues of cultural diversity in counseling theory and counseling practice. A major challenge to counseling processes in a culturally diverse world was that for most of its history in the United States, counseling, in both its assumptions and its techniques had ignored cultural differences or treated them as unimportant (L. A. Clark, 1987). Theories of counseling did not acknowledge the cultural distinctiveness of most people in the United States or the racial and ethnic traditions that shaped their behavior and affected their approaches to learning and decision making (Herr, 1998). Too often, culturally different students were treated as deficient, inferior, or abnormal, rather than as distinct in their socialization. In response to such inappropriate behavior toward cultural differences, Vontress (1970), among others, talked about the issues involved when White counselors counseled African-American students, how cultural differences affect the establishment of rapport between counselors and students, and the fact that "sensitivity to issues of racial and ethnic diversity must be factored in as an important variable in counseling theory, practice, and research" (C. C. Lee, 2001b, p. 581).

During the ensuing decades, growing attention has been directed to embedding scholarship about ethnic and racial differences into counseling theory and practice. Such perspectives do not embrace deficit models; rather, they provide affirmations of the worldviews of different cultural groups and the implications of these for counseling process. Virtually all counselor education programs now have one or more courses, practicum experiences, or other methods by which to prepare professional school counselors to work effectively and sensitively in a culturally diverse world. Professional school counselor training now includes studies of how appraisal, ethics, interventions, and counseling competencies/standards are affected by cultural diversity (Sue, Arredondo, & McDavis, 1992). The refinement and application of these perspectives will be a constant presence in the training of professional school counselors throughout the 21st century.

VOICES FROM THE FIELD 2.1   **SERVING A DIVERSE AND CHANGING STUDENT POPULATION**

Today's world is growing ever smaller, thanks to modern advances in technology. But it is also growing smaller because of the diversity that continues to add to the depth of our communities and bring types of people who rarely interacted previously into the same sphere. In my experience at a suburban Baltimore public high school, the importance of keeping up with cultural changes and the growth that is occurring is critical to our field. Those cultural changes are not only ethnic or racial group changes, but also socioeconomic differences and family structure, among others. As professional school counselors, it is imperative that we understand our stakeholders and the perspectives from which they are coming in the best ways that we can in order to understand how to help them most effectively.

When a school's demographics begin to change, many structural implications need to be considered. For example, my school has a rising need for interpreters and for persons who can translate documents into different languages. In order to most effectively communicate with some students and many parents, we need to do so in their native language. There are many complex and detailed educational issues of which parents/guardians and students need to be aware. It is particularly challenging to tell a parent/guardian about a student's academic difficulties or behavioral concerns if the parent/guardian is better versed in a different academic structure or has different expectations of the school's role compared to the parent's role and, on top of that, speaks a different language. It may not be necessary to know the details of other countries' school structures, but it is essential to keep in mind that a family may have very different expectations of your role as a professional school counselor than you do.

Socioeconomic changes within a school's population also require sensitivity and continued growth on the part of professional school counselors. If a school becomes less affluent, new issues such as residency concerns, homelessness, and the need for students to have jobs are important for counselors to keep in mind. If a community becomes more affluent, other issues, like access to cars, drugs, and career opportunities or connections, need to be considered. All of these issues affect our students in unique ways, but if counselors do not learn about the community being served, students and families may not receive needed services.

Changing family structure is another factor that must be taken into consideration by counselors. Today, family structures are diverse—and often different from the "one mother, one father" model. In many instances,

(Continued)

counties or districts have policies about which parents have access to student records and who is able to make educational decisions, so professional school counselors need to be aware of the changes students' families undergo. Counselors must also be sensitive to those differences and learn about how those changes affect the students.

It is critical for professional school counselors to be aware of diverse student characteristics so adjustments can be made in our buildings to best serve students. Cultural proficiency requires that counselors *not* treat everyone exactly the same and *not* be blind to the differences or the changes. Instead, cultural proficiency requires professional school counselors to be aware of and sensitive to changes and differences while working to always serve students and their families in ways that will be most beneficial.

Source: Kami Wagner, Professional School Counselor, Mt. Hebron High School, Howard County Public School System, Maryland

The Latter Decades of the 20th Century

During the 1980s and into the 1990s, much of the legislative activity in the nation did not directly address school counseling; it focused on the need for professional school counselors to deal with issues such as child abuse, drug abuse prevention, and dropout prevention. Legislation supporting career guidance continued under new guises as well. Among the major legislation defining school guidance and counseling, with a primary emphasis on career guidance, was the Carl D. Perkins Vocational Education Act of 1984, the Carl D. Perkins Vocational and Applied Technology Act of 1990, and the subsequent amendments to these acts. These were the major federal sources of funding for guidance and counseling in the schools through the 1980s and early 1990s. In 1994, Congress passed the School to Work Opportunities Act, which reinforced the importance of career guidance and counseling as students contemplate their transition from school to employment. Throughout the 1980s and 1990s, the National Occupational Information Coordinating Committee (NOICC), created by congressional legislation as a joint effort of the U.S. Departments of Education, Defense, and Labor, provided career development and guidance program information and resources to elementary, middle, and secondary schools. Unfortunately, the NOICC was disbanded in 2000.

However, in 2003, the National Career Development Guidelines Project was commissioned by the U.S. Department of Education's Office of Vocational and Adult Education. By 2005, the Guidelines Revision Project had reconceived the original NOICC Career Development Guidelines, aligned them with the goals of the No Child Left Behind Act (NCLB), and created a website by which information on the new guidelines; learning activities; and strategies for K–12 students, teachers, counselors, parents, and administrators and the business community could be delivered.

In 1995, the Elementary School Counseling Demonstration Act, which was expanded and reauthorized in 1999, represented the first major legislative departure in more than a decade from the emphasis on career guidance and related topics. This legislation, providing $20 million, assisted schools in making counseling services more accessible and in creating a more positive ratio of professional school counselors to students. Given the reduction of direct support for school counseling during the 1980s and 1990s at the state and national levels, the current statistics indicate that, rather than a ratio of 1 counselor to every 250 students, as recommended by the American Counseling Association (ACA) and the American School Counselor Association (ASCA), in 2006 the ratio across the United States averaged 1 professional school counselor to every 561 students. The state with the lowest counselor-to-student ratio was Wyoming (1:212), while the highest ratio was in California, where there is 1 professional school counselor per 920 students (ACA, 2009). There were, however, some hopeful signs that more professional school counselors and innovative counseling programs were developing.

For example, by the beginning of the 21st century, the Elementary School Counseling Demonstration Act had been expanded to include secondary schools and the word *Demonstration* was dropped. The Elementary and Secondary School Counseling Program is a discretionary program administered by the U.S. Department of Education to provide competitive grants to school districts that demonstrate the greatest need for new or additional counseling services or the greatest potential for replication or dissemination or that propose the most innovative program. For fiscal year 2004, some $33.8 million in federal funds were expended to meet the goals of the act. The more wide-ranging affirmation of the need for professional school counselors is embedded in NCLB, signed into law in January 2002. This comprehensive legislation requires that states adopt a specific approach to testing and accountability to lead to higher achievement for all children, take direct action to improve poorly performing schools, raise the qualifications of teachers, and make many other changes in schools to make them accountable for student achievement. The need for and support of school counseling is evident in many parts of the legislation relating to dropout prevention, career counseling, drug and alcohol counseling, safe and drug-free schools, facilitation of the transition of students from correctional institutions back to community schools, identification of and services for gifted and talented students, and children who are neglected or delinquent or otherwise at risk of academic and social failure. These many legislative actions suggest the importance of counseling as a process that complements and is integral to the success of instructional methods and goals and, as such, allows, if not encourages, school districts to have professional school counselors engage in many complex tasks. A time line of significant events in the history of school counseling is provided in Table 2.1.

TABLE 2.1   A School Counseling Historical Time Line

Year	Event
1895	George Merrill developed the first systemic guidance program in San Francisco.
1908	Jesse B. Davis organized a program of vocational and moral guidance in the schools of Grand Rapids, Michigan.
1908	Eli W. Weaver, a high school principal in Brooklyn, New York, authored *Choosing a Career*.
1908	Frank Parsons founded the Vocational Bureau of the Civic Services, a vocational counseling program that was soon expanded to schools in Boston.
1908	Clifford Beers, a former patient in a mental institution, wrote *A Mind That Found Itself*, which helped illuminate the plight of patients with mental disorders.
1909	Parsons's book *Choosing a Vocation* was published posthumously; it established the principles and methods counselors should follow to provide vocational guidance in schools.
1913	The National Vocational Guidance Association (NVGA) was founded at a meeting in Grand Rapids, Michigan. The NVGA became the first professional counseling organization and later became one of the four founding divisions of the American Counseling Association. Today, the NVGA is known as the National Career Development Association (NCDA).
1920s	This decade saw the rise of the student personnel, social work, children's rights, mental health, measurement, and Progressive Education movements.
1926	William Henry Burnham became a pioneering advocate for elementary school counseling by publishing *Great Teachers and Mental Health*.
1926	New York became the first state to require certification for guidance workers.
1929	New York became the first state to have full-time guidance personnel in the State Department of Education.
1930	Arthur J. Jones wrote *Principles of Guidance*.
1938	The Vocational Education Division in the U.S. Office of Education established the Guidance and Personnel Branch.
1939	The *Dictionary of Occupational Titles* (*DOT*) was published.
1942	Carl Rogers published *Counseling and Psychotherapy*.
1948	The *Occupational Outlook Handbook* was published by the U.S. Bureau of Labor Statistics.
1952	The American Personnel and Guidance Association (APGA) was established. Today, the APGA is known as the American Counseling Association (ACA).
1952	The American School Counseling Association (ASCA) was founded.
1953	The ASCA became the fifth division of APGA.
1953	The Pupil Personnel Services Organization was created in the U.S. Office of Education.
1953	*School Counselor* was created as the journal of the ASCA.
1957	The APGA created the American Board for Professional Standards in Vocational Guidance.
1957	The Soviet Union launched *Sputnik I*, the first human-made satellite to orbit the earth.
1958	The National Defense Education Act passed, expanding the training and hiring of school counselors.
1959	James B. Conant authored *The American High School Today*, suggesting a ratio of 1 school counselor for every 250–300 students.

(Continued)

TABLE 2.1   A School Counseling Historical Time Line (Continued)

Year	Event
1962	C. Gilbert Wrenn published *The Counselor in a Changing World*, which influenced the school counseling profession in the years to follow.
1964	NDEA Title A was passed, which extended counseling to elementary schools.
1976	The Career Education Act integrated career education into schools.
1988	Gysbers and Henderson published *Developing and Managing Your School Guidance Program*, which focused the profession on comprehensive, developmental school counseling programs.
1994	The School to Work Act was passed, reinforcing career guidance and counseling.
1995	The Elementary School Counseling Demonstration Act was passed to assist elementary schools in providing counseling services
1997	The ASCA published *The National Standards for School Counseling Programs*, providing benchmarks for school counseling programs to promote student competency in the academic, career, and personal/social domains
2002	The No Child Left Behind Act was signed into law.
2003	*The ASCA National Model: A Framework for School Counseling Programs* was published.
2005	The ASCA published the second edition of the *National Model* and focused on foundations, management system, delivery system, and accountability.

VOICES FROM THE FIELD 2.2   **MY 30-YEAR JOURNEY IN SCHOOL COUNSELING**

As a retired school counselor and current teacher of graduate school students in school counseling, I often look back at my 30-year journey in school counseling and try to find things of value to share with my students. In the mid-1970s, I started out in high school counseling. At that time, the main focus was on career exploration and crisis counseling and whatever else the administration of the school wanted counselors to pursue. I was ever so lucky to have supervisors in the counseling department that encouraged all their counselors to become part of counseling associations and to attend programs that would help in our professional growth. At the same time, various grants were pursued, so school counselors could get all types of resources for their schools. In the summer, counselors were encouraged to work on various curriculum writing projects that could be shared with other counselors from the county school system.

As I observed the school environment in which I worked, I realized that there were many needs of the students not being met by our current counseling program. I was given the opportunity by my principal and supervisor to visit other schools in other school districts in order to bring back ideas that might be usable at our site. After some of the counselors in the county heard about this experience, they also wanted to be a part of it. So began a different

type of professional development that proved beneficial to many schools and counselors. At the same time, many counselors were attending annual conferences and were bringing back ideas from other states and countries.

Society as a whole was changing during the 1980s, and more and more materials were being published on career activities, decision making, drug abuse, diversity, and, oh yes, accountability. We also saw a push from our administrations to be more precise in our child abuse reporting and to develop ways of charting dropouts and the prevention methods we were using. This, of course, brought about the question of what uniform evaluation methods we could use across the school system.

Workshops were developed in our county to produce a uniform school counseling program given to all students, while also addressing the diverse needs of students within schools. It was a wonderful time for counseling. Principals and staff were seeing how a sequential program in a school could elevate the level of learning for all students, while helping individual students to develop a plan that would make them more successful in everyday life. School counselors were given financial support in order to develop programs and to train students to help others in their school (e.g., peer facilitators).

During the 1990s, not only did the counseling profession change, but also the school administrative profession changed. This caused a paradigm shift in the counseling profession. In Maryland, more and more counties were embracing site-based management. This gave principals more power to direct the programs in their schools. School counselors then had to present their program to the principal and see how that program fit in with the school's mission. It was also the age in middle schools of "Teams!" This was very positive, in that the counselor was a part of the "Team" and therefore a major player in presenting counseling curriculum to a whole grade level. It initiated a collaborative environment with the staff of the schools that promoted counseling. In the high schools, however, counseling staffs often were more focused on counting credits, registering students, and completing other tasks that took them away from the classroom and other counseling-related programs.

When the ASCA's *National Standards* and *National Model* came to the forefront in the late 1990s and the first decade of 2000, principals began to look at their school's counseling program to see how it could become a program that could have a more detailed role in the achievement and success of all students. Again, across the nation, principals could see a more uniform method of delivering counseling objectives. Principals especially liked the data-driven methods of evaluation because they could use them in reports and put them in various aspects of the school program. Technological innovations helped show the impact of the counseling program. Principals also could see a yearly plan from their counselors that would allow principals to see how important counselor time was and to make a case for not assigning counselors to noncounseling duties.

Society is continually changing, and today professional school counselors are facing many challenges. Every year new administrators and counselors are coming into the schools, each with their own ideas and feelings about counseling. In our schools today, we have many different generations, each with its own perspectives on how school counseling should move forward. The following challenges are a few of the issues that should be looked at by our associations, advocates, and legislative representatives:

1. As economic difficulties arise, more and more pressure will be put on principals to determine what the staffing in a counseling program will be.
2. More and more, counselors will need to affect the "climate of the school" in a positive manner, showing the importance of the program.
3. New students going into counseling need to recognize the impact they can have and convey to students that the future is full of hope and possibilities.

As I look back on my experience in counseling, I see how far school counselors have come and how hard they must work to not slide back to where we were in the 1970s, given the frequent pendulum swings of educational changes. Professional school counselors and their programs have a great deal to offer a society in need of transformation and direction.

Source: Mary Keene, Retired Professional School Counselor, Baltimore County Public Schools, Maryland; Affiliate Professor, School Counseling Program, Loyola University Maryland

CONTINUING AND FUTURE ISSUES FOR THE SCHOOL COUNSELING PROFESSION

Space limitations prohibit a comprehensive analysis of all of the trends cited in each of the decades discussed. For example, the use of computers in guidance and counseling began in the 1960s, with the first computer-assisted career guidance system becoming operational in 1965. In 1964, the Association for Counselor Education and Supervision (ACES) published the *ACES Standards for Counselor Education in the Preparation of Secondary School Counselors,* the forerunner to standards developed by the Council for the Accreditation of Counseling and Related Educational Programs (CACREP). In the 1970s, pressure mounted for accountability in guidance and counseling. During the 1970s and 1980s, models were developed that envisioned school guidance and counseling as an integrated, planned, and systematic K–12 program, rather than a loosely connected set of services (Gysbers & Henderson, 2006; Herr, 2002; Lapan, 2001).

Such efforts were designed, among other reasons, to clarify the expected results or outcomes of guidance and counseling programs in the schools. To that end, in 1997, ASCA published *The National Standards for School Counseling Programs* (C. Campbell & Dahir, 1997). These standards argued that school counseling programs should facilitate three broad areas of student development: academic development, career development, and personal/social development. Within these three areas are nine standards, each of which includes a list of student competencies or desired learning outcomes that define the specific types of knowledge, attitudes, and skills students should obtain as a result of effective school counseling programs. Among their other purposes, the *National Standards* were intended to clarify appropriate and inappropriate aspects of the counselor role. The basic point was that the role of school counselors needs to be focused on addressing student needs, not performing noncounseling quasi-administrative tasks. Further, implementation of the *National Standards* and, more specifically, the three broad areas of student development—academic, career, and personal/social development—requires counselor competencies that are important assets in furthering student development and in achieving educational goals. These counselor competencies should not be ignored or misused if local programs are to be comprehensive, professional, and provided for all students (ASCA, 2005a).

In 2003, the ASCA published *The National Model for School Counseling Programs* to help professional school counselors implement the *National Standards* and focus school counseling programs on four primary areas: foundation, management system, delivery system, and accountability. The *National Model* was published in a second edition in 2005 and is expanded upon in far greater detail in Chapter 3. The *National Model* has served to focus both what goals professional school counselors across the United States accomplish and how they do so through systemic and comprehensive developmental programs.

In the quest for clarity, professionalism, and accountability of professional school counselors, in addition to the substantial program of content and delivery identified in the *National Standards* and *National Model,* the National Career Development Guidelines, briefly mentioned previously, have provided another source of program content and delivery, particularly for the career development segment of the ASCA's *National Standards.* The National Career Development Guidelines also address three broad areas of student development: personal/social development, educational achievement and lifelong learning, and career management. The three domains organize the content of the guidelines in 11 goals and in 3 learning stages: knowledge acquisition, application, and reflection (www.acrnetwork.org). These guideline domains, goals, indicators and learning stages can be the basis for a K–12 or K–adult career development program, its delivery, and its evaluation.

The school counseling profession continues to grow and develop through the daily efforts of tens of thousands of professional school counselors; professional counseling associations, such as the ASCA, ACA, and ACES; private, nonprofit organizational initiatives, such as the Education Trust and College Board: and governmental programs. But the school counseling profession is not without current and future issues and challenges.

In spite of the important contributions to the nation's schools and to its students made by professional school counselors, there continue to be basic issues that confront professional school counselors and school counseling programs. Some of these issues have been articulated by Paisley and Borders (1995), including the

> lack of control school counselors have over their day-to-day work activities. . . . [S]chool counselors, for example, are [often] directly accountable to school principals and the school system's director of school counseling. . . . These two . . . supervisors may have very different agendas about the counselor's role in the school. . . . There is a second fundamental issue [for school guidance and counseling], the ongoing confusion and controversy about the appropriate focus for its practitioners. . . . [T]he first [issue] concerns their role in the delivery of a comprehensive developmental program [although] despite its centrality to the profession . . . such a program has rarely been implemented; and the second philosophical role question . . . is "What is counseling in the schools?" . . . The distinction between counseling and therapy is never clear, and it often seems to have little relevance. (pp. 151–152)

Herr (1998) has suggested that the future role of professional school counselors is based on several pivotal concerns. Admittedly, different school counseling programs and the regulations of different state departments of education promote or require different approaches to address these issues. These concerns are presented in abridged form with added commentary.

1. *The degree to which school counseling programs are systematically planned; tailored to the priorities, demographics, and characteristics of a particular school district or building; and clearly defined in terms of the results to be achieved rather than the services to be offered.*

The ASCA (2005a) and, indeed, other blue-ribbon panels and national organizations have increasingly advocated for planned programs of school counseling. Such planned programs are intended to clarify the expected outcomes of such programs and how these outcomes will be achieved, to maximize the efficient use of resources committed to school counseling, to prevent or modify student risk factors and promote social and educational competence, and to provide a structure by which to assess whether professional programs of school counseling are meeting the goals assigned to them. The development of the *ASCA National Model* is a large step forward in addressing this and other issues.

> 2. *The degree to which school counseling programs [that] begin in the elementary school or in the secondary school [are] truly . . . longitudinal (K to 12) and systematically planned.*

For much of the latter part of the 20th century, as both secondary school counselors and, increasingly, elementary school counselors have been employed in schools, there has been support in the professional literature for longitudinal (i.e., vertically articulated) programs of school counseling. Essentially, the advocates of such approaches have argued that students at every educational level have concerns, problems, and environmental circumstances that affect their behavior and productivity in school. While the issues and tasks that students experience vary developmentally from kindergarten through grade 12, they are important at each developmental level and deserve the attention of professional school counselors and planned programs tailored to their needs.

> 3. *The degree to which school counseling programs are seen as responsible for the guidance of all students or for only some subpopulations of students, such as those at risk.*

A debate that has recurred throughout the history of professional school counseling has focused on whether school counseling programs should serve all students or only selected groups of students (e.g., potential dropouts, those in crisis, those who are disruptive and act out). This issue has to do with how best to use the limited number of professional school counselors and to maximize their positive effects on students. The subquestions focus on whether all students need the attention and support of professional school counselors and whether subgroups of students who would benefit most from such services can be identified. Among the underlying assumptions are that many students can get along effectively without the help of professional school counselors, that many students receive positive support and resources from their parents or other persons in their environment that replace the need for a professional school counselor, and that a school should direct its resources to those students who cannot get adequate guidance outside of school or who are most in need of such support.

> 4. *The degree to which school counseling programs include teachers, other mental health specialists, community resources, parent volunteers, and families as part of the delivery system.*

Because the ratio professional school counselors to students is so high (e.g., 1:500 or more) in many schools, it is necessary to broaden the network of persons who can augment the work of professional school counselors. Thus, in many schools, teachers, parents, and others are trained to perform specific functions (e.g., completing academic scheduling, coordinating a career resource center, helping students use educational and career resources, providing group guidance topics or workshops) that free professional school counselors to deal with student problems for which they, specifically among school employees, are qualified (e.g., individual counseling, group work). In such situations, professional school counselors coordinate, train, and support other persons who augment and extend the outreach of their functions.

> 5. *The degree to which school counseling programs are focused on precollege guidance and counseling; counseling in and for vocational education and the school-to-work transition; counseling for academic achievement; and counseling for students with special problems such as bereavement, substance abuse, antisocial behavior, eating disorders, and family difficulties (single parents, stepparents, blended family rivalries).*

The issue here is whether the school counseling program in a particular school offers a range of interventions that address the academic, career, and personal/social needs of all students or whether the program emphasis is on a restricted range of students or topics (e.g., college-bound students, students in crisis).

> 6. *The degree to which professional school counselors should be generalists or specialists; members of teams or independent practitioners; and proactive or reactive with regard to the needs of students, teachers, parents, and administrators.*

This issue has to do with how professional school counselors should be educated and how they should function in a school. Should they be trained to view children or adults in holistic terms and thus be prepared to deal with any type of problem they experience? Or should they be trained in a subspecialty (e.g., career, discipline, family, testing, substance abuse) and melded into a team of specialists who can combine to serve the needs of a particular individual? A further question is whether professional school counselors should be essentially passive and wait for students, parents, or teachers to come to them or be assertive in marketing their program and providing services, work-shops, and so forth in multiple and visible forms and potentially outside of counselors' offices.

7. *The degree to which professional school counselors employ psychoeducational models or guidance curricula as well as individual forms of intervention to achieve goals.*

As professional school counseling has evolved during the past 100 years, so has the range of techniques available for use. In addition, the knowledge bases that students need to acquire for purposes of self-understanding, educational and career planning, interpersonal effectiveness, conflict resolution, and decision making have expanded. The question is, Given pressures for efficiency and accountability, can such knowledge, and the associated attitudes and skills, be best conveyed to students by individual counseling? Or are these types of knowledge best conveyed through group work or a guidance curriculum (e.g., workshops, units in classrooms) that is likely to disseminate this information more evenly to all students?

8. *The degree to which the roles of professional school counselors can be sharpened and expanded while not holding counselors responsible for so many expectations that their effectiveness is diminished and the outcomes they affect are vague.*

Clearly, the role of professional school counselors is complex and comprehensive. The range of concerns and problems that professional school counselors are expected to address continues to grow as the dynamics of the larger society affect the readiness and behavior of students in schools. Thus, these questions must be addressed: What can counselors do best? For what outcomes should they be held accountable? How should their workload be balanced and to what end? Which current duties should be eliminated and which emphasized? How can the responsibilities of professional school counselors be made explicit and achievable?

9. *The degree to which professional school counselors have a reasonable student load, 250 or less, so that they can know these students as individuals and provide them personal attention.*

If one of the important aspects of professional school counselors' role is to help students personalize their education and make individual plans pertinent to their abilities, interests, and values, how is that best done when a professional school counselor is responsible for 400 to 1,000 students? Is the answer providing more group work; making more use of technology; shifting selected functions of

professional school counselors to other persons in the school or community, such as teachers, parents, or mental health specialists; limiting the responsibilities of professional school counselors to a specific and defined set of functions; or lowering the counselor-to-student ratio to the recommended 1:250?

One possible response, now lost in the history of professional school counseling, is the Carnegie Foundation for the Advancement of Teaching's book *High School: A Report on Secondary Education in America* (Boyer, 1983). This report was unequivocal in its support of guidance services and student counseling as critical needs in American high schools. According to the report's conclusions,

> The American high school must develop a more adequate system of student counseling. Specifically, we recommend that guidance services be significantly expanded; that no counselor should have a caseload of more than 100 students. Moreover, we recommend that school districts provide a referral service to community agencies for those students needing more frequent and sustained professional assistance. (Boyer, 1983, p. 306)

This very important, but long overlooked, recommendation has increased urgency in today's school environment, which is fraught with pressures for students and for those who teach and counsel them. It suggests that the needs of many students go beyond the capacity of the school to address and that there is a communitywide responsibility to coordinate and use all of the mental health resources available on behalf of the needs of the student population.

10. *The degree to which professional school counselors effectively communicate their goals and results to policy makers and the media both to clarify their contributions to the mission of the school and to enhance their visibility as effective, indeed vital, components of positive student development.*

This issue relates to how professional school counselors should use knowledge about what interventions work effectively, for which student problems, and under what conditions to help policy makers understand more fully their role. In this sense, professional school counselors must be spokespersons for their field, able to interpret their goals, their skills, and the added value they bring to positive student development and to the mission of the school.

VOICES FROM THE FIELD 2.3   A 30-YEAR PERSPECTIVE ON SCHOOL COUNSELING

In the early 1970s, when I completed my Masters of Education program in what was then "Guidance and Counseling" and entered the profession of "Guidance Counseling," my primary goal was "How do I get students who are upset to come see me?" The answer was "visibility, connections, and relationships." With that in mind, my first year as a "guidance counselor" began. I remained in my first school placement for eight years, during which time there was a growing awareness that simply providing responsive services to students who requested them was clearly not enough. In a school, one can see trends (e.g., developmental, seasonal, social, societal, economic, etc.) that can be addressed through a developmental and comprehensive plan of action. Therefore, after a couple of years, I began to assess the needs of the school community to ensure that I could deliver activities to all students that met those needs. This began to change my view of how to implement "guidance and counseling" in a school setting. Prevention became important in the delivery of services. Classroom guidance and group counseling took on new meanings as I began to see how a proactive approach could change the climate in a school.

Over the years, various models were constructed that answered the needs of professional school counselors who shared the vision that school counseling is for all students. These models included a data-driven, needs-based program, allowing a wide variety of delivery methods; the incorporation of counseling, coordination, and consultation; a focus on specific goals; and a system of accountability that gave school counselors the needed framework on which to build. I began to look at all of the day-to-day things in which I was involved and realized that all of these activities supported the three overall domains crafted by the ASCA (C. Campbell & Dahir, 1997). The ASCA's *National Model* (2005a) has provided a more organized structure and identified the professional school counselor as having an integral role in the achievement and success of all students.

This paradigm shift did not come without obstacles. Some of these challenges were as follows: (1) If schools are solely for student learning, how can a professional school counselor convince others that what they do has a direct impact on student achievement? (2) If a school counseling program is based on data and evaluated using data, what data should we be collecting, how are they tied to student achievement, and how can they be measured? (3) How can a school counseling program be marketed to principals and the public in order to ensure "our seat at the table" as a contributing, indispensable educator? None of these answers has come easily. There is a constant need to educate other professionals regarding the role of the professional school counselor. Other professionals continue to judge counselors based solely on *how many students they see, how many students went to college*, and the like. That professional school counselors contribute to students, staff, and the school climate is not easily observed—and not

easily measured. The barriers that school counselors remove to ensure students can learn often go unnoticed. Hence, marketing and accountability continue to be a need for professional school counselors, as they continue to make a difference in schools. It is difficult at times for school counseling interns to implement a comprehensive school counseling program, since often they work with only a limited percentage of the student population and their part-time schedule precludes daily follow-up. In such cases, I recommend that interns create a mini-program for a smaller group of students with whom they work. Often, it is easier to see the results of your efforts with that smaller group.

One of the programs that has strongly influenced my thinking as an educator and professional school counselor over the years is Positive Behavioral and Support Interventions (PBIS), a schoolwide behavior system based on the theory of response to intervention (RTI). It is an approach or framework for redesigning and establishing teaching and learning environments. RTI was designed primarily to address the academic needs of students with disabilities, but it is really an approach for addressing the behavioral needs of all students. Both RTI and PBIS offer a range of interventions that are systematically applied to students based on their demonstrated level of need and address the role of the environment as it applies to development and improvement of behavior problems. Both approaches implement their programs through a system of tiered interventions. This tiered-intervention approach has been extremely helpful to me as I implement a comprehensive school counseling program. Each approach delimits critical elements to be in place at each tier. There are three tiers:

- Tier 1, or the universal tier, includes programs and interventions that address *all* students;
- Tier 2, or the targeted tier, includes programs and interventions for students in smaller groups who have demonstrated the need for additional supports; and
- Tier 3, or the intensive tier, includes a more in-depth analysis of the data on and individual interventions for students who have not responded to tier 1 or tier 2.

This model also fits well as school counselors implement the ASCA *National Model*. The universal tier (tier 1) includes all of the activities and programs developed for all students. Prevention, psychoeducation, advisement, and coordination of programs are included in this tier. The targeted tier (tier 2) includes counseling and consultation for students who need additional supports. The intensive tier (tier 3) includes the coordination of wraparound services with other interventionists to meet the needs of students who require individual services in and outside of the school. A pictorial representation of the tiered approach is shown in Figure 2.1. I share this model because it has helped me to visualize my program around a graphic organizer and it reminds me daily that I need to be creating a plan that addresses all students and includes a differentiated approach for a variety of issues.

(Continued)

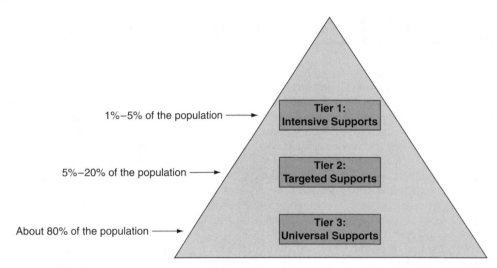

FIGURE 2.1 A model for understanding a professional school counselor's responsibilities to all students in a comprehensive school counseling program.

In summary, I consider the delivery of a school counseling program to be as much about a philosophy as about an approach. Once you begin to see how the school counseling program positively affects a school, you begin to recognize how indispensable a comprehensive, developmental school counseling program is in helping to fulfill the mission and vision of the school.

Source: Marcia Lathroum, School Counselor Specialist, Maryland State Department of Education; Affiliate Faculty, School Counseling Program, Loyola University Maryland

TRADITIONAL AND EMERGING PRACTICES

The work of the transformed professional school counselor is multifaceted and stems from several essential "realizations," which are discussed next. Following the realizations are 10 current and emerging practice areas that influence the implementation of school counseling services in various parts of the country. It is essential to note that, depending on the school community's needs and the skills of the professional school counselor, some of these "roles" may predominate in a given school or even at certain times of the school year. However, necessary boundaries must be in place to ensure that no single role predominates universally. A comprehensive, developmental school counseling program requires substantial attention to balance in order to meet the needs of *all* students.

Realizations Guiding the Transformation of the Professional School Counselor's Role

The first important realization is that, of all the education professionals, professional school counselors receive the most extensive specialized training in consultation and collaboration and in team and relationship building. It follows therefore that professional school counselors are among those most able and qualified not only to build collaborative relationships in order to fully implement a comprehensive, developmental school counseling program, but also to move school reform work and task groups in positive directions, leading to changes that will benefit all students. That is, professional school counselors are in an excellent position to facilitate systemic changes that will eliminate barriers to student academic, career, and personal/social success.

Over the past several decades, many professional school counselors and counselor educators have come to realize that the job descriptions and role responsibilities, coupled with the work and caseload realities, are overwhelming for all but the superhuman. Add to this the challenge professional school counselors face in taking a leadership role in school reform, and experienced professionals would justifiably throw up their hands.

This leads to the second realization: Professional school counselors can't do it all alone. Societal problems are creating developmental and clinical problems for children and youth in record numbers, and most citizens and stakeholders are expecting school personnel to effectively address these issues. Children are developing serious psychological problems at younger ages and in greater numbers; teachers are leaving the field in droves, and fewer college students are choosing teaching as a professional career; professional school counselor caseloads and workloads are expanding; and governments and citizens demand improved test scores in high-stakes testing programs. In addition, school violence is all too common, technology is changing rapidly, and the challenges stemming from an increasingly diverse student population are growing. How can one person, a professional school counselor, possibly do it all?

One person can't do it all—and shouldn't be expected to. For too long, the "lone ranger" attitude has pervaded the profession. In transforming the profession, counselors must look to resources beyond themselves: community agencies, local business partners, teachers, parents, grandparents, and, yes, even the students themselves, among many other possible partners. If school conflict and violence are increasing, professional school counselors can partner with students, teachers, and organizations to implement a teacher- or student-led developmental conflict resolution curriculum and peer mediation program, while also tapping community organizations to provide workshops on personal safety. If substance abuse is a problem, professional counselors can partner with community mental health and substance abuse professionals, teachers, parents, and students to implement a substance abuse curriculum taught by teachers. Counselors can run groups for students who abuse substances and for children of alcoholics and can harness the resources of local businesses and organizations such as the local Mothers Against Drunk Driving chapter to offer continuing programs to help parents and their children cope with substance abuse. If children's reading scores are below expectations, professional counselors can partner with community organizations, grandparents, parents, and educators to hold book drives to procure books for use by preschoolers and school-aged children; organize community "read-ins" at local bookstores or the school or public library; facilitate coordination of a parent and grandparent volunteer reading program; and even ask older students to volunteer some time before or after school to listen to and help a younger child read.

The common denominator is that someone has to take the initiative to get things started, and the professional school counselor has the systemic, collaborative, and human relationship skills to do it. Many traditional thinkers will reflexively argue that these are not the kinds of things that professional school counselors do—or should do. But think about it: Which of the partnering examples mentioned above does not fit perfectly into the goals of a comprehensive, developmental school counseling program? The key is that the examples describe different ways to achieve the goals, rather than having a professional school counselor counsel one child at a time or go into the classroom to teach

one or several guidance lessons on these topics. While these traditional interventions are effective in their own way, the partnering plans use the gifts and talents of many other people who are more than willing to help, if invited to do so.

The third realization guiding the transformation of the professional school counselor's role is that well-organized and well-run, comprehensive, developmental school counseling programs are greatly needed in today's schools and do work (see Chapter 4 for outcomes studies on school counselor interventions). Furthermore, if a professional school counselor fails to implement a comprehensive program in a school, no one else will. Establishing such a program must become the professional school counselor's top priority. Some schools lack a comprehensive program because of poorly trained and unmotivated counselors or counselors who believe their job is merely to put out fires, provide long-term individual therapy for a select group of students in need, or complete office work. When a counselor spends nearly all of his or her time providing one type of service, a comprehensive program does not exist. The exception is when a school has multiple professional school counselors engaging in specialties, but even in this case, professional school counselors expend a lot of effort integrating and coordinating their services in a comprehensive manner.

This leads to the fourth realization: All professional school counselors have strengths and weaknesses and therefore may provide services of varying levels of quality to varying populations. Thus, in many ways, specialization makes sense and is most efficient, but only if the remaining portions of a comprehensive, developmental school counseling program are provided by other qualified individuals. It is here that the argument recycles to the discussion of partnering, including other professional school counselors, school personnel, or community resources. For professional school counselors, the key is to know what they are good at and to specialize in those areas without upsetting the balance of the school counseling program. Counterbalancing is provided by counselor, school, and community collaboration.

The fifth and final realization is that many students are not getting what they need from our educational and mental health systems (Substance Abuse and Mental Health Services Administration [SAMHSA], 2008). Some professional school counselors view their role as something like "triage," which in medical terms means to sort, prioritize, or allocate the treatment of patients. Although this holds true in most instances, like it or not, professional school counselors will encounter many students for whom they are the last and only hope. This is why school counselor training is so broad and comprehensive and includes topics such as human and career development, counseling techniques and multicultural issues, appraisal, and special services. If counselors do not have the skills and knowledge to help those students, those students will likely not get help. This is also why professional school counselors need to become social advocates and members of their local, state, and national professional organizations. Oftentimes, working with an individual who has nowhere else to turn is like sticking a finger in the dike. A look to the left and right will often show other professionals using their fingers to plug a hole. By joining with other professional counselors in the same area, state, and nation and speaking with a united voice in advocating for the needs of students, professional school counselors are seeking solutions not only for the students they are working to help, but also for all students—those whom colleagues are seeking to serve and those who will seek help in the future. The counseling profession is based on the belief that all human beings have worth and dignity (ACA, 2005a). Professional school counselors seek to create systemic solutions for students who are oppressed and marginalized so that their paths of development will also lead to successful life opportunities.

Although many of the services provided by professional school counselors are well known and accepted, others are gaining wider acceptance in various parts of the country and world. The purpose of this book is to explore not only what professional school counselors *do*, but also what they *could do*. There are a number of important roles and practices that appear to have value to the transformation of school counseling. These 10 practices or initiatives will be reviewed briefly here and serve as a prelude to the chapters that follow.

The School Counselor as a Professional

By now, you have noticed the use of the term *professional school counselor*. This is the term preferred by the ASCA (ASCA, 1999a) and adopted by numerous counselor educators and professional school counselors around the world. It means something! Professional school counselors are first and foremost representatives of their profession. How one professional school counselor behaves, good or bad, reflects on all professional school counselors. School counseling literature is replete with articles emphasizing the importance of ethical, professional practice (e.g., Bodenhorn, 2006; Froeschle & Moyer, 2004; Guillot-Miller & Partin, 2003; Gysbers, Lapan, & Jones, 2000; L. S. Johnson, 2000; Lazovsky, 2008; Merlone, 2005; C. W. Mitchell & Rogers, 2003; Moyer & Sullivan, 2008; White-Kress, Drouhard, & Costin, 2006; Worsham, 2005).

Professional school counselors practice as professionals in three major ways. First, professional school counselors are aware of the history of guidance and counseling, as well as the pressing issues guiding future transformations. When one is trying to know where one is going, it is generally helpful to know where one has been. Second, professional school counselors use effective techniques and practices implemented through legal, ethical, and professional means.

Belonging to a profession requires one to adhere to the highest standards of that profession.

Third, professional school counselors maintain membership in professional organizations at the local, state, and national levels. At the national level, the ACA and the ASCA are the professional and political forces supporting the mission of professional school counselors. Each of these has branches or divisions in most states, and many local areas have affiliated chapters. All are ready to welcome professional school counselors and students-in-training into the profession, but it is the counselors' responsibility to join and support these efforts. It is estimated that almost 90% of doctors belong to the American Medical Association (AMA) and 70% of licensed psychologists join the American Psychological Association (APA). Each organization has a powerful political and professional voice. Less than 20% of eligible counselors belong to either the ACA or the ASCA. Until counselors develop an allegiance to the profession to a degree commensurate with that of psychologists and doctors, their political and professional voices will remain background noise. Being a professional school counselor means committing to the mission of the professional organizations. The money contributed annually to these organizations is small compared to the professional and political gains benefiting students and colleagues.

The Professional School Counselor as an Agent of Diversity and Multicultural Sensitivity

Referred to as the Fourth Wave, multicultural counseling and development is a strong influence on the counseling field today (e.g., J. R. Adams, Benshoff, & Harrington, 2007; Day-Vines & Day-Hairston, 2005; Day-Vines, Patton, & Baytops, 2003; Graham & Pulvino, 2000; Hijazi, Tatar, & Gati, 2004; Holcomb-McCoy, 2001, 2004, 2005; Holcomb-McCoy, Harris, Hines, & Johnston, 2008; Moore-Thomas & Day-Vines, 2008; J. A. Nelson, Bustamante, Wilson, & Onwuegbuzie, 2008; ParK–Taylor, Walsh, & Ventura, 2007; Rayle & Myers, 2004; Satcher & Leggett, 2007; Schwallie-Giddis, Anstrom, Sanchez, Sardi, & Granato, 2004; Shin, Daly, & Vera, 2007; Smith-Adcock, Daniels, Lee, Villalba, & Indelicato, 2006; Varjas et al., 2007; Villalba, Brunelli, Lewis, & Orfanedes, 2007; F. C. Williams & Butler, 2003; Yeh, 2001). With U.S. demographic projections estimating that the trend toward a more diverse U.S. population will continue for decades, the demographics of teachers and professional school counselors, who are mainly White and female, will most likely also shift. Regardless, current professional school counselors must retool, and future professional school counselors must enter the field prepared to address the developmental and counseling needs of a diverse student population. Although professional school counselors are, by and large, ahead of other education professional groups, the multicultural counseling movement is helping professional school counselors lead the way toward a more diverse, tolerant, and sensitive educational environment.Chapter 6 addresses this essential area of practice, and multicultural issues are infused throughout the other chapters of this book.

The Professional School Counselor as a Leader and Advocate for Academic and Social Justice

In some ways, this entire book is about preparing the professional school counselor to be an advocate for social justice, but Chapters 1, 6, 7, and 8 specifically address the issue. Professional school counselors have an ethical responsibility to help students minimize or eliminate barriers to educational performance and career and personal/social development. Sometimes these barriers and inequities exist in federal and state laws, regulations, and funding mechanisms; sometimes in the policies and procedures of local school systems; and sometimes in the hearts and minds of students, their parents, the community, and, yes, even teachers, administrators, and professional school counselors. Professional school counselors seek to address barriers and inequities, wherever they may exist, for the benefit of all. Fortunately, professional school counseling literature is beginning to give substantial attention to this emerging role (e.g., Amatea & West-Olatunji, 2007; Baggerly & Borkowski, 2004; Bemak & Chung, 2004, 2005; Britzman, 2005; Brooks-McNamara & Pedersen, 2006; J. E. Field & Baker, 2004; K. A. S. Howard & Solberg, 2006; Lambie, 2005; McCall-Perez, 2000; Miranda, Webb, Brigman, & Peluso, 2007; N. Mitchell, 2005; Ratts, DeKruyf, & Chen-Hayes, 2007; C. B. Stone, 2000; Trusty & Brown, 2005; Villalba, Akos, Keeter, & Ames, 2007). If a single student is oppressed and treated unfairly, no one in that society can claim equity.

The Professional School Counselor as a Developmental Classroom Guidance Specialist

Professional school counselors are aware of recent national (ASCA, 2005a), state, and local standards that guide implementation of a comprehensive, developmental school counseling program. They have specialized expertise in planning and evaluating comprehensive programs (e.g., Akos, Cockman, & Strickland, 2007; Brigman & Campbell, 2003; Britzman, 2005; D. Brown & Trusty, 2005a; Dahir, 2001; Fitch & Marshall, 2004; Foster, Young, & Hermann, 2005; Geltner & Clark, 2005; Gysbers, 2004; Gysbers & Henderson, 2001; Herr, 2001; Lapan, Gysbers, & Petroski, 2003; Lenhardt & Young, 2001; Nicholson & Pearson, 2003; Paisley, 2001; Rowley, Stroh, & Sink, 2005; Sink, 2005b;

Sink & Stroh, 2003; Sink & YilliK–Downer, 2001; S. L. Smith, Crutchfield, & Culbreth, 2001). Although many have not been teachers before entering the profession (Quarto, 1999), professional school counselors provide developmental educational and guidance instruction to classes and other large groups and prepare their lessons much as classroom teachers do. This means they write measurable objectives and plan interesting activities to meet the diverse learning needs of the students. Perhaps most important, professional school counselors must assess the effectiveness of their instruction and evaluate the outcomes of the comprehensive program (Lapan, 2001; Trevisan & Hubert, 2001). Chapters 3, 8, 9, and 13 address these issues in detail.

The Professional School Counselor as a Provider of Individual and Group Counseling Services

While it may come as no shock to hear that the professional school counselor will continue to provide specialized group and individual counseling in the schools, the nature of the problems that bring students to counseling today differs from in years past. Today, students are much more likely to need assistance with special issues, exhibit clinical symptoms, or show resistance, all requiring a different approach. The professional literature for school counselors is addressing these changes (e.g., Abrams, Theberge, & Karan, 2005; Arman & McNair, 2000; Auger, 2005; Bardick & Bernes, 2005; Cook & Kaffenberger, 2003; Erford, 1999; Eschenauer & Chen-Hayes, 2005; Gibbons & Goins, 2008; S. K. Johnson & Johnson, 2005; Kress, Gibson, & Reynolds, 2004; Lambie, 2004; Lambie & Sias, 2005; Moyer & Nelson, 2007; M. Oliver, Nelson, Cade, & Cueva, 2007; D. C. Ray, Armstrong, Warren, & Balkin, 2005; S. L. Ray, 2004; Rayle, 2005; Shillingford, Lambie, & Walter, 2007; Steen, Bauman, & Smith, 2007; Steen & Kaffenberger, 2007; Stout & Frame, 2004; Webb & Myrick, 2003).

Chapter 10 briefly reviews the developmental facets so essential to the implementation of individual counseling and group work within a comprehensive approach to school counseling. Chapter 16 focuses on what professional school counselors need to know about clinical disorders and psychopathology to help ensure their students get appropriate help. Some view professional school counselors of the future as serving in a school-based clinical role; undoubtedly, some professional school counselors are providing services to clinically diagnosed students already. Other school systems have hired licensed clinicians to provide counseling services (often receiving third-party reimbursement in the process), confining professional school counselors to those "noncounseling" functions of their role or, in a few instances, cutting school counseling positions altogether. While many professional school counselors, having received appropriate education, experience, and supervision, are licensed to provide clinical counseling services by state licensing boards, the practice of what some see as mental health counseling in the schools is likely to remain a professional issue receiving much attention and discussion.

The Professional School Counselor as a Career Development and Educational Planning Specialist

Many states now require that individual educational and career plans be developed for every high school student to serve as a guide for entering higher education or the workforce. School counseling claims career development as its roots, and many secondary professional school counselors become specialists in career and lifestyle development. The trend is for elementary, middle, and secondary school counselors to provide more emphasis in this area as well. Chapter 11 provides an overview of the important developmental issues requiring attention. School reform and accountability movements in the United States demand that professional school counselors focus on academic performance and achievement. This is commensurate with the *National Model for School Counseling Programs* (ASCA, 2005a) and the goals of a comprehensive developmental school counseling program (e.g., Auger, Blackhurst, & Wahl, 2005; Baggerly & Osborn, 2006; Barker & Satcher, 2000; Blackhurst, Auger, & Wahl, 2003; Carnevale & Desrochers, 2003; Dykeman et al., 2003; Feller, 2003; Gibbons, Borders, Wiles, Stephan, & Davis, 2006; Gibbons & Shoffner, 2004; Jarvis & Keeley, 2003; L. K. Jones, Sheffield, & Joyner, 2000; Kolodinsky et al., 2006; S. M. Lee, Daniels, Puig, Newgent, & Nam, 2008; Mosconi & Emmett, 2003; Niles, Erford, Hunt, & Watts, 1997; O'Shea & Harrington, 2003; Rosenbaum & Person, 2003; Tang, Pan, & Newmeyer, 2008; Trusty & Niles, 2003; Trusty, Niles, & Carney, 2005; Turner et al., 2008; Wahl & Blackhurst, 2000).

The Professional School Counselor as a School and Community Agency Consultation/Collaboration Specialist

Chapter 12 addresses the basics of consultative/collaborative models used with individuals and organizations, as well as how to engage parents in the educational process. Consultation has long been a part of the professional school counselor's role, but collaboration makes the professional school counselor a more active and vested participant in the problem-solving process, whether working with individuals or organizations (Keys, 2000). Collaboration has been receiving considerable attention recently in school counseling literature (e.g., Amatea, Daniel, Bringman, & Vandiver, 2004; Bemak, 2000; C. Bradley, Johnson, Rawls, & Dodson-Sims, 2005; C. Brown, Dahlbeck, & Sparkman-Barnes, 2006; Bryan,

2005; Bryan & Holcomb-McCoy, 2004; K. M. Davis & Lambie, 2005; Dimmitt, 2003; Fusick & Bordeau, 2004; Giles, 2005; Kahn, 2000; Keys, 2000; N. Mitchell & Bryan, 2007; Palladino Schultheiss, 2005; Porter, Epp, & Bryant, 2000; Taylor & Adelman, 2000).

In the future, working hand in hand with parents will become more important to all education professionals because supportive parents are more likely to have successful students. For example, students who have at least one parent actively involved in their academic life are more likely to get high grades and less likely to get suspended. More than half of all Americans believe parents encounter circumstances when help is needed to raise their children. Interestingly, the parents are not viewed as irresponsible so much as overwhelmed at the time (U.S. Department of Education, 2008).

The Professional School Counselor as a School Reform and Accountability Expert

Another topic addressed throughout the book is the professional school counselor as an agent of school reform. School reform hinges on an understanding of what is and isn't working—a process called accountability. While Chapter 13 introduces the topics of needs assessment and program evaluation, Chapter 4 provides a synopsis of counseling and guidance outcomes research. Although one can take heart in knowing that there is validation for much of what professional school counselors do, what amazes many experienced counselors is the relative dearth of outcomes studies related to school counseling. For example, in comparison with other functions outlined in this book, outcomes assessment has traditionally received the least attention, although recent efforts are addressing this problem (e.g., Astramovich, Coker, & Hoskins, 2005; Bauman, 2006; Blacher, Murray-Ward, & Uellendahl, 2005; Brigman, 2006; Brott, 2006; D. Brown, Galassi, & Akos, 2004; D. Brown & Trusty, 2005a; Carey & Dimmitt, 2006; Carey, Dimmitt, Hatch, Lapan, & Whiston, 2008; Curcio, Mathai, & Roberts, 2003; Curry & Lambie, 2007; Eder & Whiston, 2006; Ekstrom, Elmore, Schafer, Trotter, & Webster, 2004; Eschenauer & Chen-Hayes, 2005; Farber, 2006; D. K. Hughes & James, 2001; Isaacs, 2003; S. K. Johnson & Johnson, 2003; McDougall & Smith, 2006; D. Miller, 2006; Myrick, 2003b; Poynton & Carey, 2006; Rowell, 2005, 2006; Sabella, 2006; Scarborough, 2005; Sink & Spencer, 2005, 2007; Sink & Stroh, 2006; Studer, Oberman, & Womack, 2006; Whiston & Aricak, 2008; Zinck & Littrell, 2000). This becomes another essential task for your generation of professional school counselors. Much more outcomes research and results evaluation of school counseling activities and services are greatly needed to determine the effectiveness of what is currently done and to lead the school counseling field in new directions.

The Professional School Counselor as a Safe Schools, Violence Prevention, At-Risk Specialist

Recent sensational news stories have created powerful "safe schools" and "at-risk" movements in the United States, and professional school counselors are positioned to play a pivotal role. In an equivalent fashion, the professional interest in school counseling literature has kept pace with societal interest (e.g., Arman, 2000; Auger, Seymour, & Roberts, 2004; Beale & Scott, 2001; Bernes & Bardick, 2007; Bryant & Milsom, 2005; Buckley, 2000; Canfield, Ballard, Osmon, & McCune, 2004; Cantrell, Parks-Savage, & Rehfuss, 2007; Carlson, 2003; Carney, 2008; Cole, Cornell, & Sheras, 2006; Cunningham & Singh Sandhu, 2000; Del Prete, 2000; Edwards & Mullis, 2003; Esters & Ledoux, 2001; Fein, Carlisle, & Isaacson, 2008; Flom & Hansen, 2006; Froeschle, Smith, & Ricard, 2007; Fryxell & Smit, 2000; Gibbons & Studer, 2008; Glasser, 2000a; Hall, 2006; Hanish & Guerra, 2000; Hazler & Carney, 2000; Hernandez & Seem, 2004; Jacobsen & Bauman, 2007; J. L. Johnson, Sparks et al., 2006; King, Price, Telljohann, & Wahl, 2000; Kruczek, Alexander, & Harris, 2005; Lambie, 2005; Lambie & Sias, 2005; S. M. Lee & Smith-Adcock, 2005; McAdams & Schmidt, 2007; McFarland & Dupuis, 2001; Minden, Henry, Tolan, & Gorman-Smith, 2000; Riley & McDaniel, 2000; Schaefer-Schiumo & Ginsberg, 2003; Suh & Satcher, 2005; Theberge & Karan, 2004; Vera, Shin, Montgomery, Mildner, & Speight, 2004; Watkins, Ellickson, Viana, & Hiromoto, 2006).

Chapter 14 addresses the professional school counselors' responsibility in counseling students at risk. It is hard to underestimate the importance of these components in the future of school counseling. Conflict and violence are prevalent in schools and society, and the developmental and intervention components of a comprehensive school counseling program can address these problems on multiple levels.

The Professional School Counselor as an Advocate for Students with Special Needs

Over five million students aged 6 to 21 years receive special education services in the public schools (U.S. Department of Education, 2005a). The movement known as inclusion has resulted in numerous students with significant emotional and learning problems being returned to the regular education classroom and being taught by regular teachers with little or no training to instruct children with special needs (Lockhart & Keys, 1998). Though the research has demonstrated neutral to positive outcomes for special

education students, the impact on regular education students and teachers is largely unknown.

Professional school counselors are often the designated (and sometimes lone) advocates for children with special needs and their parents in an intricate and often intimidating education bureaucracy. It follows that the more professional school counselors know about testing and special programs, including special education and the requirements of Section 504 of the Rehabilitation Act, the more effective their advocacy will be (e.g., Assouline, Nicpon, & Huber, 2006; de Barona & Barona, 2006; Durodoye, Combes, & Bryant, 2004; Erford, 1995, 1996a, 1996b, 1997, 1998; Erford, Peyrot, & Siska, 1998; Frye, 2005; Gentry, 2006; Greene, 2006; Kaffenberger, 2006; Milsom, 2006; Milsom & Hartley, 2005; Milsom & Peterson, 2006; J. S. Peterson, 2006; Reis & Colbert, 2004; Scarborough & Gilbride, 2006; Taub, 2006; V. Thomas & Ray, 2006).

It is essential that professional school counselors know all there is to know about school system standardized testing programs, the child study process, special education eligibility procedures and planning, Section 504 eligibility procedures and modifications, and group and individual assessment procedures and interpretation strategies. Professional school counselors who know the laws, ethics, policies, procedures, and loopholes serve as effective advocates for students, families, and schools. Chapter 15, which focuses on special education, serves as a primer on this subject.

LIVING THE TRANSFORMED ROLE

The question becomes not whether the role of the professional school counselor will continue its transformation, but what shape this transformation will involve. This book focuses on the importance of a comprehensive program and some important areas of professional practice, each of which has a great deal to offer a school community. But for a professional school counselor alone in a school to focus on only one of these practice areas would result in an ineffective program, or at least a program that is not comprehensive and that will not address many needs. Likewise, professional school counselors who attempt to focus on all practice areas will probably become overwhelmed. No one can do it all. School counseling services involve a complex interplay of student and school community needs with counselor strengths. Balance is needed, and it is quite possible that a professional school counselor who is "unsuccessful" in one school venue can be very successful in another venue in need of his or her particular strengths and talents. Thus, the transformed role of the professional school counselor will be multifaceted, but flexible and practical.

It is helpful to think of the transformed role in terms of the confluence of rivers. When two or more rivers join, the resulting flow is dependent on a complex interplay of factors, including the volume of water (e.g., school, societal, and individual needs) and topographical features (e.g., services and resources). If the water volume of various rivers is heavy and the topography flat and featureless, a messy flood occurs! However, if the topography allows for channeling and measures of control such as deep collecting pools, which make for calm appearances, or even steep, narrow walls with a rocK–strewn path, which can lead to an appearance of controlled turbulence, the situation can be managed. In many ways, skilled, competent professional school counselors can make a huge difference in very important ways. Likewise, professional school counselors who partner with stakeholders to provide a pool of resources and services can often calm the flow or at least channel it in some positive directions. Either way, the needs of many students, parents, educators, and citizens will be addressed in a proactive manner.

Another helpful way of looking at this complex interplay is through the metaphor of nets of various sizes. A comprehensive, developmental school counseling program with its focus on large-group guidance and prevention-based programs is the first and highest net attempting to catch students and keep them on track developmentally. But as fate would have it, some students' needs are more serious and not necessarily developmental in nature, thus requiring intervention services. The next level of netting attempting to catch students in need may be group counseling with students or consultation or collaboration with parents and teachers. While many students are put back on track through effective implementation of these services, some require additional interventions (nets) that are more individualized. Individual counseling or referral to qualified mental health professionals when lack of time or skill requires it serves as that next level of netting. However, even after individualized services, some students will still be present with unmet needs. These students are the ones who in the past have been described as "falling through the cracks" and require a more systemic service delivery approach. This is where school-community-agency partnering and social and academic advocacy come in. These systemic interventions (nets) are essential to ensure that the needs of all children in our society are addressed.

ON BECOMING A PROFESSIONAL SCHOOL COUNSELOR: YOUR DESTINY

Among the many important components of a school counseling program and functions of the professional school counselor, the professionals authoring the chapters of this book have advocated for the development of data-driven and comprehensive developmental school counseling programs and the establishment of school-community partnerships. We have underscored the importance of social advocacy in removing systemic barriers to student academic performance and career and personal/social development. We have made clear that professional school counselors must attain and maintain a high degree of skill and competence in the various components of a comprehensive program to ensure that all students can succeed.

Transformations are visible at both surface and deeper levels. The lessons of this book will be wasted if readers simply make cosmetic changes to program and profession. The transformations advocated in this book cut to the core of our mission as educators and counselors, indeed to the very essence of why we wanted to become professional school counselors.

Most professional school counselors get into the profession because they love to work with children or adolescents, want to make an important difference in students' daily lives, and believe in the power of education as an equalizing social force. Welcome to a profession in which you can do all that and more! But before you begin that journey, take a moment to visualize, in your mind's eye, what you see yourself doing as a professional school counselor.

Many professional school counselors in training picture themselves counseling a student in a one-on-one setting or, perhaps, a small group of students. While this is certainly part of what a professional school counselor does, it is but a single facet. The professional school counselor provides a comprehensive school counseling program that is very broad and very deep—so broad and so deep that many counselor educators struggle to prepare professional school counselors who can "do it all." From a realistic perspective and as described earlier, this may not be possible for all counselors (or perhaps any). The job of the professional school counselor is complex and involves a complicated interplay of what the school community's needs are and the strengths and weaknesses of the individual counselor.

As you make your way through this book, try to picture yourself performing the described practices and implementing the suggested strategies. It is likely that your strengths and weaknesses as a counselor and learner, as well as your past life experiences, will make some practices feel natural, while others may feel uncomfortable. This is the normal developmental process of becoming a professional school counselor.

Please do enjoy your wondrous journey in becoming a professional school counselor and transforming the school counseling profession—a journey on which hundreds of thousands have preceded you, but which will be as distinct and fulfilling a path as you choose to make it. Enjoy the struggles. Serve the students, their families, your colleagues, and the community. But most of all, always remember in your heart why you wanted to become a professional school counselor!

Summary/Conclusion

Professional school counseling in the United States rests on a rich heritage of ideas, techniques, and implementation approaches. The profession has evolved in response to institutional changes such as immigration; national defense; social and school reform; economic circumstances, such as poverty and programs for the economically disadvantaged; the integration of culturally diverse students who had been previously segregated in some parts of the nation; and growing knowledge about student development—changes that have shaped concepts of education and the role of school counseling.

The historical roots that have spawned the need for counselors in schools and the future issues that remain to be fully resolved at the beginning of the 21st century suggest that the role of the professional school counselor is not a rigid and static set of functions. Rather, it is a role in a constant state of transformation in response to the changing demands on American schools and the factors and influences that affect the growth and development of America's children and youth.

Across the 100 years or so that make up the history of school counseling in the United States, the questions and issues have changed. However, there is no longer a question of whether professional school counseling will survive or whether it is relevant to the mission of the school. The questions today are how to make its contribution more explicit, how to distribute its effects more evenly across school and student groups, and how to deploy these precious professional resources in the most efficient and effective manner. These are the challenges that this generation of professional school counselors faces.

Activities

1. Interview a school social worker, school psychologist, or community-based mental health worker to find out what role his or her profession plays in student development.
2. Research a culture different from your own and brainstorm possible counseling issues someone from this culture may experience.
3. Talk to a professional school counselor or a school administrator to find out some of the noncounseling tasks counselors are often asked to perform in a school. Develop a plan of action to advocate for using counselor time for counseling and not for noncounseling-related tasks.

3

The ASCA National Model: Developing a Comprehensive, Developmental School Counseling Program

Bradley T. Erford

Editor's Introduction: A comprehensive, developmental school counseling program is an essential part of any K–12 educational program and has been effectively addressing developmental and prevention needs for several decades. It is responsible for supporting student educational performance and forms the foundation for career and personal/social development. The ASCA *National Standards* and *National Model* are reviewed in this chapter, as are practical program implementation issues, including other school personnel partners. A thorough understanding of a comprehensive, developmental school counseling program sets the stage for comprehending the role of the varied professional school counselor services presented in subsequent chapters.

THE ASCA *NATIONAL STANDARDS* AND *NATIONAL MODEL*

In 1997, the American School Counselor Association (ASCA) published *The National Standards for School Counseling Programs* (C. Campbell & Dahir, 1997) to provide a standardized basis for the creation of comprehensive, developmental, preventive school counseling services. The nine standards, three each in the domains of academic, career, and personal/social development, were accompanied by suggested student competencies (i.e., knowledge and skills to be acquired) and led to the development of comprehensive, developmental school counseling curricula by school systems around the country. The ASCA *National Standards* were a historical landmark that gave direction to a profession floundering for a unified identity and role in school reform. While the *National Standards* can be implemented through nearly any component of the school counseling program, many professional school counselors today implement much of this developmental model through developmental classroom guidance lessons, which are covered in depth in Chapter 9, and responsive services, covered in Chapter 10. For now, please peruse the ASCA *National Standards* provided in the executive summary of the ASCA National Model (www.ascanationalmodel.org) and become well acquainted with these domains, standards, and competencies. They likely will form the basis of your school counseling program whether you work in an elementary, middle, or high school.

Shortly after publication of the ASCA *National Standards* (C. Campbell & Dahir, 1997), leaders in the school counseling field realized that producing curricular standards and competencies was only the first step in transforming the school counseling profession. A developmental curriculum is essential to educating students and provides the "what," but it falls short of the "how." At the same time, the Education Trust's Transforming School Counseling Initiative was gaining steam in school counselor education and public school venues. This initiative emphasized systemic, data-driven services and programs to address achievement disparities, particularly between racial or socioeconomic subpopulations, as well as more specific attention to issues of social advocacy and justice (see Chapter 1). To expand on and integrate the ASCA *National Standards* into a comprehensive framework that addressed the "how" of school counseling, the ASCA (2003a) published *The ASCA National Model: A Framework for School Counseling Programs*, which is now in its second edition (ASCA, 2005a). This model focused professional school counselors on a more comprehensive, systemic approach to four core elements or mechanisms for student success—foundation, delivery, management, and accountability—and four infused themes—leadership, advocacy, systemic change, and collaboration and teaming. The *ASCA National Model* borrowed heavily from several existing and effective approaches (e.g., Gysbers & Henderson, 2006; Myrick, 2003b). In doing so, professional school counselors were encouraged to switch from the traditional focus on services for some select needy students to program-centered services for every student in the school and, by extension, their families and community.

THEMES OF THE *ASCA NATIONAL MODEL*

The *ASCA National Model* (2005a) encouraged professional school counselors to focus on local student needs and on the local political context and to use data to identify and meet these needs, as well as to document program effectiveness. It emphasized four important themes: leadership, advocacy, collaboration and teaming, and systemic change. *Leadership* describes the activities of professional school counselors within the school and beyond to enact systemwide changes to facilitate student success. Professional school counselors work diligently to ensure that all students have access to rigorous academic programs and to close achievement gaps among student groups, particularly minorities and the materially poor.

Advocacy involves the systematic identification of student needs and accompanying efforts to ensure that those needs are met. Professional school counselors help every student to achieve academic success by setting high expectations, providing needed support, and removing systemic barriers to success. Chapter 7 provides in-depth information on how professional school counselors can develop leadership and advocacy skills.

Collaboration and teaming require that professional school counselors work with a wide array of stakeholders within the school, school system, and community.

Collaborative efforts should focus on providing students access to rigorous academic programs and on other factors leading to academic success. Teaming with parents, educators, and community agencies to develop effective working relationships is critical to this goal. Chapter 12 addresses collaboration and consultation in depth.

Systemic change encompasses schoolwide changes in expectations, instructional practices, support services, and philosophy with the goal of raising achievement levels for all students. A focus on data-driven programming allows professional school counselors to identify areas in need of improvement, leading to alterations in systemic policies and procedures that empower students and lead to higher performance and greater opportunities for postsecondary success. Chapter 8 provides professional school counselors with a primer on creating systemic changes in schools. These four themes are woven throughout the *ASCA National Model* (2005a), but the heart of a comprehensive, developmental school counseling program is the four primary program components: program foundation, delivery system, management system, and accountability.

PROGRAM FOUNDATION

The *program foundation*, the "what" of a comprehensive school counseling program, makes clear what every student will know and be able to do and includes emphases on the school counseling program's beliefs and philosophies, mission, domains (i.e., academic, career, personal/social), standards, and competencies (ASCA, 2005a). These domains, standards, and competencies are amply described in the ASCA *National Standards* (C. Campbell & Dahir, 1997) and form the foundation of a comprehensive, developmental school counseling program.

Likewise, an important focus of Chapter 8 is the systemic changes reflected in a school system's and school counseling program's beliefs, philosophy, and mission. The school counseling program must be based upon a set of principles and beliefs that will direct the implementation of program components and services. Through collaboration and teamwork, professional school counselors help build a consensus among stakeholders as to the principles and beliefs that will guide the program. The purpose and vision of a program are established through development of a program mission statement, which aligns with the overall mission of the school system, as well as those of the individual schools. Again, these facets of program foundation will be expanded upon in Chapter 8.

IMPLEMENTING A COMPREHENSIVE, DEVELOPMENTAL SCHOOL COUNSELING PROGRAM AT THE ELEMENTARY SCHOOL

A comprehensive, developmental guidance program is the cornerstone of an effective school counseling program and includes delivering a school guidance curriculum, individual student planning and counseling services, responsive counseling services, and systems support services. The total guidance program must be able to show the results of that program, not just serve as a list of what I accomplish on a day-to-day basis. A comprehensive, developmental school counseling program allows me to be in touch with *each student* in each class at least every other week. In addition to allowing me time to teach the students specific concepts and skills identified by my school system, it allows students the opportunity to set a time to meet with me regarding any issues they may be experiencing. It allows me to be approachable and accessible to all students, parents, and staff members.

In my school system, the Elementary Guidance Essential Curriculum, which drives my classroom guidance program, was developed by current professional school counselors. Its purpose is to provide all students, K through 5, with the knowledge and skills appropriate to each grade's developmental level. The three domains identified by the ASCA—academic, personal/social, and career—are embedded in the curriculum. Beginning with kindergarten and continuing through fifth grade, identified ASCA competencies and concepts are scheduled to be taught at specific times in the school calendar based on the developmental assets (strengths) and abilities of students in each grade. Each grade level builds upon the previous grade level (vertical articulation) in terms of the concepts taught. For example, the personal safety topic taught in kindergarten is "Stranger Safety and Teasing." In first grade, the personal safety concept taught in September is "Teasing and Bullying"; then personal safety is revisited in April with the concept of "Good and Bad Secrets and Touches," when students are deemed to be more developmentally ready to handle this topic. In the fourth and fifth grades, personal safety concepts include "Internet Safety," "Sexual Harassment," "Peer Pressure," and "Child Sexual Abuse," all developmentally advanced, but appropriate concepts.

This continuum within each grade and across grades K–5 provides all students the content necessary to attain the knowledge, attitudes, and skills related to each ASCA domain in a systematic and systemic manner (meaning a child can move within our county and still be aligned with the next concept being taught in the classroom by the school counselor). Each professional school counselor then creates lessons based on the developmental levels within each class, allowing us to differentiate classroom guidance instruction much like classroom teachers differentiate content area instruction, while addressing students with special needs or learning disabilities and even the personality of the class and classroom teacher. If I need to revisit a particular concept or skill, I am able to do so. At the teacher or an administrator's request, I can develop a lesson to help that particular class with any concepts needing to be strengthened in order to prevent future problems or to address current concerns. Our school also has an annual, supplemental focus (e.g., Character Education, Habits of Mind, Keys to Success), which I am able to either embed into lessons that are part of the existing Elementary Guidance Essential Curriculum or include as part of my comprehensive, developmental guidance program. Finally, as part of the classroom guidance program, I must always assess the effectiveness of my lessons. I do this by consulting with teachers to see that overall student progress is noted. This service definitely allows me to get "the biggest bang for the buck" in terms of having face-to-face time with each student.

The two biggest challenges in delivering the Elementary Guidance Essential Curriculum are limited amounts of time and the need to keep parents informed of the concepts being taught in classroom guidance so that they can reinforce these skills at home. I insist on being part of the Cultural Arts schedule in that it *guarantees* me a scheduled time each week in each classroom. I request that classroom teachers remain in the classroom during my lesson so that they can supplement the lesson and so that, as teachable moments arise in the classroom, they can reflect back on my lesson with the class. I consider it a loose form of "co-teaching," but an effective one. In order to keep parents informed of the concepts being taught in classroom guidance, I include a brief description of the concept being covered with each grade level in our monthly school newsletter. I also purchased a stamp with my name and "Guidance Lesson" imprinted on it. Each paper I use as part of the classroom guidance lesson is imprinted with this stamp so that parents know that that particular paper was part of my lesson.

Individual student planning and counseling services assist students in establishing personal goals and developing future plans. At the beginning of each marking period, I issue a needs assessment to the teachers as a form of data collection on children and needs they may have. I usually know of students and their particular needs, but the needs assessment brings students to my attention whom I may not be aware of as having problems. At the elementary level, I meet with students struggling academically, behaviorally, or socially. Sometimes I meet with the students individually or with those students experiencing the same types of issues in a small group. We discuss the problems the students are experiencing and list ways they can work on the problems. Goals are set and revisited within an established time. With elementary-aged students, I find that putting problems, possible solutions, and goals on paper helps them to remember what they are to be working on and provides teachers and parents with information on what the students are working on. Contracts are often developed as a way to keep the students, the parents, and the teacher "in the loop" in terms of expectations and progress. Each time we meet, the worksheet or contract provides us a "talking point" on which to focus. Often, older students and I will review tests, benchmark assessments, and even state test scores to help establish the most meaningful goals for each particular student. In order for this service delivery model to be effective, the students and their progress must be monitored in a consistent manner, and communication with the teacher and the home is imperative.

Responsive counseling services include consulting with teachers, parents/guardians, other professional school staff (e.g., special educators, administrators), and community resource groups to identify ways to best help students and their families. Such services also include small-group counseling, where, again through a needs assessment and my knowledge of the student body, small groups are developed and services are delivered based on similar student needs. Each small group runs between six and eight weeks, once permission is obtained from the parent/guardian. I survey the teachers, parents, and students (if developmentally appropriate) to see which skills students in the small group would *benefit most* from acquiring. Small-group lessons are then developed based on this information and other skills I deem necessary. Small groups are run according to traditional group counseling methods. After the completion of the group, students self-assess, and teachers and parents/guardians are again surveyed to see if growth has taken place. I then reflect on what

went well with the group as a whole, what didn't work well, and what I would repeat again. This reflection piece is critical in moving forward with small-group counseling. Again, the challenge in delivering this service comes with scheduling. Whenever possible, I schedule groups during lunch so that students do not miss instruction or recess. I have also scheduled groups that deal with academic needs during reading instructional time as part of a three-group rotation.

Responsive counseling services also include crisis counseling as needed to provide staff and students and their families with support during emergencies. It may be short term or long term in nature and is based on the presented emergency. I also make referrals to outside agencies/resources as needed and follow up frequently with the person or family involved in the emergency. Referrals to other resources also fall into the responsive services delivery model for concerns such as depression, suicide ideation, academic difficulties, and other individual or family issues.

The final cornerstone of my comprehensive, developmental guidance program is systems support services. These include seeking ways to continue my personal professional development and growth through taking postgraduate classes, attending workshops/in-services, participating in professional learning communities, and being a member of professional associations (local and national). It also includes my providing staff and parents with up-to-date information and workshops on topics that are helpful to those two groups (based on a needs assessment distributed during fall parent–teacher conferences or administrative directive). Finally, systems support services include consulting, collaborating, and teaming with all stakeholders for the students in my school, including teachers, support staff members, parents/guardians, and outside community members and agencies.

Source: Kim K. Baicar, National Board Certified School Counselor, Broadneck Elementary School, Anne Arundel County Public Schools, Maryland

DELIVERY SYSTEM

The *delivery system* is the "how" of the comprehensive, developmental school counseling program. As professional school counselors implement their programs, they use delivery systems that include attention to the guidance curriculum (e.g., systematic, developmental classroom guidance lessons; parent workshops), individual student planning (i.e., assistance in establishing personal goals and future plans), responsive services (i.e., individual or small-group counseling, crisis response, consultation, peer facilitation, referrals), and systems support (i.e., program maintenance through professional development, systemic consultation/collaboration, management functions). These delivery systems are often called program components.

Program components provide methods of service delivery that operationalize program goals. Each program component can include direct and indirect services. *Direct services* are frequently targeted to students. Typical direct service activities are individual counseling, small-group counseling, and classroom guidance. *Indirect services* support direct services and are the foundation of a system-focused school counseling program. Typical indirect services include consultation, coordination, team building, leadership, and advocacy. This system focus puts into action the "new vision of school counseling" (see Chapter 1).

For effective service delivery of a comprehensive school counseling program, professional school counselors must possess the knowledge and skills to implement both the direct and the indirect services detailed for each program component. For example, group counseling is one method of service delivery within the responsive services program component. This service delivery method is frequently used to address recurring needs identified in individual sessions, needs assessments, and consultations with parents and/or teachers. Planning and implementing group counseling services requires a cadre of group leaders with knowledge and skills in such areas as teamwork, coordination, consultation, group skill building, and organizational skills. If any of these skills or knowledge bases is not developed, even the best-intended small-group counseling services might go awry. Therefore, in planning activities in each program component area, it is critical for professional school counselors to carefully inventory their knowledge and skills. Deficits in knowledge and skills are opportunities for professional development. In this way, service delivery within the comprehensive school counseling program reflects student needs and is not compromised by limited professional school counselor knowledge or skills.

Moreover, professional school counselor knowledge and skills development should not be limited to service delivery that is primarily counseling related, where the professional school counselor provides direct service to students. The professional school counselor needs to possess knowledge and skills even in areas where the primary service to students is indirect and focused on classroom and academic performance. Consultation with teachers on issues of curriculum development, classroom management, and classroom assessment is critical even though professional school counselors' primary role is not teaching in the classroom all day. The professional school counselor's knowledge and competence in these skill areas, applied through consultation services, delivers a direct service to teachers and an indirect service to students. This also broadens the school counselor's skill base to facilitate delivery of curriculum in both the classroom and other large-group settings.

Thus, within the framework of a comprehensive school counseling program various components provide multiple levels of service that build on and connect with each other. The professional school counselor is involved in both direct and indirect service activities that target the developmental needs of the school community.

Gysbers and Henderson's (2006) enumeration of comprehensive school counseling program components is widely used and consists of four program components: guidance curriculum, individual student planning, responsive services, and systems support. Each program component encompasses both direct and indirect service delivery.

The remainder of this section elaborates on these four program components as adopted by the *ASCA National Model*. For each program component, suggestions are shared on both "how to do it" (techniques/strategies for successful implementation) and "why do it" (expected benefits).

Guidance Curriculum

The guidance curriculum provides services to large groups. For example, classroom guidance consists of units on age-appropriate topics presented by either the professional school counselor or the classroom teacher in consultation with the professional school counselor. Each unit typically consists of multiple classroom lessons. Coordination and facilitation of peer helper programs may be related to the guidance curriculum, as may parent workshops.

Classroom guidance units are not independent; they may be linked to classroom guidance units at other grade levels and/or integrated into the school's core curriculum. Scope and sequence across grade levels is an important classroom guidance consideration. For example, self-esteem is a common classroom guidance unit. An effective, comprehensive school counseling program articulates self-esteem classroom lessons at various grade levels, increasing in cognitive and affective complexity in the upper grade levels. A self-esteem unit in one grade level builds and expands on the content presented at the previous grade level. Classroom guidance also includes activities specific to one grade level, such as senior-year events and transition orientation (e.g., for kindergarten students and incoming ninth-graders).

An advantage of classroom guidance is that it enables service delivery to a large number of individuals that addresses topics in a preventive manner. Many professional school counselors report that classroom guidance provides the opportunity to "get to know" students. This eases the transition when professional school counselors need to intervene for individual student issues. Developmental classroom guidance is reviewed in detail in Chapter 9.

Individual Student Planning

Individual student planning addresses the need for all students to plan and monitor their academic progress. Individual or small-group appraisal includes using test information and other student data to help to develop goals and plans. The comprehensive school counseling program offers an integrated and holistic method for students to assess and become knowledgeable about their abilities, interests, skills, and achievement. Test information is linked with other data to help students to develop immediate goals and plans (e.g., course selection), as well as long-range goals and plans (e.g., college, career).

During *individual advisement*, the professional school counselor helps students plan for and realize their goals. Students need direction in understanding, applying, and analyzing self-appraisal information in conjunction with social, career, and labor market information. This will help them plan for and realize their educational, career, and personal goals.

Responsive Services

Effective, comprehensive school counseling programs incorporate both direct and indirect services within the program component of *responsive services*. These services address both proactive and reactive goals. The methods of service delivery for responsive services are individual counseling, group counseling, consultation, referral, crisis response, and peer facilitation.

INDIVIDUAL COUNSELING Individual counseling sessions meet both proactive and reactive student needs. Given the complex and wide-ranging issues confronting students today, expertise in individual counseling is required, as is continuous updating of one's knowledge and skill repertoire through professional development. Some professional school counselors may overrely on individual counseling because it is often easier to provide, deliver, and/or schedule individual counseling sessions than various other interventions. This view may be shared by others in the school community, who assert that individual counseling is more sensitive to both the classroom routine and the overall school schedule.

The perspective on individual counseling promoted by the "new vision" of school counseling is that, if professional school counselors spend too much time with a few students, they will be perceived as "therapists" and probably shortchange most of the student body. Extensive time devoted to individual counseling means less time for services included in program components that can address common needs of a larger proportion of the student body. Professional school counselors need to effectively collaborate with community mental health professionals without engaging in the role of "therapist at school." A large proportion of a professional school counselor's day needs to be spent outside of or beyond the school counseling office. Individual counseling as an effective intervention is addressed in Chapter 10.

SMALL-GROUP COUNSELING Small-group activities respond both proactively and reactively to student needs (see Chapter 10). *Group counseling* and psychoeducational counseling services offer a variety of small-group experiences on relevant topics or issues such as study skills, effective relationships, bereavement, and postsecondary planning. Group counseling allows professional school counselors to address issues common to several students at one time, and comprehensive group counseling services can be offered throughout the academic year. This can help students perceive participating in group counseling as a "normal" or expected school experience.

Each group counseling activity consists of several sessions with a small group of students who explore their ideas, attitudes, feelings, and behaviors. Student insight and/or learning can come from group leaders, other group members, and/or the synergy of the group. Outcomes research studies document that small-group counseling frequently is effective, especially when focused on academic or personal development topics. Professional school counselors also conduct group counseling services for others in the school community, such as parenting groups or new teacher support groups. Because one group serves several individuals, group counseling is a time- and cost-efficient method of service delivery.

CONSULTATION *Consultation* is an indirect service in which professional school counselors collaborate with administrators, teachers, or parents to help them with student issues or concerns. Consultation is a cooperative process in which the professional school counselor (serving in the role of consultant) helps others in the school community to think through problems and to develop skills that make them more effective in working with students. Thus, consultation is a process of directly working with a second party (the consultee) to indirectly help a third party (the student).

When consulting with administrators, professional school counselors most typically discuss program or curriculum planning, academic or behavioral interventions for students, and school climate and work-related concerns. Common consultation activities with teachers include presenting in-service programs and working with an individual student's or a class's difficulties. When parents are the consultees, concerns about a student's academic, behavioral, or social development typically are shared. Assuming that professional school counselors cannot meet each and every one of the intense, complex counseling needs of students today, an effective consulting relationship with referral agency personnel is critical.

When serving as a consultant, professional school counselors need to follow all the steps of the consultation process: identify a purpose, establish a goal, plan strategies to meet that goal, and assign responsibilities to carry out that goal. No matter who is the target of the consultation, the goal of a consultation intervention is the same: Consultees will learn information and enhance skills that they can use to interact more effectively with others, especially with students.

REFERRAL   *Referral* enlists the services of other professionals to assist school counselors. Many students today are confronted with complex issues compounded by family, peer pressure, developmental, and societal situations; it is not practical for professional school counselors to be the sole service provider for these students. As a result, professional school counselors enlist the services of other school personnel (e.g., school psychologist, school nurse, school social worker) and/or community agency personnel to address some student issues.

CRISIS RESPONSE   *Crisis response* to critical and acute situations that require immediate intervention is an important counselor function. Crisis situations usually call for such immediate intervention because of their sudden onset. Crisis counseling interventions include individual counseling, group counseling, and/or the managing and coordinating of the services of others. The purpose of crisis response interventions is to diffuse a situation, serve school community members affected by the situation, and initiate a healing process. This may require direct services by the professional school counselor. However, professional school counselors may not be the only service providers in a crisis situation. Therefore, they may also need to coordinate the efforts of others.

Professional school counselors may lead or contribute to a committee review and update of the school's crisis response plan to ensure it is current and accurate. Many school administrators rely on the professional school counselor to annually lead a discussion on crisis situation roles and responsibilities among members of the school community.

In crisis situations, professional school counselors may also provide indirect services such as collaboration and referral. Often, crisis response also involves additional resources and individuals beyond the school counseling department staff.

PEER FACILITATION   Creating a peer helper program involves training students to use helping skills to assist other students. Professional school counselors provide leadership in the systematic training of peer helpers, which includes teaching them interpersonal skills and preparing them for helping roles. Peer helper programs extend services to more students and develop leadership skills among students. They also empower students to learn more about themselves and each other. Peer helper programs can be provided as part of the classroom curriculum or as an extracurricular activity.

Systems Support

Systems support provides ongoing support in the administration and management of the comprehensive school counseling program. Program management and operations involve planning and connecting the numerous initiatives of service delivery, as well as data analysis and "fair share" responsibilities. Community outreach and advisory boards become mechanisms for input to, feedback on, and evaluation of the comprehensive school counseling program's activities when sufficient information on the program is shared with them. Program management includes the tasks needed to support the program. Professional school counselors expand their knowledge and skills by participating in professional development.

For many systems support service delivery methods, the professional school counselor works with others to support and enhance interventions and program activities for students, rather than directly interacting with students. Systems support program elements emphasize the interconnectedness of systems that affect students' lives. Professional school counselors need to document systems support program components in order to ascertain "the actual benefit of cooperative ventures as they impact school-focused goals" (Bemak, 2000, p. 326).

PROGRAM MANAGEMENT AND OPERATIONS   Planning and administrative tasks support the activities of a comprehensive school counseling program. These may include securing and allocating resources, providing for staffing needs and training, and dealing with facility constraints. Coordination activities frequently draw upon the leadership and advocacy dimensions of the professional school counselor's role as counselors plan and coordinate numerous services and initiatives. Professional school counselors also serve as the liaison between the school and community agencies. Effective coordination in a comprehensive school counseling program requires interfacing with the entire school community.

Data analysis is a key facet of program management and involves analysis of student achievement data and school counseling program evaluations (see Chapter 13). Professional school counselors are particularly interested in identifying gaps in student achievement, sharing the data and information with colleagues, and developing individual and systemic interventions to address these needs. *"Fair share" responsibilities*, the final facet of program management, acknowledge that professional school counselors are full participants on the school's educational team and, as such, equitably participate in necessary responsibilities, even though these responsibilities may not be part of counselor training. For example, teachers and administrators often have "bus duty," so counselors should also contribute a fair share of their time to such activities.

PROFESSIONAL DEVELOPMENT   Ongoing *professional development* congruent with the needs of the school community is critical. Relevant skill development and knowledge updating prepare the professional school counselor to continuously facilitate the implementation of a comprehensive school counseling program. Professional development encompasses in-service training, postgraduate education, and membership in professional associations.

CONSULTATION, COLLABORATION, AND TEAMING

Collaboration and advocacy themes are frequently implemented through partnering with parents, educators, and community organizations, as well as through participating on school district committees, on community advisory councils, and in parent and community outreach activities. As mentioned above with regard to responsive services, consultation and collaboration with parents, teachers, and others support the school system mission by facilitating feedback on student, system, and community needs.

VOICES FROM THE FIELD 3.1	COUNSELING IN AN INDEPENDENT/PRIVATE SCHOOL

The presence of professional school counselors in private and independent schools is a relatively new phenomenon. With its roots in career and vocational assessment and placement, school counseling was once thought to be the realm of the public sector because the perception among educators at independent schools often is "all our students are going to college." While there is a longer tradition of college counseling in independent schools, counseling for personal/social issues in independent schools traditionally was more often left to coaches, advisors, and teachers. With smaller class sizes and mandatory athletics, teachers and coaches did have a lot of contact with students. What teachers and coaches did not have was professional counseling training, and as the psychosocial issues facing students and schools have become more complex, more and more independent schools have hired professional school counselors.

One of the advantages of being a professional school counselor in an independent school setting is that students and educators actually require less unlearning of what counselors *used to* do because, for the most part, there did not *used to* be a counselor. If an independent school did employ a counselor, it was often as a "therapist in residence," so the first challenge in implementing the new vision is to help the administration and the school community understand the professional school counselor's role in serving the whole community, rather than a few students with special needs who are better served by outside mental health professionals. Because the needs of the whole community are so great, I have found independent school communities to be very open to a broader understanding of the school counselor's role across the curriculum. Some of this work is directly with students through classroom guidance, group and individual counseling, peer education, parenting programs, and so on. But much of the work is often indirect—helping those teachers, advisors, and coaches who already do have significant access to students learn the skills that can make those relationships more productive and beneficial. In this sense, the "new vision" of counseling supports the old model of helping the teachers and coaches develop the skills they need to help the students of today. While there are certainly crises that counselors need to react to in independent schools, our primary focus is definitely proactive, preventive, and focused on early intervention.

Like public school counselors, independent school counselors are not sitting in their offices waiting to react to the next crisis or for a "client" to wander in. Professional school counselors are very visible in the halls, lunchrooms, and classrooms. As packed as students' and teachers' schedules are in independent schools, much of our "checking in" happens between classes. During class times, counselors visit classes with a very proactive and developmental curriculum. Our middle school counselor visits small health classes quarterly with a developmental curriculum that mixes group guidance and counseling. In my lower school, the counselor supports teachers with character education programs and presents various counseling units to various grades. Our upper school counselor trains 11th-grade peer educators who teach a guidance curriculum to younger students. The counselors sponsor annual mandatory parent–student dialogue evenings for students and parents in grades 4–12 on topics ranging from bullying to substance abuse to healthy relationships. While we have done much with transition from lower school and middle school, this year we introduced a four-day, three-night senior retreat program designed to help students with the personal and emotional transition from high school to college and beyond.

As you look toward a career in school counseling, remember the fertile ground that independent schools offer for building, sometimes from the ground up, a truly developmental and comprehensive counseling program. Being truly independent of state and local curricula and expectations really does give professional school counselors in independent schools freedom to shape school counseling as it ought to be. Graduate students in my introductory-level course often ask if this new vision of counseling really happens in schools because that has not always been their experience in the public sector. I say that I can speak only for my school, but, yes, it really happens, and it really works.

Source: John Mojzisek, Director of Counseling, The Gilman School; Affiliate Professor, School Counseling Program, Loyola University Maryland

MANAGEMENT SYSTEM

The *management system* element accounts for the "when," "why," and "on what authority" of a comprehensive school counseling program (ASCA, 2005a). It comprises management agreements (i.e., what accomplishments professional school counselors are accountable for during the school year), the advisory council, the use of data (for student monitoring and the closing of achievement/social disparities), action plans, the school counseling program calendar, and the use of time.

Management Agreements

The use of *management agreements* is somewhat controversial, but such agreements are meant to help both professional school counselors and school administrators to understand the goals of a school counseling program and to remove barriers to effective implementation of services to meet those goals. The ASCA (2005a) provided sample program management agreements for both the secondary and the elementary levels. These agreements are short and to the point, but they represent a basic understanding of responsibilities and program management.

Advisory Council

Advisory councils provide a mechanism for input, feedback, and evaluation of the school counseling program's activities for a wide range of individuals. The community advisory council, also known as the *school counseling program advisory committee (SCPAC)*, serves as a sounding board and steering committee. The most important factor to consider when constituting an SCPAC is influence. The professional school counselor must seek to include individuals who can influence and hold the confidence of school and school system decision makers, generally the principal and central office administrators. Including influential members on the SCPAC will ease the way in obtaining necessary programmatic changes as well as resources.

From a personnel perspective, it is essential for the principal to be a member of the SCPAC. The principal can hear firsthand the ideas and planning that go into recommendations for improvement, as well as the rationale for any additional funding that may be needed. In addition to the professional school counselor(s), at least several influential teachers and parents should be included. Political linkages to parent–teacher organizations often play to the advantage of a professional school counselor, as these members can serve as conduits to and from the organizations. The members can inform the SCPAC of various constituencies' concerns and provide information back to those constituencies regarding

actions recommended by the SCPAC or the blockage of the recommended actions.

To round out the committee, an influential school resource person (e.g., school psychologist, special education teacher, reading specialist) and influential community organization and business leaders should be included. Individuals from community organizations and businesses are useful for providing an external perspective, as well as partnerships and external funding and resources.

The SCPAC should convene at least twice annually—and more frequently if the program is new or undergoing major changes. The primary role of the SCPAC is to review the results of needs assessments, make recommendations for program development, review accountability data and outcomes research generated by staff, and locate internal and external funding sources for program development. Locating funding sources often requires the cooperation of the building principal; this is where it pays off to include the principal on the committee, as well as other individuals who can influence the principal's decision making. Thus, the SCPAC can serve a practical and political function, making it a top priority on the professional school counselor's agenda.

Use of Data

Professional school counselors monitor student progress and collect and disaggregate data to identify systemic issues that interfere with equity in achievement. School counselors also collect, analyze, and disseminate program evaluation and "closing the gap" data and analyses. Data collection, analysis, and program evaluation procedures will be covered in much greater detail in Chapter 13.

Action Plans

Action plans are detailed strategies for achieving important outcomes. The ASCA (2005a) outlines the components of both school guidance curriculum action plans and closing the gap action plans. School guidance curriculum action plans contain the following information:

- Domain and standard to be addressed: academic, career, personal/social;
- Student competency to be addressed;
- Description of the actual school counseling activity the school counselor or counseling team will provide;
- Assurance the curriculum is provided for every student;
- Title of any packaged or created curriculum that will be used;
- Timeline for completion of the activity;
- Name of the individual responsible for delivery;
- Means of evaluating student success using pre-post tests, demonstration of competency, or product;

- Expected result for students stated in terms of what will be demonstrated by the students; and
- Indication that the plan has been reviewed and signed by the administrator. (p. 54)

Closing the gap action plans are similar, but are generated from a data-driven approach that identifies some existing discrepancy in students' achievement.

Calendars

Planning is an essential component of any program management system. Indeed, if one does not plan for something to occur, it usually won't! Thus, professional school counselors are strongly encouraged to produce weekly, monthly, and annual calendars. Calendars can

> Identify grade levels, dates and activities . . . Be published and distributed to appropriate persons . . . Be posted on a weekly or monthly basis . . . Be compared to locally established goals for time spent in the delivery of system components . . . Be utilized to allocate time for data analysis and program evaluation . . . Be used when designing and determining system priorities . . . Be shared with the principal as an indicator of leadership, advocacy, and foresight in the school counselor's professional approach. (ASCA, 2005a, pp. 57–58)

Use of Time

How much time do professional school counselors spend providing various services or implementing components of the school counseling program? How much time should they spend? These are questions of use of time, ordinarily answered through what is commonly known as a service assessment or through collection of a time log. Service assessment is reviewed in greater detail in Chapter 13.

The *National Model* also identifies appropriate responsibilities that professional school counselors should engage in and inappropriate activities that they should avoid (ASCA, 2003b, p. 168). For example:

1. Designing individual student academic programs . . . [NOT] registering and scheduling all new students.
2. Counseling students with excessive tardiness or absenteeism . . . [NOT] signing excuses for students who are tardy or absent.
3. Counseling students with disciplinary problems . . . [NOT] performing disciplinary actions.

4. Collaborating with teachers to present guidance curriculum lessons . . . [NOT] teaching classes when teachers are absent.
5. Interpreting student records . . . [NOT] maintaining student records.
6. Ensuring student records are maintained in accordance with state and federal regulations . . . [NOT] clerical record keeping.
7. Assisting the school principal with identifying and resolving student issues, needs and problems . . . [NOT] assisting with duties in the principal's office.

ACCOUNTABILITY SYSTEM

Accountability answers the all-important question of "How are students different as a result of the program?" Accountability is provided by professional school counselors through results reports, performance standards, and program audits. A *results report* comprises outcomes assessments that document changes in students and other stakeholders through systematic analysis of their performance within various program components. An example might be academic performance changes as a result of participation in a study skills group. Monitoring changes in perceptions, processes, and attitudes can also provide helpful evidence of professional school counselor effectiveness. *Performance standards* for professional school counselors include all local job and program expectations that help to assess one's skill in implementing a comprehensive, developmental school counseling program. *Program audits* are conducted to ensure that a school's comprehensive, developmental program aligns with some set of standards, whether at the local or state level, or with the *ASCA National Model*. Such alignment is deemed critical in addressing the needs of all students. All of these accountability processes are aimed at program evaluation and continuous quality improvement. Each of these facets of program accountability is explained in detail in Chapter 13.

Applications of the *ASCA National Model* (2005a) and its facets can be seen in every chapter in this book. The *National Model* presents professional school counselors with a cogent starting point for implementing comprehensive, developmental programs that will benefit all students and with a solid framework on which to build responsive, proactive, comprehensive, developmental school counseling programs. These programs ensure that all students are exposed to rigorous academic curricula, treated equitably and with dignity, and held to high academic standards that enhance postsecondary career opportunities.

But the *ASCA National Model* is not without its critics. Some of this criticism is based upon the lack of outcomes data supporting the model. That is not to say that the model is not effective, just that studies supporting its use have yet to emerge. Counseling researchers will continue to strive for resolution of this concern over the next decade or so. Regardless, keep in mind that implementation of the model is above all a team effort; students, parents, and education professionals all have their roles to play. The final section in this chapter reviews some of the school professionals and staff members with whom the professional school counselor often partners.

THEORY INTO PRACTICE 3.2

THE EFFECTS OF IMPLEMENTING THE ASCA *NATIONAL STANDARDS* AND *ASCA NATIONAL MODEL* SYSTEMWIDE

The ASCA *National Standards* and *ASCA National Model* have played an important role in my work as the Coordinator of School Counseling in Howard County Public Schools in Maryland. Until late 1997, I was a school counselor at the elementary and middle school levels when I applied for the Coordinator of School Counseling position. By this time, I had worked in two different counties in Maryland and never felt that I had been clear on what an effective school counseling program should entail. I believe it was fate that led me to be asked to read a draft version of the ASCA *National Standards* two weeks before my interview for the new position. This draft helped provide a framework for all the elements that I wanted to bring to the interview, and I am sure it was a factor in the awarding of this supervisory position to me. So, of course, when the ASCA *National Standards* were officially published in 1997, and the *ASCA National Model* in 2003, both gave me the vision and tools for the school counseling program in the Howard County Public Schools.

In my opinion, the *ASCA National Model* has brought many positive changes to school counseling. In a time of tight budgets, limited resources, and accountability, the *ASCA National Model* helped school counseling align with school improvement efforts and made the school counselor an integral player in these efforts. The following are some of the changes in Howard County that were the result of using the *ASCA National Model* as our framework:

1. **A Focus on Quality Instead of Quantity** Many school systems, including Howard County, had school counselors collecting tally-mark data to show how many students they met with each day, how many groups they ran, how many classrooms they visited, and so on. While this gives quantitative data, it did nothing to show the effectiveness of the school counseling program. We immediately began to make a shift toward using effectiveness data to drive our programs. It doesn't matter if the school counselor sees every single student in the building if the counselor isn't effective in the interaction.

2. **Essential Curriculum in School Counseling** A team of counselors developed an essential curriculum in school counseling that focused on academic, career, and personal/social development. They used the *ASCA National Model* as the basis for their work. This essential curriculum helped us change the focus from what the counselor does to what students should know and be able to do as a result of the school counseling program. It also gave consistent goals and objectives for students, regardless of the school they attended.

3. **Program Planning** Counselors were asked to create a yearly plan that showed how their school counseling program aligned with the school improvement efforts. All school counseling programs have some similar elements, but each program is unique based on the needs of the school. Each plan contains milestones and evaluation components to measure program effectiveness.

4. **The Use of Data** This was one of the biggest changes that resulted from our use of the *ASCA National Model*. Counselors were asked to use data to make decisions about their programs. The data included pre- and post-activity surveys, attendance data, office referral data, suspension data, and test scores. We challenged counselors to develop more strategies to help improve academic achievement in our students.

5. **Professional Development** An increased importance was placed on professional development to help train our counselors. With all of the changes in our school counseling program, there were many opportunities for professional development. The counselors in Howard County are fortunate that monthly professional development meetings are part of the culture in our county. These meetings are critical in helping counselors to integrate the components of the *ASCA National Model* into their work.

6. **A Reduction in Noncounseling Duties** Since our school counselors now had a written yearly plan to

show what students should know and be able to do and data to show their effectiveness, it became easier to show that they didn't have the time to do some of the noncounseling duties they had typically been assigned. Our counselors were relieved of their duties as accountability coordinators for testing, which had traditionally taken a large chunk of time from their school counseling program.

Has it been easy to implement the *ASCA National Model* in our school counseling program? Yes and no. I have found that like most initiatives, it takes time and consistent effort to develop the buy-in among the school counselors. Those counselors who were trained in counseling programs

where the *ASCA National Model* was taught generally come in and hit the ground running. The counselors who were trained before the *ASCA National Model* was developed fall into two categories: those who embrace the change and move forward and those who resist the change and hope it will go away. While those in the last group are a challenge, they have had no choice but to join the new way of school counseling because the *ASCA National Model* has increased the importance of having an effective school counseling program in each of our schools.

Source: Lisa Boarman, Coordinator of School Counseling, Howard County Public Schools, Maryland

ROLES OF OTHER SCHOOL PERSONNEL IN THE COMPREHENSIVE SCHOOL COUNSELING PROGRAM

While a great deal of this book focuses on the role of the professional school counselor, it is important to emphasize that the counselor is but one player in a team effort. Without collaborative partnerships with other school personnel and community agencies, it is quite likely that a professional school counselor trying to stand alone will fall flat on his or her face. While establishing viable community partnerships is an important and evolving role of the professional school counselor and will be explored further in Chapter 12, this section will focus on school-based personnel who can become valuable partners in the comprehensive school counseling program.

Teachers

Few people can make or break the school counseling program like classroom teachers can. Teachers can serve as valuable allies of professional school counselors in many ways. First, teachers are often the implementers of developmental guidance lessons, and in large part, their competence and enthusiasm can determine the fate of numerous goals and learning objectives. Therefore, it becomes necessary to properly prepare and motivate teachers to help students to reach the established competencies. An unmotivated teacher can block access to students and derail a comprehensive program. Therefore, a golden rule of school counseling is "Always treat your teachers with respect and kindness (especially when they don't reciprocate)." Failing to do so will affect not only your relationship with that teacher, but also often your access to that teacher's students.

Teachers also serve as excellent referral sources for children in need of counseling services. Teachers not only see their students daily, but also see the friends of students

in need. A tuned-in teacher misses little and can effectively encourage troubled youth to seek needed help. In addition, teachers are a valuable source of information for needs assessments and program evaluations. Their input is vital to understanding the needs of a school community, as well as the effectiveness of the school counseling program interventions.

It may seem strange to start this section off with teachers, rather than the principal, but while principals often have more policy-making authority at the school level, teachers hold the power over what does and does not happen in the classroom. A seasoned professional school counselor understands this and seeks to bond strongly with all teachers. In summary, if you take good care of your teachers, your teachers will take good care of you.

Resource Teachers

Resource teachers take many forms in different states, but generally include special education teachers, reading specialists, speech and language pathologists, and behavior intervention specialists. Special education teachers are especially important to connect with in schools because special education students are often underserved by professional school counselors. Connecting with special education teachers is one way to ensure that *all* students receive comprehensive school counseling services. Students in need of special education often require specialized services related to social and study skills, and their teachers are often open to program-related suggestions to meet these needs. Like professional school counselors, resource teachers have special expertise that makes them invaluable consultants and referral sources. The experienced professional school counselor explores the specific strengths of these professionals and does not hesitate to call upon them when the need arises.

Principals and Assistant Principals

Principals and their assistants contribute to many important facets of the comprehensive school counseling program. They frequently assign individuals to the Guidance Advisory Council and provide support and leadership to that committee when necessary. The principal provides resources and contributes to the working environment, while defending the counselor from role diffusion and "noncounseling" tasks—although this is a bit like the fox guarding the henhouse. Administrators can also play a vital role in facilitating needs assessments and evaluations of the comprehensive school counseling program, as well as communicating to the public the importance of a developmental program.

School Psychologists

School psychologists are specially trained to provide psychological services in a school environment. In many states, school psychologists are relegated to simply providing psychoeducational testing to determine a child's eligibility for special education or Section 504 services. However, many school systems have greatly expanded the school psychologist's role to allow for consultation with parents and school personnel, case management of special needs children, and counseling with severely behavior-disordered or emotionally disturbed students. Developing a strong collaborative relationship with the school psychologist is an excellent strategy for beginning to address the needs of a school's most serious cases. School psychologists and counselors are often on the front lines together when it comes to intervening with dangerous and suicidal students.

School Social Workers (Visiting Teachers, Pupil Personnel Workers)

School social workers (sometimes called visiting teachers or pupil personnel workers, depending on the state or locale) often conduct sociological assessments for child study proceedings and work with needy families to secure social, financial, and medical services. They are frequently invaluable sources of information on families and communities and serve as liaisons between the school and public heath facilities.

School Nurses

School nurses provide a wide range of health services, depending upon the state. Nurses monitor the medications taken by students in school and often facilitate teacher feedback on the effectiveness of those medications when requested by physicians. Nurses also conduct hearing and vision screening and are a valuable ally of professional school counselors on developmental matters such as hygiene, personal safety, and physical and sexual development. School nurses also frequently come in contact with students with anxiety disorders, depression, eating disorders, reproductive issues, and phobias and can serve as valuable referral and information sources.

Secretaries

The climate of a school often rises and falls with the quality of the secretarial staff. Secretaries are usually the first contacts parents have with the school or school counseling program—and you never get a second chance to make a first impression. Experienced administrators and professional school counselors make clear their expectations for how secretaries and other staff are to treat the public—including the students. Secretaries are often among the first to encounter parents and students in crisis, and the respectfulness, sensitivity, and efficiency with which they handle these situations speak volumes about the school climate. Finally, one need not be employed in an office environment long to realize that a secretary can make you look very good—or very incompetent. Always treat your secretary with great respect.

Summary/Conclusion

The ASCA *National Standards* and *ASCA National Model* have had a positive effect on the identity and service delivery proficiency of professional school counselors. The *National Standards* provide a guide for implementing curricular goals and competencies across the domains of student academic, career, and personal/social development. The *National Model* provides a framework for describing, implementing, and evaluating a comprehensive, developmental school counseling program. The model includes four themes that are infused throughout the program: leadership, advocacy, collaboration and teaming, and systemic change.

However, the heart of the program is the four primary program components: program foundation, delivery system, management system, and accountability. The program foundation, the "what" of a comprehensive school counseling program, makes clear what every student will know and be able to do as a result of the school counseling program and includes the program's beliefs and philosophies, mission, domains (i.e., academic, career, personal/social), standards, and competencies. The delivery system is the "how" of the comprehensive, developmental school counseling program. As professional school counselors implement their programs, they include the guidance curriculum, individual student planning, responsive services (e.g., individual and group counseling, referral, consultation), and systems support (e.g., professional development, collaboration). The management system accounts for the "when," "why," and "on what authority" of program implementation and includes management agreements, school counseling program advisory committees (SCPACs), use of data, action plans, calendars, and use of time. The SCPAC is a diverse group of stakeholders and can be helpful in guiding the program in positive directions through understanding and meeting the needs of the school community. The SCPAC can also play an important role in securing resources and demonstrating accountability. Accountability answers the all-important question of "How are students different as a result of the program?" It includes results reports, performance standards, and program audits.

Finally, the roles of other school personnel as they impact the comprehensive school counseling program were discussed. Professional school counselors should develop partnerships with teachers, resource teachers, administrators, school psychologists, school social workers, school nurses, and secretaries to help facilitate and smoothly implement the comprehensive school counseling program.

4

Outcomes Research on School Counseling Interventions and Programs

Susan C. Whiston and Robert F. Quinby

Editor's Introduction: The science of school counseling involves empirical study of the methods, techniques, and procedures used by professional school counselors in their day-to-day work. The transformation of the profession must be guided by knowledge and understanding of what works, rather than by what or how much of something is done. Effective practices raise a profession to new heights, and it is with this focus that we explore what is known about the effectiveness of school counseling practices. As you will see, while some evidence exists regarding effective service provision, much more evidence is needed to document effectiveness and establish school counseling as an accountable profession. The transformed professional school counselor understands the vital nature of this mission and establishes collaborative partnerships to conduct field-based action research and outcomes evaluation to benefit students and the profession.

OUTCOMES RESEARCH IN SCHOOL COUNSELING

As we explore the practice of professional school counseling, it is important to examine whether the services professional school counselors provide are actually helpful to students. Although professional school counselors may believe certain approaches are effective, others—such as school board members, administrators, parents, and legislators—want documented evidence that reflects the effectiveness of school counseling. Furthermore, many of these individuals not only want confirmation that school counseling services are beneficial to students, but also want evidence that these services are cost-effective. In some school districts, professional school counseling positions may be eliminated unless there is empirical support documenting the effectiveness of professional school counselor activities. As school funding often is limited, a principal may want research indicating that hiring a professional school counselor is a good investment.

Another reason to conduct research related to the effectiveness of professional school counseling programs is the movement toward evidence-based practice. A few years ago the U.S. Department of Education (2005b) made it a goal to transform education into an evidence-based field. Evidence-based practices in education are those interventions or teaching methods used within a school that have empirical support. In determining whether a certain approach or intervention meets the criteria for evidence-based practices, individuals often look at the outcomes research conducted related to that approach or intervention. Outcomes researchers seek to understand the end results or effects on students of some practice or intervention. Outcomes research in the field of professional school counseling analyzes whether school counseling programs or components of such a program result in positive outcomes for students.

In addition to providing accountability information on the effects of school counseling interventions and services, outcomes research can provide pertinent clinical information that informs professional school counselors. Counseling outcomes research can be a useful resource because it is designed to identify which approaches and activities produce positive changes for students. Outcomes research can aid professional school counselors in selecting counseling interventions and guidance activities that have been shown to be effective. Some have argued that without empirical information, practitioners are making uninformed decisions. Lambert (1991) contended that without a thorough knowledge of the counseling outcomes research, a practitioner cannot ethically counsel. He argued that counselors are ethically bound to provide the best services to their clients, and without a thorough knowledge of the research, they will not know what has been shown to be the "best." Given the significant responsibilities that professional school counselors have, it is important they choose interventions that are effective.

However, it is not always easy to be a good consumer of outcomes research. Outcomes research is published in a wide variety of journals, and it is often difficult for professional counselors to keep abreast of relevant findings. In addition, it is sometimes difficult to decipher results and identify valid and reliable findings that are pertinent to counseling practice. This chapter is designed to assist counselors by summarizing the outcomes research related to school counseling activities. Whiston (2002) argued that it is critical for professional school counselors to be informed about outcomes research and know which activities are supported or not supported by research. By summarizing the research in this area, this chapter gives professional school counselors the empirical knowledge they need when making decisions about what works best with which students. The chapter also is designed so that accountability information and outcomes research can be communicated to other constituents (e.g., school boards and principals). In examining outcomes research, this chapter addresses the following set of questions: Is professional school counseling effective? Which students benefit from school counseling interventions? What are the effective methods for delivering school counseling programs? Does a fully implemented school counseling program make a difference?

IS PROFESSIONAL SCHOOL COUNSELING EFFECTIVE?

The question of whether professional school counseling is effective cannot be answered using the results of just one study. No single study can examine the multitude of duties performed by professional school counselors at all the different grade levels. Therefore, answering the question concerning the effectiveness of school counseling services requires an examination of the accumulation of school counseling research. One valuable resource is research reviews on professional school counseling. There are two types of research reviews: The first is the more common qualitative review, where researchers examine the studies and summarize the findings and trends; the second is based on meta-analytic techniques, where researchers seek to quantify the results by calculating an overall effect size (e.g., the mean of the control

group subtracted from the mean of the experimental group and divided by the standard deviation of the control group). Cohen (1988) offered a helpful rule-of-thumb guideline for interpreting effect sizes derived from this formula: .20 is considered a small effect, .50 is considered a moderate effect, and .80 or higher is considered a large effect.

Results from qualitative reviews are generally supportive of the effectiveness of school counseling activities. Borders and Drury (1992) examined research studies and professional statements from counseling organizations published between 1960 and 1990. They concluded that school counseling interventions have a substantial impact on students' educational and personal development. Their review cited a number of studies that indicated students who received school counseling services showed improvements in terms of their academic performance, attitudes, and behaviors. In a systematic review of outcomes research in professional school counseling, Whiston and Sexton (1998) concluded that a broad range of activities professional school counselors perform results in positive changes in students. They found, however, that not all school counseling activities have been empirically investigated.

In addition to general reviews of school counseling research, a few qualitative reviews have focused on specific student populations. Gerler (1985) found support for elementary school counseling programs, whereas St. Claire (1989) found support for some programs and strategies used by professional middle school counselors. N. S. Wilson (1986) focused specifically on the effects of professional school counseling interventions with underachieving and low-achieving students and concluded that professional school counseling interventions have a positive influence on these students' grade point averages. All of these reviews, however, were conducted in the 1980s, which indicates there is a need for more-current systematic reviews of the research.

Meta-analytic reviews, as stated earlier, provide a quantitative measure of the degree to which school counseling interventions and programs are effective. A recent meta-analysis conducted by Whiston, Rahardja, Eder, and Tai (2008) provided some quantitative evidence concerning the degree to which school counseling interventions are effective. These researchers examined the school counseling literature since 1980 and found 117 school counseling studies, both published and unpublished (e.g., dissertation), that contained sufficient data to calculate an effect size (ES). The ES is calculated by subtracting the mean of the control group from the mean of the treatment group and dividing the result by the pooled standard deviation and indicates whether the students receiving the school counseling intervention did better or worse on the outcomes measure than the students who did not receive the intervention during the time of the study. In examining these 117 studies, Whiston et al. identified

153 school counseling interventions that involved 16,296 students. In terms of the effectiveness of all school counseling interventions, these researchers found an average unweighted ES of .46; however, when weighting the ES by the methods proposed by Hedges and Olkin (1985), they found a significant ES of .30. An ES of .30 is somewhat small, but it does indicate that on measures used in the studies, students who received a school counseling intervention were almost a third of a standard deviation above those who did not receive the intervention. Whiston et al. also found that school counseling interventions were not homogeneous and that there was variation among the interventions, which reflects the fact that some interventions are more effective and that others have much smaller ESs.

There are four other meta-analytic reviews that have some relationship to school counseling. Sprinthall (1981) found that primary prevention programs were effective; however, this meta-analysis included only six studies. A more comprehensive review of primary prevention strategies is that of S. B. Baker, Swisher, Nadenichek, and Popowicz (1984). The ESs varied, but a conservative estimate of ES was .55, which would indicate that prevention activities are moderately effective. Two other meta-analyses have examined the effects of counseling or psychotherapy in school settings. In the first (H. T. Prout & DeMartino, 1986), the researchers found a moderate effect size (ES = .58), whereas the second meta-analysis (S. M. Prout & Prout, 1998) found these types of interventions were very effective (ES = .97). It should be noted that these last two meta-analytic reviews (H. T. Prout & DeMartino, 1986; S. M. Prout & Prout, 1998) included interventions conducted by both professional school counselors and school psychologists.

If the results from these various meta-analytic reviews are combined, there appears to be support for the conclusion that school counseling interventions are moderately to highly effective. The qualitative reviews are also generally positive. As a caveat, however, these conclusions are based on a somewhat limited number of studies. Another concern noted by Whiston et al. (2008) was that many of the studies evaluating the effectiveness of school counseling have methodological limitations.

WHICH STUDENTS BENEFIT FROM SCHOOL COUNSELING INTERVENTIONS?

Professional school counselors work with students at different grade levels, and there is some evidence that school counseling interventions may have a differential effect on students at different ages. Whiston et al. (2008) found that outcomes studies in the past 25 years have focused most on elementary school counseling; that is, 46% of the interventions researched were with elementary students, 21% were

with middle or junior high school students, and 28% were with high school students. Whiston et al. found a weighted ES of .26 for school counseling interventions with elementary students, an ES of .42 for interventions with middle and junior high school students, and an ES of .34 for interventions with high school students. This meta-analytic study's findings that professional school counseling interventions are most effective with middle school students is somewhat inconsistent with Nearpass's (1990) finding that interventions with upper-level high school students are more effective than interventions with younger high school students, who are closer in age to middle school students. H. T. Prout and DeMartino (1986) also concluded that older students seem to benefit more from counseling or therapeutic interventions than younger students do; however, S. M. Prout and Prout's (1998) study found that psychotherapeutic interventions with elementary students produced the greatest gains. Additionally, Gerler (1985) found that elementary school counselors' interventions have a positive effect on elementary students. Hence, the findings regarding the effectiveness of school counseling at different levels are somewhat mixed and are probably related to differences in interventions at different levels. For example, although Whiston et al. (2008) found an overall ES of .26 for elementary school counseling interventions, they also found considerable differences among ESs, depending on the types of interventions used with elementary students. In outcomes research, often the most interesting and useful findings are related to what works with which types of students, rather than being the result of combining diverse interventions (e.g., individual counseling, group counseling, classroom guidance) to find a general measure of effectiveness.

Concerning this area of research, a factor to consider is which students use school counseling services. Mahoney and Merritt (1993) examined ethnic differences in the utilization of school counseling services. They found that a higher percentage of African-American students than White students considered counselors to be important in helping them make their educational plans. Furthermore, African-American students, particularly males, were more likely to seek school counseling services to overcome academic weaknesses than were White students. The researchers also found this same trend concerning African-American students' increased usage of counseling resources related to job and educational placement. Bradshaw, Buckley, and Ialongo (2008) conducted a study of the usage of school-based services among urban children who were identified as having early onset educational and mental health problems. They found that students who displayed symptoms of early onset educational and mental health problems had high rates of using school-based mental health services, as compared to

| VOICES FROM THE FIELD 4.1 | THE IMPORTANCE OF USING EMPIRICALLY BASED RESEARCH IN THE SCHOOLS |

Empirically based and data-driven research related to the field of school counseling is a critical cornerstone for building a foundation of "efficacy" for our profession. School counselors impact the lives of students, parents, colleagues, and the community through academic, career and postsecondary, social and emotional, and developmental counseling and advising. As we are able to validate the level of that impact through outcomes that have empirically proven results, our profession will benefit by having the leverage of accountability to argue for the placement of more counselors in more schools, lower student-to-counselor ratios, and more time to implement direct counselor-related services to our students and parents.

Source: Greg W. Chaffin, Counseling Department Chair, Bloomington High School North, Monroe County Community School Corporation, Bloomington, Indiana

---

students who did not appear to have either educational or mental health problems. Of the groups analyzed, they found that those students who experienced educational or externalizing difficulties had particularly high rates of service usage (Bradshaw et al., 2008). They suggested that the early identification of both educational and mental health problems is critical for the prevention of subsequent academic difficulties and behavioral problems.

Increasingly, professional school counselors are required to serve *all* students in a school. Questions related to which students benefit from school counseling activities are probably not as important as questions related to how professional school counselors can deliver a school counseling program effectively to all students. The next section of this chapter examines the research related to the methods of delivering school counseling programs and the effectiveness of the different modalities.

WHAT ARE THE EFFECTIVE METHODS FOR DELIVERING SCHOOL COUNSELING PROGRAMS?

The field of school counseling increasingly is moving toward providing a systematic program. Professional school counselors do not solely focus on helping select students find scholarships and helping other students who are experiencing a crisis. The role of professional school counselors is to implement a comprehensive program for all students that is a key component of the larger school's purpose and mission.

For example, Sink and Stroh (2003) found that elementary students who attended schools with a comprehensive school counseling program for at least five years had slightly higher achievement scores than did students who attended schools with no systematic guidance program. In providing a school counseling program, counselors typically employ a variety of interventions and activities; hence, it is important to know which delivery methods result in the most positive benefits for students. As an example, professional school

counselors may want to know whether it is more effective to counsel using groups or whether students benefit more from individual counseling. The American School Counselor Association (ASCA; 2005a) has developed its *National Model*, which suggests four components within the delivery system of a school counseling program (i.e., guidance curriculum, individual student planning, responsive services, and systems support). These four areas of program delivery will be used to organize our examination of the outcomes research on the effectiveness of these areas and on the particular types of activities that tend to be most effective.

Guidance Curriculum

Gysbers and Henderson (2006) suggested that professional school counselors incorporate guidance curriculum activities into their daily work with students. According to the ASCA (2005a), the guidance curriculum involves structured developmental lessons designed to assist all students in achieving the desired guidance competencies and to provide them with the knowledge and skills appropriate for their developmental level. In recent years, there appear to be a number of curriculum materials developed for school counselors. As an example, Rowley, Stroh, and Sink (2005) surveyed 86 school counselors who listed 94 guidance curricular materials that they were using. In making decisions about how to invest their time, professional school counselors need to consider whether there is evidence that these guidance curriculum programs produce positive benefits for students.

Borders and Drury (1992) concluded that classroom guidance activities were effective; however, Whiston and Sexton (1998) did not find clear empirical support for classroom guidance activities. Whiston et al. (2008) identified 44 studies that evaluated guidance curriculum activities that had an overall weighted ES of .35. Hence, students who were in schools where guidance curriculum materials were implemented tended to score about a third of a standard deviation better than those students who did not receive these types of classroom and group activities. Of the guidance curriculum interventions evaluated, 40% were used with elementary school students, 26% with middle school students, 26% with high school students, and 7% with a mixture of students or with parents. Interestingly, although much of the research on guidance curriculum interventions is with elementary students, it seems that middle or junior high school students benefited the most (ES = .46) from guidance curriculum offerings. Whiston et al. also found that high school students seemed to benefit, with an average ES of .39, while the ES for elementary students was somewhat smaller (ES = .31).

Recently, the National Panel for Evidence-Based School Counseling (Carey, Dimmitt, Hatch, Lapan, & Whiston, 2008) used the outcome research coding protocol to evaluate the effectiveness of two widely used guidance programs (i.e., Student Success Skills and Second Step). The panel is an independent body that seeks to provide thorough and unbiased reviews of school counseling practices. Student Success Skills is a structured group and classroom guidance approach to teaching cognitive/metacognitive skills, social skills, and self-management skills to students in grades 5 through 9. The outcomes studies the panel used in evaluating Student Success Skills were Brigman and Campbell (2003), C. A. Campbell and Brigman (2005), and Webb, Brigman, and Campbell (2005). The coding protocol used required the panel to evaluate the programs' outcomes studies in seven domains. Concerning Student Success Skills, the panel found the program to have either "promising" or "strong" evidence in all domains except persistence of effect. The panel encouraged researchers to conduct additional research related to Student Success Skills and advised researchers to examine the long-term effects of the program on students' cognitive and social skills. It appears that the developers of the Student Success Skills program are continuing to evaluate its effectiveness. Brigman, Webb, and Campbell (2007) found that students who participated in the Student Success Skills program had higher mathematics achievement scores, as compared to students who did not participate, and their teacher found that their behavior improved after participating in the program.

The National Panel for Evidence-Based School Counseling (Carey et al., 2008) was more positive in its evaluation of Second Step: A Violence Prevention Curriculum (Committee for Children, 1997a, 1997b). Second Step is a social and emotional learning curriculum for students in kindergarten through eighth grade. The panel reviewed seven research studies related to Second Step and determined there was "strong" evidence in all of the research domains. Furthermore, Second Step has been endorsed by the U.S. Department of Education as an exemplary program.

Related to guidance curriculum activities at the elementary level, Rowley et al. (2005) found that elementary counselors were most likely to use guidance curriculum materials related to the personal/affective domain. Whiston et al. (2008) found that professional school counseling interventions designed to increase self-esteem had limited impact on students' self-esteem. In a well-designed study, Schlossberg, Morris, and Lieberman (2001) found that counselor-led developmental guidance units presented in ninth-grade classrooms have the potential to improve students' expressed behavior and general school attitudes, while also addressing their developmental needs.

Classroom guidance activities are a major emphasis of school counseling programs in some school districts; yet the research in this area could be more extensive. Rowley et al. (2005) found that with a few exceptions (e.g., the Missouri Comprehensive Guidance and Counseling Program), professional school counselors are predominately using curricular materials that have not been well researched. They recommended the development and evaluation of guidance curriculum materials that meet the needs of students and correspond to the ASCA's *National Standards for School Counseling Programs* (C. Campbell & Dahir, 1997). We concur with this recommendation and believe the development of empirically supported guidance curriculum materials is a crucial step in transforming school counseling.

Individual Student Planning

Individual student planning involves professional school counselors coordinating ongoing systemic activities designed to assist students in individually determining personal goals and developing plans for their future (ASCA, 2005a). Whiston et al. (2008) found only 10 studies that addressed individual planning, and the majority of these were with high school students. The overall weighted ES was statistically significant (ES = .26).

According to Gysbers and Henderson (2006), professional school counselors often design individual planning around educational and career/vocational planning. In addition, one of the three areas in the ASCA's *National Standards for School Counseling Programs* (C. Campbell & Dahir, 1997) is career development. In addition, Scruggs, Wasielewski, and Ash (1999) found that both students and parents would like professional school counselors to put more emphasis on career guidance and development activities. Therefore, it is important to examine the research related to effective career guidance and counseling activities.

There is support for the effectiveness of career counseling with clients at various developmental levels from both narrative reviews (Whiston & Oliver, 2005; Whiston & Rahardja, 2008) and meta-analyses (L. W. Oliver & Spokane, 1988; Whiston, Sexton, & Lasoff, 1998). The meta-analyses differ somewhat on the degree to which career interventions are effective. The first meta-analysis

(L. W. Oliver & Spokane, 1988) indicated career interventions were highly effective, whereas the meta-analysis of more current research (Whiston et al., 1998) found career interventions to be moderately effective. These two meta-analyses were consistent in finding that individual career counseling (vocational classes) were the most effective methods of delivering career counseling services.

Another meta-analysis found that counselor-free interventions are not effective and that interventions involving a counselor are significantly more efficacious (Whiston, Brecheisen, & Stephens, 2003). This finding is particularly important because many schools have purchased computerized career guidance programs or encourage students to use career resources on the Internet. Whiston et al.'s (2003) finding clearly indicated that students do not gain much when they use these resources alone; however, students do benefit from the use of computerized career guidance systems when they are integrated with other activities involving a counselor.

Within the area of individual planning, a major focus of many professional school counselors, particularly those at the high school level, involves encouraging and assisting students in entering college. Longitudinal studies indicate that almost half of the students who pursue an associate's or bachelor's degree do not achieve that goal in the 8 to 10 years after graduating from high school (Trusty & Niles, 2003, 2004). Trusty and Niles found that coursework was predictive of college success and encouraged professional school counselors at the middle school level to devote more energy to career and academic development interventions. Whiston et al. (1998) found that career interventions were more effective at the junior high/middle school level than at the high school level. A commonly used program for middle school students in various countries, the Real Game, was evaluated by Dimmitt (2007) with a large sample ($N = 617$) of middle school students from the United States. Dimmitt found that those students who participated in the Real Game scored higher in the domains of self-efficacy, school engagement, and prosocial behaviors, as compared to those who did not participate.

In conclusion, professional school counselors can feel confident in reporting that career development activities are generally effective. Rowley et al. (2005) found that at the secondary level, professional school counselors are increasingly using guidance curriculum materials to address the career/vocational domain. This is a positive development because previous research had indicated this domain was often neglected in school counseling programs.

Responsive Services

Responsive services concern the role of the professional school counselor in assisting students with immediate issues that are usually affected by life events or situations in the students' lives (ASCA, 2005a). Gysbers and Henderson (2006) suggested this component of a school counseling program concerns attending to students' issues or problems. Typical modalities employed in responsive services activities are individual counseling, group counseling, referral, and peer assistance programs.

In examining the school counseling research, Whiston et al. (2008) found 58 studies that examined 73 interventions that were classified as being responsive services. Once again, the weighted overall ES of .35 indicated that those who received the responsive services scored a little more than a third of a standard deviation above those who did not receive the interventions. It should be noted that elementary children seemed to particularly benefit from these services, with an ES of .40. Surprisingly, they found that only 10 studies evaluated different approaches to responsive services with middle or junior high school students, and these studies resulted in an ES of .22. It is perplexing that so few studies have been conducted with this early adolescent population when these students are often experiencing physiological changes, social pressures, and behavioral problems. Whiston et al. (2008) found the evaluation of 20 responsive services interventions with high school students, and these studies produced an ES of .35.

INDIVIDUAL AND GROUP COUNSELING Administrators, teachers, and parents sometimes question whether the time students spend in individual or group counseling is worth the time away from classrooms and other responsibilities. The research findings are mixed on whether it is more effective for a professional school counselor to provide responsive services primarily through group interventions or through individual counseling. S. M. Prout and Prout (1998) found that most research studies concerning counseling and psychotherapy in schools examined group approaches. Whiston et al. (2008) found that group interventions were often evaluated (e.g., more than 45 studies) and produced a weighted ES of .36; only three studies investigated individual counseling, and the average weighted ES for these few studies was .07. N. S. Wilson (1986) found evidence that group counseling was more effective than individual counseling in increasing the academic performance of low-achieving and underachieving students, whereas Nearpass (1990) found that individual counseling is generally more effective than group counseling. Wiggins and Wiggins (1992) found that counselors who predominately used individual counseling were more effective than those counselors who predominately used classroom guidance activities. This finding, however, should be interpreted cautiously because of methodological problems with the study.

There are indications that individual counseling does not have to be lengthy to be effective. Littrell, Malia, and

Vanderwood (1995) concluded that three approaches to brief individual counseling were effective with secondary students. There is also empirical support for using brief counseling approaches with students with learning disabilities (R. Thompson & Littrell, 1998). In terms of working with young children, Bratton, Ray, Rhine, and Jones (2005) found that play therapy can be quite effective, particularly when the treatment involves a humanistic approach.

Group counseling seems a prevalent approach among professional school counselors, as Steen, Bauman, and Smith (2007) found that 87% of the professional school counselors in their study reported facilitating groups in their schools. In a recent study, Steen and Kaffenberger (2007) found that a small group for fourth and fifth graders resulted in language arts grades increasing by at least one letter grade for a majority of them. In summarizing research on group counseling with students in schools, Gerrity and DeLucia-Waack (2007) and Riva and Haub (2004) concluded that these groups are generally helpful to students. In a meta-analysis of group interventions, Hoag and Burlingame (1997) found that groups conducted in schools were significantly less effective than those conducted in clinical settings. This may be due to the fact that school counselors have a plethora of responsibilities and often cannot devote the same time and energy to facilitating groups as clinicians in clinical settings can. This raises an important point about whether some principals and administrators understand the benefits of systematic group interventions and whether this lack of understanding may result in professional school counselors being directed toward other duties. Kulic, Horne, and Dagley (2004) found that about a third of the group counseling studies published between 1990 and 2000 utilized treatment manuals and projected that manual-based approaches are increasingly being evaluated. This probably will be beneficial to professional school counselors, as it appears that in the coming years, they will have access to group protocols that are empirically supported.

As a result of a number of incidents, there is an increasing interest in school violence and empirically supported treatment to decrease aggressive and angry behaviors. In a meta-analysis of the effects of school-based programs on aggressive behavior, S. J. Wilson, Lipsey, and Derzon (2003) found that behavioral counseling approaches had the largest ESs and therefore were the most effective approaches. Gansle (2005) conducted a meta-analysis of school-based interventions regarding anger management. Interestingly, 25% of the studies were conducted either in alternative schools or in combined alternative and traditional school settings. They found that with outcomes that measured externalizing symptoms and anger, longer treatments were associated with better outcomes. Although

school counselors often have limited time to conduct groups, it appears from Gansle's meta-analysis that, if the goal is reduction in school violence, then longer group interventions may be worth the investment. In addition, there is research that indicates that groups designed to assist students whose parents have divorced can have positive effects (Stathakow & Roehrle, 2003; Whiston & Sexton, 1998). In conclusion, the support for group counseling is primarily with younger students, and further exploration is required before conclusions can be drawn about the effectiveness of group approaches with high school students.

PEER MEDIATION   In recent years, there has been an increased interest in peer mediation programs. Some of the earlier reviews of research in this area indicated that there was empirical support for peer counseling and peer mediation programs at both the elementary and the secondary levels (Borders & Drury, 1992; Whiston & Sexton, 1998). Whiston et al. (2008) found that peer mediation interventions were effective, with a weighted ES of .39; however, many of the outcomes measures that were used involved assessing peer mediators' knowledge of the mediation process and did not involve measuring whether the peer mediation process had any effect on reducing conflict. This is consistent with McGannon, Carey, and Dimmitt's (2005) findings that students who provide the peer counseling often benefit to a larger degree from the service than do the students who are receiving the counseling. S. J. Wilson et al. (2003) found that peer mediation programs had a small impact on aggressive behavior and that, as indicated in the previous section, there are more-effective treatment approaches for aggressive behavior. Hence, professional school counselors should not assume there is conclusive empirical support for peer mediation programs; more research is certainly needed in this area.

BULLYING PROGRAMS   The issue of bullying is a pressing problem that has become prevalent in school settings (Ma, Stewin, & Mah, 2001). Skiba and Fontanini (2000) reported that as many as 20% of students in the United States say they have been bullied. To respond to this issue, several researchers have developed and studied the effectiveness of bullying prevention programs. Perhaps one of the most widely known antibullying program is the Olweus Bullying Prevention Program. In recent studies of this program, Olweus (2005) found reductions in bullying behavior that approached around 50%. At implementation sites, he also noted a reduction in antisocial behavior and improvements in the social climate of the school. In another study of public middle schools in which the Olweus Bullying Prevention Program had been implemented, N. S. Bauer,

Lozano, and Rivara (2007) found the program had no effect on students' reports of being victimized. However, they did find that White students were more likely to report victimization. N. S. Bauer et al. (2007) also found that students were more likely to perceive other students as intervening on behalf of victims after the Olweus program had been implemented.

Another popular antibullying program is Bullybusters. This psychoeducational program, targeting students in grades K–8, has been implemented in many schools across the United States (Newman-Carlson & Horne, 2004; Orpinas & Horne, 2006). Some of the initial studies of the implementations of Bullybusters found a 20% reduction in the number of bullying incidents reported in the first year (Beale, 2001). Another study of Bullybusters focused on the teachers implementing the program and noted several increases in their level of self-efficacy and ability to respond to incidences of bullying (Newman-Carlson & Horne, 2004). The study also found that the focused effort to increase these teachers' skills resulted in a reduction of bullying behaviors in the students whom the teachers taught.

Still another program, PeaceBuilders, is a violence prevention program designed for grades K–5 (Flannery et al., 2003). In a study of the effectiveness of this program, Flannery et al. noted significantly higher ratings of social competence among K–2 students who received the intervention and moderately higher levles of social competence for students receiving the intervention in grades 3–5. Furthermore, in this study students in grades 3–5 who received the intervention were reported to be less aggressive, and all students who received the intervention had higher self-reported ratings concerning peace-building behaviors. Flannery et al. also found that many of these effects, particularly regarding improvements in social competence and reductions in aggressive behavior, persisted over time. Finally, Jenson and Dieterich (2007) studied the effects of the Youth Matters program on elementary school students in an urban school district. In this study, they found self-reported incidents of bully victimization decreased at higher rates for students at intervention sites versus students at controlled sites. Although a number of bullying prevention programs currently exist, there remains significant room for the continued implementation and evaluation of such programs to address the rampant problem of bullying.

PARENT EDUCATION The benefits of parent training and family counseling are well established in the counseling and psychotherapy outcomes research (Kaminski, Valle, Filene, & Boyle, 2008; Kazdin, 1997; Lundahl, Nimer, &

Parsons, 2006). Furthermore, there is some evidence that with low-achieving and underachieving students, the effectiveness of the counseling is significantly related to the amount of parental involvement in the counseling process (N. S. Wilson, 1986).

A movement to provide mental health services, social services, and "wrap-around" services in school-based centers is growing across the country (Anderson-Butcher & Ashton, 2004; Center for Mental Health in Schools, 1999). These centers often provide health and mental health services to students and their families. Professional school counselors and professional organizations need to consider the role they are going to play in providing these services. In some communities, professional school counselors may be viewed as having primarily clerical responsibilities and will not be involved in the parent education and family counseling services provided through these centers. If professional school counselors ignore this trend of others providing mental health services in school settings, then in the future professional school counselors may have little involvement with mental health issues and family counseling.

Systems Support

According to the ASCA (2005a), comprehensive school counseling programs are similar to other programs and require management activities in order to establish, maintain, and enhance them. It is more difficult to ascertain the effectiveness of systems support activities, and there is little research in this area. Although some professional school counselors might argue that consultation is often related to assisting students and might fall under the umbrella of responsive services, we are discussing consultation research as a systems support mechanism.

Consultation is typically considered an indirect method of providing psychologically oriented services. There is empirical support for the effectiveness of consulting as a means of remediating problems (J. J. Murphy, 1999; Zins, 1993). Professional school counselors are often involved in consultative activities with parents, teachers, and other education professionals. Professional school counselors often consult with teachers, and Otwell and Mullis (1997) found that a consultation workshop held with teachers resulted in more students being referred for counseling. D. C. Ray (2007) compared the effects of play therapy, teacher consultation, and a combination of play therapy and consultation. Working with ethnically diverse students, Ray was interested in which of the three approaches had the most impact on reducing teacher–child relationship stress. All three approaches reduced teacher–child relationship stress, but their results were not significantly different from one another. Amatea, Daniel,

Professional school counselors have always been of the belief that the jobs we do make a difference for students. We have not, however, always had the data, nor have we collected and provided data, to prove that this was so. Thankfully, with the advent of *No Child Left Behind*, which has brought about a new age of accountability, there is far more attention being paid to what is happening in schools that truly positively impacts student learning. In difficult economic times, programs that are not shown to make a difference either are being or are in danger of being cut. It is therefore imperative for every school counselor to be a part of collecting data, not only to

prove that their role in the school makes a difference with academic achievement, but also to know what the research is showing regarding the best use of counselor time and what classroom curricula are empirically shown to be effective. School counselors, now more than ever before, must make informed decisions and must be accountable. It is our responsibility to our own programs. as well as to our profession.

Source: Marilyn Agee, Concord East Side School Counselor and Elementary Counselor Coordinator, Concord Community Schools, Elkhart, Indiana

---

Bringman, and Vandiver (2004) described a three-year consultation project designed to promote strong working alliances among professional school counselors, teachers, and students' families. They held family–school problem-solving meetings that focused on developing plans to assist students by involving their parents in a nonblaming and respectful manner.

There are some indications that the verbal responses of professional school counselors were very similar whether they were conducting counseling sessions or consultation sessions (Lin, Kelly, & Nelson, 1996). One of the few differences these researchers found was that professional school counselors provided more information and asked fewer open and closed questions when they were consulting, as compared to when they were counseling. In terms of skills that increase the effectiveness of consultation, Gresham and Kendell (1987) found problem identification to be the most important process variable. Zins (1993) found a direct approach to be most effective in enhancing consultees' problem-solving skills. He recommended that counselors directly train consultees in problem-solving, communications, and intervention techniques. He further recommended that counselors overtly model for their consultees the problem-solving process.

There are many systems support activities that professional school counselors perform in order to implement their comprehensive school counseling program. This is a somewhat more difficult area to research, but we have a few suggestions. For example, does the amount of clerical support in professional school counseling programs have an influence on student outcomes? Do different types of scheduling software have an influence on the time professional school counselors spend with students? Are there differences in systems support procedures in high-performing schools versus low-performing schools?

In conclusion, it does appear that research related to systems support might also facilitate the transformation of school counseling programs.

DOES A FULLY IMPLEMENTED SCHOOL COUNSELING PROGRAM MAKE A DIFFERENCE?

In the previous section of this chapter, the efficacy of components and activities of a school counseling program were reviewed. As the field moves toward comprehensive, developmental school counseling programs, it is important to examine the research related to school counseling programs, and particularly the implementation of the *ASCA National Model* (ASCA 2003a, 2005a). Walsh, Barrett, and DePaul (2007) found that newly hired elementary counselors' activities did correspond to the guidelines suggested in the *ASCA National Model*. On the other hand, Whiston and Wachter (2008) found that on the average, high school counselors reported spending 27% of their time in nonprogram activities.

In order to determine the effectiveness of professional school counseling programs, it is essential to examine the degree to which these programs make a difference in students' lives. Sink and Stroh (2003) found that the academic achievement scores of elementary students who consistently attended schools with a comprehensive school counseling program were significantly higher than those of students who were attending schools with no systematic guidance program. This positive finding regarding academic achievement is further substantiated because the researchers' sample was quite large—5,618 third and fourth graders. The importance of a well-designed school counseling program was also underscored by Fitch and Marshall (2004). These researchers used achievement test scores to determine high-achieving and low-achieving schools and found that professional school counselors in high-achieving schools spent more time in program management and coordination. Furthermore, high-achieving schools were more likely to have implemented a school counseling program that aligned with national and state standards.

Lapan and his colleagues have conducted a number of studies related to whether more fully implemented school counseling programs are better for students. Lapan, Gysbers, and Petroski (2003) surveyed 22,601 seventh graders regarding their feelings of safety and other educationally related outcomes. Students attending middle schools with more fully implemented, comprehensive programs reported (1) feeling safer in school, (2) having better relationships with their teachers, (3) thinking their education was more relevant and important to their future, (4) being more satisfied with the quality of education at their school, and (5) earning higher grades. Lapan, Gysbers, and Sun (1997) compared schools with more fully implemented guidance programs to schools with a less programmatic approach. The students from schools with more fully implemented programs were more likely to report that (1) they had earned higher grades, (2) their education better prepared them for the future, (3) they had more career and college information available to them, and (4) their schools had a more positive environment. In another study, Gysbers, Lapan, and Blair (1999) found that school counselors from programs that were more fully implemented rated themselves as having higher levels of engagement with and more visibility in the community. In addition, although the results were somewhat mixed, those schools with more fully implemented guidance programs reported a reduction in the performance of nonguidance tasks, such as clerical or student supervision duties.

In the state of Utah, education personnel established the Utah Comprehensive Guidance Program in 1993. In a large study of schools in Utah, D. E. Nelson, Gardner, and Fox (1998) found that students in highly implemented, comprehensive guidance programs were more positive about their peers and felt their school had better prepared them for employment or further education, as compared to those students in schools designated as low in terms of implementing a guidance program. In addition, students in schools with highly implemented guidance programs tended to be more satisfied with the guidance they received, as compared to those in schools with a low implementation rating. In a recent study, D. E. Nelson, Fox, Haslam, and Gardner (2007) examined student perceptions toward conceptual areas connected with comprehensive guidance programs. The authors measured percentages of positive responses from both middle school and high school students in regard to a number of domains (e.g., School Climate, Exposure to Career Information). Nelson et al. found that students viewed the areas of School Climate and Personal Student Academic Planning most favorably. Additionally, they found generally positive responses on the measures of Student Involvement with Counseling and Quality of Help for Students from Counselors and Other Staff. Of the areas measured, the fewest positive responses were found in regard to Exposure to Career Information. In their review, Nelson et al. (2007) also compared performance by students at high-implementation schools versus performance by students at matched low-implementation schools on other outcome measures (e.g., ACT scores). The researchers found that students from high-implementation schools did better than did those in their matched low-implementation schools, with significant mean differences in performance. In addition, in comparing matched high- and low-implementation schools on the Iowa Tests of Basic Skills and Iowa Tests of Educational Development, Nelson et al. found that eighth graders from high-implementation middle schools showed performance superior to that of the comparison groups, albeit with small differentiation in mean differences between comparison groups.

One of the issues to be addressed in providing a comprehensive school counseling program is counselor-to-student ratios. The *ASCA National Model* (2003a, 2005a) recommended a counselor-to-student ratio of no more than 1:250. Carrell and Carrell (2006) sought to examine whether decreases in elementary counselor-to-student ratios influenced student outcomes. This study is important because the study design eliminated factors on which schools may differ (e.g., socioeconomic levels). Their results indicated that schools with higher counselor-to-student ratios were more likely to have higher numbers of students with recurring disciplinary problems.. In another study of counselor-to-student ratios, Whiston and Wachter (2008) found that low-achieving schools tended to have larger counselor-to-student ratios than did high-achieving schools. They classified high schools as being high achieving versus low achieving based on students' scores on Indiana's state achievement tests. Schools whose scores fell in the lower third of the distribution were classified as low achieving, and schools whose scores fell in the upper third of the distribution were classified as high achieving. Thus, there is increasing research that demonstrates that lower professional school counselor-to-student ratios positively influence a number of student outcomes.

Summary/Conclusion

Reviews of outcomes research in professional school counseling generally indicate that school counseling activities have a positive effect on students. The reviewers, however, vary somewhat on the degree to which they believe there is empirical support for professional school counseling interventions. Meta-analytic reviews of school counseling interventions indicate that school counseling activities are moderately to highly effective. The conclusion that many school counseling interventions are effective may be heartening to professional school counselors, but we would suggest that it is an important time to communicate these findings to principals, parents, school board members, and legislators. Furthermore, these stakeholders should be informed that smaller counselor-to-student ratios are associated with better student outcomes.

This review of the school counseling outcomes research indicates that many school counseling interventions produce positive effects, but that not all interventions produce beneficial results for students. Therefore, professional school counselors need to be cautious in selecting activities. For example, at the elementary level, some guidance curriculum activities designed to increase self-esteem did not necessarily increase self-esteem. Moreover, many of the guidance curriculum activities at the elementary level produced comparatively small positive ESs.

On the other hand, a number of school counseling activities were supported by research. More fully implemented, comprehensive school counseling programs were found to result in better outcomes than were nonsystematic approaches to school counseling activities. Studies suggest that within a comprehensive school counseling program, responsive services at the elementary level seem to be particularly effective, whereas guidance curriculum activities appear to be more effective at the junior high/middle school and high school levels. Middle and junior high school students seem to benefit greatly from individual planning activities. Furthermore, counselor involvement in career development activities is also supported, and schools should be discouraged from relying on counselor-free interventions (e.g., computer programs).

Surveys of professional school counselors indicate most of them are using guidance curriculum materials that have not been researched. The Center for School Counseling Outcome Research (see the following section on "Resources") is a clearinghouse for the evaluation school counseling research and can assist professional school counselors in finding empirically supported guidance curriculum programs. It also appears that, based on the research, professional school counselors at the middle school level should consider integrating more guidance curriculum activities into their school counseling programs.

In terms of providing responsive services to assist students who are experiencing some difficulties in school, there is support for both individual and group counseling. In particular, there is increasing research related to group counseling in the schools. A number of studies seem to indicate that longer group counseling interventions tend to be more effective than briefer ones. There also are indications that more empirical studies are being conducted of systematic group counseling programs, so professional school counselors should monitor research in this area.

There are mixed findings regarding the effectiveness of peer mediation programs. Peer programs require significant time, and professional school counselors need to examine whether the results are worth that time investment. As professional school counselors have many responsibilities, it is important to focus on implementing strategies that will be helpful to the students in their schools.

In conclusion, this analysis of the outcomes research on school counseling indicates that there is considerable need for more and better research in this area. Whiston et al. (2008) found that the majority of studies in their meta-analysis did not contain sufficient information about the treatment that would allow for replication of the study. They also found that many of the studies used outcomes measures that were author developed and often used only once. Whiston (2002) noted the lack of psychometrically sound outcomes measures suitable for school counseling research studies. Better and more research is needed because the lack of systematic and rigorous research may put the field in peril. Education is frequently the focus of public interest, and currently there is close scrutiny of educational practices. The public is no longer interested in funding educational programs without substantial evidence that these programs contribute to increased student learning. This is a critical time for professional school counselors and researchers to join together and provide more compelling documentation concerning the positive effects that school counseling programs have on children and adolescents. There is also a particular need to examine the cost-effectiveness of school counseling services. Without additional empirical support, some schools may eliminate professional school counseling programs

Readers need to consider ways they can contribute to outcomes research on school counseling. Professional school counselors should encourage professional organizations to devote funds to research projects and should welcome researchers into their schools. In addition, practicing professional school counselors can identify methods for evaluating themselves and their own programs and share these results with other professional school counselors. Students in the field of school counseling might consider taking additional research classes so they are prepared to contribute to the knowledge base and become involved in research projects related to school counseling during and after their graduate studies. The future of professional school counseling is at risk unless there is a shared commitment to conducting research that clearly documents how professional school counselors make a positive difference in students' lives.

Activities

1. Begin the basic process of a research project on a topic related to school counseling. What topic would you like to gather data and information about? Would you use a qualitative or quantitative study? What would you hope or expect to find?
2. Choose an intervention you would like to implement in a school setting. Search the literature for empirically based outcomes studies pertaining to that intervention. What did you learn about this intervention from the literature? How will this affect your approach to implementing this intervention in a school setting?

3. Call a local school to find out if the counseling department offers counseling groups. Interview the professional school counselor who facilitates the groups. Has he or she noticed a difference in the student population since the program began? Ask what studies are conducted or what documentation is collected to demonstrate program outcomes and effectiveness. How might this intervention be effectively implemented in all schools?

Resources

Center for School Counseling Outcome Research (University of Massachusetts Amherst)

http://www.umass.edu/schoolcounseling/index.htm

What Works Clearinghouse (U.S. Department of Education, Institute of Educational Sciences)

http://ies.ed.gov/ncee/wwc

SAMHSA's National Registry of Evidence-Based Programs and Practices

http://www.nationalregistry.samhsa.gov

5

Ethical, Legal, and Professional Issues in School Counseling

Lynn Linde

Editor's Introduction: Before moving into the "how to" portion of this book, we must address some ethical, legal, and professional issues. Always remember that professional school counselors are first and foremost representatives of the school counseling profession. How you conduct yourself personally and professionally reflects on your colleagues. Knowledge and understanding of the issues reviewed in this chapter are but a starting point. Keep up to date with the laws, ethics, policies, and procedures that govern professional practice. The implementation of your professional responsibilities will require your undivided attention every day of your professional life.

One of the greatest challenges facing most professional school counselors daily is how to appropriately handle the many different ethical and legal situations they encounter. Due to the nature of school counseling, counselors must be prepared to help students who have a variety of problems. It is often difficult to know all that one needs to know. Fortunately, there are a number of resources and sources of information that can help guide counselors as they strive to assist students in an ethical and legal manner. The professional associations for counselors have created ethical standards for professional behavior and provide a wealth of current information, resources, and training. Federal and state governments continually enact laws and regulations that affect counselors, and the courts in the state and federal judicial branches hand down decisions that directly affect counselors' behavior. In addition, state boards of education and local school systems create policies, guidelines, and procedures that professional school counselors must follow. Each of these areas will be covered in detail in the sections that follow.

PROFESSIONAL ASSOCIATIONS AND CREDENTIALING ORGANIZATIONS

The American Counseling Association (ACA) is the professional association for all types of counselors. Its mission is to enhance the quality of life in society by promoting the development of professional counselors, advancing the counseling profession, and using the profession and practice of counseling to promote respect for human dignity and diversity. The ACA is a partnership of associations representing professional counselors who enhance human development. It comprises 19 divisions, which represent specific work settings or interest areas within the field of counseling; about 50 state or affiliate branches; and 4 regions, which represent major geographical areas. The ACA influences all aspects of professional counseling through its programs, committees, and functions. This includes the credentialing of counselors and accreditation of counselor education programs, ethical standards, professional development, professional resources and services, and public policy and legislation.

The ACA has 15 standing committees, which address much of the professional business of the association. One of those is the Ethics Committee, which is responsible for updating the ethical standards for the association and investigating ethical complaints. When joining the ACA, one must sign a statement agreeing to abide by the *ACA Code of Ethics* (2005a). This is covered in more detail in the next section. The other committees are Awards, Bylaws and

Policies, Cyber-Technology, Financial Affairs, Human Rights, International, Interprofessional, Nominations and Elections, Professional Standards, Public Awareness and Support, Public Policy and Legislation, Publications, Research and Knowledge, and Strategic Planning. Each year task forces are created to address time-limited concerns and business for the association; there are currently 10 task forces. Task forces last for one year unless it is determined that additional time is needed, in which case they must be reappointed.

The ACA and its affiliates offer many training and professional development opportunities through state, regional, and national conferences, workshops, and learning institutes. *The Journal of Counseling and Development,* the ACA journal, and the journals published by its divisions cover current research, professional practices, and other information valuable to the practicing counselor. Its monthly newsletter, *Counseling Today,* includes information about what is going on in the field, as well as covering special topics and providing notes about members and a governmental relations update. The ACA also publishes books about counseling and current trends and topics in the field, some of which are used as textbooks in counseling courses. ACA staff are available for consultation on a variety of issues, represent the ACA before Congress and other organizations, and advocate for counselors and professional counseling. The ACA has recently developed email newsletters targeted to different types of counselors, provides continuing education for members through the web, and offers liability insurance as a member benefit for students. In summary, the ACA touches all counselors' lives, from the training they receive, to the requirements they must achieve to be credentialed, to the way in which they conduct themselves (regardless of the type of counseling practiced), to the professional development in which they engage.

The American School Counselor Association (ASCA) is a semiautonomous division of the ACA and addresses school counseling issues. The ASCA "supports school counselors' efforts to help students focus on academic, personal/social and career development so they achieve success in school and are prepared to lead fulfilling lives as responsible members of society" (ASCA, 2005a, p. 1). The ASCA targets its efforts toward professional development, publications and other resources, research, and advocacy specifically for professional school counselors. It publishes its journal, *Professional School Counseling,* six times a year and a bi monthly magazine, *The School Counselor.* The ASCA sends its members several email newsletters and alerts on various topics pertaining to school counseling. It also offers its members liability insurance as part of membership. The ASCA has a number of committees that perform the work of the association. One

of the main focuses of the ASCA is *The ASCA National Model for School Counseling: A Framework for School Counseling Programs* (2005a). The *National Model* provides the framework for a comprehensive, data-driven school counseling program; more information about the model can be found in Chapter 3 and on the ASCA's webpage at www.ascanationalmodel.org.

The National Board for Certified Counselors (NBCC) began as a corporate partner of the ACA and is now an autonomous organization. Headquartered in Greensboro, North Carolina, the NBCC is the only national credentialing organization for professional counselors; all other licenses and certifications are granted through state and local entities. The NBCC has established the National Certified Counselor (NCC) credential and several specialty-area certifications. The National Counselor Exam (NCE) must be passed as part of the process for becoming nationally certified. The NCE is also frequently required by state counseling licensure boards for professional counselor licensure or certification.

The Counsel for Accreditation of Counseling and Related Educational Programs (CACREP) also began as a corporate partner of the ACA and is now an autonomous organization. CACREP is responsible for establishing state-of-the-art standards for counselor education programs. CACREP standards address program objectives and curricula, faculty and staff requirements, program evaluation, and other requirements for accreditation. Currently, more than 198 school counseling programs and 561 programs in all in the United States are CACREP accredited. Students who graduate from CACREP programs are usually in an advantageous position to be hired because their programs include 48 graduate credit hours and 700 hours of field placement.

ETHICAL STANDARDS AND LAWS

Counselors are sometimes confused by the difference between ethical standards and laws and what one should do when these appear to be in conflict with each other. It may be helpful to take a look at the origin of both. Ethical standards are usually developed by professional associations to guide the behavior of a specific group of professionals. According to Herlihy and Corey (2006), ethical standards serve three purposes: to educate members about sound ethical conduct, to provide a mechanism for accountability, and to serve as a means for improving professional practice. Ethical standards change and are updated periodically to ensure their relevance and appropriateness.

Ethical standards are based on generally accepted norms, beliefs, customs, and values (Fischer & Sorenson, 1996). The *ACA Code of Ethics* (2005a) is based on

Kitchener's five moral principles of autonomy, justice, beneficence, nonmaleficence, and fidelity (Forester-Miller & Davis, 1996). Autonomy refers to the concept of independence and the ability to make one's own decisions. Counselors need to respect the right of clients to make their own decisions based on their personal values and beliefs and must not impose their values on clients. Justice means treating each person fairly, but it does not mean treating each person the same way. Rather, counselors should treat clients according to client needs. Beneficence refers to doing good or what is in the best interests of the client. In counseling, it also incorporates the concept of removing conditions that might cause harm. Nonmaleficence means doing no harm to others. And fidelity involves the concepts of loyalty, faithfulness, and the honoring of commitments. This means that counselors must honor all obligations to the client, starting with the relationship.

Laws are also based on these same, generally accepted norms, beliefs, customs, and values. However, laws are more prescriptive, have been incorporated into a legal code, and carry greater sanctions or penalties for failure to comply. Both laws and ethical standards prescribe appropriate behavior for professionals within a particular context in order to ensure that the best interests of the client are met. When the two appear to be in conflict with each other, the professional must attempt to resolve the conflict in a responsible manner (Cottone & Tarvydas, 2007). Counselors must make their clients aware of the conflict and their ethical standards. But because there are greater penalties associated with laws, counselors will often follow the legal course of action if there is no harm to their clients. Many ethical standards recognize that other mandates must be followed and suggest that counselors work to change mandates that are not in the best interests of their clients. In the absence of laws or other legal directives, courts may look to the established standards of behavior of a profession to determine liability (Wheeler & Bertram, 2008).

Within the ACA, there are multiple codes of ethics. The ACA has the *ACA Code of Ethics* (2005a), to which its members must adhere. Additionally, several divisions, including the ASCA, have their own codes of ethics; also, the Association for Specialists in Group Work (ASGW) has developed guidelines for best practices in group work. These codes of ethics and guidelines parallel the *ACA Code of Ethics*, but speak more directly to the specialty area. The ASCA's *Ethical Standards for School Counselors* (2004a) discuss what ethical behavior consists of for those who work in a school setting and deal with issues specific to students, parents, colleagues, and the community.

Many counselors belong to multiple organizations, each of which has its own code of ethics. They may also hold credentials from organizations or state credentialing boards that have a code of ethics as well. It is often hard to know which code takes precedence. While each professional will have to make that determination individually, the answers to these two questions provide general guidelines. First, in what setting is the professional practicing, and is there a code that applies specifically to that setting? Second, in what capacity is the professional operating? Additionally, all the codes are similar, and all concern behaving in an appropriate, professional manner; operating in the best interests of the client; and practicing within the scope of one's education, training, and experience. If a counselor is doing all of that, then the existence of multiple codes of ethics should not be a significant issue.

ACA Code of Ethics

The ACA revises the *ACA Code of Ethics* at least every 10 years. The sixth and most recent revision became effective in August 2005. There are several significant changes from the *1995 ACA Code of Ethics and Standards of Practice*. The most obvious change is that the Standards of Practice, which described in behavioral terms the aspirational ethics set forth in the code, are no longer separate, but have been incorporated into the body of the code. Each section of the code now begins with an introduction, which sets the tone for that section and is a beginning point for discussion (ACA, 2005a). Parts of the *ACA Code of Ethics* have been updated to reflect current thinking and practice in the field, and several new issues have been added. Additionally, a glossary of terms has been added.

The issue of culture and diversity is critical in this iteration of the code. The preamble to the 2005 *ACA Code of Ethics* begins with the assertion that "members must recognize diversity and embrace a cross-cultural approach in support of the worth, dignity, potential, and uniqueness of people within their social and cultural contexts" (2005, p. 3). Multicultural and diversity issues were infused into this code, as opposed to being a separate section, and the section on diagnosis cautions counselors to view problems within a cultural context. These changes further support the need to view counseling in a cultural context. The concept of family must also be viewed from a cultural context; in many cultures, family includes many more people than those to whom one is biologically connected. This concept is reflected in the change from the term *family* to *support network* in the code, thus reflecting the reality of our clients' worlds.

The 2005 *ACA Code of Ethics* states that it serves five main purposes:

1. The *Code* enables the association to clarify to current and future members, and to those served by members, the nature of the ethical responsibilities held in common by its members.

2. The *Code* helps support the mission of the association.
3. The *Code* establishes the principles that define ethical behavior and best practices of association members.
4. The *Code* serves as an ethical guide designed to assist members in constructing a professional course of action that best serves those utilizing counseling services and best promotes the values of the counseling profession.
5. The *Code* serves as the basis for processing of ethical complaints and inquiries initiated against members of the association. (ACA, 2005a, p. 3)

The 2005 *ACA Code of Ethics* (see Appendix A) addresses the responsibilities of professional counselors toward their clients, colleagues, workplace, and themselves by delineating the ideal standards for one's behavior. All members are required to abide by the *ACA Code of Ethics*, and action will be taken against any member who fails to do so. In effect, as these are the standards of the profession, all professional counselors are held to the *ACA Code of Ethics* by the mental health community, regardless of whether they are members of the association.

The *ACA Code of Ethics* is divided into eight areas: The Counseling Relationship; Confidentiality, Privileged Communication, and Privacy; Professional Responsibility; Relationships with Other Professionals; Evaluation, Assessment, and Interpretation; Supervision, Training, and Teaching; Research and Publication; and Resolving Ethical Issues. Each of these areas details the responsibilities and standards for that area. In general, the *ACA Code of Ethics* discusses respecting one's clients and the backgrounds they bring to the counseling setting; maintaining professional behavior with clients and other professionals; practicing with the best interests of clients in mind; and practicing within the limits of one's training, experience, and education. The last section provides direction for members resolving ethical dilemmas.

ASCA Ethical Standards for School Counselors

The ASCA's *Ethical Standards for School Counselors* (2004a) begin with a preamble, which affirms each individual's right to be treated with respect and dignity, to receive information and support, to understand the meaning of one's choices and the impact these choices have upon future opportunities, and to be afforded the right to confidentiality. The *Ethical Standards for School Counselors* define expected behavior in seven areas. Section A discusses responsibilities to students and includes Responsibilities to Students; Confidentiality; Counseling Plans; Dual Relationships; Appropriate Referrals; Group Work; Danger to Self or Others; Student Records;

Evaluation, Assessment and Interpretation; Technology; and Student Peer Support Program. Section B discusses responsibilities to parents and guardians and includes Parent Rights and Responsibilities and Parents/Guardians and Confidentiality. Section C discusses responsibilities to colleagues and professional associates and includes Professional Relationships and Sharing Information with Other Professionals. Section D discusses responsibilities to the school and community and includes Responsibilities to the Schools and Responsibility to the Community. Section E discusses responsibilities to self and includes Professional Competence and Diversity. Section F discusses responsibilities to the profession and includes Professionalism and Contribution to the Profession. Section G discusses maintenance of standards.

Like the *ACA Code of Ethics*, the ASCA standards discuss putting each student's best interests first, treating each student as an individual and with respect, involving parents as appropriate, maintaining one's expertise through ongoing professional development and learning, and behaving professionally and ethically.

Both the ACA and the ASCA have developed guides to ethical decision making that can be used when a counselor is concerned about a particular situation and needs to determine if an ethical dilemma exists. The ACA's model involves seven steps: (1) identify the problem, (2) apply the *ACA Code of Ethics*, (3) determine the nature and dimensions of the dilemma, (4) generate potential courses of action, (5) consider the potential consequences of all options and choose a course of action, (6) evaluate the selected course of action, and (7) implement the course of action (Forester-Miller & Davis, 1996).

C. B. Stone (2005) has taken the ACA model and applied it to the school setting. She named the nine-step model the STEPS Model for School Settings. The steps are as follows:

1. Define the problem emotionally and intellectually;
2. Apply the ACA and ASCA ethical codes and the law;
3. Consider the students' chronological and developmental levels;
4. Consider the setting, parental rights, and minors' rights;
5. Apply the moral principles;
6. Determine your potential courses of action and the consequences, and choose one;
7. Evaluate the selected action;
8. Consult; and
9. Implement the course of action. (pp. 17–19)

As Stone and others caution, counselors using either of these models or any other ethical decision-making model will not necessarily come to the same conclusion. There is seldom one correct way of handling any given situation, and each counselor brings different background, values, and belief systems to each dilemma. However, if one reflects on the moral principles and continues to practice with these in mind, it is likely that the dilemma can be resolved in the client's best interests.

Remley and Herlihy (2010) suggested four self-tests to consider, once a decision has been made. First, in thinking about justice, would you treat others this same way if they were in a similar situation? Second, would you suggest this same course of action to other counselors? Third, would you be willing to have others know how you acted? And last, do you have any lingering feelings of doubt or uncertainty about what you did? If you cannot answer in the affirmative to the first three tests and in the negative to the fourth test, then perhaps the decision was not ethically sound. It is always appropriate and ethically sound to consult with a colleague when working through a dilemma to ensure that all aspects of the issue have been examined and that all possible problems have been discussed. Remley and Huey (2002) developed an ethics quiz for school counselors that is one tool professional school counselors can use to test their knowledge of ethical codes and to reflect on their professional conduct.

SOURCES OF INFORMATION AND GUIDANCE

While ethical standards provide an important foundation for guiding counselor behavior, there are a number of other sources of information with which counselors must become familiar if they are to maintain the highest standards of ethical and legal behavior. Each of these other sources is described below.

The Court System

Counselors are affected by three main types of laws: statutory law, which is created by legislatures and interpreted by courts; constitutional law, which results from court decisions concerning constitutional issues; and common law, which results from court decisions on issues not governed by statutes. There are 51 U.S. court systems—the court systems for the 50 states and the federal system. Both state and federal courts can issue decisions affecting counselors, and both are usually composed of tiers. The structure of state courts varies, but generally consists of trial courts—which include courts of special jurisdiction such as juvenile court and small claims court—and courts of appeal. All states have a court that is the final authority to which cases may be appealed. The name of this court varies across states. In Maryland and New York, it is called the court of appeals; in

West Virginia, it is called the supreme court of appeals; in other states, it is called the superior court. One must be careful in reading state court decisions to note which court rendered the decision, as the names are not consistent across states. Certain cases from the highest court in each state may be appealed to the U.S. Supreme Court. Decisions from state courts are binding only on persons living within that state, but may serve as persuasive precedent for a similar case in another state.

The federal court system is a three-tiered system. The approximately 100 U.S. district courts form the first tier of the federal system. They are general trial courts that hear cases involving federal law, disputes between citizens that involve over $75,000, and disputes where the United States is a party (Fischer, Schimmel, & Kelly, 1999). There are 13 circuit courts of appeals. Decisions issued by a circuit court of appeals are binding only on those states within that court's jurisdiction. However, decisions issued by one circuit court may influence the decision rendered by a court in another circuit when the same issue arises. Parties may request the U.S. Supreme Court, the highest court in the country, to review rulings by circuit courts of appeals.

Statutory Law

Statutory law is the body of legislation passed by the U.S. Congress and state legislatures. Much of the structure of education and health services and many of the policies that govern their implementation are found within these statutory mandates. The U.S. Congress has authority to pass legislation related only to those powers specified in the Constitution, and it has enacted a number of laws that affect counselors who work both in schools and in other settings under its power to provide for the general welfare. The majority of legislation influencing schools and counselors is passed by state legislatures and is of two types: legislation passed to implement federal legislation and new, state-specific legislation. State laws may be more restrictive than federal legislation, but may never be less restrictive.

State and Local Agencies

Most state departments of education have the ability to enact regulations that are binding on the school districts within the state. The state's board of education passes regulations that encompass areas not addressed through state legislation or that add detail to state legislation such as implementation plans and more specific definitions. State agencies, including education departments, also develop policies, which are often detailed explanations of how to implement specific laws. Last, state agencies may issue guidelines, which are actually suggestions about how to address a specific issue. Unlike regulations and policies, guidelines are not mandates and do not have to be followed. However, because they do represent an agency's current thinking regarding a particular issue, local policies generally do not deviate too far from them.

Although it is not a regulation, the state attorney general may issue an opinion or advice of counsel. This guidance is frequently issued in response to a new court case or law or to the request of a state agency. The advice or opinion is the attorney general's legal interpretation of what that law or case means for the agency or agencies affected and usually suggests what the agency needs to do

to comply. The advice or ruling is often incorporated into policy or guidelines by the agency.

Local school systems and agencies may also develop their own policies, procedures, and guidelines. School systems, in particular, often take state regulations and policies and rewrite them to reflect their specific local situation; these are often then adopted by the local board of education. Local mental health departments or agencies may also further define state policies and procedures to reflect their jurisdiction-specific needs. Finally, individual schools or centers may have additional policies or guidelines in place for certain issues that further direct the manner in which a professional school counselor must act.

VOICES FROM THE FIELD 5.1   ETHICAL CONSIDERATIONS IN THE SCHOOLS

The professional school counselor is faced with a number of ethical situations on a daily basis. While ethical standards and practices are clearly established by the professional organizations that guide us (i.e., the ACA and ASCA), I have found that the situations I am often presented with as a school counselor fall into a gray area. This point was illustrated by a recent school counseling intern; as we handled a tricky abuse case, she asked, "At what point will I just know what to do?" While I believe you never just know, it is my opinion that counselors must rely on their training and stay abreast of policies, regulations, and current practices. This being noted, it is with time and many experiences with challenging situations, as well as having established a network of professional counselors and/or supervisors with whom to consult, that I believe one becomes effective in dealing with the ethical, legal, and professional aspects of this profession.

To be effective, it is imperative to know when you "don't know" what to do. Not knowing does not imply or suggest ineptitude; however, acting when you really "don't know" can be risky and even unethical. Certainly, experience can breed confidence, but it remains important for each counselor to continually stay up to date and also to take time to reflect on his or her actions. As a new counselor, each action I took was slow and deliberate. I reviewed policy and consulted with supervisors and other colleagues on each and every case. Decisions today come more quickly, but I continue to be deliberate in my judgment and consult frequently with colleagues to assure I am acting in the best "ethical" interest of the student.

Understanding your role in any given situation is also an important consideration. Professional school counselors have a unique position within the school building and are bound often by a different standard of ethics. This can be further complicated as, by instinct, many school counselors see themselves as "helpers." The professional school counselor functions and "helps" within certain legal and ethical

standards set forth by professional organizations, as well as by the school systems in which we are employed. Being effective is often different from "helping." One must continually examine attempts to be "helpful" for the sake of helping. For example, counselors sometimes find themselves in ethical dilemmas with staff members by sharing perhaps too much information in an effort to help or by functioning outside of their role as a school counselor and inadvertently "counseling" fellow staff members who seek advice. Balancing the desire to help with the ethics of the job can be tricky, but it is necessary.

It is important to remember that we serve students first, yet are responsible for having relationships with many stakeholders in that student's life such as teachers, administrators, staff, parents, and the community. It can be complicated to juggle the demands of running an effective program, while balancing the unique needs of the people whom we ultimately serve. It is important to educate all stakeholders about the role of the professional school counselor, including ethical and professional responsibilities. This should be done frequently, informally during collaboration with staff and formally during in-service opportunities.

Recently, at a system counseling department chair meeting, I was asked to facilitate a discussion about ethics and the school counselor. The engagement level of the participants was high, as this topic lends itself easily to great discussion. The biggest piece of advice that resulted after reviewing many articles and ethical standards is to consult your colleagues when in doubt. Many counselors admitted that they are sometimes hesitant for fear that a colleague might see them as ineffective. The ASCA and ACA highly recommend peer consultation in times of confusion, and consultation actually can serve to protect you legally. If your actions are found to be questionable, courts or review boards often ask, "Would another counselor have acted the same way?" While middle and secondary counselors often use their team or department as a sounding board, elementary counselors are frequently the sole counselor in the school and must branch out. Many school systems allow networking opportunities via planned professional development or meetings. The system where I am employed establishes counseling cluster groups to meet monthly for this purpose.

The job of a professional school counselor is multifaceted because it is results-based. It is not about how much a school counselor does in a given day, but rather how effective the actions of the school counselor have been. Counselors need to hold themselves to a high standard of accountability with regard to each action and remain attuned to the ethical, legal, and professional implications in their day-to-day interactions.

Source: Jennifer Elsis, Professional School Counselor, Bodkin Elementary School, Anne Arundel County Public School System, Maryland

---

MAKING DECISIONS

Failure to understand the law—and by extension, policies, procedures, and guidelines—is not an acceptable legal defense. It is incumbent on the professional school counselor to become familiar with all the various sources of information and guidance that are available in order to carry out his or her responsibilities in an ethical and legal manner. Fortunately, there are many ways of staying abreast of current information.

In most work settings, with the exception perhaps of private practice, counselors have a supervisor or other person in authority who can help them become familiar with the regulations, policies, and guidelines relevant to that setting. Most schools and many community agencies have administrative manuals that incorporate all these sources of information into continually updated binders. The ACA newsletter highlights issues and hot topics in counseling, as do other professional journals and newsletters. There are also a number of commercially available newsletters that cover recent court rulings and their impact in different work settings. The Internet has become an invaluable tool for finding current information and resources. Guillot-Miller and Partin (2003) identified over 40 sites that include information relevant to ethical and legal practices for counselors. Professional associations for counselors and other mental health professionals, institutions of higher education, state and federal government agencies, government-funded organizations, and professional and legal publishers all continuously update their websites and are good sources of current information.

There may be times when mandates appear to be in conflict with each other. In such cases, common sense should prevail. There may be a therapeutically logical reason to follow one particular mandate, rather than another one. Counselors should follow the logical course of action and document what they did and why. For example, if a counselor is working with a suicidal student, but believes that telling the parents will result in an abusive situation, the counselor should handle the situation as an abuse case and tell Child Protective Services about the suicidal behavior. Additionally, if following a particular policy, guideline,

or regulation is not in the best interest of the students in the counselor's work setting, as per the ethical standards, the counselor should work to change the mandate.

Two other issues are sometimes confusing for counselors. The first concerns the different ways in which counselors in different settings operate. Some mandates—and particularly those that are the result of federal or state legislation or court cases—cover all counselors. For example, child abuse and neglect laws apply to all counselors regardless of the setting in which they work. But the implementation of some mandates, particularly as they become policy and guidelines, may look very different in different settings. Schools have perhaps the greatest number of mandates under which staff must operate, yet professional school counselors seldom need permission to see students (Remley & Herlihy, 2010), particularly if there is an approved, comprehensive, developmental counseling program. A mental health counselor employed by an outside center or agency, but working either in a school or in a school-based health center, needs signed, informed consent to see those same students. In some cases, local school systems have mandated an opt-in program, which is a program that requires signed, informed consent for students to participate in different aspects of the comprehensive guidance program. In such cases, professional school counselors working in nearby systems or even schools may operate very differently.

The second issue concerns counselors who hold multiple credentials. A counselor may work as a professional school counselor, but hold state certification or licensure and work as a mental health counselor outside of school. The counselor may need permission to do something as a professional school counselor, but not need permission to do the same thing as a mental health counselor, or vice versa. Under which set of mandates should the counselor operate?

The solution to both of these issues is the same: Employees must follow the mandates that apply to their work setting. Counselors are required to operate under the mandates of the system that employs them or, in the case of volunteers, the mandates of the entity under whose auspices they are working. If a counselor is employed by a school system as a counselor, then he or she must follow the mandates of the local school system. Teachers who have

VOICES FROM THE FIELD 5.2 | **DECISIONS ARE NOT ALWAYS BLACK AND WHITE**

Many school counseling programs require school counselors to take an ethics course or receive training regarding ethical decision making. In this training, various scenarios are discussed and standards of conduct are reviewed. I left my ethics course feeling relieved that I had a specific set of guidelines to adhere to when faced with difficult situations. In addition to making sure I understood the ethical guidelines established by the American School Counseling Association, I became familiar with state and local laws and policies that affected school counselors. As I set up my first office, I made sure to have these current guidelines and laws at my fingertips. However, I soon learned that every ethical situation did not have a specific black-and-white answer. For example, the parent of one of the students on my caseload did not believe in school counseling and specifically asked me to not ever meet with his son. After learning from a teacher that this student was having suicidal thoughts, I was faced with the ethical dilemma of meeting with this student and going against the parent's consent or not following my county's mandated protocol for suicide threats. According to the ASCA, there are guidelines about obtaining parent consent and there are guidelines about taking appropriate actions to prevent student harm. Trying to decide which guideline to follow was difficult. I consulted with my colleagues and principal, and together we came up with a plan. I learned the value of consulting with my colleagues.

When working with adolescent students, topics such as sexual experiences, sexually transmitted diseases, and pregnancy come up during individual counseling sessions, and school counselors find themselves facing ethical dilemmas surrounding issues of confidentiality. It is important to stay informed about local laws, policies, and procedures within your own state, as these laws and policies surrounding confidentiality can vary. I have had students share with me that they are questioning their sexual orientation. There are no specific guidelines, laws, or policies that speak specifically

to counseling gay, lesbian, or questioning students in a school setting, other than to be nonjudgmental. These situations call for school counselors to apply ethical guidelines to individual situations based on interpretation. Sometimes these ethical dilemmas are the result of directives given to school counselors by administrators and principals that may be in conflict with specific guidelines school counselors have to follow according to policies and procedures set by their county or their professional organization. In these situations, having established resources such as the county's Office of School Counseling to consult with and get support from is key in making the right decision. It is vital that school counselors enter the field with an established plan for making ethical decisions that should include examining local and state guidelines, laws, policies, and procedures, as well as consulting with colleagues and outside resources if necessary, as no two situations are the same.

Another aspect of acting ethically responsible when working with students is examining your own core values and beliefs. I work in a community where going to a two- or four-year college after high school is not the top priority for many of the families. Many of these families run successful small businesses and want their children to work for their business right out of high school. Although my own belief is that obtaining a college degree should be a goal for every student, I need to be respectful of the hopes and dreams of the families I serve and of each individual student's postsecondary career goals. Being consciously aware of the differences between your own core values and beliefs and the values and beliefs of a particular family you are serving can ensure you are taking extra precaution to remain objective so that you can guide students into making choices that are right for them.

Source: Tracy MacDonald, Professional School Counselor, Chesapeake Bay Middle School, Anne Arundel County Public School System, Maryland

---

a degree in counseling or another related mental health degree, but who continue to be employed as teachers, do not have the same protections as counselors because they are not employed in a mental health capacity. They need to check their system's policies carefully to see if they are covered by any protections such as confidentiality.

ADDITIONAL LEGAL CONSIDERATIONS

In developing an ethical stance, professional school counselors must take all of the aforementioned sources of information into account. However, there are several other

influences that must be considered (Herlihy & Corey, 2006; Hopkins & Anderson, 1990; C. B. Stone, 2005; Wheeler & Bertram, 2008). Each counselor brings to every counseling relationship the sum of his or her experiences, education, and training. Each also brings to the setting that which makes him or her unique: that is, values, morals, and spiritual influences. Who a counselor is strongly influences the stance he or she takes on issues. Professional school counselors must continually be aware of how their own beliefs and values impact the way they think about issues, the students and their needs, and the options that they perceive to be available. Counselors must also continually examine their behavior in light of cultural bias and multicultural understanding. When deciding on a course of action for their clients, counselors must always try to do what is in the best interests of the clients.

Professional Competence

In addition to being knowledgeable about mandates, as was previously discussed, there are a number of further steps counselors should take to ensure ethical and legal behavior. Several of these are mentioned in the ethical standards, but it is important to reemphasize them. As reported in Cottone and Tarvydas (2007) and Wheeler and Bertram (2008), counselors should

- Maintain professional growth through continuing education. While counselors must attend continuing education opportunities to renew national credentials, state credentials, or both, it is important to stay current with theories, trends, and information about clients and different populations.
- Maintain accurate knowledge and expertise in areas of responsibility. Information changes so quickly that counselors must ensure they are providing quality and effective services to their clients. One way of achieving this goal is through professional development, but counselors may also gain information through reading, consultation with colleagues, supervision, and other means.
- Accurately represent credentials. As stated in the ethical standards, counselors should claim only those credentials they have earned and only the highest degree in counseling or a closely related mental health field. Counselors who hold doctorates in non–mental health fields should not use the title "doctor" in their work as a counselor. This is a particular problem in school settings where counselors earn doctorates in administration and supervision, or related fields, but continue to work as counselors and use the title "doctor" in their job. Furthermore, counselors should not imply in any way that their credentials allow them to work in areas in which they are not trained.
- Provide only those services for which they are qualified and trained. The easiest way for counselors to get into trouble professionally is to provide services for which they are not qualified, either by training or by education. This is particularly true when using counseling techniques. Counselors should have training in using a particular technique before using it. Reading about a technique is not equivalent to implementing it under supervision. Professional school counselors should also not try to work with students whose problems go beyond their expertise. If a professional school counselor is put in a situation where there are no other

counselors to whom to refer the student, the counselor should consult with colleagues and ask for supervision to ensure the effectiveness of the counseling.

"Can I Be Sued?" and "What Is Malpractice?"

The answer to "Can I be sued?" is, of course, yes. Anyone can be sued for almost anything, particularly in our litigious society. But the more important question is "Will I be found guilty?" The answer to this question is much more complex.

If professional school counselors fail to exercise *due care* in fulfilling their professional responsibilities, they can be found legally liable for harm caused to an individual by such failure. A court may find negligence if the duty owed to the client was breached in some way, resulting in injury or damages. In counseling, it is more common for counselors to be sued for malpractice. Malpractice, the area of tort law that concerns professional conduct, has been defined as "negligence in carrying out professional responsibilities or duties" (Wheeler & Bertram, 2008, p. 34). Generally, for a counselor to be held liable in tort for malpractice, four conditions have to be met (C. B. Stone, 2005): A duty was owed to the client (now the plaintiff) by the counselor (now the defendant); the counselor breached the duty; there is a causal link between the breach and the client's injury; and the client suffered some damage or injury.

An example of negligence would be a counselor who failed to report an abuse case. The counselor had a duty to the client and failed to fulfill that duty. With malpractice, the client suffers due to lack of skill or appropriate behavior on the part of the counselor. An example of malpractice would be a counselor who used hypnosis to treat a client with an eating disorder when the counselor was not trained to use the technique of hypnosis. The situation would be further complicated if this technique was not recognized as being particularly effective for treating eating disorders.

The standard of practice will be used in any liability proceeding to determine if the counselor's performance was within accepted practice. The standard of practice question is "In the performance of professional services, did the counselor provide the level of care and treatment that is consistent with the degree of learning, skill and ethics ordinarily possessed and expected by reputable counselors practicing under similar circumstances?" (ACA, 1997, p. 9).

The standard of practice will be established through the testimony of peers. These peers are called as expert witnesses because they are considered to be experts in the field under question. For professional school counselors, the expert witnesses will be other school counselors (C. B. Stone, 2005). The standard of practice is an ever-evolving level of expectation and is influenced by two major factors: education and experience. The standard is not an absolute one, but rather a variable one. It will be much higher for a counselor who has practiced for a number of years and pursued advanced graduate training or professional development than it will be for a counselor in the first year of practice immediately following graduate school. The more training and experience a counselor possesses, the higher the standard to which the counselor will be held accountable. The assumption is that a counselor should know more each year he or she practices through experience and training and should therefore be held to a higher standard with each additional year. Using this standard of practice, a counselor will usually be found guilty of malpractice if one or more of the following situations occur (Wheeler & Bertram, 2008):

- The practice was not within the realm of acceptable professional practice.
- The counselor was not trained in the technique used.
- The counselor failed to follow a procedure that would have been more helpful.
- The counselor failed to warn and/or protect others from a violent client.
- The counselor failed to obtain informed consent from the client.
- The counselor failed to explain to the client the possible consequences of treatment.

Several professional publications (Wheeler & Bertram, 2008) have reported that sexual misconduct is the primary reason that liability actions are initiated against counselors. School staff, counselors, and other mental health professionals have been accused of committing sexual abuse or misconduct. It may be that other problems, such as failure to use a more appropriate technique, are actually more common, but that most clients lack the ability to recognize therapeutic problems and may just have a general sense that "it isn't working or helping" and choose to terminate.

While the number of professional school counselors who are sued is increasing, the number still remains very small. Parents are more likely to request their child not be included in certain guidance program activities or to complain to the principal or central administration about a program or behavior. In rare cases, parents may sue. The majority of cases against school counselors have been rejected by the courts (Fischer & Sorenson, 1996). In school settings, violating or failing to follow school system mandates will get a professional school counselor in trouble faster than almost any other behavior. Depending on the counselor's action, the system may choose to reprimand the professional school counselor. In extreme cases, the counselor's employment may be terminated. Professional school counselors must also be knowledgeable about their communities. They may have a legal right to implement certain programs or conduct certain activities, but if the community is not supportive of those activities, they are going to face opposition.

When a professional school counselor is faced with any legal action, the first thing the counselor should do is call a lawyer and then let the counselor supervisor, if there is one, know. Most agencies, clinics, practices, and schools are accustomed to dealing with such legal issues and may even have a procedure for what to do. Professional school counselors should never attempt to reason with the student or contact the student's lawyer without advice of counsel. It is important to not provide any information to, or discuss the case with, anyone except the counselor's lawyer or the person designated to help the counselor. Just as professional school counselors advise clients to get professional mental health help when they have personal problems, counselors must get legal help when they have legal problems.

Subpoenas

Many counselors will receive a subpoena at some point in their professional career. Counselors, and particularly professional school counselors, probably receive subpoenas most often in cases involving custody disputes, child abuse or neglect allegations, and special education disputes and these subpoenas can be brought forward on behalf of, or against, the counselor's client/student. In most cases, one of the parties in such a dispute believes that the counselor may have some information that will be helpful to his or her case. Professional school counselors need to pay attention to subpoenas because they are legal documents. At the same time, they need to consider whether the information being requested is confidential because professional school counselors may be limited in what they can share. Under no circumstances should the counselor automatically comply with the subpoena without discussing it first with the client (or the student's parents in the case of a minor child), the client's attorney, or both or without consulting the agency's or school system's attorney. According to the ACA (1997), a counselor should take the following steps when receiving a subpoena:

1. Contact the client or the client's attorney, and ask for guidance. If you work for a school system, contact the school system's attorney to seek guidance.
2. If the above-mentioned parties advise you to comply with the subpoena, discuss with the student, family or attorney the implications of releasing the requested information.
3. Obtain a signed informed-consent form to release the records. That form should specify all conditions of release: what, to whom, and so forth.
4. If the decision is made to not release the records, cooperate with the client's attorney in filing a motion to quash (or in some areas, asking for a protective order). This will allow you to not comply with the subpoena.

5. Maintain a record of everything you and the client's attorney did; keep notes regarding all conversations and copies of any documents pertaining to the subpoena.

An attorney who wants information may also ask a judge to issue a court order. A court order permits the release of confidential information, but does not mandate its release (ACA, 1997). If both a subpoena and a court order are received, the counselor must release the information with or without the client's consent. Failure to do so may result in the counselor's being held in contempt of court.

There are two important things to remember about subpoenas: do not panic, and do consult an attorney. Subpoenas are legal documents, but you have enough time to consider the implications of releasing the information and to seek legal advice.

CONFIDENTIALITY

For clients to feel free to share sometimes sensitive and personal information during a counseling session, they must feel that they can trust the counselor not to share what is disclosed during sessions with anyone else without their permission. This sense of trust and privacy, called confidentiality, is essential for counseling to be successful. Confidentiality is the cornerstone of counseling and is what separates the counseling relationship from other relationships where information is shared. Confidentiality belongs to the client, not to the counselor. The client always has the right to waive confidentiality and allow the counselor to share information with a third party.

Counseling minors presents particular challenges with respect to the issue of confidentiality. Every state sets the age of majority; for most states, it is 18 years of age. Most students are minors and therefore not legally able to make their own decisions. Thus, these students have an ethical right to confidentiality, but the legal right belongs to their parents or guardian (Remley & Herlihy, 2010). Approximately twenty states protect professional school counselor–client confidentiality through statutes (Cottone & Tarvydas, 2007), but many include significant restrictions.

Professional school counselors often ask what to do if parents want to know what is discussed during counseling sessions with their children. Legally, parents, and only parents, have the right to know what is being discussed. However, the child might not want the information shared with the parent. Section B.5.b, Responsibility to Parents and Legal Guardians, of the *ACA Code of Ethics* states

> Counselors inform parents and legal guardians about the role of counselors and the confidential nature of the counseling relationship.

Counselors are sensitive to the cultural diversity of families and respect the inherent rights and responsibilities of parents/gaurdians over the welfare of the children/charges according to law. Counselors work to establish, as appropriate, collaborative relationships with parents/guardians to best serve clients. (ACA, 2005a, p. 8)

Section B. 2 of the ASCA *Ethical Standards for School Counselors* states

> The professional school counselor:
>
> a. Informs parents/guardians of the counselor's role with emphasis on the confidential nature of the counseling relationship between the counselor and student.
> b. Recognizes that working with minors in a school setting may require counselors to collaborate with students' parents/guardians.
> c. Provides parents/guardians with accurate, comprehensive and relevant information in an objective and caring manner, as is appropriate and consistent with ethical responsibilities to the student. (ASCA, 2004a, p. 3)

These statements leave counselors with a dilemma. To resolve this dilemma, Remley and Herlihy (2010) suggested that the counselor first discuss the issue with the child to determine if he or she is willing to disclose the information to the parent. If the child will not disclose, then the counselor should try to help the parent understand that the best interests of the child are not served by disclosure. If this does not work, then the counselor should schedule a joint meeting with the parent and child to discuss the issue. If the parent still is not satisfied, then the counselor may have to disclose the information without the child's consent. Some counselors would suggest that this type of situation may be reflective of some deeper family issue. While the parent or guardian has a legal right to the information, there may be an underlying "family secret" that the parent does not want known, and the counselor should be sensitive to any difficulties the child may be demonstrating. Or this situation may be the result of cultural differences, and the counselor needs to be more aware of and sensitive to the family's traditions and beliefs.

Many counselors suggest that at the beginning of the first session of each new counseling relationship, the professional school counselor should discuss confidentiality with the student, explain what it means, and point out the limits of confidentiality. Some counselors choose to hang a sign on the wall of their office that outlines this information as a reinforcement to what is discussed in the first session. While this issue appears to be simple on the surface, in reality it is a very complex issue that has generated a significant amount of research and professional discourse. As the use of technology increases in counseling settings, the discussions will continue and expand. There are significant challenges to keeping electronic information confidential.

Limits to Confidentiality

These provisions are included in the *ACA Code of Ethics* (2005a, p. 2):

- Section B.1.a: "Counselors respect client rights to privacy. . . ."
- Section B.1.c: "Counselors do not share confidential information without client consent or without sound legal or ethical justification."
- Section B.1.d: "At initiation and throughout the counseling process, counselors inform clients of the limitations of confidentiality and seek to identify foreseeable situations in which confidentiality must be breached."

There are several instances in which counselors must break confidentiality. These are delineated within Section B.2.a of the *ACA Code of Ethics* and Section A.7 of the ASCA *Ethical Standards for School Counselors*. The most important of these is the "duty to warn." When a counselor becomes aware that clients are in danger of being harmed, as in instances of abuse, or that clients are likely to harm themselves or someone else, the counselor can break confidentiality and tell an appropriate person.

The duty-to-warn standard was first set out in the 1976 court decision in *Tarasoff v. Regents of the University of California*. In this case, the client, a graduate student, told his psychologist about his intent to kill a girl (named Tarasoff) who had rejected his advances. The psychologist told the campus police and his supervisor, but did not warn the intended victim or her family. The majority of the California Supreme Court ruled that the psychologist had a duty to warn a known, intended victim. This case established the legal duty to warn and protect an identifiable victim from a client's potential or intended violence and has been the basis for many other court decisions across the country. In the ensuing decades, some cases have extended the duty-to-warn standard to include types of harm other than violence and foreseeable victims in addition to identifiable victims. Section B.2.a of the *ACA Code of Ethics* now reads: "The general requirement that counselors keep information confidential does not apply when disclosure is

required to protect clients or identified others from serious and foreseeable harm. . ." (ACA, 2005a, p. 2).

Several other situations constrain the limits of confidentiality, as delineated in the *ACA Code of Ethics* (2005a):

- *Subordinates.* Confidentiality is not absolute when subordinates, including employees, supervisees, students, clerical assistants, and volunteers, handle records or confidential information. Every effort should be made to limit access to this information, and the assistants should be reminded of the confidential nature of the information they are handling.
- *Treatment teams.* The client should be informed of the treatment team and the information being shared.
- *Consultation.* The professional school counselor always has the right to consult with a colleague or supervisor on any case. In such instances, the counselor should provide enough information to obtain the needed assistance, but should limit any information that might identify the client.
- *Group and families.* In group or family counseling settings, confidentiality is not guaranteed. The counselor may state that what goes on in the sessions is confidential, and the members may agree. However, because there is more than one client in the group, it is impossible to guarantee confidentiality.
- *Third-party payers.* Information will sometimes have to be sent to a mental health provider, insurance company, or other agency that has some legitimate need for the information. The counselor will disclose this information only with the client's permission.
- *Minors.* There are special considerations regarding confidentiality and minors that will be discussed in detail in the next section.
- *Contagious, life-threatening diseases.* Unlike the duty-to-warn standard, the ACA ethical standards state that the counselor is justified in disclosing information about a client to an identifiable third party if that party's relationship with the client is such that there is a possibility of contracting the disease and the client does not plan on telling the third party. It should be noted that the word used is *justified*, not *should* or *must*. This wording leaves it up to the counselor to decide if the third party is at risk and must be warned.
- *Court-ordered disclosure.* Subpoenas were previously discussed. Even if ordered to reveal confidential information by a judge, counselors should limit what they reveal to what is absolutely necessary.

In summary, confidentiality is a very complex issue, but essential to the effectiveness of counseling. Clients have an ethical right to confidentiality, and counselors must make every effort to ensure this right. However, there are specific cases where it is not only permissible, but also essential to break confidentiality to protect the client or to protect others from the client.

Confidentiality and Privileged Communication

The term *confidentiality* is used in discussions about counseling, while the term *privileged communication* is the legal term to describe the privacy of the counselor–client communication. Privileged communication exists by statute and applies only to testifying in a court of law. The privilege belongs to the client, who always has the right to waive the privilege and allow the counselor to testify. Clients have an ethical right to confidentiality, and the ethical standards for the mental health professions detail the boundaries of confidentiality. Privileged communication is more limited, and federal, state, and local mandates determine its parameters. Whether a client–counselor relationship is considered privileged communication varies widely across jurisdictions. Even within a jurisdiction, a counselor in private practice may be covered by privileged communication provisions, but the school counselors who work in that same jurisdiction may not be. It is essential that counselors become familiar with their local mandates and policies to determine the extent to which privileged communication applies to their situation.

MINOR CONSENT LAWS

All states have a minor consent law that allows certain minors to seek treatment for certain conditions, usually involving substance abuse, mental health, and some reproductive health areas. These laws are based on federal law, 42 U.S.C. § 290dd-2, and federal regulation, 42 C.F.R. Part 2, which reference the confidentiality of patient records for drug and alcohol abuse assessment, referral, diagnosis, and treatment. These federal mandates further prohibit the release of these records to anyone without the client's informed consent and include clients under the age of 18 years even if they are in school and living with parents or guardians.

Over the past 10 years, there has been a movement to increase the number of student assistance teams and student assistance programs (SAPs) in schools. These teams usually consist of an administrator, one or more student services professionals (e.g., professional school counselor, school social worker, pupil personnel worker, school psychologist, or school nurse), and teachers and may include a substance abuse assessor from a local agency or similar professional. School staff refer students who are suspected of having a substance abuse problem to this team. The team members are trained to deal with substance abuse issues and, if they believe the student has a substance abuse problem, will have the student assessed and referred for appropriate assistance.

The controversy surrounding this program concerns the role of parents or guardians in this process. Under the federal law, the student can go from referral through completion of treatment without the parents' or guardians' knowledge. Substance abuse professionals are divided regarding whether it is possible to successfully treat students who abuse substances without the family's involvement. Other professionals have concerns about the ability of young adolescents to seek treatment without any family knowledge or involvement.

As the federal law has been incorporated into state statutes, states have taken different approaches to deciding to whom this law applies and for what. In general, the patient must be old enough to understand the problem, the treatment options available, and the possible consequences of each option. Some states have no age limits and maintain that a minor has the same capacity as an adult to consent to certain services. On the other hand, some states have decided on a specific age, usually 12 years and older, at which the minor may consent to mental health treatment, reproductive or substance abuse services, and treatment for sexually transmitted infections (STIs) and Human Immunodeficiency Virus/Acquired Immune Deficiency Syndrome (HIV/AIDS). According to the Guttmacher Institute's *State Policies in Brief* (2005a, 2005b, 2009)(see Table 5.1), 25 states and the District of Columbia allow all minors to consent to all contraceptive services, 21 states allow minors to consent to contraceptive services in one or more circumstances, and 4 states have no law covering contraceptive services for minors. Thirty-two states and the District of Columbia allow minors to consent to prenatal treatment when pregnant, whereas 18 states have no law. All 50 states and the District of Columbia allow minors to consent to treatment for STIs and HIV/AIDS. Seventeen states and the District of Columbia allow, but do not require, the doctor to inform the parent about mental health services, and 29 do not, while the other four states allow contact under some circumsatnces. Twenty-one and the District of Columbia allow general medical care, and 29 do not. Three states and the District of Columbia allow abortion services, 40 require parental consent and/or notification, and seven have no law

There is tremendous variation across the 50 states in what is permissible under the law. There is also some question as to the applicability of this law to school settings. The laws clearly cover medical personnel and certain conditions. A school nurse is covered, but a professional school counselor or school psychologist may not be covered. It is critical that counselors and other student services personnel become familiar with the minor consent law in the state in which they work to ensure compliance. Staff must also investigate local

TABLE 5.1   An Overview of Minor Consent Law as of April 1, 2009

Minors May Consent To:

State	Contraceptive Services	STI Services	Prenatal Care	Adoption	Medical Care For Minor's Child	Abortion Services
Alabama	All[†]	All*	All	All	All	Parental consent
Alaska	All	All	All		All	▼ (Parental consent)
Arizona	All	All		All		Parental consent
Arkansas	All	All*	All		All	Parental consent
California	All	All	All	All		▼ (Parental consent)
Colorado	All	All	All	All	All	Parental consent
Connecticut	Some	All		Legal counsel	All	All
Delaware	All*	All*	All*	All	All	Parental notice[‡]
Dist. of Columbia	All	All	All	All	All	All
Florida	Some	All	All		All	Parental notice
Georgia	All	All*	All	All	All	Parental notice
Hawaii	All*,[†]	All*,[†]	All*,[†]	All		
Idaho	All	All[†]	All	All	All	Parental consent
Illinois	Some	All*	All	All	All	▼ (Parental notice)
Indiana	Some	All		All		Parental consent
Iowa	All	All				Parental notice
Kansas	Some	All*	Some	All	All	Parental notice
Kentucky	All*	All*	All*	Legal counsel	All	Parental consent
Louisiana	Some	All*		Parental consent	All	Parental consent
Maine	Some	All*				All
Maryland	All*	All*	All*	All	All	All
Massachusetts	All	All	All		All	Parental consent
Michigan	Some	All*	All*	Parental consent	All	Parental consent
Minnesota	All*	All*	All*	Parental consent	All	Parental notice
Mississippi	Some	All	All	All	All	Parental consent
Missouri	Some	All*	All*	Legal counsel	All	Parental consent
Montana	All*	All*	All*	Legal counsel	All	▼ (Parental notice)
Nebraska	Some	All				Parental notice
Nevada	Some	All	Some	All	All	▼ (Parental notice)
New Hampshire	Some	All[†]	Some	All[Ω]		
New Jersey	Some	All*	All*	All	All	

(Continued)

TABLE 5.1   **An Overview of Minor Consent Law as of April 1, 2009** (*Continued*)

Minors May Consent To:

State	Contraceptive Services	STI Services	Prenatal Care	Adoption	Medical Care For Minor's Child	Abortion Services
New Mexico	All	All	All	All		▼ (Parental consent)
New York	All	All	All	All	All	
North Carolina	All	All	All			Parental consent
North Dakota		All*,†		All		Parental consent
Ohio		All		All		Parental consent
Oklahoma	Some	All*	All*	All†	All†	Parental consent and notice
Oregon	All*	All	All*,Φ			
Pennsylvania	Some	All	All	Parental notice	All	Parental consent
Rhode Island		All		Parental consent	All	Parental consent
South Carolina	All◊	All◊	All◊	All	All	Parental consent
South Dakota	Some	All				Parental consent
Tennessee	All	All	All	All	All	Parental consent
Texas	Some	All*	All*			Parental consent
Utah	Some	All	All	All	All	Parental consent and notice
Vermont	Some	All		All		
Virginia	All	All	All	All	All	Parental consent
Washington	All	All†	All	Legal counsel		
West Virginia	Some	All		All		Parental notice
Wisconsin		All				Parental consent
Wyoming	All	All		All		Parental consent
Total	25+DC	50+DC	32+DC	28+DC	30+DC	3+DC

▼ Enforcement permanently or temporarily enjoined by a court order; policy not in effect.

  Notes: "All" applies to minors 12 and older unless otherwise noted. "Some" applies to specified categories of minors (those who have a health issue, or are married, pregnant, mature, etc.) The totals include only those states that allow all minors to consent.

* Physicians may, but are not required to, inform the minor's parents.

† Applies to minors 14 and older.

‡ Applies to minors younger than 17.

Ω A court may require parental consent.

Φ Applies to minors 15 and older.

◊ Applies to mature minors 15 and younger and to minors 16 and older.

Source: Reproduced with permission of the Guttmacher Institute: *State policies in brief: An overview of minor consent law as of April 1, 2009.*

policies. A state law may allow a professional school counselor to address reproductive issues and substance abuse without parental consent or notification, but a local policy may prohibit such counseling. The laws cover minors seeking advice and/or treatment. If a minor is not seeking help, then the law may not apply, and the counselor would follow other policies or procedures in dealing with these issues.

The legal issues aside, this is the law that raises a tremendous number of ethical issues for counselors. There are a number of professionals who question the ability of young adolescents, in particular, to access these services without the family's involvement. Should a counselor help a 13-year-old who abuses substances seek treatment without the family's knowledge? How successful will the adolescent's recovery be? What about a 15-year-old who is abusing drugs and engaging in risky sexual behaviors? What is the counselor's ethical responsibility? The problem this law presents for many counselors is that it allows them to assist adolescent clients legally, but may conflict with their personal beliefs. Some professionals believe behaviors such as these can cause harm to the client and therefore they have a duty to warn that supersedes all other responsibilities. Other counselors work with the adolescent to help him or her involve the family, whereas still others believe that telling the family will work against the adolescent's obtaining help.

Another issue is that many parents do not understand that their children can seek treatment in these areas without parental consent. Parents will be understandably angry and distrustful when they discover their child has an STI or abuses substances and the counselor knew and did not tell them about it. Counselors need to be prepared to deal with the aftermath of such discoveries. They need to think through their positions on these issues very carefully and be honest with clients about their beliefs. Counselors should not wait until they are faced with a situation to figure out where they stand on an issue.

RECORDS AND PERSONAL NOTES

Educational Records

Educational records are all the records of a student's achievement, attendance, behavior, testing and assessment, and school activities, as well as any other such information that the school collects and maintains on a student. Schools frequently divide student records into cumulative records, health records, special education records, and confidential records, including psychological evaluations. In reality, this is done for the convenience of the school; all these records are considered to be part of the educational record. The only exceptions are

personal notes, reports to Child Protective Services for abuse or neglect, and, in some states, reports from law enforcement agencies regarding students' arrests for reportable offenses.

The inspection of, dissemination of, and access to student educational records must be handled in accordance with the Family Educational Rights and Privacy Act (FERPA) of 1974 (20 U.S.C. § 1232g). This law, which is often referred to as the Buckley Amendment, applies to all school districts, pre-K–12 schools, and postsecondary institutions that receive federal funding through the U.S. Department of Education. Nonpublic schools that do not accept federal funding are exempt from this law. New regulations for FERPA were enacted in January 2009. The new regulations provide clarity for those who need to understand and administer FERPA and make important changes to improve school safety, access to data for research and accountability purposes, and the safeguarding of educational records (Family Educational Rights and Privacy Act (FERPA), 2008).

FERPA requires that schools or systems annually send a notice to parents or guardians regarding their right to review their children's records and to file a complaint if they disagree with anything in the record. The system has 45 days in which to comply with the parents' request to review the records. There are penalties, including loss of federal funding, for any school or system that fails to comply. The law also limits who may access records and specifies what personally identifiable information can be disclosed without informed consent—that is, what constitutes directory information or pubic information. Under FERPA, only those persons "with a legitimate educational interest" can access a student's record. This includes the new school when a student transfers. The sending school may send the records without the parents' consent, but should make every attempt to inform the parent that it has done so. The major exception to this limitation relates to law enforcement; the school must comply with a judicial order or lawfully executed subpoena. The school must also make whatever information is needed available to the school's law enforcement unit. In emergencies, information relevant to the emergency can be shared (see www.ed.gov/print/policy/gen/guid/fpco/ferpa/index.html). All states and jurisdictions have incorporated FERPA into state statutes and local policies, with some degree of variance among them on such aspects as what constitutes directory information.

The right of consent transfers to the student at 18 years of age or when the student attends a postsecondary institution. The law does not specifically limit the rights of parents of students over 18 who are still in secondary school. The new regulations clarify that information about a student in a postsecondary institution can be shared with his or her parents under any circumstance if the student is claimed on the parents' income tax forms or in a health or safety emergency, regardless of the student's tax or dependency status.

The Protection of Pupil Rights Amendment (PPRA) of 1978, often called the Hatch Amendment, gives parents additional rights. It established certain requirements when surveys are given to students in pre-K–12 schools; it does not apply to postsecondary schools, as students can consent on their own. If the survey is funded with federal money, informed parental consent must be obtained for all participating students in elementary or secondary schools if they are required to take the survey and questions about certain personal areas are asked. PPRA also requires informed parental consent before a student undergoes any psychological, psychiatric, or medical examination, testing, or treatment or any school program designed to affect the personal values or behavior of the student. Further, PPRA gives parents the right to review instructional materials in experimental programs.

The No Child Left Behind Act of 2001 (NCLB) included several changes to FERPA and PPRA and continued to increase parents' rights. The changes apply to surveys funded either in part or entirely by any program administered by the U.S. Department of Education. NCLB made minor changes to the seven existing survey categories and added an additional category. PPRA now requires that

- Schools and contractors make instructional materials available for review by parents of participating students if those materials will be used in any U.S. Department of Education–funded survey, analysis, or evaluation.
- Schools and contractors obtain written, informed parental consent prior to students' participation in any U.S. Department of Education–funded survey, analysis, or evaluation if information in any of the following listed areas would be revealed:
- Political affiliations or beliefs of the parent or student;
- Mental and psychological problems of the family or student;
- Sex behavior or attitudes;
- Illegal, antisocial, self-incriminating, or demeaning behavior;
- Critical appraisals of other individuals with whom the student has close family relationships;
- Legally recognized privileged or analogous relationships such as those of lawyers, ministers, and physicians;
- Religious practices, affiliations, or beliefs of the parent or student (added by NCLB); and
- Income other than such information as is required to determine eligibility or participation in a program. (20 U.S.C. § 1232h)

The new provisions of PPRA also apply to surveys not funded through U.S. Department of Education programs. These provisions give parents the right to inspect, on request, any survey or instructional materials used as part of the curriculum if created by a third party and involve one or more of the eight aforementioned areas. Parents also have the right to inspect any instrument used to collect personal information that will be used in selling or marketing. Parents always have the right to not grant permission or to opt their child out of participating in any activity involving the eight previously delineated areas. PPRA does not apply to any survey that is administered as part of the Individuals with Disabilities Education Improvement Act (IDEA).

As can be seen from the previous discussion, there are many constraints in schools to assessing, testing, and surveying students. Because individual school systems or districts may have further defined this legislation, it is essential that professional school counselors become familiar with the requirements of the policies and procedures for their specific school system.

The word *parents* has been used in the preceding discussion about student records. The law does recognize the right of students over 18 years of age to access their own records and accords them the same rights as parents of students under 18 years of age. However, the law does not specifically limit the right of parents whose child is over 18 of age to also access that child's records, particularly in cases where the child is still living at home and is financially dependent on the parents. The law also gives noncustodial parents the same rights as custodial parents. Unless there is a court order in the child's file that limits or terminates the rights of one or both parents, both parents have the same access to the child's records. School personnel must also provide copies of records such as report cards to both parents if requested.

The word *parent* is used to reference the legal guardian of the child, who may not be the biological or adoptive parent of the child, but rather some other legally recognized caregiver. Stepparents and other family members have no legal right to the student's records without court-appointed authority, such as adoption or guardianship. This is particularly problematic in situations where a relative provides kinship care; that is, the relative has physical custody 24 hours a day, 7 days a week, but no legal custody of the child. Legally, this person providing kinship care has no educational decision-making rights for the child and cannot access that child's records or give consent. The crack epidemic and HIV/AIDS have created a situation where millions of children under 18 years of age are involved in informal kinship care situations. The American Bar Association (2009) estimates that over 6 million children, or approximately 1 in 12, are currently living in a household headed by grandparents or other relatives. Only 21 states have enacted legislation enabling the caregiver to enroll a child in school and/or extracurricular activities without formal guardianship (American Bar Association, 2009). Kinship care may be the best situation for children, but these situations present significant legal implications for schools.

Outside agencies may not access the records of any student without the signed consent of the parent. Some states have worked out interagency agreements wherein a parent signs one form that designates which records may be shared with which agencies, making individual forms unnecessary. Local policies dictate whether signed informed consent is needed to share information at school team meetings such as SAP, Individualized Education Program, or student services meetings when personnel from outside agencies are regular members of the team.

Personal Notes

Most counselors keep two types of notes: counseling notes and personal notes. Counseling notes record their interactions with their students and may include such information as when the student was seen, the reason for the session, the outcome, and the expected follow-up. Counselors probably do not keep counseling notes on all their students, given counseling caseloads, but may keep counseling notes for those students they see individually or in group. These notes are covered under FERPA and may be considered part of the educational record.

Personal notes, or sole possession notes, are written by professional school counselors to serve as an extension of their memories and to record impressions of the client or the counseling session. As such, they are not considered part of the educational record. These notes must remain "in the sole possession of the maker" and cannot be shared with anyone except "a substitute maker." A substitute maker is someone who takes over for the counselor in the counselor's position, in the same way a substitute teacher takes over for the regular teacher. A substitute maker is not the counselor who becomes responsible for the child the next year or in the next school.

The important point to remember about personal notes is that such notes must remain separate from the educational record. Once any information in the personal notes is shared, it is no longer confidential. If professional school counselors keep their personal notes in their offices, they should keep them separate from all other records and secured, such as in a locked file cabinet. Some counselors go so far as to keep them in their car or house, but this is not necessary unless there are problems with security in their office. As technology is more commonly used in counseling offices, professionals may prefer to keep their personal notes on the computer. However, that is not a good idea unless the counselor can absolutely guarantee that no one can access the program or break through firewalls. Even keeping the personal notes on disk is questionable. Stories of computer hackers breaking codes and paralyzing websites for hours are frequently reported in the news. It is preferable to keep personal notes separate and to not tell anyone they exist, even if there is nothing of particular interest in them. The information is confidential, and the professional school counselor needs to ensure its security. Information from the personal notes would be shared only in those cases when there is a clear duty to warn or when a judge requires that confidentiality be broken and the information shared.

THE HEALTH INSURANCE PORTABILITY AND ACCOUNTABILITY ACT OF 1996

The Health Insurance Portability and Accountability Act of 1996 (HIPAA) required that the U.S. Department of Health and Human Services (HHS) adopt national standards for the privacy of individually identifiable health information, outlined patients' rights, and established criteria for access to health records. The requirement that HHS adopt national standards for electronic health-care transactions was also included in this law. The resulting Privacy Rule was adopted in 2000 and became effective in 2001. The Privacy Rule sets national standards for the privacy and security of protected health information. It specifically excludes any individually identifiable health information that is covered by FERPA. Thus, health records in schools that fall under FERPA are specifically excluded from HIPAA. However, in reality, the situation is not quite that simple, particularly in the area of special education. Many schools receive mental, physical, and emotional health assessments of students that have been conducted by outside providers whose practices are covered by HIPAA regulations. In previous years, such assessments and reports automatically became part of the educational record. This may no longer be the case, particularly if the provider requests that the report not be redisclosed. As HIPAA continues to impact health information, school systems must develop policies and procedures to address any potential conflicts between FERPA and HIPAA. Professional school counselors must be aware of these issues and any school policies.

CHILD ABUSE

Another issue professional school counselors must deal with that has clear legal mandates is child abuse and neglect. Efforts to recognize and intervene in child abuse cases began in the late 1800s and were modeled on the laws prohibiting cruelty to animals. In 1961, *battered child syndrome* was legally recognized, and by 1968, all 50 states had laws requiring the reporting of child maltreatment. In 1974, the National Child Abuse Prevention and Treatment Act became federal law. The act was later reauthorized with changes and renamed the Keeping Children and Families Safe Act of 2003. The law defined child abuse as physical or mental injury, sexual abuse or exploitation, negligent treatment, or maltreatment of a child under the age of 18 or the age specified by the child protection law of the state in question, by a person who is responsible for the child's welfare, under circumstances that indicate that the child's health or welfare is harmed or threatened (42 U.S.C. § 5101).

The law is very clear regarding who must report child abuse and neglect cases. Every health practitioner, educator, human services worker, and law enforcement officer must report suspected abuse or neglect, generally within 24 to 72 hours of first "having reason to suspect." It is incumbent on the person who first suspects the abuse or neglect to call Child Protective Services to report it. The oral report must be followed up by a written report in most cases. Each state may have slightly different procedures for reporting; some states allow up to seven days for submission of the written report and identify different agencies to which the report must be made. What does not change is the legal mandate to report.

There is no liability for reporting child abuse, even if a subsequent investigation determines no evidence that abuse or neglect occurred, unless the report is made with malice. However, most states do have serious penalties for failure to report. These penalties may include loss of certification or license, disciplinary action, or termination of employment.

Parents or guardians have no rights to information during this process. The school or other entity making the report should not inform the parents that a report is being made. It is the responsibility of the department of social services and the law enforcement agency to contact the parent and conduct the investigation. It is critical that professional school counselors and other professionals understand the laws regarding child abuse and neglect cases and follow the procedures exactly. It should be emphasized that the person submitting the report does not have to prove that abuse has occurred; it is enough to have reason to suspect it.

Professional school counselors are sometimes put in an awkward position when another staff member is the first person to suspect abuse, but he or she is not willing to make the report and asks the counselor to do it. In such a case, if the staff member will not make the report, the professional school counselor should do it, but should apprise the administrator of the circumstances surrounding the

report. Regardless of who submits the report, the student will need support and assistance throughout the process. Lambie (2005) suggested that "the counselor use sound and appropriate counseling skills" (p. 257) and assure the student of his or her concern.

SUICIDE

For many years, the standard that was used in the profession for dealing with potential suicide cases was that set out in the *Tarasoff* decision, which was previously discussed. As a result of the *Tarasoff* ruling, counselors had a duty to warn if there was a foreseeable victim. According to Remley and Herlihy (2010), subsequent court decisions interpreted the case differently; some judges ruled that the duty exists even when there is no foreseeable victim, or if the client unintentionally injures the victim, a class of persons to which the victim belongs, bystanders, and other individuals. In general, when dealing with a potentially suicidal client, the professional school counselor would conduct a lethality assessment, determine the seriousness of the threat, and then, based on the seriousness of the threat, decide whether the duty to warn was applicable.

The *Eisel* case in Maryland changed the standard for many school counselors. In that case, two middle school students became involved in Satanism and, as a result, became obsessed with death and self-destruction. Friends of Nicole Eisel went to their school counselor and told her that Nicole was thinking about killing herself. This counselor consulted with Nicole's school counselor. Both professional school counselors spoke with Nicole, who denied thinking about killing herself. Shortly thereafter, on a school holiday, Nicole's friend, who attended another school, shot Nicole and killed herself in the park behind the school. Mr. Eisel sued the school, the school system, and the professional school counselors. After the circuit court dismissed the case, Mr. Eisel appealed to the court of appeals, which in its decision of October 29, 1991, stated: "Considering the growth of this tragic social problem in the light of the factors discussed above, we hold that school counselors have a duty to use reasonable means to attempt to prevent a suicide when they are on notice of a child or adolescent student's suicidal intent" (*Eisel v. Board of Education*, 1991).

On the facts of this case as developed to date, a trier of fact could conclude that the duty included warning Mr. Eisel of the danger. The case was remanded back to the circuit court to decide the issue of liability for both the school system and the professional school counselors. The case finally concluded eight years after it began with a finding that the school system and the professional school counselors had acted appropriately, given the circumstances, their training, and the policies in place at the time.

However, the court's decision had a major impact on professional school counselors in the state of Maryland. This decision removed the counselor's ability to determine whether the duty to warn is applicable. As a consequence, professional school counselors in Maryland must always tell the parent whenever there is any indication from a child or someone else that the child is thinking about suicide, regardless of the seriousness of the threat. Further, they must inform the principal or the principal's designee. Many of Maryland's school systems now apply this procedure to all student services personnel employed by the school system.

While this case is legally binding only on professional school counselors in Maryland, it has become the standard used in subsequent cases. For example, a federal circuit court in Florida made a similar ruling in 1997 in *Wyke v. Polk County School Board*, and several other courts are following suit. But courts in other states have rejected the *Eisel* decision and have found in favor of the school systems. Professional school counselors must be aware of the policies within their system. Some courts clearly are ruling in favor of the duty to warn, as opposed to counselor discretion.

Summary/Conclusion

If one were to survey practicing counselors regarding the "hot issues" in counseling, the list would likely include eating disorders, HIV/AIDS, self-mutilation, autism and Asperger's syndrome, bullying, harassment, changing family structures, mobility, cultural diversity, sexual orientation, depression, loss and grief, students with special needs, emotional disturbance, gangs, and a host of other topics. So how does a counselor help the 13-year-old who believes he is gay? Or the 16-year-old who is starving herself to death? Or the incarcerated parent who wants the professional school counselor to read his letters to his children in school because the mother will not let him have any contact with his children?

Here are some final words of wisdom to help guide you as a professional school counselor:

- Always document in writing what you did and why you did it.
- If you did not follow a policy, document why you did not (e.g., you did not call the parent in a suicide case because it was handled as an abuse case).

- Know federal, state, and local laws, regulations, policies, and guidelines.
- Consult with a colleague or supervisor when you have questions or doubts.
- Read and use resources.
- Consult with a lawyer when appropriate.

Professional school counselors must be prepared to deal with these issues and more every day of their professional lives. Many of these areas do not have clear laws, regulations, court cases, or policies to guide counselors toward legal and ethical behavior. Professional school counselors need to try to do what is in the best interest of their clients and to help their clients see what that is. They must advocate for their students because frequently they will be the only support that these students have. Professional school counselors must never stop believing and having faith that what they do makes a difference in the lives of children.

6

Culturally Competent School Counselors: Affirming Diversity by Challenging Oppression

Cheryl Holcomb-McCoy and Stuart F. Chen-Hayes

Editor's Introduction: The transformed professional school counselor is culturally competent, respectful of human diversity, and a school leader in ensuring that oppressive systemic barriers to academic, career, and personal/social development are removed. To achieve this goal, professional school counselors must explore and know their own culture and biases and then open themselves to, and seek to understand, the cultures of the diverse populations they serve. This chapter includes a Professional School Counselor Multicultural Competence Checklist and several dilemmas and vignettes to help you on your journey to becoming multiculturally competent.

Vignette 1

Janice is a middle-class, Jewish professional elementary school counselor in a wealthy suburban school district. In recent years, there has been a large influx of multilingual working-class Taiwanese students of indigenous ethnicity and Buddhist faith into her school. Because these students never self-refer for counseling and because she has never attended the local Buddhist temple or consulted with spiritual leaders of the local Taiwanese Buddhist community, Janice erroneously assumes they have no school or family concerns.

Vignette 2

John, a White, middle-class professional urban high school counselor, is puzzled as to why there is an achievement gap at his school with Native American, African-American, and Latino/a students, 90% of whom qualify for free and reduced lunch, who are overrepresented in special education classes, and who are accepted to college and universities at a significantly lower rate than White and Asian students are. He wonders what can be done to change the attainment gap that is evident because few of the school's poor and working-class Latino/a, African-American, and Native American students who are accepted into college graduate with diplomas.

Vignette 3

Kay, an African-American professional middle school counselor in a rural school district, feels uncomfortable providing developmental school counseling lessons to a class of students recently immigrated from Central America, all of whom qualify for free and reduced lunch. Kay cannot speak Spanish, and the only Spanish-speaking staff member is a custodian.

Vignette 4

Ricardo, an upper-class, Latino professional urban middle school counselor, avoids academic, career/college, and especially personal/social counseling with students whom he perceives as being lesbian, bisexual, gay, or transgendered because he fears they will "out him" as a gay Latino.

The dilemmas faced by the professional school counselors in the above scenarios have become increasingly more commonplace. This is due in part to the fact that never before has the American population been as multiethnic, multicultural, and multilingual as it is today (Marshall, 2002). For instance, in 2005–2006 Latino students accounted for 19.8% of all public school students, up from 12.7% in 1993–1994. During this same period, African-American student enrollment rose slightly, from 16.5% to 17.2%, while White student enrollment fell sharply, from 66.1% to 57.1% (Fry 2007). The current racial/ethnic distribution of students in public schools in the United States is about 1% Native American, 5% Asian/Pacific Islander, 20% Latino/a, 17% African-American, and 57% White/European (National Center for Education Statistics [NCES], 2006). These figures are expected to change as the number of students of color enrolling in school increases each year, with the largest increases in student population among Latino/as and Asian/Pacific Islanders. For instance, while today one of every eight residents of the United States is Latino, it is projected that Latinos could account for one of every five residents by 2035, one of every four by 2055, and one of every three by 2100 (Saenz, 2009).

Based on these rapidly changing demographics, the skills of affirming diversity and challenging oppression are key components of the professional school counselor's transformed role. In fact, knowledge and skill about multiculturalism as a key component of the school counseling profession is no longer viewed as desirable, but is mandatory. Professional school counselors, like other school professionals, are becoming more aware of the need to be knowledgeable about the manner in which students' diverse characteristics affect the learning process and, more importantly, how students are differentially affected in their schools based on ethnicity, race, language, disability status, social class, and other cultural identities.

In many school districts, professional school counselors are preparing themselves for their diverse clientele by taking courses in foreign languages, enrolling in extensive multicultural counseling training, and consulting with leaders from diverse communities. Professional school counselors are also beginning to play a major role in school reform initiatives and efforts to improve the academic achievement of historically oppressed students (by, e.g., the Education Trust). At the same time, it is unclear whether professional school counselors are effective in their work with students from oppressed backgrounds. Some research has even suggested that professional school counselors maintain the status quo in terms of educational outcomes for minority students (Perna et al., 2008).

In response to the increasingly diverse caseloads of professional school counselors, the American School Counselor Association (ASCA; 1999b) adopted the following position statement on multicultural counseling:

Cross/multicultural counseling: the facilitation of human development through the understanding and appreciation of cultural diversities. ASCA recognizes cultural diversities as important factors deserving increased awareness and understanding on the part of all school personnel, especially the school counselor. Counselors may use a variety of strategies not only to increase the sensitivity of students and parents to culturally diverse persons and enhance the total school and community environment, but also to increase the awareness of culturally diverse populations.

In addition, in the 2004 revision of the ASCA's *Ethical Standards for School Counselors*, multicultural, diversity, and anti-oppression competencies are addressed as follows in Section E.2, Diversity:

The professional school counselor:

a. Affirms the diversity of students, staff and families.

b. Expands and develops awareness of his/her own attitudes and beliefs affecting cultural values and biases and strives to attain cultural competence.

c. Possesses knowledge and understanding about how oppression, racism, discrimination and stereotyping affects her/him personally and professionally.

d. Acquires educational, consultation and training experiences to improve awareness, knowledge, skills and effectiveness in working with diverse populations: ethnic/racial status, age, economic status, special needs, ESL or ELL, immigration status, sexual orientation, gender, gender identity/expression, family type, religious/spiritual identity and appearance. (ASCA, 2004a, p. 4)

Considering the ethical and professional obligations of professional school counselors to be culturally competent, this chapter's main objectives are to (1) clarify the language and terminology used when discussing multicultural competence, affirming diversity, and challenging oppression; (2) discuss the need for culturally competent professional school counselors; (3) offer ways in which professional school counselors can integrate multiculturalism in their school counseling programs; (4) offer a checklist that can be used to assess professional school counselors' multicultural competence; (5) provide case studies of actual professional school counselors challenging multiple oppressions through closing achievement and opportunity gaps; and (6) offer vignettes that can be used to facilitate one's development of competence when working with students' multiple cultural identities and challenging oppression.

For clarification, the term *culturally diverse* is used throughout this chapter to denote distinctions in "the lived experiences and the related perceptions of and reactions to those experiences, that serve to differentiate collective populations from one another" (Marshall, 2002, p. 7). These distinctions are affected directly by the complex interactions of racial/ethnic classification, social status, historical and contemporary circumstances, and worldview. Racial/ethnic designations are used throughout the chapter when discussing cultural diversity, and other factors such as social class, gender, religion, sexual orientation, language, disability, and immigration status have been incorporated into various discussions. Racial/ethnic and social class identities have been highlighted throughout the chapter because of their historical correlations with the achievement, opportunity, and attainment gaps that persist among cultural groups in U.S. schools (Education Trust, 2005b).

MULTICULTURAL AND ANTI-OPPRESSION TERMINOLOGY

Much of the frustration in understanding multiculturalism and anti-oppression theory is due to misuse of and confusion about the terminology. In a classic article, S. D. Johnson (1990) suggested that more time be devoted to clarifying multicultural terminology in counselor education graduate programs. In his study of counselor trainees' ability to make distinctions between the concepts of race and culture, he found that trainees offered definitions that were "badly confounded, containing vague and simplistic notions of culture and race" (p. 49). Culture, race, ethnicity, and various types of oppression are contrasted in this section.

The term *culture* has been defined in a variety of ways. Decades ago, Goodenough (1981) described culture as consisting of the following components: (1) the ways in which people perceive their experiences of the world so as to give it structure; (2) the beliefs by which people explain events; (3) a set of principles for dealing with people, as well as for accomplishing particular ends; and (4) people's value systems for establishing purposes and for keeping themselves purposefully oriented. More recently, and drawing from a more traditional perspective, Wehrly (1995, p. 4) described culture as

"a dynamic construct that includes the values, beliefs, and behaviors of a people who have lived together in a particular geographic area for at least three or four generations." Culture has also been described narrowly, to include only an individual's ethnicity or nationality, and broadly, to include an individual's economic status, gender, religion, and other demographic variables. Banks and McGee Banks (2005) defined culture as the way in which people interpret, use, and perceive artifacts, tools, or other tangible cultural elements. And Geertz (1983) suggested that members of a specific culture do not experience their culture as a humanly constructed system. Instead, they experience culture as the way things are and the way things should be. This phenomenon is generally referred to as *ethnocentrism*. In other words, individuals within a cultural group tend to believe that their ideas about the world are simply "common sense."

Similar to *culture*, *race* is a term that has been defined in various ways. For behavioral scientists, race has been used to denote genotypically homogeneous human groupings (Kluckhohn, 1985). However, according to Baba and Darga (1981), the practice of racial classification by biological characteristics is practically impossible. Within psychology and counseling, researchers across subfields have studied race and ethnicity, generating a variety of distinct literatures that were well-integrated. One empirical literature now demonstrates that race shapes individuals' psychological experiences. We now know from this research that racial identity can be an important predictor of attitudes, beliefs, motivation, and performance (Major & O'Brien, 2005; Sellers & Shelton, 2003; Steele, 2007). *Merriam-Webster's Collegiate Dictionary* (2007, p. 1024) defines *race* (or racial group) as a "family, tribe, people, or nation belonging to the same stock." Ponterotto and Pederson (1993) suggested that, although the race construct has been discredited as a scientific and biological term, it remains an important political and psychological concept. Markus (2008) captured the construct of race as

a dynamic set of historically derived and institutionalized ideas and practices that (1) sorts people into ethnic groups according to perceived physical and behavioral human characteristics; (2) associates differential value, power, and privilege with these characteristics and establishes a social status ranking among the different groups; and (3) emerges (a) when groups are perceived to each other's world view or way of life; and/or (b) to justify the denigration and exploitation (past, current or future) of, and prejudice toward, other groups. (p. 654)

It is critical for professional school counselors to remember that race has been and continues to be used in schools to carry out such practices as segregation; the stereotyping of groups by students' academic achievement; tracking; the identification of students for special education; and low teacher expectations for students of color, particularly students of color who are also poor, have disabilities, or are English language learners.

In contrast to race, *ethnicity* was defined by Schaefer (1990, p. 27) as "a group set apart from others because of its national origin or distinctive cultural patterns." It is within this ethnic identity that an individual is socialized to take on the group's values, beliefs, and behaviors. McGoldrick and Giordano (1996) referred to ethnicity as

> [a] common ancestry through which individuals have evolved shared values and customs. It is deeply tied to the family, through which it is transmitted. . . . The concept of a group's "peoplehood" is based on a combination of race, religion, and cultural history and is retained, whether or not members realize their commonalities with one another. The consciousness of ethnic identity varies greatly within groups and from one group to another. (pp. 1–2)

Oppression, in contrast to other terms in this chapter, can be defined in an equation: **Oppression = prejudice × power**. Here, prejudice means maintaining incorrect conscious or unconscious attitudes, feelings, and beliefs to the effect that members of a cultural group are inferior or that a group's cultural differences are unacceptable (Arnold, Chen-Hayes, & Lewis, 2002). Power is the ability to control access to resources and includes control of, or over, the images of what is culturally appropriate. Power and power over are maintained and used on individual, cultural, and systemic levels (Arnold et al., 2002; Hardiman & Jackson, 1997).

I. M. Young (1990) further expanded the definition of oppression by delineating five conditions of an oppressed group: exploitation, marginalization, powerlessness, cultural imperialism, and violence. *Exploitation* refers to the steady transfer of the results of the labor of one social group to the benefit of another. *Marginalization* refers to the process by which individuals or groups of people are permanently confined to lives of social marginality because they are not attractive or not perceived as "acceptable" to people in the dominant culture. Young emphasizes that marginalization is particularly harmful, since it means people are both expelled from participation in social life and subjected to material deprivation. *Powerlessness* is defined as

having to take orders without having the right to give them. *Cultural imperialism* refers to the dominance of one group's experiences and culture and its establishment as the norm. Young claimed that cultural imperialism occurs when the experiences and perspectives of oppressed groups seem "invisible" to the dominant group. Paradoxically, the oppressed group is stereotyped and marked out as the "other." *Violence* is a manifestation of oppression because of the social context, which makes violence possible and, in some cases, acceptable. Violence is systemic because it is often directed at members of oppressed groups simply because they are members of that group.

Other forms of oppression include individual, cultural, systemic, internalized, and externalized oppression. *Individual oppression* is behavior based on conscious or unconscious negative assumptions about people who are culturally or racially different. Examples are telling jokes, staring at someone "different," and targeting a person for a crime solely because of his or her skin color. *Cultural oppression* occurs when the standards of appropriate actions, thought, and expression of a particular group are seen as negative (overtly or covertly). As a result, a member of the oppressed group must change his or her behavior to be accepted by the dominant group. An example of cultural oppression is the recognition of heterosexuality as the only sexual orientation in a school's curriculum. *Systemic/ institutional oppression* includes unequal power relationships in institutions that result in the inequitable distribution of resources. It can include inflexible policies and procedures unresponsive to cultural differences. Systemic oppression can involve the use of power to limit others based on their race, cultural background, or both. Examples include women and ethnic minorities being paid less for work comparable to that of White men (Arnold et al., 2002; Hardiman & Jackson, 1997). *Internalized oppression* is characterized by an individual believing the stereotypes about his or her group and then acting accordingly (Chen-Hayes, 2005). *Externalized oppression*, on the other hand, occurs when an individual targets members of nondominant groups for oppression, violence, coercion, and control based on a belief (conscious or not) that members of the nondominant group are inferior or otherwise deserving of control, coercion, or violence (Chen-Hayes, 2005). Table 6.1 lists common forms of oppression.

School counselors can find evidence of oppression in K–12 school data. School data (e.g., achievement scores, grades) can illustrate groups of students that are achieving and those that are not. Likewise, data can indicate inequities among groups of students regarding college application rates, graduation rates, dropout rates, suspension rates, attendance rates, percentages of students in special education, and percentages of students identified as

TABLE 6.1   Forms of Oppression That Are Found Throughout Society, Including K–12 Schools

Ableism: Prejudice multiplied by power used by temporarily able-bodied persons against persons with disabilities (physical, developmental, or emotional) that limits their access to individual, cultural, and systemic resources.

Ageism: Prejudice multiplied by power used by persons aged 18–49 against children and youth and persons aged 50+ that limits their access to individual, cultural, and systemic resources.

Beautyism: Prejudice multiplied by power used by persons with dominant standards of beauty against persons with obesity or persons with other nondominant appearances that limits their access to individual, cultural, and systemic resources.

Classism: Prejudice multiplied by power used by wealthy and upper-middle-class persons against poor, working-class, or lower-middle-class persons that limits their access to individual, cultural, and systemic resources.

Familyism: Prejudice multiplied by power used by persons in traditional family configurations against single persons, single parents, same-gender parents, same-gender couples, divorced persons, couples who live together, and adoptive/foster families that limits their access to individual, cultural, and systemic resources.

Heterosexism and Transgenderism: Prejudice multiplied by power used by heterosexuals and traditionally gendered persons against lesbian, bisexual, gay, two-spirit, intersex, and transgendered persons that limits their access to individual, cultural, and systemic resources.

Linguicism: Prejudice multiplied by power used by dominant-language speakers against nonspeakers or persons who speak with an accent that limits their access to individual, cultural, and systemic resources.

Racism: Prejudice multiplied by power used by Whites against people of color or multiracial people that limits their access to individual, cultural, and systemic resources.

Religionism: Prejudice multiplied by power used by members of a dominant religious group (e.g., in the United States, Christians) against nondominant religious, spiritual, or nonreligious persons and groups (Jews, Muslims, Hindus, Jains, Buddhists, Earth-Centered Spiritualists, Pagans, atheists, agnostics) that limits their access to individual, cultural, and systemic resources.

Sexism: Prejudice multiplied by power used by men or boys against women or girls that limits their access to individual, cultural, and systemic resources.

Source: Multicultural Counseling Class Lecture, by S. F. Chen-Hayes, 2005, Bronx, New York: Lehman College of the City University of New York.

gifted/talented. These are examples of achievement, opportunity, and attainment gaps. *Achievement gaps* are the differences in academic performance among groups of K–12 students based on ethnicity/race, gender, social class, disability status, language status, and other variables. *Opportunity gaps* are the differences in resources given to K–12 students in terms of quality of instruction, college preparatory curriculum, quality of teachers, access to a school counseling program with specific indicators of skill development, access to career and college development skills and counseling, and other opportunities that differentiate who is able to graduate from college and obtain satisfying, well-paying careers. And *attainment gaps* are the differences among groups who attain particular status in schools (e.g., graduation, college admission) based on data disaggregated by ethnicity/race, gender, social class, disability, and language identities, among others. As school counselors monitor data (Chen-Hayes, 2005; Dimmit, Carey, & Hatch, 2007; Holcomb-McCoy, 2007), they can formulate action plans, create interventions, and gather results of their effectiveness in challenging the

oppression manifested in achievement, opportunity, and attainment gaps.

Multicultural and Social Justice Counseling

It is the lack of clear and consistent definitions of terms that leads to the question "What is multicultural counseling?" Locke (1990) referred to multicultural counseling as a counseling relationship in which the counselor and client differ as a result of socialization in unique cultural or racial or ethnic environments. However, C. E. Vontress (1988) noted, "[I]f the counselor and client perceive mutual cultural similarity, even though in reality they are culturally different, the interaction should not be labeled cross-cultural counseling" (p. 75). It has also been debated whether or not to narrowly define multicultural counseling as a relationship between two or more ethnically or racially diverse individuals. According to Arredondo and D'Andrea (1995), the definition of multicultural counseling provided by the Association for Multicultural Counseling and Development (AMCD) relates to "five major cultural groups in the United States and its territories: African/Black, Asian, Caucasian/European, Hispanic/Latino, and Native American or indigenous groups which have historically resided in the continental United States and its territories" (p. 28).

Other counseling professionals and professional organizations, including the Council for Accreditation of Counseling and Related Educational Programs (CACREP), view multicultural counseling from a universal perspective and include characteristics of not only race and ethnicity, but also gender, lifestyle, religion, sexual orientation, and so on (CACREP, 2009). CACREP's definition further emphasizes the implication of a pluralistic philosophy. The term *pluralistic* in the accreditation procedures manual and application is used to "describe a condition of society in which numerous distinct ethnic, racial, religious, and social groups coexist and cooperatively work toward interdependence needed for the enhancement of each group" (CACREP, 2009, p. 61).

More recently, the terms *social justice counseling* and *social justice perspective* have been used in the literature instead of multicultural counseling (D'Andrea & Heckman, 2008). Social justice counseling, according to Crethar, Rivera, and Nash (2008), addresses issues related to both individual and distributive justice. They also suggested that social justice counseling involves the promotion of equity, access, participation, and harmony. Holcomb-McCoy (2007) argued that professional school counselors should shift to more of a social justice perspective in order to challenge the achievement inequities found in many schools. She suggested that professional school counselors are in the perfect position to advocate for social justice and challenge systemic social injustices (e.g., overrepresentation of African-American students in special education, underrepresentation of Latino and African-American students in gifted and honors courses). Her social justice framework for school counselors includes six components: (1) counseling and planning interventions (e.g., empowerment-based counseling), (2) consulting (e.g., parent and teacher consultation), (3) connecting schools, families, and communities, (4) collecting and using data to identify inequities, (5) challenging bias, and (6) coordinating student services to support and emphasize rigor and academic success for all students. According to Holcomb-McCoy, a school counselor is able to work from a social justice perspective if each of these six areas is emphasized in a counseling program.

Multicultural Competence

Perhaps one of the greatest challenges confronting the multicultural counseling movement is determining how to operationalize multicultural counseling competence. Since the 1970s, a growing body of literature has addressed the need for multicultural competence in counseling and in the training

of future counselors (K. Achenbach & Arthur, 2002; Stuart, 2004). Multicultural theorists have defined cultural competence as a specific area of competence that includes (1) cultural awareness and beliefs, (2) cultural knowledge, and (3) cultural skills. Cultural competence is achieved when a counselor possesses the necessary skills to work effectively with clients from various cultural backgrounds. Hence, a counselor with a high level of multicultural counseling competence acknowledges client–counselor cultural differences and similarities as significant to the counseling process. On the other hand, a counselor with a low level of multicultural competence provides counseling services with little or no regard for the counselor's or client's ethnicity or race.

Over the past four decades, the literature related to the impact of cultural/racial/ethnic factors on the counseling process has grown (Ivey, D'Andrea, Ivey, & Simek-Morgan, 2007; D. W. Sue & Sue, 2003). And research has provided increasing evidence that multicultural counseling training is associated with greater self-perceived multicultural competence (Kiselica, Maben, & Locke, 1999), including greater cultural self-awareness (Heppner & O'Brien, 1994) and increased cultural knowledge and skills (Manese, Wu, & Nepomuceno, 2001). Constantine (2001) found that previous multicultural counseling training, along with an integrative theoretical orientation and higher levels of empathic attitudes, was related to higher levels of sophistication in conceptualizing a cross-cultural counseling case/scenario.

To highlight the importance of becoming a culturally competent professional counselor, the American Counseling Association (ACA) formally endorsed the Multicultural Counseling Competencies (D. W. Sue, Arredondo, & McDavis, 1992), and the American Psychological Association endorsed the multicultural guidelines. Both of these documents were aimed at setting multicultural counseling standards for mental health professionals. In addition, the 2005 *ACA Code of Ethics* includes numerous multicultural counseling competency concepts (Pack-Brown, Thomas, & Seymour, 2008).

In addition to the three-dimensional framework of multicultural competence (i.e., attitudes, skills, and knowledge), other perspectives regarding multicultural competence have been offered. In another article, Holcomb-McCoy and Myers (1999) suggested that there could possibly be more than three dimensions to multicultural counseling competence. They proposed that one must also have knowledge of multicultural terminology and racial identity–development theories. Pope-Davis, Reynolds, Dings, and Ottavi (1994) suggested that multicultural competence in counseling is "an appreciation of and sensitivity to the history, current needs, strengths, and resources of communities and individuals who historically have been underserved and underrepresented by psychologists" (p. 466). Ridley, Mendoza, Kanitz, Angermeier, and Zenk (1994) proposed a conceptualized model of cultural sensitivity that is based on perceptual schema theory. Ridley and colleagues described cultural sensitivity as the ability of counselors to "acquire, develop, and actively use an accurate cultural perceptual schema in the course of multicultural counseling" (p. 130).

S. Sue (1998) offered a more scientific approach to cultural competence. He suggested that cultural competence consists of three characteristics: being scientifically minded, having skills in dynamic sizing, and being proficient with a particular cultural group. *Being scientifically minded* stresses the counselor's ability to form hypotheses, rather than reaching premature conclusions about the status of culturally different clients. The second characteristic, *having skills in dynamic sizing*, reinforces the importance of the counselor's skill in knowing "when to generalize, when to individualize, and finally when to be exclusive" (p. 446). The counselor's ability to use dynamic sizing decreases his or her tendency to use stereotypes, while still embracing the client's culture. In other words, the use of dynamic sizing is one's ability to appropriately categorize experiences and behaviors. Third, the characteristics of *being proficient with a particular cultural group* include the counselor's expertise or knowledge of the cultural groups with which he or she works, sociopolitical influences, and specific skills needed to work with culturally different clients.

THE NEED FOR CULTURALLY COMPETENT SCHOOL COUNSELORS

As stated previously, professional school counselors are faced with the challenge of providing services that enhance the academic, career, and personal/social development of all students. One of their major challenges, however, is the need to create developmental school counseling programs that help to close attainment, achievement, opportunity, and funding gaps among groups of students in K–12 schools. These gaps exist not only in terms of standardized test scores, but also in areas such as Advanced Placement (AP) course participation and test taking, high school graduation rates, college entrance and graduation rates, and earned income. For instance, scores on the 2003 version of the National Assessment of Educational Progress (NAEP; U.S. Department of Education, 2003) revealed the continued achievement gaps between African-American and Latino/a students and their White peers. Scores on the reading portion of the test at the fourth-grade level showed that 75% of White students scored at the basic level or above, whereas only 44% of Latino/a students and only 40% of African-American students did so.

The achievement, attainment, funding, and opportunity gaps are demonstrated in other ways as well. For instance, the Education Trust (2005b) reported that African-American and Latino/a students were underrepresented on several different measures of academic and career/college achievement. Students of color were underrepresented in AP test taking, as compared to their percentage of the population (e.g., African Americans—17% of student population, 5% of AP calculus tests; Latinos—20% of student population, 8% of AP biology tests; Whites—57% of students, 72% of AP calculus tests, 67% of AP biology tests). High school graduation rates showed that about 72% of White students who began high school in 1997 graduated in 2001, whereas only 52% of Latino students and 51% of African-American students graduated within four years. Finally, of those students who enrolled in college in the fall of 1998, 59% of White students graduated in four years; in contrast, only 36% of Latino students and only 40% of African-American students graduated in four years. Discussions regarding professional school counselors' role in addressing these inequities and disparities in student achievement and career/college access and achievement are relatively new in the school counseling literature. The Education Trust's Transforming School Counseling Initiative (TSCI) sparked a dialogue among school counseling professionals regarding how professional school counselors can assist in closing the gaps between student groups (Education Trust, 2005b).

INTEGRATING MULTICULTURAL AND ANTI-OPPRESSION TOPICS IN SCHOOL COUNSELING PROGRAMS

Professional school counselors can play a pivotal role in combating oppression and assisting culturally diverse students in achieving success in academics, in career and college attainment, and in personal, social, and cultural skills. To begin, however, professional school counselors must recognize that traditional school counseling is embedded in White or European culture and that this limits its cross-cultural utility (Bolyard & Jensen-Scott, 1996). Professional school counselors typically lack the specific training necessary to address the problems and effects of oppression and multiple cultural identities because most counselor education programs do not offer consistent training (e.g., coursework, field experiences) in anti-oppression work and cultural history and in the related awareness, knowledge, and skills needed to work effectively with multiple cultural groups and identities.

To effectively assist students of historically oppressed backgrounds, professional school counselors must engage in interventions that create social environments for students that support social justice. The concept of social

VOICES FROM THE FIELD 6.1 THE CRITICAL NEED FOR MULTICULTURALLY COMPETENT SCHOOL COUNSELORS

There is a real need for culturally competent counselors because, regardless of the school setting, a counselor will have a student population that is diverse. At the same time, there tends to be more White, middle-income, and female counselors. If these counselors are not culturally competent, then they tend to "check out" on students because they don't know what to do or how to work with students. As a result, counselors are frustrated and rely on

biases and faulty assumptions about students. Their biases and worldviews get in the way of meeting the needs of all students. And students "check out" on counselors because they realize that counselors do not understand them, and then students don't see counselors as a viable resource.

Source: Dr. Julia Bryan, Counselor Educator, University of Maryland

---

justice is central to the practice of multicultural school counseling. Social justice refers to equity, equality, and fairness in the distribution of societal resources (Flynn, 1995). Social justice includes a focus on the structures and outcomes of social processes and how they contribute to equality. The professional school counselor's role is to develop practices that contribute to social justice. For instance, professional school counselors might reach out to community members and organizations to develop school counseling services that are closely aligned with the community's goals for its students and families. More importantly, professional school counselors should be involved in community organizing that mobilizes people to combat common community problems and increases community members' voices in schools. For example, a professional school counselor, as an advocate for improved housing for low-income parents in her school, might attend city council meetings with local community members and lobby for a new housing policy.

There is a limited amount of literature on strategies and interventions specifically designed for culturally diverse students. However, this section will include an overview of how multicultural topics and/or diversity topics can be integrated into existing school counseling programs. To begin, empowerment-focused interventions will be described. These have been suggested in the literature as a means of promoting the well-being of culturally diverse persons. Next, discussions of how multicultural topics may be integrated into typical professional school counselor delivery modes and functions (e.g., individual counseling, group counseling, assessment, consultation, and data collection and sharing) will be offered.

Empowerment-Focused Interventions

Empowerment is a construct shared by many disciplines (e.g., community development, psychology, economics). How empowerment is understood or defined varies among

these perspectives. Rappaport (1987) noted that it is easy to define empowerment by its absence, but difficult to define in action, as it takes on different forms in different people and contexts. As a general definition, empowerment is a process of increasing personal, interpersonal, or political power so that individuals, families, and communities can take action to improve their situations. It is a process that fosters power (i.e., the capacity to implement) in disenfranchised and powerless groups of people, for use in their own lives, their communities, and their society, by acting on issues that they define as important. Interestingly, the word *empowerment* can be disempowering when it is understood to mean the giving of power by the powerful to the powerless. Therefore, the appropriate role of the professional school counselor is to help students and parents build their own power base.

Empowerment is multidimensional, social, and a process. It is multidimensional in that it occurs within sociological, psychological, and economic dimensions. Empowerment also occurs at various levels, such as individual, group, and community. Empowerment, by definition, is a social process, as it occurs in relationship to others. It is a process that is similar to a path or journey, one that develops as we work through it. One important implication of this definition of empowerment is that the individual and community are fundamentally connected.

Although the literature on empowerment theory describes empowerment as a method that can incorporate multiple levels of intervention, most of the current work has focused on individual or interpersonal empowerment (Gutierrez, 1995). The literature has discussed methods and strategies for moving individuals to a point where they feel a sense of personal power. One such strategy is the development of critical consciousness (Zimmerman, 2000). *Critical consciousness* has been described as involving three psychological processes: (1) *group identification*, which includes identifying areas of common experiences and concern with a particular group; (2) *group consciousness,* which involves understanding the differential status of power of groups in society; and (3) *self and collective efficacy,* which is described as perceiving one's self as a subject (rather than an object) of social processes and as capable of working to change the social order. For individuals to understand that their problems stem from a lack of power, they must first comprehend their group's status in society, as well as the overall structure of power in society. At the individual level, professional school counselors can help students feel empowered by facilitating discussions about their group identifications and helping them to understand how their group membership has affected their life circumstances. Students can empower themselves by taking responsibility for their own learning, by increasing their understanding of the communities in which they live, and by understanding how they as individuals are affected by current and potential policies and structures. Equipped with this greater understanding and with new confidence in themselves, students can develop new behavior patterns and perspectives.

An empowerment approach to working with students requires that professional school counselors provide students with the knowledge and skills needed to think critically about their problems and to develop strategies to act on and solve problems (C. C. Lee, 2001a). Professional school counselors and students must work collaboratively to help students take charge of their lives. For instance, professional school counselors might help facilitate the problem solving and decision making of students by building on their strengths. Rather than counselor-assumed student problems, the focus should be on problems identified by the students. The problem-solving process can include problem identification, the selection of one problem, the choosing of a goal to solve or minimize the problem, the identification of available resources to assist in goal attainment, and the generation of activities to achieve the goal.

Individual Counseling

Individual counseling is a mode of counseling that most professional school counselors are trained in their graduate training programs to implement. Individual counseling theories and techniques, however, tend to be based on traditional, Eurocentric theories that are often inappropriate for students of diverse cultural backgrounds. According to D'Andrea and Daniels (1995), one of the most serious problems in school counseling is that "most counseling theories and interventions, which are commonly used in school settings, have not been tested among students from diverse student populations" (p. 143). Very few counseling

approaches have been specifically designed and validated for use with specific cultural groups. For this reason, professional school counselors should seek and develop individual counseling strategies that are effective with culturally diverse students.

Professional school counselors should also be aware of the pervasive influence that culture has on the counseling process (Holcomb-McCoy, 2007). In the school setting, counselors should be aware of the impact of culture on students' ways of thinking, belief systems, definitions of self, decision making, verbal and nonverbal behavior, and time orientation. For instance, some non-Westernized cultures place more emphasis on "being" than on "doing." In the Native American and Asian cultures, self is not seen as an entity separate from the group or from nature. In addition, African Americans and other nonmainstream Western cultures see family as an extended unit that does not necessarily limit itself to "blood" relatives. These varied cultural beliefs and practices can be significant in the individual counseling process and have profound effects on the behavior of children and adolescents. Perusse and Goodnough (2004) contributed an edited text full of individual counseling suggestions using a transformative approach across multiple domains (academic, career, and personal/social) and cultural groups.

Group Counseling

When implementing groups in schools, multiculturally competent school counselors must be able to facilitate the cultural development of group members. This can be done by understanding and acknowledging the reality that students are socialized within a society in which some groups have a history of suffering stereotypes, prejudice, oppression, and discrimination. When setting up groups, professional school counselors should consider how students from differing cultural backgrounds are likely to relate to each other and to the group leader. Professional school counselors should be familiar with the literature on selecting and planning for culturally diverse groups (e.g., D. Anderson, 2007; Asner-Self & Feyissa, 2002; Baca & Koss-Chionino, 1997). For instance, when reviewing the strengths of same-sex and same-race groups, A. Brown and Mistry (1994) noted that these groups have advantages when the group task is associated with issues of personal identity, social oppression, and empowerment.

Professional school counselors who lead groups must remember that students bring diverse patterns of behavior, values, and language to groups. Students might bring experiences of oppression and particular feelings about themselves, their group identity, and the larger society to the group. When problems of dissatisfaction or conflict among group members occur, the professional school counselor should

VOICES FROM THE FIELD 6.2   KEEP FOCUSED ON THE GOAL

When it comes to working with parents in schools, culture plays a major role, and a counselor cannot assume that strategies that work with one set of parents will work for another. The important idea to keep in mind is that all families, regardless of race, culture or socioeconomic status, want their children to succeed.

Source: Ileana Gonzalez, Professional School Counselor, Broward County, Florida

remember that the issues may be caused by cultural differences, not by an individual member's personal characteristics or flaws in the group process. Perusse and Goodnough's (2004) edited text on leadership and advocacy in school counseling contains multiple ideas for group counseling, including culturally competent small- and large-group outlines in academic, career, and personal/social development.

Consultation

Despite the attention focused on multicultural counseling, less emphasis has been placed on the significance of culture in the consultation process. Consulting is a significant responsibility for professional school counselors (Ingraham, 2000; Ramirez & Smith, 2007). Given the vast amount of time professional school counselors spend consulting with parents, teachers, and administrators of diverse backgrounds, a discussion of the multicultural competence of school-based consultants is warranted. Professional school counselors acting in the role of consultant should be sensitive to the cultural differences among the three parties in the consultation process: consultant, consultee, and client. Professional school counselors who consult with culturally different teachers and parents should ensure that such teachers or parents understand that their input is welcomed and in many cases is necessary for the success of the intervention. It is just as important, however, to consider the cultural differences of the client. Although the consultation process involves indirect contact with the client, the consultant should not forget that the client is the focus of the consultee's problem; therefore, the culture of the client will have an impact on the change process.

School-based consultants should also focus on conceptualizing the problem or concern of the consultee (e.g., parent, teacher) within a cultural context. Assessing the influence of culture on the consultee's and client's perception of the problem and interpersonal interactions is critical to the consultation process. For instance, a Taiwanese student who is overly concerned about involving her parents in her college choice should not be considered immature by a teacher because of his or her own cultural beliefs. Because

the Taiwanese culture emphasizes parental respect, the consultant must ensure that the student is not penalized for behaving in a culturally appropriate manner.

School-based consultants should be able to identify and challenge a consultee's stereotypical beliefs and biases because, ultimately, these faulty perceptions can affect the consultation outcomes. Prejudicial attitudes within the consultation process may be manifested in outright rejection or the provision of inadequate interventions. Clearly, school-based consultants need to be vigilant in order to detect and deal with negative racial attitudes, negative cultural attitudes, or both (M. R. Rogers, 2000). By identifying the consultee's biased and prejudicial statements or assumptions, the school-based consultant is more apt to be able to eliminate negative cultural attitudes that might possibly affect the consultee's or client's problem. Oftentimes, for example, teachers will consult with a professional school counselor but fail to recognize their own biased beliefs that are directly or indirectly creating a problem for a student.

Assessment

Given the prevalence of standardized achievement and aptitude tests in today's schools, it is imperative that professional school counselors understand the cultural appropriateness of assessment instruments used frequently in schools (Rhodes, Ochoa, & Ortiz, 2005). The assessment of students from diverse backgrounds is complex and needs to be performed with professional care and consideration. Professional school counselors should be able to evaluate instruments for cultural bias and identify other methods for assessing culturally diverse students. In addition, professional school counselors should be competent in relaying assessment results to culturally diverse students and parents. It is important to remember, however, that there is not one instrument that is totally unbiased. Therefore, professional school counselors should know that their judgments in assessing the cultural appropriateness of an instrument and providing unbiased interpretations are key in the process of culturally sensitive assessment. Biased interpretations, for instance, of a student's test results can lead to inappropriate decisions regarding a student's needs. Professional school counselors must always be cognizant of the presence of unjust assessment practices, which lead to tracking students of color and poor students in low-performing classes, excluding racially or culturally diverse students from gifted and talented programs, and disproportionately identifying students of color for special education services.

Finally, professional school counselors should be aware of the testing options for English language learners. Generally, the options for these students are to have a test translated, use an interpreter for the test, use a test that is norm-referenced in their first language, or use a bilingual test administrator. Professional school counselors must challenge linguicism (Chen–Hayes, Chen, & Athar, 2000) and ensure that bilingual students receive a fair and appropriate testing environment, as well as an opportunity to present a fair representation of their skills, abilities, and aptitudes.

School Counseling/Guidance Curriculum Lessons

School counseling/guidance curriculum lessons are used to relay information or to instruct a large group of students in the classroom. These lessons, based on the *ASCA National Model* (2005a), are an effective way for professional school counselors to address cultural sensitivity and issues pertaining to race, gender, sexual orientation, disabilities, or any diversity-related issue (Bruce, Shade, & Cossairt, 1996). Perusse and Goodnough (2004) included multiple school counseling curriculum lessons on culturally diverse aspects of academic, career, and personal/social development, looking at multiple oppressions including ableism (Coker, 2004), racism (Bailey & Bradbury-Bailey, 2004), sexism (C. B. Stone, 2004), heterosexism (S. D. Smith & Chen–Hayes, 2004), and multiple oppressions (Jackson & Grant, 2004) as they affect K–12 students. Adams, Bell, and Griffin (1997) published an entire text on how to focus on teaching multiple issues of oppression in social justice skills training.

Professional school counselors can help students become more culturally sensitive by implementing school counseling/guidance curriculum lessons focused on affirming differences, using accurate multicultural terminology, exploring one's biases, learning about ethnic/racial identity–development models, understanding diverse worldviews, and challenging the various oppressions. In addition to the above resources, sample classroom school counseling curriculum lessons might include the following activities related to multicultural issues:

1. Students are given case studies of students dealing with racism, classism, heterosexism, ableism, linguicism, sexism, multiple oppressions, and so forth. They are then asked to discuss the feelings of the students featured in the case studies and ways to solve problems dealing with oppressive behavior—and particularly solutions for challenging systemic barriers that keep certain groups of students from achieving access and success.

2. Students are asked to define *stereotype* and then brainstorm stereotypes that students have or have heard about different groups of people. They then discuss the dangers of stereotypes and where students can go to find accurate information about persons of diverse cultural identities.

3. Students are asked to interview a classmate or classmate's family members about their experiences with prejudice, power, and various forms of oppression. This activity is followed by a large-group discussion of themes that have emerged and the similarities and differences with various oppressions.

4. Students invite diverse persons from the community to discuss their personal ethnic/racial/cultural histories. This activity can be done in a large auditorium with 60 to 65 students. Students should have prepared questions for the panelists about how they have dealt with prejudiced people, racism, and oppression.

5. Students read *A People's History of the United States* (Zinn, 2003), or excerpts from it, and then do a family history explaining how their ancestors, as well as current members, have been subject to, or have subjected others to, oppression based on ethnicity, race, gender, social class, language, immigration status, disability, and other identities.

School Counseling Program Coordination

Professional school counselors provide a variety of services directly and indirectly to students, parents, and teachers. At the same time, professional school counselors are responsible for coordinating school counseling program activities and services that involve individuals and programs outside the school. Professional school counselors' coordinating activities may range from coordinating a peer mediation program to coordinating family counseling services. Multicultural aspects of coordination include being sensitive to the diverse needs of those persons inside the school and in the community. Professional school counselors should coordinate schoolwide programs relevant to the needs of all students, particularly those from culturally diverse backgrounds. Schoolwide programs that develop the skills needed to affirm all cultures and to handle conflict resolution promote respect for various worldviews.

Also, professional school counselors should take the time to meet and develop relationships with referral sources that are representative of their school's communities. D. A. Atkinson and Juntunen (1994) recommended that professional school counselors be familiar with services offered both in ethnic/racial communities and in the larger community. For instance, a professional school counselor in a community with a large percentage of Muslim students should contact and begin a working relationship with local mosques. Or a professional school counselor seeing out lesbian, bisexual, gay, and transgendered students should contact and assess the services provided by local agencies that specialize in working with gay and lesbian youth and their families, such as Parents and Friends of Lesbians and Gays (PFLAG; www.pflag.org) and the Gay, Lesbian, Straight Education Network (GLSEN; www.glsen.org).

Data Collection and Sharing

Collecting and analyzing meaningful data about the characteristics and academic performance of students and about school organization and management helps highly diverse schools "identify achievement gaps, address equity issues, determine the effectiveness of specific programs and courses of study, and target instructional improvement" (Lachat, 2002, p. 3). Data are collected, analyzed, and interpreted to make school counseling program improvements, as well as total school improvements. The use of data to effect change within the school system is integral to ensuring that every student receives the benefits of the school counseling program. To create a data-driven school counseling program, professional school counselors must work with administrators, faculty, and advisory council members to analyze data in order to create a current picture of students and the school environment. This picture focuses discussion and planning around students' needs and the professional school counselor's role

in addressing those needs. Professional school counselors should be proficient in the collection, analysis, and interpretation of student achievement and related data. Professional school counselors monitor student progress through four types of data: (1) achievement data, (2) attainment data, (3) school culture data, and (4) standards- and competency-related data.

Student achievement data measure students' academic progress and include grade point averages, standardized test scores, academic standards–based test scores, and SAT/ACT scores, Attainment data measure those factors that the literature has shown to be correlated to academic achievement and include these data fields: gifted and talented patterns, transition patterns, special education identification, promotion and retention rates, course enrollment patterns, and graduation rates. School culture data include data regarding attendance, suspensions and expulsions, faculty-to-student relationships, school climate, student attitudes, and dropout rates. Standards- and competency-related data measure student mastery of the competencies delineated in the *ASCA National Model* (2005a) and can include the percentage of students who have a four-year plan on file, the percentage of students who have participated in job shadowing, the percentage of students who have set and attained academic goals, and the percentage of students who have applied conflict resolution skills.

Professional school counselors who strive to be culturally competent disaggregate data by variables to see if there are any groups of students who may not be doing as well as others. These data often shed light on issues of equity and focus the discussion on the needs of specific groups of students. Although there are many variables by which data may be separated, the common fields include gender, ethnicity/race, socioeconomic status, home language,

---

THEORY INTO PRACTICE 6.1

SOCIAL JUSTICE: USING DATA TO ADDRESS REFERRAL INEQUITIES

A professional middle school counselor in a rural district in Arizona becomes increasingly disturbed by the number of teacher referrals she has received regarding the behavior and/or social/personal concerns of Native American students. She decides to collect and analyze her counseling referrals by the race of the student. The data confirm her suspicion that more Native American than White students have been referred to her. Next, she decides to analyze the data by the referring teacher. Her results indicate that there are four teachers that repeatedly refer Native American students for counseling. After discussing the data with her

administrator, they decide to review and analyze school achievement and attainment data by race. They find that Native American students have lower achievement scores in all academic areas. The school counselor and administrator decide to present the data to the school. The administrator meets individually with the four teachers who disproportionately refer Native American students for counseling. The administrator shares the data with each of the four teachers, and they discuss ways that these teachers can take a more proactive and strengths-based approach with Native American students.

disability, attendance, grade level, and teacher(s). To determine whether specific programs are not working for certain students—underachieving students, students with excessive absenteeism, and dropouts—data can be disaggregated by the courses taken or even by the teachers who taught them in order to identify and consider relevant school influences. The performance of students with similar personal characteristics can be disaggregated to determine which courses, instructional strategies, and so forth are most effective with them. Differences between student grades and scores on standardized tests can be reviewed to determine whether there are lags in course content or poor preparation for some types of tests (Lachat, 2002) (see Theory into Practice 6.1).

CASE STUDIES OF PROFESSIONAL SCHOOL COUNSELORS CHALLENGING OPPRESSION IN K–12 SCHOOLS

In this section, case studies of professional school counselors who have used the previously discussed strategies for becoming culturally competent will be highlighted.

Case Study 1

Having learned about the Education Trust's Transforming School Counseling Initiative and the importance of professional school counselors focusing on academic success for all students, James Martinez, a bilingual, Puerto Rican professional middle school counselor, asked his assistant principal for data measuring the results of academic services for students who were failing three or more classes. James was overwhelmed with the response. The assistant principal not only gave him the data on students' failing grades, but also wanted to give him more data on other issues. Based on the data, James developed a program to monitor the performance progress of students who were failing and advocated for equitable academic services to support students' diverse learning needs. When the superintendent and the school board wished to know exactly what it was that professional school counselors do, he sent his newly created brochure on school counseling programs and services offered at Peekskill Middle School to the administrators, along with handouts on transformative school counseling programs and a summary data collection used to challenge academic inequities.

Case Study 2

Winnie Lisojo, a Puerto Rican, bilingual/bicultural professional school counselor, was concerned about the academic success of the Puerto Rican and Dominican students at the school where she performed her internship and worked as a bilingual teacher. She realized that systemic linguicism was occurring. Winnie found that Puerto Rican students were often transferred into English as a second language (ESL) classrooms simply because they possessed Latino/a surnames and without any screening of their language abilities. After months of advocating for a change in the policy of ESL inclusion, Winnie convinced the principal to place students on the basis of their language skills, rather than simply sorting them by surnames. Students, parents, administrators, and staff all benefited from her challenging linguicism.

Case Study 3

Theresa Wyre-Jackson, a Bronx high school counselor of Caribbean descent, realized that her school was focusing on "at-risk" students who were failing, as opposed to her preferred focus on "at-promise" students in order to build on their strengths and potential for academic, career, and college success. As she collected data on academic success at her school, she challenged her students and her teaching colleagues to strive for high expectations and high achievement. She created a series of workshops to directly challenge the internalized and externalized racism, classism, and heterosexism adversely affecting students and teachers. Through her school advocacy efforts, she created dissatisfaction with the status quo and instead created an environment in which *all* students learned to challenge oppressive myths.

Case Study 4

Inez Ramos, a professional school counselor at Health Opportunities High School in the Bronx, is Latina and bilingual and a strong student advocate. At a public meeting, she openly questioned the New York City Board of Education chancellor as to why he was not providing more financial and administrative support for the academic and emotional needs of K–12 students, particularly poor children of color. Her question was replayed on several New York City television stations and resulted in her being asked to discuss her concerns with the chancellor.

Case Study 5

Kimmerly Nieves, a middle-class professional middle school counselor of Puerto Rican descent in Westchester County, New York, works at Albert Leonard Middle School. Roughly 50% of the school's student body consists of poor ethnic/racial minorities, including African-American and Latino/Chicano students, and the other 50% is made up of White and Jewish students of middle- and upper-middle-class backgrounds. The staff was primarily White or Jewish. Kimmerly developed multicultural school counseling lessons and implemented them at her school. She found support from administrators, staff, and a diverse range of parents in her school. She found that many of the White teachers embraced her efforts to increase academic success for all students. Her unwavering work in support of the concept that the cultural identities of all learners must be affirmed by all members of the school for greater academic success has modeled multicultural and anti-oppression competencies for the community. Her outreach to students and parents of color in particular was critical in demonstrating trust and credibility on the part of professional school counselors—and all educators—in ensuring academic success for all students.

INCREASING PROFESSIONAL SCHOOL COUNSELORS' MULTICULTURAL COMPETENCE

As DeLucia-Waack, DiCarlo, Parker-Sloat, and Rice (1996) stated, "[M]ulticulturalism is best viewed as a process or a journey rather than a fixed end point" (p. 237). Because this is a process, it is important for counselors to have a variety of learning experiences that enhance multicultural competence. This section offers five ways in which professional school counselors can increase their level of multicultural competence: investigate one's own cultural or ethnic heritage; attend workshops, seminars, and conferences on multicultural and diversity issues; join counseling organizations focused on cultural and social justice equity competency; read literature written by culturally diverse authors; and become familiar with multicultural education literature.

Investigate One's Own Cultural or Ethnic Heritage

Researchers and counselor educators have documented the importance of self-awareness as a requirement for working with others (G. Corey, Corey, & Callanan, 2006).

Self-awareness is essential to becoming multiculturally competent. Speight, Myers, Cox, & Highlen (1991) suggested that the acceptance of others' cultures and differences increases as one's self-knowledge increases. For this reason, many multicultural counseling courses and training seminars focus on increasing trainees' self-awareness.

Professional school counselors should explore their ethnic identity, racial identity, and other cultural identities. For many White counselors, this is a difficult process because they often don't see themselves as having an ethnicity or affiliation with a racial identity. However, almost everyone can trace his or her family history, values, and experiences, with the exception of some persons who have been adopted or have no access to family members. For some, this can mean exploring the values of their family of origin or examining written histories of their families' "roots." In addition to exploring one's family history, White counselors should spend time exploring the concept of White privilege and the issues that result from such privilege. For instance, White counselors should have an opportunity to explore what it means to be White, the benefits of White privilege, and the guilt associated with being a member of the dominant racial culture in terms of power and privilege in the United States.

Attend Workshops, Seminars, and Conferences on Multicultural and Diversity Issues

For many professional school counselors, one course in multicultural counseling is not the answer to their lack of multicultural competence. In addition to the content learned in the course, most counselors need additional training when they are employed. Given the importance of multiculturalism in counseling, most counseling organizations have developed special workshops, weekend seminars, and annual conference presentations that cover issues related to multiculturalism, various oppressions, and creative approaches for working with diverse clientele.

Join Counseling Organizations Focused on Cultural and Social Justice Equity Competencies

It is important that professional school counselors not only attend workshops and seminars related to multiculturalism and diversity, but also join organizations that are focused primarily on increasing multicultural and social justice equity competencies. Such counseling organizations as the AMCD, Counselors for Social Justice (CSJ), and the Association for Gay, Lesbian, Bisexual, and Transgendered Issues in Counseling (AGLBTIC) are dedicated to combating oppression and increasing cultural sensitivity in the counseling profession.

Read Literature Written by Culturally Diverse Authors

Literature can be a useful tool in learning about other cultures. Through reading about other cultures, the professional school counselor's worldview is broadened, and he or she is introduced to the present and past realities of people of those cultural groups. Cornett and Cornett (1980) indicated that the reading experience encourages readers to engage in critical thinking when they begin to realize how selectively some U.S. historical and sociopolitical events have been and still are reported. One of the authors uses Zinn's (2003) *A People's History of the United States* to teach multicultural counseling because it uses a narrative format to present the personal and systemic stories that illustrate how ethnic, racial, social class, and gender oppressions have been intertwined for centuries in the United States and how members of oppressed groups and their allies have resisted and continue to resist oppression in the forms of racism, classism, and sexism in the United States and the rest of the Americas.

It gives a powerful understanding to how affirming diversity is not enough; culturally competent professional school counselors must also be advocates for social justice and equity.

Become Familiar with Multicultural Education Literature

It is imperative that professional school counselors stay abreast of the literature and research pertaining to multicultural education. The teacher education profession has a long history of exploring teachers' lack of multicultural competence and their biased behavior in the classroom. For professional school counselors to play a pivotal role in changing some of the institutional barriers for ethnic minority students, they must be aware of the most current research related to multicultural pedagogy and curriculum.

PROFESSIONAL SCHOOL COUNSELOR MULTICULTURAL COMPETENCE CHECKLIST

Perhaps one of the first steps to becoming a multiculturally competent professional school counselor is determining areas of personal improvement needed. Figure 6.1 is a checklist that can be used by professional school counselors to determine areas for additional multicultural counseling training and exploration. Based on the AMCD's Multicultural Counseling Competencies (Arredondo et al., 1996) and multicultural education literature, the checklist encompasses those behaviors, knowledge, and awareness that have been noted as important for culturally competent work in school settings. The checklist can be completed by professional school counselors and counselors in training annually to monitor progress and needs for further exploration. In addition, professional school counselors in training benefit from the use of case studies of actual professional school counselors who have created culturally competent schools through challenging oppression and from the use of practice vignettes.

Practice Vignettes

Another step in the process of developing multicultural counseling competence is for professional school counselors to openly question their thoughts and behaviors when working with ethnic minority students: "What additional knowledge, awareness, or skills do I need to effectively work with this student?" "Am I effective when working with students of this particular ethnic background?" "How

Directions: Check whether you are COMPETENT or NOT COMPETENT on each of the following items.

	Competent	Not Competent

Multicultural Counseling

1. I can recognize when my beliefs and values are interfering with providing the best services to my students.

2. I can identify the cultural bases of my communication style.

3. I can discuss how culture affects the help-seeking behaviors of students.

4. I know when a counseling approach is culturally appropriate for a specific student.

5. I know when a counseling approach is culturally inappropriate for a specific student.

6. I am able to identify culturally appropriate interventions and counseling approaches (e.g., indigenous practices) with students.

7. I can list barriers that prevent ethnic minority students from using counseling services.

8. I know when my helping style is inappropriate for a culturally different student.

9. I know when my helping style is appropriate for a culturally different student.

10. I can give examples of how stereotypical beliefs about culturally different persons impact the counseling relationship.

11. I know when my biases influence my services to students.

12. I know when specific cultural beliefs influence students' responses to counseling.

13. I know when my helping style is inappropriate for a culturally different student.

Multicultural Consultation

14. I know when my culture is influencing the process of consultation.

15. I know when the culture of the consultee (e.g., parent, teacher) is influencing the process of consultation.

16. I know when the race and/or culture of a student is a problem for a teacher.

17. I can initiate discussions related to race/ethnicity/culture when consulting with teachers.

18. I can initiate discussions related to race/ethnicity/culture when consulting with parents.

Understanding Racism and Student Resistance

19. I can define and discuss White privilege.

20. I can discuss how I (if European/American/White) am privileged based on my race.

21. I can identify racist aspects of educational instruction.

22. I can define and discuss prejudice.

23. I can identify discrimination and discriminatory practices in schools.

24. I am able to challenge my colleagues when they discriminate against students.

25. I can define and discuss racism.

26. I can discuss the influence of racism on the counseling process.

27. I can discuss the influence of racism on the educational system in the United States.

28. I can help students determine whether a problem stems from racism or biases in others.

29. I understand the relationship between student resistance and racism.

30. I am able to discuss the relationship between student resistance and racism.

31. I include topics related to race and racism in my classroom guidance units.

32. I am able to challenge others' racist beliefs and behaviors.

33. I am able to identify racist and unjust policies in schools.

FIGURE 6.1 Professional school counselor multicultural competence checklist. (*Continued*)

Directions: Check whether you are COMPETENT or NOT COMPETENT on each of the following items.

	Competent	Not Competent

Understanding Racial and/or Ethnic Identity Development

34. I am able to discuss at least two theories of racial and/or ethnic identity development.

35. I can use racial/ethnic identity development theories to understand my students' problems and concerns.

36. I can assess my own racial/ethnic identity development in order to enhance my counseling.

37. I can assist students who are exploring their own racial/ethnic identity development.

38. I can develop activities that enhance students' racial/ethnic identity.

39. I am able to discuss how racial/ethnic identity may affect the relationships between students and educators.

Multicultural Assessment

40. I can discuss the potential bias of two assessment instruments frequently used in the schools.

41. I can evaluate instruments that may be biased against certain groups of students.

42. I am able to use test information appropriately with culturally diverse parents.

43. I can advocate for fair testing and the appropriate use of testing of children from diverse backgrounds.

44. I can identify whether or not the assessment process is culturally sensitive.

45. I can discuss how the identification stage of the assessment process might be biased against minority populations.

46. I can use culturally appropriate instruments when I assess students.

47. I am able to discuss how assessment can lead to inequitable opportunities for students.

Multicultural Family Interventions

48. I can discuss family counseling from a cultural/ethnic perspective.

49. I can discuss at least two ethnic groups' traditional gender-role expectations and rituals.

50. I can anticipate when my helping style is inappropriate for a culturally different parent or guardian.

51. I can discuss culturally diverse methods of parenting and discipline.

52. I can discuss how class and economic level affect family functioning and development.

53. I can discuss how race and ethnicity influence family behavior.

54. I can identify when a school policy is biased against culturally diverse families.

Social Advocacy

55. I know of societal issues that affect the development of ethnic minority students.

56. When counseling, I am able to address societal issues that affect the development of ethnic minority students.

57. I can work with families and community members in order to reintegrate them into the school.

58. I can define "social change agent."

59. I am able to be a "social change agent."

Directions: Check whether you are COMPETENT or NOT COMPETENT on each of the following items.

	Competent	Not Competent

60. I can discuss what it means to take an "activist counseling approach."

61. I can intervene with students at the individual and systemic levels.

62. I can discuss how factors such as poverty and powerlessness have influenced the current conditions of at least two ethnic groups.

63. I am able to advocate for students who are being subjected to unfair practices.

64. I know how to use data as an advocacy tool.

Developing School–Family–Community Partnerships

65. I can discuss how school–family–community partnerships are linked to student achievement.

66. I am able to develop partnerships with families that are culturally different than me.

67. I am able to develop partnerships with agencies within my school's community.

68. I can define a school–family–community partnership.

69. I am able to discuss more than three types of parent involvement.

70. I am able to encourage the participation of ethnic minority parents in school activities.

71. I am able to work with community leaders and other resources in the community to assist with student (and family) concerns.

Understanding Cross-Cultural Interpersonal Interactions

72. I am able to discuss interaction patterns that might influence ethnic minority students' perception of inclusion in the school community.

73. I can solicit feedback from students regarding my interactions with them.

74. I can verbally communicate my acceptance of culturally diverse students.

75. I can nonverbally communicate my acceptance of culturally diverse students.

76. I am able to assess the manner in which I speak and the emotional tone of my interactions with culturally diverse students.

77. I am able to greet students and parents in a culturally acceptable manner.

78. I know of culturally insensitive topics or gestures.

Multicultural Career Assessment

79. I can develop and implement culturally sensitive career development activities where materials are representative of all groups in a wide range of careers.

80. I can arrange opportunities for students to have interactions with ethnic minority professionals.

81. I am able to assess the strengths of multiple aspects of students' self-concepts.

82. I can discuss differences in the decision-making styles of students.

83. I can integrate my knowledge of varying decision-making styles when implementing career counseling.

84. I can integrate family and religious issues in the career counseling process.

85. I can utilize career assessment instruments that are sensitive to cultural differences of students.

86. I can discuss how "work" and "career" are viewed similarly and differently across cultures.

87. I can discuss how many career assessment instruments are inappropriate for culturally diverse students.

FIGURE 6.1   (*Continued*)

Directions: Check whether you are COMPETENT or NOT COMPETENT on each of the following items.

	Competent	Not Competent

Multicultural Sensitivity

88. I am able to develop a close personal relationship with someone of another race.

89. I am able to live comfortably with culturally diverse people.

90. I am able to be comfortable with people who speak another language.

91. I can make friends with people from other ethnic groups.

Source: "Assessing the Multicultural Competence of School Counselors: A Checklist," by C. Holcomb-McCoy, 2004, *Professional School Counseling, 7,* pp. 178–186. Copyright 2004 by ASCA. Reprinted with permission.

are my beliefs, values, and biases affecting the counseling process with this student?" Professional school counselors who answer these questions are better able to understand their level of multicultural competence and need for further multicultural counseling training.

In addition to questioning their thoughts and behaviors, professional school counselors can use case studies and practice vignettes to begin discussions with colleagues. Following are three vignettes that involve sensitive cultural issues arising in a school. The task of the reader is to think about how to work with the student(s), parents, and teachers involved and to determine his or her own level of multicultural competence. These vignettes can be used for large- and small-group discussions with other counselors who are seeking to improve their multicultural competence.

Vignette 1

Brandon is a 15-year-old student at a high school in a predominately upper-middle-class White suburb. Brandon has lived most of his life in this community, but has recently begun hanging out in the African-American section of the suburb and has announced that he has converted to Islam from Christianity. Brandon is biracial: his mother is White and his father is African American. His parents are concerned about Brandon because he has become very angry at his parents' supposedly "White lifestyle" and has asked to live with his father's parents. His parents want you, the professional school counselor, to talk to Brandon about their concerns.

Vignette 2

You are a professional school counselor at a diverse elementary school. The ethnic/racial composition of the student population is 41% White, 25% African American, 25% Asian, 5% Latino/a, and 2% Native American; 33% of the students are on free or reduced lunch; 29% of the students are English language learners; and 22% of the students have one or more learning, physical, developmental, or emotional disabilities. The ethnic/racial make-up of the teaching staff is 95% White and 5% "other," and all are at least working class or middle class. There are no teachers who speak English as a second language, and some teachers have physical and emotional disabilities. Since the student population has become increasingly diverse, you have become more cognizant of teachers making racist, classist, linguicist, and ableist jokes and stereotypical comments about students of color, poor and working-class students, English language learners, and students with disabilities in the teachers' lounge. You have become very uncomfortable with the comments.

Vignette 3

Maria is a bilingual, Mexican 11th grader with severe asthma and obesity and is eligible for free and reduced lunch at the high school in which you are a professional school counselor. Maria has just received her SAT scores, which are very high (i.e., a 1250 total on Critical Reading and Mathematics). She has also received several letters from competitive colleges and universities. Nevertheless, Maria tells you that she doesn't want to go to college. Instead, she would like to find a job so that she can help her family financially.

Summary/Conclusion

With the increasingly diverse student population of today's schools, there is a critical need for professional school counselors who are able to provide effective school counseling programs that offer both culturally competent and anti-oppressive programs to all students to help close achievement, opportunity, and attainment gaps in K–12 schools. As professional school counselors work with larger numbers of students of color and students of other multiple cultural identities, they need to adjust their perceptions and school counseling programs to address these students' diverse needs. This chapter has focused on several ways in which professional school counselors can integrate cultural competence; anti-oppression work; and multiple cultural identity awareness, knowledge, and skills into school counseling programs in order to increase student success and demonstrate school counselor cultural competence. This chapter is only an introduction; the goal for professional school counselors is to continue the journey of developing greater cultural competence. Engagement in the process of developing cultural competence and affirming diversity through challenging oppression provides professional school counselors an unparalleled opportunity to achieve personal and professional growth and demonstrable skills to better the lives of all students through data-driven school counseling programs.

This chapter began with an introduction to important multicultural and anti-oppression terminology because it is imperative that professional school counselors first know how to define and conceptualize cultural and oppressive incidents that occur in schools. In addition, a brief discussion of how cultural and anti-oppression practice might be integrated into components of developmental school counseling programs was provided. Considering that a major goal for professional school counselors is learning how to discuss oppression and cultural topics freely and openly in school settings, this chapter included case studies and practice vignettes to stimulate dialogue among counselors as to how they might react to or resolve issues related to oppressive school practices, students' cultural differences, or both. Continuous dialogue regarding issues of oppression in schools should be initiated by professional school counselors.

Professional school counselors who want to assess their multicultural competence can complete the Professional School Counselor Multicultural Competence Checklist included in this chapter. This checklist is unique in that it includes 11 dimensions of professional school counselor multicultural competence: multicultural counseling, multicultural consultation, understanding racism and student resistance, understanding racial and/or ethnic identity development, multicultural assessment, multicultural family interventions, social advocacy, developing school–family–community partnerships, understanding cross-cultural interpersonal interactions, multicultural career assessment, and multicultural sensitivity.

Overall, this chapter has provided an introduction to multicultural counseling in schools and the ways in which oppressive beliefs and practices impact student success. It is important to note, however, that it is impossible to prepare in advance for all the different experiences one might encounter in schools. Instead, professional school counselors need to acquire the knowledge and skills that will allow them to critically assess and intelligently address the various challenges encountered by students and their families.

Activities

1. Collaborate in a small group to outline a developmental school counseling lesson plan with specific activities and content on the awareness, knowledge, and skills needed by students and staff to combat at least two of the oppressions discussed in this chapter. Link this activity to the *ASCA National Model* or your state's school counseling model and specific state learning standards/outcomes for a specific grade and building level (e.g., 5th-grade elementary students, 8th-grade middle school students, 10th-grade high school students).

2. Discuss the multicultural demographics (ethnicity/race, gender, sexual orientation, disability status, social class, language status, religious/spiritual identity, and other variables), as well as the multicultural competence levels of the teaching and school counseling staff, of the K–12 schools that you attended. How will you be similar or different when you are working as a professional school counselor?

3. Go to the Education Trust's website (www.edtrust.org), and find a piece of local or national data that best illustrates the racism and classism involved in a current achievement, opportunity, or attainment gap facing poor and working-class students or students of African American, Latino/a, or Native American ethnic/racial identity, including students who are English language learners, students with disabilities, or both. Once you have located the piece of data, what would you do as a culturally competent professional school counselor to challenge systemic barriers in a school that has that type of gap?

7

Leadership and Achievement Advocacy for Every Student

Stuart F. Chen-Hayes, Emily M. Miller, Deryl F. Bailey, Yvette Q. Getch, and Bradley T. Erford

Editor's Introduction: Key to the transformation of the school counseling profession is the professional school counselor's skill in providing both leadership and advocacy for social justice, thus ensuring academic, career, and college access equity (also known as achievement advocacy). Transformative school counseling programs deliver measurable achievement competencies to all students via group and individual counseling, ASCA model and college access lesson plans, parent and guardian workshops, and annual educational planning for every student.

The school counseling profession, in the span of less than 10 years, has put leadership and advocacy into a central place for all professional school counselors (American School Counselor Association [ASCA], 2005a; Bryan, 2005; Bryan, Holcomb-McCoy, Moore-Thomas, & Day-Vines, 2009; Chen-Hayes, 2007; Council for Accreditation of Counseling and Related Educational Programs [CACREP], 2009; Ratts, DeKruyf, & Chen-Hayes, 2007). While some school professionals refer to students "at risk," it is more empowering and focuses on strengths instead of deficits to believe that all students are "at promise" (Swadener & Lubeck, 1995). This change in language helps school counseling programs to lead and advocate and to challenge some adults' beliefs that not all students can achieve high levels of K–12 school success or graduate from college. School counseling programs using a strengths-based, "nondeficient" leadership and advocacy model are educational leaders providing measurable equity, achievement results, and success for all students (ASCA, 2005a; Hatch & Chen-Hayes, 2008). In particular, students of color, poor and working-class students, students with disabilities, and students who are English language learners (ELLs) have not received equal academic, career, and college access, opportunities, and resources for success from school counseling programs or K–16 schools as a whole (ASCA, 2005a; Bryan et al., 2009; Education Trust, 2005a; Vela-Gude et al., 2009; see also Chapters 1 and 6).

Professional school counselors who develop and implement transformative school counseling programs based on the *ASCA National Model* (ASCA, 2005a) strive to empower and advocate for students from historically oppressed populations that have been defined by their ethnicity, race, social class, language, disability, sexual orientation, gender, gender identity/expression, appearance, immigration status, family type, spirituality/religion, and so forth, as outlined in the ASCA's *Ethical Standards for School Counselors* (2004a). A results-based, transformative school counseling program uses systemic achievement advocacy to benefit all students (Hatch & Chen-Hayes, 2008). When professional school counselors develop and maintain a school counseling program based on advocacy and leadership with specific competencies and outcomes that demonstrate how professional school counselors help students to succeed in academic, career/college, and personal/social achievement domains, they empower teachers, parents, guardians, and students to speak out and change unjust institutional and systemic practices. The transformed professional school counselor leads and advocates to remove barriers to student performance and overcome social injustice through modeling and teaching social and achievement advocacy and leadership strategies and through implementing both a transformative school counseling program and a strong school counseling public awareness and support program. Creating public awareness of and support for the school counseling program helps clarify for all stakeholders the transformative results for all students in grades K–12 (see Chapters 1 and 6).

Unfortunately, some achievement and opportunity gaps are maintained even under the guise of reform. Some school systems, hoping to encourage positive change, invite charismatic leadership speakers whose goal is to motivate educators to make a difference in the lives of all children. Most often, this peaked motivation to serve all students dissipates. Shortly after the start of classes, educators can be found conducting business as usual and, at the end of the year, wondering why so many students are failing, suspended, expelled, dropping out, or disappearing. A building leader once explained this phenomenon as follows: "If you always do what you've always done, you'll always get what you've always gotten." This statement demonstrates why achievement and opportunity gaps exist between various groups of students.

Achievement gaps are the disparities in academic performance found among different groups of students based on ethnicity/race, gender, ability/disability, social class, and language status (monolingual, bilingual, ELL). Access (opportunity) gaps are the disparities in who receives school counseling programs, services, a high-level college preparatory curriculum, honors courses, Advanced Placement and International Baccalaureate coursework (International Baccalaureate, 2009), college counseling, the best teachers—and who does not—usually based on ethnicity/race, gender, ability/disability, social class, and language status (e.g., monolingual, bilingual, ELL) (Bryan et al., 2009; Chen-Hayes, 2007; Vela-Gude et al., 2009). Achievement, access, attainment (e.g., who graduates from college with a diploma and who does not, based on cultural and economic group), and funding gaps (e.g., who gets the most money for schools based on tax levies and who gets the least) exist between students of color and White students as well as between students from low-income families (often students of color) and students from middle- and upper-income families (Brennan, 1999; Bryan et al., 2009; Chen-Hayes, 2007; Vela-Gude et al., 2009).

Why are these gaps between various groups of students so wide if all students can learn? In some cases, students of color had no access to school counselors, or school counselors were dismissive of their academic, career, and college access potential (Bryan et al., 2009; Vela-Gude et al., 2009). Many school systems, however, have taken bold steps to reform and have demonstrated that students of color and students from low-income households can excel academically (Brennan, 1999). The Education Trust, for example, annually honors school districts and individual schools that have closed significant achievement and opportunity gaps throughout the United States (Education Trust, 2005b), and the National Office for School Counselor Advocacy (NOSCA) at the College Board offers annual Inspiration Awards for individual high schools with demonstrable increases in college access and attendance rates (College Board, 2008b). Brennan (1999) reported that students from low-income families can match the achievement of students from high-income families "stride for stride" and that in increasing numbers of school districts, many poor students outperform students from affluent families. According to a report released by the Education Trust (1999), *Dispelling the Myth: High Poverty Schools Exceeding Expectations*, successful high-poverty schools demonstrated the following characteristics:

1. Extensive use of state/local standards to design curriculum and instruction, assess student work, and evaluate teachers;
2. Increased instructional time for reading and mathematics;
3. Substantial investment in professional development for teachers focused on instructional practices to help students meet academic standards;
4. Comprehensive systems to monitor individual student performance and to provide help to struggling students before they fall behind;
5. Parental involvement in efforts to get students to meet standards; and
6. Accountability systems with real consequences for adults in the school.

Therefore, in high-poverty schools, professional school counselors must use advocacy, leadership, systemic change, and collaboration skills (ASCA, 2005a) and services to help close achievement and access gaps for every student. For example, school counseling programs should use state and local standards to design curriculum and instruction and assess student learning. School counseling programs can be major contributors by integrating student learning styles and other learning modalities. Professional school counselors can work with academic intervention teams and other educators collaboratively in school leadership teams to monitor student progress weekly and determine what needs to be done by all adults in schools to ensure that there is educational equity and that high standards are achieved by every K–12 student. Professional school counselors can collaboratively design and implement professional development workshops for teachers, administrators, and parents and guardians to increase awareness of achievement, access, attainment, and funding gaps and devise specific advocacy and leadership strategies, skills, and outcomes for systemic change in schools.

Professional school counselors play a pivotal role in monitoring student performance. Professional school counselors assist students with career and college curriculum offerings and decision making, as well as with personal and social concerns. For example, some professional high school counselors resist and resent scheduling classes. While professional school counselors should not be high-paid clerks, professional school counselors must be engaged as educational leaders and advocates, ensuring that all students receive outstanding teaching and that no students are marginalized or tracked with teachers who lack credentials or who do not believe all students can learn at high levels. Thus, during the master schedule creation process, professional school counselors need to ensure that all K–12 students are receiving a college and career preparatory curriculum with high levels of mathematics, science, and literacy courses that will allow them to be both career- and college-ready (Trusty & Niles, 2003). Professional school counselors also can encourage parents' and guardians' involvement by ensuring that they are notified immediately when students begin to experience academic concerns in school and can assist families with these difficulties using a strengths-based advocacy perspective (Ratts, DeKruyf, & Chen-Hayes, 2007).

This chapter focuses on professional school counselors as leaders and achievement advocates who promote systemic changes in schools and communities through transformative school counseling programs that provide measurable achievement results based on the *ASCA National Model* (2005a), the Education Trust's National Center for Transforming School Counseling (2005b), and the National Office for School Counselor Advocacy at the College Board (College Board, 2008b). Professional school counselors as leaders and advocates assist in eliminating barriers that have traditionally impeded the growth and performance of all students, particularly students of color, poor and working-class students, students who are ELLs, and students with disabilities.

PROFESSIONAL SCHOOL COUNSELORS AS LEADERS

Leadership is one of the four overarching themes of the *ASCA National Model* (2005a) and is inextricably tied to advocacy. Being an advocate requires strong leadership skills, especially when advocating for broad, systemic change. A leader is someone who has a "vision" for change, can communicate that vision effectively to others, and can help to direct supporters in working toward creating the desired change; the process requires considerable planning and dedication (Dollarhide, Gibson, & Saginak, 2008).

Although professional school counselors are encouraged by the *ASCA National Model* (2005a) to act as leaders specifically to ensure that all students have the benefit of receiving challenging academic coursework that will prepare

them for a variety of postsecondary opportunities, schools provide school counselors with countless additional opportunities to take on leadership roles. Whether it is working to close an achievement gap, increasing awareness about an important issue, teaching students how to be leaders, being a model for responsible and healthful behavior, or helping to create a safe and welcoming school environment, school counselors have a responsibility to lead the way in improving their school environment so that all students can learn (Dollarhide, 2003).

Bolman and Deal (1997) posited four kinds of leadership: structural leadership, human resources leadership, political leadership, and symbolic leadership. All four leadership domains are integral to effective leadership in schools (Dollarhide, 2003). These leadership styles can be used one at a time, or, when appropriate, a few may be combined to achieve the desired result. Structural leadership comprises the nuts and bolts of an effective leadership campaign. It involves creating an organized plan for change, as well determining how to best put that plan into action, such as by implementing results reports and action reports (ASCA, 2005a).

Human resources leadership may come most naturally to school counselors, as it necessitates implementing the beliefs around equity that most school counselors possess. This kind of leadership requires school counselors to empower and motivate every K–12 student for academic, career, and college success. At the heart of human resources leadership is the capacity to form positive working relationships and demonstrate trust and support of others' abilities to help enact change.

Political leadership may be the most difficult kind of leadership for some school counselors, as it has the potential for dissension (Dollarhide, 2003). Political leadership requires the integration of advocacy, an understanding of how systems work, and the ability to make a strong and convincing argument, establish compromises, and connect with people in power. Political leadership is most likely to lead to conflict because it directly involves changing unfair organizational or systemic structures that are in place, a task that may unsettle those in power who are content with the status quo. Yet this is the key leadership skill needed to close achievement and opportunity gaps in schools successfully.

Finally, symbolic leadership is the public relations component. Symbolic leadership involves creating and communicating a vision of change to others to gain supporters and allies. Professional school counselors aiming to make important changes must communicate their belief to others in a persuasive, inspiring, sincere, and relevant way to effectively close gaps and ensure equity and access for every K–12 student.

These four leadership domains are rarely used all at the same time. Nonetheless, all are necessary for effective school counseling leadership. Professional school counselors need to be competent in each of these contexts and to be able to use each type of leadership appropriately as they work to create equitable change in schools and school counseling programs.

In conjunction with an awareness of and expertise in the four types of leadership, a successful leader must master other important skills. One essential aspect of leadership, as well as advocacy, is being proactive (ASCA, 2005a). For example, professional school counselors can continually monitor their school's climate and data to identify and address achievement gaps or unfair school policies or practices in areas such as attendance, disciplinary issues, referrals to the school counseling department, grades, test scores, college-going rates, and college entrance exam scores (C. B. Stone & Dahir, 2007). Rather than waiting for complaints or obvious acts of discrimination, a leader will maintain an ongoing awareness of the school climate and environment so that problems can be pinpointed and remedied proactively, using specific data points and intervening with specific developmental school counseling lessons and group and individual counseling strategies. In addition to being proactive, to be successful leaders, professional school counselors must build strong alliances and work cooperatively with other important stakeholders, including building leaders, teachers, parents and guardians, and community members. It is much easier for school counselors to effect systemic change and exert political leadership if they have rapport with influential stakeholders who can assist and support them in the process.

Dollarhide et al. (2008) conducted a qualitative study that observed the leadership efforts of new school counselors. The results of the study indicated what may lead to successful or unsuccessful leadership attempts. School counselor participants who were successful in their leadership efforts had specific commonalities: They held themselves accountable for achieving their goals, were able to convey their vision and garner support and validation for their work, reframed resistance as a learning experience, persevered through resistance, and found ways to improve their leadership abilities throughout the process. School counselor participants who were unable to achieve their leadership goals also had similarities: They did not seek the support of others or were unable to gain support, did not hold themselves accountable for their leadership efforts, set goals that required resources and access beyond what they were able to procure, did not strive to improve any deficits in their leadership abilities, and allowed others to define their role as a school counselor, rather than defining it themselves.

Based on the results of the study, Dollarhide et al. (2008) recommended these leadership strategies for new counselors: Start by setting reasonable and realistic leadership goals, approach the work with determination, resolve to work through resistance, build a strong support system, seek supervision and support from supervisors and colleagues, and be clear about the role of a school counselor. Although this study had limitations including a small sample size, the results and recommendations provide useful leadership pointers for professional school counselors.

Ultimately, it is the responsibility of all school counselors to evaluate their leadership strengths and weaknesses and work to improve in any areas of concern. Because leadership and advocacy are so intertwined, school counselors must develop leadership skills to effectively advocate for systemic change (ASCA, 2005a).

WHAT ARE ADVOCACY AND ACHIEVEMENT ADVOCACY?

Similar to leadership, advocacy is the intentional effort to change existing or proposed policies, practices, and learning environments on behalf of all students and families (Ezell, 2001). Osborne et al. (1998) presented a model of advocacy congruent with the aforementioned definitions. Their model encouraged counselors to take individual or collective actions on behalf of all students in order to promote justice and improve academic and environmental conditions.

For professional school counselors, achievement advocacy is defined as ensuring high levels of academic, career, college, and personal/social skills are fostered in every K–12 student in a school counseling program with specific results. All K–12 students need a school counseling program to advocate on their behalf at some point during their K–16 school career. But are all professional school counselors ready, willing, and able to implement school counseling programs focused on achievement advocacy for all students? How are professional school counselors transforming the profession and the perception and roles of school counselors and school counseling programs to create positive achievement results for every K–12 student? It is essential for school counselors to advocate as change agents for equity by speaking out against policies or practices that have been "business as usual" and have contributed to achievement, opportunity, attainment, and funding gaps.

History of Advocacy

Advocacy has been an important part of counseling for decades. In the early 1970s, Dworkin and Dworkin (1971) issued a call to action for counselors to become leaders in social change, rather than sideline cheerleaders. Professional school counselors serve as academic, career, college, and personal/social advocates for all students and their families, with extra programmatic attention and counseling and lesson plan interventions for students who demonstrate academic, career/college, and personal/social concerns (ASCA, 2005a; Chen-Hayes, 2007).

Too often, professional school counselors become overwhelmed with administrative concerns (e.g., bus and hall duties, discipline, attendance, testing, lunch monitoring, relentless paperwork, schedule changes, constant crises) to the point of becoming entrenched in the system. As a result, professional school counselors who should be advocating for all students and encouraging changes in the system end up "gatekeepers of the status quo," supporting and maintaining an inequitable system that harms entire groups of students, because they cannot figure a way out from under the inappropriate roles and job responsibilities that take them away from counseling—delivering lesson plans, workshops, activities, and educational planning—for all students (Hart & Jacobi, 1992).

R. M. House and Martin (1998) suggested that professional school counselors not support and maintain such ineffective systems, but instead become "catalysts and leaders focused on removing the institutional barriers that continue to result in an achievement gap between poor and minority youth and their more advantaged peers" (p. 284). House and Martin also encouraged professional school counselors to be "dream-makers," rather than "dream-breakers." Achievement advocacy must be infused throughout the counselor education curriculum if new professional school counselors are to be properly prepared for their roles as educational change agents (CACREP, 2009).

The Importance of Advocacy: Challenging the Barriers

Student populations in public and private schools across the United States have changed dramatically over the past few decades. The percentage of students of color has increased substantially along with that of bilingual and multilingual students, with many lacking fluency in English (U.S. Department of Education, 2005c). Additionally, the percentage of students identified as low-income or poor has increased (Education Trust, 2004). By the year 2020, children of color will make up over 50% of public school students, and they already are the dominant group in most major cities, in older suburbs, and in many rural areas in the United States.

Professional school counselors serve as advocates for all students and their families, especially those students for whom achievement, opportunity, attainment, and funding gaps continue to grow—namely, students who are African American, Latino/a, Native American, from low-income households, students who are ELLs, and students with disabilities. While high school graduation rates for Whites, African Americans, and Latinos have improved and the gains made by African-American students have narrowed the gap with White students, the gap between White and Latino/a students has remained constant, especially at the high school level, and the gap between White and Native American students is even larger than the White/African American gap (U.S. Department of Education, 2005c). Specifically, out of every 100 White kindergartners, 94 graduate from high school. Out of every 100 African-American kindergartners, 88 graduate with a high school diploma. Out of every 100 Latino/a kindergartners, 62 earn a high school diploma, and fewer than 60 of 100 Native American kindergartners earn a high school diploma.

To be outstanding advocates for all students, professional school counselors and their colleagues must understand their own biases, recognize potential harm when dealing with culturally diverse students and parents, and be open to change in personal worldviews. When professional school counselors and other educators have developed multicultural competencies, they can understand the social and political forces operating around and within the school community. When professional school counselors and other educators recognize their own inappropriate and potentially harmful beliefs, attitudes, actions, and inactions, they can see how these work against their students. They then can change their attitudes and behaviors in order to advocate for students and challenge inappropriate practices and barriers that disproportionately harm students of color, poor students, students with disabilities, and students who are ELLs. If this recognition does not occur, professional school counselors and their colleagues may never be a proactive force for social change, equity, and achievement advocacy.

With these changes come new challenges for professional school counselors who believe that all students can learn. Becoming sensitive to multicultural issues in school counseling (see Chapter 6) is an important step for a professional school counselor who hopes to be an advocate for every student. Instead of maintaining a stereotypical view of the student that focuses on the student's family as the source of academic concerns, a socially responsive professional school counselor recognizes external oppressive forces built into the social, economic, and political framework of the school as potential sources of these academic concerns. The student's problem may be a response to various oppressions, poverty, or some other factor related to the inequities that exist in schools, communities, or society in general. This redirects the professional school counselor's response to one of empowering the student and the school counseling program to discover ways to deal with the problem and formalize an action plan for success within the system (ASCA, 2005a).

The professional school counselor needs to advocate for and encourage change within the school community so that all students feel safe and are served academically and socially. All students, parents, and guardians must have full access to career and college development information and curricula throughout their K–12 experience. This approach, part of a transformative school counseling program, helps the professional school counselor move beyond treating problems or issues as single incidents (ASCA, 2005a).

ADVOCACY COUNSELING IN SCHOOLS

Advocacy counseling involves efforts by professional school counselors to advocate for and with clients on both the microlevel and the macrolevel (Gibson, 2010; Ratts et al., 2007). On the microlevel, school counselors might advocate on behalf of students within the school system or teach them self-advocacy skills so they can advocate for themselves. However, because not all issues can be adequately addressed on the microlevel, school counselors might also intervene on the macrolevel to advocate for the needs of students in some larger context (e.g., community) in order to effect more broad-based change. As such, school counselors must be aware not only of the climate of their school, but also of the climate of their community so that change can be enacted at the most appropriate level (Bemak & Chung, 2005). For instance, if a problem exists within a school, as well as within the larger community, schoolwide change will result only in limited improvement for students. Under these circumstances, the advocacy-oriented counselor will also work in the community to mobilize efforts to ameliorate the situation.

To assist counselors in advocating for and with clients on both the microlevel and the macrolevel, four members of the American Counseling Association (ACA)—Dr. Judy Lewis, Dr. Mary Smith Arnold, Dr. Reese House, and Dr. Rebecca Toporek—developed the ACA Advocacy Competencies, a document that describes the skills important for counselors to possess in order to advocate for their clients and students (see Figure 7.1 and Table 7.1). According to the ACA advocacy competencies, there are three domains where counselors can advocate for change: client/student advocacy, school/community advocacy, and the public arena advocacy (Gibson, 2010; Ratts et al., 2007). There are two levels within each domain; one level involves advocating with a stakeholder or system and another level involves advocating on behalf of a person or system.

The two levels within the client/student advocacy domain are client/student empowerment and client/student advocacy (Gibson, 2010; Ratts et al., 2007). Client/student empowerment involves teaching clients self-advocacy skills, helping clients develop a strategy or plan for self-advocacy, and assisting clients in becoming knowledgeable and aware of their situations and identifying the skills and assets that they can use in the advocacy process. Although the primary goal is for the client or student to advocate on his or her own behalf, the school counselor serves as a mentor and assistant throughout the process. Professional school counselors might use this level to help students become more assertive, address a bullying situation, improve their communication skills, ensure college and career access materials are available in multiple languages, and work through conflicts. Parents and guardians can also be empowered by providing them with resources and information to help them through any confusing school paperwork or processes so

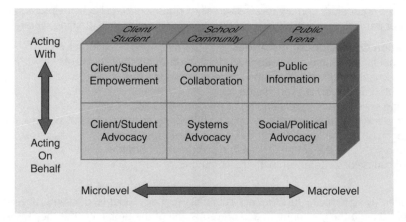

FIGURE 7.1 The American counseling association advocacy competencies.

Source: Lewis, J., Arnold, M. S., House, R., & Toporek, R. (2003). *Advocacy competencies* [Electronic version]. Retrieved October 3, 2006, from http://www.counseling.org/Publications

TABLE 7.1   The American Counseling Association Advocacy Competencies

Client/Student Empowerment
- An advocacy orientation involves not only systems change interventions but also the implementation of empowerment strategies in direct counseling.
- Advocacy-oriented counselors recognize the impact of social, political, economic, and cultural factors on human development.
- They also help their clients and students understand their own lives in context. This lays the groundwork for self-advocacy.

Empowerment Counselor Competencies
In direct interventions, the counselor is able to:
1. Identify strengths and resources of clients and students.
2. Identify the social, political, economic, and cultural factors that affect the client/student.
3. Recognize the signs indicating that an individual's behaviors and concerns reflect responses to systemic or internalized oppression.
4. At an appropriate development level, help the individual identify the external barriers that affect his or her development.
5. Train students and clients in self-advocacy skills.
6. Help students and clients develop self-advocacy action plans.
7. Assist students and clients in carrying out action plans.

Client/Student Advocacy
- When counselors become aware of external factors that act as barriers to an individual's development, they may choose to respond through advocacy.
- The client/student advocate role is especially significant when individuals or vulnerable groups lack access to needed services.

Client/Student Advocacy Counselor Competencies
In environmental interventions on behalf of clients and students, the counselor is able to:
8. Negotiate relevant services and education systems on behalf of clients and students.
9. Help clients and students gain access to needed resources.
10. Identify barriers to the well-being of individuals and vulnerable groups.
11. Develop an initial plan of action for confronting these barriers.
12. Identify potential allies for confronting the barriers.
13. Carry out the plan of action.

Community Collaboration
- Their ongoing work with people gives counselors a unique awareness of recurring themes. Counselors are often among the first to become aware of specific difficulties in the environment.
- Advocacy-oriented counselors often choose to respond to such challenges by alerting existing organizations that are already working for change and that might have an interest in the issue at hand.
- In these situations, the counselor's primary role is as an ally. Counselors can also be helpful to organizations by making available to them our particular skills: interpersonal relations, communications, training, and research.

Community Collaboration Counselor Competencies
14. Identify environmental factors that impinge upon students' and clients' development.
15. Alert community or school groups with common concerns related to the issue.
16. Develop alliances with groups working for change.
17. Use effective listening skills to gain understanding of the group's goals.
18. Identify the strengths and resources that the group members bring to the process of systemic change.
19. Communicate recognition of and respect for these strengths and resources.
20. Identify and offer the skills that the counselor can bring to the collaboration.
21. Assess the effect of counselor's interaction with the community.

Systems Advocacy
- When counselors identify systemic factors that act as barriers to their students' or clients' development, they often wish that they could change the environment and prevent some of the problems that they see every day.
- Regardless of the specific target of change, the processes for altering the status quo have common qualities. Change is a process that requires vision, persistence, leadership, collaboration, systems analysis, and strong data. In many situations, a counselor is the right person to take leadership.

Systems Advocacy Counselor Competencies

In exerting systems-change leadership at the school or community level, the advocacy-oriented counselor is able to:

22. Identify environmental factors impinging on students' or clients' development.
23. Provide and interpret data to show the urgency for change.
24. In collaboration with other stakeholders, develop a vision to guide change.
25. Analyze the sources of political power and social influence within the system.
26. Develop a step-by-step plan for implementing the change process.
27. Develop a plan for dealing with probable responses to change.
28. Recognize and deal with resistance.
29. Assess the effect of counselor's advocacy efforts on the system and constituents.

Public Information

- Across settings, specialties, and theoretical perspectives, professional counselors share knowledge of human development and expertise in communication.
- These qualities make it possible for advocacy-oriented counselors to awaken the general public to macro-systemic issues regarding human dignity.

Public Information Counselor Competencies

In informing the public about the role of environmental factors in human development, the advocacy-oriented counselor is able to:

30. Recognize the impact of oppression and other barriers to healthy development.
31. Identify environmental factors that are protective of healthy development.
32. Prepare written and multi-media materials that provide clear explanations of the role of specific environmental factors in human development.
33. Communicate information in ways that are ethical and appropriate for the target population.
34. Disseminate information through a variety of media.
35. Identify and collaborate with other professionals who are involved in disseminating public information.
36. Assess the influence of public information efforts undertaken by the counselor.

Social/Political Advocacy

- Counselors regularly act as change agents in the systems that affect their own students and clients most directly. This experience often leads toward the recognition that some of the concerns they have addressed affected people in a much larger arena.
- When this happens, counselors use their skills to carry out social/political advocacy.

Social/Political Advocacy Counselor Competencies

In influencing public policy in a large, public arena, the advocacy-oriented counselor is able to:

37. Distinguish those problems that can best be resolved through social/political action.
38. Identify the appropriate mechanisms and avenues for addressing these problems.
39. Seek out and join with potential allies.
40. Support existing alliances for change.
41. With allies, prepare convincing data and rationales for change.
42. With allies, lobby legislators and other policy makers.
43. Maintain open dialogue with communities and clients to ensure that the social/political advocacy is consistent with the initial goals.

Source: Lewis, J., Arnold, M. S., House, R., & Toporek, R. (2003). *Advocacy competencies* [Electronic version]. Retrieved October 3, 2006, from http://www.counseling.org/Publications

that they can adequately advocate for their children. The second level in this domain, client/student advocacy, involves direct school counselor endeavors to enact change or secure certain resources *for* students. To be an effective client advocate, counselors must create and put into action a plan for initiating change, which often involves communicating their plan to important stakeholders and gaining

supporters and allies to assist them in achieving their goal, such as ensuring that the dropout rate in a high school is cut by 75% through school counseling program interventions. This process requires all of the four leadership domains discussed earlier in this chapter.

The two levels within the school/community advocacy domain are community collaboration and systems advocacy (Gibson, 2010; Ratts et al., 2007). A professional school counselor who is involved in community collaboration will team up with community organizations to aid them in their advocacy efforts. For example, if a professional school counselor observes a startling increase in crime in his or her community, which is negatively affecting the school community and students' ability to learn and feel safe, that school counselor may consider (1) creating a bridge by meeting with local law enforcement officers and finding a way to collaboratively tackle issues in the school and (2) collecting data on ways to decrease crime through positive school interventions. Systems advocacy involves a more direct effort by counselors to change a system. Instead of allying themselves with existing organizations to help address a problem, they will spearhead the effort themselves. To be systems advocates, counselors must understand how systems work, use data to make a compelling case for change, design a plan for change, communicate their vision of change to others, work through resistance, and continually evaluate the success of their advocacy efforts.

The two levels within the public arena advocacy domain are public information and social/political advocacy (Gibson, 2010; Ratts et al., 2007). The public information level involves creating and distributing materials about important topics to the community. Professional school counselors working from this level create school counseling program websites, blogs, and wikis; write school counseling newsletters; send e-blasts; and design school counseling program brochures with helpful information for all stakeholders, including parents and guardians, about their children's development and how to address various issues (e.g., accessing community mental health resources, navigating the special education system, helping their children achieve academically and with career and college readiness). The social/political advocacy level involves contacting local and state representatives and policy makers to raise awareness about issues and work to create change on a much broader level. Professional school counselors will challenge the oppressions that are behind the achievement and opportunity gaps that result in unfair practices facing students of color (racism), poor and working-class students (classism), bilingual students (linguicism), and students with disabilities (ableism). To become an effective social/political advocate, school counselors must collaborate with other stakeholders, develop strong working relationships with influential community members, gain supporters, and join forces with local organizations addressing the same issue. Once again, developing competence in the four leadership domains is vital for successful social/political advocacy.

In addition to the ACA Advocacy Competencies, Trusty and Brown (2005) developed advocacy competencies

for professional school counselors: dispositions, knowledge, and skills necessary for professional school counselors to effectively operate as advocates for their students, schools, and communities. Four essential school counselor dispositions are highlighted: the advocacy, family support/empowerment, social advocacy, and ethical dispositions. School counselors with an advocacy disposition will welcome the opportunity to be an advocate and, as such, work through resistance and ruffle some feathers in order to achieve academic, career, and college equity for all K–12 students. School counselors with a family support/empowerment disposition will recognize the family as a key stakeholder and work to teach families how to advocate for their children and adolescents. School counselors with a social advocacy disposition advocate on behalf of others when they recognize unfair situations, as when they empower lesbian, bisexual, gay, and transgendered students, who are often stigmatized and subjected to harassment in schools. Finally, school counselors with an ethical disposition behave in accordance with applicable codes of ethics (ACA and ASCA) at all times.

Beyond possessing the necessary advocacy dispositions, professional school counselors must have the appropriate knowledge and skills to advocate (Trusty & Brown, 2005). School counselors should have knowledge of how systems work, knowledge of how to resolve conflicts, and an awareness of advocacy models they can use to structure advocacy efforts. Additionally, school counselor advocates should have or gain skills in effective communication, collaboration and teaming, problem solving, organization, and coping mechanisms, including having strong allies both at work and outside of work who can be counted on for a listening ear when the going gets tough.

Advocacy may be an arduous process and particularly draining for professional school counselors who want to be liked by everyone (Bemak & Chung, 2005). Bemak and Chung (2008) referred to this desire to be universally beloved and esteemed as the *nice counselor syndrome*, which, they theorized, resulted in school counselors supporting the current system's status quo, even when inequities such as achievement and access gaps are evident. Advocacy often requires disrupting a system, a process that can result in discontent for those who were comfortable with the existing system. As a result, professional school counselors may receive adverse responses to their actions and be viewed as nuisances. Nonetheless, school counselors must find ways to ensure that all students have access to quality education and opportunities for career and college access. Bemak and Chung (2008) suggested multiple strategies to help school counselors become more comfortable with advocacy: Use data to make a case, connect change efforts to the school's mission, do not take resistance personally, find supporters, develop a realistic plan based on data and research, remember to act ethically at all times, and, above all, trust the process. With the proper competencies, knowledge, and self-care strategies, professional school counselors can make vital changes at multiple levels thatimprove the lives of every K–12 student and society as a whole.

Empowering Students with Achievement Advocacy Skills

Professional school counselors and school counseling programs play an important role by advocating on behalf of all students and teaching them how to advocate for themselves and others. What kind of advocates do students need? Students need advocates who will recognize when student needs are not being heard or met and when students are being squashed emotionally and intellectually by the very systemic policies and procedures designed to enhance their emotional, physical, and intellectual well-being. Perhaps there is no more effective way to do this than to model advocacy behaviors. Advocacy should not end with the students. Professional school counselors should also advocate on behalf of all students, parents and guardians, teachers, and communities. In addition, people need to be taught to advocate on their own behalf (i.e., become self-advocates).

To be an effective advocate, one needs to have the conviction, knowledge, and skills to advocate (Ezell, 2001). The entire community and individual members (including professional school counselors) need to believe that all students can excel, and professional school counselors must be able to convey this belief and expectation to all students. School counselors can convey their belief that all students can excel by assisting students in recognizing inequities that exist and by taking action to change practices that are unfair or inequitable. For example, if a student is placed in a lower-level academic class, but has the potential to succeed in a more advanced class, the professional school counselor can step in and advocate on the student's behalf or advocate alongside the student. More broadly, students can be empowered to challenge tracking practices all together and insist that all students receive a high-level college and career preparatory curriculum in all classes, especially mathematics (Trusty & Niles, 2003). Advocating with the student simply means that the professional school counselor helps point out the condition; ensures the student has the necessary information to express the discrepancy; helps the student meet with the necessary parties (parents, teachers, administrators); and provides support and direction to the student before, during, and after meetings.

Professional school counselors must recognize when it is necessary for them to take the lead in advocating on behalf of students and when it is more beneficial to play a supportive role. There will undoubtedly be occasions when the professional school counselor will attempt

---

THEORY INTO PRACTICE 7.1

STUDENT FEARS OF SCHOOL COUNSELOR ACHIEVEMENT ADVOCACY

As a professional school counselor, educational leader, and student advocate, I would at times advocate for students and find students fearful about my advocacy. On one occasion, an African-American male student requested a schedule change that would have removed him from an honors-level class, placing him in an average-level class. After reviewing the student's academic records, speaking with teachers regarding his academic performance and potential, and reviewing the student's goal to attend college, I denied the student's request. I explained to the student that, when I compared his previous academic performance to his present performance (e.g., lack of effort evidenced by missed assignments and poor attendance), it was evident that his poor performance was not because he could not do the work, but because he chose not to do the work.

The student and his parents were not happy with my decision and went to the principal to appeal my decision. I was immediately summoned to the principal's office. After explaining how and why I made the decision I did (sharing with the principal the information from teachers, student records, and the student's desire to attend college), the principal informed me, "As a counselor you are oftentimes the student's last hope. Therefore, you should be advocating for the student." I was stunned that the principal could not see that I was being an advocate for the student. I was very confident that the student could handle the work in the upper-level course, and this course would strengthen the student's chances of being admitted into college. It was for this reason that I did not honor the student's request. In the end, the principal honored the student's request.

Think: Based on your knowledge of school counseling and advocacy, how would you have handled this situation? How do the professional school counselor and the principal differ in how they perceive and use advocacy? What advocacy strategies could the school counseling program develop if this situation arises in the future?

to advocate on behalf of a student, but the student and even the parents or guardians will fear the professional school counselor's help. Being an advocate for a student does not mean doing what is easy; it means doing what is right for that particular student and his or her educational goals. Too often in the case of students of color, immigrant students, poor and working-class students, and students with disabilities, low academic expectations dictate the decisions made by professional school counselors, administrators, parents and guardians, and even the students if they have bought into the adults' mistaken beliefs about their skills. Professional school counselors acting as advocates for students must explain the reason for their decisions and then stand firm. Theory into Practice 7.1, which discusses student fears of achievement advocacy, is an example of such a scenario.

Professional school counselors can help students recognize external barriers that affect their well-being and academic achievement and then assist them in formulating plans to confront these barriers (Toporek, 1999). It may be necessary for school counselors to accompany students when they initially approach the identified barriers and then gradually encourage students to take the lead in advocating for themselves. Remember, involving students in the process gives students ownership and empowers them.

Professional school counselors must actively remove barriers to student learning (R. M. House & Martin, 1998). This includes identifying cultural attitudes, stereotypes, and misunderstandings that lead to students being placed in environments that are not conducive to learning and achieving at high levels. Examples include students who are tracked into lower-level classes, students who are taught by underqualified teachers, and groups of students who are placed disproportionately in special education. Overwhelmingly, this includes young men with African-American, Latino, and Native American ethnic and racial identities. However, it is not enough for counselors to assist students and their parents in recognizing these inequities. Professional school counselors must take action to resolve the identified inequities. When advocating for removing barriers, professional school counselors need to work not just at the individual level, but also at the systemic level. By doing so, professional school counselors are simultaneously modeling social advocacy behaviors and conveying support to students and their parents and guardians.

Professional school counselors are also in a position to teach students how to advocate on their own behalf, as well as on behalf of peers. Professional school counselors can do this on a group level by teaching students how to use conflict resolution skills and peer mediation and by assisting students with organizational skills, study skills, and test-taking skills (R. M. House & Martin, 1998). Students also need to learn how to advocate for career development and college development skills in elementary, middle, and high school to ensure they are well prepared for their future. Students need to learn self-advocacy skills for two important reasons. First, it is essential that students become more active in the decisions that affect their academic careers (ASCA, 2005a). Professional school counselors can also educate students and their parents and guardians to manage the bureaucracy of the school system (R. M. House & Martin, 1998). Far too often, students or parents and guardians do not possess these skills. Parents and guardians often defer to school personnel as the authority. When schools make decisions, parents and guardians many times assume the professionals making these decisions are acting in the best interest of their children. Professional school counselors can step in and point out the inequities or injustices that are present and then assist the students and their parents or guardians through the bureaucratic labyrinth to ensure students receive what they need to succeed.

Professional school counselors assist students and their families by informing them of what resources are available in the school and community and how to access them (R. M. House & Martin, 1998). Connecting parents or guardians and children to these resources is vital. Although this can be done in a traditional group fashion, professional school counselors must recognize that some students and families may need systemic assistance in accessing resources. Professional school counseling programs need to take a leadership role in ensuring that all materials in the school are provided in languages spoken by parents and guardians and that parents, guardians, and students receive specific information on accessibility issues and accommodations that can be provided for various disabilities (e.g., learning, emotional, physical, developmental). Financial and transportation resources, as well as child care during parent/guardian–teacher nights and meetings, are also essential services to advocate for and ensure that students have family involvement in their schooling.

Finally, students need to be empowered to become leaders for life in their elementary, middle, and high school communities. Professional school counselors develop leadership academies, peer tutoring, and peer counseling programs and encourage and expect all students to participate in extracurricular activities such as student government, athletics, the arts, and academic-related subjects to increase their leadership skills, which, in turn, can provide students with a basis to learn advocacy skills. Students need to be encouraged to evaluate the success of the school and the school counseling program through anonymous surveys and needs assessments, and student representation on the school counseling program advisory committee should be ensured (ASCA, 2005a).

Empowering Parents and Guardians with Achievement Advocacy Skills

Parents and guardians often approach schools and school personnel as the "authority." When parents and guardians present issues and the school answers, parents and guardians often take that information as fact or accept that this is "just the way it is." Parents and guardians often do not understand the political or bureaucratic nature of schools (R. M. House & Martin, 1998). Professional school counselors inform parents and guardians about how the school operates. Although parents and guardians are often strong advocates for their children, collaboration between parents and guardians and professional school counselors increases the effectiveness of advocacy.

Professional school counselors help parents and guardians to maneuver through unfamiliar territories to access services. They also help parents and guardians to understand and interpret information received from the school through websites, brochures on the school and the school counseling program, bulletin boards, letters, and handouts and to understand their rights as parents or guardians. Once parents and guardians have the information they need in an understandable form, they may then need assistance in determining how and when to use that information.

Parents and guardians are often faced with many barriers, including lack of respite care or appropriate child care, repeated crises that place a strain on the family, isolation, lack of transportation, financial difficulties, work schedule conflicts, time constraints, guilt, and sometimes stigma related to disability issues (Friesen & Huff, 1990). These barriers make it difficult for parents and guardians to become involved in support groups and advocacy activities. Professional school counselors assist parents and guardians in identifying resources that will allow them to access the services they need, thereby reducing barriers to participation in the activities that are so important to their children.

Parents and guardians may need assistance in learning how to effectively communicate their needs, desires, and concerns. Such assistance may involve teaching parents and guardians the mechanics of communication, including compromise, persuasion, and negotiation (Cunconan-Lahr & Brotherson, 1996). Parents and guardians also may need assistance in identifying whom they need to include in communication efforts and what they need to communicate. Assisting parents and guardians, especially those from diverse cultural backgrounds, in recognizing the best or most appropriate time to address issues or take calculated risks is an important school counseling program objective.

Professional school counselors recognize when it is necessary to advocate on behalf of parents and guardians because parents and guardians may be reluctant to disagree with professionals they perceive as having expertise or power (Friesen & Huff, 1990). In these cases, professional school counselors collaborate with parents and guardians and educational professionals to remove barriers to achievement. Professional school counselors often recognize when educators distort or lack sensitivity to parent and guardian concerns. Professional school counselors explain the content of written reports that are meant for parent and guardian review, such as standardized test score reports and career- and college-development information and applications, especially when written in convoluted professional jargon. At these times, professional school counselors ensure that parent and guardian concerns are heard and that written reports accurately reflect the reality of complicated situations. Some parents and guardians may not possess the skills or resources to advocate on their own or their child's behalf. The professional school counselor as advocate is vital in these instances.

Oftentimes, families become more frustrated when they become more knowledgeable about their rights (Friesen & Huff, 1990). Parents and guardians may advocate on behalf of their children and run into a brick wall. When this occurs, professional school counselors may bear the brunt of parental and guardian frustrations. Professional school counselors should be candid with parents and guardians and share knowledge about the system, possible roadblocks, and possible delays or red tape that may be encountered. This precaution allows professional school counselors to maintain open communication with parents and guardians and often reduces long-term parent and guardian frustration. Parents and guardians can also be valuable members of school leadership teams and school counseling program advisory committees (ASCA, 2005a). Finally, many schools have hired a parent/guardian coordinator. Professional school counselors can easily collaborate with this person to empower parents and guardians as achievement advocates for all students in schools.

Empowering Educators with Achievement Advocacy Skills

Professional school counselors assist teachers and other educators in recognizing inequities that exist in the school system and use data to correct them (ASCA, 2005a). These inequities include differential treatment of students from low-income families and students from middle- or high-income families, students of color and White students, students who are intellectually gifted and those who are average, students with and without disabilities, and students who speak only English and students who are learning

English and speak a different native language. Professional school counselors encourage and challenge teachers to examine their own biases and practices. Challenging teachers to do this has a risk, but it is imperative to do so if school counseling programs and schools in general are to change so that all students can achieve. In many ways, teachers are the school environment, and professional school counselors must encourage teachers to create an environment that supports all students, with data and evidence showing that all students learn at high levels in every classroom.

When professional school counselors witness stereotyping and self-fulfilling prophecies in action based on ignorance and misinformation about certain groups of students, it is their duty to challenge the misinformation as systematic advocates. What should professional school counselors do when overhearing teachers making defeatist statements like "Kids from homes like that are doomed," "What do they expect us to do with 'those' children?" and "Why should I have to have a child with a disability in my class?" These statements clearly indicate biases, and these teachers do not believe that all students can learn and achieve. Professional school counselors can provide annual formal in-service training (Gysbers & Henderson, 2006) and frequent informal informational sessions or activities aimed at increasing teacher knowledge and effectiveness. Informal activities might include sharing success stories, sharing empirical research, utilizing technology (e.g., webpages, e-mail, etc.), discussing the professional school counselor's role, consulting with teachers, and using evidence-based practices collected by the Education Trust's National Center for Transforming School Counseling (2005b).

It is perhaps most important for professional school counselors to consistently model advocacy behaviors both systemically and individually. Not all teachers have the requisite skills to effectively work with students, parents and guardians, or administrators. Professional school counselors have training in communication, interpersonal relationships, problem solving, conflict resolution (M. Clark & Stone, 2000), collaboration, and team building, which enables them to promote collaboration among school personnel, thereby promoting high achievement for all students. Teachers may look to professional school counselors for assistance in solving classroom-management problems, problems with parents and guardians, specific learning issues with students, career and college development and counseling for students, and collegial support. Professional school counselors assist teachers in developing management, facilitation, and advocacy skills.

Professional school counselors provide in-service training on effective classroom-management skills and assist teachers in learning techniques to create a safe, equitable, and learner-friendly environment for all students. Professional school counselors also work with teachers to assist them in learning to more effectively communicate with parents and administrators. This training should include multicultural information so counselors can help teachers to effectively communicate and collaborate with persons from various economic, linguistic, ethnic or racial, and other cultural backgrounds and with those with disabilities. Professional school counselors can assist teachers in advocating on behalf of students and parents and guardians by providing them with strategies and skills to facilitate the development and use of advocacy skills. Unfortunately, teachers are not typically taught advocacy skills, and some may not feel that advocacy is a teacher's responsibility. To be a true advocate, one must speak out about injustice and work to abolish barriers to students' success, well-being, and academic achievement.

Professional school counselors can encourage teachers to become leaders within the school and community. Strong leaders who believe in the potential of all students can change the school environment and influence others to make changes that facilitate the inclusion and achievement of all students. Professional school counselors can inform teachers of learning opportunities and should encourage teachers to become involved in the community. It may be as simple as organizing a community service project for the year, whereby teachers participate in a project that facilitates interaction with people that they might not otherwise have an opportunity to meet. Professional school counselors can also encourage teachers to participate in school events and as extracurricular advisors for sporting events, club activities, recitals, art exhibitions, contests, and so forth. When teachers become actively involved in the school community and the larger community, they are more likely to recognize the needs, issues, and inequities that exist. Getting involved outside of regular academics provides teachers with an opportunity to network with others. In turn, students notice and appreciate teachers who take the time to attend events and may internalize these efforts as evidence that teachers believe in them and support their efforts.

Most importantly, school counseling programs ensure that specific academic, career, college, and personal/social competencies are defined and taught each year to all students. Working collaboratively with teachers as advocates to deliver developmental school counseling lessons in each of these areas is a key part of achievement advocacy. The *ASCA National Model* (2005a) delineates delivery of the school counseling curriculum as a shared task that is planned and systemic each year for each grade level. Successful school counseling programs have strong teacher input and collaboration and ensure that teachers are a vital component of the school counseling program advisory committee.

THEORY INTO PRACTICE 7.2

ASTHMA MEDICATION IN A SECURE LOCATION

When my child was entering kindergarten, I met with the school principal to discuss his medical needs and to arrange for him to have his asthma medication with him at all times. When I asked about this, I was informed, "Medications must be in a secure location at all times . . . we keep them in the school office." I persisted and explained that my child needed his rescue inhaler with him at all times. I was then informed, "State policy requires that medication must be in a secure location." At that point in time, I said, "I'm aware of that, but if necessary we can write a 504 plan to ensure he is able to keep his medication with him at all times." When I said that, the principal looked at me in a surprised manner (I could almost hear her thinking, "Oh no, informed parent here") and said, "Well, I'm sure we can work it out."

Think: How can a school counseling program help parents, guardians, and teachers understand the procedures for ensuring that children with special needs are well cared for in terms of individual and systemic advocacy policies and practices?

Empowering School Systems for Achievement Advocacy

Professional school counselors work with students, parents, guardians, teachers, administrators, and all other school personnel. Working as a team is important; the most important requirement for ensuring the success of the school counseling program is to have administrators "on board" and supporting these efforts. Some principals fail to support professional school counseling programs because of previous experiences with ineffective school counselors (Keys, Bemak, Carpenter, & King-Sears, 1998). Educating principals and other building and district leaders on the changing roles of professional school counselors and the key function of systemic achievement advocacy is important. Establishing effective relationships with building and district leaders is essential if counselors are to take advocacy-related risks as change agents in school counseling programs. Several strategies that enhance relationships between counselors and building and district leaders include maintaining a respectful demeanor, communicating effectively and often, and asking for overt signs of support for the school counseling program.

Professional school counselors can improve communication and be more effective in team building if they involve building and district leaders in school counseling activities. Professional school counselors can invite building and district leaders to attend education, career, or college information sessions; school counseling curriculum lesson planning sessions; conferences with parents and guardians; and other activities that do not breach confidentiality (ASCA, 2005a). Formal and informal meetings can also enhance communication among counselors and building leaders because they provide an opportunity not only to share information, but also to build rapport. They also offer a mechanism whereby professional school counselors can bring forward ideas and issues that affect students, teachers, and schools. Ideally, this occurs through school leadership, inquiry, and data team meetings, where the professional school counselor is an essential figure in advocating for academic achievement for all students, using data and demonstrating school counseling program results (C. B. Stone & Dahir, 2007).

Professional school counselors need to work collaboratively with all school personnel (ASCA, 2005a). To do this, counselors use skills in interpersonal communication, group process, human development, multiculturalism, assessment, leadership, advocacy, and counseling. Working collaboratively also means that all stakeholders understand the professional school counselor's role (Chen-Hayes, 2007).

Professional school counselors provide staff development training and research data to promote system change. Staff development training should emphasize the promotion of high standards and expectations for all students. Counselors can share success stories of schools that have emphasized high achievement for all students as telling examples of how important expectations are in achieving academic success. Counselors can also use these opportunities to "challenge the existence of low-level and unchallenging courses" (R. M. House & Martin, 1998, p. 289). As long as low-level courses exist, schools perpetuate old ideas that some students can achieve and others cannot. Many schools continue to disproportionately place students of color, students from low-income families, students with disabilities, and students who are ELLs in these low-level courses. Thus, the students who need the most receive the least, and their academic, career, college, and personal/social opportunities are diminished by the actions, policies, and practices of educators and administrators.

Professional school counselors need to be visible in the school and the community in delivering the school counseling program. To do this, they must be out of their offices and in the classrooms, delivering school counseling curriculum lessons, as well as in public areas of the school on a daily basis. Professional school counselors need to be seen and involved. They should be proactive and implement outreach programs to inform students about educational, career, college, and social/emotional opportunities; motivate students to achieve at high levels; dispel myths that are harmful to students; and provide opportunities for students to develop their talents (Chen-Hayes, 2007). It is difficult to predict problems that may occur if the professional school counselor is not out and about in the school, communicating with students and school personnel. Visibility and accessibility are the keys, and administrators may be more apt to provide support when they view professional school counselors and school counseling programs as active, integral players in the achievement and success of students and schools.

Professional school counselors and school counseling programs assist administrators in creating student-, parent-, and guardian-friendly schools. These schools communicate that students, parents, and guardians are valued members of the community and that their input and presence are welcome. One of the most important values to convey is that all children and adolescents are expected to excel. Creating an environment that empowers students and parents and guardians enhances communication and collaboration among students, parents, guardians, and educators. When a safe, welcoming environment is established, it is more likely that parents, guardians, and students will communicate their concerns and needs to school personnel. This open communication creates an opportunity to recognize the needs and disparities that exist in schools and provides an avenue for productive, cooperative change. Finally, administrators are welcomed as a key part of the school counseling program advisory committee (ASCA, 2005a; see Chapter 3) and assist in creating goals and objectives for the year for each grade level, as well as the benchmarks that will be used to assess the results of the school counseling program for student achievement and college access results each year.

Empowering Community Stakeholders with Achievement Advocacy Skills

Outside of the school environment, professional school counselors are presented with unique opportunities to work with the community as a whole. School counseling programs should have networks to connect parents, guardians, and students with resources that will help all students succeed (ASCA, 2005a). Professional school counselors also can assist parents, guardians, and school personnel in organizing community efforts to assist schools in instituting a higher standard for all children and adolescents. To do this, professional school counselors must be involved in the community and be aware of available organizations and resources. Professional school counselors should enlist the support of various community organizations, including civic organizations, places of worship, businesses, colleges, social service agencies, and individual volunteers. Unfortunately, important parties are often left out of the collaborative efforts of professional school counseling programs. These untapped resources include physicians, local mental health resources, politicians, lawyers, support groups, and other leaders in the community.

Connecting parents and guardians with organizations creates a network of support that can be used to change schools at a systems level. Professional school counselors encourage community involvement in education and

---

THEORY INTO PRACTICE 7.3

BUT YOU ARE DEAF! EXCLUSIONARY PRACTICES BASED ON DISABILITY

Todd and Bill, both of whom are deaf, had participated in a summer research project where they learned self-advocacy skills. More specifically, they learned how to be active participants in their Individualized Education Program meetings. Todd and Bill were getting ready to enter sixth grade. When Todd picked up his schedule, he realized he had been signed up for art as an elective. Todd went to his resource teacher and said, "I don't want art. I want music." The resource teacher said, "But you are deaf." Todd then said, "Do the other kids get to choose their elective?" The resource teacher said they did, and then Todd said, "Then my choice is music! I know that the other kids get to choose; then it is my right to choose." Todd's schedule was changed. When Todd met up with Bill, Bill was complaining that he had been assigned an art elective and he wanted music. Todd said, "Bill, remember the class this summer? You can choose music; it is your right!" Bill had his schedule changed, too.

facilitate activities that promote and provide support for students' academic achievement (Hart & Jacobi, 1992). Networking within the community facilitates the creation of quality services and opportunities for students and encourages the development of a community culture that supports and values all students and expects all students to succeed. In doing so, the professional school counseling program can play an important role in integrating the community into the schools, thereby supporting and promoting system changes that will enhance the educational opportunities for all students. Community members also play a critical role as a part of the school counseling program advisory committee and are encouraged to take an active role in shaping the implementation and evaluation of the school counseling program each year (ASCA, 2005a).

PUBLICIZING ACHIEVEMENT ADVOCATE FOR EVERY STUDENT

Both internal and external publics are important in the ongoing dialogue about the role and function of professional school counselors and school counseling programs. Internal publics include students, parents, guardians, educators, and other school system employees. External publics include those outside of the school system who have a stake in student success, including politicians, businesses, agencies, and the general community. Part of the professional school counselor's essential role in schools is to ensure that school counseling programs are defined and affirmed as supporting the academic, career, college, emotional, personal, and social success of all learners in a school and to use data to back up the results (ASCA, 2005a). If school counseling programs do not function in the role of achievement advocates for all students with demonstrable results, in an era of tight school budgets, professional school counselors may be seen as expendable. The reality is that, most recently, the media have covered professional school counselors only during times of crisis, primarily during acts of violence occurring on school grounds. Rare is the news story that discusses the proactive role professional school counselors play daily in schools through comprehensive, developmental school counseling programs. Professional school counselors need to create advisory councils that will assist in getting the word out inside and outside the school about the essential achievement advocacy function of school counseling programs.

Many superintendents, principals, teachers, and other related school personnel know little about what professional school counselors or school counseling programs do for student success. Therefore, professional school counselors and school counseling programs must undertake specific internal and external public relations strategies to spread the word about the professional school counseling program's role and mission in the school as academic success and achievement advocate for all students. The more all members of the school and community are aware of the professional school counselor's role and the school counseling program, the better the support from all stakeholders.

A strong internal and external public relations effort is essential to ensure that school counseling programs delivered by state-certified professional school counselors are seen by others as central to the school's mission of educating all students effectively. First, professional school counselors, school counseling programs, and their allies need to target external publics—such as legislators, local politicians, community-based organization workers, clergy and members of places of worship, and workers in businesses—to explain the specific benefits provided by professional school counselors through school counseling programs. Second, internal publics—such as students, teachers, administrators, parents and guardians, school social workers and psychologists, school counseling and teaching practicum and internship students, school secretaries, janitors, lunchroom personnel, and bus drivers—must be informed of the professional school counselor's role and the school counseling program's mission, services, activities, competencies, and achievement results (ASCA, 2005a) to ensure that professional school counselors are not relegated only to pushing paper, responding to crises, or providing discipline. As professional school counselors' job descriptions and roles as achievement advocates are developed and clarified, professional school counseling programs must publicize to internal and external publics their roles as academic leaders, advocates, team members and collaborators, users of data for assessment of academic success, counselors and coordinators, and vital members of the school who possess multicultural and technology competencies (Education Trust, 2000).

When professional school counselors put achievement advocacy for all students at the center of their work, they become invaluable to the mission of all schools. When they are seen as leaders, change agents, and persons able to challenge systemic and institutional barriers to learning and when they demonstrate how to use data to ensure that all students have the resources and high expectations to succeed in school through school counseling programs, everyone benefits from the refocused vision. Proactive professional school counselors who publicize their work in academic, career, college, emotional, personal, and social success for all students demonstrate how school counseling programs are successfully implementing the *ASCA National Model* (ASCA, 2005a).

From Gatekeepers of the Status Quo to Advocates for Systemic Change and Leadership in Schools

In the past, many professional school counselors and school counseling programs have been criticized for helping to maintain the status quo in schools (Hart & Jacobi, 1992). Specifically, they have been criticized for neglecting or unfairly judging students, particularly if they were (1) students of color, particularly African, African-American, Caribbean, Latino/a, or Native American students; (2) tracked in low- or middle-ability groups; (3) uninterested in or perceived as unable to handle college preparatory class material; (4) bilingual or spoke Black English or English with an accent or lacked fluency in English as a second language; (5) students with one or more developmental, emotional, physical, or learning disabilities; (6) girls seen as not needing college or careers; (7) boys seen as having too many discipline problems to be good students; (8) perceived as less than worthy of success due to being lesbian, bisexual, gay, transgendered, or gender variant; (9) from a nontraditional family; (10) immigrants; (11) seen as having a nontraditional appearance, including being overweight; or (12) from a nondominant religious or spiritual belief system. In other words, professional school counselors used various forms of oppression to unfairly sort students based on biases toward children and youth with nondominant race, class, gender, sexual orientation, gender identity or expression, disability, language, family type, religion/spirituality, and other cultural identities (Chen-Hayes, 2000; Chen-Hayes, Chen, and Athar, 2000; R. S. Johnson, 2002; Nieto, 2004).

There is a significant body of literature that includes anecdotal evidence of similar patterns on the part of many professional school counselors (Nieto, 2004). It is after incidents such as these that public awareness and support for professional school counselors and school counseling programs takes on such urgency—challenging past practices and demonstrating how professional school counselors and school counseling programs have changed to include academic success for all students and achievement advocacy as the top priority (ASCA, 2004b, 2005a). So not only do professional school counselors and school counseling programs need to publicize their changing roles and the data-based results of their successes, but also they must recognize that there is just as much work to be done with adults in schools and communities who had poor experiences with professional school counselors.

One way to overcome past difficulties is for professional school counselors and school counseling programs to take on advocacy roles for academic, career, and college success for all students. Lewis and Bradley (2000) defined the counselor's role as that of a social change agent and an advocate in schools and communities. Information about counselor advocacy efforts to foster academic success, high standards, and high aspirations for all students is welcome news to most parents, guardians, teachers, and principals. However, most remain unclear regarding the professional school counselor's role as academic success advocate for all students through a school counseling program (ASCA, 2005a).

Nieto (2004) shared outstanding school reform efforts and a set of recommendations for professional school counselors interested in public relations and support from an advocacy perspective. She stated that the best school reform promotes equity for all students through access to learning. According to Nieto (2004), positive school reform (1) is antiracist and antibias, (2) reflects the belief that all students have talents and strengths that can enhance their education, (3) is based on the notion that those most intimately connected with students need to be meaningfully involved in their education, (4) is based on high expectations and rigorous standards for all learners, and (5) is empowering and just. This framework for equitable educational reform in all schools meshes with the school counseling program's advocacy role for all students' academic success and achievement in careers and college (Bryan et al., 2009; Chen-Hayes, 2007; Ratts et al., 2007).

Savvy Ways to Send the Message of Professional School Counselors as Achievement Advocates

Professional school counseling programs have a multitude of ways in which they can promote public support and awareness. The *ASCA National Model* (ASCA, 2005a) discussed the importance of all schools' having a mission or vision statement focused on academic success and achievement for all students. The school counseling program should also have a mission statement aligned with the school's mission. The mission or vision statement then guides all functions of the school and school counseling program and is written specifically in terms of the results that all students will achieve based on participation in a school counseling program. Schmidt (2008) listed important ways to market and publicize the professional school counselor's role and function as part of a school counseling program, including (1) print and web-based brochures, (2) a professional school counselor's column in the school or local newspaper, (3) the use of websites and a school counseling program page, (4) speaking engagements at local events, and (5) classroom presentations. In addition, Schmidt (2008) advocated attention to (1) outreach in print formats, such as newsletters, handouts, bulletin boards, and disclosure statements; (2) uses of technology, including websites, interactive communications with parents and teachers via e-mail, and computer training for parents; (3) school counseling program advisory boards; and (4) partnerships formed with other community members interested in the academic, career, and interpersonal success of children, youth, and families. Each of these ideas is an effective way of spreading the word about the professional school counselor's essential role as an academic success advocate.

Similarly, the ACA's Public Awareness and Support Committee developed a comprehensive set of guidelines for promoting public awareness of and support for professional counselors. Attention to internal and external public relations, according to activities in the ACA public awareness and support packet (see www.counseling.org/Counselors), includes the need for professional school counselors to deliver speeches and presentations and to work with the media to get the word out about professional counseling programs in schools and communities. Specific suggestions that are applicable to professional school counselors include these: (1) Call or write television and radio stations and newspapers in your area to promote the latest activities of or awards for the school counseling program and the students it serves; (2) interview current and former students, parents, administrators, and teachers about the ways professional school counseling programs have made a difference in their lives; (3) create a school counseling program webpage to promote the school counseling program on the Internet; (4) create a school counseling program Listserv and encourage local media to access it for story ideas and questions related to referrals; (5) sponsor specific community or school events of a developmental nature and ask local media to cover them to publicize the school counseling program's role in prevention efforts; (6) request that professional school counselor license plates be offered by your state to promote the profession's visibility externally; and (7) advocate with local and state legislators to better fund and support school counseling programs (ACA, 2006).

Professional school counselors and school counseling programs are a vital resource in the school for all persons. Using a framework of advocacy for academic achievement for all learners, coupled with the importance of addressing career, college, emotional, personal, and social issues, professional school counselors and school counseling programs share an important message as they assist students, their families, and educators in a successful learning process in schools. Using recent models of school counseling focused on ensuring academic success and high expectations for all students, professional school counselors can convey the importance and power of school counseling programs to internal and external publics (ASCA, 2004b, 2005a; Education Trust, 2005c). Using both traditional print and technological resources, as well as public speaking opportunities both inside the classroom and in community meetings far outside the school's walls, it is easier and more important than ever to effectively publicize and support the new focused mission of professional school counselors as academic achievement advocates for all students.

CASE STUDY 7.1

Tyler and the Bully

Tyler is a seven-year-old first grader who has a growth disorder that makes him much smaller than even the smallest kindergartners. One night Tyler told his mom that his privates hurt, and on investigation, his mom found a bruise on his penis. When she asked what happened, Tyler explained that a fourth grader had kicked him while he was waiting to get on the bus after school. His mom asked if this was the only time he had been kicked, and Tyler sadly said, "No, Mom, this kid punches me in the stomach or kicks me every day." His mom asked how long this had been going on, and Tyler replied, "I don't know, a long time—it's so long I can't remember when it started." When his mom asked if he had told a teacher, Tyler replied, "Momma, that would be tattling. I'm not a tattletale!" His mom asked if there were other kids around, and Tyler said there were, but they just watched. Tyler's mom was upset and called Tyler's teacher, who said she'd talk with the professional school counselor. Tyler's grades had been sinking for some time now, and his mom was very worried about his safety and his academics. When Tyler returned home from school the next day, his mom asked him if the kid had kicked or punched him. Tyler said, "No, he had to apologize to me, and he spent, like, the whole day in the principal's office."

1. Based on your knowledge regarding school counseling, in what way(s) did the professional school counselor and administrator demonstrate advocacy for Tyler?
2. What additional steps would you have taken to ensure Tyler's safety?
3. What specific policies and procedures should be in place to handle issues of bullying and school violence?
4. Should the "principal's office" be the only remediation for the bully?
5. What systemic advocacy approaches should you take if you discover that multiple students are being bullied throughout the school and there is no "bully-proofing" program being offered in the school?

Summary/Conclusion

Historically, the rhetoric has been that all students can learn. Unfortunately, quality resources and opportunities are not allocated to all children in schools or in school counseling programs. Research substantiates that particular groups of children and adolescents in the United States are consistently provided fewer resources and substandard teachers and attend schools where administrators, teachers, and some politicians do not believe they can achieve at high levels, all resulting in achievement, access, attainment, and funding gaps (Education Trust, 2005b). These children are often inappropriately labeled "at risk." Being at risk is often situational and too often based on poor practices used by educators that fail students, rather than being the result of students failing in schools on their own. School administrators, teachers, and communities can alleviate some risk by providing all students with qualified, well-trained teachers who affirm diversity (Nieto, 2004) and who truly believe that all students can achieve at high levels, transforming students "at risk" into students "at promise" (Swadener & Lubeck, 1995).

Professional school counselors and school counseling programs are in a critical position to initiate positive changes that promote high achievement because they have great opportunities to interface with all students, teachers, school administrators, and the community. Professional school counselors and the transformative school counseling program must be a link between schools and communities. They should be visible in schools and communities and recognized as achievement advocates for all students. To be achievement advocates, professional school counselors must have the requisite advocacy skills, consultation skills, commitment, and energy necessary to work with parents, teachers, administrators, civic organizations, agencies, and the community at large and the ability to teach these skills to students in such a way that results are measurable. To truly make a difference, professional school counselors and school counseling programs must be action-oriented risk takers whose actions demonstrate belief that all students can learn and all students deserve the academic, career-development, and college-development resources to access the very best educational opportunities beyond K–12 schooling.

Professional school counselors and school counseling programs recognize that nondominant ethnic/racial identity, socioeconomic status, disabilities, and English-learning status often are used unfairly by educators to create barriers to learning and achievement success on the part of all K–12 students (Nieto, 2004). Professional school counselors and school counseling programs advocate for the elimination of barriers faced by students from all nondominant cultural identity groups (ASCA, 2004a). Children attending some low-funded schools excel because these schools have removed barriers, expect all children to succeed, and provide the necessary opportunities for achieving excellence (Brennan, 1999).

Professional school counselors position themselves as leaders and achievement advocates for every K–12 student and are an integral part of the school and the community. We challenge you to become facilitators of change, embracing the challenge inherent in becoming a risk taker as you create, develop, implement, and evaluate the results of your school counseling program. Furthermore, we challenge you to become exemplary role models for leadership and achievement advocacy for our colleagues in school counseling and other professions and to generate data showing how your school counseling program makes a difference for every student at your school.

8

Systemic, Data-Driven School Counseling Practice and Programming for Equity

Vivian V. Lee and Gary E. Goodnough

Editor's Introduction: A systemic, data-driven school counseling program is essential to K–12 education. It is responsible for supporting student achievement and forms the foundation for effective career and personal/social development interventions.

IMPLEMENTING THE NEW VISION OF SCHOOL COUNSELING

The new vision of school counseling for the 21st century focuses on social justice, which intentionally increases the social and cultural capital for all students and aids in the attainment of equitable educational outcomes, especially for marginalized populations. Inherent in this vision is a scope of work that is systemic, data driven, and aligned and integrated with the educational program in such a way that it supports the mission of schools. This vision for school counseling is a response to the demands of today's schools, which are driven by federal and state mandates and focus on issues such as complying with No Child Left Behind (NCLB), reducing dropout rates, increasing graduation rates, getting more students into college, increasing student participation and performance in rigorous courses, and increasing scores on high-stakes testing. This new mission of schools is designed to close the access, attainment, and achievement gaps (V. V. Lee, 2005, 2006: V. V. Lee & Goodnough, 2006) between all student groups and the gap between achievement and academic standards set forth for all students.

To be integral to the mission of schools, school counseling programs need to be systemic, data-driven, equity-focused, and able to produce measurable results that support the educational success of all students, especially students from underrepresented populations. A full description of the new vision of school counseling is presented in Chapter 1, which outlines the new scope of the work for school counselors and school counseling programs. To complement the new vision, this chapter will present a process that uses the role of the transformed school counseling in the practice and programming of a systemic, data-driven school counseling program (see Figure 8.1).

To ensure clarity of message and purpose, this chapter describes school counseling practice and programming as data-driven, equitable, and systemic. We believe that for change to truly occur and for gaps to be eliminated, school counselors must embrace these tenets. This is challenging and exciting work that requires a belief system rooted in equity and the courage necessary to be a culturally responsive leader and advocate. Figures 8.2 and 8.3 diagram the process of program development that is discussed in this chapter.

Program Vision—Commitment to Social Justice

Commitment to a vision of social justice and a mission of equitable educational outcomes for all students is a moral and ethical mandate for the school counseling profession. This mandate causes school counseling professionals to deeply examine their beliefs and how those beliefs impact behavior. In other words, it asks school counselors to know

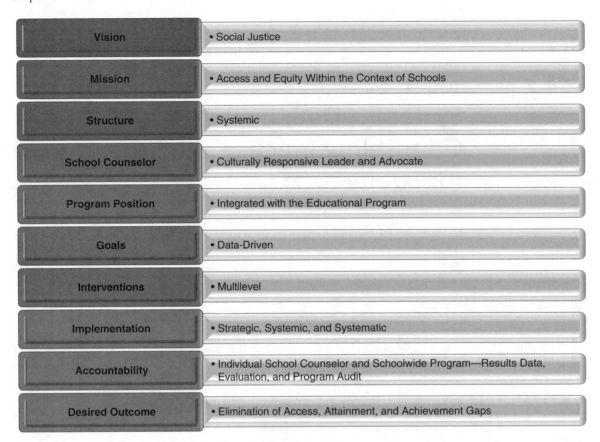

Vision	• Social Justice
Mission	• Access and Equity Within the Context of Schools
Structure	• Systemic
School Counselor	• Culturally Responsive Leader and Advocate
Program Position	• Integrated with the Educational Program
Goals	• Data-Driven
Interventions	• Multilevel
Implementation	• Strategic, Systemic, and Systematic
Accountability	• Individual School Counselor and Schoolwide Program—Results Data, Evaluation, and Program Audit
Desired Outcome	• Elimination of Access, Attainment, and Achievement Gaps

FIGURE 8.1   Systemic, data-driven school counseling programs.

what they believe in and to courageously lead and advocate through intentional behavior in their daily work on behalf of students, especially those who are traditionally marginalized and underserved. As President Barack Obama stated, the "fight for social and economic justice begins in the classroom". We would add that it also begins in the school counseling office, in the teachers' lounge, and in the hallways of any school in any district in the country. When school counselors hold these beliefs, they engage students and their parents/families and communities in ways that are meaningful and relevant. Some have questioned whether or not equity and social justice are the work of school counselors. But C. C. Lee and Hipolito-Delgado (2007, p. xiv) remind us that "improving society by challenging systemic inequities has always been a major objective of the counseling profession . . . to ensure that all individuals can participate fully in the life of a society." Indeed, such a commitment is ensconced in the preamble of the ASCA's *Ethical Standards for School Counselors* (2004a). What would such a futuristic and inclusive vision look like? At the Democratic National Convention in August 2008, presidential candidate Barack Obama gave us an idea of what that might mean. He stated, "Now is the time to finally meet our moral obligation to

provide every child a world-class education, because it will take nothing less to compete in the global economy." The notion of a "world-class education" for all provides us with that visionary hope for the future.

Equity—A Working Definition

The complement to a vision of social justice is the striving for equity. Throughout the school counseling and educational literature, there is a resounding call for "equity" in student outcomes. However, most definitions don't actually describe what working in an equitable way means. After examining multiple definitions (Coalition of Essential Schools, 2008; College Board, 2008a; Hart & Jermaine-Watts, 1996), we have developed the following working definition of equity that incorporates parts of all three:

> Equity is the elimination of systemic barriers to create a culturally responsive school/district climate. In such a climate, policies and practices build social capital, shape high expectations, and ensure access to rigorous courses necessary for college readiness, extracurricular

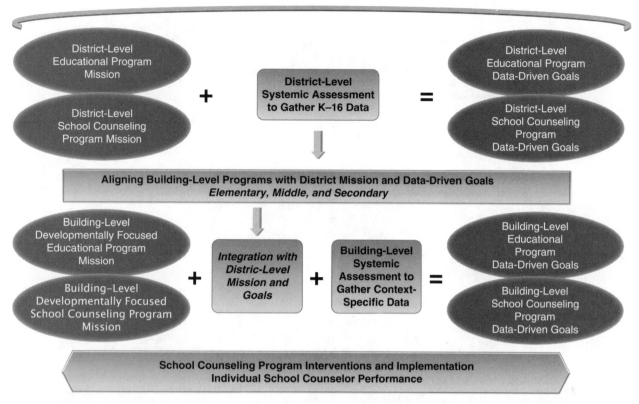

FIGURE 8.2   Vision for student outcomes.

activities, and other educational experiences. Equity is measured by participation and performance outcomes that show minimal variance due to race, income, language status, gender, or other demographic variables.

This definition highlights the four tenets that define a systemic, data-driven school counseling program. First is a belief in equity. While there is much talk about equity in school counseling and education, this reality still eludes us. Therefore, we use the word *create* in our definition to make clear that equity will not just happen: It requires action. We must intentionally become visionary leaders able to shed the bonds of "oppression [that] restrict our ability to imagine new possibilities, [and become] transformational leaders [that can] hold a proxy vision for what may be that is radically different from what is" (Coalition of Essential Schools, 2008, p. 1). Part of that difference is a school counseling leader who possesses the *courage* and *persistence* to reframe power structures through practice and programming to build social capital among those who are traditionally underrepresented.

Second, this definition makes explicit the systemic tenet. The systemic baseline or marker against which practice

and programming can be measured moves school counseling away from a solely school-based endeavor to the wider district arena. This expansion allows professional school counselors to contextualize their work from a pre-K–12 perspective, as well as across a level—for example, all high schools or middle schools.

The third tenet is data. This definition uses data to fuel equity by requiring outcomes in both participation and performance to be measured against the school/district demographic data as a baseline. In this way, data are the guiding force in identifying inequity, developing measurable goals, shaping interventions, and demonstrating accountability based on the context and demographics of a school.

Finally, each of the tenets described above is executed by a culturally responsive school counselor, the last tenet. This means that professional school counselors simultaneously work to address existing disparity and take proactive measures to help prevent further inequity, especially for underserved or underrepresented populations such as students of color and those from lower socioeconomic backgrounds. When this definition is actualized, the roles of leadership and advocacy gain primacy and direct the work of culturally responsive school counselors. Unfortunately,

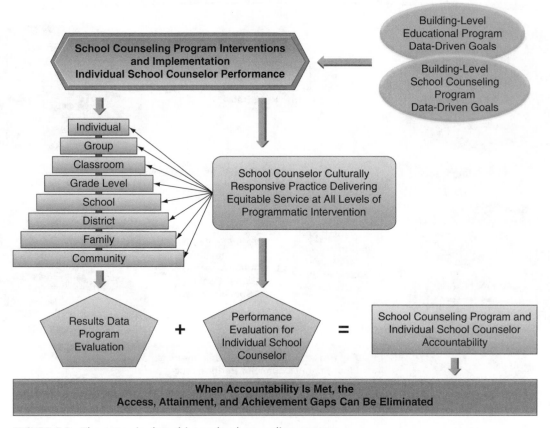

FIGURE 8.3 The systemic, data-driven school counseling process.

longitudinal data tell us that such equitable practice is not always the case in schools across our country. This ongoing unacceptable reality means that, when left to chance, equity and social justice can become hollow rhetoric. We believe that the lives of *all* students are equally worthy; therefore, this chapter makes explicit that achieving equity requires intentionality.

Program Structure—Making a Paradigm Shift to Systems

With the understanding of equity described above, the professional school counselor is poised to engage in "systems thinking" and action (Fullan, 2005). There is a real need for systemic, data-driven school counseling programs. Citing the Education Trust (1997), the *ASCA National Model* (2005a) supports data-driven approaches through "closing the gap" activities (ASCA, 2003b) and action plans. While we support these activities and plans, the complexity and persistence of educational gaps, rooted as they are in social injustice, require a broader and more in-depth response. Changing deeply

grounded inequities requires a systems-focused program that reaches deep into and across the inner workings of the system and populations of a school district and each individual school. Essentially, it requires a school counseling program to be grounded in the applied principles of systems theory. If a program is not grounded in these principles in structure and delivery, we believe it is misleading to consider it systemic. It is equally misleading to consider *systemic* to be the same as *systematic*. According to the *Merriam-Webster Collegiate Dictionary* (2004), *systematic* is defined as a methodical or orderly process, and *system* is defined as the whole or universal. Thus, without attention to the principles of systems, school counseling programs can offer interventions in a systematic fashion that are not necessarily systemic. Moreover, even if a program is called systemic, if it is not structured according to a systems theory paradigm, it is systemic in name only. Systemic, data-driven programs intentionally intervene across the entire school, with outreach to other schools in the district, to parents and families, and to the larger community, using the principles of systems theory. All of those conditions are necessary for a school counseling program to be systemic.

UNDERSTANDING SYSTEMS IN SCHOOL COUNSELING

To begin, it is essential to first acknowledge that schools are systems (Rowley, Sink, & MacDonald, 2002). Thus, the most critical point in developing and implementing effective systemic school counseling programs is that *the system*, both the structures and all of the people there, is as much the client as the individual student is (Green & Keys, 2001). A systemic focus is achieved by placing the individual at the center of the system and examining the relations between, and expectations of, larger subsystems that affect the individual, such as school, family, community, and society (see Figure 8.4). Additionally, because systemic approaches highlight the interconnectedness and interdependence of all subsystems within a school (Green & Keys, 2001; Keys & Lockhart, 1999), they are more likely to address policy and procedural barriers to access, achievement, and attainment. In today's school counseling literature, there is much written about school counselors working from both an individual and a systemic approach. This statement reflects limited understanding of systems theory. Based on the above definition, working systemically is working for the individual as well—it is an integrated and holistic approach. A mindset of working in two different ways increases the likelihood of isolated and fragmented work that lacks connection to the diverse contexts of a school environment. Moreover, when school counseling programs are developed and implemented using a systems approach based on relevant data, interventions become a strategic and intentional response to all students' academic, career, and personal/social needs and the ways in which these needs interface. Finally, a systemic, data-driven approach

supports embedding school counseling interventions across multiple levels of the educational program.

The use of multilevel interventions (V. V. Lee & Goodnough, 2006; Ripley, 2001) across the school and community was found to be among the 10 elements critical in addressing complex educational, social, and cultural challenges in striving schools (College Board, 2008b). Multilevel interventions are also a basis for the newly developed Response to Intervention (RTI) programs (see Chapter 15). Thus, systemic, data-driven school counseling programs provide a dynamic framework that easily interfaces with the structure of the school and the delivery of the educational program. Without a systemic approach that uses strategic interventions and multilevel approaches, school counseling programs struggle to align with the mission of schools and the educational program. For example, many environmental factors affecting student development and achievement are beyond student control. Among these are family influences and systemic intolerance. Systemic intolerance is often manifested in phenomena such as racism, sexism, and homophobia. These environmental factors may play a major role in shaping the attitudes, values, and behaviors of all members of a community—factors that can insidiously affect student educational success in the school environment. Consequently, professional school counselors need to address the negative effects of these environmental factors through systemic intervention.

Understanding the Role of Data

During the past decade, as the accountability movement continued to dominate and reshape public education, data became central to the work of professional school counselors. During this time of transition, new catch phrases emerged as part of a new language that provided a rationale for using data. One of those phrases was "data create the urgency for change." Despite the fact that this phrase has gained seemingly wide popularity, it can be misleading. While data certainly are important and certainly should create an urgency that drives the work of school counselors, data are only a tool of discovery and a tool to monitor and report outcomes. Using data in powerful and transformative ways can happen only when those examining the data *believe that the inequities revealed are unacceptable.* Then urgency for change can become a reality. The inequities revealed in today's social and educational data are not new. Yet the struggle to respond to the data without blaming students and their families, and without using excuses that maintain stereotypes and resistance, still remains a challenge in some school counseling offices. Fortunately, many professional school counselors embrace the use of data as the guide for challenging long-standing inequity.

FIGURE 8.4 Programmatic levels of intervention.

DATA SKILLS

The first step in using data for equity is to master the basics of data usage. Data skills are used at every step throughout the development, implementation, and outcome reporting in a school counseling program. Data skills allow the school counselor to reach into the past and present of a school and plan for the future. When used effectively, data allow the school counselor to see the school and its needs through the eyes of its diverse populations. Table 8.1 provides a list of the data skills that are essential for school counselors to master. A separate explanation of each of these skills is beyond the scope of this chapter; the process of program development based on these skills is integrated throughout the chapter.

Measuring Progress Toward Access, Attainment, and Achievement: Data and Nondata Elements

Measuring progress is a challenge because many school counselors do not have data skills and are overwhelmed by the sheer volume of data available in schools. To effectively manage data and maintain a focus on analyzing and interpreting it for equity, it is helpful to have a means to categorize or label types of data. What are these categories? Earlier in the chapter, we discussed access, attainment, and achievement gaps (V. V. Lee, 2005; & V. V. Lee & Goodnough, 2006). For each of these gaps, there are specific corresponding data elements. While each one of these categories holds specific types of data, they also reflect the interdependent and interrelated nature of systems, as we shall see later in our discussion. In-depth understanding of these interrelationships is critical in strategic planning to address equity concerns and promote systemic change.

ACCESS DATA   Access is about creating pathways to equitable engagement in the educational process for equitable outcomes. Without access, students who have traditionally not been equitably served by the educational system do not even have the chance to attain or achieve at higher levels. Thus, when attempting to close gaps, attention to the inequities in access data is a precursor. But access is multifaceted. There are both data and nondata elements of access. We will detour in this discussion to address the nondata elements of access before returning to the data elements of access, attainment, and achievement.

The nondata elements of access have direct bearing on the data elements of access. The nondata elements of access include, but are not limited to, (1) school/school counselor belief systems or cultural responsiveness and (2) school policies, practices, and procedures regarding information and student identification. These two aspects of access are highly interdependent and play a definitive role in determining whether or not school personnel (i.e., administrators, teachers, and other staff) and their school counselors *respond* to hard data elements when they reveal inequity. For example, a counselor's or teacher's or administrator's belief system about why the data look the way they do, who should or should not be in rigorous courses, or who goes to college is intertwined with his or her response to inequitable data. If counselors and other school personnel do not truly believe, deep in their hearts, that *all* students should be college ready, they will not behave in ways that promote equitable access to academic preparation by addressing corresponding policy issues. And it is likely that they will not engage in leadership, outreach, and advocacy efforts to challenge the *status quo* regardless of the data. In those cases, a school counselor's low expectations and biasing beliefs will see the data as the outcomes expected from students incapable of meeting high standards. These beliefs create and support inequitable

---

TABLE 8.1   Data Skills

The school counselor will know how to

- Identify and gain access to relevant data sources—students, school, district, state, national, and international.
- Collect relevant data.
- Analyze and interpret relevant data in order to identify inequity and trends-using disaggregated and longitudinal data.
- Establish baseline data.
- Prioritize needs at multiple levels (individual, group, classroom, grade, school, district, family, and community) as appropriate.
- Develop measurable goals with benchmarks to drive the school counseling program and the work of the individual school counselor (individual, group, classroom, grade, school, district. family, and community).
- Align goals to the school improvement plan, district goals, and state and federal mandates.
- Collect outcome data.
- Develop accountability reports and share them with stakeholders.

policies, practices, and procedures. Once these are put in place, the data will not move school counselors toward the elimination of the access, attainment, and achievement gaps regardless of the identified disparities. Thus, the nondata elements of access shape and mold the data elements of access. Moreover, the degree to which the nondata elements of access are equity focused can be considered a predictor of the outcome of the data elements of access. The data elements of access include, but are not limited to,

- Course enrollment patterns (i.e., rigorous and non-rigorous courses),
- Student participation in extracurricular and enrichment activities, and
- The presence of highly qualified teachers.

ATTAINMENT DATA   Attainment data measure the rate at which a behavior, event, or marker point is reached or completed. Often the term *achievement gap* is used to refer to gaps that are actually about attainment. For example, data elements that are often considered part of the achievement gap are course completion rates, graduation rates, college-going rates, and attendance rates. Each of these is a marker of *attainment*—a point or rate at which something is attained. While they represent different data elements, attainment and achievement are not mutually exclusive.

ACHIEVEMENT DATA   Achievement data are primarily about grades and scores. Achievement data indicate a test, class, or exam score or grade. Scores on state tests and end-of-course tests and even semester and marking period grades are all achievement data. Other well-known achievement data are grade point averages (GPAs) and PSAT, SAT, and ACT scores. But working for equity using data is not as simple as using data elements from one of these categories. As mentioned earlier, the three data categories are intertwined. For example, even if all (100%) of the seniors in a class graduate, it is still very possible that an achievement gap exists. How is that possible? There are several ways. The most striking can be revealed in their GPAs. If the GPAs of the graduating class are disaggregated and some groups of students consistently have higher GPAs than other groups, then the achievement gap is still present regardless of the fact that all the seniors graduate, thereby closing the attainment gap. It is also possible that, while 100% of the seniors graduate, there are still remaining attainment gaps in other data elements. Figure 8.5 and Theory into Practice 8.1 demonstrate how gaps that affect equity can go unnoticed unless we are sharply focused on all three types of data that impact equity.

As you can see in Theory into Practice 8.1 to work toward equity in outcomes for students requires that all three gap categories be addressed. Professional school counselors

---

THEORY INTO PRACTICE 8.1

RIGOROUS HIGH SCHOOL COURSES

If a school counseling program wanted to work toward equity by closing the gaps among students in rigorous courses, there are several pieces of data to consider in addition to the nondata elements of access.

1. **Access**

   a. Consider the nondata elements—that is, whether the learning environments are culturally responsive, how students are identified for rigorous courses, and who receives information about rigorous courses and the policies that govern entrance.

   b. Review course enrollment patterns and disaggregate the data.

   c. Identify which students are or are not enrolled in rigorous classes.

2. **Attainment**

   a. Identify which students actually finish the course. Many counselors know that students who begin rigorous courses often do not finish those courses.

Therefore, it is essential to examine not only the enrollment data, but also the course completion data. Participation has not increased until the course is completed.

   b. Disaggregate data on completion by teacher and course. Attainment data have equity implications around teacher quality, safety nets (especially for nontraditional students), culturally responsive teaching and learning environments, school peer group acceptance of rigorous course taking, and student academic preparedness.

3. **Achievement**

   a. Disaggregate course grades and/or end-of-course test scores. When disaggregated, the achievement data for those who finish the course shed light on the quality of teaching and learning that occurred in a course throughout the academic year. Ideally, the grade distribution should be equitable among all student groups and genders.

FIGURE 8.5 Building equitable AP programs.

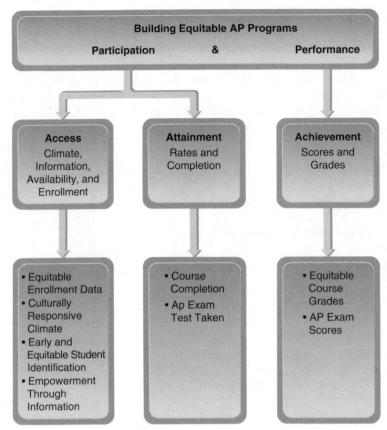

can effectively employ this method of using data when they encounter a goal in schools to increase participation and performance in a given area. The example demonstrates that the gap in participation is closed through attention to access and attainment, while the gap in performance is closed with attention to achievement. The example of taking rigorous courses (see Theory into Practice 8.1) is often associated with high school. However, this process can also be applied to middle and elementary schools. For example, in middle school it is well known that Algebra I is a gatekeeping math course. Eighth-grade students who complete Algebra I are more likely to reach the point of taking AP courses in high school; thus, it serves to significantly assist students in preparing for college (see Case Example 8.1).

Case Example 8.1

Middle School Algebra I

1. **Access**

   a. Review course enrollment patterns.
   b. Examine policies, practices, and procedures that guide entrance.
   c. Identify the process for how and when students will enter Algebra I.
   d. Disseminate information about Algebra I and the implications of taking it in eighth grade.

2. **Attainment**

   a. Finish Algebra I.
   b. Take end-of-course test.

3. **Achievement**

   a. Disaggregate end-of-course grades by group, gender, teacher, or other identifier.
   b. Disaggregate scores on end-of-course tests by group, gender, teacher, or other identifier.

In elementary school, policies and procedures for entry into gifted and talented programs or other enrichment activities can often be controversial and inequitable. Relevant equity data may be considered, as demonstrated in Case Example 8.2. Table 8.2 provides insights into the whole-school data elements required to address access, attainment, and achievement gaps.

Case Example 8.2

Elementary School Gifted and Talented

1. **Access**

    a. Review program enrollment patterns.
    b. Examine policies, practices, and procedures that guide entrance.
    c. Review the student identification process for gifted and talented programs.
    d. Disseminate information about enrichment programs.

2. **Attainment**

    a. Determine whether enrollees attain equitable academic placements in math and language arts.

3. **Achievement**

    a. Disaggregate grades and other test score-related criteria by group, gender, teacher, or other identifier.

TABLE 8.2   Whole-School Data Elements

Access
- Enrollment patterns in
  - Rigorous courses such as AP, IB, honors, and college prep, and nonrigorous courses
  - Special education
  - Gifted and talented programs
  - English for Speakers of Other Languages classes
  - Extracurricular and enrichment activities

Attainment
- Attendance
- Dropout rates
- Promotion and retention rates
- Graduation rates
- Passing rates for all subjects
- Completion rates in rigorous and nonrigorous courses
- Successful transitions to elementary, middle, and high school and to postsecondary options
- Proficiency rates in all subjects, especially math, reading, language arts, and science
- Discipline infraction rates-suspension and/or expulsion
- Parent participation rates in academic, college/postsecondary, and career activities
- Enrichment program completion rates
- College/postsecondary acceptance patterns
- College applications completed
- FAFSA completions
- Scholarship forms completed
- Test-taking rates-state assessments, college entrance exams, and career and interest inventories

(Continued)

TABLE 8.2 Whole-School Data Elements *(Continued)*

Achievement

- Grade point averages
- Scores on state tests and end-of-course tests
- Scores on AP and IB exams
- SAT, ACT, and PSAT scores
- Career assessments and interest inventory scores
- Marking period, quarter, or semester grades

Once school counselors understand how to use data for equity, as described above, they are better able to develop goals and interventions that address equity in a multifaceted manner. They no longer view goal attainment as a singular event, but rather recognize the complexity of and interrelationship among various data elements in categories of gaps. Moreover, using data in this way complements a systems theory approach to school counseling, as it emphasizes the interdependent and interrelated nature of systems. In addition to access, attainment, and achievement data, there is also *student and school demographic data*, *culture and climate data*, and *community life data*, referred to in an earlier text as part of the *Rubric of Data Elements*. These data elements can be collected in more informal ways and can substantially impact student success, as indicated in Table 8.3.

The Culturally Responsive Leader and Advocate

The transformed role of the professional school counselor delineates the knowledge and skill school counselors need to have to facilitate the development, implementation, and evaluation of a systemic, data-driven school counseling program. In addition, we believe that this work must explicitly state that the school counselor possesses multicultural competence and can effectively engage all of the diverse populations in his or her school, district, and community through culturally responsive leadership and advocacy. The transformed role of the school counselor and culturally responsive practice are outlined in Chapters 1 and 6, respectively. The reader should refer to those chapters for more complete discussion. The reader is also directed to the American Counseling Association website to locate critical resources in the development of multicultural counseling competence: (1) Multicultural Counseling Competencies and Standards, (2) Cross-Cultural Competencies and Objectives, and (3) Advocacy Competencies. Additionally, the Professional School Counselor Multicultural Competence Checklist (see Chapter 6) provides a comprehensive, hands-on tool for school counselors. The personal and professional development that can be gained through these resources shapes the foundation of equitable and ethical practice and programming in school counseling.

TABLE 8.3 Examples of Student and School Demographic Data, Culture and Climate Data, and Community Life Data		
Student and School Demographic Data	**Culture and Climate Data**	**Community Life Data**
Whole-school enrollment data	Staff-to-staff relationships	Parent involvement
Disaggregated enrollment data by student gender, grade level, race/ethnicity, English language proficiency, and disability	Student-to-student relationships	Family issues and configurations
Socioeconomic data	Student-to-staff relationships	Neighborhood/community participation
Mobility and stability of students and staff	Respect for diversity and equity agenda	Local employment patterns
Highly qualified teachers	Leadership styles	Environmental impact-military deployments, layoffs, unemployment
		Immigration and challenges in migrant communities

THEORETICAL FOUNDATIONS

School counseling programs use a wide cadre of theoretical orientations. A description of all potential theories is beyond the scope of this chapter. However, this discussion will focus on a few theories that are of critical importance to systemic, data-driven school counseling programs. The reader is directed to counseling theories books that provide a thorough description of the theories listed in Figure 8.6. The reader is challenged to apply the principles of those theories in the same ways illustrated in this discussion.

The ASCA *National Standards* (C. Campbell & Dahir, 1997) stated that the theoretical foundation for school counseling programs is rooted in developmental psychology, counseling methodology, and educational philosophy. While we agree that these three broad categories continue to be important theoretical foundations, we will label them a bit differently. Specifically, we add systems theory as a foundational aspect of systemic, data-driven school counseling programs. These four categories of theory can be integrated in a culturally responsive way to provide a holistic foundation for the academic, career, and personal/social development of students (see Figure 8.6). This foundation supports a conceptualization of human growth and development as multifaceted and complex and recognizes that environmental and societal influences affect students in the various contexts in which they live. It is essential for professional school counselors and others in the school to understand the diverse ways in which development is contextualized and expressed during the pre-K–12 educational experience.

Such an understanding breathes life into the mission of the program and emphasizes the use of data as the tool that identifies and monitors the attainment of growth and development. In a systemic and data-driven program, growth and development needs are assessed across the system. That means that professional school counselors have to reframe the notions of theory to extend beyond the wall of the counseling office and apply it to the system (see Figure 8.7). For example, Maslow's humanistic theory of development posits that humans have needs for growth—but they will not reach higher-level needs until their lower-level needs are met. These needs are, in order from most basic to most advanced, (1) physiological, (2) safety, (3) belonging/acceptance, (4) competency/achievement, and (5) actualization.

When this premise is applied to a systems approach and the system becomes the client, then school counseling interventions take on a schoolwide perspective and professional school counselors ask questions such as these:

- Do the culture, climate, policies, practices, procedures, values, attitudes, and beliefs of the school provide a culturally responsive teaching and learning environment?
- Does the environment provide a physically, emotionally, and intellectually safe place where all students can achieve to high expectations?
- Does the culture of the school promote belonging, so that all of its students, teachers, administrators, and parents/families can work collaboratively in the educational process?

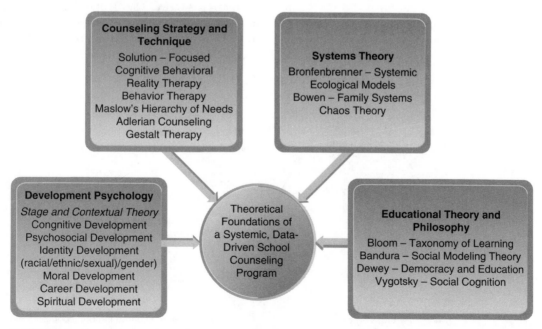

FIGURE 8.6 Theoretical foundations of a systemic, data-driven school counseling program.

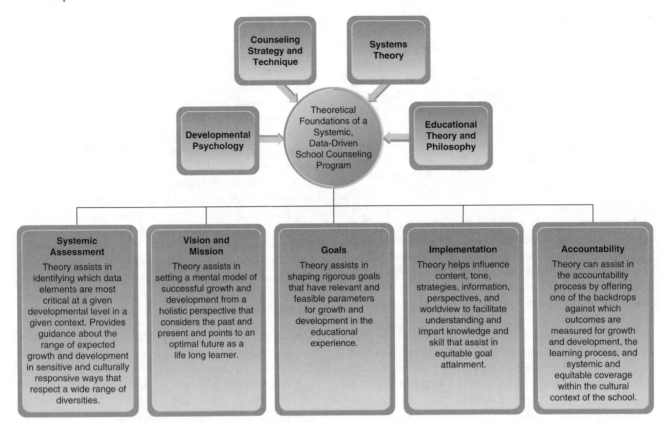

FIGURE 8.7 Applying theoretical foundations to the system.

These are but a few of the essential questions that examine whole-system growth and development. When systemic needs are ignored, a major piece of the equity equation is missing. Systems then become a force that negotiates and barters out basic human needs, rather than fighting for the equitable attainment of basic human needs for all individuals in the system. This type of intentional focus on systemic application of theory is essential if systems are to be imbued with social justice (see Figures 8.8 and 8.9).

In addition to the educational philosophy of such luminaries as Dewey (1910) and Vygotsky (1978), professional school counselors in systemic, data-driven school counseling programs need to possess a strong working knowledge of theories such as Bloom's taxonomy of

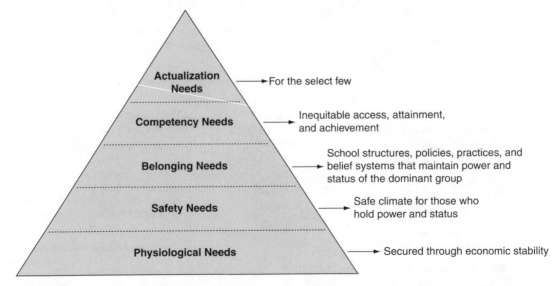

FIGURE 8.8 Maslow's hierarchy in a traditional school. Needs are met only for advantaged students.

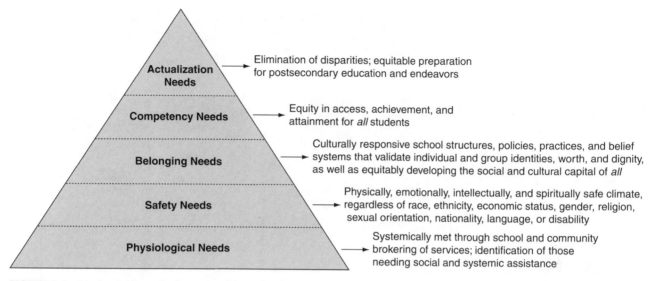

FIGURE 8.9   Maslow's hierarchy in a new vision school. All needs are met for all students.

educational objectives (1956). Anderson and Krathwohl (2001) (see Figure 8.10) proposed a revision that makes Bloom's theory even more applicable to our discussion. All students are expected to remember and understand information, and these are considered lower-order thinking skills. But, higher-order thinking skills—application, analysis, evaluation, synthesis, and creativity—are essential for each and every individual in the system. Teachers and professional school counselors need not only to possess higher order thinking skills, but also to be able to facilitate student learning at those levels. Additionally, in order to be involved in system-level discussions of policy, practice, procedures, and educational reform across the district and school, professional school counselors must understand higher-order thinking skills. For example, content in school counselor lesson plans, workshops,

classroom units, parent initiatives, vertical teaming, and schoolwide assessments must go beyond the elements of knowledge and comprehension. The learning initiatives must be rigorous in all facets of planning and delivery. This also means that rigor goes far beyond the classroom; it is about a rigorous environment for equitable success. It means that school counselors possess advanced skills and actively use them to meet the challenges of today's schools. Moreover, it means higher-order thinking skills and vision go hand in hand. For example, the skill of creativity (i.e., combining elements into a pattern not clearly there before) is vital to be able to hold a mental image of what social justice in education can be. School counseling programs must be shaped and delivered in this way if the work of school counselors is to be recognized as an essential aspect of closing gaps and promoting substantial futures for all students. When this type of systemic rigor is combined with strategic planning, school counseling programs can become a force for systemic change not only in an individual school, but also across an entire school district.

Competencies: Theory into Practice

The process of translating the cadre of theories that are integral to the systemic, data-driven school counseling program into competencies is depicted in Figure 8.11. Competencies are the behavioral indicators of theory. Therefore, we should be able to back-map all competencies used in a school counseling program to theory. This process will be described in terms that are applicable at both the district and the individual school levels.

The process begins with a review of the most relevant constructs and concepts within the cadre of theories (step 1).

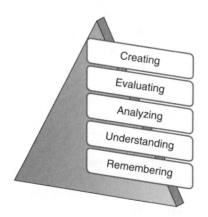

FIGURE 8.10   Taxonomy of learning.

Source: Anderson, L.W., & Krathworld D. R. (eds). (2001). A taxonomy for learning, teaching, and assessing: A revision of Bloom's Taxonomy of educational objectives. New York: Longman.

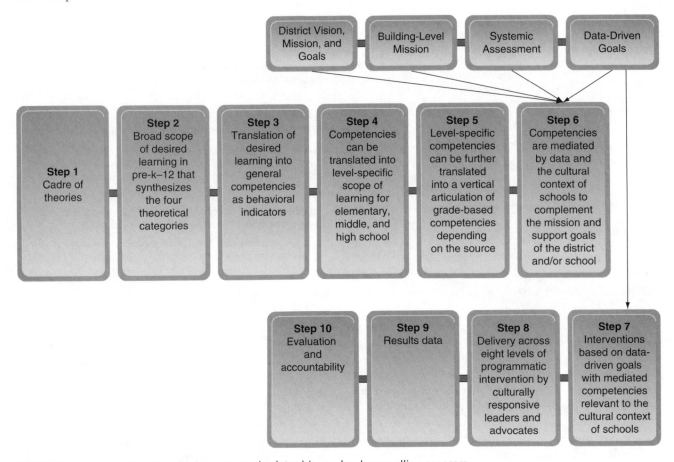

FIGURE 8.11 Translating theories into a systemic, data-driven school counselling program.

In step 1, theories are synthesized and then extended to examine potential age, context, teaching and learning, and culturally appropriate tasks for pre-K–12 students (step 2). In step 3, broad statements of potential desired learning can be established and translated into general competencies. In step 4, these competencies can be articulated across grade levels, creating a vertical articulation across building levels, or used without further specification. In schools and districts, competencies can come from multiple sources such as the *ASCA National Model* (2005a), state departments of education, local directives, or other educational venues. However, competencies can be categorized further into a more definitive grade-level articulation (step 5). This type of articulation can delineate learning at different grade levels and determine which concepts are presented both within a grade level and between grade levels.

Step 6 is critical, as it makes the difference between fitting a school or district into a set of competencies and making competencies fit a context. This a turning point in the difference between solely standards-driven programs and the data-driven programs described in this chapter. In this step, the vertical articulation of competencies is *mediated by data and the cultural context of schools* to complement data-driven goals at the district and school levels. It is also at this point in the process where the goals from Figure 8.2 and the competencies meet. Here, the entire program begins the process of becoming contextualized, making relevant the whole force of the program. As the goals continue through the strategic planning process, interventions are developed to operationalize the goals across the district or school, and the accompanying competencies reflect the context and diverse populations of the school. In Step 7, goals are defined as needs in access, attainment, or achievement, and the data elements of the goal are identified. This is essential in developing a program and interventions dedicated to equity; this is where programs go from equality-focused to equity-focused (step 7). Now that the goals, interventions, and corresponding competencies reflect the equity needs of the school building, interventions across all eight levels can be implemented (step 8). Then, as the interventions are implemented, results data are collected (step 9). Once sufficient data are collected, the process of evaluation can begin (step 10). Thus, the content of the program is delivered at all levels of intervention in a data-driven, equity-focused, and theoretically sound manner.

THE BUILDING BLOCKS OF PROGRAM DEVELOPMENT

Program Mission: Equity Within the Context of Schools

School counseling program mission statements address the overarching belief about all students and the global goals of the program. A school's or district's mission statement provides the foundation for the school counseling program and states the collective results desired for all students (S. K. Johnson & Johnson, 2003). As with goals, for the school counseling program mission to become an integral part of the overall school mission, it must reflect and parallel the basic tenets of belief and the purpose of the educational mission of the state, the district, and the school. Additionally, if the state and district have school counseling mission statements, the basic tenets and beliefs of these statements should be reflected in the school counseling program's mission statement. A clear and concise mission statement affects programmatic implementation and evaluation.

Mission statements can be written in a variety of ways. Some state a mission along with a programmatic philosophy and then state specific principles and objectives. Some include the role of the professional school counselor as advocate and collaborator focused on access to meet future societal needs. Others are longer and indicate within the statement their support of school district and state mission statements. Yet others can be written to demonstrate the linkages with national and state school counseling associations and educational missions. Regardless of how a mission statement is written, the most critical point is that it sets the foundation for the counseling program to serve all students.

Program Philosophy: The Guidance and Counseling Program of the Newport News Public Schools is dynamic, comprehensive, proactive, sequential and coordinated. It is an integral part of the total educational experience for all students and members of the school community.

The Richmond (Virginia) Public Schools' (n.d.) mission statement reads as follows:

The mission of the Richmond Public Schools counseling program is to provide a comprehensive, developmental counseling program addressing the academic, career and personal/social development of all students. School counselors are professional advocates who provide support to maximize student potential and academic achievement. In partnership with other educators, parents, or guardians and the community, school counselors facilitate the support system to ensure all students in the Richmond City school district have access to and are prepared with the knowledge and skills to contribute at the highest level as productive members of society.

The development of the school counseling mission statement is one of the collaborative team initiatives of a school counseling program advisory committee. As this group has representatives from all of the diverse populations of the community, the school counseling mission statement it develops will be sure to serve the needs of all students. The Education Trust (1996) provided a structured format for the process of creating a mission statement (adapted in Table 8.4).

TABLE 8.4 Creating a New Mission Statement

Give careful consideration to the words that will convey the new program mission:

- What? What are the essential words that describe the major focus of a systemic, data-driven school counseling program? What will the school counseling program do?
- Who? With whom? Stakeholders? For what purpose?
- Where? What is the systemic scope of the school counseling program?
- To what end? What are the desired results/outcomes of implementing the systemic, data-driven school counseling program? How are they measured? How will program accountability be demonstrated?

Source: Adapted from *National Institute for Transforming School Counseling*, Education Trust, 1996. Retrieved March 21, 2004, from www.edtrust.org.

Systemic Assessment

Creating a program that equitably serves the entire school population requires a systemic assessment. A systemic assessment is a process used to identify the needs of students and of the larger community by reaching every subsystem of that community. These subsystems include the various microsystems present (e.g., various subgroups of students, teachers, and administrators), as well as the relationships among the various microsystems. The goal of the systemic assessment is to ensure that relevant data are collected that represent the needs of all diverse populations, as identified by those populations. The purpose of conducting a systemic assessment is to use the data to drive the school counseling program so that it is relevant and serves the dynamic and ever-changing needs of a community in a culturally responsive manner. In this way, the services of the school counseling program can be said to reflect the context and demographics of the school. When the school counseling program is relevant to the needs of the school, it more easily aligns with the educational program and supports the mission of the school.

Systemic assessments employ multiple methods of data collection within the school and from external sources in the district. For example, data can be gathered by examining both school and district databases. Extending a systemic assessment to the district level allows counselors to understand the needs of their school in relation to the larger district. This perspective helps mold and shape goal development and the strategic planning process. Many data reports are available at the district level and can range from reports submitted to the state department of education on a yearly basis to more contextualized or in-house reports. Examples of these types of reports may include adequate yearly progress (AYP) reports, graduation reports, and college-going reports. More-qualitative methods such as surveys, focus groups, interviews, and observations can also be used to gather information and data.

When determining what types of data will be collected, it is essential that school counselors include access, attainment, and achievement data. By examining the various data elements in each of the three data categories, professional school counselors are more likely to get an in-depth understanding of student needs and the barriers that hinder the equitable outcomes. In addition to the data elements within access, attainment, and achievements listed earlier, student and school demographic, culture and climate, and community life data should be addressed in a systemic assessment. These areas can provide powerful information about the dynamic life of a community. Once data from the assessment are collected, they are disaggregated to provide a clear picture of the needs of all students and the school. Data can be disaggregated in many ways. Some of the most common ways to disaggregate data elements about student access, attainment, and achievement are by student group, grade, gender, socioeconomic level, English language proficiency, disability, and mobility. Once the needs are identified, data-driven goals can be developed for the systemic school counseling program. This process ensures that the school counseling program is reflective of student need.

Data-Driven Goals

The goals of a systemic, data-driven school counseling program represent a confluence of several points. First, goals represent the overall desired outcome for all students. Second, goals represent the attempt to close the gaps between student groups, as well as the difference between established standards and the reality of the data for all students in a school or district. Third, goals are influenced by national, state, district, and local school goals. National goals (e.g., AYP requirements) provide key mandates such as closing the access, attainment, and achievement gaps. For example, common goals include improving attendance and graduation rates and ensuring safe and drug-free schools. States consider these national goals in developing their strategic plans and add issues specific to their states. These state goals may originate in the state department of education, a board of regents, or gubernatorial mandates, depending on the state and those currently in political office. These additional mandates could put a focus on issues such as promoting African-American male achievement, as has been adopted in Maryland, or promoting literacy or attending to the psychological repercussions of military deployments. School districts attend to these goals, while adapting them to the specific needs, contexts, and demographics of their populations. Individual schools add or adapt additional goals based on the needs identified by their data and their mission statement.

Within the context of national, state, district, and schoolwide goals and missions, professional school counselors analyze and interpret the data collected from the systemic assessment to create the specific goals on which the school counseling program is based. Goals are developed as general, data-based statements of a desired outcome. To ensure that goals are systemic and reflect district needs, professional school counselors can team and collaborate with counselors at feeder schools to develop goals that fortify students during transitions and identify potential trouble spots. The goals then guide program implementation and individual school counselor performance.

Goals are written so that they identify concrete measures for the results and can be aligned to other schoolwide measures of student access, attainment, and achievement.

In this way, the results of the school counseling program address the needs and concerns within the delivery and outcomes of the educational program. Once goals are developed, they are prioritized and "sized" for feasibility of implementation. Goals and corresponding interventions that are relevant, feasible, and aligned with the needs of the educational program have a higher likelihood of contributing to the overall success of students. As the school's goals exist in the context of district, state, and national goals, it is appropriate that the goals of each school counseling program reflect wider concerns such as the AYP status of the school. A school counseling program that is not supportive of and that fails to address these broader needs directly through its goals and interventions is not integral to the mission of the school (i.e., it is a marginal program). Such marginalized programs and services do not serve the needs of all students.

But how are goals actually written? There are certain components that goals must contain to be able to show the metrics upon completion of the desired interventions. For example, a school that wants to increase successful transitions from elementary to middle school needs to think strategically and specifically about the needs of its students. First, the school needs to establish a baseline and determine criteria:

- What are the data elements that define a successful transition?
- Based on the criteria, how many students make a successful transition—and who are they?

Second, it must disaggregate both longitudinal data and snapshot data, if available:

- What inequities are identified?

Third, based on the inequities identified, it must write a measurable goal in a metric format:

- What is the desired percentage increase or decrease in the identified data element?
- How many students and what percentage does that desired goal represent?

This means that the goal clearly states what percentage of increase or decrease will occur after the intervention. It is important to clarify the meaning of a percentage with the number of students the percentage represents because a given percentage in one school can mean something very different in another school in terms of actual numbers of students affected. For example, in School A, a 10% increase may involve 16 students, while in School B a 10% increase

may involve 120 students—so School A is 10% ($n = 16$) and School B is 10% ($n = 120$).

A goal may be written in either of the following ways:

A broad, general goal: "Beginning with the fifth-grade class of 2012, 10% more students will make a successful transition to middle school."

A more specific goal: "African-American male fifth-grade students ($n = 48$) will increase their success in transition to middle school by 15% (baseline = 24)."

After the goal is written, the next steps in the strategic planning process can be activated, including (1) determining the feasibility of goal implementation and revisions, if needed; (2) implementing the goal; (3) collecting data; and (4) promoting advocacy and sustainability.

Integrated Educational and School Counseling Programs

The educational success of all students is a school moral obligation and therefore part of the ethical and professional responsibility of all school personnel. Fulfilling this foundational responsibility requires the creation of a culturally responsive teaching and learning environment that encourages the dreams and aspirations of all students. In this way, the educational program and the school counseling program become collaborative and intertwined forces that share an overarching goal of equitable access, attainment, and achievement for all students. It also means both programs are integrated through similar or complementary structures in which content, delivery, and reporting of results are aligned. More specifically, the systemic, data-driven school counseling program is integrated into the mission of the schools by aligning its program goals, development, implementation, and evaluation with those aspects of the educational program. Thus, alignment of the educational program and the school counseling program exemplifies a commitment to serve all students through mutually dependent goals and interventions. This mutuality has the advantage of also integrating the school counseling program into school improvement plans and initiatives, which, in turn, aligns school counseling with educational reform. For example, in many schools across the country, the goal of increasing student participation and performance in rigorous courses is paramount. To achieve this goal, administrators, teachers, counselors, students, parents, and the community are all integral in changing expectations, increasing knowledge and skill for all populations, and fostering the structural changes necessary to attain this goal.

Understanding integration of the school counseling program with the educational program can be difficult. For successful integration to occur, professional school counselors need to be familiar with the academic goals and standards of their district and state and with any other established curriculum that is used in the school, such as reading programs and conflict resolution curricula. It is also essential to understand how the educational program is delivered, the multiple ways it is implemented, and how the results are measured and reported.

EDUCATIONAL PROGRAMS ARE DELIVERED AT MULTIPLE LEVELS Reflecting on the earlier discussion about systems, recall that schools are systems (Rowley et al., 2002) and that systems are made up of individuals (Fullan, 2005). Within these systems, standards-based educational programs are delivered across the entire school using multilevel initiatives. More specifically, each academic discipline has standards and competencies implemented in the school, using multilevel initiatives. Standards and competencies are delivered not only in classrooms, but also through other initiatives such as tutoring, clubs, service learning projects, sports, student buddies, mentoring projects, honor societies, band, chorus, and fine arts initiatives. Parent contacts, collaborations with businesses, and outreach programs are all part of the overall educational program.

Significantly, the educational program is also delivered through the policies, practices, and procedures of the school. These aspects of the educational program affect the culture and climate of a school and serve as long-term environmental instructors that either promote or hinder achievement. For example, policies that affect discipline, course enrollment patterns, attendance, and participation in co- or extracurricular activities systemically impact the educational program—and therefore student outcomes. This means that to positively affect systems, purposeful interaction across all levels of the system, or *vertical integration*, is necessary to create coherence among the many unconnected and superficial innovations that can permeate a school in the name of making change (Fullan, 2005). School counseling programs, central as they are to schools achieving their academic mission, need to have a structure/delivery process that mirrors this system-level reality to fully engage this process.

SCHOOL COUNSELING PROGRAMS ARE DELIVERED AT MULTIPLE LEVELS The structure and delivery of a systemic, data-driven approach are conceptualized as *levels of programmatic intervention*. This perspective focuses on the eight levels of intervention introduced

previously—individual, group, classroom, grade, school, district, home/ family, and community/society—which are interdependent and interrelated. These levels of intervention can be viewed as concentric circles with individually based interventions in the middle. Each additional ring represents a larger and potentially more diverse population, including the larger society, as shown in Figure 8.4. The eight levels are points of intervention into the structure of the school and the community. The rationale behind this approach is that systemic transformation requires consistent and intentional intervention across all levels of the school and the community in order to affect persistent inequities. In other words, this approach is a pragmatic response to complex issues that require complex solutions. Professional school counselors cannot do the work of equity and social justice alone. Therefore, this approach fully embraces collaboration within a systems theory perspective to mold and shape *constellations of interventions* across the eight levels that can saturate a system with a desired message, knowledge, and skill. Attributing systemic change to singular school counselor interventions, especially to just distal data elements, is questionable, especially in light of the scant school counseling research. Creating constellations of interventions (multilevel) around what we do empirically know may hold greater promise, as some research is beginning to show (College Board, 2009). Additionally, these levels are basic structures for collecting and reporting data in the elementary, middle, and high schools and in the school system.

To deliver a program effectively, professional school counselors must possess the knowledge and skills to implement services at all levels of intervention so that program delivery is rigorous and is not compromised by limited professional school counselor knowledge or skill. This broader delivery of school counseling services exemplifies the systemic nature of the school counseling program.

Educational and school counseling integration is also essential from a goals and content perspective. This added dimension of integration requires professional school counselors to become familiar with the academic curriculum and to know the general aspects of the content and the specific sequence of the curriculum being taught. It does not mean that the professional school counselor teaches geometry and chemistry, but it does mean that he or she broadly knows the curriculum, as well as concepts and constructs that facilitate learning across the academic disciplines, such as critical thinking and problem solving. It also means that professional school counselors assist teachers with the delivery of the curriculum through *collaborative classroom instruction* in areas where counseling expertise can support and enhance student learning and development toward goal attainment.

For example, professional school counselors can contribute to student learning and development in specific disciplines. In civics, government, and history, issues of diversity, human rights, citizenship, conflict and war, oppression, and violence are prevalent. Professional school counselors do not have to be history experts to assist teachers with discussions and activities that help students explore these areas and relate them to their day-to-day lives. Second, language arts curricula often include consideration of careers, resume writing, alternative points of view, conflict resolution, relationships, and a host of human dramas and triumphs explored through literature. School counseling interventions that are integrated into the curriculum in these areas provide a holistic environment for learning. Third, the health curriculum is often replete with topics in which professional school counselors possess expertise. Issues such as healthy relationships, alcohol and drug prevention, sexuality, personal safety, family relationships, and wellness are all areas where professional school counselors and teachers can team and collaborate to achieve curricular goals. Fourth, while *collaborative classroom instruction* is the most obvious point of integration, integration that includes policy, practices, and procedures, as well as schoolwide culture and climate, can have a significant effect on student outcomes. Finally, integration of the educational and school counseling programs also occurs around issues like attendance, promotion and retention, extracurricular activities, transitions, and graduation.

Outcomes/Results

The multilevel structures of school produce outcomes or results that are collected and reported systemically. In the assessment climate fostered by NCLB, results are often reported at the following levels: group/subgroup, grade, school, and district. For example, individual state department of education websites provide links to school districts and individual school performance report card data (as does the Maryland Department of Education at msp.msde. state.md.us). A school counseling program that aligns with reporting categories provides a ready-made database to assist in conceptualizing and responding to the link between the educational program and the school counseling program. This linkage forms a collaborative and systemic integration in the accountability and results of both programs. When all school personnel team up and collaborate in these ways to reach collective goals, programs become integrated, and all stakeholders share in the responsibility and results. Engaging in this type of practice does require professional school counselors to ensure that they have both

proximal and distal outcomes that highlight their work as they link to more whole-school data elements to avoid minimizing their contribution (D. Brown & Trusty, 2005c).

GUIDING FOUNDATIONS

Ethical and Legal Directives

The requirement to practice ethically and legally guides the implementation of a systemic, data-driven school counseling program. Federal, state, and district mandates, as well as standards from professional organizations, guide the development, implementation, and evaluation of the school counseling program. By appropriately implementing ethical and legal directives and practicing within these guidelines, the professional school counselor and the program interventions equitably serve all students and promote the overall educational mission of the school. A full discussion of the ethical and legal guidelines professional school counselors should know is provided in Chapter 5 and should be directly applied to the discussion in this chapter.

District and School Policies

District and school policies, both spoken and unspoken, govern and shape the day-to-day operations of a school district and individual schools. Policies are used to create a "way of doing things," set the tone for the culture and climate of the school, operationalize ethical and legal mandates, and implement goals. The practices and procedures used to implement policy, though assumed necessary and beneficial, can either advantage or disadvantage all or groups of students. For example, policies affecting the points listed in Table 8.5 can either promote equity for all students or inadvertently create or maintain access, attainment, and achievement barriers. Since student and community demographics are dynamic, an ongoing analysis of policies, practices, and procedures is essential to ensure that they promote access and equity for all students. Additionally, school policies, practices, and procedures can be used to promote or mitigate environmental influences that affect students, from racism, classism, and violence to access to postsecondary opportunity.

District and school policies interface with the mission, goals, development, implementation, and evaluation of the systemic, data-driven school counseling program. Ongoing examination of school policy may point to needed revisions and changes, and professional school counselors need to be aware of the impact of policy on the school (Ripley & Goodnough, 2001). As part of the educational leadership teams in their schools, professional school counselors can be leaders and advocates who give voice to

TABLE 8.5 Student Issues Affected by School Policies, Practices, and Procedures	
Attendance	Student Recognition
Discipline	Club Membership
Tardiness	Release Time from Class for School-Sponsored Activities
Suspensions	Promotion and Retention
Makeup Work due to Illness	Transitions from One Level to Another
Student Recognition	Scholarships
Club Membership	Testing Practices
Decisions Regarding Placement in Rigorous Curricula	Communication with Families and the Community
Dissemination of Academic and Postsecondary Information	College Advising and Application Procedures

the day-to-day interpretation and application of school policy. Inequities in interpretation and application may be the result of oversights, outdated rules, or the values, attitudes, and beliefs of the policy makers that are translated into school policy and create barriers to educational access and equity. Although the role of the professional school counselor in the examination, influence, and revision of school policy is new, it is a moral imperative, as it is unprofessional for counselors, as part of the school system, to ignore aspects of the school or school counseling program that hinder educational success for all students.

PLANNING THE SCHOOL COUNSELING PROGRAM

Strategic Planning and Program Development

Throughout this chapter, we have discussed parts of a strategic plan and the use of strategic interventions as a way to match the needs of students and the community with program development and interventions for a desired outcome (D. Brown & Trusty, 2005a). The process of developing the program's structure, planning and delivering the program, and ensuring accountability is similar to that used for school improvement and educational reform, which encompasses all three domains of academic, career, and personal/social growth and development and encourages further study in this area. Moreover, using strategic interventions helps school counselors adopt a more proactive approach (D. Brown & Trusty, 2005a). The steps in the process of planning and implementing a school counseling program are outlined below and modified and demonstrated in the example shown in Figure 8.12.

- Establish a vision and a mission.
- Conduct a systemic assessment to collect data and identify need (this includes infromation from a gap analysis and program audit).

- Engage in goal development, feasibility analysis, and prioritization.
- Select and develop interventions as constellations that include both proximal and distal data elements.
- Implement and monitor interventions with established benchmarks, timelines, and responsibilities. Communicate the plan to all stakeholders.
- Collect data at both formative and summative points.
- Analyze and report findings to all stakeholders.
- Engage in advocacy efforts to translate gains into established practice codified in policy.
- Establish a strategic planning review and revision cycle at one-, three-, and five-year intervals.

The Program Calendar

A calendar for the school counseling program is an essential tool that serves a variety of purposes. First, the calendar format and structure demonstrate the systemic nature of the program in a monthly plan. Second, the calendar serves as a means of organizing interventions into a clear and intentional order. It is the written representation of the strategic plan and goals of the program. It defines the work of the counselor and presents a structure of professional activities similar to that used by other educational professionals in the school.

Calendars are organized by year, month, week, or day. Yearly calendars are global, so we recommend a monthly calendar as the format of choice for a school counseling department. The activities for each month can be laid out using the same template for each month, with the eight levels of intervention as a base. This ensures consistency of format in the delivery interventions from month to month. It also allows stakeholders to become familiar with the format of school counseling program delivery. See Table 8.6 for an outline of a calendar. Once the monthly calendar is established, individual counselors can then transfer their assignments to their own weekly and daily calendars.

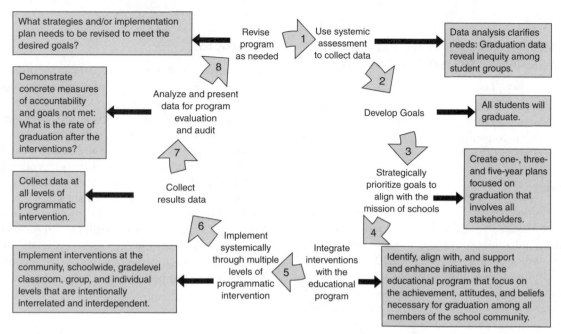

FIGURE 8.12 Vision: Social justice; Mission: Access and equity; Program: Data driven.

TABLE 8.6   A Content Outline of Activities for a Calendar for a Systemic, Data-Driven School Counseling Program

Each Month

Ongoing activities including individual

    Team meetings

    Staff planning meetings

    Individual level

    Referrals

    IEP meetings

    Section 504 meetings

    Crisis counseling

Group (should indicate the grade level[s])

Groups that are beginning, continuing, and/or ending this month

Any other targeted group activities

Classroom (collaborative classroom instruction)

Targeted interventions with classrooms in need

Grade

Transitional interventions at a particular grade level

Grade-specific interventions-preventive, developmental, remedial

School

Data collection, analysis, presentation, planning, and revision of programs and policies

    Discipline policies

    Course enrollment patterns

    Attendance policies

Interventions with all teachers

    In-service on learning styles

Interventions focused on schoolwide culture and climate

District

    Vertical and horizontal activities to address pervasive needs

Family

Parent/guardian groups

Informational/skill-building workshops

Advocacy activities for parents

Community

Task force for equity

Community advisory boards

Collaborations to promote achievement

Community educational and career mentors

Special presenters

Business sponsors for student needs

School-community partnerships

School-to-work initiatives

Professional Development Activities

Conferences and in-house trainings

School counselor building- and district-level meetings

Planning for Upcoming Events

List the activities that need to be accomplished to ensure timely and thorough planning for each upcoming intervention.

IMPLEMENTATION AT MULTIPLE LEVELS OF PROGRAMMATIC INTERVENTION

As demonstrated in Figure 8.4, school counseling program implementation can occur at multiple levels, including individual, group, classroom, grade, school, district, family, and community. Implementation at each of these levels will be described in the following sections.

Individual

This level of intervention is used to respond to crisis situations and issues specific to individual students. Importantly, individual counseling is not the key target of school counseling program interventions. Issues identified at this level provide insight into issues in the larger school that can then be further examined using specific data elements. Interventions can be developed and delivered at other programmatic levels to address issues in a preventive, developmental, and even remedial fashion. Services at the individual level include personal and crisis counseling. Most often included in this area, referral represents collaborative interventions at the community level and therefore is not a singular intervention. Additionally, issues at the individual level involve policies that are practiced schoolwide, such as policies around confidentiality, informed consent, duty to warn, and parental or guardian permission for counseling. Data around issues that necessitate the use of these policies, such as child abuse, substance abuse, and self-injurious behaviors, can inform counselors about the health and wellness of the school population, which can also be addressed at other levels in a preventive fashion. Other data that are often collected at this level include the number of students a counselor meets with, although these data are sometimes limited in value because they do not address outcomes.

Group

Efficacious use of group interventions requires examination of data elements gleaned from a systemwide assessment. This level of intervention can be either developmental or remedial and responds to data that identify specific and targeted needs across all grade levels. Group interventions can focus on specific subgroups of students or can be offered across student groups, depending on the identified needs of students. Additionally, group work is a critical level of intervention because it provides social modeling and peer support and promotes learning through a developmentally appropriate forum. Because this level of intervention serves only a small population of students, it should be intentionally interrelated to corresponding services at other levels.

Classroom

Collaborative classroom instruction can be offered in one particular class, across several classes in the school, or as part of an interdisciplinary team effort. Data are used at this level to identify classrooms and teachers in need of specific and targeted assistance with transforming the culture and climate of the teaching and learning environment in order to deliver developmental and preventive interventions that result in specific student outcomes. For example, specific collaborative classroom instruction interventions can focus on learning styles, healthy classroom relationships, or the sharing of responsibility. Likewise, they can supplement an academic unit such as diversity in history, citizenship, careers in the curriculum, or any other area that affects student performance and attainment.

Grade

Grade-level interventions specifically attend to the context of grade-level experiences (e.g., sixth grade) and transitions at developmental benchmarks (e.g., entering and leaving kindergarten, middle school, and high school). An emphasis on examining policies that affect specific grade levels is essential at this level of intervention. Because of the broader reach of this level, intervention usually involves a number of other levels of service, such as the school and community levels, and may require long-term planning as for transition events or postsecondary planning events. The ability to analyze and use disaggregated data on postsecondary plans, promotions, course enrollment patterns, and retentions helps the professional school counselor discern the influence of grade-level and transition points on these processes. Additionally, revision of grade-level policies that either support or hinder achievement is appropriate. Finally, grade-level data by subgroups (e.g., ethnicity, socioeconomic status, English language proficiency) are analyzed to develop interventions both within and between grade levels to promote achievement. An example of interventions at the grade level is transition activities—from elementary to middle school, from middle to high school, and from high school to postsecondary options. Other examples include senior activities such as postsecondary planning, resume writing, the scholarship process, the application process, and the awarding of local scholarships.

School

The school level of intervention has the greatest potential for removing systemic barriers and creating the conditions for learning at all other levels (R. L. Hayes, Nelson, Tabin, Pearson, & Worthy, 2002; R. M. House & Hayes,

2002). As far back as 1992, Gerler posited that the coordinating of systems-level interventions was the most important role of the professional school counselor. Now under accountability mandates, this level of intervention emphasizes reform as a whole-school challenge in which all stakeholders must be actively involved.

The potential of this level of intervention lies in examining the interrelatedness and interdependence of all school populations and the corresponding schoolwide disaggregated data. Interventions at this level involve the entire school, reflecting a data profile that includes policies and procedures, which are often the focus of these interventions. These interventions can also reflect areas of growth and development that are important to the entire school and focus on issues such as culture and climate. Interventions in these areas involve students, teachers, and administrators, making the interventions strong collaborative initiatives. Finally, interventions at this level can provide the support necessary to ensure success of interventions at other levels. For example, policy change at this level can be the linchpin that helps more students enroll in rigorous courses at a particular grade level.

District

Interventions at the school district level focus on connecting the work of professional school counselors to the larger district in ways that respond to both vertical and lateral districtwide issues. In the same way that particular student needs can be pervasive in a school, those same needs can be pervasive throughout a district. Work at the district level can happen in several ways. First, student need can be present across a district at elementary, middle and high schools. For example, issues around attendance, discipline, or academic achievement and attainment can be pervasive and persistent. Second, sometimes issues can be more focused on one level, but involve all or some of the schools at that level. For example, in elementary schools, where students are more likely to be referred for special education than at other levels, it may be that there is disproportionate representation across the district of one student group over another. While this is not solely an elementary school issue, a strong focus on the elementary level would be necessary to alter this situation. If there is a low college-going rate at multiple high schools across a district, it would be helpful for counselors to team and collaborate as they plan their interventions to increase the college-going rate among students. Such districtwide strategic interventions that pool the skill and resources of counselors in both vertical and horizontal teaming and collaboration can maximize time and efficiency and provide a broader perspective on the needs of students. To work effectively at this level, the professional school counselor must possess an understanding of the interrelationship between the needs of elementary, middle, and high school students and the factors that affect healthy growth and development, as well as a basic understanding of the functioning of schools at all levels. Data and gaps at this level can involve all three types: access, attainment, and achievement. The disaggregation of data at this level occurs across schools as well as within schools.

Family

Interventions at the family level assist parents and guardians in learning the skills that enable them to successfully navigate school and community services in order to gain access to resources for their children and assist their children in mastering the skills necessary for educational success. Intentional and culturally responsive outreach to marginalized parent and guardian populations can promote increased engagement of their children in the educational process and thus result in greater equity. It can also help parents and families take an active and empowered role in the school. This level of intervention uses data to intentionally assess parent need and involve parents and guardians in the school counseling program as equal partners in promoting student educational success. Data at this level most often are collected by counting how many parents attend an activity. While it is important to have data to demonstrate that increased numbers of parents participate, it is also important to collect data that can demonstrate that the knowledge and skill parents gained made a difference in the lives of their students.

Community

Interventions at the community level are used to actively involve all community stakeholders in creating broad-based partnerships for student success. This broad base can increase the likelihood that students will experience consistent expectations for success across the multiple contexts of their lives. These can include places of worship, libraries, sport and entertainment venues, and local businesses. Also important are even broader outreach and public relations efforts with local civic organizations, school boards, businesses, social services agencies, professional organizations, state departments of education, and federal bodies that contribute to the creation of standards, policies, and laws that affect schools, school counseling programs, and student achievement. Implementation of community-level interventions requires strategic planning over time. Careful planning, documentation, timely and clear communication, and shared decision making are essential. As with all other levels of intervention, using data to create urgency and drive decision making and using inquiry to continue to focus, evaluate, and revise interventions are essential and the hallmarks of a well-articulated data process. Administrative support and sanctioning (preferably codified in policy) of the collaborative efforts at this level of intervention can help prevent school counseling programs from becoming marginalized and superfluous to the mission of schools (Ripley & Goodnough, 2001). Table 8.7 provides an example of what this type of delivery, with its multiple levels of intervention, looks like in action.

EVALUATING THE SYSTEMIC, DATA-DRIVEN SCHOOL COUNSELING PROGRAM

Full and detailed attention to program evaluation and accountability, research, and best practices requires in-depth study. This brief discussion will focus on the importance of program evaluation and provide some clarification of terms. First, evaluation demonstrates accountability and establishes the credibility of professional school counselors and the school counseling program as viable contributors to the achievement of all students. This occurs when concrete measures can demonstrate that established goals were met and allows counselors to assess the impact of the program and the levels of programmatic interventions that were most successful. It also allows counselors to determine combinations of interventions that proved successful in goal attainment.

Second, evaluation demonstrates where goals were not met. Determining when goals are not met is equally as important as determining success. Unachieved goals highlight the need for further examination of needs, assessment methods, strategic planning, and selected intervention, as well as the skill level of all stakeholders involved in implementing the initiative. Also, it is important to not continue to engage in interventions that do not work.

TABLE 8.7 An Example of Multilevel Interventions at the High School Level

1. Level: High school
2. Goal: Increase the number of students entering rigorous courses by _____%
3. The levels in action:

Individual: Provide individual counseling that focuses on building aspirations, addressing stereotypes, disseminating information, carrying out academic planning, carrying out career and college planning, and reviewing high school graduation requirements and college requirements.

Group: Carry out academic planning, conduct college and career groups, focus on building aspirations for the future, and review high school and college graduation requirements.

Classroom: Cover the same topics as at the group level, but focus them more on the educational aspect of the information around academic, college, and career planning. Make sure messaging is consistent with individual and group initiatives. Target classrooms where messages of educational equity are not readily accepted.

Grade: Target grade-level information and activities to ensure optimal enrollment in rigorous courses, provide information that outlines the opportunities at each grade level, and implement culture and climate initiatives around educational and career success. Address what each grade level needs to know.

School: Collect schoolwide data related to course enrollment and completion patterns, as well as grades-all disaggregated by group, grade, gender, English language proficiency, disability, and any other salient demographics. Conduct workshops with teachers on differentiated learning, cultural responsiveness, classroom management, and belief systems.

District: Engage in vertical teaming with middle school counselors to prepare students and parents for the transition to high school and the need to take rigorous courses as it relates to postsecondary choices; provide information on graduation requirements, course selection, career choice, and building aspirations. Consult with other high schools about their difficulties or successes in increasing student enrollment in rigorous courses.

Family: Conduct workshops and outreach for parents that address all of the areas discussed above. Ensure the same information and messaging for parents along with the use of specific culturally responsive techniques that respond to multiple generational, ethnic, racial, religious, and language differences, to name a few. Engage in advocacy that opens the doors of empowerment for parents and families.

Community: Inform and engage community and business leaders in understanding the importance of equitable student participation and performance in rigorous courses and the impact successful participation has on their businesses and the community at large.

Third, it is important to make the distinction between research and school counseling program evaluation. Carey and Dimmitt (2006) define evaluation as information that allows stakeholders to assess programs and interventions in order to make better decisions within the program context. The information gained by evaluating programs and interventions is designed to answer this question: "Did this work in our context?" These authors also define research as adding "knowledge to a field of study and . . . [contributing] to the growth of a theory" (p. 417). Many professional school counselors do not have the resources to conduct stringent research studies, but do have the ability to conduct evaluations. This is an important difference between research and evaluation.

Fourth, when school counselors do engage in evaluation, Carey (2006) suggests that it is ideal for programs and interventions to be evaluated within a framework of three types of relevant outcomes: immediate, proximal, and distal. Immediate outcomes address questions such as "Did students learn what was intended?" and include outcomes tied to learning objectives, such as comprehension or changes in knowledge. Proximal outcomes answer questions such as "Did students change in ways that predict long-term changes in school behavior and performance?" and include changes in test-taking skills, college search skills, and decision-making skills. Distal outcomes answer questions such as "Did students show long-term changes in behavior and/or performance?" and include changes in graduation rates, college placement data, achievement test scores, and discipline data. Data in all three areas are important to school counselor accountability and provide clarity about school counselor impact because data elements from distal outcomes alone can be difficult to link to school counselor actions (D. Brown & Trusty, 2005a). Finally, linking these kinds of outcomes to strategic interventions can benefit school counseling practice and assist in program development.

IMPLICATIONS FOR PROFESSIONAL SCHOOL COUNSELORS

Creating systemic, data-driven school counseling programs is the ethical responsibility of all professional school counselors, including school-based directors of school counseling services and district directors of school counseling. While the knowledge and skills needed to develop and implement systemic, data-driven programs are slowly becoming accepted practice for school counseling professionals, attaining these skills and others necessary to meet the needs of all students is an ethical responsibility regardless of the stage in one's career. Implicit in this statement is the recognition that professional school counselors are self-reflective practitioners who engage in ongoing professional development to ensure they are relevant. Such a commitment ensures professional school counselors will develop the competence to implement the systemic, data-driven programs that equitably meet the academic, career, and personal/social needs of all students.

Summary/Conclusion

This chapter has offered a rationale, description, and tools useful in creating a systemic, data-driven school counseling program. To build this type of program, professional school counselors need to possess the values, attitudes, and beliefs implicit in the transformed role of the professional school counselor. Additionally, professional school counselors who possess the awareness, knowledge, and skills necessary to develop and implement such programs will ensure that school counseling is integral to the mission of the school and demonstrate the value-added worth of school counseling through concrete measures of accountability. Most importantly, the implementation of systemic, data-driven school counseling programs can form the bedrock of an effort to ensure that the needs of all students are equitably met in a learning environment that encourages academic success with cultural integrity.

Activities

1. Reflecting on your graduate training thus far, identify areas in which you need to develop greater levels of awareness, knowledge, and skill to begin the career-long process of becoming a transformed school counselor. What do you need to do to improve those skills throughout the remainder of your training and after you graduate?

2. In which level(s) of program intervention do you feel most comfortable, and which level(s) are most challenging? Why? What do you need to do to improve those skills throughout the remainder of your training and after you graduate?

Developmental Classroom Guidance

Gary E. Goodnough, Rachelle Pérusse, and Bradley T. Erford

Editor's Introduction: Whether conducted by the professional school counselor or the classroom teacher, developmental classroom guidance is a common and efficient method for implementing the comprehensive, developmental school counseling curriculum. Unfortunately, professional school counselors have not consistently focused on designing academically rigorous lesson plans, activities sensitive to diverse learners' needs, and assessment and follow-up procedures to determine the effectiveness and continuity of classroom guidance activities. The school reform movement, with its emphasis on academic performance, requires this of classroom teachers. The same is expected of the transformed professional school counselor.

In the past, professional school counselors were hired almost exclusively from the ranks of classroom teachers. It was implicitly assumed that these counselors, as former teachers, understood the role of teacher and could assume such a role. Beginning in the 1970s, states began to drop their requirements that professional school counselors be certified, experienced teachers (Randolph & Masker, 1997). It became clear to counselor educators and state officials that restricting entry into one profession (counseling) by requiring experience in a related profession (teaching) not only was a historical bias, but also served to lower the number of eligible and willing candidates for professional school counselor positions. Currently, only seven states require professional school counselors to have experience as teachers (American School Counselor Association [ASCA], 2009). Most counselor educators suggest that this movement toward opening the ranks to nonteachers has benefited the profession (Bringman & Lee, 2008).

   With the advent of comprehensive, developmental school counseling programs, professional school counselors at all levels are in the classroom. Most have responsibility for delivering their program directly, as well as indirectly, to students. Direct delivery of a school counseling curriculum means that professional school counselors have a significant role in teaching students in classrooms. Thus, professional school counselors, while increasingly not rooted in the teaching profession, nevertheless need to become knowledgeable of effective teaching methods. Clearly, this is a tall order. To become a teacher, one must receive an undergraduate degree—in some cases, a graduate degree—and then complete a teaching internship. In 43 states, many new school counselors do not have this background, but will assume significant teaching responsibilities.

   In this chapter, it is our intention to outline and discuss some pedagogically sound ways in which professional school counselors can provide for students' academic, career, and personal/social development. In so doing, it is our hope that professional school counselors will be able to better implement the classroom component of their comprehensive school counseling programs.

THE SCOPE AND RESPONSIBILITY OF THE DEVELOPMENTAL GUIDANCE SPECIALIST

The *ASCA National Model* (2005a) charges professional school counselors with the responsibility of implementing programs to assist all students in their academic, career, and personal/social development. As discussed in the previous chapter, professional school counselors intervene at multiple levels, including the classroom. Gysbers and Henderson (2006) suggested that

VOICES FROM THE FIELD 9.1   MY BIG CHANCE

"Megan, would you like to run the classroom guidance lesson next week?" my supervisor inquired after I had spent several weeks observing. *By myself? Am I ready for this? What if I mess up? What if the students become out of control?*

"Of course, sounds great!" I replied, trying to sound confident.

During the lesson, part of a curriculum series, sixth graders are to write a letter to a mentor they can look to for guidance during their teenage years. Attempting to be as prepared as possible, I studied the lesson plan over and over, trying to commit it to memory. Not much, however, could prepare me for my largest concern: the students' reactions. Even though my supervisor would be there, I wanted to show her, and prove to myself, that I could manage 25 sixth graders. *But how will I keep so many students under control?*

On the day of the lesson, I quickly ran it through my head one last time as I arrived at the classroom. *Twenty-five sixth graders staring at me. Do not mess up.* I introduced myself to the class and outlined the lesson. *Okay, going well so far.* I asked the students to explain what they had covered in the previous lesson. Silence. I reworded the question. Silence. *They can tell I am nervous. I don't know if I can do this.* I was so worried about the students being out of control, I had not considered that they might say nothing at all. Through a combination of nerves and desperation, I began to increase my energy. I walked around the room, trying to engage the students. Hands started rising into the air and the lesson gained momentum. *Phew!* After a productive discussion, I explained the letter activity and let the students work. *Were my directions clear? Do the students understand why they are doing this?*

As they finished, a few students shouted out, "Miss Krell! Come here! Read my letter!" I was shocked by the amount of pride they took in their letters and how excited they were to mail them out. At the end of the lesson, my supervisor was smiling. "That was awesome," she mouthed to me, while I let out a huge sigh of relief and let the students pass to their next class.

Source: Megan Krell, School Counseling Intern, University of Connecticut

---

local districts inevitably determine the precise percentage of time spent in delivering classroom guidance. Nevertheless, Gysbers and Henderson provided general guidelines that describe how much time is typically devoted to curriculum implementation. Using Gysbers and Henderson (2006) as a guide, the *ASCA National Model* suggests that at the elementary school level, approximately 35% to 45% of the counseling program be devoted to implementing the curriculum. At the middle school level, an appropriate amount of counselor time devoted to curriculum is 25% to 35%; and at the high school level, the recommendation is that 15% to 25% of the program time be dedicated to the guidance curriculum (ASCA, 2005a).

Although counselors are not the only professionals delivering the guidance curriculum, professional school counselors clearly commit significant resources to teaching. The ASCA (2005b), in its position statement on comprehensive school counseling programs, supports the teaching role in stating that professional school counselors "teach skill development in academic, career and personal/social areas." With the decline in the number of counselors having backgrounds as teachers, professional school counselors must develop their teaching skills if they are to fulfill their roles within comprehensive, standards-based programs. Although many learn these important skills during their internship experiences (J. S. Peterson, Goodman, Thomas, & McCauley, 2004), there is an undeniable need to address this potentially important skill during preservice trainings.

THE EFFECT OF CLASSROOM GUIDANCE ON STUDENT DEVELOPMENT

Lending credence to the discussion of the effect of classroom guidance on student achievement is a statewide study conducted in Missouri high schools (Sink, 2005a), which found that students who were in schools with a fully implemented model guidance program including classroom guidance reported higher grades, better preparation and information for future goals, and a more positive school climate. According to Holcomb-McCoy (2007), studies exist that demonstrate the positive effects of classroom guidance on specific outcome measures. In their review of the literature, Borders and Drury (1992) found studies that showed classroom guidance activities had positive effects on a variety of student behaviors, including classroom behaviors and attitudes, exam preparation, school attendance, career goals, college attendance, career planning skills, and coping skills.

With the advent of the accountability issues raised in the *ASCA National Model*, the Transforming the School Counseling Initiative, and the No Child Left Behind Act of 2001 (NCLB), there is a necessity for professional school counselors to demonstrate that their interventions are effective. Such is also the case with classroom guidance interventions. There is a move away from simply counting how many times an intervention is used and toward describing how effective an intervention is (ASCA, 2005a). One way to show effectiveness is to collect data both prior to and after the intervention, known as a pretest–posttest design. It is not enough to say that one has conducted a certain number of classroom guidance activities. Professional school counselors must demonstrate that these activities are effective and that students are different as a result (Dimmitt, Carey, & Hatch, 2007). There are many data points that can be used in a pretest–posttest design. A professional school counselor might access school files to find out about grades, standardized test scores, and graduation rate, or, once data are already collected, disaggregate the data by gender, ethnicity, and socioeconomic status. For example, if one were conducting a classroom guidance unit on bullying behavior, one might count the number of bullying incidents on the playground or the number of discipline referrals to the assistant principal before and after the unit.

Besides collecting pretest and posttest data, professional school counselors might collect content evaluation data and process evaluation data from the students and teachers in the classroom. When conducting an evaluation based on the content of the classroom guidance activity, professional school counselors might use pretest and posttest measures resembling a quiz. For younger children, professional school counselors might use a Smiley–Frowny Form or a Feelometer (LaFountain & Garner, 1998). For older children, they might use multiple-choice and open-ended questions based on the unit. For example, D. S. Young (2005) conducted a classroom guidance activity based on the portrayal of Theodore Roosevelt. His content evaluation contained 10 multiple-choice questions asking students to identify facts presented during the activity.

A process evaluation is aimed at identifying which parts of the classroom guidance activity went well and which parts can be improved on. Especially when a classroom intervention is new, it is important to get feedback from students and teachers about ways to improve the lesson the next time it is taught. A process evaluation might contain questions such as those in Figure 9.1. Some classroom guidance curriculum

---

Classroom Guidance Lesson: _____
Counselor: _____

1. I found this lesson to be: (Check one)

_____
Very   Somewhat   Not At All
Helpful   Helpful   Helpful

2. I especially enjoyed:
_____
_____

3. I think the following could be done differently:
_____
_____

4. I found the counselor to be: (Check one)

_____
Very   Somewhat   Not At All
Helpful   Helpful   Helpful

5. Overall, I would rate this lesson: (Circle one)

    1   2   3   4   5   6   7   8   9   10
    AWFUL   EXCELLENT

6. COMMENTS: _____
_____
_____
_____

FIGURE 9.1 Process evaluation.

materials have already been evaluated for effectiveness. The website for the Center for School Counseling Outcome Research (www.umass.edu/schoolcounseling), located at the University of Massachusetts, Amherst, contains research briefs and monographs based on published works that show the effectiveness of school counseling interventions. Included among those evidence-based programs are Second Step (www.cfchildren.org/ssf/ssindex), Student Success Skills (www.studentsuccessskills.com), The Real Game (www.realgame.com), and Peacebuilders (www.peacebuilders.com).

DEVELOPMENTAL THEORY

It is relevant to stress the importance of a comprehensive, developmental approach to classroom guidance. Within this framework, it has been argued that to be successful in implementing a classroom guidance curriculum, the professional school counselor must adhere to an overall theory of counseling. To this end, human development theories are most appropriate for professional school counselors to consider. Borders and Drury (1992) emphasized that developmental stages are the basis for effective counseling programs. They identified several human development theories, including those of Piaget, Erikson, Loevinger, Kohlberg, Gilligan, and Selman. In addition to these theorists, Myrick (2003a) recommended the work of Havighurst and Super. The challenge for professional

school counselors is how to translate developmental theory into practical ideas for classroom guidance. Table 9.1 contains examples of what professional school counselors might do in relation to the domains of cognitive, career, and personal/social development theory when presenting classroom guidance lessons.

Consistent among each of these theories is the concept that developmental changes occur over the life span of the individual and that achievement of each developmental task is dependent on the successful accomplishment of earlier tasks (Myrick, 2003a). Thus, professional school counselors must ensure that relevant developmental changes are addressed in a sequential, orderly manner within a pre-K-12 curriculum. Using this comprehensive, developmental model, professional school counselors avoid delivering their services in isolated units. Instead, they build on previous efforts and successes toward a meaningful outcome. As an example of this hierarchical learning, Nicoll (1994) suggested a five-stage framework, based in Adlerian psychology, for the implementation of classroom guidance programs. These five stages are (1) understanding of self and others, (2) empathy skill development, (3) communication skills development, (4) cooperation skills development, and (5) responsibility skills development. Nicoll noted that each of the five stages could be repeated throughout each grade and adapted to appropriate developmental levels. Thus, the framework would be applied in such a way that each year builds on previous years.

TABLE 9.1 Classroom Applications for Cognitive, Career, and Personal/Social Development Theory

	Developmental Theorist	Key Concepts	How It Translates to Classroom Guidance
Cognitive	Piaget	Preoperational	Use props and visual aids.
			Use actions and words to give instructions.
			Use hands-on activities.
		Concrete operational	Use actions, props, and hands-on activities.
			Use brain teasers, mind twisters, and riddles.
		Formal operational	Set up hypothetical questions.
			Have students justify two opposite points of view.
			Use song lyrics to reflect on topics.
			Teach broad concepts that are open to discussion.
	Vygotsky	Sociocultural theory, co-constructed process, cultural tools, private speech, scaffolding	Provide examples, use prompts, and give feedback.
			Encourage students to challenge themselves.
			Teach students to use tools such as homework planners and technology.
			Use peer tutoring.

(Continued)

TABLE 9.1 Classroom Applications for Cognitive, Career, and Personal/Social Development Theory *(Continued)*

	Developmental Theorist	Key Concepts	How It Translates to Classroom Guidance
Career Development	Super	Curiosity, exploration, career maturity	Plenty of materials with career-related information should be available.
			Career information should be integrated into all disciplines.
	Gottfredsen	Orientation to sex roles	Take care not to use gender-stereotyped materials.
		Orientation to social valuation	Help expand career areas outside of those typical of student's socioeconomic status.
Personal/social	Erikson	Initiative versus guilt	Allow students to choose an activity.
			Teach in small steps.
			Use costumes and props.
		Industry versus inferiority	Have students set and work toward goals.
			Delegate tasks to students to encourage responsibility.
			Use charts to keep track of progress.
		Identity versus role confusion	Invite guest speakers for career day.
			Include examples of women and people of color in your discussions.
	Kohlberg	Moral reasoning based on the ethic of justice	Conduct lessons on bullying, cheating, and peer relationships.
	Gilligan	Moral reasoning based on the ethic of care	Use themes of care as a basis to organize the curriculum: caring for self, caring for family and friends, caring for strangers and the world.

VOICES FROM THE FIELD 9.2   **USING DEVELOPMENTAL GUIDANCE AND DATA TO BUILD SCHOOL COUNSELING PROGRAMS**

School counseling must truly be comprehensive, addressing the domains of academic, personal/social, and career development. For many years, particularly in public high schools, the primary focus of school counselors was scheduling. In years past, private/independent schools had no school counseling services. The assumption was that all students in private schools were going to college, and it was the mindset of many educators to just teach the students. Today, many more students in public and private schools have serious issues and are bringing those issues inside the school building. As a result, schools have recognized that professional school counselors are integral to the school mission and that their work must be comprehensive to address the needs of the whole student.

Classroom guidance is an important piece of the developmental, comprehensive guidance program because it

helps professional school counselors connect with every student, while meeting students' academic, career, and personal/social needs. With the large caseloads of professional school counselors, classroom guidance is an important vehicle for making these connections with students. Through classroom guidance, school counselors become visible throughout the school and are able to build rapport with students, letting students know counselors are available to provide important services that will benefit them.

As a school counselor, the use of data has become critically important to me in terms of measuring the success of a comprehensive, developmental school counseling program. Since its inception, the No Child Left Behind Act has caused educators to use data to assess educational programs. Insofar as professional school counselors are concerned, we embrace data/accountability to measure and assess our school counseling programs. We need adequate training to effectively measure what is working, what is not working, and where adjustment is needed in this area of data/accountability. Through accountability, we demonstrate that professional school counselors provide useful services to students, evidence to back our mission and belief that all students can benefit from comprehensive, developmental school counseling programs that meet the academic, personal/social, and career development needs of all students.

Source: Kenneth Barrett, Professional School Counselor, Old Mill High School, Anne Arundel County Public Schools, Maryland

THE ROLE OF THE PROFESSIONAL SCHOOL COUNSELOR IN DELIVERING THE CURRICULUM

Professional school counselors implement their curricular role in three ways—through consultation, collaboration, and direct teaching. While the most visible modality is that of providing instruction directly to students and parents, professional school counselors also implement their curricular role in indirect ways (M. A. Clark & Breman, 2009). For instance, a professional school counselor might consult with a middle school team of teachers as they plan a unit on ecosystems. In working with the teachers, the professional school counselor can become a resource to help integrate guidance curriculum components into the unit. In this case, classroom teachers are teaching the school counseling curriculum and are helping to promote the career maturity of students by providing world-of-work information as one of several important parts of the unit. By becoming involved with teachers as they plan, counselors educate the educators and are able to reach a wider audience more consistently.

A second way in which professional school counselors implement their curricular role is by working collaboratively not only in the planning phase, as in the previous example, but also in the implementation phase. In this case, a high school counselor might meet regularly with the physical education (PE) teachers to plan adventure-based education. The teachers and professional school counselor could then implement the program as a team, with each professional responsible for an area of expertise. For example, the PE teacher might attend primarily to the physical fitness components of a ropes course, and the professional school counselor could attend more directly to the team-building and positive social interaction aspects of the program.

Although it is true that all members of a school community share responsibility for implementing a counseling curriculum, professional school counselors may still directly deliver a significant portion of it themselves. For instance, in this third service delivery method, counselors in an elementary school program might teach developmentally appropriate units on conflict resolution to multiple grade levels. At the high school level, they might administer interest inventories to sophomores and then follow up with interpretation and a series of carefully designed lessons to facilitate students' career growth.

Counselors, by virtue of their professional preparation, are the individuals best suited to teach the content, skills, and processes of conflict resolution. They understand the role of interests in career development and know how to foster the career maturity of high school students. For these reasons, it is not uncommon for professional school counselors to be directly involved in teaching students every day. Although it is vital to the ultimate success of the school counselors' curriculum to engage teachers and staff in supporting and reinforcing the program components, many counselors, particularly in elementary and middle schools, nevertheless spend a significant amount of time teaching.

SETTING UP AND MANAGING A CLASSROOM ENVIRONMENT

Arranging the Classroom

Classroom arrangement not only creates an atmosphere or climate for learning, but also communicates the teaching philosophy and interaction expectations of the instructor. In a practical sense, how a professional school counselor chooses to physically set up a learning environment depends on the desired interaction strategies to be used during implementation of the lesson. For example, if the goal is to get students to explore an interpersonal issue in a deep and personally meaningful way, the professional school counselor might break the students into groups of two to four and have them cluster in small circles in several areas around the room or around small tables. On the other hand, if the goal is simply to impart information on how to fill out a college application, a typical classroom-style setup may suffice. The important point is that teaching style, learning style, instructional strategies, and participant seating should combine to form an effective learning atmosphere.

Figure 9.2 contains drawings of several typical seating arrangements used by professional school counselors. A lecture hall or classroom-style setup creates a formal,

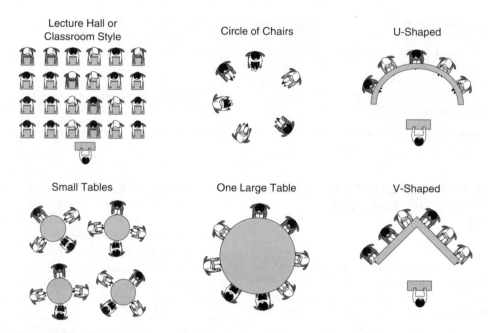

FIGURE 9.2 Classroom arrangements.

businesslike, and often cold and sterile atmosphere that leaves no question as to who is in charge. It sets the expectation that students are there to be taught and emphasizes one-way communication, with periodic pauses for questions. When discussion does occur, it is typically funneled through the instructor. The classroom-style setup lends itself to an authoritarian-instructor style, relegating student participation to secondary status. Many students take a passive role or are minimally active and engaged.

The U-shaped or V-shaped arrangement with the instructor at the open end still creates a formal or instructor-centered atmosphere indicating the instructor is in command, but it also indicates that there will be opportunities for interaction. The philosophy conveyed by the U shape is that interaction can occur between participants, even though the instructor will still function as the primary source of information.

The small-tables arrangement presents a more relaxed, informal, student-centered atmosphere where all will have the opportunity to discuss, share, explore, and problem solve. In this arrangement, the instructor is more of a facilitator and serves as a catalyst and resource to all of the small groups. The small-tables environment sets an expectation of active participation on the part of all students and is used primarily for small-group work and learning. Putting student desks into a circle or block is a modification of this arrangement.

The one-table (round or square) arrangement conveys the expectation of participation and free exchange of information. Generally, this arrangement is viewed as less formal,

although the presence of a table often inhibits maximum expressiveness. Most important, the instructor's authority and status can be deemphasized, and he or she can be viewed as a participant in the group. This arrangement has a high potential for learning because a small-group environment can be a positive force in learning and all students have the opportunity for significant involvement.

The circle-of-chairs arrangement presents a friendly, relaxed, warm atmosphere in which all participants are expected to be fully engaged. In many ways, interpersonal-social learning is dependent on the extent of participation, depth of cohesion, and quality of peer relationships. The instructor role must be conveyed as that of a group facilitator and participant who is also expected to learn from the group.

The arrangement of chairs, tables, desks, or even participants themselves will convey a learning atmosphere and instructor philosophy to all participants. The instructional objectives, strategies, and activities should lead the professional school counselor to choose an appropriate classroom arrangement.

Working with the Classroom Teacher's Rules

It is the rare professional school counselor who has his or her own classroom. More typically, counselors are in an itinerant role wherein they teach in different classrooms. As a result, professional school counselors usually present lessons to intact classroom groups. In the elementary school, these classroom groups often are taught by one teacher for the entire

day. Certain norms are already established [...]
students relative to behavior and discipli[...]
al who "comes and goes," it is importa[...]
school counselor to have an understand[...]
so that students have some consistency a[...]
pect. Typically, teachers appreciate it as w[...]
al school counselors follow the basic rul[...]
This is not to suggest that professiona[...]
must rely solely on the teachers' rules fo[...]
ment and discipline. In fact, profession[...]
usually augment and adapt some rules t[...]
style and professional role. Neverthele[ss...]
travene basic classroom rules, as this [...]
students and annoy teachers.

One of the typical roles of prof[...]
selors is that of a consultant to classroo[...]
sometimes provide help with impl[...]
management strategies and working effectively with children
who present teachers with significant challenges. It is important that professional school counselors themselves be able to
deal effectively with the wide range of students present in
classrooms and to prevent discipline problems from arising.
When problems do arise, it is imperative that professional
school counselors attend to the issues in effective ways that are
respectful to the student and his or her classmates.

Preventing Discipline Issues in the Classroom

The best way to deal with discipline issues in the classroom is
by preventing occurrences in the first place. A well-designed
lesson is essential. This includes several components, including making sure that the work is neither too hard nor too
easy, that the work is not boring, and that expectations and
instructions are clear (Geltner & Clark, 2005). Further information about presenting clear, effective lessons will be provided later in this chapter.

A good lesson is only part of the equation, however.
Geltner and Clark (2005) suggested several classroom-
management skills that are fundamentally important. The
first is getting children's attention and keeping it properly
focused. Several strategies are effective for getting and keeping children's attention. One is working to keep the whole
group alert and on task through positive strategies such as
encouragement, enthusiasm, praise, nonsarcastic humor,
and dramatic delivery. Another strategy is enlisting student
involvement in the lesson. Teachers and professional school
counselors do this by using an interesting variety of voice
tones, piquing students' curiosity, using suspense, and connecting with students' interests and fantasies.

A second general management component that prevents discipline issues from occurring is having a smooth flow

[...]rred to as *momentum.*
[...] parts, two of which will be
[...]dy availability of sufficient
[...]s will need during the les-
[...]ting to the flow of a lesson
[...]g a finite resource material.
[...]selors need to be aware of
[...]ously—what teachers refer
[...]ur head." Classroom educa-
[...] individuals are doing at any
[...]nat comes next in the lesson
[...]cks might exist for off-task
[...]g aware and knowledgeable,
[...]roblems from occurring.

[...]haviors [...]assroom

Despite educators' best efforts at prevention, children
sometimes behave in ways that educators find disruptive.
Professional school counselors know that students often
bring with them concerns from home or from peer relationships that have little to do with being in class. These
matters can make it difficult for students to benefit from
regular instruction. A discipline plan needs to take into account that there are sometimes quite understandable reasons for children's misbehavior. Counselors, as consultants,
help teachers see this and provide advice on dealing with it.
Professional school counselors working in classrooms need
to have strategies to handle problems directly.

When discipline problems arise, professional school
counselors must first decide if there is a need to deal with the
problem. They need to know what behaviors require intervention. It is important that teachers' rules be respected; still,
professional school counselors need to have a sense of their
comfort level with different types of student behavior.
Professional school counselors need to behave in such a way
as to help students understand that the responsibility for the
classroom's environment belongs to students and that professional school counselors are not police officers present to en-
force oppressive rules. This being said, it is important to have
strategies available to deal with difficult behaviors in respectful and effective ways. Having such strategies is particularly
important for professional school counselors who, by virtue
of being in the classroom, set up potentially conflicting dual
relationships with students whom they may later counsel.

There are several approaches that professional school
counselors can take in addressing discipline problems that
arise in the classroom setting. Effective approaches are based
on the notion that the professional school counselor does
not act in an authoritarian manner, but rather embodies
democratic principles. As a result of their professional

preparation and personal demeanor, most professional school counselors do not tend toward authoritarianism. A mistake often made, however, is to move toward the polar opposite of authoritarianism—that of passivity, where the professional school counselor becomes a nondisciplining "nice guy." While all professional school counselors wish to be liked by students, being passive relative to student classroom misbehavior can both undermine the respect students have toward professional school counselors and render lessons ineffective. Of the several approaches to discipline available to counselors, one developed by Driekurs will be discussed (for an in-depth discussion on classroom discipline, see Charney, 2002, or Charles and Senter, 2005).

Driekurs and Cassell (1974) classified student misbehavior according to the goals toward which students strive. Their system is reflective of Driekurs's conceptions of misbehavior derived from his work with Alfred Adler. Driekurs noted that classroom misbehavior stems from one of four student goals: seeking attention, having power, getting revenge, and showing inadequacy. Students who seek power or revenge often feel powerless or oppressed. It is particularly important to develop a healthy nonauthoritarian relationship with these students. As a result of their work in providing responsive services in the school, professional school counselors often know these students quite well and, indeed, have developed strong, healthy relationships with them. When professional school counselors have strong alliances with these students and the counselor's presence in the classroom is not authoritarian, then it is unlikely that misbehaviors stemming from the goals of power and revenge will be apparent in class. According to Driekurs, students who withdraw or show inadequacy are discouraged and need encouragement. Obviously, professional school counselors should provide such support. Dinkmeyer and McKay (1980) operationalized these principles in their book *Systematic Training for Effective Teaching*.

Attention-seeking behavior is the most common form of classroom misbehavior and the one that is most amenable to the application of logical consequences. Logical consequences are based on the belief that social reality requires certain behaviors. It is not the power of the professional school counselor or the teacher that requires students to behave in certain ways, but the requirements of a just social order. Punishment is not meted out by the authority; rather, the professional school counselor, in conjunction with the class, makes it known that certain behaviors have certain consequences. Professional school counselors using this discipline strategy do not get in power struggles with students. They refrain from judging students or thinking of them as bad, and in a caring manner, they help students realize that certain behaviors result in certain consequences. The consequences need to be logically related to the student misbehavior. It is important as well that the consequences reflect the social order, not the authority of the professional school counselor or the teacher. As such, professional school counselors do not imply any moral judgment toward the student and use a kind, but firm voice. Anger has no part in discipline (Geltner & Clark, 2005).

Professional school counselors seek to prevent discipline issues from arising by having well-designed lessons. They are aware of potential times during their lessons when children might tend toward off-task behavior, and they seek to mitigate such behavior proactively. Professional school counselors act in such a way as to be clearly perceived as being nonauthoritarian, yet neither are they passive. By embodying democratic, authoritative principles of classroom management and discipline, professional school counselors are able to enact their role as educator in a positive manner. Armed with such knowledge about the interpersonal role of the professional school counselor as educator, it is now necessary to know how to go about creating and designing a curriculum to implement.

CRAFTING A CURRICULUM

The process of developing a school counseling curriculum, while unique in some ways, is similar to that used to develop curriculum in other subject areas. While in some states subject-area curriculum decisions made at the state level, educators in other states create the entire curriculum at the local level. Locally, curricula are often developed via committees having representatives from stakeholder groups such as parents, community members, administrators, and central office staff (Landsverk, 2003). Whether at the state or local level, social studies experts play a large role in the development of a social studies curriculum. In mathematics curriculum development, the contributions of mathematicians and their professional organizations are central. Likewise, in the development of a school counseling curriculum, the professional school counselor and the extant professional literature play primary roles.

The school counseling leadership team (Kaffenberger, Murphy, & Bemak, 2006) or the school counseling program advisory committee (Gysbers, 2004; Gysbers & Henderson, 2006; see Chapter 3) develops a curriculum that supports the counseling program's vision and overall goals. Regardless of the name of the group that provides leadership to the curriculum-writing process, curriculum development is a schoolwide responsibility requiring the active commitment and involvement of administrators and teachers. Because of professional school counselors' knowledge of the subject matter, however, leadership for developing a comprehensive curriculum is often provided by, or at least shared with, the professional school counselor or guidance director. Questions such as "How do professional school counselors decide what will be taught in each grade level?" and "What factors determine the curriculum goals and priorities?" will be addressed in the next section.

The *ASCA National Model* (2005a) should be considered when crafting a curriculum. In addition to considering national standards, professional school counselors in many states incorporate standards from their state guidance and counseling models, as well as the state curriculum standards. Thirty-six states now have their own comprehensive programs (ASCA, 2009). Regardless of whether a local counseling program is guided by national standards or by a state program, a central component of the program is a theoretical foundation that fosters the academic, career, and personal/social development of students.

Within a state or national program foundation, professional school counselors, working together with a steering committee or advisory group, assess students' guidance and counseling needs as perceived by important constituencies in the school and community. Comprehensive program professionals (Gysbers, 2004; Gysbers & Henderson, 2006; see Chapter 13) recommend that a formal needs assessment be administered at the outset of a move to a comprehensive program and then readministered about every three years. In this way, the program consistently represents the perceived needs of the supporting community. During this formal needs assessment, students, parents, teachers, administrators, and the wider community are asked about their perceptions of student needs. In states where comprehensive programs exist, these formal needs assessments reflect the state's curricular priorities, and also incorporate local stakeholders' perceptions into the program.

Needs are also assessed on a regular basis in a less formal way. An example of informal needs assessment involves professional school counselors speaking regularly with teachers, students, and staff and responding to changing needs in a timely way. For instance, recently there has been an increased focus on bullying prevention and intervention. Some states (e.g., New Hampshire) have enacted legislation designed to foster systemwide prevention and intervention. Many professional school counselors assess student and staff concerns regarding bullying and assist the system and the students in creating bully-free and safe environments. On a more local scale, professional school counselors respond to myriad specific classroom and grade-level requests by teachers and administrators. These requests range from teaching social skills in a particularly difficult second-grade class to addressing sexual harassment with seventh graders. After conducting the formal needs assessment, and in conjunction with national standards and state standards, the school counseling leadership team or advisory council decides on the student outcomes appropriate for the locality (Kaffenberger et al., 2006). These student outcomes reflect what students need to

know or be able to do on graduating from high school. Many school systems use the *National Standards for School Counseling Programs* (C. Campbell & Dahir, 1997) as their outcomes. In this case, the nine standards, three each from the domains of academic, career, and personal/social development, are the outcomes. These outcomes are further broken down into a series of competencies that, when accomplished, will lead to the outcome or standard. Finally, methods of assessment are detailed. (See Figure 9.3 for a flowchart of this process.) It is important to have agreed-on methods by which to judge the attainment of competencies. This process of generating an integrated curriculum is often done in conjunction with a district's comprehensive strategic plan.

The next phase in curriculum development involves deciding how to help students meet the competencies. Professional school counselors and teachers sometimes create their own curriculum materials and sometimes use commercially available curricula. As a result of the NCLB legislation, there has been a recent emphasis in schools on using commercial curricula for which research evidence of effectiveness exists. Using these *evidence-based* curricular materials supports the efficacy of professional school counselors' classroom interventions. When schools carefully adopt a commercial curriculum that matches their outcomes and implement it in a pedagogically sound manner, students are then in a position to achieve the desired competencies. In their study of the national trends related to professional school counselors and curriculum materials, Rowley, Stroh, and Sink (2005) surveyed school districts in 12 states about the type of curricular materials they use in implementing their guidance curriculum. Although the authors do not suggest which are the best or most effective

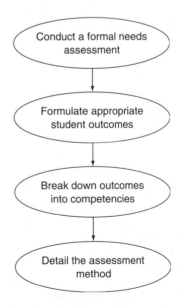

FIGURE 9.3   Steps involved in crafting a curriculum.

published curricular resources, they do provide a table that lists over 20 curricular materials currently being used by those school counselors surveyed. For a description of several commonly used commercially available curricula, see Table 9.2. Classroom guidance lesson plans can also be found in journal articles, in books, and on the Internet. Curriculum design and the creation of units and lessons will be discussed in the next section.

TABLE 9.2 Examples of Commercially Available Curricula

Second Step: Violence Prevention Curriculum. This program teaches social and emotional skills to prevent violence. The curriculum is easy to use and is unique in that it has parent education components. This research-based program focuses on the three essential competencies that students need—empathy, impulse control and problem solving, and anger management. *Second Step* is a well-articulated curriculum spanning grades pre-K–9. It is one of the very few programs that meet the strict criteria of an "evidence-based" program (Poynton & Dimmitt, 2004).

Student Success Skills (SSS). This program is designed for students in grades 4–9 includes group counseling and a classroom guidance curriculum that helps students develop cognitive, social, and self-management skills. Also an evidence-based program, *SSS* has been shown in recent studies to improve the math, reading, and social skills of students participating in the program (Brigman & Campbell, 2003).

DUSO (Developing Understanding of Self and Others). DUSO focuses on personal/social development. It is designed to help children in the primary grades understand social and emotional behavior.

Its goal is to assist children in developing positive self-images, in becoming more aware of the relationship between themselves and other people, and in recognizing their own needs and goals. *DUSO* uses listening, discussion, and dramatic play to help students focus on feelings, communication, and problem solving. Professional school counselors conduct activities with students that include stories, guided fantasies, puppetry, role plays, and music.

Kelly Bear Programs.

Violence Prevention: A skills-based, video/DVD series for grades pre-K–3 that focuses on themes of bullying, resolving disputes, and controlling oneself.

Drug Awareness and Prevention Program (DAPP): Also for grades pre-K–3, an eight-session program that promotes self-understanding, respect, empathy, positive behaviors, coping skills, resiliency, social competence, responsibility, problem-solving skills, refusal skills, and healthy living habits.

Character and Resiliency Education Skills (CARES): This program seeks to prevent problem behaviors by promoting self-awareness, social competence, empathy and kindness toward others, problem-solving and anger-management skills, healthy living choices, resiliency, refusal skills, and personal safety.

Educators for Social Responsibility (ESR) Programs.

Conflict Resolution in the Middle School: This program presents developmentally appropriate classroom activities to help students to handle conflict effectively. Skills are developed in areas such as active listening, perspective taking, negotiation, and mediation. Discussion, role plays, and journal writing are employed to assist students in increasing their understanding of conflict, learning about conflict escalation and deescalation, and exploring connections between diversity and conflicts.

Creative Conflict Resolution: This program provides elementary school teachers and counselors with ideas for responding to everyday classroom conflicts. A goal is to help teachers to turn conflict into productive opportunity.

Grounded in a theory of "peacemaking," ESR's programs are designed to help students to deal nonviolently and constructively with anger, fear, aggression, and prejudice. ESR's elementary and middle school programs are focused on addressing conflict systemwide. In implementing these programs, professional school counselors work primarily as consultants to teachers and staff.

Here's Looking at You, 2000®. This program was designed to meet students' needs in drug education, is popular with counselors, and is often used in conjunction with Drug-Free Schools grants. The lessons in *Here's Looking at You, 2000*® seek to promote protective factors and to establish positive norms among students. A major thrust of the curriculum is to foster positive attitudes and behaviors among students and the school community. The curriculum features skills for developing self-control, resisting pressure, making friends, and making and sticking to positive decisions. *Here's Looking at You, 2000*® makes use of cooperative learning teams. Cooperative learning fosters positive interdependence, individual accountability, and face-to-face interaction.

Skillstreaming. This psychoeducational program focuses on teaching students prosocial behavior through direct instruction in social skills. It uses the teaching procedures of modeling, role playing, feedback, and transfer to help students develop these skills. Separate curricula have been developed for children of preschool age, elementary age, and adolescents. In contrast to some other programs, which seek broad, self-esteem-enhancing outcomes, *Skillstreaming* teaches specific skills such as asking permission, using self-control, accepting "no," and accepting a compliment (McGinnis & Goldstein, 1997; A. P. Goldstein & McGinnis, 1997).

The PASSPORT Program: A Journey Through Emotional, Social, Cognitive, and Self-Development. This program, authored by Ann Vernon, is a prevention curriculum dedicated to helping students develop self-acceptance, build healthy relationships, solve problems, and make decisions effectively. This program integrates theory and a developmental understanding of school-age children and uses them as a foundation to teach children how to act in their own and others' best interests (Hawes, 2000; Vernon, 1998).

National Education Association (NEA) (1–800–229–4200).

> *Flirting or Hurting? A Teacher's Guide on Student-to-Student Sexual Harassment in Schools (Grades 6 Through 12)* **by Nan Stein and Lisa Sjostrom.**
>
> *Bullyproof: A Teacher's Guide on Teasing and Bullying for Use with Fourth and Fifth Grade Students* by Nan Stein and Lisa Sjostrom.

CREATING UNITS AND LESSONS

Scope and Sequence

To help students achieve the academic, career, and personal /social outcomes determined by leadership and advisory teams, professional school counselors must develop a comprehensive curriculum within their school or district. The breadth or content of the program provides its scope. Ideally, this is a pre-K–12 effort; however, in districts, it is done by building level. In these cases, elementary counselors develop the elementary curriculum, middle school counselors develop their curriculum, and high school counselors put together the secondary curriculum.

In curriculum design, it is important to ensure that grade-level learning is neither isolated from other grade levels nor redundant. This vertical articulation provides for a schoolwide or districtwide curriculum that builds skills and competencies sequentially (Kellough & Roberts, 2002). For professional school counselors, horizontal articulation is also important, particularly in schools where much of the curriculum is taught either solely by teachers or by professional school counselors and teachers collaboratively. Horizontal articulation establishes the connection between the content of the counseling curriculum and the content in other subject areas. For instance, social studies in the seventh grade might contain a unit on the medieval period, including the conflicts and battles of the time. Horizontal articulation suggests that professional school counselors weave their conflict resolution curriculum in with the social studies curriculum (and perhaps English and other curricula) for a more integrated learning experience for students.

Conceptualizing a Unit

How professional school counselors conceptualize a curriculum unit depends on the model of curriculum implementation. As suggested, professional school counselors implement their curriculum either by teaching directly or by working collaboratively with teachers to present units and lessons together. A third model of implementation involves professional school counselors consulting with teachers and having teachers teach the lessons and units.

Professional school counselors who directly teach conflict resolution might choose to adopt a schoolwide approach to implementing this competency by using commercially available, evidence-based curriculum materials. Professional school counselors using a locally developed curriculum need to understand how to create and teach high-quality units and lessons. Many elementary counselors spend a set amount of time in different grade levels; it is not uncommon for professional school counselors to devise a curriculum unit that includes one lesson per week spanning eight weeks. In this case, the professional school counselor devises eight lessons in one general competency area, with one or more student outcomes being the anticipated result. The process of creating and teaching units and lessons is an important part of the role of the professional school counselor as educator.

In many schools, particularly at the elementary level, the professional school counselor's role in developmental classroom guidance includes itinerant, classroom-to-classroom teaching. It is important for professional school counselors to organize and present their units and lessons in classrooms in a manner that is coherent, clear, and effective. To achieve this, professional school counselors engage in a level of instructional planning equivalent to that which teachers use.

LEARNING CONSIDERATIONS FOR PLANNING UNITS AND LESSONS

Professional school counselors see students as learners in a holistic sense. According to H. Gardner's (1999) theory of multiple intelligences, there are eight intelligences: linguistic, logical-mathematical, spatial, bodily-kinesthetic, naturalist, musical, intelligence about other people (interpersonal), and intelligence about ourselves (intrapersonal). Students may display significant cognitive strengths and weaknesses in one or more of these intelligences (see Table 9.3). Understanding that students enter the learning environment with multiple cognitive strengths and weaknesses implies that instruction as well as assessment should be varied. At a minimum, this suggests that instruction should seek to help students develop in cognitive, affective, and psychomotor-kinesthetic-behavioral domains. Although these domains have much overlap and are not entirely discrete, the following discussion highlights their focus.

In the cognitive domain, there are six levels or categories of cognitive understanding (Kellough & Roberts, 2002): knowledge, comprehension, application, analysis, synthesis, and evaluation. Within a lesson plan or unit, it is important to teach to and evaluate within several of the categories of the cognitive domain. In teaching conflict resolution, it might be helpful for students to have knowledge of the terms and words that describe the process of resolving conflict peacefully. Further, professional school counselors need to be sure that students show they understand the material. The domain of comprehension attends to this and is ascertained by having students explain or describe what they have learned. As an example of these first two levels, professional school counselors might devise a game-show activity to help students learn and show their understanding of terms such as *deescalation* and *negotiation*. Applying the knowledge (application) can be taught by devising scenarios and having students be able to choose which particular conflict resolution strategy might best be applied in a given situation.

In other lessons in the unit, a professional school counselor might want students to analyze the relationships among violence, bullying, and conflict by discussing and hypothesizing how to manage real conflicts that arise on the playground. A synthesis-level objective of a conflict resolution unit might have students combine knowledge learned about a specific conflict in social studies class—for example,

---

TABLE 9.3 **Gardner's Multiple Intelligences Summarized**

Linguistic intelligence involves the ability to use language (native or otherwise) to express ideas and understand the ideas of others. Poets, writers, orators, speakers, and lawyers rely on linguistic intelligence.

Logical-mathematical intelligence requires an understanding of the underlying principles of some kind of causal system or the manipulation of numbers, quantities, and operations. Scientists, logicians, engineers, and mathematicians rely on logical-mathematical intelligence.

Spatial intelligence involves the ability to represent the spatial world internally in your mind. It is important in the arts and sciences. For example, if you possess spatial intelligence and are artistic, you may gravitate toward painting, sculpture, or architecture. Surgeons, topologists, navigators, and chess players rely on spatial intelligence.

Musical intelligence involves the capacity to think musically—so much so that the music is omnipresent and free flowing. The musically intelligent are able to hear patterns, recognize them, remember them, and perhaps manipulate them.

Bodily-kinesthetic intelligence involves the ability to use your whole body or parts of your body (e.g., hands, fingers, arms) to solve complex motor problems. Such activities may involve making something or performing some action or production. Athletes, carpenters, dancers, and actors rely on bodily-kinesthetic intelligence.

Interpersonal intelligence involves understanding how to get along with other people and how to solve problems of an interpersonal nature. Teachers, clinicians, salespersons, and politicians rely on interpersonal intelligence.

Intrapersonal intelligence involves having an understanding of yourself. If you possess intrapersonal intelligence, you know what you can and cannot do and when to ask for help. You can control impulses and are self-motivated.

Naturalist intelligence involves the human ability to discriminate among and classify living things (e.g., plants, animals) and features of the natural world (e.g., clouds, rock configurations). Hunters, farmers, botanists, and chefs rely on naturalist intelligence. Children also frequently display these capabilities in classification hobbies.

the Revolutionary War—and have them act out a mediation session between the British and Americans. The final level of cognitive skill, evaluation, might be addressed by having a "courtroom" in which students sit on panels as "judges" and evaluate the effectiveness of the mediation sessions using the knowledge they have gained. All of these cognitive levels of understanding might be included as a professional school counselor plans a unit on conflict resolution.

Cognitive learning is important, but it is not the sole means through which a holistic understanding of curricular areas occurs. The affective domain is also an important aspect of instruction. It focuses on using and developing intra- and interpersonal intelligences. While some consider teaching for affective understanding more difficult to conceptualize and assess, Krathwohl, Bloom, and Masia (1964) developed a system of affective understanding that is modeled after Bloom's cognitive levels. In this system, understanding is organized on a continuum that ranges from surface-level learning to those types of affective understanding that reflect the personal internalization of values.

The five levels of affective learning are receiving, responding, valuing, organizing, and internalizing. At the receiving level, students might simply be aware of the affective aspect of a lesson. For instance, some students who were observing the courtroom scene might listen attentively to the proceedings; they are receiving affective instruction. At the responding level, we may ask the observing group to discuss how they believe the "actors" felt during their role play. The valuing domain is critical in affective learning. Again, using the example of conflict resolution, professional school counselors might focus on valuing by asking students how they feel when they are called belittling names by their peers. As such, this group brainstorming activity would be addressing students' values regarding respect. After several lessons, professional school counselors might ask students to monitor their own and others' behaviors regarding conflict, thus providing a gauge for ascertaining the depth to which affective learning (and ultimately behavioral change) has occurred.

The fourth and fifth levels in the affective domain are typically longer-term goals and may, in fact, be ultimate standards or outcomes within a comprehensive program. Nevertheless, lessons often address these levels. For instance, in the organizing domain, teaching typically refers to conceptualizing and arranging values. In our example of the Revolutionary War and conflict resolution, professional school counselors and teachers can engage students in understanding and organizing their values relative to peaceful conflict resolution and notions of liberty and fairness. Finally, we want lessons to help students internalize their beliefs and develop consistency between their beliefs and their actions. This can be done by teachers and professional school counselors during regular class meetings when students discuss and process the events of the day. (For an in-depth discussion of a classroom and schoolwide approach to developing interpersonal values and respect, see Charney, 2002.)

The final broad area of learning is the psychomotor-kinesthetic-behavioral domain. Harrow (1972) discussed four areas within this hierarchy: moving, manipulating, communicating, and creating. Because they concern skill development in areas of gross- and fine-motor coordination, moving and manipulating focus on areas of learning that are typically less relevant to the professional school counselor's curriculum. Communicating and creating are the domains that are the most salient. For instance, in a lesson on conflict resolution, students might improve their communication skills and be able to create solutions to problems that have led to conflict in the past.

In a well-designed unit, professional school counselors attend to learning and development in the cognitive, affective, and psychomotor-kinesthetic-behavioral domains. To ensure adequate attention to the levels of learning and development, professional school counselors create learning objectives for each of the instructional activities.

Learning Objectives

When the counseling curriculum is competency-based, it is necessary that the lessons result in measurable outcomes. One way to ensure attainment of outcomes is to write learning objectives for each lesson. Learning objectives focus the professional school counselor on the desired outcomes of students' participation in the lesson. To address the holistic needs relative to student development, it is helpful for professional school counselors to write objectives that are reflective of the cognitive, affective, and psychomotor-kinesthetic-behavioral domains of instruction. With this focus in mind, consider the components of thoroughly conceived and written learning objectives.

There are four parts that make up measurable learning objectives, commonly referred to as the ABCDs of learning objectives (Erford, 2010). First, the audience (A) for whom the objective is intended needs to be stated. In most cases, this is the student, although it could be the learning group or the whole class. It is not uncommon for many learning objectives to include the phrase "The student will be able to. . . ."

Second, the expected behavior (B) needs to be stated clearly. These behaviors are typically stated using descriptive verbs that address the cognitive, affective, or psychomotor-kinesthetic-behavioral outcome around which the lesson is structured. Using the example of conflict resolution again, one cognitive domain outcome might read, in part, "The student will be able to identify behaviors that lead to conflict." A learning objective that addresses affective learning at the valuing level, yet is still written in behavioral terms, might state, "Students will voice their beliefs regarding. . . ." Finally, a learning objective might be more oriented toward psychomotor-kinesthetic-behavioral outcomes. An example of this might be "The class will create a process allowing students to solve conflicts without teacher intervention."

In addition to denoting the audience and the expected measurable outcomes, learning objectives typically include the conditions (C) under which the learning will occur and be observed. This third component specifies when or how the intended behavior will be measured. One of the examples with the inclusion of this third component might read, "After observing role plays, the student will be able to identify behaviors that lead to conflict."

The fourth and final component of a well-written learning objective is the degree (D) of the expected performance, or how frequently students will need to exhibit the behavior for the objective to be considered met. If there were three role plays and students successfully identified the behaviors in two of the three, the professional school counselor needs to know whether that level of performance is considered successful. With the inclusion of the level of expected performance, the complete learning objective would read, "After observing three role plays, the student will be able to identify behaviors that lead to conflict in at least two of the three scenarios."

If students do not achieve the competency or do not achieve it at the specified rate, then the professional school counselor may decide to design a new learning activity to reach the desired outcome. See Table 9.4 for a summary of the ABCDs of learning objectives with examples from the cognitive, affective, and psychomotor-kinesthetic-behavioral domains.

TABLE 9.4   Components of Measurable Learning Objectives by Learning Domain

	Cognitive Domain	Affective Domain	Psychomotor-Kinesthetic-Behavioral Domain
Component A **Audience:** Specify the audience for whom the objective is intended	The student will . . .	Students will . . .	The class will . . .
Component B **Behavior:** Specify the expected behaviors	The student will be able to identify behaviors that lead to conflict.	Students will voice their beliefs regarding respectful behavior.	The class will create a process allowing students to solve conflicts without teacher intervention.
Component C **Conditions:** Specify the conditions under which learning will occur and be observed. How will the intended behavior be measured?	After observing role plays, the student will be able to identify behaviors that lead to conflict.	After discussing the components of respect, students will voice their beliefs regarding respectful behavior.	At the end of four meetings on playground behavior, the class will create a process allowing students to solve conflicts without teacher intervention.
Component D **Degree:** Specify the expected degree of performance. Specify what is acceptable performance.	After observing three role plays, the student will be able to identify behaviors that lead to conflict in at least two of the three scenarios.	After discussing the components of respect, at least two-thirds of the students in the class will voice their beliefs regarding respectful behavior, including both significant personal experience and considerable content from the discussion.	At the end of four meetings on playground behavior, the class will create a process allowing students to solve conflicts without teacher intervention. If it reduces the need for teacher intervention by 25%, it will be considered successful.

CONSTRUCTING DEVELOPMENTAL LESSONS AND ACTIVITIES

Lessons can be conceptualized as having three distinct parts: an introduction, the developmental activities of the lesson, and the conclusion. A well-designed lesson increases the likelihood that students will invest their energies in learning the material and that they will learn what is being taught. Further, a pedagogically sound lesson captures students' interest and allows them to extend their knowledge and competency.

Introducing Lessons

There are two important aspects to introducing a lesson to students. One is to communicate to students an overview and the overall objective of the lesson. When professional school counselors do this clearly, students develop an itinerary of their learning and know what the expected learning objectives will be. The second important aspect of lesson introduction is to help students to understand that they already know something about the topic at hand and that, during the lesson, they will be working to extend their knowledge or skills (Saphier, King, & D'Auria, 2006).

Typically, students already know some information about the areas being taught. For instance, a school counseling program may be working toward the outcome that "Students will acquire skills to investigate the world of work in relation to knowledge of self and to make informed career choices" (C. Campbell & Dahir, 1997, p. 25). Since this is a program outcome or standard, learning will have been developed at various checkpoints throughout previous grades. Therefore, it is likely that students will already have some knowledge of the required skills, as well as how to go about making informed choices. In fact, if we have vertically articulated the curriculum properly, the counseling curriculum builds in a sequential and logical manner. Let us posit that the specific eighth-grade benchmark is that students will understand their interests, motivations, skills, and abilities. Prior to the eighth grade, students likely will have had some curricular and personal experiences supportive of the benchmark. Activating this previous knowledge helps provide the groundwork for a productive educational session.

Activating previous knowledge helps students orient themselves to the lesson. It shows them that they already know some important information and that the topic at hand is not entirely new. Done well, it also motivates students and provides a continued rationale for their efforts. There are several ways school counselors can activate students' previous knowledge and, in so doing, effectively introduce a lesson.

One method frequently used is semantic mapping (Hedrick, Harmon, & Wood, 2008). In a semantic mapping exercise for the career development example, the professional school counselor might ask the class, "What motivates people to receive good grades or work hard?" The professional school counselor might list the students' responses in logical categories suggesting internal motivators (wanting to learn the material, being interested in it) and external motivators (making the honor roll, being rewarded by parents). The professional school counselor can show students what they already know on the topic and get them actively involved in the lesson.

Developmental Activities

Once students' previous knowledge has been activated and they have been oriented to the topic, they are ready to engage in the learning activity. Learning activities are student experiences that facilitate mastery of the lesson's objectives. It is essential to clearly delineate learning objectives because understanding what students are to learn not only helps professional school counselors design lessons that are most likely to accomplish that end, but also allows them to conduct meaningful assessment. There are two broad areas of understanding that can help guide professional school counselors as they design learning activities: multiple intelligences and level of activity.

As discussed earlier, students can be considered to have multiple intelligences. Given this theory, professional school counselors make efforts to structure and implement their lessons to draw on the variety of cognitive strengths and weaknesses that students may have. Schools have traditionally focused on fostering linguistic or verbal learning. For instance, both traditional, teacher-led discussions and most writing assignments draw heavily on linguistic intelligence. Although professional school counselors will want to teach to and assess students' language and verbal skills, they have a broad understanding of intelligence and design lessons likely to draw on a variety of student strengths. For instance, learning can both occur and be expressed through music. Tapping into students' musical intelligence might involve having students create a song, rap, or chant that describes the steps involved in problem solving or conflict resolution (Hoffman, 2002). Other activities can involve drawing on knowledge of self (intrapersonal intelligence). In a lesson on feelings, this intrapersonal approach might ask students to reflect on times they were sad. Interpersonal intelligence is activated when professional school counselors ask groups to work together to come up with a solution to a problem. Other avenues for learning include artistic, spatial, naturalist, logical-mathematical, and kinesthetic modalities. To access these avenues, professional school counselors often use role plays and art during lessons. Professional school counselors design a variety of activities that draw on the multiple intelligences students may possess in order to teach and assess the learning objectives.

In a similar vein, there are many types of teaching strategies relative to student activity level. These range from the teacher or expert at the front of the class to those strategies that keep all students actively involved in their learning. Generally, it is better pedagogically for the professional school counselor to keep students active as opposed to passive. This is not to suggest that professional school counselors never stand before a group of students and explain information. In fact, this may be an important aspect of some lessons. Still, this type of learning experience limits student participation to only one sense—auditory learning. Professional school counselors can increase the students' experience to two senses by adding visual activities (e.g., pictures, videos, and overheads) to their presentations (Kellough & Roberts, 2002). Although the addition of visual cues does not amount to what is considered active learning, it involves the student in more than merely listening to the teacher or counselor. The more active levels of student involvement have students simulating or engaging in direct experiences.

Using an example of teaching conflict resolution, professional school counselors might have students role-play conflict deescalation strategies to provide a simulated experience. In a lesson on connecting interests to career clusters, all students might take a computerized interest assessment individually and then work with a partner or in small groups to investigate several career clusters. Or all students might play a classroom game such as the Real Game (Jarvis, 2004) or the Real Deal (Ad Council, 2000). Many teachers and professional school counselors use cooperative learning groups (CLGs) to foster students' active learning. In CLGs, students work together, each having a specific role within the group (Kellough & Roberts, 2002). Finally, when teachers and professional school counselors use peer mediators to help resolve conflict, the type of learning students experience is direct and reflects real life. Professional school counselors are aware of the various levels of learning and strive to help students be as active as possible during lessons and units.

Conclusion, Assessment, and Follow-Up

On completing the planned developmental activities, it is important to reinforce and conclude the session's learning by summarizing the essential points of the lesson. An experienced classroom educator will usually plan for at least two to five minutes to successfully summarize and end the lesson. Many professional school counselors also prefer to have the students contribute to the summary as a way of promoting an additional learning experience and testing students' comprehension of and knowledge gained from the day's lesson. It is generally most efficient to begin the summary by restating the lesson's objective(s) and briefly reviewing how the lesson built on previously developed skills and knowledge. Next, the professional school counselor should strive to encapsulate the content of the developmental activities, highlighting the important content and experiences. Finally, experienced professional school counselors should help students to generalize the classroom experience to real-world experiences by asking students how the lessons learned can apply to life outside of the classroom or to their short- or long-term academic, career, or personal/social goals. Skilled classroom educators know that this generalization process, accompanied by real-life homework assignments, is the best way to get students to remember the classroom-based learning and transfer it to daily life.

Perhaps the most essential and overlooked part of guidance instruction is the assessment of learning objectives. For some reason, many professional school counselors develop the self-defeating perception or attitude that "What we do can't be measured or evaluated." Nothing could be farther from the truth. In fact, it is this errant attitude that has put the profession in jeopardy in this age of educational accountability and reform. Can you imagine a math, science, reading, or social studies teacher explaining that he or she can't measure what children have learned or can do as a result of his or her instruction? It sounds equally ridiculous when principals or other stakeholders hear this from professional school counselors! Of course, effective school counselors produce measurable gains in students' learning. The key, however, is to plan for assessment when the learning objectives are written, rather than after the lesson is taught.

Well-written learning objectives are the key to effective instruction and outcomes. If a learning objective is written in accordance with the model in Table 9.4, assessment is made simple because the audience, expected behavior, measurement parameters, and expected level of performance have already been specified. At this point, all the professional school counselor needs to do is collect the data as specified in the learning objective and apply the specified criterion. For example, consider the cognitive domain learning objective shown in Table 9.4: "After observing three role plays, the student will be able to identify behaviors that lead to conflict in at least two of the three scenarios." To document that the learning objective has been met, the professional school counselor must design three role plays and write out a list of behaviors leading to conflict that the student may observe. Then the scenarios are presented one at a time, and the student is asked to write at least one observable behavior for each scenario that led to the conflict. If the student is able to discern behaviors that were on the list compiled by the professional school counselor for two of the three scenarios, the learning objective has been met.

Of course, one of the real values of assessment is that it helps to inform our practice, and another is that it helps to demonstrate accountability. If assessment of learning objectives indicates student nonmastery, then it follows that the instructional process must be analyzed and improved. Were the objectives clearly stated? Were the expectations too high? Were the activities ineffective? Were the assessment criteria and strategies inappropriate? Each of these steps in the process must be visited, analyzed, and, if necessary, refined or redesigned before the lesson is repeated. Too often in education—and school counseling—professionals continue to implement ineffective curricula and even blame the unsuccessful students. Professional school counselors, as educators, must look to the processes and strategies implemented and further tailor them to the needs of the students.

Chapter 13 discusses outcome assessment procedures and program evaluation in detail, stating that those types of programmatic assessments should be conducted systematically. The assessment of learning objectives at the classroom level is just as important. Logically, if a professional school counselor successfully implements a guidance curriculum as documented by assessments of learning objectives at the classroom level and if these objectives directly relate to the school counseling program's outcomes, then the evaluation of the program will also result in success.

Finally, follow-up is an essential part of the learning process frequently disregarded by professional school counselors. Why should busy professional school counselors "waste time" on follow-up? After all, when someone has been "fixed," that's the end of the story, isn't it? Not at all! Many children require booster sessions to review and extend what they have learned. Regarding personal/social and mental health interventions, recidivism, or slipping back into old habits and behaviors, is a huge problem. If nothing else, simply checking back with students within a few days or weeks after a lesson or intervention can bolster their learning and behavioral change. Another part of follow-up may involve follow-up assessment procedures to ensure that changes in learning and behavior are continuing. Such valuable information helps the professional school counselor and classroom teacher to be responsive to potential recidivism and act accordingly.

Follow-up is a way of checking progress and shoring up support for students. It is arguably the most important, most cost-effective step in the process because it prevents all previous instructional or intervention time and effort from being wasted! In other words, choosing not to spend a few minutes on follow-up could lead to hours of wasted instructional or intervention effort. Figure 9.4 presents a flowchart of the process for constructing developmental lessons and activities.

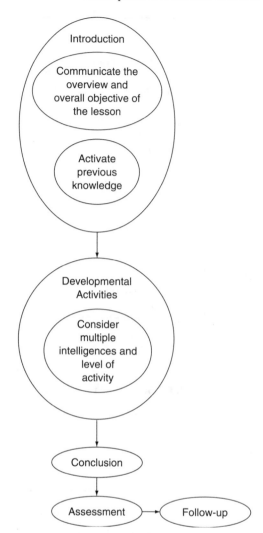

FIGURE 9.4 Constructing developmental lessons and activities.

Professional school counselors, as educators, are knowledgeable about how students learn. They are aware of students' multiple intelligences and design learning activities that attend to the development of the whole student. Lessons featuring cognitive learning are commonly taught alongside lessons that address both affective and psychomotor-kinesthetic-behavioral domains of learning. Professional school counselors design units and lessons for students at all grade levels—they carefully plan what the objectives are for the lesson and how they will both teach the lesson and evaluate learning. Figure 9.5 shows a planning outline for professional school counselors to use as they prepare their lessons. Figures 9.6, 9.7, and 9.8 show lessons and examples of counseling curriculum at the elementary, middle, and high school levels, respectively.

Title of Lesson:

Outcome or Standard:

Competency:

Learning Objective(s):

Materials:

Developmental Learning Activities:

   Introduction:

   Activity:

   Conclusion:

Assessment/Evaluation:

Follow-up:

FIGURE 9.5 Outline for effective lesson plans.

Title of Lesson: Understanding your multiple intelligences

Outcome or Standard: Students will acquire the attitudes, knowledge, and skillsthatcontribute to effective learning in school and across the life span. (C.Campbell & Dahir, 1997).

Competency: (a)Identify attitudes and behaviors that lead to successful learning; (b)Apply knowledge of learning styles to positively influence school performance.

LearningObjective: After completing the Teele Multiple Intelligences Inventory (Teele, 2000), 90% of fifth-grade students will be able to identify their top three intelligence strengths as determined by personal ratings.

Materials: One copy of the Teele Multiple Intelligences Inventory and a pencil for each student.

Developmental Learning Activities:

   Introduction: Begin with a discussion of how every student has different learning strengths and weaknesses. For example, some students would rather work in groups, others alone. Some like to think out loud, others in silence. Some like to draw a picture of how something works, others would rather act it out. Then solicit several examples of learning strengths from students (thereby connecting the current objective to previous knowledge).

FIGURE 9.6 Example of an elementary school lesson.

Activity: Pass out one copy of the Teele Multiple Intelligences Inventory to each student and read the directions for completing the inventory aloud. Because the inventory is pictorial, no reading or language skills are required. After the directions are completed, allow 15 minutes for students to complete the inventory. When time is up, explain how to transfer student responses to the scoring form and "score" the inventory. After students have scored their own inventories, have them write the titles of their top three categories (intelligences) on a sheet of paper. Use Table 8.3 of this text (Gardner's multiple intelligences) to explain to students the skills associated with their top three intelligences.

Conclusion: Next, lead students in a discussion of their interests and skills relate to each intelligence on their list and challenge students to think about what they have done to develop these abilities, and what they could do to develop these abilities to even higher levels.

Assessment/Evaluation: At the end of the session, collect student papers containing their top three intelligences and determine the percentage of fifth-grade students who have determined their top three choices. If 90% of the students complied, the objective has been met.

Follow-up: In a future session, review Gardner's eight intelligences and ask students to share events when they were using these abilities to master academic content

---

Title: Understanding Sexual Harassment

Outcome or Standard: Students will understand safety and survival skills (ASCA National Standard C within "Personal/Social Development"; C. Campbell & Dahir, 1997).

Competency: Students will learn about the relation between rules, laws, safety, and the protection of individual rights.

Learning Objective(s):

1. After group discussion and counselor-led instruction, all students will be able to identify the correct definition of sexual harassment. (This is basic *knowledge* within the cognitive domain of understanding.)
2. Subsequent to group discussions, all students will describe incidences of sexual harassment they have seen or experienced and how these incidences made them feel. (This objective supports the development of the *responding* level of affective learning.)

(Continued)

FIGURE 9.7 Example of a middle school lesson.

Materials: Large-sized paper, markers.

Developmental Learning Activity:

Introduction: The professional school counselor begins by initiating a discussion with students about respectful behavior. (This serves as groundwork to connect the current learning objectives to previous knowledge.) The professional school counselor then asks the students to brainstorm in pairs about how respectful behavior is sometimes codified in rules and laws. Pairs then share ideas with the larger group and the counselor writes the ideas on the board. (Make a connection to previous knowledge, this time regarding social studies. The activity of having students work in pairs increases the level of student involvement and is called Think, Pair, Share [Saphier & Gower, 1997].)

Activity:

1. The counselor asks students to get into groups by gender, i.e., all male and all female groups. Their task is to brainstorm examples of disrespectful behavior they have seen or heard that is directed toward one gender or the other.
2. Groups write their experiences on large sheets of paper. Then representatives from the groups tape the sheets of paper on the walls.
3. The counselor discusses the students' experiences, paying particular attention to how it feels or might feel to be the recipient of such behavior.
4. Finally, using the concepts generated, the counselor shares with the students the definition of sexual harassment (unwanted behavior directed at a person based on his or her gender). The counselor can provide examples of sexual harassment that the students have not generated (for example, see Strauss, 1994, for a thorough listing of commonly reported types of student-to-student sexual harassment).

Conclusion: The professional school counselor asks students to share ideas about how the knowledge they have generated can be used to better their environment. (This is also a lead into the follow-up activity below.)

Assessment/Evalution:

1. At the beginning of the next session when the professional school counselor meets with the group, he or she reads the students the three possible definitions of sexual harassment. Students vote by a show of hands which definition is correct. (This attends to the first learning objective and provides a time lapse so that the counselor can ascertain whether students retained the information.)
2. Accomplishment of the second learning objective is completed by the lesson itself. By observing the group's process and outcome (as demonstrated by students' verbal and written responses), the professional school counselor determines the degree to which the objective is met.

Follow-up:

In a subsequent session, the counselor has students work in mixed-gender groups to create a system of classroom and school norms regarding sexual harassment.

Title: Career Exploration and Postsecondary Planning

Outcome or Standard: Students will acquire the skills to investigate the world of work in relation to knowledge of self and to make informed career decisions (ASCA National Standard A within "Career Development"; Campbell & Dahir, 1997).

Competencies:

1. Students will develop skills to locate, evaluate, and interpret career information.
2. Students will learn about the variety of traditional and nontraditional occupations.
3. Students will develop an awareness of personal abilities, skills, interests, and motivations.

Learning Objective(s):

Using the Internet, students will be able to locate self-assessments, career assessment materials, career information, and postsecondary options in sufficient quantity and quality so that they are able to write a paper about their postsecondary choices (knowledge, application, analysis, and synthesis).

Materials: Computer lab with access to the Internet, a list of Web sites.

Developmental Learning Activities:

Introduction: The counselor introduces the topic of postsecondary planning and the importance of self-assessment in career decision making. The counselor gives an overview of the use of assessment materials and their strengths and limitations in helping select appropriate postsecondary options.

Activity:

1. Students meet in groups of four to discuss the types of postsecondary options and career choices in which they may already be interested. Each student generates at least three postsecondary options.
2. In a computer lab at a computer, students begin by taking an interest inventory online. The counselor should provide students with some Web site addresses where they can access a career quiz.
3. Students identify 10–12 careers that seem interesting and look for other relevant Web sites to explore these occupations (such as Occupational Outlook Handbook: http://stats.bls.gov/oco/).

Conclusion: Students share their experience and relate what they found to be surprising, or what reinforced earlier beliefs about themselves.

Assessment/Evaluation: In collaboration with the English teacher, students are asked to prepare a paper about their postsecondary choices and the developmental steps they could take to reach their goals. (This analysis-synthesis-level assessment is in the cognitive domain. If students accomplish this higher level task, they will have shown that they also mastered the knowledge and application-level objectives.)

Follow-up: The professional school counselor meets with the English teacher to discuss future classroom guidance units to bolster student learning and decision making in the career domain. In addition, the professional school counselor offers groups based on postsecondary options (such as a 4-year college group, a 2-year college group, a job-entry group, a military group) that will meet on a regular basis and address barriers and other issues relevant to postsecondary and career options.

FIGURE 9.8   Example of a high school lesson.

As I enthusiastically entered my first year as a middle school counselor determined to deliver an effective program, I quickly realized the many different perceptions the education community holds regarding the role of a professional school counselor. Surprisingly, few were related to school counselors delivering a meaningful program to support student development and achievement. School counselors historically provided response services focused on helping students individually. Over the years, school counselors have been working hard to change these perceptions and have developed programs that reach many students and are preventive in nature.

Some contemporary programs focus on targeted interventions for various student groups within a school. However, many of these programs are not data driven and lack methods to measure the program's success. More importantly, what about all of the students who are not in targeted student groups and therefore do not benefit from the school counseling services? It is now time to take these programs to the next level and begin implementing comprehensive, developmental school counseling programs that reach every student.

As part of a five-person dynamic school counseling team, I have had the experience of delivering a comprehensive, developmental school counseling middle school program to approximately 1,400 students per year. The program was designated a Recognized ASCA Model Program (RAMP) in 2008 by the American School Counselor Association. There are many benefits to running a program that is aligned with a nationally recognized model. The program clearly identifies and targets all stakeholders, which include students, their families, and teachers. The program goals are aligned with the overall mission of the school and address the academic, social/emotional, and career needs of all our students. The program provides direct services to students, including individual counseling, group counseling, and classroom guidance activities. Equally important, the program provides indirect services, which include regular parent communication via conferences, phone calls, and email, as well as support to all teachers when counselors attend interdisciplinary meetings and attendance meetings and respond to teachers' concerns about individual students in a timely manner. The program is data driven and is formally evaluated each year. When specific interventions or parts of the program are determined to no longer be effective, new interventions are properly researched and implemented. In addition, the program has a Guidance Advisory Council made up of counselors and teachers who meet on a monthly basis to collaboratively identify areas that need improvement and work together toward making the program better.

One of the challenges of running a comprehensive, developmental school counseling program is making sure that the program continues to run effectively every day regardless of expectations to participate in any noncounseling duties, mandatory meetings, or statewide testing. As a professional school counselor, I know that these challenges can be overcome because the school community can vividly see how students are different as a result of this program. As a relatively new school counselor, delivering a sound program has helped me to increase my skills and knowledge of school counseling and has allowed me to take part in the overall school community effort to link professional school counselors with running programs that support and enhance learning.

Source: Tracy MacDonald, Professional School Counselor, Chesapeake Bay Middle School, Anne Arundel County Public Schools, Maryland

Summary/Conclusion

Professional school counselors provide direct services to students through a number of roles, including that of classroom educator. Professional school counselors spend time in classrooms teaching developmental lessons to students. Through these lessons, counselors seek to implement a comprehensive, developmental curriculum made up of standards from the academic, career, and personal/social domains. The ultimate goal of the professional school counselor in this role is for all students to achieve the developmental outcomes that the local school counseling leadership team deems essential.

To reach this important goal, professional school counselors work with teachers to integrate the counseling curriculum with other components in the school's curriculum. Professional school counselors ensure that all students receive instruction in the counseling curriculum by teachers, by teacher–counselor teams, or by professional school counselors themselves. When professional school counselors deliver the curriculum themselves, they strive to maintain the high standards of the teaching profession. This means that they manage the classroom well and create positive learning environments for students. Most important, professional school counselors know how to design effective, interesting lessons for diverse groups of students. At times, this means starting from scratch and creating one's own unit or plan. Other times counselors incorporate lesson elements from well-researched, commercially available curricula. Whether they use their own or commercially available curricula, professional school counselors help students attain important cognitive, affective, and behavioral outcomes.

Activities

1. Think back to when you were in elementary, middle, or high school. Who was your favorite teacher? Why was he or she your favorite? How can you honor the memory of that teacher in your work as a developmental guidance classroom specialist?

2. Go to a local school and ask to observe a master teacher for a half day. Note the following:

   a. How does the teacher introduce lessons?

   b. What rules seem to be implicit in the classroom? What rules are explicit?

   c. How do students treat each other? What is your sense of the teacher's role in this?

   d. How active are students? How does the teacher help them to learn?

3. Brainstorm five classroom guidance lessons that you could develop that would be appropriate for the education level you are interested in pursuing. For one of the five lessons, create a full lesson plan. Make sure to include appropriate headings and activities for the age group with which you are working.

CHAPTER

10

Counseling Individuals and Groups in School

Debbie W. Newsome and Elisabeth S. Harper*

ditor's Introduction: Individual counseling and group counseling have long been effective tools in the professional school counselor's toolbox and continue to be so in the transformed role. It is essential that professional school counselors have a strong background in developmental counseling theory, as well as more specialized approaches—especially brief, solution-focused models. Such breadth of training reflects belief in both the developmental nature of many childhood struggles and the value of time-limited counseling interventions.

Vignette 1

Meagan, age six, is in Mrs. Hendrick's first-grade classroom. Recently, Meagan has been crying in class and withdrawing from activities. On talking with Meagan's mother, Mrs. Hendrick learns that Meagan's mother and father separated last month. Mrs. Hendrick wonders if it would be helpful for Meagan to talk with you, the professional school counselor.

Vignette 2

Since starting 10th grade, 16-year-old Eric, an African American, has been skipping classes. Consequently, his grades have dropped from Bs and Cs to Ds and Fs. One of Eric's friends stops by your office and tells you that he thinks Eric has become involved with a gang and is thinking about dropping out of school.

Vignette 3

This academic year has been especially difficult for several students on the sixth-grade team. Two students experienced the death of a parent. One student had a sister killed in an automobile accident. Another sixth grader recently lost his grandmother, with whom he had a very close relationship. Mr. Tobias, the school principal, approaches you to see if there is anything you can do to help.

Vignette 4

Andrea, age 10, is new to the school. She is Romanian and was adopted in July by an American family. She speaks limited English and has made very few friends. Andrea has heard that you are available to talk with students who are having difficulties, but she is embarrassed to approach you.

Vignette 5

Stephen, a 15-year-old Caucasian boy, is questioning his sexual orientation. Last week, somebody defaced his locker by writing "gay" and "fag" on it. He comes to you distressed, angry, and hurt, stating, "Sometimes I think I'd be better off dead."

---

*Special thanks to Sam Gladding for his contributions to the first and second editions of this chapter.

Vignette 6

Mrs. Macon, the physical education teacher, has noticed that Abby, one of her eighth-grade students, has lost weight over the course of the past quarter and is extremely thin. She tires easily in gym class, refuses to shower afterward, and is wearing sweaters even though it is warm outside. "I'm worried that Abby has an eating disorder," Mrs. Macon tells you. "What can we do?"

Professional school counselors in elementary, middle, and high school settings are likely to face issues similar to these during the course of their work. When faced with such situations, it is important to know how to respond.

Comprehensive, developmental school counseling programs provide the means for addressing students' immediate needs and concerns through the component called *responsive services*. Responsive services provide special help to students who are facing problems that interfere with their personal, social, career, or educational development. Specific interventions may be preventive, remedial, or crisis oriented. Individual counseling and small-group counseling are two activities that are classified as *responsive services* (American School Counselor Association [ASCA], 2005a; Gysbers & Henderson, 2006). Other activities that are considered part of the responsive services component include crisis counseling, referrals, consultation and collaboration, and peer facilitation.

Although the amount of time allocated for responsive services differs from school to school, general guidelines, specified in the *ASCA National Model*, have been set for different grade levels. Suggested allocations include 20% to 30% in elementary schools, 30% to 40% in middle schools, and 25% to 35% in high schools (ASCA, 2005a; Gysbers & Henderson, 2006). In this chapter, we focus on the counseling component of responsive services by describing strategies for working with individuals and groups in schools. We also provide an overview of crisis counseling and crisis intervention in schools.

INDIVIDUAL COUNSELING IN SCHOOLS

Family changes, violence, poverty, chronic illness, and interpersonal difficulties, as well as typical developmental transitions, are just a few of the myriad issues that can interfere with students' personal, social, and academic growth. When these or other concerns negatively affect a student's development and progress, individual counseling may be warranted. Professional school counselors make decisions about how to administer individual counseling services, keeping in mind that these services need to closely align with the educational mission and philosophy of educating all students to high levels of academic, career, and personal/social success (ASCA, 2005a; Eschenauer & Chen-Hayes,

2005). In the following sections, we provide a definition of counseling in school settings. We then discuss developmental factors that affect the counseling process and provide a general model for individual counseling in schools. Finally, we describe two theoretical approaches to counseling that have been used effectively in schools: solution-focused brief counseling and counseling using choice theory.

COUNSELING IN SCHOOLS DEFINED

The ASCA (2005a) defined counseling as "a special type of helping process implemented by a professionally trained and certified person, involving a variety of techniques and strategies that help students explore academic, career, and personal/social issues impeding healthy development or academic process" (p. 150). The ultimate goal of implementing counseling interventions is to promote students' personal and social growth and to foster their academic process. Some of the concerns that may be addressed in counseling include academic problems, relationship issues, grief and loss, family concerns, anger control, sexual issues, and stress management. Referrals for individual counseling may come from students, parents, teachers, or others who are involved with students. Although individual counseling cannot meet the needs of all students in K–12 schools (Eschenauer & Chen-Hayes, 2005), it represents a vital component of a comprehensive, developmental school counseling program.

Individual counseling involves a confidential relationship between a student and the professional school counselor that can last from a single session to several sessions. Not all one-on-one meetings with students are considered individual counseling (D. B. Brown & Trusty, 2005b; Schmidt, 2008). What distinguishes individual counseling from other forms of interaction is the close emotional contact between the student and the professional school counselor. Also, with individual counseling, the focus is on the student's problem or concern, and the goal is to help the student make positive changes in coping, in adapting, or in specific behaviors that are problematic (D. B. Brown & Trusty, 2005b).

Because professional school counselors are responsible for a wide range of services and because they typically serve a large number of students, teachers, and parents, it is critical for counselors to assess who will benefit from individual counseling relationships within the school setting. The *ASCA National Model* (2005a) clearly states that professional school counselors do not provide traditional therapy. Instead, they work within a developmental framework on issues that have direct relevance to educational success. If more expanded counseling services are needed, it is appropriate to engage in referral and consultation practices with outside agencies and community resources.

CASE STUDY 10.1

The Case of Carlos

Carlos, an eight-year-old third grader, was referred to the professional school counselor by his teacher for being disruptive in class. The teacher feared that Carlos was having problems in the home that might be distracting him from his schoolwork. Assisted by a Spanish translator, the professional school counselor met with Carlos and his mother and discovered that Carlos had been in the United States for only six months and that getting to the United States had been a very traumatic experience.

Six months earlier, Carlos was sitting in his school classroom in Mexico when his mother, who had abandoned the family three years earlier to move to the United States, showed up at his school and told him that they were leaving. That same day they began their journey to the United States.

Because of the language barrier between the professional school counselor and the client's mother (the mother did not speak or understand any English), the professional school counselor decided to refer the family to an agency in the community that offered bilingual counseling. Through counseling, Carlos was able to express his anxiety and stress over leaving his home for a foreign land where people spoke a foreign language and looked very different from him. Family counseling at the agency also helped build family trust and cohesion among Carlos, his mother, and his two siblings.

As Carlos's language skills increased and his anxiety decreased, he began making friends at school. His behavior improved, as did his academic progress. Throughout the process, the professional school counselor served as a link among the school, the home, and the community counseling agency, which helped ensure that all systems were working together to facilitate Carlos's developmental and educational success.

Identifying which students will benefit the most from individual counseling services can pose a tremendous challenge for professional school counselors. Additional challenges include how to integrate these services into the school day, how to conduct the counseling process, and how to evaluate the effectiveness of the interventions (Cobia & Henderson, 2007). Professional school counselors need to be proactive in making decisions about how to conduct individual counseling, with whom, at what time, and under what circumstances. As they make those decisions and deliver individual counseling services, professional school counselors will want to take into account the various developmental changes and challenges that influence the students with whom they work.

DEVELOPMENTAL CONSIDERATIONS

Counseling with children and adolescents differs in multiple ways from working with adults. Indeed, interventions that are appropriate for adult populations may be ineffective and even detrimental if applied to children. Knowledge of developmental theory can help professional school counselors make decisions about what approaches to use with students at different levels. Moreover, such knowledge helps professional school counselors make informed decisions about whether a particular behavior is developmentally appropriate or is out of the range of "normal" (Vernon, 2004).

Development is multidimensional and complex and is marked by qualitative changes that occur in many different domains (Gladding & Newsome, 2009). In this section, we provide an overview of some general developmental characteristics associated with students in elementary, middle, and high school. Readers also may wish to refer to texts that provide in-depth descriptions of child and adolescent development (e.g., Berk, 2007; Bjorklund, 2000; Vernon, 2004).

Early Childhood

Counselors working in elementary schools may work with children in kindergarten or even preschool. Children between the ages of two and six are in the *early childhood* stage, sometimes called the play years (Berk, 2007). During this period, children refine their motor skills, they begin to build ties with peers, and their thought and language skills expand rapidly. To understand the way young children think and use language, it is helpful to refer to Jean Piaget's stage-constructed theory of cognitive development. Although current research indicates that the stages of cognitive development are not as discrete and clear-cut as Piaget hypothesized, his description of cognitive development provides a relatively accurate picture of how children think and reason at different ages (Bjorklund, 2000).

According to Piaget (1963), children between two and seven years of age are *preoperational*, which means they are developing the ability to represent objects and events through imitation, symbolic play, drawing, and spoken language. They are most likely egocentric, implying that they cannot see the viewpoint of another. Preoperational children may attribute lifelike qualities to inanimate objects and have difficulty with abstract nouns and concepts such as time and space (Vernon, 2004). They are likely to engage in magical thinking and may offer imaginative explanations for things they do not understand. As children progress through early childhood, they become better able to represent and recall their feelings. As they near the end of the preoperational stage, their emotional self-regulation improves.

Erik Erikson's psychosocial theory (1963, 1968) provides another way to understand children's development. Erikson described development as a series of psychological crises that occur at various stages. The manner in which each crisis is resolved, along a continuum from positive to negative, influences healthy or maladaptive outcomes at each stage (Berk, 2007). Young children are in the process of resolving the developmental crisis of *initiative versus guilt*. *Initiative* refers to being enterprising, energetic, and purposeful. Children in this stage are discovering what kinds of people they are, particularly in regard to gender. Because of their increased language and motor skills, they are capable of imagining and trying out many new things. To navigate this period successfully, children need to be given a variety of opportunities to explore, experiment, and ask questions. Understanding adults can be instrumental in helping young children to develop self-confidence, self-direction, and emotional self-regulation.

Play is an extremely important activity for children in this age group. Through play, children find out about themselves and their world. Professional school counselors will want to use some form of play when working with young children. Play provides a way for children to express feelings, describe experiences, and disclose wishes. Although young children may not be able to articulate feelings, toys and other play media serve as the words they use to express emotions (Landreth, 2002). Materials used to facilitate play include puppets, art supplies, dolls and dollhouses, tools, and toy figures or animals.

Middle Childhood

Children between the ages of 7 and 11 are in *middle childhood*. During this time period, children develop literacy skills and logical thinking. Cognitively, they are in Piaget's *concrete operational* stage, meaning that they are capable of reasoning logically about concrete, tangible information. Concrete operational children are capable of mentally reversing actions, although they still can only generalize from concrete experiences. They grasp logical concepts more readily than before, but they typically have difficulty reasoning about abstract ideas. Children in this stage learn best through questioning, exploring, manipulating, and doing (Flavell, 1985). As a rule, their increased reasoning skills enable them to understand the concept of intentionality and to be more cooperative.

From a psychosocial perspective, children in middle childhood are in the process of resolving the crisis of *industry versus inferiority*. To maximize healthy development, they need opportunities to build up a sense of competence and capability. When adults provide manageable tasks, along with sufficient time and encouragement to complete the tasks, children are more likely to develop a strong sense of industry and efficacy (R. M. Thomas, 2005). Alternatively, children who do not experience feelings of competence and mastery may develop a sense of inadequacy and pessimism about their capabilities. Experiences with family, teachers, and peers all contribute to children's perceptions of efficacy and industry.

Negotiating relationships with peers is an important part of middle childhood. Being accepted in a peer group and having a "best friend" help children develop competence, self-esteem, and an understanding of others (Vernon, 2004). Some of the interpersonal skills children acquire during middle childhood include learning to get along with age-mates, learning the skills of tolerance and patience, and developing positive attitudes toward social groups and institutions (Havighurst, 1972). Professional school counselors can help children develop their interpersonal skills through developmental guidance activities and group counseling, as well as through individual counseling.

Adolescence

Adolescence is the period when young people transition from childhood to adulthood. During adolescence, youth mature physically, develop an increased understanding of roles and relationships, and acquire and refine skills needed for performing successfully as adults. Puberty marks the beginning of adolescence, with girls typically reaching puberty earlier than boys. For most students, *early adolescence* (ages 11–14) begins in middle school, *midadolescence* (ages 15–18) begins in high school, and *late adolescence* (18 years through young adulthood) occurs at the end of high school and continues beyond.

As young people enter adolescence, they begin to make the shift from concrete to formal operational thinking. The transition takes time and usually is not completed until at least age 15 years (Schave & Schave, 1989). Adolescents moving into the formal operational stage are able to deal with abstractions, form hypotheses, engage in mental manipulation, and predict consequences. As formal operational skills develop, adolescents become capable of reflective abstraction, which refers to the ability to reflect on knowledge, rearrange thoughts, and discover alternative routes to solving problems (Bjorklund, 2000). Consequently, counseling approaches that provide opportunities to generate alternative solutions are more likely to be effective with adolescents than with younger children.

A new form of egocentrism often emerges during adolescence, characterized by a belief in one's uniqueness and invulnerability. Egocentrism may be reflected in reckless behavior and grandiose ideas. Related to this heightened sense of uniqueness is the adolescent phenomenon of feeling constantly "on stage." It is not uncommon for adolescents to feel that everyone is looking at them, leading to increased anxiety and self-consciousness. These feelings tend to peak in early adolescence and then decline as formal operational skills improve (Bjorklund, 2000).

The onset of puberty often triggers the psychosocial crisis of *identity versus role confusion* (Erikson, 1968). A key challenge during adolescence is the formation of an identity, including self-definition and a commitment to goals, values, beliefs, and life purpose. To master this challenge, adolescents need opportunities to explore options, try on various roles and responsibilities, and speculate about possibilities. Sometimes adolescents enter a period of role confusion, characterized in part by overidentification with heroes or cliques, before they develop a true sense of individuality and recognize that they are acceptable human beings (R. M. Thomas, 2005).

Spending time with peers continues to be important throughout adolescence. As adolescents develop self-confidence and sensitivity, they base their friendships on compatibility and shared experiences. Intimate friendships increase, as do dating and sexual experimentation. Counseling may involve helping these young people deal with issues of complex relationships and decision making about the future.

It is important to keep in mind that developmental generalizations may not be applicable to all ethnic or cultural groups. For example, the search for self-identity may be delayed, compounded by a search for ethnic identity, or even nonexistent among certain groups of adolescents (Herring, 1997). Also, research on Piagetian tasks suggests that some forms of logic do not emerge spontaneously according to stages, but are socially generated, based on cultural experiences (Berk, 2007). Developmental theories provide useful guides for understanding children and adolescents; however, no theory provides a complete explanation of development, nor does any theory take into account all cultural perspectives.

Developmental knowledge helps professional school counselors build relationships, assess concerns, and design effective interventions for students at all grade levels. By understanding developmental levels and their implications, professional school counselors are better prepared to meet the needs of the children and adolescents whom they counsel and the parents and teachers with whom they consult.

A COUNSELING MODEL FOR CHILDREN AND ADOLESCENTS

Models of individual counseling can range anywhere from three to a multitude of stages (Schmidt, 2008). The model presented in this section is adapted from Orton (1997) and consists of the following phases: *building a counseling relationship, assessing specific counseling needs, designing and implementing interventions,* and *conducting evaluation and closure.* Generic and nonlinear in nature, the model can be applied to different theoretical orientations and situations, and certain phases can occur throughout the counseling process.

Building a Counseling Relationship

Key to any successful counseling experience is the development of an effective working relationship built on mutual trust and acceptance. Developing a counseling relationship sometimes takes longer with children than with adults because children may need more time to believe that an adult can help them (Orton, 1997). Essential factors involved in building a counseling relationship include establishing rapport, clarifying the counseling role, and explaining confidentiality.

ESTABLISHING RAPPORT   To build relationships successfully, professional school counselors need to tailor their responses and interactions to fit the specific needs of each student, taking into account developmental experiences, sociocultural background, and reasons for referral (McClure & Teyber, 2003). Perhaps the most important first step is being willing to enter completely into that student's world, with no preconceptions, expectations, or agenda. It is important to be fully "with" student clients, accepting them for who they are at that moment. All judgment needs to be suspended so that the counselor can remain open to what the student is sharing, either verbally or nonverbally. As the relationship is being established, listening skills are more important than questioning skills (Erdman & Lampe, 1996; C. L. Thompson & Henderson, 2007). Professional school counselors can create bridges of trust and understanding by listening carefully to what young people have to say; giving them undivided attention; and responding sensitively to feelings, reactions, and cultural cues.

It helps to be knowledgeable about a variety of rapport-building approaches. For example, play and art

VOICES FROM THE FIELD 10.1   REFLECTIONS OF A FIRST-YEAR MASTER'S STUDENT ON CONDUCTING INDIVIDUAL COUNSELING AT AN ALTERNATIVE SCHOOL DURING PRACTICUM

I completed my practicum experience at the New School, which hosts students who have been referred from their home schools because of behavior problems. Problematic behaviors range from minor classroom disruptions and peer conflicts to aggressive and sometimes violent displays of anger. During the first three weeks of my practicum, I was regularly questioned by the school's administrators, teachers, and staff: "Do you know what you're getting yourself into with *these* students?" I spent the first month at the site building relationships with administrators, teachers, and staff—and, most importantly, with the students.

I found it surprisingly easy to build rapport and empathize with the students. I expected to have to work extremely hard to tear down barriers to trust and communication to establish a counseling relationship. Interestingly enough, a smiling face and an attentive ear were more than enough to gain the students' respect. Many of the students with whom I worked had rarely had an adult willing to spend time with them and listen to their opinions, fears, anger, and experiences. Teachers and administrators were shocked when students returned to classrooms or the office talking with me calmly after walking out of a classroom, yelling profanities at the teacher, and banging lockers. This was the turning point: I'd won the teachers over.

---

media can help professional school counselors establish relationships with young children who have difficulty verbalizing. With older children, games like Jenga and "in-house" basketball can provide a nonthreatening introduction to the counseling process. Use a dry-erase whiteboard and markers with children, inviting them to draw pictures or symbols that illustrate things they would like you to know about them. As a variation, ask students to create an *About Me* collage by decoratively writing their names in the center of a piece of art paper. Then ask students to select magazine pictures that illustrate things about them, including strengths, interests, relationships, or other characteristics they want to reveal at that point, and paste them on the paper. Their choices serve as a springboard for further discussion and provide a lens for glimpsing their subjective worlds. Other children may be eager to talk, and the professional school counselor can respond accordingly by listening reflectively, summarizing, probing, and clarifying.

One of the factors that makes building a relationship with children different from building a relationship with adults is that children may have no idea what counseling is all about. They may be confused about the counseling process or reluctant to participate. In schools, students frequently are referred by teachers or parents, and it is these adults, not the students, who want change to occur. Consequently, the students may not be motivated to make changes. This is particularly true when children or adolescents are referred because of behavioral patterns that are troublesome to adults (Sommers-Flanagan & Sommers-Flanagan, 2007).

When children are "sent" to counseling, rather than self-referred, they may be resistant to the counseling process. One professional middle school counselor in a

local public school shared her strategy for working with students who have been referred by parents or teachers:

> If a child is ready to talk, I sit back, relax, and hear her story. If she is not, I'll generally do something temporarily diverting, such as say, "You know, I realize we're supposed to talk about whatever it is you've been sent here for, but do you mind if we do something else for a while? Do you see anything here that you'd like to do?" I keep lots of games and toys, art supplies, clay, etc. out and about, and almost always something will catch a child's interest. (Niedringhaus, 2000, p. 1)

When students are self-referred, resistance may not be an issue. However, in such situations the need to obtain parental consent for counseling services can become a concern. Many counselors will not counsel students without parental consent (Freeman, 2000). Professional school counselors need to be aware of state regulations, school policies, professional ethical codes, and limits of confidentiality as they make decisions about counseling individual students.

CLARIFYING THE COUNSELING ROLE   Professional school counselors are responsible for explaining to students the purpose and nature of the counseling relationship (ASCA, 2004a). Providing an age-appropriate explanation of the counseling role can help establish structure and initiate the development of a collaborative relationship. With younger students, the professional school counselor might say something like "My job is to help children with lots of different things. Sometimes people have unpleasant feelings they want to talk about. Other people might want help figuring out a problem. I wonder what I might be able to help you with?" With older students, it might be helpful to ask students to describe what they think individual counseling entails, after which the professional school counselor can provide clarification as needed.

EXPLAINING CONFIDENTIALITY During the initial phase of counseling, it is necessary to clarify confidentiality and its limits. The ASCA's (2004a) ethical standards state that professional school counselors have a responsibility to protect information received through confidential counseling relationships with students. Confidentiality should not be abridged unless there is a clear and present danger to the student, other individuals, or both. Also, professional school counselors have the responsibility of explaining the limits of confidentiality to their students and of notifying students regarding the possible necessity of consulting with others. Moreover, professional school counselors recognize that, although their primary obligation for confidentiality is to the student, that obligation must be balanced with "an understanding of the legal and inherent rights of parents/guardians to be the guiding voice in their children's lives" (ASCA, 2004a, p. 4).

The way a professional school counselor approaches the issue of confidentiality with students depends on the students' age. With young children, the counselor will want to use words that they can understand. As noted earlier, in many cases professional school counselors will not counsel with students, especially young children, before obtaining parental permission. Also, it often is in the child's best interest to consult with parents or teachers during the process. Therefore, the counselor might say to the student, "Most of the things you and I talk about in here are between you and me, unless you tell me that you are planning to hurt yourself or someone else. If you tell me something that I think your mother (father, other caregiver, teacher) needs to know, you and I will talk about it before I tell anything."

Adolescents often have a heightened concern about privacy and confidentiality in the counseling relationship (Remley & Herlihy, 2010). Professional school counselors who work with adolescents can help students understand confidentiality and its limits from the outset. Keeping this in mind, it is important for adolescents to feel free to disclose their concerns in an atmosphere of trust. Balancing issues related to trust and minor consent laws can often be challenging.

In addition to the ethical issue of confidentiality, a number of state and federal statutes affect the counselor–client relationship in school settings. Each state has its own laws that directly influence the practice of counseling in

schools (S. B. Baker & Gerler, 2008). For example, many states mandate privileged communication, which is a client's right to have prior confidences maintained during legal proceedings. If clients are under the age of 18, their parents maintain the right to privileged communication. Privilege is not absolute, and several exceptions to privilege exist, including child abuse, with those exceptions varying from state to state (Glosoff, Herlihy, & Spence, 2000). It is the professional school counselor's responsibility to stay abreast of state statutes and exceptions to privilege.

Professional school counselors also need to be aware of federal statutes that affect their work with students and limits to confidentiality. In particular, the Family Educational Rights and Privacy Act (FERPA), enacted in 1974, ensures that parents' rights to information about their children's education are honored. Part I of FERPA specifies that parents have the right to access school records about their children. Because this stipulation refers to the school's educational records, professional school counselors are advised to keep their counseling records separate from the official educational records (Wheeler & Bertram, 2008). As noted by Linde in Chapter 5, counseling notes are confidential, and the professional school counselor needs to ensure their security.

Part II of FERPA requires parental consent for medical, psychiatric, or psychological evaluations of children under 18 years, as well as for participation in school programs designed to affect a student's personal behavior or values. Thus, parental or legal guardian consent is needed when administering formal assessment instruments to students that are not administered to all students as an aspect of the school's regular curriculum. Ordinarily, this includes individualized psychological or educational testing (e.g., to determine special education or Section 504 eligibility) and specialized individual screening processes (e.g., testing for the gifted program).

It is not unusual for professional school counselors to face dilemmas regarding the requirements of confidentiality; minor students' requests for information; and counselor responsibilities to parents, teachers, and colleagues. By keeping the lines of communication open and taking responsibility for knowing state and federal law, it may be possible to prevent potential problems from arising (Freeman, 2000).

Assessing Specific Counseling Needs

Assessment is an integral part of the counseling process that can, in and of itself, be therapeutic. The purposes of assessment are to gain a better understanding of the child's needs and to establish goals for meeting those needs. Assessment methods, which can be informal or formal, help the professional school counselor understand the student's current problems within the context of his or her unique developmental and contextual history.

CASE STUDY 10.2

The Case of Gabriella

Gabriella, a second-generation Latina student in the ninth grade, has been referred to you, the professional school counselor, because she has been falling asleep in class for the past two weeks. You know Gabriella, but have not conducted individual counseling with her until now. During your initial meeting with Gabriella, she tells you that she is just tired because she has to stay up late to take care of her younger brother while her mother and stepfather are working. In a subsequent session, Gabriella reveals that the real reason she is so tired is because she is afraid to go to sleep at night. On further questioning, she reveals that her stepfather has been touching her in ways that make her uncomfortable and that during the past month he has been coming into her room at night. She insists that he has not done anything except touch her in "an embarrassing way." She now keeps her door locked at night and stays awake as long as she can, until she is sure that her stepfather has gone to bed.

- What are your responsibilities to Gabriella?
- What are your legal and ethical responsibilities in this situation?
- What would you do in this situation? What considerations should you keep in mind?
- What factors make this situation challenging?

EXPLORING STUDENT CONCERNS Whereas counselors in mental health settings conduct intake interviews to collect information about client concerns, counselors in school settings typically do not conduct formal intake interviews. Nonetheless, some form of early and ongoing assessment is warranted for accurate case conceptualization and effective intervention planning. Often, professional school counselors begin this process with an informal interview through which students' concerns are explored. Myrick (2003a) suggested that professional school counselors look for effective ways to collect information without turning the session into a fact-finding question-and-answer period. When exploring students' concerns, it is important to use active listening skills, be sensitive to nonverbal expressions, and probe gently and sensitively.

The type of information collected during early stages of assessment varies according to developmental levels and student concerns. If professional school counselors will be working with the student for more than just a few sessions, Orton (1997) suggested that information be gathered in the following areas:

- *The student's specific concerns.* The manifestation, intensity, frequency, and duration of concerns should be explored. In what settings and around what individuals are the concerns evidenced? To what extent are the concerns developmentally appropriate?
- *The student's physical, cognitive, emotional, and social development.* Depending on the situation, it may be beneficial to consult with parents and teachers to get more information about the student's medical history, cognitive functioning, and ability to express and regulate emotions. It also is helpful to gather information about socioeconomic and sociocultural factors that have influenced the student's development.
- *Relationships between the student and his or her parents, siblings, classmates, and teachers.* Understanding the nature and quality of relationships the student has with family members and peers is a key component of assessment. The degree to which these areas are explored depends on the nature of the problem. For example, if a student is not turning in homework, the professional school counselor will want to gather information about what is going on at home and in the school that may be contributing to the problem.
- *The student's school experiences, including academics, attendance, and attitude.* Academic and social successes or failures play important roles in a student's overall development. Students who experience repeated failures often have poor self-esteem and may engage in disruptive behaviors to compensate (Orton, 1997). Also, school failure may signify a learning disorder that typically requires formal testing for diagnosis.
- *The student's strengths, talents, and support system.* Implementing a strengths-based approach to assessment can help take the focus off the problem so that it is possible to begin moving more toward solutions. Solution-focused brief counseling (SFBC), which is addressed later in the chapter, places particular emphasis on assessing students' strengths. Creative activities, checklists, and various qualitative assessment methods are useful tools for evaluating strengths and supports.

INFORMAL AND FORMAL ASSESSMENT Informal assessment includes observation and qualitative assessment activities. Observation can occur in counseling sessions or in the classroom. Qualitative assessment emphasizes a holistic study of students using methods that typically are not standardized and do not produce quantitative raw scores (Goldman, 1990). A variety of qualitative assessment methods can be used with children and adolescents, including informal checklists, sentence completion activities, writing activities, decision-making dilemmas, games, art activities, storytelling, self-monitoring techniques, role-play activities, and play therapy strategies (e.g., Myrick, 2003a; J. Peterson, 2004; Vernon, 2004). Informal assessment procedures of this nature can reveal patterns of thoughts and behaviors relevant to concerns and issues. They can be especially helpful with young children, who may not know exactly what is bothering them or who lack the words to express their concerns verbally.

In some situations, professional school counselors may wish to obtain information through the use of formal assessment instruments, which require students to respond to standardized measurements. Formal instruments that have sound psychometric properties provide a way for professional school counselors to gain a somewhat more objective view of children's behaviors and attributes than do informal methods of assessment. Examples of formal assessment include standardized behavioral checklists, values scales, interest and skill inventories, self-concept measures, and personality inventories. Professional school counselors have been trained in appraisal procedures and have the ability to use these instruments effectively with students.

By evaluating counseling needs though interviews, informal assessment, and formal assessment, the professional school counselor can gain a better understanding of the student's concerns within his or her developmental and environmental context. This understanding can then be used to set goals, design and implement interventions, and conduct evaluation and closure of the counseling process.

Designing and Implementing Interventions

After a relationship has been established and initial assessment conducted with a child, what is the next step? Interventions should be developed and selected after carefully considering the student's developmental level, cultural background, personality characteristics, and particular circumstances. Other considerations that need to be taken into account are time constraints, teacher and parental support, and the counselor's level of expertise. In addition, it is important to select interventions that are evidence-informed and evidence-based (Galassi, Griffin, & Akos, 2008). If, during the course of counseling, it becomes apparent that

the student's problems are more serious and chronic, then the professional school counselor will want to refer him or her to mental health counselors or other helping professionals within the school or community (ASCA, 2005a; D. B. Brown & Trusty, 2005b). When it is necessary to refer, the professional school counselor can continue to play a significant role by working collaboratively with clinical mental health counselors and other referral sources.

INTENTIONALITY AND FLEXIBILITY Being intentional implies taking steps to set goals for counseling with the student. Being flexible refers to recognizing that no single counseling approach is best for all students or all problems. By designing interventions in ways that are both intentional and flexible, professional school counselors can personalize the intervention for the student within the context of a collaborative relationship.

One way professional school counselors can intentionally plan interventions is by asking specific questions related to the following areas (Vernon, 1993):

1. *Vision.* What could be different? How could things be better? What would be ideal?
2. *Goal setting.* What is going well? What needs to be worked on?
3. *Analysis.* What is enabling or interfering with achieving these goals? What is getting in the way of resolving the problem?
4. *Objective.* What specifically does the student want to change?
5. *Exploration of interventions.* What has already been tried and how did it work? How does the student learn best? Who will be involved in the helping process? What has research shown to be the most effective intervention for this type of concern?

In many ways, these guiding questions are similar to those that guide SFBC, an approach that we describe in further detail later in the chapter.

SELECTING INTERVENTIONS In making decisions about which interventions to use, professional school counselors can select from a wide range of theoretical approaches. Although no single theoretical approach to counseling children and adolescents has been found to be more effective than another (e.g., Bergin, 2004; Sexton, Whiston, Bleuer, & Walz, 1997), some approaches are more suited to school settings than others are. D. B. Brown and Trusty (2005b) outlined six aspects of counseling theory for professional school counselors to consider as they make decisions about interventions:

1. The degree to which the theory (or model) focuses on the *counseling relationship*, including the relationship between the counselor and students as a whole.

2. The degree to which the theory enhances *student empowerment.*

3. The amount of attention devoted to students' *overt behavior.*

4. The usefulness of the theory at students' various levels of *development.*

5. The *flexibility* of the theory to fit various student characteristics, student problems, and school counseling delivery formats.

6. The *time span* of counseling associated with the theory. (p. 292)

An additional consideration is the degree to which the theory or model takes into account issues related to diversity and cultural strengths.

Theoretical approaches that seem to be particularly effective in school settings include Adlerian counseling, reality therapy (RT)/choice theory, cognitive-behavioral counseling, and SFBC (D. B. Brown & Trusty, 2005b; Schmidt, 2008). Other models and structures that are effective with school-aged children include multimodal counseling, Gestalt techniques, and family counseling approaches (D. B. Brown & Trusty, 2005b). A variety of expressive arts techniques—including art, music, clay, puppetry, storytelling, drama, bibliotherapy, sand play, and other forms of directive and nondirective play therapy—can guide the counseling process and promote healing and growth (e.g., L. J. Bradley, Gould, & Hendricks, 2004; Gladding, 2005; Gladding & Newsome, 2009). Recently, Galassi and Akos (2007) emphasized the use of strengths-based school counseling (SBSC) approaches with students, which build on students' strengths and assets. "In SBSC, the focus is on strengths promotion rather than problem reduction, although the two latter functions do remain important in the school counselor's role. Strengths promotion often simultaneously accomplishes the twin goals of problem prevention and problem reduction" (Galassi et al., p. 177).

Professional school counselors need to select counseling approaches systematically (Schmidt, 2008), matching the approach and intervention with the presenting issue and taking developmental, cultural, and other contextual factors into account. For example, a professional school counselor working with a student with attention-deficit/hyperactivity disorder may find cognitive-behavioral approaches useful, with an emphasis on specific tasks related to organization, self-monitoring, and impulse control. For students who have difficulty completing assignments, RT (Glasser, 2000b), which focuses on the present and future rather than the past, may be the treatment of choice. Professional school counselors using this approach ask students to evaluate their actions and determine whether they want to change. Together, the student and the counselor design a plan for change that emphasizes personal control. For adolescents struggling with depression, cognitive theory (e.g., Beck & Weishaar, 2000), which focuses on recognizing automatic thoughts and their effects on emotions, may be the preferred approach.

IMPLEMENTING INTERVENTIONS After the professional school counselor and the student have collaboratively selected interventions, it is time to implement the plan. Professional school counselors can empower students by affirming their resilience, offering affirmation and encouragement, and providing acceptance and stability (J. Peterson, 2004). Depending on the situation, counselors should consult with other people in the school or family invested in the success of the intervention. It may be important to inform teachers and parents that the situation may get worse before it gets better. In some cases, it may be helpful to work with teachers on designing a behavior contract, recognizing that teachers are more likely to implement a plan they have helped create (Orton, 1997).

Conducting Evaluation and Closure

Implementation of interventions also includes working with the student to evaluate progress. Evaluation of the counseling relationship, interventions, and outcomes is an ongoing process. As with assessment, evaluation methods can be informal or formal. Informal evaluation involves observing changes in the student's thoughts, feelings, and behaviors. It also includes monitoring interactions during counseling sessions and being aware of personal responses to the child. Formal evaluation of counseling outcomes may include checklists completed by teachers and parents, grades in academic areas and in conduct, and self-reports completed by students related to the issues on which they are working (Orton, 1997).

Measuring progress in counseling can be challenging because evaluation tends to be subjective and not all counseling goals are stated in measurable terms. Finding ways to demonstrate the effectiveness of counseling is important, however, and professional school counselors are encouraged to incorporate formal and informal methods of outcome evaluation into their work with students, teachers, and parents. Single-case study experimental designs provide one effective way to conduct outcomes research evaluating the effectiveness of professional school counselors' interventions (Eschenauer & Chen-Hayes, 2005).

Closure, sometimes called termination, refers to the ending of the counseling relationship, either naturally or circumstantially (Schmidt, 2008). Gladding and Newsome (2009) indicated that it is the least researched and most neglected aspect of counseling. In school counseling, the process of ending the helping relationship deserves particular attention (Henderson, 1987). As Schmidt (2008) pointed out, "Students who see counselors for individual sessions also interact with them in other ways during the day . . . . Because these interactions are ongoing, closure of an individual counseling relationship is planned and carried out gradually" (p. 165). Closure is facilitated when professional school counselors reinforce the progress students have made, encourage them to express their feelings about ending the helping relationship, and determine resources for continued support.

Solution-Focused Brief Counseling

Brief counseling approaches, including SFBC (e.g., Bonnington, 1993; de Shazer, 1985; Metcalf, 2008; J. J. Murphy, 2008; Sklare, 2005) and systematic problem solving (Myrick, 2003a), are advocated in the school counseling literature and are particularly valuable in schools where time constraints are crucial. The successful brief counseling model is brief by design, not by accident (Bruce, 1995). Brief counseling models parallel the generic model for individual counseling presented in this chapter by encouraging students to (1) assess the problem in concrete terms; (2) examine previously attempted solutions; (3) establish a specific, short-term goal; and (4) implement the intervention. Because of its utility in school settings, a particular form of brief counseling, SFBC (Sklare, 2005), is discussed next.

OVERVIEW OF SFBC   SFBC is an approach that "has shown great promise and that allows counselors to provide effective counseling to students in less time" (Charlesworth & Jackson, 2004, p. 139). It emphasizes strengths, resources, successes, and hope and is a model that can be used with students from diverse backgrounds. Sklare (2005) attributed the SFBC model primarily to de Shazer (1985), though many other innovative practitioners have contributed to its evolution (e.g., Berg & Miller, 1992; Berg & Steiner, 2003; O'Hanlon & Weiner-Davis, 1989; Selekman, 1997; Walter & Peller, 1992). Charlesworth and Jackson (2004) cited numerous studies supporting the efficacy of SFBC in school settings. Sklare (2005) referred to research providing support for the use of SFBC with students from culturally diverse backgrounds.

CORE BELIEFS, ASSUMPTIONS, AND CONCEPTS   The core beliefs on which SFBC is based were originally proposed by de Shazer (1985) and Berg and Miller (1992) and are summarized by Sklare (2005) as follows:

- "If it ain't broke, don't fix it." Do not make an issue out of something that is not an issue for the student.

- "Once you know what works, do more of it." Once successes are identified, professional school counselors have students replicate them.
- "If it doesn't work, don't do it again." Repeating ineffective strategies does not make sense; it is more productive to try out new strategies. (pp. 9–10)

In addition to these core beliefs, Sklare (2005) presented five assumptions and four concepts that guide the SFBC model:

- *Assumption 1.* Counselors should focus on solutions, rather than problems, for change to occur.
- *Assumption 2.* Every problem has identifiable exceptions that can be discovered and transformed into solutions.
- *Assumption 3.* Small changes have a ripple effect that leads to bigger changes.
- *Assumption 4.* Student clients have the necessary resources to solve their problems.
- *Assumption 5.* Constructing goals in positive terms (what clients want to happen) is more effective than stating them in negative terms (an absence of something). For example, "I want to get to class on time" represents a positive goal; "I don't want to get in trouble" represents a negative goal.
- *Concept 1.* Avoid problem analysis. SFBC addresses what is working for students, rather than exploring the etiology of their problems.
- *Concept 2.* Be efficient with interventions. Because counseling in schools is time limited, professional school counselors want to get the most accomplished in the minimum amount of time.
- *Concept 3.* Focus on the present and the future, not the past. Past events are only highlighted in the process of finding exceptions to problems.
- *Concept 4.* Focus on actions, rather than insights. Insight requires a level of cognitive development that young students may not have. Also, insight is not necessary for change to occur.

IMPLEMENTING THE SFBC MODEL   Sklare (2005) suggested that professional school counselors begin the first session with students by explaining the SFBC approach. He provides the following as an example of what professional school counselors might say to students:

I want to let you know how this is going to work. I am going to ask you a lot of questions, and some of them are going to sound kind of crazy and will be tough to answer [for some students, informing them that the questions will be hard to answer is intriguing and challenging]. Some of the answers you give I'm going to write down on my notepad, and I'm going to use these notes to write you a message. When I finish, I will tell you what I was thinking about and read the message to you. I will make a copy of the message so you can take one with you and I can keep one. What do you think about this? (p. 20)

After the process has been explained, the next step is to help the student formulate clear goals. As assumption 5 indicates, goals need to be stated in positive rather than negative terms. Sklare (2005) classified goals as (1) positive, (2) negative, (3) harmful, and (4) "I don't know" goals. Skillful questioning on the part of the professional school counselor can help the student state positive goals that are observable, behaviorally specific, measurable, and attainable.

Professional school counselors can use a wide range of techniques to help students develop positive goals and envision solutions. Following are examples of those techniques:

- *The miracle question.*   With young children, the professional school counselor might ask, "Suppose I had a magic wand and waved it over your head and the problem was solved, what would be different? What would you see yourself doing differently?" (Sklare, 2005, p. 31). If students state wishes that are impossible (e.g., "I would not live here anymore"), the professional school counselor can ask questions like "How would things be different for you if your miracle happened?" and "What would other people notice?"
- *Identifying instances and exceptions.*   Following assumption 2, professional school counselors can ask students to think of a time when the miracle has already happened to some extent. For example, the professional school counselor might say, "Tell me about a time when you were getting along with your teacher. What was going on then?"

- *Mindmapping.*   Mindmapping refers to identifying specific behaviors that led to success in the past. Identifying concrete steps that were beneficial in the past can help students create a mental road map to guide them in the future.
- *Cheerleading.*   Supporting and encouraging students, acknowledging their accomplishments, and expressing excitement when a new behavior is successfully implemented is called cheerleading. Sklare (2005) pointed out that it is important to be genuine in cheerleading and to avoid patronizing.
- *Scaling.*   Scaling can be used to establish baselines, set goals, and measure progress. For example, the professional school counselor might ask the student, "On a scale of 0 to 10, with 10 being the day after the miracle has happened and the problem is solved, where are you right now?" Subsequent questions might be "What would it take for you to move to a ———— on the scale?" and "How would you know when you were at a ————? What would be happening?"
- *Flagging the minefield.*   Helping students anticipate obstacles that might impede their progress gives them an opportunity to consider ways to overcome those obstacles before they are encountered. Reviewing strategies in advance can help keep students from being caught off guard and can empower them to make positive choices.

SFBC is an example of one of several forms of brief counseling. Although this and other brief approaches may not be appropriate for every student in every situation, professional school counselors can incorporate models like SFBC as one way to effectively deliver individual counseling services. For a more in-depth description of the model, readers are encouraged to refer to Sklare's (2005) text, *Brief Counseling That Works: A Solution-Focused Approach for School Counselors and Administrators.* The case in Voices from the Field 10.2 illustrates ways an elementary school counselor uses SFBC in her work with students.

| **VOICES FROM THE FIELD 10.2** | **USING SOLUTION-FOCUSED BRIEF COUNSELING IN THE SCHOOLS** |

I find solution-focused brief counseling to be extremely helpful and effective in individual counseling sessions. I begin each meeting by asking the student to describe his or her feelings using a number. I have a poster hanging in my office that displays a number line and appropriate feelings for each number. For example, a "one" means extremely sad, depressed, or angry and a "ten" means that everything feels perfect! When the student pinpoints his or her feelings, I have a starting point for my session. Whether the issue is grief and loss, divorce, anxiety, self-esteem, or friendships, by using this measure, I am able to determine how they are feeling at the moment. From that point, we can work to improve this number during the session and then set goals for the week ahead.

(Continued)

Recently, I've been working individually with a nine-year-old female suffering from severe anxiety. Prior to tests, she finds herself shaking and nauseous. She also experiences headaches and will often break into hives following the stressful event. At our first meeting, I asked her to point to how she was feeling on my number line. She directed me to the 2–3 range and claimed that she has difficulty controlling herself when there is an upcoming test. Together, in our first session, we compared worries and anxiety to planting seeds. I explained to her that, when we focus on our worries and pay special attention to them, they grow—just like a seed that is given water and sunlight. Following our discussion, we talked about ways that we could spend less time focusing on anxious thoughts and

more time on ways to enjoy being at school. When asked to point to the number line at the end of the session, she had improved to a 5! She was still preoccupied with her anxiety, but began to see that focusing on it was not the answer.

In subsequent sessions with the same child, I began to focus on relaxation techniques. Together, we came up with a set of four techniques that work for her. We continue to meet and work on her ability to relax. She rates herself prior to every session and following every session, allowing both of us to evaluate the effectiveness of each activity and conversation.

Melissa Snapp, Elementary School Counselor at Lewisville Elementary School, Winston-Salem/Forsyth County Schools

Reality Therapy/Choice Theory

Reality therapy (RT), like SFBC, was designed to be brief and has been shown to be particularly effective in school settings (D. B. Brown & Trusty, 2005b; C. L. Thompson & Henderson, 2007). William Glasser, founder of reality therapy (2000b), began working with school systems in the 1960s to apply RT to education (C. L. Thompson & Henderson, 2007). Over the course of his career, he wrote several books on the topic, including *Schools Without Failure* (1969), *The Quality School: Managing Students Without Coercion* (1990), *The Quality School Teacher* (1993), and *Every Student Can Succeed* (2000). RT provides school counselors with a systematic way to address students' needs and wants, in both their personal and their educational lives. It works well in individual and small-group counseling, as well as in guidance (D. B. Brown & Trusty, 2005b). RT fits well with the *ASCA National Model's* (2005a) goal of reaching as many students as possible because it provides a brief framework to accomplish concrete improvements in areas self-identified by students and empowers them to take responsibility for their behaviors.

CORE BELIEFS, ASSUMPTIONS, AND CONCEPTS   Choice theory, also created by Glasser (1998), serves as a theoretical basis for RT. C. L. Thompson and Henderson (2007, p. 115) summarize choice theory with the following statements:

- "The only person whose behavior we can control is our own." People are responsible for themselves and their actions.
- "All long-lasting psychological problems are relationship problems that result from attempts of people to control other people." We get into trouble when we try to control others.
- "Past events have everything to do with what we are today, but we can satisfy our basic needs only in the

present and make plans for the future." RT focuses on the present and future, rather than on the past.
- "Satisfying the needs represented by the pictures in our quality world is the way we meet our needs for survival, freedom, power, fun, and love and belonging." If we can identify and attain our quality worlds—what we want our lives to be like—we will accomplish the five basic needs common to all people.
- "Total behavior is all that we do, including acting, thinking, feeling, and physiology." Regarding total behavior, we have the most control over our actions and thoughts.

QUALITY WORLD   Glasser believed that everyone has a quality world that includes images that make up the life we'd like to have, including people, things, experiences, and values (M. Seligman, 2006). People are motivated by what is in their quality worlds, so they are more likely to find satisfaction in life if they are aware of what is in their quality worlds and if those things are attainable and meet their basic needs.

FIVE BASIC NEEDS   According to Glasser (1998), people have five basic needs:

- *Belonging*—the need to give and receive love;
- *Power*—the need to feel in control of one's self, to feel competent;
- *Fun*—the need to experience pleasure and enjoy life;
- *Freedom*—the need to be without limitations, to make one's own choices; and
- *Survival*—the need to eat, breathe, and have shelter, safety, and physical comfort.

Glasser believed that by intentionally including each of these needs in their quality worlds, people are more likely to get their basic needs met.

TOTAL BEHAVIOR   According to Glasser (1998), all our behaviors are directed at satisfying our needs. He defined *total behavior* as the four parts of our overall functioning: action, thinking, feeling, and physiology. We have the most control over our actions and thoughts, which means that they are easiest to change. Therefore, in order to better satisfy our needs, we can *choose* to change our actions and thoughts. By making better choices, we end up having more control over attaining our quality worlds and meeting our five basic needs.

IMPLEMENTING THE RT MODEL   Essentially, treatment in RT involves helping students make better choices to meet their needs. C. L. Thompson and Henderson (2007, pp. 117–118) described eight steps for practicing RT with students:

Step 1.   Build the relationship. Because RT often involves some confrontation, it is important to build trust between counselor and student first.

Step 2.   The student identifies and describes the present behavior.

Step 3.   The student evaluates the present behavior and is likely to change this behavior only if the student believes that it is not working. To help the student, the counselor can ask questions such as these: "How does this behavior help you?" "How does it hurt you?" "Does it help you get along with your teacher?"

Step 4.   The student is encouraged to identify alternative behaviors he or she could try to better meet personal needs. The counselor can assist if the student is stuck, but ultimately the student is responsible for coming up with ways to replace the problem behavior with a healthier behavior.

Step 5.   The student chooses one new behavior and commits to trying it.

Step 6.   In a second session, the counselor and the student review the outcome of the student's attempt at a new behavior. If the student reports being unsuccessful, the counselor does not concentrate on why or allow the student to give excuses.

Step 7.   The student is allowed to face logical consequences, such as a lower grade on an assignment turned in late. The student is not punished.

Step 8.   Don't give up on students who have a hard time changing their behaviors. Give these students extra sessions, working with them longer than they expect you to.

Because treatment can often involve adjusting what a student includes in the quality world, it is helpful for the counselor and the student to first identify what the student's quality world includes. Questions to help understand a student's quality world include these:

- Who are the most important people in your life?
- If you become the person you want to be, what will you be like (ask for specific traits and characteristics)?
- What is something you've done that you are really proud of?
- What does it mean to be a friend?
- What are your most deeply held values?

Once these things have been identified, the school counselor can help the student evaluate whether these things are realistic and responsible—in essence, do these images match the student's five basic needs? One way professional school counselors can use RT effectively with students is by asking five questions (C. L. Thompson & Henderson, 2007):

1. What have you tried so far to help your problem?
2. How has that been working? (Are you getting what you want?)
3. What else could you try?
4. Which of these are you ready to commit to trying?
5. When can we meet again to see if your idea has helped?

C. L. Thompson and Henderson (2007) summarized RT this way: "Counselors are in the business of teaching people better ways to meet their needs. From the reality therapy point of view, counseling is a matter of learning how to solve problems, teaching people, in effect, to become their own counselors" (p. 116). Although RT may not be appropriate for all individuals, it can be effectively used to help many students with issues ranging from minor concerns to more serious problems (Glasser, 2000b).

Individual counseling represents an essential responsive service in comprehensive, developmental school counseling programs. Another powerful and effective means of helping students with situational and developmental concerns is group counseling. In school settings, group work, including group counseling, is often viewed as the intervention of choice.

GROUP COUNSELING IN SCHOOLS

Group counseling, in addition to individual counseling, represents a mode of delivering direct services to students and is an integral part of a comprehensive, developmental school counseling program (ASCA, 2005a). From a developmental and a pedagogical perspective, students often learn best from each other (Goodnough & Lee, 2004);

therefore, group settings are ideal places to conduct both preventive psychoeducational work and remedial counseling. Groups provide a social environment in which members can learn and practice new behaviors, exchange feedback, and experience support. They allow students to develop insights into themselves and others and provide an effective, efficient way of helping students deal with developmental and situational issues.

Group work is one of the professional school counselor's most specialized skills (Goodnough & Lee, 2004). It represents a central means of delivering services in a comprehensive, developmental school counseling program. In this section, ways to set up and conduct group work in school settings are described. Before examining those activities, however, the types of groups that are most prevalent in school settings are discussed.

Types of Groups

Group work in schools can be classified in several different ways (e.g., Bergin, 2004; Cobia & Henderson, 2007; Goodnough & Lee, 2004; Greenberg, 2003; Myrick, 2003a). The Association for Specialist in Group Work (ASGW; 2000) defined four types of group work: task group facilitation, group psychoeducation, group counseling, and group psychotherapy. Task groups, also called work groups, are made up of members working together on a particular assignment or task. Examples in a school setting include student assistance teams, crisis response planning groups, and peer-helper orientation groups (Jacobs & Schimmel, 2005). Group psychotherapy, which is used with people who may be experiencing severe maladjustment, chronic maladjustment, or both, is usually conducted in community mental health settings, not schools.

Our focus in this section is on the two types of groups involving students led most frequently by professional school counselors: *psychoeducational groups* and *counseling groups*. In educational settings, psychoeducational groups include guidance groups, which typically are conducted in classrooms and are described in Chapter 9, and smaller (usually fewer than 10 members), growth-oriented groups that help students learn new skills and develop an awareness of their values, priorities, and communities. Counseling groups, while also growth oriented, are designed to help individuals who are experiencing some form of stress in their lives, such as loss of a family member, family changes, or issues related to sexual identity.

Although psychoeducational and counseling groups are conceptualized here and elsewhere as two distinct entities, it is more accurate to consider them along a continuum, with psychoeducational groups tending to be more structured and content oriented and counseling groups tending to be less structured and more process oriented. In reality, any number of topics (e.g., grief and loss, stress management, school success) can be the focus of either a psychoeducational group or a counseling group. Goodnough and Lee (2004), who classify groups in schools as *developmental, remedial,* and *school climate* groups, point out that psychoeducation has a place in all types of group work, as does group processing, which refers to interpersonal interactions among members within the group (Gladding, 2008). The professional school counselor's role is to design groups intentionally and balance content and process appropriately.

PSYCHOEDUCATIONAL GROUPS Psychoeducational groups use educational methods to help students gain knowledge and skills in several domains, such as personal identity, interpersonal interaction, developmental transitions, social maturity, academic achievement, and career planning (Bergin, 2004). When young people in psychoeducational groups face natural age and stage developmental tasks together, they frequently master more than the specifically targeted skills. Interaction within the group can promote an improved sense of well-being, leading to the prevention of future problems as group members develop new resources and coping skills. The goal of psychoeducational group work in schools is to "prevent future development of debilitating dysfunctions while strengthening coping skills and self-esteem" (Conyne, 1996, p. 157).

Psychoeducational groups tend to focus on central themes that correspond with students' developmental levels (Bergin, 2004). For example, young children may benefit from friendship groups or problem-solving groups. Older children and adolescents may respond well to groups that focus on stress management, assertiveness training, or boy–girl relationships. Topics for psychoeducational groups come from several sources. In part, professional school counselors select topics based on the academic, career, and personal/social domains outlined in the planned scope and sequence of a comprehensive, developmental school counseling program. In addition, professional school counselors can select topics based on the results of needs assessment surveys distributed to students, parents, teachers, and related school personnel. Furthermore, professional school counselors can use student outcome data to make decisions about specific psychoeducational groups that will benefit their students. For example, if academic achievement has declined or if behavior referrals have increased, professional school counselors can create and implement psychoeducational groups that focus on study skills, work habits, or anger management (Paisley & Milsom, 2007).

Psychoeducational groups vary in format according to the topic and the age of the students in the group. Regardless of the specific format selected, professional school counselors will want to take a number of factors into account as they prepare to lead psychoeducational groups, including students' developmental levels, multicultural issues, school climate, and the overall purpose of the school's counseling program (Akos, Goodnough, & Milsom, 2004). Furr (2000) outlined a six-step model for psychoeducational groups that moves from a statement of purpose to a session-by-session design that includes didactic, experiential, and processing components. The model includes the following sequential steps:

1. *Stating the purpose.* Psychoeducational groups should be guided by a clear statement of the reason for the group's existence that answers the following questions: (a) What is the primary content focus of the group? (b) What population is expected to benefit from participating in this group? (c) What is the purpose of the intervention (i.e., remediation, prevention, development)? (d) What is the expected outcome of participating in the group (e.g., change in thoughts, affect, behavior, or values)?

2. *Establishing goals.* Clearly defined goals describe how a student may change as a result of the group experience. Goals need to be achievable, measurable, short term, and clearly articulated. For example, a goal for a psychoeducational group designed to help students build self-esteem might be "To develop an understanding of the relationship between self-talk and self-esteem and to learn to modify inappropriate self-talk" (Furr, 2000, p. 45).

3. *Setting objectives.* Objectives specify the steps needed to reach the group goals. To build on the previous example, an objective for reaching the goal of understanding the relationship between self-talk and self-esteem might read, "Participants will learn the definition of self-talk and be able to differentiate between positive, negative, and coping self-talk" (Furr, 2000, p. 45).

4. *Selecting content.* Group content includes didactic, experiential, and process components. *Didactic content* refers to the information that will be taught directly to group members, such as information about types of self-talk. *Experiential activities* help group members learn by doing, rather than just by listening or discussing. To help students connect the experiential and didactic components, professional school counselors use the *process component.* It is important to plan processing questions in advance, first focusing on what happened during the activity and then moving to group members' reactions to and reflections on the experience.

5. *Designing exercises.* There are multiple resources professional school counselors can access that describe group exercises that can be adapted to meet the needs of a particular group. Group exercises can generate discussion and participation, help the group focus, promote experiential learning, provide the group leader with useful information, increase group comfort, and facilitate fun and relaxation (Jacobs, Masson, & Harvill, 2006). It is important to select theoretically grounded, developmentally appropriate exercises so as to enhance the group experience, not just fill time or provide entertainment. Role playing, imagery, and creative arts are just a few examples of the types of exercises that can be used effectively in psychoeducational groups. Furr (2000, p. 41) stated, "Without exercises, the psychoeducational group would become a vehicle that only conveys information rather than changes perceptions and behavior." As stated earlier, effective group leaders take steps to fully process the exercises with the participants.

6. *Evaluating the group.* Evaluation is an important component of any group activity. *Process evaluation* refers to ongoing, session-to-session evaluation of how the group members are perceiving their experiences, whereas *outcome evaluation* measures the overall effectiveness of the group experience, particularly in regard to individual change. Additional attention to evaluation is given later in this chapter.

COUNSELING GROUPS   In addition to psychoeducational groups, professional school counselors offer counseling groups that are primarily remedial in nature. Group counseling is remedial "when it addresses topics or issues that impair the learning and development of specific groups of students" (Goodnough & Lee, 2004, p. 174). It is often employed with children who have special life-event concerns, such as the death of a family member, family changes, teenage parenting, or school failure. Group counseling is also appropriate for children who have disruptive or acting-out behavioral problems such as violent outbursts, excessive fighting, defiance, maladjustment, and an inability to get along with peers and teachers (Brantley, Brantley, & Baer-Barkley, 1996; J. R. Nelson, Dykeman, Powell, & Petty, 1996). A large body of research supports the efficacy of group counseling in schools (e.g., C. A. Campbell & Brigman, 2005; Goodnough & Lee, 2004; Riva & Haub, 2004; Shechtman, 2002; Whiston & Sexton, 1998; see Chapter 4). Group counseling can help reduce social isolation and negative emotions, as well as increase positive peer relations and a sense of belonging (Arman, 2000).

In group counseling, the affective as well as the cognitive and behavioral domains of students are emphasized. The group creates a climate of trust, caring, understanding, and support that enables students to share their concerns with their peers and the counselor. Through group experiences, members maximize the opportunity to help themselves and others. Group counseling frequently takes one of three approaches to dealing with persons and problems: crisis centered, problem centered, and growth centered (Myrick, 2003a).

Crisis-centered groups are formed due to some emergency such as conflict between student groups. These groups usually meet until the situation that caused them to form is resolved. Crisis-centered groups may also form as a result of crisis intervention for large-scale trauma that affects the school's population. For example, in the aftermath of the tragedy of a school shooting incident, crisis-centered groups can help students process their feelings and develop ways of coping. Sometimes groups that were formed because of a crisis continue to meet after the crisis has passed and develop into either problem- or growth-centered groups. For example, after a fight between fourth and fifth graders, students in one school formed a "peace group," whose initial purpose was to resolve problems among the children who had been in open conflict. As the group continued to develop, however, its purpose expanded to finding ways to identify problems in the school and to correct them in a productive way.

Crisis counseling for groups, as well as schoolwide crisis counseling, is described more completely in Chapter 14. As stated by Baker and Gerler (2008), professional school counselors do not have a choice whether to include crisis counseling in their comprehensive school counseling program; instead, "crises will seek them out, and they will be expected to respond successfully" (p. 230). Controlled simulations of potential crises and interventions can help prepare professional school counselors to cope more effectively when crises arise. The American Counseling Association (ACA) has created a Responding to Tragedy resource link on its website (www .counseling.org) that provides helpful information for such situations.

Problem-centered groups are small groups that are established to focus on one particular concern that is interfering with educational progress. Problem-centered groups, which can also be considered issue-based groups, are beneficial to students who have demands placed on them that are beyond their current ability to handle. Examples of issue-based group topics include coping with stress, resolving conflicts, making career choices, getting better grades, dealing with family changes, and ending substance abuse. Like members of crisis-centered groups, students in problem-centered groups are often highly motivated and committed to working on their situations and themselves.

Growth-centered groups focus on the personal and social development of students. Their purpose is to enable children to explore their feelings, concerns, values, and behaviors about a number of everyday subjects such as developing social competence and making transitions. Through the sharing process, "students can learn effective social skills and acquire a greater concern and empathy for the needs and feelings of others" (Orton, 1997, p. 194). Often, growth-centered groups are formed after classroom guidance lessons have been presented on a particular topic, such as managing anger or making friends. Students are identified who would benefit from additional focus on the topic through growth-centered counseling groups.

Setting Up Groups in Schools

Several factors need to be considered in planning for group work in schools. In particular, professional school counselors will want to give attention to each of the following areas:

- Collaborating with school staff and parents,
- Determining group topics,
- Planning the logistics (e.g., group size, length of sessions, scheduling, group composition),
- Recruiting and screening group members, and
- Establishing group guidelines and confidentiality.

In this section, an overview of each of these important topics is provided. Readers are encouraged to refer to the sources cited for more in-depth information on each topic.

COLLABORATING WITH SCHOOL STAFF AND PARENTS

For group work in schools to be effective, professional school counselors need to have the support of the school administration, teachers, and parents. To gain this support, professional school counselors work collaboratively with school faculty and parents to develop awareness of the centrality and importance of group counseling services in their schools (Ripley & Goodnough, 2001; Steen, Bauman, & Smith, 2007). Among the barriers to successful group work is the justifiable concern about the possibility of students missing class to participate in group sessions. Schools are held accountable for students' academic performance; consequently, it is important to demonstrate ways group counseling can enhance, rather than diminish, student performance.

Open, clear communication about the nature and purpose of a comprehensive, developmental school counseling program is the key to successful group work in schools. Professional school counselors can lead in-school workshops early in the academic year. At this time, they can explain the overall comprehensive school counseling program, which includes group counseling, an example of responsive services. Similarly, professional school counselors can introduce the program to parents through an orientation at the first Parent Teacher Association or Parent–Teacher–Student Association meeting (Greenberg, 2003). Other suggestions for communicating with faculty and parents include the following (Greenberg, 2003; Ripley & Goodnough, 2001):

- Distribute needs assessment surveys to obtain suggested topics for group counseling, suggestions for a schoolwide counseling focus, and specific parent or teacher concerns.
- Consult with teachers frequently and encourage them to let you know about particular student needs.
- Meet regularly with the principal to discuss program concerns and goals. Inform the principal of activities taking place within the program, including group work.
- Send notes to faculty announcing such things as the topics for groups that are being formed, dates of standardized testing, and general activities of the program.
- Visit classrooms to introduce yourself to students and inform them about all the services offered by the school counseling program, as well as guidelines for participation.
- Share information about group goals and objectives and, when appropriate, written materials about group topics.
- Provide outcome data to faculty and parents regarding the effectiveness of the groups that you coordinate.

- Encourage faculty and parents to give you feedback about what they have observed.
- Have a clear process for establishing groups, selecting students, scheduling sessions, and obtaining parental or guardian permission.

DETERMINING GROUP TOPICS There are several ways to make decisions about which groups to offer. As discussed earlier, administering a needs assessment survey to students, parents, and teachers is an effective way to select group topics. One approach to the survey can ask respondents to develop a list of topics they think would be helpful to discuss in small groups. Another option is for the professional school counselor to list group topics and have the respondents indicate whether they are interested (Jacobs & Schimmel, 2005). A third option is to use a confidential "counselor suggestion box" in which students place their ideas for group topics and other concerns (Stroh & Sink, 2002). Yet another way to make decisions about what groups to offer is to examine existing data. School databases about attendance, test scores, retention, and other information can provide additional sources of information about schoolwide needs (Jacobs & Schimmel, 2005; Paisley & Milsom, 2007).

Group topics are directly connected to the academic, career, and personal/social development of students. Whereas many topics (e.g., building self-esteem, establishing peer relationships) are applicable across grade levels, others (e.g., transitioning to high school, teenage pregnancy) are more developmentally specific. Also, although general topics may be applicable across grade levels, the specific manner in which they are addressed differs according to developmental level. An example of sample group topics that might be offered at various grade levels is presented in Table 10.1.

TABLE 10.1 Sample Group Topics for Elementary, Middle, and High School Students

Elementary School	Middle School	High School
Dealing with feelings	Peer pressure	Assertiveness training
Friendship	Interpersonal relationships	Dating/relationships
Academic achievement	Organizational/study skills	Test-taking anxiety
Family changes	Body image	Teen parenting
Self-esteem	Transitioning to high school	Personal identity
Career awareness	Understanding interests and skills	Career exploration and planning
Social skills	Conflict management	Managing stress
Problem solving	Being new to the school	Transitioning to college or work
Valuing diversity	Multicultural issues/sensitivity training	Gay, lesbian, bisexual issues

Note: These topics represent just a few of the many topics that professional school counselors may use in their settings.

PLANNING THE LOGISTICS (GROUP SIZE, LENGTH OF SESSIONS, SCHEDULING, GROUP COMPOSITION)

Early in the planning process, professional school counselors will want to consider several factors related to the logistics of group formation. Generally speaking, the younger the child, the smaller the number of group members and the shorter the session (Gladding, 2008; Myrick, 2003a). Children have shorter attention spans and tend to be easily distracted in a large group. With young elementary school children, it is advisable to limit the group to no more than five students (Gazda, Ginter, & Horne, 2008). When working with children as young as five or six, groups may be limited to three or four members, with sessions lasting only 20 minutes (C. L. Thompson & Henderson, 2007). With older elementary school children and preadolescents (ages 9–12), groups may consist of five to seven students and meet from 30 to 45 minutes (Gazda et al., 2008). Adolescents (ages 12–19) typically meet for one class period, which lasts between 40 and 50 minutes. Group size should be limited to no more than eight members, with six being ideal (Jacobs et al., 2006). When groups get too large, it is difficult for all members to participate, and groups are more likely to lose focus. These are "rule of thumb" guidelines; group size and session length should be based on a number of factors, including students' developmental levels, the purpose of the group, and the nature of the problems with which students are dealing (D. B. Brown & Trusty, 2005b).

Scheduling groups can be a challenging task, especially in middle and high schools. With the increased call for raising achievement on standardized testing, many teachers are understandably reluctant to release students from classes (Hines & Fields, 2002). Consequently, it is imperative to work collaboratively with teachers in designing group schedules. In some educational settings, group sessions are rotated so that students do not have to miss the same class more than once. Another option is for professional school counselors to consult with teachers to determine whether there is a time during the day when attending a group counseling session would have the least impact on student learning.

Another logistical consideration relates to the group's composition. Should the group be homogeneous or heterogeneous in regard to such factors as gender, age, and ethnicity? Decision making about group composition is complex, and there are few definitive answers. First, there is considerable disagreement regarding whether to separate groups by gender. For example, Kulic, Dagley, and Horne (2001) indicated that is helpful to separate younger children along gender lines, whereas C. L. Thompson and Henderson (2007) stated that most counselors prefer a balance of both sexes in a group unless the problem to be discussed (e.g., some sex education topics) is such that the presence of the opposite sex would hinder discussion. In regard to age, it is generally agreed that groups should be composed of members who are relatively close in age, both developmentally and chronologically (Gladding, 2008; Kulic et al., 2001). Ethnic and cultural diversity in groups is desirable unless the topic is specific to a particular group. For example, Villalba (2003) described group work with Latino/a children with limited English proficiency.

Some groups lend themselves to homogeneity with regard to the issues that are addressed. In such cases, the groups are homogeneous in that the students are experiencing similar concerns, and being together can contribute to a sense of universality (Yalom & Leszcz, 2005). Examples of homogeneous groups include groups for children whose parents are divorced and groups for adolescents questioning their sexual orientation (Stroh & Sink, 2002). However, there also are benefits to heterogeneity in membership. Group members can learn from each other about different ways of addressing problems (Goodnough & Lee, 2004). Also, heterogeneity may be desired in a group for social skills development or anger management so as to have role models in the group. In general, groups should possess some in-group heterogeneity, but not so much that group members have nothing in common (Kulic et al., 2001).

RECRUITING AND SCREENING GROUP MEMBERS

Professional school counselors recruit potential group members in several ways. One way to recruit members is to provide parents, teachers, and students with an *information statement* that describes what the group is about and what is expected of its members (Ritchie & Huss, 2000). Flyers, bulletin boards, newsletters, and word of mouth also can be used to promote group participation. Professional school counselors often have special knowledge about students, gained through long-term relationships and through communication with teachers and parents, that may allow them to identify potential group members (Hines & Fields, 2002). Also, particularly when groups are topic specific, students may volunteer to participate.

Not all students who volunteer or are referred, however, are suitable for a group. Therefore, professional school counselors will want to conduct screening interviews to determine whether the student is a candidate for group participation and whether the student wants to participate. Screening potential group members is a practice endorsed by the ACA (2005a) and by the ASGW (2000). Screenings may be conducted individually or in small groups.

During screening interviews, the professional school counselor talks with students about the group, its purpose, and expectations of its members. Students are encouraged to ask questions about the group so that they can make informed decisions about joining (M. S. Corey & Corey, 2006). Through this interactive process, the professional school counselor can assess students' motivation and level of commitment. Issues to be taken into account in making decisions about whether a student is suitable for a group include emotional readiness, willingness and ability to participate interactively, willingness to accept the rules of the group (e.g., confidentiality), and desire to be helpful to other group members (Greenberg, 2003). If a student has been referred to the group (whether self-referred or other-referred) and it appears that he or she is not ready to be in a group, Greenberg (2003) suggested that the professional school counselor consider initiating individual counseling, with one of the goals being to get the student ready to become a member of a group.

If the professional school counselor and the particular student decide that the student is ready to participate, a letter requesting permission for participation should be sent to his or her parents or guardians, assuming that notification is appropriate. The letter should include information about the type of group, the length and number of sessions, and the activities that will take place in the group, as well as the professional school counselor's contact information. Some school systems or states may have a policy mandating or recommending notification of and approval for students to participate in groups. The most recent ASCA ethical code (2004a) also states that parents and guardians should be notified if the counselor considers it appropriate and consistent with school board policy or practice (Section A.6.b). Professional school counselors will want to follow their school policy or state law in regard to parent notification (Bodenhorn, 2005; Sink, 2005a). In addition to obtaining permission from parents, professional school counselors should ask students to sign consent forms so that everyone is in agreement about the purpose of the group and the procedures involved before the group begins (Gladding, 2008).

ESTABLISHING GROUP GUIDELINES AND CONFIDENTIALITY Early in the process, professional school counselors will want to discuss group procedures and expectations with all group members. M. S. Corey and Corey (2006) recommended having a pregroup meeting designed to help members get acquainted and to prepare them for the group experience. During this time, students can be asked to sign informed consent forms. Group rules can be discussed and confidentiality clarified.

Group guidelines are needed to create the foundation for cooperative group relationships (Schmidt, 2008). In most cases, it is advisable to get students' input in establishing the ground rules so as to foster a sense of ownership and investment (Greenberg, 2003). Examples of ground rules, which can be adapted to match the developmental

level of group members and the purpose of the group, include being a good listener, participating in the group, sharing experiences and feelings, not interrupting, showing respect for group members, and maintaining confidentiality. The concept of confidentiality is especially important, as professional school counselors are bound by their professional code of ethics to protect the confidentiality of group members (Jacobs & Schimmel, 2005). Some professional school counselors ask students to sign contracts in which they agree to not discuss outside the group what happens in the group.

Professional school counselors also need to let students know that confidentiality in a group setting cannot be guaranteed. As sensitive matters are brought up during group discussion, professional school counselors can remind members about confidentiality and its limits.

Conducting Group Work

The reader may have already taken or will soon take a course in group counseling. In that course, one develops knowledge and skills related to group dynamics, effective group leadership, group stages, ways to work with different populations, and legal and ethical aspects of group work, among other topics. It would be beyond the scope of this chapter to discuss each of those areas or to provide suggestions for group sessions on various topics, although many excellent sources address the scope and practice of group work. Instead, in this section, the role and functions of group leaders in schools are outlined and suggestions for planning, implementing, and evaluating groups in schools are provided.

ROLE AND FUNCTIONS OF GROUP LEADERS "Effective group leadership is a process, never ending and cycling through stages" (DeLucia-Waack, 1999, p. 131). To be effective, group leaders must be able to function in a variety of ways at different times. Bergin (2004) described the professional school counselor's role during the group process in this way:

> During the group process, the counselor concentrates on promoting the development of group interaction, establishing rapport among group members, leading the group progressively through all four stages, and encouraging individual members' self-exploration and personal decision making. The counselor guides the group as it discusses individual and joint concerns, models appropriate attending and responding behaviors, and reinforces members for supporting one another during their individual self-exploration. In addition, the counselor confronts resistance sensitively, redirects

negative behavior, and encourages the group's efforts to become self-regulatory. The counselor safeguards the group's integrity by enforcing the rules the group establishes for itself. (p. 360)

Professional school counselors who lead groups need to develop knowledge and skills in several areas. Following are five noteworthy areas (G. Corey, 2008; Jacobs & Schimmel, 2005; Shechtman, 2002):

1. *Be clear as to the purpose of the group.* Is the group primarily a psychoeducational group or a counseling group? What goals and outcomes are desired for students who participate in the group? Group leaders need to clarify the group's purpose and help members move in that direction.

2. *Know how to relate developmental theory and counseling theory to group work.* As stated earlier in this chapter, a strong grounding in developmental theory is essential for any type of counseling work with children. It also is important for professional school counselors to apply counseling theory to the group process so that they can feel confident about the strategies they are using (Goodnough & Lee, 2004). Cognitive therapy, RT,

Adlerian therapy, and SFBC represent four theoretical approaches that have been shown to be effective in group work with students. A professional school counseling intern describes her experiences using RT with a group of fifth graders in Voices from the Field 10.3.

3. *Be knowledgeable about the topic or content being covered in the group.* Professional school counselors will want to acquire knowledge and information about a wide range of topics, including such things as stress management, grief and loss, sexual identity development, study skills, bullying, teenage parenting, divorce, stepfamilies, acculturation, and racial identity development. There are many resources available that contain a wealth of information about topics and about ways to present them at different developmental levels. It may be helpful for professional school counselors to create a portfolio that includes information about various topics, suggestions for group exercises related to those topics, and specific developmental and cultural considerations.

4. *Be creative and multisensory.* Children and adolescents respond well to activities that engage their minds and their senses. Professional school counselors can use art, drama, music, movies, and props

---

VOICES FROM THE FIELD 10.3   **REALITY THERAPY AND THE RUMOR MILL**

I have found reality therapy to be a useful model of counseling to use with students, both individually and in groups. Most recently, I was asked by a fifth-grade teacher to talk with her female students about gossiping and spreading rumors. The teacher had been approached by several parents and students about what she described as a widespread problem. I decided to talk with approximately ten girls and ask what they thought about gossiping to determine whether they viewed it as a problem and something they wanted to stop doing. They all indicated that they wanted to change their behaviors. Using the five questions of reality therapy, we worked together to define the problem and examined whether the behaviors were helping them get what they wanted. After determining that gossiping and spreading rumors were not getting them what they wanted, the girls came up with ideas for behaviors that would help them get what they wanted. They selected one behavior to "try out."

I checked back with the girls individually to see how things were progressing and to see if they needed any other ideas to try. I charted the process on the board in their classroom and showed them how they could follow that same outline when trying to solve other problems they experienced. I suggested that they revisit that process

together if they got stuck and let them know that they could contact me for more help if needed.

I also led an anger management group for sixth-grade students who self-referred. They all thought that their ways of handling anger were interfering with their lives and wanted help learning ways to manage it differently. Using RT, we explored the students' behavior and determined whether it was getting them what they wanted. Because the behaviors were not working, we came up with lists of at least five alternative behaviors. Each student decided on an idea to try. The group was six sessions long, and we spent four sessions discussing new behaviors selected to replace old behaviors. By the final group session, each student had new ideas about ways to handle anger more effectively.

Working as a professional school counselor can be challenging because of the number of students who need assistance. Working with students in groups provides a way to reach several students simultaneously. Using RT with students gives them an opportunity to change behaviors and also teaches them a process that they can employ when other concerns arise.

Cassie Cox Evans, Professional School Counseling Intern, Wake Forest University, North Carolina

to generate discussion and participation, help the group focus, and promote experiential learning (Jacobs et al., 2006). Moreover, employing a variety of creative methods provides a way to address students' different learning styles, thereby enhancing the overall group experience. Examples of creative, multisensory group activities are described in Table 10.2. For other examples, readers are referred to Gladding (2005), Greenberg (2003), and Jacobs et al. (2006).

5. *Possess multicultural understanding.* For group leaders to work effectively with all populations, they need to be culturally competent (Bailey & Bradbury-Bailey, 2007; Bemak & Chung, 2004). Multiculturally competent counselors have the self-awareness, knowledge, and skills needed to interact successfully with people from different cultural backgrounds. They recognize their own values, biases, and assumptions and are open to diverse value orientations and assumptions about human behavior (G. Corey, 2008). Multiculturally competent group leaders understand the different cultures of their group members, and they also recognize how different cultural backgrounds might affect members' participation in the group (Jacobs & Schimmel, 2005). A key aspect of multicultural group work is fostering "acceptance, respect, and tolerance for diversity within and between members" (Bemak & Chung, 2004, p. 36). Professional school counselors can refer to the

ASGW Principles for Diversity-Competent Group Workers (ASGW, 1999) for guidance in addressing issues of diversity with sensitivity and skill.

PLANNING, IMPLEMENTING, AND EVALUATING GROUPS   To maximize the group experience, it is important for leaders to plan for sessions ahead of time (Furr, 2000; Jacobs & Schimmel, 2005). An example of a six-step model for psychoeducational groups was presented earlier in the chapter. As with individual counseling, group leaders will want to balance *intentionality* (planning) with *flexibility* (being responsive to the needs of the group at a given time). When groups are focused on specific topics such as stress management, study skills, or anger management, leaders can plan the content and activities for each session in advance (Jacobs & Schimmel, 2005). Planning a series of sessions in this way is a "big picture" reminder that helps the leader keep the group focused and goal oriented.

Some general suggestions for beginning, middle, and ending sessions include the following:

- During beginning sessions, group leaders strive to create a safe environment in which members feel free to share their experiences. The creation of cohesion and trust, which begins during the initial session, contributes to the overall success of the group. Some of the activities that take place during the initial group session (unless there has already been a

---

TABLE 10.2   Introductory Group Activities

Elementary School: *Coat of Arms*

Create a coat of arms by drawing a shield and dividing it into four equal sections. Explain to children that a coat of arms tells different things about a person. Ask group members to create a shield that illustrates things they would like other people to know about them. The group leader might give specific suggestions such as "In the first section, draw or write something about your family. In the second section, draw or write something that you are really good at. In the third section, draw or write about a good book or something that you have read recently. In the last section, draw or write what you have a lot of fun doing."

Middle School: *Decorating My Bag*

Ask group members to cut out pictures representing themselves from magazines or newspapers. Tape or paste these pictures, along with other symbols, on the outside of their paper bags. Also, as part of the exercise, students can put loose pictures and symbols that they are not yet ready to share inside their bags. The students can use the bags to introduce themselves to one another in relation to the pictures and symbols on the outside of the bags. During subsequent sessions, as trust develops, provide students with opportunities to share the material inside the bags, as they see fit (Gladding, 1997).

High School: *Empty Chair Introductions*

Ask group members to think of someone whom they trust and value. This person can be a friend or family member. Ask members to stand behind their chairs, one at a time, and pretend to be that friend or family member. Then ask the student how that person would introduce the student. Next, the student, speaking as the trusted individual, introduces the "empty chair" as though the student were sitting in it. After introductions have been made, encourage group members to share what they learned about each other.

pregroup meeting) include introducing members, discussing the group's purpose, establishing ground rules, explaining confidentiality, and discussing expectations. Suggestions for activities to include in an initial session are presented in Table 10.2. Also, during the beginning sessions, leaders will want to take note of how group members relate to each other and how they relate to the purpose or content of the group (Jacobs & Schimmel, 2005).

- The format of subsequent sessions will vary according to the age of the group members and the purpose of the group. In general, it is helpful to establish a routine that is used in all group sessions (Gilbert, 2003). Following are suggested elements to include in this routine:
  1. Welcoming members individually,
  2. Reviewing group rules,
  3. Summarizing what occurred during the previous session,
  4. Focusing on the current topic or issue,
  5. Leading an experiential exercise related to the topic,
  6. Processing the exercise, and
  7. Leading a closing activity in which members describe what they have learned or how they experienced the session.

- During these "middle" sessions, general goals include moving to a deeper level where feelings are identified and shared and group cohesion, support, and awareness are increased.

- The final group session is a time of summary and termination. Goals for the final session include helping group members to focus on the future, instilling hope, and helping members to translate insights into behaviors (Corey & Corey, 2006). Termination of the group should be planned in advance, with leaders announcing two to three meetings before the final session that the group experience will be ending. Like the initial session, the final group session tends to be structured. Students discuss their feelings about the group ending and identify what they have learned from the group experience. There are a number of ways to conclude groups, many of which include a time of group celebration. Some of the tasks that may occur during the group's closing stage include the following:

  1. Reviewing and summarizing the group experience,
  2. Assessing members' growth and change,
  3. Finishing business,
  4. Applying change to everyday life,
  5. Providing feedback,
  6. Handling good-byes, and
  7. Planning for continued problem resolution. (Jacobs et al., 2006, p. 362)

Giving group members an opportunity to evaluate the group experience takes place either during the final session or during a follow-up meeting. Evaluation is needed to determine the usefulness of the group and its effect on the members (Akos & Martin, 2003; Steen et al., 2007). Group evaluation can take several forms. Brief questionnaires and surveys with incomplete statements are two ways to evaluate students' perceptions and learning. Examples of incomplete statements include the following:

The group helped me at school by _____.

One thing I learned in this group was _____.

The most helpful part about being in this group was _____.

One thing I wish we had done differently was _____, and to improve the group, I suggest _____.

In addition to asking group members to evaluate the group, professional school counselors can design pretest and posttest surveys to evaluate outcomes (Akos & Martin, 2003). Professional school counselors may also want to ask teachers, parents, or both to evaluate the group based on their observations of students after the group sessions have ended. Such evaluations are particularly helpful when the group focus was improved behavior (e.g., anger management, study skills, social skills). Finally, following up with students approximately six to eight weeks after the group has ended can provide professional school counselors with additional information about the group's impact and effectiveness.

Summary/Conclusion

Individual counseling and group counseling are important components of a comprehensive, developmental school counseling program. They represent responsive services and provide ways to address students' needs and concerns. In particular, individual counseling and group counseling are ways to help students who are facing problems that interfere with their personal, social, career, or academic development.

The manner in which professional school counselors carry out individual counseling and group work is affected by a number of factors, including the developmental characteristics of the students, personal philosophical orientations, and specific school demands. In this chapter, counseling in school settings was defined. Certain developmental characteristics of children and adolescents, particularly as they relate to the counseling process, were described. A model of individual counseling was presented, which included building a counseling relationship, assessing specific counseling needs, designing and implementing interventions, and conducting evaluation and closure. Also, because of their utility in school settings, two theoretical models of counseling, SFBC and RT, were presented. These approaches allow professional school counselors to provide effective counseling to students in a brief amount of time.

Whereas some students have needs that warrant individual counseling, a larger number of students can be reached when they participate in psychoeducational or counseling groups in schools. Psychoeducational groups use educational methods to help students gain knowledge and skills in several domains. They help group members to develop new resources and coping skills, which may prevent problems in the future. Counseling groups tend to be more remedial than psychoeducational groups and may be crisis centered, problem centered, or growth oriented.

Regardless of the type of group offered, several issues need to be considered by professional school counselors as they plan for group work. Important factors associated with setting up groups include collaborating with school staff and parents, determining group topics, making decisions about group composition and scheduling, screening students, and establishing group guidelines. Factors related to conducting groups effectively include demonstrating effective group leadership skills; planning for initial, middle, and final group sessions; and conducting group evaluation. Professional school counselors can effectively use group work, as well as individual counseling, with students to enhance development and remediate problems.

As a final note, group work in schools represents an integral domain in the *ASCA National Model* (2005a) and the Transforming School Counseling Initiative (TSCI). We encourage you to read about some of the new directions school counseling groups are taking (e.g., wellness, self-advocacy, academic achievement with African-American males), which are described in depth in the 2007 edition of *The Journal for Specialists in Group Work*. This special edition, produced by ASGW, focuses on group counseling in schools and has a plethora of information that professional school counselors will find useful.

Activities

1. Role-play an individual counseling session with an adolescent who is considering dropping out of school. Use the premises from solution-focused brief counseling or reality therapy to guide your session.
2. Develop an interview for screening members for a group topic of your choice (e.g., children from changing families, social skills, study skills).
3. Develop a psychoeducational group for young children in a school setting using Furr's six-step model for psychoeducational groups.

Helping Lab Videos

To help further your understanding of some of the topics in this chapter, go to MyHelpingLab at www.myhelpinglab.com and view the following video clips:

Counseling Individuals and Groups in Schools: Child Counseling and Psychotherapy,
Module 4 (Narrative Therapy with Children, "Using Client's Stories to Define the Problem"),
Module 9 (Play Therapy, "Using Role Plays and Projection in Play Therapy"),
Module 11 (Multimodal Therapy, "Addressing Emotions from a Structural Profile" and "Listing Coping Skills for Dealing With Emotions"), and
Module 13 (Reality Therapy, "Exploring a Client's Need for Power" and "Helping Clients Develop 'Their' Goals and Plans").

11

Promoting Educational and Career Planning in Schools

Patrick Akos, Spencer G. Niles, Emily M. Miller
and Bradley T. Erford

E ditor's Introduction: When professional school counselors provide career and educational guidance to students, they influence the future by helping clarify developmental decisions that often last a lifetime. Although educational planning and career planning have been responsibilities of professional school counselors for decades, the school reform movement has placed renewed emphasis on challenging students to pursue rigorous academic coursework, oftentimes regardless of future aspirations. In the future, professional school counselors must continue to challenge students academically, while building support systems and contingencies for exploring diverse vocational and avocational opportunities. In other words, professional school counselors must help students pursue a rigorous academic path, while supporting important developmental life-role decisions that will affect students long after high school.

BACKGROUND FOR EDUCATIONAL- AND CAREER-PLANNING INTERVENTIONS IN SCHOOLS

Providing career assistance to students has always been an integral part of the work performed by professional school counselors. During most of the 20th century, professional school counselors fostered their students' career decision making by administering and interpreting interest inventories and aptitude tests. In the 1950s, however, Donald Super (1957) proposed a developmental perspective emphasizing career development as a lifelong process. Super's theory created a paradigm shift within the career development field. Specifically, the focus of career interventions shifted from a single-point-in-time event of making a career decision to the manifestation of career behaviors over time. Super outlined career development stages and tasks, proposing that development through the life stages could be guided "partly by facilitating the maturing of abilities and interests and partly by aiding in reality testing and in the development of self-concepts" (Super, 1990, p. 207).

In addition to Super's contributions to the field, changes in the economy in the past few decades have enhanced the need for professional school counselors to focus on the area of educational planning and career development. Changes in population, economics, and technology have had the largest impact on the job market. Furthermore, an increase in the globalization of jobs has altered job titles, roles, and structure within the workplace (Feller, 2003). Of particular interest to the professional school counselor should be the shift toward jobs in technology. According to Feller, of the 30 jobs that are projected to grow the most quickly in the coming decade, one-third of them are in the field of technology. Further, because of technology and the global context, entirely new careers continue to emerge each year. Because of these advances, a focus on educational and career planning is at an all-time high and will continue to grow.

EDUCATIONAL AND CAREER PLANNING TODAY

Educational planning and career development for youth are prominent components of the current standards for developmental school counseling programs established by the American School Counselor Association (ASCA; C. Campbell & Dahir, 1997). The ASCA *National Standards for School Counseling Programs* identify as goals of comprehensive, developmental school counseling programs these three core areas of development: academic, career, and personal/social. All three areas are interrelated and occur together in multiple systems. The *National Standards* specify three important areas of student career development:

- *Standard A.*   Students will acquire the skills to investigate the world of work in relationship to knowledge of self and to make informed career decisions.
- *Standard B.*   Students will employ strategies to achieve future career success and satisfaction.
- *Standard C.*   Students will understand the relationship among personal qualities, education and training, and the world of work. (p. 16)

A complete list of competencies for each of these three standards of the career development component of the developmental school counseling program can be found in Appendix C. These competencies include the development of career awareness and employment readiness; the acquisition of career information; and the identification of, and development of skills to achieve, career goals.

Among the academic competencies in the *ASCA National Model* (2005a) are several statements on educational planning that are interconnected with those for career development. Educational planning is the means through which linkages are forged, for students as well as stakeholders, between academic achievement and postsecondary options (Hobson & Phillips, 2010). Although the interdependence of school and work is often overlooked by students, the educational-planning process, when started early enough (i.e., middle school at the latest), can help students become aware of how their school performance relates to post–high school goal achievement, thereby increasing motivation to work hard in school. For example, Trusty and Niles (2004) demonstrated the long-term impacts (e.g., completion of a bachelor's degree) of course taking in middle and high school. According to Hobson and Phillips, an effective educational-planning process eliminates making a career choice by chance because it creates a foundation for a student's career development and prosperity as a citizen. Rigorous academic coursework completed during middle school builds this foundation.

Educational planning can and should be infused into the school counseling curriculum in all grade levels. In elementary school, students should first become acquainted with the concept of educational and career planning (Trusty, Niles, & Carney, 2005) through learning about the salient relationship between school performance and the world of work and postsecondary education. When students reach middle school, where it is hoped that they are introduced to careers at a more complex level and obtain self-knowledge about their skills, interests, and values through inventories and other career activities, the stage will be set for them to start thinking in more concrete terms about their educational, career, and life goals. These goals will then form the basis for making choices about the courses they take while in middle school, as well as helping them to create a tentative blueprint for their high school course taking.

It is through this kind of sequential educational-planning process that students are continually reminded about the school–work connection. More importantly, however, this process provides students with many and varied opportunities to learn about themselves and engage in mindful planning and preparation that will help to ensure that their decisions about life after high school are made thoughtfully, in advance, and with their personal life goals in mind (Hobson & Phillips, 2010).

Others have promoted career development strengths that are needed by all. Lapan (2004) and Savickas (2004) created schema based on decades of career development research that contributed to positive career behaviors. Lapan highlighted positive expectations, identity development, person–environment fit, vocational interests, academic achievement, and social skills (work readiness behaviors). Similarly, Savickas proposed a structural model of career adaptability that includes a taxonomy of adaptive attitudes of concern, control, conviction, competence, commitment, and connection. Although a full description of these is beyond the scope of this chapter, these constructs are integrated into the programs and interventions later.

Finally, life-span, life-space theorists define *career* as the total constellation of life roles that people engage in over the course of a lifetime (Super, 1980). Career development tasks include developing the skills necessary not only for selecting and implementing an occupational choice, but also for selecting, adjusting to, and transitioning through a variety of life roles, with an emphasis on helping students develop life-role readiness (Niles, 1998). Counselors using this multisystemic approach to career development ask questions such as these: "What skills are necessary for successful performance as a student, worker, citizen, and so forth?" "What types of awareness do students need to acquire to make effective personal, educational, and career decisions?" "What knowledge is essential for students to make informed choices about life-role participation?" "What skills do I need to accomplish my desired life roles?" The *ASCA National Model* (2005a) supports this idea of life-role readiness by focusing on the holistic development of each student in the three core areas of academic, career, and personal/social development. These focuses (*ASCA National Standards*, educational planning, career development strengths, and life-role readiness) encompass the content for a K–12 educational- and career-planning program.

IMPLEMENTING SYSTEMATIC AND WELL-COORDINATED EDUCATIONAL- AND CAREER-PLANNING PROGRAMS

To help students acquire the knowledge, skills, and awareness necessary for effectively managing their career development, counselors implement systematic and well-coordinated educational- and career-planning programs (Herr, Cramer, & Niles, 2004). Counselors recognize that the piecemeal implementation of such programs limits the degree to which they can positively influence students. Moreover, an unsystematic and poorly coordinated intervention program often creates confusion about the meaning and purpose of career programs among those not directly involved in their creation and implementation. The *ASCA National Model* (2005a) is one example of a comprehensive and systematic program that can be implemented.

Specific to career development and similar to the *ASCA National Model*, a five-stage planning model for implementing systematic educational and career intervention programs was recommended by Herr et al., 2004):

Stage 1. Develop a program rationale and philosophy.

Stage 2. State program goals and behavioral objectives.

Stage 3. Select program processes.

Stage 4. Develop an evaluation design.

Stage 5. Identify program milestones. (p. 310)

An important component of stage 1 is the needs assessment, used to determine appropriate program rationales, goals, and interventions (Herr et al., 2004). The needs assessment provides benchmarks against which program outcomes can be assessed. Herr et al. emphasized the importance of incorporating teachers, students, parents, and community participants in the needs assessment to increase their understanding of, and involvement in, career development programs. Clearly, a properly conducted needs assessment provides a firm foundation on which effective educational and career intervention programs can be constructed.

An implicit theme in these recommendations is that program planners need to be sensitive to the political climate in which they operate. In some locations, not clearly connecting career development interventions to the academic curriculum or student academic achievement (e.g., educational planning) will significantly decrease the chances of program success. Also, not adequately communicating successful program outcomes will result in the program resources being vulnerable to funding cuts. If school personnel view the program as an additional burden to their already heavy workloads, then there is little chance that the program will succeed. Thus, the "marketing" of the program to all stakeholders and its coordination and integration into current goals are important aspects of program development and implementation. Clearly defined behavioral objectives that address the specific needs of program participants will be useful in marketing the program and providing outcome data demonstrating program benefits.

Another theme implicit in these recommendations for implementing systematic educational- and career-planning programs is the importance of taking a team approach to service delivery. The *ASCA National Model* (2005a) emphasizes this team approach to service delivery in the stress it places on collaboration. Working with administrators, professional and support staff, parents, and community members, the professional school counselor can add depth and variety of experience to the school's career development program. For example, in some districts, professional school counselors need to coordinate and connect with others in the school working toward career development outcomes (e.g., career development coordinators, career and technical education staff, career decisions elective instructors). Counselors may, at times, provide classroom instruction, and teachers may, at times, perform more counseling-related functions. Although there is no one prescription for how the roles and responsibilities should be defined, it is logical that counselors take the lead role in developing and implementing the programs. For example, bringing together parents and professionals within the community for a career fair would provide a much wider base of knowledge and first-hand experience about various careers than would merely using the information that the counselor could locate.

To address career development within the traditional academic curriculum, professional school counselors integrate career development interventions into the classroom. For example, students in an English class can conduct research projects to explore a potential career path. In this format, academic development (by engaging in research) and career development (by gathering occupational information) are connected with a writing assignment. Students learning about government can be introduced to presidents and legislators not only as historical figures, but also as real people who have job descriptions and earn salaries and who possess specific job qualifications. This type of integration or infusion of career- and educational-planning concepts into the curriculum enhances the academic and career development of students.

Professional school counselors are often the only professionals in the school system with specific training in career development; therefore, professional school counselors possess the knowledge of career development theory and practice necessary for formulating appropriate program interventions. Moreover, the processes typically used in program delivery relate to counselors' primary areas of expertise. These processes are counseling, assessment, career information services, placement services, consultation procedures, and referrals (National Occupational Information Coordinating Committee [NOICC], 1992).

In addition to having specific training in career development, the professional school counselor is usually the primary figure within the school who helps students with educational planning. Throughout the middle and high school years, educational planning and career development are inextricably tied to one another because decisions that are made about class choices and high school pathways often correlate with the postsecondary options that are available. Hobson and Phillips (2010) suggested that the professional school counselor discuss the following three areas with students and parents: the amount of postsecondary training the student is willing to attain, the career in which the student is currently interested, and the type of training or education that is required to attain that career.

Counselors can also play an important role in program delivery by helping teachers communicate to parents the ways in which systematic career development programs can enhance student achievement. Communicating clearly the value of programs to parents and incorporating parents into program interventions will increase the likelihood that the program will be successful. At the same time, professional school counselors can help students understand the connection between current academic activities and future careers. Again, Super's concept of career development as a lifelong process and the *ASCA National Model*'s multiple, interrelated competencies are essential.

Career Assessment

Assessment is another indispensable component of career planning and development. It is through the use of formal assessments (i.e., inventories, aptitude tests) and informal assessments (i.e., checklists, card sorts, interviews) that students begin to learn about themselves and their interests, skills, and values related to the world of work. Results from assessments also provide professional school counselors with

a starting point for guiding students in the career-planning process. Therefore, it is vital that professional school counselors remain current in their knowledge about which career assessments are suitable for use with school-aged youth, as well as possessing a general understanding of assessment so that they can make informed decisions about which assessments to use with their student population.

There are numerous career assessments on the market, and a full listing of them is beyond the scope of this chapter. Nonetheless, a variety of formal assessments appropriate for use with students will be briefly discussed to give readers a sense of the types of assessments available to professional school counselors. Kuder has a career- and educational-planning system that allows students in middle school and high school to create an online career portfolio that includes their educational plan, as well as their results from three assessments: the *Kuder Career Search with Person Match*, which helps students to identify their interests and then links them to the most fitting career cluster; the *Kuder Skills Assessment*, which helps students to identify their skills and then links them to the most fitting career cluster; and *Super's Work Values Inventory*, which helps students to identify which values are most important to them in their work. Additional information about the Kuder Career Planning System can be found online at www.kuder.com/solutions/kuder-career-planning-system.html.

The *Self-Directed Search* (SDS), created by John Holland, is an assessment that is suitable for high school students. The SDS uses the test-taker's information about his or her interests to determine personality type, which is presented in the form of a three-letter Holland code. In the results report, the individual is also given information about occupations and college majors compatible with his or her code. Information about the SDS can be accessed at www.self-directed-search.com. The *Strong Interest Inventory* (SII) is another assessment based on Holland's typology, which can be used with high school students to help them find their Holland code and learn about occupations that correspond to their code. The SII can be purchased online at www.cpp.com/products/strong/index.asp.

O*NET, a career resource center, offers career assessments related to interests, abilities, and values: The *O*NET Interest Profiler* measure users' interests based on Holland's six types, the *O*NET Ability Profiler* measures users' skills in nine areas important to many occupations, and the *O*NET Work Importance Profiler* measures users' work values in six different categories. *O*NET* also compiles information about a multitude of occupations. For each occupation, a summary is provided describing the tasks, skills, knowledge, abilities, activities, interests, values, salaries, and trends associated with that career. Students can visit online.onetcenter.org/find to explore and learn about occupations of interest. For more information on O*NET's career resources and products, visit www .onetcenter.org.

Finally, the professional school counselor must use emerging technology to sustain an educational- and career-planning program. In the past, technology was used primarily for computer-assisted career guidance systems (CACGSs), but more recently the Internet has emerged as the primary way to use technology in career development programs. This includes career assessment, career exploration, and job information websites that are easy to access and inexpensive, a handful of which will be briefly introduced in this chapter.

The *Occupational Outlook Handbook* (OOH), a well-known reference developed by the U.S. Department of Labor, provides individuals with considerable information about labor market trends for hundreds of occupations. High school students can use the OOH to research occupations of interest to them and glean information regarding the training and educational requirements needed to enter the field, as well as typical worker salaries and future job prospects. The OOH is available online at www.bls.gov/OCO. There is also a companion website for students in grades 4 through 8 (www.bls .gov/k12), which provides visitors with similar information in age-appropriate language. To search for occupations, students can click on a school subject that they enjoy, which then links them to a sampling of careers associated with that subject.

Students interested in beginning their job search can use the following websites as a jumping-off point: Quint Careers (www.quintcareers.com/job-seeker.html), the Riley Guide (www.rileyguide.com), JobHuntersBible (www .jobhuntersbible.com), CareerBuilder (www.careerbuilder .com), Monster (www.monster.com), Simply Hired (www.simplyhired.com), and Indeed (www.indeed.com). The first three websites provide visitors with guidance and tips on how to find a job on the Internet, including information about interviewing and about writing resumes and cover letters. The last four websites are job search engines.

For those students interested in attending college, the Internet hosts a plethora of helpful websites related to college admission and financial aid. For college admission information, students should be directed to Peterson's (www.petersons.com), which allows students to search for colleges that match their interests and then provides them with extensive information about each college; *U.S. News and World Report* (www.usnews.com), which creates an annual list ranking the nation's best colleges; College Board (www.collegeboard.com), which offers information on the SATs, a college search, resources to help students through the application process, a scholarship search, and financial aid resources and information; and Quint Careers (www .quintcareers.com/student.html), which has a special section for students with extensive information on college

planning, summer and seasonal jobs, internships, and financial aid. Another valuable financial aid website is run by the U.S. Department of Education (studentaid.ed.gov). It provides students with information about choosing a college and paying for their education.

There are a variety of ways that professional school counselors can integrate technology into their career development programs. For example, a classroom guidance lesson that focuses on career exploration could center on the use of technology. Students can use the Internet to take an inventory of their own career interests and then search for specific information on jobs that align with those interests. Additionally, the Internet can be used to gather information on creating cover letters and resumes when teaching students about employability skills and to coach students on the job-search process.

Developing a systematic and coordinated educational- and career-planning program across grades K–12 requires understanding the developmental tasks confronting students as they progress through school. Understanding these tasks prepares school personnel to work collaboratively in program development and implementation. A comprehensive understanding of the career development process also sets the stage for developing program interventions that are sequential and cohesive.

ELEMENTARY SCHOOL

During the elementary school years, children begin formulating a sense of competence and interests through greater interaction with the world beyond their immediate families. Interactions with peers, teachers, parents, and community members shape children's self-perceptions. Through exposure to adult life patterns via observations in schools, community activities, home, and the media, children draw conclusions about their lives. The conclusions they draw include assumptions about their current and future place in the world.

Obviously, there is tremendous variability in the quality-of-life patterns to which children are exposed. Television, for example, often provides children with examples of men and women in gender-stereotyped roles and occupations (e.g., only women working as nurses, only men working as auto mechanics, and women taking primary responsibility for homemaking and parenting). It also may provide very limited perceptions of careers for people of color. Children use this information to draw conclusions about the life patterns that are appropriate for them. As children are increasingly exposed to stereotypical behaviors and expectations of majority groups, they begin to eliminate nontraditional life patterns and narrow occupations for further consideration. The *ASCA National*

Model (2005a) addresses the discussion of traditional and nontraditional career choices in several of the career development competencies.

Gottfredson (1996) contended that a gender-based elimination process begins as early as the age of six. She also suggested that between the ages of 9 and 13, children begin to eliminate those occupations from further consideration that they perceive to be less prestigious for their social class. Variables such as race or gender stereotyping and prestige rankings interact with self-perceptions of abilities and interests, as well as family and community expectations. These influences shape the decisions young people make about potential occupational options. An additional variable that influences students' perceptions of certain careers is geography. Students who have resided in more rural locations may have been exposed to entirely different jobs than those who have grown up in urban areas.

Because elementary school children have not yet had the opportunity to fully explore their options, an important goal of career development interventions in elementary school is to counteract environmental factors that pressure students to prematurely commit to educational and occupational options (Marcia, 1989). The use of nontraditional models (e.g., male nurses and female engineers) and exposure to a broad range of occupational environments is encouraged during the elementary school years. Because gender stereotyping is prevalent in society, students in elementary school should be encouraged to examine beliefs about female and male roles in society and how the various life roles interact to shape the overall life experience. To help students develop the skills necessary for effective career planning, they are taught decision-making strategies. Another goal of career development interventions with elementary school children is to provide an environment in which each student's natural sense of curiosity can flourish (Super, 1990). Curiosity provides the foundation for exploring; children naturally express curiosity through fantasy and play. Children often engage intensely in fantasy-based play related to occupations such as physician, firefighter, teacher, and nurse. Curiosity can be guided to help students learn accurate information about themselves and their environments. For example, field trips to occupational environments related to a child's fantasy-based interests reinforce the child's sense of curiosity and stimulate further exploration and the gradual crystallization of interests (Super, 1957).

Encouraging students to participate in activities relating to their interests nurtures a sense of autonomy, the anticipation of future opportunities for exploring, and the beginning of planful behaviors (Super, 1990). When interests connect with skills and capacities, a positive self-concept emerges, which, in turn, provides the foundation for coping with the career development tasks of adolescence (Super, 1990). As children move toward adolescence, they must accomplish four major career development tasks. Specifically, they must (1) become concerned about the future, (2) increase personal control over their lives, (3) convince themselves to achieve in school and at work, and (4) develop competent work habits and attitudes (Super, Savickas, & Super, 1996).

Educational planning is also essential in elementary school. A study by Blackhurst, Auger, and Wahl (2003) found that fifth-grade students had a limited understanding of specific job skills and educational requirements for commonly known occupations, believing inaccurately that many widely known jobs require a college degree. These findings point to the possible need for professional school counselors and teachers to spend time introducing students to the training and educational requirements for a variety of popular occupations to ensure that students do not needlessly rule out potential careers early on in their lives based on faulty beliefs, as well as to make sure students are aware of the full range of postsecondary options that exist beyond four-year colleges, such as vocational and technical colleges. Raising student awareness about the training and educational requirements for occupations that interest them may also serve to heighten their motivation to do well in school.

Although important decisions about postsecondary plans will not be made until later in their education, students in elementary school should begin exploring possible career pathways and become aware of how the skills they are learning in school are used in various careers. Teachers and professional school counselors can play a key role by helping students connect the dots between the learning that occurs in school and the skills necessary for the world of work. For example, professional school counselors could collaborate with teachers to present classroom guidance lessons showing students how math skills are needed by doctors and nurses to ensure that patients receive the appropriate amount of medicine, how newspaper and magazine writers need excellent writing skills in order to convey important and interesting stories to the public, how skills learned in art are useful for architects and graphic designers, or how almost all jobs require workers to have strong interpersonal and problem-solving skills. Making these connections can provide students with increased understanding of the importance of school and a solid foundation for future educational and career goal-setting, which is an integral part of the educational-planning process.

Finally, students' performance in elementary school can have a significant influence on their future course-taking and postsecondary options. For example, if students want to take accelerated classes in middle school, their ability to do so will depend largely on their performance and behavior in elementary school (Trusty et al., 2005). Likewise, students' likelihood of doing well in accelerated high school classes depends largely on their performance in intensive middle school courses. Thus, educational planning and goal-setting play an important role even in elementary school, and it is essential that professional school counselors begin talking with parents about their hopes and plans for their children, as well as students' goals for themselves, so that students are not put at a disadvantage later in their academic careers due to poor planning.

Career Development Guidelines in Elementary School

Along with the ASCA *National Standards* covering career development, NOICC (1992) developed National Career Development Guidelines to help counselors identify developmentally appropriate goals and interventions across the life span. The specific career development competencies identified as appropriate for elementary school children fall within three categories: (1) self-knowledge, (2) educational and occupational exploration, and (3) career planning. Today, the National Career Development Guidelines are organized around personal and social development, educational achievement and lifelong learning, and career management and are available online at www.acrnetwork.org/ncdg.htm.

At the elementary school level, students develop a basic sense of self (e.g., the activities in which they enjoy participating, the things they like and do not like) that provides the foundation for career exploration activities. Students also learn how to interact effectively with others. They learn that as they grow and develop, they will take on additional responsibilities. By learning school rules, students develop a basic understanding of the importance of cooperative behavior within institutions. Erikson (1963) noted that developing a sense of initiative and industry

during the elementary school experience provides children with a solid foundation from which they clarify their identities during secondary school.

Students in the elementary grades also engage in educational and occupational exploration by developing an understanding of the importance of educational achievement. Developing a sense of personal competence and positive self-worth is an important goal for elementary school children to achieve. Erikson (1963) noted that children who do not achieve this goal will struggle as they attempt to move forward in educational and career planning.

The primary focus of career development interventions in the elementary school is awareness. Children need to develop an awareness of important self-characteristics (e.g., values, interests, and capacities). According to the *ASCA National Model* (2005a), professional school counselors need to promote self-knowledge; academic self-concept; and awareness of skills, interests, and motivations in relation to careers. They also need to receive accurate information about educational and career options. Helping children learn about a variety of occupations and the educational requirements for entering different occupations reinforces the fact that current activities relate to future options. School personnel must also work to challenge the gender and racial occupational stereotypes that confront children (e.g., see Voices from the Field 11.1 for an illustration of the career development work of a practicing elementary school counselor). Teaching children about the importance of diversity helps them learn how to interact more effectively with others in the school and community. Collectively, these interventions provide the basis for effective educational and career planning during secondary school.

THEORY INTO PRACTICE 11.1

CAREER DEVELOPMENT ACTIVITIES FOR ELEMENTARY SCHOOL STUDENTS

The possibilities for career development activities in elementary school are endless. This is the time to use creative and engaging activities to introduce students to possible occupations and raise their awareness about the diverse careers that exist. Thus, developmental classroom guidance lessons and schoolwide initiatives are the most efficient and appropriate ways to deliver this information. Because students at this level have shorter attention spans than older students, it may be helpful to limit lessons to 20–30 minutes.

Practical Ideas for Career Development Activities

- Ask students to identify and discuss the jobs that they have observed in their communities and then

add to their knowledge base by introducing a few new ones.
- Encourage students to identify the "jobs" they currently have as students and sons or daughters. They can use this self-knowledge to create a "Me and My Job" booklet that highlights their interests, as well as their "job" responsibilities at school and home.
- Fill paper grocery bags with two to five items that are associated with a specific career. Take the items out of each bag one by one and have students guess the type of worker that uses those items. For example, one bag could contain a stethoscope and blood pressure cuff to represent a doctor.

- Ask students to draw a picture of a job they might want to have when they are older.
- Give each student a letter of the alphabet and ask the students to select a job that begins with that letter, draw a picture of the job, and write three tasks or activities that are related to that occupation. Bind the students' work together to create an "Alphabet Career Book" for the school's library.
- Read a developmentally appropriate story (e.g., *Worm Gets a Job* by Kathy Caple for students in second grade and below) to a class and then have the students identify the various jobs that were discussed in the book.
- Expose students to women who work in traditionally "male" occupations and men who work in traditionally "female" occupations.
- For students in grades 3 to 5, require each student to complete an interview with an adult about his or her career. Questions should focus on what the adult does and the schooling needed to prepare for that career. After interviews have been conducted, students can share their findings with the class.
- For fifth-grade classrooms with access to computers and the Internet, have students visit the children's *Occupational Outlook Handbook* website (www.bls.gov/k12), select an occupation that interests them, and fill out a worksheet describing the job's training requirements, typical salary, and future outlook. Students can then take turns sharing their information with the rest of the class and commenting on whether the information they found made them more or less interested in the job and why.
- Engage students in a discussion about the connection between education and career planning. Ask students: "How does school help you in career planning?" After this discussion, instruct each student to choose a career and research the career online at the children's *Occupational Outlook Handbook* website (www.bls.gov/k12) to determine the skills taught in school that are needed for success in that occupation.
- Challenge students to look into the future and think about how the jobs they are currently interested in might be different in 15 to 20 years. Using a computer lab, provide students with time to research the education, training, and skills they will need to be successful in these "future careers."
- Host a career day or career week during which students' parents and members of the community visit the school to talk about their occupations. Before visitors come to speak, it is important to meet with students and develop a list of questions that they can ask speakers. These questions can then be typed up and distributed to students prior to each presentation. Following the career day, the professional school counselor can conduct a booster session during which students are asked to reflect on and process their thoughts about the careers they learned about.
- Arrange field trips to nearby businesses to help students get a sense of the types of occupations that exist in those fields (e.g., hospital, grocery store, library, bank). Like with a career day, students should develop questions to ask their tour guide before the trip, and professional school counselors should ensure that there is time for processing afterward.
- On a more global level, carve out a small amount of time during every classroom guidance lesson, whether it is career related or not, to have students identify how the skill being taught in the lesson is integral to success in the workplace and engage them in a brainstorming session to come up with the types of occupations that are most likely to need that skill to be effective.
- Provide parents with links to any websites used in the career development program so that they have the chance to explore these sites with their children at home and reinforce the learning that occurred in school.
- Using your school's behavioral and achievement data, identify students who demonstrate academic potential, but who, because they are from historically underrepresented populations or have not yet mastered essential school skills, may not be recommended for the more challenging classes in the articulation process in middle school. Work with these students, either individually or in small groups, in the fourth and fifth grades to explore their career interests, set academic goals, and develop the skills necessary to excel in school and be recommended for higher-level courses by their teachers.

VOICES FROM THE FIELD 11.1   **CAREER DEVELOPMENT IN THE ELEMENTARY SCHOOL**

I utilize career development classroom guidance lessons as well as schoolwide events to address career competencies with my elementary students. The classroom guidance lessons vary among grade levels. In kindergarten, we focus on career awareness and explore the multitude of jobs available by looking at different tools that jobs use. I link this activity to a kindergartener's job as a student and the tools used every day in class such as pencils, erasers, glue, and crayons. We also focus on nontraditional jobs by matching girls and boys to jobs such as mechanic, nurse, doctor, and teacher. I intentionally

(*Continued*)

match the genders to nontraditional jobs and then present images of real people working in the nontraditional jobs.

As students get older, I link career planning to academic goal-setting. Third-grade students focus on exploring their interests, abilities, and favorite subjects and then link them to future careers. Fourth- and fifth-grade students delve deeper into career development theory by completing interest inventories and learning about John Holland's personality theory. We incorporate technology into career planning and utilize the Bureau of Labor Statistics website to research jobs that match with their personality type. Students research the education required for a career, the job outlook, and subjects used. Video clips of nontraditional jobs are shared through media center resources. Within each career lesson, community members and parents are incorporated as students share interviews they have conducted with family members about what they like and dislike about their jobs, the subjects they use, and the education they received.

The career development lessons culminate in a schoolwide Career Week, which ignites excitement among all students about future careers. Video bios of community members are shared with the entire school population on the "Morning Show." Students are able to dress up as a favorite future career. Kindergarteners and fourth- and fifth-grade students participate in a Career Day. Approximately 20 community members are scheduled to present to these students and bring visual props or interactive materials to engage the students. The activity is then linked to academic learning through writing lessons that result in thank-you notes and summary reports of what students learned. The impact on students is tremendous as they learn how subjects in school eventually are used in careers, thereby increasing motivation to learn those skills. They also see the multitude of opportunities that are available in the world of work, which is especially valuable for students who have not been exposed to a diverse number of occupations within their family environments. Furthermore, they begin to see realistically how grades, school attendance, and good homework habits relate to getting a good job with sufficient pay. For younger students, Career Day plants the seeds for future questioning and learning in the school environment. Finally, the events connect the school community to the community at large and involve key community stakeholders in the educational process.

Source: Angela Poovey, Professional School Counselor, Dillard Drive Elementary, Wake County Public Schools, Raleigh, North Carolina

MIDDLE OR JUNIOR HIGH SCHOOL

Students at the middle or junior high school level are confronted with a more sophisticated set of developmental tasks than they experienced during their elementary school years. The stormy experience of transitioning from childhood to adolescence presents a challenge to the young person. Physiological and social development leads the early adolescent to take strides toward independence; these strides, however, are often accompanied by feelings of insecurity, conflict, fear, and anxiety. Dramatic changes in cognition and the intensification of affect contribute to a "fluctuating sense of self" (Vernon, 1998, p. 10). As a result of their advancing development, middle or junior high school students are preoccupied with belonging and are influenced significantly by same-gender peers. Thus, the personal and social developmental tasks experienced by middle or junior high school students influence the delivery of career development interventions. The primary focus of these interventions is to help students crystallize and articulate their identities. Counselors need to challenge students to become involved in the career development process, while offering supportive assistance as students acquire additional information about self and career.

Middle or junior high school students demonstrate a growing understanding of the world of work. Often, this progress is the result of students' participating in school activities, hobbies, and part-time work. Herr et al. (2004) reported several important facts pertaining to the career development of middle or junior high school students. For example, they noted that boys and girls at age 13 tend to be equally knowledgeable about highly visible occupations and can link at least one school subject to a job. Most students at this age indicate that they have at least started the process of thinking about a future job. Interestingly, their choices for future jobs tend to be occupations requiring college degrees or lengthy training periods beyond high school, rather than jobs now held by the majority of the workforce.

For students who do wish to attend college, it is essential that they begin talking about these plans with their parents and the appropriate school staff while in middle or junior high school so that they can take classes that will adequately prepare them for the rigorous courses (i.e., college prep) they will need to take once they reach high school (Hobson & Phillips, 2010). Failure to begin planning in middle or junior high school can have substantial repercussions for students' postsecondary options. Equally relevant are the students who do not have any postsecondary plans or goals. These students will be at a distinct disadvantage later on in their academic career if they find that they have not achieved high enough grades or taken the necessary classes to prepare themselves for the occupation or continuing education they desire (Trusty et al., 2005). This is why a focus on educational planning is necessary during the seventh and eighth grades. Hobson and Phillips (2010) addressed the notion of balancing the high career aspirations of students with the influence of others.

They suggest that the professional school counselor can play a role in coaching students as they make course selections, while attempting to attend to both the dominance of their parents and the influence of their peers.

Variability in career development among middle or junior high school students points to the importance of being clear about the societal expectations placed on students in middle or junior high school. As these students transition between Super's (1980) growth and exploration stages, they encounter the task of crystallizing occupational preferences. They are expected to develop a realistic self-concept and to learn more about opportunities (Super, 1980). Specifically, middle or junior high school students are required to learn about themselves and the world of work and then translate this learning into an educational plan for the remainder of their secondary school education. Through educational planning, students make important choices about their future careers. For example, during the eighth grade, a student is expected to identify a specific pathway of academic classes that will lead to certain possibilities on graduation. To make an educational plan, it is important for the student to have already developed some self and career awareness. Without sufficient coursework or achievement, he or she may find that the postsecondary option that was desired is no longer available because requirements were not met early on in the educational-planning process.

Super et al. (1996) stated the following about the crystallization process: "When habits of industriousness, achievement, and foresight coalesce, individuals turn to daydreaming about possible selves they may construct. Eventually, these occupational daydreams crystallize into a publicly recognized vocational identity with corresponding preferences for a group of occupations at a particular ability level" (p. 132). Thus, to establish an appropriate course of action for high school and beyond, educational- and career-planning interventions during middle or junior high school must be directed toward helping students cope successfully with the tasks of crystallizing and specifying occupational preferences (Super et al., 1996). Although research has shown that career identity will change several times in the future, students bring interests discovered in elementary school to career thinking in middle or junior high school.

Career Development Guidelines in Middle or Junior High School

Middle or junior high school students learn that a positive self-concept is crucial for effective career planning. Developing a positive self-concept is facilitated by increased competence. They develop more-sophisticated interpersonal skills and gain a greater understanding of human growth and development.

Middle or junior high school students must also develop specific competencies in educational and occupational exploration to advance in their career development. For example, the link between school activities and future opportunities first developed during elementary school must continue to be strengthened. Guest speakers representing a variety of occupations can discuss the relationship between learning and work. Specific subject areas can be linked to occupational success. The importance of life-long learning for occupational success can also be stressed. To reinforce the importance of academic achievement, professional school counselors can inform students about the positive correlation between the level of academic attainment and the amount of income workers earn. Teaching students how to locate, understand, and use career information fosters independent activity in educational and career planning. To this end, students can be taught the Holland (1992) occupational codes as a means for developing self-understanding and organizing occupational information.

The primary focus of career development interventions during middle or junior high school is exploration. Career exploration can take place in numerous ways. Through classroom guidance on self-exploration (e.g., using Holland's [1992] theory), students can use computers to take the Career Key (L. K. Jones, 2004) and learn more about their own personality types. On discovering their types, students may look through a list of correlating career options and begin to explore these options through activities such as career days, job shadowing, and Internet searches. Students can be encouraged to explore by learning more about themselves not only as that knowledge pertains to important characteristics (e.g., interests, skills, values), but also in terms of considering the life roles that are important now and that are likely to be important in the future. Moreover, students learn the skills necessary for accessing and using educational and occupational information. These competencies are essential for moving forward with educational and career planning in high school.

During the middle or junior high school years, an educational and career portfolio is started for every student. Included in this portfolio are interest inventories, career exploration information and activities, educational-planning materials, results from Internet searches, resources acquired at career fairs or job shadowing, and any other information that will add to the student's career development process. Using this portfolio, the student and professional school counselor can meet throughout the year and discuss the career development process using easy-to-access information that is specific to the student. Although this portfolio is started during middle or junior high school, it should be passed on to the high school counselor and maintained throughout the high school years. It is during the high school years that items in the portfolio will reflect more specific career choices.

CAREER DEVELOPMENT ACTIVITIES FOR MIDDLE OR JUNIOR HIGH SCHOOL STUDENTS

Professional school counselors working at the middle or junior high school level need to help students determine their career interests, skills, and values so that they have enough self-awareness when they reach high school to create suitable educational plans. Middle or junior high school is the ideal time to engage students in educational planning, career exploration, awareness, information gathering, and future goal-setting.

Practical Ideas for Career Development Activities

- Administer a career interest inventory, skills assessment, and values inventory (see the section on assessment at the beginning of this chapter for specific instruments that may be helpful in this process) to students. These inventories can be found online, in paper form, or through computer-assisted career programs and software (e.g., Career Futures or Choices Explorer [www.bridges.com], Kuder Career Planning System [www.kuder.com/solutions/kuder-career-planning-system.html], Career Cruising [www.careercruising.com], and Coin Educational Products [www.coinedu.com/products/middle.cfm]). Using the results from these inventories, help students pinpoint one or two career clusters that are of interest to them to begin exploring in more detail.
- Present a classroom guidance lesson to students in the computer lab introducing them to the host of available online resources to help them learn about careers. Ask students to research one occupation on each website and write down their findings.
- Ask students to make a list of the occupations they think women most commonly work in and the occupations they think men most commonly work in and have them share their lists with the class. Teach students about nontraditional career opportunities and how certain jobs have been stereotyped and discriminated against as "male jobs" or "female jobs." Present common myths related to nontraditional jobs, as well as information about the realities of these jobs. End with a discussion about the implications of such stereotyping.
- Inform students about the importance of educational and career goal-setting. Create a goal-setting worksheet that asks students to list two educational goals and two career goals that they have for themselves. For each goal they set, provide space for them to list

the specific steps they will need to take to achieve each of their goals. Allow sufficient time for students to share some of their goals with the class and ask them what they can begin doing in the next few days or weeks to start working toward their goals.

- Deliver a classroom guidance lesson on the connection between school and work and then assign students the task of conducting one informational interview with a professional in the community to learn about the professional's work environment and the skills learned in school that lead to success in that occupation.
- Prepare a presentation introducing students to the wide range of postsecondary possibilities (e.g., four-year college, community college, vocational school, job training) and provide a sampling of occupations corresponding to each pathway. Engage students in a discussion about how their performance in middle or junior high school and high school has a significant influence on the possibilities that will be available to them upon graduation from high school.
- Introduce students to the concepts of lifestyle and life roles and have them write down how they currently spend their time and what their current life roles are, as well as what they would like their lifestyle to be like and what life roles they think will be important to them when they are adults. Make sure to explain the variety of factors that make up a lifestyle, how different people prefer different lifestyles, and how money is only one part of the equation. Provide students with examples of the kinds of lifestyles associated with well-known careers (e.g., a doctor's lifestyle, a teacher's lifestyle, a banker's lifestyle). Once students have completed this task, ask them to research careers of interest to them and see how many they can find that would allow them to support their desired lifestyle and fulfill the life roles that are important to them.
- Collaborate with teachers to find ways to integrate career development activities into students' core classes. For example, professional school counselors could team up with science teachers to present information about science-related careers and the education necessary to pursue those careers.

- Host a career day or career fair where students have the opportunity to meet and hear from professionals who work in a diverse range of occupations.
- Work with students to begin creating a career portfolio, either on the computer or in a binder, to house the results from their assessments, as well as any other important documents, activities, projects, or research that they accumulate throughout middle or junior high school that will aid them in the career and educational decision-making process once they reach high school.

VOICES FROM THE FIELD 11.2　CAREER PLANNING AT THE MIDDLE SCHOOL

As a first-year counselor in the only middle school in a small school district, I've faced many challenges. Our school counseling program is making progress toward reflecting the ideals of the *ASCA National Model*, which means we often spend time advocating for our role and have to find time to dedicate to our students when we have many other responsibilities that take up a great deal of our time. One issue we have struggled with is determining how to devote sufficient time to career development outside of the standard high school program planning. In today's society, middle school counselors must advocate for time with students dedicated to career development and exploration because of the challenging job market our students will face.

In the first few months of the year, I had limited opportunities to conduct classroom guidance lessons and small-group counseling sessions on academic or personal/social topics with my seventh graders. However, when I requested time to discuss career exploration with the students, no one questioned the meaningfulness of this type of lesson, especially because I included a career interest inventory that would help students determine the careers in which they might be successful. Additionally, there was full administrative and staff support for attending a career fair hosted at the state university across town.

These career exploration activities may have been the first meaningful exposures our students had in understanding the importance of discussing careers because of the immediacy of decisions they will make regarding high school program planning. While middle school students may developmentally be able to make the connection between school and future work, we struggled to get all students to understand the value of these experiences. Middle school students are too often negatively influenced by their peers, and unfortunately the overall composition of the class dictates how successful many activities can be. These facts are important to keep in mind when planning and executing career development activities, and it was a hard lesson I had to learn during my first year. However, by collecting data, both before and after conducting the career development activities, it was possible for me to determine how to improve the lessons and make them even more meaningful for all students. This will make it easier to advocate for time with students when the amount of time allotted for counselors to work with students is becoming increasingly more limited with the standards placed on schools today.

Source: Megan A. Kingsley, Professional School Counselor, Buford Middle School, Charlottesville City Schools, Virginia

HIGH SCHOOL

As students transition from middle or junior high school to high school, they focus more directly on the task of identifying occupational preferences and clarifying career and lifestyle choices. According to Super (1957), the tasks of crystallizing, specifying, and implementing tentative career choices occur during early (ages 12–15), middle (ages 16–18), and late (ages 18–24) adolescence.

When adolescents complete the relevant training and preparatory experiences, they then implement their occupational choices by acquiring positions in their specified occupations. In today's dynamic job world, the ability to adapt to various work environments may be the most important people skill. Thus, the key elements of a successful school-to-work and school-to-school transition involve being able to implement and adjust to career choice(s).

It is important to note that the majority of secondary school students in the United States enter work immediately on leaving high school or do not attend or finish college. Thus, a majority of adolescents must acquire workforce readiness to cope successfully with their school-to-work transition. The definition of *workforce readiness* changes with the times. Until recently, this term may have focused solely on helping adolescents acquire training for a specific job, but today employers are more concerned with "finding youth who can read and write, have a good attitude, are motivated, are dependable, follow directions, and can be good team members" (Krumboltz & Worthington, 1999, p. 316). Obviously, academic skills, interpersonal skills, and the willingness to engage in lifelong learning have emerged as important skills for youth to acquire if they are to be successful workers. Most current job skills are transferable to other occupations and contexts.

THEORY INTO PRACTICE 11.3

SCHOOL TRANSITION

The transition to work or postsecondary education is a prominent theme in the career development literature. However, professional school counselors at the elementary, middle or junior high, and high school levels should also consider the opportunity to support students and promote successful transitions between levels of schooling. For example, the transition to middle or junior high school is an opportunity to support students in adopting the new roles they take on and in taking advantage of the new autonomy to choose classes and extracurricular activities. Similarly, as students create high school plans in eighth grade, professional school counselors can engage students in self and career awareness in choosing curricular paths and elective choices.

Hansen (1999) argued for expanding school-to-work career development interventions to include student development in addition to the more traditional emphasis on workforce development. Hansen pointed to curricula such as the Missouri Life Career Development System, the Minnesota Career Development Curriculum, and a model developed by the Florida Department of Education titled A Framework for Developing Comprehensive Guidance and Counseling Programs for a School-to-Work System as excellent examples of comprehensive career development interventions to help youth prepare for the transition from secondary school to work. The *ASCA National Model* (2005a) reinforces many of these ideas through its career development competencies. In particular, several of the competencies emphasize the transition from school to work and the relationship between learning and work (e.g., each student should demonstrate an understanding of the value of lifelong learning and have the skills necessary to adjust to career transitions).

S. B. Baker and Gerler (2008) emphasized the importance of providing "transition enhancement" assistance to secondary school students as they progress toward further education, training, or employment. They recommended that, because such transitions are a regular part of high school students' development, counselors view transitions as a process, rather than as events or a sequence of events. The basic needs of students coping with the transition process can be classified into the categories of support, awareness, and skills. Because most adolescents have lived their lives primarily in the arenas of home and K–12 schools, postsecondary work, training, and education present new challenges and experiences. Professional school counselors can aid in normalizing the transition process by providing reassurance to students that, although somewhat frightening, these new opportunities will present them with normal challenges and that many of the competencies they have developed thus far will be useful to them as they move forward.

When conceptualized as a process, the skills required for coping with the school-to-work and school-to-school transition are linked to the elementary and middle or junior high school career development competencies discussed previously. That is, transition skills build on the self-awareness, occupational awareness, and decision-making skills students have developed throughout their educational experience. Transition skills also build on the basic educational competencies related to reading, writing, and arithmetic (S. B. Baker & Gerler, 2008). For example, composing a resume and cover letter requires self-awareness, occupational awareness, and writing skills. Performing effectively in a job or college interview requires skill in oral communication and interpersonal communication. Acquiring information about jobs, colleges, and training programs requires research, technology, and reading skills. Transition skills can also be expanded to include skills related to stress and anxiety management. The ASCA takes the position that counselors in the school must assume the primary (but not sole) responsibility for fostering these skills in students. Providing career guidance to students is one of the most important contributions professional school counselors make to a student's lifelong development. Thus, proactively bolstering students' readiness to cope with the career development tasks they are likely to encounter is a primary component of the professional school counselor's role. Likewise, counselors must be competent in developing and delivering strategies to help students who encounter difficulty in coping with career development tasks.

Much of Super's research focused on understanding how adolescents can develop their readiness to cope effectively with the various career development tasks confronting them. The term initially used by Super (1957) to describe this process was *career maturity*. Because the career development tasks confronting adolescents emerge from expectations inherent in academic curricula and society (e.g., those of family and teachers), the career development process during this life stage is more homogeneous than in adulthood. That is, the school system expects students to make career decisions at specific points in the curriculum (e.g., eighth graders choose an academic program that they will study in high school). Because the timing of these tasks can be predicted, career development practitioners can provide a systematic set of interventions to foster adolescent career development.

Savickas (1999) noted the importance of orienting students to the tasks they will face and the decisions they will make during their secondary school years. Discussing the items on career development inventories such as the *Career Maturity Inventory* (Crites, 1978) or the *Adult Career Concerns Inventory* (Super, Thompson, & Lindeman, 1988) is one technique that Savickas suggested for helping secondary school students consider the career development tasks they will encounter as they move through high school. Students need to develop awareness of the choices they will make throughout high school and beyond. Additionally, Savickas suggested that a positive attitude toward making educational and career plans, a willingness to become actively involved in the career development process, the relevant competencies and motivation to acquire information about the world of work, and decision-making abilities are some of the competencies high school students need in order to manage their career development effectively.

Other researchers such as Marcia (1989) have also identified important variables for adolescent career development. Marcia focused on two variables—crisis/exploration and commitment—as central to the career development process during adolescence. Crisis/exploration refers to the process of sorting through identity issues; questioning parentally defined goals, values, and beliefs; and identifying personally appropriate alternatives regarding career options, goals, values, and beliefs. Commitment refers to the extent to which the individual is personally involved in, and expresses allegiance to, self-chosen aspirations, goals, values, beliefs, and career options (Muuss, 1998). The degree to which adolescents resolve the tasks associated with crisis/exploration and commitment provides the conceptual structure for Marcia's (1989) taxonomy of adolescent identity. This taxonomy comprises four identity statuses: (1) identity diffused or identity confused, (2) foreclosed, (3) moratorium, and (4) identity achieved.

The *identity-diffused* person has yet to experience an identity crisis or exploration and has not made any personal commitment to an occupation or to a set of goals, values, and beliefs. The *foreclosed* person has yet to experience an identity crisis or exploration, but has committed to an occupation and to a set of goals, values, and beliefs (usually due to indoctrination or social pressure by parents or significant others). This type of foreclosure is premature because it has occurred without exploring

and struggling with the basic existential questions related to identifying one's values, beliefs, goals, and so on. The *moratorium* person is engaged in an active struggle to clarify personally meaningful values, goals, and beliefs. Committing to a particular set of values, goals, and beliefs has been placed "on hold" until the process of identity clarification is more complete. The *identity-achieved* person has sorted through the process of identity clarification and resolved these issues in a personally meaningful way. Moreover, as a result of exploring and resolving identity issues, the identify-achieved person commits to an occupation and a personal value system.

Rather than being a singular process of exploring and committing to a set of values, goals, and beliefs, identity formation occurs across several domains such as occupation, religion, politics, ethnicity, and sexuality, among others. In many respects, these domains parallel Super's (1980) notion of life-role self-concepts (e.g., worker, leisurite, student, and homemaker) and reinforce Hansen's (1999) call for holistic career development interventions in the schools. Additionally, the individual's identity status within each domain is not static, but rather an ongoing process involving back-and-forth movement across stages. Marcia (1989) noted that, although any of the identity statuses can become terminal, the foreclosed person experiences the greatest risk of closed development. Thus, career development interventions for early adolescents and adolescents (who, by definition, enter into these life stages with a relatively diffused identity) should be carefully designed to foster exploration and identity development related to the career domain.

Educational planning culminates in high school. During this time period, students must begin to make serious decisions about their future. This process should entail formulating an educational plan delineating the steps students will need to take to achieve their postsecondary career/educational goals (Hobson & Phillips, 2010). According to Rosenbaum and Person (2003), educational plans should list a variety of possible postsecondary paths so that students are not locked into one option and also so that they have an alternative in case one of their plans does not work out. The high school component of educational planning is crucial because a lack of preparation could lead to a rocky or unsuccessful transition for students as they move from school to work or school to school. Beyond working with students and parents to create educational plans, professional school counselors can help with the educational-planning process in high school by connecting students with opportunities to more fully investigate, learn about, and prepare for the preliminary goals they have set for themselves (e.g., elective classes, job shadowing, summer enrichment programs, informational interviews).

THEORY INTO PRACTICE 11.4

CAREER DEVELOPMENT ACTIVITIES FOR HIGH SCHOOL STUDENTS

It is crucial that high school students begin the process of tentatively crystallizing their career and educational goals so that they can begin serious consideration of possible postsecondary paths. Professional school counselors can play a valuable role in this process by providing students with opportunities to learn about their options, as well as about the skills and academic performance necessary to pursue those options.

Practical Ideas for Career Development Activities

- Administer interest inventories to students that provide them with information about careers and college majors potentially suitable for them (e.g., Holland's assessment, the *Self-Directed Search*). Have students research two or three careers and college majors that sound interesting to them.
- Help all students create a four-year educational plan (this is a requirement of many public schools). Use students' postsecondary goals and results from career assessments to help guide course selection.
- Inform students that different occupations require different levels of education. In a computer lab, show students a few helpful career websites and ask them to locate occupations that require certain degrees. For example, encourage students to find two occupations requiring a high school diploma, two occupations requiring vocational/technical school experience, two occupations requiring a bachelor's degree, two occupations requiring a master's degree, and two occupations requiring a doctoral degree. Engage students in a discussion about how knowing specific educational requirements for various occupations might guide their choice of courses in high school.
- Present a lesson on decision making to students and teach them a specific decision-making model. Inform students that sound decision-making skills will enable them to make educated choices about their postsecondary plans. Break students into small groups, provide each group with a decision-making scenario, and encourage each group to resolve the situation in the scenario using the decision-making model. Once students have shared their work with the rest of the class, initiate a discussion about how the decision-making model could be used to help them choose a college or a career.
- Run counseling groups for students on topics related to career development and educational planning (e.g., choosing a college, succeeding in college, finding a job, choosing a career).
- Connect with local companies and professionals to provide students with job shadowing opportunities.
- Collaborate with English teachers to present lessons to 11th and 12th graders on how to write a resume and cover letter.
- Host a mock interview day for 11th and 12th graders. Bring in members of the community to conduct brief mock interviews with students, as well as providing them with feedback. Prior to this event, make sure to collaborate with teachers to disseminate information to all 11th and 12th graders about interview preparation, tips, and best practices.
- Advertise local job and college fairs, or host your own.
- Invite college representatives to visit campus and hold information sessions for interested students.
- Hold information sessions about financial aid and scholarship opportunities for students interested in attending college.
- Offer job workshops to assist students in finding and applying for jobs.
- If the high school you work at has a career resource center, create a scavenger hunt to orient students to the career and educational information and resources available to them.

VOICES FROM THE FIELD 11.3   **CAREER DEVELOPMENT AND EDUCATIONAL PLANNING IN THE HIGH SCHOOL**

In working with high school students, I have discovered that they are aware that long-term academic and career development is necessary; however, they often lack knowledge of how to start this process and what career exploration resources are available. As a high school counselor, my focus is usually twofold: help the student to better understand his/her personal attributes, interests, and aptitudes, while also introducing the specifics of career exploration (e.g., career searching, job readiness, career development resources). I think one of the biggest challenges school counselors face is helping students gain an accurate knowledge of the "basics" surrounding a particular career (e.g., starting salary, education needs, typical workday). For example, I want my students to understand that, if becoming a doctor or a lawyer is a career aspiration for them, then they must be willing to attain a significant amount of postsecondary training. I also find that a large percentage of students' career exploration tends to be shaped by parental/environmental influences and salary aspirations. Encouraging students to see beyond salary numbers in career investigation is a major task for school counselors because I see that students often limit their career exploration to careers that have been historically known for their higher-end salaries (e.g., doctors, lawyers, professional athletes), and environmental influences usually promote this type of focus. Thus, using available career exploration tools to expand students' perspectives, as well as introducing them to the plethora of occupational fields, is one of my primary jobs as a professional school counselor.

In reality, career development sometimes gets overshadowed by other counselor responsibilities such as academic planning and/or responsive services; thus, it is important that school counselors be creative in the ways in which they introduce career development strategies to students. Utilizing resources that are easily accessible through technology gives students an opportunity to do some level of self-directed career exploration, which I have found to be critical, given the time constraints school counselors sometimes face. Collaboration between the school counselor and the school's career development coordinator (CDC) can be another valuable tool for school counselors when implementing a comprehensive career development program. At my school, I tend to facilitate the self-awareness piece and introduce students to career exploration resources, and the CDC coordinates more of the practical components of career exploration by organizing career fairs, bringing in guest speakers, and collaborating with the local business alliance. Time restraints and other responsibilities are a reality in the day-to-day work of school counselors; thus, it is critical, when establishing a comprehensive career development program, that we expand upon what has been historically done in regard to career development with our students and utilize emerging resources.

Source: Brooke Comer, Ninth-Grade Counselor, Athens Drive High School, Wake County Public Schools, Raleigh, North Carolina

Career Development Guidelines in High School

The extensive body of literature related to adolescent career development helps professional school counselors identify appropriate career development goals and interventions for high school students. High school students continue the momentum gained in self-knowledge during the middle or junior high school years. They acquire a more sophisticated understanding of the importance of developing a positive self-concept that serves as a basis for career planning. They also continue developing more sophisticated interpersonal skills during the high school years.

High school students grow increasingly aware of the relationship between educational achievement and career planning as the need to choose postsecondary educational and career options moves from being a remote event to one that is more immediate. Through work and extracurricular experiences, high school students increase their understanding of the need for positive attitudes toward work and learning. They increase their skills in locating, evaluating, and interpreting career information, and they develop and begin to refine job search skills.

Throughout high school, adolescents also continue to develop and refine their decision-making skills. The approaching inevitability of participation in multiple life roles provides motivation for additional clarification of life-role salience. Life-role structure issues (Super et al., 1996) become more realistic topics of importance for adolescents. Finally, the need to consider the approaching end of high school requires secondary school students to continue to be active participants in their own career planning.

In essence, high school provides the opportunity for adolescents to build on the career development competencies they acquired during middle or junior high school. As life after high school moves from being remote to more immediate, adolescents must learn to assume greater responsibility for their career planning. Participation in multiple life roles becomes a serious component of the career-planning process. Some adolescents are relatively well prepared for the life roles they will assume after high school. Others need substantial assistance to prepare for life after secondary school.

MULTICULTURAL IMPLICATIONS

When designing a K–12 educational- and career-planning program, students' cultural backgrounds are a salient and an important part of the process. Although within-group variance is an important factor, generally cultural values are an important lens. For example, the impact of gender on career circumscription in elementary school was highlighted. Another example is the concept of decision making as an independent process. This may be typical of European Americans, but is often not true of many other cultures. Individuals from other cultures may make decisions in a more collective or linear manner.

Studying the cultural values of the client is a necessity. Specifically, having an understanding of the client's time orientation, problem-solving strategies, and view on social relationships becomes an essential factor in discussing careers. For example, an Asian-American client may have interests and abilities in the education field, but his or her father may insist that the client enter the field of engineering. For this Asian-American client, decisions may be made in accordance with the wishes of the father because of the culture's lineal view on relationships. The professional school counselor must be aware of how culture intersects with and influences all aspects of career and educational planning in elementary, middle or junior high, and high school to be able to promote development that is congruent with the client's culture. One example of this is the concept of life-role readiness and salience.

Developing Life-Role Readiness and Salience

An approach to addressing academic, career, and personal/social development emphasizes the importance of developing students' life-role readiness. The life-role readiness concept is based on developmental approaches to school counseling (Myrick, 2003a). According to Myrick, developmental approaches contain objectives and activities directed to the following eight content areas:

1. Understanding the school environment,
2. Understanding self and others,
3. Understanding attitudes and behavior,
4. Making decision and solving problems,
5. Developing interpersonal and communication skills,
6. Developing school success skills,
7. Achieving career awareness and engaging in educational planning, and
8. Developing community pride and involvement.

Each of these content areas focuses on specific life roles. For example, *understanding the school environment* focuses on the life role of student, *developing community pride and involvement* focuses on the life role of citizen, and *achieving career awareness and engaging in educational planning* focuses on the life role of worker. Counseling activities within each content area are essentially intended to help students cope with the task of identity formation within the context of developing life-role readiness. *Life-role readiness* can be defined as the possession of the knowledge, attitudes, and skills necessary for effective life-role participation in a multicultural society. For example,

among other things, effective parenting requires basic knowledge about child development, a positive attitude toward parenting as a life role, and the skills necessary for providing basic child care. Likewise, life-role readiness related to the leisure role requires basic knowledge about specific leisure activities, a positive attitude toward leisure as a life role, and the basic skills necessary for participating in specific leisure activities.

Developmental school counseling interventions should include learning opportunities that foster the development of the knowledge, attitudes, and skills necessary for effective life-role participation (i.e., life-role readiness). By providing these learning opportunities within a context that is sensitive to cultural diversity, professional school counselors help students avoid adherence to the cultural uniformity myth and cultural ethnocentrism. That is, students learn to appreciate and value cultural differences in life-role behavior. For example, the life role of sibling may be different for a White adolescent than for a Hispanic adolescent. Perhaps a student's ethnicity and family traditions will call for duties and responsibilities that are unique.

Encouraging students to discuss life-role salience is useful because life-role salience provides the motivating force behind the development of life-role readiness (Super et al., 1996). If a life role is important to someone, then it is likely that the individual will engage in the behaviors necessary to prepare to take on that life role. Likewise, when salience is low, there is often little motivation to develop the requisite behaviors for effective participation in that role.

Addressing the issue of life-role salience, Super (1980) noted that work is only one role among many that individuals play. He identified the primary roles of life (e.g., student, worker, citizen, homemaker) and noted that some roles are more important than others at particular points in time. For example, some adolescents attend high school, work in part-time jobs, and are also parents. For a majority of adolescents, the life role of peer is paramount in middle or junior high and high school. Others devote a majority of their time to leisure, student, and family-of-origin activities. Developing life-role readiness requires secondary school students to identify their salient life roles and to examine the relationship between their goals and their current life-role activities.

Obviously, patterns of life-role salience are significantly influenced by immediate contextual factors (e.g., family, cultural heritage, level of acculturation) and distal contextual factors (e.g., economics, environmental opportunities for life-role participation). Contextual factors, therefore, contribute to patterns of life-role salience among secondary school students. However, many students lack an awareness of the ways in which contextual factors (such as the dominant culture and the student's culture of origin) interact with identity development to shape life-role salience (Blustein, 1994).

Often, students simply "inherit" patterns of life-role salience that are passed on from the dominant culture. Such inheritances can be problematic when they are embedded with beliefs based on gender and racial stereotypes. For instance, researchers have consistently found gender differences that coincide with traditional gender-role expectations in life-role salience (e.g., women participating more in home and family and expecting more from this life role than men do [Niles & Goodnough, 1996]). Women for whom the worker role has high salience are placed at an obvious disadvantage in the workforce by such traditional expectations. Also, men limit their opportunities for participating in the home and family when they adhere to traditional expectations for life-role salience. By raising their awareness of the influence of the dominant culture on life-role salience, students will be less likely to allow beliefs reflecting racist and sexist attitudes to influence their beliefs about life-role salience.

To foster the development of life-role readiness, professional school counselors can encourage students to address several topics. First, counselors at the elementary school level can introduce students to the primary roles of life (e.g., student, worker, family member, citizen). After developing life-role awareness in the elementary school, middle or junior high school students can be encouraged to identify the life roles that are important to them (i.e., their life-role salience). Second, students can identify the contextual factors (e.g., family, culture, economics, new occupational options) influencing their life-role salience. Third, middle or junior high and high school students can be encouraged to participate in specific activities that foster the development of life-role readiness. Together, these topics provide a conceptual framework around which counseling interventions that facilitate life-role readiness in a multicultural society can be constructed.

Using a group guidance format, students can examine their current life-role salience by responding to such questions as these: "How do you spend your time during a typical week?" "How important are the different roles of life (e.g., student, worker, citizen) to you?" "What do you like about participating in each of the life roles?" "What life roles do you think will be important to you in the future?" "What do you hope to accomplish in each of the life roles that will be important to you in the future?" "In which life roles do members of your family participate?" "What do your family members expect you to accomplish in each of the life roles?"

Professional school counselors can also use a group guidance format to help students identify the life roles they are currently spending most of their time emotionally committed to and expect to be important to them in the future. With regard to the latter, counselors can help students construct strategies for preparing for their salient life roles. For example, if the life role of parent is expected to be salient in the future, students can discuss ways to plan and prepare for that role. Counselors can also encourage students to examine areas of potential role conflict and discuss strategies for coping with excessive demands from multiple life roles.

Discussions related to the influence of the dominant culture on life-role salience can also lead to discussions that focus on how students' cultural backgrounds influence their viewpoints on life-role salience. Professional school counselors can emphasize how different cultures often influence the values individuals seek to express in life roles (e.g., seeking to express self-actualization in work for the student from a Eurocentric cultural background or seeking to express cultural identity in work for the student from an Asian background). By discussing the ways in which culture influences life-role salience, students become aware of how their cultural backgrounds influence their life-role salience, and they learn about differing patterns in role salience across cultures.

INTERVENTION Through group guidance and classroom discussions, students can explore the various cultural prescriptions that are generally assigned to specific life roles. In these discussions, counselors can encourage students to identify how they perceive and interpret the role expectations emanating from their cultures of origin and how these expectations influence their decisions as to whether a particular life role is important. Particular attention can be paid to exploring how these expectations influence students' understandings of the behaviors required for effective role performance.

Borodovsky and Ponterotto (1994) suggested one specific activity that may provide opportunities for discussing these topics. They identified the family genogram as a useful tool for exploring the interaction among family background, cultural prescriptions, and career planning. The genogram provides a tool for tracking career decisions across generations and identifying sources of important career beliefs and life themes that students have acquired.

This technique can be expanded to address the same topics for other life roles. By using the genogram, professional school counselors can encourage students to identify the beliefs and life themes pertaining to specific life roles (e.g., parent and citizen) that they have acquired from members of their immediate and extended families. Counselors can also use the information provided by the students to contrast the influences on life-role salience emanating from group-oriented cultures with influences from more individualistic cultures. Terms such as *cultural assimilation* and *cultural accommodation* can be introduced in these discussions. The effects of gender-role stereotyping on life-role salience can also be examined here and challenged in these discussions. The goal of these interventions is to increase student awareness of the factors influencing their beliefs about the primary roles of life.

Knowing which life roles are salient and how contextual factors influence one's life-role salience is a starting point for developing life-role readiness. Professional school counselors must also encourage students to participate in activities that foster further development of life-role readiness. Super's (1957, 1977) theory is also useful in this regard. Super suggested that by actively planning for career decisions, exploring occupational options, gathering occupational information, learning how to make occupational decisions, and reality-testing tentative occupational choices, individuals develop their readiness for participating in the life role of worker.

These same behaviors can be applied to other life roles. To develop readiness for the life role of student, college-bound secondary school students must plan for the academic tasks they are likely to encounter (e.g., choosing a program of study, registering for college entrance examinations, knowing when to begin the process of college selection). They must also engage in a thorough exploration of postsecondary school options. In the process of exploring, students must gather information relevant to the academic options they are considering. Once options are explored and information is gathered, students are then ready to make tentative academic plans and decisions. As students implement their decisions (e.g., entering an academic program intended to prepare them for college, narrowing a list of prospective colleges), they begin the process of reality-testing their choices. The postimplementation feedback they receive (e.g., grades) informs them as to the appropriateness of their current plans and indicates ways in which their plans may need to be revised (e.g., a high school student who plans on majoring in engineering in college, but who earns poor grades in science may need to explore, gather information, make decisions, and reality-test options related to nonscience majors).

An educational- and career-planning portfolio is an effective tool for helping students engage in purposeful planning, exploring, information gathering, decision making, and reality testing related to the life roles of student and worker. This can be expanded to a "life-role portfolio" by addressing students' readiness for life roles beyond those of student and worker. Students can be encouraged to plan, explore, and gather information for each of the major life roles.

For example, students who anticipate one day being a parent can plan for this role by considering how parenting interacts with other roles. Students can explore different styles of parenting by interviewing parents about their parenting practices and philosophies. Students can also gather information about the skills required for effective parenting (perhaps by taking a parenting class). Through these activities, students can learn about the factors that are important to consider in making decisions about parenting. Finally, students can reality-test their interest in parenting through participating in child care activities. Thus, the life-role portfolio stimulates counselor and student meetings focused on planning, exploring, information gathering, decision making, and reality testing vis-à-vis the major life roles. When the portfolio is used over successive years, it also provides developmental documentation of activities and decisions related to major life roles.

This expanded use of the planning portfolio is an example of a counseling activity that is intended to help students cope with the task of identity formation within the context of developing life-role readiness. It also provides additional opportunities for discussing contextual influences on life-role salience. Regardless of the life role, it is important that professional school counselors be sensitive to the cultural diversity among their students.

Summary/Conclusion

According to the *ASCA National Model* (2005a), one of the primary roles of any professional school counselor is to facilitate a career development program. A major goal of professional school counseling programs is to facilitate student development toward effective life-role participation. Professional school counselors must initiate appropriate developmental guidance activities in elementary school (e.g., self-awareness, curiosity) and facilitate culmination of this process with assistance in the transition to school, work, and a variety of life roles. Professional school counselors can enhance students' life-role readiness by helping students develop life-role awareness and by encouraging them to examine their life-role salience and the contextual factors that influence it. To foster the continued development of life-role readiness, professional school counselors can encourage students to engage in planning, exploring, information gathering, decision making, and reality testing vis-à-vis the major roles of life. In addition, the program should anticipate adaptations to various cultural backgrounds and the utilization of technology. By systematically addressing these topics throughout grades K–12, professional school counselors facilitate the development of life-role readiness in their students and increase the probability that students will cope successfully with life-role tasks in school and beyond.

Activities

1. Develop a career exploration activity for the grade level of your choice using technology.
2. Plan a classroom guidance session for elementary students that discusses traditional and nontraditional occupations.
3. Plan a career development group for high school students that focuses on employability skills.

12

Consultation, Collaboration, and Parent Involvement

Bradley T. Erford*

Editor's Introduction: Consultation and collaboration are efficient interventions that not only allow professional school counselors to address the issue at hand, but also provide a model for consultees and collaboratees to take responsibility for solving their own problems in the future. The collaborative model encompasses the establishment of partnerships with parents and community organizations to solve systemic problems and remove barriers to student performance. The practices of collaboration and partnering hold tremendous potential for the transformation of the school counseling profession. Professional school counselors are in a wonderful position to build bridges between students who are in need of necessary community resources, be they human or material. Students whose parents are involved in and supportive of their educational journey achieve higher levels of performance and are better adjusted socially and emotionally. Collaboration, outreach, and school–community partnering are processes meant to get parents and the community involved in the educational enterprise. Although these processes may diverge from a traditional role, the transformed role of the professional school counselor makes such initiatives crucial. The discerning professional school counselor will also note that many of the suggestions may require only an initial impetus followed by delegation of responsibilities to colleagues and volunteers, thus preventing professional school counselors from perpetually investing valuable time and resources over the long term.

THE COUNSELOR AS CONSULTANT: CASE EXAMPLES

Samantha is a kindergarten student in Mrs. Miller's class at River Falls Elementary School. Samantha has few friends and limited social skills. She is often bossy and frequently demands to have things her own way. Mrs. Miller has met with little success in helping Samantha respond more appropriately. Running short of ideas for how to intervene, she refers Samantha to the professional school counselor.

Alberto is a ninth-grade student who is having difficulty with math class and is in danger of failing the course. Although his other courses are challenging, he is managing passing grades. Mr. Long, Alberto's math teacher, feels Alberto's behavior contributes to his problem with math. According to Mr. Long, Alberto interrupts him and his classmates frequently. Alberto is rude in class, generally making sarcastic comments to Mr. Long and the other students. Most of his classmates consider him to be a big annoyance. Alberto has started to cut class. On the surface, Alberto exhibits an "I don't care" attitude. Mr. Long recently referred Alberto to the school's Student Support Team. Alberto's professional school counselor is a team member.

---

*In the first edition of this text, portions of this chapter were written by Susan G. Keys, Alan Green, Estes Lockhart, Peter F. Luongo, Gayle Cicero, and Pat Barton.

Westwood Middle School is located in a culturally diverse urban area. A recent increase in discipline referrals for aggressive behavior has prompted Westwood's School Improvement Team to make the promotion of school safety an important goal for the year. Westwood's principal, Ms. Johnson, has charged the school's four professional school counselors with taking the lead in developing a comprehensive school violence prevention program.

These cases represents typical referrals that a professional school counselor at the elementary, middle, or high school level might receive in the normal course of his or her work. The professional school counselor represents an important resource for teachers who are confronted by students for whom the usual methods of instruction and discipline are often less than successful. Parents and family members also seek support from the professional school counselor when confused or uncertain about what is normal development or expected behavior and how to help their child when personal, interpersonal, or academic difficulties arise. Administrators also use the professional school counselor's expertise when looking to solve problems involving individual students, as well as problems that affect larger groups of students, family members, and staff. In each of these cases, the professional school counselor may respond using a number of different roles—counselor, consultant, program developer and coordinator, or classroom educator—and in all likelihood will use a combination of roles to provide assistance to teachers, staff, families, and students.

This chapter looks in detail at one of these roles: the counselor's consultant role. The *ASCA National Model* (American School Counselor Association [ASCA], 2005a) points to the importance of consultation and collaboration services in a comprehensive, developmental school counseling program. Collaboration and consultation are effective methods for intervening in developmental student issues by working with essential people in the student's life (e.g., parents, teachers). Furthermore, consultation and collaboration have been important services provided by counselors for decades, across many settings (D. Brown, Pryzwansky, & Schultz, 2000; Dinkmeyer & Carlson, 2001; Kahn, 2000; Kampwirth, 2002). In schools, the collaborative approach to consultation currently predominates because it allows the professional school counselor to become an active agent of change even after a course of action has been agreed to by all parties (Dinkmeyer & Carlson, 2001; Dougherty, 1999; Kampwirth, 2002). How might professional school counselors, as collaborators and consultants, approach the problem-solving process in each of the above cases? What models of consultation might professional school counselors draw on? How do professional school counselors integrate their expertise with the skills and knowledge of

other problem solvers? This chapter explores these and other questions as a way of discovering more about the professional school counselor's very important consultant role.

BACKGROUND

Gilbert Wrenn's (1962) landmark report on the condition of school counseling, *The Counselor in a Changing World*, strongly urged that consultation with teachers, parents, and administrators be considered an essential element of the professional school counselor's role and function. With the emergence of the developmental guidance and counseling movement in the 1970s, consultation became a widely accepted function (Schmidt, 2008). The professional school counselor's responsibility for large numbers of students added impetus to the adoption of a consultation focus. Although the American Counseling Association (ACA) and the ASCA recommend a student-to-counselor ratio of 250:1, only a few school systems have been able to maintain this standard. Providing individual counseling services becomes prohibitive when faced with unrealistic student-to-counselor ratios. Through consultation, professional school counselors can assist more students by working directly with those individuals who have frequent contact with students—teachers and family members. Professional school counselors as consultants also work with other professionals and family members when planning broad-based prevention and intervention programs.

CONSULTATION MODELS

Keys, Bemak, Carpenter, and King-Sears (1998) noted that models of consultation can be distinguished by the type of interaction that occurs between the consultant and the person or persons seeking the consultant's help. They described three types of interaction as triadic-dependent, collaborative-dependent, and collaborative-interdependent.

The Triadic-Dependent Model: Traditional Expert-Directed Consultation

Traditionally, consultation is thought of as a problem-solving process that involves a helpseeker, referred to as a consultee (e.g., teacher, administrator, family member); a helpgiver (i.e., consultant); and a third person who is the focus of concern (i.e., client or student). This three-party relationship is referred to as triadic. In this type of relationship, the consultant provides services indirectly to the client through the consultant's work with the consultee (see Figure 12.1).

Counseling, in contrast, is considered a direct student service, since the professional school counselor works

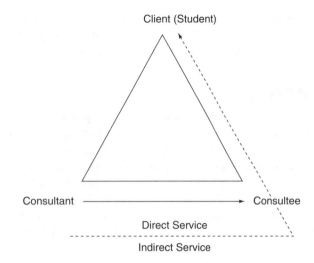

FIGURE 12.1 Consultation as indirect service to the client.

FIGURE 12.2 Consultation as a triadic-dependent relationship.

in direct contact with the student. In some situations, the professional school counselor may combine different types of services; in effect, the counselor may consult with teachers or family members of a student (indirect service to the student) and provide the same student with one-on-one or group counseling services (direct service to the student).

In the triadic-dependent model, the consultant is viewed as the expert from whom the consultee seeks assistance to remediate a problem with the client (see Figure 12.2). In effect, the consultee is dependent on the consultant's advice and recommendations. The consultant works through the consultee to bring about change for the client. Although the expectation is that the consultation ultimately ends in improved achievement, affect, attitude, or behavior for the student, the immediate recipient of this service is the administrator, teacher, or family member, not the student. The immediate goal of the consultation might be increasing the skills, knowledge, and objectivity of the consultee so that the consultee is better able to implement an intervention plan designed to achieve change for the student.

Many consultations that professional school counselors conduct with teachers and family members fall under the triadic-dependent relationship category. Using this model, the professional school counselor would meet with a teacher or family member (or both) to assess their perspectives on the student's problem. The professional school counselor might collect additional data through observations, consultations with other teachers or professionals, and meetings with the student. As a consultant, the professional school counselor makes recommendations to the consultee, with the consultee being the one responsible for implementing the prescribed plan. The consultant's recommendations

may include interventions that focus on change for the client, the consultee, and the system. R. Parsons (1996) referred to this as client-focused, consultee-focused, and system-focused consultation. In actuality, a consultation could result in recommendations for changes in all three areas.

Bergan and Kratochwill's (1990) behavioral consultation is an example of a triadic-dependent consultation model. Within this model, the consultant, as a behavioral expert, draws on principles of behaviorism to help define the problem, identify environmental conditions that maintain the problem, generate solutions that result in changes in behavior for the client or the consultee, and change the social context within which the client or consultee functions. Professional school counselors who help teachers and family members acquire the skills and knowledge necessary to implement a behavior management plan draw on this particular consultation model (Sterling-Turner, Watson, & Moore, 2002; Sterling-Turner, Watson, Wildmon, Watkins, & Little, 2001). Watson, Watson, and Weaver (2010) proposed a four-step behavioral consultation model that is similar to other models of collaboration and consultation: (1) problem identification, (2) problem analysis, (3) plan implementation, and (4) plan evaluation. During plan implementation, behavioral contracting, positive reinforcement, and response cost are strategies that might be implemented. Each of these strategies would result in client-focused change. However, if the consultant needed to spend time educating the teacher or family member about how to implement these procedures, then the consultation would include both client-focused and consultee-focused interventions. Table 12.1 includes helpful suggestions for conducting effective triadic-dependent consultations with parents and teachers.

TABLE 12.1   Suggestions for Conducting Effective Triadic-Dependent Consultation

Make sure the environment for the consultation is comfortable and professional.

Quickly establish the purpose of the consultation, identifying the client (usually the student) and defining the problems or issues of concern.

Try to minimize anxiety and maximize cooperation quickly. Maintain a friendly, professional demeanor even in the face of angry or emotional consultees. Do not become defensive.

Give the consultee the opportunity to tell his or her story. Be supportive, help as necessary, and listen actively.

Get to the point efficiently and avoid educational or psychological jargon.

Establish clear boundaries for the consultee (usually the parent or teacher) so that the student, not the consultee, becomes the focus of problem identification and intervention.

Probe for any factors or conditions that may be relevant to effective treatment planning, including what the consultee has tried previously and any condition that may contraindicate a potential intervention.

Focus on the student's behavior, not the student. Reframe the presenting behaviors in terms of student needs to provide alternative perspectives to consider in treatment. Often, understanding the goal of behavior helps adults to better help the student meet those needs.

Classroom observation can be a helpful way of collecting additional information about the context surrounding student behavior and performance.

Dougherty (1999) suggested four questions that must be addressed for interventions to be understood and effective: (1) What are we going to do? (2) How are we going to do it? (3) When and where are we going to do it? (4) How well did we do?

Be sure to develop a working relationship with the consultee as an equal partner in the endeavor. Try to have the consultee suggest potential interventions and evaluation plans.

Provide resources (e.g., books, handouts, websites) that can help the consultee better understand the issues and interventions.

Be sure to schedule follow-up procedures during the initial consultation. All interventions must be tracked and evaluated. When consultees fail to achieve the desired results, they may assume that either they are incompetent or the consultant is incompetent. Follow-up and evaluation ensure an atmosphere of cooperation and continued addressing of issues until a successful resolution is reached. Most counseling interventions require adjustments or even a completely different approach.

Document in writing contacts with consultees or others involved with the issue.

Case Example: Samantha

How might a professional school counselor who functions as a consultant within the triadic-dependent model respond to Mrs. Miller in the case of Samantha? After receiving Mrs. Miller's initial referral, the counselor–consultant will take several steps to develop a more thorough understanding of Samantha and Mrs. Miller's concerns. These could include the following:

- An initial consultation session with Mrs. Miller to better define the problem and assess how she and the other students typically respond when Samantha is disruptive and demanding.
- Observation of Samantha in Mrs. Miller's classroom to further identify occasions when Samantha is disruptive and demanding and to see firsthand

any patterns that may exist in how others respond to Samantha. The consultant may also spend time observing Samantha in less structured situations such as the lunchroom and playground to determine if the same behaviors exist in these contexts.

- A meeting with Samantha to determine her perception of the problem and further assess her social skills development.

The consultant will integrate all information and in a subsequent consultation session (or sessions) with Mrs. Miller will recommend strategies Mrs. Miller might use to encourage Samantha to exhibit more positive behavior in the classroom. These strategies could include teaching Mrs. Miller new techniques for positive reinforcement and how

(Continued)

to use modeling to teach Samantha new social skills. The consultant might also recommend that Samantha participate in small-group counseling sessions (with the consultant then functioning as counselor) focused on social skill development. Because follow-up and accountability are essential to successful outcomes, the consultant will monitor the student's progress and maintain contact with Mrs. Miller to determine the intervention's effectiveness.

THEORY INTO PRACTICE 12.1

IMPLEMENTING THE TRIADIC-DEPENDENT MODEL

As a professional school counselor serving the needs of four nonpublic schools, my caseload far exceeds the numbers suggested by the ASCA. This being the case, consultation makes up a significant portion of my daily work. One of the most common types of consultation that I engage in is behavioral consultation.

Will is a sixth-grade student whose teacher, Mrs. Jones, approached me because of Will's trouble with organization. To begin the consultation process, I set up a meeting with Mrs. Jones and a second one with her and Will's parents, Mr. and Mrs. Brown. In my meeting with Mrs. Jones, I discovered that she was most concerned about the lack of follow-through that appears to be going on at home. She shared that once things go home, she never sees them again. Homework, tests, and even field trip permission forms rarely come back to school with Will. In fact, Will almost missed the sixth grade's first field trip because of this. Along with this concern, she shared that Will typically leaves her class with the wrong books when they switch classes. Will also becomes easily distracted and appears off task frequently when he is in her classroom. Mrs. Jones shared that the other teachers who see Will throughout the day share her concerns.

In between the meeting with Will's teacher and the meeting with Will's teacher and parents, I observed Will in the classroom setting to get a better understanding of the issues at hand. Before Will's parents came to school for the meeting, Mr. Brown contacted me to voice some concerns. He wanted me to be aware of the fact that he and his wife were concerned that Mrs. Jones wasn't very organized. They believed that Mrs. Jones's relaxed methods of organization were not helping their son to be an effective student. He said that they had not been notified about Will's difficulties prior to when we set up our meeting. Mr. Brown also shared that he thought it would be a good idea for his son to work on anger management skills in weekly counseling sessions with me.

I began the meeting with Will's parents and teacher by thanking everyone for coming and agreeing to find a way to all work together to help Will meet his potential. After giving Mrs. Jones and Mr. and Mrs. Brown a chance to voice their concerns, I shared what I had observed during my classroom observation. We discussed what Mrs. Jones and Mr. and Mrs. Brown had tried in the past to help Will. With the input I received from Will's parents and teacher, along with my observation, we shared the following suggestions:

- Seat Will in a place where he will be close to the teacher.
- Create a nonverbal signal for the teacher to give to Will to refocus him.
- Provide an extra desk to help Will learn how to organize (keep supplies in one, books in the other).
- Give Will time during homeroom or lunch recess to organize his desk.
- Provide redirection for Will instead of issuing demerits on the first offense.
- Get Will color-coded folders and book covers so that he can quickly grab what he needs when it's time to switch classes.
- Keep lines of communication open between school and home. Parents and teacher can e-mail each other to provide updates and evaluate how well the plan is working.
- Write homework on the board and give time for students to copy it down at the beginning of class.
- Have teachers initial the homework book after Will copies homework down; have parent initial it when homework is complete.
- Give Will a folder specifically for papers that he needs to show his parents.
- When possible, give Will a choice of when to complete his homework (e.g., after school, after dinner, before basketball practice).
- Provide counseling sessions focusing on anger management and organizational skills.

At the end of the meeting, we planned to meet again in two weeks to evaluate how well the plan was working once it was implemented. At our follow-up meeting, Mrs. Jones shared that she had noticed significant changes in Will's organizational skills and off-task behaviors. She was happy with his progress and saw no need to revise the plan, but would continue to implement my suggestions. Mr. and Mrs. Brown wanted more consistent feedback from Mrs. Jones, but aside from that, they were pleased with Will's progress and saw no need to meet again unless things changed for the worse. I closed the meeting by asking both Mrs. Jones and Mr. and Mrs. Brown to contact me in the future with updates or further concerns.

Katie Young, Professional School Counselor, Montgomery County Intermediate Unit, Nonpublic School Services Division, Pennsylvania

The Collaborative-Dependent Model: Partnership and Problem Solving

In a collaborative-dependent relationship, the helping process departs from a view of the consultant as a solitary expert. The consultee continues to depend on the consultant's (1) problem-solving expertise, (2) knowledge of normal and abnormal development, and (3) skills for effecting client and systemic change. In a collaborative-dependent relationship, the consultant also recognizes and engages the knowledge and expertise of the consultee regarding both the student's and the system's strengths and weaknesses, the contextual factors that influence the student, and the student's reaction to previously attempted interventions (see Figure 12.3).

Creating a partnership relationship is important to this process. Consultants who work within a collaborative-dependent relationship may educate consultees about the problem-solving process itself, as well as facilitating how the actual problem-solving process unfolds. Importantly, and in some ways in contrast to a triadic-dependent model, the collaborative professional school counselor is seen not as an expert, but as a partner in defining the problem, implementing interventions, and providing evaluation and follow-up services. Together, the consultant and the consultee establish mutual goals and objectives for the student and develop an intervention plan. The consultee is responsible for implementing the intervention plan with either the student and the classroom system (if the consultee is a teacher) or the student and the family system (if the consultee is a family member). The consultant and the consultee depend on the knowledge and skills each person brings to the problem-solving process.

A collaborative-dependent consultation relationship may focus on help for a specific client (student-focused

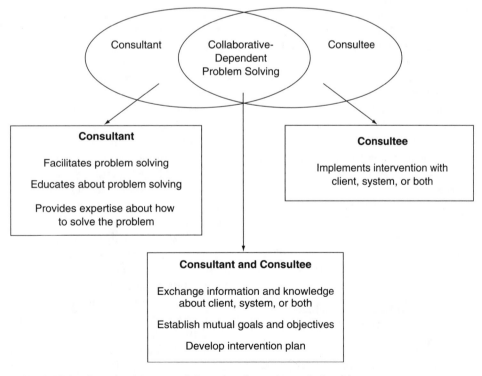

FIGURE 12.3 Consultation as a collaborative-dependent relationship.

Case Example: Alberto

As a member of the school's Student Support Team, the professional school counselor participates in the initial review meeting for Alberto's case. Other participants include the referring teacher, Mr. Long; the school's assistant principal; a special education resource teacher; the school psychologist; the school nurse; and the school social worker. Alberto's academic record indicates that math has been a consistent area of weakness for Alberto; however, he has always managed passing grades. No special education services have been provided in the past, and the team does not feel a referral for such services is warranted. After reviewing case information, the team makes two recommendations: (1) that Alberto be invited to participate in an after-school math tutoring session and (2) that Mr. Long and the professional school counselor work on helping Alberto develop a more positive classroom demeanor.

After meeting with Mr. Long and visiting his class during math time, the professional school counselor, functioning as a consultant, meets with Mr. Long again to establish mutual goals and to develop an intervention plan. Mr. Long is well recognized in the school for his expertise as a math teacher. The consultant is careful to convey respect for Mr. Long's expertise and to support his interest in helping Alberto to be successful in his classroom. The consultant stresses the need for the two of them to agree on a mutual goal and plan for helping Alberto.

When visiting in Mr. Long's classroom, the consultant observes that Mr. Long has the students compete as teams in weekly math quizzes. The team that scores the most points earns a homework pass for one night. This competition seems to make Alberto uncomfortable, with a noticeably higher rate of disruptive behavior occurring at these times. During the consultation session, the consultant shares this observation about Alberto with Mr. Long. Together, they devise a plan for how students can practice their math skills (the reason for the competition) in a way that supports cooperative learning and minimizes stress for Alberto, as well as for the other students. This system-focused intervention will be implemented by Mr. Long, the consultee. The consultant will remain in contact with Mr. Long in an assessment or accountability role to ascertain if the solution is bringing about a change in Alberto's behavior.

consultation), on help for the consultee (consultee-focused consultation), or more broadly on change within the organizational context or system (system-focused consultation). Schein's (1969) classic process model illustrates system-focused consultation. As a process consultant, the professional school counselor, using Schein's (1969) model, approaches problem solving by examining six different variables critical to the organizational system: (1) communication patterns, (2) group members' roles and functions, (3) processes and procedures for group problem solving and decision making, (4) group norms and group growth, (5) leadership and authority, and (6) intergroup cooperation and competition. Within a process consultation model, the focus of change is the organizational system, with the consultant contributing expertise on assessment and interventions related to system change. These variables are also relevant for the consultant who wants to bring about change in a family system.

The Collaborative-Interdependent Model: Addressing Issues with Multiple Causes Across Multiple Contexts

Triadic-dependent and collaborative-dependent consultation models are helpful when seeking change for an individual client or family or for a single organizational system related to normal developmental problems. But when problems are more complex—as is particularly the case with the multicausal and multicontextual problems of youth who are at risk—these more traditional models are too limited in scope to provide comprehensive solutions. A collaborative-interdependent relationship is a useful alternative.

Collaboration is "an interactive process that enables groups of people with diverse expertise to generate creative solutions to mutually defined problems" (Idol, Nevin, & Paolucci-Whitcomb, 1994, p. 1). This model emphasizes an interdependent problem-solving process in which family members, educators, counselors, youth, and members of the broader community contribute as equal participants (see Figure 12.4). Unlike previously discussed models that rely heavily on the counselor–consultant as an expert, a collaborative-interdependent model does not presume that any one person has sufficient knowledge or information to understand the problem and develop and implement solutions. Ultimately, it is the sharing and transferring of knowledge and information among all problem solvers that enables the group to determine and implement a more comprehensive plan (Keys et al., 1998). The plan may include change for an individual student, new knowledge and skills for team members (including the consultant), and change for the organizational system.

FIGURE 12.4 Consultation as a collaborative, interdependent relationship.

Each person in the group is interdependent on the expertise of the other group members in formulating and executing the problem-solving plan.

Friend and Cook (1996) described consultation as a process and collaboration as the style of interaction within the process. Collaboration refers to how people interact during the problem-solving process. Professional school counselors who use collaboration work within a team framework. To have convened a team, however, does not necessarily mean that the team functions collaboratively. Keys et al. (1998) cautioned that, although family members, teachers, and other professionals and community members may share information about a problem and may have knowledge of what each is doing to solve the problem, they are not necessarily functioning collaboratively unless they actively involve each other in carrying out their functions. The interdependence of a collaborative style extends to all phases of the problem-solving process—problem identification, goal-setting, strategy development and implementation, and evaluation.

Friend and Cook (1996) defined several distinguishing features of a collaborative style of interaction:

- Collaboration is *voluntary.* People who come together to solve complex problems must want to collaborate for a collaborative style of interaction to occur. Collaboration cannot occur merely because it has been mandated by an administrator.

- Collaboration requires *parity* among all participants. Parity suggests that each participant has an equal voice in decision making and that all team members value equally each member's input. This characteristic is often the most difficult to support in the school

setting. Administrative oversight in some schools precludes parity. In some schools, the school-based professionals often decide outcomes before the team even assembles, with the team more of a rubber stamp of what the "school experts" feel should be done, rather than an interactive body that values the expertise of family and community members. Attitudes and assumptions by some school professionals about those who are economically disadvantaged or culturally diverse may also prohibit parity. Professional school counselors–consultants need to pay particular attention to issues of parity and seek to provide balance in the crucial discussions among teachers, administrators, and students and their families.

- Collaboration depends on *shared responsibility* for decision making. In a school context, shared responsibility suggests that it is not the school (e.g., teachers) alone or the family members alone or the community alone that is responsible for "fixing the problem." Each participant has a role in identifying the problem, setting objectives, implementing solutions, and evaluating outcome. Not all team members necessarily contribute equally to the implemented solution, nor is the division of labor necessarily equal across all members. The degree to which any team member contributes is directly dependent on the need for that individual's skills and expertise.

- Collaboration is based on *mutual goals* and a *shared accountability* for outcomes. All participants must agree on what the team is to accomplish. Commitment from each member is critical. Each member may contribute a different expertise to achieve the desired outcome, but the desired end result must be supported by all partners. Responsibility for outcomes—successes as well as disappointments—is shared by all members.

- Individuals who collaborate *share their resources* without dictating how these resources are to be used. How to best use resources becomes a part of the collaborative decision-making process.

What is the consultant's role in helping professionals and family members function collaboratively? First, the consultant can model a collaborative style when interacting with teachers and family members. Engaging others as equals in the problem-solving process sends a clear message that the consultant does not perceive himself or herself as "the expert." Additionally, the consultant encourages a collaborative process by (1) seeking others' perspectives, (2) being open to new ways of conceptualizing problems, (3) integrating others' suggestions in intervention plans, (4) reinforcing others' ideas, (5) being flexible in how he or she defines and executes his or her own role, and (6) assisting a team in establishing group norms that reflect collaboration.

Case Example: Westwood Middle School

To address the needs of Westwood Middle School, the four professional school counselors develop a violence prevention work group consisting of local higher education institution partners, relevant community resource agencies, family members, and school staff—including administrators, teachers, and student support personnel. The purpose of the group is to develop a useful and comprehensive solution to the violence and aggressive behavior problems at Westwood Middle School.

Since the discipline referral problem at Westwood Middle is an ongoing issue, the work group develops a violence prevention initiative that includes primary and secondary prevention strategies. After reviewing data and collaboratively brainstorming, the group finds that the students need to develop positive social, problem-solving, and anger management skills. Skill development will occur through (1) classroom guidance lessons, jointly planned and delivered by the professional school counselors and teachers; (2) activities integrated within the broader educational curriculum, delivered by classroom teachers; (3) small-group counseling sessions, led by the professional school counselors and other student services personnel, including the school psychologist, school social worker, and school-based mental health clinicians; and (4) educational classes for students and family members provided at the local community center, with community center staff co-leading evening training sessions with the school counseling staff.

The work group also recommends staff development on school safety, including the integration of skill training into the broader curriculum, strategies for responding to volatile students, and skills for classroom management. Staff development sessions will be jointly planned and implemented by a professional school counselor, teacher, student support staff, and community representatives from the work group. A school newsletter for family members will highlight all prevention efforts. Family members who participate in the work group will advise about how best to disseminate program information to families and how to engage family members in training and workshop opportunities. The work group invites community leaders to join them in developing employment opportunities for youth.

The work group consults with the school's administrative staff on redesigning the school's discipline referral process so that a student referred for a discipline problem is automatically involved in identifying more productive ways of behaving. This process also ensures

that a student referred for a discipline problem is referred to the Student Support Team for further evaluation and that an intervention plan is designed specifically for that student. Intensive counseling sessions with the professional school counselor or a school-based mental health clinician may be part of the intervention plan.

Each member of the work group is involved in all phases of the problem-solving process—from problem and need identification through evaluation. Each member assumes multiple roles based on his or her particular area of expertise. Communication among work group members, role sharing, and shared accountability for outcomes underscore the group's interdependence and collaborative nature. For example:

- In addition to the previously mentioned skills training and counseling services, *professional school counselors* provide leadership within the work group by coordinating the group's work, establishing norms for a collaborative group process, modeling collaborative behavior, and recommending program evaluation procedures.
- The *school-based mental health clinician* and other *community mental health practitioners* help the group identify contributing mental health problems and facilitate the referral of students and family members who are in need of more intensive services to community-based services. These clinicians also participate with professional school counselors and student support staff members in providing training for school staff about risk factors and warning signs for mental health problems.
- *Faculty members* in the departments of counseling, social work, and school psychology at a nearby university provide the work group with information about theoretical models and "best practices" for primary and secondary intervention. These professionals also provide leadership for the work group in exploring grant funding to support prevention initiatives and in ensuring linkage of this smaller program with broader partnership initiatives between the school system and their respective departments.
- *Teacher* representatives team with professional school counselors and mental health clinicians to implement staff development workshops. The teacher work group representatives also provide leadership to the group on how best to integrate

school violence prevention skill training within the broader curriculum.

- *Family members* in the group serve as liaisons between the work group and other parents to communicate the goals and strategies of this initiative to the broader community. Family members also help to identify neighborhood leaders who can provide the work group with information about community needs.

Through this team process, the professional school counselor functions as one of many *collaborative consultants*. Each member of the team joins his or her expertise with the expertise of other members to develop and implement a comprehensive prevention plan. Work group members function interdependently, both during the team process itself and when enacting their roles during the implementation of the comprehensive prevention plan.

THEORY INTO PRACTICE 12.2

IMPLEMENTING THE COLLABORATIVE-INTERDEPENDENT MODEL

During my school counseling internship at a public elementary school, I recall when a collaborative-interdependent relationship was both a practical and a beneficial approach. As a new counselor, I did not presume that I yet had sufficient knowledge and experience with a particular student to execute the most comprehensive and beneficial problem-solving plan. Furthermore, those interacting with this student on a daily basis would need to be privy to any information available and possibly work as a team after a plan was in place to later support the student.

The collaboration process began when a fourth-grade teacher explained to me that her student was acting in a bizarre and confused manner. The teacher also observed that the student appeared disheveled and dirty. Her student relocated from a neighboring school to this school about five months earlier when the student's home burned down and she lost everything. At this juncture, I collaborated with the rest of the fourth-grade team who interacted with the student on a regular basis, and there was consensus among the fourth-grade teachers about the student's condition—and no viable ideas about how to help the student.

I continued the process by observing the student within the classroom setting during different intervals of the day on two different occasions. I saw a young lady who was, indeed, disheveled and who quite possibly hadn't bathed in some time. She appeared very tired and maintained a glazed-over expression, possibly from something more extreme than fatigue and boredom. I later approached the student, inviting her to speak with me. The student didn't ask why or about what I wished to speak with her, and she welcomed the invitation.

It was during this meeting that she told me about seeing ghosts and how the ghosts visit her at home, speak to her, and are angry with her. She presented as emotionally disconnected and depressed. As part of the interview, I asked her if she had thoughts about hurting herself. She said she had thoughts of cutting her hair off and then cutting her head off. After some gentle prodding, she revealed she would use her mom's large kitchen knife.

I stayed with this young lady until my supervising school counselor arrived, after asking the student if we could invite the professional school counselor to be with us. At this point, because of comments the student made, I was concerned about possible sexual abuse and suicidal ideation. My supervisor and I agreed strongly that this student needed an immediate suicide assessment and needed to be supervised by a guardian, parent, or responsible adult until the assessment was completed and a plan was in place to assure the safety and well-being of this child. The principal and teachers were notified, the parents were contacted, and the student was transported to an appointment with a local youth service bureau staffed by clinical mental health professionals (e.g., psychologists, counselors, social workers) who were briefed on the situation.

From that moment on, the expertise of all of these professionals was used to help and support this student. This collaborative-interdependent process—involving teachers, myself, my school counselor supervisor, the principal, the student's parents, and clinical mental health professionals from the local off-site youth services agency—proved beneficial as we met to develop a comprehensive treatment plan to best serve the complex needs of this at-risk student.

Brigitte Scheerer, School Counselor Intern, Loyola University Maryland

CONSULTATION PROCESS

As indicated in the previous discussion of consultation models, effective consultation in a school setting requires skill in problem solving and an ability to form collaborative relationships with other experts, including family members. A consultant who works within a school setting must also be astute about the systemic issues that affect the consultant's ability to fully implement his or her role and function. This section describes these issues through a six-step system-based process model for school consultation (see Table 12.2). Although each step is presented sequentially, the process is not linear and may involve repeated patterns and cycles.

Step 1: Enter the System

In addition to having physically entered the school building, the professional school counselor as consultant needs to be psychologically ready to enter the organizational system that exists within the building. Both the professional school counselor who is new to the building and the seasoned professional school counselor need to enter the school's system with a mind-set that is (1) flexible in its approach to problem solving, (2) committed to establishing collaborative relationships, and (3) motivated to encourage the types of systemic changes that may be needed to promote student learning.

Many professional school counselors enter the building ready to provide direct counseling services to students

TABLE 12.2 System-Based Process Model for School Consultation

Step	Components
Enter the system	Enter the system physically and psychologically
	Clarify role perceptions
	Perceive self as a direct and an indirect service provider
	Understand the goals of the system
Joining the system	Learn system rules and metarules
	Observe positions of power
	Build alliances
	Establish communication with subsystems
	Maintain objectivity
Initiate problem solving	Create group norms based on parity, mutual goals, shared decision making, shared resources, and shared expertise
Frame change	Identify goals
	Determine outcome measures
	Empower participants as change agents
	Think multisystemically
	Encourage flexible roles and permeable boundaries
	Protect change
Evaluate change	Monitor progress
	Assess outcomes
	If no progress occurs or if change is in an undesired direction, assess reasons
	Protect change
Facilitate change	Debrief
	Terminate consultation services for identified student
	Maintain relationships with other professionals
	Reinitiate consultation process for new students and problems

most in need. Counseling is an important role for the professional school counselor. In fact, many professional school counselors would probably view counseling as their most important role. The problems confronting many student-clients, however, may require a more comprehensive plan that engages the multiple systems (school, classroom, peer, family, neighborhood–community) that are a part of the student's life. Consultation provides a means through which the professional school counselor can access the range of systems necessary for long-term change. Hence, it is important for professional school counselors to perceive their role broadly—a role that includes both direct counseling services and the indirect services of consultation. Being ready to enter the school system and encouraging system-focused changes presupposes an indirect service orientation.

As the consultant enters the school's system, it is important to understand the goals of the system and how these goals relate to the consultant's role. Schools exist to support the academic achievement of students. Test scores and other measures of academic success drive what happens in schools. The consultant who can directly link his or her program to the school's mission will have an easier time gaining support from faculty and administrators. It is also important for the consultant to have a clear understanding of the school's perception of his or her role. A misperception of that role by the consultant, school administrator, faculty, or family member can create expectations for different types of services. Failure to meet these unrecognized expectations can place the consultant at a disadvantage. Clarifying these expectations, therefore, is an important step in the entry process.

Step 2: Join the System

Leaving at the school door all expectations that faculty and administrators "should" recognize how much the consultant has to offer is an important part of joining the school system. Schools are very busy places. Teachers are under enormous pressure to produce "educated" students. Earning the respect of teachers, administrators, and family members is an important part of joining the system. Consultants can begin to acquire this respect—can, in effect, "join with the school system"—by attending to the six points that follow.

LEARN THE SYSTEM RULES AND METARULES Knowing the policies and procedures that govern professional behavior within the system is essential. The consultant will need to know (1) the larger school system's policies and procedures related to a number of issues, including confidentiality, reporting of abuse, and parental notification about service delivery, as well as (2) the specific school's interpretation of how these policies and procedures are implemented at the school level. For example, it might be school board policy that parents are to be notified of a change to the student's

educational plan, including the addition of counseling services, before instituting the changes. How that policy is carried out at the school level could differ from school to school. One school might ask the student to deliver a written message to the parents, another school might notify the parents in writing by mail, and still another school might allow a brief grace period before notifying parents.

It would be easy for the consultant if all of the school rules were written in a manual that the consultant could read. Many are, but as is apparent from the previous discussion, having a written policy or rule does not mean it is interpreted and executed similarly across all schools. Many unwritten and unspoken rules, or *metarules*, also exist that can be learned only through interaction with the system. Metarules exist in how teachers manage their classrooms, and these rules can differ from teacher to teacher. Some teachers resent interruptions, preferring not to have students leave the classroom for counseling services or not to have other professionals enter the room during class time. Other teachers may be more open to the ebb and flow of students' movement, more willing to excuse students from their classes, and quite comfortable with other professionals entering the room to speak with them or observe a student.

OBSERVE EXPLICIT AND IMPLICIT POSITIONS OF POWER Nothing, be it an academic program or a counseling and consultation service, works well in a school without the principal's support. It is important for the consultant to join with, and maintain sufficient contact with, the school principal. Demonstrating how the consultant's work directly relates to the principal's agenda is an important avenue for gaining acceptance and support from the principal. Allotting ample consultation time with the principal allows the consultant to maintain lines of communication and act as a support to the principal. This will often involve learning the principal's schedule and putting in extra time to be able to catch up with the principal when he or she is available. Valuing the principal's contributions and recognizing the principal as an essential collaborator constitute an important part of joining the school system.

Not all people in a school who occupy a position of power have an accompanying title that suggests such status. All experienced school professionals know that most school secretaries occupy an implicit power position within the school. Some control who has access to the principal, and others are an important communication link between teachers and parents—and possibly between the consultant and parents. In some schools, other professionals in the building may hold a certain teacher or teachers in high esteem. Such teachers can enhance or jeopardize change, depending on whether or not they support the initiative.

The consultant who is not accepted by these power figures may find it difficult to accomplish his or her mission.

BUILD ALLIANCES THROUGH SHARED AGENDAS, RECOGNITION OF INDIVIDUAL STRENGTHS, AND SUPPORTIVE ACTIONS Having the principal's support does not necessarily mean the consultant will have the support of others in the building. As suggested earlier, the need for others to perceive a common agenda between themselves and the consultant is critical to the consultant's acceptance. Forming an alliance with those who hold explicit and implicit positions of power is an important strategy. Taking the time to get to know others, to offer assistance that may make others' jobs easier or help them to be more successful, and to explicitly recognize others' strengths are helpful ways of offering support and building alliances. Such actions must be conveyed and perceived as sincere and genuine.

Some alignments can be a serious hidden danger for consultants. For example, certain teachers might be in conflict with the school principal over any number of issues. If the principal sees the consultant aligning with these individuals, then the consultant unknowingly can experience resistance from the principal and those aligned with the principal. Being aware of staff alignments around issues affecting counseling and consultation services is an important part of the joining process.

In general, the consultant must be sensitive to giving the impression of aligning with any one group against another. In some instances, the school could perceive the consultant and family to be aligned against the school. If the consultant and family meet and make school-related decisions that are then conveyed to the teacher or administrator, the rest of the school understandably could feel left out. It is important for the consultant to be cautious about forming alignments with families that position the consultant and family against the school. It is important for the consultant to work toward collaboration with staff and families, rather than fragmentation.

ESTABLISH COMMUNICATION WITH MEMBERS OF ALL RELEVANT SUBSYSTEMS The school as a system is made up of several subsystems—administrative, staff, faculty, parental, student-peer, and community. Each of these subsystems may also be composed of smaller subsystems. For example, special education faculty and regular education faculty could be subunits within the larger faculty subsystem. When working with students with complex needs, interventions may need to involve several, or even many, layers of subsystems. Getting to know and be known by members of these different subsystems can be an important first step in establishing a working relationship.

Face-to-face contact through consultation services; attendance at staff, parent–teacher, and community meetings; participation in classroom activities; and announcements about services provided by the consultant in the school newsletter can provide avenues for connecting with subsystems. Developing an awareness of the types of issues that might create friction between subsystems is also important. Special education and regular education teachers will need to work together when implementing inclusive procedures for students. Collaboration may be hindered, however, by territorial issues and role rigidity. The consultant can provide a neutral perspective as subsystems strive to overcome the barriers that prohibit problem solving.

MAINTAIN OBJECTIVITY Joining with a system can take time. Acceptance by a few may precede acceptance by many. The consultant may do everything right, and still some members of the system may resist accepting the consultant as a team member and may impede full implementation of the consultant's services at the school. This can be frustrating and discouraging. The consultant may begin to resent the challenges presented by the school. Reframing challenges as opportunities and seeing resistance as a systemic reaction to change, rather than a personal affront, are important if the consultant is to maintain objectivity. A loss of objectivity as the consultant is in the process of joining with the system could threaten the consultant's ability to eventually effect client, consultee, and systemic change.

STAY "ONE DOWN" Teachers, administrators, and the consultant all act as helpers in the school setting. Many schools have a number of individuals in addition to the professional school counselor who deliver some type of mental health services. These might include social workers, school health nurses, crisis intervention counselors, and school psychologists. To work effectively, the consultant needs to work in a way that is not threatening to anyone's territory. Also, the consultant who is trying to acquire acceptance by a system has a harder time gaining acceptance if other professionals perceive his or her interactions as intimidating. Consultants who seek acceptance by the faculty or family subsystem need to minimize status differences between themselves and teachers and family members. Acknowledging the expertise of the other person, seeking advice, asking for assistance, and being open to trying new approaches are all ways the consultant can overtly recognize another person's skills and knowledge and covertly maintain a "one-down" position.

Step 3: Initiate Problem Solving

After entering and joining the school system, the consultant is in a position to initiate problem solving. This begins the working stage of the process model. The stages of problem solving remain the same regardless of whether the consultant is implementing a triadic-dependent, collaborative-dependent, or collaborative-interdependent type of relationship. As indicated, problem complexity often determines which consultation model the consultant uses.

The consultant begins the problem-solving phase of the consultation process by collecting information to assist in identifying the problem. This could mean working directly with the student, meeting with teachers and family members, and participating as part of a problem-solving team. Collecting and integrating available data about the student and the broader system occur at this stage of the process. The focus of problem solving could be an individual student, such as Samantha from our earlier example; or the consultee, such as Mrs. Miller, who needed to learn new skills; or a classroom system, as in Mr. Long's math class; or the broader systemic issue of increased violence and aggression at Westwood Middle School. Regardless of the focus, a thorough understanding of the student's, consultee's, or system's needs, including strengths and weaknesses, is an important part of a comprehensive assessment of the problem.

The opportunity to function as a consultant within a team context occurs frequently in today's schools. In addition to specific content knowledge about a particular problem, the consultant brings to the team knowledge of group dynamics and an ability to facilitate group process. Most school teams are task oriented; group process issues, so central to the ability of a team to function collaboratively, are often unnoticed or ignored. Without an attention to process, it will be difficult for a collaborative dynamic to emerge. Without strong process skills, it will be difficult for the consultant to become an integrated part of the school system and difficult for the consultant to establish a collaborative identity.

The consultant can use his or her expertise to facilitate a team's movement through the developmental stages of group process. The consultant can work to (1) establish collaborative group norms, (2) encourage cooperative rather than competitive behavior, (3) explicitly recognize the expertise of all participants, and (4) create communication patterns that allow all to participate equally in the problem-solving process. Establishing a collaborative team process might also require educating the school administrator about collaboration and acquiring the administrator's support prior to initiating this type of team process.

Step 4: Frame Change

During this fourth step of the process, the consultant works with others to set goals and shape an action plan for accomplishing goals that is realistic and that can be executed reasonably by those involved. A collaborative style of interaction continues as team members (if the consultant is working in a group context) or individuals (if the consultant is working with an individual teacher or family member) ascertain their roles in supporting client change. When framing change, the consultant may find the following points helpful.

1. ***Identify goals.***   After a thorough assessment of the problem in the initial problem-solving phase, appropriate goals are identified. These could include outcomes for the student, the consultee, and the system. Establishing concrete objectives further refines and defines each goal statement. Goals and objectives for students will need to be connected to academic achievement to be consistent with the school's larger mission.

2. ***Determine outcome measures.***   The measures and methods to be used in the evaluation process need to be considered prior to conducting the actual evaluation. Clarifying how outcomes will be measured at this point in the process also helps ensure that goals have been appropriately operationalized.

3. ***Empower participants as change agents.***   Some teachers and family members may feel less able to be or less committed to being part of a solution. Family members may blame the school for the problem, while some teachers may feel that the student's problems are a result of poor parenting. The consultant needs to reframe problems so that the emphasis is on common goals and how each person can help, rather than who is at fault. Affirm teacher and family strengths, and use these strengths as part of the change process. Create hope that change can be accomplished. When the consultation is student focused, it is important for the consultant to remember that, while client change may be the explicit outcome, change in the consultee or system might be a first step toward change for the student.

4. ***Think multisystemically.***   Many of the students with whom the consultant will work have very complex problems, with no single easy solution. Change for the individual is often predicated on change in the systems within which the individual is embedded. This would suggest that to be comprehensive, an action plan would need to include more than interventions targeting the individual. A word of caution is important here: A school that is open to viewing the student as the identified problem may not be open to examining staff or family actions that affect the student. Such a change in focus could result in a great deal of resistance. The consultant will need to

proceed prudently, being careful to offer suggestions tentatively. Earlier work in forming alliances and building a collaborative ethic will help support such efforts. In some cases, the consultant may work separately with a particular teacher or parent to help shape a change in the classroom and family subsystems.

5. *Encourage flexible roles and permeable boundaries.* When people assemble to solve problems, quite often they bring with them a particular notion of how change should occur and what their role is or is not in that process. Creative solutions often reside in being able to step outside of such preconceived notions. Initially, the professional counselor may have viewed his or her role primarily as one of direct service. To redefine that role to include consultation—using a variety of models—suggests flexibility. In another instance, a teacher may see himself or herself primarily as someone who conveys academic material within a specific discipline. Asking the teacher to conduct or co-lead classroom activities focused on social-emotional issues would encourage role flexibility. As people begin to collaborate, the boundaries that often separate and restrict professionals and families can become more permeable and less rigid.

6. *Plan to protect change.* Creating expectations about what might happen once participants enact the plan for change is a way to protect the change effort from failure. The wise consultant lets participants know ahead of time what they might expect; for instance, things might get worse before they improve. Strategize about what to do if the unexpected happens. Protect change by creating a system of shared accountability; make sure the action plan identifies who is responsible for what and describes benchmarks for evaluating progress. Recognize persistence, and remember the importance of linking student change to academic achievement. Creating mechanisms for ongoing communication and sources of support is also important.

Step 5: Evaluate Change

Monitoring progress and determining whether goals have been accomplished are tasks that are part of the evaluation process. Consistent with the shared accountability ethic of collaboration, those involved in the intervention are potential participants in the evaluation. Collecting data, summarizing and recording information, and developing mechanisms for sharing data are all tasks that can be shared.

The evaluation should assess if change has occurred, and if so, the degree to which it has occurred. If no change is noted or if undesired change has occurred,

the consultant can help assess the reason for a lack of progress and make recommendations for revising the intervention. Decisions about continuing the intervention are also made at this time.

Step 6: Facilitate Closure

Bringing the consultation relationship to closure can be a very different process for the school-based consultant who remains in the school than for a consultant who physically leaves the building at the end of the consultation. In the former case, although the intervention for a particular client may have ended, the consultant remains in relationships with the professionals in the building. Debriefing with consultees allows an opportunity to reflect on not only achieved outcomes, but also the process of working together. Debriefing provides an opportunity for the consultant and other team members to assess how well they collaborated as a group.

SCHOOL CONSULTATION AND COLLABORATION WITH DIVERSE POPULATIONS

While substantial attention has been given to issues of multicultural diversity in the counseling profession in general, infusion of multicultural research and practices into the area of collaboration and consultation has been slow in coming. In spite of a lack of research and even a lack of emphasis on cross-cultural consultation in training programs, most educational professionals perceived that they had the necessary skills and training to work effectively with culturally and linguistically diverse students (Roache, Shore, Gouleta, & de Obaldia Butkevich, 2003). But within the literature, some approaches and modified consultation strategies have emerged that may help professional school counselors to even more effectively address the needs of culturally diverse youth, as well as their families and teachers.

Tarver-Behring and Ingraham (1998) defined *multicultural consultation* as "a culturally sensitive, indirect service in which the consultant adjusts the consultation services to address the needs and cultural values of the consultee, the client, or both" (p. 58). Ingraham (2000) further defined *cross-cultural consultation* as a facet of multicultural consultation in which the consultant and consultee share dissimilar ethnic, socioeconomic, or linguistic characteristics. So even though the professional school counselor and parent may speak the same language and be of the same ethnicity, socioeconomic differences may indicate that cross-cultural modifications may be necessary for effective consultation to occur.

While the basic processes of multicultural collaboration or consultation are virtually identical to the processes discussed above, the framework or lens of the professional school counselor must account for cross-cultural issues that may impede the effectiveness of interventions. Ingraham (2000) proposed a multicultural school consultation framework to focus school professionals on the important facets of effective cross-cultural consultation. Her model consists of five components:

1. *Domains of consultant learning and development* involve knowledge and skill requirements in eight competence domains, including

   Understanding one's own culture . . . Understanding the impact of one's own culture on others . . . Respecting and valuing other cultures . . . Understanding individual differences within cultural groups and multiple cultural identities . . . Cross-cultural communication/multicultural consultation approaches for rapport development & maintenance . . . Understanding cultural saliency and how to build bridges across salient differences . . . Understanding the cultural context for consultation . . . Multicultural consultation and interventions appropriate for the consultee(s) and client(s). (p. 327)

2. *Domains of consultee learning and development* involve the knowledge, skills, confidence, and objectivity to deal with diverse circumstances.
3. *Cultural variations in the consultation constellation* involve cultural similarity between and among the consultant, consultee, and client.
4. *Contextual and power influences* involve societal influences, balance of power issues, and "cultural similarity within a differing cultural system" (p. 327).
5. *Hypothesized methods for supporting consultee and client success* involve knowledge, skills, and strategies of various supportive interventions in areas such as how to frame problems. This component also encompasses the professional school counselor's commitment to professional development.

Competence in the area of multicultural consultation is essential to the effective functioning of the professional school counselor in a diverse society. Increasingly, the literature is addressing the importance of understanding the consultation process through a multicultural lens (Ingraham, 2000; Sheridan, 2000), immigration (Maital, 2000), acculturation and bilingual educational services (B. S. C. Goldstein & Harris, 2000), and bicultural educational issues (Lopez, 2000). From time to time, professional school counselors may need to work with interpreters, and schools need to be proactive in locating, collaborating with, and training interpreters to better meet the needs of linguistically diverse students and their families (Lopez, 2000; Rogers et al., 1999).

In general, the effectiveness of collaboration and consultation approaches relies on the consultant and consultee participating as equal partners. But one should not expect the approaches discussed in this chapter to be equally effective with consultees from all cultures. Indeed, D. R. Atkinson and Lowe (1995) concluded that more directive styles of consultation, as opposed to more indirect collaboration styles, may be more effective with consultees from some cultures, such as Asian Americans. As great diversity exists in society and in the school population, great diversity must exist in the professional school counselor's intervention approaches to collaboration and consultation.

COLLABORATIVE CONSULTATION: REACHING OUT TO THE BROADER COMMUNITY

Students with complex problems are typically involved in the broader community of core social institutions. Core social institutions are those enduring structures whose mission is to provide the basic level, the core, of public services. These services for children include child welfare services, to protect children, and the juvenile justice system, to protect the public from children's misdeeds (Luongo, 2000).

The collaborative consultation model has to engage and be responsive to this context and advocate for the integration of basic services. When children simultaneously appear in multiple systems, and the evidence is that there is a 30% to 40% overlap in population among core social institutions serving children (Loeber & Stouthamer-Loeber, 1998), simply connecting the different professionals in the system is insufficient. Collaborative consultation supports an integrative approach that demands a shared responsibility for defining, planning, and moving with good intent for the student. This is an outcomes focus and places a premium on collaboration across systems of care. Helping professionals, no matter what core social institution they represent (public education, by definition, is a core social institution), need to be unburdened of the routine administrative responses to children's needs so that they can concentrate on creative and joint responses to complex needs. Through collaborative consultation, the definition of *helping* moves away from the narrow confines of any one core social institution to the focus of what these institutions can do together for children in question.

To create an effective, integrated network of community–school professionals, professional school counselors (as collaborative consultants) need to be familiar with other core social institutions—how they function and who in these systems represent potential partners. Bringing these potential partners together to create positive outcomes for students expands the consultant's role to include a community liaison function. While partnering with community resources is essential to effective school counseling programs, it is perhaps even more vital that educators partner with parents and involve them deeply in their children's education. It is this essential topic that becomes the focus of the remainder of this chapter.

INVOLVING PARENTS IN EDUCATION

Today, schools harbor a population of students with academic, personal, and social problems that create barriers to academic success. Complex and multifaceted issues are forcing professional school counselors to assess and redefine their current roles. While schools have traditionally stood alone in their mission to educate children, children are arriving in the classroom with needs that far exceed traditional educational methods. As health care organizations continue to limit services offered, including mental health services, it has become critical for professional school counselors to work with other human service professionals to meet their students' wide-ranging needs (Ponec, Poggi, & Dickel, 1998).

Professional school counselors are well positioned to act as proactive change agents in the school setting. Training in group processes and an understanding of the cycle of change are necessary skills acquired in counselor training. School reform has redefined the roles of many school professionals, including professional school counselors. All must become actively engaged in strengthening relationships among schools, families, and communities.

True collaboration includes jointly agreeing to identify and address specific problems and areas of service. This description goes far beyond talking about problems, learning about resources, and coordinating service delivery. When true collaboration exists, all parties equally share the outcomes. This process requires consensus building and may not be imposed hierarchically. Collaborators must learn about each other's roles and explain their own. Expertise in the process of goal-setting is critical. Through

collaboration, professional school counselors will gain a clearer understanding of what other agencies can contribute and how they function (resources and procedures). By developing personal relationships, people will become more willing to respond and work together for all children. They must remind themselves that their leadership efforts will improve the academic achievement of students.

Schools are in the business of education, and this generation of professional school counselors must be trained to work effectively with others to meet the needs of students and their families. It is critical to understand the system in which one works. Professional school counselors need to collect and analyze data when identifying needs and creating partnerships.

Braback, Walsh, Kenny, and Comilang (1997) described schools as conservative, with many gatekeepers, rules, regulations, and structures that make collaboration difficult. They further stated that staff members are often threatened by the appearance of other professionals. Professional school counselors need to help staff members to recognize the benefits of developing relationships with other agencies and service providers. Because it is necessary for families and outside agencies to know the rules and regulations with a special sensitivity to hierarchy and the structure of the system, professional school counselors are positioned best to facilitate collaborative efforts (Ponec et al., 1998).

A number of studies have underscored the challenges to school–agency collaboration, as well as curative factors. For example, Ponec et al. (1998) conducted a study to explore, understand, and describe the therapeutic relationship shared among professional school and community counselors engaged in collaborative relationships. Although mutual concerns focused on confidentiality and the responsibility of financial obligations, community counselors expressed the value of personal interaction and identified time (specifically, a nine-month cyclical school calendar) as an impediment to those interactions. The authors of this study concluded that it is only through the enhancement of communication that the ability to be effective helping professionals can be advanced. Personal knowledge, interaction, a perception of professionalism, and teamwork will develop and enhance the collaborative effort.

VOICES FROM THE FIELD 12.1   **STAYING CONNECTED THROUGH COLLABORATION AND PARTNERING**

As a relatively new professional school counselor who has worked at the high school, middle school, and elementary school levels, I have found collaboration to be a particularly vital part of the job. This past year I was working at four

schools and with many students of different grade levels. I would have missed a lot of pertinent information about those students had I not proactively communicated with their teachers and families, with administrators and other staff members, and with staff from community resources and agencies. The information included things that sometimes did not come up during my individual counseling sessions with the students, including information about academics, social and emotional issues, and events going on in the students' lives. In the limited time allotted for counselor–student sessions, the students sometimes neglected to talk about certain things that were going on in their lives, or they might simply not have been thinking about them (and, therefore, did not express them) at that particular time, or sometimes they did not see the information as important. Communicating with professionals and family members who were important in these students' lives added invaluable perspectives on these students' "worlds."

Teachers see students almost every day and, therefore, are excellent judges and sources of information on how students are doing. In my experience, teachers saw more than just the academic side of things. They also were privy to information about, and observed, a student's relationships with friends and other significant people in the student's life. Teachers were able to notice when something was different with a student and when that student might need help.

School administrators often saw yet a different side of students. Administrators had information about difficulties a student may have experienced. Some administrators had frequent contact with parents via school functions, meetings, or phone calls or by living in the same community and, therefore, had a good sense of what the students' home lives were like.

I found that families frequently had still a whole different perspective on how their children were faring. They saw their children outside of school, had known them for the longest time, and knew them well. Families also were usually keenly aware of changes in children's behavior, especially at home or in social settings outside the school.

Other school personnel working in areas or programs such as Healthy Start or probation services and people staffing community resource programs also proved to be vital resources for me. They were a great help in finding out what resources were available to students and what steps needed to be taken to get those services to the students. For example, this past year I worked closely with a woman from a Healthy Start program whom I went to often when I needed to match specific resources available in the community to the needs of a particular student. She was able to provide detailed information about resources in the community and had the firsthand experience to anticipate which community resource would, in fact, be a good fit with a particular type of problem.

Without collaborating with teachers, administrators, families, other school staff members, and professionals in the community, I would not have been able to work as effectively with the students. With collaboration, I was able to piece together a more complete picture of the student and develop a truer sense of the problems that student was experiencing. We mutually drew from each other's expertise, and collectively we were able to generate a number of possible approaches to working with a student. By staying in constant communication, we were able to better select those approaches that worked, monitor the student, and better evaluate how that approach was succeeding. Working together helped the students more than any one of us working alone. I found that helping students to the best of *my* ability meant working as a team.

Megan Earl, Professional School Counselor, Lake County Office of Education, Safe Schools Healthy Students, Middletown, California

SCHOOL OUTREACH AND CHANGING FAMILY NEEDS

Schools have traditionally engaged in outreach strategies such as the fall open house and parent–teacher conferences. Other strategies such as parent resource centers, home visits, and positive phone calls are less common. Doing a better job of making schools more family-friendly is within the reach of all educators. In particular, professional school counselors are in a key position to increase opportunities for parents to be involved in and supportive of their child's education. Today's parents seem to fall into one of three categories:

1. Parents who are able to, and do, prepare their children for success in school on their own. They initiate contact with the school and take the steps to maintain a continuous line of communication with the school. Working with such parents requires little effort on the part of the professional school counselor and school officials.

2. Parents who want to help their children be successful in the school setting, yet do not take the steps necessary to do so. Sometimes the reticence may be due to a lack of knowledge of what to do; sometimes it may be due to a lack of resources. These are the parents to reach out to and continuously encourage. Often, professional school counselors encounter parents with no health insurance or no transportation or with rigid work schedules and demands. Counselors must use their listening skills to hear and respond to these parents' needs.

3. Parents (a small percentage) who do not have the skills or interest necessary for involvement in their child's school success. These are the truly challenging families who are often living at the subsistence level and who may be involved with multiple agencies and organizations, all attempting to intervene to assist the family toward independence. Counselors' consultation, coordination, and collaborative skills are put to the test with these families.

TABLE 12.3 Possible Types of Parental Involvement

Type of Involvement	Sample Activities
1. Parenting	Parent education workshops
	Home visits at transition points
2. Communicating	Yearly conference with every parent
	Weekly folder of student work sent home
3. Volunteering	Parent room or family center
	Class parent
4. Learning at home	Information on homework policies
	Summer learning packets or activities
5. Making decisions	Active PTA or PTO
	District-level councils and committees
6. Collaborating with community	Service to community
	Service integration through partnerships

The great majority of parents care about their children's education. They understand that an education is their child's ticket to success in the job market and the avenue to a better lifestyle than, perhaps, they were able to provide. Job and family demands, however, engage much of parents' time, often to the exclusion of school involvement. Parents in low socioeconomic groups and those who speak English as a second language also tend to shy away from school involvement. Professional school counselors should view such families as a welcome challenge to their communication skills and creative thought processes and invite these parents to become involved in the school. Table 12.3 suggests some ways in which parent involvement in school and community activities can be accomplished.

Parent involvement initiatives around the world have been effective in improving achievement and a wide variety of childhood adjustment difficulties (Jordan, Snow, & Porche, 2000; Westat & Policy Studies Associates, 2001). Parent involvement in the home makes an even greater difference in achievement than parent involvement at school (Christenson & Sheridan, 2001; Izzo, Weissberg, Kasprow, & Fendrich, 1999; Trusty, 1999). Thus, the challenge and impetus for professional school counselors and educators in general must be to actively engage parents and guardians in the academic lives of their children.

Correlative studies have indicated that parental involvement predicts student achievement (Jimerson, Engeland, & Teo, 1999; Keith et al., 1998), student attendance, dropouts (Wright & Stegelin, 2003), and student attitudes and behaviors (R. M. Clark, 1993). As a more

specific example, when parents are trained to help increase their children's achievement at home, significant improvements have been documented. Darling and Westberg (2004) reported that parents who were trained to teach their children how to read using guided exercises and questioning produced significantly better results than did parents who simply listened to their children read—which most do.

The research on parental involvement indicates that most involved parents are White, married mothers with higher levels of education and socioeconomic status (Griffith, 1998; Grolnick, Benjet, Kurinski, & Apostoleris, 1997). Parent involvement is far more common in elementary schools than in high schools (Eccles & Harold, 1996), with the transition from elementary to middle school resulting in an average decline in parent participation of nearly 50% (Manning, 2000). However, some research indicates that when educators deliberately seek out, encourage, and invite parent involvement, factors such as educational and socioeconomic levels are eliminated as differentiating factors. Studies have explored what motivates parents to become involved in schools and student achievement (e.g., Benson, 2004). Table 12.4 provides some suggestions for increasing parent involvement in student achievement and the schools. Of course, a major benefit of parent involvement is frequently greater parental satisfaction with the quality of education their children are receiving (Applequist & Bailey, 2000).

Not surprisingly, all of the research literature does not back the effectiveness of parent involvement on academic achievement. For example, Mattingley, Prislin, McKenzie, Rodriquez, and Kayzar (2002) conducted a meta-analysis of more than 40 studies evaluating parent

---

TABLE 12.4   A Dozen Strategies for Increasing Parent Involvement

1. Focus on student achievement (academic and otherwise) as a school and extended community.
2. Acknowledge parent contributions at school or community events, as well as through print and personalized expressions of gratitude.
3. Be specific in giving directions so that parents understand exactly what you expect them to do.
4. Use varied and repeated types of communications to solicit volunteers. These may include personal, phone, or written contacts by educators, other parent volunteers, and even students. Recruitment must be a continuous process.
5. Include parents in the planning and decision-making stages of programs to enhance feelings of ownership.
6. Find out what parents are interested and skilled in doing so that volunteer activities will match parent needs, interests, and skills.
7. Develop a school climate that is positive, inviting, and interactive. Make the school a place that parents want to be.
8. Provide (at least) monthly opportunities for parents to visit the school and interact with the educators and parent volunteers.
9. Provide parents with resources and information that help them to help their children learn at home.
10. Encourage the rest of the family (e.g., grandparents, aunts, uncles, siblings), neighbors, employers, and community leaders to get involved.
11. Select a coordinator of volunteer activities to keep everyone moving in sync. This can be a parent volunteer.
12. Provide niceties (e.g., refreshments, name tags) and remove barriers to participation (e.g., provide transportation and/or babysitting).

---

involvement, finding little empirical support for such claims. However, it is important to note that flaws/overgeneralizations in research methodologies (e.g., the studies were primarily correlational studies, rather than causative-comparative studies) of the 40-plus studies led to this conclusion, not necessarily ineffective results. Henderson's (1987) classic study is often cited as conclusive evidence of the effectiveness of parent involvement in student achievement, but Mattingly et al. (2002) correctly point out that less than half of the studies Henderson reviewed explored the effect of interventions and that only one out of every five of the reviewed studies was published in a refereed journal. Likewise, White, Taylor, and Moss (1992), reviewing 172 research studies, found the evidence of effectiveness of parent involvement unconvincing. Much better research is needed in this area before conclusive results can be stated with confidence. Better research is likely to occur soon, given that parent involvement was one of six targeted and funded areas in the No Child Left Behind Act.

Opportunities for parent involvement in the school (and school counseling program) include serving on an advisory committee; staffing registration or special events tables; presenting at career fairs or career programs; providing character education or social skills training (after brief training by the professional school counselor; Cuthbert, 2001); grandparents days; coffee or tea gatherings with teachers, counselors, or administrators; computer training days; parent visitation days; special events days (e.g., field day, cookout, talent show); awards assemblies; ice cream socials; community fund-raising dinners; parent workshops; field trips; and parent–child events (e.g., father–son, mother–daughter, father–daughter, mother–son, grandparent, etc.)—among many others. The limits to parent involvement are primarily the limits of creativity and time.

COMMUNICATING EFFECTIVELY WITH PARENTS AND GUARDIANS

Although parents and school personnel often seem to have similar goals, both can set up roadblocks to effective communication. Berger (2000) identified six parental roles that inhibit their ability to communicate with schools, albeit often unintentionally: Protector, Inadequate-me, Avoidance, Indifferent parent, Don't make waves, and Club-waving advocate. These roles can potentially become roadblocks to successful communication. Likewise, schools often unintentionally install roadblocks to successful communication. Berger also identified five roles that educators might assume to hamper communication between home and school: Authority figure, Sympathizing-counselor, Pass-the-buck, Protect-the-empire, and Busy teacher. School staff must treat parents and guardians as partners in education, involving each to maximize the potential of all students. Professional school counselors need to connect to and develop authentic relationships with educators and parents who adopt these counterproductive roles in order to help both groups get what they most desire, a quality education for their students and children. The bottom line is that educators and parents must be helped to adopt what Blue-Banning, Summers, Frankland, Nelson, and Beegle (2004) called the six themes of collaborative family–professional partnerships: communication, commitment, equality, skills, trust, and respect.

Although job and family demands, as well as cultural and socioeconomic backgrounds, pose a temporary roadblock to school involvement, most parents want guidance from schools on ways to support their children's learning. Contact by the professional school counselor is often the first step toward making parents feel welcome in the school during student registration, back-to-school nights, new-families gatherings, and so on. In addition, contact with parents can often be made by letter, website, e-mail, phone call, text message, blog pages or home visit. For example, text messaging or e-mailing a parent/guardian to notify him or her of a child's missing assignment or the need to prepare for an important examination is a fast and efficient way of communicating. Likewise, teachers can post study guides or assignments on websites that students or parents/guardians can access. Technology can make learning and communication more efficient, but parents/guardians, students, and educators must work together to make it so.

Most schools today are concerned about communicating with parents. Many schools provide newsletters and flyers to distribute information to families. This one-way communication is quite common. Ideally, schools will consider some methods of two-way communication, allowing parents an opportunity to express ideas and concerns, give feedback, and interact with school personnel. Some examples of two-way communication are phone calls; e-mail; home visits; text messages; conferences; breakfast with a grade-level team, professional school counselor, or administrator; and community meetings to discuss a particular topic or concern.Educators cannot wait for parents to make the first contact, but must communicate with all families about school programs and procedures, individual student progress, and ways parents can help their children at home.

Although teachers remain the first line of defense in the communication effort, professional school counselors continue to be critical in maintaining ongoing dialogue with families. They may inform parents of special concerns regarding their child, provide updates on their child's progress with modifications and interventions, coordinate workshops to increase parents' skills, or assist in connecting families to needed community-based services.

Through parent workshops, parents learn the importance of two-way communication. If families are to be truly involved as partners in their children's education, they must learn the skills of listening to their children and expressing their concerns regarding their children's learning success. Teachers, as well, need to develop good listening

and communicating skills to effectively convey their students' progress. Together, teachers, parents, and professional school counselors make an effective team to support children's learning success.

Many of the following strategies for communicating with families are outlined in the U.S. Department of Education publication *Reaching All Families* (2008). They may be used by professional counselors to open lines of communication with parents and clarify the counselor's role in the school setting:

- *Welcome letter.* Generally sent home by teachers at the beginning of the school year, this letter provides a good opportunity to include the counselor's introduction, as well as to underscore the partnership of parent, teacher, and counselor in meeting the needs of the whole child.
- *Home–school handbook.* Most schools publish a handbook of general school policies and procedures. This is another forum for defining the professional school counselor's role and function.
- *Information packets.* These packets provide more-detailed information about the role of the counselor in the school setting. The packets may include information on school policy and procedures, as well as on services offered by the school. By adding pertinent telephone numbers, this packet becomes an easy reference for parents to access needed people, programs, and services.
- *Calendars.* Weekly, monthly, or annual calendars highlight counselor-planned or -coordinated meetings and events for parents. They may also include encouraging and informative parenting tips, upcoming community events, family resources, and appropriate television shows and movies. They should be simply designed, only one page in length, and posted on the refrigerator door or family bulletin board for easy reference.
- *School newsletter.* Counselors often maintain a regular column in the school newsletter. This is another opportunity to connect with parents by providing parenting and child development tips from a variety of resources. It is important to use clear, simple language that avoids educational or counseling jargon in these articles and to address the needs of the audience.
- *Open house.* Publicity, planning, and preparation are keys to the success of this annual school event. Counselors can help market the event during other contacts with parents. They should plan to greet the families as they arrive and prepare a formal presentation to explain their role in the school. Counselors will want to encourage parents to contact them and to

participate in planned activities for parents held throughout the year. In addition, the counselor may want to have a display table of parent and community resource brochures and other items of interest to families.

- *New-families meeting.* Most new families have registered their children prior to the first day of school. Holding a new-families meeting during the week before school begins will enable the counselor to connect with these families on a personal basis. The counselor might also give the families a tour of the school, introduce the families to the students' teachers, and answer other questions regarding school procedures and practices. This meeting can serve as a prelude to new-student group sessions held after the start of school.
- *School–parent compacts.* These are voluntary agreements between the home and school to define goals, expectations, and shared responsibilities of schools

and parents as partners. Although this is a requirement of schools receiving federal Title I funds, it is a good practice for all schools to build partnerships that help students achieve high standards. Compacts need to be used in combination with other family involvement activities, not as the only way schools communicate with parents.

- *Positive phone calls.* Traditionally, parents have received a phone call from the school when there was a problem. Imagine the impact of a telephone call from the school that carries information that is positive! This kind of call opens lines of communication, helps parents feel hopeful, and encourages everyone to believe that all children can learn. To be most beneficial, parents need to receive at least two to three positive phone calls over the course of the school year. Counselors can assist and support teachers and administrators in this important effort.

VOICES FROM THE FIELD 12.2   **REPORT CARD TIME**

I work in an all-boys private high school. Usually after first-quarter interim grades are sent home, I will receive numerous phone calls from worried parents concerned about their sons' failing grades. Since we have a web-based program that allows parents to track their sons' academic progress for each subject, I inquire as to whether or not they've been utilizing this resource. If they have not, I recommend they do so. I encourage them to contact their sons' teachers through either e-mail or telephone. In most cases, these suggestions address the situation. However, there are occasions where I will recommend a parent conference to include all teachers because the issues are broad in scope, extending to most subjects. The purpose in arranging such a meeting is to allow all parties (e.g., parents, teachers, support staff, outside mental health professionals) an opportunity to share their insights. It is also a way to see if any problems are isolated to a particular teacher/subject or are common among all classes. My intention is that together we can identify the needs of the student, develop a plan to meet those needs, and establish relationships that will allow for ongoing, effective communication.

I believe that parents are the primary teachers of their children, and therefore it is critical that they have an opportunity to share their knowledge, insights, and experience regarding their sons. Because it is extremely difficult to choose a time that assures attendance of all parties, the parents and I decide on a date and time to meet. In most cases, the meeting begins 10 minutes after the end of the school day and is usually scheduled for a Tuesday, Wednesday, or Thursday. I have found that

Mondays and Fridays are not conducive for gathering as many parties as possible. If a teacher cannot attend because of a scheduling conflict, I ask that he or she contact the parents directly.

We meet in the guidance conference room, which provides a professional environment devoid of interruptions. I begin by welcoming all in order to create a relaxed and hospitable atmosphere. Invited members introduce themselves and state their relationship with the student. In advance, I inform the parents that they will speak first to give their impression as to the issues, concerns, and needs regarding their son. Each teacher has an opportunity to discuss the student's academic progress regarding homework; tests and quizzes; class participation, which includes behavior; and any other general impressions regarding attitude. The first teacher provides for the parents a copy of the current academic progress report. The parents then have an opportunity to ask questions in order to seek clarification. After all questions have been thoroughly addressed, the next teacher does the same until all have had the opportunity to share. Teachers will relay to parents strategies that they will continue or introduce in the classroom to address any concerns that were raised. By listening to one another, teachers may be exposed to other effective strategies used by fellow teachers. Each teacher can decide with the parents how communication will occur regarding the student.

After all have shared, the teachers are thanked for their time and insights and are dismissed. The parents and I continue the meeting to discuss and process privately what

(Continued)

has just transpired. I will ask them what insights they have gained, and we will discuss any common themes. I will share with the parents my insights regarding student performance and behavior. I will talk about my role and what services I can provide. For example, at one such meeting the student's need for organizational skills came to light. The following day I met with the student to discuss strategies with him such as time management, locker and book bag arrangement, use of a daily planner, and prioritization. I then follow up with all parties by sending an e-mail summarizing the points of concern, the strategies identified, and the format for evaluation and follow-up. I have found this process of parent–teacher conferences to be most effective.

Charles J. Belzner, Professional School Counselor, Mount Saint Joseph High School, Baltimore, Maryland

Summary/Conclusion

It is unlikely that school resources are going to increase over time to the extent necessary to provide optimal professional school counselor-to-student ratios. The challenges facing counselors are many, with too many students to serve and too few resources. Through consultation, professional school counselors facilitate positive growth for students by working directly with teachers and family members and the systems within which these groups live and work. By helping to expand the skills and knowledge of these significant others, professional school counselors, as consultants, extend the reach of their services. Consultation efforts that focus on changing the nature and functioning of a system—be it a school or family system—provide the most promising prevention potential for large numbers of students.

Many professional school counselors have been trained primarily as direct service providers. Changing the mind-set—getting ready to enter the system as an agent of change—presupposes a change in orientation from direct to indirect service provider. A professional school counselor's primary focus is prevention, which can be accomplished most effectively by maximizing the consultation function.

Connecting school, family, and community continues to be a nationwide challenge. Professional school counselors are uniquely positioned to provide both traditional and innovative services to meet the needs of children and families. As we move forward in the 21st century, professional school counselors' use of technology and other innovative approaches will provide new opportunities and forums for schools and parents to connect and communicate.

Activities

1. Spend some time in a school setting. What examples of consultation and collaboration do you witness? How effective do they appear to be?
2. Imagine you are a professional school counselor and a teacher comes to you with concerns regarding one of her students, who has been acting out in class. Perform a consultation role play to come up with a plan of action for this teacher. What model of collaboration did you use? Why?
3. Pretend you are a new professional school counselor. Create a list of steps you would take to acclimate to your new school. With whom would you attempt to build relationships? Compare your list with that of another member of your class. What similarities and differences are evident between your lists? Discuss these with your partner.

13

Accountability: Evaluating Programs, Assessing Needs, and Determining Outcomes

Bradley T. Erford

Editor's Introduction: Education reform movements have made accountability a central responsibility of all educators, including professional school counselors. But accountability is not just tallying the number of students seen for individual or group counseling or how much time has been spent in direct or indirect services. At its core, accountability addresses several issues: needs assessment, program (process) evaluation, service assessment, outcomes studies, and performance appraisal. Each of these important facets of accountability is addressed in this chapter.

ACCOUNTABILITY IN SCHOOL COUNSELING

One of the cornerstones of the *ASCA National Model* (2005a) is accountability. Accountability involves responsibility for professional actions—in other words, for the effectiveness of one's actions. In the more specific context of school counseling program accountability, this may involve

- Identifying and collaborating with stakeholder groups (e.g., a school counseling program advisory committee, parents/guardians, teachers, students);
- Collecting data and assessing needs of students, staff, and community;
- Setting goals and establishing objectives based on data and determined need;
- Implementing effective interventions to address the goals and objectives;
- Measuring the outcomes or results of these interventions;
- Using these results for program improvement; and
- Sharing results with major stakeholder groups such as administration, teachers and staff, parents and guardians, students, school boards, community and business leaders, school counselors, and supervisors. (Isaacs, 2003; Loesch & Ritchie, 2004; Myrick, 2003b)

It is undeniable that accountability and assessment have, in general, been given greater visibility in both the extant counseling literature and the day-to-day functioning of the average professional school counselor over the past 10 years. Indeed, calls for greater accountability from professional school counselors have been occurring since at least the mid-1970s (Nims, James, & Hughey, 1998). This increased focus on accountability is due to numerous contemporary factors, including the education reform movement, the rise in high stakes and other standardized testing programs, federal and state legislation (e.g., the No Child Left Behind Act (NCLB), Title I, the Individuals with Disabilities Education Improvement Act, Section 504 of the Rehabilitation Act), data-driven transformative initiatives, and outcomes-driven practice emphases. It is the professional and ethical responsibility of professional school counselors to ensure that the comprehensive school counseling services offered to stakeholder groups are truly effective. Given the impetus of school reform, the time is right for professional school counselors to partner with administration and key stakeholders to promote accountability and provide effective services to ensure the academic success of all students (C. B. Stone & Clark, 2001).

The focus of this chapter is on the wide-ranging accountability functions of the professional school counselor, including needs assessment, program evaluation, and interpretation of assessment results. The content of this chapter is among the most important in terms of understanding the needs of a school community and a school counseling program's effectiveness (i.e., answering that critical question, "Why do we need school counselors?"). This information will also allow professional school counselors to speak the language of decision makers, thus allowing social and academic advocacy for children with special needs or those encountering systemic barriers to academic, career, or personal/social success. Finally, every professional school counselor should be constantly asking and gathering information to answer the question, "Is what I'm doing working with this student?" As with nearly every counselor function, conducting accountability studies has

its advantages and disadvantages. Table 13.1 lists some of these. Consider these and others as you peruse the remainder of this chapter.

More to the point, accountability in the school counseling program must address five primary questions using the five accountability measures noted in parentheses following each question: (1) Is a comprehensive, standards-based program in place? (program [process] evaluation or audit) (2) What are the needs of the school's student population when compared to these standards? (needs assessment) (3) What services were implemented to address the identified needs and standards? (service assessment) (4) What was the result of the implemented services? (results or outcomes studies) (5) How well is the professional school counselor performing? (performance evaluation/appraisal). This chapter will focus on each of these questions.

In this age of school reform and accountability, program evaluation is more important than ever. Traditionally, however, professional school counselors for many reasons have failed to hold their programs and services accountable or to provide evidence that activities undertaken were achieving intended results (Lombana,

---

TABLE 13.1 Advantages and Disadvantages of Accountability Studies

Advantages

1. Data is almost always better than perception when it comes to guiding decision making about programs, practices, and interventions.

2. Accountability studies help demonstrate necessity, efficiency, and effectiveness of counseling services.

3. Accountability studies can help identify professional development and staff development needs.

4. Professional school counselors can network to share program results, thereby spreading the word about effective practices.

5. Conducting accountability studies is a professional responsibility and demonstrates one's commitment to personal and professional improvement.

6. Accountability results can serve a public relations function by informing educators and the public of a school counseling program's accomplishments.

Challenges

1. Outcome measures and surveys take some training and skill (sometimes including consultation with experts) to develop.

2. It takes time and resources to do quality outcomes research and evaluation, time and resources that could be dedicated to additional service delivery.

3. Many do not understand the nature and purpose of accountability (e.g., impact of school counseling program on student outcome data) because of misperceptions or previous "bad" experiences (e.g., evaluations by principals or others not skilled in counseling, having to "count" every minute or service).

4. Data are sometimes "overinterpreted" or given undue meaning (e.g., the facts may not support the conclusion). All studies have limitations that must be considered when arriving at conclusions.

5. Comprehensive evaluations are seldom conducted. More often, bits and pieces of evaluative information are collected and the "big picture" is often incomplete.

1985). Some complain that the nature of what school counselors do is so abstract and complicated as to render the services and results unmeasurable. Others are so busy attempting to meet the needs of students that they shift time that should be spent in evaluation to responsive interventions. Some lack an understanding of the methods and procedures needed to conduct accountability studies. Still others are unsure of the effectiveness of the services provided and shy away from accountability unless forced to do so by supervisors.

Whatever the reason, the end result is a glaring lack of accountability that poses dangers for the future of the profession. Each of the above reasons contributes to a shirking of professional and ethical responsibility to ensure that the services provided to students, school personnel, and parents are of high quality and effective in meeting intended needs. Think about it from a business perspective. How long would a business last if it continued to engage in indiscernible or ineffective activities, the value of which was unknown to the business's consumers, managers, or employees? Such businesses are selected out for extinction! The same may hold true for professional school counselors. Without accountability data to back up service provision, school counseling services could be among the first "nonessential services" to go during budget cutbacks. The key is to document and determine the worth of all aspects of the comprehensive school counseling program.

The evaluation of a comprehensive school counseling program involves program (process) evaluation, needs assessment, service assessment, results (outcomes) evaluation, and personnel evaluation. Each component is essential in holding school counseling programs accountable.

PROGRAM (PROCESS) EVALUATION

Program evaluation (also sometimes called process evaluation or program auditing) is akin to the measurement concept of content validity (which is a systematic examination of a test's content) in that it is a systematic examination of a program's content. In short, the audit or evaluation of a program involves determining whether there is written program documentation and whether the program is being implemented appropriately in various locales. A program audit frequently provides an analysis of each facet of the comprehensive school counseling program (Bowers & Colonna, 2001; S. K. Johnson & Johnson, 2003). Auditing the program will often point to areas of programmatic strengths and weaknesses. The *ASCA National Model* (2005a) provided a sample program audit aligning with model components. For example, sample criteria included whether "a statement of philosophy has been written for the

school counseling program" and whether that statement "addresses every student's right to a school counseling program" (p. 66). The ASCA suggested that program criteria be evaluated using the following response choices: "None: meaning not in place; In progress: perhaps begun, but not completed; Completed: but perhaps not implemented; Implemented: fully implemented; Not Applicable: for situations where the criteria does not apply" (p. 66). In practice, a program audit should be conducted near the end of each academic year. Reports derived from the audit should address program strengths, areas in need of improvement, and long- and short-term improvement goals (ASCA, 2005a). The areas in need of improvement and goals also are derived from a needs assessment. These goals then drive program development procedures and activities during subsequent years.

NEEDS ASSESSMENT

At least two primary purposes underlie the use of a needs assessment in school counseling programs. First, needs assessment helps professional school counselors understand the needs of various subpopulations of a school community. These subpopulations may include teachers, parents, students, administrators, community organizations, local businesses, and the general citizenry. Subpopulations may also include groups of students experiencing achievement gaps or differential access to rigorous academic programming. Each of these groups holds a stake in the success of the total educational enterprise. Second, needs assessment helps establish the priorities that guide the construction of a comprehensive, developmental school counseling program, as well as continuous quality improvement of the program. In this way, a needs assessment assesses not only what currently is, but also what should be. Assessing the needs of a school community provides a trajectory for addressing what the community values and desires to pursue. Two types of needs assessments are commonly conducted within school counseling programs: data-driven needs assessments and perceptions-based needs assessments.

Data-Driven Needs Assessments

Data-driven decision making deals with demonstrated need and impact, not perceived needs. It begins with an analysis of school-based performance data. Given the prominence of high-stakes testing and large-scale testing programs required under NCLB, schools are frequently provided with aggregated and disaggregated performance results. *Aggregated* means that all student results are lumped together to show total grade-level or school-wide (average) results. Aggregated data are helpful in understanding how the average students perform in a given class, grade, or school, but tell very little about the diversity of learner performance or needs and nothing about how various subgroups or subpopulations performed. In Table 13.2, the aggregated results are represented by the "Total Grade" line at the top for a school with 100 fifth graders.

To fully understand how to use school performance data, professional school counselors must become proficient in understanding norm-referenced and criterion-referenced score interpretation. While a comprehensive explanation of score interpretation is beyond the scope of the book and typically encountered by counselors in an ●ssessment or testing course, what follows can be considered a very basic primer on interpretation of norm-referenced scores.

Note that in the example in Table 13.2, the mean national percentile rank was 50. A percentile rank is most easily understood if one visualizes a lineup of 100 individuals, all with certain characteristics in common; in this case, they are all fifth-grade math students. Importantly, when interpreting percentile ranks, the first student in the line is the lowest-performing student, and the 100th student is the highest-performing student. A student's place indicates his or her relative standing compared to other fifth-grade math students across the country (thus the term *national percentile rank*). For example, a student scoring at the 79th percentile performed better than 79% of the fifth graders in the national norm group or was the 79th student standing in the line of 100 students. Likewise, a student performing at the 5th percentile would be standing in the fifth place in line and has outperformed only 5% of the fifth graders in the nationwide norming group.

A *quartile* is a commonly used interpretive statistic that divides the percentile rank distribution into four segments. The first quartile includes percentile ranks ranging up to and including 25, the lowest quarter of a distribution and designated Q_1. The second quartile (Q_2) includes percentile ranks ranging from 26 to 50. The third quartile (Q_3) includes percentile ranks ranging from 51 to 75. The fourth quartile (Q_4) includes percentile ranks ranging from 76 and up, the highest quarter of the distribution. Some test publishers also use an interpretive statistic known as stanines. Stanines, short for "standard nine," divide a normal distribution into nine segments, although in a manner quite different from quartiles. Stanines actually represent one-half standard deviation units. So while each quartile represents 25% of the population, stanines may represent varying percentages

TABLE 13.2   Aggregated and Disaggregated Results From a Typical Large-Scale Math Achievement Test for a Total-School Fifth-Grade Level

	n	NPR	% in Quartile			
			Q_1	Q_2	Q_3	Q_4
Total Grade	100	50	19	31	26	24
Male	48	45	22	34	26	18
Female	52	56	10	31	31	28
Asian	8	72	0	25	38	38
Black	31	37	29	52	13	6
Hispanic	8	43	25	50	25	0
White	52	58	9	30	33	28
Other	1	44	0	100	0	0
Low SES	48	31	36	38	23	3
Non Low SES	52	71	5	24	36	35
English (second language)	3	43	0	67	33	0
English (primary language)	97	51	19	30	27	24
Special Education	10	25	60	20	20	0
Non Special Education	90	58	11	31	32	26

Note: n = number of students in sample; NPR = national percentile rank; "% in Quartile" means the percentage of the sample that performed in a given quartile; SES = Socioeconomic Status.

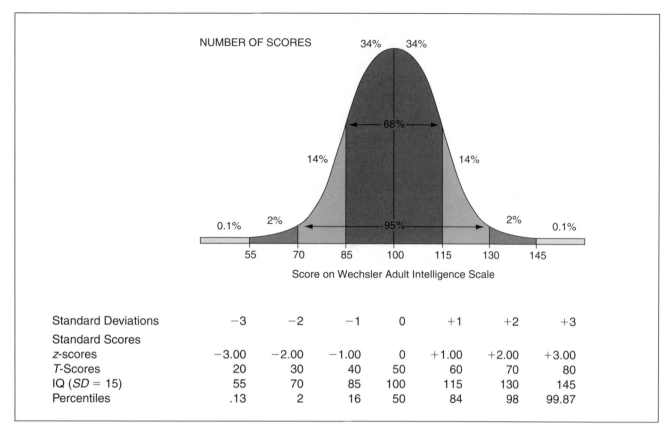

FIGURE 13.1 The normal curve and related standardized scores.

of the population. The first stanine represents the lowest level of performance, and the ninth stanine represents the highest level of performance. Importantly, parents, teachers, and students will understand performance most easily and most accurately when using percentile ranks. Other standardized scores can require some sophistication and may lead to errors in interpretation. Figure 13.1 provides a graphic of the normal curve and commonly used standardized scores the professional school counselor may encounter. Note that each of these standardized scores can be converted into percentile ranks for easy explanation to parents, teachers, and students. Erford (2008) provides a thorough explanation of standardized scores.

Disaggregated means the data have been broken down by subpopulations so that performance differences between and among groups can be analyzed. Usually, this analysis involves intergroup differences (e.g., male vs. female, race, ethnicity, special education

vs. regular education status). Most test publishers can provide this information on request, broken down by school, by grade level, and even by individual classes. Differences can be determined using statistical methods or informal comparison. Seeing differences in disaggregated data helps professional school counselors to provide hard evidence of gaps in student performance, rather than relying on perceptions. It also provides direction for the types of strategies and interventions needed to close these achievement gaps. Returning to the data provided in Table 13.2, one can see several noticeable gaps in achievement. First, students from the low socioeconomic status (SES) group performed at the 31st percentile rank, on average, while students from the non-low SES group performed at the 71st percentile rank, on average. Second, there is a noticeable difference between the average math performance for Black and Hispanic students (37th and 43rd percentile ranks, respectively), as compared to Asian and White students (72nd and 58th percentile ranks, respectively). Third, females outperformed males, on average (56th and 45th percentile ranks, respectively). From these comparisons of disaggregated data, discussions can ensue and strategies can be developed to decrease the math performance gap. But importantly, it all starts with the data—thus the name data-driven. In this way, data provide the impetus and drive behind school improvement plans and responsive school counseling programs.

Perceptions-Based Needs Assessments

In contrast to a data-driven needs assessment, a more traditional approach to needs assessment is more content and perception driven. Professional school counselors are often interested in what teachers, parents, and students perceive as primary needs to be addressed in a developmental way.

FREQUENCY OF CONDUCTING A NEEDS ASSESSMENT

While it may seem tempting to design and conduct a global needs assessment on an annual basis, such an endeavor would be a massive administrative undertaking, likely resulting in findings being outdated by the time changes are made to the total program. It is probably best to follow a continuous cycle of assessing programmatic needs. This will allow ample time for program development and improvements over the course of the cycle. For example, the *ASCA National Model* (2005a) designates the areas of academic, career, and personal/social development as cornerstones of a comprehensive, developmental guidance program; therefore, it makes sense that school community needs can be assessed according to these components on a rotating basis. For a new program or one undergoing tremendous renovations, years 1 and 2 of a six-year cycle can be spent conducting needs assessment and implementing programmatic changes to address horizontal and vertical articulation issues surrounding student academic development. Years 3 and 4 can be spent addressing student career development needs; years 5 and 6 can focus on student personal/social issues. On the other hand, the six-year cycle could rotate among the three domains, addressing half of the domain issues every three years (i.e., year 1: academic, year 2: career, year 3: personal/social, year 4: academic, year 5: career, year 6: personal/ social). A program in good condition and requiring only fine-tuning may be put on a three-year continuous improvement cycle. The main point here is that assessing needs is part of a much bigger endeavor—that of implementing curricular changes in order to continuously improve the comprehensive, developmental counseling program. Implementing curricular changes can be quite time intensive and simply a waste of time if not guided by accurate needs assessments and program outcomes

research. An effective program uses this information to fine-tune its efforts in data-driven decision making.

POPULATIONS TO BE ASSESSED   In the broadest sense, any stakeholder group can provide helpful information about the needs of a school community. However, it is most practical and efficient to seek out those who are informed and likely to respond. Teachers, administrators, students, and parents are the most likely to be informed about school issues and needs and, under most circumstances, will be the primary stakeholder groups surveyed during a needs assessment. Valuable information can be garnered from community organizations, local businesses, and the general citizenry as well. It is just more difficult to obtain a large response sampling from these groups. Information from these stakeholders is probably best obtained through personal contacts and interviews.

Return rate is another factor in the needs assessment process. Return rate is the percentage of surveys returned of all those sent out. As in any research sampling procedure, the higher the return rate, the lower the sampling error; this leads to greater confidence in the accuracy of the results. In this way, counselors help control for nonresponse bias. Return rate is generally maximized when the participants are a "captive audience." For example, if a social skills needs assessment of fourth-grade students is conducted in the classroom, the response rate should be nearly 100%. On the other hand, if a needs assessment for parents is sent home, the professional school counselor may be lucky to receive 25% to 50% of the questionnaires back. Whenever possible, surveys should be distributed and collected immediately during faculty meetings, class meetings, and parent gatherings.

Triangulation of needs across populations should be attempted when possible; that is, the highest priority needs should be those agreed to by all or most populations assessed. This ensures that the school community's needs, not an individual's agenda, drive the developmental guidance curriculum. For instance, if a principal has decided to place a high priority on social skills, but teachers, parents, and students indicate this is a low priority—and far below other issues such as school safety, substance abuse, and study skills—the triangulated responses of the teachers, parents, and students can provide compelling evidence to guide the program's focus.

DESIGN ISSUES IN AN EFFICIENT NEEDS ASSESSMENT
Designing an efficient needs assessment is essential to meaningful results. While some advocate for a comprehensive needs assessment simultaneously assessing all goals and topics associated with a comprehensive developmental

guidance program, others have found it more helpful to focus the assessment on specifically defined topics or issues that are being updated or altered. This chapter will focus on the latter method.

L. A. Stone and Bradley (1994) recommended seven methods for determining needs: questionnaires and inventories, analysis of records, personal interviews, counseling statistics, classroom visits, use of outside consultants, and systematic evaluation of the guidance program. Perhaps what is most important is that the needs assessment use objective methods for data gathering and analysis. It is essential to understand that different questions are addressed by different methodologies. Although all of these methods are important and useful, questionnaires (formal or informal surveys) are most commonly used (Schmidt, 2008) and will be focused on here. Importantly, while open-ended questionnaires are generally easier to design and yield rich and diverse information, such questionnaires are usually more difficult to tabulate, interpret, and translate into goals and objectives. Also, consider that the younger a student is, the lower the demands must be for reading comprehension and written responses.

From a return-rate perspective, it is good practice to try to design a needs assessment that is only one or two pages in length and can be completed in less than five minutes. The content of the needs assessment should be topical (e.g., social skills, changing families, substance abuse, college application procedures), rather than service related (e.g., individual counseling, group counseling, consultation). As will be explained later, the professional school counselor should keep in mind that services are simply methods for meeting needs, not needs in themselves. Of course, the topics should be related to the program goals as described in the *ASCA National Model* (2005a) and in local or state standards so that priority status can be given to addressing the most pressing needs of the school in comparison to these standards. A good needs assessment directly translates into program development.

In general, the following steps form the basis of an efficient needs assessment:

1. Decide what you need to know.
2. Decide on the best approach to derive what you need to know.
3. Develop the needs assessment instrument or method.
4. Enlist the support of colleagues and a few individuals from the target groups to review and try out items for understanding.
5. Implement the final version with the target groups.
6. Tabulate, analyze, and interpret the results.
7. Translate the results into programmatic goals and objectives.

The design of the scale itself deserves some mention. The survey should ask for the name of the individual completing the form (unless the form is to be completed anonymously). Teacher surveys may ask for the grade level, the number of students in class, or other pertinent information. Parent surveys should ask for the names of the parent's children in case their response to the survey requires contact by the counselor. Student surveys should ask for the student's grade and homeroom teacher's name. Questions or response stems should be short, to the point, and easily understood. The reading level of the items should also be appropriate for the target audience. Figures 13.2, 13.3, and 13.4 show examples of topic-focused needs assessments for teachers (student interpersonal skills), students (academic development), and parents (student tolerance for diversity of sexual orientation), respectively.

Substantial consideration also should be given to the response format. If the purpose of the survey is to determine the importance or frequency of a potential problem, it is generally best to use a multipoint scale with three to five choices. For example, Figure 13.2 asks about the frequency of display of interpersonal skills, so the response choices "Rarely," "Sometimes," "Frequently," "Most of the time," and "Almost always" are appropriate. Note that the response choices "Never" and "Always" do not appear. It is rare that behaviors never or always occur; to include these descriptors may force responses to the center of the distribution and truncate the range of results. Also notice how each category has a descriptor. Thankfully, gone are the days in survey construction when a survey listed the response categories of 0, "Rarely," and 4, "Almost always," and then provided the center points of 1, 2, and 3 with no accompanying descriptors. The reliability problems of such a scale are obvious: Will all respondents agree on what 1, 2, and 3 represent? Certainly not! All choice categories must be accompanied by verbal descriptors.

Figure 13.4 asks parents to rate the importance of seven sexual orientation tolerance items. Notice that the scale responses move from "Not important" (because in this case it is possible that a parent may perceive a total absence of importance) to "Very important." Such a scaling choice format allows parents to register incremental perceptions of importance. Alternatively, the scaling choice format could have simply stated "Yes" or "No," but to do so would have significantly truncated parent perceptions and forced an all-or-nothing response, thus complicating rather than simplifying the interpretation of the needs assessment.

Another important response component of a needs assessment is a frequency count. Suppose a professional school counselor would want to not only assess the

Grade you teach _____   Number of students in your homeroom _____   Teacher's name _____
Please place an X in the boxes that you agree with. Do the students in your class:

	Rarely	Sometimes	Frequently	Most of the time	Almost always	About how many of your students need help in this area?
1. Complain of others teasing them?						
2. Complain about problems on the playground?						
3. Complain about problems with others during less structured class time?						
4. Work well in cooperative groups?						
5. Show respect for other students?						
6. Show respect for adults?						
7. Identify feelings of frustration with other students?						
8. Express feelings of frustration with other students?						
9. Have trouble making friends?						
10. Have trouble keeping friends?						

Thank you for taking the time to complete this!

FIGURE 13.2   Elementary teacher needs assessment of interpersonal skills.

importance of an issue, but also determine how many students were likely in need of services to address the problems stemming from the issue. When possible, the needs assessment should be designed to include an indication of whether the student should be targeted for intervention. In Figure 13.3, notice how the far right-hand column asks for a "Yes" or "No" response to the statement "I need help with this." An affirmative

response targets the student for intervention to address a self-perceived weakness.

Figure 13.2 asks teachers, "About how many of your students need help in this area?" The teachers' responses will indicate the type of intervention required. For example, if the teacher determines that 25 out of 26 students require intervention, the professional school counselor may decide to implement a series of group guidance

Student Name and Grade: _____

Below is a series of questions. Answer these questions by placing a check mark in the appropriate boxes.

	Almost never	Seldom	Sometimes	Often	Almost always	I need help with this	
						Yes	No
Are you an active participant in class discussions and activities?							
Do you look forward to going to class every day?							
Do you double-check assignments before turning them in for a grade?							
Do you complete lengthy assignments on time?							
Do you ask for help as soon as you don't understand an assignment?							
Do you use a variety of learning strategies when performing school tasks?							
Do you take immediate responsibility for your actions, whether positive or negative?							
Do you enjoy working independently in class?							
Do you enjoy working in cooperative groups in class?							
Do you willingly share what you have learned with your peers when they don't seem to know or understand?							

Thanks for your help!

FIGURE 13.3 Secondary-level student needs assessment for academic development.

lessons or consult with the teacher in this regard. If only a handful of students in each of several classes requires intervention, the counselor may opt for a small-group counseling program to address the needs. If only one or a few individuals are identified, the counselor may attempt to address the difficulties through teacher or parent consultation or through time-limited individual counseling services.

Finally, Figure 13.4 asks for a frequency count of those students who parents believe could benefit from a program dealing with tolerance for diversity of sexual

My child is in (check one) ☐ 9th grade ☐ 10th grade ☐ 11th grade ☐ 12th grade	Very important	Important	Somewhat important	A little important	Not important
1. How important is it to be aware of the school's mission statement as it pertains to tolerance for students who are gay or lesbian?					
2. How important is it for students to exhibit tolerance for students who are gay or lesbian?					
3. How important is it that diversity in sexual orientation not be a cause of verbal conflict in the school?					
4. How important is it that diversity in sexual orientation not be a cause of physical conflict in the school?					
5. How important is it that "jokes" regarding sexual orientation be eliminated from the school community?					
6. How important is it that slang words and other inappropriate references to students who are gay or lesbian be eliminated in the school community?					
7. How important is it that students who are gay or lesbian feel safe and secure in the school community?					
8. I believe my child could benefit from a program on this topic.	Yes _____ No _____				
9. I believe other students could benefit from a program on this topic.	Yes _____ No _____				
10. I believe parents could benefit from a program on this topic.	Yes _____ No _____				

FIGURE 13.4 Parent needs assessment of tolerance for diversity of sexual orientation in the student body (Targeted group: Parents of sophomore students).

orientation. Such information gives impetus for a schoolwide program that is either developmental or preventive in nature.

Tallying or computing the information from a needs assessment is simple and has been alluded to in the preceding paragraphs. Tallying simply involves counting the number of students who may benefit from intervention. Computing the results of a needs assessment is probably best accomplished by assigning a number value to each response category and averaging all responses for a given item. In Figure 13.3, assume that the response categories are assigned the following values: "Almost never" = 0, "Seldom" = 1, "Sometimes" = 2, "Often" = 3, and "Almost always" = 4. For item 1, "Are you an active participant in class discussions and activities?" simply add all student response values and divide by the number of responses. Therefore, if 25 students completed the needs assessment and 2 students marked "Almost never" ($2 \times 0 = 0$), 4 students marked "Seldom" ($4 \times 1 = 4$), 10 students marked "Sometimes" ($10 \times 2 = 20$), 5 students marked "Often" ($5 \times 3 = 15$), and 4 students marked "Almost always" ($4 \times 4 = 16$), simply sum the points ($0 + 4 + 20 + 15 + 16 = 55$) and divide by the number of student responses (sum of 55 divided by 25 students = 2.20) to compute the average frequency rating (2.20). Although this assumes a ratio scale and is somewhat nebulous from a statistical interpretation perspective (i.e., what does a 2.20 really mean?), it does offer a reasonable estimate of the average frequency of a behavior, or importance of an issue, in comparison with the other issues under study.

CONVERTING NEEDS TO PROGRAM GOALS AND OBJECTIVES If the needs assessment was designed correctly, translating the results into goals and learning objectives is relatively easy. The first step is to prioritize the needs in order of their importance and their relation to existing components of the program. Prioritization can be accomplished most easily by using the tallying, computing, and triangulation strategies mentioned. Next, the needs must be matched with, or translated into, the goals included in the *ASCA National Model* (2005a) or in state and local standards. Finally, the goals are operationalized through development of learning objectives. (See Chapter 9 for an excellent nuts-and-bolts discussion of how to write learning objectives.)

A reasonable goal stemming from the needs assessment shown in Figure 13.2 would be "To increase students'

interpersonal and friendship skills." Notice how the wording of a goal is nebulous and not amenable to measurement as stated. In developing learning objectives related to goals, particular emphasis is given to specific actions that are measurable. For example, a possible objective stemming from this goal could be "After reading *Frog and Toad* by Arnold Lobel and answering discussion questions, 80% of the students will be able to recognize at least two qualities (describing words) to look for in a friend." Another possible objective might be "After reading *Frog and Toad* by Arnold Lobel and answering discussion questions, 80% of the students will be able to identify at least one issue that may cause problems among friends." Notice how the objectives designate the audience, the stated behavior, how the behavior will be measured, and the level of expected performance.

A reasonable goal from the assessment shown in Figure 13.4 might be "To create a school environment that is tolerant of gay and lesbian students." A possible learning objective stemming from this goal might be "After participating in a series of class sessions focusing on school policies and respect for sexual diversity, 85% of the students will recognize that tolerance toward gay and lesbian students is an integral part of a school's mission and essential to harassment-free life at school." Again, notice how the objective designates the audience, the stated behavior, how the behavior will be measured, and the level of expected performance.

SERVICE ASSESSMENT

Service assessments are sometimes requested by guidance supervisors and demanded by superintendents and school boards to document how counselors are spending their time. Two types of service assessments are commonly used: event–topic counts and time logs. Event–topic counts involve the professional school counselor's documenting each time an individual is contacted or provided with a counseling service and the nature of the topic addressed. In this way, professional school counselors can keep a weekly or monthly tally of the number of students seen not only for global individual counseling, but also specifically for individual counseling for depression, anxiety, behavior, changing family, social skills, anger management, or conflict resolution issues. Such data are quite impressive when aggregated and presented to a school board to indicate that "38,961 individual counseling sessions were held with students last year."

A time log is sometimes kept by professional school counselors to document the amount of time spent in various counseling and non-counseling-related activities. For example, some administrators may wish to know the percentage of time counselors actually spend doing group counseling or teacher consultation at the high school level. Time logs require professional school counselors to document and categorize their activities for every minute of the workday. In states with mandates for providing direct service activities (e.g., elementary professional counselors must spend at least 50% of their time in the direct service activities of individual counseling, group counseling, and group guidance), time logs may be necessary to document compliance for funding purposes.

While service assessments do a wonderful job of telling what or how much a professional school counselor is doing, such assessments give no information about the quality or effectiveness of counselor interventions. The important question becomes "What happens as a result of professional school counselors choosing to use their time this way?" After all, what will a professional school counselor who spends 80% of his or her time doing group and individual counseling, but has ineffective counseling skills, really accomplish? For this kind of information, we must conduct outcomes studies.

VOICES FROM THE FIELD 13.1   ALL THAT I DID

The shift from *"all that I do"* to *"the results of my interventions are demonstrated by . . ."* is one of the toughest issues facing professional school counselors in public education. How is it that highly trained professionals have been taught to measure their professional worth by naming activities and tasks, but failing to speak of the impact of their programs and services? This shift, I believe, is the most critical to ensure that school counseling programs and services truly support all children's success in school.

The misconception that data, numbers, and bottom-line measurements don't mix with school counseling is largely an antiquated mind-set that is dampening the forward movement of the profession. Professional school counselors continue to resist articulating the value of their services by ignoring the absolute necessity of bottom-line results. The benefits of school counseling services are quantifiable and not a mystery that can be understood only through feelings and abstract representations.

As a system-level school counseling supervisor, I see the resistance to accountability in my day-to-day work. Shifting from tools that count activities and hours to measurable outcomes has created discomfort, as school counselors are anxious about not reporting all that they do. Further, the idea of linking results data to performance evaluations has not been received easily. As I grapple with why this is so unnatural for a group of professionals that pride themselves on being change agents, I wonder how much is fear and how much can be attributed to systemic influences. Specifically, I often consider how much reinforcement the system provides for school counselors to continue business as usual. Clearly, educational institutions can be resistant to changes and have established rigid hierarchies, rules, and policies to protect the *status quo*. For professional school counselors, this means doing business as usual and not fully involving themselves in the accountability measures associated with school reform efforts. It is tough to negotiate the system norms and work in new ways, while maintaining important relationships within the schools.

Perhaps one solution is assisting professional school counselors in negotiating systems successfully and teaching advocacy and leadership skills to drive needed changes. This can be accomplished through continuous professional development and mentoring from peers and supervisors. Some strategies that have been useful in transforming the work of school counselors in my experience include informal mentoring sessions (individual and small group), leadership courses designed for professional school counselors, data training workshops, and weekly electronic announcements across the system to convey a vision that includes high levels of accountability. These strategies must be coordinated, strategic, and linked to systemwide goals and rating tools. While none of the identified strategies is highly effective in isolation, layering strategies and building a pool of competent advocates drive the needed energy to shift to a more accountable culture. It takes a refreshed culture to shift the paradigm to one that embraces accountability as a natural and healthy aspect of school counseling.

I hold an idealistic view that professional school counselors will serve all children well as accountability is embraced by all those working in the profession. Measuring the actual results of interventions will ensure that targeted interventions are effective and allow the school counselor to acknowledge, in tangible terms, the payoff. Further, effectively measuring outcomes allows interventions to be adjusted for optimal results. In other words, no longer is it enough to just "do an intervention" because it was planned; rather, the current question is whether to continue an intervention because the data support that it is working. It is no longer enough to do what we do and talk about all that we've done; it is time to assess what we've done and use that information to inform and modify our future work!

Source: Gayle Cicero, Coordinator of School Counseling, Anne Arundel County Public Schools, Maryland.

RESULTS OR OUTCOMES EVALUATION

Results evaluation (sometimes called outcomes evaluation) answers the question "How are students different as a result of the program?" (S. K. Johnson & Johnson, 2003). There is much confusion in the field regarding what program assessment is and what it isn't. Table 13.3 shows a list of some of these issues. Most important among these is the ongoing, cyclical nature of evaluation. The assessment loop shown in Figure 13.5 provides a helpful way to visually conceptualize program evaluation and how outcome studies can be used to improve programs.

Many educators view assessment as a discrete component, but it is actually an integrated part of a continuous process for program improvement. All assessment procedures must have the institution's mission in mind because the institutional values and needs will determine the focus of study. Questions of worth and effectiveness are derived from a confluence of values, needs, goals, and mission, and these questions lead to the determination of what evidence must be collected. For example, consider an elementary school counseling program that recently implemented a study skills curriculum in grades 3–5 using classroom guidance lessons. A reasonable research question might be "How is student academic performance/achievement different as a result of the new study skills curriculum?" The elementary school counselor and teachers may collect several types of evidence to answer this question (performance data on tests, homework completion, parent survey of amount of time spent, or work and study habit improvements). Likewise, a high school counseling team may be interested in knowing "Is the recently modified educational

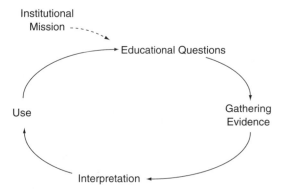

FIGURE 13.5   The assessment cycle.

and career planning curriculum using small psychoeducational groups and individual planning sessions over a three-year period accomplishing the ASCA career domain competencies?" Again, the counseling team would plan for the collection of evidence to answer this question.

Evidence may exist in many places, but it is typically derived using preplanned measures or from the performances or products students engage in during program activities. Once information has been gathered, it must then be interpreted, and conclusions must be drawn from it regarding the program's or activity's worth, strengths, and weaknesses. Finally, the interpretations and conclusions must be used to change the program or parts of the program to improve it.

Notice how the loop in Figure 13.5 never stops—it represents a continuous process in which assessment results are interpreted and fed back into the improvement process. As assessment information is used to prompt programmatic changes, so goal-setting and the posing of new questions about the revised program begin anew. Most professional school counselors fail in the assessment loop because they gather evidence and then stop, believing that the program has been evaluated and the job finished. Why spend valuable time collecting evidence and not use it to improve what you are doing?

Important Assessment Terms

A number of terms associated with research and evaluation are important to understand. *Evaluation* is the measurement of worth and indicates that a judgment will be made regarding the effectiveness of a program. The experienced researcher knows that being very specific about what you are measuring and how you are measuring it is the key to successful results. This was made clear in the section on writing learning objectives in Chapter 9. Too often, professional school counselors are not specific about what they are trying to accomplish and become frustrated when they fail to measure what they may or may not have achieved. If a person doesn't know where she

---

TABLE 13.3   The "Is" and "Isn't" of Assessment

Assessment of school counseling programs is

- A way to answer important program-related questions.
- The responsibility of an accountable professional school counselor.
- A cooperative endeavor with other SCPAC members and stakeholders.
- Ongoing and evolving.
- A means to a better end—better education for *all* students.

Assessment of school counseling programs isn't

- The evaluation of an individual professional school counselor.
- An assault on the professional school counselor's freedom.
- A mandate for standardized tests or curricula.
- All figured out.

is heading, she must either get specific directions (write a specific, measurable objective) or be satisfied with wherever she ends up (perhaps an ineffective program)!

Evidence is any data that will help make judgments or decisions and can be quantitatively or qualitatively derived. *Formative evaluation* is evaluative feedback that occurs during the implementation of a program, whereas *summative evaluation* is feedback collected at a specified endpoint in an evaluation process (Worthen, Sanders, & Fitzpatrick, 1997). Although summative evaluation is conducted most frequently, formative evaluation has the advantage of allowing corrective action to occur if an implemented program is shown to be off course. This makes sense when you consider that some programs are expensive (in time and money) to implement. If you know after one-third of the program has been implemented that desired results are not occurring, then midcourse corrections can be made to tailor the program to the audience and desired outcomes.

A *stakeholder* is anyone involved in or potentially benefiting from the school counseling program (Erford, 2008). Stakeholders may include students, parents, teachers, professional school counselors, administrators, community organizations, and local businesses, among others. A *baseline* is any data gathered to establish a starting point. It is essential to know where students are so you can tailor interventions to help facilitate their development. *Inputs* are any resources (e.g., personnel, material) that go into a program; *outcomes* are what stakeholders can do as a result of the program.

A *pretest* is a measure administered before a program is implemented, and a *posttest* is a measure administered after the program or intervention has been completed (Erford, 2008). If a study calls for both a pretest and a posttest, usually there is tremendous overlap in their content because the goal is to determine changes in the individual or group as a result of participating in the program. Any changes that occur in the examinee between administration of the pretest and the posttest are usually attributed to the program activities.

Sources of Evidence

Both people and products merit discussion as potential sources of evidence. Almost anyone—students, teachers, staff, administration, parents, employers, graduates, community resource people, and so on—can serve as a helpful source of evidence. Numerous products from data collection methods can also be used. A short list includes portfolios, performances, use of ratings from external judges or examiners, observations, local tests, purchased tests, student self-assessments, surveys, interviews, focus groups, and student work. Each of these sources or products can produce helpful evaluative data, but what is collected will result from the specific question to be answered.

Practical Program Evaluation Considerations

Erford (2008) provided practical guidelines for conducting accountability studies. To be of practical value, assessment must be connected to real program concerns, as well as the core values of the school or program. Avoid overwhelming the data collectors, focus on only one or several important questions at a time, and always select measures that will yield reliable and valid scores for the purposes under study. Oftentimes, ineffective program outcomes stem from poor or inappropriate measurement rather than faulty programming. Be sure to involve the relevant stakeholders and use a variety of approaches. Perhaps most important, do not reinvent the wheel—use what you are already doing to generate useful data about program effectiveness. Also, don't be afraid to call on outside experts to consult on the development and evaluation of a program.

It is good advice to start small and build on what is found to work; the methods and goals of individual programs are celebrated, and successes can be shared by professional school counselors across programs. This often leads to a cross-pollination effect that yields both diversity of approach and homogeneity of results. In other words, over time, professional school counselors will learn from each other what works and implement these strategies with their own populations after necessary refinements based on the needs of a differing school community. Different can still be effective!

Assessing Outcomes Through a Hierarchical Aggregated Process

As mentioned earlier, aggregation is the combining of results to provide a more global or generalized picture of group performance. While such a practice may deemphasize subgroup or individual performance, aggregation can also be a valuable tool when it comes to evaluating how well school counseling programs meet higher-level standards, such as the ASCA *National Standards* (C. Campbell & Dahir, 1997). Due to their more abstract or generalized wording, standards (sometimes called goals) are difficult, if not impossible, to directly measure. This is why curriculum development begins with a statement of standards (goals) that are then further described through a series of outcomes (sometimes called competencies). While more specific and well defined, these outcomes are still ordinarily not amenable to direct measurement in the classic sense. Instead, educators rely on educational objectives (sometimes called behavioral objectives), such as those discussed in Chapter 9. Objectives are written in such specific, measurable terms that everyone (e.g., teacher, student, parent, professional school counselor) can tell when an objective has been met. The use of objectives, outcomes, and standards constitutes an aggregated hierarchical model and is an important way that professional school counselors can demonstrate the effectiveness of a school counseling program. Figure 13.6 provides an example of this aggregated hierarchical model.

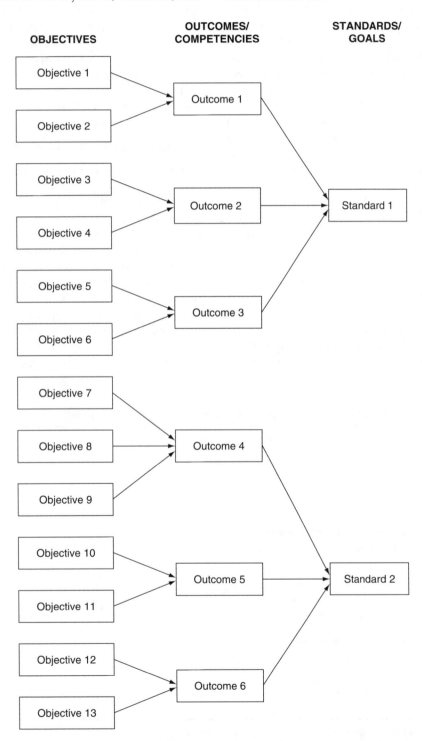

FIGURE 13.6 Aggregated hierarchical model for evaluating the effectiveness of a school counseling program.

In Figure 13.6, note the alignment of objectives to outcomes to standards. Objective 1 measures Outcome 1, which is aligned with Standard 1. Likewise, Objective 13 measures Outcome 6, which is aligned with Standard 2. Such a hierarchical structure allows the professional school counselor to conclude that meeting the lower-order objectives provides evidence that higher-order outcomes and standards have been successfully met. For example, assume the professional school counselor provides evidence that Objectives 1 through 6 have been met. By extension, if Objectives 1 and 2 were met, then Outcome 1 was met. If Objectives 3 and 4 were met, then Outcome 2 was met. If Objectives 5 and 6 were met, then Outcome 3 was met. Because Outcomes 1 through 3 were met, the professional school counselor has provided evidence that Standard 1 was met. Success! In addition, areas of curricular strength have been identified.

Again referring to Figure 13.6, now consider a second example in which Objectives 7 through 10 were met, but Objectives 11 through 13 were not met. By extension, if Objectives 7 through 9 were met, then Outcome 4 was met. If Objective 10 was met, but Objective 11 was not met, then Outcome 5 either was not met or, more accurately, was only partially met. If Objectives 12 and 13 were not met, then Outcome 6 was not met. Now, because of some inconsistent results, interpretation is a bit cloudier. It is most appropriate to conclude that Standard 2 was only partially met because Outcome 4 was met, Outcome 5 was partially met, and Outcome 6 was not met. Given the inconsistency of the outcomes, it would be inappropriate to conclude that Standard 2 had been met; it would be equally inappropriate to conclude that Standard 2 had not been met. A conclusion of "partially met" identifies the hierarchical set of standard, outcomes, and objectives as a curricular area in need of improvement, additional attention to or revision of the criteria for successful performance, or both. From these examples, one can see that an aggregated hierarchical model can be a valuable curriculum evaluation method. It also underscores the importance of a measurable objective as the building block of an effective developmental curriculum (see Chapter 9).

Designing Outcome Studies

While any data collected on counselor effectiveness can be helpful, in most instances, professional school counselors should measure outcomes or results by designing a research-type study. Importantly, a bit of forethought and planning can lead to much more meaningful conclusions. Research studies are typically empirical in nature and involve providing some control over how students are assigned to counseling interventions and the timing and circumstances under which data are collected. D. T. Campbell and Stanley (1963) explored helpful, easy-to-implement designs, and several of these designs that may be particularly useful to professional school counselors have been included in Table 13.4. Although a comprehensive treatise on this topic is beyond

---

TABLE 13.4   Common Designs Used for Outcomes Research

Nonexperimental Designs

1. Pretest–posttest single group design		O I O
2. Case study		I O
3. Static-group comparison	group 1	O
	group 2	I O

Quasi-Experimental Designs

4. Two-sample pretest–posttest design	R O
	R I O
5. Nonequivalent control group design	O I O
	O O
6. Time series design	O O O I O O O

True Experimental Designs

7. Randomized pretest–posttest control group design	R O I O
	R O O
8. Randomized posttest only control group design	R I O
	R O

Note: R = participants are randomly assigned to groups; I = intervention (implemented treatment or program); O = observation or other data collection method.

the scope of this book, the following are some of the relevant points professional school counselors should consider when designing outcome studies. Counselors generally receive an entire course in research and evaluation that can be useful in this context. The interested reader should consult Erford's *Research and Evaluation in Counseling* (2008) for a helpful source on research methodology and statistical analysis written specifically for counselors.

Answering several questions can help the professional counselor determine which research design to use:

1. *Has the treatment already been implemented?* So much for planning ahead! If the intervention has not already occurred, one has many possible options. If the intervention has already occurred, one is relegated to a nonexperimental design, probably a case study or static-group comparison design. It is critical to think about outcomes assessment in the early stages of planning for an intervention and certainly before the intervention has begun!

2. *Can I randomly assign participants to treatment conditions?* If the answer is yes, outstanding! Control over the random assignment of participants is critical to implementing true experimental designs. If one does not have control over assignment of participants, the professional school counselor must choose a quasi-experimental or nonexperimental design.

3. *Can I conduct (one or several) pretests, posttests, or both?* Usually, measuring the dependent variable both before (pretest) and after (posttest) is desirable, although certainly not essential.

The answers to these questions will help the professional school counselor choose the most useful and powerful design. For example, if the answers to the three questions are no, yes, and yes, respectively, the professional school counselor may opt for an experimental design (i.e., design 7 or 8 in Table 13.4). If the answers are yes, no, and posttest only, one is relegated to a nonexperimental design (e.g., design 2 or 3 in Table 13.4). As one can no doubt surmise, outcome studies require some level of planning early on in program development. Accountable professional school counselors plan ahead.

Most true experimental designs involve randomization of participants, which also randomizes various sources of error, allowing for the control of numerous threats to internal validity. True experimental designs allow causative conclusions to be reached. This is a big advantage when the professional school counselor wants to know conclusively if interventions caused significant improvements in students. For example, if a professional school counselor wants to know if a group intervention designed to improve study skills and academic performance was effective, he or she could use the randomized pretest–posttest control group design (design 7 in Table 13.4). The counselor would begin by randomly assigning students into two optimal-sized groups, designated control and treatment, and determining a data collection method (e.g., test, survey, or observation) to measure an outcome of interest (e.g., academic achievement, study skills, social skills). The counselor would begin by administering the "test" (a dependent variable called the pretest) to all participants in both the control and the treatment conditions. Next, the counselor would implement the intervention (e.g., group counseling experience) with the treatment group, but not with the control group. (*Note:* The control group would either experience nothing or undergo a group counseling experience for some issue other than academic performance, study skills, social skills, etc.) On conclusion of the treatment (program, intervention), the professional school counselor would again administer the test (this time called the posttest) to participants in both groups. It would be expected that no change in the control group participants' scores would be observed (i.e., no statistically significant difference between pretest and posttest scores). However, if the group counseling experience was successful, it would be expected that a significant change would be observed in the treatment group (e.g., higher posttest scores than pretest scores, higher grades at the end of group than at the beginning). Of course, the other designs in Table 13.4 also could be used with this or other examples. However, quasi-experimental and nonexperimental designs do not allow the professional school counselor to conclude that the treatment was the "cause" of the changes noted in the participants. Thus, in many ways, results or outcomes from studies with experimental designs are more valuable and powerful.

A lot of thought must be given to the design of the outcome measure used. Often, nonsignificant results are due not to the intervention, but to the selection of an outcome measure not sensitive enough to demonstrate the effect of the treatment. Some outcome measures can be easily obtained because they are a matter of record (e.g., grade point average, percentage grade in math class, number of days absent, number of homework assignments completed) or already exist in published form (e.g., Conners Parent Rating Scale–Revised [CPRS–R], Achenbach System of Empirically Based Assessment [ASEBA], Beck Depression Inventory [BDI–II], Children's Depression Inventory [CDI]). Available outcome measures are plentiful. Still, sometimes professional school counselors need to design an outcome measure with sufficient sensitivity and direct applicability to the issue being studied (e.g., adjustment to a divorce, body image, social skills, math self-efficacy). When professional school counselors need to develop an outcome measure from scratch, the basics of scale development covered above in the discussion of needs assessments can be helpful. In addition, Weiss (1998) provided a dozen principles the assessor should consider:

1. Use simple language.
2. Ask only about things that the respondent can be expected to know.
3. Make the question specific.
4. Define terms that are in any way unclear.
5. Avoid yes–no questions.
6. Avoid double negatives.
7. Don't ask double-barreled questions [e.g., two questions in one].
8. Use wording that has been adopted in the field.
9. Include enough information to jog people's memories or to make them aware of features of a phenomenon they might otherwise overlook.
10. Look for secondhand opinions or ratings only when firsthand information is unavailable.
11. Be sensitive to cultural differences.
12. Learn how to deal with difficult respondent groups. (pp. 140–142)

These principles apply to most types of data collection procedures. Professional school counselors can use a wide range of procedures, each with advantages and disadvantages. Table 13.5 presents descriptions of several of the most common methods of data collection used by professional school counselors.

TABLE 13.5   Common Data-Collection Methods

1. *Interviews* of the professional school counselor, key personnel, or members of stakeholder groups can provide valuable data. Interviews can be structured, semistructured, or unstructured. Structured interviews present a formal sequence of questions to interviewees, with no variation in administration, thus generating clear evidence of strengths and weaknesses. Unstructured formats allow for follow-up deeper exploration and are commonly used in qualitative studies. Usually, multiple respondents are required for patterns and conclusions to emerge. Face-to-face interviews are generally better than phone interviews, although usually more costly and inconvenient. Careful consideration must be given to question development, and interviewers must guard against introducing bias.

2. *Observations* can also be classified as informal or formal. Informal observations tend to yield anecdotal data through a "look-and-see" approach. Formal or structured observations usually involve a protocol and predetermined procedures for collecting specific types of data during a specified time period. Structured procedures tend to minimize bias. As an example of observation, professional school counselors can be observed implementing a developmental guidance lesson by a supervisor or peer.

3. *Written questionnaires, surveys, and rating scales* are usually paper-and-pencil instruments asking a broad range of questions (open ended, closed ended, or both). Questionnaires and rating scales typically ask for factual responses while surveys generally solicit participant perceptions. By far the greatest weakness of this data collection method is that many participants do not complete or return the instrument (i.e., low return rate). It also requires a certain level of literacy. Few respondents take the time to write lengthy responses, so it is usually best to keep the questions simple and closed ended with the opportunity for participants to expand a response if needed. Multiscaled response formats (e.g., Likert scales) often provide more helpful results than yes–no questions. E-mailed or online versions of these instruments are becoming more commonly used.

4. *Program records and schedules* are a naturally occurring and helpful source of evaluation data. If stored on a computer in a database format, this kind of data is particularly accessible, and a professional school counselor is well advised to consider this ahead of time when determining how best to maintain electronic records and schedules. Archives should also be kept in good order to facilitate record searches. In particular, professional school counselors should keep previous program improvement documents and outcome study reports.

5. *Standardized and educator-made tests* provide objective sources of measurable student performance and progress in the academic, career, and personal–social domains. Individual, classroom, and schoolwide tests can be extremely helpful and powerful measures. Tests exist that measure academic achievement, depression, anxiety, substance use, distractibility, career indecision, and myriad other student behaviors. Likewise, professional school counselors can design and develop tests to measure student behaviors and characteristics, much like teachers design tests to measure academic achievement.

6. *Academic performance indicators* may include a student's grade point average or classroom grade but also includes daily work behaviors and habits (e.g., attendance, homework completion, disruptions) and attitudes (e.g., academic self-efficacy, attitude toward school).

7. *Products and portfolios* are real-life examples of performance. A product is anything created by a student (or the professional school counselor) that stemmed from a program standard (e.g., artwork, composition, poster). A portfolio is a collection of exemplar products that can be evaluated to determine the quality of an individual's performance.

TABLE 13.6   Steps to Developing an Action Research Plan

1. *Identify and clarify the research question*. The main focus of this step should be to make improvements in practice or troubleshoot and correct existing problems.
2. *Gather data*. In action research, the data are gathered using only a specific or particular group of individuals; thus, the sample and population are identical. Using more than one method of gathering data (e.g., triangulation) is suggested in order to provide a more thorough picture of the situation.
3. *Analyze and interpret data*. Any of the aforementioned methodologies (Table 13.4) may be used to collect and analyze the data.
4. *Create an action plan*. One of the main goals of action research is to understand and improve practice in applicable settings. The way to accomplish this goal is to plan and create the steps necessary to alter or improve the situation. The action plan should support and validate the data gathered.
5. *Evaluation and reflection*. Once an action plan is created, the next step is to critically and periodically evaluate the plan's effectiveness. Evaluation can be accomplished by validation through testing the claims of improvements in practice (e.g., Do the action plan changes implemented produce the desired outcomes?). Self-evaluation of participants can also be used as a tool for reflection and validity.

Source: From B. Erford, *Research and Evaluation in Counseling*, 1E. © 2008 Wadsworth, a part of Cengage Learning, Inc. Reproduced by permission. www.cengage.com/permissions

Action Research

Action research allows professional school counselors to focus on changing social, ecological, or client conditions in particular situations or settings by creating a study and intervention to explore and solve a particular problem, usually in the client's environment. Designed and conducted by practitioners or researchers, action research involves the analysis of data to improve practice and solve practical problems. Action research presents the professional school counselor with a number of advantages over traditional experimental research procedures because action research requires minimal training; helps develop effective, practice-based solutions for practical problems; and creates a collaborative atmosphere where professionals work together to address and improve conditions affecting students. Table 13.6 reviews the steps ordinarily considered when developing an action research plan. A more lengthy discussion and case examples of action research can be found in Erford (2008).

THEORY INTO PRACTICE 13.1

USING DATA

As an elementary school counselor, I try to use data whenever possible to support my interventions. I believe that it is important to keep track not only of what I do as a counselor but also of how effectively I am meeting the needs of my students. Although I often feel like I don't have enough time to collect data for everything I do, I try to work it into my schedule as much as possible. There are often simple ways to collect data that do not take a whole lot of time.

I run a small guidance group entitled "Let's Pay Attention." The group targets second-grade students who have a hard time paying attention, completing work, listening to the teacher, or staying in their seat. A few months into the new school year, I ask teachers to refer students who fall into this category. My school uses a schoolwide discipline program that involves moving student "clips" (clothespins) on a colored chart: Green—Good job, Yellow—Warning, Blue—Lose recess, Orange—Call home, Red—Go to Principal. Teachers refer students who frequently move their clip. Last year I ran two second-grade

"Let's Pay Attention" groups, each with four group members. Teachers reported how many times each student moved his or her clip in the month of November. There were 18 days of school in that month. Most students in a classroom moved their clips 1–2 times in the month; some moved their clips far more frequently than others, such as those listed in Table 13.7.

During the first group session of each small-group counseling experience, I read the book *Ethan Has Too Much Energy* by Lawrence Shapiro. After discussing the story, I asked the students to think about how they were like Ethan. Then each student came up with his or her own personal goal based on suggestions that the teacher had given me (i.e., completing center work, staying in seat, following directions). I took pictures of the students completing their goal. For instance, for completing work I took a picture of the student working at his desk. This picture was placed on the student's desk as a reminder of the goal. They also received a chart to track their progress toward their goal. Students received stickers on their chart

(Continued)

TABLE 13.7   Results of a School-wide Monitoring Program

Student	Number of Times Clip was Moved in Month
Garrett	10
Dan	11
James	8
Aaron	9
Sean	11
Thomas	9
Emma	7
Joshua	10

energy in their bodies. Each week when the students came to group, I would show them a graph of the amount of stickers they had earned. They were able to see whether or not they were making progress. Each week I talked with the students to set an individual goal for the following week.

At the end of the group, I used the sticker chart data to determine if the students had made progress and if my group was effective in helping students become more focused learners. Table 13.8 and Figure 13.7 show the students' progress toward their individual goals.

Based on these results, I saw that four students made progress, one student remained the same, and three students' behavior actually declined. I can see that the students who were working on completing their work improved the most during the course of the group. Aaron, who was working on staying in his seat, also improved somewhat. However, the students who were working on listening to the teacher and following directions either did not improve or seemed to get worse.

These results can tell me a number of things about the group. I know that the group was most effective for helping students stay in their seat and complete their work.

to indicate when they had achieved the goal. I kept track of how many stickers the students earned each day.

In the subsequent six group sessions, the students learned about and practiced techniques for listening, following directions, improving visual/auditory memory, keeping the body still, and releasing tension and extra

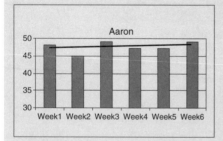
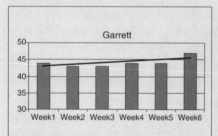
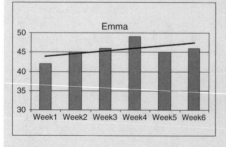
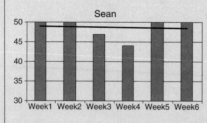
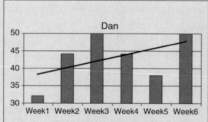
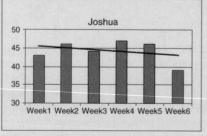
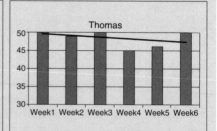
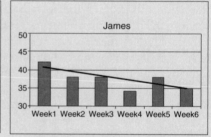

FIGURE 13.7   Monitoring individual student progess toward meeting personal goals.

TABLE 13.8 Monitoring Student Progress Toward Meeting Personal Goals

Student	Personal Goal	Week 1	Week 2	Week 3	Week 4	Week 5	Week 6
Garrett	Completing Work	44	43	43	44	44	47
Dan	Completing Work	32	44	50	44	38	50
James	Listening to Teacher	42	38	38	34	38	35
Aaron	Staying in Seat	48	45	49	47	47	49
Sean	Listening to Teacher	50	50	47	44	50	50
Thomas	Following Directions	50	49	50	45	46	50
Emma	Completing Work	42	45	46	49	45	46
Joshua	Following Directions	43	46	44	47	46	39

However, it does not tell me which part of the group caused the improvement in behavior. The data also tell me that I need to adjust what I am doing in the group in order to focus more on listening and following directions in order to help those students better achieve their goals. But again, it's hard to tell what caused the decline in student behavior. It could just be that the teachers were more aware of when the students were not listening or following directions.

Regardless, this year when I run the group again, I will try to fine-tune my groups in order to better help the students who are working on listening and following directions, while at the same time continuing to help students who need to stay in their seats and complete their work.

Source: Emily M. Bryant, Professional Elementary School Counselor, Monocacy Elementary Center and Amity Primary Center, Daniel Boone Area School District, Pennsylvania.

Reporting the Results

Although professional school counselors, or perhaps an outside consultant, may write the majority of a report, the school counseling program advisory committee (SCPAC) should be involved at every step of the process. A comprehensive report may be helpful for SCPAC analysis purposes; however, a one- to two-page executive summary should also be prepared for release to building administrators, system administrators, and the school community. Loesch and Ritchie (2004) suggested that dissemination of school counseling program results could occur through a written report, a verbal presentation, a multimedia presentation, journal articles, a website posting, a videotape, posters, text messaging, e-mail, or a newspaper article. For example, many schools now have websites or electronic newsletters. The written executive summary could be added to these publications. Likewise, some schools send out e-mail blasts or text message bursts to parents electing to receive information through those electronic modes. A brief message could be posted directing parents to the written or electronic source for the full report. However, it is important to remember that not all parents may have these technologies and that those who do may not check these sources in a timely manner. Thus, some redundancy across sources or postings should occur to ensure everyone can obtain access to at least the executive summary, if desired.

Regardless of the vehicle for dissemination, results of the program outcomes should be released to relevant stakeholder groups at regular intervals after the results have

been reviewed by the SCPAC, professional school counselors, and administration. As mentioned, the results of the outcome studies are used to make substantive program improvements that then prompt more questions to be studied—and the process cycles again and again. This cycle is essential to the transformation and continuous quality improvement of any comprehensive developmental school counseling program.

PERFORMANCE APPRAISAL

The effectiveness of a school counseling program often relies on the competence and efficiency of its implementers. While an entire book could be written on procedures for assessing the performance of professional school counselors, this section will provide but a few guiding principles. It is not an exaggeration to say that the services provided by, and responsibilities of, the professional school counselor are among the most complex of any school employee. The advanced, specialized training certainly demands that individuals placed in a position to evaluate the counselor must also have equivalent training and advanced supervision skills. Thus, while the experiences and training of principals often provide a useful vantage point from which to evaluate teachers and secretarial staff, principals seldom have the training and counseling supervision experience to evaluate counselors effectively. That is not to say that principals lack the ability to provide helpful information regarding counselor performance. It is an infinitely better practice, however, to have counselor supervisors coordinate and participate in the appraisal of counselor performance. One facet of a professional school counselor's performance appraisal that a principal or other noncounselor administrator may be able to contribute to is evaluation of the professional school counselor's skill when providing a classroom-based developmental guidance lesson. The criteria for any evaluation always should be available well in advance. Figures 13.8 and 13.9 provide sample instructional evaluations adapted for the purpose of assessing a

Observee: _____ Observer: _____ Date: _____				

Directions: Circle the number for each statement corresponding with your observation. Please write in any additional comments. *Key:* NA = not applicable; NI = needs improvement; S = satisfactory; VS = very satisfactory.

Presentation of Introductory Material

	NA	NI	S	VS
1. Indicated the purpose of the presentation.	NA	NI	S	VS
2. Provided preview/overview of presentation.	NA	NI	S	VS
3. Connected today's content to previous presentations or experiences.	NA	NI	S	VS

Body of Presentation

4. Content was arranged in a logical order.	NA	NI	S	VS
5. Assessed throughout presentation to determine if information was understood.	NA	NI	S	VS
6. Gave examples to help students understand ideas and/or to tie subject to prior knowledge that students possessed.	NA	NI	S	VS
7. Summarized important ideas throughout presentation.	NA	NI	S	VS

Conclusion of Presentation

8. Asked questions to see what students understood/learned, any misconceptions they might have, and what needed to be retaught/covered again.	NA	NI	S	VS
9. Summarized main concepts in presentation.	NA	NI	S	VS
10. Dealt effectively with any problems/questions that came up in the presentation.	NA	NI	S	VS
11. Previewed what will be covered next time, linking it to the current presentation.	NA	NI	S	VS
12. Evaluated what students learned to see if objectives were met.	NA	NI	S	VS

Overall Instructional Presentation

13. The material presented was important and aligned with content standards/competencies.	NA	NI	S	VS
14. Distinctions were made between fact and opinion, as appropriate.	NA	NI	S	VS
15. Statements were supported with reference to authoritative sources, as appropriate.	NA	NI	S	VS
16. Presented and encouraged divergent viewpoints.	NA	NI	S	VS
17. Included an appropriate amount of content for the available time period.	NA	NI	S	VS
18. All materials were ready.	NA	NI	S	VS
19. Presentation began on time.	NA	NI	S	VS
20. Presentation ended on time.	NA	NI	S	VS
21. Presentation time was used efficiently.	NA	NI	S	VS

Clarity of Presentation

22. Defined any new items, concepts, and/or principles.	NA	NI	S	VS
23. Explained why problems are solved using certain processes or techniques.	NA	NI	S	VS
24. Used clear and relevant examples to explain major ideas and connect them to students' prior knowledge.	NA	NI	S	VS

FIGURE 13.8 Instructional evaluation of a developmental guidance lesson.

Verbal Communication

25. Spoke clearly and could be easily heard.	NA	NI	S	VS
26. Raised and lowered voice to emphasize points and provide variety.	NA	NI	S	VS
27. Minimized use of speech distracters (e.g., ahh, OK).	NA	NI	S	VS
28. Speech rate was appropriate (neither too fast nor too slow.)	NA	NI	S	VS
29. Invited participants to share.	NA	NI	S	VS
30. Answers and asks questions clearly.	NA	NI	S	VS
31. Gives students feedback when appropriate.	NA	NI	S	VS

Nonverbal Communication

32. Kept appropriate eye contact with students throughout presentation and when listening to student questions and responses.	NA	NI	S	VS
33. Mannerisms were comfortable and inviting, allowed students to participate (not too formal or casual).	NA	NI	S	VS
34. Facial and body movements matched speech and/or expressed intentions.	NA	NI	S	VS
35. Listened attentively to students' questions and comments.	NA	NI	S	VS

Classroom Management

36. Kept participants' attention.	NA	NI	S	VS
37. Encouraged everyone to participate.	NA	NI	S	VS
38. Was able to keep control of the group.	NA	NI	S	VS
39. Respected and valued all members of the group and differences between members.	NA	NI	S	VS

professional school counselor's skill in the classroom or less formal sessions.

Most professional school counselor performance appraisals are composed of a rating system that aggregates or averages responses across a variety of categories of work-related responsibilities. Generally, these rating schemes involve some indication of "Satisfactory" or "Unsatisfactory" performance in each of the targeted skill categories. Some performance appraisal forms allow greater differentiation in ratings—for example, "Unsatisfactory," "Inconsistently meets expectations," "Consistently meets expectations," and "Consistently exceeds expectations." This latter differentiation is particularly useful when incentives such as merit pay are in effect.

Numerous formats are used for professional school counselor performance appraisal. In fact, nearly all school systems tailor forms and criteria to their specifications and needs. Some are particularly comprehensive models, using a multipoint rating system. Figures 13.10 and 13.11 are actual performance appraisal documents from public school systems. Although briefly stated and somewhat open to interpretation, notice how the indicators and competencies serve as discussion points for an ongoing professional development dialogue between counselor and supervisor. Such discussions are meant to highlight a professional school counselor's strengths and weaknesses and guide

him or her in the direction of needed improvement. This dialogue eventually results in a rating of "Satisfactory" or "Unsatisfactory" in each category under investigation; then an overall rating is determined, generally for retention purposes. While performance appraisals do sometimes affect retention and dismissal of counselors, the truth is that the number dismissed for unsatisfactory performance is very small. Thus, the primary focus of the appraisal system should be, and in most instances is, to enhance the quality and competence of all those evaluated.

Many school systems have undertaken the task of revealing exemplary practices at the school level. Figure 13.12 is such an attempt, as it provides both a vision for school counselors and expectations for other school personnel regarding the implementation of a comprehensive, developmental school counseling program. The *ASCA National Model* (2005a) provided 13 school counselor performance standards, each with several subcomponents. These standards are presented in an adaptive format in Figure 13.13, with a response format similar to those discussed above. It is essential that professional school counselors held to performance standards such as these provide additional evidence and comments to give an appropriate context for those supervisors ultimately making evaluative decisions. Regardless of the evaluation system used, it is critical that the focus be on development of higher levels of counselor skills.

Anne Arundel County Public Schools | Office of School Counseling

Professional School Counselor Observation

Name	School	Grade(s)
Date	Time in/out	Number of Students/ Participants

Objective:

To assist in determining the degree to which the professional school counselor is implementing a comprehensive, data-driven school counseling program that is preventive in design and developmental in nature toward achieving the school's identified goals.

Counseling Domain Observed:

☐ Academic Development   ☐ Career Development   ☐ Personal/Social Development

Delivery System Observed:

☐ **School Guidance Curriculum:** Classroom Instruction, Parent Workshop

☐ **Individual Student Planning:** Individual/Small Group Appraisal or Advisement

☐ **Responsive Services:** Individual/Small Group Counseling, Peer Facilitation, Crisis Response

☐ **System Support:** Professional Development, Teaming, Consultation, Collaboration

Pre-Observation Conference:

A pre-observation conference is highly recommended and should include the following questions for professional dialogue:

1	What is the intended outcome of the activity?
2	How was the target audience chosen?
3	How does this activity address the National Standards for School Counseling?
4	What, if any, specific concerns do you have with regard to the activity?
5	How will students be different as a result of their participation in the activity?

AACPS · Office of School Counseling · DPS/JH 2750/24 (New 10/08) page 1

FIGURE 13.9   Anne Arundel County Public Schools professional school counselor observation.

Professional School Counselor Observation cont.

6. How will you measure the impact/results of this activity?

7. What type of feedback will assist you in growing as a professional school counselor?

Observation and Feedback

Indicator	Evidenced	Not Evidenced	Comments
The activity has a clear focus aligned with the National Standards for School Counseling.			
The activity aligns with and supports the school's Improvement Plan and/or the AACPS School Counseling Program Essential Curriculum.			
The activity is designed to support the specific needs of the students/participants.			
The students/participants demonstrate an understanding of the content/focus as a result of participating in the activity.			
The school counselor informs students or participants of the goals, techniques, confidentiality and rules of the activity.			
The school counselor effectively manages behavior in order to facilitate a safe learning environment.			
The school counselor demonstrates effective interpersonal skills with students and/or participants.			
The school counselor utilizes perception, process, or results data to evaluate the effectiveness of the activity.			

Commendations/Recommendations:

_____   _____
Observer's Signature   Date

_____   _____
School Counselor's Signature   Date

AACPS · Office of School Counseling · DPS/JH 2750/24 (New 10/08) page 2

Source: Anne Arundel County Public Schools

Anne Arundel County Public Schools | Division of Human Resources

Evaluation of Unit I—Professional School Counselors

Employee	Employee ID#
Title	School/Office
Completed by	

Goal-setting/Performance Review Conference Dates	*Required NLT*	November 30	January 31	April 30	June 30
	Actual (1)_____		(2)_____	(3)_____	(4)_____

The professional school counselor implements a comprehensive, data driven school counseling program that is preventive in design and developmental in nature to serve the academic, career and personal/social needs of students in addressing the school's identified goals. Toward that end, The American School Counseling Association recommends the majority of the school counselor's time be spent in direct service to all students so that every student receives maximum benefits from the program. The operational structure includes four elements that are Interdependent and define a comprehensive school counseling program.

A. Performance Standards	5 Outstanding Performance	4 Highly Effective	3 Standards Met/ Satisfactory	2 Needs Improvement/ Marginal	1 Standard Not Met/ Unsatisfactory	0 Not Assigned	Supporting Statement
I. Foundation: This serves as the ground upon which the school counseling program is built and includes beliefs, philosophy, mission statement, and the ASCA standards for all three domains (academic, social/emotional, and career). A strong foundation is critical to ensuring the school counseling program is an essential and integrated component of the total educational program for student success.							
1 Exhibits values that support the achievement of all students							
2 Participates in continuous and relevant professional growth.							
3 Addresses all domains (academic, career, personal/ social) through the school counseling program.							
4 Participates in the development and implementation of a written mission statement aligned with the district and school mission that addresses advocacy for the equity, access, and success of every student.							

AACPS · DPS/JH 1330/160 (New 10/08) **1 of 3**

Distribution: Copies to   1—Human Resources   2—Employee   3—Principal or Supervisor

Employee Initials

FIGURE 13.10 Anne Arundel County Public Schools professional school counselor evaluation.

Evaluation of Unit I—Professional School Counselors

A. Performance Standards	5 Outstanding Performance	4 Highly Effective	3 Standards Met/ Satisfactory	2 Needs Improvement/ Marginal	1 Standard Not Met/ Unsatisfactory	0 Not Assigned	Supporting Statement
II. Delivery System: Four components define the delivery system of a comprehensive school counseling program: Essential Curriculum, Individual Student Planning, Responsive Services, and System Support. The delivery is the how of the implementation process.							
1 Delivers the Essential Curriculum to all students as outlined in the AACPS timeline.							
2 Works with individuals and/or small groups to analyze and evaluate students interests, abilities, etc.							
3 Provides responsive counseling services through consultation, individual & small group counseling, crisis counseling, referrals, and peer facilitation.							
4 Develops, maintains, and updates (based on needs) a master calendar of school counseling events to ensure students, parents/guardians, school staff, and administrators know what, when, and where school counseling programs and activities are scheduled.							
III. Management System: This system describes the processes needed to effectively manage the school counseling program, including use of data and action plans that maximize learning for all students. Attention to recommended time allocations is necessary, and carefully planned calendars serve as an indicator that the program is well managed. The management system identifies the "when, why, by whom and on what authority" of the comprehensive school counseling program.							
1 Establishes a written management agreement that aligns with the time allocations suggested by the National Model, i.e. 80% of time is spent delivering services to students, staff, and parents							
2 Implements a school counseling program that is built upon relevant data, assessing both short and long term needs.							
3 Implements Targeted Intervention plans that are data-driven and include student outcomes that are aligned with the district strategic plan.							
4 Functions collaboratively as a team member by partnering with staff, parents, and community, eg. participation on Advisory Councils, School improvement Teams, IDT, Student Assistance, MSAP, Human Relations, and district level committees.							

AACPS · DPS/JH 1330/160 (New 10/08) **2 of 3**

Employee Initials

(Continued)

Evaluation of Unit I—Professional School Counselors

	5	4	3	2	1	0	
A. Performance Standards	Outstanding Performance	Highly Effective	Standards Met/ Satisfactory	Needs Improvement/ Marginal	Standard Not Met/ Unsatisfactory	Not Assigned	**Supporting Statement**

IV. Accountability System:

School counselors must collect and use data that support and link the school counseling program to students' academic success. An evaluation of the school counseling program must answer the question, "How are students different as a result of the school counseling program?" Further, a significant contribution to the system-level or School Improvement Plan must be evident. This means that results should be fully aligned with the district strategic plan and outcomes to support goals must be quantifiable and substantial regarding the number of students affected.

		5	4	3	2	1	0	
1	Demonstrates significant program impact through perception and results data.							
2	Uses appropriate baseline data to set clear targets that are quantifiable and linked to the district strategic plan.							
3	Advocates for systemic change that supports optimal student achievement within schools.							
4	Regularly reviews results data to continually adjust and improve school counseling services.							

Total Score for HR Use **0** **Grand Total**

B. Additional Job-Related Information

C. Future Objectives for Consideration

D. Overall Evaluation	**Overall Comments**
☐ *Outstanding* ☐ *Highly Effective* ☐ *Satisfactory* ☐ *Marginal* ☐ *Unsatisfactory*	

Signatures

Person Evaluated	Date	Evaluator	Date

AACPS · DPS/JH 1330/160 (New 10/08) **3 of 3**

Distribution: Copies to   1—Human Resources   2—Employee   3—Principal or Supervisor

Employee Initials

Source: Anne Arundel County Public Schools

_____   _____
Name   Professional Assignment

A complete description of the teacher evaluation process of the Howard County Public Schools is provided in the Guide to Teacher Evaluation and Professional Development.

Please place the appropriate letter   Circle either **Tenured** or **Nontenured**
Symbol in the box next to the objective:

S - Satisfactory
U - Unsatisfactory

School counselors and administrators must note that staff members selecting a differentiated supervision option as part of the professional development and evaluation process will receive a final overall evaluation rating of SATISFACTORY unless the staff member and administrator rewrite the Professional Development and Evaluation Objectives form prior to January 31.

1. **INTERPERSONAL SKILLS**
   Relates Effectively with Students
   Develops Collaborative Relationships with Administrative, Teaching, and Support Staff
   Fosters Positive Relationships with Families and Community Members
   Comments:

2. **PLANNING AND PREPARATION/MANAGEMENT**
   Demonstrates Knowledge of Guidance and Counseling Theory and Strategies
   Demonstrates Knowledge of Students
   Selects Appropriate Counseling/Instructional Goals
   Demonstrates Knowledge of Resources
   Designs Coherent Counseling/Instruction
   Assesses Students' Needs Effectively
   Comments:

3. **THE CLASSROOM ENVIRONMENT/SCHOOL ENVIRONMENT**
   Establishes a Culture for Learning
   Manages Counseling/Classroom Procedures Effectively
   Manages Student Behavior Effectively
   Organizes Physical Space Appropriately
   Comments:

(Continued)

FIGURE 13.11 Howard County Public School System school counselors evaluation form.

☐ 4. **DELIVERY OF INSTRUCTION/PROGRAM IMPLEMENTATION**
Communicates Clearly and Accurately
Uses Questioning and Discussion Techniques Effectively
Engages Students in Learning Activities Directed to Guidance Goals (Comar 13A05050) and Student Needs
Provides Effective Feedback to Students
Demonstrates Flexibility and Responsiveness
Comments:

☐ 5. **PROFESSIONAL RESPONSIBILITIES**
Reflects on Guidance and Counseling
Supports and Maintains Accurate Records
Communicates with Families
Shows Professionalism
Grows and Develops Professionally
Comments:

☐ Overall Rating   ☐ See attachments (Attachments are required for all overall ratings of unsatisfactory.)

_____   _____
Counselor's Signature & Date   **Designated Evaluator's Signature & Date**

_____
Principal's Signature & Date

Note: Must be given to counselor within five school days after it is signed by the principal and no later than the last duty day.

Distribution: Principal, Employee, Personnel File

HOWARD COUNTY PUBLIC SCHOOL SYSTEM
Framework for Excellence in Guidance and Counseling

DOMAIN 1	**INTERPERSONAL SKILLS**

INDICATOR 1A   RELATES EFFECTIVELY WITH STUDENTS
Knowledge of students
Interactions with students
Communication skills

INDICATOR 1B   DEVELOPS COLLABORATIVE RELATIONSHIPS WITH ADMINISTRATIVE, TEACHING, AND SUPPORT STAFF
Respect and rapport
Communication skills
Conflict resolution

INDICATOR 1C   FOSTERS POSITIVE RELATIONSHIPS WITH FAMILIES AND COMMUNITY MEMBERS
Respect and rapport
Communication skills
Conflict resolution

DOMAIN 2	**PLANNING AND PREPARATION/MANAGEMENT**

INDICATOR 2A   DEMONSTRATES KNOWLEDGE OF GUIDANCE AND COUNSELING THEORY AND STRATEGIES
Content
Application in a school setting

INDICATOR 2B   DEMONSTRATES KNOWLEDGE OF STUDENTS
Developmental needs of students and characteristics of age groups
Students' varied approaches to learning
Students' skills and knowledge
Students' interests and cultural heritage

INDICATOR 2C   SELECTS APPROPRIATE COUNSELING/INSTRUCTIONAL GOALS
Value
Clarity

Indicator 2D   DEMONSTRATES KNOWLEDGE OF RESOURCES
Resources for counseling
Resources for student support

INDICATOR 2E   DESIGNS COHERENT COUNSELING/INSTRUCTION
Long/short term planning
Integrated with individual school improvement planning
Learning/informational activities
Counseling/instructional groups
Counseling/instructional materials and resources

(Continued)

INDICATOR 2F	ASSESSES STUDENTS' NEEDS EFFECTIVELY
	Prevention and intervention appropriate to specific grade levels
	Use in designing or modifying guidance program appropriately

DOMAIN 3	**THE CLASSROOM ENVIRONMENT/SCHOOL ENVIRONMENT**

INDICATOR 3A	ESTABLISHES A CULTURE FOR LEARNING
	Development of life skills and career connections
	Expectations for learning and achievement

INDICATOR 3B	MANAGES COUNSELING/CLASSROOM PROCEDURES EFFECTIVELY
	Managing counseling/instructional groups
	Managing materials and supplies
	Performing non-instructional duties
	Supervising volunteers and paraprofessionals

INDICATOR 3C	MANAGES STUDENT BEHAVIOR EFFECTIVELY
	Expectations
	Monitoring student behavior
	Response to student misbehavior

INDICATOR 3D	ORGANIZES PHYSICAL SPACE APPROPRIATELY
	Safety and accessibility
	Respect for confidentiality
	Welcoming and inviting environment

DOMAIN 4	**DELIVERY OF INSTRUCTION/PROGRAM IMPLEMENTATION**

INDICATOR 4A	COMMUNICATES CLEARLY AND ACCURATELY
	Directions and procedures
	Oral and written language

INDICATOR 4B	USES QUESTIONING AND DISCUSSION TECHNIQUES EFFECTIVELY
	Quality of questions
	Discussion techniques
	Student participation

INDICATOR 4C	ENGAGES STUDENTS IN LEARNING ACTIVITIES DIRECTED TO GUIDANCE GOALS (Comar 13A05050) AND STUDENT NEEDS
	Variety of guidance interventions
	Materials, activities, technology, and assignments
	Relevant and thoughtful applications
	Counseling/instructional groups
	Lesson/unit structure and pacing
	Transitions across grades/schools/community

INDICATOR 4D	PROVIDES EFFECTIVE FEEDBACK TO STUDENTS
	Quality: accurate, substantive, constructive, and specific
	Equitability
	Timeliness
INDICATOR 4E	DEMONSTRATES FLEXIBILITY AND RESPONSIVENESS
	Adjustment of counseling strategies
	Response to students
	Persistence

DOMAIN 5	PROFESSIONAL RESPONSIBILITIES
INDICATOR 5A	REFLECTS ON GUIDANCE AND COUNSELING
	Accuracy
	Use in future guidance and counseling planning
INDICATOR 5B	SUPPORTS AND MAINTAINS ACCURATE RECORDS
	Record keeping
	Standards of confidentiality/security
INDICATOR 5C	COMMUNICATES WITH FAMILIES
	Information about the counseling/instructional program
	Information about individual students
	Opportunities for involvement in the counseling/instructional program
	School and community resources
INDICATOR 5D	SHOWS PROFESSIONALISM
	Student advocacy
	Collaborative problem solving
	Relationships with business and community
	Following federal, state, and local policies and procedures
	Adherence to the Code of Ethics of the American Counseling Association
INDICATOR 5E	GROWS AND DEVELOPS PROFESSIONALLY
	Enhancement of content knowledge and counseling skills
	Service to the school, district, and profession

Source: Reprinted by permission of the Howard County Public School System, Ellicott City, MD, 21042. Reproduction or use of this document without the written permission of Howard County Public Schools is expressly prohibited.

Exemplary School Counseling Programs

Vision for School Counseling Programs

The school counseling program, in collaboration with faculty, parents, and community, will provide all students with the attitudes, knowledge, and skills for lifelong success. The comprehensive school counseling program integrates academic, career, and personal/social development and focuses on issues relevant to *all* students.

Students will participate in a planned, developmentally age-appropriate, and sequential school counseling program that is based on the National Standards for School Counseling. The program will prepare students to become effective learners, achieve success in school, and develop into contributing members of our society.

A. School-Level Factors Impacting Student Learning/Social Emotional/Healthy Development

The school counseling program is set up and run in a manner that supports student achievement.

Component I: Academic Support

ALWAYS EVIDENT	SOMEWHAT EVIDENT	NOT EVIDENT	FACTORS
O	O	O	1. The school counseling office requires the school counselors to learn about the strengths and interests of students and to use this information to identify appropriate strategies for accelerating student learning.
O	O	O	2. At the secondary level, the school administration includes a school counselor in facilitating and encouraging student movement to classes at the level of most appropriate challenge, including Honors, G/T and AP classes.
O	O	O	3. The school administration ensures that students with special needs receive the appropriate support from school counselors to accelerate student learning.
O	O	O	4. At the high school level, the school administration, in collaboration with the school counselor, schedules all 10th and all 11th grade students to take the PSAT. Students use the results to identify areas in which they need additional preparation.
O	O	O	5. At the high school level, counselors ensure that all diploma-seeking students are strongly encouraged to take the SAT.

Component II: Program Development and Evaluation

ALWAYS EVIDENT	SOMEWHAT EVIDENT	NOT EVIDENT	FACTORS
O	O	O	1. The school counseling program is aligned with school improvement goals and is written on the School Counseling Program Plan. The School Counseling Plan should be approved by the principal.
O	O	O	2. The school counseling program uses a planning process to define needs, priorities, and program objectives.
O	O	O	3. The school counseling program educates the school staff, parents, and the community about the school counseling program through a public information program.
O	O	O	4. The school counseling program evaluates the effectiveness of individual activities and the overall program in meeting desired student outcomes.
O	O	O	5. The school counseling program continues to seek feedback from students, parents, and staff about the services provided by the counseling office.
O	O	O	6. The school counselor(s) meet on a regular basis within the department and with administration to assess the progress of the school counseling program.
O	O	O	7. School counselors provide differentiated services to help all students develop academic identities that foster achievement.

Component III: Staff Assignments

ALWAYS EVIDENT	SOMEWHAT EVIDENT	NOT EVIDENT	FACTORS
O	O	O	1. The Office of Student Services ensures that school counselors are certified by an accredited institution in the area of school counseling.
O	O	O	2. Administrators use the staffing parameters to develop a plan to keep the counselor's involvement in non-counseling duties to a minimum.

FIGURE 13.12 Howard County Public Schools exemplary school counseling programs.

Howard County Public Schools
School Counseling

ALWAYS EVIDENT	SOMEWHAT EVIDENT	NOT EVIDENT	FACTORS
o	o	o	3. Administrators ensure that the counselors are provided sufficient access to students so that time is available to implement effective school counseling program activities.
o	o	o	4. At the secondary level, counselor assignments in the department are made in such a way that counselor expertise and workload are taken into consideration.
o	o	o	5. At the high school level, administrators select highly competent counselors to serve as instructional team leaders.

Component IV: Materials and Resources

ALWAYS EVIDENT	SOMEWHAT EVIDENT	NOT EVIDENT	FACTORS
o	o	o	1. The Office of Student Services in conjunction with the school administration ensures that school counselors have multicultural instructional materials that reflect the ethnic and gender diversity of the school's students.
o	o	o	2. The Office of Student Services in conjunction with the school administration provides appropriate technology and ensures that school counselors use it to enhance student learning.
o	o	o	3. The Office of Student Services in conjunction with the school administration requires staff members to use professional development standards and resources and ensure that all professional development results in improving the learning of all students.
o	o	o	4. School Administrators, in collaboration with the school counseling office, ensure that all school counselors participate in ongoing leadership development.

Component V: Community Outreach/Involvement

ALWAYS EVIDENT	SOMEWHAT EVIDENT	NOT EVIDENT	FACTORS
o	o	o	1. The school leadership team collects data on the school climate and collaborates with the school counselor to make the climate welcoming and inviting for all visitors.
o	o	o	2. School counselors support the school-wide vision for parent/family involvement that supports student achievement in their children's education.
o	o	o	3. The school leadership team and the office of school counseling ensure that communication about the school counseling program for non-English speaking parents/families is available through written translations and oral interpreter services.
o	o	o	4. The school counselor has a process for identifying parents/families that are not partners in their children's education.
o	o	o	5. The school counselor has a process for analyzing the data and the reasons for the noninvolvement of identified parents/families.
o	o	o	6. Based upon the data analysis, the school counselor develops a plan for engaging families in their children's education.
o	o	o	7. The school counselor uses Central Office resources for additional support for parent/family involvement in their children's education.
o	o	o	8. The school counselor has a well-defined process for gathering and responding to feedback on practices for involving parent/families in their children's education.
o	o	o	9. The school counselor has a process to inform parents/families about the school counseling program and student progress. The process fosters two-way communication and ensures participation that is representative of the school community.

(Continued)

ALWAYS EVIDENT	SOMEWHAT EVIDENT	NOT EVIDENT	FACTORS
O	O	O	10. When necessary, the school counselor uses the services of ESOL Community Liaisons and the Office of International Student Services to facilitate family and community involvement in the education of students.
O	O	O	11. The school counselor develops and maintains educational partnerships that include support for improving achievement.

B. Educator-Level Factors Impacting Student Learning/Social Emotional/Healthy Development

Exemplary school counselors form a partnership with students and their families to promote the personal and social development of students in order to help students achieve high levels of cognitive development. They use research-based best practices to plan and implement lessons that effectively meet the needs of all learners.

Component I: Personal Development of Students

ALWAYS EVIDENT	SOMEWHAT EVIDENT	NOT EVIDENT	FACTORS
			All school counselors help students develop a positive academic identity. They…
O	O	O	1. Make it a daily habit to tell students, individually and collectively, that they are capable and competent learners. (Domain 3A)
O	O	O	2. Take explicit steps to know and understand students as individual learners. (Domain 3A)
O	O	O	3. Involve students in goal setting, self-assessment, and reflection. (Domain 2F-3)
O	O	O	4. Ensure that students know how they learn best and how to use that information to master their academic subjects. (Domain 2B-2)
O	O	O	5. Assist students with developing the character traits that will help them to be successful in school, as well as other settings. (Domain 3A-2, 3A-3, and 3C-1)
O	O	O	6. Use appropriate data about students' current level of personal development to plan future lessons. (Domain 2B-2)

Component II: Social Development of Students

ALWAYS EVIDENT	SOMEWHAT EVIDENT	NOT EVIDENT	FACTORS
			All school counselors help students become part of a community of learners. They…
O	O	O	1. Make all students feel welcome and that they are a part of a community of learners. (Domain 1A)
O	O	O	2. Give students a variety of purposes for being a part of a community of learners. (Domain 1A)
O	O	O	3. Create a physically, emotionally, and socially secure learning environment that encourages students to ask questions about what they are learning, especially when they are confused or not certain about what to do. (Domain 3D-1, 4B-3)
O	O	O	4. Create a learning environment that encourages high expectations, enables students to experience success, provides students with a sense of belonging, and promotes shared responsibility for the achievement of all. (Domain 2D-2)
O	O	O	5. Use appropriate indicators of the degree to which the student functions socially as a part of the community of learners to plan future school counseling programs. (Domain 2D-2)

Howard County Public Schools
School Counseling

Component III: Cognitive Development of Students

ALWAYS EVIDENT	SOMEWHAT EVIDENT	NOT EVIDENT	FACTORS
			All school counselors help students develop learning-to-learn skills. They ...
O	O	O	1. Use a variety of instructional strategies to keep students engaged in classroom guidance lessons. (Domain 2E)
O	O	O	2. Give students a variety of specific purposes for learning that connect to students' personal goals and interests. (Domain 2E)
O	O	O	3. Model and teach students how to use specific thinking skills. (Domain 2A-1)
O	O	O	4. Engage students in instructional activities that infuse and celebrate diverse cultural backgrounds. (Domain 2B-4, 4C-3)

Component IV: Prevention and Intervention

ALWAYS EVIDENT	SOMEWHAT EVIDENT	NOT EVIDENT	INDICATORS
			All school counselors provide a program which focuses primarily on prevention and intervention. They ...
O	O	O	1. Implement a comprehensive and balanced program. (Domain 2E)
O	O	O	2. Use the *Essential Curriculum for School Counseling* to develop thorough plans for units and individual lessons. (Domain 2C, 2E)
O	O	O	3. Involve students in personalized educational and career planning. (Domain 3A, 4C)
O	O	O	4. Provide individual counseling in a systematic and timely manner. (Domain 2B, 2E)
O	O	O	5. Provide small group counseling. (Domain 2E, 4C)
O	O	O	6. Provide classroom guidance to ALL students to address developmental needs. (Domain 4C)
O	O	O	7. Use effective techniques and strategies appropriate to counseling in the school setting. (Domain 2A)
O	O	O	8. Are aware of the needs of all sub-groups of the student population and seek to provide services to meet their needs. (Domain 2B)

Component V: Consultation

ALWAYS EVIDENT	SOMEWHAT EVIDENT	NOT EVIDENT	INDICATORS
			All school counselors use consultation skills to enhance the academic achievement of our students. They ...
O	O	O	1. Foster collaboration among school and community resources and service providers to enable students to learn as effectively as possible. (Domain 1C, 5D)
O	O	O	2. Collaborate with families to support learning and achievement in school by providing parent education and/or parent support groups. (Domain 1C, 5C)
O	O	O	3. Participate on school-based problem-solving teams. (Domain 5D)
O	O	O	4. Consult and collaborate with other staff members regarding academic development, career development, and personal/social development. (Domain 1B, 5C)
O	O	O	5. Provide parents and students with information about private and public medical, social, and mental health service providers. (Domain 5C)
O	O	O	6. Maintain a communication system that effectively collects and disseminates information about students to other professionals as appropriate. (Domain 1C, 5B)
O	O	O	7. Develop and maintain positive working relationships with representatives of community resources. (Domain 1C, 5D)

(Continued)

ALWAYS EVIDENT	SOMEWHAT EVIDENT	NOT EVIDENT	INDICATORS
O	O	O	8. Assess accurately students' and their families' need for referrals. (Domain 2F, 5C)
O	O	O	9. Facilitate an articulation between instructional levels which provides a smooth transition for students. (Domain 4C)

Component VI: Assessment

ALWAYS EVIDENT	SOMEWHAT EVIDENT	NOT EVIDENT	INDICATORS
			All school counselors use best practices for sharing assessment information. They ...
O	O	O	1. Interpret tests and other appraisal results to students, staff, and parents. (Domain 5C)
O	O	O	2. Use other sources of student data as assessment tools for the purpose of educational planning. (Domain 2D)

Component VI: Professionalism/Professional Development

ALWAYS EVIDENT	SOMEWHAT EVIDENT	NOT EVIDENT	FACTORS
			All school counselors practice professionalism in school counseling. They ...
O	O	O	1. Adhere to ethical and professional standards for school counseling. (Domain 5D)
O	O	O	2. Seek out opportunities for continuing professional development provided by the Office of School Counseling. (Domain 5E)
O	O	O	3. Comply with federal, state, and local policies and procedures. (Domain 5D)
O	O	O	4. Participate on the School Improvement Team, Instructional Intervention Team, and Student Assistance Team. (Domain 5E)

Source: Howard County Public Schools

Standard 1: The professional school counselor plans, organizes, and delivers the school counseling program.	Does Not Meet	Does Meet	Exceeds
1.1 A program is designed to meet the needs of the school.			
1.2 The professional school counselor demonstrates interpersonal relationships with students.			
1.3 The professional school counselor demonstrates positive interpersonal relationships with educational staff.			
1.4 The professional school counselor demonstrates positive interpersonal relationships with parents or guardians.			
Standard 2: The professional school counselor implements the school guidance curriculum through the use of effective instructional skills and careful planning of structured group sessions for all students.			
2.1 The professional school counselor teaches school guidance units effectively.			
2.2 The professional school counselor develops materials and instructional strategies to meet student needs and school goals.			
2.3 The professional school counselor encourages staff involvement to ensure the effective implementation of the school guidance curriculum.			
Standard 3: The professional school counselor implements the individual planning component by guiding individuals and groups of students and their parents or guardians through the development of educational and career plans.			
3.1 The professional school counselor, in collaboration with parents or guardians, helps students establish goals and develop and use planning skills.			
3.2 The professional school counselor demonstrates accurate and appropriate interpretation of assessment data and the presentation of relevant, unbiased information.			
Standard 4: The professional school counselor provides responsive services through the effective use of individual and small-group counseling, consultation, and referral skills.			
4.1 The professional school counselor counsels individual students and small groups of students with identified needs and concerns.			
4.2 The professional school counselor consults effectively with parents or guardians, teachers, administrators, and other relevant individuals.			
4.3 The professional school counselor implements an effective referral process with administrators, teachers, and other school personnel.			

(Continued)

FIGURE 13.13 A sample performance appraisal using the ASCA School Counselor Performance Standards.

Standard 5: The professional school counselor provides system support through effective school counseling program management and support for other educational programs.			
5.1 The professional school counselor provides a comprehensive and balanced school counseling program in collaboration with school staff.			
5.2 The professional school counselor provides support for other school programs.			
Standard 6: The professional school counselor discusses the counseling department management system and the program action plans with the school administrator.			
6.1 The professional school counselor discusses the qualities of the school counselor management system with the other members of the counseling staff and has agreement.			
6.2 The professional school counselor discusses the program results anticipated when implementing the action plans for the school year.			
Standard 7: The professional school counselor is responsible for establishing and convening an advisory council for the school counseling program.			
7.1 The professional school counselor meets with the advisory committee.			
7.2 The professional school counselor reviews the school counseling program audit with the council.			
7.3 The professional school counselor records meeting information.			
Standard 8: The professional school counselor collects and analyzes data to guide program direction and emphasis.			
8.1 The professional school counselor uses school data to make decisions regarding student choice of classes and special programs.			
8.2 The professional school counselor uses data from the counseling program to make decisions regarding program revisions.			
8.3 The professional school counselor analyzes data to ensure every student has equity and access to a rigorous academic curriculum.			
8.4 The professional school counselor understands and uses data to establish goals and activities to close the gap.			

Standard 9: The professional school counselor monitors the students on a regular basis as they progress in school.			
9.1 The professional school counselor is accountable for monitoring every student's progress.			
9.2 The professional school counselor implements monitoring systems appropriate to the individual school.			
9.3 The professional school counselor develops appropriate interventions for students as needed and monitors their progress.			
Standard 10: The professional school counselor uses time and calendars to implement an efficient program.			
10.1 The professional school counselor uses a master calendar to plan activities throughout the year.			
10.2 The professional school counselor distributes the master calendar to parents or guardians, staff and students.			
10.3 The professional school counselor posts a weekly or monthly calendar.			
10.4 The professional school counselor analyzes time spent providing direct service to students.			
Standard 11: The professional school counselor develops a results evaluation for the program.			
11.1 The professional school counselor measures results attained from school guidance curriculum and closing the gap activities.			
11.2 The professional school counselor works with members of the counseling team and with the principal to clarify how programs are evaluated and how results are shared.			
11.3 The professional school counselor knows how to collect process, perception, and results data.			
Standard 12: The professional school counselor conducts a yearly program audit.			
12.1 The professional school counselor completes a program audit to determine the degrees to which the school counseling program is being implemented.			
12.2 The professional school counselor shares the results of the program audit with the advisory council.			
12.3 The professional school counselor uses the yearly audit to make changes in the school counseling program and calendar for the following year.			

(Continued)

Standard 13: The professional school counselor is a student advocate, leader, and collaborator and a systems change agent. 13.1 The professional school counselor promotes academic success of every student.			
13.2 The professional school counselor promotes equity and access for every student.			
13.3 The professional school counselor takes a leadership role within the counseling department, the school setting, and the community.			
13.4 The professional school counselor understands reform issues and works to close the achievement gap.			
13.5 The professional school counselor collaborates with teachers, parents, and the community to promote academic success of students.			
13.6 The professional school counselor builds effective teams by encouraging collaboration among all school staff.			
13.7 The professional school counselor uses data to recommend systemic change in policy and procedures that limit or inhibit academic achievement.			

Source: Adapted with permission from the American School Counselor Association. Further reproduction prohibited.

Summary/Conclusion

Accountability involves the demonstration of responsibility for professional actions. Professional school counselors demonstrate accountability by providing evidence that answers five primary questions. First, is a comprehensive, standards-based program in place? A program evaluation (or audit) should be conducted annually near the end of the school year to determine whether a written school counseling program is being fully implemented.

Second, what are the needs of the school's student population when compared to these standards? A needs assessment can be implemented using one of two primary methods. A data-driven needs assessment evaluates needs demonstrated through derived information. Aggregated results are broken down (disaggregated) so they can be examined on the subgroup level. Such analysis is critical to demonstrate whether all students are given access to rigorous academic coursework and are benefiting from the curriculum. A perceptions-based needs assessment determines what primary stakeholder groups (e.g., teachers, parents, students) perceive as needs. These perceptions can be gathered through a variety of methods, but some form of quantifiable result is preferred so that various perceived needs can be compared and prioritized.

Third, what services were implemented to address the identified needs and standards? A service assessment

provides an accounting of who did what, how much, and for how long. This type of evidence is helpful in demonstrating that professional school counselors are using their time to provide valuable (or even not so valuable) services and is often requested by administrations and school boards. Unfortunately, service assessment is more of a process evaluation (i.e., how one spends one's time), rather than an outcomes evaluation (i.e., what valuable result has occurred by spending one's time that way). In other words, time is a process variable. Results stem from the actions one performs, given the precious commodity of time.

Fourth, what was the result of the implemented services? Some argue that results or outcomes studies are the most valuable facet of accountability. The assessment loop shows that the purpose of evaluation is continuous quality improvement. Data are collected to evaluate actions and interventions so that judgments can be made on the worth or value of services and programs. Often, traditional research designs can yield the most helpful and authoritative information about program or event quality. Because of the broad-ranging nature of standards and competencies, professional school counselors attempting to demonstrate the effectiveness of a developmental curriculum should use an aggregated hierarchical model in which evidence is collected at the objectives level to demonstrate whether higher-order competencies and standards have been met.

Fifth, how well is the professional school counselor performing? As a condition of employment, professional school counselors undergo periodic performance evaluation or performance appraisal. The purpose of this process is to determine the performance of the individual, rather than that of the program. Of course, if there is only one professional school counselor in the school, the individual appraisal often also reflects program quality. Professional school counselors should be aware of the evaluation criteria well in advance of any assessment, and such processes should be aimed at developing higher-level counseling skills and competencies.

Accountability applies to every facet of a school counseling program. The better prepared a professional school counselor is to engage in accountability activities, continuously collect evidence, and report on program performance, the more valuable he or she is to the school, school system, and profession. Being responsible for one's actions and the quality of services provided is an important ethical and professional responsibility.

Activities

1. Develop a preliminary needs assessment for a school in your community. What type of method did you use (questionnaire, classroom visits, etc.)? What types of needs were addressed in your assessment? How will this assessment influence the development of your program?
2. Interview a professional school counselor regarding the use of needs assessment. Ask to view a needs assessment recently given and what learning objectives were derived from student responses.
3. Conduct a role play with a partner in which you are the school counselor and your partner is an administrator. Using assessment and accountability, convince the administrator that your school counseling program is an important aspect of student academic success.

14

Systemic Approaches to Counseling Students Experiencing Complex and Specialized Problems

Bradley T. Erford, Vivian V. Lee, Debbie W. Newsome and Elana Rock*

Editor's Introduction: Students experiencing academic failure and personal/social problems present a substantial dilemma for schools, families, and communities. This dilemma also presents an extraordinary example of how the transformed professional school counselor can collaborate with and coordinate school and community organizations and resources to benefit these students in need. After a brief introduction recapping the state of affairs for students in the United States, a case is made for professional school counselors as "coordinators of interdisciplinary resources" to collaborate and develop partnerships with community agencies and organizations providing overlapping services with school personnel. Specialized issues in working with specific populations of students also will be introduced (e.g., loss, divorce, dropout prevention, suicide, threat assessment). Perhaps most important, professional school counselors must help educators support students, rather than blaming and punishing them or their parents.

THE CHANGING NEEDS OF STUDENTS AND FAMILIES

American society and the world in general have changed so much in the past few decades that educators at all levels have struggled to keep pace. While technological innovations and socially progressive movements have yielded many positive and exciting outcomes, the unintended consequences at times seem overwhelming. Rising levels of poverty, substance abuse, and domestic violence are but a few of the major problems presently affecting society (National Institutes of Health, 2005).

Society's fast-paced changes have resulted in myriad mental health dilemmas. Consider but a few of the staggering statistics. Glied and Cuellar (2003) reported that 20% of all children and adolescents have significant emotional impairment requiring treatment, but only about one out of five of these affected children and adolescents actually receives treatment. This is a particularly critical statistic, given that almost half of all students with emotional problems drop out of school. The American Psychiatric Association (APA, 2000) estimated that clinical depression afflicts 3 to 6 million children, contributing to widespread social and emotional problems, including suicide. Suicide continues to be the third leading cause of death among American adolescents. More than 2,000 adolescents kill themselves each year, and approximately 10,000 to 20,000 adolescents attempt suicide annually (D. Brown, 1996). Finally, about 30% to 50% of school-aged children referred to community mental health agencies experience conduct problems and behavior disorders, the most common of which is Attention-deficit/ Hyperactivity Disorder (AD/HD), which is estimated to exist in 3% to 5% of school-aged children (APA, 2000).

---

*The first edition chapter, "A New Perspective on Counseling At-Risk Youth," was written by Fred Bemak, Rita Chi-Ying Chung, and C. Sally Murphy. Much of their outstanding work on systemic approaches to working with at-risk youth was continued in this third edition chapter.

Many children with AD/HD are served in the public schools either through special education or under Section 504 of the Rehabilitation Act of 1973; students with AD/HD constitute a large subgroup of the more than 5 million students who annually receive special education services (U.S. Department of Education, 2005c).

All in all, there is an increasing trend toward mental and emotional problems among American students, perhaps stemming from rapid societal and technological changes. These problems have been compounded by government funding procedural changes and shortages of affordable community-based mental health services (Luongo, 2000; National Institute of Mental Health [NIMH], 2005). As so often has been the case, governments and citizens have turned to the schools to help resolve societal difficulties. Fortunately, professional school counselors can play an essential role in the amelioration of many of these mental health concerns.

Twenty-first-century society has the potential to learn from the past and improve on what has been done in previous centuries. This is especially true in light of technological innovations, globalization, dramatic improvements in health care, economic prosperity, and increased consciousness about cultural diversity. Yet, U.S. reports continue to show increasing numbers of youth who are alienated and disconnected from the positive aspects and opportunities of society and have difficult and negative experiences in schools, communities, and families. The result is an increasing quantity of youth who are struggling to mature and develop into contributing members of society.

In previous decades, students experiencing complex problems in the United States were identified as socially and culturally deprived, with a focus on impoverished and minority youth who were labeled as disadvantaged. As the realization dawned on policy makers and professionals working with youth, families, communities, and schools that children and adolescents experiencing complex problems came from all socioeconomic classes and ethnic and racial backgrounds, the characterization of this population changed to include those youth identified as disengaged and not connected to mainstream institutions and society at large. They were not just the minority or urban poor students. They originated in urban, suburban, and rural neighborhoods; were rich and poor; were immigrants and native born; had one or two parents living at home; and came from any racial and ethnic background. They came from the best schools and communities that the United States had to offer, as well as the poorest, most decayed neighborhoods. Anyone could be exposed to community, school, and family violence; family dysfunction; drugs and alcohol; teenage suicide; or problems with peers. It is critical to understand that in the United States, students who experience complex problems are quite diverse. Given the growing numbers of these youth, despite numerous programs to address their problems, it is clear that overall intervention and prevention strategies have been limited in their success.

The *ASCA National Model* (American School Counselor Association, 2005a) proposes that the academic, career, and personal/social needs of all children be addressed through comprehensive school counseling programs that focus on systemic change, advocacy, leadership, and collaboration. Helping to address the holistic needs of children requires sound foundational skills in each of these primary areas. This chapter begins by presenting current perspectives and policy implications for working with students experiencing complex problems. The chapter goes on to review some new, innovative, and culturally responsive strategies for working with these students; examines reasons why the needs of this population have not been fully addressed; discusses the accountability for program failure; and provides systemic recommendations for professional school counselors. Finally, the chapter provides information for working with specific subpopulations of students experiencing problems, multicultural implications, and transition issues across grade levels.

RESILIENCY: FOCUSING ON WHAT'S RIGHT, RATHER THAN WHAT'S WRONG

Risk factors are characteristics of students that place them at higher risk of developing mental disorders, academic problems, or personal/social difficulties. It is important to realize that a single risk factor leads to only a slight increase in risk, while multiple factors exponentially increase one's risk status. While risk factors are sometimes helpful when implementing prevention or early intervention models, resilience factors are ordinarily more important to assess because resilience involves characteristics that allow an individual to rebound from adversity or maintain equilibrium of positive functioning when exposed to traumatic events or environmental stressors. The Search Institute (Scales, 2005) published a list of 40 developmental assets helpful to professional school counselors using a resilience-based or wellness approach to counseling, broken into eight organizing categories.

I. Support: (1) family support, (2) positive family communications, (3) other adult relationships, (4) caring neighborhood, (5) caring school climate, (6) parent involvement in schooling;

II. Empowerment: (7) community values youth, (8) youth as resources, (9) service to others, (10) safety;

III. Boundaries and Expectations: (11) family boundaries, (12) school boundaries, (13) neighborhood boundaries, (14) adult role models, (15) positive peer influence, (16) high expectations;

IV. Constructive Use of Time: (17) creative activities, (18) youth programs, (19) religious community, (20) time at home;

V. Commitment to Learning: (21) achievement motivation, (22) school engagement, (23) homework, (24) bonding to school, (25) reading for pleasure;

VI. Positive Values: (26) caring, (27) equality and social justice, (28) integrity, (29) honesty, (30) responsibility, (31) restraint;

VII. Social Competence: (32) planning and decision-making, (33) interpersonal competence, (34) cultural competence, (35) resistance skills, (36) peaceful conflict resolution;

VIII. Positive Identity: (37) personal power, (38) self-esteem, (39) sense of purpose, (40) positive view of personal future.

Professional school counselors can help students develop increased resilience or protective factors by helping to build parent, peer, and school support mechanisms (O'Donnell, Schwab-Stone, & Muyeed, 2002). Brooks (2006) proposed that resilience-enhancing school environments help students develop social competence, caring relationships, high expectations, and opportunities for meaningful interactions, while creating partnerships with families and communities. In short, school environments that surround students with nurturing, caring relationships help them to develop the sense of security and self-respect that foment the success experiences and positive outcomes that create resilience. Professional school counselors play a leadership role in creating the systemic changes that lead to nurturing, caring environments and educators (ASCA, 2005a). While we are well aware of the problems students encounter inside and outside of schools, we are more concerned with pursuing solutions for students now and in the future, and resiliency models hold promise for helping students during current and future times of trouble.

IDENTIFYING AND CATEGORIZING STUDENTS WITH COMPLEX PROBLEMS

Although attempts to address at-risk youth have been long-standing, remarkably as we move into the 21st century, there is still ongoing debate and controversy over defining this population. For the purpose of this chapter, students are at risk when they lack the familial, community, cultural, institutional, and societal supports necessary to develop and grow in an environment that is safe, positive, healthy, and conducive to personal, social, cultural, intellectual, spiritual, economic, and physical development. The absence of these supports inhibits the potential for development as a person and the potential for choices and opportunities necessary to contribute as a productive member of society. Healthy growth and development for youth must include the context of the family and other social networks; environment; health and nutrition; opportunities for spiritual development; and a positive interaction with the surrounding community, society, and culture within which one lives. The quality of a child's or an adolescent's physical, mental, emotional, social, spiritual, and economic health significantly correlates to being at risk; therefore, prevention and intervention program design and implementation must include a holistic framework.

We prefer to avoid using the term *at-risk* when possible because use of that term leads to five potential problem areas. First, when using this term, there is a danger of discounting resiliency. Potential strengths, coping abilities, and strategies for handling the variables that constitute being at risk are disregarded with the shift in focus to pathology, problems, and weaknesses. Second, the label *at-risk* has strong negative associations and stigmatizes youth. Chances of moving out of at-risk status are nominal, leaving many youth labeled for their entire childhood and adolescence. Third, when youth are identified as being at risk during adolescence, the prospect of being at risk is no longer a question, but becomes a fact. This leaves far less opportunity for designing prevention programs that would affect these youths' future, given the permanency associated with the label being designated during adolescence. It determines that being at risk, in essence, means "deep trouble," which has implications for how we regard, treat, and conceive of this population. A fourth problem with categorizing youth at risk is that the term has been used as a catchall phrase that does not differentiate the risk level one is facing or the conditions, causes, or problem behaviors associated with that risk. This generalization of the term does not help in defining the problems or the strategies best employed to address them. Fifth, there is no sensitivity to or awareness of cultural differences related to at-risk behavior. For example, some cultures (including various cultural minorities in the United States) have far greater tolerance for youth behaviors than other cultures do. This has been differentiated as "broad socialization," or more open and tolerant practices that minimize social constraints, versus "narrow socialization," where obedience and conformity to community norms are demanded, thus reducing experimentation and sensation-seeking behaviors.

Cultures can be further differentiated as child centered and not child centered. In child-centered cultures, there is greater acceptance of children and support in developing personal, family, and community social skills within a social context, resulting in youth demonstrating higher levels of achievement and greater self-reliance. In contrast, non-child-centered cultures prioritize individuality over the family and community at large and have less tolerance for children. In non-child-centered cultures, children are shown to be more aggressive, to feel rejected and disengaged more often, and, subsequently, to be more independent. In turn, the adults in non-child-centered cultures exhibit greater hostility toward and less compassion for people in need, and their response to problems is in a reactive crisis mode that many of the schools, communities, and families in the United States face today. These problems contribute to confusion in characterizing and identifying youth with complex problems and are reflected in the lack of effective programming to reduce problems such as teenage pregnancy, substance abuse, violence, juvenile delinquency, gangs, school dropout, and school failure.

SYSTEMIC APPROACHES TO WORKING WITH STUDENTS EXPERIENCING COMPLEX PROBLEMS

Historically, the definition of *at-risk* has been based on one of four approaches: predictive, descriptive, unilateral, or school factors, with each approach having its flaws (Hixson & Tinzmann, 1990). For example, the predictive approach is based on a deficit model that emphasizes what is wrong or missing in the individual student, family, or community. The descriptive method focuses on after-the-fact reporting and therefore addresses the issue after the behavior has occurred. The unilateral technique assumes that all students are at risk by virtue of living in today's society. Finally, the school factors approach states that schools are solely accountable and therefore absolves parents of any responsibility.

To further illustrate, look more closely at the categorization of students solely by the criterion of academic achievement and success. When considering the large and growing number of immigrant and refugee students entering the United States, it is increasingly apparent that psychosocial adjustment, acculturation, and psychological well-being are not reflected solely by academic performance. Yet when complex problems experienced by students are standardized and measured by academic success, it is not reflective of the complex and demanding issues faced by this population (Bemak & Chung, 2002). Designating immigrant and refugee students or any students by virtue of their academic success automatically limits the area of concern to schools, neglecting other aspects of the students' lives, rather than examining the issues within a social context that would include collaboration with parents, community agencies, businesses, and government agencies. This, in turn, places the onus of responsibility for intervention and prevention strictly on school personnel, leading to the conclusion that problems are related only to the confines of the brick and mortar of a school building. These assumptions are not only misleading, but also egregiously incorrect.

Helping students with complex problems cuts across several disciplines, including mental health, education, public health, substance abuse, business, social services, juvenile justice, and child and family services. Many professionals working within these various systems are disheartened by failures to reach these students. They are frustrated, burned out, and even angry at the lack of responsiveness to honest intervention attempts. These attitudes frequently result in schools, programs, and society giving up on those youth in most need and in trouble. In fact, a culture has emerged that blames the child in more subtle and sophisticated ways and molds itself into a 21st-century version of "blaming the victim." This defeatist attitude is observed in principals and other educators who want certain children out of their school, programs that identify children and adolescents as "too difficult" to benefit from their good services, families that are labeled and stigmatized as "unreachable," and neglected communities that are considered dangerous and "too far gone."

These negative attitudes toward students with complex problems are fueling the trend toward containment, punishment, and banishment, rather than treatment and prevention. The emphasis is on a "quick fix," rather than an in-depth examination of the problem from family, community, and societal perspectives. For example, Americans are more concerned with metal detectors than community prevention models, as demonstrated after the flurry of public school shootings in different parts of the United States (Keys & Bemak, 1997). The emphasis on punishment not only results in resentment toward and disregard of the disenfranchised youth of today, but also marginalizes and segregates youth for whom there is little hope and on whom society has essentially given up. This is a dangerous proposition and will ultimately result in disenfranchised students who lead difficult and frustrating lives and who lack the skills and knowledge to participate in society in healthy, positive ways. Even more alarming is that a significant number of these youth will contribute to growing social problems and become an economic and social burden in the country.

Contrary to this subtle, but growing, movement is the contention that all children can be reached. But this requires a dramatic step in redefining the programs to fit the changing needs of youth in trouble. Rather than reject and abandon youth who do not respond to traditional programs, it is critical that professionals develop new and innovative strategies for working with families, communities, and schools to reach those children now regarded as unreachable. This requires support on multiple levels: new ways of training professionals at the university level to work with these students; innovative programming that goes beyond what we currently propose; policy changes; an emphasis on prevention and intervention, rather than crisis management; interdisciplinary cooperation to address the complexity of the problems that youth face (Bemak & Keys, 2000); and a shift in attitude from control and punishment to intervention and prevention. Underlying this support is the firm belief and hope in the dignity and possibility of each child and adolescent.

SYSTEMS FAILURES: WHO IS TO BLAME?

There are a large number of facilities in the United States that have the potential to effectively serve at-risk youth. For example, there are 85,000 public and 25,000 private elementary and secondary schools; 400 national organizations (e.g., Boy Scouts, 4H, YMCA); 17,000 community-based programs; and 6,000 libraries, recreational centers, and police departments that provide programs for youth (Dryfoos, 1998). Even so, schools today, despite valiant efforts to prevent students from dropping out, still encounter a 6% dropout rate in urban areas and a 4% rate in suburban areas (U.S. Bureau of Census, 2008). The inability to reach these students reflects the inadequacy of programming strategies, rather than a belief that these students are hopeless and won't respond to programming.

For a number of years, at-risk youth have been blamed for their problems, whether done consciously or more subtly. The general consensus has been that youth fail our programs, rather than programs failing our youth. This has perpetuated a system of hopelessness and acceptance of failure and directly contradicts a reevaluation of current prevention and intervention methodologies that have a substantial rate of failure, yet continue to be funded. We contend that youth do not fail, but that programs and systems have a long-standing record of failing these students. By blaming children and adolescents who are already powerless, programs are not only negligent in protecting our youth, but also add to and perpetuate the existing problems faced by this population. If we truly want to help our youth engage in future opportunities, we can no longer blame the youth, but must critically evaluate our intervention strategies and

admit that they may not be effective; at the same time, we must move beyond the blame and work to redesign successful interventions.

To address the complexity of problems that interrelate with youth, peer groups, family, school, and community, it is critical that we not only reexamine our current strategies, but also redesign and develop new workable interventions. Advocates have strongly argued for service integration (e.g., Bemak, 2000; Taylor & Adelman, 2000), given the complexity of interrelated problems facing youth, rather than addressing discrete problem areas. Many programs and interventions with students experiencing complex difficulties focus on problem areas that are categorized by distinct behaviors. This results in intensive and expensive programs that are aimed at specific issues such as substance abuse, teenage pregnancy, anger management, juvenile delinquency, school failure, or suicide risk.

Programs that are narrow in focus and aim to address isolated problems fail the students in need of services for more complex issues. It is important to adapt intervention strategies to the complex needs of the target population from the perspective of an interagency response that is not limited to schools. Furthermore, professional school counselors are in a pivotal position to lead this endeavor, given that they are based in schools. Schools have the potential to be the focal point for all youth during childhood and adolescence.

WHY HAVEN'T NEEDS OF STUDENTS EXPERIENCING COMPLEX PROBLEMS BEEN ADDRESSED?

There are five major reasons for the lack of commitment to the needs of students with complex problems. First, funding priorities have not been focused on this population within the broader context of multiple problems. Funding of intervention and prevention programs must be reevaluated, and cross-disciplinary, research-based, interagency funding must be supported. Simplifying the problems of youth with complex problems into discrete categories is insufficient, yet many funding initiatives remain limited in scope or breadth. Second, it is difficult to change systems. Professional school counselors and other professionals should study systems change theory and practice, learning how to move resistant systems that are set in their ways. Third, the nation does not have a consensual moral commitment to working with this population. As discussed previously, the current national trend in the United States emphasizes punishment and excommunication from one's community or society, rather than intervention strategies that aim to reengage youth into mainstream cultures.

A fourth reason for the lack of commitment to students with complex problems is the absence of societal, institutional, and community commitment to address these problems for a disengaged and essentially powerless population. Neither is there a true commitment reflected in school, state, and federal policies. For example, schools that are measured by student performance on standardized tests may prefer that problem students in jeopardy of failing those exams transfer to another school or leave school entirely. Essentially, this translates into education for some of our students, not all. Finally, graduate-level university training of professionals often lacks innovation and responsiveness to addressing modern-day concerns of students with complex problems as part of the curriculum. This can be seen in training for professional school counselors, which rarely focuses specifically on this population of students in courses such as career counseling, group counseling, individual counseling, family counseling, and human growth and development or during practicums and internships when counselors in training have the opportunity to work in agencies that serve this population. With these reasons in mind, the remainder of the chapter reviews some of the specific issues students may present to professional school counselors that lead to more complex problems and academic challenges.

WORKING WITH YOUTH WITH SPECIFIC PROBLEMS

There are many issues that lead students to struggle academically or emotionally. This section identifies and addresses several of the more prominent issues that professional school counselors must prepare themselves to address, including crisis intervention, suicide, school violence, substance abuse, divorce, teen pregnancy, delinquency, and peer conflict. This list is by no means comprehensive, nor is the treatment given to each topic in this chapter. What follows is meant to educate and provide some strategies for assessing or intervening with students experiencing these issues.

Responding to Crisis Situations

During the past two decades, there has been a heightened awareness of the need for crisis intervention in schools. Crises in schools can affect a single student, a small group of students, or the entire school. Experiences of violence, disaster, and trauma can leave students without sufficient resources to cope. Crises that may affect the school community include suicide, loss, medical emergencies, family trauma, school shootings, gang activities, abuse, and natural disasters (e.g., hurricanes, floods, earthquakes, tornadoes). Professional school counselors play a key role in planning and implementing crisis response in schools. Consequently, professional school counselors need to understand what constitutes a crisis, know how to intervene effectively, and be able to help implement a response plan to schoolwide crises (ASCA, 2000; D. B. Brown & Trusty, 2005b).

DEFINITION OF CRISIS   The term *crisis* has been defined in many ways (e.g., Gilliland & James, 2005). The Chinese characters that represent *crisis* mean both "danger" and "opportunity." A crisis represents danger because it initially is experienced as an intolerable difficulty that threatens to overwhelm the individual. Unless the person obtains relief, the crisis potentially can cause severe psychological, cognitive, physical, and behavioral consequences. In contrast, the term represents opportunity because, during times of crisis, individuals are usually more receptive to help. Prompt, skillful interventions not only may prevent the development of sustained problems, but also may help individuals to develop new coping patterns, thereby increasing their ability to adapt and function in the future.

The concept of crisis is not simple or straightforward. With all crises, stress is a major component (Steigerwald, 2010a). However, individuals experience stress in different ways, with some students having stronger coping skills, resources, and support systems than others. An event that is perceived as relatively minor by one student, such as failing an exam or being "dumped" by a girlfriend, may be perceived as a crisis by another student. Also, the timing and intensity of the crisis, as well as the number of other stressors the student is experiencing, can impact the complexity of the crisis situation (Gladding & Newsome, 2009).

CRISIS INTERVENTION   *Crisis intervention* differs from counseling in several ways. Crisis intervention refers to the immediate action a professional school counselor takes to "provide the support and direction that the student in crisis cannot provide for him or herself" (Steigerwald, 2010a, pp. 830–831). It is an action-oriented approach designed to help students cope with a particular life situation that has thrown them off course. Goals of crisis intervention include helping the student to defuse emotions, organize, and interpret what has happened; to integrate the traumatic event into his or her life story; and to interpret the event in a way that is meaningful (Bauer, Sapp, & Johnson, 2000). Crisis intervention is time limited and should not be confused with more long-term postcrisis counseling, which may be needed and which usually necessitates referral to other helping professionals. Trusty and Brown (2005, pp. 262–263) and Steigerwald (2010b, p. 840) suggested several guidelines for school counselors to follow in crisis counseling. These are summarized in Table 14.1.

TABLE 14.1   Crisis Counseling Guidelines

---

1. *Respond immediately.* The longer students wait for counseling to occur, the more difficult it is to cope with the crisis.
2. *Be directive at first.* Environmental interventions may be necessary, especially when there are safety concerns. Being directive and caring provides structure, predictability, safety, and comfort to the students.
3. *Listen actively and nonjudgmentally as students tell their stories.* Attempt to view the crisis from their perspective. Pay close attention to feelings and help normalize them. Emotions typically associated with crisis include confusion, sadness, loss of control, loss of self-worth, stigma, loneliness, fear of mortality, guilt, and anger.
4. *Follow a holistic approach.* Observe and assess the physical, behavioral, emotional, and cognitive domains of the student in crisis.
5. *Begin work where the student is experiencing the most impairment.*
6. *Get the facts surrounding the crisis.* The counselor needs to understand the situation to assess the student's reactions.
7. *Sustain relationships and resources.* Help students keep lines of communication open and use family, peer, school, and community resources for support. Watch for isolation behavior.
8. *Keep a multicultural awareness of the student's expressions of emotions, perspectives, and behaviors.*
9. *Do not offer false reassurance.* Students who have experienced crises face difficult tasks. Work toward generating realistic hope.
10. *Help students take action.* Helping students move from the victim role to the actor role is a key component of crisis counseling.
11. *Determine whether the effects are long-lasting and whether a referral for further assessment and counseling is needed.*
12. *Do not work in isolation.* Involve the student's support system and work with a consultant or supervisor.
13. *Continue to develop knowledge and skills in crisis intervention by reading current literature about the topic and by participating in crisis training workshops.* Such workshops are sponsored by the American Red Cross and the National Organization for Victim Assistance (NOVA).

CRISIS RESPONSE PLANS   At times, a crisis affects a large number of students, and a systematic response from the school is required (ASCA, 2000; Trusty & Brown, 2005). Examples of crises that may dictate a systemic response include student homicide or suicide, unexpected death, and natural disasters. Although crises are, unfortunately, an uncontrollable aspect of school life, the manner in which school professionals respond to crisis can be controlled. Professional school counselors often play leadership roles in helping schools develop and implement a systemic crisis plan, which is comprehensive, is well planned, mobilizes resources, and operates quickly (Steigerwald, 2010b).

Crisis response plans should exist both on a district level and on an individual-school level. Professional school counselors may be members of the district and school critical response teams or solely members of the school-level response team. In either case, the professional school counselor takes a leadership role in the prevention, intervention, and postincident support of school critical responses (ASCA, 2000). In this role, professional school counselors provide individual and group counseling; consult with administrators, teachers, parents, and professionals; and coordinate services within the school and the community (Allen et al., 2002; ASCA, 2000).

Crisis plans need to be put in place before a crisis occurs. Crisis response planning committees and crisis response teams (CRTs) are instrumental in planning for, coordinating, and implementing a systemic crisis response. Gilliland and James (2005) recommended the following minimum requirements for a school crisis plan:

- *Physical requirements:* Identify locations for temporary counseling offices. An operations/communications center should be identified where crisis intervention procedures are monitored, needs are assessed, and information for the media is disseminated. Also suggested are a break room, a first-aid room, and an information center designed to handle media personnel and to facilitate parent communication.
- *Logistics:* Address specific areas that need consideration as an intervention plan is implemented. For example, attention needs to be given to the manner in which on-site and off-site communication will take place. Other logistics that need attention include providing (a) procedural checklists to ensure that the intervention plan is being followed, (b) building plans for emergency personnel, and (c) food and drink for crisis personnel.
- *Crisis response:* A sequential plan for crisis response includes gathering and verifying the facts, assessing the impact of the crisis to determine what assistance

is needed, providing triage assessment to determine who is most in need of immediate attention, providing psychological first aid as a first-order response, having a model in place, providing crisis intervention, and following through by briefing, debriefing, and demobilizing. (pp. 553–558)

It is essential for professional school counselors to be familiar with their district and school crisis response plans. If no such plan is in place, professional school counselors will want to work with administrators and other school personnel to create and implement a plan to respond to crises. Moreover, professional school counselors can be instrumental in leading workshops in the school and community to communicate the plan to others. A helpful resource that provides information and guidance for crisis planning is *Crisis Communications Guide and Toolkit* (www.nea.org/crisis), produced by the National Education Association (NEA, 2002).

VOICES FROM THE FIELD 14.1   CRISIS MANAGEMENT FOR THE HOLIDAYS

It was a Sunday evening and I had just finished decorating my Christmas tree and wrapping the last Christmas gifts when I got a phone call from one of the principals with whom I work. She went on to explain, "Katie, we have a big problem. Mr. Smith just murdered Mrs. Smith and is on the loose. We don't have many more details, but we think that one of their children may have witnessed it." My job as a professional school counselor is somewhat unique in that I am assigned to four nonpublic schools, but even with my high caseload, I never expected to have a crisis like this one on my hands. After taking a minute to digest the information that I had just received, I knew that I needed to get in touch with my supervisor to come up with a plan of how we could best help the school community that would be experiencing immeasurable shock and grief. This particular school is part of a very tightly knit community where it is rare to find a person whose grandfather or grandmother didn't also grow up in the town. We knew that there would be a ripple effect throughout not only the school, but also the community and that the rumor mill would be swirling.

Mr. and Mrs. Smith had three children together and two of them attended my school. Along with their children, the Smiths had seven nieces and nephews and many more family friends who attended the same school. Mrs. Smith had been active with the Home and School Association, was a homeroom mother, and also volunteered lots of time working at the school. She was well known and loved by students and teachers alike. I knew that I would need a lot of help from my colleagues in handling this situation. I am fortunate that I work for an organization that employs 19 professional school counselors, all of whom can be on call for crisis situations.

On Monday morning, eight additional counselors arrived at the school with me. We came up with a plan of how to respond. First thing in the morning, we would meet with all of the teachers and staff members to answer any questions and let them know of our plan for the day. Two counselors went down to handle the parents who we knew would show up wanting their questions answered and reassurance that the children were safe at school, even though Mr. Smith was on the loose. Two counselors stayed in the office for any student, staff member, or parent who needed to talk. One counselor walked around and checked in with the teachers, maintenance man, lunch moms, and so on. The rest of us went around to the classrooms to dispel rumors and process what we could with the classes. The upper grades knew more and had heard more about the situation so it follows that more time was spent with the older students. In the Smith boys' classes, we discussed not only their feelings and concerns, but also what to do when the boys returned to school.

Needless to say, instead of going to my other schools that week, I spent every day at this school. On the day of the funeral, another counselor and I went to the viewing to be there for the students and teachers and to express our sorrow for the family. At the funeral, we had a counselor available to sit with each grade (1–8) in case anyone had to leave the chapel due to distress. Afterward, we went back into the classrooms to process any feelings that came up during the funeral. The funeral was the last day of school before Christmas break began. The Smith boys were due back at school after the break, so I arranged to be at the school on their first day back.

As I'm sure was true for many involved in this crisis, that Christmas was a difficult one for me. It was hard to leave what was happening at work behind. It was hard to stop thinking about the children whose mother was no longer there for them on Christmas morning because she was dead due to the actions of their father, who was now in jail.

In the weeks that followed, I got in touch with one of the local hospital's grief support programs to get resource information for the family. The mother of Mrs. Smith got custody of the Smith boys and wanted to do everything she could to help her grandchildren. I provided counseling referrals for the grandmother, as she had lost her daughter. I got in touch with a certified trauma specialist and arranged for her to do a training session with the faculty and staff so that they would know more about what grief looks like in children and learn ways that they could support the Smith boys. Many hours were spent on the phone speaking with parents who knew Mrs. Smith well. Some of my time was also spent consulting with the Smith children's teachers about

(Continued)

the children's well-being and capacity for completing school work. I offered counseling to the students who were relatives or close family friends of the Smiths. For the second half of the school year, most of my one day per week at this school was spent responding to this crisis situation in one way or another.

Nearly ten months later, it appears as if the school community is healing. When this crisis first happened, there was national media coverage of this case, and not all of it was accurate. Every once in awhile the local news stations cover this story again, and this attention is difficult for the family and for the school community because it reopens the wounds that have begun to heal. I expect that when Mr. Smith's trial begins, the rumors will once again begin circulating throughout the school and uncomfortable feelings will surface. There is a chance that the healing that this school community has achieved until this point may be halted or set back.

Source: Katie Young, Professional School Counselor, Montgomery County Intermediate Unit, Nonpublic School Services Division, Pennsylvania.

Suicide

Suicide is a real problem in schools, particularly high schools, and professional school counselors need to be prepared to assess suicidal ideation, behaviors, and risk, as well as being ready to intervene decisively. As discussed in Chapter 5, some states and many school systems require that professional school counselors inform parents or guardians of students demonstrating suicidal thoughts or behaviors. One is well advised to take all threats seriously and be very familiar with state laws and regulations, as well as local school system policies and procedures. Although the next section focuses on assessment of suicidal threat, a comprehensive explanation of how to intervene in cases of student suicidal threat is well beyond the scope of this book. While the student is in the school, it is common practice to be sure the student is in the company of an adult at all times and that contact is made with a parent or guardian as soon as possible. Many school systems require that the parent pick the child up from school. Professional counselors can be valuable consultants to parents, facilitating transitions to treatment with mental health professionals, community agencies, or psychiatric inpatient facilities. Professional school counselors are well advised to find out the scope of community services available to students in crisis to develop a referral network that can be acted on instantaneously.

ASSESSING SUICIDAL IDEATION AND BEHAVIORS

Professional school counselors should pay close attention to student suicidal ideation and behaviors during an initial interview and revisit the issue periodically during the course of treatment. Nearly all suicides are avoidable. A current and thorough understanding of the prevalence statistics across population demographics is essential to effective practice. A brief presentation can be found in Table Table 14.2, and professional counselors are encouraged to delve more deeply into this area of the literature.

Predicting who will attempt suicide is extremely difficult, which is why experienced professional school counselors take every student with suicidal ideation very seriously. Depressed, suicidal students may appear at minimal risk one day and the next day may experience a situational, environmental stressor or a frustrating, negative interpersonal encounter that leads to an attempted suicide. D. C. Clark and Fawcett (1992) reported that 57% to 86% of suicides are related to depression and alcoholism, so pay particularly close attention to students with these conditions, with expressions of hopelessness and helplessness being key indicators.

In addition to assessing risk of suicide, professional school counselors should assess for resiliency and protective factors, activities, or people in a student's life that provide responsibilities, meaning, and hope for the student (Sanchez, 2001). Such factors may include significant supportive relationships (e.g., parents or relatives, friends, co-workers) or purpose (e.g., work or school, caregiving responsibilities).

When assessing suicidal risk, it is essential to determine both the existence and the intensity of suicidal thoughts and behaviors and to respond quickly and decisively with a treatment plan to immediately address student needs and safety. Table 14.3 presents the seven areas Stelmacher (1995) recommended as the focus during an interview for determining suicidal risk.

Several instruments have been published that professional school counselors may find useful adjuncts to the interview when assessing suicidal ideation and behaviors. These include the Suicide Probability Scale (SPS; Cull & Gill, 1992), Beck Scale for Suicide Ideation (BSSI; Beck & Steer, 1991), Beck Hopelessness Scale (BHS; Beck & Steer, 1993), and Suicide Ideation Questionnaire (SIQ; Reynolds, 1988). The SIQ was specifically designed for use with school-aged youth. Professional school counselors who use these instruments must use caution because of the potential for clients to underreport the severity of suicidal thoughts and behaviors. In addition, checklists and rating scales rarely differentially weight suicide risks. Thus, at most, scores should be used as helpful guidelines. As with most psychological tests, students who respond openly and honestly generally yield

---

TABLE 14.2 Demographic Parameters, Clinical Conditions, and Suicide Risk

---

Suicide is the 11th leading cause of death in the United States.

Suicide is the 3rd leading cause of death in the 15- to 24-year-old range and the 7th leading cause of death in the 5- to 14-year-old range.

Females are more likely to attempt suicide; males are more likely to complete a suicide attempt, generally because they choose more lethal means (e.g., guns).

73% of all suicides are completed by White males. Of these, the highest prevalence occurs in the over-85-years-old category.

Married clients are at lower risk of suicide than single, divorced, or widowed clients.

Parents responsible for minor children are at lower risk.

Individuals who have attempted suicide are more likely to make future attempts.

Clients with depression who have experienced a recent loss (e.g., divorce, separation) are at greater risk of suicide.

Certain personality factors may increase risk (e.g., perfectionism, impulsivity, pessimism, aloofness, dependency).

Clients with personality disorders (e.g., Borderline PD, Antisocial PD) account for about one-third of completed suicides.

Firearms account for nearly one-half of all suicides. Hanging, strangulation, and suffocation are the next three most lethal means. Taking most poisons and medications have low levels of lethality.

Of counselors in professional practice, about 70% have treated a client who attempted suicide, and 28% had a client who committed suicide.

Source: Statistics from *America's Children: Parents Report Estimated 2.7 Million Children with Emotional and Behavioral Problems*, by the National Institute of Mental Health, 2005, retrieved September 2, 2005, from www.nimh.nih.gov/healthinformation/childhood_indicators.cfm

accurate scores and interpretations; those who respond in a guarded or deceitful manner do not.

Violence and Threat Assessment

Several highly publicized school shootings have heightened public interest, and fears, related to school safety. Thankfully, such instances are rare, but unfortunately other types of school violence are not rare. Compared with a generation ago, students today are more likely to bring a weapon to school, fight on school grounds, and bully or harass other students.

BULLYING, HARASSMENT, ABUSE, AND DATING VIOLENCE Hazler and Denham (2002) noted that at-risk

---

TABLE 14.3 Seven Facets of Suicidal Risk Determination and Some Related Brief, Important Queries

---

1. *Verbal communication.* Has the student verbalized suicidal thoughts overtly or subtly? Are there themes of escape, self-mutilation, or self-punishment? Has the student ever thought of hurting herself?
2. *Plan.* Does the student have a plan or idea about how he may kill himself? Is the plan concrete, detailed, and specific? Is it feasible? Does it contain provisions to prevent rescue?
3. *Method.* Has the student chosen a specific method of self-harm? Firearms are the most lethal and commonly used method by students who complete suicide.
4. *Preparation.* Has the student obtained the means to carry out the plan? Has he written a note or contacted others to resolve old business, put finances in order, given away possessions, or "said good-bye"? Preparation is a good index of the seriousness of a suicidal attempt.
5. *Stressors.* What are the student's past, present, and future stressors (e.g., loss, employment, illness)? What are important loss-related anniversary dates?
6. *Mental state.* What is the student's degree of hopelessness? Is the student impulsive, using alcohol, or both? Is the student despondent, angry, or distraught? Particular concern is warranted during periods of remission (e.g., uplifted spirits) because this may indicate a decision to commit suicide was made and the plan is progressing.
7. *Hopelessness.* What is the student's level of perceived hopelessness? To what degree is death viewed as the only way to relieve pain? This area is particularly important to assess when students do not verbalize suicidal thoughts.

Source: Based on "Assessing Suicidal Clients," by Z. T. Stelmacher, in *Clinical Personality Assessment: Practical Approaches,* edited by J. N. Butcher, 1995, New York: Oxford University Press, pp. 336–379.

status stemmed from isolation from societal, cultural, school, family, or peer interactions and institutions. Such isolation may lead to victimization and perpetuation of violence in the forms of bullying and harassment, abuse and neglect, and suicide. A form of peer-on-peer abuse, bullying and harassment occur throughout American society (Hazler, 1998) and the world (P. K. Smith et al., 1999) and may serve as a contributing factor to homicide (Heide, 1999) and suicide (Carney, 2000). While these potentially devastating results have been infrequently observed, the more insidious long- and short-term influences of bullying and harassment may impact not only victims, but also perpetrators and bystanders (Janson, 2000).

Bullying and harassment are caused when an imbalance of power (e.g., social, physical, emotional) is created. It is maintained when others, including adults or peer bystanders, do not act to balance the inequalities (Hazler, Miller, Carney, & Green, 2001). Failure of adults and bystanders to act encourages perpetuation of the abusers' reputation as strong individuals and the victims' reputation as weak. The quickest way to interrupt the cycle of bullying or harassment is for adults and peers to intervene. Thus, teaching adults and peers the importance of intervening and how to effectively intervene is a critical role the professional school counselor can undertake. Bullying and harassment have become so problematic in schools that a number of states have passed antibullying and antiharassment legislation or regulations prohibiting these behaviors—accompanied by stiff consequences for school system employees who do not intervene appropriately. This area of prevention and intervention becomes a huge opportunity for teaching advocacy skills. Importantly, this includes "indirect" forms of harassment and bullying, such as spreading vicious, hurtful rumors or socially excluding a victim—called relational aggression.

Physical and sexual abuse and neglect are also widespread problems in society, often resulting in devastating long-term emotional problems, including anxiety, depression, substance abuse, and other serious psychiatric disturbances. Emotional and social isolation is particularly problematic with individuals who have been abused or neglected—a result of the embarrassment and secrecy endemic to the acts. This social and emotional isolation is not restricted to children who are directly abused; children who witness domestic abuse, as when their mother is battered, have similar isolative reactions (Weitzman, 1998). But violence in significant or intimate relationships is no longer related only to the home and kept behind closed doors.

Dating violence has experienced an unfortunate rise over the past decade and affects many teenagers. D. E. Howard and Wang (2003) reported that about 10% of high school girls reported dating violence, with the occurrence increasing to more than 15% in seniors. The Centers for Disease Control and Prevention's (2000) estimates ranged from 9% to 65%, depending on definitions and methodologies used; likely estimates of prevalence were 22% of high school seniors and 32% of college students. Victims of dating violence displayed increased risks of suicidal thoughts and actions, substance use, depression, and risky sexual behavior (D. E. Howard & Wang, 2003; Silverman, Raj, Mucci, & Hathaway, 2001).

THREAT ASSESSMENT   Violent acts committed on school property increased sharply during the 1980s, but, contrary to popular opinion, have been steadily declining since 1993 (Borum, 2000; Rollin, Kaiser-Ulrey, Potts, & Creason, 2003). Sensationalized school shootings in various parts of the United States have created a quite different public perception. One of the benefits of this attention is an increased research focus on the topic, both scholarly and governmental, particularly by the Federal Bureau of Investigation (FBI) and the U.S. Secret Service. Both of these agencies have developed protocols and procedures that have been used by school crisis management and public safety specialists. Their reports can be accessed, respectively, at www.fbi.gov/publications/school/school2.pdf and www.ustreas.gov/USSS. While much of what follows was developed to understand school shooters, a great deal of the information generalizes to less drastic forms of school violence.

From the outset, it is important for professional school counselors to understand that there is no foolproof profile of violent youth or list of risk factors that allows certain identification of youth as violent. Indeed, the research is clear that the majority of youth who display multiple risk factors never become violent offenders. Likewise, many violent offenders do not display many of the risk factors commonly considered by experts to indicate increased risk. Violence, by its nature, is unpredictable. Also, an exclusive focus on identification, to the exclusion of prevention and intervention, is misguided. Threat assessment, developmental programming, prevention, and intervention are all part of a comprehensive school safety program. Threat assessment is an important facet that will be expounded on below. The developmental, prevention, and intervention facets will be addressed at the end of this section and later in this chapter in the section that deals with conflict resolution and peer mediation.

Historically, mental health practitioners have been no better at predicting violent behavior in clients than informed nonprofessionals have been; recent innovations have improved predictability somewhat, although the accuracy is very far from perfect. Importantly, violence is brought on by multiple factors, not just one, making it a complex problem, from both diagnostic and treatment perspectives.

Most violent students are not planful, although exceptions certainly exist. Violent students often feel desperate and panic stricken, fearing that others want to hurt them. Striking out violently is a means of defense and, at times, retribution. In general, males aged 15 to 24 have a higher risk of violence. Race is not ordinarily associated with violence risk, but students with lower socioeconomic status have higher associated risks. Students with thought disorders (e.g., hallucinations, delusions) and disorders of impulse (e.g., AD/HD, conduct disorder) present with higher degrees of risk. Of course, those with a history of violent acts are at greater risk for future violent acts (F. R. Wilson, 2004). Environmental risk factors include unstable family and peer relationships, association with criminal or sexual predators, association with antisocial peers, educational problems, and living in an urban environment.

Specific to school shooting incidences, motivation includes revenge for social isolation and bullying. The FBI reported that attackers frequently engage in "behaviors of concern," although not necessarily aberrant behaviors, prior to the incident. Most of the time, the attacker revealed his plan to at least one other person not involved in the attack, and most had access to guns and previous experience using guns. Finally, although the notion of a school shooter as a loner is often true, this is certainly not always the case.

The FBI defines a threat as intent to do harm or act out violently against someone or something. It classifies threats of violence into four categories.

1. *Indirect threats* are ambiguous and vague, but with implied violence. The phrasing of an indirect threat ordinarily suggests that a violent act may occur, not necessarily that it will occur.
2. *Veiled threats* do not specifically threaten violence, but strongly infer the possibility.
3. *Conditional threats* warn of violence if certain conditions or demands are not met (e.g., extortion).
4. *Direct threats* are clear, straightforward, and explicit warnings of a specific act against a specific target.

The FBI also presented guidelines for determining the seriousness of a threat. *Low-level threats* are vague and indirect, lack realism, and pose minimal risks to the victim or public. The specific content of a low-level threat ordinarily leads to the conclusion that the student is unlikely to carry out the threatened act of violence. *Medium-level threats* are somewhat more direct, concrete, and plausible than low-level threats are, but frequently they do not appear entirely realistic. Some evidence of rudimentary planning is often apparent (e.g., place, time, method), but the plan lacks detail, and preparations to fulfill the plan are absent. Often students making a medium-level threat will state "I mean it" to convey a seriousness to the threat. A *high-level threat* is direct, specific, and plausible, with a serious and imminent danger to the safety of the victim or public. Plans have been made and concrete steps have been taken to prepare for the act (e.g., obtaining weapon). High-level threats almost always require the involvement of law enforcement officials.

When assessing threat, the FBI suggests a "four-pronged assessment model" involving attention to the student's personality, family dynamics, school dynamics, and social dynamics. Table 14.4 provides specific facets of each of these areas that the professional school counselor should attend to during a threat assessment. The literature is replete with suggestions for helping to mitigate and minimize violence. Table 14.5 provides a short list.

The U.S. surgeon general reported that commitment to school, intelligence, intolerance toward deviance, and a positive social orientation were important protective factors (U.S. Public Health Service Office of Surgeon General, 2001). Adult mentoring programs have also had positive effects (Catalano, Loeber, & McKinney, 1999), as have programs designed to enhance positive social interaction, decision making, and problem solving. Finally, one cannot overemphasize the essential impact that a hopeful and rewarding future career can play in bolstering the motivations and attitudes of adolescents.

| VOICES FROM THE FIELD 14.2 | VERBAL THREATS AND THE LANGUAGE OF VIOLENCE |

A greater use of violent language may also be considered a societal trend or crisis that professional school counselors will have to face. More and more students resort to the use of verbal threats to express their frustration and anger. If children are not taught appropriate ways to express anger, some may feel that the only way they can really express their strong emotions is to threaten violence against their entire class or specific groups of people. Others may "wish that they wouldn't wake up sometimes." I have had teachers and administrators report to me that students have said these things when they have been in trouble during class or when they are harassed by their peers. It amazes me that students realize that this language will result in grand amounts of attention. While assessing the severity of a threat, the majority of the time students tell me that they were just angry or that they didn't really mean what they said. Most students do not realize how seriously adults, and the school system as a whole, must interpret

(Continued)

these comments. Even after the realization of the consequences for this expression of anger or frustration, some students will repeatedly use these statements to express their anger.

When informing parents of their child's statements, parents usually seem to be extremely concerned. Some say they think it may be an attention-getting tactic. Whatever it may be, I reassure parents that this is not something that children typically say and that they may want to consider arranging for therapy outside of school or having the child evaluated by another professional. Most parents are extremely receptive to this information, although I have encountered some who do not view the event to be significant enough to warrant additional mental health attention for their child. Along with the many types of harassment, threats seem to be more commonly used by today's youth.

Source: Lacey Wallace, Professional School Counselor, Manor View Elementary, Anne Arundel County Public Schools, Maryland

---

TABLE 14.4   The FBI's Four-Pronged Assessment Model for Conducting a Threat Assessment

Prong 1: Personality of the Student

- Leakage (intentional or unintentional revelation of clues to an impending violent act)
- Low tolerance for frustration
- Poor coping skills
- Lack of resiliency
- Failed love relationship
- "Injustice collector" (resentment over real or perceived injustices)
- Signs of depression
- Narcissism (self-centeredness)
- Alienation
- Dehumanizes others
- Lack of empathy
- Exaggerated sense of entitlement
- Attitude of superiority
- Exaggerated or pathological need for attention
- Externalizes blame
- Masks low self-esteem
- Anger-management problems
- Intolerance
- Inappropriate humor
- Seeks to manipulate others
- Lack of trust
- Closed social group
- Change in behavior
- Rigid and opinionated
- Unusual interest in sensationalized violence
- Fascination with violence-filled entertainment
- Negative role models
- Behavior appears relevant to carrying out a threat

Prong 2: Family Dynamics

- Turbulent parent–child relationship
- Acceptance of pathological behavior
- Access to weapons
- Lack of intimacy
- Student "rules the roost"
- No limits or monitoring of TV and Internet

Prong 3: School Dynamics (from the student's perspective)

- Student's attachment to school
- Tolerance for disrespectful behavior (bullying)
- Inequitable discipline
- Inflexible culture
- Pecking order among students
- Code of silence
- Unsupervised computer access

Prong 4: Social Dynamics

- Media, entertainment, technology
- Peer groups
- Drugs and alcohol
- Outside interests
- The copycat effect

Source: From *The School Shooter: A Threat Assessment Perspective*, by the Federal Bureau of Investigation, 2005. Retrieved September 2, 2005, from www.fbi.gov/publications/school/school2.pdf

Substance Abuse

Substance abuse is a substantial problem in society and has reached an alarming level among children and adolescents. The Substance Abuse and Mental Health Services Administration (SAMHSA; 2008) estimated than nearly one-third of youth aged 12 to 20 drank alcohol in the previous month and as many as 10% of youth in this age group abused, or were dependent on, alcohol. Clients with substance abuse problems ranged between 12% and 30%, depending on the treatment setting. While substance abuse counselors receive specialized training in the assessment, diagnosis, and treatment of substance disorders and professional school counselors may serve more as referral sources than as providers of actual treatment in the school

context, professional school counselors must, at the very least, become proficient in substance abuse assessment to ensure that students get much-needed services. Similar to the assessment of suicidal thoughts and behaviors, assessment of substance abuse is best conducted early in the counseling process so that a comprehensive treatment program can be implemented.

Fortunately, self-reports of substance use are pretty reliable (F. G. Miller, 2001), although certainly not with all clients. During an initial interview, it is important to explore with the student any and all medications and substances being taken, including over-the-counter, prescription, alcohol, and illegal substances. Such a survey of substances helps the professional school counselor to understand potential for abuse, as well as whether use of

---

TABLE 14.5   Suggestions for Preventing Violence and Intervening with Violent Youth

1. Increase the quality and frequency of peer contacts.
2. Create a sense of hope and feelings of togetherness in the school and community.
3. Teach and role-play interpersonal and social skills in real-life situations.
4. Establish a clear districtwide policy for exploring and dealing with allegations of violence, bullying, harassment, abuse, and neglect.
5. Encourage participation in mentoring programs (e.g., Big Brother, Big Sister).
6. Develop and train a threat assessment team in each school.
7. Establish a peer mentoring program in the school to address needs of new and socially isolated students.
8. Collaborate with law enforcement, faith leaders, and representatives of social service agencies.
9. Create a school climate of trust between adults and students.
10. Help parents, guardians, and other adults in the life of the child make systematic connections in the community. Socially and emotionally isolated students often have socially and emotionally isolated caretakers.
11. Above all, provide supportive intervention services to potential offenders. This connection with a caring professional school counselor may make all the difference!

such substances may cause side effects of concern. The most recent edition of the *Physician's Desk Reference* is an excellent source of information on drugs and side effects.

Because self-report of substance use is fairly reliable, professional school counselors often use a straightforward interviewing approach. Table 14.6 includes some commonly asked questions that professional school counselors can include in an initial interview to directly assess for substance use and abuse. Another brief, but classic interview method designed for alcohol abuse screening, but which can be easily adapted to other substances, uses the acronym CAGE (Mayfield, McLeod, & Hall, 1974):

C – Have you ever felt you need to **Cut down** on your drinking?

A – Have people **Annoyed** you by criticizing your drinking?

G – Have you ever felt bad or **Guilty** about drinking?

E – Have you ever had a drink first thing in the morning to steady your nerves or get rid of a hangover (**Eye opener**)?

Client responses to a brief screening device such as CAGE can lead the professional counselor to suspect alcohol or other drug abuse and use more formalized or systematic data collection procedures. While there are a number of tests designed to assess for substance abuse issues, the most popular for use with adolescents is the Substance Abuse Subtle Screening Inventory–Adolescent 2 (SASSI–A2; F. G. Miller, 2001).

Grief Work and Children from Changing Families

Any time you experience a loss, you grieve. Sometimes the grief passes in a few moments, such as when a student gets an unexpected poor grade on an exam or when a teenage girl is informed she will not be allowed to carouse with her friends at the mall because Grandma is coming for a visit. Other times, the loss is so profound that recovery may take months, years, or longer. For example, when a parent or sibling dies or when parents separate or divorce, children and adolescents often experience a long emotional road before accepting the loss and moving on. Sometimes these youngsters never do recover properly. Professional school counselors encounter children with grief reactions quite frequently, so some mention of strategies and interventions is appropriate. Most grief reactions share commonalities. This section will focus on helping mitigate grief reactions in youth from changing families, the grief-inducing circumstance most commonly encountered by school-aged youth. First, a review of relevant extant literature will be presented, followed by strategies and interventions. Importantly, most of the interventions are applicable to work with groups or individuals.

UNDERSTANDING THE EFFECTS OF DIVORCE   There is a large, rich literature base on children of divorce. A generally accepted conclusion of this research is that most children adjust well to divorce, although, on average, older children experience more negative outcomes (Amato, 2000). Importantly, Amato (2000) and Heatherington (1999) reported that the majority of children from divorced families are emotionally well adjusted, contrary to popular cultural mythology. However, there are a number of risk and resiliency factors that play into the mix. Grych and Fincham (2001) and Whiteside and Becker (2000) identified interparental conflict as the primary risk factor associated with negative outcome. Heatherington (1999) found gender, poor-quality parenting, and lack of contact with the father to be additional risk factors. It is essential to understand from the outset that these factors are family process variables, not family structure variables (Demo & Acock, 1996; Voydanoff & Donnelly, 1998). That is, negative emotional and social outcomes can be expected of

---

TABLE 14.6   Useful Questions When Screening for Potential Substance Abuse

1. Do you take any over-the-counter medications? If yes . . . What is it called? What do you take it for? How much? How often? Side effects?
2. Do you take any prescription medications? If yes . . . What is it called? What do you take it for? How much? How often? Side effects?
3. Do you take any other drug or substances? If yes . . . What is it called? What effect does it have on you? How much? How often? Side effects? When did you start?
4. Do you drink alcohol? If yes . . . What kind? How much? How often? How does it affect you? When did you start?
5. With whom do you drink (take drugs)?
6. Has drinking (taking drugs) caused you problems (financial, legal, family, friends, at work)?
7. Has anyone ever suggested you have a problem with drinking (taking drugs)? Who? What makes them say this?
8. Have you ever tried to quit? Successful for how long? What happened (withdrawal, symptoms, relapse)?

children from nondivorced families if many of these risk factors are evident. In other words, it is not difficult to imagine or conclude that many children growing up in an intact family in which the parents are in conflict, provide low-quality parenting, or have an uninvolved father would be at a disadvantage. Still, when compared to peers from nondivorced families, adolescents from divorced families demonstrate, on average, more depression, greater conflict with parents, poorer school performance, and higher levels of aggression and disruptive behavior (Demo & Acock, 1996).

Numerous resiliency and protective factors have been observed to ameliorate the potential negative effects of divorce. Protective factors are characteristics or environmental facets that serve as buffers against stressors and harmful forces. In some ways, protective factors are on the opposite end of the spectrum from risk factors. Researchers have identified a number of resiliency or protective factors associated with positive outcomes for children of divorce, including interparental cooperation and diminished conflict following the divorce (Whiteside &

Becker, 2000), competent parenting from custodial parents (Amato, 2000; Emery, Kitzman, & Waldron, 1999; Heatherington, 1999; Krishnakumer & Buehler, 2000), and contact with and competent parenting from nonresidential parents (Amato & Gilbreth, 1999; Bauserman, 2002). Relationships and activities outside of the family also frequently serve as important buffers. Having a trusting relationship with a nonparental adult (Masten & Coatworth, 1998) and peers and having positive school experiences may all play a protective role.

While divorce continues to be a troubling societal issue and its effects on children can be grief inducing, emotionally draining, and even at times traumatic, it is critical for professional school counselors to understand that 75% to 80% of children and young adults from divorced families do not experience major psychological problems (e.g., depression), aspire to and achieve career or higher educational goals, and enjoy intimate relationships as adults (Amato, 2000; Larmann-Billings & Emery, 2000; McLanahan, 1999). Indeed, some researchers (Kelly & Emery, 2003) have concluded that factors prior to the

---

VOICES FROM THE FIELD 14.3   **CUSTODY AND THE PROFESSIONAL SCHOOL COUNSELOR**

Although divorce is not necessarily a current societal issue, the experiences children face as a result of divorce are becoming more complex. In the past, the majority of children may have stayed together under the custody of one parent. Recently, children are more frequently separated among their parents, where a mother may have custody of one child and a father may have custody of two of the children. Sometimes these children may even be separated by thousands of miles. Children are no longer losing only a parent as a result of divorce; in some cases, they are also losing half of their once existing family. More and more fathers are gaining custody of children, whereas in the past we may have seen more mothers with custody, and parents are remarrying multiple times, which may lead to complicated step-sibling situations.

I have reviewed incoming folders of new students to find restraining orders against a parent due to violent threats or acts against the other parent. I have read restraining orders due to one parent's attempt to kidnap the children from the other parent. As a professional school counselor, it is extremely important to note the situations of these students to be sure that the number one duty is fulfilled, to keep children safe. These aggressive and threatening parental relationships can have a significant impact on a child's well-being.

Complex custody issues have made my job as a professional school counselor especially complicated. Since divorce is so common in our society, custody battles may be just as common. I find it extremely important to review divorce documents discussing custody to ensure that I do not divulge information to a noncustodial parent. As parents contact me on a daily basis, I have to be aware of which parent has access to educational information and the right to make educational decisions for their children. Already, I have encountered a woman who has been remarried for all six years of her child's life, yet the stepfather is not the legal guardian. It is necessary to request that the mother be present when educational decisions are made or that legal documentation of the stepfather's guardianship be provided.

These are just a handful of the current issues that children may experience as a result of new trends of divorce. They bring about a number of cautionary practices that are necessary to ensure our students' safety. New interventions and practices must be employed to meet the needs of this student population.

Source: Lacey Wallace, Professional School Counselor, Manor View Elementary, Anne Arundel County Public Schools, Maryland

divorce, such as the degree of marital conflict or the child's ability to adjust to emotional and social circumstances, may be more indicative of long-term social adjustment and mental health.

A PRIMER ON GRIEF WORK   Various researchers and authors have discussed reactions to grief as a developmental process proceeding through stages similar to those discussed by Kübler-Ross (1969) in her classic work, *On Death and Dying*:

- *Stage 1: Shock and denial*—the individual is in disbelief that the event has occurred. Anxiety is heightened, but ordinarily decreases as fears are pinpointed.
- *State 2: Anger*—a period of rage is generally accompanied by an awareness of unfair treatment. Individuals often ask questions such as "Why me?" or "What did I do to deserve this?"
- *Stage 3: Guilt*—feelings arise that the individual may have contributed to the situation or done something to deserve it. Some may try to bargain with others (including God) to change what has happened. Generally, fear and anger decrease as fewer conditions for forgiveness are set.
- *Stage 4: Hopelessness/Depression*—individuals experience loneliness and feelings of sadness and hopelessness. This is often the longest stage and ordinarily becomes so uncomfortable that the individual becomes motivated to move on.
- *Stage 5: Acceptance*—the stage involves moving on from the event and readjusting to one's new life situation. Fears and anxieties are frequently harnessed and used as energy to propel the individual in new directions.

Many of the physical symptoms associated with grief reactions are similar to those of depression: fatigue, loss of or increase in appetite, loss of concentration, feelings of hopelessness and isolation, frequent sighing or breathlessness, and aches and pains. The intensity of the grief experience is usually determined by a combination of factors, including one's relationship to the person who was lost (e.g., parent, spouse, cousin, neighbor), the intensity of or ambivalence toward that relationship, the dependency or security provided by that relationship, how the loss occurred (e.g., single vs. multiple events, knowledge ahead of time), one's personality (e.g., hardiness, resilience, mental illness), history of dealing with grief experiences, and individual characteristics (e.g., sex, age, cultural determinants). A number of obstacles to effective grieving have been identified, including sudden

loss (e.g., no warning, no chance to say good-bye), lack of finality or uncertain loss (possibility that things may still work out), lack of support, and the perception that grief is a weakness and should be avoided or denied.

Helping students deal with grief is a common service provided by professional school counselors. If the student is experiencing "complicated grief," specialized counseling services are usually required, and an immediate referral should be made. But in the context of developmental grief reactions, the professional school counselor should continuously remind the student that the symptoms and reactions are normal and that life and emotional health will get better in time. Professional school counselors can help students resolve the four primary tasks of grieving (Worden, 2002). The first task is to accept the reality of the loss, usually by talking about the loss and integrating the reality of the situation on both the intellectual and the emotional levels. The second task is to experience (not avoid) the pain of the grief. Worden referred to this task as the "bleeding stage" of grief, when the student must experience the pain of the grief reaction internally and externally. The third task is adjusting to life without the lost object or condition. This usually involves accepting help from others, acknowledging limitations, and performing new coping skills and activities on one's own. The final task involves emotionally relocating the loss and moving on with life. This requires students to reinvest energy from the lost relationship into new relationships or activities, as well as to find an appropriate place for the loss inside one's emotional psyche.

While helping students to resolve these tasks of grieving, professional school counselors should use good listening and communication skills, use questions sparingly, and honor silence when possible. Try to adjust to and connect with their mood or emotional state and be fully attentive to them. Help them to talk about the loss at a pace comfortable to them. Provide a safe place for and encourage emotional release (e.g., crying, raging, ranting, complaining) and offer assistance in practical as well as emotionally supportive ways. Help students to maintain helpful routines and encourage them to find a way to resolve the loss. Encourage social support (e.g., peers, caring adults), bibliotherapy, and journal writing. Also help the students keep busy in meaningful activities (including volunteering) and take care of their physical health. Finally, professional school counselors should always be alert for signs of complicated grief or other signs of trouble (e.g., extreme behavior changes, suicidal or homicidal ideation, changes in eating or sleeping habits, substance abuse). Refer these students to community mental health practices as appropriate.

IN TIMES OF CRISIS

Many of our students view school as "home." During times of hardship, school is the place where students feel a sense of structure, acceptance, and belonging. The faculty and staff work hard to help students feel connected to their school, and all of us (professional counselors, teachers, administrators, custodians, nurse, psychologist, school resource officer, school probation officer) work together to ensure that all of our students have at least one adult in the building who they feel a connection with and can approach in times of need. We also work with outside agencies that send clinical counselors into the school to meet with identified students and attend our meetings to report progress so that we can do our part to help the students achieve desirable goals.

On a schoolwide level, students are polled and asked to identify adults in the building who they feel a connection with and can go to in times of need. Additionally, the faculty and staff are asked to identify students, from a list of the total school population of over 1,500 students, with whom they have a connection. Any students who are not identified are then recognized and looked in on by faculty members to help them establish some kind of connection.

Additionally, as a school, we have set up programs to help students feel connected to their school. This year we had a freshmen connection day before the school year started and offered games, prizes, food, face painting, and so on to the freshmen who attended the event. We had a big turnout of students and faculty, and the event helped students meet other students and faculty members to help with the transition and ease the apprehension of attending high school.

Also, students have the same homeroom advisor each year in an effort to make nonacademic connections with adults. We provide remediation classes and after-school sessions for students who have not been successful with standardized tests needed as a graduation requirement, as well as academic tutoring for all students. Our pupil personnel worker has been instrumental in working with students who have high absentee rates, and as a result, our attendance rates have risen over the past couple of years. Furthermore, we work closely with our Parent Teacher Student Association (PTSA) so that teachers and parents can work together to help students stay on the path to success. All of these strategies help students with complex problems persist in school, as well as forming a bond with someone in the school setting.

As a counselor at the high school level, my roles are very diverse. I embrace every opportunity I have to connect with students, since most students want to know someone cares and will listen and help to steer them in the right direction. Many of my students who could benefit from treatment do not receive any outside of the school setting, so I may be the first line of defense in helping to steer them in a direction to get the help that they need or in providing limited services within the school. Establishing rapport is key, and presenting lessons in the classroom, being present in the hallways and cafeteria, attending after-school activities, running groups, and meeting with students individually are all ways I connect with students and build a strong rapport. Providing career and vocational counseling and assisting with the college application process are important in helping students establish realistic goals. Also, I run a group with students with complex problems and incorporate creative arts into the counseling process. I have seen much success with these students, as the arts helps them express their feelings and thoughts so that we can work toward achieving individual goals, such as overcoming obstacles, being successful in school, and receiving a high school diploma.

In conclusion, many of our students turn to the school in times of crisis and look to the faculty and staff to assist during these times. A couple of years ago, a sibling of a former student was killed on her way to school. The deceased student's older brother, who had graduated several years earlier, came to school that day to find support and comfort from those members of the faculty with whom he had built a strong rapport. He is just one example of the many students who return to school for numerous reasons to visit faculty/staff members and maintain that connection that developed during the years they attended school. As a professional school counselor, I am an advocate for students and do what I can to empower students, offer them support, and connect them with resources available in the community to help them to overcome obstacles and reach their goals and become successful members of society.

Source: Tricia Uppercue, Professional School Counselor, Aberdeen High School, Harford County Public Schools, Aberdeen, Maryland

Another current issue children may be forced to deal with is the reality of a parent's deployment to another country to serve in war. Although war is not necessarily a new concept for the United States, it is something that our country has not had to face in a number of years. The War in Iraq has greatly affected us here at home, but one particular way in which is has affected our country is one that most may not think of on a daily basis. Working on a military base has provided me with ample opportunity to witness the effects of the war on the families and children of America. Not only is at least one student in every classroom experiencing this separation from a parent, but also they are experiencing the fear of losing a parent to death, on a daily basis.

There was a student who visited the nurse three times in one day, complaining of a stomach ache, but did not wish to go home sick. When the nurse called home to ask the parent if she thought it would be appropriate to pick her child up from school, she disclosed that her husband was scheduled to return home from Iraq two nights prior, yet they still had not heard any news. The nurse immediately approached me to discuss the situation. These psychosomatic symptoms are common for children who are experiencing stress of all different kinds. However, many children are not able to understand the connection between their mental and physical states. I spent some time with the student shortly afterwards to "see how her year was going so far." During this time, she brought her father up a number of times. I asked a handful of open questions about her favorite memories with dad, what she loved most about him, and drew him a picture to send to Iraq. Later that day, I stopped into her classroom to see how she was feeling. I asked her how she was feeling, and she looked at me with a smile and chimed, "My stomach doesn't hurt any more." A precious memory, to be sure!

I have conversed with a handful of parents whose spouses were deployed. They report feelings of hopeless and feel lost without their significant other. Parents request information to facilitate talking to their children about deployment and information about local parent support

groups. Parents also request that I check in with their children to process the changes at home with them. As I have seen so far, most children are sad, yet extremely resilient. The parents may be the ones with greater concerns that also need to be tended to in every way possible. Parent support groups, workshops, and student groups are only a few of the avenues to attend to these needs of the community.

When parents return from war there are even more needs of both children and parents to be addressed. Soldiers may return with physical and mental wounds. A lack of medical and mental health attention may also be an issue. A parent with Posttraumatic Stress Disorder can affect a child in many ways. A mother called me this year to inform me of her husband's violent streak due to PTSD. Her husband had become physically and verbally aggressive toward her, and her son had witnessed these acts. This boy was so confused as to what had changed his father's demeanor from calm and passive to aggressive and argumentative. How can we expect children to understand the effects that war has on a person? These are just a few of the effects today's war has on the children and families of American soldiers.

The current issues facing today's youth reinforce the need for and importance of professional school counselors. Although working with this high-needs population feels like a whirlwind at times, it is also an extremely fulfilling experience. The sense of making a difference in the lives of children is always apparent when working with this population. Despite the frantic pace and the feeling that there are not enough hours in a day to address the needs of all of the students in my school, there is not a day that goes by that I have not addressed a serious issue that a child is very concerned about. What would these children do without a professional school counselor? That is the question that reminds me that the stress and busy days are worth it. After all, I am here for the children.

Source: Lacey Wallace, Professional School Counselor, Manor View Elementary, Anne Arundel County Public Schools, Maryland

Dropout Prevention

Because students who experience academic failure drop out at significantly high rates, a large part of successful programming involves dropout prevention. Recent research has identified a number of factors that contribute to or reduce dropout risk in students (Lehr, Johnson, Bremer, Cosio, & Thompson, 2004). Some risk

factors are fixed and not subject to change. However, many of the factors associated with dropout risk are alterable, including high rates of absenteeism and tardiness, low grades, a history of course failure, limited parental support, low participation in extracurricular activities, alcohol or drug problems, negative attitudes toward school, high levels of mobility, and grade retention. In addition, there are factors that provide protection to students with other risk factors; these preventive factors relate to increased likelihood of persisting in school despite difficulties. Some preventive factors include more time in general education for students with disabilities, provision of tutoring services, training for competitive employment and independent living, and attendance at schools that maintain high expectations for all students. In addition, students with complex problems who remained in school reported participating in a "relevant" high school curriculum, receiving significant support from teachers, perceiving positive attitudes from teachers and administrators, and benefiting from improvements in curriculum and instruction (e.g., additional assistance, better teaching, more interesting classes, better textbooks).

Taking risk factors and preventive factors into account, most dropout interventions seek to enhance students' sense of belonging in school; foster the development of relationships with teachers, administrators, and peers; improve academic success; address personal problems through counseling; and provide skill-building opportunities in behavior and social skills. Reviews of effective dropout intervention programs found that most of these interventions could be categorized according to the following types (Lehr, Hansen, Sinclair, & Christenson, 2003).

- Personal/affective (e.g., retreats designed to enhance self-esteem, regularly scheduled classroom-based discussion, individual counseling, participation in an interpersonal relations class)
- Academic (e.g., provision of special academic courses, individualized methods of instruction, tutoring)
- Family outreach (e.g., strategies that include increased feedback to parents or home visits)
- School structure (e.g., implementation of school within a school, redefinition of the role of the homeroom teacher, reduced class size, creation of an alternative school)
- Work related (e.g., vocational training, participation in volunteer or service programs)

Professional school counselors can help develop and implement schoolwide dropout prevention programs, using risk screenings to identify students at highest risk and promoting some of the key components related to school completion. Table 14.7 lists key intervention components synthesized from the research on dropout prevention and increasing school completion (Lehr et al., 2004) that are particularly appropriate for initiation or support by professional school counselors.

Conflict Resolution and Peer Mediation Program Development

Most schools implement some systemic or developmental program to help students mediate and resolve conflict. The development of any conflict resolution or peer mediation program or intervention should reflect the unique contextual needs of the school or district to be served. Climate assessment and strategies for systemic change are integral to program development, as are diversity considerations in the recruitment, selection, and training of peer mediators, in circumstances where a school system implements a peer mediation program.

ASSESSING CLIMATE Prior to proposing a conflict resolution–peer mediation program, careful assessment of school culture and climate is essential. It is particularly relevant to gain an understanding of the atmosphere of competition versus collaboration that characterizes most schools, as well as the systemic patterns, policies, and procedures that sustain and promote imbalances in power and the prejudice and discrimination directed at any disenfranchised population. It is also necessary to understand the structure of competition in the school. The ultimate goal of competition is to win, thus creating a loser. Winning rarely results in maintaining good relationships, understanding each other's perspectives, or accepting the legitimacy of others' needs and feelings. Conversely, in a cooperative win–win environment, there exists a commitment to developing mutual goals beneficial to all, while preserving positive relationships that honor and respect multiple perspectives (D. W. Johnson & Johnson, 1995b).

The implementation of a cooperative school environment in which to manage conflict seems appropriate, given the positive effects of cooperative learning on cognitive and social development. However, opponents of school conflict resolution programs believe that these programs cover the real causes of conflict without focusing on the policies and practices of the adults who hold power. Essentially, the opponents of peer mediation and conflict resolution programs seem to be advocating attention to the issues that create intractable conflict (i.e., resolution resistant conflict). These issues are woven into the fabric of educational practices and contribute to the inequity that fuels the inevitable conflict of differing attitudes, values, and beliefs. For example, academic tracking and inconsistent policies and practices in attendance, discipline, and entrance into extracurricular activities can create inequities for students from low-income and underserved populations, based on policies that sort and select students, often diminishing access to and equity in educational opportunity. Student and parent/guardian awareness of these inequities causes

---

TABLE 14.7   Key Dropout Prevention Interventions

Provide environmental support:

- Help provide a structured environment that includes clear and equitably enforced behavioral expectations.
- Monitor the occurrence of risk behaviors, regularly collect data, and measure the effects of timely interventions.

Provide counseling support:

- Provide individual behavioral assistance.
- Help students address personal and family issues through counseling and access to social services.
- Help students with personal problems (e.g., on-site health care, availability of individual and group counseling).
- Develop students' problem-solving skills and enhance skills to meet the demands of the school environment.
- Provide conflict resolution and violence prevention programs to enhance effective interpersonal skills.

Enhance relationships and affiliation:

- Incorporate personalization by creating meaningful and supportive bonds between students and teachers and among students.
- Create a caring and supportive environment (e.g., use of adult mentors, expanding role of homeroom teachers, organizing extracurricular activities).
- Promote additional opportunities for the student to form bonding relationships and include tutoring, service learning, alternative schooling, and out-of-school enhancement programs.
- Foster students' connections to school and sense of belonging to the community of students and staff (e.g., clubs, team activities, intraschool competition, retreats).

Provide/support vocational programming:

- Provide vocational education that has an occupational concentration.
- Provide career counseling and life-skills instruction.
- Coordinate the academic and vocational components of participants' high school programs.
- Communicate the relevance of education to future endeavors (e.g., offer vocational and career counseling, flexible scheduling, and work-study programs).

Bolster outside influences:

- Recognize the importance of families in the success of their children's school achievement and school completion.
- Link with the wider community through systemic renewal, community collaboration, career education, and school-to-work programs.

---

conflict as students and parents/guardians strive to meet their needs satisfactorily.

Using Maslow's need theory, conflict theorists suggest that need is a motivating factor in intractable conflict and will go on indefinitely, as human needs are not negotiable (Conflict Information Consortium, 2000a). Most relevant to schools is conflict over the need for identity, a salient factor in racial, ethnic, gender, and family conflicts (Conflict Information Consortium, 2000b). Of additional concern are issues of dominance that reflect a power structure and hierarchy of "one up, one down" or "one group up, one group down." Students are keenly aware of inequities in power. When conflict arises and is peer mediated, the two disputants may come to an agreement to fight no more, but the underlying unmet needs have not been addressed. Unless students believe their needs can be met satisfactorily, the conflict will continue (Conflict Information Consortium, 2000c). However, if the issues that undergird intractable conflict are brought to light by a peer mediation program and are addressed from an institutional perspective, then the program takes an active role in institutional change, and the process becomes part of the framework of a transformed school climate and culture. This affords students a venue for meeting their needs while saving face (Conflict Information Consortium, 2000d). This process suggests the need for conflict resolution training for all members of the school community. Teachers cannot impart feelings and principles of empowerment to their students if they feel estranged from their colleagues and the school in which they work. Transformation of school culture and climate is a slow process that requires careful assessment of the unique structure and assumptions of a school, but it is well worth the effort.

SYSTEMIC CHANGE Resolving conflicts and preventing violence are interrelated (D. W. Johnson & Johnson, 1995a). The relationship between initiatives addressing conflict resolution and youth violence reduction warrants attention to a systemic change model that targets youth violence. Hazler (1998) suggested that successful school programs recognize violence as a developmental issue, with various grade-level interventions that are both preventive and remedial. Then, efforts to create a high level of personal and community awareness and participation in conflict resolution and peer mediation programs can stimulate collective power and share information about similarities and differences that is useful in formulating solutions. Efforts of the collective whole lead to change in daily patterns of the majority of the school, rather than isolated changes for only a few. Given that change is difficult, invitational strategies that involve all concerned stakeholders in planning and implementing change, address formal and informal policies, give attention to the needs of diverse constituents, and personalize and maintain involvement of all parties are essential. Student involvement in the change process broadens role expectation beyond the classroom setting. These opportunities encourage more-genuine renegotiated relationships and roles between students and school personnel. As teachers broaden their roles in systemic change initiatives, they become empowered and actively involved in redefining the school culture and climate.

Administrative support is vital to systemic change efforts, as principals are responsible for promoting the overall school mission through the efforts of school personnel. Therefore, administrators need to trust that change efforts will be carried out appropriately through a process defined by clear goals and objectives that foster and complement existing efforts and priorities. Because multilevel interventions reach beyond the school, the inclusion of families and the school community is essential.

DIVERSITY CONSIDERATIONS IN RECRUITMENT, SELECTION, AND TRAINING OF PEER MEDIATORS Peer mediation programs are used in many schools either as stand-alone programs or in conjunction with other initiatives. Because these programs put students in leadership roles, it is essential that peer mediators represent the multiple diversities of the school. In this way, programs demonstrate an appreciation for the dynamic worldview and cultural complexity of students and school personnel (Graham & Pulvino, 2000). In this way, initiatives are inclusive and contribute to a balance in power as both an institutional and a programmatic objective. Specifically, when developing new programs and revising existing peer mediation programs to reflect the pluralistic composition of schools, examination of three factors—recruitment, selection, and training—is necessary. The diverse populations of schools—differentiated by age, race or ethnicity, disability, socioeconomic status, and academic ability—need to be reflected in programming. The basic goal in addressing difference is to assist students and school personnel in recognizing diversity as a resource, not a point of contention.

Empowering students to be leaders and role models is an essential step toward creating and maintaining a school environment that prevents harassment and violence (Wessler & Preble, 2003). Some groups of students who feel disenfranchised from the school community distance themselves from participation in extracurricular activities. As a result, traditional methods of recruitment prove unsatisfactory. Individual solicitations to students with low participation in school activities are advisable. Individual solicitation communicates interest in a particular student or group and may be helpful coming from a teacher who has a close relationship with a student or group or from a teacher whom students respect (Day-Vines, Day-Hairston, Carruthers, Wall, & Lupton-Smith, 1996). Moreover, enlisting the assistance of teachers helps to enlighten these teachers on the institutional issues that prevent some students from participating in school activities. On a cautionary note, only students who are likely to be selected should be encouraged because creating hopeless situations can be as detrimental as exclusion.

Selection of student mediators should reflect a cross section of the student population. Multiple criteria in terms of student attributes are suggested, including leadership skills, maturity, communication skills, responsibility, perspective taking, empathy, and problem-solving skills. High academic achievement is not necessarily a prerequisite for selection. Students with average grades and some who are considered at risk may well possess the desirable skills. A heterogeneous configuration of mediators makes the service more approachable.

The varying levels of racial or ethnic identity development among students are another salient factor to consider. It is critical that program coordinators be familiar with the stages of racial or ethnic identity development for students of color and White students. Coordinators need to be aware of and understand the impact of their own racial or ethnic identity development and the potential challenges that selecting for diversity may present to them and other members of the school community.

Throughout the literature, training is equated to the acquisition of lifelong skills that can be generalized beyond the school environment. Multicultural sensitivity should be integrated throughout the training process, as students should not always mediate conflicts between students from only their own racial or ethnic background (Day-Vines et al., 1996). Training for awareness of ways members of different groups view conflict and mediation within a cultural, family, and community context is essential to understanding the pattern of behavior and avoiding inaccurate assumptions and conclusions. Additionally, patterns of speech and issues specific to the special needs of non-English-speaking students or students for whom English is a second language must be considered in peer mediation training to avoid bias and discrimination, as well as to encourage the use of mediation services by all students.

PEER MEDIATION PROGRAM IMPLEMENTATION
Regardless of the initiative or combinations of initiatives, implementation that is strategically planned, artfully carried out, and well documented is essential. This is especially important because the results of conflict resolution initiatives and peer mediation programs can be directly linked to schoolwide data as initiatives that assist in creating a safe school environment for learning. The specifics of implementation may vary from school to school and district to district, depending on who coordinates the initiatives. The professional school counselor may or may not coordinate the initiatives. Either way, program implementation can be conceptualized as a cyclical process including the development of a mission statement, the collection of data used to set goals, the prioritizing of goals, the provision of training for skill development, an implementation schedule, evaluation, and follow-up. Additionally, careful examination of policies, practices, and procedures that affect the development and implementation of and access to these initiatives is important to ensure they reflect the spirit of the initiatives under construction. For example, inconsistencies in discipline referrals and patterns of punishments can undermine even carefully planned efforts to build peaceable schools and peer mediation programs.

Throughout every step of program revision or development, it is essential to enlist the input of all stakeholders. The use of multiple levels of input in a variety of venues that move beyond a onetime newsletter sent home, a community speaker, or several morning announcements can increase the level of ownership a school community feels in conflict resolution and peer mediation initiatives.

TRAINING FOR PROGRAM COORDINATORS   As with any important role in the school, the responsibility of coordinating peer mediation programs and conflict resolution initiatives requires specific training. A study of Safe and Drug-Free School coordinators revealed a desire for strategies and information that are practical, easy to use,

and able to be directly applied (King, Wagner, & Hedrick, 2001). Some of these strategies include improving student success; preventing alcohol, tobacco, and other drug use; building school–community–parent partnerships; and resolving conflicts safely. Well-trained coordinators can take a leadership role and provide the school community with this practical information, as well as initiating appreciation of cultural diversity and challenging the beliefs of disenfranchised students.

STUDENT ACCESS TO SERVICES   As with other programs, careful examination of policies that govern program access helps ensure that programs serve the entire school community. For example, schoolwide policies establishing when and how mediation takes place should be publicized to all members of the school community. Individual teachers or staff members should not deny students access to the mediation process. Administrative support in establishing policy lends credibility to peer mediation as an integral part of the total school program and creates consistent student access. Moreover, it sends a message of the shared values, attitudes, and beliefs that form the foundation of the school culture and climate.

PROGRAM EVALUATION   The lack of empirical data documenting the consistent effectiveness of peer mediation and conflict resolution programs is problematic in schools where limited funds mandate programmatic outcomes such as student achievement. As the focus of accountability through concrete measure increases, it is incumbent on school-based peer mediation and conflict resolution coordinators to document results. The importance of conducting evaluations for conflict resolution and peer mediation programs cannot be overstated. As professional school counselors work to link school counseling programs to the mission of schools, evidence of concrete measures that contribute to creating a safe leaning environment is essential.

Regular program evaluation reports should be completed and presented to all school personnel. Program evaluations should specify the impact conflict and violence within the school have on the culture and climate of the school and student academic achievement (e.g., adequate yearly progress). Program evaluation reports should be completed regularly and presented to all school personnel to keep them up to date and informed.

MULTICULTURAL IMPLICATIONS OF CONFLICT RESOLUTION AND PEER MEDIATION PROGRAMS
According to the U.S. Department of Health and Human Services (2008), African-American and Hispanic males

who attend large inner-city schools that serve very poor neighborhoods are at the greatest risk of becoming victims or perpetrators of school violence. These youths become more familiar with violence as it is socially constructed (K. M. Williams, 2001). Generally, racial-minority youth not only represent families from the lowest socioeconomic level, but also live in lower-income communities. Thus, these youth are much more vulnerable to the oppressions and negative afflictions plaguing society today. This can escalate the potential for these youth to adopt self-destructive, especially violent, attitudes and behaviors (Brinson, Kottler, & Fisher, 2004). But suburban and rural youth are no longer immune to school violence. An incisive look into American culture reveals some disturbing realities that influence youth, including poverty, disintegrating families, child abuse, romanticized violence, materialism, and pressure to achieve (Long, Fabricus, Musheno, & Palumbo, 1998). These social injustices in our society are believed to be the antecedents of most forms of school violence (Casella, 2001; Coleman & Deutsch, 2000). Moreover, Casella (2001) suggested race, gender, social status, sexual identity, prejudice, and fear are also central to varying forms of violence. Alcohol and drug abuse (R. L. Peterson & Skiba, 2001; Sandhu, 2000) and gang affiliation (Sandhu, 2000) also contribute to youth violence.

Some authors believe that to be truly effective, conflict resolution and violence prevention efforts must "adjust" to the diverse cultural, ethnic, and socioeconomic influences of society and involve every segment of society (e.g., families, neighborhoods, civic and social organizations, government and private institutions, businesses, cities, states, schools, justice systems, health professionals). Within the school setting, that translates into emphasizing the need to educate students in a global context and use education to bridge the divides between groups of people (Carter, 2004). Carter stated that "bridging the divides" between groups of people "requires attention not only to teaching about differences, such as language, culture, and religion, but also to exploring areas of deep cultural understanding" (p. 2). Brinson et al. (2004) asserted that there is also a lack of emphasis on cross-cultural conflict resolution, particularly within peer mediation and process curriculum approaches to conflict resolution. Therefore, not only must schools implement programs that educate and promote violence prevention, but also they must teach students how to manage and resolve conflicts through multiple contexts that move beyond merely tolerating diversity to seeking out and celebrating the rich dimensions of multiple diversities. All students need to learn alternatives to using violence for resolving their disputes (Bucher & Manning, 2003) and to learn to become peacemakers (D. W. Johnson & Johnson, 2002) in a pluralistic society.

EFFECTIVE SYSTEMIC INTERVENTION FOR STUDENTS WITH COMPLEX PROBLEMS

Schools alone no longer have the capacity to handle the multileveled problems facing today's students with complex problems. The extent and degree of problems presented by these students require a multidisciplinary and multileveled response that goes far beyond isolated school interventions and professional school counselors (Bemak, 2000). Complex problems of this nature require a redefined role for the professional school counselor, one that allows counselors to reach out to other resources in the community and in homes. We would term this aspect of the new role for the professional school counselor the coordinator of interdisciplinary resources (CIR) and shift the focus of the position from that of a primary intervention specialist to that of a facilitator of multiple resources.

There are nine key recommendations for shifting the role and responsibilities of the professional school counselor to ensure effective counseling of youth with complex problems:

1. *Develop authentic partnerships.* Although fostering partnerships with community agencies, businesses, families, universities, police departments, recreational centers, and so on is important, it oftentimes does not truly address the problems of at-risk youth. Partnerships have become fairly stable components of school outreach programs, but are frequently established merely for the sake of saying that schools have collaborative relationships. In fact, many of the partnership relationships retain the status quo, rather than developing new and innovative strategies to address the complex problems presented by youth at risk. Therefore, partnerships must be forged without traditional institutional boundaries and examine unique ways that multiple partners can cooperatively address the difficulties of children and adolescents who are experiencing problems.

2. *Facilitate interdisciplinary collaboration.* The modern-day problems of at-risk youth are far too complex to be addressed in any one system. Thus, to expand on the first recommendation, professional school counselors should assume the role of CIR to facilitate interdisciplinary school collaboration with community agencies, government, businesses, and families to generate comprehensive approaches to multifaceted problems. This requires moving beyond partnerships with one institutional or parental body and fostering cross-disciplinary collaboration.

3. *Maintain a strong multicultural focus.* Racial and ethnic demographics are changing in the United States, creating a growing ethnic minority population

(Aponte & Crouch, 2000); therefore, problems manifested by youth must be considered from a cultural perspective. Too often, at-risk youth populations are defined and addressed by the nature of their problems, without considering the cultural distinctions among the youth when designing prevention and intervention programs. It is important to underscore the need for a concerted awareness of cultural differences in worldviews, especially when working with youth with complex problems.

4. *Be a systems change agent.*   To better serve the needs of youth, professional school counselors must assume the role of change agent (Bemak, 1998; C. C. Lee, 1998). Professional school counselors are in an ideal position to understand what needs to change to provide successful support and educational services for youth with problems. Rather than simply "hearing" about those problems from students and parents, we recommend that professional school counselors take an active role in challenging inequities, injustices, and harmful practices within the school context.

5. *Empower students.*   Truly empowering students means giving up power (Bemak, 2000). This is particularly important within the school setting when working with children and adolescents who are facing obstacles. Thus, professional school counselors should help empower students and their families while modeling and promoting collaboration.

6. *Look for short-term successes.*   One way to ensure failure with students who face myriad problems is to demand unrealistic goals. This is done regularly in schools where students who are angry are told not to be angry, students who are not studying are told simply to study, and students with low grades are commanded to work harder and improve their grades. We argue that professional school counselors must pave the way in establishing short-term realistic goals as measures of success, particularly when working with at-risk youth. Building on these short-term positive experiences will provide a building block to longer-term success.

7. *Become an advocate.*   Advocacy is a key ingredient in working with youth at risk. Traditionally, many of the disenfranchised youth are without anyone to fight for their rights and dreams. The professional school counselor is in a unique position to intimately know the child or adolescent and the system. Furthermore, the professional school counselor has access to important systemic information regarding the child. Given their unique position, professional school counselors must assume the role of advocate, challenging policies, practices, and procedures that perpetuate failure for the at-risk population.

8. *Research and document outcomes.*   It is not sufficient to justify the success of prevention and intervention programs with anecdotal reports. Professional school counselors must assume a leadership role in documenting and disseminating information on the efficacy of programs through publishing and presenting their findings, both within the school system and externally at state and national forums (Bemak, 2000). Clear outcomes and dissemination of findings will help tailor successful program strategies, create a base for future funding, and facilitate better job descriptions and responsibilities for professional school counselors.

9. *Assume responsibility for successes and failures.*   It is important that professionals model the demands made on youth to assume responsibility for their lives. Professional school counselors, institutions, agencies, and other professionals must become more accountable for their work with these youth. It is important to acknowledge and accept when intervention strategies are flawed and therefore discontinue using such interventions. At the same time, professional school counselors need to recognize and implement effective intervention strategies. Although this sounds straightforward, there is a history of systems blaming the child or adolescent for failures and creating a culture of victimization, rather than assuming responsibility for ineffective interventions.

Summary/Conclusion

It is clear that the issues encountered by youth with complex problems in the United States continue to present serious problems for schools, families, and communities. It is essential that professional school counselors design innovative service systems to effectively address the complex and multifaceted needs of these youth. It is clear that many of the existing prevention and intervention programs are ineffective and unsuccessful, given the high numbers of disengaged and marginalized youth. Therefore, a new approach to working with this population is critical.

The professional school counselor is in a unique position to assume a leadership role in more effectively working with children and adolescents with complex problems. As a CIR, advocate, social change agent, multicultural expert, and documenter of successful programs, the professional school counselor is well positioned to make a difference. Professional school counselors must shift the blame from the youth to ensure that the service system and programs assume responsibility and that youth are supported, rather than punished. These paradigm shifts will be critical in changing the trajectory of youths' lives. It is an opportune time to change the course of a growing number of youth in the United States, and the professional school counselor is an ideal professional to become a leader in this process.

Activities

1. Interview a high school counselor regarding his or her approach to working with students with complex problems. How does he or she identify these students? What techniques does he or she find to be helpful in dealing with these students?

2. Create a program for use in either a primary or a secondary school to reach at-risk youth. How would you define the population? How do you plan to reach your desired population? What messages would you try to convey to them? Why would such a program be important to implement in schools and communities?

3. Design an outline for a violence prevention program for an elementary, middle, or high school. What message would you attempt to convey to the students? What programs and activities would you ask the students to participate in?

4. Observe a school cafeteria during lunch hour. What types of conflicts do you notice? How are these conflicts resolved?

5. Conduct a role play involving a professional school counselor and two students who are involved in a conflict. What conflict resolution strategy was used? How well did it work?

15

The Professional School Counselor and Students with Disabilities

Elana Rock and Erin H. Leff*

E ditor's Introduction: Advocating for the needs of all students is a primary responsibility of the transformed professional school counselor. For too long, students with special needs have been identified and served through special programs without appropriate attention given to their developmental academic, career, and personal/social needs. This chapter focuses on what professional school counselors can do to effectively advocate for and serve students with special needs.

POOR OUTCOMES FOR STUDENTS WITH DISABILITIES

> Each person has the right to receive the information and support needed to move toward self-direction and self-development and affirmation within one's group identities, with special care being given to students who have historically not received adequate educational services: students of color, low socio-economic students, students with disabilities and students with nondominant language backgrounds. (ASCA, 2004a)

Considered a population requiring "special care," students with disabilities face a number of barriers to successful school and postschool outcomes. According to recent national data (U.S. Department of Education, 2008), the most common disabilities, which affect more than 90% of those school-aged students with disabilities, are learning disabilities, emotional/behavioral disorders, mild mental retardation, language disorders, and other health impairments, including Attention-Deficit/Hyperactivity Disorder (ADHD). Overall, more than 6 million school-aged children in the United States are receiving special education and related services for an eligible disability, most often one that interferes with behavior and academic performance. In addition to the effects of the disorders themselves, students with disabilities have not always received adequate educational services and supports.

As a result, students with disabilities have significant problems making academic progress in schools. They earn lower grades, are retained more often, and often fail to graduate with a diploma. In addition, students with disabilities drop out at significantly higher rates than do students without disabilities. Currently, the dropout rates range from 15% of students with visual impairments to 56% of students with emotional/behavioral disorders (U.S. Department of Education, 2008). Regarding adult outcomes, adults who were students with disabilities have lower rates of postsecondary educational involvement (including vocational training) and higher rates of unemployment and underemployment (National Council on Disability, 2004).

---

*The authors acknowledge the significant contribution of Estes J. Lockhart to the first edition of this text chapter. May he rest in peace.

These poor outcomes are particularly disheartening when considering the fact that approximately 90% of students receiving special education services have "mild" or high-prevalence disabilities (U.S. Department of Education, 2008). Most of these students have average cognitive ability and lack significant physical or sensory impairments that might further interfere with functioning. Notably, over 96% of these children are educated in regular public schools, with nearly half spending the majority of their time in typical classrooms. The great majority of students with disabilities are capable of positive school and adult outcomes, including college and competitive employment, despite a long history of poor outcomes in these areas.

The U.S. Department of Education has recognized the poor outcomes for students with disabilities and articulated requirements in an effort to ensure improved progress. In its 2004 reauthorization of the Individuals with Disabilities Education Act (titled the Individuals with Disabilities Education Improvement Act and also referred to as the IDEA), Congress noted that

> [d]isability is a natural part of the human experience and in no way diminishes the right of individuals to participate in or contribute to society. Improving educational results for children with disabilities is an essential element of our national policy of ensuring equality of opportunity, full participation, independent living, and economic self-sufficiency for individuals with disabilities. (IDEA, 2004)

Students with disabilities are capable of becoming and expected to become contributing members of society, providing they receive the appropriate supports necessary for positive school and adult outcomes. To achieve these ends, Congress mandated the delivery of special education and related services in the IDEA (2004) and has required accountability measures for students with disabilities through the No Child Left Behind Act (NCLB) of 2002.

The IDEA (2004) states that 30 years of research and experience have demonstrated that the education of children with disabilities can be made more effective by

> having high expectations for such children and ensuring their access to the general education curriculum in the regular classroom, to the maximum extent possible, in order to . . . meet developmental goals and, to the maximum extent possible, the challenging expectations that have been established for all children; and . . . be prepared to lead productive and independent adult lives, to the maximum extent possible.

SERVING STUDENTS WITH DISABILITIES

According to the IDEA, educational programming for a child with a disability requires an individualized approach to all identified needs. In order to identify and serve each student with a disability, a multidisciplinary team is constituted. Each team includes the parent(s), at least one general educator (if the child may be participating in general education), at least one special educator, related service providers, transition services participants (for students age 16 years and older), and the student whenever appropriate. In addition, the parent or school may bring in other individuals who have knowledge or special expertise regarding the student. For example, a child with a learning disability may have a multidisciplinary team consisting of the student, parent, school principal, general educator, special educator, professional school counselor, speech pathologist, psychologist, and occupational therapist.

The team is initially responsible for determining whether a newly referred student requires assessment. If assessment is warranted, the team determines what assessments are needed, orders the assessments, reviews the findings, and determines whether the student is eligible for special education services because he or she meets the criteria for "a child with a disability." Once the student is found eligible for special education and related services, the team is responsible for developing the student's Individualized Education Program (IEP), identifying all necessary services and supports required to meet areas of identified need, determining the student's placement, and implementing the IEP.

As a member of the multidisciplinary team, the professional school counselor may have many roles and potential responsibilities associated with programming and delivering services for children with disabilities. These responsibilities may be to the team (e.g., for assessment, development of the IEP, and implementation planning), directly to the child (e.g., counseling services, career development), or indirectly to the child through work with others on the team (e.g., parent training, consultation with educators, clinical support).

The American School Counselor Association (ASCA), in its position paper on students with special needs (2004b), described various roles of the professional school counselor regarding these students:

> When appropriate, interventions in which the professional school counselor participates may include but are not limited to:
>
> • Leading school counseling activities as a part of the comprehensive school counseling program

- Providing collaborative services consistent with those services provided to students through the comprehensive school counseling program
- Serving on the school's multidisciplinary team that identifies students who may need assessments to determine special needs within the scope and practice of the professional school counselor
- Collaborating with other student support specialists in the delivery of services
- Providing group and individual counseling
- Advocating for students with special needs in the school and in the community
- Assisting with the establishment and implementation of plans for accommodations and modifications
- Providing assistance with transitions from grade to grade as well as post-secondary options
- Consulting and collaborating with staff and parents to understand the special needs of these students
- Making referrals to appropriate specialists within the school system and in the community.

It is clear that there are many roles in which professional school counselors support students with disabilities. Table 15.1 lists the most frequent roles reported by professional school counselors working with students with disabilities.

Despite clear expectations for the delivery of services by professional school counselors and for counselors' involvement in the multidisciplinary team process, many master's-level school counseling programs do not adequately prepare counselors for these responsibilities. Many professional school counselors report having little, if any, coursework dealing with the needs of students with disabilities (McEachern, 2003). In addition, even professional school counselors who have taken coursework on programming for students with disabilities often report feeling underprepared or unprepared for the delivery of services to the children in their schools (Dunn & Baker, 2002; Milsom, 2002).

This chapter discusses the legal mandates involving the delivery of counseling-related services to children with disabilities. It then examines the roles of professional school counselors, including relevant responsibilities, service delivery options, and best practices in delivering services in areas associated with the needs of school-aged students with disabilities. Since many of the professional school counselors' responsibilities to students with disabilities are the same as or similar to their responsibilities to students without disabilities, emphasis in this chapter will be placed on those processes not discussed elsewhere in this text.

FEDERAL LEGISLATION

The federal laws that articulate and protect the rights of students with disabilities can be grouped into one of two categories: education laws or civil rights laws. The special

---

TABLE 15.1   Frequent Roles for Counselors Working with Students with Disabilities

From 75% to 83% of professional school counselors reported involvement in each of these roles:

- Provide individual/group counseling
- Make referrals
- Serve on multidisciplinary team
- Counsel parents and families
- Advocate for students
- Assist with behavior modification plans
- Provide feedback for team

From 40% to 60% of professional school counselors reported involvement in each of these roles:

- Provide self-esteem activities
- Serve as consultant to parents/staff
- Provide social skills training
- Assist with transition plans

Source: "Students with Disabilities: School Counselor Involvement and Preparation," by A. S. Milsom, 2002, *Professional School Counseling,* 5, 331–339.

education law most widely applied in schools is the IDEA (2004). It was originally entitled the Education for All Handicapped Children Act when it was first enacted in 1975. The IDEA provides federal funding and requires states to guarantee a free appropriate public education (FAPE) to students who need special education and related services because of an eligible disability. There are other education laws that also affect the delivery of special education programs and services. Among them are Title I of the Elementary and Secondary Education Act (ESEA) and NCLB (see U.S. Department of Education, 2002).

The most widely applied civil rights law is Section 504 of the Rehabilitation Act of 1973 (commonly referred to as Section 504). Although it provides no federal funding, Section 504 mandates that programs receiving federal funding under other laws may not exclude an otherwise qualified individual with a disability from participation in these programs. It also requires that individuals with disabilities be provided reasonable accommodations that will allow them to access these programs. The Americans with Disabilities Act (ADA) of 1990 is another civil rights act whose school-related provisions are nearly identical to Section 504 of the Rehabilitation Act. The ADA extends the protection from discrimination because of disabilities to all public and private schools, except for religious schools, whether or not they receive federal financial assistance.

Understanding the differences between the IDEA and Section 504 is of practical importance for the professional school counselor. Professional school counselors often act as consultants for school staff, family, and outside agency representatives to help them understand how the legal rights of a student with a disability are appropriately addressed within an educational setting. As Bowen and Glenn (1998) stated, "In order to provide appropriate remedial and preventative services, counselors must more fully understand the present legislative requirements, characteristics, terminology and related counseling needs associated with exceptional learners" (p. 17).

The major difference between the IDEA and Section 504 is one of focus. The IDEA focuses on educational remediation, whereas Section 504 focuses on prevention of discrimination. The IDEA attempts to address gaps in skills or abilities by ensuring the provision of appropriate services and modified instruction for students in need of special education. Section 504, on the other hand, attempts to level the playing field for those students whose disabilities may not directly affect their academic abilities but who may require accommodation to access the educational program.

For example, a student with a learning disability served under the IDEA may require special instruction in reading, as well as related services such as speech therapy or counseling, to learn. In contrast, a student with cerebral palsy qualified under Section 504 may be achieving at grade level in all academics, but still need accommodations such as being allowed to dictate responses rather than write them, due to his or her limited fine motor skills.

Individuals with Disabilities Education Improvement Act (IDEA)

The IDEA is the major special education law governing identification, evaluation, program, placement, and the provision of a FAPE for school-aged students determined to have a disability falling in one of 13 identified categories. This law provides that eligible students receive "special education," which is defined as "specially designed instruction, at no cost to parents, to meet the unique needs of a child with a disability, including instruction conducted in the classroom, in the home, in hospitals and institutions, and in other settings" (IDEA, 2004). Table 15.2 includes the definitions of each of the categories of disabilities that may entitle a child to receive special education under the IDEA. As can be seen from the definitions in Table 15.2, the IDEA requires that disabilities affect educational performance. While a student with a disability may need, or at least benefit from, some interventions or special instruction, if the disability has minimal or no negative effect on learning, the student would not qualify as eligible for special education under the IDEA. However, he or she might be eligible for reasonable accommodations or supports under Section 504 if his or her impairment substantially limits a major life activity.

When a student is determined to be eligible for services under the IDEA, the school system is required to provide a FAPE. It is important to remember that the law specifically states that the education must be "appropriate." This standard has been adopted by most states. *Appropriate* does not mean *best*, and loosely using the term *best* when the school team means appropriate can cause significant problems. While professional school counselors and other professionals will try to do their best in providing services, they will not always provide the maximum or most beneficial services to an individual student. When the word *best* is used, it can lead to parental expectations of a range of services that are not required under the law or necessary for the student to learn. This increased level of services might be helpful in assisting the student to reach optimal performance; however, the IDEA does not require optimal programming, only appropriate programming that enables a child to make reasonable educational progress. In addition, the professional school counselor needs to be clear that the law requires school

TABLE 15.2   Handicapping Conditions Under the IDEA

Autism means a developmental disability significantly affecting verbal and nonverbal communication and social interaction, generally evident before age 3, that adversely affects a child's educational performance. Other characteristics often associated with autism are engagement in repetitive activities and stereotyped movements, resistance to environmental change or change in daily routines, and unusual responses to sensory experiences. The term does not apply if a child's educational performance is adversely affected primarily because the child has an emotional disturbance, as defined below. A child who manifests the characteristics of autism after age 3 could be diagnosed as having autism if the criteria above are satisfied.

Deaf-blindness means concomitant hearing and visual impairments, the combination of which causes such severe communication and other developmental and educational needs that they cannot be accommodated in special education programs solely for children with deafness or children with blindness.

Deafness means a hearing impairment that is so severe that the child is impaired in processing linguistic information through hearing, with or without amplification, that adversely affects a child's educational performance.

Developmental delay means a significant cognitive delay in a child age 3 to 9 not accounted for by another handicapping condition.

Emotional disturbance means a condition exhibiting one or more of the following characteristics over a long period and to a marked degree that adversely affects a child's educational performance:

A. An inability to learn that cannot be explained by intellectual, sensory, or health factors.

B. An inability to build or maintain satisfactory interpersonal relationships with peers and teachers.

C. Inappropriate types of behavior or feelings under normal circumstances.

D. A general pervasive mood of unhappiness or depression.

E. A tendency to develop physical symptoms or fears associated with personal or school problems.

The term includes schizophrenia. The term does not apply to children who are socially maladjusted, unless it is determined that they have an emotional disturbance.

Hearing impairment means an impairment in hearing, whether permanent or fluctuating, that adversely affects a child's educational performance but that is not included under the definition of deafness in this section.

Mental retardation means significantly subaverage general intellectual functioning, existing concurrently with deficits in adaptive behavior and manifested during the developmental period, that adversely affects a child's educational performance.

Multiple disabilities means concomitant impairments (such as mental retardation–blindness, mental retardation–orthopedic impairment, etc.), the combination of which causes such severe educational needs that they cannot be accommodated in special education programs solely for one of the impairments. The term does not include deaf-blindness.

Orthopedic impairment means a severe orthopedic impairment that adversely affects a child's educational performance. The term includes impairments caused by congenital anomaly (e.g., clubfoot, absence of some member, etc.), impairments caused by disease (e.g., poliomyelitis, bone tuberculosis, etc.), and impairments from other causes (e.g., cerebral palsy, amputations, and fractures or burns that cause contractures).

Other health impairment means having limited strength, vitality, or alertness, including heightened alertness to environmental stimuli, that results in limited alertness with respect to the educational environment, that is due to chronic or acute health problems such as asthma, ADD or ADHD, diabetes, epilepsy, a heart condition, hemophilia, lead poisoning, leukemia, nephritis, rheumatic fever, or sickle cell anemia and adversely affects a child's educational performance.

Specific learning disability means a disorder in one or more of the basic psychological processes involved in understanding or in using language, spoken or written, that may manifest itself in an imperfect ability to listen, think, speak, read, write, spell, or do mathematical calculations, including conditions such as perceptual disabilities, brain injury, minimal brain dysfunction, dyslexia, and developmental aphasia. The term does not include learning problems that are primarily the result of visual, hearing, or motor disabilities; of mental retardation; of emotional disturbance; or of environmental, cultural, or economic disadvantage.

Speech or language impairment means a communication disorder such as stuttering, impaired articulation, a language impairment, or a voice impairment that adversely affects a child's educational performance.

Traumatic brain injury means an acquired injury to the brain caused by an external physical force, resulting in total or partial functional disability or psychological impairment, or both, that adversely affects a child's educational performance. The term applies to open or closed head injuries resulting in impairments in one or more areas such as cognition; language; memory; attention; reasoning; abstract thinking; judgment; problem solving; sensory, perceptual, and motor abilities; psychosocial behavior; physical functions; information processing; and speech. The term does not apply to brain injuries that are congenital or degenerative, or to brain injuries induced by birth trauma.

Visual impairment including blindness means an impairment in vision that, even with correction, adversely affects a child's educational performance. The term includes both partial sight and blindness.

Source: Congressional Research Service. (2005). Individuals with Disabilities Education Act (IDEA). P.L. 108-446. Washington, DC: U.S. Government Printing Office.

systems to educate students, not to rehabilitate them. Rehabilitation services sometimes are provided, but only for the purpose of educating or helping students make a transition from secondary school to a useful career path, not for rehabilitation in and of itself.

The provision of FAPE generally involves two types of services, special education and related services. Special education is provided by special educators, as well as general educators and paraprofessionals in consultation with special educators. The IDEA identifies a continuum of placements where students may receive their instructional services, related services, or both. They range from full-time regular class placement to part-time regular class placement to services provided in residential schools and hospitals. Most students with disabilities are educated in regular education classes for a majority of the school day (U.S. Department of Education, 2008).

Once found eligible for special education, students are entitled to receive not only special education instruction, but also related services, accommodations, and supports that meet their needs and enable them to benefit from their educational program. In a few statutorily specified instances, some related services—for example, speech—can be considered special education instruction. In these circumstances, the child can receive an IEP that includes only the related services. In general, however, a child must need special education instruction to be found eligible under the IDEA.

For a child to receive special education and related services under the IDEA, a multidisciplinary team must complete a multistep process. The process involves a series of statutorily defined steps, including identification, screening, notification and consent, assessment, eligibility determination, IEP development, and implementation. Table 15.3 provides an outline of the special education process.

Section 504 and the Americans with Disabilities Act (ADA)

Section 504 of the Rehabilitation Act of 1973 specifically focuses on students with disabilities in school and their right to access all services and programs available to students without disabilities (U.S. Department of Education, 2005d). A student is eligible under Section 504 if the student has a physical or mental impairment that substantially limits one or more major life activities. Major life activities include caring for oneself, walking, talking, seeing, hearing, performing manual tasks, breathing, learning, and working. Thus, for example, students who are educationally able but physically disabled, such as typically achieving students with severe asthma or cerebral palsy, would be qualified individuals under Section 504. All students found eligible for services under the IDEA, then, are also qualified individuals under Section 504 because they have a substantial impairment of a major life function—learning. This is important because this means that special education students may not be excluded from school activities such as assemblies, field trips, vocational programs, sports teams, or clubs simply because they have disabilities.

A student is also qualified under Section 504 if he or she has a record of having such an impairment or is regarded as having such an impairment. To "have a record of having, or be regarded as having such an impairment," means that the student has had a disability or has been believed to have a disability for a significant period of time even though the student no longer has a disability or did not, in fact, ever have a disability. An example would be someone who does not meet the criteria for autism, but who has been classified as having autism in the past. However, if a person not qualified to diagnose physical or mental disorders tells a parent or some other person that

TABLE 15.3 Outline of Steps in the Special Education Process

Identification. A parent, guardian, state educational agency, other state agency, or local school system may initiate a request for initial evaluation for eligibility for special education (referral).

- Referral must be made to the IEP team of the child's home school (the public school to which the child is zoned), even if he or she attends another public or a private school.
- Referral should be in writing and clearly specify that it is a referral for special education services. It should provide parents' and child's names, address, and phone number.
- Referral should include area(s) of concern—for example, problems with reading, problems attending and learning, and so forth.

Screening. A multidisciplinary team (e.g., parent, guardian, regular educator, special educator, administrator) reviews the records and history of the child's learning problem(s) to determine if there is a need for individualized assessment.

- The parent will be asked to provide basic and historical information to determine possible areas of impairment.
- The parent will be asked to allow review of records (e.g., medical, school) and sign consents to obtain any needed information.
- The parent will be asked to complete screening interviews or data forms.
- The evaluation team will determine if assessments are needed and in what areas.
- If the team does not believe assessment is necessary, the parent may request mediation or due process.

Notification and consent. If screening identifies a need for further assessment, the team notifies parents and requests written consent for all areas to be assessed.

- Parents must be notified in advance of any possible assessments.
- Parents must sign written consent for all assessments.
- Parents must receive 10 days' notice of all meetings.

Assessment. Professionals (e.g., special educators, psychologists, audiologists) administer tests individually to the student in a nondiscriminatory manner (considering dominant language, etc.).

- Assessments should be completed in every area of suspected problem(s).
- Assessments typically include educational and other areas (e.g., psychological, related health, visual acuity).
- For each area of suspected disability, particular assessments are usually required, and these assessments are performed by assessment-specific evaluators. For example, a suspected learning disability requires at least an educational assessment and a psychological (cognitive) assessment, with the possible need for a speech-language or other assessment. The required evaluators are a special educator, psychologist, and speech-language pathologist, respectively.
- If a parent disagrees with the results of an assessment, the parent may request that the school fund an independent evaluation.
- Initial assessments are to be completed within 60 days of receipt of parental consent.

Eligibility Determination. The multidisciplinary team considers all assessment results and determines if the child meets the criteria for a disability under one of the eligible categories.

- The team (including parent) reviews all assessment results.
- With parent input, the team determines whether the child meets eligibility criteria for one (or more) disability areas.
- If the team determines that the child does not meet eligibility requirements and the parent disagrees, the parent can request mediation or due process.

IEP Development. The team (including the parent) collaboratively (1) develops goals to meet the student's needs and (2) determines all required services and supports needed to provide FAPE. IEPs must include

- Present levels of performance in academic and functional areas.
- A statement of measurable annual goals.
- A description of how the child's progress toward meeting the goals will be measured.
- A statement of the special education and related services and supplementary aids and services to be provided.
- An explanation of the extent, if any, to which the child will not participate with nondisabled children in regular classes and activities.
- A statement of any appropriate accommodations.
- The start date for services.
- The anticipated frequency, location, and duration of services and modifications.
- Beginning not later than age 16, transition goals.

Implementation. The team, including the parent, determines the least restrictive environment (LRE) in which the student's IEP can be implemented.

- This occurs only after all the components of the IEP, described above, have been developed.
- Each successive removal from a less restrictive placement to a more restrictive placement (e.g., from full-time regular class placement to part-time resource room) needs to be justified.
- Placement in LRE includes placing the student, if at all possible, in the home school. It also means placement with age-appropriate peers.
- Students need not be assigned to a particular placement to obtain a service. Any service can be provided in any placement.
- LRE is individually determined for each child—not by disability type, severity, program availability, or cost.

---

the student has a disability, the student is not considered as "having a record of, or as being regarded as having, an impairment." Diagnosis must be conducted by a qualified practitioner. These phrases protect students from discrimination (i.e., exclusion) who otherwise might be excluded from services should subsequent changes in the qualifying criteria occur, despite having received accommodations or services as a person with a disability in the past.

To determine whether a student is protected under Section 504, an evaluation is conducted or existing records are reviewed. Public school districts receiving federal financial assistance are required by Section 504 regulations to provide a FAPE, parallel to the IDEA requirement, to students with disabilities in their jurisdiction. A FAPE under Section 504 consists of "regular or special education and related aids and services that . . . are designed to meet individual educational needs of handicapped persons as adequately as the needs of nonhandicapped persons are met" and are provided in accordance with Section 504 requirements relevant to educational setting, evaluation and placement, and procedural safeguards. While there is a clear overlap regarding the use of the words *special education* in both the IDEA and Section 504, in practice, students who require special education are served under the IDEA, and students who require only accommodations and support are typically served under Section 504.

Decisions about what educational and related services are appropriate for a child under Section 504 must be made by a placement group that includes persons knowledgeable about the child, the meaning of evaluation data, and placement options (IDEA, 2004). Students who are found eligible under Section 504 receive a Section 504 Plan. A Section 504 Plan is frequently patterned after an IEP, although it tends to contain less detail. The Section 504 Plan describes the services the student is to receive under Section 504, along with the accommodations the student needs in order to access the educational program. The services that may be provided under Section 504 include

counseling services, physical recreational athletics, transportation, health services, recreational activities, special interest groups or clubs sponsored by the recipients, referrals to agencies which provide assistance to handicapped persons, and employment of students, including both employment by the recipient and assistance in making available outside employment. (IDEA, 2004)

Schools are also required to provide reasonable accommodations under Section 504. Just as the IDEA (2004) requires the provision of "appropriate" but not necessarily the best services, Section 504 requires schools to provide only reasonable accommodations. Some examples of the types of accommodations that schools are typically required to provide include "auxiliary aids" such as "taped texts, interpreters or other effective methods of making orally delivered materials available to students with hearing impairments, readers in libraries for students with visual impairments, classroom equipment adapted for use by students with manual impairments, and other similar services and actions." In addition, the eligible student does not have to provide one's own "attendants, individually prescribed devices, readers for personal use or study, or other devices or services of a personal nature".

Section 504 is a civil rights statute that addresses discrimination in access to programs and services, not remediation of learning. Eligibility under Section 504 is not limited to a specific list of disabilities as is IDEA eligibility, nor is there a defined list of educational requirements and related services. In this sense, Section 504 provides more flexibility in that any physical or mental impairment could potentially create eligibility. Impairments frequently resulting in eligibility under Section 504 are AD/HD (the most often cited diagnosis in schools under Section 504), medical conditions, physical impairments, behavioral or emotional disorders, addictions, communicable diseases, and chronic medical conditions. Examples of students who might be covered under Section 504, but not the IDEA, include students with alcohol or drug problems who are not currently using or abusing substances, allergies or asthma, environmental illnesses, communicable diseases, and conduct disorders. A comprehensive compliance guide for elementary and secondary schools regarding Section 504 is available online at www.edlaw.net/service/guidcont.html.

Family Educational Rights and Privacy Act (FERPA)

In the role of case manager, professional school counselors are likely to encounter issues regarding confidentiality of records and other communications referred to them. FERPA, a federal law, defines access to and confidentiality of student educational records. FERPA also is sometimes referred to as the Buckley Amendment, in honor of its sponsor, Senator James Buckley. Under FERPA, parents have rights to control access to academic records until the student is 18 years old, at which time the rights are transferred to the student. Thus, under FERPA, an 18-year-old student must sign a release of information for a professional school counselor to share written records with anyone, including a service provider outside the system.

For the professional school counselor serving students with disabilities, three issues in FERPA are of particular importance:

1. Parents have a right to inspect and review all educational records of the student. Essentially, once a written document from any source is placed in the school file, parents have a right to inspect it. Further, they have a right to decide if the school may share the report in the future. In general, written permission must be obtained before an educational record can be shared.
2. FERPA defines what an educational record is and what a professional school counselor or anyone else may call a personal confidential file. Virtually every piece of paper, including all professional mental health reports, relating to a student in a school is an educational record. For professional school counselors to call any written documents in their possession personal confidential notes, they must not have shared the information with anyone at any time. For example, if a professional school counselor at a multidisciplinary meeting pulls out his or her notes and reads from them, the notes become educational records and cease to be confidential counselor notes.

3. Under FERPA, the parent has a right to challenge what is in the school records and to have any information that can be proven to be inaccurate or misleading removed.

Another issue of confidentiality facing professional school counselors who keep records on students with disabilities is that of safekeeping for the confidential files. Most counselors may believe that the files are safe in their offices. It is important, however, for the counselor to ensure that the records are locked up and that only the counselor (and supervisor) has keys that will allow access to the records. A good website that provides information and excellent copyright-free materials on all of the specific disabilities, education laws and regulations, parent rights and responsibilities, and other resources is www.nichcy.org.

RELATED SERVICES FOR STUDENTS WITH DISABILITIES UNDER THE IDEA AND SECTION 504

Students may receive related services under both Section 504 and the IDEA. Related services are noninstructional, ancillary services that are not part of the regular instructional program, but may be required for the successful implementation of a student's instructional program under the IDEA or Section 504. The IDEA (2004) definition of related services is "transportation, and such developmental, corrective, and other supportive services...as may be required to assist a child with a disability to benefit from special education" (Statute: Title I / A / 602 / 26 [http://idea.ed.gov/explore/view/p/%2Croot%2Cstatute%2CI%2CA%2C602%2C26%2C]). These services include audiology, counseling, early identification and assessment, interpreting services, medical services (for diagnostic and evaluation purposes only), occupational therapy, orientation and mobility services, parent counseling and training, physical therapy, psychological services, recreation, rehabilitation counseling, school nurse services, social work services, speech-language services, and transportation (IDEA, 2004). In some instances, individual aides also are provided to assist students with school functioning.

School counseling services, when provided under the IDEA or Section 504, are listed on the IEP or Section 504 Plan as a related service. Related services can be provided on a direct basis, or they can be delivered indirectly using a consultation model with a teacher or family member. For example, the professional school counselor might instruct the teacher in how to reinforce social skills in class, rather than holding social skills training sessions individually with the student. The professional school counselor also might consult with the classroom teacher on how best to preempt or defuse the angry outbursts of a student with disabilities.

Recent data indicate that one in five students receiving special education also receives mental health services, an increase of nearly seven percentage points over the number 15 years earlier (Wagner, Newman, & Cameto, 2004). While mental health services may be provided by a number of different professionals in schools (e.g., psychologists, social workers, professional school counselors, mental health assistants, behavioral specialists), professional school counselors are increasingly being considered important resources in the delivery of services to students with emotional, behavioral, or social needs affecting their learning.

The IDEA (2004) specifically includes as related services for students with disabilities the following three service areas that are often performed by professional school counselors: counseling services, parent counseling and training, and rehabilitation counseling services. The following information on these three related service areas is provided by the National Dissemination Center for Children with Disabilities (2001) in collaboration with the U.S. Department of Education's Office of Special Education Programs.

Counseling Services

Counseling services, according to the ASCA (2004b), focus on the needs, interests, and issues related to various stages of student growth. Professional school counselors may help students with personal and social concerns such as developing self-knowledge, making effective decisions, making healthy choices, and improving responsibility. Counselors may also help students with future planning related to setting and reaching academic goals, developing a positive attitude toward learning, and recognizing and utilizing academic strengths. Other counseling services may include parent counseling and training and rehabilitation counseling (i.e., counseling specific to career development and employment preparation). Counseling services are services provided by qualified social workers, psychologists, professional school counselors, or other qualified personnel (IDEA, 2004).

Parent Counseling and Training

Parent counseling and training is an important related service that can help parents enhance the vital role they play in the lives of their children. When necessary to help an eligible student with a disability benefit from the educational program, parent counseling and training can include "assisting parents in understanding the special needs of their child, providing parents with information about child development, and helping parents to acquire the necessary skills that will allow them to support the implementation of their child's IEP or IFSP [individualized family service plan]" (IDEA, 2004).

Rehabilitation Counseling Services

Rehabilitation counseling services are

> services provided by qualified personnel in individual or group sessions that focus specifically on career development, employment preparation, achieving independence, and integration in the workplace and community. . . . The term also includes vocational rehabilitation services provided to a student with disabilities by vocational rehabilitation programs funded under the Rehabilitation Act of 1973, as amended. (IDEA, 2004)

According to the Council on Rehabilitation Education (2003–2004), a rehabilitation counselor is a counselor who possesses the specialized knowledge, skills, and attitudes needed to collaborate in a professional relationship with people who have disabilities to help them to achieve their personal, social, psychological, and vocational goals. To this end, rehabilitation counseling services generally may include assessment of a student's attitudes, abilities, and needs; vocational counseling and guidance; vocational training; and identifying job placements.

TRANSITION SERVICES UNDER THE IDEA

The professional school counselor may have a variety of responsibilities in providing transition services to students with disabilities. According to the IDEA (2004), the term *transition services* means a coordinated set of activities for a child with a disability that

1. Is designed to be within a results-oriented process that is focused on improving the academic and functional achievement of the child with a disability in order to facilitate the child's movement from school to postschool activities, including postsecondary education, vocational education, integrated employment (including supported employment), continuing and adult education, adult services, independent living, or community participation.
2. Is based on the individual child's needs, taking into account the child's strengths, preferences, and interests.

3. Includes instruction, related services, community experiences, the development of employment and other postschool adult living objectives, and when appropriate, acquisition of daily living skills and the provision of a functional vocational evaluation.

Beginning not later than the first IEP to be in effect when the child is 16 years old, and updated annually thereafter, each student's IEP must include

1. Appropriate, measurable postsecondary goals based on age-appropriate transition assessments related to training, education, employment, and, where appropriate, independent living skills;
2. The transition services (including courses of study) needed to assist the child in reaching those goals; and
3. Beginning not later than one year before the child reaches the age of majority under state law, a statement that the child has been informed of the child's rights under the IDEA, if any, that will transfer to the child on reaching the age of majority.

In addition to the provision of programming for transition services and of related services as described above, there are other support services required for students with disabilities that may involve the professional school counselor. These areas include some types of assessment, interpretation of assessments, positive behavioral support services, case management, advocacy, collaboration with other pupil support specialists, social skills training, activities to improve self-esteem, support for high school completion, dropout prevention, self-determination training, vocational programming, career development, evaluation of college options, and referral to outside agencies. These support services and other IEP responsibilities are defined briefly in Table 15.4.

PROVIDING SERVICES TO SUPPORT STUDENTS WITH DISABILITIES

Professional school counselors have many responsibilities, which can be roughly divided into three categories. First are the counselor's responsibilities to the multidisciplinary team in developing and implementing a response to intervention (RTI) process to identify students at risk, providing assessments, collaborating on the eligibility decision-making process, and developing counseling goals and objectives. Second are the counselor's responsibilities to the child in the provision of direct services, including counseling services, vocational guidance, and transition programming. Third, professional school counselors have indirect responsibilities to support the

child by providing case management, consulting with teachers, training parents, or developing community-based resources that can assist the child after his or her graduation.

Multidisciplinary Team Responsibilities

DEVELOPING AND USING RESPONSE TO INTERVENTION

According to a 2008 position statement, the ASCA views professional school counselors as stakeholders in the development and implementation of the RTI process. RTI is a multitier approach to help students in both general and special education who are struggling academically and behaviorally through early identification and support. All children begin the RTI process by participating in high-quality instruction coupled with screening for potential problems in the regular education classroom. Learners experiencing academic and behavoral problems then receive interventions at increasing levels of intensity to address problems and return their learning trajectory to normal levels. These early intervention services are provided by school personnel from various disciplines, including classroom teachers, special educators, and specialists. Student progress is monitored and assessed to determine both performance and learning rate. Duration and intensity of interventions are based on each student's response to the interventions and outcomes data.

Professional school counselors address the needs of struggling students by designing and implementing intervention plans and assess the effectiveness of these interventions by collecting outcomes data. Professional school counselors assist in the RTI process by

- Providing all students with a standards-based guidance curriculum to address universal academic, career and personal/social development
- Analyzing academic and behavioral data to identify struggling students
- Identifying and collaborating on research-based intervention strategies that are implemented by school staff
- Evaluating academic and behavioral progress after interventions
- Revising interventions as appropriate
- Referring to school and community services as appropriate
- Collaborating with administrators about RTI design and implementation
- Advocating for equitable education for all students and working to remove systemic barriers (ASCA, 2008)

TABLE 15.4   **Definitions of Typical Services Performed by Professional School Counselors for Children with Disabilities As Required Under the IDEA**

Advocacy. Actively supporting the rights of individual children with disabilities, including referral, active participation in team processes, promotion of the rights and needs of students, and support for service delivery by self and others.

Assessment. Determining current performance and identifying areas of need for social or emotional functioning in school; evaluation in other areas, including substance abuse, social skills, self-determination, self-esteem, and career development.

Career counseling. The process of assisting individuals in the development of a life-career with focus on the definition of the worker role and how that role interacts with other life roles (National Career Development Association [NCDA], 1997).

Clinical case management. Coordinating counseling and delivery of other services for students with disabilities. Note that in its 2004 position statement, the ASCA (2004b) recommended against serving as case manager for students for whom a counselor is not delivering direct services.

Clinical support. Providing supervision and support of certified or trained assistants who are assisting in the delivery of related services, including mental health associates, interns, special educators, paraprofessionals, assistants, or others.

Collaboration. Working with other team members (e.g., educators, parents, other related service personnel) to deliver required services and supports to students with disabilities.

Crisis intervention. Providing intervention for emergent situations, including acting out behavior, suicide risk, panic attacks, or other urgent needs.

Decision making. Contributing to team consensus on the eligibility of a child for special education services under the current federal definitions of disability categories. Working with the team to determine required services and supports or accommodations as well as LRE where the student can receive an appropriate education.

Discipline and manifestation determination. Responding to serious discipline issues warranting possible suspension and expulsion. In cooperation with the multidisciplinary team, determining whether the behavior at issue was a manifestation of the disability and the need for alternative placement or supports.

Dropout prevention. Identifying students at high risk for dropping out and providing interventions aimed at engaging these students in school activities, promoting attendance, improving school functioning, and accessing other supports (e.g., mentors) as appropriate.

Direct services. Providing counseling to individuals or groups of students to address specific behavioral or emotional needs. May include social skills training, self-determination, career development, clinical support, grief work, and brief family counseling.

IEP development. Participating in designing measurable goals and identifying services and supports to address each area of need that interferes with functioning in school.

IEP team membership. Participating in screening, assessment, eligibility determination, IEP development, and progress monitoring for students with disabilities on the counselor's case load. Attending IEP meetings or providing written recommendations concerning the nature, frequency, and amount of counseling service to be provided to the child.

Parent counseling and training. Helping families access services in the school and community providing information on disability and disability management and supporting the implementation of their child's IEP. This may also involve helping the parent gain skills needed to support IEP goals and objectives at home.

Positive behavioral support. Collecting data on a student's interfering behaviors to determine patterns of occurrence and to identify the function of the behavior. Generation of strategies designed to replace inappropriate behavior with more appropriate behaviors meeting the same function. Devising a system of prevention and intervention emphasizing positive behavior change methods.

Referral. Completing screening or other identification procedures to help identify students in need of special education. Referring individual children, as needed, to the multidisciplinary special education team for eligibility determination.

Safekeeping of confidential records. Ensuring compliance with the IDEA and other laws (e.g., FERPA) concerning access to and contents of confidential records of students receiving special education.

Self-determination training. Helping students acquire the skills necessary to direct their own lives. Skills in this area include self-awareness; identification of strengths, limitations, and interests; identification and programming of goals; self-advocacy; and goal-directed activity.

Transition program planning. Participating in the development and implementation of a transition plan for case load students with disabilities who are 14 years old or older, including an individual's and family's postschool goals specific to postsecondary education, employment, and independent living. Providing linkages to adult services, supported employment, independent living options, and postsecondary education supports as appropriate.

ASSESSING STUDENTS WITH DISABILITIES Professional school counselors serving students with disabilities often provide wide-ranging assessment services (see Table 15.5). In addition, professional school counselors may be asked to explain the assessments conducted by others. Usually, the reason professional school counselors are asked to review the assessment reports of others is because of time conflicts preventing the assessor from attending meetings. The professional school counselor can prepare for this eventuality through training or by asking the report writer, usually the school psychologist or educational diagnostician, for a briefing on the specific report prior to the day of the multidisciplinary meeting. The key guideline for the professional school counselor to consider while carrying out this function is to review only what is written in the report and never attempt to add to the interpretation of data stemming from someone else's report.

Professional school counselors sometimes perform a complete assessment or a portion of an assessment. The professional school counselor must be trained in the administration of any assessment instruments used. Whenever assessing a student, the professional school counselor will need written parental permission to assess. Professional school counselors also need to be aware that in school systems, disagreements over who may use a testing instrument may arise among professionals who do assessments. Professional school counselors who find themselves in such conflicts will have to determine whether administering a specific assessment instrument is worth being in conflict with a colleague.

Professional school counselors often do assessments of social skills and career skills and frequently deliver or consult on the delivery of training on these skills. In assessing social skills, most programs have a preintervention screening measure, or pretest. Using the pretest along with implementing the social skills program provides an indicator of the treatment success.

In particular, the professional school counselor may be asked to assess a student's social, emotional, or behavioral functioning in school. One method is to use a behavior checklist that has parent, teacher, and student forms. The results of the assessment are the answers given by the parent, teacher, and student that the professional school counselor may then interpret, report, or both.

An example of this type of assessment instrument is the Child Behavior Checklist (CBCL), part of the Achenbach System of Empirically Based Assessment (ASEBA) by Achenbach and Rescorla (2001). The CBCL has become one of the most widely used instruments for assessing children's behavior, with separate norms for males and females and for different age groups from age 6 to 18 years. A direct observation form, teacher rating form, semistructured interview form, and youth self-report are also available. The CBCL has six scales—Affective Problems, Anxiety Problems, Somatic Problems, Attention Deficit/Hyperactivity Problems, Oppositional Defiant Problems, and Conduct Problems—oriented to the American Psychiatric Association's (2000) *Diagnostic and Statistical Manual of Mental Disorders*. In addition, the CBCL provides descriptive measures in nine observable behavioral areas. Other instruments are available to address more specific areas of social, emotional, or behavioral functioning. For example, there are substance abuse, depression, social skills, self-esteem, and anxiety rating scales available. Most of these instruments require only training on the instrument for the professional school counselor to become adept at using them, as long as they are not being used to evaluate or diagnose, but rather to describe how the student perceives the situation or how others perceive the student's situation.

Another form of assessment the professional school counselor may find useful is that of measuring the attitudes of students without disabilities toward students with disabilities. Students who do not have disabilities are found, in

---

TABLE 15.5   Assessment Functions of Professional School Counselors Serving Students with Disabilities

1. Carry out and/or interpret functional behavioral assessments.
2. Interpret educational skill assessments.
3. Carry out and/or interpret curriculum-based assessments.
4. Explain psychological testing, including cognitive ability, emotional status, and behavior measures.
5. Carry out and/or interpret counseling assessments, including social skill, emotional status, and behavioral measures.
6. Carry out structured observations of the student.
7. Carry out a student records review.
8. Help stress the need for assessing student strengths.
9. Assess peer attitudes toward students with disabilities.
10. Collaborate with others using portfolio-, performance-, and curriculum-based assessments.

general, to have less than desirable attitudes toward students with disabilities, and these attitudes can affect how much cooperative and beneficial interaction they have with students with disabilities (Salend, 1994). Professional school counselors can play a key role in helping the peers of students with disabilities develop a positive attitude toward these students.

There are two other assessments that are seeing increased usage because of 1997 changes to the IDEA. When disciplinary actions by school personnel will result in extended periods of removal from school for a student (after the first removal beyond 10 cumulative school days in a school year or after a removal that constitutes a change in placement), the IDEA requires that the IEP team meet within 10 days to make a manifestation determination. If a manifestation is evident, the team must then conduct a functional behavioral assessment (FBA) and develop a behavior intervention plan (BIP). If a behavior intervention plan already exists, the team must review and revise it as necessary to ensure that it addresses the behavior on which disciplinary action is predicated. The FBA and the development of BIPs are discussed in detail later.

POSITIVE BEHAVIORAL SUPPORT   A significant percentage of students identified as having emotional disturbance, behavioral disorders, or AD/HD demonstrate behaviors that interfere with their learning or the learning of their peers. Under the IDEA, the IEP team is charged with specific responsibilities in relation to the support of such students and others with similarly disruptive or problematic behaviors (e.g., students with autism, traumatic brain injury, mental retardation, learning disabilities).

There are three primary occasions that require the provision of *positive behavioral supports* (PBSs) under the IDEA. They are (1) the development of schoolwide systems of PBS, (2) PBS to individual students, and (3) PBS after a serious behavior (IDEA, 2004). The professional school counselor has roles in each area. In the creation of schoolwide systems of PBS, the counselor can serve on the school improvement team, help provide staff development activities, or otherwise provide assistance in general school programming for student well-being. By taking a leadership role in developing systems of schoolwide support, the school counselor can facilitate improvement for all students in the building in areas of appropriate behavior and reduction of problem behaviors (e.g., substance abuse, vandalism, bullying) and can help support increased learning for all.

In the second and third areas for providing PBS, the counselor is likely to be more directly involved in the collection of information for the FBA and the development of the BIP. In some schools, psychologists or behavior specialists typically conduct FBAs; in other systems, a behavioral support team collaboratively conducts them. This team is usually composed of a special education teacher, a regular teacher, a professional school counselor, a school psychologist, and an administrator. Sometimes professional school counselors are given the role of carrying out or interpreting FBAs. In these cases, the professional school counselor will want to attend training on the process. Most school systems provide their own training and have a required process for carrying out assessments. A general description of the process is provided later.

Schoolwide Systems of PBS.   The first approach for providing PBSs is the establishment of general, schoolwide policies and procedures that promote positive behavior among all students, commonly referred to as schoolwide positive behavior support (SWPBS; Osher, Dwyer, & Jackson, 2004; Sprague & Golly, 2004; Sugai, Horner, & Gresham, 2002). According to the National Technical Assistance Center on Positive Behavioral Interventions and Supports (U.S. Department of Education, 2005e), the SWPBS process emphasizes the creation of systems that support the adoption and durable implementation of evidence-based practices and procedures that fit within ongoing school reform efforts.

Comprehensive behavior management systems are very effective at improving school climate, decreasing instances of office referral by 50%, and preventing 80% of problematic student behaviors, including antisocial behavior; vandalism; aggression; later delinquency; and alcohol, tobacco, and other drug use. In addition, positive changes in academic achievement and school engagement have been documented using an SWPBS approach in concert with other prevention interventions (Sprague & Walker, 2004).

There are several major components in the development of effective schoolwide systems. These crucial elements are often constructed in a staff development program or incorporated into a model system that is developed, implemented, evaluated, and modified on a regular basis by school staff. Data are collected regularly and used to evaluate progress and monitor system implementation. The seven components are as follows:

1. An agreed-on and common approach to discipline,
2. A positive statement of purpose,
3. A small number of positively stated expectations for all students and staff,
4. Procedures for teaching these expectations to students,
5. A continuum of procedures for encouraging displays and maintenance of these expectations,

6. A continuum of procedures for discouraging displays of rule-violating behavior, and

7. Procedures for monitoring and evaluating the effectiveness of the discipline system on a regular and frequent basis. (U.S. Department of Education, 2005e)

One example of a process-based model for comprehensive behavior management systems is the PAR model (Rosenberg & Jackman, 2003). In this model, collaborative teams of teachers, school administrators, related service personnel, and parents work together within a prescriptive workshop format to come to consensus on an individualized, schoolwide, comprehensive approach to discipline. They collaboratively develop, implement, and evaluate plans and strategies to prevent the occurrence of troubling behavior, respond to instances of rule compliance and noncompliance in a consistent fashion, and resolve many of the issues that underlie or cause troubling behavior.

Another system, the Best Behavior Program (Sprague & Golly, 2004), provides a standardized staff development training program aimed at improving school and classroom discipline and associated outcomes. The Best Behavior Program addresses whole-school, classroom, individual student, and family collaboration practices and is intended to be used in combination with other evidence-based prevention programs such as Second Step: A Violence Prevention Curriculum (Committee for Children, 2002a). Representative school team members are trained to develop and implement positive school rules, direct teaching of rules, positive reinforcement systems, data-based decision making at the school level, effective classroom management methods, curriculum adaptation to prevent problem behavior, and functional behavioral assessment and positive behavioral intervention plans.

PBS to Individual Students. PBSs are used when an individual student's behavior interferes with his or her learning or that of others. When a student with a disability exhibits disruptive or problematic behavior, the IEP team must consider the need for a targeted intervention that includes appropriate strategies and support systems (Quinn, Gable, Rutherford, Nelson, & Howell, 1998). This targeted intervention involves the completion of an FBA and the development of a BIP to address the specific target behaviors. The rationale for an FBA is that identifying the function of a student's behavior—specifically what the student seeks to receive or avoid by engaging in the behavior—helps the IEP team develop proactive instructional strategies (such as a positive behavior management program or strategies) that address behaviors interfering with learning. The use of BIPs has wide applicability to individuals with serious challenging behaviors and has been demonstrated to reduce problem behavior by 80% in

two-thirds of the cases. The FBA/BIP process has also been used to successfully reduce disruptive classroom behaviors in students with mild disabilities in a general education classroom (e.g., Roberts, Marshall, Nelson, & Albers, 2001).

Unlike with other types of assessment, the goal of an FBA is the identification of the function of a student's misbehavior and the development of information on the conditions that give rise to the behavior, as well as the conditions likely to sustain or decrease the behavior. This information is directly applicable to the generation of strategies to prevent the occurrence of the behavior and to substitute more appropriate behaviors when similar conditions arise. The steps in the FBA process include (1) the clear identification and description of the problematic behavior, (2) the identification of the conditions and settings in which the behavior does and does not occur, (3) the generation of a hypothesis regarding the "function" of the behavior for the child, and (4) the testing of the hypothesized function of the behavior by manipulating the environmental antecedents and consequences. An excellent overview of the FBA process, including completed samples, is available on the Multimodal Functional Behavioral Assessment website (mfba.net).

To document the existence of the target behavior, team members first collect data on the occurrences of the behavior in a variety of environments and under a number of differing conditions. Data need to be collected on the situation in which the behavior is demonstrated, such as the setting, time of day, environmental conditions, and group membership (situation demands). Data also need to be collected on the specific requirements expected of the child at that point in time (setting demands). Data are typically collected via an ABC log, which is a narrative listing of antecedents (what occurs immediately before the target behavior), the description of the behavior, and consequences (what occurs immediately after the behavior). When conducting ABC observations, it is important to identify class or setting demands, describe what is occurring, describe student behavior, describe the response (from teacher or environment), identify next antecedent (and repeat), and take copious anecdotal notes. It also helps to compute percentage of time on task or percentage of work completed, if possible. An example of an ABC log is presented in Table 15.6.

The ABC data in Table 15.6 allow for the clear examination of the student's behavior. The ABC log reveals that some of Kerri's problematic behavior can be described as "calling out answers" and "arguing with teacher," both more objective targets than "disruptive behavior." Other data to collect include amount of work turned in, discipline referrals, grade report, frequency of time-outs or

TABLE 15.6 ABC Log for Kerri, a Student with Disruptive Classroom Behaviors

Time:	9:30 a.m.
Setting:	Social studies class with Mr. Pepper
Setting demands:	Group discussion with teacher-directed questioning
Participants:	Class of 28 students in Grade 4

Antecedent	Behavior	Consequence
Teacher (T) asks question.	Kerri says, "Ooh, ooh" and waves hand.	T calls on Kerri.
T asks another question.	Kerri calls out answer.	T says, "Raise your hand," and says answer is correct.
Jon (student) asks question.	Kerri calls out answer.	T says, "Kerri, that is incorrect."
T says, "Kerri, that is incorrect."	Kerri argues with T that she read it in a book.	T says, "You are wrong. The correct answer is _____."
T says, "The correct answer is _____."	Kerri says sarcastically, "Like you know anything, Pepper!"	T says, "You've disrupted class one too many times. Go to the principal's office!"

direct intervention, and educational history regarding the demonstration of similar behaviors.

In addition to the ABC data collection, a variety of individuals are asked to complete an interview regarding the possible behavioral targets. Parents, teachers, and other school staff would be asked questions about problematic behavior that occur in their interaction with the student, the conditions under which it occurs, and what the individual has done to address the behavior in the past. In addition, the student should be interviewed to examine his or her perception of the behavior and its benefit to him or her. Interview data should include a description of the problematic behavior, settings where it occurs, frequency, intensity, duration, previous interventions used, and effect on the student. The Center for Effective Collaboration and Practice (www.air.org/cecp/fba) has copyright-free samples of interview instruments available for FBAs, along with ABC charts and scatterplots to record frequency of behavior. Additional forms and completed FBA samples are available from the Center for Evidence-Based Practice (challengingbehavior.fmhi.usf.edu/fba.htm) and Special Connections, at the University of Kansas (www.specialconnections.ku.edu).

To select a specific target behavior to address, the team considers the existing problems that were revealed from the interviews and ABC data. Potential target behaviors must be described objectively and must be repeatable, controllable, and measurable. These elements are essential for verifying that the behavior is within the conscious control of the student, as well as quantifiable by the observer. To be measurable, a behavior typically must have a clear beginning and end point, contain movement, or produce a product that can be measured. Therefore, "throwing objects" would be an appropriate target behavior, whereas "aggressive behavior" would not. Similarly, "laziness, off-task behavior, and daydreaming" are not measurable targets, but "failure to complete work" can be measured. Only one or two behaviors are targeted at any one time. If necessary, the team can generate a list of behaviors and ask members to rank order them by priority level. A useful hierarchy is Severity Level I: Physically dangerous to self or others; Severity Level II: Interfering with work or learning of self or others; and Severity Level III: Inappropriate for age or grade placement or likely to cause increasing problems in the future.

Next, by examining situations where the target behavior does and does not occur, team members can identify variables that may predict the behavior (e.g., from Kerri's example in Table 15.6, the teacher asking a general question to the class) or consequences that may sustain it (e.g., the teacher paying attention to Kerri's call-outs and arguing with her). In addition, by seeing where the behavior does *not* occur, the team can explore possible functions for the student. For example, in other data collections conducted with different teachers and in different instructional settings, it became obvious that Kerri did not call out in class activities that included cooperative learning groups (but did actively assume a group leadership role).

The next step is to synthesize the available data to determine the possible function of the behavior for the student. Functions of behavior may relate to involvement with others (interactive functions), such as requests for attention (e.g., social interaction, play interaction, affection, permission to engage in an activity, action by receiver, assistance, information/clarifications, objects, food); negations/protests (e.g., cessation, refusal); declarations/comments about events or actions (e.g., about objects/persons, about errors/mistakes, affirmation, greeting, humor); or declarations about feelings/anticipation (e.g., boredom, confusion, fear, frustration, hurt feelings, pain, pleasure). Functions of behavior also may be noninteractive in that they provide internalized effects. For example, noninteractive functions can be habitual or for self-regulation, rehearsal, pleasure, or relaxation or tension release.

In our example, interview data were collected from Kerri as well as from her divorced parents. Her mother reported extreme difficulty getting Kerri to follow directions without a struggle. Her father reported no difficulty, as he "laid down the law" with no room for negotiation or discussion. He reported that he was surprised her male teacher had problems with her, as Kerri should respond immediately to the teacher as she does her father. Based on the synthesis of all of the available data, the team hypothesized that the function of her behavior may be to seek power or control.

Once the function of the behavior is hypothesized, the next step is to manipulate the environment to test the hypothesis. For example, if a student's behavior was hypothesized as seeking attention from peers, the team might construct a strategy to collect data at times where peer response was or was not forthcoming and to determine if the hypothesis was supported.

Once the function of the behavior is identified, the team can begin to craft a BIP. This document is used to provide information to educators and parents to address the student's target behavior. Typically, problematic behavior is addressed by (1) identifying ways to prevent or minimize the occurrence of the behavior, (2) providing appropriate methods to change the behavior, and (3) assisting the student in building more appropriate behaviors to meet the same function as the inappropriate behaviors did.

To reduce instances or prevent the occurrence of the behavior, strategies may be provided to help teachers and parents restructure the setting demands where the behavior occurs. For example, a teacher may use "Every Student Responds" (whole-class response) techniques to reduce the times when he or she calls on a single student for a response. Similarly, a parent may be advised to tell a child, "Come to the table now," instead of asking, "Are you ready for dinner?"

Next, the BIP often includes a specific behavior change plan to address problem behavior as it occurs. For example, Kerri's BIP might include the use of extinction procedures for call-outs to be combined with a DRL (differential reinforcement of lower rates of behavior) strategy. By ignoring the call-outs, Kerri's teacher stops reinforcing problem behavior, and the DRL provides reinforcement to Kerri as she meets preset (and increasingly lower) goals for number of call-outs per time period.

Finally, the BIP typically includes strategies to help the student learn more appropriate ways to achieve the same objective. For example, a student like Kerri who seeks control or power may be provided with choices and opportunities for appropriate leadership within the classroom or in other school activities.

Sugai et al. (2000) provided an excellent resource for school staff and administrators on the procedures for implementing the FBA process in schools. To implement the FBA and BIP processes effectively in schools, teams typically follow a series of steps:

1. Identify the case manager responsible for the overall management of the plan.
2. Describe the expected outcomes and goals for the plan.
3. Identify the problem.
4. Conduct the FBA.
5. Identify expected outcomes and goals.
6. Develop interventions.
7. Identify barriers to plan implementation.
8. Specify the interventions used to achieve the goals.
9. Specify the person or people responsible for specific interventions.
10. Specify a review date.
11. Implement the BIP.
12. Collect follow-up data on the effects of the BIP.
13. Review data and modify the plan as necessary.

PBS After a Serious Behavior. The third situation requiring PBS is when a student has been suspended or expelled because of problem behavior. According to the IDEA, FBAs and BIPs are required in connection with disciplinary removals of students receiving special education services or for any combination of school removals totaling 10 days. The IEP team must meet within 10 days to determine whether a manifestation exists, and if so, then conduct the FBA and formulate a BIP. If a BIP already exists, the team must review and revise it as necessary to ensure that it addresses the behavior on which disciplinary action is predicated. This process follows the same series of steps described earlier, but it is obviously less preventive in nature, as the student has already demonstrated seriously problematic behavior, warranting the school removal.

COLLABORATION AND GROUP DECISION MAKING
Professional school counselors often will serve on multidisciplinary teams for determining eligibility and planning programs for students with disabilities. While the laws are different with regard to the formation, membership, and

responsibilities of multidisciplinary teams under the IDEA and Section 504, the professional school counselor's role is the same whether at a meeting operating under the IDEA or under Section 504. The professional school counselor must be a supportive member of a group decision-making process whose goal is to enable a student with a disability to learn. A primary task of the professional school counselor is to help the multidisciplinary team understand the whole student, especially the individual assets of the student that are sometimes not readily apparent in paper reviews. Assets such as good character, perseverance, mood, gross- or fine-motor coordination, special talents, desire to help others, motivation, sports skills, leadership qualities, unique experiences, supportive relationships, enriching hobbies, vocational experiences, close family ties, and membership in organizations need to be brought before the multidisciplinary group planning an individualized program for the student.

All professional school counselors should consider whether peer tutoring or other generally available services would address the student's needs without the student's having to be labeled as having a disability. Most schools use some type of prereferral team process that attempts to address the student's performance problems prior to seeking eligibility for special services. On the other hand, no student may be refused the opportunity to receive special education under the IDEA when qualified. Professional school counselors should always keep in focus the fact that the student's learning needs are the main purpose of the multidisciplinary meeting.

Once a student has been deemed eligible, the IEP team will determine the appropriate constellation of services to address the student's needs. If a student needs counseling services, this responsibility sometimes will be assigned to the professional school counselor. In other situations, a psychologist or social worker will provide the services. Sometimes the goals are written so that any one of these three professionals can provide the service, and the professionals determine among themselves who will take the responsibility. It is important that the provider of the service have the necessary training and availability.

MANIFESTATION MEETINGS Manifestation hearings are multidisciplinary team meetings convened because a student has been excluded for disciplinary reasons from his or her educational program for more than 10 days during a school year. The meeting must occur within 10 days of the student's removal from school. The purpose of the manifestation meeting is for the team to determine whether the student's behavior was caused by, or had a direct and substantial relation to, the student's disability. It is important to remember that the student's competency is not at issue

in a manifestation meeting. In other words, manifestation is not a determination of whether the student understood if his or her actions were right or wrong; rather, the meeting is purely intended to determine whether there was a causal connection between the student's disability and the behavior.

If the team decides that the behavior was caused by, or was directly related to, the student's disability, the student is reinstated. If the team determines that the student's disability did not cause the behavior, the student may be suspended or expelled unless the team finds one of two situations occurred: 1) if the student's IEP was not properly implemented or 2) if the team determines that the IEP did not provide the student with a FAPE (and therefore additional or different services should be included in the IEP).

Under the IDEA, if a student with a disability is removed from school for more than 10 days, he or she must continue to receive programs and services that will allow him or her to progress toward meeting the goals on the IEP and in the general curriculum. These programs and services may be provided through home teaching or at a different location, such as an alternative education setting. Under Section 504, if the problem behavior is not a result of the student's disability, then the student may be excluded, and there is no requirement to continue his or her educational services during the period of exclusion.

In some instances, a student's behavior may relate to a disability and still result in a removal from school for up to 45 school days. This can occur if (1) the student is involved in a drug offense, (22) the student is involved in a weapons offense, or (3) the student's behavior inflicted serious bodily injury.

The professional school counselor can be an important player in the manifestation hearing, particularly when the student's disability is emotionally based or has strong emotional or behavioral aspects (e.g., AD/HD, emotional disturbance, or autism). The team may look to the professional school counselor to help it better understand the nature of the emotionally or behaviorally based disability. This can place the professional school counselor in a difficult position if other staff members disagree with his or her perspective. For example, the student might have physically or verbally assaulted a staff member in a fairly serious manner. When this happens, the counselor can lose the trust or respect of staff by simply focusing on the manifestation issue without acknowledging the effect of the assault on the staff member, whether or not it was a manifestation of the student's disability.

DETERMINING NEED FOR COUNSELING SERVICES FOR STUDENTS WITH DISABILITIES When considering individual counseling for a student, the professional school counselor should work with the family and staff to construct a list of the social, emotional, or behavioral issues and concerns affecting the student's educational performance. Assessments (including the FBA, if available) and interviews can provide important information on the extent and nature of the problems. A review and prioritization of this information can help the team to clarify the problem, identify ways to involve parents and other staff (e.g., teachers, other related service providers), recognize the need for implementation in multiple settings, and reveal the extent of this need and its impact on the types and amounts of services needed.

It is important for the professional school counselor to help the team remain focused on the purpose of school counseling as a related service for children with disabilities—that is, to enable the student to learn. It is easy to slip into discussing counseling interventions that might be helpful for the student, but that are not required for the student to learn. For example, the parents of a child with a learning or emotional disability might feel that counseling could reduce the child's anxiety. However, unless such a reduction in anxiety is needed for the child to be able to learn, it should not be included in the IEP.

Counseling goals usually fall under the area of social-emotional or behavioral needs, though they may include transition goals as mandated by law for students over age 16. Typical areas addressed by counseling goals include anger management, stress/anxiety management, respect for authority, compliance with school rules, self-determination/life planning, career awareness/vocational development, coping skills/frustration tolerance, interpersonal skills, family issues regarding postschool outcomes, and self-esteem.

COUNSELOR CONCERNS ABOUT PROVIDING IEP SERVICES The IEP team, as a group, determines what services the student is to receive, the frequency of the services, and who is to provide the services. No one individual can change the components of an IEP. Sometimes the professional school counselor may feel this is not the appropriate time to provide the service, these are not the appropriate services to provide, or the training to carry out the task appropriately is lacking. Any of these issues could produce an ethical dilemma for the professional school counselor. In these situations, the professional school counselor must follow the IEP as written until it is changed. At a meeting to revise the IEP, the concerns can be raised, and the team will have the opportunity to revise the IEP to appropriately address them. Under the 2004 provisions of the IDEA, nonsubstantive changes can be made to the IEP without another meeting.

It is also important that professional school counselors remain cognizant of the limits of their role and ensure that they do not perform activities outside their area of qualification. In particular, counselors should be careful not to assume responsibilities that are typically within the purview of psychologists or social workers or that are specifically assigned to others by the IEP. In some instances, IEP counseling goals will indicate that the counselor, psychologist, or social worker may provide the service. In that situation, the providers can decide who will implement the IEP. If a student's IEP calls for counseling services and the professional school counselor is unable to provide them, the school may contract with another counselor to provide the services or may rewrite the IEP so that a psychologist can provide the services.

IEP Development

WRITING COUNSELING IEP GOALS Goals are the core components of an IEP. They are intended to establish what the IEP team—including the parent and the child, when appropriate—thinks the student should accomplish in a year. These goals are based on the needs of the student as determined by relevant assessments and on the student's present levels of academic achievement and functional performance. The IDEA requires goals to address all areas of identified needs in academic and functional skill areas. Functional skills may include adaptive skills, classroom behavior, social-interpersonal skills, self-determination, and vocational skills. The IDEA specifically requires that the IEP team, in developing goals, consider the strengths of the child; the concerns of the parents for enhancing the education of their child; the results of the initial or most recent evaluation of the child; and the academic, developmental, and functional needs of the child. The goals are to be designed to enable the student to be involved in and make progress in the general education curriculum and to address all of the student's other educationally related needs that result from the disability. Since goals are focused on the student's expected achievement in one year's time, goals are generally written in broad, but measurable, terms.

For each area of identified need, at least one goal should be written. If there are multiple areas, the team may decide to prioritize the issues and first address those issues it considers most important. Following are guidelines on how to develop effective goals:

Each annual goal should include five components: (1) *direction* of change desired, (2) *deficit* or *excess*, (3) *present* level, (4) *expected* level, and (5) *resources* needed.

The direction of change is one of the following: (1) *increase* (e.g., social skills, impulse control, self-determination), (2) *decrease* (e.g., hitting, temper tantrums, call-outs, days absent), or (3) *maintain* (e.g., attention span, attendance).

The deficit or excess is the general area that is identified as needing special attention. Examples of areas in which deficits may occur include work completion, ability to follow staff directions, frustration tolerance, coping, impulse control, and peer relationships. Examples of areas in which excesses may occur include physical aggression, activity level, talking out, and anxiety level.

The present level ("from" _____) is a description of what the student does now in the area of deficit or excess; it is his or her present performance level. Examples of present level include working with a peer for two minutes, completing 40% of class work, arguing with teacher when corrected, remaining on task with direct adult supervision, and following directions with repeated prompts.

The expected level ("to" _____) is where the student can reasonably be expected to be, or what he or she can reasonably be expected to attain, at the end of one year, if the needed resources are provided. Each expected level must be specific to the individual student and must be based on where the student is at present and what is realistic to expect from him or her in a year's time if the needed resources are provided. Examples of expected level include working with a peer cooperatively for 10 minutes, following teacher directions the first time given, responding appropriately to redirection/correction, remaining on task for 15 minutes with no reminders, using appropriate language in school, and asking for help or a break when needed.

The resources needed describe the special methods, techniques, materials, situations, equipment, and so forth that will be needed to enable the student to reach the expected levels of performance. Examples of resources include positive reinforcement, a point system, individual counseling, parent training, and job coaching.

Table 15.7 provides sample goals with all essential components.

EVALUATION PROCEDURES IEPs must include evaluation procedures and schedules for determining, at least on an annual basis, whether the goals and objectives are being achieved. The evaluation procedure selected must be appropriate for the behavior or skill in question. Put another way, not every behavior or skill can be evaluated through "teacher or therapist observation." Some of the evaluation procedures that might be used for different objectives include direct observation, formal or informal assessments, and permanent products.

Direct observation by counselors and teachers provides a continuous and potentially valuable source of assessment information regarding student performance and may be used in all areas of instruction, including academic and social behavior. Observation can vary in its degree of formality and specificity, but when used to evaluate student progress, it must be objective. Observational methods that are both objective and structured include event recording (e.g., number of call-outs), duration recording (e.g., time on task), interval recording (e.g., whether the student kept his hands to himself for each 15-minute period), and time sampling (e.g., whether the student was in her seat each time the timer went off). Evaluation methods may also use formal and informal tests (e.g., the ARC's Self-Determination Scale) or permanent

---

TABLE 15.7 Sample Goal Statements

1. Jon will decrease destructive behavior from an average of five incidents per week to no destructive acts through reinforcement of positive behavior and individual counseling.
2. Chandra will increase coping skills from screaming and crying to asking for help appropriately through modeling, strategy instruction, and positive reinforcement.
3. Lin will increase ability to follow class and school rules from 30% compliance to 90% compliance through group counseling, positive reinforcement (point sheet), and the use of a peer buddy.
4. Keith will increase peer relationships from rejection by peer group members to inclusion in group activities through social skills training and the use of group contingencies.
5. Davon will decrease arguing with adults and peers from a mean of 13 times per day to zero times through the use of extinction and individual or group counseling.
6. Keisha will increase social behavior from daily hitting, kicking, and throwing objects to no hitting, kicking, or throwing objects through modeling, positive reinforcement for appropriate social behaviors, and structured, small-group interaction.

TABLE 15.8 Sample Objectives

1. Given a 10-minute cooperative learning activity, Rodney will participate with peers without leaving the group in two of three trials. Evaluation procedure: Peer group log; Schedule: Daily.
2. Given a verbal direction from the teacher, Jay will comply within 1 minute 80% of the time. Evaluation procedure: "Follows Directions" points on point sheets; Schedule: Weekly.
3. When included in a small group of peers, Julie will exhibit consideration for others by taking turns, sharing, and refraining from physical aggression in three of four opportunities. Evaluation procedure: "Peer" points on daily point sheet; Schedule: Weekly.
4. Given bus tokens, Jose will arrive for school on time 95% of school days. Evaluation procedure: Attendance record review; Schedule: Weekly.
5. When demonstrating signs of anxiety and prompted by a teacher, Thomas will verbally identify the cause of his distress and at least one strategy for resolution. Evaluation procedure: Event recording; Schedule: Weekly.

products (e.g., a point sheet, percent work completed, homework returned, attendance record).

The frequency of data collection should be determined by (1) the importance of the objective in question and (2) the amount of additional staff time that it takes. As a guideline, evaluative data should generally be collected at least every week. It is these data that must be reported on regular IEP report cards. Table 15.8 provides examples of objectives written in measureable terms that include evaluation procedure and schedule.

SPECIFYING IEP SERVICES The IDEA further requires that the IEP include a statement of the special education and related services and supplementary aids and services, based on scientifically based practices, to the extent practicable, to be provided to or on behalf of the child. In addition, the IEP must describe the student's participation in regular education programs, a list of the projected dates for the initiation of services, and the anticipated duration of services.

The frequency and intensity of counseling sessions are determined at the IEP meeting. Services will vary significantly according to an individual child's needs. Sometimes, for example, a student's needs require weekly sessions, either to help the student learn a new coping skill or to help the student stay emotionally stable and support his or her access to education. In other situations, the student may need to be seen less frequently, for monitoring only. In any counseling relationship, there also may be situations requiring that the counselor see the student when in crisis in addition to the time allotted on the IEP. A counselor is able to provide more services than the IEP dictates, but not less.

With the professional school counselor's input, the IEP team may also determine whether required services are provided individually or in group sessions. In other situations, the team will leave that decision to the judgment of the service provider. Also, the IEP team determines whether the service is delivered directly or via consultation with another staff member or parent.

Individualized Transition Program Planning

As noted above, the IDEA requires the IEP team to create a transition plan for a student with a disability by the time the student is 16 years old. Section 504 has no transition requirements. Students must be invited to IEP meetings when their transition plans are discussed. Representatives of programs such as vocational rehabilitation services also are to be invited to transition planning meetings if the parent consents. Sometimes the state's department of rehabilitation services can provide diagnostic services while the student is in school and can then offer training for a career, money to assist in obtaining educational or support services, or linkages to adult services as needed after graduation.

The transition plan is intended to address all areas of the student's life after high school, including postsecondary education, career, independent living, recreation, and community involvement. Counselors can help the team by assessing student career interests; developing appropriate transition goals; providing resources and connections to adult services as needed; and helping the student with personal adjustment, self-concept development, self-determination training, career exploration, and job coaching. Professional school counselors might also help plan and implement a school-to-work program or internship for the student.

Since a transition plan focuses on the individual's present needs and stated preferences, assessment is required. Typically, the assessment includes interest inventories, interviews of the student and parents (to determine expectations regarding employment, education, and living arrangements after high school), review of work history and work habits, review of progress toward graduation and postsecondary acceptance, self-determination assessment, and other information specific to the individual student as needed (e.g., assessment of functional living skills, vocational assessment, interpersonal skill assessment). In many schools, the professional school counselor provides some or most of this assessment information to the team.

The individualized transition plan (ITP) is developed after information is collected on the student's and family's hopes and expectations for the future and synthesized with assessment results, as described earlier. For example, the goals and needs addressed in a transition plan for Ryan, a 16-year-old 11th-grade student with learning and behavioral disorders, might include

- Obtaining a part-time paid job in the community;
- Selecting and applying to a two-year college or vocational program;
- Shadowing workers in three areas of career interest: elevator maintenance, cable installation, and computer networking;
- Identifying community-based counseling agencies to assist in addressing life stresses after high school; and
- Participating in church-related youth activities on a monthly basis.

Transition planning also includes goals relating to personal development, independence, self-determination, social skill development, or other needs for adult independent functioning (e.g., self-care, accepting criticism, cooking, resume development). For example, if a student plans to live independently in an apartment, then he or she may need goals in some or all of the following areas:

- Identify living options in the community,
- Describe processes and requirements for renting an apartment,
- Secure employment to financially support the goal,
- Budget for the cost of living by oneself,
- Demonstrate skills for maintaining an apartment, and
- Identify and access needed community resources.

Secondary Transition Programming

In addition to the development of an ITP for each student over age 16 with an IEP, the IDEA requires transition programming to support the needs of the students and enable them to meet their specific goals. Research has documented many "best practices" in transition. The following list of recommended practices is synthesized from the literature and is intended to be integrated into secondary programs serving students with disabilities (Sitlington, Clark, & Kolstoe, 2000): vocational training, parent involvement, interagency collaboration, social skills training, paid work experience, follow-up employment services, integrated settings, community-based instruction, vocational assessment, community-referenced curriculum, career education curricula and experience, employability skills training, and academic skills training.

While not every school can or will provide all of the recommended transition practices, there are a number of strategies that can be incorporated into any school program and that often involve the secondary school counselor. Hughes et al. (1997) identified the following socially validated transition support strategies: identify and provide social support, identify environmental support and provide environmental changes, promote acceptance, observe the student's opportunities for choice, provide choice-making opportunities, identify the student's strengths and areas needing support, teach self-management, and provide opportunities to learn and practice social skills.

An excellent resource for schools and professionals serving secondary students with disabilities is the National Alliance for Secondary Education and Transition (NASET). NASET is a voluntary coalition of 30 national organizations representing general education, special education, career and technical education, youth development, postsecondary education, workforce development, and families. NASET was formed specifically to promote high-quality and effective secondary education and transition services by identifying what youth need in order to achieve success in postsecondary education and training, civic engagement, meaningful employment, and adult life. NASET has identified benchmarks that reflect quality secondary education and transition services for all students in its Standards for Secondary Education and Transition. The standards focus on five areas relating to the transition of students with disabilities to adult living: schooling, career preparatory experiences, youth development and youth leadership, family involvement, and connecting activities. These standards are available online at www.ncset.org/teleconferences/docs/TransitionToolkit.pdf.

HIGH SCHOOL PROGRAMMING The professional school counselor has an essential role in providing support for appropriate curricular programming for secondary students with disabilities. Recent data indicate that students with disabilities have increased significantly the number of academic courses they are taking in mathematics, science, and foreign language (Wagner et al., 2004). This is likely a positive effect of the increased requirements for access to the general curriculum under NCLB. It is unknown whether this access, in and of itself, will be sufficient to enable students with disabilities to pass high-stakes testing for graduation, now required in virtually every state. It will be essential to monitor student progress carefully over the next few years to determine what additional supports and services are required to enable students with disabilities to graduate with a standard diploma.

Another concern recently noted has been the significant decrease in the numbers of students taking vocational courses (Wagner et al., 2004). This is likely a result of the increase in courses taken in the general curriculum by students with disabilities. This is a large concern, however, as vocational programming can significantly increase positive postsecondary outcomes (Wagner, Blackorby, Cameto, & Newman, 1993).

As Wagner et al. (2004) noted, "An overriding emphasis on academics, to the exclusion of vocational and other kinds of nonacademic instruction, could be mismatched to the goals of some students with disabilities." Professional school counselors should advocate for curricular programming to address individual student needs and help families to realistically determine whether goals should relate primarily to postsecondary education or to employment and independent living.

POSTSECONDARY EDUCATIONAL PROGRAMMING   As noted above, students with disabilities attend college and other postsecondary educational programs at rates far below those of their nondisabled peers. One of the greatest needs for these students is to have others hold high expectations for their continued education, including attendance at four-year universities, two-year colleges, technical schools, and community colleges. There are excellent resources available to help students identify appropriate colleges, seek reasonable accommodations, and access support services (e.g., mental health services) while attending postsecondary educational programs. Some examples include the following:

1. DO-IT (Disabilities, Opportunities, Internetworking, and Technology), at the University of Washington (www.washington.edu/doit/Resources/postsec.html)
2. Post-ITT (Postsecondary Innovative Transition Technology), supported by the U.S. Department of Education's Office of Special Education and Rehabilitative Services (www.postitt.org/indexs.html)
3. HEATH Resource Center (Higher Education and Adult Training for People with Disabilities), a national clearinghouse on postsecondary education for individuals with disabilities (www.heath.gwu.edu)

Professional school counselors can help students with disabilities significantly by providing them and their parents specialized information regarding readiness for college, including accommodations for the SAT-I or ACT exams, information on disability disclosure during the application process, methods to interview effectively, ways to document a disability at the postsecondary level, information on how to identify available accommodations at various colleges, and tips for finding a "good match" for a specific student's special needs.

Following are general tips on supporting students with learning disabilities in the transition to college:

1. Teach students about their disability and compensatory strategies. Students should understand the nature of their learning problems. Specifically, they should be aware of their academic strengths and weaknesses, accommodations that allow them to circumvent their learning problems, and other study skills and learning strategies.
2. Teach students to self-advocate. Students become self-advocates when they (1) demonstrate an understanding of their disability, (2) are aware of their legal rights, and (3) can competently and tactfully advocate for their rights and needs to those in positions of authority.
3. Teach students about the law. After high school, students with disabilities are no longer entitled to special services, only equal access. Students need to know that it is their responsibility to self-identify and provide documentation supporting their need for accommodations that is sufficient to meet their school's criteria. They must request necessary accommodations, be familiar with college requirements, make programming decisions with the assistance of an advisor, monitor their own progress, request assistance when needed, and meet the same academic standards as all other students.
4. Help students select postsecondary schools wisely. Although choosing the right college is important for any student, it takes on added significance when the student has a learning disability. (Skinner & Lindstrom, 2003)

CAREER COUNSELING   Career counseling for students with disabilities requires the professional school counselor to understand the implications of the disability for a potential career. The school counselor must encourage and support, while remaining realistic. Computerized career programs can easily be used with assistive technology like screen readers to enable students with disabilities to explore various career possibilities and requirements independently. The professional school counselor who is knowledgeable about training opportunities through private and public agencies and about resources in general, including financial resources, can be helpful to students with disabilities. There are excellent resources for career exploration online, including these:

1. Kids & Youth Pages from the U.S. Department of Labor at www.dol.gov/dol/audience/aud-kidsyouth.htm
2. Occupational Outlook Handbook at www.bls.gov/oco
3. Teenager's Guide to the Real World—Careers at www.bygpub.com/books/tg2rw/careers.htm
4. Job and Career Resources for Teenagers at www.quintcareers.com/teen_jobs.html

In addition to the websites intended for the general population, there are a number of excellent resources specifically developed for students with disabilities. Partners in Employment is a free online course designed to help people with developmental disabilities find meaningful jobs and plan a career. In this course, available at www.partnersinpolicymaking.com/employment/index.html, participants create a resume or portfolio of their strengths, skills, and interests; learn how to network and identify potential employers; prepare for an interview; and gain an understanding of the hiring process.

An additional resource is a comprehensive course, complete with lesson plans, entitled Life Skills for Vocational Success, available at www.workshopsinc.com/manual/TOC.html. This course includes lessons intended for students with disabilities on wide-ranging competencies, including developing listening skills, avoiding destructive behaviors, getting along with co-workers, having a good attitude, and keeping sexual behavior out of the workplace.

VOCATIONAL/CAREER PLANNING   In many school systems today, online programs and software are used to assist students in career planning. Typically, they include interest inventories and career-trait surveys. In addition, some programs provide decision-making support to students to help them identify job values, personal strengths, and coursework related to professions of interest (e.g., the Career Decision-Making System [CDM]). There are also online tools that assess student interests, aptitudes, and personality styles. A good resource is www.QuintCareers.com, which provides reviews of free and low-cost online career assessment tools, including the name and link to each assessment, the measures obtained, the relative ease of use, and the level of detail of the results. In addition, QuintCareers provides a qualitative rating of the overall utility of each assessment based on their own and their clients' experiences.

In addition to computerized testing for vocational interests, there are typically either school system staff or local agency staff trained to do vocational aptitude testing of students with disabilities. In fact, in many school systems, all secondary students with IEPs complete a lengthy vocational assessment at a vocational school or center.

Other information necessary for vocational/career planning includes interview data from parents regarding their expectations and dreams for their child, the student's stated career goal and history of work experience, reports of the student's work habits and behaviors, and observation of the student's functioning at the work site.

The involvement of staff from the state office of rehabilitative services is essential in obtaining linkages to adult services, determining funding for postsecondary educational or vocational programs, and assisting families with ongoing transition needs beyond high school. For some students with disabilities (including even those who are high functioning), providing information on how to access Social Security Insurance and Social Security Disability Insurance (www.ssa.gov) can allow these students to attend adult vocational training programs, access job coaching and other adult services (e.g., Ticket to Work Program), pay for college, or defer income to pay for disability-related expenses (e.g., Plan for Achieving Self-Support [PASS]).

VOCATIONAL TRAINING   Another strategy employed to improve outcomes after high school for individuals with disabilities is vocational training. The School-to-Work Opportunities Act, passed in 1994, focuses on coordinated efforts between schools and the community to design and provide an appropriate, individualized education for individuals with disabilities, including those with emotional and behavior disorders, that smoothly and successfully moves them from the school environment to the work environment. This act and other school efforts focus on providing students with the skills that employers seek. Thus, while still in school, students are provided with specific job training and experiences through vocational work placements, job coaching, and other related activities.

SELF-DETERMINATION   The Division on Career Development and Transition of the Council for Exceptional Children (CEC) defines *self-determination* as a combination of skills, knowledge, and beliefs that enable a person to engage in goal-directed, self-regulated, autonomous behavior. These skills enhance individuals' abilities to take control of their lives and assume the role of successful adults. Research has found that helping students acquire and exercise self-determination skills is a strategy that leads to more positive educational outcomes, including higher rates of employment, postsecondary education, and independent living (S. Field, Martin, Miller, Ward, & Wehmeyer, n.d.).

Elements of self-determination include self-awareness, self-evaluation, choice and decision making, goal-setting and attainment, problem solving, self-advocacy, and IEP planning. Professional school counselors can utilize some of the following strategies to assist students in developing their self-determination skills:

- Use a structured curriculum to directly teach skills and attitudes. A good compilation of curriculum descriptions can be found on the Self-Determination Synthesis Project website at www.uncc.edu/sdsp/sd_curricula.asp.
- Use assessments to determine student needs (e.g., the ARC's Self-Determination Scale is available free

online at the Beach Center on Disability of the University of Kansas, at www.beachcenter.org).

- Prepare students for the IEP planning and implementation process. Expect and support active student participation and leadership in their IEPs. (Resources for student participation in the IEP process are available through the National Dissemination Center for Children with Disabilities at www.nichcy.org.)
- Meet with students weekly to discuss their goal attainment and help them to implement strategies.
- Provide students with information on their disabilities. Help students to describe their needs to others and appropriately request needed accommodations.
- Help students to access available resources, especially online, to assist with college, career, leisure, and living planning. (See, e.g., the National Center on Secondary Education and Transition at www.youthhood.org.)
- Help students adjust strategies, schedules, or supports in collaboration with their teachers or family members to help them to attain their goals.
- Encourage families to promote choice and decision making.
- Allow for student selection of course electives and program of study.

There are excellent resources, including staff development materials, curricula, and lesson plans, available online to promote self-determination in students with disabilities. Following are some examples of electronic resources:

- The Person-Centered Planning Education Site (PCPES), at www.ilr.cornell.edu/ped/tsal/pcp, was developed by the Employment and Disability Institute at Cornell University. The PCPES provides coursework and staff development activities in such areas as transition planning, community membership, and self-determination.
- The Self-Determination Synthesis Project (www.uncc.edu/sdsp), at the University of North Carolina, provides information on exemplary programs, reviews existing research on self-advocacy models for students with disabilities, and develops and disseminates an array of products, including a directory of self-advocacy model programs.
- The Council for Exceptional Children and the University of Minnesota Institute on Community Integration collaboratively developed *Student-Led IEPs: A Guide for Student Involvement*, a 2001 publication useful for working with secondary students with disabilities (available at www.cec.sped.org/bk/catalog2/student-led_ieps.pdf).

| VOICES FROM THE FIELD 15.1 | ADVOCACY FOR STUDENTS WITH DISABILITIES |

The role of the professional school counselor encompasses many areas of the educational experience. As a professional school counselor, it is important to advocate for the needs of all students, which includes students with disabilities. This sometimes creates the feeling of a "baptism by fire" in the first year of practice for a new professional school counselor. Many times the counselor is unclear about his or her responsibilities, or the child study (special education) team is unclear in communicating their expectations. However, it is the responsibility of the professional school counselor to be able to have an honest and courageous dialogue to understand the team's expectations. Quite often both the professional school counselor and the team members have the same goals in mind, but go about a plan of attack in *very* different ways. Once the professional school counselor and the team are in synch with each other, the effectiveness of the team can grow exponentially.

The professional school counselor is the consistent common bond between the family of a student with a disability and the school community. It is the responsibility of the professional school counselor to create a relationship with the student and synthesize that relationship with the

student's educational needs. The professional school counselor advocates for that student's needs within the team process and throughout every school day. When the special education team meets, it expects the professional school counselor to be familiar with the student in and out of the classroom, as well as with the student's personal or family concerns. Many times it is the information provided by the professional school counselor that explains behaviors or reactions that members of the team would not necessarily see because they lack context.

When the special education process begins, the counselor may be the only professional in the meeting with prior knowledge of the student. It is the professional school counselor that must inform the team of the student's strengths and weaknesses. It is also the role of the school counselor to understand the criteria the team must use to evaluate the student's placement in special education. The school counselor needs to be able to see from both viewpoints—the observed qualities of the student versus the actual special education criteria—and translate that vision into a well-thought-out conclusion. Many times the team will look to the professional school counselor as the person to span the gap between home and school and to deliver appropriate information to the family. The professional school counselor has the ability to integrate the special education information into a more "user friendly" explanation for families and students. It is for this reason that the professional school counselor must understand the special education process, in addition to NCLB and the IDEA.

When the professional school counselor has a strong relationship with students with special needs, it makes the IEP process more cohesive. The goals and objectives that each child has on his or her IEP can be supported by the professional school counselor and evaluated for effectiveness. Also, there may be goals that need to be met with the help of the professional school counselor, such as individual counseling, group counseling, and transition planning. The professional school counselor can implement a number of strategies to become an effective supporter of that student. Sometimes the professional school counselor is integral in providing education to the school community regarding certain disabilities, rather than providing a direct service to the student; other times the professional school counselor does both. Regardless of the role that the professional school counselor needs to adopt, it is in the best interest of the student that the responsibility be met efficiently and effectively and with empathy.

As you become a professional school counselor, it is important to understand your role as an advocate for all students. Many times you will be called upon to be the expert: the advocate, the translator, the supporter, and the policy specialist. However, it is within these roles that we support our school and the community. As a professional school counselor, you may be involved in the team process of writing IEPs and BIPs or of sitting in on manifestation meetings; the perspective that the counselor has is fundamental for these documents to be effective. In my professional school counseling career, I have had many positive moments working with the special education team and the parents for the good of the student. As you move into this role, my hope is that you can maximize the capacity of the team in your building that supports students with special needs in all domains and that you can witness the immense growth of students who are supported by this process.

Source: Maryellen Beck, Professional School Counselor, George Fox Middle School, Anne Arundel County Public School System, Maryland

INFORMATION ABOUT THE SPECIAL EDUCATION PROCESS AND THE RIGHT OF APPEAL

Many families seek information about special education services for students with disabilities. For instance, parents may want to know what will happen to their child during an evaluation, what will happen with the evaluation results, or what information is included in the IEP. Parents may question whether they should seek their own evaluations, worry about going to a meeting without their own legal representatives, or want to know if there are any safeguards or appeals if they disagree with the process.

Many excellent organizations provide assistance to families, educators, agency workers, and professional school counselors who are seeking additional information. Four national organizations are listed in Table 15.9.

States also have parent advocacy groups and public law organizations that are focused on providing parents a range of assistance. The professional school counselor can identify these organizations in a local area, but for a listing of parent resources by state, go to www.taalliance.org/centers.

The IDEA and Section 504 require that families be given a statement of their rights and means of appeal at regular points in the process. This includes information on the multiple means to address any disagreement with the identification, classification, program, or services developed for or provided to the student. At multidisciplinary team meetings, families are given a booklet on these rights and asked to sign a paper saying they have received such a booklet. In some instances, the parents may resolve their concerns without using these dispute resolution processes by appealing directly to the school principal or district supervisory personnel. However, the IDEA and Section 504 have more formal processes to resolve disagreements.

Under the IDEA, the first step in the dispute resolution process is the resolution session. The resolution session provides an opportunity to resolve issues without having to use the due process system. Parties may agree not to conduct the resolution session. Parents' other approaches to dispute resolution are mediation and due process. Due process is a hearing process where parents and the school district present their disagreement to an impartial hearing officer, who then issues a legal decision resolving the matter. Appeals from the hearing officer's decision can go to state or federal court. There is a similar requirement for due process hearings under Section 504.

In addition to these processes, the IDEA and Section 504 include complaint investigation processes. In these situations, state or federal offices assign investigators who determine whether appropriate laws and regulations have been followed, and if not, they order that corrective actions be taken.

GENERAL ISSUES FOR PROFESSIONAL SCHOOL COUNSELORS SERVING STUDENTS WITH DISABILITIES

Clearly, there are numerous ways in which professional school counselors will come into contact with students with disabilities. Although there are significant similarities in serving students with and without disabilities in schools, there are a few areas where special sensitivity is required or where special considerations are necessary in serving youth with disabilities.

Cultural Considerations

High stress can be felt by the parents of a child with a disability in families from all cultural backgrounds. However, the professional school counselor needs to be sensitive to cultural considerations because families from different cultures may approach identification of a child with a disability differently, particularly regarding the level of protection and independence afforded.

In some cultures, the disability of a family member is too private to share, and some families feel that discussion about the disability with anyone outside the family would be shameful. In other cultures, a high value on learning and achievement may create added pressure on a student. In still other cultures, those identified by mainstream society as having disabilities are not seen as disabled. Sometimes attempting to physically help a child with a disability can present a challenge because in some cultures the degree of physical touch implies respect or disrespect.

When collaborating with or counseling families of students from different cultures, the professional school counselor must consider the language differences and the cultural views of those involved. This process can be improved with the help of a friend of the family who is from the same culture, who can be an interpreter of both the language and the culture. It is critical for the professional school counselor to hear the "real" needs and priorities of the family and attempt to address them. To the extent possible, professional school counselors must place themselves in the position of the families. Before the professional can begin to meet the needs of families and children with disabilities, he or she must understand how family needs are shaped by the context of their subculture (M. Seligman & Darling, 1989). Among groups where there is a strong religious presence, a clergy member can provide support for a student with a disability, and this aid may be more readily accepted than assistance offered by the counselor would be.

The professional school counselor can help the family of diverse students cope with the maze of bureaucracy that public education may present to someone from another culture. For parents of a student with a disability, fears often exist because of language issues; those in the school system may not understand the needs of their child, and the parents may not understand how best to acquire services for their child. The CEC (www.cec.sped.org) has a Division for Culturally and Linguistically Diverse Exceptional Learners that can be a resource for the professional school counselor addressing the needs of a student with a disability from another culture. The American Counseling Association maintains a division of multicultural counseling, the Association for Multicultural Counseling and Development, referred to in Chapter 5, which could also provide resources.

TABLE 15.9 Organizations Assisting Parents and Guardians with Appeals

1. The National Association of State Directors of Special Education (NASDSE; www.nasdse.org) facilitates state agency efforts to maximize educational outcomes for individuals with disabilities.
2. The Council for Exceptional Children (CEC; www.cec.sped.org) is the professional organization for special education with divisions and councils that address many aspects involved in educating students with disabilities. Professional school counselors will probably find subdivisions such as the Council for Children with Behavioral Disorders, the Division of Career Development and Transition, the Division for Culturally and Linguistically Diverse Exceptional Learners, and the Division for Research most helpful.
3. The National Dissemination Center for Children and Youth with Disabilities (NICHCY; www.nichcy.org) is a national information and referral center that provides information and fact sheets on disabilities and disability-related issues for families, educators, and other professionals.
4. The ERIC Clearinghouse on Disabilities and Gifted Education (ericec.org; the searchable database is now at www.eric.ed.gov) provides research and publications related to individuals with disabilities. ERIC also maintains a National Parent Information Network.

Summary/Conclusion

The professional school counselor's role with the student who has a disability is still emerging, even though the laws addressing students with disabilities have been around since the early to mid-1970s. Professional school counselors have always served students with disabilities; however, it was usually with services similar to those given to regular education students who might be experiencing a problem. When professional school counselors addressed the clinical needs of students with disabilities, it was most often to provide appropriate referral sources. Today, professional school counselors are being called on to play a major role in delivering a broad array of counseling services to students with disabilities. Thus, professional school counselors must have a clear understanding of the laws that govern eligibility of and service delivery to those students.

Professional school counselors are well trained to provide counseling services to students with disabilities and their families—in part because professional school counselors have a strong tradition of training in developmental counseling. Professional school counselors have traditionally focused on integrating social and academic skills and prefer working collaboratively, rather than in isolation. Increasingly, counselors are seeking additional training and taking on greater mental health and case management roles. The ASCA (2004b) has responded by issuing a position paper on appropriate and inappropriate roles for professional school counselors serving students with disabilities. One of the main concerns of the ASCA is that counselors not be put in positions that will harm their counseling relationships and thus their effectiveness. The ASCA leaves open the opportunity for professional school counselors to address any issue that falls in the counselor's arena, and it seeks to promote a role for the school counselor to work collaboratively and in a transdisciplinary mode when serving students with disabilities. It is possible that a new subspecialty in school counseling could develop in response to the increasing needs of students with disabilities. For example, perhaps special education and student services may jointly fund positions providing a school team with a professional school counselor specially trained in the areas discussed in this chapter.

The number of students with disabilities has grown, and counseling services will be essential for many of them. Contracting outside mental health services can be expensive, but it may be necessary for schools to address these needs. How this will affect the school counseling profession is unclear, but those school counselors today who seek additional training in clinical counseling and collaborative team problem solving to better serve students with disabilities may be blazing a path for future professional school counselors.

Activities

1. Interview a school administrator regarding how the IDEA and NCLB have affected his or her school policies. What changes were made to accommodate students with special needs? How effective have these adjustments been?
2. Create an example of an SWPBS system. What positive expectations would you convey to all students and staff? How would you encourage positive behaviors and discourage negative behaviors? How would you monitor and evaluate the effectiveness of your program?
3. Bobby is a fourth-grade student identified with a serious emotional disturbance. He is aggressive and having difficulty getting along with peers. Create three sample goal statements that could be included on his IEP.

16

Helping Students with Mental and Emotional Disorders

Carol J. Kaffenberger*

E ditor's Introduction: Whereas the historical roots of professional school counseling lie in developmental counseling theories, societal changes are contributing to substantial increases in psychopathology among school-aged children. A professional school counselor's ability to treat students with emotional disorders depends on education, training, and experience, as well as local school board policies and procedures; however, all future professional school counselors living the transformed role must know the characteristics and diagnostic criteria for common disorders of childhood and adolescence. Such knowledge is essential to one's ability to make timely and appropriate referrals, as well as to facilitate school-based services to supplement mental health treatment. This chapter introduces the vast array of mental disorders that professional school counselors may encounter in their work with students. In addition, each section addresses common treatment interventions and discusses their relevance to the professional school counselor. Whether referring, treating, collaborating, or advocating, professional school counselors must be aware of this information to interface with and make appropriate referrals to the medical and mental health communities and help the students to achieve academic and social success at school.

The professional school counselor's primary responsibility is to support the educational mission of schools—to help all students be academically successful. The No Child Left Behind Act (NCLB) of 2001 and the school reform movement have increased the pressure on schools to focus on academic performance and achievement for *all* students (U.S. Department of Education, 2001). Unfortunately, a number of factors interfere with the achievement of that goal. Environmental and mental health issues impact children and make it difficult for schools to provide them an appropriate education. As a result, schools are increasingly expected to deal with the emotional and mental health concerns of students.

This chapter will briefly review the history of the professional school counselor's role in serving students with mental and emotional disorders, the role professional school counselors can play in the diagnosis and treatment of these mental disorders in light of the transformation of the school counseling profession, the nature and prevalence of mental disorders most often diagnosed in students, and the implications for the future.

PREVALENCE OF MENTAL HEALTH ISSUES IN YOUTH

The prevalence of mental health issues in children and adolescents is increasing and is considered a mental health crisis in the United States (American Psychological Association, 2004). One in five children and adolescents has a

---

*The first and second editions of this chapter were coauthored by Dr. Linda Seligman, may she rest in peace.

mild to moderate mental health issue, and 1 in 20 has a serious mental or emotional illness (U.S. Department of Health and Human Services, 2000). Of the children between the ages of 9 and 17 who have a serious emotional illness, only 20% receive mental health services (Hoagwood, 1999; Kataoka, Zhang, & Wells, 2002; Kazdin, 2008; U.S. Department of Health and Human Services, 2000). In addition to the increased prevalence of mental illness, children are presenting with mental health concerns at a younger age. The rate of unmet needs among Latino youth and uninsured children is even greater than that among White and publicly insured youth (Kataoka et al., 2002), and the needs of children living in rural areas are also largely unmet due to lack of access and availability (Mohatt, Adams, Bradley, & Morris, 2006).

Adolescent suicide rates are another indicator of the severity of mental health concerns. Suicide is the third leading cause of death for adolescents, after accidents and homicide (National Institute of Mental Health, 2000; Shaffer & Pfeffer, 2001). The 2003–2004 incidence of suicide increased by 8% after a 28.5% decline between 1990 and 2003 (Lubell, Kegler, Crosby, & Karch, 2008). It is estimated that 7% of adolescents who develop a major depressive disorder will commit suicide (National Institute of Mental Health, 2000) and that 90% of teens who commit suicide have a mental disorder (Shaffer & Pfeffer, 2001). Adolescents who use alcohol or illicit drugs are three times more likely than nonusing adolescents to attempt suicide (Substance Abuse and Mental Health Services Administration, 2002a).

The high incidence of violent, aggressive, and disruptive behavior in children is another reflection of children's emotional difficulties (Luongo, 2000). Approximately one-third to one-half of referrals of young people to mental health agencies are for behavioral and conduct problems primarily occurring in school (Atkins et al., 1998). Approximately 3% to 5% of children are thought to have Attention-Deficit/Hyperactivity Disorder (AD/HD) (American Psychiatric Association, 2000).

FACTORS CONTRIBUTING TO THE HIGH INCIDENCE OF EMOTIONAL DISTURBANCE

Environmental factors such as the breakdown of the family, homelessness, poverty, and violence in the community place increased stress on families and contribute to an increase in mental health needs (Keys, Bemak, & Lockhart, 1998; Lockhart & Keys, 1998). The number of children living in poverty has steadily increased. It is estimated that 23% of all homeless families include children and that the

number of homeless children is in excess of 1 million (National Coalition for the Homeless, 2008). Poverty, as well as exposure to violence and substance use in the community, puts children at greater risk for developing mental disorders and experiencing emotional difficulties, thus making it more difficult for them to attend school regularly and succeed academically (Weist, 1997).

Particularly at risk are children from diverse ethnic and cultural groups, who have a higher incidence of mental disorders and are overrepresented in special education programs (Coulter, 1996; Kataoka et al., 2002; Santos de Barona & Barona, 2006). Children and adolescents of color have been unserved or underserved and have had their emotional difficulties overlooked or misdiagnosed (Kress, Erikson, Rayle, & Ford, 2005). Diagnostic tools and procedures that have been developed for Euro-American populations may not be appropriate for diagnosing emotional difficulties in children from other cultures (Kress et al., 2005; Mezzich et al., 1999).

Low-cost mental health services available in the community are limited, thereby putting added pressure on schools to provide those services (Keys & Bemak, 1997; Luongo, 2000). Additionally, lack of transportation, poor insurance coverage, limited after-school office hours, and understaffing at mental health agencies all serve as barriers to young people receiving mental health services (Kazdin, 2008; Weist, 1997). Services that are available often are fragmented, and typically no one agency takes responsibility for providing or coordinating care.

The Individuals with Disabilities Education Act (IDEA) was originally authorized in 1975 (as the Education for All Handicapped Children Act) to ensure that all children with disabilities would have their educational needs met in schools (Cortiella, 2006). Changes introduced in 2004, when the IDEA was reauthorized, require that students be served in regular education classrooms and that expectations for students with disabilities be increased. Under the IDEA, the process of identifying students with disabilities is now called response to research-based interventions (RTI) (Burns, Jacob, & Wagner, 2008). RTI requires that research-based teaching strategies be used and documented for all children and that student progress be monitored, allowing for more intense services for students who do not make adequate progress. The American School Counselor Association's (ASCA's) position statement on RTI identifies a significant role for professional school counselors in providing research-based interventions through classroom guidance, small-group and individual counseling, consultation, and data-gathering activities (ASCA, 2008). The box on the next page provides an example of how school counselors can be involved with RTI.

SCHOOL COUNSELOR INVOLVEMENT WITH RESPONSE TO INTERVENTION

Ms. Houseman, the school counselor, participated in a Child Study Committee meeting to discuss Jimmy Rodriquez's progress in the second grade. Jimmy's progress has been monitored since first grade, when his teacher grouped him with others who were struggling with learning letters and sounds and with word recognition. Jimmy made some progress with Tier I classroom interventions. Now in grade two, by the end of the first marking period Jimmy's progress seems to have slowed down. Not only is Jimmy struggling with reading skills and basic classroom performance skills, but also he is having some trouble getting along with others. The Child Study Committee determined that Jimmy's failure to make adequate progress requires a Tier II intervention. Jimmy will see the reading teacher once a week and will be put in a small group with Ms. Houseman. Before Ms. Houseman begins to work with Jimmy, she reviews evidence-based counseling interventions and chooses one that she believes will help Jimmy with his attitude toward school, learning, and problems he is experiencing with peers. Ms. Houseman and the reading teacher will both document Jimmy's progress throughout the second and third marking periods and report back to the Child Study Committee in April.

Professional school counselors are often members of the school's special education team and should be involved with the RTI process for all children (Burns et al., 2008; Santos de Barona & Barona, 2006). The IDEA requires that school counselors be well versed in the nature of, and requirements for, psychological assessment and services.

Section 504 of the Rehabilitation Act of 1973 protects students who have a physical or mental disability that substantially limits a major life activity (N. Hayes, 2002; U.S. Department of Health and Human Services, 2004). Section 504 provides program modifications that are different from special education services. This legislation, too, has increased professional school counselors' involvement with students' mental health needs. Students who are eligible for Section 504 accommodations require modifications to their learning environment so that they will have access to educational opportunity. Examples of students who might be eligible for Section 504 services include a student with leukemia who requires a shorter school day and homebound instruction; a student with AD/HD who might benefit from modifications to assignments, special seating, and permission to take frequent breaks; and a child with dysgraphia who requires special testing accommodations. In some school districts, professional school counselors chair the Section 504 committee and are responsible for working with parents, teachers, and students to develop

VOICES FROM THE FIELD 16.1   A PERSPECTIVE FROM A SCHOOL COUNSELING INTERN

Before going back to school to pursue my counseling degree, I was a special education teacher. During my first year of teaching, I had a self-contained classroom with students who had a variety of disabilities ranging from autism and mental retardation to emotional disorders and learning disabilities. My students did not receive any support from the school counselor. The school counselor could have helped me understand and meet the psychosocial needs of my students. It seemed like such a missed opportunity that the school counselor was not involved with me or my classroom. Realizing that I could not meet all of the psychosocial and educational needs of my students, I decided to pursue a degree in school counseling with a personal mission of supporting all the students, including those students with mental or learning disorders.

The professional school counselor's role in serving students with mental and learning disorders is to help negotiate the most appropriate services for students by collaborating with stakeholders: teachers, parents, administrators, and students.

The professional school counselor is often the first person to hear about the concerns of parents and teachers regarding a particular child. It has been my experience that sometimes parents bring their concerns to the school, and other times the school is the first to notice a problem. The counselor's role is a delicate one when a disorder is affecting a student's school performance and the parents are unaware. The professional school counselor is often the person who communicates the school's concern to the parents and provides information regarding how the school can support the student. The professional school counselor needs to be a member of the multidisciplinary team and therefore able to communicate to the parent how the school is able to help the child.

As a counseling intern at the end of my program, I see counseling theories and best practices in action. The professional school counselor needs to have an understanding of how to affect all students in his or her building. On a daily basis, my counseling supervisor interacts with students who have mental and learning disabilities. I also observe as she provides support for parents and teachers as they consider the possibility that their students will need specialized services. Having knowledge and understanding of these disabilities is a benefit to any professional school counselor—and the students.

As I make this transition into my role as a professional school counselor, I will never forget my special education experiences. I want to be the professional school counselor

that the special education teachers consider a valuable, contributing team member. How ideal to have the support of a professional school counselor who understands the many ways disabilities affect students and can contribute to developing psychosocial interventions for these students.

Source: Robin Hudspeth, School Counseling Intern, George Mason University

---

and implement appropriate accommodations (ASCA, 2004c).

Failure to address the emotional and mental health concerns of students has a cost. Most mental health issues in adulthood are known to begin during childhood or adolescence (Berglund, Demler, Jin, Merikangas, & Walters, 2005). Estimates suggest that 48% of students with emotional problems drop out of school and that students with severe emotional problems miss more days of school than students in any other disability category. Children with mental or emotional disorders are at an increased risk of substance abuse (Substance Abuse and Mental Health Services Administration, 2002b). Forty-three percent of children using mental health services also have a substance abuse disorder. It is estimated that 66% of males and 75% of females in the juvenile justice system have one or more mental disorder diagnoses (President's New Freedom Commission on Mental Health, 2003).

THE PROFESSIONAL SCHOOL COUNSELOR'S ROLE

The role of professional school counselors is in a period of transformation (ASCA, 2005a; Bemak, 2000). Part of the ongoing debate focuses on how professional school counselors should address the mental health and emotional issues of students and how that role fits into a comprehensive school counseling program as framed by *The ASCA National Model: A Framework for School Counseling Programs* (2005a). The mental health needs of students have not always been the concern of professional school counselors. School counseling in the 1950s and 1960s emphasized a personal growth model that promoted individual development (Keys, Bemak, & Lockhart, 1998; Paisley & Borders, 1995). Currently, most school counseling programs are based on a comprehensive developmental model that focuses on prevention and meeting the needs of the whole child and that emphasizes the educational goals of counseling services and programs.

While many professional school counselors, influenced by the direction of ASCA and the National Center for Transforming School Counseling at the Education

Trust, affirm the educational goals of their school counseling programs, others argue that professional school counselors are not doing enough to meet the complex needs of children who are at risk (Keys, Bemak, & Lockhart, 1998). They claim that professional school counselors are not allowing sufficient individualization of services and are focused on student competencies, rather than individual mental health needs (Gysbers & Henderson, 2006). Leaders in the counseling field argue that the role of school counselors is still evolving (Bemak, 2000; Paisley & Borders, 1995). Others (Dryfoos, 1994; Keys, Bemak, & Lockhart, 1998) believe that new delivery systems for providing school-based mental health services are required (Bemak, Murphy, & Kaffenberger, 2005). For example, Dryfoos (1994) envisioned *full-service* schools where community mental health resources combine forces with schools and other agencies to provide adequate mental health services for students. Other alternative service models include providing evidence-based interventions through the use of technology such as CD-ROMs, webcasts, and the Internet (Kazdin, 2008).

Barriers to Providing Mental Health Services in Schools

The ability of professional school counselors to meet the needs of students with mental health issues is limited by several factors, including workload ratio of students to counselors, local policy, fragmented programs, and lack of expertise (Bemak, 2000; Keys & Bemak, 1997). The first barrier is the number of noncounseling duties that professional school counselors are asked to shoulder (ASCA, 2005a). Overworked professional school counselors with a host of other school responsibilities, both of a counseling and of a noncounseling nature, are unable to provide adequate counseling services or consult with parents and mental health professionals to serve students with chronic and serious mental health needs.

The second barrier that interferes with a counselor's ability to serve the mental health needs of students is the fragmentation and duplication of services and programs (Bemak, 2000; Bemak et al., 2005).

School- and community-based services and programs often have been developed in isolation, without consideration of existing services and programs. Lacking knowledge and awareness of collaborative opportunities, both school and community settings miss the opportunity to provide comprehensive and coordinated services.

The third barrier is the discrepancy that exists between professional school counselors' need to understand mental disorders and their knowledge base (Lockhart & Keys, 1998; L. Seligman, 2004). Not all professional school counselors possess the knowledge, experience, and expertise needed to recognize and address the mental health needs of students. Counselor education programs have typically prepared professional school counselors to understand the developmental needs of students, but have not provided the training required to recognize and treat mental disorders affecting children, adolescents, and their families.

In spite of these barriers that schools and professional school counselors encounter when addressing the mental health needs of students, the reality is that the most common point of entry into the mental health system is through the schools. One study found that 60.1% of all youth who received mental health services entered the system through the school (Farmer, Burns, Phillips, Angold, & Costello, 2003). Unfortunately, this same study found that entering the mental health services system through the schools was also least likely to result in involvement with other services, such as community mental health or private care.

Current and Future Trends in the Way Services Are Provided

If schools are to achieve their educational mission, new service models will be required of professional school counselors (ASCA, 2005a; Bemak, 2000; Bemak et al., 2005; Keys, Bemak, & Lockhart, 1998). The way mental health services are provided for children and the role of the professional school counselor are beginning to change (Flaherty et al., 1998). The U.S. Department of Education, the U.S. Department of Health and Human Services, and private managed health-care organizations are encouraging preventive health care as a way of ultimately reducing the need for future costly care, remediation, and intervention (Power, DuPaul, Shapiro, & Parrish, 1998). Schools are the logical place for programs that seek to both prevent and ameliorate mental health problems in students and their families. As a growing number of public schools privatize, various counseling service models have been developed Some schools have increased their use of community and

private resources by hiring psychiatrists and using outside consultants to provide direct treatment, psychotherapy, and psychopharmacology to students (Bostic & Rauch, 1999). In increasing numbers of schools, the counseling functions are either shared between the professional school counselor and outside agencies or contracted out completely.

Flaherty et al. (1998) described an ideal service model in which professionals from different disciplines collaborate to promote mental health in children and adolescents. The team would be composed of professionals representing school health, mental health, and education. Most schools already have child study teams charged with managing the special education evaluation process. The collaborative interdisciplinary teams proposed by Flaherty et al. would expand the membership of special education teams to include professionals from community agencies who would develop and implement programs for individuals and for schools. Interdisciplinary teams could also provide a vehicle for educating staff and students about mental health issues (Weist, 1997). High levels of collaboration and coordination will be required to effect necessary systems-level change (Bemak, 2000).

The effectiveness of new community-based mental health services and comprehensive guidance programs is being assessed. One study evaluated the effectiveness of high school counseling programs statewide and found that students who attend schools with fully implemented mental health programs are more academically successful and have a greater sense of belonging and safety than do those who do not (Lapan, Gysbers, & Sun, 1997). Another study showed that comprehensive community-based services to children cut state hospital admissions and inpatient bed days by between 39% and 79% and reduced average days of detention by 40% (Substance Abuse and Mental Health Services Administration, 1995).

The discussion of how best to provide services to students is ongoing. What is clear is that, to efficiently and effectively use the limited resources available to meet the needs of students, a high level of collaboration will be required (Bemak et al., 2005). Collaboration among mental health professionals is even more important when fiscal concerns threaten to reduce services to students (J. M. Allen, 1994). To maximize their effectiveness, professional school counselors need to develop interdisciplinary and interagency relationships and practices and a working knowledge of the role and function of the other mental health professions in schools and in the community (Bemak, 2000; Bemak et al., 2005; Farmer et al., 2003; Flaherty et al., 1998).

Professional school counselors must increase their knowledge, skills, and expertise regarding mental health issues of students in order to assume a more collaborative role (Bemak, 2000; Lockhart & Keys, 1998). They must be knowledgeable about the criteria in the fourth edition of the *Diagnostic and Statistical Manual of Mental Disorders–Text Revision* (*DSM–IV–TR*; American Psychiatric Association, 2000) criteria, the symptoms of mental disorders, and the appropriate treatment recommendations for all children, including the culturally and linguistically diverse (Santos de Barona & Barona, 2006; L. Seligman, 2004). They must understand psychological evaluation processes, be able to explain them to school staff, and communicate with other mental health professionals.

WHAT PROFESSIONAL SCHOOL COUNSELORS NEED TO KNOW ABOUT MENTAL AND EMOTIONAL DISORDERS

With the increased prevalence of mental health and emotional issues in children and adolescents, professional school counselors need to take an increasingly active role in understanding these disorders and facilitating services. The professional school counselor is often the first person contacted by parents or teachers when concerns about children arise. Professional school counselors must understand normal social, emotional, cognitive, and physical development. In addition, it is essential that they possess a working knowledge of the range of mental disorders and mental health issues affecting young people. Professional school counselors need to be familiar with the diagnostic criteria for those mental disorders that are commonly found in young people, even though professional school counselors may not be responsible for diagnosing mental disorders. Professional school counselors will need to be knowledgeable about diagnostic tools and intervention strategies appropriate for culturally and ethnically diverse students (Santos de Barona & Barona, 2006). Professional school counselors can play a pivotal role in raising awareness concerning mental disorders, identifying students who are experiencing significant emotional difficulties, collaborating with the child study team on response-to-intervention strategies, recommending school-based interventions, interpreting diagnostic information for parents, and making referrals. Counselors' awareness of diagnostic information also will be invaluable to parents, teachers, and administrators as initial treatment decisions are being made.

Mental health professionals, including psychologists, psychiatrists, social workers, and licensed professional counselors, regularly use the *DSM–IV–TR* (American Psychiatric Association, 2000) to diagnose emotional, behavioral, and mental disorders in children and adolescents. In general, school psychologists did not use the *DSM* until the 1987 publication of the revised third edition, the *DSM–III–R*, but for the last 10 to 15 years, they have viewed diagnosis as one of their essential skills (A. E. House, 1999). By 1994, when the fourth edition of the *DSM* was published, the expectations of the school's role in the diagnostic process had increased, and many professional school counselors recognized that they, too, needed to be familiar with the diagnostic criteria for mental disorders in young people. Changes in the way mental health services were provided to children and increased pressure to provide special education services to children required that schools develop more sophisticated ways of diagnosing educational and behavioral disorders. *DSM* criteria are now accepted as the standard, and workshops, training, and textbooks guiding the use of *DSM* criteria proliferate (A. E. House, 1999).

While the *DSM* is gaining greater credibility among mental health professionals, a debate about the relevance of *DSM* criteria to people of other cultures and ethnicities is increasing (Dana, 2001; R. Gardner & Miranda, 2001; Kress et al., 2005; Mezzich et al., 1999; Santos de Barona & Barona, 2006). Beginning in the late 1980s, researchers began the discussion of the relevance of *DSM* criteria to people of other cultures and ethnicities. In spite of good-faithl efforts on the part of those who prepare the *DSM*, working groups, collaborative task forces, and independent researchers found the most recent version, the *DSM–IV–TR*, does not reflect "cultural or racial difference in symptoms, syndromes" (Dana, 2001, p. 131). The *DSM–IV–TR* (American Psychiatric Association, 2000) addressed ethnic and cultural considerations and warned that *DSM* diagnostic criteria may not be appropriately assessed unless the cultural frame of reference is considered. In this edition of the *DSM*, the American Psychiatric Association also provided three types of information related to cultural considerations: (1) a discussion within the text description of each disorder of known cultural variance, (2) a discussion in Appendix I of culture-bound syndromes, and (3) an outline (also contained in Appendix I) of cultural formation.

Professional school counselors are not expected to, nor have most of them been trained to, make diagnoses using the *DSM* criteria. While professional school counselors may not make formal diagnoses and will probably not provide primary services to students diagnosed with a mental disorder, they often are expected to identify young people in need of mental health services; to consult with other school-based mental health professionals such as school psychologists and social workers; to make referrals to outside community agency resources such as psychiatrists, psychologists, social workers, and mental health counselors;

and to decipher mental health reports for school personnel and parents. Once an outside referral has been made, professional school counselors, with the parents' permission, may be asked to provide input from the school, including observations, behavioral checklists, and sample schoolwork. When parents, professional school counselors, teachers, and mental health therapists work together successfully, the results can be very beneficial for children. Although professional school counselors typically will not provide therapeutic services to students with severe mental disorders, having a working knowledge of the diagnosis of mental disorders and understanding ways that diagnostic criteria may not be relevant to students from other cultures or students of color can greatly enhance the effectiveness of professional school counselors' interactions with students, teachers, and parents (R. Gardner & Miranda, 2001; Lockhart & Keys, 1998).

Diagnosis and Treatment Planning

The *DSM–IV–TR* (American Psychiatric Association, 2000) includes a multiaxial system of diagnosis, one that involves an assessment of a person on five different axes or areas. Each of these axes refers to a different domain of information that aids the clinician in planning treatment for the person being assessed. Axis I, Clinical Disorders and Other Conditions That May Be the Focus of Clinical Attention, describes clinical disorders such as conduct disorders, eating disorders, anxiety disorders, and mood disorders. Axis II, Mental Retardation and Personality Disorders, encompasses mental retardation and enduring, maladaptive personality disorders. Axis III, General Medical Conditions, includes general medical conditions or physical symptoms. Axis IV, Psychosocial and Environmental Problems, pertains to psychosocial and environmental problems such as educational, family, and occupational stressors. Axis V, Global Assessment of Functioning, indicates a person's global assessment of functioning by assigning a number on a scale of 1 to 100, with 100 indicating superior functioning and 1 indicating persistent and severe danger of hurting self or others.

A multiaxial approach to assessment is used to facilitate a comprehensive and systematic evaluation of a person. Professional school counselors usually will not be involved in the assessment process, but will benefit from understanding how the multiaxial system is used in the diagnosis of an emotional or mental disorder. For example, when assessing an adolescent for depression, the clinician should know about all areas of this young person's life. This adolescent might have a medical condition such as cancer, or the adolescent's parents may have recently been divorced. It is helpful to be able to assess the child or adolescent for various issues other than the primary diagnosis to create a treatment plan that is tailored for the individual's issues and experiences, rather than just for "depression." A sample *DSM* multiaxial diagnosis is presented in Case Study 16.1.

According to the *DSM–IV–TR* (American Psychiatric Association, 2000), 13 types of disorders are often diagnosed in infancy, childhood, or adolescence. What follows is a description of those disorders, as well as disorders more likely to be diagnosed in adulthood, but also frequently diagnosed in children and adolescents. Specific characteristics of each disorder, intervention strategies, prognosis, and relevance to the professional school counselor are presented.

CASE STUDY 16.1

Demonstrating a *DSM–IV–TR* Multiaxial Diagnosis

Anna, a seven-year-old girl, was evaluated for an episode of depressed mood, sleeping problems, irritability, loss of weight, and reduced energy level. Anna's symptoms had been present for nearly two months. Her parents could hardly get her to wake up in the morning. She refused to dress or bathe and had been absent from school for two weeks. On further evaluation, it was discovered that Anna's dog, Max, was killed about two months ago, right around the time that Anna's symptoms began. Recently, Anna had begun to tell her parents that she wished the car could have hit her also so that she could be with Max.

Anna's multiaxial diagnosis is

Axis I	296.22 Major Depressive Disorder, Single Episode, with Melancholic Features
Axis II	V71.09 No diagnosis on axis II
Axis III	None reported
Axis IV	Death of family pet
Axis V	50

MENTAL DISORDERS USUALLY FIRST DIAGNOSED IN INFANTS, CHILDREN, OR ADOLESCENTS

Mental Retardation

Mental retardation typically is described in terms of a person's failure to demonstrate skills that are age-, culture-, and situation-appropriate, reflected by an intelligence quotient (IQ) that is much lower than that found in the normal population (Baumeister & Baumeister, 2000). Mental retardation has a pervasive impact on cognitive, emotional, and social development (L. Seligman, 2006). It is diagnosed from results of individual intelligence tests, such as the Wechsler Intelligence Scale for Children, Fourth Edition (WISC–IV; Wechsler, 2001) or the Stanford-Binet Intelligence Scale, Fifth Edition (SBIS–5; Roid, 2003). According to the *DSM–IV–TR,* the criteria for diagnosis of mental retardation include onset prior to age 18; subaverage intellectual functioning reflected by an IQ two standard deviations below the mean (WISC–IV or SBIS–5 full scale IQ of 70 or less); and impaired adaptive functioning in at least two areas, such as communication, social skills, interpersonal skills, self-direction, leisure, functional academic skills, safety, and work (House, 1999). Although people with an IQ that is in the 71–84 range are not typically diagnosed with mental retardation, they, too, are likely to have academic and other difficulties related to their below-average intellectual abilities. The *DSM–IV–TR* describes people in this group as having a condition called borderline intellectual functioning.

The impact of mental retardation is directly related to the degree of intellectual impairment. Four degrees of retardation are defined by the *DSM* as follows: Mild retardation is diagnosed when the IQ score is in the range of 50–55 to 70, moderate retardation is diagnosed when the IQ score is in the range of 35–40 to 50–55, severe retardation is diagnosed when the IQ score is in the range of 20–25 to 35–40, and profound retardation is diagnosed when the IQ score is below 20–25.

According to Baumeister and Baumeister (2000), the American Association of Mental Retardation (AAMR) has recently modified the classification of mental retardation. The new system advocates a multidimensional approach to identification, involving intellectual functioning and adaptive skills, psychological and emotional considerations, and etiology, as well as environmental considerations. The language used for students with mental retardation has also been modified to be more sensitive to the negative connotation of the term *retarded* and to encourage such terms as *developmental* or *cognitive disabilities.*

Mental retardation is usually diagnosed in infancy or early childhood, although mild retardation may not be identified until the child reaches school age. It is estimated that 1% to 2% of the general population can be diagnosed with mental retardation, although estimates can vary depending on definitions and populations studied (American Psychiatric Association, 2000; National Institute of Mental Health, 2000). Of those people meeting the criteria for mental retardation, 85% are diagnosed with mild retardation (Rapoport & Ismond, 1996). Boys are three times more likely than girls to be diagnosed with this disorder (Dulmus & Wodaraski, 1996).

Recent advances in knowledge have been made concerning the genetic, physiological, and neurological bases of mental retardation (State, King, & Dykens, 1997), which may have implications for the future diagnosis and treatment of this disorder. Approximately 25% to 30% of people with mental retardation have identifiable biological causes of the disorder, such as genetic and chromosomal abnormalities, prenatal and perinatal difficulties, or acquired childhood diseases. Down syndrome is the most widely known genetic type of mild or moderate retardation (A. S. Davis, 2008). Severe and profound retardation commonly have a neurological origin and may be associated with more than 200 physical disorders, including cerebral palsy, epilepsy, and sensory disorders. When mental retardation lacks identifiable biological causes, it is thought to be the result of some combination of inherited cognitive impairment and environmental deprivation (Baumeister & Baumeister, 2000).

Children and adolescents diagnosed with mental retardation usually receive special education services under the IDEA (Macmillan, Gresham, Spierstein, & Bocian, 1996). Prior to the passage of Public Law 94-142 (the precursor to IDEA) in the 1970s, children who had previously been categorized as trainable and custodial were excluded from free public education (Hardman, Drew, & Egan, 1996). Today, public education is available to all children, regardless of the nature and degree of their impairment; thus, many children with mild mental retardation are found in the public schools.

The characteristics of children, adolescents, and adults with mental retardation vary greatly, depending on their level of impairment and on their environment. These clients often present with aggressive, overactive, or self-injurious behaviors (Kronenberger & Meyer, 1996). Although children with Down syndrome display fewer behavior problems overall than other children with mental retardation do, these children still exhibit maladaptive behaviors, particularly stubbornness (Ly & Hodapp, 2002). Because of their cognitive limitations, they tend to be concrete in their thinking, reasoning, and problem solving. Developmental delays are common, with such milestones as walking and talking generally reached later than average.

Learning new tasks requires more practice and guidance for people with mental retardation than for their chronological counterparts (L. Seligman, 2006).

Children with mild disabilities present with a wide variety of cognitive abilities and need to be evaluated with these differences in mind (A. S. Davis, 2008). Inclusion requires that most children with mild disabilities be educated in the regular classroom (Elias, Blum, Gager, Hunter, & Kress, 1998). Many students with mild disabilities are academically successfully in the regular classroom, but lack the social skills needed to interact with peers and adults.

INTERVENTION STRATEGIES   Early intervention is essential for treatment of children with mental retardation (L. Seligman, 2006). Early intervention includes systems, services, and supports designed to enhance the development of young children, minimize the potential of developmental delays and the need for special education services, and enhance the capacities of families as caregivers (B. L. Baker & Feinfield, 2003). Family, group, and individual counseling can be effective in promoting the child's or adolescent's positive self-regard and in improving social, academic, and occupational skills Behavior modification has long been the treatment modality of choice for people with mental retardation (Baumeister & Baumeister, 2000).

PROGNOSIS   Mental retardation has implications for a person's entire life span (L. Seligman, 2006). Adults with a mild level of retardation often live independently and maintain a job with minimal supervision. People with a moderate level of retardation may be able to live independently in group-home settings and gain employment in sheltered workshops. Those with severe and profound retardation often reside in public and private institutions.

RELEVANCE TO SCHOOL COUNSELORS   Professional school counselors are often members of multidisciplinary teams that attempt to develop appropriate educational plans for students with mild retardation. In so doing, they may engage in advocacy, consultation, diagnosis, assessment, development of a delivery system, and provision of support services for students, parents, and teachers (Wood Dunn & Baker, 2002). Professional school counselors may play a role in helping families understand and accept the diagnosis and make the transition to an appropriate school program. Professional school counselors may be asked to provide social skills training for students with mental retardation. It also is important for professional school counselors to help educate the other students about mental retardation in order to promote their understanding and tolerance. It is suggested that professional school counselors be familiar with the overall procedural safeguards of the IDEA and characteristics unique to students with disabilities. Professional school counselors who are more able to understand the challenges for students with disabilities are also able to provide the students, parents, and teachers with accurate information (Wood Dunn & Baker, 2002).

Learning, Motor Skills, and Communication Disorders

Learning, motor skills, and communication disorders are diagnosed in children when they are functioning significantly below expectations in a specific area, based on their age, cognitive abilities, and education, and when their level of functioning is interfering with daily achievement and functioning (L. Seligman, 2006). Significant discrepancies between functioning and performance are typified by achievement in a given area that is 20 to 30 standard score points below the child's intelligence as measured by standardized achievement tests and intelligence tests. Diagnosis of these disorders also requires that other factors that may be primary contributors to the learning problems, such as lack of educational opportunity, poor teaching, impaired vision or hearing, and mental retardation, be ruled out (A. R. Young & Beitchman, 2002). Specific learning disabilities (SLDs) reflect a disorder in one or more of the basic learning processes, which may manifest itself in an impaired ability to listen, think, speak, read, write, spell, or do mathematical calculations (A. R. Young & Beitchman, 2002). SLDs, referred to as learning disorders in the *DSM–IV–TR*, are believed to affect approximately 10% of the population, but are diagnosed in only about 5% of students in public schools in the United States (Rapoport & Ismond, 1996). The *DSM–IV–TR* identified three types of learning disorders: mathematics disorder, reading disorder, and disorder of written expression, characterized by significant difficulties in academic functioning in each of those areas. Reading disorder is diagnosed in approximately 4% of the school-aged population; 60% to 80% are boys. Children with reading disorder have difficulty decoding unknown words, memorizing sight-word vocabulary lists, and comprehending written passages. Estimates of the prevalence of mathematics disorder range from 1% to 6% of the population (American Psychiatric Association, 2000). Children with mathematics disorder have difficulty with problem solving, calculations, or both (L. Seligman, 2006). Disorder of written expression is rarely found in isolation; in most cases, another learning disorder is also present (American Psychiatric Association, 2000). Children with disorder of written expression have difficulty with handwriting, spelling, grammar, and the creation of prose (L. Seligman, 2006). Care must be taken to distinguish these disorders from underachievement, poor teaching, lack of opportunity, and cultural factors.

Communication disorders are defined as speech and language impairment. This category is narrowly defined as impairments in language, voice, fluency, or articulation that are not a result of sensory impairment or developmental delay (C. R. Johnson & Slomka, 2000). Four communication disorders are identified in the *DSM–IV–TR*: expressive language disorder, mixed receptive-expressive language disorder, phonological disorder, and stuttering. Like nearly all sections in the *DSM–IV–TR*, this section also includes a not otherwise specified (NOS) diagnosis for disorders that belong in this category, but do not fully meet the diagnostic criteria for any of the specific disorders (C. R. Johnson & Slomka, 2000). Expressive language disorder and mixed receptive-expressive language disorder are diagnosed when language skills are significantly below expectations based on nonverbal ability and interfere with academic progress. Phonological disorder involves "failure to use developmentally expected speech sounds that are appropriate for the individual's age and dialect" (American Psychiatric Association, 2000, p. 65). Stuttering is diagnosed when speech fluency interferes with the child's ability to communicate or make good academic progress. Characteristic errors include repetitions of sounds, syllables, and words; broken words; and the production of words with excessive tension (C. R. Johnson & Slomka, 2000). Professional school counselors should be sure that an unusual speech pattern is not primarily the result of an inadequate education or a family or cultural environment before diagnosing a communication disorder. A referral to a speech and language specialist can facilitate this discrimination.

Learning, motor skills, and communication disorders are currently thought to involve perinatal or neonatal causes (D. Johnson, 1995). Other causes for these disorders are being investigated. Changes in the communication skills of individuals with the human immunodeficiency virus (HIV) and the resultant disease, the acquired immunodeficiency syndrome (AIDS), are being recognized and studied (McCabe, Sheard, & Code, 2002). Lead poisoning or head trauma in childhood might also contribute to learning disorders. Specific infections, such as a particular type of meningitis, have also been related to later learning difficulties (C. R. Johnson & Slomka, 2000). Approximately 35% to 40% of boys with learning disorders have at least one parent who had similar learning problems (Snowling, 2002; A. R. Young & Beitchman, 2002). Learning disorders are also associated with low socioeconomic status, poor self-esteem, depression, and perceptual deficiencies Children with these disorders often are unhappy in school, have negative self-images and social difficulties, and

show increased likelihood of dropping out of school (L. Seligman, 2006). High school students with learning disabilities are reported to have lower educational and career aspirations than do their peers (A. R. Young & Beitchman, 2002). Depression, anxiety, AD/HD, and disruptive behavior disorders often coexist with learning disorders. In addition, a wide assortment of social skill deficits has been found in children with learning and communication disorders (Barnes, Friehe, & Radd, 2003; A. R. Young & Beitchman, 2002).

INTERVENTION STRATEGIES The primary educational strategies for these disorders (L. Seligman, 2006) include behavioral, cognitive-behavioral, and psychoeducational interventions (C. R. Johnson & Slomka, 2000). Children who demonstrate a significant discrepancy between intelligence and achievement, with achievement usually being 20 to 30 standard score points below measured intelligence, may be eligible to receive special education services. An Individualized Education Program (IEP) is developed by the school according to the requirements of the IDEA Cortiella, 2006; U.S. Department of Education, 1999). The IEP specifies areas of weakness, strategies for addressing the deficit areas, measurable behavioral goals, and criteria for determining whether goals have been successfully met. A. R. Young and Beitchman (2002) suggested teaching strategies that include paying attention to sequencing; using drill-repetition-practice; segmenting information into parts or units for later synthesis; controlling task difficulty using prompts and cues; making use of technology (e.g., computers); systematically modeling problem-solving steps; and using small, interactive groups (A. R. Young & Beitchman, 2002). Frequently, social and emotional goals such as improved interpersonal relations and increases in motor or attention on-task behaviors are included in the IEP. Interventions, including counseling, individualized teaching strategies, and accommodations, and social skills training can lead to positive outcomes (Silver, 1995).

PROGNOSIS Learning disorders continue to have an impact on people's lives throughout adolescence and adulthood (L. Seligman, 2006; A. R. Young & Beitchman, 2002). When learning disorders are undiagnosed and untreated, they can lead to extreme frustration, loss of self-esteem, inadequate education, underemployment, and more serious mental disorders (Silver, 1995). Functioning of the family affects the prognosis of a child with learning problems. A "healthy" family may cope adequately in parenting a child with a learning disorder; however, families described as "disorganized" and "blaming" have more difficulty responding to the child's needs and providing appropriate support and intervention (C. R. Johnson & Slomka, 2000).

RELEVANCE TO PROFESSIONAL SCHOOL COUNSELORS

Professional school counselors frequently serve on child study and special education committees tasked with screening children for learning disorders. Through their contact with children, teachers, and parents, professional school counselors are often the first to be aware of how learning problems are impacting the child's performance in the classroom, in the home, and with peers. Professional school counselors may be required by the IEP to provide some individual or small-group counseling to the child, to help parents and children understand and cope with the diagnosis of a learning disorder, and to implement accommodations. Because children with learning disorders frequently have coexisting issues such as poor social skills, low self-esteem, negative attitudes toward school, behavioral difficulties, and family problems, professional school counselors can expect to be involved with students, teachers, and parents in a collaborative role.

Collaboration between professional school counselors and speech and language pathologists (SLPs) is important when helping students with communication disorders. It is suggested that the professional school counselor and SLP work together to develop appropriate accommodations, such as in materials, activities, and instructional discourse, for these students during classroom group guidance lessons. Professional school counselors can also coordinate support groups for students with communication disorders, as well as see these students individually and meet with families (Barnes et al., 2003).

Pervasive Developmental Disorders

The increase in the diagnosis of Pervasive Developmental Disorders (PDDs) is attributed to many factors. Some of these factors include more sensitive diagnostic procedures, a rise in appropriate referrals, ambiguity in diagnostic criteria, administrative mandates to use psychiatric diagnoses to ensure reimbursement for professional services in medical settings, categorical funding for children with autism by state and county health and social service agencies, and educational placement in categorical programs, as well as changing biological and environmental influences on the etiology of developmental disorders (Mulick & Butter, 2002). PDDs are diagnosed in approximately 10 to 20 people per 10,000 (Lord & Rutter, 1994), although the addition of Asperger's disorder will likely substantially increase this rate. Males with these disorders outnumber females by a ratio of approximately 2.5:1 (J. C. Harris, 1995; Sigman & Capps, 1997). Five subtypes of PDD are included in the *DSM–IV–TR*: (1) autistic disorder, (2) Asperger's disorder, (3) childhood disintegrative disorder, (4) Rett's disorder (Rapin, 1999), and (5) PDD–NOS.

Children with PDDs are characterized by impaired social behavior and impaired communication, as well as abnormalities of routine behavior (S. L. Harris, 2000). They usually exhibit a flat affect (lack of facial expression; emotionless), poor eye contact, and minimal social speech. Additionally, these children often show repetitive, stereotyped body movements such as rocking, waving, or head banging (S. L. Harris, 2000). They generally do not seek parental attention or involvement with peers and rarely engage in imitative or interactive play (J. C. Harris, 1995). Language impairment is present in most people with PDDs.

Autistic disorder is present in 2 to 20 of every 10,000 people and causes significant deficits in socialization, communication, and behavior (American Psychiatric Association, 2000; Sigman & Capps, 1997). The symptoms of autistic disorder are evident by age three. Mental retardation accompanies this diagnosis 75% of the time. The ability to communicate varies widely in children diagnosed with autistic disorder. Some are mute, whereas others do eventually develop near-age-appropriate language skills. Generally, they do not form close relationships with others, preferring to engage in repetitive interactions with inanimate objects.

Rett's disorder and childhood disintegrative disorder are less prevalent than autistic disorder. Both are characterized by normal development in early childhood (for a period of 5 months to 4 years for Rett's disorder and for 2 to 10 years for childhood disintegrative disorder), followed by a steady deterioration. In the case of Rett's disorder, the result is ultimately severe or profound retardation. Rett's disorder is diagnosed only in females (M. Campbell, Cueva, & Hallin, 1996; S. L. Harris, 2000). Childhood disintegrative disorder results in significant regression in at least two of the following areas: language, social skills, elimination, play, and motor skills. Asperger's disorder is generally the mildest of the PDDs, which often makes it particularly difficult to diagnose. Asperger's is diagnosed in 0.05 % of children (Centers for Disease Control and Prevention, 2008). Like autistic disorder, Asperger's disorder is characterized by impaired social skills and repetitive or stereotypical behaviors, but it is not characterized by the delayed language development and impairment in communication skills found in people with other PDDs. Behavioral symptoms to consider with Asperger's include preoccupation with one or two areas of interest, tactless comments, inability to understand feelings, and difficulty with change in routine (Cooley, 2007). Typically, children with Asperger's disorder have average to above-average intelligence, whereas in other forms of PDD, there is often mental retardation (S. L. Harris, 2000). Forty percent of children with Asperger's have other mental disorders such as AD/HD, depression, and anxiety disorder in adolescents (Centers for Disease Control and Prevention, 2008. Boys are diagnosed with Asperger's disorder five times more frequently than are girls (American Psychiatric Association, 2000).

PROGNOSIS For most children, the PDDs will last a lifetime. Although early intervention for many young children with autistic disorder, Asperger's disorder, and PDD–NOS has produced major developmental changes, the technology and knowledge of effective treatment approaches have not yet reached the point where the majority of children diagnosed with PDDs make the degree of change that allows them to blend imperceptibly into their peer group (S. L. Harris, 2000). Those with Asperger's disorder have the best prognosis; many succeed in becoming self-sufficient (L. Seligman, 2006). Children with Rett's disorder and childhood disintegrative disorder will most likely be placed in residential treatment facilities due to the progressive nature of these disorders. Early intervention seems to be the most important factor for a positive outcome (M. Campbell, Schopler, Cueva, & Hallin, 1996).

INTERVENTION STRATEGIES Children with PDDs will need a combination of special education services that may include speech and language therapy, as well as physical therapy. These children may also require the services of neurologists, medical specialists, and behavioral therapists. While these children could benefit from social and communication skills, there are some difficulties in having children with PDDs in social skills groups. For example, there are the anxieties intrinsic in group learning situations, the natural difficulty of the subject matter (i.e., social interaction and social understanding), and the typically high oral language load in social skills group work, compounded by the difficulties that the children have in generalizing their new skills into their real-life experiences (C. Smith, 2001). Instead, C. Smith (2001) suggested using social stories, a short-story form (20–150 words), to inform and advise the child about a social situation. Some of the benefits of social stories are that they focus on immediate social difficulties, they can be more personalized than a traditional social skills group, they are easily produced and shared by those involved with the child, and they focus on real-life situations (C. Smith, 2001). Behavioral treatments have been found to be particularly effective in helping children with autistic disorders (M. Campbell, Schopler et al., 1996). Social skills and social communication training have been beneficial for children with autistic disorder and Asperger's disorder.

RELEVANCE TO PROFESSIONAL SCHOOL COUNSELORS Having a child with a PDD in the family places a considerable strain on every family member. Siblings typically have problems with friends, feel lonely, and worry about their sibling. Marital problems in the parents are also common. Most children with PDDs will receive special education services; however, the professional school counselor may play an important role in helping siblings cope, as well as helping parents access supportive resources. The professional school counselor can help teachers make classroom modifications and help students with milder forms of PDD, such as Asperger's, learn the routines that will contribute to their success in the classroom. Parents may also benefit from structured behavioral training programs that help them learn how to help their child.

Additionally, professional school counselors may need to provide educators with resources as the expectation that students with PPDs will be included in regular education classrooms increases. In-service training for teachers can provide time for learning about the nature of the PDDs; for discovering the preferences, priorities, and concerns of the children with PDDs; and for adapting curriculum and instruction to match the learning strengths, needs, and interests of these students (Dow & Mehring, 2001).

Attention-Deficit Disorders and Disruptive Behavior Disorders

Attention-deficit disorders and disruptive behavior disorders include Attention-Deficit/Hyperactivity Disorder (AD/HD), Conduct Disorder (CD), and Oppositional Defiant Disorder (ODD), as well as disruptive behavior disorder NOS. Children with AD/HD or CD also often have learning disorders. Children with ODD or CD often have AD/HD.

AD/HD AD/HD is found in as many as 50% of children seen for counseling or psychotherapy (Cantwell, 1996). The *DSM–IV–TR* divides AD/HD into three types: predominately hyperactive-impulsive type, predominately inattentive type, and combined type. By definition, AD/HD has an onset prior to age seven; is present in two or more settings (such as home and school); and interferes with social, academic, or occupational functioning. For a diagnosis of AD/HD, symptoms need to be present for at least six months (American Psychiatric Association, 2000) and may include failure to give close attention to details, difficulty sustaining attention, poor follow-through on instructions, failure to finish work, difficulty organizing tasks, misplacement of things, distraction by extraneous stimuli, and forgetfulness. Children with hyperactive and impulsive symptoms are usually diagnosed at a younger age than are children with symptoms of the inattentive type of AD/HD. The diagnosis of AD/HD is made through medical, cognitive, and academic assessments, as well as parents' and teachers' input on behavioral rating scales (Cantwell, 1996) such as the Conners-3 Rating Scales (Conners, 2008).

The current prevalence rates for AD/HD range from 3% to 7% of children (American Psychiatric Association, 2000; Cantwell, 1996; Jensen et al., 1999; National Institutes of Health, 1998). Conduct disorders, AD/HD, and developmental language and reading disorders are typically diagnosed early and more commonly in males (Zahn-Waxler, Shirtcliff, & Maraceau, 2008). AD/HD is diagnosed in boys two to nine times more frequently than in girls (American Psychiatric Association, 2000). AD/HD is diagnosed in 44% of children receiving special education services (Bussing, Zima, Perwien, Belin, & Widawski, 1998). Recent meta-analyses of gender differences have also pointed to diagnostic differences. Girls with AD/HD had lower ratings on hyperactivity, inattention, impulsivity, and externalizing of problems and greater intellectual impairment and internalizing of problems than boys did (Gershon, 2002). However, more research is needed to clarify gender and ethnic differences in students with AD/HD.

The diagnosis and treatment of AD/HD remain controversial (National Institutes of Health, 1998). Dramatic increases in diagnostic rates of AD/HD have raised questions about the accuracy of the diagnoses and have led to particular concern that lively and active boys may often be misdiagnosed with this disorder (L. Seligman, 2006). Correspondingly, concerns have been raised as to whether stimulant medication prescribed for treatment of this disorder is overused (Gruttadaro & Miller, 2004). One study of children diagnosed with AD/HD in four communities concluded that of the 5.1% of the population of children meeting the AD/HD criteria, only 12.5% were being treated with psychostimulant medication (Jensen et al., 1999). However, this study also found that a number of children not meeting the AD/HD criteria were being inappropriately treated with medication. This study supports the conclusion that children are both undermedicated and overmedicated for AD/HD. Adding further support to this view is a study by Hoagwood, Kelleher, Feil, and Comer (2000) that found that only 50% of the children diagnosed with AD/HD were receiving adequate and appropriate care.

Prognosis. The prognosis for improvement of AD/HD via treatment is good. Studies by DuPaul, Guevremont, and Barkley (1992) and Whalen and Henker (1991) indicated that behavioral interventions allowed most children with AD/HD to reduce off-task and distractible behaviors. The effectiveness of psychostimulant

medications such as methylphenidate (Ritalin or Concerta), Adderall, Strattera, and dextroamphetamine (Dexadrine) continues to be supported by research despite an ongoing debate concerning the use of these medications.

Intervention Strategies. The most commonly used interventions with children diagnosed with AD/HD are behavioral strategies and the use of stimulant medication (National Institutes of Health, 1998; L. Seligman, 2006). Cognitive-behavioral strategies have been used to improve social skills in children with AD/HD and to address on-task behaviors (Cousins & Weiss, 1993; Rapport, 1995). Social skills training programs focus on such skills as improving awareness of appropriate interpersonal distance, starting and maintaining a conversation, identifying the main idea of a conversation, and accepting and giving compliments (L. Seligman, 2006). Group therapy has also been used effectively to help children with AD/HD improve self-esteem and communication and develop social skills.

Training for parents is considered to be essential to successfully addressing AD/HD in children. Training involves helping parents recognize and encourage socially competent behaviors, teach self-evaluation strategies, model good communication skills, establish appropriate limits, and provide consistent rewards and consequences (Anastopoulos & Farely, 2003). Programs like Systematic Training for Effective Parenting (STEP; Dinkmeyer, 1975) and support groups like Children and Adults with Attention-Deficit/Hyperactivity Disorder (CHADD) may also be useful (L. Seligman, 2006). Multifaceted approaches such as school-based community support programs (Hussey & Guo, 2003) that target elementary-aged students and aim to increase family involvement and support of the school and to improve social and behavioral functioning, as well as attendance and academic achievement, also seem to be effective in reducing AD/HD behaviors. Ultimately, the goal for children with AD/HD is to learn self-monitoring behaviors (L. Seligman, 2006). Self-monitoring is encouraged through behavioral strategies such as praise to reinforce desirable behaviors, proximity (standing near the student), and the use of token economies. Token economies consist of providing children with tokens or points for appropriate behaviors that can be exchanged later for rewards (DuPaul et al., 1992).

One of the most controversial strategies for treating AD/HD is the use of psychostimulant medication. Researchers continue to investigate the benefits and risks of using this medication to treat AD/HD (National Institutes of Health, 1998). Effective medications are thought to stimulate the production of the neurochemicals that facilitate brain functioning (L. Seligman, 2006). Contrary to the misconception that these children are hypersensitive or hyperattentive, neurodevelopmental research suggests that AD/HD is actually a problem of underarousal (Barkley, 1996). Methylphenidate (Ritalin) and dextroamphetamine (Dexadrine) are the most frequently prescribed medications. Newer medications such as Adderall, which is long acting and has less drop-off action; a sustained release version of methylphenidate (Concerta); and a stimulant-free medication, Strattera, are also being used. The Nation's Voice on Mental Illness (NAMI) concluded after conducting a task force investigation that psychotropic medications should be used to treat children only when the benefits outweigh the risks (Gruttadaro & Miller, 2004). The task force went on to recommend that evidence-based treatments be identified, through research, and used to treat mental disorders in children.

DISRUPTIVE BEHAVIOR DISORDERS The *DSM–IV–TR* describes two disruptive behavior disorders: Conduct Disorder (CD) and Oppositional Defiant Disorder (ODD). Prevalence rates for all disruptive behavior disorders are approximately 10% (Tynan, 2008). For CD, the prevalence is 6% to 16% of males and 2% to 9% of females under the age of 18 years (American Psychiatric Association, 2000; Tynan, 2006). Prevalence rates for ODD are 2% to 16% for males and females.

CD is a more serious disruptive behavior disorder than ODD or AD/HD. Left untreated, ODD may develop into a conduct disorder. A diagnosis of CD requires the presence of repeated and persistent violations of the basic rights of others or violations of major age-appropriate societal norms or rules (L. Seligman, 2006). CD is diagnosed when 3 of 15 criteria grouped into the following four categories are present: aggression against people and animals, destruction of property, deceitfulness or theft, and serious violation of rules. CD is divided into childhood-onset and adolescent-onset types. The adolescent-onset type is diagnosed when no symptoms are present before the age of 10, whereas the childhood-onset type is diagnosed if symptoms appear before that age. The prognosis for the childhood-onset type is worse than for the adolescent-onset type (Webster-Stratton & Dahl, 1995). If the symptoms of CD have not remitted by age 18, the diagnosis of CD is usually replaced with the diagnosis of antisocial personality disorder. Approximately 50% of children with CD are also diagnosed with AD/HD (Tynan, 2006). Mood disorders, anxiety disorders, substance use, low verbal intelligence, learning disorders, dropping out of school, delinquency, and violent behavior are common in young people with CD (Snyder, 2001; Tynan, 2008).

ODD is described as a pattern of negativistic, hostile, and defiant behaviors lasting at least six months. According to the *DSM–IV–TR*, characteristic behaviors include losing one's temper, arguing with adults, defying or refusing to comply with adults' requests, deliberately annoying people, being angry and resentful, being easily annoyed by others, blaming others for one's own negative behavior, and being vindictive. Younger children may have temper tantrums, engage in power struggles, have low tolerance for frustration, and be disobedient (Tynan, 2008; Webster-Stratton & Taylor, 2001). Older children will argue, threaten, show disrespect for adults, destroy property in a rage, and refuse to cooperate. The presence of ODD is positively correlated with having low socioeconomic status and growing up in an urban location. ODD is more common in boys, and the symptoms first appear by the age of eight (Tynan, 2008).

Prognosis. Disruptive behavior disorders are difficult to treat, and even with the use of evidence-based treatment, young people with this diagnosis often experience long-term consequences (Tynan, 2008). However, the prognosis for ODD is more promising than for CD. Prognoses for disruptive behavior disorders appear to be best when there has been late onset, early intervention (Tynan, 2008), and long-term intervention (Webster-Stratton & Taylor, 2001). The most critical element of successful treatment is parents' support and participation.

CASE STUDY 16.2

Defiance in the Teenage Years

A 15-year-old female was brought to counseling by her parents. They reported that over the past year or so, she had changed; she has a quick temper and is hostile and argumentative; she has disobeyed her parents repeatedly to meet her boyfriend at a local shopping mall; she blames her teachers for her poor grades in some subjects, but will not ask them for help; and she has even been teasing her four-year-old sister, whom she used to adore. Family, as well as teachers, report that she is difficult and uncooperative, but cannot provide an explanation for the change. A physical examination revealed no medical problems.

Principal Diagnosis: Oppositional Defiant Disorder

Intervention Strategies. Intervention for children with disruptive behavior disorders should be multifaceted. Four types of intervention strategies are suggested: individual counseling, family interventions, school-based interventions, and community interventions (Cooley, 2007; Tynan, 2006). Residential or day treatment programs may be recommended when the child or adolescent poses a danger to self or others. School-based interventions include early education, classroom guidance units, classroom instruction, home visits, and regular meetings with parents.

Relevance to Professional School Counselors. Of all the categories of mental disorders, professional school counselors will have the greatest need to be knowledgeable about AD/HD and disruptive behavior disorders. Classroom teachers and other school personnel, as well as parents, may look to the professional school counselor for guidance concerning how to effectively work with children diagnosed with these disorders. In fact, Jensen et al. (1999) found that children with AD/HD were more likely to receive mental health counseling and school-based interventions than medication. Children are not usually diagnosed with AD/HD and disruptive behavior disorders until they enter school. Teachers and professional school counselors will want to work closely with parents to help them understand these disorders and make appropriate referrals to medical and mental health professionals who can make the diagnosis. Since AD/HD and disruptive behavior disorders frequently coexist, the diagnosis and decisions about interventions will require a high degree of collaboration among physicians, psychologists, classroom and special education teachers, professional school counselors, and parents. Children with disruptive behavior disorders may qualify for special education or Section 504 services.

Recent studies have examined the relationship between low reading achievement and the development of CD in young children (Bennett, Brown, Boyle, Racine, & Offord, 2003) and the relationship of perceived school culture, self-esteem, attachment to learning, and peer approval to the development of disruptive behavior problems in adolescents (DeWit et al., 2000). This research is encouraging the development of a range of school-based and family-focused prevention programs targeting young children (Webster-Stratton & Taylor, 2001). There are two approaches to early prevention. One is to provide social skills, problem-solving, and anger management training to the entire school population through a developmental curriculum. Second Step: A Violence Prevention Curriculum (Committee for Children, 2002b) is an example of such a developmental program. The second approach to prevention is to identify high-risk students and provide a small-group curriculum for them. Fast Track (Bierman et al.,

2002) is an example of a research-based program delivered to identified high-risk first graders. By the end of the third grade, 37% of the program participants were free of serious conduct-problem dysfunctions. The efficacy of both of these approaches will continue to be evaluated, but the implications for professional school counselors are clear. Using either approach, the professional school counselor will play a central role in the delivery of such programs. See the box below for an example of the professional school counselor's role in supporting students with a disruptive behavior disorder.

THE SCHOOL COUNSELOR'S ROLE IN DETERMINING THE EXTENT OF DISRUPTIVE BEHAVIOR

Robert's seventh-grade homeroom teacher has come to talk with the professional school counselor about Robert's behavior. By midterm in the first marking period, Ms. Sandhouse has already documented a series of behavioral issues including Robert being argumentative with teachers, not getting along with peers, annoying students he sits next to, and not taking responsibility for his behavior. Ms. Sandhouse has spoken with Robert's parents by phone and concluded that they do not know how to control Robert's anger other than to punish him and were unable to help the teacher come up with a plan. The professional school counselor listens carefully to the teacher's report and considers a variety of explanations. Robert could be having trouble adjusting to middle school, or perhaps something is going on at home. After speaking with the school counselor, the teacher will implement a more consistent behavior plan with Robert to see if that will make a difference. The school counselor offers Ms. Sandhouse suggestions on how to avoid power struggles and help Robert to increase his self-control. The teacher will also keep a log of his outbursts, noting what has worked and what the triggers seem to be, and establish a behavior contract. They will also meet in person with the parents to share their concerns and ask for parent support for the plans they are implementing. The professional school counselor will ask for parent permission to work with Robert on research-based anger management strategies and will begin by building a positive alliance with Robert. The school counselor considers that Robert may have a disruptive behavior disorder, but before such a diagnosis can be made, the efforts of the teacher and school counselor will need to be documented. Once the teacher and school counselor have more information, they will consider the possibility of asking for a Child Study Team meeting and recommending a psychoeducational evaluation.

Eating Disorders in Children and Adolescents

Feeding and eating disorders of early childhood include two disorders that can interfere with a child's development, social functioning, or nutritional health: pica and rumination disorder. Pica and rumination disorder are especially likely to be diagnosed in children with mental retardation and are often associated with PDDs. Typically, these disorders will be diagnosed before a child enters school, but professional school counselors should be aware of them nonetheless.

Pica is characterized by the ingestion of nonfood substances (A. E. House, 1999). Mouthing and eating non-nutritive substances is not uncommon in children under the age of two; therefore, the diagnosis of pica should not be made before that age unless the behavior is judged to be problematic (Motta & Basile, 1998). Rumination disorder is characterized by persistent regurgitation and rechewing of food (A. E. House, 1999). Typically, rumination disorder is diagnosed in infants and very young children after a period in which a normal eating pattern has been established. Prevalence rates and risk factor assessments have been established based on samples of Caucasian adolescents and, therefore, do not accurately reflect the nature of eating disorders in other ethnic populations (Jacobi, Hayward, de Zwaan, Kraemer, & Agras, 2004).

Anorexia Nervosa (AN) and Bulimia Nervosa (BN) are eating disorders that are diagnosed in adults, as well as in children and adolescents. Prevalence rates of 0.5% to 2% have been reported for AN and 1% to 3% for BN (Roth & Fonagy, 1996) in late adolescent and young adult populations. Prevalence rates for AN and BN have increased during the last 50 years (Wakeling, 1996), and the incidence of eating disorders among elementary-aged children is also increasing. Approximately one-third of adults with an eating disorder report that their disorder began between the ages of 11 and 15 (National Association of Anorexia Nervosa and Associated Disorders [ANAD], 2000.) The most common risk factors for eating disorders in adolescence include early childhood eating and gastrointestinal problems, body dissatisfaction, depression or anxiety, and low self-esteem (Jacobi et al., 2004; Polivy & Herman, 2002). Other factors sometimes associated with eating disorders are environmental stressors, cognitive distortions such as obsessive thoughts, and weak identity formation. Caution must be used in the application of these risk factors to diverse cultural groups. For instance, body dissatisfaction is not a risk factor for females in many cultures (Katzman & Lee, 1997). The causes of eating disorders and the role culture plays in the manifestation of eating disorders are being debated. Recently, researchers (Keel & Klump, 2003) challenged the belief that eating disorders

are culture-bound syndromes, concluding that a strong genetic link exists. Eating disorders in both males and females are associated with sports or occupational choice (Carlat, Carmago, & Herzog, 1997); people in occupational or avocational roles that require low weight, such as in ballet, theater, and many sports, are at an elevated risk of developing an eating disorder.

Anorexia Nervosa, according to the *DSM–IV–TR*, involves a person's refusal to maintain normal body weight or failure to gain weight at what would be an expected rate. For adolescents diagnosed with AN, the *DSM–IV–TR* criteria specify a body weight that is 85% or less than the normal weight for the person's age and size. Other symptoms include great fear of becoming overweight, a disturbed body image, dread of loss of control, and, in females, the cessation of menstrual cycles. In prepubescent girls, the disorder may be associated with apprehension about puberty. Two types of AN have been identified: restricting type (more common) and binge-eating/purging type (American Psychiatric Association, 2000). The restricting type is associated with dieting, fasting, or excessive exercise. The binge-eating/purging type is associated with binge eating, purging, or both, accompanied by a very low weight.

Purging is accomplished through self-induced vomiting or the misuse of laxatives, diuretics, or enemas. The onset of AN is commonly between the ages of 10 and 30. However, 85% of the people with this disorder first meet the diagnostic criteria for the disorder between the ages of 13 and 20 (Kaplan, Sadock, & Grebb, 1994). Physiological consequences of AN include dry skin, edema, low blood pressure, metabolic changes, potassium loss, and cardiac damage that can result in death (Maxman & Ward, 1995).

Individuals diagnosed with BN engage in behaviors similar to those of persons with the binge-eating/purging type of AN, but do not meet the full criteria for that disorder, usually because their weight is more than 85% of normal. According to the *DSM–IV–TR*, BN involves an average of two episodes a week of binge eating (usually accompanied by compensatory behavior such as vomiting, fasting, laxative use, or extreme exercise) for at least three months. Physiological reactions to purging include dental cavities and enamel loss, electrolyte imbalance, cardiac and renal problems, and esophageal tears (ANAD, 2000). Bingeing is associated with dysphoric mood, stress, and unstructured time. People usually binge alone and can consume 3,000 calories in a single binge (Maxman & Ward, 1995).

PROGNOSIS   The prognosis for women with AN is mixed (Löwe et al., 2001). Maxman and Ward (1995) reported that 44% of people with AN recover completely through treatment, 28% are significantly improved, and 24% are

CASE STUDY 16.3

Eating Disorders in Childhood

Marie, age 11, aspired to be a model. She exercised daily and ate very little. Her weight had dropped from 120 lb to 95 lb; at 5 ft 5 in., she looked gaunt and tired. Nevertheless, she continued to perform well at school and at home and was never disobedient. She had few friends, but reported that she was so busy studying that she had little time for socializing. Part of her reluctance to socialize with others stemmed from some unusual behaviors she manifested. She would often wave her arm as though she were swatting flies. She also emitted sounds and words, including obscenities. Marie reported that she could not control these behaviors. Marie was in a special class because of severe difficulty with reading; her reading ability was nearly 2 standard deviations below the norm for her age.

Diagnoses: Anorexia Nervosa, Tourette's disorder, and a reading disorder

not helped or deteriorate. Approximately 5% of people with AN die as a result of the disorder (Maxman & Ward, 1995; Morrison, 1995). The prognosis for BN is somewhat better (Kaplan et al., 1994). Treatment that follows recommended guidelines can have a positive impact on eating patterns, typically reducing binge eating and purging by a rate of at least 75% (L. Seligman, 2006). A positive prognosis is associated with the following factors: good functioning prior to occurrence of the disorder, a positive family environment, the client's acknowledgment of hunger, greater maturity, higher self-esteem, higher educational level, earlier age of onset, lower weight loss, shorter duration of the disease, little denial of the disorder, and absence of coexisting mental disorders.

INTERVENTION STRATEGIES Primary intervention strategies for eating disorders involve a complete medical assessment and multifaceted therapy (L. Seligman, 2006). Behavioral therapy has been effective in promoting healthy eating and eliminating purging and other destructive behaviors. Cognitive therapy can help the individual gain an understanding of the disorder, improve self-esteem, and gain a sense of control. Group therapy has been used effectively to treat people diagnosed with AN and BN, with family therapy included as an important component of the treatment plan, especially for children and adolescents.

RELEVANCE TO PROFESSIONAL SCHOOL COUNSELORS
Given that 86% of adults with eating disorders report that the disorder began before age 20, professional school counselors will need to have knowledge of the risk factors and symptoms of eating disorders and will need to consider how culture may influence the development of an eating disorder (ANAD, 2000; Krentz & Arthur, 2001). Research (Leon, Fulkerson, Perry, Keel, & Klump, 1999) indicates that prevention programs and early detection

in elementary and middle school may be the best defense against the development of an eating disorder during adolescence. Professional school counselors can enlist the help of classroom teachers by increasing their knowledge of eating disorder risk factors and encouraging strategies that promote healthy behaviors (Piran, 2004). Schoolwide antibullying programs can go a long way in protecting students' self-esteem, body image, and identity development.

Professional school counselors may become aware of students who are regularly eating little or no lunch, engaging in ritualized eating patterns, or purging. It is not uncommon in schools to have other students, influenced by the weight loss of youth with AN or BN, begin to experiment with restricted eating patterns. Working with classroom teachers, the school nurse, and the parents, the professional school counselor can help students and their families become aware of dangerous eating patterns and the long-term consequences of eating disorders. Children and adolescents who are diagnosed with eating disorders will need to have long-term medical and mental health interventions. However, professional school counselors can assist these students in school, support the efforts of their mental health counselors, and help parents and families find resources.

Tic Disorders

The *DSM–IV–TR* identifies four tic disorders: Tourette's disorder, chronic tic disorder, transient tic disorder, and tic disorder NOS. Tics are defined as recurrent, nonrhythmic series of movements and sounds (of a nonvoluntary nature) in one or several muscle groups. Tics are usually divided into simple and complex tics of a motor, sensory, or vocal nature (American Psychiatric Association, 2000). Examples of motor tics are eye blinking, neck jerking, facial grimacing, and shrugging. Vocal tics include coughing, clearing one's throat, grunting, sniffing, and barking. Tic symptoms are typically worse under stress, are less noticeable when the child is distracted, and diminish entirely during sleep (L. Seligman, 2006). Tic disorders are more common in boys and have an elevated incidence in children with other disorders such as AD/HD, learning disorders, PDDs, anxiety disorders, and obsessive-compulsive disorder (Coffey et al., 2000; Gadow, Nolan, Sprafkin, & Schwartz, 2002; Kadesjo & Gillberg, 2000; Kurlan et al., 2002).

Tourette's disorder is characterized by a combination of multiple motor tics and one or more vocal tics that have been present for at least one year. These involuntary movements have been reported to occur as frequently as 100 or more times per minute (Leckman & Cohen, 1994). Tourette's disorder often begins with simple eye blinking. Over time, the tic behaviors become persistent and occur at multiple sites in the body. These tics commonly interfere with academic performance and social relationships. Tourette's is diagnosed in 4 or 5 children per 10,000 and tends to run in families.

Budman, Bruun, Park, Lesser, and Olson (2000) reported sudden, explosive outbursts of behavior in children and adolescents with Tourette's disorder. These explosive outbursts are recognizable by their stereotypic features, which include the abrupt onset of unpredictable and primitive displays of physical aggression, verbal aggression, or both that are grossly out of proportion to any provoking stimuli, often threatening serious self-injury or harm to others. Explosive outbursts in children can be distinguished from the more common "temper tantrum" by their magnitude and intensity. These outbursts occur at an age when such symptoms are no longer regarded as age appropriate (Budman et al., 2000).

PROGNOSIS Tic severity peaks at approximately 10 to 11 years and declines in early adolescence (Coffey et al., 2000). One study of the treatment of tic disorders compared the effectiveness of behavioral interventions with that of medication (A. A. Peterson, Campise, & Azrin, 1994). Habit-reversal techniques showed a 90% reduction in tics as compared to medication, which showed only a 50% to 60% reduction. Coffey et al. (2000) conducted a study examining whether a substantial decline in the prevalence rate of tic disorders occurs from childhood to adulthood, suggesting that tic disorders may follow a remitting course. Results of this study found that early adolescence is the time of remission of tics and Tourette's disorder– associated impairment.

INTERVENTION STRATEGIES The treatment of tic disorders currently includes identification of any underlying

stressors; cognitive-behavioral methods for stress management; education of children and families about the disorder; advocacy with education professionals; and collaborative work with physicians, if pharmacological interventions are necessary (Towbin, Cohen, & Lechman, 1995). The first steps include gathering enough information about the symptoms to make an accurate diagnosis and educating the parents and the child about the course of the disorder and the influence of stress (Towbin et al., 1995). Behavioral strategies such as self-monitoring, relaxation training, and habit-reversal training may be recommended after baseline data concerning the nature and frequency of the tic are collected (Kronenberger & Meyer, 1996). The current psychological treatment of choice for tics is habit reversal, which essentially addresses the tic as a behavior. The principal stages in habit reversal involve relaxation and introduction of a competing response (O'Connor, 2001). Social skills training has also been used successfully to offset the negative impact of tic disorders on peer relationships. While behavioral interventions may sometimes attenuate the frequency and severity of the above-mentioned explosive outbursts, these symptoms often increase relentlessly without medication intervention (Budman et al., 2000). Pharmacological treatment is used only for children who do not respond to behavioral strategies (Towbin & Cohen, 1996).

RELEVANCE TO PROFESSIONAL SCHOOL COUNSELORS
The professional school counselor may be the first professional consulted about the development of tic behaviors in a child. A counselor who is knowledgeable about this disorder will be able to provide sources of referral and information to parents and teachers during the diagnostic period. Once the diagnosis has been made, the professional school counselor can provide suggestions concerning classroom modifications to reduce stress, rewards for behavioral control, and adjustment of academic expectations. Professional school counselors may also be able to provide the social skills training to help children deal with the peer relationship problems that frequently result from tic disorders.

Elimination Disorders: Encopresis and Enuresis

Encopresis and enuresis are characterized by inadequate bowel or bladder control in children whose age and intellectual level suggest they can be expected to have adequate control of these functions. Many children diagnosed with these disorders have no coexisting mental disorders (Rapoport & Ismond, 1996). For the diagnosis to be made, the encopresis or enuresis cannot be associated with a general medical condition, with the exception of constipation (Mikkelsen, 2001; L. Seligman, 2006).

Encopresis is the voluntary or involuntary passage of feces in inappropriate places (S. Murphy & Carney, 2004). This diagnosis would not be made in a child younger than four years (Mikkelsen, 2001). "Antisocial or psychopathological processes may be behind deliberate incontinence" (Rapoport & Ismond, 1996, p. 172). There sometimes is an association between encopresis and ODD or CD. Sexual abuse and family pressure have also been associated with this disorder. The most effective treatment strategies involve medical, educational, and therapeutic interventions. Encopresis with constipation responds to treatment more quickly than does encopresis without constipation (Rockney, McQuade, Days, Linn, & Alario, 1996). Encopresis may continue for some time, but it is rarely chronic (Shaffer & Waslick, 1995). According to Mikkelsen (2001), the long-standing conventional treatment regimen, which encompasses educational, behavioral, dietary, and physiological components, has not been surpassed as a primary treatment modality.

Enuresis is the involuntary or intentional inappropriate voiding of urine, occurring in children over the age of five (Butler, 2004; Rapoport & Ismond, 1996). The nocturnal-only subtype is the most common form of this disorder. Nocturnal enuresis can be caused by high fluid intake at night before bedtime, urinary tract infection, emotional stress, sexual abuse, chronic constipation, or a family history of enuresis (Silverstein, 2004). Traumatic events during a sensitive stage in the development of bladder control (two to three years of age) have been found to be related to the later development of nocturnal enuresis (Butler, 2004; Mikkelsen, 2001). Behavioral interventions are the most successful (L. Seligman, 2006). Behavioral treatment in the form of a bell-and-pad method of conditioning is usually considered the first line of intervention (Mikkelsen, 2001). Spontaneous remission occurs in many children.

RELEVANCE TO PROFESSIONAL SCHOOL COUNSELORS
Parents are likely to consult professional school counselors about their child's enuresis, most often manifested as "bedwetting." Parents will need information and education about the nature of this disorder and how to deal with it. Education may help alleviate parents' anxiety about the course of the disorder (L. Seligman, 2006). Parents should be encouraged to rule out medical causes of the bedwetting; if a diagnosis of enuresis is made, professional school counselors can help parents cope. Encopresis is a less common, but often more serious disorder than enuresis. Counselors suspecting this diagnosis in a student should recommend a medical evaluation as the first step in treatment.

Separation Anxiety Disorder

Separation Anxiety Disorder (SAD) is diagnosed in 4% to 5% of children and young adolescents (A. E. House, 1999; Masi, Mucci, & Millepiedi, 2001). SAD is the sole *DSM–IV–TR* anxiety disorder diagnosed only in children and adolescents under the age of 18 (A. E. House, 1999). This disorder is characterized by excessive distress on separation from primary attachment figures. Children diagnosed with SAD must have three or more of the following symptoms present for at least four weeks prior to age 18: worry about caregivers' safety, reluctance or refusal to go to school or be separated from caregivers, fear about being alone, repeated nightmares involving separation themes, and somatic complaints. SAD is more common in girls than boys (Masi et al., 2001), and 50% to 75% of children diagnosed with SAD come from low-socioeconomic-status homes. Children with SAD typically spend a great deal of time in the school clinic complaining of minor illnesses, will ask to go home (Popper & Gherardi, 1996), and have more negative thoughts and lower estimations of their ability to cope than do children without this disorder (Bögels, Snieder, & Kindt, 2003). School refusal is a prominent symptom in 75% of children diagnosed with the disorder (Masi et al., 2001). Adolescents exposed to domestic violence and living in abusive homes are at particular risk for developing SAD (Pelcovitz, Kaplan, DeRosa, Mandel, & Salziner, 2000). Children with a history of SAD are at a 20% increased risk of developing adolescent panic attacks (Hayward, Wilson, Lagle, Killen, & Taylor, 2004).

PROGNOSIS   A study conducted by Last, Perrin, Hersen, and Kazdin (1992) reported a high rate (96%) of recovery from SAD with treatment. A history of the disorder is reported by many adults being treated for other disorders. Childhood SAD may be a precursor to early-onset panic disorder (Goodwin, Lipsitz, Chapman, Mannuzza, & Fyer, 2001), adult anxiety disorders (Klein, 1994), and mood disorders (Popper & Gherardi, 1996). Additionally, a family history of emotional disorders seems to be related to a poor prognosis for children with SAD (Kearney, Sims, Pursell, & Tillotson, 2003).

INTERVENTION STRATEGIES   Treatment strategies can best be determined when the underlying cause of the disorder is understood, particularly whether it stems from insecurity and change in the home environment or is linked to negative experiences in the school setting. The first treatment strategy should be psychoeducational, involving the education of the parents and child (if he or she is old enough) about the symptoms, the consequences, and management strategies (Masi et al., 2001). Encouraging the child to face new situations and being positive may be enough to allow the child to return to school and participate in anxiety-producing situations.

SAD is considered a type of phobia; therefore, behavioral strategies such as systematic desensitization may be the most effective treatment (L. Seligman, 2006). Systematic desensitization, which is a cognitive-behavioral approach, involves rewards being given for successive approximations toward the goal (Weems & Carrion, 2003). Since getting the child back in school is frequently the goal, this strategy would involve rewarding the child for being driven to the school, then entering the school, and finally going into the classroom. Working closely with the parents and school personnel on consistent strategies will be essential. Family therapy may also be necessary, especially when family enmeshment is present.

RELEVANCE TO PROFESSIONAL SCHOOL COUNSELORS
Professional school counselors will most likely encounter children with SAD through referrals from the school nurse or other personnel in the school clinic. Parents also may be aware of the symptoms of this disorder and may seek the counselor's help. Children are more likely to demonstrate symptoms of the disorder during the first few weeks of school and particularly in the early years of school (kindergarten and the primary grades). Professional school counselors can help parents distinguish between mild and transient symptoms associated with difficulty adjusting to school and true SAD. When SAD, the symptoms of school refusal, or both are present, professional school counselors can play an important role in helping to plan and implement systematic desensitization. Professional school counselors can also provide parents with encouragement and support to leave their children at school and provide children with the help they need to stay in school.

Selective Mutism

Selective mutism is a disorder characterized by a person's consistently not speaking in selected social contexts, such as at school (A. E. House, 1999), but speaking in other situations, such as at home (Popper & Gherardi, 1996). The symptoms of selective mutism are not usually related to other communication difficulties such as lack of familiarity with the language, as would be the case for immigrant students (Krysanski, 2003). Selective mutism usually begins before age five and occurs in 30 to 80 people per 100,000 (Popper & Gherardi, 1996). Family dysfunction is often implicated in this disorder (L. Seligman, 2006). Approximately 97% of children diagnosed with selective mutism also had symptoms of an anxiety disorder, usually

social phobia (Black & Uhde, 1995; Krysanski, 2003). The child with this disorder is often lonely and depressed, and the mother is often overinvolved or enmeshed.

PROGNOSIS The prognosis for successful treatment of selective mutism is excellent. Popper and Gherardi (1996) reported that half the children treated are able to speak in public by age 10. The prognosis is especially good for young children; however, the prognosis for children over the age of 10 who still exhibit symptoms of this disorder is less hopeful. Older children are often teased by peers or inappropriately managed by teachers and therefore inadvertently encouraged to maintain the behaviors (Krysanski, 2003).

INTERVENTION STRATEGIES The most effective treatment strategies are behavioral interventions designed to increase communication and teach social skills that help the child overcome feelings of fear and shyness (Kehle, Madaus, Baratta, & Bray, 1998; Krysanski, 2003), such as the use of reinforcements, shaping or prompting, self-modeling, and response initiation procedures. Play therapy can be used to help children overcome the symptoms and to provide a nonverbal way of communicating. Family therapy is also helpful in addressing the role families might play in perpetuating or reinforcing the symptoms.

RELEVANCE TO PROFESSIONAL SCHOOL COUNSELORS
Professional school counselors will want to understand the characteristics of this disorder and may be helpful to parents and school personnel in deciding whether a referral to an outside agency is necessary. Because selective mutism has an impact on school performance and because school is often the place where children with this disorder choose not to speak, selective mutism will often come to the attention of school personnel before parents or others notice it. Professional school counselors may be part of the treatment team once selective mutism is diagnosed, may facilitate treatment by providing a safe environment in which the child can begin to speak in school, and can help teachers to use effective behavioral strategies to encourage speech.

Reactive Attachment Disorder

Reactive Attachment Disorder (RAD) is an uncommon disorder that begins before the age of five years and is characterized by children manifesting severe disturbances in social relatedness (L. Seligman, 2006). The style of social relating among children with RAD typically occurs in one of two extremes: (1) indiscriminate and excessive attempts to receive comfort and affection from any available adult, even relative strangers, or (2) extreme reluctance to initiate or accept comfort and affection, even from familiar adults and especially when distressed (Haugaard & Hazan, 2004). Children with this disorder are those whose attachments to their primary caregivers have been disrupted, leading to impairment of future relationships. Neglect, abuse, or grossly inadequate parenting, otherwise known as pathogenic care, is thought to cause this disorder (P. K, Coleman, 2003; Hanson & Spratt, 2000; Haugaard & Hazan, 2004; Sheperis, Renfro-Michel, & Doggett, 2003). Studies have considered the relationship between RAD and behavioral problems among preschool children; RAD may reflect the roots of ODD and CD (Lyons-Ruth, Zeanah, & Benoit, 1996). In older children and adolescents, the behaviors associated with RAD present as withdrawing from others, acting out aggressively toward peers, being socially awkward, and exhibiting sexual promiscuity, as well as being the frequent victim of bullying (Haugaard & Hazan, 2004). According to Sheperis et al. (2003), some additional symptoms of RAD include low self-esteem; lack of self-control; antisocial attitudes and behaviors; aggression and violence; and a lack of ability to trust, show affection, or develop intimacy. Behaviorally, these children are often self-destructive, suicidal, self-mutilative, and self-defeating (Sheperis et al., 2003). P. K. Coleman (2003) suggested that behaviors such as tantrums, recklessness, risk taking, bullying, stealing, abuse of pets, hoarding of food, and deception are also believed to be associated with RAD; however, these problem behaviors are not currently considered a part of the *DSM–IV–TR* criteria.

INTERVENTION STRATEGIES   Early intervention is the key to treating RAD. Recent research based on Bowlby's theory of attachment has focused on the ways in which secure and insecure attachment patterns evolve and affect children (L. Seligman, 2006). Bowlby and others have found that without treatment, failure to achieve a secure and rewarding attachment during the early years can impair people's ability to form rewarding relationships throughout their lives.

Once the medical needs of the child are addressed, behavioral programs to improve feeding, eating, and caregiving routines can be implemented (L. Seligman, 2006). It will be important to provide caregivers with training so that they know how to provide infants and children with a nurturing environment. Speltz (1990), for example, developed a parental training program based on behavioral and attachment theory that might be useful to parents of children with RAD. Beneficial treatments of RAD should include (1) proper diagnosis at an early age; (2) placement in a secure and nurturing environment; (3) instruction for the parents in empirically based parenting skills; (4) emphasis on family functioning, coping skills, and interaction; and (5) working within the child's and family's more naturalistic environments, as opposed to their more restrictive and intrusive settings (Hanson & Spratt, 2000; Sheperis et al., 2003).

RELEVANCE TO PROFESSIONAL SCHOOL COUNSELORS Professional school counselors will need to be aware of the diagnostic criteria for RAD because a connection has been found between insecure attachment and both subsequent behavior and impulse-control problems and poor peer relationships in young children (Zeanah & Emde, 1994). RAD may be associated with eating problems; developmental delays; and abuse, neglect, and other parent–child problems. In addition, it is important to distinguish RAD from other diagnoses with related symptoms, such as CD and depression, because effective treatment for RAD and these other disorders can be quite different (Haugaard & Hazan, 2004).

OTHER DISORDERS DIAGNOSED IN CHILDREN AND ADOLESCENTS

Mental disorders reviewed up to this point in the chapter are those that typically begin during the early years and are diagnosed primarily or exclusively in young clients. However, many other mental disorders, more likely to be diagnosed in adults, can also be found in children and adolescents. The most common of these include mood disorders, substance-related disorders, psychotic disorders, and several anxiety disorders (Obsessive-Compulsive Disorder [OCD], Posttraumatic Stress Disorder [PTSD], Generalized Anxiety Disorder [GAD], and Adjustment Disorders). These disorders will be reviewed next.

Mood Disorders

Although the diagnostic criteria for mood disorders in adults and children are the same, children and adolescents diagnosed with mood disorders typically have symptoms that differ from those of adults (Emslie & Mayes, 2001; L. Seligman, 2006). Rather than manifesting the classic symptoms of depression, children tend to externalize their feelings and may be irritable, often presenting with somatic complaints. Adolescents are more likely to present with the more familiar symptoms of depression, similar to those of adults, including feelings of sadness and guilt, social withdrawal, and perhaps even thoughts of suicide.

Suicide is rare in children, but increases in prevalence through adolescence (Shaffer & Pfeffer, 2001), with current

CASE STUDY 16.4

Depression in Adolescence

A 17-year old girl was evaluated for an episode of depressed mood, sleeping problems, irritability, loss of weight, and reduced energy level. Symptoms had been present for nearly a month, since her best friend was killed by a car. Her parents could hardly get her up in the morning. She refused to dress or bathe and had been absent from school for 2 weeks. She repeatedly told her parents that she wished she could die so that she could be with her friend. No previous emotional difficulties were reported.

Principal Diagnosis: Major depressive disorder, single episode

estimates as high as one out of five students seriously considering taking his or her own life (Kann et al., 2000). The rate of suicide among African Americans has always been lower than that among Whites, but has been increasing in adolescent males. Attempted suicide is greater among Hispanic adolescents than among African Americans and Whites. Native American adolescents have a very high rate of suicide. Mood disorders, disruptive behavior disorders, and anxiety disorders increase the risk of suicidal ideation and attempts in both sexes. Approximately 90% of adolescents who commit suicide had been diagnosed with a psychiatric disorder for at least two years. Given the high correlation of mood disorders and suicide attempts, it is important to identify young people with mood disorders and begin treatment. Yet it is estimated that 70% of children and adolescents with serious mood disorders are either undiagnosed or inadequately treated (Lewinsohn, Rohde, Seeley, Klein, & Gotlib, 2000).

Major depressive disorder, characterized by at least two weeks of severe depression, is diagnosed in 0.4% to 2.5% of children and 0.4% to 8.3% of adolescents (Birmaher, Ryan, Williamson, Brent, & Kaufman, 1996). Major and minor depression has been reported in 14% of adolescents 15 to 18 years old (Kessler & Walters, 1998). Dysthymic disorder, a milder, but more pervasive form of depression that lasts for at least one year, is diagnosed in 0.6% to 1.7% of children and 1.6% to 8% of adolescents. Bipolar disorder, characterized by episodes of depression and episodes of mania or hypomania, is difficult to diagnose in children and adolescents (Emslie & Mayes, 2001). Prevalence rates for adolescents are thought to be as high as 1%, but the estimates for young children are likely lower (Coyle et al., 2003).

PROGNOSIS Psychotherapy and psychoeducational interventions have been shown to be effective in treating depression in children and adolescents. A cognitive-behavioral group treatment intervention, Coping with Depression for Adolescents (CWDA), has demonstrated significant positive outcomes (G. N. Clark, DeBar, & Lewinsohn, 2003). A meta-analysis conducted by Weisz, Weiss, Han, Grander, and Morton (1995) found that psychotherapy was effective in alleviating the symptoms of 77% of children diagnosed with depression. However, a less optimistic outlook offered by one longitudinal study demonstrated that early-onset depression often persists and is associated with mental illness in adulthood (Weissman et al., 1999).

INTERVENTION STRATEGIES Treatment of children and adolescents with mood disorders is similar to that of adults; cognitive and behavioral interventions are emphasized. Psychoeducational programs (Evans, Van Velsor, & Schumacher, 2002) focus on improving social skills and encouraging rewarding activities. Although medications are used successfully to treat depression in adults, the effective and safe use of antidepressant medications with children and adolescents has not been established (Coyle et al., 2003; Emslie & Mayes, 2001). Nevertheless, medication is often used with children and adolescents to relieve depression.

RELEVANCE TO PROFESSIONAL SCHOOL COUNSELORS Professional school counselors will encounter many sad children and adolescents. It will be particularly important for counselors to understand the diagnostic criteria for mood disorders so they can distinguish situational sadness from a mental disorder, especially given the differences between adult and childhood depression. Mood disorders in children are frequently overlooked and misdiagnosed (Evans et al., 2002). Given the increased risk of suicide behavior linked to mood disorders, this is a diagnosis that professional school counselors will need to be educated about. Professional school counselors will want to consult with parents, teachers, and other mental health professionals if a diagnosis of a mood disorder is suspected, given the evidence that early diagnosis and treatment are associated with better outcomes.

Substance-Related Disorders

Professional school counselors and other mental health professionals generally have considerable concern about the use of alcohol, tobacco, and other harmful substances by children and adolescents. Children who live with parents with Substance-Related Disorders are at particularly high risk of developing these disorders themselves (Rapoport & Ismond, 1996). Professional school counselors need to have current and accurate information about substance use, abuse, and dependence to work effectively with students, teachers, and parents.

Substance-use disorders are unlike most other mental disorders in at least two ways. First, drug abuse and dependence rely on an external agent (the drug) and vary depending on the availability of drugs. Second, substance-use disorders always involve a willing host (the user), who is an active instigator and participant in creating the disorder (Newcomb & Richardson, 2000). Substance-Related Disorders, according to the *DSM–IV–TR*, include two substance-use disorders (substance dependence and substance abuse), as well as a variety of substance-induced disorders that stem from substance abuse or dependence. It is important to differentiate among the types of Substance-Related Disorders (Rapoport & Ismond, 1996). Substance abuse is characterized by maladaptive use of substances, leading to significant impairment or distress. People may fail to fulfill their obligations or may have social or legal problems related to their substance use. Substance dependence is more severe than substance abuse and often includes not only distress and impairment, but also the development of tolerance and symptoms of withdrawal.

Determining whether a young person is using substances is often difficult. Children and adolescents commonly deny substance use for fear of punishment. Substance-use disorders have a high comorbidity with other mental disorders, such as mood disorders, impulse control disorders, and learning disorders in children and adolescents (A. E. House, 1999). Consequently, diagnosing Substance-Related Disorders in young people may be complicated by a pre- or coexisting condition (Rapoport & Ismond, 1996).

PROGNOSIS Many factors are related to a good prognosis for Substance-Related Disorders (L. Seligman, 2006). A stable family situation, early intervention, the lack of accompanying antisocial behavior, and no family history of alcohol use are indicators of a positive outcome (Frances & Allen, 1986). However, Newcomb and Richardson (2000) suggested several areas that work together to influence drug use and abuse. These areas are the cultural, societal environment (i.e., school, peers, and family); psychobehavioral factors (i.e., personality, attitudes, and activities); and biogenetic factors. Furthermore, Lambie and Rokutani (2002, p. 355) proposed 10 risk factors that predict or precipitate Substance-Related Disorders: (1) poor parent–child relationships; (2) mental disorders, especially depression; (3) a tendency to seek novel experiences or take risks; (4) family members or peers who use substances; (5) low academic motivation; (6) absence of religion/religiosity; (7) early cigarette use; (8) low self-esteem; (9) being raised in a single-parent or blended family; and (10) engaging in health-compromising behaviors. It has been found that adolescents who concurrently possess five or more of these qualities are at an extremely high risk for developing substance-use problems. Childhood anxiety disorders and depression have also been identified as potential risk factors affecting the development and course of substance-use disorders (Kendall, Safford, Flannery-Schroeder, & Webb, 2004). According to Wu et al. (2004), there is a strong association between alcohol abuse and suicide attempts. This relationship may involve the disinhibitory effects of acute alcohol intoxication, the increase in vulnerability for depression resulting from chronic alcohol abuse, and the possible use of drugs or alcohol as self-medication for depressive symptoms (Wu et al., 2004). Abusing substances poses significant health risks such as overdose, suicide, aggression, violent behavior, and other psychopathology (McClelland, Elkington, Teplin, & Abram, 2004).

INTERVENTION STRATEGIES Prevention through substance-abuse education, recognition of risk factors, and early detection and treatment are the most important strategies for dealing with substance-use disorders in children and adolescents (Newcomb & Richardson, 2000). Accurate screening for substance use is the first step in intervention. Home drug-test kits are available to parents who wish to assess their child's drug use. The presence of other mental disorders should be assessed as part of any intervention (A. E. House, 1999). Treatment models vary and may be distinguished by their duration, intensity, goals, degree of restrictiveness, and participant membership. Contemporary treatments may be viewed on a continuum that ranges from brief outpatient therapy to intensive inpatient treatment (Newcomb & Richardson, 2000). Treatment may include detoxification, contracting, behavior therapy, self-help groups, family therapy, change in a person's social context, social skills training, and nutritional and recreational counseling (Newcomb & Richardson, 2000). Specific treatment strategies recommended for adolescents by A. B. Bruner and Fishman (1998) include family intervention, remedial education, career counseling, and community outreach. Additionally, McClelland et al. (2004) suggested that treatment programs for youth target the specific needs of adolescents: level of cognitive development, family situation, and educational needs. Treatment programs must target all substances of abuse, especially marijuana, and address comorbid mental disorders. Unfortunately, appropriate drug treatment resources and facilities for children and adolescents who are economically disadvantaged are scarce (Bruner & Fishman, 1998).

RELEVANCE TO PROFESSIONAL SCHOOL COUNSELORS

Professional school counselors have an important role to play in the prevention of substance use. A survey conducted by the National Center on Addiction and Substance Abuse (Califano & Booth, 1998) concluded that the turning-point year, marking the most dramatic increase in exposure and drug use, is 12 to 13. The survey also concluded that there is a large gap between students' and school principals' perceptions of the prevalence of drug use. Students say drugs are everywhere, whereas principals say the problem is virtually nonexistent. Another study concluded that parents are largely unaware of the extent to which their adolescents are involved in major risk behaviors such as use of alcohol, LSD (lysergic acid diethylamide), cocaine, and marijuana (T. L. Young & Zimmerman, 1998). These findings indicate a need for continued proactive substance-use educational programs at the elementary and middle school levels, as well as an aggressive parent education component in these programs. To serve as a resource to school personnel and parents in the detection and treatment of substance use and to be a credible resource to students, professional school counselors will need to obtain accurate and up-to-date information about levels of substance use in their community, detection of substance use, and available community resources.

Lambie and Rokutani (2002) suggested that professional school counselors can be the first line of defense in detecting student troubles that may require specialized treatment not offered in the school setting. Some visible indicators of possible substance-related problems are deterioration of academic performance, increased absenteeism and truancy, fighting, verbal abuse, defiance, and withdrawal (Lambie & Rokutani, 2002). Professional school counselors have four functions in working with students with possible substance-abuse issues: (1) identify the possible warning signs of student substance abuse; (2) work with the youth to establish a therapeutic relationship; (3) support the family system to promote change; and (4) be a resource for and liaison among the student, the family, the school, and community agencies and treatment programs (Lambie & Rokutani, 2002).

Psychotic Disorders

Psychotic Disorders in children are rare (L. Seligman, 2006). Approximately 1 child in 10,000 is diagnosed with schizophrenia. These disorders have both internalizing features (e.g., flat affect, social withdrawal) and externalizing features (e.g., impulsivity, inattention) (S. R. Smith, Reddy, & Wingenfeld, 2002). The symptoms of psychotic disorders in children are the same as in adults: hallucinations, delusions, loose associations, and illogical thinking. The most common symptoms of schizophrenia in childhood are auditory hallucinations and delusions, along with illogical conversation and thought patterns (McClellan, McCurry, Speltz, & Jones, 2002). Schizophrenia in children and adolescents is difficult to diagnose because of the comorbidity with other disorders such as mood and cognitive (organic) mental disorders. Given the complexities of psychotic disorders, children and adolescents with these disorders are often difficult to identify, leading to possible delays in treatment (S. R. Smith et al., 2002). Psychotic disorders are commonly misdiagnosed in youths, due in part to clinicians not following the diagnostic criteria and in part to the relative rarity of these disorders in children (Kumra et al., 2001; McClellan et al., 2002).

PROGNOSIS Bellack and Mueser (1993) reported a fairly positive prognosis for young people diagnosed with psychotic disorders when they are treated with a combination of family therapy and medication. Seventeen percent of children who received both family therapy and medication relapsed, as compared to 83% of children receiving only medication. Biederman, Petty, Faraone, and Seidman (2004) found that, within one sample, psychotic symptoms lasted an average of three years and were present during an average of 27% of the children's and adolescents' lives.

INTERVENTION STRATEGIES Asarnow, Tompson, and McGrath (2004) suggested two phases within the treatment process: (1) acute and (2) stabilization and maintenance. The acute phase emphasizes pharmacological treatment. The stabilization and maintenance phase emphasizes the continuation of medication management supplemented with psychosocial and community treatment strategies. These include family psychoeducational interventions, individual psychotherapy, social skills training, and cognitive remediation (Asarnow et al., 2004). Treatment for children and adolescents with psychotic disorders should include family therapy, medication, counseling, and special education (L. Seligman, 2006). Social skills training, including the teaching of appropriate behaviors, interpersonal interactions, playing with peers, and effective communication, should be included as part of treatment.

Working with the family will also be important to promote a positive attitude, make modifications to the home environment, and teach parents effective coping skills. A positive and encouraging home environment can reduce the likelihood that a psychotic disorder will recur.

RELEVANCE TO PROFESSIONAL SCHOOL COUNSELORS
Due to the small number of children diagnosed with psychotic disorders, it is unlikely that professional school counselors will encounter many children with these disorders. It is important for professional school counselors to remember that loose associations in speech and illogical thinking are not unusual before the age of seven and probably are not indicative of the symptoms of psychosis. However, professional school counselors do need to be aware that the frequency of schizophrenia increases from age 11 to late adolescence, when it reaches adult prevalence rates (Volkmar, 1996). Professional school counselors may be involved in the implementation and delivery of special education services as part of an IEP for young people with psychotic disorders that may include social and emotional goals.

Obsessive-Compulsive Disorder

Approximately 1 in 200 children and adolescents meets the criteria for Obsessive-Compulsive Disorder (OCD; March & Leonard, 1996). OCD is more common in children than in adults (Gothelf, Aharonovsky, Horesh, Carty, & Apter, 2004). The symptoms for children are the same as for adults; most children with OCD present with obsessions about germs, external threats, or disease and exhibit rituals of washing or checking. Other common compulsions include touching, counting, hoarding, and repeating. A high rate of comorbidity between OCD and tic disorders (Rapoport, Leonard, Swedo, & Lenane, 1993), anxiety disorders, and bipolar disorder (Masi et al., 2001) has been reported. The most frequent age of onset among young patients treated for OCD at the National Institute of Mental Health was seven years; the average age at onset was 10.2 years (March & Leonard, 1996).

INTERVENTION STRATEGIES Children with OCD respond to cognitive-behavioral interventions. The primary intervention strategy is exposure to obsessions, with accompanying prevention of compulsions, to promote systematic desensitization (March & Leonard, 1996). Medication also is often used as part of the treatment plan. The family should be included in treatment because the family may have developed maladaptive coping strategies for dealing with the distressed child (Rapoport et al., 1993).

RELEVANCE TO PROFESSIONAL SCHOOL COUNSELORS
Professional school counselors may be the first consulted by teachers and parents concerning the symptoms of OCD. Counselors can provide information about the disorder and may be instrumental in helping parents determine whether a referral is warranted. When a diagnosis of OCD is made, professional school counselors can help structure the school modifications and interventions.

Posttraumatic Stress Disorder

The criteria for Posttraumatic Stress Disorder (PTSD) are the same for children as for adults, although the disorder may be manifested differently due to differences in cognitive and emotional functioning (L. Seligman, 2006). The essential feature of PTSD is symptom development following direct personal experience of a traumatic event, witnessing a traumatic event, or learning of such an experience with someone interpersonally close (Cook-Cottone, 2004). The *DSM–IV–TR* describes the following criteria for a diagnosis of PTSD: great fear and helplessness in response to the event; persistent reexperiencing of the event; loss of general responsiveness; and symptoms of arousal and anxiety, such as sleep disturbances, anger, or irritability. Children might have nightmares, present with a flat affect, or act withdrawn. It is often difficult for children to express their feelings about the traumatic experience except through play (Kronenberger & Meyer, 1996).

Traumatic stressors can be naturally occurring (e.g., a hurricane) or man-made (e.g., terrorism). Trauma can occur in intimate physical and emotional proximity, occur physically distant and strike emotionally close (e.g., *Challenger* tragedy, September 11), or occur physically close and emotionally distant (witnessing the fatal accident of a stranger). The stress can be acute, as in a rape, or chronic, as through years of repeated sexual abuse (Cook-Cottone, 2004).

In the past, children were thought to be resilient to the impact of traumatic events. Much has been learned about PTSD in the last 10 years through research focused on children who have been victims of natural disasters, war, violent crime, community violence, and sexual abuse (Cooley-Quille, Boyd, Frantz, & Walsh, 2001; Nader, Pynoos, Fairbanks, al-Ajeel, & al-Asfour, 1993; Thabet, Abed, & Vostanis, 2004; Wolfe, Sas, & Wekerle, 1994). Although adolescents exhibit symptoms of PTSD similar to those of adults, including depression, anxiety, and emotional disturbance, children's symptoms are more likely to be behavioral or physical (Cook-Cottone, 2004). Children who have experienced sexual abuse often exhibit inappropriate sexual behaviors. According to Cook-Cottone (2004), preschoolers' PTSD symptoms are expressed in nonverbal channels, which include acting out or internalized behaviors, nightmares and disturbed sleep patterns, developmental regression, and clinging behavior. In school-age children, symptoms continue to be expressed behaviorally and may include regressions, anxious attachment, school refusal, weak emotional regulation, and an increase in externalizing or internalizing behavioral expression (e.g., fighting with peers, withdrawal from friends, poor attention, decline in academic performance). Physiological complaints such as stomachaches and headaches are also common in children. Adolescents often present with a sense of foreshortened future, self-injurious behaviors, suicidal ideation, conduct problems, dissociation, depersonalization, and possibly substance abuse (Cook-Cottone, 2004).

PROGNOSIS Symptoms of trauma-related disorders often decrease without treatment within three months of the event (L. Seligman, 2006). With treatment, the prognosis usually is also very good for recovery from symptoms that have not spontaneously remitted, especially for people whose functioning was positive before exposure to trauma, whose onset of symptoms was rapid, whose symptoms have lasted less than six months, whose social supports are strong, and who have received early treatment (Kaplan et al., 1994). According to Ozer and Weinstein (2004), children who perceive that they have strong social support, who are able to talk about the traumatic event and feelings associated with the event, and who have safe schools and cohesive family environments have a better chance at decreasing their PTSD symptoms more quickly. Kaplan et al. (1994) reported that overall, 30% of those with trauma-related disorders recover completely, 40% have mild symptoms, 20% have moderate symptoms, and 10% do not improve through treatment.

INTERVENTION STRATEGIES Effective treatment for children and adolescents is similar to treatment for adults diagnosed with PTSD. Treatment should begin as soon as possible after the event (L. Seligman, 2006). Preventive treatment, even before symptoms emerge, is recommended. When treatment for PTSD is required, a multifaceted approach emphasizing cognitive-behavioral strategies seems to work best. The goal of treatment is to help the person process the trauma, express feelings, increase coping and control over memories, reduce cognitive distortions and self-blame, and restore self-concept and previous levels of functioning. Group therapy involving people who have had similar traumatic experiences can be especially helpful in reducing feelings of being isolated and being different. However, the group leader should ensure that the sharing of memories does not have a retraumatizing effect.

Additionally, therapeutic interventions should be based within the school setting only when (1) comprehensive assessment has been completed; (2) it is determined that school-based support is the appropriate, least restrictive level of intervention; (3) parents have been informed of all treatment options; (4) the child is experiencing adequate adjustment and academic success with intervention; and (5) consultation, supervision, and referral are readily utilized by the professional school counselor (Cook-Cottone, 2004).

RELEVANCE TO PROFESSIONAL SCHOOL COUNSELORS Professional school counselors will be called on to provide support to students, staff, and parents in the event of a trauma that affects individuals and school communities. When a student or teacher or parent dies, when there is a natural disaster in the community, or when a violent crime has been committed, professional school counselors will be called on to provide group and individual interventions that offer accurate information, give people a place to ask questions and talk about the trauma, and screen for symptoms of PTSD. Professional school counselors will need to be aware of the differences between unhealthy and healthy responses to traumatic events and to be able to provide resources to students and families when a therapeutic intervention is deemed necessary or is requested. Professional school counselors should encourage and lead school administrators to develop crisis intervention plans to deal with traumatic events affecting school communities. The professional school counselor should have a solid working knowledge of the etiological and diagnostic implications of PTSD, the therapeutic options, and, when needed, ways to facilitate school reintegration of a child who has suffered a traumatic event (Cook-Cottone, 2004).

Generalized Anxiety Disorder

The diagnosis known as overanxious disorder of childhood is now included in the diagnosis of Generalized Anxiety Disorder (GAD) because the symptoms of pervasive anxiety are the same regardless of the person's age. GAD is characterized by feelings of worry or anxiety about many aspects of the person's life and is reflected in related physical symptoms such as shortness of breath and muscle tension that are difficult to control (Wicks-Nelson & Israel, 2003). To meet the diagnostic criteria, symptoms of this disorder must persist for a minimum of six months (American Psychiatric Association, 2000) and must have a significant impact on the person's functioning. Comorbidity of GAD with other disorders is common. SAD was present in 70% of children who had been diagnosed with GAD, while 35% met the criteria for both GAD

I believe that the professional school counselor is crucial to the success of students with mental health issues. Despite the increasing need and the IDEA mandates for mental health services within the school system, no additional funding or personnel have been supplied to meet student needs. I believe that through a comprehensive school counseling program, I am the ideal provider and coordinator for students with mental health issues. I regularly work with students with a variety of mental health issues, including anxiety, depression, Attention-Deficit/Hyperactivity Disorder, autism spectrum disorders, and other mental health issues. I use a variety of strategies to promote the success of students with mental health issues, including prevention activities, early intervention activities, coordination (e.g., resource identification, education, advocacy, collaboration), and direct treatment. The school environment is ideal for the implementation of mental health services due to student access, the existing student–counselor relationship, and the ability to monitor and follow up on these services.

As a first step to promote positive mental health, I teach children appropriate social, emotional, academic, and career skills through classroom, small-group, and individual lessons. These prevention services can assist students in modifying behaviors, thoughts, and feelings that will lead to building relationships, career development, educational fulfillment, and personal success. As a professional school counselor, I am often the first person to be asked about a student concern by school staff and parents. With an understanding of common mental health issues and typical child development, I can help to identify and provide referrals for the assessment of mental health issues. Early intervention will lead to improved outcomes for students with mental health issues. I can monitor the student's progress and

facilitate the ongoing referral, coordination, and transition of services as necessary among schools and settings.

As a professional school counselor, I can provide support, advocacy, and education for the child, family, and educators as they participate in assessments by explaining results and any mental health issues. With the knowledge of both educational and mental health issues, I can identify and advocate for the child to receive the best services, both within and outside the school system, as early as possible. I can also identify possible educational, social, and emotional accommodations; provide research-based treatment approaches and strategies; and coordinate treatment with other professionals. The services that the child will receive require coordination by a professional that understands both the mental health and the educational areas in order to promote the best treatment possible.

I believe that the professional school counselor can provide treatment for children with mental health issues. I can select research-based treatments to help students with and without disabilities learn new appropriate skills and practice those skills in the school setting, and I can provide these treatments early and often for children in a naturalistic setting. As a school counselor, I am a familiar person, and unlike other mental health professionals, I am on-site, at school, and able to handle many day-to-day student needs and personal crises. While school counselors will still need to refer more serious mental health issues for assessment, many mental health services can be provided by the professional school counselor in the school setting.

Source: Judy Trigiani, Professional School Counselor, Spring Hill Elementary School, McLean, Fairfax County Public Schools, Virginia

---

and AD/HD (Last, Strauss, & Francis, 1987). A child with GAD usually experiences anticipatory anxiety that is generalized to include situations requiring appraisal or performance, but is not associated with a specific stimulus. GAD is the most common anxiety disorder in adolescents (D. B. Clark, Smith, Neighbors, Skerlec, & Randall, 1994).

PROGNOSIS People who receive cognitive-behavioral therapy for GAD frequently show significant and consistent improvement, although few will be free of all symptoms. Roth and Fonagy (1996) found that 60% maintained their improvement at a six-month follow-up.

INTERVENTION STRATEGIES As with other anxiety disorders, cognitive-behavioral strategies are the most effective treatments (Ollendick & King, 1998). The goal of treatment

is to lessen the extent of the anxiety and the overarousal that accompanies it by teaching children to cope with anxiety using a variety of strategies such as identification and modification of anxious self-talk, modeling, education about emotions, relaxation techniques, and homework (Kendall, Chu, Pimentel, & Choudhury, 2000).

RELEVANCE TO PROFESSIONAL SCHOOL COUNSELORS
Professional school counselors will undoubtedly encounter students exhibiting symptoms of GAD. Professional school counselors may be able to suggest stress management strategies to students and can help parents understand this disorder. Professional school counselors can offer guidance units and small-group counseling sessions to students coping with anxiety, as well as workshops to help their parents. Used in collaboration with treatment by mental health

professionals, these psychoeducational strategies may afford considerable ongoing help to students coping with GAD.

Adjustment Disorders

Adjustment disorders are fairly common in adults, as well as in young people (Rapoport & Ismond, 1996). Adjustment disorders are characterized by a relatively mild maladaptive response to a stressor that occurs within three months of that event. Stressors may include experiences such as changing schools, parental separation, or illness in the family. The maladaptive response may include anxiety or depression, as well as behavioral changes. This diagnosis can be maintained only for six months beyond the termination of the stressor or its consequences. If symptoms remain after that time, the diagnosis must be changed.

PROGNOSIS The short-term and long-term prognoses for an adjustment disorder are quite good if the disorder stands alone. When other disorders are also diagnosed, the prognoses are less optimistic.

INTERVENTION STRATEGIES Most adjustment disorders improve spontaneously without treatment when the stressor is removed or attenuated. However, counseling can facilitate recovery (L. Seligman, 2006). Treatment should focus on teaching coping skills and adaptive strategies to help people avert future crises and minimize poor choices and self-destructive behaviors (Maxman & Ward, 1995). A crisis-intervention model is most effective. This model focuses on relieving the acute symptoms first and then promoting adaptation and coping. A typical crisis-intervention model includes the following steps: understand the problem, view the problem in context, contract with the client for change, apply interventions, reinforce gains, and terminate treatment (Wells & Giannetti, 1990).

RELEVANCE TO PROFESSIONAL SCHOOL COUNSELORS
Professional school counselors are in an excellent position to provide students with the supportive strategies required to cope with the symptoms of an adjustment disorder. Professional school counselors regularly are asked to provide crisis intervention to students dealing with the death of a loved one, a divorce, or some other family crisis. Professional school counselors can also help parents understand the effect the stressor is having on their children.

Summary/Conclusion

Clearly, professional school counselors need to increase their knowledge of the symptoms, diagnosis, and treatment of mental disorders to meet the needs of all students. Requirements of the IDEA and Section 504 regulations, an increased number of students with mental health concerns, and the reform movement calling for full-service schools demand that professional school counselors expand their repertoire of diagnostic skills and knowledge and work collaboratively with other educational and mental health professionals in schools and the community (ASCA, 2005a; Bemak, 2000; Lockhart & Keys, 1998; Santos de Barona & Barona, 2006). Additional training in special education procedures, Section 504 regulations, diagnostic assessment, multiculturalism, and the *ASCA National Model* will enhance professional school counselors' clinical knowledge and skills (ASCA, 2005a; Dana, 2001; Santos de Barona & Barona, 2006; Wicks-Nelson & Israel, 2003). Currently, to qualify for endorsement by the Council for Accreditation of Counseling and Related Educational Programs (CACREP), counselor education programs must include coursework that covers issues related to the development and functioning of children and adolescents, such as eating disorders, abuse, attention-deficit disorders, and depression (CACREP, 2009).

The role of the professional school counselor is changing. Counselor education programs, as well as school districts, need to continue to be responsive to the changing nature of school counseling programs and the clinical challenges professional school counselors face. For professional school counselors to expand their role to include greater application of clinical knowledge and skills and increased collaboration with community and other mental health treatment programs, school districts may need to reconceptualize the role of the professional school counselor (Bemak, 2000). Recognition of the importance of the clinical aspect of the professional school counselor's role may necessitate realignment of duties, affording counselors the opportunity to use their clinical skills to more effectively help their students and families. In addition, professional school counselors must continue to make appropriate referrals to medical and mental health practitioners and to work with teachers, parents, and students to help students achieve and develop in spite of clinical issues.

Further Readings and Resources

Baumberger, J. P., & Harper, R. E. (2007). *Assisting students with disabilities: A handbook for school counselors.* Thousand Oaks, CA: Corwin Press.

Cooley, M. L. (2007). *Teaching kids with mental health and learning disorders in the regular classroom: How to recognize, understand and help challenged (and challenging) students succeed.* Minneapolis, MN: Free Spirit Publications.

Cortiella, C. (2006). *NCLB and IDEA: What parents of students with disabilities need to know and do.* Minneapolis, MN: University of Minnesota, National Center on Educational Outcomes.

House, A. E. (1999). *DSM–IV diagnosis in the schools.* New York: Guilford Press.

Jones, W. P. (1997). *Deciphering the diagnostic codes: A guide for school counselors.* Thousand Oaks, CA: Corwin Press.

Kazdin., A. E., & Weisz, J. R. (2003). *Evidence-based psychotherapies for children and adolescents.* New York: Guilford Press.

Morrison, J., & Anders, J. F. (2000). *Interviewing children and adolescents: Skills and strategies for effective DSM–IV diagnosis.* New York: Guilford Press.

Seligman, L. (1998). *Selecting effective treatments: A comprehensive, systematic guide to treating mental disorders* (rev. ed.). San Francisco: Jossey-Bass.

Smith, S. (2006). *IDEA 2004: A parent handbook for school age children with learning disabilities.* Bloomington, IN: Authorhouse.

Trolley, B. (in press). *The school counselor's guide to special education.* Thousand Oaks, CA: Corwin Press.

Wicks-Nelson, R., & Israel, A. C. (2003). *Behavior disorders of childhood.* Upper Saddle River, NJ: Prentice Hall.

Activities

1. Choose one of the mental or emotional disorders found in the *DSM–IV–TR* and find several current research articles that describe the school's role in helping students who have this disorder.

2. Interview a school psychologist or special educator in a local school. Find out the percentage of students in the school that have been diagnosed with mental or emotional disorders. Also inquire about how these students are handled within the system (i.e., inclusion, separate classes all day).

3. Home drug-testing kits are often easy to locate. Examine a home drug-testing kit and determine if it would be a simple for parents to use when they suspect their child of using drugs.

4. Interview a professional school counselor about his or her involvement with students with mental disorders or learning problems. Ask about the counselor's role with child study, local screening, and Section 504. Determine how the school counselor supports parents and teachers that have students with mental health and learning disorders.

REFERENCES

Abrams, K., Theberge, S. K., & Karan, O. C. (2005). Children and adolescents who are depressed: An ecological approach. *Professional School Counseling, 8,* 284–292.

Achenbach, K., & Arthur, N. (2002). Experiential learning: Bridging theory to practice in multicultural counseling. *Guidance and Counseling, 17,* 39–46.

Achenbach, T. M., & Rescorla, L. A. (2001). *Manual for the Achenbach System of Empirically Based Assessment (ASEBA).* Burlington: University of Vermont, Research Center for Children, Youth, and Families.

Achieve, Inc. (2004). *American Diploma Project: Ready or not, creating a high school diploma that counts.* Washington, DC: Author.

Achieve, Inc. (2005). *Rising to the challenge: Are high school graduates prepared for college and work?* Washington, DC: Peter D. Hart Research Associates/Public Opinion Strategies.

Adams, J. R., Benshoff, J. M., & Harrington, S. Y. (2007). An examination of referrals to the school counselor by race, gender, and family structure. *Professional School Counseling, 10,* 389–398.

Adams, M., Bell, L. A., & Griffin, P. (Eds.). (1997). *Teaching for diversity and social justice: A sourcebook.* New York, NY: Routledge.

Ad Council. (2000). *The real deal.* New York, NY: Author.

Akos, P., Cockman, C. R., & Strickland, C. A. (2007). Differentiating classroom guidance. *Professional School Counseling, 10,* 455–463.

Akos, P., Goodnough, G. E., & Milsom, A. S. (2004). Preparing school counselors for group work. *Journal for Specialists in Group Work, 29,* 127–136.

Akos, P., & Martin, M. (2003). Transition groups for preparing students for middle school. *Journal for Specialists in Group Work, 28,* 139–154.

Allen, J. M. (1994). *School counselors collaborating for student success* (Report No. EDO-CG-94-27). Greensboro, NC: ERIC Clearinghouse on Counseling and Student Services. (ERIC Document Reproduction Service No. ED377414)

Allen, M., Burt, K., Bryan, E., Carter, D., Orsi, R., & Durkan, L. (2002). School counselors' preparation for and participation in crisis intervention. *Professional School Counseling, 6,* 96–101.

Amatea, E. S., Daniel, H., Bringman, N., & Vandiver, F. M. (2004). Strengthening counselor–teacher–family connections: The family–school collaborative consultation project. *Professional School Counseling, 8,* 47–55.

Amatea, E. S., & West-Olatunji, C. A. (2007). Joining the conversation about educating our poorest children: Emerging leadership roles for school counselors in high-poverty schools. *Professional School Counseling, 11,* 81–89.

Amato, P. R. (2000). The consequences of divorce for adults and children. *Journal of Marriage and the Family, 62,* 1269–1287.

Amato, P. R., & Gilbreth, J. G. (1999). Non-resident fathers and children's well-being: A meta-analysis. *Journal of Marriage and the Family, 61,* 557–573.

American Bar Association. (2009). *Kinship care may lead to increased behavioral well-being.* Retrieved April 6, 2009, from www.abanet.org/child/sept08.pdf

American Counseling Association. (1997, May 31). *Know your rights: Mental health, private practice and the law* [ACA national videoconference]. Alexandria, VA: Author.

American Counseling Association. (2005). *ACA code of ethics.* Alexandria, VA: Author.

American Counseling Association. (2006). *Public awareness ideas and strategies for professional counselors.* Alexandria, VA: Author.

American Counseling Association. (2009). *Publications.* Retrieved April 26, 2009, from www.counseling.org/publications

American Psychiatric Association. (2000). *Diagnostic and statistical manual of mental disorders* (4th ed., Text rev.). Washington, DC: Author.

American Psychological Association. (2004). *Report on the Task Force on Psychology's agenda for child and adolescent mental health.* Washington, DC: Author.

American School Counselor Association. (1993). *The American School Counselor Association position statements.* Alexandria, VA: Author.

American School Counselor Association. (1999a). *Role statement.* Retrieved July 1, 2002, from www.schoolcounselor.org/role.htm

American School Counselor Association. (1999b). *Position statements.* Retrieved July 1, 2002, from www.schoolcounselor.org/pubs/position.htm

American School Counselor Association. (2000). *Position statement: Critical incident response in schools.* Retrieved May 18, 2005, from www.schoolcounselor.org

American School Counselor Association. (2003a). *The ASCA national model: A framework for school counseling programs.* Alexandria, VA: Author.

American School Counselor Association. (2003b). The ASCA national model: A framework for school counseling programs. *Professional School Counseling, 6,* 165–168.

American School Counselor Association. (2004a). *Ethical standards for school counselors.* Alexandria, VA: Author.

American School Counselor Association. (2004b). *Position statement: The professional school counselor and students with special needs.* Retrieved August 20, 2005, from www.schoolcounselor.org/content.asp?contentid5218

American School Counselor Association. (2004c). *Position statement: Special-needs students.* Retrieved December 12, 2008, from www.schoolcounselor.org/content.asp?contentid=218

American School Counselor Association. (2005a). *The ASCA national model: A framework for school counseling programs* (2nd ed.). Alexandria, VA: Author.

American School Counselor Association. (2005b). *State certification requirements.* Retrieved May 24, 2005, from www.schoolcounselor.org/content.asp?contentid5242

American School Counselor Association. (2008). *Position statement: Response to intervention.* Retrieved December 12, 2008, from http://asca2.timberlakepublishing.com/content.asp?contentid=557

American School Counselor Association. (2009). ASCA website. Retrieved April 15, 2009, from www.schoolcounselor.org

Anastopoulos, A. D., & Farely, S. E. (2003). A cognitive-behavioral training program for parents of children with attention-deficit/hyperactivity disorder. In A. E. Kazdin & J. R. Weisz (Eds.), *Evidence-based psychotherapies for children and adolescents* (pp. 187–203). New York, NY: Guilford Press.

Anderson, D. (2007). Multicultural group work: A force for developing and healing. *Journal of Specialists in Group Work, 32,* 224–244.

Anderson, L. W., & Krathwohl, D. R. (Eds.). (2001). *A taxonomy for learning, teaching, and assessing: A revision of Bloom's taxonomy of educational objectives.* New York, NY: Longman.

Anderson-Butcher, D., & Ashton, D. (2004). Innovative models of collaboration to serve children, youths, families, and communities. *Children and Schools, 26,* 39–53.

Aponte, J. F., & Crouch, R. T. (2000). The changing ethnic profile of the United States in the twenty-first century. In J. F. Aponte & J. Wohl (Eds.), *Psychological interventions and cultural diversity* (2nd ed., pp. 1–19). Needham Heights, MA: Allyn & Bacon.

Applequist, K. L., & Bailey, D. B. (2000). Navajo caregivers' perceptions of early intervention services. *Journal of Early Intervention Services, 23,* 47–61.

Arman, J. F. (2000). In the wake of tragedy at Columbine High School. *Professional School Counseling, 2,* 218–220.

Arman, J. F., & McNair, R. (2000). A small group model for working with elementary school children of alcoholics. *Professional School Counseling, 3,* 290–293.

Arnold, M. S., Chen–Hayes, S. F., & Lewis, J. (2002, June). *Unlearning oppression: Learning skills to challenge the barriers of racism, classism, and other "-isms."* Paper presented at the Education Trust Summer School Counseling Academy, Chicago, IL.

Arredondo, P., & D'Andrea, M. (1995, September). AMCD approves multicultural counseling competency standards. *Counseling Today,* 28–32.

Arredondo, P., Toporek, R., Brown, S., Jones, J., Locke, D. C., Sanchez, J., & Stadler, H. (1996). *Operationalization of the multicultural counseling competencies.* Alexandria, VA: Association for Multicultural Counseling and Development.

Asarnow, J. R., Tompson, M. C., & McGrath, E. P. (2004). Annotation: Childhood-onset schizophrenia: Clinical and treatment issues. *Journal of Child Psychology and Psychiatry, 45,* 180–194.

Asner-Self, K. K., & Feyissa, A. (2002). The use of poetry in psychoeducational groups with multicultural and multilingual clients. *Journal of Specialists in Group Work, 27,* 136–160.

Association for Specialists in Group Work. (1999). ASGW principles for diversity-competent group workers. *Journal for Specialists in Group Work, 24,* 7–14.

Association for Specialists in Group Work. (2000). Association for Specialists in Group Work: Professional standards for the training of group workers. *Journal for Specialists in Group Work, 25,* 327–342.

Assouline, S. G., Nicpon, M. F., & Huber, D. H. (2006). The impact of vulnerabilities and strengths on the academic experiences of twice-exceptional students: A message to school counselors. *Professional School Counselors, 10,* 14–24.

Astromovich, R. L., Coker, J. K., & Hoskins, W. J. (2005). Training school counselors in program evaluation. *Professional School Counseling, 9,* 49–54.

Atkins, M. S., McKay, M., Arvanitis, P., London, L., Madison, S., Costigan, C., . . . Webster, D. (1998). An ecological model for school-based mental health services for urban low-income aggressive children. *Journal of Behavioral Health Services Research, 5,* 64–75.

Atkinson, D. A., & Juntunen, C. L. (1994). School counselors and school psychologists as school–home–community liaisons in ethnically diverse schools. In P. Pedersen & J. C. Carey (Eds.), *Multicultural counseling in schools: A practical handbook* (pp. 103–119). Needham Heights, MA: Allyn & Bacon.

Atkinson, D. R., & Lowe, S. M. (1995). The role of ethnicity, culture, knowledge, and conventional techniques in counseling and psychotherapy. In J. C. Ponterotto, J. M. Casas,

L. A. Sazuki, & C. M. Alexander (Eds.), *Handbook of multicultural counseling* (pp. 387–414). Newbury Park, CA: Sage.

Auger, R. (2005). School-based interventions for students with depressive disorders. *Professional School Counseling, 8,* 344–352.

Auger, R. W., Blackhurst, A. E., & Wahl, K. H. (2005). The development of elementary-aged children's career aspirations and expectations. *Professional School Counseling, 8,* 322–329.

Auger, R. W., Seymour, J. W., & Roberts, W. B., Jr. (2004). Responding to terror: The impact of September 11 on K–12 schools and schools' responses. *Professional School Counseling, 7,* 222–230.

Baba, M. L., & Darga, L. L. (1981). The genetic myth of racial classification. In M. S. Collins, I. W. Wainer, & T. A. Bremmer (Eds.), *Science and the question of human equality* (pp. 1–19). Boulder, CO: Westview Press.

Baca, L. M., & Koss-Chionino, J. D. (1997). Development of a culturally responsive group counseling model for Mexican American adolescents. *Journal of Multicultural Counseling and Development, 25,* 130–141.

Baggerly, J., & Borkowski, T. (2004). Applying the ASCA national model to elementary school students who are homeless: A case study. *Professional School Counseling, 8,* 116–123.

Baggerly, J., & Osborn, D. (2006). School counselors' career satisfaction and commitment: Correlates and predictors. *Professional School Counseling, 9,* 197–205.

Bailey, D. F., & Bradbury-Bailey, M. (2004). Respecting differences: Racial and ethnic groups. In R. Perusse & G. E. Goodnough (Eds.), *Leadership, advocacy, and direct service strategies for professional school counselors* (pp. 157–186). Belmont, CA: Brooks/Cole-Thomson Learning.

Bailey, D. F., & Bradbury-Bailey, M. E. (2007). Promoting achievement for African American males through group work. *Journal for Specialists in Group Work, 32,* 83–96.

Baker, B. L., & Feinfield, K. A. (2003). Early intervention. *Current Opinion in Psychiatry, 16,* 503–509.

Baker, S. B., & Gerler, E. R., Jr. (2008). *School counseling for the twenty-first century* (5th ed.). Upper Saddle River, NJ: Pearson Prentice Hall.

Baker, S. B., Swisher, J. D., Nadenichek, P. E., & Popowicz, C. L. (1984). Measured effects of primary prevention strategies. *Personnel and Guidance Journal, 62,* 459–464.

Banks, J. A., & McGee-Banks, C. A. (Eds.), (2005). *Multicultural education: Issues and perspectives* (5th ed.). Hoboken, NJ: John Wiley.

Banks, J. A., & McGee Banks, C. A. (1989). *Multicultural education.* Needham Heights, MA: Allyn & Bacon.

Bardick, A. D., & Bernes, K. B. (2005). A closer examination of bipolar disorder in school-age children. *Professional School Counseling, 9,* 72–77.

Barker, J., & Satcher, J. (2000). School counselors' perceptions of required workplace skills and career development competencies. *Professional School Counseling, 4,* 134–139.

Barkley, R. A. (1996). Attention deficit hyperactivity disorder. In E. J. Mash & R. A. Barkley (Eds.), *Child psychopathology* (pp. 63–112). New York, NY: Guilford Press.

Barnes, P. E., Friehe, M. J. M., & Radd, T. R. (2003). Collaboration between speech-language pathologists and school counselors. *Communication Disorders Quarterly, 24*(3), 137–142.

Bauer, N. S., Lozano, P., & Rivara, F. P. (2007). The effectiveness of the Olweus bullying prevention program in public middle schools; A controlled trial. *Journal of Adolescent Health, 40,* 266–274.

Bauer, S. R., Sapp, M., & Johnson, D. (2000). Group counseling strategies for rural at-risk high school students. *High School Journal, 83,* 41–50.

Bauman, S. (2006). Using comparison groups in school counseling research: A primer. *Professional School Counseling, 9,* 357–366.

Baumeister, A. A., & Baumeister, A. A. (2000). Mental retardation: Causes and effects. In M. Hersen & R. T. Ammerman (Eds.), *Advanced abnormal child psychology* (2nd ed.). Mahwah, NJ: Lawrence Erlbaum.

Bauserman, R. (2002). Child adjustment in joint-custody versus sole-custody arrangements: A meta-analytic review. *Journal of Family Psychology, 16,* 91–102.

Beale, A. V., & Scott, P. C. (2001). "Bullybusters": Using drama to empower students to take a stand against bullying behavior. *Professional School Counseling, 4,* 300–305.

Beck, A. T., & Steer, R. A. (1991). *Beck Scale for Suicide Ideation (BSSI) manual.* San Antonio, TX: Psychological Corporation.

Beck, A. T., & Steer, R. A. (1993). *Beck Hopelessness Scale (BHS) manual.* San Antonio, TX: Psychological Corporation.

Beck, A. T., & Weishaar, M. E. (2000). Cognitive therapy. In R. J. Corsini & D. Wedding (Eds.), *Current psychotherapies* (6th ed., pp. 241–272). Itasca, IL: F. E. Peacock.

Bellack, A., & Mueser, K. T. (1993). Psychosocial treatment for schizophrenia. *Schizophrenia Bulletin, 19,* 317–336.

Bemak, F. (1998). Interdisciplinary collaboration for social change: Redefining the counseling profession. In C. C. Lee & G. R. Walz (Eds.), *Social action: A mandate for counselors* (pp. 279–292). Alexandria, VA: American Counseling Association & ERIC/CASS.

Bemak, F. (2000). Transforming the role of the counselor to provide leadership in educational reform through collaboration. *Professional School Counseling, 3,* 323–331.

Bemak, F., & Chung, R. C. (2002). Multicultural counseling with immigrant students in schools. In P. B. Pedersen & J. Carey (Eds.),

Multicultural counseling in schools. Needham Heights, MA: Allyn & Bacon.

Bemak, F., & Chung, R. C. (2004). Teaching multicultural group counseling: Perspectives for a new era. *Journal for Specialists in Group Work, 29,* 31–42.

Bemak, F., & Chung, R. C-Y. (2005). Advocacy as a critical role for urban school counselors: Working toward equity and social justice. *Professional School Counseling, 8,* 196–202.

Bemak, F., & Chung, R. C-Y. (2008). New professional roles and advocacy strategies for school counselors: A multicultural/social justice perspective to move beyond the nice counselor syndrome. *Journal of Counseling and Development, 86,* 372–381.

Bemak, F., & Keys, S. (2000). *Violent and aggressive youth: Intervention and prevention strategies for changing times.* Thousand Oaks, CA: Corwin Press.

Bemak, F., Murphy, S., & Kaffenberger, C. (2005). Community-focused consultation: New directions and practice. In C. Sink (Ed.), *Contemporary school counseling: Theory, research and practice* (pp. 206–228). Boston, MA: Houghton Mifflin.

Bennett, K. J., Brown, K. S., Boyle, M., Racine, Y., & Offord, D. (2003). Does low reading achievement at school entry cause conduct problems? *Social Science and Medicine, 56,* 2443–2448.

Benson, F. (2004). *Empowering teachers with best instructional practices.* New York, NY: New Millenium.

Berg, I. K., & Miller, S. (1992). *Working with the problem drinker.* New York, NY: Norton.

Berg, I. K., & Steiner, T. (2003). *Children's solution work.* New York, NY: Norton.

Bergan, J., & Kratochwill, T. (1990). *Behavioral consultation and therapy.* New York, NY: Plenum Press.

Berger, E. H. (2000). *Parents as partners in education.* Upper Saddle River, NJ: Merrill.

Bergin, J. J. (2004). Small-group counseling. In A. Vernon (Ed.), *Counseling children and adolescents* (3rd ed., pp. 355–390). Denver, CO: Love.

Berglund, P. A., Demler, O., Jin, R., Merikangas, K. R., & Walters, E. E. (2005). The nature of panic disorders and agoraphobia. In D. H. Barlow & M. G. Craske (Eds.), *Mastery of your anxiety and panic* (pp. 21–32). New York, NY: Oxford University Press.

Berk, L. E. (2007). *Development through the lifespan* (4th ed.). Boston, MA: Pearson Allyn & Bacon.

Bernes, K. B., & Bardick, A. D. (2007). Conducting adolescent violence risk assessments: A framework for school counselors. *Professional School Counseling, 10,* 419–427.

Biederman, J., Petty, C., Faraone, S. V., & Seidman, L. (2004). Phenomenology of childhood psychosis: Findings from a large sample of psychiatrically referred youth. *Journal of Nervous and Mental Disease, 192,* 607–613.

Bierman, K. L., Coie, H. D., Dodge, K. A., Greenberg, M. T., Lochman, J. E., McMahon, R. J., & Pinderhughes, E. E. (2002). Evaluation of the first 3 years of the Fast Track prevention trial with children at high risk for adolescent conduct problems. *Journal of Abnormal Child Psychology, 30,* 19.

Birmaher, B., Ryan, N. D., Williamson, D. E., Brent, D. A., & Kaufman, J. (1996). Childhood and adolescent depression: A review of the past 10 years: Part II. *Journal of the American Academy of Child and Adolescent Psychiatry, 35,* 1575–1583.

Bjorklund, D. F. (2000). *Children's thinking: Developmental function and individual differences* (3rd ed.). Belmont, CA: Wadsworth.

Blacher, J. H., Murray-Ward, M., & Uellendahl, G. E. (2005). School counselors and school assessment. *Professional School Counseling, 8,* 337–343.

Black, B., & Uhde, T. W. (1995). Psychiatric characteristics of children with selective mutism: A pilot study. *Journal of the American Academy of Child and Adolescent Psychiatry, 34,* 847–856.

Blackhurst, A. E., Auger, R. W., & Wahl, K. H. (2003). Children's perceptions of vocational preparation requirements. *Professional School Counseling, 7,* 58–67.

Bloom, B. (n.d.). *Bloom's taxonomy.* Retrieved February 2, 2005, from www.au.af.mil/au/awc/awcgate/edref/bloom.htm

Bloomfield, M. (1915). *Readings in vocational guidance.* Cambridge, MA: Harvard University Press.

Blue-Banning, M., Summers, J. P., Frankland, H. C., Nelson, L. L., & Beegle, G. (2004). Dimensions of family and professional partnerships: Constructive guidelines for collaboration. *Exceptional Children, 70,* 167–184.

Blustein, D. (1994). "Who am I?" The question of self and identity in career development. In M. L. Savickas & R. W. Lent (Eds.), *Convergence in career development theories* (pp. 139–154). Palo Alto, CA: Consulting Psychologists Press.

Bodenhorn, N. (2005). American School Counselor Association ethical code changes relevant to family work. *Family Journal, 13,* 316–320.

Bodenhorn, N. (2006). Exploratory study of common and challenging ethical dilemmas experienced by professional school counselors. *Professional School Counseling, 10,* 195–202.

Bögels, S. M., Snieder, N., & Kindt, M. (2003). Specificity of dysfunctional thinking in children with symptoms of social anxiety, separation anxiety, and generalized anxiety. *Behavior Change, 20,* 160–169.

Bolman, L. G., & Deal, T. E. (1997). *Reframing organizations: Artistry, choice, and leadership* (2nd ed.). San Francisco, CA: Jossey-Bass.

Bolyard, K. L., & Jensen-Scott, R. L. (1996). Worldview and culturally sensitive crisis intervention. In J. L. DeLucia-Waack (Ed.), *Multicultural counseling competencies: Implications for training and practice* (pp. 217–236). Alexandria, VA: Association for Counselor Education and Supervision.

Bonnington, S. B. (1993). Solution-focused brief therapy: Helpful interventions for school counselors. *School Counselor, 41*, 126–128.

Borders, L. D., & Drury, S. M. (1992). Comprehensive school counseling programs: A review for policymakers and practitioners. *Journal of Counseling and Development, 70*, 487–498.

Borodovsky, L. G., & Ponterotto, J. G. (1994). A family-based approach to multicultural career development. In P. Pedersen & J. Carey (Eds.), *Multicultural counseling in schools* (pp. 195–206). Boston, MA: Allyn & Bacon.

Borum, R. (2000). Assessing violence risk among youth. *Journal of Clinical Psychology, 56*, 1263–1288.

Bostic, J. Q., & Rauch, P. K. (1999). The 3 R's of school consultation. *Journal of the American Academy of Child and Adolescent Psychiatry, 38*, 339–341.

Bowen, M. L., & Glenn, E. E. (1998). Counseling interventions for students who have mild disabilities. *Professional School Counseling, 2*, 16–25.

Bowers, J. L., & Colonna, H. A. (2001). *Tucson Unified School District guidance and counseling program handbook.* Tucson, AZ: Tucson Unified School District.

Boyer, E. L. (1983). *High school: A report on secondary education in America.* New York. NY: Harper & Row.

Braback, M., Walsh, M., Kenny, M., & Comilang, K. (1997). Interprofessional collaboration for children and families: Opportunities for counseling psychology in the 21st century. *Counseling Psychologist, 25*, 615–636.

Bradley, C., Johnson, P., Rawls, G., & Dodson-Sims, A. (2005). School counselors collaborating with African American parents. *Professional School Counseling, 8*, 424–427.

Bradley, L. J., Gould, L. J., & Hendricks, C. B. (2004). Using innovative techniques for counseling children and adolescents. In A. Vernon (Ed.), *Counseling children and adolescents* (4th ed., pp. 75–110). Denver, CO: Love.

Bradshaw, C. P., Buckley, J. A., & Ialongo, N. S. (2008). School-based service utilization among urban children with early onset educational and mental health problems: The squeaky wheel phenomenon. *School Psychology Quarterly, 23*, 169–186.

Brantley, L. S., Brantley, P. S., & Baer-Barkley, K. (1996). Transforming acting-out behavior: A group counseling program for inner-city elementary school pupils. *Elementary School Guidance and Counseling, 31*, 96–105.

Bratton, S. C., Ray, D., Rhine, T., & Jones, L. (2005). The efficacy of play therapy with children: A meta-analytic review of treatment outcomes. *Professional Psychology: Research and Practice, 36*, 376–390.

Brennan, J. (1999). *They can and they do: Low income students and high academic achievement.* Retrieved July 1, 2005, from www.edtrust.org/Low_Income.html

Brewer, J. M. (1942). *History of vocational guidance.* New York, NY: Harper & Brothers.

Brigman, G. (2006). Research methods in school counseling: A summary pattern for the practitioner. *Professional School Counseling, 9*, 421–425.

Brigman, G., & Campbell, C. (2003). Helping students improve academic achievement and school success behavior. *Professional School Counseling, 7*, 91–98.

Brigman, G. A., Webb, L. D., & Campbell, C. (2007). Building skills for school success: Improving the academic and social competencies of students. *Professional School Counseling, 10*, 279–288.

Bringman, N., & Lee, S. M. (2008). Middle school counselors' competence in conducting developmental classroom lessons: Is teaching experience necessary? *Professional School Counseling, 11*, 380–385.

Brinson, J. A., Kottler, J. A., & Fisher, T. A. (2004). Cross-cultural conflict resolution in the schools: Some practical intervention strategies for counselors. *Journal of Counseling and Development, 82*, 294–301.

Britzman, M. J. (2005). Improving our moral landscape via character education: An opportunity for school counselor leadership. *Professional School Counseling, 8*, 293–295.

Brooks, J. (2006). Strengthening resilience in children and youths: Maximizing opportunities through the schools. *Children and Schools, 28*, 69–76.

Brooks-McNamara, V., & Pedersen, L. (2006). Practitioner inquiry: A method to advocate for systemic change. *Professional School Counseling, 9*, 257–260.

Brott, P. E. (2006). Counselor education accountability: Training the effective professional school counselor. *Professional School Counseling, 10*, 179–188.

Brown, A., & Mistry, T. (1994). Group work with mixed membership groups: Issues of race and gender. *Social Work with Groups, 17*, 5–21.

Brown, C., Dahlbeck, D. T., & Sparkman-Barnes, L. (2006). Collaborative relationships: School counselors and non-school mental health professionals working together to improve the mental health needs of students. *Professional School Counseling, 9*, 332–335.

Brown, D. (1996). Brown's values-based, holistic model of career and life-role choices and satisfaction. In D. Brown & L. Brooks (Eds.), *Career choice and development* (3rd ed., pp. 337–368). San Francisco, CA: Jossey-Bass.

Brown, D., Galassi, J. P., & Akos, P. (2004). School counselors' perception of the impact of high stakes testing. *Professional School Counseling, 8*, 31–39.

Brown, D., Pryzwansky, W. B., & Schultz, A. C. (2000). *Psychological consultation: Introduction to theory and practice* (5th ed.). Needham Heights, MA: Allyn & Bacon.

Brown, D., & Trusty, J. (2005a). School counselors, comprehensive school counseling programs, and academic achievement: Are school counselors promising more than they can deliver? *Professional School Counseling, 9*, 1–8.

Brown, D. B., & Trusty, J. (2005b). *Designing and leading comprehensive school counseling programs: Promoting student competence and meeting student needs.* Belmont, CA: Thomson Brooks/Cole.

Brown, D., & Trusty, J. (2005c). The ASCA national model, accountability, and establishing causal links between school counselors' activities and student outcomes: A reply to Sink. *Professional School Counselor, 1*, 13–15.

Bruce, M. A. (1995). Brief counseling: An effective model for change. *School Counselor, 42*, 353–363.

Bruce, M. A., Shade, R. A., & Cossairt, A. (1996). Classroom-tested guidance activities for promoting inclusion. *School Counselor, 43*, 224–231.

Bruner, A. B., & Fishman, M. (1998). Adolescents and illicit drug use. *Journal of the American Medical Association, 280*, 597–598.

Bryan, J. (2005). Fostering educational resilience and achievement in urban schools through school–family–community partnerships. *Professional School Counseling, 8*, 219–227.

Bryan, J., & Holcomb-McCoy, C. (2004). School counselors' perceptions of their involvement in school–family–community partnerships. *Professional School Counseling, 7*, 162–171.

Bryan, J., Holcomb-McCoy, C., Moore-Thomas, C., & Day-Vines, N. (2009). Who sees the school counselor for college information? A national study. *Professional School Counseling, 12*, 280–291.

Bryant, J., & Milsom, A. (2005). Child abuse reporting by school counselors. *Professional School Counseling, 9*, 63–71.

Bucher, K. T., & Manning, M. L. (2003, January/February). Challenges and suggestions for safe schools. *Clearing House, 76*, 160–164.

Buckley, M. A. (2000). Cognitive-developmental considerations in violence prevention and intervention. *Professional School Counseling, 4*, 60–70.

Budman, C. L., Bruun, R. D., Park, K. S., Lesser, M., & Olson, M. (2000). Explosive outbursts in children with Tourette's disorder. *Journal of the American Academy of Child and Adolescent Psychiatry, 39*, 1270–1276.

Burns, M. K., Jacob, S., & Wagner, A. (2008). Ethical and legal issues associated with using response-to-intervention to assess learning disabilities. *Journal of School Psychology, 46*, 263–279.

Bussing, R., Zima, B. T., Perwien, A. R., Belin, T. R., & Widawski, M. (1998). Children in special education: Attention deficit hyperactivity disorder, use of services, and unmet need. *American Journal of Public Health, 88*, 1–7.

Butler, R. J. (2004). Childhood nocturnal enuresis: Developing a conceptual framework. *Clinical Psychology Review, 24*, 909–931.

Califano, J. A., & Booth, A. (1998). *1998 CASA national survey of teens, teachers, and principals.* New York, NY: National Center on Addiction and Substance Abuse at Columbia University.

Campbell, C. A., & Brigman, G. (2005). Closing the achievement gap: A structured approach to group counseling. *Journal for Specialists in Group Work, 30*, 67–82.

Campbell, C., & Dahir, C. (1997). *The national standards for school counseling programs.* Alexandria, VA: American School Counselor Association.

Campbell, D. T., & Stanley, J. C. (1963). *Experimental and quasi-experimental designs for research.* Boston, MA: Houghton Mifflin.

Campbell, M., Cueva, J. E., & Hallin, A. (1996). Autism and pervasive developmental disorders. In J. M. Wiener (Ed.), *Diagnosis and psychopharmacology of childhood and adolescent disorders* (2nd ed., pp. 151–192). New York, NY: Wiley.

Campbell, M., Schopler, E., Cueva, J. E., & Hallin, A. (1996). Treatment of autistic disorder. *Journal of the American Academy of Child and Adolescent Psychiatry, 35*, 134–141.

Canfield, B. S., Ballard, M. B., Osmon, B. C., & McCune, C. (2004). School and family counselors work together to reduce fighting at school. *Professional School Counseling, 8*, 40–46.

Cantrell, R., Parks-Savage, A., & Rehfuss, M. (2007). Reducing levels of elementary school violence with peer mediation. *Professional School Counseling, 10*, 475–481.

Cantwell, P. D. (1996). Attention deficit disorder: A review of the past 10 years. *Journal of the American Academy of Child and Adolescent Psychiatry, 35*, 978–987.

Carey, J. (2006, November). *Evaluation is not a four letter word: How to know whether or not what you are doing is working.* Paper presented at the Colorado School Counselors Association, Denver, CO.

Carey, J., & Dimmitt, C. (2006). Resources for school counselors and counselor educators: The Center for School Counseling Outcome Research. *Professional School Counseling, 9*, 416–420.

Carey, J. C., Dimmitt, C., Hatch, T. A., Lapan, R. T., & Whiston, S. C. (2008). Report of the national panel for evidence-based school counseling: Outcome research coding protocol and evaluation of student success skills and second step. *Professional School Counseling, 11*, 197–206.

Carlat, D. J., Carmago, C. A., & Herzog, D. B. (1997). Eating disorders in males: A report on 135 patients. *American Journal of Psychiatry, 154*, 1127–1132.

Carlson, L. A. (2003). Existential theory: Helping school counselors attend to youth at risk for violence. *Professional School Counseling, 6*, 310–315.

Carnevale, A. P., & Desrochers, D. M. (2003). Preparing students for the knowledge economy: What school counselors need to know. *Professional School Counseling, 6*, 228–237.

Carney, J. V. (2000). Bullied to death: Perceptions of peer abuse and suicidal behavior during adolescence. *School Psychology International, 21*, 213–223.

Carney, J. V. (2008). Perceptions of bullying and associated trauma during adolescence. *Professional School Counseling, 11*, 179–188.

Carrell, S. E., & Carrell, S. A. (2006). Do lower student to counselor ratios reduce school disciplinary problems? *Contributions to Economic Analysis and Policy, 5*(1), 1–12.

Carter, G. R. (2004, February). *Connecting the world of education: Is it good for the kids?* (Editorial). Retrieved December 23, 2004, from www.ascd.org

Casella, R. (2001). What is violent about "school violence"?: The nature of violence in a city high school. In J. N. Burstyn, G. Bender, R. Casella, H. W. Gordon, D. P. Guerra, K. V. Luschen, . . . & Williams, K. M. (Eds.), *Preventing violence in schools: A challenge to American democracy* (pp. 15–46). Mahwah, NJ: Erlbaum.

Catalano, R. F., Loeber, R., & McKinney, K. C. (1999, October). *School and community interventions to prevent serious and violent offending* (OJJDP Juvenile Justice Bulletin). Retrieved from www.ncjrs.org/pdffiles1/ojjdp/177624.pdf. Washington, DC: Office of Juvenile Justice and Delinquency Prevention.

Center for Mental Health in Schools. (1999). *School–community partnerships: A guide.* Los Angeles, CA: Author.

Centers for Disease Control and Prevention, National Center for Injury Prevention and Control. (2000). *Dating violence.* Available at www.cdc.gov/ncipc/factsheets/datviol.htm

Centers for Disease Control and Prevention. (2008). *Autism spectrum disorders overview.* Retrieved December 11, 2008, from www.cdc.gov/ncbddd/autism/overview.htm

Charkow, W. B. (1998). Inviting children to grieve. *Professional School Counseling, 2*, 117–122.

Charles, C. M., & Senter, G. W. (2005). *Building classroom discipline.* New York, NY: Longman.

Charlesworth, J. R., & Jackson, C. M. (2004). Solution-focused brief counseling: An approach for school counselors. In B. T. Erford (Ed.), *Professional school counseling: A handbook of theories, programs, and practices* (pp. 139–148). Austin, TX: PRO-ED.

Charney, R. S. (2002). *Teaching children to care* (2nd ed.). Greenfield, MA: Northeast Foundation for Children.

Chen-Hayes, S. F. (2000). Social justice advocacy with lesbian, bisexual, gay, and transgendered persons. In J. Lewis & L. Bradley (Eds.), *Advocacy in counseling: Counselors, clients, and community* (pp. 89–98). Greensboro, NC: CAPS & ERIC/CASS.

Chen-Hayes, S. F. (2005). *Multicultural counseling class lecture.* Bronx, NY: Lehman College of the City University of New York.

Chen-Hayes, S. F. (2007). The ACCESS Questionnaire: Assessing school counseling programs and interventions to ensure equity and success for every student. *Counseling and Human Development, 39*(6), 1–10.

Chen-Hayes, S. F., Chen, M., & Athar, N. (2000). Challenging linguicism: Action strategies for counselors and client-colleagues. In J. Lewis & L. Bradley (Eds.), *Advocacy in counseling: Counselors, clients, and community* (pp. 25–36). Greensboro, NC: CAPS & ERIC/CASS.

Christenson, S. L., & Sheridan, S. M. (2001). *Schools and families: Creating essential connections for learning.* New York, NY: Guilford Press.

Clark, D. B., Smith, M. G., Neighbors, D. B., Skerlec, L. M., & Randall, J. (1994). Anxiety disorders in adolescence: Characteristics, prevalence, and comorbidities. *Clinical Psychology Review, 14*, 113–137.

Clark, D. C., & Fawcett, J. (1992). Review of empirical risk factors for evaluation of the suicidal patient. In B. Bongar (Ed.), *Suicide: Guidelines for assessment, management, and treatment* (pp. 16–48). New York, NY: Oxford University Press.

Clark, G. N., DeBar, L. L., & Lewinsohn, P. M. (2003). Cognitive-behavioral group treatment for adolescent depression. In A. E. Kazdin & J. R. Weisz (Eds.), *Evidence-based psychotherapies for children and adolescents* (pp. 120–134.). New York, NY: Guilford Press.

Clark, L. A. (1987). Mutual relevance of mainstream and cross-cultural psychology. *Journal of Consulting and Clinical Psychology, 55*, 461–470.

Clark, M., & Stone, C. (2000, May). Evolving our image: School counselors as educational leaders. *Counseling Today*, 21 & 46.

Clark, M. A., & Breman, J. C. (2009). School counselor inclusion: A collaborative model to provide academic and social-emotional support in the classroom setting. *Journal of Counseling and Development, 87*, 6–11.

Clark, R. M. (1993). Homework-focused parenting practices that positively affect student achievement. In N. F. Chavkin (Ed.), *Families and schools in a pluralistic society* (pp. 85–105). Albany: State University of New York Press.

Coalition of Essential Schools. (2008). *CES school benchmarks: Transformational leadership.* Retrieved April 26, 2009, from www.essentialschools.org/cs/cestop/print/ces_docs/643?x-r=disp

Cobia, D. C., & Henderson, D. A. (2007). *Handbook of school counseling* (2nd ed.). Upper Saddle River, NJ: Merrill/Prentice Hall.

Coffey, B. J., Biederman, J., Geller, D. A., Spencer, T. J., Kim, G. S., Bellordre, C. A., . . . & Mariola, M. S. (2000). Distinguishing illness severity from tic severity in children and adolescents with Tourette's disorder. *Journal of the American Academy of Child and Adolescent Psychiatry, 39,* 556–561.

Cohen, J. (1988). *Statistical power analysis for the behavioral sciences* (2nd ed.). Hillsdale, NJ: Erlbaum.

Coker, J. K. (2004). Alcohol and other substance abuse: A comprehensive approach. In R. Perusse & G. E. Goodnough (Eds.), *Leadership, advocacy, and direct service strategies for professional school counselors* (pp. 284–327). Belmont, CA: Brooks/Cole-Thomson Learning.

Cole, J. C., Cornell, D. G., & Sheras, P. (2006). Identification of school bullies by survey methods. *Professional School Counseling, 9,* 305–313.

Coleman, P. K. (2003). Reactive attachment disorder in the context of the family: A review and call for future research. *Emotional and Behavioral Difficulties, 8,* 205–216.

Coleman, P. T., & Deutsch, M. (2000). *Cooperation, conflict resolution, and school violence: A systems approach* (Choices Briefs No. 5). New York, NY: Columbia University, Institute for Urban and Minority Education.

College Board. (2008a). *The NOSCA components of college counseling: Preparation, planning and admissions.* Washington, DC: Author.

College Board. (2008b). *Inspiration and innovation: 10 effective counseling practices from the College Board's Inspiration Awards schools.* Washington, DC: Author.

College Board. (2009). *National Office for School Counselor Advocacy equity belief statement.* Retrieved from http://apcentral.collegeboard.com/apc/public/homepage/22794.html

Commission on Chapter 1. (1992). *Making schools work for children in poverty.* Washington, DC: Author.

Committee for Children. (1997a). *Second Step: A violence prevention curriculum, grades 1–3* (2nd ed.). Seattle, WA: Author.

Committee for Children. (1997b). *Second Step: A violence prevention curriculum, grades 4–5* (2nd ed.). Seattle, WA: Author.

Committee for Children. (2002a). *Second Step: A violence prevention curriculum* (3rd ed.). Seattle, WA: Author.

Committee for Children. (2002b). *Second Step: A violence prevention program.* Available at www.cfchildren.org

Conant, J. B. (1959). *The American high school today: A first report to interested citizens.* New York, NY: McGraw-Hill.

Conflict Information Consortium. (2000a). *Denial of identity.* Retrieved March 2, 2002, from www.colorado.EDU/conflict/peace/problem/denyid.htm

Conflict Information Consortium. (2000b). *Domination conflicts.* Retrieved March 2, 2002, from www.colorado.EDU/conflict/peace/problem/domination.htm

Conflict Information Consortium. (2000c). *The denial of other human needs.* Retrieved March 2, 2002, from www.colorado.EDU/conflict/peace/problem/needs.htm

Conflict Information Consortium. (2000d). *Treatment list 2: Treating core conflict problems.* Retrieved March 2, 2002, from colorado.EDU/conflict/peace/!treating_core.htm

Conners, C. K. (2008). *Manual for the Conners-3 Rating Scales.* North Tonawanda, NY: Multi- Health Systems.

Constantine, M. G. (2001). Theoretical orientation, empathy, and multicultural counseling competence in school counselor trainees. *Professional School Counseling, 4,* 342–348.

Conyne, R. K. (1996). The Association for Specialists in Group Work training standards: Some considerations and suggestions for training. *Journal for Specialists in Group Work, 21,* 155–162.

Cook, J. B., & Kaffenberger, C. J. (2003). Solution shop: A solution-focused counseling and study skills program for middle school. *Professional School Counseling, 7,* 116–121.

Cook-Cottone, C. (2004). Childhood posttraumatic stress disorder: Diagnosis, treatment, and school reintegration. *School Psychology Review, 33*(1), 127–139.

Cooley, M. L. (2007). *Teaching kids with mental health and learning disorders in the regular classroom: How to recognize, understand and help challenged (and challenging) students succeed.* Minneapolis, MN: Free Spirit Publications.

Cooley-Quille, M., Boyd, R. C., Frantz, E., & Walsh, J. (2001). Emotional and behavioral impact of exposure to community violence in inner-city adolescents. *Journal of Clinical Child Psychology, 30*(1), 199–206.

Corey, G. (2008). *Theory and practice of group counseling* (7th ed.). Belmont, CA: Brooks/Cole-Thomson Learning.

Corey, G., Corey, M. S., & Callanan, P. (2006). *Issues and ethics in the helping professions* (5th ed.). Pacific Grove, CA: Brooks/Cole.

Corey, M. S., & Corey, G. (2006). *Groups: Process and practice* (7th ed.). Pacific Grove, CA: Brooks/Cole.

Cormany, R. B., & Brantley, W. A. (1996). It's our problem: An administrator looks at school guidance. *School Counselor, 43,* 171–173.

Cornett, C. E., & Cornett, C. F. (1980). *Bibliotherapy: The right book at the right time.* Bloomington, IN: Phi Delta Kappa Educational Foundation.

Cortiella, C. (2006). *NCLB and IDEA: What parents of students with disabilities need to know and do.* Minneapolis, MN: University of Minnesota, National Center on Educational Outcomes.

Cottone, R. R., & Tarvydas, V. M. (2007). *Ethical and professional issues in counseling* (3rd ed.). Upper Saddle River, NJ: Merrill/Prentice Hall.

Coulter, W. A. (1996, April). *Alarming or disarming? The status of ethnic differences with exceptionalities.* Paper presented at the annual convention of the Council for Exceptional Children, Orlando, FL.

Council for Accreditation of Counseling and Related Educational Programs. (2009). *CACREP accreditation standards and procedures manual.* Alexandria, VA: Author.

Council on Rehabilitation Education. (2003–2004). *Accreditation manual.* Available from www.core-rehab.org

Cousins, L., & Weiss, G. (1993). Parent training and social skills training for children with attention-deficit hyperactivity disorder: How can they be combined for greater effectiveness? *Canadian Journal of Psychiatry-Revue Canadienne de Psychiatrie, 38,* 449–457.

Cowley, W. H. (1937). Preface to the principles of student counseling. *Educational Record, 18,* 218–234.

Coyle, J. T., Pine, D. S., Charney, D. S., Lewis, L., Nemeroff, C. B., Carlson, G. A., . . . & Hellander, M. (2003). Depression and Bipolar Support Alliance consensus statement on the unmet needs in diagnosis and treatment of mood disorders in children and adolescents. *Journal of the American Academy of Child and Adolescent Psychiatry, 42,* 1494–1503.

Cremin, L. A. (1964). The progressive heritage of the guidance movement. In E. Landy & L. Perry (Eds.), *Guidance in American education: Backgrounds and prospects* (pp. 11–19). Cambridge, MA: Harvard University Graduate School of Education.

Crethar, H. C., Rivera, E. T., & Nash, S. (2008). In search of common threads: Linking multicultural, feminist, and social justice counseling paradigms. *Journal of Counseling and Development, 86,* 269–278.

Crites, J. O. (1978). *Theory and research handbook for the Career Maturity Inventory.* Monterey, CA: CTB-McGraw Hill.

Cull, J. G., & Gill, W. S. (1992). *Suicide Probability Scale.* Los Angeles, CA: Western Psychology Service.

Cunconan-Lahr, R., & Brotherson, M. (1996). Advocacy in disability policy: Parents and consumers. *Mental Retardation, 34,* 352–358.

Cunningham, N. J., & Singh Sandhu, D. (2000). A comprehensive approach to school–community violence prevention. *Professional School Counseling, 4,* 126–133.

Curcio, C. C., Mathai, C., & Roberts, J. (2003). Evaluation of a school district's secondary counseling program. *Professional School Counseling, 6,* 296–303.

Curry, J., & Lambie, G. W. (2007). Enhancing school counselor accountability: The large group guidance portfolio. *Professional School Counseling, 11,* 145–148.

Cuthbert, B. (2001). Involving and responding to parents: Opportunities and challenges. In P. Henderson & N. Gysbers (Eds.), *Implementing comprehensive school guidance programs: Critical leadership issues and successful responses* (pp. 79–87). Greensboro, NC: ERIC–CASS.

Dahir, C. A. (2001). The national standards for school counseling programs: Development and implementation. *Professional School Counseling, 4,* 320–327.

Dana, R. H. (2001). Clinical diagnosis of multicultural populations in the United States. In L. A. Suzuki, J. G. Ponterotto, & P. J. Meller (Eds.), *Handbook of multicultural assessment: Clinical, psychological, and educational applications* (2nd ed., pp. 101–132). San Francisco, CA: Jossey-Bass.

D'Andrea, M., & Daniels, D. (1995). Helping students to learn to get along: Assessing the effectiveness of a multicultural developmental guidance project. *Elementary School Guidance and Counseling, 30,* 143–154.

D'Andrea, M., & Heckman, E. F. (2008). Contributing to the ongoing evolution of the multicultural counseling movement: An introduction to the special issue. *Journal of Counseling and Development, 86,* 259–260.

Darling, S., & Westberg, L. (2004). Parent involvement in children's acquisition of reading. *Reading Teacher, 57,* 774–776.

Davis, A. S. (2008). Children with Down Syndrome: Implications for assessment and intervention in the school. *School Psychology Quarterly, 23,* 271–281.

Davis, K. M., & Lambie, G. W. (2005). Family engagement: A collaborative, systemic approach for middle school counselors. *Professional School Counseling, 9,* 144–151.

Day-Vines, N. L., & Day-Hairston, B. (2005). Culturally congruent strategies for addressing the behavioral needs of urban, African American male adolescents. *Professional School Counseling, 8,* 236–243.

Day-Vines, N. L., Day-Hairston, B. O., Carruthers, W. L., Wall, J. A., & Lupton-Smith, H. A. (1996). Conflict resolution: The value of diversity in the recruitment, selection, and training of peer mediators. *School Counselor, 43,* 392–410.

Day-Vines, N. L., Patton, J. M., & Baytops, J. L. (2003). Counseling African American adolescents: The impact of race, culture, and middle class status. *Professional School Counseling, 7,* 40–51.

de Barona, M. S., & Barona, A. (2006). School counselors and school psychologists: Collaborating to ensure minority students receive appropriate consideration for special educational programs. *Professional School Counseling, 10*, 3–13.

Del Prete, T. (2000). Unsafe schools: Perception or reality. *Professional School Counseling, 3*, 375–377.

DeLucia-Waack, J. L. (1999). What makes an effective group leader? *Journal for Specialists in Group Work, 24*, 131–132.

DeLucia-Waack, J. L., DiCarlo, N. J., Parker-Sloat, E. L., & Rice, K. G. (1996). Multiculturalism: Understanding at the beginning of the process, rather than the ending. In J. DeLucia-Waack (Ed.), *Multicultural counseling competencies: Implications for training and practice* (pp. 237–243). Alexandria, VA: Association for Counselor Education and Supervision.

Demo, D. H., & Acock, A. C. (1996). Family structure, family process, and adolescent well-being. *Journal of Research on Adolescence, 6*, 457–488.

De Shazer, S. (1985). *Keys to solution in brief therapy.* New York, NY: Norton.

Dewey, J. (1910). *How we think.* Retrieved July 6, 2005, from spartan.ac.brocku.ca/~lward/Dewey/Dewey_1910a/Dewey_1910_toc.html

DeWit, D. J., Offord, D. R., Sanford, M., Rye, B. J., Shain, M., & Wright, R. (2000). The effect of school culture on adolescent behavior problems: Self-esteem, attachment to learning, and peer approval of deviance as mediating mechanisms. *Canadian Journal of School Psychology, 16*, 15–38.

Dimmitt, C. (2003). Transforming school counseling practice through collaboration and the use of data: A study of academic failure in high school. *Professional School Counseling, 6*, 340–349.

Dimmitt, C. (2007). *The Real Game evaluation results.* Amherst, MA: Center for School Counseling Outcome Research.

Dimmitt, C., Carey, J. C., & Hatch, T. (2007). *Evidence-based school counseling: Making a difference with data-driven practices.* Thousand Oaks, CA: Corwin Press.

Dinkmeyer, D. (1975). *Systematic Training for Effective Parenting.* Circle Pines, MN: American Guidance Service.

Dinkmeyer, D., & Carlson, J. (2001). *Consultation: Creating school-based interventions* (2nd ed.). Philadelphia, PA: Brunner-Routledge.

Dinkmeyer, D., & McKay, G. (1980). *Systematic Training for Effective Teaching.* Circle Pines, MN: American Guidance Service.

Dollarhide, C. T. (2003). School counselors as program leaders: Applying leadership contexts to school counseling. *Professional School Counseling, 6*, 204–208.

Dollarhide, C. T., Gibson, D. M., & Saginak, K. A. (2008). New counselors' leadership efforts in school counseling: Themes from a year-long qualitative study. *Professional School Counseling, 11*, 262–271.

Dougherty, A. M. (1999). *Psychological consultation and collaboration in school and community settings* (3rd ed.). Pacific Grove, CA: Brooks/Cole.

Dow, M. J., & Mehring, T. A. (2001). Inservice training for educators of individuals with autism. *Autistic Spectrum Disorders: Educational and Clinical Interventions, 14*, 89–107.

Driekurs, R., & Cassell, P. (1974). *Discipline without tears.* New York, NY: Hawthorne Books.

Dryfoos, J. G. (1994). *Full-service schools: A revolution in health and social services for children, youth and families.* San Francisco, CA: Jossey-Bass.

Dryfoos, J. G. (1998). *Safe passage: Making it through adolescence in a risky society.* New York, NY: Oxford University Press.

Dulmus, C. N., & Wodaraski, J. S. (1996). Assessment and effective treatments of childhood psychopathology: Responsibilities and implications for practice. *Journal of Child and Adolescent Group Therapy, 6*, 75–99.

Dumont, F., & Carson, A. (1995). Precursors of vocational psychology in ancient civilizations. *Journal of Counseling and Development, 73*, 371–378.

Dunn, N. A., & Baker, S. B. (2002). Readiness to serve students with disabilities: A survey of elementary school counselors. *Professional School Counseling, 5*, 277–284.

DuPaul, G. J., Guevremont, D. C., & Barkley, R. A. (1992). Behavioral treatment of attention-deficit hyperactivity disorder in the classroom: The use of the attention training system. *Behavior Modification, 16*, 204–225.

Durodoye, B. A., Combes, B. H., & Bryant, R. M. (2004). Counselor intervention in the post-secondary planning of African American students with learning disabilities. *Professional School Counseling, 7*, 133–140.

Dworkin, E. P., & Dworkin, A. L. (1971). The activist as counselor. *Personnel and Guidance Journal, 49*, 748–754.

Dykeman, C., Wood, C., Ingram, M. A., Pehrsson, D., Mandsager, N., & Herr, E. L. (2003). The structure of school career development interventions: Implications for school counselors. *Professional School Counseling, 6*, 272–279.

Eccles, J. S., & Harold, R. D. (1996). Family involvement in children's and adolescents' schooling. In A. Booth & J. F. Dunn (Eds.), *Family–school links: How do they affect educational outcomes?* (pp. 3–34). Mahwah, NJ: Erlbaum.

Eder, K. C., & Whiston, S. C. (2006). Does psychotherapy help some students? An overview of psychotherapy outcome research. *Professional School Counseling, 9*, 337–343.

Education Trust. (1996). *National Center for Transforming School Counseling.* Retrieved March 21, 2004, from www.edtrust.org

Education Trust. (1997). *The national guidance and counseling reform program.* Washington, DC: Author.

Education Trust. (2000). *National initiative for transforming school counseling summer academy for counselor educators proceedings.* Washington, DC: Author.

Education Trust (2004). *Edwatch online 2004 state summary reports.* Retrieved August 15, 2005, from www2.edtrust.org/edtrust/summaries2004/USA.pdf

Education Trust. (2005a). *Achievement in America: 2005* [Computer diskette]. Washington, DC: Author.

Education Trust. (2005b). *The Education Trust's National Center for Transforming School Counseling initiative.* Retrieved April 14, 2005, from www2.edtrust.org/EdTrust/Transforming1School1Counseling

Education Trust. (2005c). *Mission statement.* Retrieved August 19, 2005, from www2.edtrust.org/EdTrust/Transforming1School1Counseling/main

Edwards, D., & Mullis, F. (2003). Classroom meetings: Encouraging a climate of cooperation. *Professional School Counseling, 7,* 20–28.

Eisel v. Board of Education, 597 A.2d 447 (Md. Ct. App. 1991).

Ekstrom, R. B., Elmore, P. B., Schafer, W. D., Trotter, T. V., & Webster, B. (2004). A survey of assessment and evaluation activities of school counselors. *Professional School Counseling, 8,* 24–30.

Elam, D., McCloud, B., & Robinson, S. (2007). *New directions for culturally competent school leaders: Practices and policy considerations* (Policy Brief). Tampa: University of South Florida, David C. Anchin Center.

Elias, M. J., Blum, L., Gager, P. T., Hunter, L., & Kress, J. S. (1998). Group interventions for students with mild disorders: Classroom inclusion approaches. In K. C. Stoiber & T. R. Kratochwill (Eds.), *Handbook of group intervention for children and families* (pp. 220–235). Boston, MA: Allyn & Bacon.

Emery, R. E., Kitzman, K. M., & Waldron, M. (1999). Psychological interventions for separated and divorced families. In E. M. Hetherington (Ed.), *Coping with divorce, single parenting, and remarriage* (pp. 233–254). Mahwah, NJ: Erlbaum.

Emslie, G. J., & Mayes, T. L. (2001). Mood disorders in children and adolescents: Psychopharmacological treatment. *Biological Psychology, 49,* 1082–1090.

Erdman, P., & Lampe, R. (1996). Adapting basic skills to counsel children. *Journal of Counseling and Development, 74,* 374–377.

Erford, B. T. (1995). Reliability and validity of the Conners' Teacher Rating Scale–28 (CTRS–28). *Diagnostique, 21*(1), 19–28.

Erford, B. T. (1996a). Reliability and validity of mother responses to the Disruptive Behavior Rating Scale–Parent Version (DBRS–P). *Diagnostique, 21*(2), 17–33.

Erford, B. T. (1996b). Analysis of the Conners' Teacher Rating Scale–28 (CTRS–28). *Assessment, 3*(1), 27–36.

Erford, B. T. (1997). Reliability and validity of scores on the Disruptive Behavior Rating Scale–Teacher Version (DBRS–T). *Educational and Psychological Measurement, 57,* 329–339.

Erford, B. T. (1998). Technical analysis of father responses to the Disruptive Behavior Rating Scale–Parent Version (DBRS–P). *Measurement and Evaluation in Counseling and Development, 30,* 199–210.

Erford, B. T. (1999). A modified time-out procedure for children with noncompliant or defiant behaviors. *Professional School Counseling, 2,* 205–210.

Erford, B. T. (Ed.). (2008). *Research and evaluation in counseling.* Boston, MA: Houghton Mifflin.

Erford, B. T. (2010). How to write learning objectives. In B. T. Erford (Ed.), *Professional school counseling: A handbook of theories, programs and practices* (2nd ed., pp. 279–286). Austin, TX: PRO-ED.

Erford, B. T., Peyrot, M., & Siska, L. (1998). Analysis of teacher responses to the Conners' Abbreviated Symptoms Questionnaire (ASQ). *Measurement and Evaluation in Counseling and Development, 31,* 2–14.

Erikson, E. H. (1963). *Childhood and society.* New York, NY: Norton.

Erikson, E. H. (1968). *Identity: Youth and crisis.* New York, NY: Norton.

Eschenauer, R., & Chen-Hayes, S. F. (2005). The transformative individual school counseling model: An accountability model for urban school counselors. *Professional School Counseling, 8,* 244–248.

Esters, I., & Ledoux, C. (2001). At-risk high school students' preferences for counselor characteristics. *Professional School Counseling, 4,* 165–170.

Evans, J. R., Van Velsor, P., & Schumacher, J. E. (2002). Addressing adolescent depression: A role for school counselors. *Professional School Counseling, 5,* 211–219.

Ezell, M. (2001). *Advocacy in the human services.* Belmont, CA: Wadsworth.

Family Educational Rights and Privacy Act. (FERPA). (2008). Family Educational Rights and Privacy Act; Final Rule. Retrieved April 15, 2009 from http://www.ed.gov/legislation/FedRegister/finrule/2008-4/120908a.pdf

Fantuzzo, J. W., Davis, G. Y., & Ginsberg, M. O. (1995). Effects of parent involvement in isolation or in combination with peer tutoring on student self-concept and mathematics achievement. *Journal of Educational Psychology, 87,* 272–281.

Farber, N. K. (2006). Conducting qualitative research: A practical guide for school counselors. *Professional School Counseling, 9,* 367–375.

Farmer, E. M. Z., Burns, B. J., Phillips, S. D., Angold, A., & Costello, E. J. (2003). Pathways into and through mental health services for children and adolescents. *Psychiatric Services, 54*(1), 60–66.

Federal Bureau of Investigation. (2005). *The school shooter: A threat assessment perspective.* Retrieved September 2, 2005, from www.fbi.gov/publications/school/school2.pdf

Fein, A. H., Carlisle, C. S., & Isaacson, N. S. (2008). School shootings and counselor leadership: Four lessons from the field. *Professional School Counseling, 11,* 246–252.

Feller, R. W. (2003). Aligning school counseling, the changing workplace, and career development assumptions. *Professional School Counseling, 6,* 262–271.

Field, J. E., & Baker, S. (2004). Defining and examining school counselor advocacy. *Professional School Counseling, 8,* 56–63.

Field, S., Martin, J., Miller, R., Ward, M., & Wehmeyer, M. (n.d.). *Self-determination for persons with disabilities: A position statement of the Division on Career Development and Transition.* Available from dcdt.org/pdf/self_deter.pdf

Fischer, L., Schimmel, D., & Kelly, C. (1999). *Teachers and the law* (5th ed.). White Plains, NY: Longman.

Fischer, L., & Sorenson, G. P. (1996). *School law for counselors, psychologists, and social workers* (3rd ed.). White Plains, NY: Longman.

Fitch, T. J., & Marshall, J. L. (2004). What counselors do in high-achieving schools: A study on the role of the school counselor. *Professional School Counseling, 7,* 172–177.

Flaherty, L. T., Garrison, E. G., Waxman, R., Uris, P. F., Keys, S. G., Glass-Siegel, M., & Weist, M. D. (1998). Optimizing the roles of school mental health professionals. *Journal of School Health, 68,* 420–424.

Flannery, D. J., Vazsonyi, A. T., Liau, A. K., Guo, S., Powell, K. E., Atha, H., . . . Embry, D. (2003). Initial behavior outcomes for the PeaceBuilders universal school-based violence prevention program. *Developmental Psychology, 39,* 292–308.

Flavell, J. H. (1985). *Cognitive development* (2nd ed.). Englewood Cliffs, NJ: Prentice Hall.

Flom, B. L., & Hansen, S. S. (2006). Just don't shut the door on me: Aspirations of adolescents in crisis. *Professional School Counseling, 10,* 88–91.

Flynn, J. P. (1995). Social justice in social agencies. In R. C. Edwards (Ed.), *Encyclopedia of social work.* Washington, DC: National Association of Social Workers.

Forester-Miller, H., & Davis, T. (1996). *A practitioner's guide to ethical decision making.* Retrieved August 4, 2005, from www.counseling.org/Content/NavigationMenu/RESOURCES/ETHICS/APRACTIONERSGUIDETOETHICALDECISION-MAKING/Practioner_s_Guide.htm

Foster, L., Young, J. S., & Hermann, M. (2005). The work activities of professional school counselors: Are the national standards being addressed. *Professional School Counseling, 8,* 313–321.

Frances, R. J., & Allen, M. J. (1986). The interaction of substance-use disorders with nonpsychotic psychiatric disorders. In A. M. Cooper, A. J. Cooper, A. J. Frances, & M. H. Sacks (Eds.), *The personality disorders and neuroses* (pp. 425–437). Philadelphia, PA: Lippincott.

Freeman, S. J. (2000). *Ethics: An introduction to philosophy and practice.* Belmont, CA: Wadsworth.

Friend, M., & Cook, L. (1996). *Interactions: Collaboration skills for school professionals* (2nd ed.). White Plains, NY: Longman.

Friesen, B., & Huff, B. (1990). Parents and professional school counselors as advocacy partners. *Preventing School Failure, 34,* 31–35.

Froeschle, J., & Moyer, M. (2004). Just cut it out: Legal and ethical challenges in counseling students who self-multilate. *Professional School Counseling, 7,* 231–235.

Froeschle, J. G., Smith, R. L., & Ricard, R. (2007). The efficacy of a systematic substance abuse program for adolescent females. *Professional School Counseling, 10,* 498–505.

Fry, R. (2007). *The changing racial and ethnic composition of U.S. public schools.* Washington, DC: Pew Hispanic Center.

Frye, H. N. (2005). How elementary school counselors can meet the needs of students with disabilities. *Professional School Counselor, 8,* 442–450.

Fryxell, D., & Smit, D. C. (2000). Personal, social, and family characteristics of angry students. *Professional School Counseling, 4,* 86–94.

Fullan, M. (2005). *Leadership and sustainability: Systems thinkers in action.* Thousand Oaks, CA: Corwin Press.

Furr, S. R. (2000). Structuring the group experience: A format for designing psychoeducational groups. *Journal for Specialists in Group Work, 25,* 29–49.

Fusick, L., & Bordeau, W. C. (2004). Counseling at-risk Afro-American youth: An examination of contemporary issues and effective school-based strategies. *Professional School Counseling, 8,* 102–115.

Gadow, K. D., Nolan, E. E., Sprafkin, J., & Schwartz, J. (2002). Tics and psychiatric comorbidity in children and adolescents. *Developmental Medicine and Child Neurology, 44,* 330–338.

Galassi, J. P., & Akos, P. (2007). *Strengths-based school counseling: Promoting student development and achievement.* Mahwah, NJ: Erlbaum.

Galassi, J. P., Griffin, D., & Akos, P. (2008). Strengths-based school counseling and the ASCA national model. *Professional School Counseling, 12,* 176–182.

Gansle, K. A. (2005). The effectiveness of school-based anger interventions and programs: A meta-analysis. *Journal of School Psychology, 43*, 321–341.

Gardner, H. (1999). *The disciplined mind.* New York, NY: Simon & Schuster.

Gardner, R., & Miranda, A. H. (2001). Improving outcomes for urban African American students. *Journal of Negro Education, 70*, 255–263.

Gates, B. (2005, March 3). Fixing obsolete high schools. *Washington Post*, 3B.

Gazda, G. M., Ginter, E. J., & Horne, A. M. (2008). *Group counseling and group psychotherapy: Theory and application* (2nd ed.). Boston, MA: Allyn & Bacon.

Geertz, C. (1983). *Local knowledge.* New York, NY: Basic Books.

Geltner, J. A., & Clark, M. A. (2005). Engaging students in classroom guidance: Management strategies for middle school counselors. *Professional School Counseling, 9*, 164–166.

Gentry, M. (2006). No child left behind: Gifted children and school counselors. *Professional School Counseling, 10*, 73–81.

Gerler, E. R. (1985). Elementary school counseling research and the classroom learning environment. *Elementary School Guidance and Counseling, 20*, 39–40.

Gerler, E. R., Jr. (1992). Consultation and school counseling. *Elementary School Guidance and Counseling, 26*, 162.

Gerrity, D. A., & DeLucia-Waack, J. L. (2007). Effectiveness of groups in the schools. *Journal for Specialists in Group Work, 32*, 97–106.

Gershon, J. (2002). A meta-analytic review of gender differences in ADHD. *Journal of Attention Disorders, 5*(3), 143–154.

Gibbons, M. M., Borders, L. D., Wiles, M. E., Stephan, J. B., & Davis, P. E. (2006). Career and college planning needs of ninth graders—as reported by ninth graders. *Professional School Counseling, 10*, 168–178.

Gibbons, M. M., & Goins, S. (2008). Getting to know the child with Asperger syndrome. *Professional School Counseling, 11*, 347–352.

Gibbons, M. M., & Shoffner, M. F. (2004). Prospective first-generation college students: Meeting their needs through social cognitive career theory. *Professional School Counseling, 8*, 91–97.

Gibbons, M. M., & Studer, J. R. (2008). Suicide awareness training for faculty and staff: A training model for school counselors. *Professional School Counseling, 11*, 272–276.

Gibson, D. M. (2010). Advocacy counseling: Being an effective agent of change for clients. In B. T. Erford (Ed.), *Orientation to the counseling profession: Advocacy, ethics, and essential professional foundations* (pp. 340–358). Upper Saddle River, NJ: Prentice Hall.

Gilbert, A. (2003). Group counseling in an elementary school. In K. R. Greenberg (Ed.), *Group counseling in K–12 schools: A handbook for school counselors* (pp. 56–80). Boston, MA: Allyn & Bacon.

Giles, H. C. (2005). Three narratives of parent–educator relationships: Toward counselor repertoires for bridging the urban parent–school divide. *Professional School Counseling, 8*, 228–235.

Gilliland, B. E., & James, R. K. (2005). *Theories and strategies in counseling and psychotherapy* (5th ed.). Needham Heights, MA: Allyn & Bacon.

Gladding, S. T. (1997). The creative arts in groups. In H. Forester-Miller & J. A. Kottler (Eds.), *Issues and challenges for group practitioners* (pp. 214–239). Denver, CO: Love.

Gladding, S. T. (2005). *Counseling as an art: The creative arts in counseling* (3rd ed.). Alexandria, VA: American Counseling Association.

Gladding, S. T. (2008). *Group work: A counseling specialty* (5th ed.). Upper Saddle River, NJ: Prentice Hall.

Gladding, S. T., & Newsome, D. W. (2009). *Community and agency counseling* (3rd ed.). Upper Saddle River, NJ: Merrill/Prentice Hall.

Glasser, W. (1998). *Choice theory.* New York, NY: HarperCollins.

Glasser, W. (2000a). School violence from the perspective of William Glasser. *Professional School Counseling, 4*, 77–80.

Glasser, W. (2000b). *Reality therapy in action.* New York, NY: HarperCollins.

Glied, S., & Cuellar, A. E. (2003). Trends and issues in child and adolescent mental health. *Health Affairs, 22*(5), 39–50.

Glosoff, H. L., Herlihy, B., & Spence, E. B. (2000). Privileged communication in the counselor–client relationship. *Journal of Counseling and Development, 78*, 454–462.

Goldman, L. (1990). Qualitative assessment. *Counseling Psychologist, 18*, 205–213.

Goldstein, A. P., & McGinnis, E. (1997). *Skillstreaming the adolescent.* Champaign, IL: Research Press.

Goldstein, B. S. C., & Harris, K. C. (2000). Consultant practices in two heterogeneous Latino schools. *School Psychology Review, 29*, 368–377.

Goodenough, W. H. (1981). *Culture, language, and society.* Menlo Park, CA: Benjamin/Cummings.

Goodnough, G. E., & Lee, V. V. (2004). Group counseling in schools. In B. T. Erford (Ed.), *Professional school counseling: A handbook of theories, programs, and practices* (pp. 173–182). Austin, TX: PRO-ED.

Goodwin, R., Lipsitz, J. D., Chapman, T. F., Mannuzza, S., & Fyer, A. J. (2001). Obsessive-compulsive disorder, separation anxiety co-morbidity in early onset panic disorder. *Psychological Medicine, 31,* 1307–1310.

Gothelf, D., Aharonovsky, O., Horesh, N., Carty, T., & Apter, A. (2004). Life events and personality factors in children and adolescents with obsessive-compulsive disorder and other anxiety disorders. *Comprehensive Psychiatry, 45,* 192–198.

Gottfredson, L. S. (1996). Gottfredson's theory of circumscription and compromise. In D. Brown & L. Brooks (Eds.), *Career choice and development: Applying contemporary theories to practice* (3rd ed., pp. 179–232). San Francisco, CA: Jossey-Bass.

Graham, B. C., & Pulvino, C. (2000). Multicultural conflict resolution: Development, implementation, and assessment of a program for third graders. *Professional School Counseling, 3,* 172–181.

Green, A., & Keys, S. (2001). Expanding the school counseling paradigm: Meeting the needs of the 21st century student. *Professional School Counseling, 5,* 84–95.

Greenberg, K. R. (Ed.). (2003). *Group counseling in K–12 schools: A handbook for school counselors.* Boston, MA: Allyn & Bacon.

Greene, M. J. (2006). Helping build lives: Career and life development of gifted and talented students. *Professional School Counseling, 10,* 34–42.

Gresham, F. M., & Kendell, G. K. (1987). School consultation research: Methodological critique and future research direction. *School Psychology Review, 16,* 306–316.

Griffith, J. (1998). The relation of school structure and social environment to parent involvement in elementary schools. *Elementary School Journal, 99,* 53–80.

Grolnick, W. S., Benjet, C., Kurinski, C. O., & Apostoleris, N. H. (1997). Predictors of parent involvement in children's schooling. *Journal of Educational Psychology, 89,* 538–548.

Gruttadaro, D. E., & Miller, J. E. (2004). *NAMI Policy Research Institue task force report: Children and psychotropic medications.* Arlington, VA: Nation's Voice on Mental Illness.

Grych, J. H., & Fincham, F. O. (2001). *Interparental conflict and child development: Theory, research and applications.* Cambridge, England: Cambridge University Press.

Guillot-Miller, L., & Partin, P. W. (2003). Web-based resources for legal and ethical issues in school counseling. *Professional School Counseling, 7,* 52–60.

Gutierrez, L. (1995). Understanding the empowerment process: Does consciousness make a difference? *Social Work Research, 19,* 229–237.

Guttmacher Institute. (2005a). *State policies in brief: Minors' access to contraceptive services.* Washington, DC: Author.

Guttmacher Institute. (2005b). *State policies in brief: Sex and STD/HIV education.* Washington, DC: Author.

Guttmacher Institute. (2009). *State policies in brief: Minors' access to contraceptive services.* Washington, DC: Author.

Gysbers, N. C. (2004). Comprehensive guidance and counseling programs: The evolution of accountability. *Professional School Counseling, 8,* 1–14.

Gysbers, N. C., & Henderson, P. (2001). Comprehensive guidance and counseling programs: A rich history and a bright future. *Professional School Counseling, 4,* 246–256.

Gysbers, N. C., & Henderson, P. (2006). *Developing and managing your school guidance program* (4th ed.). Alexandria, VA: American Counseling Association.

Gysbers, N. C., Lapan, R. T., & Blair, M. (1999). Closing in on the statewide implementation of a comprehensive guidance program model. *Professional School Counseling, 2,* 357–366.

Gysbers, N. C., Lapan, R. T., & Jones, B. A. (2000). School board policies for guidance and counseling: A call to action. *Professional School Counseling, 3,* 349–355.

Hall, K. R. (2006). Using problem-based learning with victims of bullying behavior. *Professional School Counseling, 9,* 231–237.

Hanish, L. D., & Guerra, N. G. (2000). Children who get victimized at school: What is known? What can be done? *Professional School Counseling, 4,* 113–119.

Hansen, L. S. (1999). Beyond school-to-work: Continuing contributions of theory and practice to career development of youth. *Career Development Quarterly, 47,* 353–358.

Hanson, R. F., & Spratt, E. G. (2000). Reactive attachment disorder: What we know about the disorder and implications for treatment. *Child Maltreatment, 5,* 137–145.

Hardiman, R., & Jackson, B. W. (1997). Conceptual foundations for social justice courses. In M. Adams, L. A. Bell, & P. Griffin (Eds.), *Teaching for diversity and social justice: A sourcebook* (pp. 16–29). New York, NY: Routledge.

Hardman, M. L., Drew, C. J., & Egan, M. W. (1996). *Human exceptionality: Society, school, and family* (5th ed.). Needham Heights, MA: Allyn & Bacon.

Harris, J. C. (1995). Psychiatric disorders in mentally retarded persons. In G. O. Gabbard (Ed.), *Treatments of psychiatric disorders* (pp. 95–122). Washington, DC: American Psychiatric Press.

Harris, S. L. (2000). Pervasive developmental disorders: The spectrum of autism. In M. Hersen & R. T. Ammerman (Eds.), *Advanced abnormal child psychology* (2nd ed., pp. 315–333). Mahwah, NJ: Erlbaum.

Harrow, A. (1972). *A taxonomy of the psychomotor domain: A guide for developing behavioral objectives.* New York, NY: McKay.

Hart, P. J., & Jacobi, M. (1992). *From gatekeeper to advocate: Transforming the role of the school counselor.* New York, NY: College Entrance Examination Board.

Hart, P., & Jermaine-Watts., J. (1996). Introduction: Framing our minds to set our sights. In R. Johnson (Ed.), *Setting our sights: Measuring equity in school change*. Los Angeles, CA: Achievement Council.

Hatch, T., & Chen-Hayes, S. F. (2008). School counselor beliefs about ASCA model school counseling program components using the SCPSCS. *Professional School Counseling, 12*, 34–42.

Haugaard, J. J., & Hazan, C. (2004). Recognizing and treating uncommon behavioral and emotional disorders in children and adolescents who have been severely maltreated: Reactive attachment disorder. *Child Maltreatment, 9*, 154–160.

Havighurst, R. J. (1972). *Developmental tasks and education* (3rd ed.). New York, NY: McKay.

Hawes, D. J. (2000). Resource: The PASSPORT program: A journey through emotional, social, cognitive, and self-development. *Professional School Counseling, 3*, 229–230.

Haycock, K. (2009, February). *Access and success in higher education: Can we do more?* Oklahoma Open Enrollment Conference, El Reno, OK. Retrieved February 20, 2009, from www2.edtrust.org/EdTrust/Product+Catalog/recent+presentations.htm

Hayes, N. (2002). *To accommodate, to modify, and to know the difference: Determining placement of a child in Special Education or "504."* Retrieved November 15, 2008, from www.newhorizons.org/spneeds/inclusion/law/hayes.htm

Hayes, R. L., Dagley, J. C., & Horne, A. M. (1996). Restructuring school counselor education: Work in progress. *Journal of Counseling and Development, 74*, 378–384.

Hayes, R. L., Nelson, J. L., Tabin, M., Pearson, G., & Worthy, C. (2002). Using school-wide data to advocate for student success. *Professional School Counseling, 62*, 86–95.

Hayward, C., Wilson, K. A., Lagle, K., Killen, J. D., & Taylor, C. B. (2004). Parent-reported predictors of adolescent panic attacks. *Journal of the American Academy of Child and Adolescent Psychiatry, 4*, 613–620.

Hazler, R. J. (1998). Promoting personal investment in systematic approaches to school violence. *Education, 119*, 222–231.

Hazler, R. J., & Carney, J. V. (2000). When victims turn aggressors: Factors in the development of deadly school violence. *Professional School Counseling, 4*, 105–112.

Hazler, R. J., & Denham, S. A. (2002). Social isolation of youth at risk: Conceptualization and practical solutions. *Journal of Counseling and Development, 80*, 403–409.

Hazler, R. J., Miller, D., Carney, J. V., & Green, S. (2001). Adult recognition of school bullying situations. *Educational Research, 43*, 133–146.

Heatherington, E. M. (1999). Social capital and the development of youth from divorced, nondivorced, and remarried families. In W. A. Collins & B. Laursen (Eds.), *Relationships as developmental contexts: The Minnesota symposium on child psychology* (Vol. 30, pp. 177–210). Mahwah, NJ: Erlbaum.

Hedges, L. V., & Olkin, I. (1985). *Statistical methods for meta-analysis.* Orlando, FL: Academic Press.

Hedrick, W. B., Harmon, J. M., & Wood, K. (2008). Prominent content vocabulary strategies and what secondary preservice teachers think about them. *Reading Psychology, 29*, 443–470.

Heide, K. M. (1999). *Young killers: The challenge of juvenile homicide.* Thousand Oaks, CA: Sage.

Henderson, P. A. (1987). Terminating the counseling relationship with children. *Elementary School Guidance and Counseling, 22*, 143–148.

Heppner, M. J., & O'Brien, K. M. (1994). Multicultural counselor training: Students' perceptions of helpful and hindering events. *Counselor Education and Supervision, 34*, 4–18.

Herlihy, B., & Corey, G. (2006). *ACA ethical standards casebook* (6th ed.). Alexandria, VA: American Counseling Association.

Hernandez, T. J., & Seem, S. R. (2004). A safe school climate: A systematic approach and the school counselor. *Professional School Counseling, 7*, 256–262.

Herr, E. L. (1979). *Guidance and counseling in the schools: Perspectives on the past, present, and future.* Falls Church, VA: American Personnel and Guidance Association.

Herr, E. L. (1998). *Counseling in a dynamic society: Contexts and practices in the 21st century* (2nd ed.). Alexandria, VA: American Counseling Association.

Herr, E. L. (2001). The impact of national policies, economics, and school reform on comprehensive guidance programs. *Professional School Counseling, 2*, 236–245.

Herr, E. L. (2002). School reform and perspectives on the role of school counselors: A century of proposals for change. *Professional School Counseling, 5*, 220–234.

Herr, E. L., Cramer, S. H., & Niles, S. G. (2004). *Career guidance and counseling through the lifespan* (6th ed.). Boston, MA: Allyn & Bacon.

Herring, R. D. (1997). *Multicultural counseling in schools.* Alexandria, VA: American Counseling Association.

Hijazi, Y., Tatar, M., & Gati, I. (2004). Career decision-making difficulties among Israeli and Palestinian Arab high-school seniors. *Professional School Counseling, 8*, 64–72.

Hines, P. L., & Fields, T. H. (2002). Pregroup screening issues for school counselors. *Journal for Specialists in Group Work, 27*, 358–376.

Hixson, J., & Tinzmann, M. B. (1990). *Essay: Who are the "at-risk" students of the 1990s?* Retrieved January 5, 2002, from www.ncrel.org/sdrs/areas/rpl_esys/equity.htm

Hoag, M. J., & Burlingame, G. M. (1997). Evaluating the effectiveness of child and adolescent group treatment: A meta-analytic review. *Journal of Clinical Child Psychology, 26,* 234–246.

Hoagwood, K. (1999). *Summary sheet: Major research findings on child and adolescent mental health.* Washington, DC: National Institute of Mental Health.

Hoagwood, K., Kelleher, K. J., Feil, M., & Comer, D. M. (2000). Treatment services for children with AD/HD: A national perspective. *Journal of the American Academy of Child and Adolescent Psychiatry, 39,* 198–206.

Hobson, S. M., & Phillips, G. A. (2010). Educational planning. In B. T Erford (Ed.), *Professional school counseling: A handbook of theories, programs, & practices* (2nd ed., pp. 325–340). Austin, TX: PRO-ED.

Hoffman, E. (2002). *Changing channels: Activities promoting media smarts and creative problem solving for children.* St. Paul, MN: Redleaf Press.

Holcomb-McCoy, C. (2001). Exploring the self-perceived multicultural counseling competence of elementary school counselors. *Professional School Counseling, 4,* 195–201.

Holcomb-McCoy, C. (2004). Assessing the multicultural competence of school counselors: A checklist. *Professional School Counseling, 7,* 178–186.

Holcomb-McCoy, C. (2005). Investigating school counselors' perceived multicultural competence. *Professional School Counseling, 8,* 414–423.

Holcomb-McCoy, C. (2007). *School counseling to close the achievement gap: A social justice framework for success.* Thousand Oaks, CA: Corwin Press.

Holcomb-McCoy, C., Harris, P., Hines, E., & Johnston, G. (2008). School counselors' multicultural self-efficacy: A preliminary investigation. *Professional School Counseling, 11,* 166–178.

Holcomb-McCoy, C., & Myers, J. E. (1999). Multicultural competence and counselor training: A national survey. *Journal of Counseling and Development, 77,* 294–302.

Holland, J. L. (1992). *Making vocational choices* (2nd ed.). Odessa, FL: Psychological Assessment Resources.

Hopkins, B. R., & Anderson, B. S. (1990). *The counselor and the law* (3rd ed.). Alexandria, VA: American Counseling Association.

House, A. E. (1999). DSM–IV *diagnosis in the schools.* New York, NY: Guilford Press.

House, R. M., & Hayes, R. L. (2002). School counselors: Becoming key players in school reform. *Professional School Counseling, 5,* 249–256.

House, R. M., & Martin, P. J. (1998). Advocating for better futures for all students: A new vision for school counselors. *Education, 119,* 284–291.

Howard, D. E., & Wang, M. Q. (2003). Risk profiles of adolescent girls who were victims of dating violence. *Adolescence, 38*(149), 1–14.

Howard, K. A. S., & Solberg, V. S. H. (2006). School-based social justice: The Achieving Success Identity Pathways program. *Professional School Counseling, 9,* 278–287.

Hughes, C., Kim, H., Hwang, B., Killian, D. J., Fischer, G. M., Brock, M. L., . . . Houser, B. (1997). Practitioner validated secondary transition support strategies. *Education and Training in Mental Retardation and Developmental Disabilities, 32,* 201–212.

Hughes, D. K., & James, S. H. (2001). Using accountability data to protect a school counseling program: One counselor's experience. *Professional School Counseling, 4,* 306–310.

Hussey, D. L., & Guo, S. (2003). Measuring behavior change in young children receiving intensive school-based mental health services. *Journal of Community Psychology, 31,* 629–639.

Hutson, P. W. (1958). *The guidance function in education* (2nd ed.). New York, NY: Appleton-Century-Crofts.

Idol, L., Nevin, A., & Paolucci-Whitcomb, P. (1994). *Collaborative consultation.* Austin, TX: PRO-ED.

Individuals With Disabilities Education Improvement Act. (2004). Retrieved August 28, 2005, from www.ed.gov/policy/speced/guid/idea/idea2004.html

Ingraham, C. L. (2000). Consultation through a multicultural lens: Multicultural and cross-cultural consultation in schools. *School Psychology Review, 29,* 320–343.

International Baccalaureate Organization. (2009). *International Baccalaureate.* Retrieved April 27, 2009, from www.ibo.org

Isaacs, M. L. (2003). Data-driven decision making: The engine of accountability. *Professional School Counseling, 6,* 288–295.

Ivey, A. E., D'Andrea, M., Ivey, M. B., & Simek-Morgan, L. (2007). *Counseling and psycho-therapy: A multicultural perspective* (6th ed.). Boston, MA: Allyn & Bacon.

Izzo, C. V., Weissberg, R. P., Kasprow, N. J., & Fendrich, M. (1999). A longitudinal assessment of teacher perception of parent involvement in children's education and school performance. *American Journal of Community Psychology, 27,* 817–839.

Jackson, M., & Grant, D. (2004). Equity, access, and career development: Contextual conflicts. In R. Perusse & G. E. Goodnough (Eds.), *Leadership, advocacy, and direct service strategies for professional school counselors* (pp. 125–153). Belmont, CA: Brooks/Cole-Thomson Learning.

Jacobi, C., Hayward, C., de Zwaan, M., Kraemer, H., & Agras, W. S. (2004). Coming to terms with risk factors for eating disorders: Application of risk terminology and suggestions for a general taxonomy. *Psychological Bulletin, 130,* 19–65.

Jacobs, E. E., Masson, R. L., & Harvill, R. L. (2006). *Group counseling: Strategies and skills* (5th ed.). Belmont, CA: Thompson Brooks/Cole.

Jacobs, E., & Schimmel, C. (2005). Small group counseling. In C. Sink (Ed.), *Contemporary school counseling: Theory, research, and practice* (pp. 82–115). Boston, MA: Houghton Mifflin/Lahaska.

Jacobsen, K. E., & Bauman, S. (2007). Bullying in schools: School counselors' responses to three types of bullying incidents. *Professional School Counseling, 11*, 1–9.

Janson, G. (2000). *Exposure to repetitive abuse: Psychological distress and physiological reactivity in bystanders as compared to victims* (Unpublished doctoral dissertation, Ohio University).

Jarvis, P. S. (2004). Educators use career "games" to teach lifelong career management skills. *Techniques: Connecting Education and Careers, 79*, 34–49.

Jarvis, P. S., & Keeley, E. S. (2003). From vocational decision making to career building: Blueprint, real games, and school counseling. *Professional School Counseling, 6*, 244–251.

Jensen, P. S., Kettle, L., Roper, M. T., Sloan, M. T., Dulcan, M. K., Hoven, C., . . . Payne, J. (1999). Are stimulants overprescribed? Treatment of AD/HD in four U.S. communities. *Journal of the American Academy of Child and Adolescent Psychiatry, 38*, 797–804.

Jenson, J. M., & Dieterich, W. A. (2007). Effects of a skills-based prevention program on bullying and bully victimization among elementary school children. *Prevention Science, 8*, 285–296.

Jimerson, S., Engeland, B., & Teo, A. (1999). A longitudinal study of achievement trajectories: Factors associated with change. *Journal of Educational Psychology, 9*, 116–126.

Johnson, C. D., & Johnson, S. (2003). Results based guidance: A systems approach to student support. *Professional School Counseling, 6*, 180–185.

Johnson, C. D., & Johnson, S. K. (2001). *Results-based student support programs: Leadership academy workbook.* San Juan Capistrano, CA: Professional Update.

Johnson, C. R., & Slomka, G. (2000). Learning, motor, and communication disorders. In M. Hersen & R. T. Ammerman (Eds.), *Advanced abnormal child psychology* (2nd ed., pp. 371–385). Mahwah, NJ: Erlbaum.

Johnson, D. (1995). Specific developmental disorders. In M. Hersen & R. T. Ammerman (Eds.), *Advanced abnormal child psychology* (pp. 95–122). Washington, DC: American Psychiatric Press.

Johnson, D. W., & Johnson, R. T. (1995a). *Reducing school violence through conflict resolution.* Alexandria, VA: Association for Supervision and Curriculum Development.

Johnson, D. W., & Johnson, R. T. (1995b). Teaching students to be peacemakers: Results of five years of research. *Peace and Conflict: Journal of Peace Psychology, 1*, 417–438.

Johnson, D. W., & Johnson, R. T. (2002, February). Teaching students to resolve their own and their schoolmates' conflicts. *Counseling and Human Development, 34*(6), 1–12.

Johnson, J., Arumi, A. M., & Ott, A. (2006). *Reality check 2006: Is support for standards and testing fading?* New York, NY: Public Agenda. Retrieved April 21, 2009, from www.publicagenda.org/files/pdf/rc0603.pdf

Johnson, J., Farkas, S., & Bers, A. (1997). *Getting by: What American teenagers really think about their schools.* New York, NY: Public Agenda.

Johnson, J. L., Sparks, E., Lewis, R., Niedrich, K., Hall, M., & Johnson, J. (2006). Effective counseling strategies for supporting long-term suspended students. *Professional School Counseling, 9*, 261–264.

Johnson, L. S. (2000). Promoting professional identity in an era of educational reform. *Professional School Counseling, 4*, 31–40.

Johnson, R. S. (2002). *Using data to close the achievement gap: How to measure equity in schools* (2nd ed.). Thousand Oaks, CA: Corwin Press.

Johnson, S. D. (1990). Toward clarifying culture, race, and ethnicity in the context of multicultural counseling. *Journal of Multicultural Counseling and Development, 18*, 41–50.

Johnson, S. K., & Johnson, C. D. (2003). Results-based guidance: A systems approach to student support programs. *Professional School Counseling, 6*, 180–185.

Johnson, S. K., & Johnson, C. D. (2005). Group counseling: Beyond the tradition. *Professional School Counseling, 8*, 399–400.

Jones, A. J. (1930). *Principles of guidance.* New York, NY: McGraw-Hill.

Jones, A. J. (1934). *Principles of guidance* (2nd ed.). New York, NY: McGraw-Hill.

Jones, L. K. (2004). *The Career Key.* Retrieved May 1, 2005, from www.careerkey.org

Jones, L. K., Sheffield, D., & Joyner, B. (2000). Comparing the effects of the Career Key with Self-Directed Search and Job-OE among eighth-grade students. *Professional School Counseling, 3*, 238–247.

Jordan, G. E., Snow, C. E., & Porche, M. V. (2000). Project EASE: The effect of a family literacy project on kindergarten students' early literacy skills. *Reading Research Quarterly, 35*, 524–546.

Kadesjo, B., & Gillberg, C. (2000). Tourette's disorder: Epidemiology and comorbidity in primary school children. *Journal of the American Academy of Child and Adolescent Psychiatry, 39*, 548–555.

Kaffenberger, C. J. (2006). School reentry for students with a chronic illness: A role for professional school counselors. *Professional School Counseling, 9,* 223–230.

Kaffenberger, C. J., Murphy, S., & Bemak, F. (2006). School counseling leadership team: A statewide collaborative model to transform school counseling. *Professional School Counseling, 9,* 288–294.

Kahn, B. B. (2000). A model of solution-focused consultation for school counselors. *Professional School Counseling, 3,* 248–254.

Kaminski, J. W., Valle, L. A., Filene, J. H., & Boyle, C. L. (2008). A meta-analytic review of components associated with parent training program effectiveness. *Journal of Abnormal Child Psychology, 36,* 567–589.

Kampwirth, T. J. (2002). *Collaborative consultation in the schools: Effective practices for students with learning and behavior problems* (2nd ed.). Upper Saddle River, NJ: Prentice Hall.

Kann, L., Kinchen, S. A., Williams, B., Ross, J. G., Lowry, R., & Grunbaum, J. A. (2000). Youth risk behavior surveillance: United States, 1999. *Journal of School Health, 70,* 271–285.

Kaplan, H., Sadock, B., & Grebb, J. (1994). *Synopsis of psychiatry* (7th ed.). Baltimore, MD: Williams & Wilkins.

Kataoka, S. H., Zhang, L., & Wells, K. B. (2002). Unmet need for mental health care among U.S. children: Variation by ethnicity and insurance status. *American Journal of Psychiatry, 159,* 1548–1555.

Katzman, M. A., & Lee, S. (1997). Beyond body image: The integration of feminist and transcultural theories in the understanding of self starvation. *International Journal of Eating Disorders, 22,* 385–394.

Kazdin, A. E. (1997). Psychosocial treatments for conduct disorder in children. *Journal of Child Psychology and Psychiatry and Allied Professions, 38,* 161–178.

Kazdin, A. E. (2008). Evidence-based treatments and delivery of psychological services: Shifting our emphases to increase impact. *Psychological Services, 5,* 201–215.

Kearney, C. A., Sims, K. E., Pursell, C. R., & Tillotson, C. A. (2003). Separation anxiety disorder in young children: A longitudinal and family analysis. *Journal of Clinical Child and Adolescent Psychology, 32,* 593–598.

Keel, P. K., & Klump, K. L. (2003). Are eating disorders culture-bound syndromes? Implications for conceptualizing their etiology. *Psychological Bulletin, 129,* 747–769.

Kehle, T. J., Madaus, M. R., Baratta, V. S., & Bray, M. A. (1998). Augmented self-modeling as a treatment for children with selective mutism. *Journal of School Psychology, 36,* 247–260.

Keith, T. Z., Keith, P. B., Quirk, K. J., Speeduto, J., Santillo, S., & Killings, S. (1998). Longitudinal effects of parent involvement on high school grades: Similarities and differences across gender and ethnic groups. *Journal of School Psychology, 36,* 335–363.

Kellough, R. D., & Roberts, P. L. (2002). *A resource guide for elementary school teaching* (5th ed.). Upper Saddle River, NJ: Merrill.

Kelly, J. B., & Emery, R. E. (2003). Children's adjustment following divorce: Risk and resilience perspectives. *Family Relations, 52,* 352–362.

Kendall, P. C., Chu, B. C., Pimentel, S. S., & Choudhury, M. (2000). Treating anxiety disorders in youth. In P. C. Kendall (Ed.), *Child and adolescent therapy: Cognitive behavioral procedures* (pp. 235–287). New York, NY: Guilford Press.

Kendall, P. C., Safford, S., Flannery-Schroeder, E., & Webb, A. (2004). Child anxiety treatment: Outcomes and impact on substance use and depression at 7.4-year follow-up. *Journal of Consulting and Clinical Psychology, 72,* 276–287.

Kessler, R. C., & Walters, E. E. (1998). Epidemiology of DSM–III–R major depression and minor depression among adolescents and young adults in the National Comorbidity Survey. *Depression & Anxiety, 7,* 3–14.

Keys, S. G. (2000). Foreword: Special edition: Collaborating for safe schools and safe communities. *Professional School Counseling, 3,* iv–v.

Keys, S. G., & Bemak, F. (1997). School–family–community linked services: A school counseling role for the changing times. *School Counselor, 44,* 255–263.

Keys, S. G., Bemak, F., Carpenter, S. L., & King-Sears, M. F. (1998). Collaborative consultants: A new role for counselors serving at-risk youth. *Journal of Counseling and Development, 76,* 123–133.

Keys, S. G., Bemak, F., & Lockhart, E. J. (1998). Transforming school counseling to serve the mental health needs of at-risk youth. *Journal of Counseling and Development, 76,* 381–388.

Keys, S. G., & Lockhart, E. J. (1999). The school counselor's role in facilitating multi-systemic change. *Professional School Counseling, 3,* 101–107.

King, K. A., Price, J. H., Telljohann, S. K., & Wahl, J. (2000). Preventing adolescent suicide: Do high school counselors know the risk factors? *Professional School Counseling, 3,* 255–263.

King, K. A., Wagner, D. I., & Hedrick, B. (2001). Safe and drug-free school coordinators' perceived needs to improve violence and drug prevention programs. *Journal of School Health, 71,* 236–241.

Kiselica, M. S., Maben, P., & Locke, D. C. (1999). Do multicultural education and diversity appreciation training reduce prejudice among counseling trainees? *Journal of Mental Health Counseling, 21,* 240–255.

Klein, R. G. (1993). Clinical efficacy of methylphenidate in children and adolescents. *Encephale, 19,* 89–93.

Klein, R. G. (1994). Anxiety disorders. In M. Rutter, E. Taylor, & L. Hersov (Eds.), *Child and adolescent psychiatry: Modern approaches* (pp. 351–374). Cambridge, MA: Blackwell.

Kluckhohn, C. (1985). *Mirror for man: The relation of anthropology to modern life.* Tucson: University of Arizona Press.

Kolodinsky, P., Schroder, V., Montopoli, G., McLean, S., Mangan, P. A., & Pederson, W. (2006). The career fair as a vehicle for enhancing occupational self-efficacy. *Professional School Counseling, 10,* 161–167.

Krathwohl, D. R., Bloom, B. S., & Masia, B. B. (1964). *Taxonomy of educational objectives: Book 2. Affective domain.* New York, NY: Longman.

Krentz, A., & Arthur, N. (2001). Counseling culturally diverse students with eating disorders. *Journal of College Student Psychotherapy, 15,* 7–21.

Kress, V. E., Erikson, K. P., Rayle, A. D., & Ford, S. J. W. (2005). The *DSM–IV–TR* and culture: Consideration for counselors. *Journal of Counseling and Development, 83,* 97–104.

Kress, V. E., Gibson, D. M., & Reynolds, C. A. (2004). Adolescents who self-injure: Implications and strategies for school counselors. *Professional School Counseling, 7,* 195–201.

Krishnakumer, A., & Buehler, C. (2000). Interparental conflict and parenting behaviors: A meta-analytic review. *Family Relations, 49,* 25–44.

Kronenberger, W. G., & Meyer, R. G. (1996). *The child clinician's handbook.* Needham Heights, MA: Allyn & Bacon.

Kruczek, T., Alexander, C. M., & Harris, K. (2005). An after-school counseling program for high-risk middle school students. *Professional School Counseling, 9,* 160–163.

Krumboltz, J. D., & Worthington, R. (1999). The school-to-work transition from a learning theory perspective. *Career Development Quarterly, 47,* 312–325.

Krysanski, V. L. (2003). A brief review of selective mutism literature. *Journal of Psychology, 137,* 29–40.

Kübler-Ross, E. (1969). *On death and dying.* New York, NY: Collier Books.

Kulic, K. R., Dagley, J. C., & Horne, A. M. (2001). Prevention groups with children and adolescents. *Journal for Specialists in Group Work, 26,* 211–218.

Kulic, K. R., Horne, A. M., & Dagley, J. C. (2004). A comprehensive review of prevention groups of children and adolescents. *Group Dynamics: Theory, Research, and Practice, 8,* 139–151.

Kumra, S., Sporn, A., Hommer, D. W., Nicolson, R., Thaker, G., Israel, E., . . . Rapoport, J. L. (2001). Smooth pursuit eye-tracking impairment in childhood-onset psychotic disorders. *American Journal of Psychiatry, 158,* 1291–1298.

Kurlan, R., Como, P. G., Miller, B., Palumbo, D., Deeley, C., Andersen, E. M., . . . McDermott, M. P. (2002). The behavioral spectrum of tic disorders: A community-based study. *Neurology, 59,* 414–420.

Lachat, M. A. (2002). *Data-driven high school reform: The breaking ranks model.* Hampton, NH: Center for Resource Management.

LaFountain, R. M., & Garner, N. E. (1998). *A school with solutions: Implementing a solution-focused/Adlerian-based comprehensive school counseling program.* Alexandria, VA: American School Counselor Association.

Lambert, M. J. (1991). Introduction to psychotherapy research. In L. E. Beutler & M. Crago (Eds.), *Psychotherapy research: An international review of programmatic studies* (pp. 1–23). Washington, DC: American Psychological Association.

Lambie, G. W. (2004). Motivational enhancement therapy: A tool for professional school counselors working with adolescents. *Professional School Counseling, 7,* 268–276.

Lambie, G. W. (2005). Child abuse and neglect: A practical guide for professional school counselors. *Professional School Counseling, 8,* 249–259.

Lambie, G. W., & Rokutani, L. J. (2002). A systems approach to substance abuse identification and intervention for school counselors. *Professional School Counseling, 5,* 353–359.

Lambie, G. W., & Sias, S. M. (2005). Children of alcoholics: Implications for professional school counseling. *Professional School Counseling, 8,* 266–273.

Landreth, G. (2002). *Play therapy: The art of the relationship* (2nd ed.). New York, NY: Brunner-Routledge.

Landsverk, R. A. (2003). Families, schools, communities learning together: Connecting families to the classroom. Retrieved March 29, 2009, from www.eric.ed.gov/ERICDocs/data/ericdocs2sql/content_storage_01/0000019b/80/1b/3b/43.pdf

Lapan, R. T. (2001). Results-based comprehensive guidance and counseling programs: A framework for planning and evaluation. *Professional School Counseling, 4,* 289–299.

Lapan, R. (2004). *Career development across the K–16 years: Bridging the present to satisfying and successful futures.* Alexandria, VA: American Counseling Association.

Lapan, R. T., Gysbers, N. C., & Petroski, G. F. (2003). Helping seventh graders be safe and successful: A statewide study of the impact of comprehensive guidance and counseling programs. *Professional School Counseling, 6,* 186–197.

Lapan, R. T., Gysbers, N. C., & Sun, Y. (1997). The impact of more fully implemented guidance programs on the school experiences of high school students: A statewide evaluation study. *Journal of Counseling and Development, 75,* 292–302.

Larmann-Billings, L., & Emery, R. E. (2000). Distress among young adults in divorced families. *Journal of Family Psychology, 14,* 671–687.

Last, C. G., Perrin, S., Hersen, M., & Kazdin, A. E. (1992). *DSM–III–R* anxiety disorders in children: Sociodemographic and clinical characteristics. *Journal of the American Academy of Child and Adolescent Psychiatry, 31,* 1070–1076.

Last, C. G., Strauss, C., & Francis, G. (1987). Comorbidity among childhood anxiety disorders. *Journal of Nervous and Mental Disease, 175,* 726–730.

Lazovsky, R. (2008). Maintaining confidentiality with minors: Dilemmas of school counselors. *Professional School Counseling, 11,* 335–346.

Leckman, J. F., & Cohen, D. J. (1994). Tic disorders. In M. Rutter, E. Taylor, & L. Hersov (Eds.), *Child and adolescent psychiatry: Modern approaches* (pp. 455–466). Cambridge, MA: Blackwell.

Lee, C. C. (1997, January). Empowerment through social action. *Counseling Today, 5,* 26.

Lee, C. C. (1998). Counselors as agents of social change. In C. C. Lee & G. R. Walz (Eds.), *Social action: A mandate for counselors* (pp. 3–14). Alexandria, VA: American Counseling Association & ERIC/CASS.

Lee, C. C. (2001a). Culturally responsive school counselors and programs: Addressing the needs of all students. *Professional School Counseling, 4,* 257–261.

Lee, C. C. (2001b). Defining and responding to racial and ethnic diversity. In D. C. Locke, J. E. Myers, & E. L. Herr (Eds.), *The handbook of counseling* (pp. 581–599). Thousand Oaks, CA: Sage.

Lee, C. C., & Hipolito-Delgado, C. P. (2007). Introduction: Counselors as agents of social change. In C. C. Lee (Ed.), *Counseling for social justice* (2nd ed., pp. xiii–xxviii). Alexandria, VA: American Counseling Association.

Lee, S. M., Daniels, M. H., Puig, A., Newgent, R. A., & Nam, S. K. (2008). A data-based model to predict postsecondary educational attainment of low-socioeconomic-status students. *Professional School Counseling, 11,* 306–316.

Lee, S. M., & Smith-Adcock, S. (2005). A model of girl's school delinquency: School bonding and reputation. *Professional School Counseling, 9,* 78–87.

Lee, V. V. (2005, August). *Teaming and collaborating to challenge the realities that impact student success.* Washington, DC: College Board.

Lee, V. V. (2006, June). *Using data to build equitable access, achievement and attainment in AP, IB, honors and college preparatory courses.* Paper presented at the 2006 Education Trust Summer Academy, Deerfield Beach, FL.

Lee, V. V., & Goodnough, G. E. (2006, October). *Systemic advocacy: A model for school counseling practice and supervision.* Paper presented at the North Atlantic Regional Counselor Education and Supervision Conference, Lake George, NY.

Lehr, C. A., Hansen, A., Sinclair, M. F., & Christenson, S. L. (2003). Moving beyond dropout prevention to school completion: An integrative review of data-based interventions. *School Psychology Review, 32,* 342–364.

Lehr, C. A., Johnson, D. R., Bremer, C. D., Cosio, A., & Thomson, M. (2004). *Essential tools—Increasing rates of school completion: Moving from policy and research to practice: A manual for policymakers, administrators, and educators.* Retrieved August 28, 2005, from www.ncset.org/publications/essentialtools/dropout/default.asp

Lenhardt, M. C., & Young, P. A. (2001). Proactive strategies for advancing elementary school counseling programs: A blueprint for the new millennium. *Professional School Counseling, 4,* 187–194.

Leon, G. R., Fulkerson, J. A., Perry, C. L., Keel, P. K., & Klump, K. L. (1999). Three to four year prospective evaluation of personality and behavioral risk factors for later disordered eating in adolescent girls and boys. *Journal of Youth and Adolescence, 28,* 181–197.

Lewinsohn, P. M., Rohde, P., Seeley, J. R., Klein, D. N., & Gotlib, I. H. (2000). Natural course of adolescent major depressive disorder in a community sample: Predictors of recurrence in young adults. *American Journal of Psychiatry, 157,* 1584–1591.

Lewis, J. A., & Bradley, L. (Eds.). (2000). *Advocacy in counseling: Counselors, clients, and community.* Greensboro, NC: CAPS & ERIC/CASS.

Lin, M., Kelly, K. R., & Nelson, R. C. (1996). A comparative analysis of the interpersonal process in school-based counseling and consultation. *Journal of Counseling Psychology, 43,* 389–393.

Littrell, J. M., Malia, J. A., & Vanderwood, M. (1995). Single session brief counseling in a high school. *Journal of Counseling and Development, 73,* 451–458.

Locke, D. C. (1990). A not so provincial view of multicultural counseling. *Counselor Education and Supervision, 30,* 18–25.

Lockhart, E. J., & Keys, S. G. (1998). The mental health counseling role of school counselors. *Professional School Counseling, 1,* 3–6.

Loeber, R., & Stouthamer-Loeber, M. (1998). Development of juvenile aggression and violence: Some common misconceptions and controversies. *American Psychologist, 53,* 242–259.

Loesch, L. C., & Ritchie, M. H. (2004). *The accountable school counselor.* Austin, TX: PRO-ED.

Lombana, J. H. (1985). Guidance accountability: A new look at an old problem. *School Counselor, 32,* 340–346.

Long, J. J., Fabricus, W. V., Musheno, M., & Palumbo, D. (1998). Exploring the cognitive and affective capacities of child mediators in a "successful" inner-city peer mediation program. *Mediation Quarterly, 15,* 289–302.

Lopez, E. C. (2000). Conducting instructional consultation through interpreters. *School Psychology Review, 29,* 378–388.

Lord, C., & Rutter, M. (1994). Autism and pervasive developmental disorders. In M. Rutter, E. Taylor, & L. Hersov (Eds.), *Child and adolescent psychiatry: Modern approaches* (pp. 596–593). Cambridge, MA: Blackwell.

Löwe, B., Zipfel, S., Buchholz, C., Dupont, Y., Reas, D. L., & Herzog, W. (2001). Long-term outcomes of anorexia nervosa in a prospective 21-year follow-up study. *Psychological Medicine, 31*, 881–890.

Lubell, K. M., Kegler, S. R., Crosby, A. E., & Karch, D. (2008). Suicide trends among youths and young adults aged 10–24 years—United States, 1900–2004. *Journal of the American Medical Association, 299*, 283–284.

Lundahl, B. W., Nimer, J., & Parsons, B. (2006). Preventing child abuse: A meta-analysis of parent training programs. *Research on Social Work Practice, 16*, 251–262.

Luongo, P. F. (2000). Partnering child welfare, juvenile justice, and behavioral health with schools. *Professional School Counseling, 3*, 308–314.

Ly, T. M., & Hodapp, R. M. (2002). Maternal attribution of child noncompliance in children with mental retardation: Down syndrome versus other causes. *Journal of Developmental and Behavioral Pediatrics, 23*, 322–329.

Lyons-Ruth, K., Zeanah, C. H., & Benoit, D. (1996). Disorder and risk for disorder during infancy and todlerhood. In E. J. Mash & R. A. Barkley (Eds.), *Child psychopathology* (pp. 457–491). New York, NY: Guilford Press.

Ma, X., Stewin, L. L., & Mah, D. L. (2001). Bullying in school: Nature, effects, and remedies. *Research Papers in Education, 16*, 247–270.

Macmillan, D. L., Gresham, F. M., Spierstein, G. N., & Bocian, K. M. (1996). The labyrinth of IDEA: School decisions on referred students with sub-average general intelligence. *American Journal of Mental Retardation, 101*, 161–174.

Mahoney, J. S., & Merritt, S. R. (1993). Educational hopes of black and white high school seniors in Virginia. *Journal of Educational Research, 87*, 31–38.

Maital, S. L. (2000). Reciprocal distancing: A systems model of interpersonal processes in cross-cultural consultation. *School Psychology Review, 29*, 389–400.

Major, B. N., & O'Brien, L. T. (2005). The social psychology of stigma. *Annual Review of Psychology, 56*, 393–421.

Manese, J. E., Wu, J. T., & Nepomuceno, C. A. (2001). The effect of training on multicultural counseling competencies: An exploratory study over a ten year period. *Journal of Multicultural Counseling and Development, 29*, 31–40.

Manning, M. L. (2000). Benchmarks of student-friendly middle schools. *Education Digest, 66*(2), 21–26.

March, J. S., & Leonard, H. L. (1996). Obsessive compulsive disorder in children and adolescents: A review of the past 10 years. *Journal of the American Academy of Child and Adolescent Psychiatry, 34*, 1265–1273.

Marcia, J. E. (1989). Identity and intervention. *Journal of Adolescence, 12*, 401–410.

Markus, H. R. (2008). Pride, prejudice, and ambivalence: Toward a unified theory of race and ethnicity. *American Psychologist, 63*, 651–670.

Marshall, P. L. (2002). *Cultural diversity in our schools.* Belmont, CA: Wadsworth/Thomson Learning.

Masi, G., Mucci, M., & Millepiedi, S. (2001). Separation anxiety disorder in children and adolescents: Epidemiology, diagnosis and management. *CNS Drugs, 15*, 94–104.

Masten, A., & Coatworth, J. D. (1998). The development of competence in favorable and unfavorable environments: Lessons from research on successful children. *American Psychologist, 53*, 205–220.

Mattingley, D. J., Prislin, R., McKenzie, T. L., Rodriquez, J. L., & Kayzar, R. (2002). Evaluating evaluations: The case of parental involvement programs. *Review of Educational Research, 72*, 549–576.

Maxman, J. S., & Ward, N. G. (1995). *Essential psychopathology and its treatment* (2nd ed.). New York, NY: Norton.

Mayfield, D., McLeod, G., & Hall, P. (1974). The CAGE questionnaire: Validation of a new alcoholism screening instrument. *American Journal of Psychiatry, 131*(10), 1121–1123.

McAdams III, C. R., & Schmidt, C. D. (2007). How to help a bully: Recommendations for counseling the proactive aggressor. *Professional School Counseling, 11*, 120–128.

McCabe, P., Sheard, C., & Code, C. (2002). Acquired communication impairment in people with HIV. *Journal of Medical Speech-Language Pathology, 10*, 183–199.

McCall-Perez, Z. (2000). The counselor as advocate for English language learners: An action research approach. *Professional School Counseling, 4*, 13–22.

McClellan, J., McCurry, C., Speltz, M. L., & Jones, K. (2002). Symptom factors in early-onset psychotic disorders. *Journal of the American Academy of Child and Adolescent Psychiatry, 41*, 791–798.

McClelland, G. M., Elkington, K. S., Teplin, L. A., & Abram, K. M. (2004). Multiple substance use disorders in juvenile detainees. *Journal of the American Academy of Child and Adolescent Psychiatry, 43*, 1215–1224.

McClure, F. H., & Teyber, E. (2003). *Casebook in child and adolescent treatment: Cultural and familial contexts.* Pacific Grove, CA: Brooks/Cole.

McDougall, D., & Smith, D. (2006). Recent innovations in small-n designs for research and practice in professional school counseling. *Professional School Counseling, 9*, 392–400.

McEachern, A. G. (2003). School counselor preparation to meet the guidance needs of exceptional students: A national study. *Counselor Education and Supervision, 42,* 314–325.

McFarland, W. P., & Dupuis, M. (2001). The legal duty to protect gay and lesbian students from violence in school. *Professional School Counseling, 4,* 171–179.

McGannon, W. M., Carey, J., & Dimmitt, C. (2005). *The current status of school counseling outcome research.* Amherst, MA: Center for School Counseling Outcome Research.

McGinnis, E., & Goldstein, A. P. (1997). *Skillstreaming the elementary school child.* Champaign, IL: Research Press.

McGoldrick, M., & Giordano, J. (1996). Overview: Ethnicity and family therapy. In M. McGoldrick, J. Giordano, & J. K. Pierce (Eds.), *Ethnicity and family therapy* (2nd ed., pp. 1–27). New York, NY: Guilford Press.

McLanahan, S. S. (1999). Father absence and children's welfare. In E. M. Heatherington (Ed.), *Coping with divorce, single parenting and remarriage: A risk and resiliency perspective* (pp. 117–146). Mahwah, NJ: Erlbaum.

Merlone, L. (2005). Record keeping and the school counselor. *Professional School Counseling, 8,* 372–376.

Merriam-Webster's Collegiate Dictionary (11th ed.). (2007). Springfield, MA: Merriam-Webster.

Metcalf, L. (2008). *Counseling toward solutions: A practical solution-focused program for working with students, teachers, and parents* (2nd ed.). West Nyack, NY: Center for Applied Research.

Mezzich, J. E., Kirmayer, L. J., Kleinman, A., Fabrega, H., Parron, D. L., Good, B. J., . . . Manson, S. M. (1999). The place of culture in *DSM–IV. Journal of Nervous and Mental Disease, 187,* 457–464.

Mikkelsen, E. J. (2001). Enuresis and encopresis: Ten years of progress. *Journal of the American Academy of Child and Adolescent Psychiatry, 40,* 1146–1158.

Miller, C. H. (1961). *Foundations of guidance.* New York, NY: Harper & Brothers.

Miller, D. (2006). How collaboration and research can affect school counseling practices: The Minnesota story. *Professional School Counseling, 9,* 238–244.

Miller, F. G. (2001). *The SASSI-A2 manual.* Springfield, IN: SASSI Institute.

Milsom, A. S. (2002). Students with disabilities: School counselor involvement and preparation. *Professional School Counseling, 5,* 331–339.

Milsom, A. (2006). Creating positive school experiences for students with disabilities. *Professional School Counseling, 10,* 66–72.

Milsom, A., & Hartley, M. T. (2005). Assisting students with learning disabilities transitioning to college: What school counselors should know. *Professional School Counseling, 8,* 436–441.

Milsom, A., & Peterson, J. S. (2006). Introduction to special issue: Examining disability and giftedness in schools. *Professional School Counseling, 10,* 1–2.

Minden, J., Henry, D. B., Tolan, P. H., & Gorman-Smith, D. (2000). Urban boys' social networks and school violence. *Professional School Counseling, 4,* 95–104.

Miranda, A., Webb, L., Brigman, G., & Peluso, P. (2007). Student success skills: A promising program to close the academic achievement gap for African American and Latino students. *Professional School Counseling, 10,* 490–497.

Mitchell, C. W., & Rogers, R. E. (2003). Rape, statutory rape, and child abuse: Legal distinctions and counselor duties. *Professional School Counseling, 6,* 332–339.

Mitchell, N. (2005). Academic achievement among Caribbean immigrant adolescents: The impact of generational status on academic self-concept. *Professional School Counseling, 8,* 209–218.

Mitchell, N., & Bryan, J. A. (2007). School–family–community partnerships: Strategies for school counselors working with Caribbean immigrant families. *Professional School Counseling, 10,* 399–409.

Mohatt, D. F., Adams, S. J., Bradley, M. M., & Morris, C. D. (Eds). (2006). *Mental health and rural America: 1994–2005.* Washington, DC: U.S. Department of Health and Human Services, Health Resources and Services Administration, Office of Rural Health Policy.

Moore-Thomas, C., & Day-Vines, N. (2008). Culturally competent counseling for religious and spiritual African American adolescents. *Professional School Counseling, 11,* 159–165.

Morrison, J. (1995). DSM–IV *made easy.* New York, NY: Guilford Press.

Mosconi, J., & Emmett, J. (2003). Effects of a values clarification curriculum on high school students' definition of success. *Professional School Counseling, 7,* 68–78.

Motta, R. W., & Basile, D. M. (1998). Pica. In L. Phelps (Ed.), *Health-related disorders in children and adolescents: A compilation of 96 rare and common disorders* (pp. 524–527). Washington, DC: American Psychological Association.

Moyer, M., & Nelson, K. W. (2007). Investigating and understanding self-mutilation: The student voice. *Professional School Counseling, 11,* 42–48.

Moyer, M., & Sullivan, J. (2008). Student risk-taking behaviors: When do school counselors break confidentiality? *Professional School Counseling, 11,* 236–245.

Mulick, J. A., & Butter, E. M. (2002). Educational advocacy for children with autism. *Behavioral Interventions, 17,* 57–74.

Murphy, G. (1955). The cultural concept of guidance. *Personnel and Guidance Journal, 34,* 4–9.

Murphy, J. J. (1999). Common factors of school-based change. In M. A. Hubble & B. L. Duncan (Eds.), *The heart and soul of change: What works in therapy* (pp. 361–386). Washington, DC: American Psychological Association.

Murphy, J. J. (2008). *Solution-focused counseling in middle and high schools* (2nd ed.). Alexandria, VA: American Counseling Association.

Murphy, S., & Carney, T. (2004). The classification of soiling and encopresis and a possible treatment protocol. *Child and Adolescent Mental Health, 9,* 125–129.

Muuss, R. E. (1998). Marcia's expansion of Erickson's theory of identity formation. In R. Muuss & H. Porton (Eds.), *Adolescent behavior and society: A book of readings* (5th ed., pp. 260–270). New York, NY: McGraw-Hill.

Myrick, R. D. (2003a). *Developmental guidance and counseling: A practical approach* (4th ed.). Minneapolis, MN: Education Media Corporation.

Myrick, R. D. (2003b). Accountability: Counselors count. *Professional School Counseling, 6,* 174–179.

Nader, K. O., Pynoos, R. S., Fairbanks, L. A., al-Ajeel, M., & al-Asfour, A. (1993). A preliminary study of PTSD and grief among the children of Kuwait following the Gulf Crisis. *British Journal of Clinical Psychology, 32,* 407–416.

National Association of Anorexia Nervosa and Associated Disorders. (2000). *Facts about eating disorders.* Retrieved December 13, 2008, from www.anad.org/22385/index.html

National Career Development Association. (1997). *Career counseling competencies.* Retrieved August 20, 2005, from www.ncda.org/about/polccc.html

National Center for Public Policy and Higher Education. (2000). *Measuring up 2000.* Washington, DC: Author.

National Coalition for the Homeless. (2008). *Homeless families and children* (NCH Fact Sheet #12). Retrieved November 15, 2008, from www.nationalhomeless.org/publications/facts/families.html

National Commission on Excellence in Education. (1983). *A nation at risk: The imperative for educational reform.* Retrieved April 21, 2009, from www.ed.gov/pubs/NatAtRisk/index.html

National Council on Disability. (2004). *Improving educational outcomes for students with disabilities.* Retrieved August 28, 2005, from www.ncd.gov/newsroom/publications/2004 educationoutcomes.htm

National Dissemination Center for Children with Disabilities. (2001). *Related services: News digest 16* (2nd ed.). Retrieved August 20, 2005, from www.nichcy.org/pubs/newsdig/nd16txt.htm

National Education Association. (2002). *Crisis communications guide and toolkit.* Washington, DC: Author.

National Institute of Mental Health. (2000). *Depression research at the National Institute of Mental Health.* Bethesda, MD: Author.

National Institute of Mental Health. (2005). *America's children: Parents report estimated 2.7 million children with emotional and behavioral problems.* Retrieved September 2, 2005, from www.nimh.nih.gov/healthinformation/childhood_indicators.cfm

National Institutes of Health. (1998). *NIH consensus statement: Diagnosis and treatment of attention deficit hyperactivity disorder* (Vol. 16, no. 2). Bethesda, MD: Author.

National Institutes of Health. (2005). *The national children's study.* Retrieved September 2, 2005, from www.nationalchildrensstudy.gov

Nearpass, E. L. (1990). Counseling and guidance effectiveness in North American high schools: A meta-analysis of the research findings. *Dissertation Abstracts International: Section A. Humanities and Social Sciences, 50,* 1984.

Nelson, D. E., Fox, D. G., Haslam, M., & Gardner, J. (2007). *An evaluation of Utah's comprehensive guidance program: The fourth major study of Utah's thirteen-year program.* Retrieved January 21, 2009, from www.schools.utah.gov/cte/documents/guidance/publications/Research_AnEvaluationUtahsCCGP2007.pdf

Nelson, D. E., Gardner, J. L., & Fox, D. G. (1998). *Contrast between students in high implementation and low implementation high schools in the Utah Comprehensive Guidance Program.* Salt Lake City, UT: Institute for Behavioral Research in Creativity.

Nelson, J. A., Bustamante, R. M., Wilson, E. D., & Onwuegbuzie, A. J. (2008). The School-wide Cultural Competence Observation Checklist for School Counselors: An exploratory factor analysis. *Professional School Counseling, 11,* 207–217.

Nelson, J. R., Dykeman, C., Powell, S., & Petty, D. (1996). The effects of a group counseling intervention on students with behavioral adjustment problems. *Elementary School Guidance and Counseling, 31,* 21–33.

Newcomb, M. D., & Richardson, M. A. (2000). Substance-use disorders. In M. Hersen & R. T. Ammerman (Eds.), *Advanced abnormal child psychology* (2nd ed., pp. 467–492). Mahwah, NJ: Erlbaum.

Newman-Carlson, D., & Horne, A. M. (2004). Bully busters: A psychoeducational intervention for reducing bullying behaviors in middle school students. *Journal of Counseling and Development, 82,* 259–267.

Newport News Public Schools. (2002). *Secondary counselor handbook.* Retrieved March 28, 2005, from sbo.nn.k12.va.us/guidance/handbooks/counshandbook.pdf

Nicholson, J. I., & Pearson, Q. M. (2003). Helping children cope with fears: Using children's literature in classroom guidance. *Professional School Counseling, 7*, 15–19.

Nicoll, W. G. (1994). Developing effective classroom guidance programs: An integrative framework. *School Counselor, 41*, 360–364.

Niedringhaus, J. J. (2000). *Counseling children: Some practical suggestions.* Unpublished manuscript.

Nieto, S. (2004). *Affirming diversity: The sociopolitical context of multicultural education* (4th ed.). Boston, MA: Pearson/Allyn & Bacon.

Niles, S. G. (1998). Developing life-role readiness in a multicultural society: Topics to consider. *International Journal for the Advancement of Counseling, 20*, 71–77.

Niles, S. G., Erford, B. T., Hunt, B., & Watts, R. (1997). Decision-making styles and career development in college students. *Journal of College Student Development, 38*, 479–488.

Niles, S. G., & Goodnough, G. E. (1996). Life-role salience and values: A review of recent research. *Career Development Quarterly, 45*, 65–86.

Nims, D., James, S., & Hughey, A. (1998). The challenge of accountability: A survey of Kentucky school counselors. *Kentucky Counseling Association Journal, 17*, 31–37.

O'Connor, K. P. (2001). Clinical and psychological features distinguishing obsessive-compulsive and chronic tic disorders. *Clinical Psychology Review, 21*, 631–660.

O'Donnell, D. A., Schwab-Stone, M. E., & Muyeed, A. Z. (2002). Multidimensional resilience in urban children exposed to community violence. *Child Development, 73*, 1265–1282.

O'Hanlon, W. H., & Weiner-Davis, M. (1989). *In search of solutions: A new direction in psychotherapy.* New York, NY: Guilford Press.

Oliver, L. W., & Spokane, A. R. (1988). Career-intervention outcome: What contributes to client gain? *Journal of Counseling Psychology, 35*, 447–462.

Oliver, M., Nelson, K. W., Cade, R., & Cueva, C. (2007). Therapeutic letter writing from school counselors to students, parents, and teachers. *Professional School Counseling, 10*, 510–515.

Ollendick, T. H., & King, N. J. (1998). Empirically supported treatments for children with phobic and anxiety disorders: Current status. *Journal of Clinical Child Psychology, 27*, 156–167.

Olweus, D. (2005). A useful evaluation design, and effects of the Olweus bullying prevention program. *Psychology, Crime, and Law, 11*, 389–402.

Orpinas, P., & Horne, A. M. (2006). *Bullying prevention: Creating a positive school climate and developing social competence.* Washington, DC: American Psychological Association.

Orton, G. L. (1997). *Strategies for counseling with children and their parents.* Pacific Grove, CA: Brooks/Cole.

Osborne, J. L., Collison, B. B., House, R. M., Gray, L. A., Firthe, J., & Lou, M. (1998). Developing a social advocacy model for counselor education. *Counselor Education and Supervision, 37*, 190–202.

O'Shea, A. J., & Harrington, T. F. (2003). Using the Career Decision-Making System–Revised to enhance students' career development. *Professional School Counseling, 6*, 280–287.

Osher, D., Dwyer, K., & Jackson, S. (2004). *Safe, supportive and successful schools: Step by step.* Longmont, CO: Sopris West Educational Services.

Otwell, P. S., & Mullis, F. (1997). Counselor-led staff development: An efficient approach to teacher consultation. *Professional School Counseling, 1*, 25–30.

Ozer, E. J., & Weinstein, R. S. (2004). Urban adolescents' exposure to community violence: The role of support, school safety, and social constraints in a school-based sample of boys and girls. *Journal of Clinical Child and Adolescent Psychology, 33*, 463–476.

Pack-Brown, S. P., Thomas, T. L., & Seymour, J. M. (2008). Infusing professional ethics into counselor education programs: A multicultural/social justice perspective. *Journal of Counseling and Development, 86*, 296–302.

Paisley, P. O. (2001). Maintaining and enhancing the developmental focus in school counseling programs. *Professional School Counseling, 4*, 271–277.

Paisley, P. O., & Borders, L. D. (1995). School counseling: An evolving specialty. *Journal of Counseling and Development, 74*, 150–152.

Paisley, P. O., & Milsom, A. (2007). Group work as an essential contribution to transforming school counseling. *Journal for Specialists in Group Work, 32*, 9–17.

Palladino Schultheiss, D. E. (2005). University-urban school collaboration in school counseling. *Professional School Counseling, 8*, 330–336.

Park-Taylor, J., Walsh, M. E., & Ventura, A. B. (2007). Creating healthy acculturation pathways: Integrating theory and research to inform counselors' work with immigrant children. *Professional School Counseling, 11*, 25–34.

Parsons, F. (1909). *Choosing a vocation.* Boston, MA: Houghton Mifflin.

Parsons, R. (1996). *The skilled consultant: A systematic approach to the theory and practice of consultation.* Boston, MA: Allyn & Bacon.

Pelcovitz, D., Kaplan, S. J., DeRosa, R. R., Mandel, F. S., & Salziner, S. (2000). Psychiatric disorders in adolescents exposed to domestic violence and physical abuse. *American Journal of Orthopsychiatry, 70*, 360–369.

Perna, L. W., Rowan-Kenyon, H. T., Thomas, S. L., Bell, A., Anderson, R., & Li, C. (2008). The role of college counseling in shaping college opportunity: Variations across high schools. *Review of Higher Education, 31,* 131–159.

Perusse, R., & Goodnough, G. E. (Eds.). (2004). *Leadership, advocacy, and direct service strategies for professional school counselors.* Belmont, CA: Brooks/Cole-Thomson Learning.

Peterson, A. A., Campise, R. L., & Azrin, N. H. (1994). Behavioral and pharmacological treatments for tic and habit disorders: A review. *Journal of Developmental and Behavioral Pediatrics, 15,* 430–441.

Peterson, J. (2004). The individual counseling process. In A. Vernon (Ed.), *Counseling children and adolescents* (3rd ed., pp. 35–74). Denver, CO: Love.

Peterson, J. S. (2006). Addressing counseling needs of gifted students. *Professional School Counseling, 10,* 43–51.

Peterson, J. S., Goodman, R., Thomas, K., & McCauley, A. (2004). Teachers and non-teachers as school counselors: Reflections on the internship experience. *Professional School Counseling, 7,* 246–255.

Peterson, R. L., & Skiba, R. (2001, July/August). Creating school climates that prevent school violence. *The Social Studies, 92,* 167–175.

Piaget, J. (1963). *The origins of intelligence in children.* New York: Norton.

Piran, N. (2004). Teachers: On "being" (rather than "doing") prevention. *Eating Disorders, 12,* 1–9.

Polivy, J., & Herman, C. P. (2002). Causes of eating disorders. *Annual Review of Psychology, 27,* 187.

Ponec, D. L., Poggi, J. A., & Dickel, T. A. (1998). Unity: Developing relationships between school and community counselors. *Professional School Counseling, 2,* 95–102.

Ponterotto, J. G., & Pederson, P. B. (1993). *Preventing prejudice: A guide for counselors and educators.* Newbury Park, CA: Sage.

Pope-Davis, D. B., Reynolds, A. L., Dings, J. G., & Ottavi, T. M. (1994). Multicultural competencies of doctoral interns at university counseling centers: An exploratory investigation. *Professional Psychology: Research and Practice, 25,* 466–470.

Popper, C. W., & Gherardi, P. C. (1996). Anxiety disorders. In J. M. Wiener (Ed.), *Diagnosis and psychopharmacology of children and adolescent disorders* (2nd ed., pp. 294–348). New York, NY: Wiley.

Porter, G., Epp, L., & Bryant, S. (2000). Collaboration among school mental health professionals: A necessity, not a luxury. *Professional School Counseling, 3,* 315–322.

Power, T. J., DuPaul, G. J., Shapiro, E. S., & Parrish, J. M. (1998). Role of the school-based professional in health-related services. In L. Phelps (Ed.), *Health-related disorders in children and adolescents* (pp. 15–26). Washington, DC: American Psychological Association.

Poynton, T. A., & Carey, J. C. (2006). An integrative model of data-based decision making for school counseling. *Professional School Counseling, 10,* 121–130.

Poynton, T., & Dimmitt, C. (2004). *An evidence-based violence prevention curriculum for elementary school children.* Retrieved May 25, 2005, from www.umass.edu/schoolcounseling/briefs.htm

President's New Freedom Commission on Mental Health. (2003). *Final report to the President.* Washington, DC: Author. Retrieved November 15, 2008, from www.mentalhealthcommission.gov/reports/FinalReport/FullReport-03.htm

Prout, H. T., & DeMartino, R. A. (1986). A meta-analysis of school-based studies of psychotherapy. *Journal of School Psychology, 24,* 285–292.

Prout, S. M., & Prout, H. T. (1998). A meta-analysis of school-based studies of counseling and psychotherapy: An update. *Journal of School Psychology, 36,* 121–136.

Quarto, C. J. (1999). Teachers' perceptions of school counselors with and without teaching experience. *Professional School Counseling, 2,* 378–383.

Quinn, M. M., Gable, R. A., Rutherford, R. B., Nelson, C. M., & Howell, K. W. (1998). *Addressing student problem behavior: An IEP team's introduction to functional behavioral assessment and behavioral intervention plans* (2nd ed.). Washington, DC: Center for Effective Collaboration and Practice, American Institutes for Research.

Ramirez, S. Z., & Smith, K. A. (2007). Case vignettes of school psychologists' consultations involving Hispanic youth. *Journal of Educational and Psychological Consultation, 17,* 79–93.

Randolph, D. L., & Masker, T. (1997). Teacher certification and the counselor: A follow-up survey of school counselor certification requirements. *ACES Spectrum, 57*(4), 6–8.

Rapin, I. (1999). Autism in search of a home in the brain. *Neurology, 52,* 902–904.

Rapoport, J. L., & Ismond, D. R. (1996). *DSM–IV training guide for diagnosis of childhood disorders.* Levittown, PA: Brunner/Mazel.

Rapoport, J. L., Leonard, H., Swedo, S. E., & Lenane, M. C. (1993). Obsessive compulsive disorder in children and adolescents: Issues in management. *Journal of Clinical Psychiatry, 54,* 27–29.

Rappaport, J. (1987). Terms of empowerment/examples of prevention: Toward a theory for community psychology. *American Journal of Community Psychology, 15,* 121–144.

Rapport, M. D. (1995). Attention-deficit hyperactivity disorder. In M. Hersen & R. T. Ammerman (Eds.), *Advanced abnormal child psychology* (pp. 353–375). Hillsdale, NJ: Erlbaum.

Ratts, M. J., DeKruyf, L., & Chen-Hayes, S. F. (2007). The ACA advocacy competencies: A social justice advocacy framework for professional school counselors. *Professional School Counselors, 11*, 90–97.

Ray, D. C. (2007). Two counseling interventions to reduce teacher–child relationship stress. *Professional School Counseling, 10*, 428–440.

Ray, D. C., Armstrong, S. A., Warren, E. S., & Balkin, R. S. (2005). Play therapy practices among elementary school counselors. *Professional School Counseling, 8*, 360–365.

Ray, S. L. (2004). Eating disorders in adolescent males. *Professional School Counseling, 8*, 98–101.

Rayle, A. D. (2005). Cross-gender interactions in middle school counselor–student working alliances: Challenges and recommendations. *Professional School Counseling, 9*, 152–155.

Rayle, A. D., & Myers, J. E. (2004). Counseling adolescents toward wellness: The roles of ethnic identity, acculturation, and mattering. *Professional School Counseling, 8*, 81–90.

Reis, S. M., & Colbert, R. (2004). Counseling needs of academically talented students with learning disabilities. *Professional School Counseling, 8*, 156–167.

Remley, T., & Herlihy, B. (2010). *Ethical, legal, and professional issues in counseling* (3rd ed.). Upper Saddle River, NJ: Merrill/Prentice Hall.

Remley, T., & Huey, W. C. (2002). An ethics quiz for school counselors. *Professional School Counseling, 6*, 3–11.

Rey, J. M. (1993). Oppositional defiant disorder. *American Journal of Psychiatry, 150*, 1769–1778.

Reynolds, W. M. (1988). *Suicide Ideation Questionnaire.* Lutz, FL: Psychological Assessment Resources.

Rhodes, R. L., Ochoa, S. H., & Ortiz, S. O. (2005). *Assessing culturally and linguistically diverse students: A practical guide.* New York, NY: Guilford Press.

Ribak-Rosenthal, N. (1994). Reasons individuals become school administrators, school counselors, and teachers. *School Counselor, 41*, 158–164.

Richmond Public Schools. (n.d.). *Guidance and school counseling services making a difference.* Retrieved July 6, 2005, from www.richmond.k12.va.us/guidance/mission.cfm

Ridley, C. R., Mendoza, D. W., Kanitz, B. E., Angermeier, L., & Zenk, R. (1994). Cultural sensitivity in multicultural counseling: A perceptual schema model. *Journal of Counseling Psychology, 41*, 125–136.

Riley, P. L., & McDaniel, J. (2000). School violence prevention, intervention, and crisis response. *Professional School Counseling, 4*, 120–125.

Ripley, V. V. (2001, October). *From position to program: Supervision in context.* Paper presented at North Atlantic

Region Association for Counselor Education and Supervision National Conference, Amherst, MA.

Ripley, V. V., & Goodnough, G. E. (2001). Planning and implementing group counseling in a high school. *Professional School Counseling, 5*, 62–65.

Ritchie, M. H., & Huss, S. N. (2000). Recruitment and screening of minors for group counseling. *Journal for Specialists in Group Work, 25*, 146–156.

Riva, M. T., & Haub, A. L. (2004). Group counseling in the schools. In J. L. DeLucia-Waack, D. A. Gerrity, C. R. Kalodner, & M. T. Riva (Eds.), *Handbook of group counseling and psychotherapy* (pp. 309–321). Thousand Oaks, CA: Sage.

Roache, M., Shore, J., Gouleta, E., & de Obaldia Butkevich, E. (2003). An investigation of collaboration among school professionals in serving culturally and linguistically diverse students with exceptionalities. *Bilingual Research Journal, 27*, 117–136.

Roberts, M. L., Marshall, J., Nelson, J. R., & Albers, C. A. (2001). Curriculum-based assessment procedures embedded within functional behavioral assessments: Identifying escape-motivated behaviors in a general education classroom. *School Psychology Review, 30*, 264–278.

Rockney, R. M., McQuade, W. H., Days, A. L., Linn, H. E., & Alario, A. J. (1996). Encopresis treatment outcome: Long-term follow-up of 45 cases. *Journal of Developmental and Behavioral Pediatrics, 17*, 380–385.

Rogers, C. R. (1942). *Counseling and psychotherapy: Newer concepts in practice.* New York, NY: Houghton Mifflin.

Rogers, M. R. (2000). Examining the cultural context of consultation. *School Psychology Review, 29*, 414–418.

Rogers, M. R., Ingraham, C. L., Bursztyn, A., Cajigas-Segredo, N., Esquival, G., Hess, R., . . . Nahari, S. G. (1999). Providing psychological services to racially, ethnically, culturally, and linguistically diverse individuals in the schools: Recommendations for practice. *School Psychology International, 20*, 243–264.

Roid, G. H. (2003). *The Stanford-Binet Intelligence Scale–5th Edition (SBIS).* Itasca, IL: Riverside.

Rollin, S. A., Kaiser-Ulrey, C., Potts, I., & Creason, A. H. (2003). A school-based violence prevention model for at-risk eighth grade youth. *Psychology in the Schools, 40*, 403–416.

Rosenbaum, J. E., & Person, A. E. (2003). Beyond college for all: Policies and practices to improve transitions into college and jobs. *Professional School Counseling, 6*, 252–261.

Rosenberg, M. S., & Jackman, L. A. (2003). Development, implementation, and sustainability of comprehensive school-wide behavior management systems. *Intervention in School and Clinic, 39*, 10–21.

Roth, A., & Fonagy, P. (1996). *What works for whom?* New York, NY: Guilford Press.

Rowell, L. L. (2005). Collaborative action research and school counselors. *Professional School Counseling, 9,* 28–36.

Rowell, L. L. (2006). Action research and school counseling: Closing the gap between research and practice. *Professional School Counseling, 9,* 376–384.

Rowley, W. J., Sink, C. A., & MacDonald, G. (2002). An experiential and systemic approach to encourage collaboration and community building. *Professional School Counseling, 5,* 360–365.

Rowley, W. J., Stroh, H. R., & Sink, C. A. (2005). Comprehensive guidance and counseling programs' use of guidance curricula materials: A survey of national trends. *Professional School Counseling, 8,* 296–304.

Sabella, R. A. (2006). The ASCA National School Counseling Research Center: A brief history and agenda. *Professional School Counseling, 9,* 412–415.

Saenz, R. (2009). *Latinos and the changing face of America.* Washington, DC: Population Reference Bureau. Retrieved August 21, 2009 from www.prb.org/Articles/2004/LatinosandtheChangingFaceofAmerica.aspx

St. Claire, K. L. (1989). Middle school counseling research: A resource for school counselors. *Elementary School Guidance and Counseling, 23,* 219–226.

Salend, S. J. (1994). Strategies for assessing attitudes toward individuals with disabilities. *School Counselor, 41,* 338–342.

Sanchez, A. (2001). *Rainbow boys.* New York, NY: Simon & Schuster.

Sandhu, D. S. (2000). Alienated students: Counseling strategies to curb school violence. *Professional School Counseling, 4,* 81–85.

Santos de Barona, M. & Barona, A. (2006). School counselors and school psychologists: Collaborating to ensure minority students receive appropriate consideration for special educational programs. *Professional School Counselor, 10*(1), 3–13.

Saphier, J., King, M., & D'Auria, J. (2006). Three strands form strong school leadership. *Journal of Staff Development, 27,* 51–57.

Satcher, J., & Leggett, M. (2007). Homonegativity among professional school counselors: An exploratory study. *Professional School Counseling, 11,* 10–16.

Savickas, M. L. (1999). The transition from school to work: A developmental perspective. *Career Development Quarterly, 47,* 326–336.

Savickas, M. (2004). Toward a taxonomy of human strengths: Career counseling's contribution to positive psychology. In W. Walsh (Ed.), *Counseling psychology and optimal human functioning* (pp. 229–249). Mahwah, NJ: Erlbaum.

Scales, P. (2005). Developmental assets and the middle school counselor. *Professional School Counseling, 9,* 104–111.

Scarborough, J. L. (2005). The School Counselor Activity Rating Scale: An instrument for gathering process data. *Professional School Counseling, 8,* 274–283.

Scarborough, J. L., & Gilbride, D. (2006). Developing relationships with rehabilitation counselors to meet the transition needs of students with disabilities. *Professional School Counseling, 10,* 25–33.

Schaefer, R. T. (1990). *Racial and ethnic groups* (4th ed.). Glenview, IL: Scott, Foresman/Little.

Schaefer-Schiumo, K., & Ginsberg, A. P. (2003). The effectiveness of the warning signs program in educating youth about violence prevention: A study with urban high school students. *Professional School Counseling, 7,* 1–8.

Schave, D., & Schave, B. F. (1989). *Early adolescence and the search for self: A developmental perspective.* New York, NY: Praeger.

Schein, E. (1969). *Process consultation: Its role in organizational development.* Reading, MA: Addison-Wesley.

Schlossberg, S. M., Morris, J. D., & Lieberman, M. G. (2001). The effects of a counselor-led guidance intervention on students' behaviors and attitudes. *Professional School Counseling, 4,* 156–174.

Schmidt, J. J. (2008). *Counseling in schools: Comprehensive programs of responsive services for all students* (5th ed.). Boston, MA: Allyn & Bacon.

Schwallie-Giddis, P., Anstrom, K., Sanchez, P., Sardi, V. A., & Granato, L. (2004). Counseling the linguistically and culturally diverse student: Meeting school counselors' professional development needs. *Professional School Counseling, 8,* 15–23.

Scruggs, M. Y., Wasielewski, R. A., & Ash, M. J. (1999). Comprehensive evaluation of a K–12 counseling program. *Professional School Counseling, 2,* 244–247.

Selekman, M. D. (1997). *Pathways to change: Brief therapy solutions with difficult adolescents.* New York, NY: Guilford Press.

Seligman, L. (2004). *Diagnosis and treatment planning in counseling* (3rd ed.). New York, NY: Kluwer.

Seligman, L. (2006). *Selecting effective treatments: A comprehensive, systematic guide to treating mental disorders* (3rd ed.). San Francisco, CA: Jossey-Bass.

Seligman, M., & Darling, R. (1989). *Ordinary families, special children: A systems approach to childhood disability.* New York, NY: Guilford Press.

Sellers, R. M., & Shelton, J. N. (2003). Racial identity, discrimination, and mental health among African Americans. *Journal of Personality and Social Psychology Review, 2,* 18–39.

Sexton, T. L., Whiston, S. C., Bleuer, J. C., & Walz, G. R. (1997). *Integrating outcome research into counseling practice and training.* Alexandria, VA: American Counseling Association.

Shaffer, D., & Pfeffer, C. R. (2001). Practice parameter for the assessment and treatment of children with suicidal behavior. *Journal of the American Academy of Child and Adolescent Psychiatry, 40* (Suppl. 7), 24S–51S.

Shaffer, D., & Waslick, B. (1995). Elimination disorders. In G. O. Gabbard (Ed.), *Treatments of psychiatric disorders* (pp. 219–228). Washington, DC: American Psychiatric Press.

Shechtman, Z. (2002). Child group psychotherapy in the school at the threshold of a new millennium. *Journal of Counseling and Development, 80,* 293–299.

Sheperis, C. J., Renfro-Michel, E. L., & Doggett, R. A. (2003). In-home treatment of reactive attachment disorder in a therapeutic foster care system: A case example. *Journal of Mental Health Counseling, 25,* 76–88.

Sheridan, S. M. (2000). Considerations of multiculturalism and diversity in behavioral consultation with parents and teachers. *School Psychology Review, 29,* 389–400.

Sheridan, S. M., Welch, M., & Orme, S. F. (1996). Is consultation effective? A review of outcome research. *Remedial and Special Education, 17,* 341–354.

Shillingford, M. A., Lambie, G. W., & Walter, S. M. (2007). An integrative, cognitive-behavioral, systemic approach to working with students diagnosed with attention deficit hyperactive disorder. *Professional School Counseling, 11,* 105–112.

Shin, R., Daly, B., & Vera, E. (2007). The relationships of peer norms, ethnic identity, and peer support to school engagement in urban youth. *Professional School Counseling, 10,* 379–388.

Sigman, M., & Capps, L. (1997). *Children with autism: A developmental perspective.* Cambridge, MA: Harvard University Press.

Silver, L. B. (1995). Learning disorders. In G. O. Gabbard (Ed.), *Treatments of psychiatric disorders* (pp. 123–140). Washington, DC: American Psychiatric Press.

Silverman, J. G., Raj, A., Mucci, L. A., & Hathaway, J. E. (2001). Dating violence against adolescent girls and associated substance abuse, unhealthy weight control, sexual risk behavior, pregnancy, and suicidality. *Journal of the American Medical Association, 286,* 1263–1288.

Silverstein, D. M. (2004). Enuresis in children: Diagnosis and management. *Clinical Pediatrics, 43,* 217–221.

Sink, C. (Ed.). (2005a). *Contemporary school counseling: Theory, research, and practice.* Boston, MA: Houghton Mifflin/Lahaska.

Sink, C. A. (2005b). Comprehensive school counseling programs and academic achievement—A rejoinder to Brown and Trusty. *Professional School Counseling, 9,* 9–12.

Sink, C. A., & Spencer, L. R. (2005). My Class Inventory—Short Form as an accountability tool for elementary school counselors to measure classroom climate. *Professional School Counseling, 9,* 37–48.

Sink, C. A., & Spencer, L. R. (2007). Teacher version of the My Class Inventory—Short Form: An accountability tool for elementary school counselors. *Professional School Counseling, 11,* 129–139.

Sink, C. A., & Stroh, H. R. (2003). Raising achievement test scores of early elementary school students through comprehensive school counseling programs. *Professional School Counseling, 6,* 350–364.

Sink, C. A., & Stroh, H. R. (2006). Practical significance: The use of effect sizes in school counseling research. *Professional School Counseling, 9,* 401–411.

Sink, C. A., & Yillik-Downer, A. (2001). School counselors' perceptions of comprehensive guidance and counseling programs: A national survey. *Professional School Counseling, 4,* 278–288.

Sitlington, P. L., Clark, G. M., & Kolstoe, O. P. (2000). *Transition education and services for adolescents with disabilities* (3rd ed.). Boston, MA: Allyn & Bacon.

Skiba, R., & Fontanini, A. (2000). *Bullying prevention: What works in preventing school violence.* Bloomington, IN: Indiana Education Policy Center. (ERIC Document Reproduction Service No. ED470431)

Skinner, M. E., & Lindstrom, B. D. (2003). Bridging the gap between high school and college: Strategies for the successful transition of students with learning disabilities. *Preventing School Failure, 47,* 132–137.

Sklare, G. B. (2005). *Brief counseling that works: A solution-focused approach for school counselors and administrators* (2nd ed.). Thousand Oaks, CA: Corwin Press.

Smith, C. (2001). Using social stories to enhance behavior in children with autistic spectrum difficulties. *Educational Psychology in Practice, 17,* 337–345.

Smith, P. K., Morita, Y., Junger-Tas, J., Olwers, D., Catalano, R., & Slee, P. (Eds.). (1999). *The nature of school bullying: A cross-cultural perspective.* New York, NY: Routledge.

Smith, S. D., & Chen-Hayes, S. F. (2004). Leadership and advocacy for lesbian, bisexual, gay, transgendered, and questioning (LBGTQ) students: Academic, career, and interpersonal success strategies. In R. Perusse & G. E. Goodnough (Eds.), *Leadership, advocacy, and direct service strategies for professional school counselors* (pp. 187–221). Belmont, CA: Brooks/Cole-Thomson Learning.

Smith, S. L., Crutchfield, L. B., & Culbreth, J. R. (2001). Teaching experience for school counselors: Counselor educators' perceptions. *Professional School Counseling, 4,* 216–224.

Smith, S. R., Reddy, L. A., & Wingenfeld, S. A. (2002). Assessment of psychotic disorders in inpatient children and adolescents: Use of the Devereux Scales of Mental Disorders. *Journal of Psychopathology and Behavioral Assessment, 24,* 269–273.

Smith-Adcock, S., Daniels, M. H., Lee, S. M., Villalba, J. A., & Indelicato, N. A. (2006). Culturally responsive school counseling for Hispanic/Latino students and families: The need for bilingual school counselors. *Professional School Counseling, 10,* 92–101.

Snowling, M. J. (2002). Reading and other learning difficulties. In M. Rutter, E. Taylor, & L. Hersov (Eds.), *Child and adolescent psychiatry: Modern approaches* (4th ed., pp. 682–696). Cambridge, MA: Blackwell.

Snyder, H. (2001). Child delinquents. In R. Loeber & D. P. Farrington (Eds.), *Risk factors and successful interventions* (pp. 173–195). Thousand Oaks, CA: Sage.

Sommers-Flanagan, J., & Sommers-Flanagan, R. (2007). *Tough kids, cool counseling* (2nd ed.). Alexandria, VA: American Counseling Association.

Spaulding, F. E. (1915). Problems of vocational guidance. In M. Bloomfield (Ed.), *Readings in vocational guidance.* Cambridge, MA: Harvard University Press.

Speight, S. L., Myers, L. J., Cox, C. E., & Highlen, P. S. (1991). A redefinition of multicultural counseling. *Journal of Counseling & Development, 70,* 29–36.

Speltz, M. (1990). The treatment of preschool conduct problems: An integration of behavioral and attachment concepts. In M. Greenburg, D. Cicchetti, & E. M. Cummings (Eds.), *Attachment in the preschool years* (pp. 399–426). Chicago, IL: University of Chicago Press.

Sprague, J. R., & Golly, A. (2004). *Best behavior: Building positive behavior supports in schools.* Longmont, CO: Sopris West Educational Services.

Sprague, J. R., & Walker, H. M. (2004). *Safe and healthy schools: Practical prevention strategies.* New York, NY: Guilford Press.

Sprinthall, N. A. (1981). A new model for research in the science of guidance and counseling. *Personnel and Guidance Journal, 59,* 487–493.

State, M. W., King, B. H., & Dykens, E. (1997). Mental retardation: A review of the past 10 years. Part II. *Journal of the American Academy of Child and Adolescent Psychiatry, 36,* 1664–1671.

Stathakow, P., & Roehrle, B. (2003). The effectiveness of intervention programmes for children of divorce—A meta-analysis. *International Journal of Mental Health Promotion, 5,* 31–37.

Steele, C. M. (2007). A threat in the air: How stereotypes shape intellectual identity and performance. *American Psychologist, 52,* 613–629.

Steen, S., Bauman, S., & Smith, J. (2007). Professional school counselors and the practice of group work. *Professional School Counseling, 11,* 72–80.

Steen, S., & Kaffenberger, C. J. (2007). Integrating academic interventions into small group counseling in elementary school. *Professional School Counseling, 10,* 516–519.

Steigerwald, F. (2010a). Crisis intervention with individuals in the schools. In B. T. Erford (Ed.), *Professional school counseling: A handbook of theories, programs, and practices* (2nd ed., pp. 829–841). Austin, TX: PRO-ED.

Steigerwald, F. (2010b). Systemic crisis intervention in the schools. In B. T. Erford (Ed.), *Professional school counseling: A handbook of theories, programs, and practices* (2nd ed., pp. 843–849). Austin, TX: PRO-ED.

Stelmacher, Z. T. (1995). Assessing suicidal clients. In J. N. Butcher (Ed.), *Clinical personality assessment: Practical approaches* (pp. 366–379). New York, NY: Oxford University Press.

Stephens, W. R. (1970). *Social reform and the origins of vocational guidance.* Washington, DC: National Career Development Association.

Sterling-Turner, H. E., Watson, T. S., & Moore, J. W. (2002). The effects of direct training and treatment integrity on treatment outcomes in school consultation. *School Psychology Quarterly, 17,* 47–77.

Sterling-Turner, H. E., Watson, T. S., Wildmon, M., Watkins, C., & Little, E. (2001). Investigating the relationship between training type and treatment integrity. *School Psychology Quarterly, 16,* 56–67.

Stone, C. B. (2000). Advocacy for sexual harassment victims: Legal support and ethical aspects. *Professional School Counseling, 4,* 23–30.

Stone, C. B. (2004). School counselors as leaders and advocates in addressing sexual harassment. In R. Perusse & G. E. Goodnough (Eds.), *Leadership, advocacy, and direct service strategies for professional school counselors* (pp. 353–380). Belmont, CA: Brooks/Cole-Thomson Learning.

Stone, C. B. (2005). *School counseling and principles: Ethics and law.* Alexandria, VA: American School Counselor Association.

Stone, C. B., & Clark, M. (2001). School counselors and principals: Partners in support of academic achievement. *National Association of Secondary School Principals Bulletin, 85*(24), 46–53.

Stone, C. B., & Dahir, C. A. (2007). *School counselor accountability: A MEASURE of student success* (2nd. ed.). Upper Saddle River, NJ: Pearson Merrill/Prentice Hall.

Stone, L. A., & Bradley, F. O. (1994). *Foundations of elementary and middle school counseling.* White Plains, NY: Longman.

Stout, E. J., & Frame, M. W. (2004). Body image disorder in adolescent males: Strategies for school counselors. *Professional School Counseling, 8,* 176–181.

Stroh, H. R., & Sink, C. A. (2002). Applying APA's learner-centered principles to school-based counseling. *Professional School Counseling, 6,* 71–78.

Stuart, R. B. (2004). Twelve practical suggestions for achieving multicultural competence. *Professional Psychology: Research and Practice, 35,* 3–9.

Studer, J. R., Oberman, A. H., & Womack, R. H. (2006). Producing evidence to show counseling effectiveness in the schools. *Professional School Counseling, 9,* 385–391.

Substance Abuse and Mental Health Services Administration. (1995). *Cost of addictive and mental disorders and effectiveness of treatment.* Washington, DC: Author.

Substance Abuse and Mental Health Services Administration. (2002a). *Substance use and the risk of suicide among youths.* Washington, DC: Author. Retrieved February 16, 2005, from oas.samhsa.gov/2k2/suicide/suicide.html

Substance Abuse and Mental Health Services Administration. (2002b). *Report to Congress on the prevention and treatment of co-occurring substance abuse disorders and mental disorders.* Rockville, MD: Author. Retrieved November 15, 2008, from www.samhsa.gov/reports/congress2002/chap1ucod.htm#3

Substance Abuse and Mental Health Services Administration. (2008). Facts on Children's Mental Health. Retrieved November 15, 2008, from www.samhsa.gov/reports/congress2002/chap1ucod.htm#3

Sue, D. W., Arredondo, P., & McDavis, R. J. (1992). Multicultural competencies/standards: A pressing need. *Journal of Counseling and Development, 70,* 477–486.

Sue, D. W., & Sue, D. (2003). *Counseling the culturally different: Theory and practice* (3rd ed.). New York, NY: Wiley.

Sue, S. (1998). In search of cultural competence in psychotherapy and counseling. *American Psychologist, 53,* 440–448.

Sugai, G., Horner, R. H., Dunlap, G., Hieneman, M., Lewis, T. J., Nelson, C. M., . . . Wilcox, B. (2000). Applying positive behavior support and functional behavioral assessment in schools. *Journal of Positive Behavior Interventions, 2,* 131–143.

Sugai, G., Horner, R. H., & Gresham, F. M. (2002). Behaviorally effective school environments. In M. R. Shinn, H. M. Walker, & G. Stoner (Eds.), *Interventions for academic and behavior problems: Preventive and remedial approaches* (2nd ed., pp. 315–341). Bethesda, MD: National Association of School Psychologists.

Suh, S., & Satcher, J. (2005). Understanding at-risk Korean American youth. *Professional School Counseling, 8,* 428–435.

Super, D. E. (1957). *A psychology of careers.* New York, NY: Harper & Row.

Super, D. E. (1977). Vocational maturity in midcareer. *Vocational Guidance Quarterly, 25,* 294–302.

Super, D. E. (1980). A life span, life space approach to career development. *Journal of Vocational Behavior, 16,* 282–298.

Super, D. E. (1990). Career and life development. In D. Brown & L. Brooks (Eds.), *Career choice and development: Applying contemporary theories to practice* (2nd ed., pp. 197–261). San Francisco, CA: Jossey-Bass.

Super, D. E., Savickas, M. L., & Super, C. M. (1996). The life span, life-space approach to careers. In D. Brown & L. Brooks (Eds.), *Career choice and development: Applying contemporary theories to practice* (3rd ed., pp. 121–178). San Francisco, CA: Jossey-Bass.

Super, D. E., Thompson, A. S., & Lindeman, R. H. (1988). *Adult Career Concerns Inventory: Manual for research and exploratory use in counseling.* Palo Alto, CA: Consulting Psychologists Press.

Swadener, B. B., & Lubeck, S. (Eds.). (1995). *Children and families "at promise": Deconstructing the discourse of risk.* Albany: State University of New York Press.

Sweeney, T. J. (2001). Counseling: Historical origins and philosophical roots. In D. C. Locke, J. Myers, & E. L. Herr (Eds.), *The handbook of counseling* (pp. 1–13). Thousand Oaks, CA: Sage.

Tang, M., Pan, W., & Newmeyer, M. D. (2008). Factors influencing high school students' career aspirations. *Professional School Counseling, 11,* 285–295.

Tarasoff v. Regents of the University of California, 17 Cal. 3d 425, 551 P.2d 334 (Cal. 1976).

Tarver-Behring, S., & Ingraham, C. L. (1998). Culture as a central component to consultation: A call to the field. *Journal of Educational and Psychological Consultation, 9,* 57–72.

Taub, D. J. (2006). Understanding the concerns of parents of students with disabilities: Challenges and roles for school counselors. *Professional School Counselors, 10,* 51–57.

Taylor, L., & Adelman, H. (2000). Connecting schools, families, and communities. *Professional School Counseling, 3,* 298–307.

Teachers for a New Era. (2001). *Announcement and prospectus and executive summary.* Retrieved February 20, 2009, from teachersforanewera.org/index.cfm?fuseaction=home.prospectus

The Education Trust. (1999). *Dispelling the myth: High poverty schools exceeding expectations.* Washington, DC: Author.

Thabet, A. A. M., Abed, Y., & Vostanis, P. (2004). Comorbidity of PTSD and depression among refugee children during war conflict. *Journal of Child Psychology and Psychiatry, 45,* 533–542.

Theberge, S. K., & Karan, O. (2004). Six factors inhibiting the use of peer mediation in a junior high school. *Professional School Counseling, 7,* 283–290.

Thomas, R. M. (2005). *Comparing theories of child development* (6th ed.). Belmont, CA: Wadsworth.

Thomas, V., & Ray, K. E. (2006). Counseling exceptional individuals and their families: A systems perspective. *Professional School Counseling, 10,* 58–65.

Thompson, C. L., & Henderson, D. A. (2007). *Counseling children* (7th ed.). Belmont, CA: Thomson Brooks/Cole.

Thompson, R., & Littrell, J. M. (1998). Brief counseling for students with learning disabilities. *Professional School Counseling, 2,* 60–67.

Toporek, R. L. (1999, June). Advocacy: A voice for our clients and communities: Developing a framework for understanding advocacy in counseling. *Counseling Today,* 34–35, 39.

Towbin, K. E., & Cohen, D. J. (1996). Tic disorders. In J. M. Wiener (Ed.), *Diagnosis and psychopharmacology of childhood and adolescent disorders* (2nd ed., pp. 349–369). New York, NY: Wiley.

Towbin, K. E., Cohen, D. J., & Lechman, J. F. (1995). Tic disorders. In G. O. Gabbard (Ed.), *Treatments of psychiatric disorders* (pp. 201–218). Washington, DC: American Psychiatric Press.

Traxler, A. E., & North, R. D. (1966). *Techniques of guidance.* New York, NY: Harper & Row.

Trevisan, M. S., & Hubert, M. (2001). Implementing comprehensive guidance program evaluation support: Lessons learned. *Professional School Counseling, 2,* 225–228.

Trusty, J. (1999). Effects of eighth-grade parental involvement on late adolescents' educational experiences. *Journal of Research and Development in Education, 32,* 224–233.

Trusty, J., & Brown, D. (2005). Advocacy competencies for professional school counselors. *Professional School Counseling, 8,* 259–265.

Trusty, J., & Niles, S. G. (2003). High-school math courses and completion of the bachelor's degree. *Professional School Counseling, 7,* 99–107.

Trusty, J., & Niles, S. G. (2004). Realized potential or lost talent: High-school variables and bachelor's degree completion. *Career Development Quarterly, 53,* 2–13.

Trusty, J., Niles, S. G., & Carney, J. V. (2005). Education-career planning and middle school counselors. *Professional School Counseling, 9,* 136–143.

Turner, S. L., Conkel, J. L., Starkey, M., Landgraf, R., Lapan, R. T., Siewert, J. J., . . . Huang, J. (2008). Gender differences in Holland vocational personality types: Implications for school counselors. *Professional School Counseling, 11,* 317–326.

Tynan, W. (2006). *Conduct disorder.* Retrieved December 6, 2008, from www.emedicine.com/ped/TOPIC2793.htm

Tynan, W. (2008). *Oppositional defiant disorder.* Retrieved December 6, 2008, from www.emedicine.com/ped/TOPIC2791.htm

U.S. Bureau of Census. (2008). *The official statistics.* Washington, DC: Author.

U.S. Department of Education, Office of Special Education and Rehabilitative Services. (1999). *IDEA '97 amendments, final regulations.* Retrieved April 1, 2005, from www.ed.gov/policy/speced/reg/regulations.html

U.S. Department of Education. (2001). *The No Child Left Behind Act of 2001.* Retrieved January 3, 2005, from www.ed.gov/policy/elsec/leg/esea02/index.html

U.S. Department of Education. (2002). *No Child Left Behind.* Retrieved August 20, 2005, from www.ed.gov/nclb/landing.jhtml?src5pb

U.S. Department of Education (2003). *National Assessment of Educational Progress (NAEP).* Washington, DC: Author.

U.S. Department of Education. (2005a). *Digest of educational statistics.* Washington, DC: Author.

U.S. Department of Education. (2005b, February). *FY 2006 program performance plan.* Washington, DC: Author.

U.S. Department of Education, National Center for Education Statistics. (2005c). *The condition of education 2005.* Washington, DC: Author.

U.S. Department of Education, Office for Civil Rights. (2005d). *Regulations enforced by the Office for Civil Rights (Section 504).* Retrieved August 20, 2005, from www.ed.gov/policy/rights/reg/ocr/index.html

U.S. Department of Education, Office of Special Education Programs. (2005e). *IDEA 2004 resources.* Available at www.ed.gov/policy/speced/guid/idea/idea2004.html

U.S. Department of Education, National Center for Education Statistics. (2006, May). *Statistics in brief.* Washington, DC: Author.

U.S. Department of Education, Office of Educational Research and Improvement. (2008). *Reaching all families: Creating family friendly schools.* Washington, DC: Author.

U.S. Department of Health and Human Services. (2000). *Report of the Surgeon General's Conference on Children's Mental Health: A national action agenda.* Rockville, MD: Author.

U.S. Department of Health and Human Services, U.S. Public Health Service, Office of Surgeon General. (2001). *Youth violence: A report of the surgeon general.* Washington, DC: Author.

U.S. Department of Health and Human Services. (2004). *Your rights under Section 504 of the Rehabilitation Act.* Washington, DC: Author. Retrieved July 9, 2005, from www.hhs.gov/ocr/504.html

U.S. Department of Health and Human Services. (2008). U.S. Department of Health and Human Services home page. Retrieved November 27, 2008, from www.hhs.gov

U.S. Department of Labor, Manpower Administration, Bureau of Employment Security. (1939). *Dictionary of occupational titles.* Washington, DC: Author.

U.S. Department of Labor, Bureau of Labor Statistics. (1949). *Occupational outlook handbook.* Washington, DC: Author.

U.S. Department of Labor, National Occupational Information Coordinating Committee. (1992). *The national career development guidelines project.* Washington, DC: Author.

Varjas, K., Graybill, E., Mahan, W., Meyers, J., Dew, B., Marshall, M., . . . Birckbichler, L. (2007). Urban service providers' perspectives on school responses to gay, lesbian, and questioning students: An exploratory study. *Professional School Counseling, 11,* 113–119.

Vela-Gude, L., Cavazos, J., Johnson, M. B., Fielding, C., Cavazos, A. G., Campos, L., & Rodriguez, I. (2009). "My counselors were never there": Perceptions from Latino college students. *Professional School Counseling, 12,* 272–279.

Vera, E. M., Shin, R. Q., Montgomery, G. P., Mildner, C., & Speight, S. L. (2004). Conflict resolution styles, self-efficacy, self-control, and future orientation of urban adolescents. *Professional School Counseling, 8,* 73–80.

Vernon, A. (1993). *Developmental assessment and intervention with children and adolescents.* Alexandria, VA: American Counseling Association.

Vernon, A. (1998). *The PASSPORT program: A journey through emotional, social, cognitive, and self-development.* Champaign, IL: Research Press.

Vernon, A. (2004). Working with children, adolescents, and their parents: Practical application of developmental theory. In A. Vernon (Ed.), *Counseling children and adolescents* (4th ed., pp. 1–34). Denver, CO: Love.

Villalba, J. A. (2003). A psychoeducational group for limited-English proficient Latino/Latina children. *Journal for Specialists in Group Work, 38,* 261–276.

Villalba, J. A., Akos, P., Keeter, K., & Ames, A. (2007). Promoting Latino student achievement and development through the ASCA national model. *Professional School Counseling, 10,* 464–474.

Villalba, J. A., Brunelli, M., Lewis, L., & Orfanedes, D. (2007). Experiences of Latino children attending rural elementary schools in the southeastern U.S.: Perspectives from Latino parents in burgeoning Latino communities. *Professional School Counseling, 10,* 506–509.

Volkmar, F. R. (1996). Childhood and adolescent psychosis: A review of the past 10 years. *Journal of the American Academy of Child and Adolescent Psychiatry, 35,* 843–851.

Vontress, C. E. (1970). Counseling blacks. *Personnel and Guidance Journal, 48,* 713–719.

Vontress, C. E. (1988). An existential approach to cross-cultural counseling. *Journal of Multicultural Counseling and Development, 16,* 73–83.

Voydanoff, P., & Donnelly, B. W. (1998). Parents' risk and protective factors as predictors of parental well-being and behavior. *Journal of Marriage and Family, 60,* 344–355.

Vygotsky, L. S. (1978). *Mind in society: The development of higher psychological processes.* Cambridge, MA: Harvard University Press.

Wagner, M., Blackorby, J., Cameto, R., & Newman, L. (1993). *What makes a difference? Influences on postschool outcomes of youth with disabilities.* Menlo Park, CA: SRI International.

Wagner, M., Newman, L., & Cameto, R. (2004). *Changes over time in the secondary school experiences of students with disabilities: A special topic report of findings from the National Longitudinal Transition Study-2 (NLTS2).* Menlo Park, CA: SRI International. Available at www.nlts2.org/pdfs/changestime_compreport.pdf

Wahl, K. H., & Blackhurst, A. (2000). Factors affecting the occupational and educational aspirations of children and adolescents. *Professional School Counseling, 3,* 367–374.

Wakeling, A. (1996). Epidemiology of anorexia nervosa. *Psychiatry Research, 62,* 3–9.

Walsh, M. E., Barrett, J. G., & DePaul, J. (2007). Day-to-day activities of school counselors: Alignment with new directions in the field and the ASCA national model. *Professional School Counseling, 10,* 370–378.

Walter, J. L., & Peller, J. E. (1992). *Becoming solution-focused in brief therapy.* New York, NY: Brunner/Mazel.

Watkins, K. E., & Ellickson, P. L., Vaiana, M. E., & Hiromoto, S. (2006). An update on adolescent drug use: What school counselors need to know. *Professional School Counseling, 10,* 131–138.

Watson, S., Watson, T., & Weaver, A. (2010). Direct behavioral consultation: An effective method for conducting school collaboration. In B. T. Erford (Ed.), *Professional school counseling: A handbook of theories, programs & practices* (2nd ed.). Austin, TX: pro-ed.

Watson, T. S., Butler, T. S., Weaver, A. D., & Foster, N. (2004). Direct behavioral consultation: An effective method for promoting school collaboration. In B. T. Erford (Ed.), *Professional school counseling: A handbook of theories, programs, and practices* (pp. 341–347). Austin, TX: PRO-ED.

Webb, L. D., Brigman, G. A., & Campbell, C. (2005). Linking school counselors and student success: A replication of the Student Success Skills approach targeting the academic and social competence of students. *Professional School Counseling, 8,* 407–413.

Webb, L. D., & Myrick, R. D. (2003). A group counseling intervention for children with attention deficit hyperactivity disorder. *Professional School Counseling, 7,* 108–115.

Webster-Stratton, C., & Dahl, R. W. (1995). Conduct disorders. In M. Hersen & R. T. Ammerman (Eds.), *Advanced abnormal child psychology* (pp. 333–352). Hillsdale, NJ: Erlbaum.

Webster-Stratton, C., & Taylor, T. (2001). Nipping early risk factors in the bud: Preventing substance abuse, delinquency, and violence in adolescence through interventions targeted at young children (0–8 years). *Prevention Science, 2*(3), 165–192.

Wechsler, D. (2001). *Wechsler Intelligence Scale for Children–4th edition.* San Antonio, TX: Psychological Corporation.

Weems, C. F., & Carrion, V. G. (2003). The treatment of separation anxiety disorder employing attachment theory and cognitive behavior therapy techniques. *Clinical Case Studies, 2,* 188–198.

Wehrly, B. (1995). *Pathways to multicultural counseling competence: A developmental journey.* Pacific Grove, CA: Brooks/Cole.

Weiss, C. (1998). *Evaluation* (2nd ed.). Upper Saddle River, NJ: Prentice Hall.

Weissman, M. M., Wolk, S., Goldstein, R. B., Moreau, D., Adams, P., Greenwald, S., . . . Wickramaratne, P. (1999). Depressed adolescents grown up. *Journal of the American Medical Association, 282,* 1701–1713.

Weist, M. (1997). Expanded school mental health services: A national movement in progress. In T. Ollendick & R. Prinz (Eds.), *Advances in clinical child psychology* (Vol. 19, pp. 319–352). New York, NY: Plenum Press.

Weisz, J. R., Weiss, B., Han, S. S., Grander, D. A., & Morton, T. (1995). Effects of psychotherapy with children and adolescents revisited: A meta-analysis of treatment outcome studies. *Psychological Bulletin, 117,* 450–468.

Weitzman, S. (1998). *Upscale violence: The lived experience of domestic abuse among upper socioeconomic status* (Unpublished doctoral dissertation, Loyola University, Chicago).

Wells, R., & Giannetti, V. (1990). *Handbook of the brief psychotherapies.* New York, NY: Plenum Press.

Wessler, S. L., & Preble, W. (2003). *The respectful school: How educators and students can conquer hate and harassment.* Alexandria, VA: Association for Supervision and Curriculum Development.

Westat & Policy Studies Associates. (2001). *The longitudinal evaluation of school change and performance in Title I schools.* Washington, DC: U.S. Department of Education.

Whalen, C. K., & Henker, B. (1991). Therapies for hyperactive children: Comparisons, combinations, and compromises. *Journal of Consulting and Clinical Psychology, 59,* 126–137.

Wheeler, A. M., & Bertram, B. (2008). *The counselor and the law: A guide to legal and ethical practice* (5th ed.). Alexandria, VA: American Counseling Association.

Whiston, S. C. (2002). Response to the past, present, and future of school counseling: Raising some issues. *Professional School Counseling, 5,* 148–155.

Whiston, S. C., & Aricak, O. T. (2008). Development and initial investigation of the School Counseling Program Evaluation Scale. *Professional School Counseling, 11,* 253–261.

Whiston, S. C., Brecheisen, B. K., & Stephens, J. (2003). Does treatment modality affect career counseling effectiveness? *Journal of Vocational Behavior, 62,* 390–410.

Whiston, S. C., & Oliver, L. (2005). Career counseling process and outcome. In W. B. Walsh & M. Savickas (Eds.), *Handbook of vocational psychology* (3rd ed., pp. 155–194). Hillsdale, NJ: Erlbaum.

Whiston, S. C., & Rahardja, D. (2008). Vocational counseling process and outcome. In S. D. Brown & R. W. Lent (Eds.), *Handbook of counseling psychology* (4th ed., pp. 444–461). New York, NY: Wiley.

Whiston, S. C., Rahardja, D., Eder, K., & Tai, W. L. (2008). *School counseling outcome: A meta-analytic examination of interventions.* Unpublished manuscript, Indiana University, Bloomington.

Whiston, S. C., & Sexton, T. L. (1998). A review of school counseling outcome research: Implications for practice. *Journal of Counseling and Development, 76,* 412–426.

Whiston, S. C., Sexton, T. L., & Lasoff, D. L. (1998). Career intervention outcome: A replication and extension. *Journal of Counseling Psychology, 45,* 150–165.

Whiston, S. C., & Wachter, C. (2008). *School counseling, student achievement, and dropout rates: Student outcome research in the state of Indiana* (Special Report). Indianapolis: Indiana State Department of Education.

White, K. R., Taylor, M. J., & Moss, V. T. (1992). Does research support claims about the benefits of involving parents in early intervention programs? *Review of Educational Research, 62,* 91–125.

White-Kress, V. E., Drouhard, N., & Costin, A. (2006). Students who self-injure: School counselor ethical and legal considerations. *Professional School Counseling, 10,* 203–209.

Whiteside, M. F., & Becker, B. J. (2000). Parent factors and the young child's post divorce adjustment: A meta-analysis with implications for parenting arrangements. *Journal of Family Psychology, 14,* 5–26.

Wicks-Nelson, R., & Israel, A. C. (2003). *Behavior disorders of childhood.* Upper Saddle River, NJ: Prentice Hall.

Wiggins, J. D., & Wiggins, A. H. (1992). Elementary students' self-esteem and behavioral ratings related to counselor time-task emphases. *School Counselor, 39,* 377–381.

Williams, F. C., & Butler, S. K. (2003). Concerns of newly arrived immigrant students: Implications for school counselors. *Professional School Counseling, 7,* 9–14.

Williams, K. M. (2001). "Frontin' It": School violence, and relationships in the hood. In J. N. Burstyn, G. Bender, R. Casella, H. W. Gordon, D. P. Guerra, K. V. Luschen, . . . K. M. Williams (Eds.), *Preventing violence in schools: A challenge to American democracy* (pp. 95–108). Mahwah, NJ: Erlbaum.

Williamson, E. G. (1965). *Vocational counseling: Some historical, philosophical, and theoretical perspectives.* New York, NY: McGraw-Hill.

Wilson, F. R. (2004, September). *Assessing violence risk: An ecological analysis.* Paper presented at the Association for Assessment in Counseling 2004 National Assessment Conference, Charleston, SC.

Wilson, N. S. (1986). Counselor interventions with low-achieving and underachieving elementary, middle, and high school students: A review of literature. *Journal of Counseling and Development, 64,* 628–634.

Wilson, S. J., Lipsey, M. W., & Derzon, J. H. (2003). The effects of school-based intervention programs on aggressive behavior: A meta-analysis. *Journal of Consulting and Clinical Psychology, 71,* 136–149.

Wolfe, D. A., Sas, L., & Wekerle, C. (1994). Factors associated with the development of posttraumatic stress disorder among child victims of sexual abuse. *Child Abuse and Neglect, 18,* 37–50.

Wood Dunn, N. A., & Baker, S. B. (2002). Readiness to serve students with disabilities: A survey of elementary school counselors. *Professional School Counseling, 5,* 277–284.

Worden, J. W. (2002). *Grief counseling and grief therapy: A handbook for the mental health practitioner* (3rd ed.). New York, NY: Springer.

Worsham, H. (2005). The constants: Change and professional growth. *Professional School Counseling, 9,* 173–174.

Worthen, B. B., Sanders, J. R., & Fitzpatrick, J. L. (1997). *Program evaluation: Alternative approaches and practical guidelines* (2nd ed.). New York, NY: Longman.

Wrenn, C. G. (1962). *The counselor in a changing world.* Washington, DC: American Personnel and Guidance Association.

Wright, K., & Stegelin, D. A. (2003). *Building school and community partnerships through parent involvement* (2nd ed.). Upper Saddle River, NJ: Merrill/Prentice Hall.

Wu, P., Hoven, C. W., Liu, X., Cohen, P., Fuller, C. J., & Shaffer, D. (2004). Substance use, suicidal ideation and attempts in children and adolescents. *Suicide and Life-Threatening Behavior, 34,* 408–420.

Wyke v. Polk County School Board, 129 F.3d 560 (11th Cir. 1997).

Yalom, I. D., & Leszcz, M. (2005). *The theory and practice of group psychotherapy* (5th ed.). New York, NY: Basic Books.

Yeh, C. J. (2001). An exploratory study of school counselors' experiences with and perceptions of Asian-American students. *Professional School Counseling, 4,* 349–356.

Young, A. R., & Beitchman, J. H. (2002). Reading and other specific learning difficulties. In P. Howlin & O. Udwin (Eds.), *Outcomes in neurodevelopmental and genetic disorders* (pp. 405–438). New York, NY: Cambridge University Press.

Young, D. S. (2005). Today's lesson by . . . Roosevelt? The use of character portrayal in classroom guidance. *Professional School Counselor, 8,* 366–371.

Young, I. M. (1990). *Justice and the politics of difference.* Princeton, NJ: Princeton University Press.

Young, T. L., & Zimmerman, R. (1998). Clueless: Parental knowledge of risk behaviors of middle school students. *Archives of Pediatrics and Adolescent Medicine, 152,* 1138–1139.

Zahn-Waxler, C., Shirtcliff, E. A., & Maraceau, K. (2008). Disorders of childhood and adolescence: Gender and psychopathology. *Annual Review of Clinical Psychology, 4,* 275–303.

Zeanah, C. H., & Emde, R. N. (1994). Attachment disorders in infancy and childhood. In M. Rutter, E. Taylor, & L. Hersov (Eds.), *Child and adolescent psychiatry: Modern approaches* (pp. 490–504). Cambridge, MA: Blackwell.

Zimmerman, M. A. (2000). Empowerment theory: Psychological, organizational and community levels of analysis. In J. Rappaport & E. Seidman (Eds.), *Handbook of community psychology* (pp. 43–64). New York, NY: Plenum.

Zinck, K., & Littrell, J. M. (2000). Action research shows group counseling effective with at-risk adolescent girls. *Professional School Counseling, 4,* 50–59.

Zinn, H. (2003). *A people's history of the United States: 1492–present* (Rev. ed.). New York, NY: Perennial Classics.

Zins, J. E. (1993). Enhancing consultee problem-solving skills in consultative interactions. *Journal of Counseling and Development, 72,* 185–190.

NAME INDEX

SUBJECT INDEX

A

ABCDs of learning objectives, 167–168
ABC logs, 328–329
Ableism, 94
Abortion services, 83–84
About Me collages, 183
Absenteeism, 306
Abuse, 297–298
ACA. *See* American Counseling Association (ACA)
ACA Code of Ethics, 70, 71–73, 80, 81, 95
ACA Code of Ethics and Standards of Practice, 72–73
Academic achievement
  accountability for, 12
  at-risk students and, 291
  counseling program effect on, 66–67
  educational/career planning and, 203, 205, 217
  expectation of, 15
  gap in, 2–3
  international comparisons of, 4–6
  parental involvement and, 40, 240–241
Academic development, 30–31
  needs assessment for, 253
  outcomes research on, 63
Academic domain, 46
Academic justice, 39
Academic skills, in transition to work/postsecondary education, 214
Acceptance, 187, 304
Access gaps
  assessment of, 144
  data on, 134–135
  definition of, 111
  parent/guardian empowerment and, 121
Accountability, 1, 15–18, 245–287
  advantages and disadvantages of studies in, 246
  challenges in, 13
  classroom guidance and, 155–156
  of counselors, 12
  counselors as experts in, 40–41
  definition of, 53
  evaluation and, 152
  lack of, 247
  leadership and, 113
  outcomes research and, 58
  practical guidelines for evaluating, 258
  resistance to, 256
  for school-level interventions, 151
  shared, in collaboration, 229
  standards-based, 6–7
  for students with complex problems, 312
Accountability systems, 53–54
ACES Standards for Counselor Education in the Preparation of Secondary School Counselors, 30
Achenbach System of Empirically Based Assessment (ASEBA), 326
Achievement advocacy, 113, 114
  community stakeholders in, 124–125
  empowering students with, 119–120
  by parents/guardians, 121
  publicizing, 125–127

school systems in, 123–124
student fears of, 119
by teachers, 121–122
Achievement data, 101, 135–138, 144
Achievement gaps, 110–111
  data on, 101, 135
  definition of, 94, 111
  disaggregated data on, 249–250
Action, in total behavior, 191
Action plans, 52–53, 132
Action research, 263
Adderall, 354–355
Adequate yearly progress (AYP), 7, 144
AD/HD. *See* Attention-deficit/hyperactivity disorder (AD/HD)
Adjustment disorders, 369
Adlerian psychology, 162, 187
Administrative duties, 114
Administrators. *See also* Principals
  in community-level interventions, 152
  consultation with, 49
  empowering for achievement advocacy, 123–124
Adolescence
  confidentiality and, 184
  development in, 181–182
  educational/career planning in, 210–213
  middle school career planning and, 210
Adoption, 83–84
Adult Career Concerns Inventory, 215
Advanced Placement programs, 17, 135, 136
Adventure-based education, 159
Advisory councils, 52
Advocacy
  ACA Competencies in, 115–119
  for academic content, 8–9
  for achievement, 113, 114, 119–128
  ASCA National Model on, 45
  client/student, 115–117
  counseling, 115–125
  in counseling practice, 12, 14–15
  data-driven, 14
  definition of, 113
  dispositions for, 118
  history of, 113–114
  importance of, 114–115
  leadership and, 112–113
  proactive, 113
  public arena, 115
  publicizing, 125–127
  school/community, 115, 116, 117–118
  school systems in, 123–124
  social justice, 39
  social/political, 117
  for special needs students, 41
  by students, 119–120
  for students with complex problems, 312
  by students with disabilities, 336
  for students with disabilities, 325, 338–339
  systems, 116–117
  by teachers, 121–122
  Transforming School Counseling Initiative on, 9–10
Affective domain, 166–167

Affirmation, 187
African-Americans. *See also* Multicultural issues
  achievement gap among, 249–250
  demographics of, 91
  in school integration, 26–27
  utilization by, 60–61
  view of family in, 98
Ageism, 94
Agencies
  collaboration with, 238
  community, in systems support, 50
  local/state, 74–75
Agendas, shared, 234
Age of majority, 80
Aggregated data, 247–249, 258–260
Aggression, 64, 303, 343. *See also* Violence
Alcohol abuse, 296, 301–302, 364–365. *See also* Substance abuse
Alienation, 289
Alignment
  consultation and, 234
  of counseling programs and school goals, 12, 145–146
  program audits and, 53
  of standards with objectives, 259–260
Alliance building, 234
AMCD (Association for Multicultural Counseling and Development), 94–95, 104
American Association of Mental Retardation (AAMR), 349
American Board for Professional Standards in Vocational Guidance, 25
American College Personnel Association, 24, 25
American Counseling Association (ACA), 70–71, 194, 223–227
  Advocacy Competencies, 115–119
  on counselor-student ratios, 28
  on multicultural competence, 138
  on multicultural counseling, 340
  Multicultural Counseling Competencies, 95
  on subpoenas, 79–80
American Diploma Project, 9
American High School Today (Conant), 25
American Personnel and Guidance Association (APGA), 24–25
American Psychological Association, 95
American School Counselor Association (ASCA), 9. *See also National Standards for School Counseling Programs, The* (ASCA)
  codes of ethics, 72, 73–74
  on confidentiality, 80
  counseling definition by, 179
  on counseling students with disabilities, 315–316
  Counselor Performance Standards, 283–286
  on counselor-student ratios, 28, 223
  founding of, 24
  on group counseling permission, 197
  on multicultural counseling, 91
  on professionalism, 38
  publications of, 71
  on response to intervention, 343–344
Analysis, 166
Anger management, 64

415

JAPAN
53 Kasumigaseki
54 Fujioka

INDIA
55 Royal Calcutta

HONG KONG
56 Royal Hong Kong

SINGAPORE
57 Singapore Island

MALAYSIA
58 Royal Selangor

INDONESIA
59 Bali Handara

AUSTRALIA
60 Royal Melbourne
61 Royal Adelaide
62 Royal Sydney

NEW ZEALAND
63 Paraparaumu

SOUTH AFRICA
64 Durban Country Club
65 Royal Johannesburg

MOROCCO
66 Royal Rabat

THE
WORLD ATLAS OF
GOLF COURSES

THE
WORLD ATLAS OF
GOLF COURSES

BOB FERRIER

HAMLYN

Half title page: *The beautiful 5th hole at Muirfield Village, Jack Nicklaus' creation in his home state of Ohio.*

Title page: *The difficult 16th hole at Augusta, one of the most famous golf courses in the world and the permanent home of the U.S. Masters tournament.*

Above: *Cypress Point, and two of its famous holes – the 16th and 17th – showing to good effect the dramatic Monterey scenery.*

Published in 1990
by The Hamlyn Publishing Group Limited
a division of The Octopus Publishing Group,
Michelin House, 81 Fulham Road, London SW3 6RB

ISBN 0 600 56806 7

Produced by Mandarin Offset
Printed in Hong Kong

CONTENTS

INTRODUCTION

Golf is a solitary, subjective game, a fact enhanced by the truths that every golf course is different from the other, no golf hole ever plays twice in quite the same way, and no single golf shot can be repeated exactly. The weather, if nothing else, will see to all of that. True, golf courses have a few basic elements in common – trees, greens, hazards and, throughout most of the world, grass on the fairways. But they inhabit a wide variety of landscape – moorland, heathland, linksland, meadowland, parkland. They have prospered in humdrum suburbs and along magnificent cliff tops. Some of the greatest are public courses – Pebble Beach, Carnoustie, St Andrews. Some of the greatest are entirely and severely private – Augusta, Muirfield.

In establishing 'greatness', a treacherous quality, among the world's golf courses, we have tried to use certain basic criteria. Perhaps the most important is balance, and that is perhaps best expressed in the philosophy of Donald Ross, the Dornoch man who emigrated to the United States and over a span of some 40 years proved himself an outstanding designer involved in hundreds of golf courses. He believed that 'The championship course should call for long and accurate tee shots, accurate iron play, precise handling of the short game, and finally, consistent putting. These abilities should be called for in a proportion that will not permit excellence in one department of the game to affect too large deficiencies in another'. The championship course should ask the player from time to time to take risks, rewarding him if he is successful and punishing him if he is not; the reward should be in proportion to the size of the risk, and the punishment should reflect the extent of a failure to overcome it. The holes should have variety of length and direction, straight holes, dog-legs either way, uphill, downhill and so on, with varied green sizes and shapes, and hazards. The scenic quality of the course and its surroundings should add to the pleasure of the player, and the course should have history to sustain it.

In designing golf courses, the architect must work to the same norm as does the handicap committee of the club – that of the scratch golfer. All our references to the playing of these great golf courses have been based on the abilities of the scratch golfer – indeed, the championship golfer. If this is necessarily unfair to the average golfer, who is more likely to have a handicap of 18, nevertheless the average player can get immense pleasure from these courses even if he does not play them from the championship tees.

Our selection has been based on the observations, experiences, convictions of the most respected players, architects and observers of the great game, and from our own persuasions, prejudices and total golf experience. We trust that among them will be your favourites.

Bob Ferrier

Michael Allen on the 16th tee during the Scottish Open, held on the King's course at Gleneagles, the premier Scottish golf 'resort'. Allen, an American, went on to win the tournament.

THE AMERICAS

Golf imitates life in North America, where the vast mass of the United States, the energy and vision of its people, the sheer affluence of its society, have made it golf's world leader.

There was 18th century golf, in colonial America, at Savannah and Charleston, but the game was formalised in the 1880s; half a dozen select clubs formed the U.S. Golf Association. Canada was slightly ahead. Royal Montreal, 1873, is the oldest extant American club.

The game then expanded hugely in the 1920s, and again in the 1950s and subsequently, with the televising of great championships and champions such as Ben Hogan, Arnold Palmer, Jack Nicklaus, Lee Trevino and Tom Watson. The result is that there are several million golfers in the U.S., playing at clubs which range from the highly exclusive and fearsomely expensive, to the hundreds of public courses. In North America, golf is everyman's game.

The variety of terrain – desert, mountain, prairie, forest, beach – has enabled American golf architects to produce imaginative and often beautiful courses, the financing of which has often been sustained by sophisticated hotel and resort development, and property sales.

By contrast, the game in South America has remained aristocratic and expensive and is perhaps most advanced in the countries which consider themselves to be most 'European' – Argentina and Chile.

View from the tee of the short but treacherous 16th hole at Augusta where many a contender's challenge has come to nothing.

SHINNECOCK HILLS

Of all the great championship courses in America, Shinnecock Hills is the least known and the least played. Yet, it has a most distinctive place in the history of American golf. It was one of the five founding clubs which in December 1894 formed the Amateur Golf Association of America, which quickly became the American Golf Association, and then the United States Golf Association.

The other founding clubs were the St Andrews Club of New York, The Country Club, at Brookline, near Boston, the Newport Golf Club of Rhode Island and the Chicago Golf Club at Wheaton. Samuel Parrish from the Shinnecock club became the first treasurer of the USGA. The following year, they were able to stage the first Open and Amateur championships, at the Newport Club, and in 1896 it was Shinnecock's turn.

The club had its origins in a visit made to Biarritz by three Long Island gentlemen of means, wintering in France in 1890–91. They were William K. Vanderbilt, Edward S. Mead and Duncan Cryder. They came across young Willie Dunn, a Scottish professional who had

Willie Anderson, a dour Scot, shows a nice line in bent left elbows. A dominant force in the U.S. Open, Anderson in 1903–5 became the only man to take the title three years in a row.

ambitions as an architect and who was designing 18 holes at Biarritz. It was arranged that Dunn should cross to Southampton – a fashionable summer resort at the eastern end of Long Island – when he had finished at Biarritz, and find a piece of land suitable for a course he would then design.

Dunn arrived in March 1891 and was taken on a tour of the Southampton area, eventually settling on a treeless area of scrubland among low-lying sandhills by the south shore of Great Peconic Bay, and only a couple of miles from the ocean. The site was to provide a course unique in American golf. It was within a few minutes of the Southampton resort, and hard by the railroad which had brought the area within 2½ hours of Manhattan, a good 100 miles away.

SHINNECOCK HILLS						
Card of the course						
1	399 yards	par 4	10	412 yards	par 4
2	221 yards	par 3	11	159 yards	par 3
3	454 yards	par 4	12	470 yards	par 4
4	379 yards	par 4	13	367 yards	par 4
5	498 yards	par 5	14	445 yards	par 4
6	450 yards	par 4	15	399 yards	par 4
7	185 yards	par 3	16	513 yards	par 5
8	336 yards	par 4	17	167 yards	par 3
9	418 yards	par 4	18	425 yards	par 4
3,340 yards	par 35		3,357 yards	par 35	
Total 6,697 yards par 70					

Indian Reservation

Dunn recruited a crew of 150 Indians from the nearby Shinnecock reservation, from which the club took its name, and

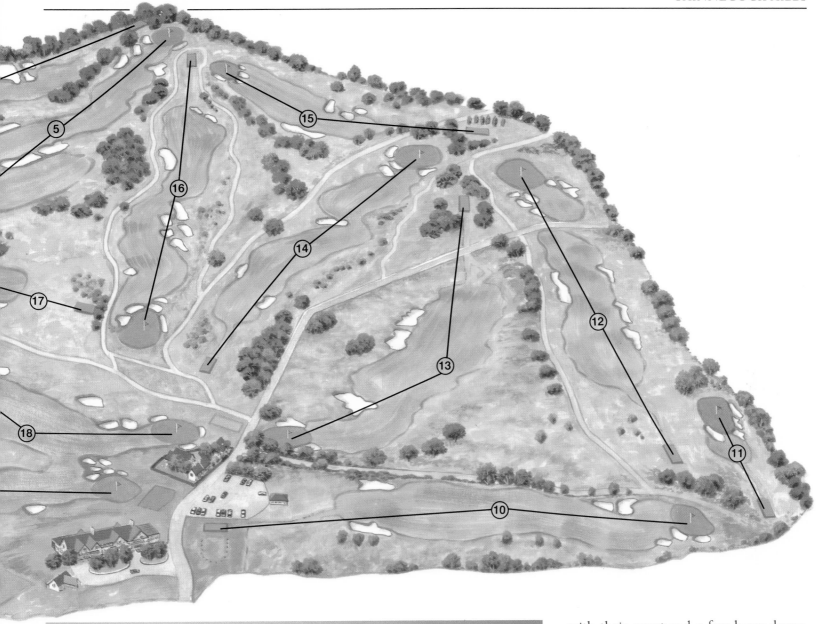

with their sweat and a few horse-drawn drags, by mid-summer he had cleared out a 12-hole course. Fairways and greens were certainly much less cosmetic than their modern counterparts, but Vanderbilt and his friends were delighted. His faith in the venture was justified. By September, 44 members had bought all the available debentures and the club was incorporated. Southampton took to the game avidly, so much so that within a year, they were extending their course to 18 holes and had opened their grandiose clubhouse, the work of one Stanford

Stanford White's clubhouse overlooks the 9th and 18th greens, and is fronted by a natural grandstand for the final green.

White, an eminent architect of the day. White produced a great white rambling palace, which still stands on its rise dominating the Southampton area. It had grill rooms, showers, comfortable locker rooms and was the very last word in luxury. It was the first true American golf clubhouse.

'Newport Swells'
In general, the first American golfers were drawn from the upper reaches of society the '400', men who might winter in Europe and spend their summers or summer weekends away from the heat of the city. Southampton and the 'Hamptons' out on Long Island, and Newport were the most swank of these summer

resorts, providing cottages and villas for the privileged. When the five clubs which formed the USGA took to meeting for play, the St Andrews boys – the famous Apple Tree Gang – were more than abashed when they saw the Shinnecock

fellows and the 'Newport swells' decked out in uniforms of red coats, white knickers and gaiters.

A New Course

Dunn's original course was less than 5,000 yards long. It was lengthened over the years. But by 1931, when part of the club's land had been lost to a new highway, and with the coming of the steel shaft era, it was time for change. Dick Wilson, a highly capable architect with an impressive body of work to his credit, was invited to modernise the course. This he did brilliantly by, in the first place, sitting down and considering what he had – a course no more that two miles from an Atlantic Ocean which produced a regular supply of salty south-west winds; an open, sandy terrain with a good deal of rolling movement in it; virtually no trees, certainly no trees 'in play' as they are in almost all American courses; severe rough; and crisp light turf, reminiscent of Scottish links turf.

Wilson designed a course that demands solid, accurate driving, as all great courses must. His fairways are undulating, often with ridges that have to be carried or passed for the player to reach the optimum position for the second shot. The second shots demand a variety of clubs, and to greens often protected by swales and dips at the fronts or sides, as the old links courses were; and the greens are defended by strong bunker positionings. The rough is of long, clinging grass.

The four short holes, so often an indication of a course's quality, are very fine, and closely trapped. All of them lie across the prevailing wind to varying degrees. Wilson artfully arranged that all the shorter par-4 holes play into the prevailing wind, while the longer par-4 holes play down the wind. The 15th hole, at 399 yards, is a good example. It plays more or less east to west, a dog-leg to the right with a rash of bunkers in the angle. If the drive carries a rise in the fairway by the angle, it will find a valley from which the shot to the green is fairly straightforward. But to get there, the drive must be long and true.

With no more than occasional primping and polishing since, Wilson's design remains thoroughly modern. The late

Above: *Raymond Floyd, the oldest champion (43 years, 9 months, 11 days), plays an old-fashioned running chip on his way to victory at Shinnecock Hills in the U.S. Open of 1986.*

Left: *Shinnecock Hills hosted the U.S. Open in 1896 and 1986. This hole, the 1st, could be at Sunningdale or at any first-rate sand-based inland course in England.*

Thirties and World War II saw Shinnecock suffer a decline; but the club and the course were saved by re-financing in 1948; and Ben Hogan, having visited it in the early 1960s, declared it 'one of the finest courses I have played'. Pulled out to 6,900 yards – not overlong for a modern championship course – it proved itself in the U.S. Open of 1986. The course shrugged off the onslaught of the world's finest players.

On the first day, when the wind blew, not one player could better the par of 70, and only one player was under par at the end of 72 holes. That player was one of the most talented, most mature of American professionals, a previous winner of the U.S. Masters and the U.S. PGA and a future American Ryder Cup captain – Raymond Floyd, aged 43, who scored 279. Shinnecock Hills was alive and well, unscarred and at peace with the world.

THE NATIONAL

The National Golf Links of America vies with its near neighbour at Shinnecock Hills as the least-known, least-played great golf course in America. Yet the National is nothing less than a monument and at the same time a milestone. It is a monument to a remarkable man, Charles Blair Macdonald, and it represents a milestone in American golf architecture, having set a style for American courses that still holds good, at least in the golfing public's mind, today. So critical was Macdonald to so many aspects of the early game in America, and in particular its courses, that he demands some consideration.

Charles Blair Macdonald, from Chicago, was sent by a wealthy father to the University of St Andrews in 1872. Still in his teens, he became enchanted by the game of golf, sitting at the feet of, and occasionally playing with, Old Tom Morris and other leading players. As the years passed, he became a very good player. In his prime Macdonald was a big man – powerful, intelligent, intolerant, aggressive, a man to have his own way. Back home in the Middle West he hustled his friends and extracted cash from them in order to start the Chicago Golf Club – building a course at Wheaton, to the west of the city. He went on to represent the club at the foundation of the U.S. Golf Association in 1894 and became the first official amateur champion.

When designing the Chicago club, one of the first in the country with 18 holes, Mcdonald had the course measure 6,200 yards, the same length at that time as the Old Course at St Andrews, which he worshipped. Golf course design in the U.S. at the end of the last century was fairly basic, often carried out by anyone who could spin a tale of his talents to the committee of one of the dozens of clubs which were springing up all over the place. Often it meant the 'architect' spending a day on the site, putting down markers for tees and greens, with straight fairways, bunkers thrown across them some 150 yards out, and flat greens with bunkers on either side, the whole thing

Charles Blair Macdonald, who studied at St Andrews, helped form the U.S. Golf Association, became the first U.S. Amateur Champion and built the classic National golf links on Long Island.

laid out on a piece of open farmland, or parkland. Macdonald was less than satisfied with this.

He had been greatly impressed by the subtle features of St Andrews and other great links courses in Scotland and by the way the more famous holes offered the golfer options in the playing of them. He came to believe that he could design holes that would equal or even improve on these features, and that indeed he should design and build the first great American golf course. It would be definitive, a classic. Thus in the early years of the 20th century Macdonald made several trips to Britain, making notes and collecting drawings of the outstanding holes on the major links courses of Scotland and England. At the same time, he searched along the eastern seaboard states for a suitable site. He found it some three miles from Shinnecock and Southampton, at the end of Long Island – more than 200 acres of rolling duneland, on a point between Sebonac and Petonic Bays.

A Taste of Scotland

On this ground, he built his masterpiece. Several of its holes are closely reminiscent, if not quite copies, of British holes. The National's 3rd might well be Prestwick's 17th (Macdonald gave his the same fanciful name, 'The Alps'), with a blind second shot over high dunes to a sharply contoured green, with a bunker guarding its front. The 4th, named after North Berwick's 'Redan', is also a par-3 with its green angled across the line of shot, and screened by a bunker. And the National's 7th, named 'St Andrews', is a lookalike of the famous 17th on the Old Course. A large area of scrubby bunkers and wasteland takes the place of the old railway sheds on the drive, while the infamous Road Hole bunker, centre-left of the front of the green, is repeated. The 13th, a fine par-3 over water, has copies of the Hill and Strath bunkers fronting St Andrews' 11th – Macdonald naming his hole the 'Eden'.

The outstanding feature of the National, apart from the positive movement which Macdonald put into the ground, is the strategic quality of the design. On every tee shot, including those of the short holes, the golfer has an alternative line and an alternative target area. There is, however, one notable exception, the 14th, a hole that has been copied all over the world. Macdonald used it on other courses which he designed. It is a drive and pitch hole of 359 yards, but the drive, over water, must be precisely placed into one small area to clear bunkering on the right, stay short of rough and bunkering on the left, and open the dog-leg approach to the right to a circular green surrounded by sand. It is the perfect illustration of penal golf – the drive must be hit in one direction and to one length. There is no alternative. It is a lovely but demanding golf hole.

A Powerful Test in the Wind

Construction of the National started in 1907, the course was in play in 1909, but thereafter Macdonald made constant revisions, fine-tuning many of the holes. It

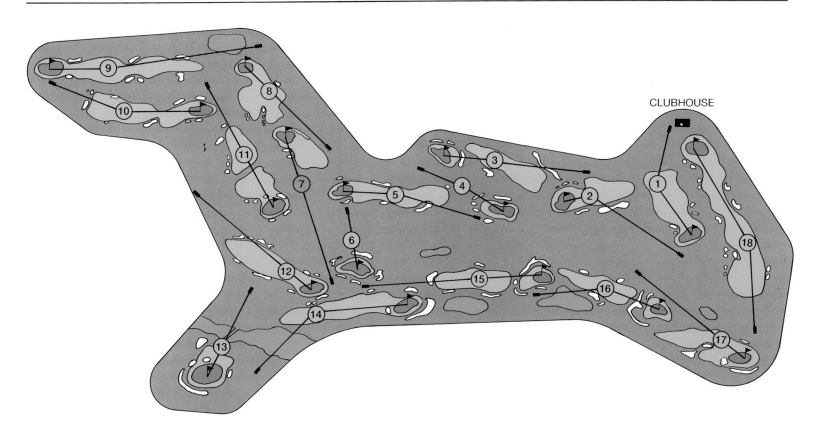

CLUBHOUSE

Right: *View of the tee of the formidable 3rd hole, which requires a long, accurate tee shot and a blind approach over high dunes.*

			THE NATIONAL		
			Card of the course		
1	320 yards	par 4	10	457 yards	par 4
2	271 yards	par 4	11	431 yards	par 4
3	426 yards	par 4	12	437 yards	par 4
4	196 yards	par 3	13	170 yards	par 3
5	476 yards	par 5	14	359 yards	par 4
6	130 yards	par 3	15	392 yards	par 4
7	478 yards	par 5	16	401 yards	par 4
8	390 yards	par 4	17	368 yards	par 4
9	540 yards	par 5	18	503 yards	par 5
	3,227 yards	par 37		3,518 yards	par 36
		Total 6,745 yards par 73			

can now play at 6,700 yards and with the wind blowing, as it almost always is from Long Island Sound to the north, or the Atlantic Ocean to the south, the National is a powerful test of golf.

From the moment of its birth, dozens of golf architects have made the pilgrimage out to Long Island. Perhaps its remoteness has been responsible for the fact that the first Walker Cup match, in 1922, between the amateurs of the United States and of Great Britain and Ireland has been the only major event staged at the National. However, its design and construction, a product of the keen observations and vivid imagination of Charles Blair Macdonald, brought a new dimension to golf architecture in the United States, demonstrated how the natural movement of land can be used to great effect, and showed the way to a succession of other great U.S. courses.

OAK HILL

The East course of the Oak Hill Country Club at Rochester, New York State, may just be as close to perfection as any course in America. Perfection in this sense means that the course is beautifully balanced as to the shot values inherent in every hole, that its layout is varied and attractive and that the course is without any weakness, yet is never either overpowering or pretentious. Oak Hill is simply excellent.

The club dates from 1901, but the course on its present site dates from 1926, and was designed by Donald Ross, the architect of Pinehurst. It retains many of his signatures – the slightly raised greens with honest gradients, the little swales and valleys around the greens, inviting a variety of chip shots, the bunker set short of the green to make judgement of distance that much more difficult, yet fairways bunkers contoured so that ambitious recovery shots are possible. One club member at the time of its construction was Dr John R. Williams, a local physician with a compelling interest in botany. He raised hundreds of seedlings, developed 28 different varieties of oak tree and was responsible for planting the

Above: *In the 1989 U.S. Open Curtis Strange (seen here on the 72nd green) retained the trophy, but a drenched Oak Hill restricted him to a two-under-par 278.*

new course, and consequently giving it its name. Now the property is said to carry more than 30,000 trees: presumably someone has counted them.

A Tough Challange

Oak Hill is an honest golf course, but it demands that the golfer get down to work at once. The 1st hole is a tight par-4 of 445 yards with a creek, which wanders through the entire property, crossing the fairway in front of the green. The green is small and closely trapped. The 2nd hole is a medium-length par-4 of around 400 yards, but with a desperately narrow landing zone for the tee shot and bunkered on either side. The 3rd is a par-3 of more than 200 yards. It is an opening sequence which offers few favours.

The climax to the course is even more severe. The three closing holes are par-4s of 441, 463 and 449 yards, and the 18th is particularly indicative of the problems they pose. At around 260–270 yards, the fairway turns to the right. In the angle of the turn is a huge bunker of florid outline. From there the hole runs uphill to a slightly raised green – three huge bunkers on the right and another on the left front

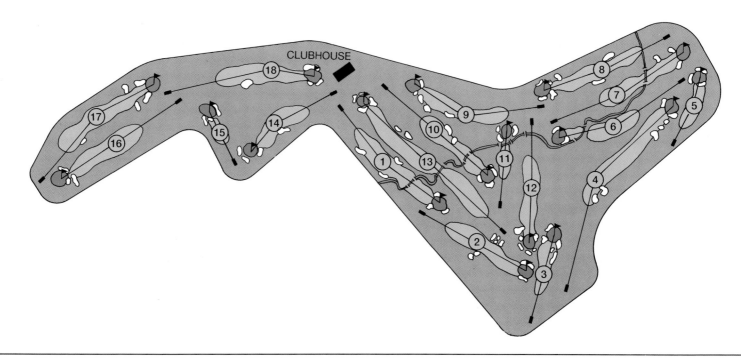

creating a less than generous entrance to the putting surface.

In 1956 Cary Middlecoff won Oak Hill's first (and his second) U.S. Open championship with a score of 281. In 1968, Lee Trevino won the Open with 69, 68, 69, 69 for a 275, equalling the Open's record low aggregate at five under par and becoming the first man to play every round under par in the U.S. Open. Rain had softened the Oak Hill course, making its 6,962 yards controllable. Trevino was playing in only his second Open, but it was clear to the keener observers of the game that here was a very special talent, perfectly illustrated by his manful play on the 72nd hole. He drove into the left rough, advanced the ball but still in the rough, then hit a defiant wedge shot a few feet from the flag, and holed out.

Oak Hill and the USGA seemed embarrassed. The course needed to be

OAK HILL					
Card of the East course					
1	445 yards	par 4	10	420 yards	par 4
2	390 yards	par 4	11	192 yards	par 3
3	206 yards	par 3	12	380 yards	par 4
4	571 yards	par 5	13	602 yards	par 5
5	180 yards	par 3	14	327 yards	par 4
6	440 yards	par 4	15	163 yards	par 3
7	443 yards	par 4	16	441 yards	par 4
8	432 yards	par 4	17	463 yards	par 4
9	416 yards	par 4	18	449 yards	par 4
3,525 yards	par 35		3,437 yards		par 35
Total 6,962 yards par 70					

less benevolent. Architects George and Tom Fazio were retained to tighten things up and they changed some holes in the middle of the course, notably the 5th, 6th, 15th and 18th, in time for the PGA Championship of 1980. However, change

Above: *The testing 449-yard 18th viewed from the green, the bunker on the inside angle of the elbow in the background. Ian Woosnam (joint second) birdie putts the 72nd hole in the 1989 U.S. Open.*

does not always mean improvement. Traditionalists like Trevino and Tom Watson were critical of them. The course was only a couple of yards longer, and in the 1980 event, in good conditions, Jack Nicklaus scored 70, 69, 66, and 69 for a 274, giving him victory by seven (!) strokes from Andy Bean, and setting yet another Oak Hill record score.

When conditions are right, Oak Hill, as any other course in the world, cannot resist the talents of the world's finest players; but for all that it remains a beautiful, stylish golf course on a lovely, gently rolling property, and is well worthy of the greatest champions.

BALTUSROL

The fairways of Baltusrol march along in stately fashion, more than half of the holes running straight while the doglegs are always less than severe. Its noble woodland never crowds the player. Its greens are neither ancient dwarf nor contemporary giant, and all are reasonably contoured. The use of water as a hazard is restrained – a small lake fronting the 4th green, and a narrow stream coming into play on another five holes. Yet, despite a pervasive and pleasing sense of grand understatement, Baltusrol's chief attribute is variety – not only in the demands the course makes in its range of shots into the greens, but also in the fact that while half a dozen of its holes require no more than a drive and a pitch, the 17th, at a hulking 623 yards, is the longest hole in U.S. championship golf. Altogether, every aspect at Baltusrol is grand, and every prospect pleases.

The club, at Springfield, New Jersey, and no more than a one hour drive from Manhattan, takes its name from a wealthy farmer of Dutch extraction, a Mr Baltus Roll, who owned the land more than 150 years ago. In 1831, he was dragged out of his house on a nearby hillside by two thieves, who murdered him in the presence of his wife in the belief that there was money hidden in the house. Towards the end of the century, the Baltusrol lands, still being farmed, were owned by one Louis Keller, a gentleman who founded and published the *New York Social Register*. He had been smitten by the game, playing with his smart society friends at Newport and Southampton, and resolved to have his own golf course.

U.S. Open 1980: winner Jack Nicklaus plays out of the back bunker on the 4th, where Robert Trent Jones scored an ace after remodelling the hole.

In 1885 he extracted an initiation fee of $10 from several of his cronies (Baltusrol charges have increased somewhat) and in no time had nine holes in play. By 1921, the club had enough extra land to invite A.W. Tillinghast to design 36 holes.

Baltustol had already become prominent in the affairs of American golf, and was sufficiently well thought of to have staged two U.S. Opens, in 1903 and 1915. The first of these was won by Willie Anderson, the club's first professional, who won four Opens in the space of five years. Only Bobby Jones, Ben Hogan and Jack Nicklaus were to equal his record of four Championships. The second was won by Jerome Travers, the wealthy Long Islander who won two Opens and four U.S. Amateur championships. The time had come for Baltusrol to advance, and in Tillinghast they selected one of the two outstanding golf course designers of the first quarter of the 20th century. The

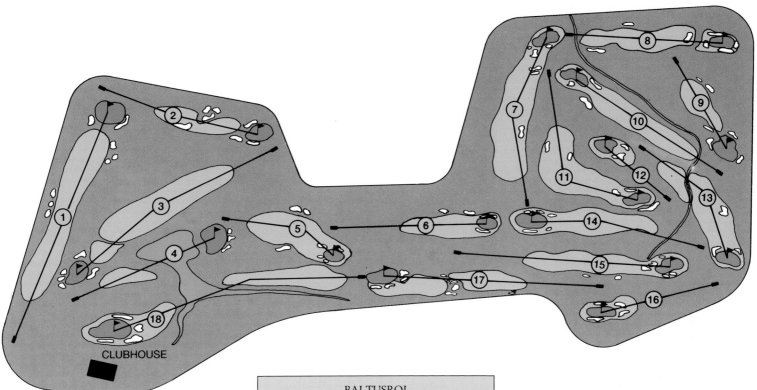

CLUBHOUSE

BALTUSROL					
Card of the Lower course					
1	469 yards	par 4	10	449 yards	par 4
2	390 yards	par 4	11	410 yards	par 4
3	438 yards	par 4	12	193 yards	par 3
4	194 yards	par 3	13	383 yards	par 4
5	388 yards	par 4	14	399 yards	par 4
6	470 yards	par 4	15	419 yards	par 4
7	470 yards	par 4	16	214 yards	par 3
8	365 yards	par 4	17	623 yards	par 5
9	206 yards	par 3	18	524 yards	par 5
	3,390 yards	par 34		3,632 yards	par 36
	Total 7,022 yards par 70				

other was Donald Ross, and the two men could hardly have been less alike; Ross, the quiet Scot of Presbyterian inclination who designed courses almost until the day he died, and Tillinghast, the *bon viveur* who ended his days as an antique dealer in Hollywood and had amongst other things been a magazine editor and a dabbler in photography and, whatever he was doing, had always enjoyed a dram or two.

Tillinghast built powerful but fair golf courses, among them Winged Foot in New York and Five Farms at Baltimore. His driving lines might be tight, but they were never penal. He believed that a 'controlled shot to a closely guarded green is the surest test of any man's golf'. His greens might be closely guarded but they never had ridiculous slopes, and he would quite often place fairway bunkers centrally, some 20 or 30 yards short of the green, demanding that the player make a positive carry over. Moreover, he used water for hazards only when it was already there – naturally.

Tillinghast's Baltusrol shares with Merion and Oakmont the distinction of having staged six U.S. Open Cham-

pionships. However, it has been revised over the years, and for the 1954 event Robert Trent Jones was called in to strengthen the course. The story of Jones at Baltusrol is almost too good to be true, but not too good not to be re-told. He re-worked Tillinghast's short 4th – paradoxically a water hole. It became a shot over water to a green narrow from front to back, wide from left to right. The water came right up to the putting surface, which was edged by a stone wall. The green sloped from left to right, from front to back, and was screened by tall, mature trees – all oddly reminiscent of the 12th at Augusta. The carry could be as much as

200 yards from the back tee. The club officials and the USGA people thought that Jones had made it much too difficult. He disagreed and offered to pay for any subsequent changes that might be necessary. He led the club president, the chairman of the USGA championship committee, and Johnny Farrell, Baltusrol's famous professional, to the tee and they all hit shots. When it came to Jones' turn he hit a shot that rolled straight into the hole, and said: 'As you see gentlemen, this hole is not too tough'!

Ed Furgol won the '54 Championship with 284. In 1967, Jack Nicklaus won with a record 275 and a last round of 65. In 1980, Jack Nicklaus won again with yet another record 274, which included a round of 63. No man ever enjoyed a victory more than this one. Jack sat in the Press Centre for hours afterwards, saying: 'I don't want this day to end'.

If the conditions are right, the modern champions can overwhelm any course, even one longer than 7,000 yards, like the modern Baltusrol. But for all that Baltusrol undoubtedly remains as one of America's finest parkland courses.

THE COUNTRY CLUB

The Country Club at Brookline, now a suburb of Boston, Massachussetts, is by way of being an American institution. It was established in 1860, and was the first of its kind. It saw no need, therefore, to qualify its title – it was and is simply 'The' Country Club. In the early days, horses were the thing – exercising them, racing them, a bit of polo from time to time. ... It was 30 years before the club laid out six holes of golf, but that was enough in the 1890s to permit it to become a founder member, as one of the five original clubs, of the United States Golf Association. The club's match with Royal Montreal, first played in 1898, was the world's first golf match between teams of different countries. But above all else, The Country Club became a shrine of American golf because of the U.S. Open Championship of 1913. It was then that the local boy, Francis Ouimet, aged 20, the Massachussetts Amateur Champion, defeated the Englishmen Harry Vardon and Ted Ray, who were beyond any reasonable doubt the two finest players in the world.

Earlier American Opens had been dominated by British-born, if American-resident, professionals who, it must be said, were scarcely outstanding players. True, a couple of years earlier, young Johnny McDermott had become the first U.S.-born champion; but Ouimet, on that cold, wet September Saturday in 1913 began an American domination of world golf that lasted for more than half a century. The Country Club produced other champions but Ouimet's victory is an almost unique instance of one single event having an immense and permanent effect on an entire sport. The nearest parallel in golf might be the victory of the Japanese team in the Canada Cup (now World Cup) of 1957, and the effect it had on the game over there.

Ouimet went on to have a remarkably fulfilled life. He was twice Amateur Champion of the U.S., a Walker Cup player and American Walker Cup captain. He became President of the USGA and the first non-British captain of the

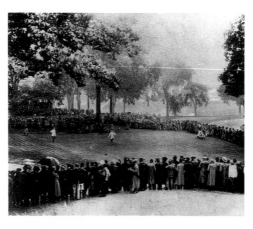

Francis Ouimet, crouching on the left, lines up the winning putt of the fateful U.S. Open of 1913, when he beat the British favourites, Harry Vardon (nearest Ouimet) and Ted Ray, in a play-off.

Royal and Ancient club. He had a prosperous business career as a stockbroker in Boston and throughout his life maintained a simple country boy image. Few in golf have ever been more highly regarded.

The Country Club is not an imperious, breath-taking course. Rather, it is old-fashioned to the point of being almost homely. But when the USGA, with a keen sense of history, took their championship back to Brookline, 50 years on from Ouimet, the course was far more sophisticated than the open spread the young Francis knew. The horses had gone. Trees and heavily-wooded areas on the property were now very much in play and time had put the stamp of maturity on one of the world's great courses. However, in 1963 history repeated itself. Again there was a three-way tie, and a play-off, this time involving Julius Boros, Jackie Cupit and Arnold Palmer. Palmer, at the height of his powers, was expected to make a breakfast of the others. But during the night before the play-off, he was stricken with some kind of food poisoning, and next day came to the tee weak as a kitten. The outcome was Boros 70, Cupit 73 and Palmer 76. And when the USGA went back to Brookline yet again, in 1988, there was yet another tie.

This time, Curtis Strange beat Nick Faldo in the play-off.

In all of these great events, the 17th hole has played an extraordinary and eventful role. Ouimet made a birdie there on his final round, helping to set up the tie with the Englishmen. The hole is 365 yards, slightly dog-legged to the left, with a bunker in the angle. From there it is uphill to the green. In the play-off round, with Ray out of it, Ouimet played nicely

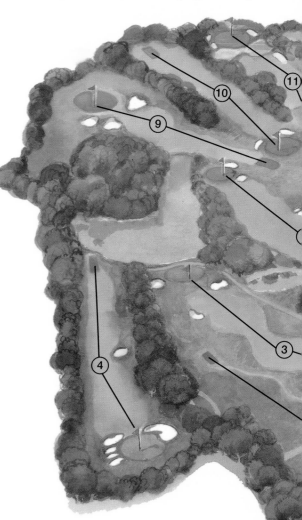

down the fairway, pitched on the green and made his birdie. Harry Vardon, on the other hand, pressing for the birdie he needed – he was a stroke down to Francis – caught the bunker with his drive, scored five, and lost the Open. In 1963 at the 71st hole – Palmer bogeyed, Cupit double-bogeyed, while Boros birdied to set up the play-off. And in 1988, Strange three-putted the 71st, to allow the tie, while Faldo, in the play-off round, over-shot the green with his second – a fateful hole indeed.

For the '88 Open, the USGA had invited Rees Jones, younger son of Robert Trent Jones, the most famous of modern golf architects, to revise the course. The original design dates back to 1909, and Jones quickly saw that the course would have to be strengthened for modern championship players. Searching through the club's archives, he found some of the early work plans and talked to the oldest members and staff as to what they could remember of the original layout. Taking all of this into account, Jones came to the conclusion that he should virtually restore the old course, but in a modern context. He thus created a course that was some 700 yards longer than the Ouimet course.

Jones also discovered that the 17th green of 1913 was long gone. Because of road widening, a new green had been built in 1958, so he set about building a new green, closely guarded by front bunkers and rather flat at the back. His work certainly sustained the critical quality of the hole.

Curtis Strange plays a bunker shot at the 17th in his playoff with Nick Faldo in the 1988 U.S. Open at The Country Club. His greenside play and holing-out work were important factors in his victory.

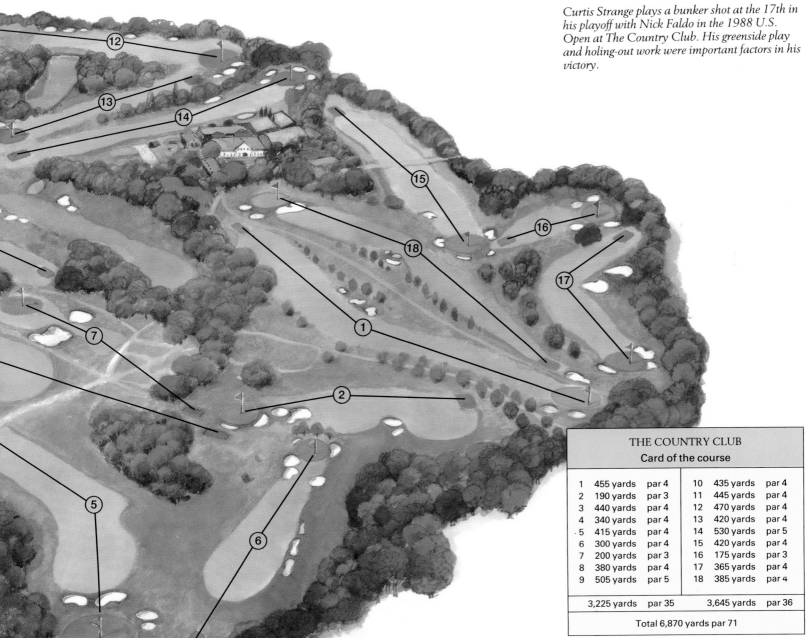

THE COUNTRY CLUB					
Card of the course					
1	455 yards	par 4	10	435 yards	par 4
2	190 yards	par 3	11	445 yards	par 4
3	440 yards	par 4	12	470 yards	par 4
4	340 yards	par 4	13	420 yards	par 4
5	415 yards	par 4	14	530 yards	par 5
6	300 yards	par 4	15	420 yards	par 4
7	200 yards	par 3	16	175 yards	par 3
8	380 yards	par 4	17	365 yards	par 4
9	505 yards	par 5	18	385 yards	par 4
	3,225 yards	par 35		3,645 yards	par 36
	Total 6,870 yards par 71				

OAKMONT

Behind every great venture is a singular man. So it was with the creation of the course at Oakmont, a village some dozen miles north of Pittsburgh, and one Henry Clay Fownes (pronounced 'phones'), its architect, creator and the first president of the Oakmont Country Club. Perhaps in this case two men should get the credit – the second being Henry's son, William. Henry, a successful Pittsburgh industrialist and near-contemporary of Andrew Carnegie, took up golf in 1899 when he was already in his forties. Playing on the short, modest courses of the Pittsburgh Field Club and the Highland Country Club, he became adept enough to qualify for the U.S. Amateur Championship of 1901.

His son, William C. Fownes Jr, was introduced to the game with his father and surpassed him. He won the U.S. Amateur Championship of 1910, played at The Country Club, Brookline, beating Chick Evans in the semi-final after being two down with three to play. He qualified for the championship 25 times in 27 years, served for many years on U.S. Golf Association committees, and was USGA president in 1926 and 1927.

Father Henry soon came to see that Pittsburgh needed a 'proper' golf course, and by 1903 he had put together a syndicate to finance such a venture. The word was out that he was seeking a suitable piece of land, within reach of the city. Eventually a friend, George S. Macram, who lived in Oakmont village, reported that a 225 acre plot nearby was available. Fownes bought it. A railroad cut through the property, but the Fowneses simply ignored that – they threw a bridge over the tracks, and laid out holes on either side. And much later, when the Pennsylvania Turnpike, one of America's earliest super-highways, threatened the course, it was routed alongside the railroad track, so that the Oakmont course was left virtually untouched.

An 18-Hole Purgatory

On the morning of 15 September 1903 the first sod was broken by the Fownes workforce of 150 men and 25 mule teams, and six weeks later, before the hard northern winter had set in, 12 holes had been cleared, tees and greens had been built, greens and fairways seeded and a drainage system put in place. The

following spring a further six holes were prepared, and by the autumn of 1904 Oakmont was in play.

It was immediately clear that the Fowneses, father and son alike, took a puritanical, hair-shirted attitude to the game of golf. Their creed was that any shot less than perfect must be punished.

Father Fownes had most of the existing trees ripped out to give the landscape that 'empty', British-links appearance. (Since those early years there has been some planting, but Oakmont retains an open look.) Within a year or so of its opening, Oakmont boasted some 350 bunkers. Since the course was 6,600 yards in length, at a time when the world of golf was only just becoming accustomed to the Haskell wound ball, which was replacing the gutty, and 25 years before the steel shaft, it must have been purgatory. It

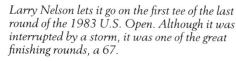

Larry Nelson lets it go on the first tee of the last round of the 1983 U.S. Open. Although it was interrupted by a storm, it was one of the great finishing rounds, a 67.

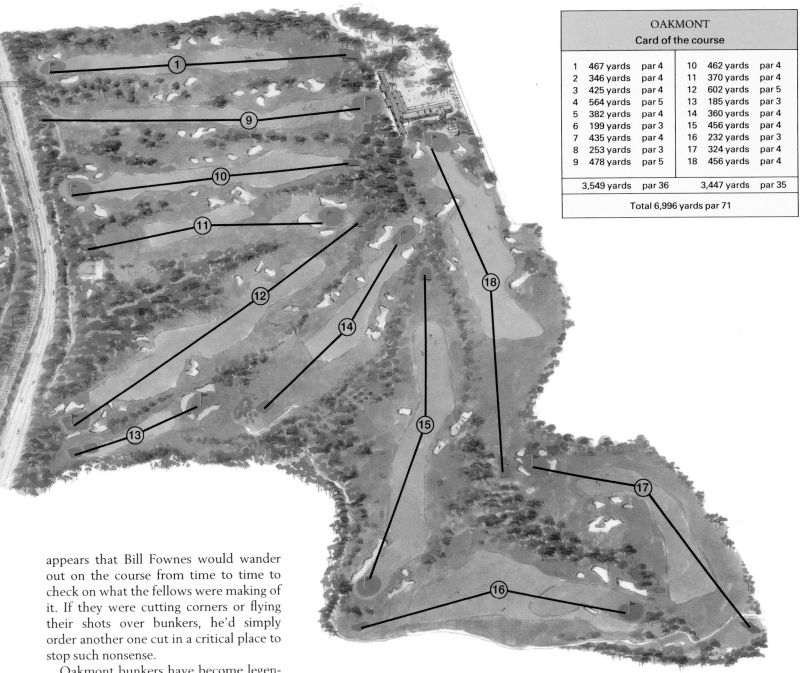

OAKMONT					
Card of the course					
1	467 yards	par 4	10	462 yards	par 4
2	346 yards	par 4	11	370 yards	par 4
3	425 yards	par 4	12	602 yards	par 5
4	564 yards	par 5	13	185 yards	par 3
5	382 yards	par 4	14	360 yards	par 4
6	199 yards	par 3	15	456 yards	par 4
7	435 yards	par 4	16	232 yards	par 3
8	253 yards	par 3	17	324 yards	par 4
9	478 yards	par 5	18	456 yards	par 4
	3,549 yards	par 36		3,447 yards	par 35
	Total 6,996 yards par 71				

appears that Bill Fownes would wander out on the course from time to time to check on what the fellows were making of it. If they were cutting corners or flying their shots over bunkers, he'd simply order another one cut in a critical place to stop such nonsense.

Oakmont bunkers have become legendary in American golf, and not just for their numbers. The 8th hole boasts 'the Sahara' bunker which is 75 yards long and 35 yards wide and needed eleven truck loads of sand to fill. It guards the left fairway of this par-3 of 253 yards and then runs up to and along the left side of the green. But most famous of all are the 'Church Pews', a block of eight lateral bunkers like lines of infantry, separating the 3rd and 4th fairways, in each case neatly nailing pulled drives.

Even more memorable in terms of the Fownes's penal design philosophy was the

'Oakmont Rake'. The course had been built on heavy clay soil. From a drainage point of view it was not feasible to build deep bunkers after the fashion of British links. The Oakmont bunkers, shallow as they were, were loaded with heavy river sand. Starting in 1920, the Fowneses had the bunkers furrowed by special rakes that had teeth 2 in long and 2 in apart. As a result the heavy sand stood up neatly in ridges, like a ploughed field, and left the

golfer no option but to splash the ball a few yards out with a routine shot.

The Fastest Greens in America
But more lethal than anything in thwarting the great champions have been the Oakmont greens. They have been described as the fastest, the truest, the most difficult in America. To make them fast in the early days the Fownes had them rolled

with a 1500-pound roller, which required eight men to pull. The grass was cut to 3/32 in (about 2.5 mm). The wonder was that they were able to retain grass on such greens, especially in high summer.

Bill Fownes became president in 1935, when his father died, and served until 1949, a year before his own death. Before that, although a committee had taken over the running of the club, Bill remained chairman of the greens committee. Over the years, 'his' greens have taken a fearful toll. In the U.S. Open of 1927, against a par of 72/288, Tommy Armour's winning score was 301. In the 1935 Open, Sam Parks, a Pittsburgh man who knew Oakmont intimately, won with 299, the only man under 300. In the previous decade, U.S. Open-winning scores at other venues had often been well under these totals. In the 1929 U.S. Amateur, on the 14th green, Chick Evans three-putted without even lipping the cup – then holed out with the handle of his umbrella!

Postwar Softening

By 1953, when Oakmont held its first postwar U.S. Open, things were different. The club committee and the USGA agreed to make Oakmont slightly less malevolent: some fairways in the driving area were widened; the number of bunkers was reduced to less than 200, and now they had fine white silicone sand.

Above: *The first age of Nicklaus. Jack, crewcut, hefty and immensely powerful, lets fly in the U.S. Open of 1962, when he beat Arnold Palmer in a play-off, 71 to 74.*

Right: *The well-guarded 18th green makes a fitting climax to this hugely difficult course. Even in his annus mirabilis, the great Hogan was only one under par when winning the 1953 U.S. Open.*

Below: *Arnold Palmer, caught in the 'Church Pews' bunkers at Oakmont in the 1983 U.S. Open, goes for a typically aggressive, swashbuckling recovery.*

Perhaps most important of all was that 1953 was the enchanted year of Ben Hogan. He came to Oakmont as the Masters Champion, and promptly played a first round of 67 which broke the back of the competition. He won the championship by six strokes from Sam Snead, with 283 – five under par and at no time in the entire year (he went on to win the British Open) was the marvelously ruth-

less precision of his shotmaking better illustrated than in the last three holes of his final round. At the 16th, a par-3 of 232 yards, he hit a four-wood into the heart of the green – two putts for a 3. At the 17th, a par-4 of some 300 yards, he drove the green – again, two putts for 3. At the 18th, a very powerful finishing par-4 of 456 yards, the second half of the hole uphill to the green, he hit an immense drive, a mid-iron a few feet to the right of the flagstick, and holed the putt – for a 3.

In the 1973 Championship, Johnny Miller, with a scarcely credible 63, played the lowest last round the Open had known, and some said the finest round of golf ever played. In the 1983 championship, Larry Nelson played the final 36 holes in 65, 67 for a record 132. It took such feats of derring-do to win the championships for these men. But in each case, at each championship, torrential rain had taken all the fire out of the Oakmont greens over the two closing rounds. Oakmont is a fearsome course. It has been described as 'the toughest golf course in the world'. It may well be overwhelming, but is it fair? 'Fairness', in the philosophy of the Fownes, 'has nothing to do with it'.

MERION

Merion is a classic, a treasury of design, imagination, craftsmanship and style. The demands it makes of the golfer are all there for him to see, with nothing hidden. But they are rigorous indeed. It is an exacting test for any class of player, and in that respect recalls the great Scottish links course at Muirfield.

The Merion Golf Club and its championship East course at Ardmore, a fashionable suburb of Philadelphia, emerged from the Merion Cricket Club, which was founded during the Civil War. As golf became popular in America, club members first used the estate of one Clement A. Griscomb for this new game; but in 1896 the club purchased 100 acres three quarters of a mile from the cricket ground and laid out nine holes. Four years later another nine were added, and on this course the U.S. Women's Amateur Championships of 1904 and 1909 were played. However, with the advent and spread of the Haskell ball from the turn of the century, it was clear that the course would quickly become obsolete. Consequently, the Merion members bought an abandoned farm at the town of Ardmore for a new course, though the property was less than stunning and included an old stone quarry long out of use, dense with trees and shrubbery.

Contrary to the fashion of the day, the design of the course was vested in a committee of five members, which in-cluded Hugh Irvine Wilson, an immigrant Scot, graduate of Princeton, local insurance broker and adequate golfer. The committee made several visits to The National, at Southampton on Long Island, where it became clear that Wilson had a special feeling for design. They sent him over to Scotland and, as Charles Blair Macdonald had done, he spent several months making drawings and maps, talking to people and looking around. When he went to work on Merion East, he copied not specific golf holes that he had seen, but concepts. For example in front

The tell-tale board hails David Graham's near-immaculate 67 – this birdie putt on the last hole grazed the cup – on the final round of his 1981 U.S. Open Championship at Merion.

of his 17th green a – ferocious par-3 – he left a big depression like the Valley of Sin in front of the 18th at St Andrews. And he used the quarry to create the climax of his round – holes 16, 17 and 18 playing over it.

The White Faces of Merion

When Wilson's work was completed in 1912, Merion East was seen to be a course of high distinction and beauty. It was built on open parkland with just enough trees to soften and enhance the landscape. There were 128 bunkers, beautifully shaped – the famous 'white faces of Merion' – some of them graced with islands of tall, spiky grass. Wilson used baskets rather than flags atop the flagsticks, an idea he was supposed to have found at Sunningdale (qv), but which actually originated in a Scottish custom of using lobster pots!

Above: *View to the par-4 16th green across the overgrown quarry, whose size enforces a long-iron or fairway wood approach shot.*

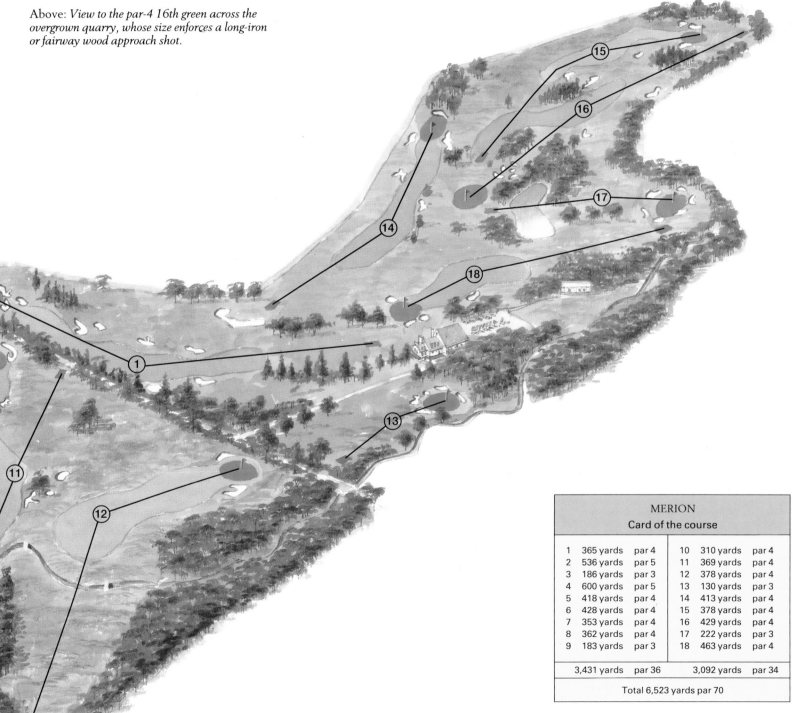

MERION					
Card of the course					
1	365 yards	par 4	10	310 yards	par 4
2	536 yards	par 5	11	369 yards	par 4
3	186 yards	par 3	12	378 yards	par 4
4	600 yards	par 5	13	130 yards	par 3
5	418 yards	par 4	14	413 yards	par 4
6	428 yards	par 4	15	378 yards	par 4
7	353 yards	par 4	16	429 yards	par 4
8	362 yards	par 4	17	222 yards	par 3
9	183 yards	par 3	18	463 yards	par 4
3,431 yards		par 36	3,092 yards		par 34
Total 6,523 yards par 70					

Merion has persisted in holding its place in the forefront of championship golf in America – it has staged more national championships than any other course – even though its off-course facilities leave a lot to be desired.

The course has always defied the greatest players of the day. At the first Open played there in 1934, Olin Dutra won with 293, 13 over par. In 1950, Ben Hogan, Lloyd Mangrum and George Fazio tied on 287, 7 over par. In fact, it was not until the Championship of 1981 that par was broken – by five players. Overnight rain had made the greens receptive, and the championship was distinguished by the final round of David Graham of Australia – a 67.

Make or Break on the Greens

Wilson's greens at Merion hold the key. Ample when receiving a long shot, small when receiving a pitch, beautifully shaped, artfully contoured, sometimes on two levels, sloping with the shot or against it, at their optimum speed they are as fast as the greens at Oakmont.

The first hole runs from the clubhouse towards Ardmore Avenue. The entire hole, which turns to the right, can be seen from the tee and it is no more than a drive and pitch. But the drive must be exactly right, placed between flanking bunkers in the driving zone to open up the widest approach to the green. It may look innocuous, but placement of every shot is essential – it is the essence of Merion. Across Ardmore Avenue is something quite different: a hulking 536-yard par-5 along the most slender of fairways. With a drive that must carry a brook, with Wilson's bunkering artfully placed at key points along the left side and with out-of-bounds hard along the right.

The 3rd is a par-3 over a valley to a plateau green; and then we are into a 600 yard par-5. This one has a slightly wider fairway, but presents a comprehensively defended green. A narrow brook crosses in front and the rest of the green is ringed with five bunkers.

The sequence of holes 10, 11 and 12 is fascinating, proving yet again that sheer length need not be a primary factor in golf-course design, even considering the sophistication of contemporary golfers and their equipment. The 10th is 310 yards downhill. It bears to the left and its major defences are at the turn, on the left. The rectangular green is inclined across the approach shot. An enormous, optimistic drive will probably find trouble of its own making rather than the putting surface, and the trick is to drive far enough and find a place on the right side of the fairway.

The 11th, at 369 yards, is the 10th in reverse. The second shot is critical. The drive is down into a valley, then up to a pear-shaped green and over a stream which also runs along the right side of the green; a very strong bunker covers the left front and centre. The hole is famous above all for being the very last championship hole that Bobby Jones played. He stood on the green eight up with eight to play against Gene Homans in the final of the U.S. Amateur Championship of 1930. He had already won the British Amateur at St Andrews, the British Open at Hoylake and the U.S. Open at Interlachen (Minnesota). Two putts on Merion's 11th green made Jones immortal – the only man to win all four of these championships in one year.

Yet perhaps the most famous holes at Merion are the last three, playing as they do across the quarry and making a frightening finish to the round. The 16th is celebrated Quarry Hole. It is 429 yards and the downhill teeshot must be held short of the quarry. The second shot will require a 4-iron or something stronger to carry the quarry, and reach up the hill to the split-level green. The 17th is a par-3 of 222 yards, requiring a very big shot should it be into the wind. The shot is across the quarry to a green set lower than the tee, but with twin levels neatly framed by five bunkers. Here, Ben Hogan holed a birdie putt of 50 feet in the 1950 Open Championship play-off.

A long and perfect drive on the 18th, 463 yards, will carry the corner of the quarry, than demand a long shot across a dip in the ground to a raised green.

Tall, spiky grass adds whiskers to many of Merion's 'white faces'. Here Jerry Pate escapes from the left-hand greenside bunker at the par-4 10th.

PINE VALLEY

According to Pine Valley records, the club had its origins in the fact that a group of golfers from the Philadelphia Country Club, at Bala, Pennsylvania, occasionally took what was then the Reading Railroad to play nearer the ocean at the Atlantic City Country Club. A Philadelphia hotelier, George A. Crump, was the leader of this happy band. En route one day, Crump noticed a piece of land along the railroad that he thought would be suitable for golf, and he and Howard Perrin, who was to become the first president of the Pine Valley club, investigated. They spent some days tramping over the property. It was virgin forest of pine, swamps and dense undergrowth, but on sandy soil and with a good deal of movement in the land. Crump, by some inexplicable miracle, saw it as the perfect landscape for an 'inland links'!

He formed a syndicate and persuaded 18 of his friends to contribute $1000 each – enough, they felt, to build 18 holes. In 1912 they bought 184 acres of the land from Sumner Ireland, its owner, and by January 1914 the *Philadelphia Inquirer*, a friendly newspaper always ready to publicise the venture, was able to report: 'The land there, comprising 184 rolling acres is, or was, the highest ground in southern New Jersey, 200 feet at points above the sea level, being more than 100 years ago the home to the Delaware Indians. It is the watershed between the Tuckahoe and Delaware rivers. The first blow of the axe was struck there last February; in the ten months since, $40,000 has been spent by the holding company under the direction of George A. Crump, chairman of the greens committee, to whom more than any other man is due the credit for the wonders wrought'.

PINE VALLEY					
Card of the course					
1	427 yards	par 4	10	146 yards	par 3
2	367 yards	par 4	11	392 yards	par 4
3	181 yards	par 3	12	344 yards	par 4
4	444 yards	par 4	13	448 yards	par 4
5	232 yards	par 3	14	184 yards	par 3
6	388 yards	par 4	15	591 yards	par 5
7	567 yards	par 5	16	433 yards	par 4
8	319 yards	par 4	17	338 yards	par 4
9	427 yards	par 4	18	428 yards	par 4
3,352 yards	par 35		3,304 yards	par 35	
Total 6,656 yards par 70					

A Labour of Love

Like an Old Testament prophet marching into the wilderness, Crump abandoned the good life, and took to a spartan bungalow he erected on site. There he literally hacked out one of the greatest golf courses in America. He directed the felling of trees, the clearing of stumps, the building of dams to form lakes, the run of the fairways and the positioning of greens; he lived on the site of the course for the best part of six years.

Crump died rather suddenly in January 1918, after a short illness. He had spent some $250,000 of his own money with little thought of repayment. When he died, 14 holes had been finished and his estate left enough to complete the last four. Hugh Wilson, admired for his work particularly at Merion, and his brother Allen directed the work on these final holes, and by the end of 1918 the club had the complete set of 18.

Before then, the world of golf had come

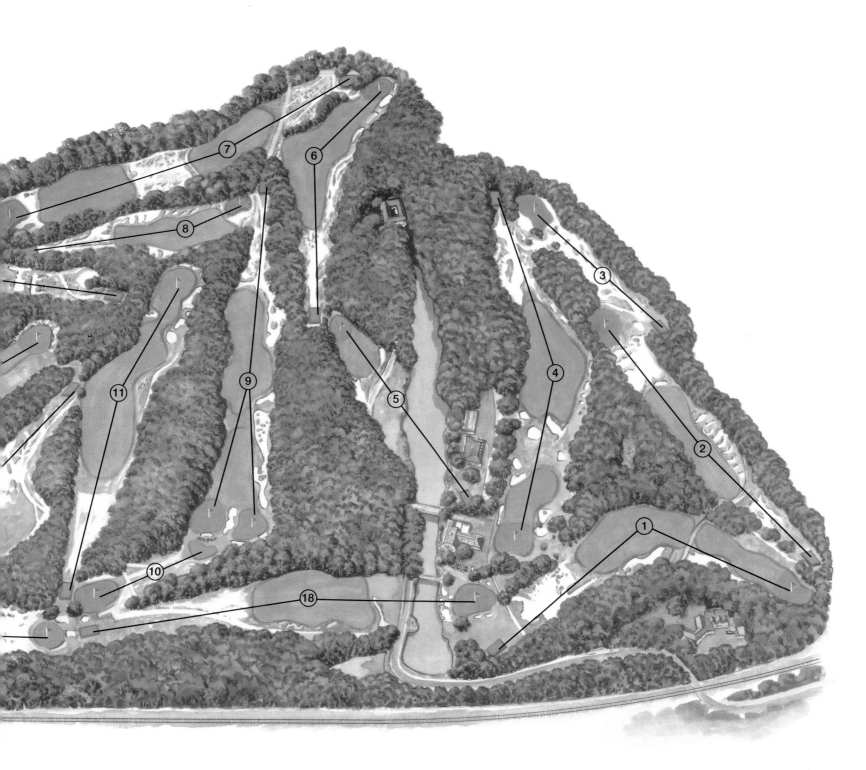

to realise that Pine Valley was an extraordinary golf course. Donald Ross of Dornoch and Pinehurst, one of golf's greatest architects, said plainly: 'This is the finest golf course in America.' Ben Sayers of North Berwick said on first seeing it: 'Why, it is Colt and Sunningdale!,' without knowing that Harry Colt, the distinguished British architect who was largely responsible for Sunningdale and other fine courses, had been imported by Crump to check on his routing and bunkering. Yet Colt made very few changes to Pine Valley. And Francis Ouimet, Charles Blair Macdonald, Walter Travis, Jerome Travers, Chick Evans, and Jim Barnes, all outstanding players of the time, sang its praises.

Pine Valley was blessed by another outstanding personality to follow George Crump. John Arthur Brown, a Philadelphia lawyer, joined the club just after the first World War, became president in 1929 and served for more than 30 years,

Pine Valley – there are simply large expanses of sand where on other courses fairways would be, and sandy areas surrounding greens. And all this sand is unraked – indeed, unrakeable: there is just too much of it. You simply take your chances with the lie.

Pine Valley is fierce but fair; fierce in the sense that it is absolutely penal ('it's not penal', said one victim, 'it's a penitentiary') in giving the golfer a single option on each shot, one route only, and punishing him severely if he fails; and fair, if any golf course can or should be described as fair, if the shots are played properly and sensibly. Then, its rewards are reasonably forthcoming. Bernard Darwin, the famous golf correspondent of *The Times* and an able (though irascible) player as a young man, was level par after seven holes. After a good drive to the 8th, he found himself 12 over par when he had holed out, and immediately became a spectator. There are even more horrifying stories of high scoring. John Brookes, a member and at one time president of the

guiding the club through some dire financial times during the Depression. Pine Valley has always been a golf club, nothing more. It has never held a major championship. For one thing, the members have not sought such a thing; for another, the layout of the course prohibits the movement of large crowds. At the Walker Cup Match of 1936 a gallery of some 3,000 was more than the club could easily handle.

Islands in a Sea of Sand

The Pine Valley course is set in a forest of pine and larch and oak. There are two good-sized lakes on the property. Each hole exists in isolation from the others – the design philosophy being that the golfer is obliged to play from one island to another; the islands are set in a sea of sand. This is the ultimate manifestation both of golf as a point-to-point game, and

of penal design. The golfer plays from a tee to an area of fairway which has been tailored to receive his drive and hold it there, in the correct place for his next shot. This may well be to a green which is entirely surrounded by sand. On a long par-4 or a par-5 hole, the second shot may be to another island, or peninsula, of sand. Thus there are few bunkers as such at

Right: The par-3 14th hole is a beautiful one-shotter over water. Here Montogomerie and Sigel (U.S.) shake hands during the 1985 Walker Cup match.

Left: The 14th, at 184 yards, is the last of Pine Valley's gorgeous short holes. With 50 feet of water and bunkering fronting the green, and more water at back left, it demands rare confidence and precision from the tee.

Burning Tree Club in Washington D.C., once played the 14th hole in 44 recorded strokes.

Pine Valley is a beautiful monster. The very essence of this golf course is that both the idea of it and the fact of it can overwhelm the golfer. He will find no solace in trying to persuade himself that it looks tougher than it is. It is not. It is just as tough as it looks. More than anything it is a test of a golfer's courage. If he brings a negative, defensive attitude to the course, the sandy wastes with their little bushes and shrubs and deep footprints will devour him. If he brings an arrogant, aggressive attitude to Pine Valley, the same thing will happen. But if he brings a positive attitude to the course, a sound reliable swing and some decent current form, he may find that the carries are after all not so fearsome and that there is much

pleasure to be found out there.

Most golf courses, on less inspiring land and designed by less inspired people, might have six very good holes, six good holes and six less than good holes. Pine valley has 18 gorgeous holes. The course has a splendid opening of four holes that swing back to the clubhouse. The very first stroke of the very first hole provides a declaration of what the player must digest at Pine Valley – a wasteland of sand spreading out 100 yards or so in front of the tee. The fairway island is ample, and contains the angle of the dog-leg to the right. Most of the rest of the way there is

The 'most awesome challenge' at Pine Valley, the 232-yard par-3 5th where only 'God can make a three'. The drive carrys a wide creek and a belt of scrub to a two-level green.

fairway to a raised green. On the 2nd hole the approach shot is the key. The drive should carry 175 yards onto a long, rectangular fairway island. The hole is 367 yards, not overlong, but the second shot must carry up to a green raised on top of a ridge, so that escarpments of sand beneath it face the player. The 3rd, a par-3 of 181 yards, has an elevated tee, and plays down to a waisted green, which is tilted to the left. Between tee and green lies nothing but an ocean of sand. The 4th is a long par-4 of 444 yards. It turns sharply to the right and there is sand in front of the tee, but Crump left 40 yards or so of fairway short of the green, for the golfer lacking a bit of length.

So the course goes on, one jewel following another. The 5th hole is a marvel, but perhaps no more than a first among equals in the one-shot holes. It is a

hulking 232 yards; when the wind is against him even the highest class of player will need a wood off the tee. The first half of the hole is over a lake, the second half over a modest piece of fairway, then a swatch of sand and then a raised green.

Hell's Half Acre

The par-5s are huge. They must be the only pair of par-5s that do not require bunkering in the ordinary sense. The 7th, at 567 yards and known as the Sahara, for fairly obvious reasons, is of sand, with three islands, one to receive the drive, one to receive the second shot and one containing the green. Between the first and second islands, a stretch of more than 100 yards, lies 'Hell's Half Acre'. The green is completely surrounded by sand and thus, it is said, no

man has ever reached it in two strokes.

The 15th on the other hand, at 591 yards, requires a drive briefly over a lake and onto the only continuous fairway on the course. All the way to the green it goes, up an avenue of pine, but narrowing insidiously as it approaches a small green.

The 13th is an exceptional hole, with less of the rigidity of some on the course. It provides an element of strategic choice – being one of the four final holes completed by Hugh Wilson. The hole is a strong, 448 yards par-4, played out to an island fairway. It turns to the left, and the drive must be to the centre or right to give

The 17th is only 338 yards long but is uphill all the way and the final 70-odd yards to the green are virtually desert scrub. This view from the green was taken during the 1985 Walker Cup.

a sight of the green. The heroic approach, directly on to the putting surface, must carry sand all the way. To the front right-hand side, there is an area of fairway to receive the approach if the drive was short. This route leaves a pitch to the flagstick and the hope of one putt. Most reasonable men would be content to score four on this hole, however they did it, and would not be devastated to score five. The course then has an appealing finish. The 17th is 338 yards, but it is uphill and played across water to a rather small green. The 18th is a fine, attractive final hole of 428 yards, played to an island fairway, then across water and yet more sand to one of Pine Valley's larger greens.

Pine Valley is unique: it is as penal as Oakmont; it is as beautiful as Augusta or Muirfield Village. It is one of the world's greatest courses.

PINEHURST

The resort village of Pinehurst, more or less midway between Charlotte and Raleigh in the sandhills of North Carolina, is a paradise. Surely no community in the world, St Andrews in Scotland included, is more obsessed with the game of golf, and Pinehurst's No 2 course is its masterpiece. The eminence of Pinehurst and its development as a shrine of world golf, with seven courses and a permanent resident population of little more than 3,000, is linked to the lives of famous men, to the village of Dornoch in Scotland and to fate.

James Tufts of Boston and the American Soda Fountain Company did not enjoy the best of health and at the end of the last century had taken to spending much of the bleak New England winters in the much drier, milder climate of North Carolina. With the idea of developing at Pinehurst a winter resort that other New Englanders might find attractive, he bought, at one dollar an acre, some 5,000 acres of almost barren timberland, and had an unpretentious course laid out on land that, though little appreciated at the time, was ideal for golf – its sandy subsoil and short crisp fairway grasses being about as close to links conditions as anyone could hope for.

In 1900 came two events of deep and lasting significance for Pinehurst. First, Harry Vardon, the great English champion who later in the year was to win the U.S. Open, came to the village in the

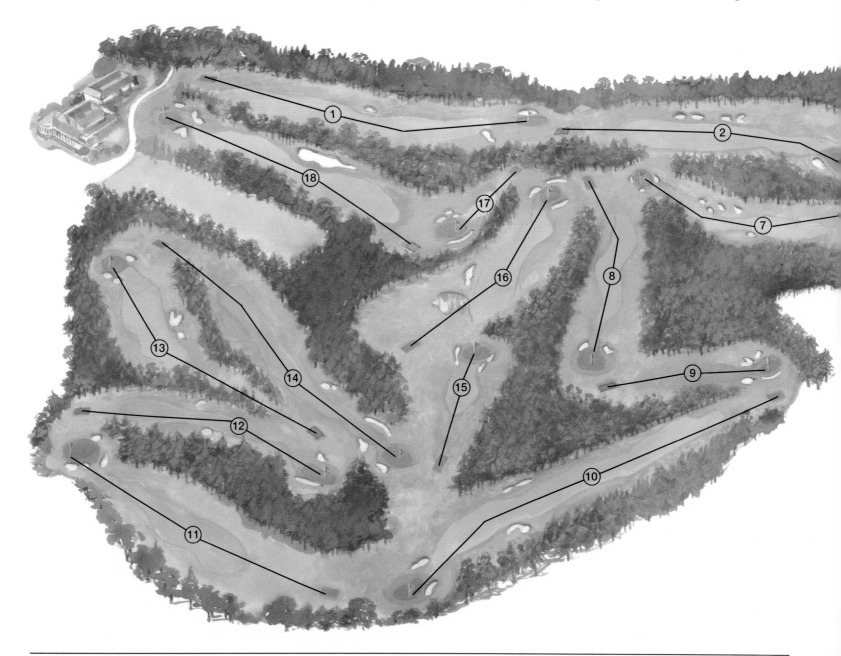

PINEHURST					
Card of the No. 2 course					
1	396 yards	par 4	10	578 yards	par 5
2	441 yards	par 4	11	433 yards	par 4
3	335 yards	par 4	12	415 yards	par 4
4	547 yards	par 5	13	374 yards	par 4
5	445 yards	par 4	14	436 yards	par 4
6	212 yards	par 3	15	201 yards	par 3
7	401 yards	par 4	16	531 yards	par 5
8	487 yards	par 5	17	190 yards	par 3
9	166 yards	par 3	18	432 yards	par 4
	3,430 yards	par 36		3,590 yards	par 36
	Total 7,020 yards par 72				

spring and played four exhibition rounds. The artistry of the great man, the simplicity with which he swung the club and his unerring control over his shots made a powerful impression on the locals and visitors alike. Second, later that year Donald Ross arrived to become Pinehurst's new professional and greenkeeper.

Links with Royal Dornoch

Donald James Ross was born in 1873 in Dornoch, a lovely Highland village of little more than 1,000 souls, some 50 miles north of Inverness in Scotland. He was apprenticed to a local carpenter and became an enthusiastic and talented golfer. Golf had been played at Dornoch for hundreds of years, but in 1877 the Dornoch Golf Club was formed at the instigation of an exceptional local man, John

The well guarded green on the 5th, a long and difficult par-4. The tee shot should be down the right half of the fairway to allow a clear way into the angled green.

Sutherland, and in 1886, Sutherland invited Old Tom Morris from St Andrews to define 18 holes of 'championship quality' at Dornoch. Sutherland arranged for young Ross to go to St Andrews and learn the clubmaking craft from Old Tom. He spent two years there.

At this point, Robert Wilson, a professor at Harvard University, visited Dornoch and became a pupil of Donald Ross. He told the young Scot of the tremendous interest in golf in America, and encouraged him to emigrate. Thus in 1898, Ross knocked on the Wilson door in Cambridge, Massachussetts and went to work at the Oakley Club, in nearby Waterstown. Here, our Bostonian James Tufts completes the chain. He observed Ross in action, admired his conduct and was impressed by his feelings for the traditions of golf and his attitude to course design. He invited Ross to become the winter professional at Pinehurst, and the young Scot arrived there in December of 1900. Ross got to work on improving the existing course, and in his very first year had started to lay out Pinehurst No 2. At the same time, Tufts had instituted a tree-planting programme.

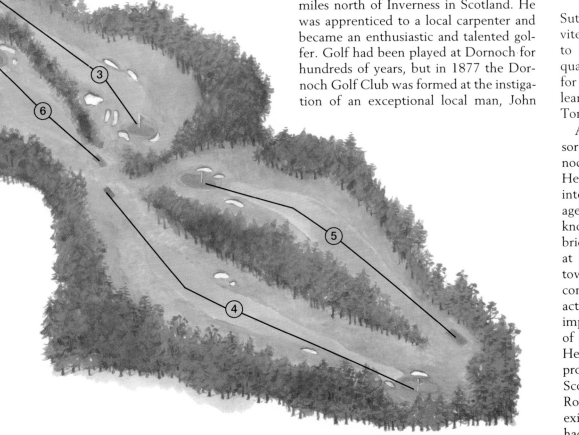

Ross's Triumph

Ross finished Pinehurst No 2 in 1907, in the sense that 18 holes were completed reaching to not quite 6,000 yards; but he continually improved and polished his work over the years as better greenkeeping and maintenance methods and equipment became available. The course as we know it today is a triumph, a links in a forest. It has a par of 72 at around 7,000 yards, and demands of the golfer virtually every shot in this repertoire. It has in abundance what we now think of as Ross characteristics: rather small greens with subtle rather than severe contouring, and with verges and swales around them to demand finesse when chipping the ball or playing a pitch-and-run to the flag.

Ross wanted golf to be a pleasure, not a penance. Unlike Fownes at Oakmont, Charles Blair Macdonald at The National, or – above all – George Crump at Pine Valley, Ross did not feel that a hazard should necessarily be penal. Rather, the player should have the possibility of redeeming his wayward shot with the chance to play an imaginative recovery. Ross's thinking was that a championship course should demand 'long and accurate

Above: *The delightful 17th hole is a medium length one-shotter whose pine-fringed green is bunkered everywhere, except the left front.*

Right: *The par-5 4th curves gently left on its uphill journey to the green, which is normally reachable in two good shots. The World Golf Hall of Fame (opened in 1974) is beyond the green.*

tee shots, accurate iron play, precise handling of the short game, and consistent putting'. He built all of these requirements into Pinehurst and other fine courses with which he was involved, such as Oak Hill, Seminole, Oakland Hills and Scioto, where Nicklaus learned the game.

Donald Ross built two further 18-hole courses at Pinehurst, but Pinehurst No 2 remained his favourite: the 'fairest test I have ever designed'. The 1st hole is a par-4 of 396 yards turning slightly left; a reasonable hole which should give anyone a comfortable start to the round. The 2nd is another par-4, this time of 441 yards turning slightly to the right and slightly less reasonable, and the 3rd, at 335 yards, is a very closely guarded drive and pitch hole. Thus the course leads the golfer into

its treasures with progressively more testing holes. The 4th is 547 yards, a big par-5 uphill to the green at the most distant corner of the course, but it is the par-4s which hold the key to scoring.

The course has an interesting finish, full of birdie opportunities for the accomplished player. The 15th is a short hole of 201 yards, a straight shot to a fairly open green. No 16 is a par-5 of some 531 yards, with a drive over a pond – the only water hazard on the course. On a direct line, the tee shot here calls for a carry of 180 yards over the water, but Ross provides an alternative fairway line to the right. No 17 is another par-3 of 190 yards, and the last hole is 432 yards, back up to the elegant, spacious clubhouse.

Although the sandy ground has given it the flavour of a links, Pinehurst No 2 is in an odd way the summation of the American parkland course. The pine trees, which are never overbearing, nevertheless screen each hole from its neighbour; isolating the player from the world as a links never does. All in all, it is an entirely stimulating experience, particularly when the blossom blooms in the Carolina springtime.

OAKLAND HILLS

'I'm glad I brought this course, this monster, to its knees'. Thus spoke Ben Hogan at the presentation ceremonies of the 1951 U.S. Open Championship at Oakland Hills, which he won with a final round of 67. His remark has passed into the folklore of the game. Whether or not Oakland Hills is a monster is a moot point. Certainly at the time it was a brutal course, and Hogan's win, like Hogan's comment, remains something of a milestone in the game.

Oakland Hills, in Birmingham, Michigan, on the edge of 'greater' Detroit, was built in 1917, the club having been formed by wealthy executives of the Ford Motor Company. The course was designed by Donald Ross of Pinehurst fame. In 1918 Walter Hagen became the head professional on a handsome retainer. But after he won the U.S. Open of 1919 he decided that a club job, however rewarding, was not to be compared with the delights of exhibition matches and public appearances awaiting him all over the world, and he quit.

The course was considered a fine Ross design and a good test, and it staged the Opens of 1924, when Cyril Walker, the little Englishman originally from Hoylake,

beat Bobby Jones into second place; and of 1937, which was won by Ralph Guldahl, for a few short seasons just about the best player in America. By the time of the next Open, scheduled for 1951, the members felt that the course needed 'modernisation' – in those days the host club and not the USGA was responsible for course preparation. The architect, Robert Trent Jones – some of the players thought that he was the monster – was called in, and he made clear that his intention was that the course should 'catch up with the players'. Jones had studied the play and collected data at several earlier Opens. He was convinced that contemporary players, now with steel shafts and much improved golf balls, were simply gobbling up golf courses which dated from the 1920s.

Thus Jones filled in all the fairway bunkers in the 200–220 yards range – the players were simply driving over them. He cut new bunkers 230–260 yards out from the tees, and allowed the rough to grow in on either side of the fairway so that the landing zone for tee shots in some cases was little more than 20 yards across. And the bunkering around the greens was tightened, the result being a course that

OAKLAND HILLS Card of the South course					
1	446 yards	par 4	10	459 yards	par 4
2	521 yards	par 5	11	420 yards	par 4
3	202 yards	par 3	12	567 yards	par 5
4	439 yards	par 4	13	173 yards	par 3
5	442 yards	par 4	14	468 yards	par 4
6	368 yards	par 4	15	388 yards	par 4
7	408 yards	par 4	16	408 yards	par 4
8	458 yards	par 4	17	201 yards	par 3
9	227 yards	par 3	18	459 yards	par 4
3,511 yards par 35			3,543 yards par 35		
Total 7,054 yards par 70					

punished the slightest error severely, demanded extreme accuracy, and rewarded rational thinking in the sense that players would prosper if they slavishly followed the only route to each hole that Jones was prepared to allow.

Hogan opened his '51 Open with a 76, a round of some indecision and uncertainty in the face of Jones' changes. But he improved every round and, deciding that attack was the only way to subdue the monster, he tore into the course and produced a brilliant last round of 67. He later called it the finest round of his career. He finished it with an arrogant, defiant flourish. The 18th hole is 459 yards, turning to the right. Hogan hit an immense drive, then a mid-iron that stopped 15 feet from the flagstick, and holed the putt.

After the controversy over the difficulty of the course for that Championship, the USGA increasingly took responsibility for the preparation of all their championship courses. But there is no doubt that Trent Jones produced the makings of a very good course – even a great one, the more so that it has now matured impressively. At 7,054 yards it is a big, open parkland course, not over-wooded, featuring two lakes and a stream and

The 16th hole at Oakland Hills, par 4, 408 yards, demanding a brave and accurate second shot across or around water. Andy North and T. C. Chen on the green during the U.S. Open of 1985, which North won.

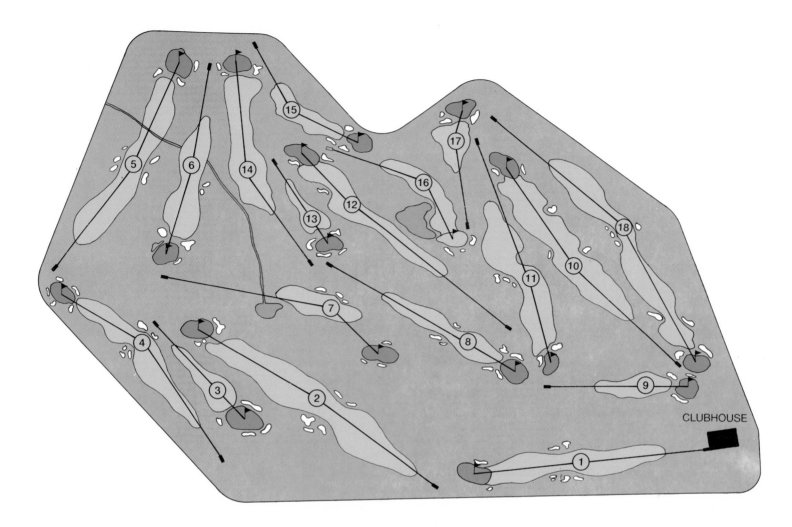

many fiendish par-4 holes, only two of them shorter than 400 yards. It has kept the modern professionals reasonably in check. Gene Littler's Open total in 1961 was 281, the same as Guldahl's 24 years earlier, and little worse than Andy North's 279 in 1985.

Oakland Hills has produced shots of high courage and of low, tragic farce. In the 1972 PGA Championship Gary Player, with three holes to play, was level with Jim Jamieson — the latter already on the 18th. Player's tee shot on 16, a drive and pitch hole, was wildly sliced into rough which had been trampled by spectators. The hole played properly is a drive out to the 250 yards mark (the hole was 408 yards), then a half-right turn to pitch along the length of the green. The putting surface is screened at the front and along the right side by a good-sized lake. Player's drive had left him in the rough 150 yards from the flagstick, with a blind shot which had to clear a copse of willow trees,

T. C. Chen playing the 5th, a hole he will never forget. In the last round of the 1985 U.S. Open, he was four strokes ahead of the field, but on this chip shot actually struck the ball twice, scoring eight on the hole.

travel far enough to cross the lake, then somehow get down onto the green without running into the bunkers immediately behind it — one of them exactly in line with his shot and the flagstick. Player hit a

9-iron. The ball stopped four feet from the flag. He holed the putt, the birdie winning him the championship.

In the U.S. Open of 1985, T.C. Chen of Taiwan, who had led after three rounds, was four strokes ahead of Andy North and eight under par with 14 holes to play. It was surely Chen's championship. At the 5th hole (442 yards) Chen drove into perfect position. Astonishingly, and for no apparent reason, he then hit a 4-iron at least 30 yards off line into heavy rough. Chen's third shot left him a yard or two short of the green, but still in heavy rough. Now came the most bizarre shot imaginable. Chen chopped down on the ball with his wedge. The ball popped up in front of him and the blade of the wedge, in following through, struck the ball for a second time. Penalised, he eventually took eight on the hole and Andy North went on to win the championship. T.C. Chen finished second, one stroke behind.

MUIRFIELD VILLAGE

The course that Jack built should be one of the wonders of the world, for surely no golfer in the world knows more about the playing of great holes and great courses than Jack Nicklaus. His lovely course at Dublin, Ohio, just to the north of Columbus, Jack's home town, was ready for play in 1976, but the concept dates from 1966 when Nicklaus, sitting on the clubhouse verandah at Augusta National, said to a friend, Ivor Young: 'Wouldn't it be great to have something like this in Columbus?'

Nicklaus has never had any qualms about spending vast amounts of money on various projects. He has charged immense fees for his design work, he has never been particularly thrifty, and he has always been his own man. In the 1960s, he was under the management of Mark McCormack and his company. When Jack told Mark about his notion of building a course in the Columbus area, Mark said: 'Forget it'. He took the view that Nicklaus might as well stand on a street corner setting fire to 100 dollar bills. But Nicklaus is a stubborn perfectionist. He went ahead, and after many dramas and disappointments managed to cobble together the finance needed. On 27 May 1974, Nicklaus drove the first ball at the opening ceremony. The costs to that point were four million dollars – 'That would not even get you started today', he said recently. Certainly, 16 years on, you'd have to multiply that sum by, say, a factor of 5.

Muirfield Village, completely dissimilar to the original Muirfield after which it was named, is on steeply rolling land, providing a succession of valleys along which the fairways run. Nicklaus has written: 'From the player's standpoint, everything is well-defined. You know exactly where you have to go and what you have to do. Your short game is tested if you miss a green, but there is not one place on the whole golf course that anyone is going to say is unfair. Golf to me is a game of precision more than power, and I think the course reflects that'.

Nicklaus, with the help of fellow designers Desmond Muirhead and Pete Dye, set out to build a course that would meet three essential requirements. Firstly, it should stretch the abilities of the world's best players in tournament conditions. (Nicklaus' Memorial Tournament is played at Muirfield Village in May.) Secondly it should provide good vantage points to the crowds attending the tournament, and thirdly it should accommodate 'lesser' men, the members of the club that he would form. Since the course opened there have been changes, large and small, nearly 100 in all.

The most extensive changes have taken place at the 11th. Its original design saw a

MUIRFIELD VILLAGE					
Card of the course					
1	446 yards	par 4	10	441 yards	par 4
2	452 yards	par 4	11	538 yards	par 5
3	392 yards	par 4	12	158 yards	par 3
4	204 yards	par 3	13	442 yards	par 4
5	531 yards	par 5	14	363 yards	par 4
6	430 yards	par 4	15	490 yards	par 5
7	549 yards	par 5	16	204 yards	par 3
8	189 yards	par 3	17	430 yards	par 4
9	410 yards	par 4	18	437 yards	par 4
3,603 yards	par 36		3,503 yards	par 36	
Total 7,106 yards par 72					

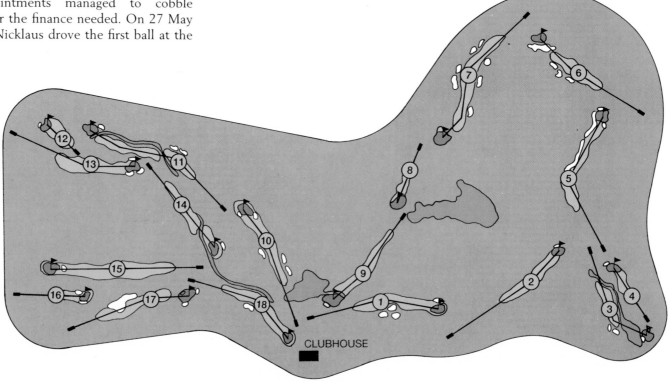

stream cutting across the fairway from left to right at about 320 yards from the tee, then running along the right side of the fairway up to the green; it then turned left and fed into a lake, which covered the entire front of the green. When Nicklaus played the hole he realised that from the landing area of the drive, in the fairway, the lake could not be seen. He had it filled and now a narrow stream crosses in front of the green. The cost of that one operation was about $200,000!

On the tenth anniversary of his Memorial Tournament, Nicklaus wrote of golf: 'I believe it is a much better game played downhill than up. You drive from a high tee at the first, second, third, fourth and fifth, on seven you drive over a valley which has the same effect. On seven, eight and nine you drive from elevated tees, on ten you drive over a valley even though you are rising and on eleven, twelve, thirteen and fourteen you hit from a high tee. There is not one tee shot that you are actually hitting uphill. In fact, there are only two second shots on the whole golf course that are uphill'.

Larry Nelson and Lanny Wadkins against Sandy Lyle and Bernhard Langer in the 1987 Ryder Cup. Nelson hits at the 16th, a par 3 reminiscent of the 16th at Augusta.

There are only 70 bunkers at Muirfield Village, not an excessive number, but it seems that Nicklaus in designing the course succumbed to the obsession that contemporary American designers have with water hazards. Water is in play at no fewer that eleven holes. At the 2nd, a creek crosses the fairway, runs along the right side of it then swings behind the green. At the 3rd, a stream crosses the fairway from the right, then opens out into a lake fronting the entire green. The hole is 392 yards and the green split level. On the 5th hole, a par-5 of 531 yards, a brook runs right up the centre of the second half of the fairway, before passing the green to the left. A stream crosses the sixth fairway and there is a pond in front of the green. Seven and eight are dry holes, but on nine, one of Muirfield's tightest driving holes, all along the right

side of a narrow fairway the ground falls away into woods and once more a stream crosses close to the green. At ten the drive crosses a pond. On the big par-5 11th, as we have seen, again there is water, all along the right side and again crossing in front of the green. The 12th, a par-3 of 158 yards, like the 16th at Augusta National, is over water all the way. And holes 14, 15 and 18 have streams, although they do not come into play as the other water hazards.

Finally, there are three separate tees at each hole, some fifty yards apart – marvellously cosmetic, but surely ruinous on the greenkeeping budget. But that's Nicklaus. Often the members' tee will be fifty yards ahead of the tournament tee. And in providing good vantage points for spectators at his tournament, with little or no expense spared, Nicklaus has done it very well, with mounds and ridges put in place along the fairways, and amphitheatres around the greens. Quite simply Muirfield Village is a magnificent achievement and a great course maintained in mint condition.

AUGUSTA NATIONAL

The Augusta National is the best-known golf course in the world. The Augusta Masters is the best-known golf tournament in the world. Millions of viewers throughout the world, not all of them golfers, see the tournament played on this distinctive course each spring as all the sporting nations of the world link into the American television coverage.

The course is immaculately maintained. Acres of closely-cropped green and luxuriant turf swaddle the property, while magnificent Georgia pines soar 100 feet in the air, forming avenues and backdrops for the holes. The tournament is played in April, in the soft Georgia springtime, and if the weather has behaved and the gardening staff have got their timing right, the entire course will be a flood of flowering shrubs which give names to the golf holes – azalea, dogwood, redbud, camellia, flowering peach, magnolia and so on.

However, the Masters has its critics. They claim that it cannot be called a championship, unless you want to call it a 'closed' championship. Certainly it has a restricted field. Most players qualify to play through established criteria; but many, including up to a dozen amateurs, are invited at the whim of, not a national association but a hugely conservative, often arrogant club. Indeed, Hord Hardin, the present tournament chairman, who could be described as a traditionalist, has been dubbed 'Lord' Hardin by many American journalists. But, in fairness, the Augusta club has never claimed the Masters to be anything other than an invitational tournament.

Bobby Jones's Legacy

When Bobby Jones retired from competitive championship play in 1930, having won the Amateur and Open Championships of both Britain and the United States that year, he had very clear ideas regarding the design of golf holes – ideas which he had amassed in 10 years of play on both sides of the Atlantic. He had often thought of building a course which would incorporate these ideas and he

AUGUSTA NATIONAL Card of the course							
1	Tea Olive	400 yards	par 4	10	Camellia	485 yards	par 4
2	Pink Dogwood	555 yards	par 5	11	White Dogwood	455 yards	par 4
3	Flowering Peach	360 yards	par 4	12	Golden Bell	155 yards	par 3
4	Flowering Crab Apple	205 yards	par 3	13	Azalea	465 yards	par 5
5	Magnolia	435 yards	par 4	14	Chinese Fir	405 yards	par 4
6	Juniper	180 yards	par 3	15	Firethorn	500 yards	par 5
7	Pampas	360 yards	par 4	16	Redbud	170 yards	par 3
8	Yellow Jasmine	535 yards	par 5	17	Nandina	400 yards	par 4
9	Carolina Cherry	435 yards	par 4	18	Holly	405 yards	par 4
		3,465 yards	par 36			3,440 yards	par 36
		Total 6,905 yards par 72					

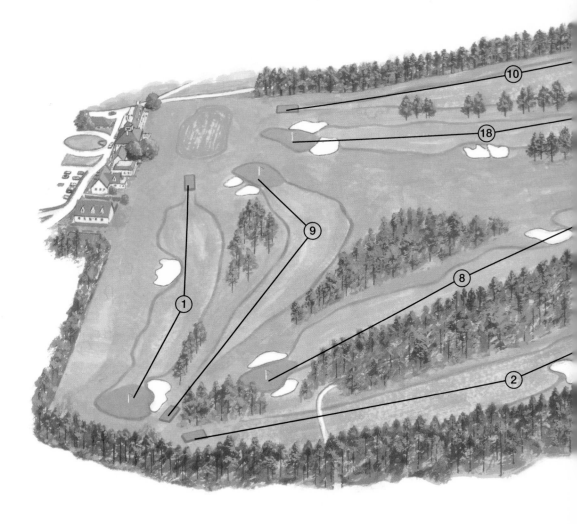

discussed this with a few of his friends.

Jones, from Atlanta, knew the small town of Augusta, 100 miles away – he married an Augusta girl – and often played winter golf there. He also knew Clifford Roberts, a New York merchant banker, who spent time every winter in Augusta. Thus when 'Fruitlands', a famous nursery, came up for sale, Jones and Roberts snapped it up, all 365 acres, at Depression prices. It seemed perfect terrain for the course Jones had in mind. He then had the good sense to retain Dr Alister Mackenzie, a Scot who had emigrated to America and given up medicine in favour of golf-course design, to lay out the course. They proved ideal partners. Jones had been impressed by the size of the double greens at St Andrews, and by the speedy links greens he had found in Scotland and England – sand-based, close-cropped, subtly contoured and fast, very fast. Mackenzie knew them well, and was of the same mind. He had designed Royal Melbourne West in 1926 (see page 186), and Cypress Point in 1928 (see page 52), and was at the height of his powers.

Jones had visualised a club of which his friends, drawn from all over the country, would be members. It would be for winter golf, open only from November to April, and only for golf: there were to be no swimming pools and no tennis courts.

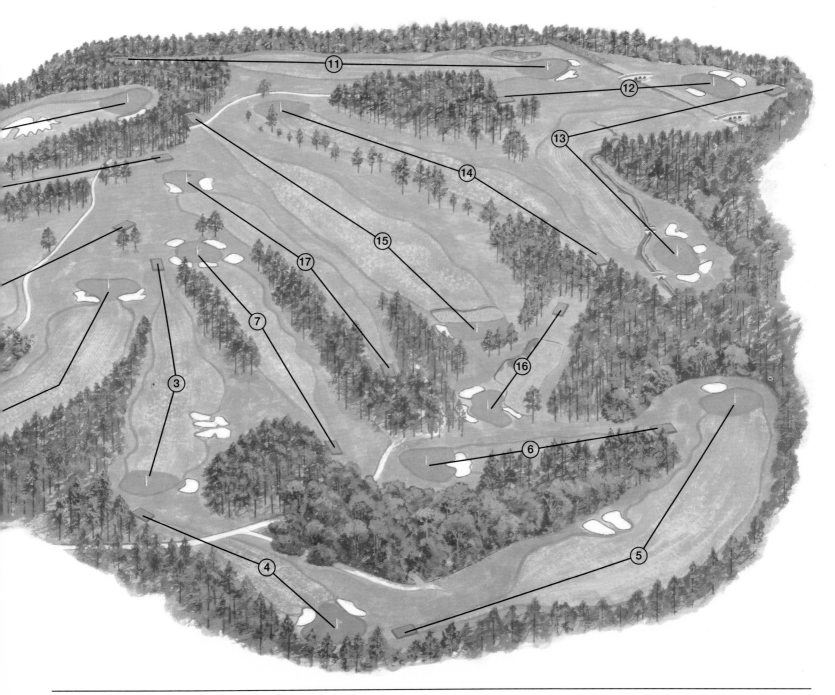

Left: *Part of Amen Corner, the 13th at Augusta National, the beautiful par-5 'Azalea' hole, with its tiara of bunkers behind and the famous Rae's Creek in front.*

Right: *Spain's José-Maria Olazábal hits a tee shot at the short 12th on the first day of the 1989 Masters. The small green is fiercely guarded by bunkers and at front by a creek.*

He made it clear to Mackenzie that he wanted a course which his friends could play and enjoy, yet at the same time one that would test tournament players. The property they had to work with is in the rough shape of a square, with a pleasant but small pre-Civil War mansion serving as the clubhouse on the north side. From there the property falls a good 100 feet down to Rae's Creek, running along the bottom boundary. The downslope is gentle and most of the holes run across rather than up and down the slope. Nowhere do two successive holes run in the same direction, and seldom do they slope excessively from side to side.

When Jones and Mackenzie had finished, they had the 'ultimate' American meadowland course. Nevertheless, its critics have strong reservations about Augusta as a true championship test. There is no rough on the course – at least, no rough as the Scots or Irish or anyone else might know it. Under Augusta's towering pines, there might be a few needles, but little else to inhibit a full recovery shot. Also, the fairways are ridiculously wide, so that sluggers can blast away off the tees to their hearts'

content. And there is an odd absence of bunkers at Augusta – fewer than 50 in all, and only 10 of these in the fairways. Thus far it seems ready made for a careful 15-handicap player!

Lightning-fast Greens
But then there are the greens. Many of them are raised a foot or two and plateaued. All of them are enormous, with extremely steep slopes, and for the Masters they are lightning-fast. It is the greens that hold the key to scoring at

Augusta – more so than almost anywhere else. Its critics say that since putting takes up 50 per cent of the strokes in the theoretical round of golf, it should constitute no more than 50 per cent of any course's challenge. At the Masters, they claim it is much more than that – some would call it 100 per cent of the challenge, since the tee to green requirement is basically little more than that the player should be able to hit the ball a long way.

Many changes have been made over the years to the original design. One of the most important, made by Jones himself, was to switch the two halves of the course, the original outward half now being the inward half. In addition, the 10th, 11th, 13th, 15th, 16th and 18th, in particular have been strengthened.

'Amen Corner'
The inward half of the Augusta National course, as set up for the Masters, merits

The 10th hole. It is here, on the final afternoon of the Masters, that the fun really begins for it is then, on the homeward stretch, that nerves are as much an ally as skill.

some study. The 10th hole is a downhill drive. A ridge runs along the centre of the fairway, the hole turning slightly right to left. A drive lined up on the right half will be thrown further right, leaving a second shot of inordinate length to the green. A drive with a line only just left of centre will be thrown forward and down to the left, to a pocket of fairway which will put 20 yards on the shot, give the player a flat and level stance and a clear look at the green. The 11th hole, now 455 yards, has a lake along its left side and part of its front calling for an audacious second shot of great accuracy. Often played defensively.

The 12th is one of the world's great par-3 holes. It measures 155 yards. It plays to a green which is quite wide, but narrow from front to back. Rae's Creek crosses in front, pushing up towards the putting surface. A frontal bunker is squeezed between water and putting surface and there are two bunkers off the

The beautifully manicured and fast greens of the par-5 15th with the 16th behind. With water to carry on the second shot this is a formidable hole, but reachable in two for the long hitters.

back of the green, with its backcloth of shrubs and tall pines. The pin is often cut on a direct line with front and back bunkers. There may be only a handful of yards between flagstick and water. Behind the green are flowering shrubs and a wall of tall pine trees. And up there, above the green, tree-top high, is wind, the great unknown factor. The player will be hitting a high pitch to this hole, to a really minute target area. If only he could know what the wind will do to his shot, if indeed there is any wind: there's little point in throwing up strands of grass in the air here. So this 12th hole, severe enough in its basic parts, becomes an enigma wrapped in a mystery.

The drive on the 465-yard 13th hole is

like that on the 10th (and unlike many other Augusta tee shots) in that it demands some precision. The hole dog-legs sharply to the left. The perfect drive will be long, with a drawn tail on it, up the left side of the fairway. The creek runs along most of the left side of the hole, crossing in front of the green. The fairway slopes down towards the creek. But if the drive is played precisely, it will carry past the corner and, drawn to the left, will find yet again a pocket of fairway which gives a flat and level lie; on the inside of the angle, this position represents the shortest route to the hole. The second is the gambler's shot. Can he carry that brook and hit the big, two-tiered green and have two comfortable putts for his birdie? Or should he play short and hope to make his birdie with an accurate pitch and a single putt? These three holes are known collectively as Amen Corner, and many of the US Masters tournaments have been won and lost here.

A Tough Finish

The 14th fairway slopes left to right, but the main defences of the hole are the mounds and slopes on the very big green – one of the most difficult on the course. The 15th is a straight par-5 of 500 yards, the drive up to and over a crest, then a second to a crowned green which lies across the shot and is protected by a lake covering its entire front. The second shot is the gamble, of course, like its equivalent on 13. Can the water be carried? Some years back, at the top of the rise on the 15th, some mounds were put in place on the right side to reduce the advantage the long hitters had when their shots would bound on far down the slope. But nowadays the best players will usually be hitting some kind of iron shot to the green. Indeed, the big hitters must beware their approach running through the green and into the lake at the 16th.

The 170-yard 16th, with a fairway consisting almost entirely of water, has

Sandy Lyle's stupendous 7-iron second shot soars out of the fairway bunker on the 72nd hole at Augusta in 1988. It finished 10 feet above the pin and his birdie putt clinched the Masters.

been a turning point in many a Masters. So it was in 1988, when Sandy Lyle won. His victory is best remembered for the epic 7-iron shot he played from the fairway bunker at the very last hole which set up the birdie he needed to win. Yet the birdie he made on the 16th was no less critical. Having lost his lead at Amen Corner, he hit a 7-iron shot some 15 feet above the hole. The fast, downhill putt had a break of a good 18 inches, from left to right, but Lyle rolled it smoothly into the centre of the hole.

The main difficulty on the 17th hole, 400 yards, is in judging distance on the second shot – a pitch to a green slightly above the player – particularly when the pin is behind one of the two front

bunkers. The 18th hole, 405 yards, is uphill all the way, the final drive out of a tunnel of pine trees, the hole turning to the right past fairway bunkers on the left (where Lyle was trapped in 1988), up to the two-level 18th green sloping wickedly towards the player.

The exploits of the great players have highlighted this inward half, some of them scarcely credible: the famous 'double-eagle' of Gene Sarazen in 1935, when he holed his second shot, a 4-wood, at the 15th to tie Craig Wood before winning the play-off; Byron Nelson making up six shots on leader Ralph Guldahl at Amen Corner in 1937 by means of a birdie at the 12th and an eagle at the 13th; Ben Hogan, then 54 years old, coming home in a flawless 30 shots in 1967; Gary Player winning in 1978 with a preposterous last round of 64, including seven birdies; Jack Nicklaus calculating coldly that a final round of 65 might just win him the Masters, and doing it in 1986.

OLYMPIC

Olympic Lakeside is the ultimate American parkland course. So heavily forested is it that the trees must be considered as much a hazard as any bunker or stream. The golfer will find himself playing from tees so over-arched by trees as to be almost claustrophobic, and he will be asked to drive along precise lines down narrow, forbidding chutes between huge stands of pine and cypress, eucalyptus and even some California redwoods, many of them growing to 80 feet. The Olympic fairways are so heavily screened by dense walls of these giants that the golfer seems to be walking along a series of trenches, each hole unvisible from its neighbours. Not surprisingly it can seem an almost spooky place.

The other pronounced characteristic of this formidable course is the sloping fairways – almost all of them tilt from one side to the other, every one is a dog-leg of varying degree, and the slopes throw the ball to the *outside* of the angles. Yet the history of the Lakeside course and the Olympic Club show that it never was a natural parkland. The club made it so.

The Olympic Club of San Francisco originated in the middle of the last century as a gymnastic club, and then developed to embrace almost all sports. The 'Athletic' club in all the major U.S. cities was an American institution. These clubs had, and still have, city premises providing swimming pools, billiards, handball, racquets, fencing, shooting and the like, and of course restaurants. In the golden days of amateurism, before the advent of professionalism and more recently, of televised sport, they would produce teams in football, basketball and ice-hockey which could compete at the highest level; and they produced many Olympic athletes.

The San Francisco club had splendid city headquarters by the time America entered the First World War, but even then a growing demand for golf could be satisfied only when it took over the ailing Lakeside Country CLub. Lakeside's property on the west side of the city, close by the ocean, ran to 365 acres of barren, treeless ground with a ridge running through the property and an existing but indifferent course, laid out early in the century by three immigrant Scottish professionals.

Lakeside and Ocean

Willie Watson, yet another Scot, who had designed the Minikahda club in Minneapolis, was retained to lay out two courses, one on either side of the ridge – one, 'inland', Lakeside; the other, on the seaward side of the ridge, Ocean. Savage storms in 1926 washed out some of the holes, and Sam Whiting, at that time professional and greenkeeper to the club, designed and built two new courses and completely altered the face of the landscape by planting 43,000 trees, three-quarters of them on the Lakeside course. A quarter of a century later they had grown to make Lakeside a forest and every one of its fairways a tree-lined avenue.

The sea mist that rolls in regularly on the prevailing wind from the Pacific Ocean, often covering the entire city,

Ben Hogan, watched by Sam Snead, lines out a drive in practice for the 1955 U.S. Open in San Francisco. Hogan, seeking a record fifth Open win, lost a play-off to club pro Jack Fleck.

OLYMPIC Card of the course					
1	530 yards	par 5	10	412 yards	par 4
2	400 yards	par 4	11	427 yards	par 4
3	220 yards	par 3	12	386 yards	par 4
4	428 yards	par 4	13	185 yards	par 3
5	456 yards	par 4	14	417 yards	par 4
6	434 yards	par 4	15	147 yards	par 3
7	288 yards	par 4	16	604 yards	par 5
8	135 yards	par 3	17	517 yards	par 5
9	424 yards	par 4	18	338 yards	par 4
3,315 yards	par 35		3,433 yards	par 36	
Total 6,748 yards par 71					

makes San Francisco a damp town, and Lakeside has, not surprisingly, little difficulty in growing grass. Its problems are in controlling growth, and the Lakeside rough can be dense and tough. The tilted fairways will carry a carelessly-hit ball into the trees and the rough, and recovery from these places often means a scrambling shot out to the nearest point of the fairway – in effect, a shot lost. Ben Hogan experienced just that in the play-off to the 1955 U.S. Open, against Jack Fleck, an unknown touring pro from a public course in Iowa. Just as Hogan finished his fourth round and seemed to have won a record fifth Championship, Fleck tied him with a brilliant last round of 67, scoring two birdies over the four final holes. In the play-off Hogan, one stroke behind, hooked his drive into fierce rough on the 18th hole and scored six on the hole. Fleck was champion.

Lakeside's rough can be unmanageable, as Arnold Palmer found when the Open next came to Olympic in 1966. The 16th is a huge par-5 of more than 600 yards which turns progressively to the left in a crescent shape. Palmer drove into the left rough and, Arnold being Arnold, elected to play a 3-iron out of that jungle. He failed. The hole cost him six. He dropped seven shots over the last nine to Billy Casper, tied the championship and lost the play-off!

Olympic Lakeside is an unrelenting course, even a disquieting course. There is

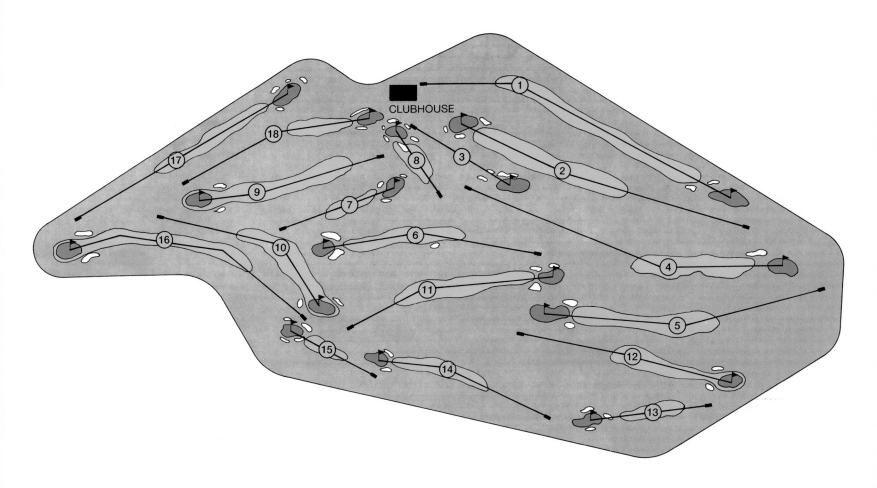

only one fairway bunker, on the 6th, and there is no water hazard. Yet the sloping fairways with the cambers going the wrong way, the severe rough and the small, closely-bunkered greens make it very exacting. The 18th hole somehow personifies the entire course. It is a mere 338 yards, played downhill, perhaps with an iron, to a slight fairway which falls off to the right and has a minute green, totally surrounded by bunkering, with a very narrow entrance.

Yet for all its degree of difficulty and somewhat strange atmosphere, Lakeside is lovely, green and fresh, and although quite different in personality and concept from its California neighbours at Pebble Beach and Cypress Point, it stands beside and equal to them as one of the world's great golf courses.

The approach to the 18th – the shot to the tiny green has to run the gauntlet of four bunkers. Scott Simpson (centre left) strides to the 72nd and victory in the 1987 U.S. Open.

CYPRESS POINT

The Monterey Peninsula contains three great courses: Cypress Point, the somewhat older Pebble Beach, and Robert Trent Jones's 1966 addition, the frighteningly difficult Spyglass Hill. Three courses of such quality side by side brings to mind the Kent coast and its string of three great English links of Prince's, Royal St George's and Royal Cinque Ports – but in what a different landscape!

The Monterey Peninsula is punched out into the Pacific Ocean by the descending thrust of the Santa Lucia mountains on the south side of Monterey Bay, just over 100 miles south of San Francisco. Records of the area date from the middle of the 16th century, but the city of Monterey dates from 1770, when a formal mission was set up. The original Del Monte Hotel dates from 1878, and boasted tennis courts, polo fields, a racecourse, steeplechase track and stables – and from 1897 the golf course, the first 18-hole course in California.

The peninsula is a place of surf booming against high cliffs at high tide, surging among low rocks at low tide. It is a place of quite dazzling beauty, of green forests sweeping down to the shore, of startling silver sandhills, of pine and eucalyptus, of sealions basking on offshore rocks, of deer meandering out of the forests, and of Monterey cypress. Set in this landscape, Cypress Point offers a catalogue of breathcatching delights.

Origins

The club's origins are curiously similar to Pebble Beach's. Its first moving spirit was Marion Hollins, who by the early 'Twenties was a champion amateur golfer selling real estate for the Del Monte company. The lady was obviously a crackerjack personality on and off the course. She had been a beaten finalist in the U.S. National Women's Amateur Championship in 1913, defeated by an English girl, Gladys Ravencroft, the British champion of the previous year, but had come back to win in 1921 when she defeated the famous Alexa Stirling of Atlanta by 5 and 4. Miss Hollins had been very active in promoting the Women's National, a fine 'women-only' course at Glen Head on Long Island. She then discovered California, fell in love with it and moved to Monterey. There she joined Byington Ford, a former mayor of nearby Carmel – then little more than a village – and Roger Lapham, a member of a prominent San Francisco shipping family. The trio paid Del Monte Property Company $150,000 for 175 acres.

The first architect chosen for the work was Seth Raynor, a disciple of Charles Blair Macdonald; but he died unexpectedly, of pneumonia. Marion Hollins wisely, and luckily, was able to appoint Dr Alister Mackenzie to take over the work. Mackenzie had just done some impressive work in Australia, and was to do more, subsequently, at Augusta National in Georgia. The Cypress Point Golf Club opened in August 1928, and had passed the 100 mark in membership commitments when the Depression struck. Not surprisingly there were many withdrawals and the club started up with but 40 members. Plans for a grandiose

Dr Alister Mackenzie – seen here (right) on the 1st fairway at St Andrews – created a masterpiece at Cypress Point. It was here that Bobby Jones asked Mackenzie to design the Augusta National.

Marion Hollins, one of the founders of Cypress Point, is seen here (left) with Alexa Stirling after beating her in the final of the 1921 U.S. Women's Amateur Championship.

clubhouse were scrapped and a more modest building set up. Today, Cypress Point is an exclusive private club of some 250 members, drawn from all over the United States and beyond.

'The Ground Determines the Play'

In the context of golf-course design, Mackenzie produced a work of genius; although, without diminishing his achievement, it can be said that his raw material was quite exceptional. The terrain he was offered included deep pine

CYPRESS POINT Card of the course			
1	421 yards par 4	10	480 yards par 5
2	548 yards par 5	11	437 yards par 4
3	162 yards par 3	12	404 yards par 4
4	384 yards par 4	13	365 yards par 4
5	493 yards par 5	14	388 yards par 4
6	518 yards par 5	15	143 yards par 3
7	168 yards par 3	16	231 yards par 3
8	363 yards par 4	17	393 yards par 4
9	292 yards par 4	18	346 yards par 4
3,349 yards par 37		3,187 yards par 35	
Total 6,536 yards par 72			

forests, huge soaring dunes of the whitest sand, crisp turf and a stretch of cliffs which offered him the chance to create spectacular holes right by the ocean. Mackenzie made the most of it. He believed in the aphorism that 'the ground determines the play', and the creed of 'Nipper' Campbell that 'the best golf course is built into the landscape you've got'. Mackenzie immediately recognised that he was never going to improve on this landscape. He could do no more than rejoice in it, and perhaps complement it.

His Cypress Point features two successive par-5 holes and two successive par-3 holes, which has lead to some pedantic criticism, but at the same time the un-answerable: 'But what holes!'. His 16th hole of 231 yards has come to be one of the most photographed of all the world's golf holes. There are students of the game prepared to argue that of all the thousands of golf holes ever made, this one is simply the best.

The 16th tee is perched on the edge of a cliff. Across a little bay, usually surging with Pacific surf, lies a promontory on the very point of the Monterey Peninsula, where the green is set, guarded by four bunkers. Open fairway skirts round the head of the bay to the left, offering an alternative route. By driving to the left and thus short of the green, the golfer then has to seek his par-3 by pitching or chipping close enough to the flagstick to be able to make a single putt. On such an exposed headland the wind will always be a major calculation, but if ever a single shot favoured the brave it is this one.

The element of strategic design inherent in the 16th is repeated at the 17th. Strategy in design is the simple business of giving the golfer an option, an alternative solution to his problem. It challenges him to make the difficult shot, the dangerous carry over a corner of rough, sand dune, lake or even ocean, as at Cypress or Pebble Beach, with his reward a much

Above: The 16th at Cypress Point. Considered by many as the most beautiful golf hole in the world, it demands a shot of 231 yards across the Pacific Ocean, no less.

Right: The 17th, another clifftop hole illustrating Monterey golf – the cliffs, wind-tilted trees, solitary strategic pins and greens backed by sand, cypresses and ocean.

less taxing, shorter second shot. If he is also given a shorter, easier way, it is liable to be one which makes the next shot longer, or more difficult.

At the 17th hole, a 393-yard dog-leg to the right, the challenge is again in a tee shot driven across a bay to a cliff-top fairway. The second shot is complicated by a cluster of cypress trees growing in the right centre of the fairway. Thus the ideal drive may well be the more conservative one of playing to the left of these trees and trying to fade the ball around them on the left, but not overrunning the fairway. That would give an open route to the green, hard by the cliff top. Driving to the right of these trees gives a much shorter approach shot, but demands a much longer, more dangerous drive which must carry further, over the bay and the cliff and avoiding the ice-plant which lines the top of the cliff and the edge of the fairway.

Thus Mackenzie gave the golfer some

latitude as to where to go and how to get there; rather than facing him with the penal 'This way – or else' attitude that many designers had adopted. And Mackenzie had come to see that the design of greens was of major importance in the overall testing of the player. Varying the pin position, defending the pin position, and making it more inviting meant varying of the type of approach shot required. Careful contouring of the greens had the same effect. So, we find that Mackenzie greens more and more are raised, sloped, tilted, often multi-tiered and carefully 'sized', all in relation to the incoming shot. All of these factors inherent in the Monterey terrain made it quite unnecessary for Cypress to be any longer than its 6,500 yards.

A Fair Test

On the 1st hole, for instance, the green slopes quite sharply. On the 2nd, a par-5 of 548 yards, the drive must carry over a large area of rough on the left and avoid out-of-bounds on the right. The second shot must dodge fairway bunkers, and for a hole of such yardage Mackenzie has quite properly left a fairly large, flat green. The 3rd is a classic par-3 of 162 yards, tee and green on the flat but the front right half and side of the green is closely trapped, permitting some very difficult pin positions near this bunker. On the par-5 5th the green is plateaued

and two-tiered; this is a lovely hole of 491 yards, uphill through the pine forest with a rolling fairway and lovely banks of silver sand. The 6th is a bigger par-5 at 518 yards. Its green, framed by tall, solitary pines and six handsome bunkers, is small, since it will almost certainly be receiving a short pitch, and slopes from right to left.

The 8th green has three levels and, that disposed of, there is a splendid view from the ninth tee of the ocean and over half of the course. The 9th hole at 292 yards, brought out a certain impishness in the good Doctor Mackenzie. It plays downhill with dunes on both sides. The green is long, sloping and set across the fairway. The front left side is closed by a bunker, and there is sand and high grass all around at the back. Again, the architect gives the golfer a choice: go for the green, hoping to sneak on through that narrow gap, or play short and pitch up to the flag.

Holes 10 to 14 work their way through

Right: The 15th, a short hole to rival the 7th at Pebble Beach – at 143 yards it seems a simple pitch along the cliffs and across a rocky inlet, but then the wind comes into play.

Below: The 5th green is approached from a fairway studded with strategically placed bunkers, while the two-tiered green is itself defended at right front and left rear.

open duneland in which almost every green has a backcloth of tall pine trees. The 12th (404 yards) and the 14th (388 yards) are particularly fine holes. The first of these is a dog-leg to the right with a bunker and massed dunes covering the angle of the turn. The 14th green brings us close to the cliffs again and to the remarkable 15th hole, a par-3 of 143 yards. This is a gem which has often had its sparkle taken away, quite unjustly, by the 16th. The hole plays along the cliff tops, crossing an inlet to a little green that is almost overwhelmed by six bunkers, the dreaded Cypress ice-plant, a huge barrier of cypress trees behind, not to mention the Pacific Ocean foaming around below.

Finally, the 18th tee turns its back on the spectacular Pacific coastline and plays back to the pleasant clubhouse over 346 yards away, a drive and pitch for the competent player, but a drive that must thread through a channel of trees, and a pitch that must hold a very fast green.

Cypress Point, a magnificent golf course, basks in a strange anonymity. It has been a supporting course for the old Crosby Pro-Am played at Pebble – Crosby, by the way, had one of the very few holes-in-one made at Cypress's 16th – and staged the 1981 Walker Cup matches, but has otherwise sought no championships and no publicity. To play there is a privilege.

PEBBLE BEACH

In the context of golf, indeed of sport, the Pebble Beach course is a massive achievement. Of all the thousands of golf courses around the world, it would surely be given a place in the top half-dozen in the assessment of knowledgeable and honourable men. Embedded in the same landscape as Cypress Point, only a mile or so away – California is singularly blessed with 36 such holes almost side by side – Pebble Beach is some years older, its history rooted in a different time.

After the transcontinental railway had been established, a spur line was opened in 1880 to serve the Hotel Del Monte and the Monterey peninsula, 100 miles south of San Francisco. The intention was that the hotel would become the core of a resort that would be the Newport of the West, and its expansive Victorian splendours soon attracted the wealthy society from San Francisco and Los Angeles and, increasingly, points further east. The hotel and the land were owned by the Southern Pacific Railroad Company, and the riding trails and carriage drives through the forests of the peninsula were the prime leisure activities. There was also a modest golf course.

Morse and Neville
In 1914 Samuel A. Morse, an Easterner, a Yale man and a nephew of the inventor of the code and the telegraph, came to Monterey to work with the Pacific Improvement Company, a real-estate subsidiary of the Southern Pacific. He was instructed to dispose of all the railroad's real-estate holdings and, very smartly forming the Del Monte Property Company, bought the land, some 7,000 acres, for $1.3 million for himself. Morse had more than a little vision. He decided that a golf course would be critical to the marketing of his development and that the existing course was inadequate. He discovered that one Jack Neville, who was working for Pacific Improvement as a real-estate salesman, was a golfer good enough to have won the California State Championship twice.

Neville was from Oakland, where his father was a member of the Claremont Country Club, at which his brother George and such famous golfing personalities as Macdonald Smith and Jim Barnes all worked at one time. Morse decided to entrust the design and building of the new course to Neville, realising that the young man knew enough about the game to get the work done.

For three weeks Neville walked the property, establishing in his mind the routing of the holes. Then, accompanied by Sam Morse, and starting at the original Del Monte Lodge, he staked out the tees and greens.

The Cliff-edge Masterpiece
The first two holes ran eastward from the lodge, out of sight of the ocean. The 1st was 385 yards, the second a good par-5 of just over 500 yards – two perfectly fine golf holes, but less than memorable. Then Neville turned towards the sea with another rather routine par-4 of 368 yards curving slightly to the left.

However, the next brings us to the ocean and starts a run of holes along the cliffs to the 10th which make Pebble Beach the greatest 'ocean' course in the world. The holes are simply magnificent. The 4th is only 325 yards, but it gives an inkling of some of the excitements to come. The tee shot is over a cross bunker

Jack Neville, many times California State champion, shows some dandy style some 80 years ago, but his chief claim to immortality is as the designer of peerless Pebble Beach.

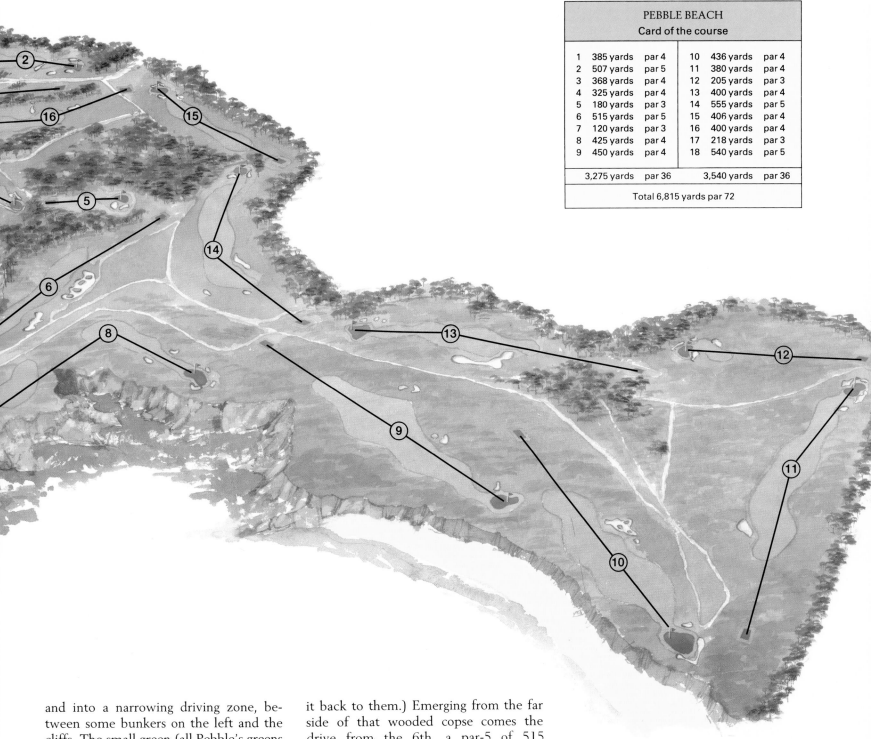

and into a narrowing driving zone, between some bunkers on the left and the cliffs. The small green (all Pebble's greens are small by modern standards) is surrounded by bunkers and is squeezed close to the cliff tops.

The 5th, a one-shot hole of 180 yards, turns away from the water and runs uphill into a wooded area. (Neville would have preferred to run it along the cliff top, but Morse had sold a critical plot of land there and could not persuade the owner to sell

it back to them.) Emerging from the far side of that wooded copse comes the drive from the 6th, a par-5 of 515 thrilling yards which explodes out to the cliff tops again, above Stillwater Cove, with a second shot that must sweep up to the great plateau on the peninsula spearing out into Carmel Bay, and the green that is placed there. Along the very edge of this stunning promontory, lies the 7th hole, a par-3 of only 120 yards — the shortest hole on any American cham-

pionship course, and none the worse for that. The green, set below the tee, is ringed with a maze of bunkers, an infinitesimal target, a rectangle no more than eight yards across, and subject to all the winds the Pacific can blow.

The 8th, 425 yards, is one of the world's great two-shotters. The course is now returning from that big headland

Above: *The 9th green and, beyond, the 10th fairway. These two magnificent par-4s demand the strictest accuracy in both tee and approach shots.*

Left: *Not for the nervous – the sea-girt chasm that cuts into the direct line between the 8th fairway and the green, in the foreground.*

which houses six and seven and the tee is on the very edge of the cliff. The drive must carry up a slope onto an unseen plateau. It must not be hit too far, as you will discover when you get up there: not far beyond the rise the ocean has carved a huge chunk out of the fairway, which skips around it on the left. The direct shot to the green is over that monstrous chasm, requiring a carry of perhaps 180 yards. In this classic shot (as with the second shot to the 13th at Pine Valley, where a similar carry must be made over sand) lies the brutal challenge of the hole: how much of the angle to cut off, which line dare you take? Too far right, even by the slightest margin, and you will be in the ocean; too far left, and you will be hard pressed to reach the green, which again is small and bunkered on both sides and to the back.

The 9th is a difficult par-4 running downhill, its fairway tilted towards the cliffs. Two high-backed bunkers cover the left side at about 230 yards from the tee, at which point the fairway is no more than 30 yards wide. The 10th hole follows the same pattern, breaking slightly to the right in driving range, where a very long bunker on the left at the top of the fairway compresses it even more than that at the ninth. Three-quarters of the green is bunkered, leaving only a narrow entrance, just short of which is a swale of thick grass. The second shot should carry all the way to the putting surface. These are very severe holes – in the final round of the U.S. Open in 1972, in very windy conditions, Jack Nicklaus at the 10th drove clean over the cliff onto the beach, which was a lateral water hazard. Nicklaus took a drop and penalty, hit his next with a 2-iron and holed out rather thankfully for six.

Pebble's Great Finish

The 10th green is the most distant point from the clubhouse and the course then turns back inland through woodlands of cypress, oak, eucalyptus and Monterey pine, before returning to the ocean at the 17th and 18th holes. The 17th is a compelling one-shot hole of 218 yards. In that same final round of the 1972 U.S. Open, Nicklaus hit a 1-iron into the wind here. The ball took one bounce, hit the flagstick, and flopped down six inches away! But beyond doubt the greatest single shot ever played at this hole was the little wedge shot which Tom Watson holed from off the green in the last round of the 1982 U.S. Open Championship. For the 17th Watson smashed out a 2-iron tee shot which soared high, turned to the left with just a suggestion of a hook in it and finished pin-high but in long grass just off the green. Fortunately it had skipped between two bunkers and the lie was good. As Watson looked it over, his caddie said: 'Get it close'. Watson replied: 'I'm not going to get it close – I'm going to make it'. And he did. He popped-up the ball softly with a sand wedge, it landed on the green and ran straight towards the hole. When it fell in, Watson, seldom a demonstrative fellow, set off on a mad dance around the green. The shot was to win him the U.S. Open Championship.

The 540-yard 18th, one of golf's great finishing holes, curves steadily to the left along the cliff tops. A decision is required as to how much of the angle to cut off with the tee shot. Ultra-greedy players will quickly find themselves on the beach. The ocean is hard along the left side. In the driving zone on the right bunkers and trees menace the fairway; beyond them is out-of-bounds. Trees encroach in the second-shot area around 50 yards short of the green, which is set above the player. Shots over the green are likely also to go over the cliffs. In short, the 18th requires a combination of brute force and fine judgement. In 1982 Watson birdied it with a 3-wood, 7-iron, 9-iron and a superb 20-foot putt.

Pebble Beach Today
Jack Neville's original design has stood up well since the course opened in 1918. True, tees have been extended, bunkers fiddled with. Neville in fact had asked a contemporary, Douglas Grant, who was also good enough to be state champion, to check on his original bunkering. And for the 1929 U.S. Amateur Championship, the first played on the Pacific coast, H. Chandler Egan, a Chicago man who had been U.S. Champion in 1904 and 1905, re-modeled the greens and generally stiffened up the course. This championship was memorable for the fact that, for the only time in his U.S. Amateur career,

Bobby Jones lost a first-round match. He had come all the way from Atlanta – by train of course – only to lose to Johnny Goodman. And Jones was U.S. Open Champion! The press coverage was enormous: it was one of the biggest sports stories of the year, and the publicity did nothing to harm Pebble Beach.

But it was the presentation of the Bing Crosby National Pro-Am tournament, televised, and with Pebble Beach the anchor course and neighbouring Cypress Point and Spyglass Hill the supporting courses, that really established Pebble in the consciousness of world golf. The tournament is played in late January or early February, when the weather can be as capricious as in the west of Scotland, but no one seems to mind. Crosby started his pro-am event in 1936 for charity and so that his Hollywood and other friends might have some fun. In 1947 he moved it from Rancho Santa Fe in Los Angeles up to Monterey. After his death, there was something of a hiatus and, sadly, the Crosby name is no longer in the title. The event is now sponsored by A.T. & T., and the players chase prize-money of the order of $700,000. In a similar way, the world of business did not leave Pebble Beach untouched. It had always been a public course, with privileges for guests of the Del Monte Lodge. After Samuel Morse died in 1969, things were not as they used to be. Del Monte Properties became Pebble Beach Corporation, which was later bought by 20th Century Fox. Maximising the plant became the policy, profit became the key word. Golf cart tracks were laid, more and more players were 'processed' around the course and the $100 green fee loomed ahead. If all of this did little for the condition of the course, it had little impact on Neville's grand design. Pebble Beach remains one of international golf's shrines, and entirely worthy of Robert Louis Stevenson's much-quoted description of the peninsula as 'the most felicitous meeting of land and sea in creation'.

The 18th green. The long scimitar-shaped fairway curving around the bay makes for one of the finest finishing holes in championship golf.

BANFF

If ever a course qualified for greatness on the grounds of beauty and dramatic setting alone, it would be Banff Springs in Alberta, in the foothills of the Rocky Mountains. This is not to say that these are its only qualities. Banff Springs, from the point of view of its design and the pleasures and challenges its varied holes offer the golfer, is by any judgement a great course – but the place, its setting, its whole environment, is breathtaking.

It was built as an adjunct to the huge Banff Springs Hotel, the Canadian Pacific Railway's luxury Shangri-la resort, on the line that presently runs west from Calgary to Lake Louise and threads through the Kicking Horse Pass on the way to Vancouver and the Pacific Coast. The initial course, of nine holes, was constructed in 1911, and a further nine were added during the Great War with the labour of German prisoners of war.

In 1927, Stanley Thompson, the prominent Canadian designer with whom Robert Trent Jones served an apprenticeship, was asked to re-make the course. Thompson was dealing essentially with a wooded strip along the bank of the Bow River, squeezed between the latter and the towering mass of Mount Rumble. He cut down trees by the hundred, blasted tons of rock out of the mountain, imported topsoil from the east and positioned a maze of bunkers on the course – 144 in all. No fewer than 28 of them were in play on the 18th hole! Clumps of bunkers, set into the fairways at critical distances, were a Thompson feature at

The world famous Devil's Cauldron hole is the 8th on the championship course and the 4th on the Rundle. Picturesque and very difficult this 171-yard par-3 has an elevated green and water in abundance.

Banff Springs. In 1989 a further nine holes were added, making three nine-hole courses: Sulphur, Randle and Tunnel (the newest nine).

The course is nicely wooded with conifers, although not oppressively so – save perhaps along the stretch from the 5th to the 10th, where the fairways are simply avenues in isolation. A critical factor when playing this extraordinary course is judgement of distance, and judgement of exactly how far the ball will fly at this altitude, just as it is on the

BANFF				
Card of the Championship course				
1	411 yards	par 4	10	351 yards	par 4
2	394 yards	par 4	11	514 yards	par 5
3	372 yards	par 4	12	138 yards	par 3
4	578 yards	par 5	13	474 yards	par 5
5	414 yards	par 4	14	220 yards	par 3
6	174 yards	par 3	15	398 yards	par 4
7	514 yards	par 5	16	420 yards	par 4
8	171 yards	par 3	17	230 yards	par 3
9	424 yards	par 4	18	429 yards	par 4
3,452 yards	par 36		3,174 yards	par 35	
Total 6,626 yards par 71				

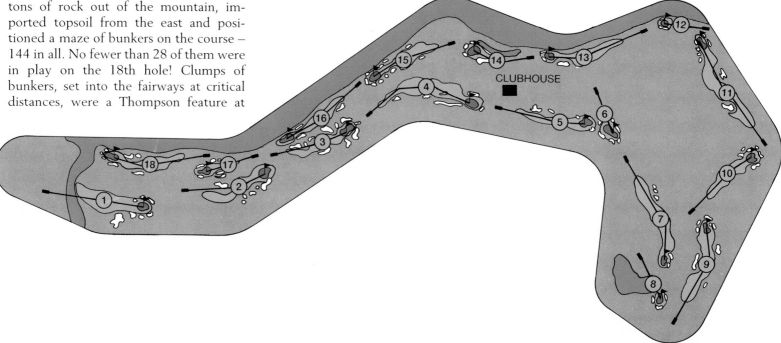

is a very interesting hole, a par-5 which dog-legs to the right – twice. Named 'Windy', it goes 578 yards along a mounded fairway with the left side favoured, the better to see 'round the corner', and into the rather small green. The 7th too is intriguing, in that it is a straight par-5 of 514 yards, pressed in on the right by the cliffs of Mount Rumble with a little kick to the right at the end onto a green well screened by trees.

The most famous hole on the course, renowned far beyond Banff, is the 'Devil's Cauldron', the 8th and a par-3 of 171 yards. It is played from a high tee over a little natural lake, which the Scots might call a 'lochan', to a green embedded in a forest, surrounded by bunkers and raised slightly above a ledge of fairway between its front edges and the lake. To hold the green, a shot must be long and high so that it will flop down vertically to hold the putting surface. The terror intrinsic in the hole is largely environmental – the high tee, the lake, the woodland behind the minute green, and the massive wall of mountain behind it can overwhelm the golfer.

The 12th hole, named 'Papoose' is another par-3 also over water; this time an inlet of the Bow River, but at 138 yards is a very different proposition. The 14th is almost a replica, also over water, but a stronger hole at 220 yards. Banff's finish is a thrilling run along the bank of the Bow which forms the right side boundary of the last four holes. Three stiff par-4s and a single shotter of 230 yards demand some concentration. On the 16th Thompson has put in a fairway bunker with a siting reminiscent of the Principal's Nose bunker on the 16th at St Andrews, tempting the player to line his drive out between it and the river. But concentration on golf, on the swing and on the playing of the game may be difficult at Banff. In the presence of the landscape, the environment and the wild life, the quality of the golf may become secondary and for once, the obsessed golfer will not mind – Banff is a wonderful place.

Alpine courses of Switzerland or the Rand courses in the Transvaal of South Africa. At Banff's 4,000 feet, the light can be sharp and clear, so that there is foreshortening of targets, which can look closer than they really are. On the other hand, in the thin air the ball will fly much further; club selection takes on a whole new dimension in a game at Banff.

The old Banff clubhouse is set close to the confluence of the Bow and the Spray rivers. However, a new clubhouse has been built in the centre of the course and a shuttle bus runs continuously between it and the hotel. In the spring and early summer, when the mountain snows melt, the Bow and Spray can be very lively rivers indeed. And the prospect from the 1st tee (of the championship course) can be daunting. It is set above a minor precipice over the Spray, and the tee shot must carry directly across the river, some 100 yards wide, then into an alleyway of trees and reach or pass a crest at about 200 yards, where a ridge comes in from the right. The first green has a reasonably wide entrance. The 2nd and 3rd holes are reasonable par-4s, splashed all over with Thompson's big, ornate bunkers, but reasonableness ends about here. The 4th

ROYAL MONTREAL

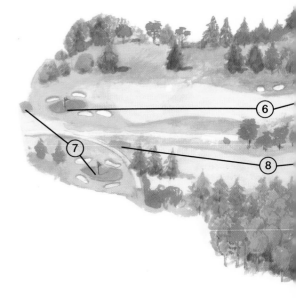

The Royal Montreal Golf Club is the oldest in North America. It was formed in 1873, fifteen years before the first of the U.S. clubs, St Andrews, in Yonkers, New York. As such, Royal Montreal is appropriately aristocratic and very proud of the substantial contribution it made to Canadian golf during its infant years. It founded the Royal Canadian Golf Association. Its annual match with The Country Club, of Brookline, Mass., was the first international encounter between countries, pre-dating even the England-Scotland amateur match. It inaugurated the first national championship, the womens' amateur of 1901, followed by the mens' amateur in 1902, and it staged the very first Canadian Open Championship in 1904.

The club was formed by 16 wealthy Montrealers, a Scot or two among them. One of the prime movers was Alexander Dennistoun, who presented the club with a medal which is still played for. Rather like Charles Blair Macdonald and the U.S. National Amateur Championship, Dennistoun contrived, perhaps connived, to have his name engraved on the medal as the first winner.

Move to a New Site

A public park, Fletcher's Field on the slopes of Mount Royal, was the club's starting point. But in 1896 a new site was needed, and one was found at Dixie, to the west of the city, which became good enough to stage five Canadian Opens. However, the inevitable growth of Montreal meant that another move was necessary by the 1950s. Fortunately the club found a property at Ile Bizard big enough to provide 45 holes. They first sought the services of Robert Trent Jones, by this time famous for his treatment of Oakland Hills for the U.S. Open of 1951 and for even more grandiose and controversial ventures. Jones at the time was overcommitted and declined the invitation. Consequently, the club turned to Dick Wilson, a plain-spoken engineer who had had many design and construction successes, most of them in Florida and other U.S. southern states.

Fortunately for the club, Wilson was a qualified civil engineer: the land had to be cleared of rocks, tree trunks, boulders and dead matter and its swampland drained and channelled off into two lakes, the larger of which was destined to have four

holes played over it. Wilson produced the nine-hole Black course and two of 18: the Red and the championship Blue.

Huge Greens

From a design point of view, Royal Montreal's Blue championship course has two unusual features. There is an absence of fairway bunkering – only 11 in all – and the greens are huge. Wilson was not one for the dramatic excavations or massive landscaping of a Trent Jones. The Blue course is by no means flat, but the ground moves gently, pleasantly contoured; the fairways, nicely aligned, sauntering quietly across a tree-dotted rather than wooded landscape. And Wilson turned his back on length for length's sake – at its championship length the course was no more than 6,738 yards with a par of 70.

In fact Wilson made the size of his greens the penal element in his course design. At around 12,000 square feet they were double the size of the average championship greens, some of them running 40 yards from front to back. They

The 17th is one of the most attractive and shortest holes at Royal Montreal. A tricky 133-yard par-3, it captures the essence of Dick Wilson's design work, with its clever use of sand, trees and water.

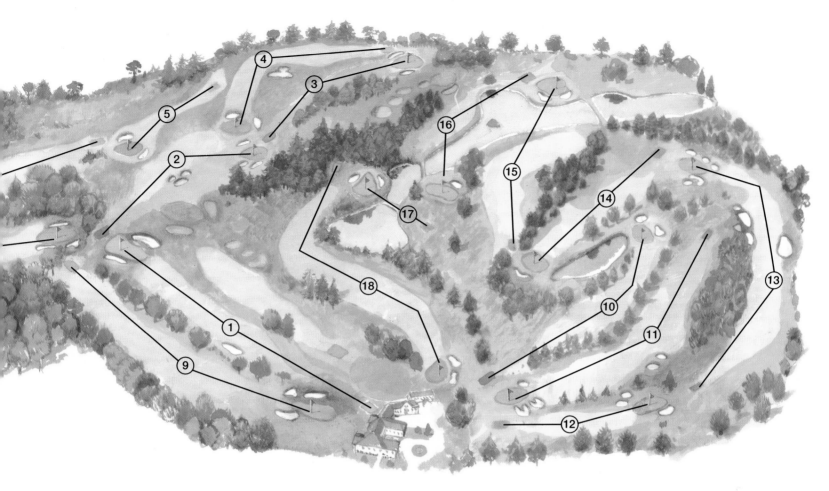

were all closely trapped – he used 48 greenside bunkers in all. They widened out from front to back, but from front to back there was sometimes a two or three club difference. Thus the approach shot and its club selection were the tests – under-clubbing might result in the golfer having to face a putt of 100 feet! The shot into the green was the key shot, and it required the golfer to steel himself to attack and strike boldly, knowing that the shot would be longer than it seemed and that he would have to force the ball, perhaps against his inclination, to the heart of the green and beyond.

Waist Deep in Water

One factor which is inhibiting at Ile Bizard is that over the four final holes, five shots across water are required – the second shot to 15, both drive and second at 16, and drives at 17 and 18. When the wind blows, which it does most of the time at Ile Bizard, these shots can be challenging. Perhaps no man was ever challenged more than Pat Fitzsimons, a young U.S. professional playing in the 1975 Canadian Open, the last played at Royal Montreal. The 16th requires a drive over the spur of a lake which covers the entire left side of the fairway, then a second shot back across the water. The hole is a par-4 of 433 yards and Fitzsimons, seeking to cut off as much of the angle as he could, hooked his drive not into the water but onto a tiny island some 10 yards from the bank. The ball was visible and still in play. So Fitzsimons sent his caddie in to test the water, which was found to be waist deep. An attempt by the caddie to carry him across having failed, Fitzsimons waded across himself, hit a 4-iron from the island to the green and took two putts for his par – perhaps one of the greatest pars in the history of the game! So elated was the dripping Fitzsimons that he birdied the 17th and 18th holes, scored 73 for a 140 total after 36 holes and made the cut.

That '75 Open was won by Tom Weiskopf at the first hole of a play-off with Jack Nicklaus. Testament to the quality of

ROYAL MONTREAL Card of the course					
1	434 yards	par 4	10	452 yards	par 4
2	375 yards	par 4	11	438 yards	par 4
3	364 yards	par 4	12	193 yards	par 3
4	440 yards	par 4	13	533 yards	par 3
5	179 yards	par 3	14	361 yards	par 4
6	570 yards	par 5	15	420 yards	par 4
7	143 yards	par 3	16	433 yards	par 4
8	397 yards	par 4	17	133 yards	par 3
9	423 yards	par 4	18	450 yards	par 4
	3,325 yards	par 35		3,413 yards	par 35
		Total 6,738 yards par 70			

Royal Montreal's course, its world rating and the club's stature in the international game is the fact that the championship was secured with a score of 274, only six strokes under par, and that the ten leading players were: Tom Weiskopf, Jack Nicklaus, Gay Brewer, Arnold Palmer, Bruce Crampton, J.C. Snead, Gary Player, Bob Wynn, Lee Trevino and Ken Still.

CLUB DE GOLF MEXICO

Golf architects, most of the time, are ordinary men living in the ordinary world of three-dimensions. But there are times when they are extraordinary men, living in an extraordinary world of four dimensions. The fourth dimension is altitude. It has affected the work of the golf course designer at, for example, the Swiss Alps, where the course at Crans-sur-Sierre is at 5,000 feet, or on the Johannesburg courses of the Rand of Transvaal, at 6,000 feet, or even the central plateau of Mexico, which reaches 7,500 feet in the region of Mexico City. At these altitudes, the golf ball flies and flies, often 20 per cent further than it would at sea level. Thus the yardage of the Club de Golf Mexico, probably Mexico's finest course, is initially frightening: 7,166 yards, is difficult to reconcile with a par of 72.

An Elitist Sport

Yardage and altitude apart, Club de Golf Mexico is a big powerful course, demanding the most careful striking and intense concentration. And despite its yardage, it demands accuracy even more than power. Golf in Mexico, of course, has had an irregular history. As in all Latin American countries, it has been seen as an elitist sport, and certainly social circumstances have made it very much a minority game.

But its aficionados are an influential minority, as the story of the Club de Golf illustrates.

The creation of the club and the course was orchestrated by Percy Clifford, six times amateur champion of Mexico and three times Open champion. With the blessing of Miguel Alemán, the President of Mexico at the time, Clifford found the ground he wanted at Tlalpán, about an hour's drive from Mexico City. It was part of a dense woodland of cedar, pine and cypress. Clifford retained Lawrence Hughes to plan the course – the latter's connection with golf course design running all the way back to the Dornoch of Donald Ross. Clifford, it should be noted, had been to college in England, and had seen the best of the English and Scottish courses. He thus had definite ideas about design and about building courses which would entail a minimum of maintenance expenditure. Similarly, Lawrence Hughes, in his teens, had worked with his

CLUB DE GOLF MEXICO Card of the course				
1	431 yards par 4	10	390 yards par 4
2	559 yards par 5	11	569 yards par 5
3	429 yards par 4	12	174 yards par 3
4	384 yards par 4	13	461 yards par 4
5	165 yards par 3	14	222 yards par 3
6	438 yards par 4	15	580 yards par 5
7	220 yards par 3	16	374 yards par 4
8	562 yards par 5	17	412 yards par 4
9	360 yards par 4	18	436 yards par 4
3,548 yards par 36		3,618 yards par 36
Total 7,166 yards par 72			

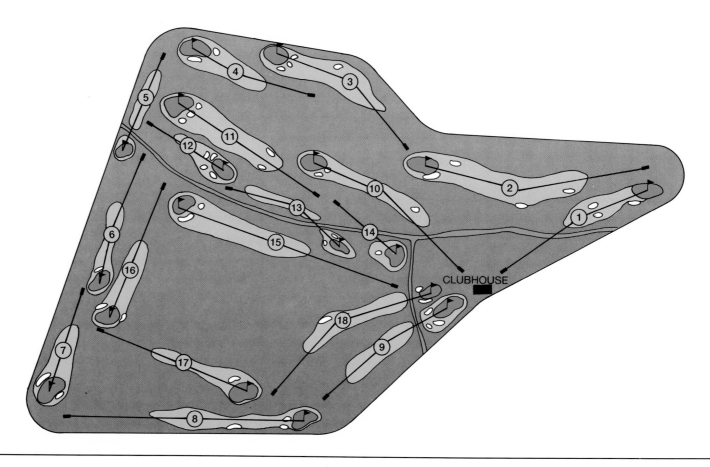

father, a construction supervisor with Ross in his dozens of courses throughout the States. Thus he too had some definite ideas about golf course design.

Shangri-la

In 1946, Hughes met Johnny Dawson, a U.S. Amateur Championship finalist and a Walker Cup player. Dawson was convinced that there were underground springs that would make golf feasible in the Palm Springs desert area, and enlisted Hughes as a designer. Between them they produced the Thunderbird CC in 1947, the first of the post-war golf/property developments in the area. Eldorado and La Quinta were to follow and Palm Springs in time became a golfing Shangri-la. From Palm Springs and work in San Diego, it was a short hop for Hughes to

The 18th green viewed from the creek, which threatens the over-ambitious drive. This is one of seven holes on the course requiring shots over one of the branches of the creek.

get to Mexico, and he and Clifford had produced the Club de Golf by 1951. Significantly, Hughes went on to design a dozen or more courses in Mexico, while by 1980 Clifford had been involved in putting together practically half of the courses in the country.

The course they built at Tlalpán is powerful and in many ways forbidding. It is carved out of a solid forest so that trees become the main hazards, with woodland lining each side of every fairway. There is a creek which winds through the course and is in play on seven holes, although it is

likely to be dry. Only one of the four short holes is less than 200 yards. Of the four par-5 holes, the 15th is 580 yards. There is not too much movement in the ground and, rather surprisingly, almost all the holes are straight, and when they do turn, they turn only slightly. The course is notable for an almost complete absence of fairway bunkering – understandable since a shot off the fairway is in the trees, and is a stroke almost certainly lost.

Evidence of the quality of Club de Golf Mexico came early in its life – the course twice staging the World Cup; Harry Bradshaw and Christy O'Connor winning for Ireland in 1958 and Arnold Palmer and Jack Nicklaus winning for the United States in 1967 – Palmer taking the individual title with an impressive 275, twelve strokes under par.

CAJUILES

Paul 'Pete' Dye was born in Ohio in 1925, and after college became a life-insurance salesman in Indianapolis and a fine amateur golfer, winning the Indiana State Championship in 1958. He also served some time as chairman of the greens committee at the country club of Indianapolis during a complete replanting of the course. Dye was so successful as an insurance salesman that he could afford to leave the business in 1959 and set up as a golf course designer. He worked modestly in the Midwest until 1963, when he and his wife Alice, also a first-rate golfer, toured the championship courses of Scotland. Dye was immensely impressed by the small greens, pot bunkers and sleepers

The 17th green, like others at Cajuiles, is walled with coral on the seaward side. The 18th hole, whose tee is behind the trees fringing the green, involves a drive across the runway.

(railroad ties), which he saw on these Scottish courses.

Although such features were quite out of fashion in contemporary American design, Dye started to apply them to his work. It was work that was to have a significant effect on the whole of golf course architecture. When Hilton Head Island off the coast of South Carolina was beginning to develop as a resort, Dye's Harbour Town course was opened in 1969 – Jack Nicklaus helping out, almost in the role of an apprentice. Harbour Town, and Dye's reputation, was confirmed when Arnold Palmer won the first Heritage Classic tournament, played on the course that year and shown on national television.

Two years later, in 1971, Dye presented to the world one of the most spectacular courses ever built, the Campo de Golf Cajuiles, at La Romana in the

south-east corner of the Dominican Republic. Comparisons with Pebble Beach and Cypress Point are inevitable, since four holes on the outward half and four holes on the inward half are played along, beside, above or over the ocean. Dye had been invited to build a 'special' course by the developer of a luxury resort complex of some 7,000 acres and he saw it as 'the chance of a lifetime' to create a seaside course – few architects get that chance.

Holes 1, 2 and 4, surprisingly, are par-4s of less than 400 yards, and with the trade wind prevailing from the east, are drive and pitch holes. The 5th is a long,

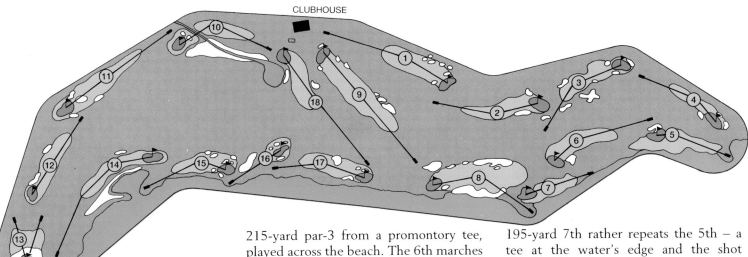

215-yard par-3 from a promontory tee, played across the beach. The 6th marches parallel with the ocean front, playing over a rise, then down to a small green. The 195-yard 7th rather repeats the 5th – a tee at the water's edge and the shot entirely across sand. The 8th tee is again pushed out into the ocean, and the drive must carry a slice of water over the angle. This 385-yard hole turns left and goes down to a sea-level green behind a huge bunker.

The 9th leaves the shore and the course swings up in a big curve to the 13th, a freakish par-3 to a green literally surrounded by sand and shaded by fur trees. The 14th, the last par-5 at 500 yards, has a bunker along its entire right side, and an ocean inlet screening the green. The 15th and 17th could well be the 17th at Cypress Point – drives across a bay, a dog-leg to the right and the challenge lying in deciding how much of the angle should be cut off. Both greens are heavily protected.

CAJUILES					
Card of the course					
1	380 yards	par 4	10	380 yards	par 4
2	380 yards	par 4	11	548 yards	par 5
3	530 yards	par 5	12	430 yards	par 4
4	320 yards	par 4	13	170 yards	par 3
5	215 yards	par 3	14	500 yards	par 5
6	450 yards	par 4	15	380 yards	par 4
7	195 yards	par 3	16	185 yards	par 3
8	385 yards	par 4	17	435 yards	par 4
9	520 yards	par 5	18	440 yards	par 4
3,375 yards	par 36		3,468 yards	par 36	
Total 6,843 yards par 72					

There is no option but to go for the green at the par-3 7th. Short and to the left is the sea; short and to the right is a gigantic bunker masquerading as a fairway.

MID OCEAN

Bermuda is a coral jewel set in an azure sea. The island is enchanting, and on the grounds of beauty alone its Mid Ocean golf course must rank with the best of them. A member of the British Commonwealth, Bermuda has long been a haunt of the American tourist – New York is only 90 minutes away by air, and Boston is even closer. The Mid Ocean course lies along the southern shore of the island and the lovely property could be described as a parkland course of modest length – 6,547 yards and a par of 71 – moving attractively over a landscape of valleys and crests, through dense woods and flowering shrubs.

Mid Ocean has been compared with Cypress Point and Turnberry, although in truth few of its holes run hard by the ocean as they do at the two other courses. On the other hand, no place in Bermuda is far from the sea, and Charles Blair Macdonald, its designer, took his holes as close to the cliffs above Bermuda's stunning beaches as he dared. Macdonald designed the course in 1924 (he died in

The par-3 13th is the most demanding of Mid Ocean's short holes, not so much in its subtlety but in the powerful shot that it requires, often in ocean breezes.

1928 at the age of 72), and Robert Trent Jones updated it in 1953.

Macdonald was a pioneer of American golf. Having studied at St Andrews as a young man, he had come to love the Scottish approach to the game and to course design, and he preached it incessantly on his return to the States. His greatest work was the National Links of

America (q.v.), at Southampton, L.I., where on a piece of scrubland he built what was the nearest thing to a links in the U.S. at that time. One distinctive characteristic of his design and routing at Mid Ocean, which of course was totally different ground with which to work, was the number of high or elevated tees, which let the player drive down into a valley and often hit his second shot uphill.

The 1st hole, 'Atlantic', is a par-4 of 404 yards running down from the clubhouse and turning left. The 2nd is a dogleg to the left of 465 yards, rated a par-5, and the 3rd is a straightforward one-shotter of 190 yards. Thus Macdonald, noted for his penal attitude to the game – 'if a golfer made mistakes, he should be punished', he said – gave Mid Ocean a friendly start.

MID OCEAN Card of the course					
1	404 yards	par 4	10	404 yards	par 4
2	465 yards	par 5	11	487 yards	par 5
3	190 yards	par 3	12	437 yards	par 4
4	350 yards	par 4	13	238 yards	par 3
5	433 yards	par 4	14	357 yards	par 4
6	360 yards	par 4	15	496 yards	par 5
7	164 yards	par 3	16	376 yards	par 4
8	339 yards	par 4	17	220 yards	par 3
9	406 yards	par 4	18	421 yards	par 4
3,111 yards	par 35		3,436 yards	par 36	
Total 6,547 yards par 71					

The 4th, at 350 yards, is tighter than the yardage might suggest, because of a narrow, mounded fairway and a key bunker to the right. The 5th is beyond any doubt one of the world's great golf holes, using a principle of design that has been repeated with variations on literally hundreds of golf courses throughout the world. From a very high tee, it calls for a drive over Mangrove Lake. The hole then doglegs and runs left to a big, but quite well-guarded green. The trick here is in deciding on the line of the drive, how much of the lake to cut off and then having the confidence to drive along the chosen line. The hole is only 433 yards, yet if the golfer decides on the short carry and plays straight ahead or to the right, he will not reach the green with his second shot. If he goes for the long carry, regardless of what the wind may be doing, he may not succeed in carrying the water. So the tee shot at the 5th hole is a question of optimism or pessimism, fear or courage, judgement and confidence.

The 5th hole at Mid Ocean and one of the classic design questions which its architect, Charles Blair Macdonald, loved to ask of golfers – how much of the dog-leg to cut off.

On the other hand, the 6th, 7th and 8th are somewhat undemanding – 6 and 8 have raised greens in the old Scottish fashion – and water is in play at the 9th, where the drive must cross a lake. For that matter, the par-3 7th, at 164 yards, is also played over a lake.

Holes number 10, 11, 12, 13 and 15 are the heart of the course, and its most difficult stretch. Numbers 11 and 15 are par-5s and 13 is a par-3 of 238 yards. On each of these holes the drive is very tight, with bunkered dog-leg angles and trees crowding the fairway. And the 14th fairway slopes from right to left, with a cluster of bunkers on the left awaiting a ball that might dribble down towards them. The hole is 357 yards, just a drive and a pitch you might say. But even on its 'easy' holes, Mid Ocean has a sting.

The drive on 16 is uphill. The 17th, par-3 at 220 yards, is named 'Redan' after the North Berwick hole, although the only thing the two have in common is a green set across the line of the shot. The 18th is a fine and fair finishing hole of 421 yards, played from a tee set high above the beach and the cliffs, up towards the huge white clubhouse. For 20 years, this was the place of business and social life of Archie Compston, a rumbustious professional from the West Midlands of England who once tackled Walter Hagen in a 72-holes challenge match at Moor Park, London, and won by 18 and 17.

In conclusion, Mid Ocean is always in prime condition, with Bermuda grass, the strong, sharp, broad-bladed grass, growing in summer and the finer bent grasses thriving during the winter. Its verdant colours are offset by the pink and white houses on the island and the deep blues of the western Atlantic lapping its shores. Quite simply, Mid Ocean is both lovely and unique.

LAGUNITA

The Lagunita Country Club in the suburb of El Hatillo in Caracas, Venezuela, is typical of latter-day South American country clubs – country clubs in the sense that they have very comfortable premises with cocktail bars and restaurants, a variety of sporting facilities with emphasis on the golf course, the essential swimming pool, and the whole complex locked into extensive real estate development. Lagunita dates from 1956, when a group of local businessmen bought rather more than one square mile of land on which to develop some very expensive housing. However, they also retained Louis Sibbett (Dick) Wilson to build a golf course for them on the plot.

Dick Wilson was an almost direct contemporary of Robert Trent Jones and for 15 years throughout the 'Fifties and into the 'Sixties they were the two outstanding architects in America. Unlike Jones, who had made a careful and academic study of all the disciplines involved in the business – landscaping, surveying, agronomy, horticulture, hydraulics and grass – Wilson was proud of his practical background and the fact that he could actually build as well as design a golf course.

A native of Philadelphia, Wilson moved to Florida in the early 'Thirties, made it his base and created an impressive body of work in that state alone. Other than in the Bahamas, he did little work outside the U.S., although what he did was of the highest class – Royal Montreal, Villa Real in Cuba and Lagunita.

Lagunita is a private club with more than 1,000 members. Wilson's course is laid out like a boomerang, with the clubhouse in the centre of the inner

Right: *The 12th is one of the most treacherous holes on the course. The huge green is well defended by a lake which runs right up to the putting surface.*

Far right: *The 18th green has a narrow entrance and is well guarded by bunkers on both sides. It is a straight, uphill hole into the prevailing wind.*

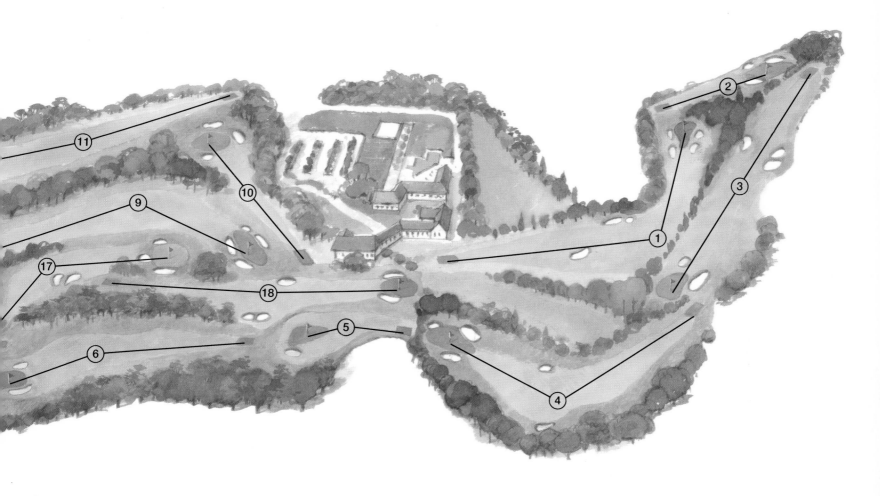

curve. The 1st hole is a big par-5 at 535 yards, with a double turn to the left. There is an out of bounds along the left side into a rather deep quarry, which makes it daring to try to carry over the second angle. Besides, Wilson defended that line with big greenside bunkers.

The 2nd, at 205 yards, is the first of Lagunita's five par-3 holes. The course has only three par-5s, hence a total par of only 70, but the par-3s are long and balance up the overall yardage to 6,895 yards. The 3rd hole, a straight full-length

par-4 of 470 yards, has out of bounds to its left as it turns and starts a swing back round the outer rim of the course to the 8th hole. The 4th hole is rather forbidding. It is 455 yards with a 90 degree turn to the right. A clutch of three bunkers in the angle and trees mean that the corner cannot be cut, and what is left is a long shot to a green with a narrow entrance and bunkered at the sides and rear.

The 8th, the longest short hole at 220 yards, may be almost a little unfair – the front being almost closed off by bunkering. The stretch of holes from 12 to 15, however, is very fine – all strong par-4s beautifully defended; and the 12th green, demanding a most difficult second shot, has a lake at front and right side. The 16th, the shortest hole on the course at 170 yards, has a large green, very fast, with sand at each corner. And the 18th is a good finishing hole of 440 yards. It runs straight uphill to the clubhouse and is well bunkered in the fairway and by the green.

Lagunita is a finely-designed, sharp test of golf for championship players. It is true

and honest, with all hazards visible. When the World Cup of 1974 was played at Lagunita, and won by Bobby Cole and Dale Hayes for South Africa, only three players bettered the 72-hole aggregate. They were Cole, the individual winner, who was also South African Open Champion, Hale Irwin who was U.S. Open Champion, and the leader of the world stroke averages that year, Masishi Ozaki.

LAGUNITA					
Card of the course					
1	535 yards	par 5	10	210 yards	par 3
2	205 yards	par 3	11	510 yards	par 5
3	470 yards	par 4	12	445 yards	par 4
4	455 yards	par 4	13	420 yards	par 4
5	190 yards	par 3	14	435 yards	par 4
6	405 yards	par 4	15	425 yards	par 4
7	380 yards	par 4	16	170 yards	par 3
8	220 yards	par 3	17	390 yards	par 4
9	590 yards	par 5	18	440 yards	par 4
3,450 yards		par 35	3,445 yards		par 35
Total 6,895 yards par 70					

THE JOCKEY CLUB

Argentina is probably the most power-ful golf country in South America, with a hundred or more courses and a history of excellent international golfers, such as Jose Jurado, Tony Cerda, Roberto de Vicenzo and Vicente Fernandez. The game, as so much else, was taken there by the Scots and English who were involved in the management and operation of the railways, the tramways, and the gas, water and power services earlier in the century. But in Argentina, as throughout South America, golf has remained a game for the affluent, and has never begun to rival the great god, football.

For all that, just as the country has produced great players, so it can boast fine courses; and none greater than the Red course of the Jockey Club in Buenos Aires. The club has two courses adjoining its racetrack and polo fields at San Isidro – a suburb on the north side of Buenos Aires, edging the shore of the River Plate and therefore rather flat.

In the early 'Thirties, when they de-cided to go for 36 holes of golf, the Jockey Club had the good sense to go for the best, and briefed Dr Alister Mackenzie of Royal Melbourne, Cypress Point and Au-gusta National renown. To get some movement into the land Mackenzie in-dulged in a good deal of earth-moving, building swales and mounds and raising greens, and called for a programme of planting of trees and shrubs. Across the Rio de la Plata, Mackenzie also at this time built the Golf Club of Uruguay in Montevideo and the Punta del Este Golf Club. Of the Red and Blue courses in Buenos Aires, the Red – the 'Colorado' – was to be the championship course, although at 6,699 yards it was by no means long, even in 1935 when it opened. Sadly, Mackenzie did not see the finished product as he died in 1934.

On two occasions the Jockey Club's Red course has staged the World Cup. In 1962, the American team of Sam Snead and Arnold Palmer won, but the indi-vidual title went to Roberto de Vicenzo, on a score of 276. In 1970, the Australian team of Bruce Devlin and David Graham

The elegant clubhouse and part of the two courses of the Jockey Club, in the centre of Buenos Aires. The 1970 World Cup was played on the Red course, with only 19 players breaking par over 72 holes.

won, but the individual title again went to Roberto de Vicenzo, with a 269.

The 1st hole runs straight and directly away from the clubhouse for 437 yards, into an alleyway of trees. The bunkering on the left side of the fairway and the green suggests that this hole should be played entirely along the right. The 2nd is a jinky little 345 yards, and is anything but simple. A large eucalyptus tree on the right, 100 yards out, shuts off half of the target area from the tee. A big bunker on the left at 220 yards tightens it even further, and another bunker covers the front of a small green. The 3rd at 154 yards, has a bunker left front biting into the putting surface – a Road Hole type of bunker. The 4th and 5th run along the edge of the Club's property with an out-of-bounds down the left – a par-5 and a par-4 with ten bunkers between them.

Another of Mackenzie's techniques for compensating for the lack of movement in the ground, and perhaps the lack of yardage available to him, was bunkering and contouring the greens. The par of 72 is well won here!

The inward half is substantially more

severe. The 11th hole, at 518 yards, needs a long drive to get to the turn. Once that is done, bunkers to the left and right of a green which is overhung with trees on the left, make it very difficult to attack the hole. And the 13th hole is probably at the same time the simplest and the most difficult on the course. It is a straight, very narrow 440 yards to an extremely narrow green. The 15th, the last of the par-5s, has an out-of-bounds along the left, turns to the left, is heavily bunkered on the right and plays to a green surrounded by three bunkers! This Red course at the Jockey Club is a course of considerable difficulty. It is also one of distinction – indeed, one of the finest in all of South America.

The 17th green with the 16th in the background. The famous golf architect Alister Mackenzie was employed to give character to a course which was on very flat ground, hence the introduction of mounds and contouring combined with subtle bunkering.

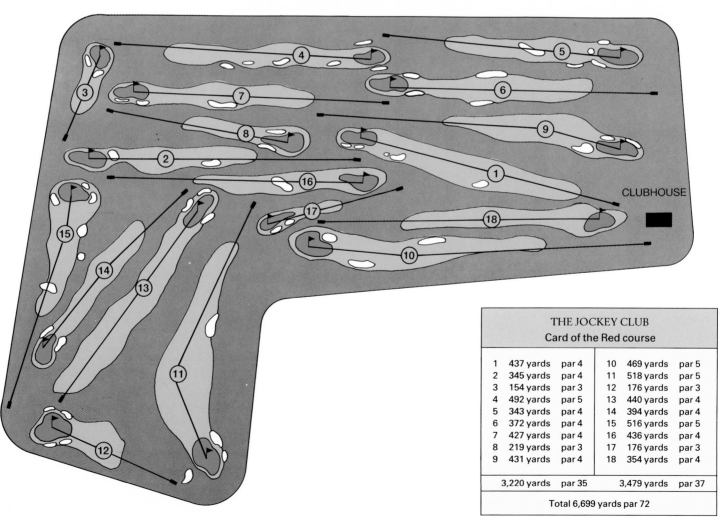

CLUBHOUSE

THE JOCKEY CLUB				
Card of the Red course				
1	437 yards	par 4	10	469 yards	par 5
2	345 yards	par 4	11	518 yards	par 5
3	154 yards	par 3	12	176 yards	par 3
4	492 yards	par 5	13	440 yards	par 4
5	343 yards	par 4	14	394 yards	par 4
6	372 yards	par 4	15	516 yards	par 5
7	427 yards	par 4	16	436 yards	par 4
8	219 yards	par 3	17	176 yards	par 3
9	431 yards	par 4	18	354 yards	par 4
3,220 yards	par 35		3,479 yards	par 37
Total 6,699 yards par 72				

EUROPE

Golf in Europe in the Nineties could be compared with the game in America in the Sixties – it is enjoying a second coming. Included in this are the successes of British and/or European teams – men, women, amateurs, professionals – against the Americans. Also there are a complete generation of professionals who have proved themselves outstanding international champions – Severiano Ballesteros of Spain, Bernhard Langer of West Germany, Sandy Lyle of Scotland and Nick Faldo of England – and consequently a massive increase of the media coverage of golf has made it a major sport in Europe as it always has been in the U.K.

In Scotland, the home of golf, and in the British Isles generally, the game remains relatively inexpensive, a game of the people. Its main problem in small, over-crowded Britain has been the shortage of land to meet an incessant demand for new courses.

In continental Europe, the game has always been expensive, aristocratic, even esoteric, but while remaining expensive it has expanded in dramatic fashion. Golf course architects were busy as could be throughout Europe and into the Near East as governments and entrepreneurs alike saw golf as a critical factor in support of tourism, and as in America, of hotel, resort and property development. Thus the coasts and islands of Spain and Portugal had courses galore and became the Florida of Europe. And still to be developed is the growth of the game in Eastern Europe, and dare one say it, in the U.S.S.R.

The 16th green at Turnberry during the 1986 Open Championship. The swales, humps and bumps of this true linksland course are only too evident.

ROYAL ST GEORGE'S

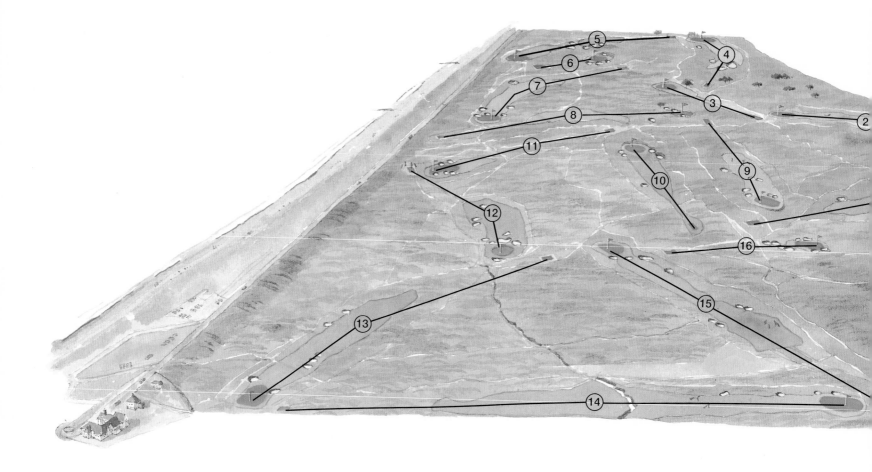

Royal St George's at Sandwich is the classic links course; its immense sand dunes hard by the sea, undulating fairways and severe bunkering give the impression that it is isolated from the world: on no other course in England can a golfer feel so happily abandoned to the game and to an environment which can seem to be a vast wilderness. In still summer sunshine it is a place of beauty and joy. In storms rolling in unimpeded off the North Sea, it can reduce the strongest tournament player to despair.

The origins of the course and the club, as so often in the litany of these great golf courses, can be traced to a single individual – Dr Laidlaw Purves. An Edinburgh man who had played his golf at the old Bruntsfield club there, he became an eye specialist at Guy's Hospital in London. He began playing at Wimbledon,

which like so many other courses in the 1880s was becoming crowded as England enjoyed its first golf boom. Purves and Henry Lamb, the Wimbledon secretary, decided to look further afield. There are various tales of how Purves came upon the huge linksland at Sandwich. One has it that Purves and a couple of friends climbed to the top of the tower of St Clement's church in Sandwich and saw the promised land – a huge expanse of dunes by the sea which in time became three great golf courses side by side: St George's in the centre (1887), Royal Cinque Ports on the southward side, towards Deal (1892), and Prince's to the north, on the Ramsgate side (1904).

Laidlaw Purves and his group leased 320 acres from the Earl of Guildford and promptly laid out their course, named St George's as England's riposte to Scot-

land's St Andrews, in what was an entirely contemporary links style – in those days, course designers were still much addicted to the blind shot over a mountainous sandhill, as at Prestwick, perhaps with a forbidding bunker cut in the face of it and with greens cut into hillsides. There was also a farmhouse on the land which served as a makeshift clubhouse, but much use was made of the Bell Hotel in Sandwich – and is to this day – following the Scottish tradition of golf being associated with inns.

Within five years the Royal and Ancient had noted that this extraordinary new golf course at Sandwich 'might be suitable for big tournaments'. They sent a four-man delegation to look at the course; and in 1894, a mere seven years since the founding of the club, St George's staged the first of its many Open Cham-

ROYAL ST GEORGE'S Card of the course					
1	445 yards	par 4	10	399 yards	par 4
2	376 yards	par 4	11	216 yards	par 3
3	214 yards	par 3	12	362 yards	par 4
4	470 yards	par 4	13	443 yards	par 4
5	422 yards	par 4	14	508 yards	par 5
6	156 yards	par 3	15	467 yards	par 4
7	529 yards	par 5	16	165 yards	par 3
8	415 yards	par 4	17	425 yards	par 4
9	387 yards	par 4	18	458 yards	par 4
	3,414 yards	par 35		3,443 yards	par 35
		Total 6,857 yards par 70			

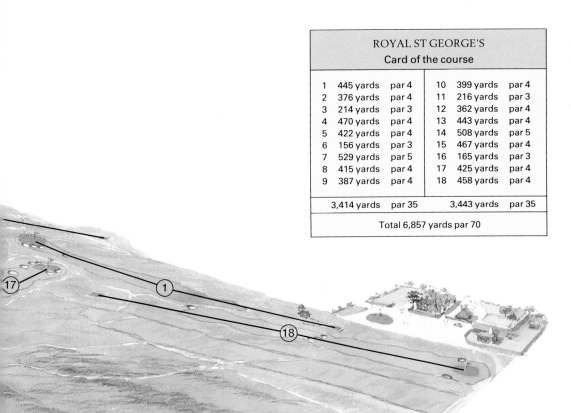

pionships. The first ever played in England, it was won by J.H. Taylor, aged 24, who was to win a total of five championships in all and be confirmed as one of golf's greatest players before the First World War.

Cotton's Triumph

From 1894 to 1949 St George's, often called simply 'Sandwich', staged nine Open championships, with the list of winners showing such illustrious names as Harry Vardon, Walter Hagen, Henry Cotton and Bobby Locke. Perhaps the most significant of these victories was Cotton's in 1934. For 11 years American golfers, in particular Bobby Jones and Hagen, had dominated the championship. At Sandwich Cotton shattered the entire field with opening rounds of 67 and 65. His second round record brought golf the famous 'Dunlop 65' ball. What is often overlooked is that Cotton, in his first qualifying round that week, scored 66, a well-nigh perfect round of golf. He was nine strokes ahead after 36 holes, ten ahead after the third round and finally won by five strokes after a nervous last-round 79. It would be another 12 years before an overseas player won the championship again.

Bobby Locke beat Harry Bradshaw in a play-off in 1949, but the post-war Championship was becoming so large in terms of crowds and cars, so demanding of access and accommodation, that Sandwich fell out of favour. The cramped, narrow streets of the medieval town, with its toll bridge over the river, made the course virtually inaccessible. It was ignored for 32 years, but then, with the highways from London to the coast much improved, Sandwich bypass opened and a back road to Deal modernised with the help of the R. and A., Sandwich came back with a flourish in 1981. The club played host to 114,522 spectators for the week and victory went to a young Texan, Bill Rogers. Architect Frank Pennink had been brought in to bring the course up to

Roger Wethered drives at the 11th at Royal St George's in his Walker Cup match in 1930 against Bobby Jones. Jones, seen on the tee beside the caddie, won 9 and 8 – he never lost a Walker Cup match.

the mark, and he removed most of the blind shots, re-positioned a green or two, stretched some tees and checked on St George's bunkers – not many more than 100, but all of them in prime positions.

A Muirfield of the South

Royal St George's is not so much a St Andrews as a Muirfield of the south, although it is even more rugged. They share a quality of spaciousness, of being not in any way overlooked, of being adrift in an immense and ancient landscape.

Perhaps the triangle of holes 13, 14 and 15 contains the very essence of this course, requiring play in three 'different' winds. The 13th is the first of four big par-4 holes over the final six. It is 443 yards long and turns slightly to the left. There are bunkers on the right at the outside of the turn, at 240 and 265 yards. The drive to the left of them must cross a diagonal line of rough country and small

Above: *Sandy Lyle in one of St George's man-deep bunkers. Lyle won the Open Championship of 1985 at the Sandwich links, the first 'home' winner since Tony Jacklin in 1969.*

Left: *The monstrous sand trap at the 4th hole at Royal St George's, one of the most intimidating courses on the Open Championship rota.*

sandhills. The line is desperately important. An over-ambitious shot, too far to the left, can find disaster in that ground.

At 508 yards, the 14th hole is the last par-5. It runs straight, with an out-of-bounds fence hard along the right side (Prince's Golf Club is beyond the fence) and a broad stream, known as the 'Suez Canal', running across the fairway at 320 yards from the back tee. There is very rough ground to the left of this fairway and bunkers string along the left-hand

side forward to the green, which is extremely flat and almost an extension of the fairway.

In winning the 1975 PGA Championship over this course, Arnold Palmer played one of the greatest rounds of his life – a 71 in a freezing gale on the last day. He played that 14th hole with a drive, a 3-iron shot under the wind, and one short putt.

Sandy Lyle, in the last round of his Open in 1985, played it rather differently. He drove into heavy rough on the left. His recovery shot advanced him a mere 80 yards. He then hit a 2-iron shot a fulminating 220 yards to the green and holed the putt of 45 feet. And when he hit a lovely 6-iron second to the 15th – one of the classic par-4 holes in British golf – he 'suddenly realised I had a real chance of winning'. He did, and was the first Scot to win the Open since Tommy Armour in 1931.

ROYAL LYTHAM AND ST ANNES

Visually, the Royal Lytham and St Annes course is the most modest, you might almost say, of all the British championship courses; yet it is linksland at its best. Its environment is urban. There are no massive sand dunes as at Birkdale or St George's; no panoramas of island and estuary, as at the West of Scotland courses, Troon and Turnberry; no grand sweep of bay as at St Andrews.

In fact, the course is a mile or so from the sea, with the Lytham-Blackpool railway line defining the seaward side of the course. Its other boundaries are overlooked by private properties, which has the golfing purist shuddering, but which

may well be considered a pleasure by the owners. Above all, Lytham calls for courage, nerve, confidence and accuracy from the tees and it has in abundance the one absolute quality that distinguishes links golf from any other – its greens will receive the running approach shot.

The St Annes-on-Sea Land and Building Company was formed in 1874 by a group of Lancashire businessmen with the simple but imaginative intention of building a new resort town between Lytham and Blackpool's south shore. They did it. And they persuaded the railway company to build them a fine station, and after some teething troubles,

St Annes prospered – the present town having grown out of the square mile of land which the company leased in 1874.

The initiative in getting the golf club started came from Alexander Doleman, a Musselburgh schoolmaster, who had opened a school in Blackpool. He was a golfer talented enough to play in the 1870 Open at Prestwick, with the Morrises and

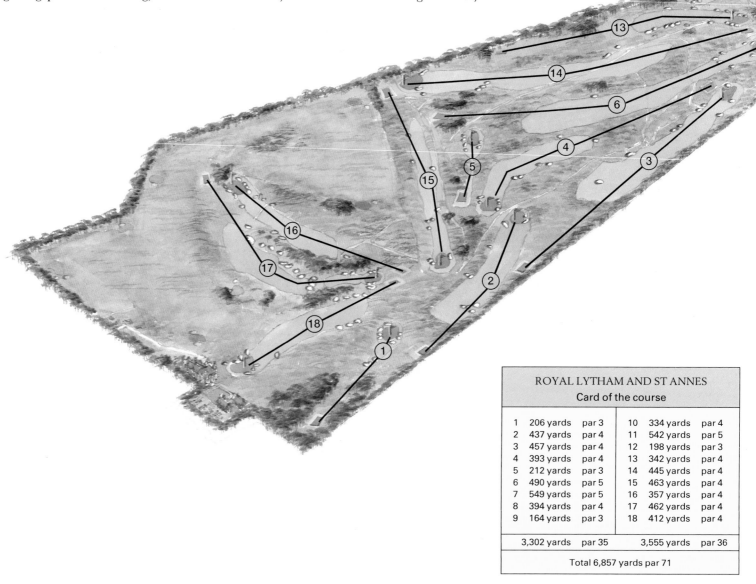

ROYAL LYTHAM AND ST ANNES					
Card of the course					
1	206 yards	par 3	10	334 yards	par 4
2	437 yards	par 4	11	542 yards	par 5
3	457 yards	par 4	12	198 yards	par 3
4	393 yards	par 4	13	342 yards	par 4
5	212 yards	par 3	14	445 yards	par 4
6	490 yards	par 5	15	463 yards	par 4
7	549 yards	par 5	16	357 yards	par 4
8	394 yards	par 4	17	462 yards	par 4
9	164 yards	par 3	18	412 yards	par 4
3,302 yards	par 35		3,555 yards	par 36	
Total 6,857 yards par 71					

Right: *The lovely rhythm of Tony Jacklin brought him the Open title of 1969, his purple patch caught here in his crucial tee shot at the 72nd at Royal Lytham. The following year he won the U.S. Open by seven shots.*

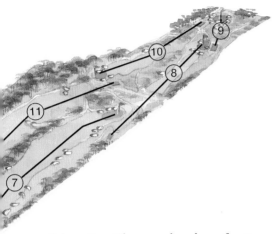

Below: *Peter Thomson, the urbane, five-times Open Champion, plays a bunker shot at Fairhaven, qualifying for the 1958 Open, which he won after a playoff with David Thomas.*

Straths of the time, and in the first Amateur Championship played at Hoylake in 1885. Although the club quickly laid out 18 holes, and indeed had a separate nine for the ladies, there were problems with the St Annes-on-Sea Land and Building Company, who were not very interested in extending what was a

rather short initial lease. Thus by 1891, with the club in a healthy state and a membership of around 400, it was decided that it was time to find a more permanent site. In 1897, the club moved to its present location and into a splendid clubhouse, reported to have cost £8,000 – an impressive sum at the time. The 1897 course cost £2,500 to build and is generally thought to be the work of George Lowe, who came from Hoylake in 1888 to be the club's first professional. Subsequently, such famous architects as Herbert Fowler, Harry Colt and G.K. Cotton made changes to firm up and 'modernise' the course.

Lytham has stood up well to the modern game and its list of Open Champions could not be more impressive: Bobby Jones in 1926, Bobby Locke in 1952, Peter Thomson 1958, Bob Charles 1963, Tony Jacklin 1969, Gary Player 1974 and Severiano Ballesteros in 1979 and 1988. All of them might well have agreed that on this course, the foundation of the round would have to be built on

the outward half, and any birdies made there would have to be protected on the inward half – for the last half dozen holes represent perhaps the toughest sustained finish in championship golf.

An Opening Par-3
A Lytham oddity is that the first hole is a par-3 of 206 yards. It is played out of a grove of trees, so judging the wind is difficult on this opening shot. The 2nd and 3rd holes are strong par-4s. The railway running hard down the right side is an intimidating factor. These three holes run straight out, but the 4th turns back on them and together with the short 5th and long 6th, 'triangulates' back towards the railway line. The 4th is 393 yards, but turns to the left and is likely to be into wind. The 5th is a long one-shotter of 212 yards from a raised tee to a mounded green – a difficult tee shot this, especially in wind.

Now we have another Lytham oddity: successive par-5s, of 490 yards and 549 yards, both considered prime birdie holes. The 8th, at 394 yards, takes us nearer to the end of the course and the one area of Lytham which has some rolling, if modest, sand hills; while the 9th, 164 yards, is a pitch down from a plateau to a bowl green ringed by 10 bunkers. The 10th, at 334 yards, is only a drive and pitch hole – although the drive is into a narrow, broken fairway.

The Long Road Home
The 11th is really the start of a long and grinding road home. It is 542 yards, dog-leg left, with two deep bunkers in the angle at 256 yards out. A drive over these bunkers gives the player some hope of being on the green in two. To the right of them, the second shot becomes longer and longer. The short 12th is rather like the first hole in that it is 198 yards and played out of a spinney of trees, which again make the wind difficult to assess. The green is set across the shot, and there is a road and an out-of-bounds uncomfortably close to it. The 13th is something of a catch-your-breath hole of 342 yards, but now we are into the king-sized finish.

All the finishing holes, without exception, feature very narrow fairways with vigorous bunkering and set the sternest

Above: *The 16th at Royal Lytham, 356 yards and a blind tee shot, is known as the 'car park' hole. In the 1979 championship, Severiano Ballesteros drove far to the right amongst parked cars, was allowed a free drop, pitched to the green and holed for a birdie!*

Left: *Severiano Ballesteros exults in his chip shot from the back left of the last green, on the last round of the 1988 championship at Royal Lytham. The ball nudged the hole, stopped a few inches away, and made his victory certain.*

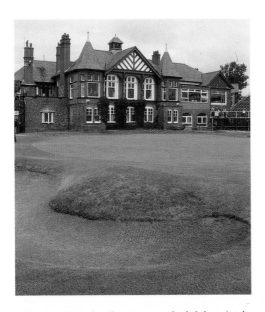

This enormous bunker protects the left-hand side of the 18th green; in the background the fine Royal Lytham clubhouse.

examination of driving patterns and angles. The 15th, at 468 yards and as often as not into the wind, is one of the most demanding par-4 holes in championship golf. The 16th, at 356 yards, is more manageable, but needs a blind drive over tumbling ground, while the green and its approaches feature no fewer than 11 bunkers. It was at this hole in 1979 that Ballesteros drove into a car park on the right, dropped clear without penalty, pitched to the green and holed the putt for a wonderfully preposterous birdie.

Jones's Historic Mashie Shot
The 17th hole, of 462 yards, is a marvellous golf hole, intrinsically and because of its place in the Lytham sequence. It dog-legs to the left some 300 yards from the tee. All along the left side are bunkers. At the 300 yards mark, a broad swathe of rough crosses the fairway, containing another rash of bunkers. The green is quite large by Lytham standards. It was on this hole in 1926 that Bobby Jones, in winning the first of his three Open Championships, hit one of golf's most famous shots. Trapped in a shallow bunker on the left, 175 yards from the green, he found a clean lie. Jones picked the ball off the sand cleanly and found the green with his mashie to secure a par-4. Al Watrous, playing with Jones and level with him for the Championship, was so unnerved that he three-putted, and finished second. To this day, a plaque marks the bunker from which Jones played the shot.

The last hole at Lytham seems to be a microcosm of the whole golf course. At first glance it seems almost nondescript, running on to a flat green which runs right under the clubhouse windows. At 412 yards, it was lengthened by some 25 yards for the 1988 Championship, but can be considered short for a finishing hole. However, it is in fact a superb driving hole. Across the fairway in the driving zone are two diagonals of bunkers; there are clumps of bushes in the right rough, so that the landing area for the tee shot is terribly confined. It demands a drive that is long, finely calculated and straight, and no champion has ever played it better than did Tony Jacklin in winning his Open Championship in 1969.

ROYAL BIRKDALE

If ever a piece of land seemed designed exclusively for the hand of the golf architect, it was surely the coast of Lancashire running north from Liverpool along Liverpool Bay and the Irish Sea to the town of Southport. Tumbling sand dunes, heather, pine forest, willow scrub; and the railway tracks, which seem almost mandatory for British links courses, marking the boundaries of some holes, and serving a litany of famous courses – all of this has given us West Lancs., Formby, Southport & Ainsdale, Hillside and Royal Birkdale. And the greatest of these is Royal Birkdale.

The course is laid out through a great wasteland of sand dunes, the design following the valleys between them. The original course, dating from 1889, is generally thought to have been the work of George Lowe; but problems arose with the renewal of the lease and in 1897 the founding fathers moved to the present site. In 1931 Southport Corporation bought the land and leased it to the club for 99 years. The present clubhouse was then built, and Fred Hawtree and J.H. Taylor re-modeled the course. Royal Birkdale was now ready for the modern age of steel shafts.

In 29 years from 1954, it staged six Open Championships and two Ryder Cup matches. It has also presented the Curtis Cup match, the Walker Cup match, British and English championships and several major professional tournaments. And its Open champions form a distinguished hierarchy: Peter Thomson

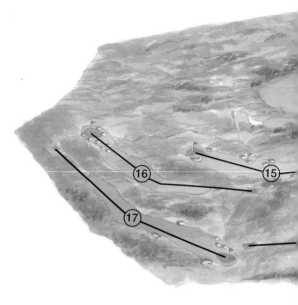

Arnold Palmer, wearing his storm gear on the 2nd tee during the first round of the 1961 Open at Royal Birkdale, the first of his successive wins which did much to rejuvenate the championship.

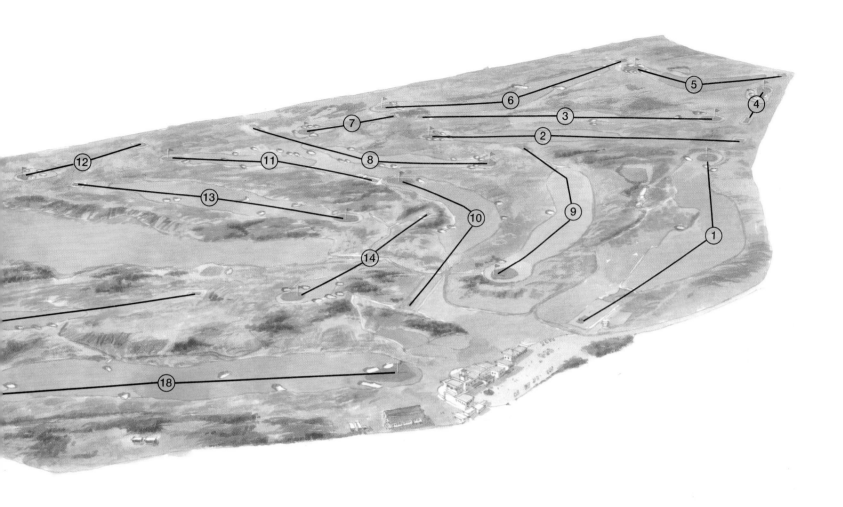

ROYAL BIRKDALE

(twice), Arnold Palmer, Lee Trevino, Johnny Miller and Tom Watson.

While the Birkdale fairways, rising and falling, have a good deal of movement in them, there is an absence of those small mounds and pimples such as we find at St Andrews or Troon or St George's, which can make a lottery of the bounce of the ball. The sand dunes are huge, giving both shelter to the fairways and splendid vantage points for spectators. One particular feature of the course has been the siting of the greens and their defences. There are no blind shots at Birkdale. But the greens in general have been planted tightly into the dunes. All of them have impish little slopes running off the putting surfaces, all of them are closely bunkered and many of them – the 2nd, 6th, 15th and 17th, for example – are all but surrounded by plantations of willow scrub. Thus missing the green at Birkdale, even by a few feet, can bring retribution most foul!

In championship trim, Royal Birkdale

ROYAL BIRKDALE					
\multicolumn{6}{c}{Card of the course}					
1	448 yards	par 4	10	395 yards	par 4
2	417 yards	par 4	11	409 yards	par 4
3	409 yards	par 4	12	184 yards	par 3
4	203 yards	par 3	13	506 yards	par 5
5	346 yards	par 4	14	199 yards	par 3
6	490 yards	par 5	15	543 yards	par 5
7	154 yards	par 3	16	414 yards	par 4
8	458 yards	par 4	17	525 yards	par 5
9	414 yards	par 4	18	472 yards	par 4
3,339 yards	par 35		3,647 yards	par 37	
\multicolumn{6}{c}{Total 6,986 yards par 72}					

runs to just under 7,000 yards with a par of 72. On the outward half the course has two par-3 holes and no par-5. On the inward half, it has four par-5s packed into the final six holes, ready made for high drama and deeds of derring-do in tight championship finishes. Two such were shots to the last green, 200 yards away,

finding the narrow entrance between the flanking bunkers. Peter Thomson did it in 1965 and Tom Watson did it in 1983, each man winning his fifth championship. Each played a 2-iron, and Thomson won by two strokes, Watson by one. Watson said afterwards that it was the best 2-iron shot he had ever played.

Palmer's Heroics

Birkdale is man-sized on the outward half: six of its par-4 holes are 400 yards or better. Yet it always seems to produce better than man-sized champions. In the Open of 1961 a gale flattened Birkdale on the second day; tented areas were devastated, and fairways were in part under water. But Arnold Palmer gave an astonishing display of power and control in keeping the ball under the wind, hitting 1-iron shots that never rose more than six feet off the ground. He was three under par after five holes and eventually finished with a remarkable 73.

At the 15th hole (now the 16th) of the last round, Palmer hit a shot that is immortalised by a plaque marking the spot. The hole is 414 yards and Palmer drove off the fairway into the heavy right rough in the elbow of the fairway. The green, raised on a plateau, has two bunkers on either side and four short of the green. Palmer would have to extract his ball from the rough and advance it by a good 150 yards through the air to reach the putting surface. He gave the ball the most immense smash with a 6-iron, and from this awful rough it flew all the way, finishing 15 feet from the flagstick. He won the championship by a stroke from Dai Rees.

The most interesting (and difficult) hole on the outward half is the 6th, a big, 490-yard par-5 which turns to the right. At the angle, a long, mounded bunker crosses most of the fairway, leaving a gap of only a few yards on the left, while rough closes out the right end of the bunker. Playing safely short of it leaves a very long second shot to a large but raised green, bunkered and backed by willow scrub. On the other hand, to carry the bunker means a giant shot, and even in perfect conditions few will manage it. Similarly, trying to sneak past the left end of the bunker will require a drive of impressive length and accuracy.

Of the par-5s, the 13th at 506 yards is perhaps the most open. From a high tee the hole plays straight along a fairly flat fairway, with a ditch on the left. The pretty green is in a little canyon, with high dunes and willow scrub on three sides. The 15th is an immense hole: at 543 yards, it demands a very long drive to give the player any chance of carrying a screen of eight bunkers with his second shot to get anywhere near a green which has a closely trapped entrance. The 17th, at 525 yards, is almost as forbidding. The drive must find a rather narrow fairway set between huge sand ridges. The green is long and rather narrow; it will receive a running shot, but it gives the impression

This tranquil shot of the 13th hole, taken during an early round of the British Ladies' Championship of 1986, illustrates Royal Birkdale's ranging sand dunes and valley fairways, not to mention its famous willow scrub.

Johnny Miller holes out to win the 1976 Open at Royal Birkdale with a closing 66. An inspirational player, Miller had also scored a final low round, a record 63, in winning the 1973 U.S. Open Championship at Oakmont.

that it is slightly sunken, and it too has willow scrub pressing close.

Enter Ballesteros

In one sense, the Royal Birkdale championship of 1976, won by Johnny Miller, was a portent of things to come. It was a year of heatwave – part of the course had caught fire during the second day – and playing conditions were perfect. It was also the year that Severiano Ballesteros, 19 years old, played his first Open. He played the first 36 holes in 69, 69 with all the brio of a man enjoying Sunday morning golf. He went into the last round leading the championship by two strokes from Miller. They were paired together on that last round, and Miller, hardened championship player that he was, was not about to let this young Spaniard take any liberties with him. Playing relentlessly attacking golf, Miller was out in 33, round in 66, and took the championship by six strokes from Ballesteros and Jack Nicklaus. But for many the moment of the championship came at the 13th hole in the final round, when Miller chipped in from off the green and Seve Ballesteros skipped across the green and smilingly shook his hand.

FORMBY

The course of the Formby Golf Club is a lovely, unsung link in that necklace of courses that runs from the northern fringes of Liverpool to Southport. But Formby, even if it is more unassuming than most, is second to none of them. The club dates from 1881, making it one of the oldest of Lancashire clubs, and it could scarcely have had a more modest beginning. The minutes of the original meeting remain and show that ten 'gentlemen' met at the Rev. Lonsdale Formby's Reading Room on the 11th of December 1884. Mr William McIver, who was to become the first captain of the club, took the chair. They resolved to call it the Formby Golf Club, the number of members being restricted to 25. Subscription was one guinea and the 'Links should be open for play on 1st October, closing on the Saturday nearest 15th April following'. So it was winter golf they had in mind, in spite of the fact that, at that moment, they did not have a course – they thought they would rent Mr William Halewood's 'Warren' as their links at a rental of £10 per season, but only £5 'for the unexpired portion of this season'!

The Warren was rough grazing land, with sandhills and scrub, in the general area of the present first and second holes, adjoining the railway line, and the 18th. McIver had shooting rights over it – the area was infested with rabbits. Formby's start was certainly primitive! Nine holes were knocked out, with greens no more than extensions of the fairways, and with little more than a year gone, it was agreed that membership could rise to 40, and a wooden shanty was raised as a 'clubhouse' (built by a member for less than £3). The most significant fact of that first year came when Formby was asked to support the initiative of the Royal Liverpool Club, which had suggested to the Royal and Ancient that an Amateur Championship should be established. Two delegates from each of the supporting clubs, including Formby, met to organise the event, played for the first time that year, 1885,

Formby is a classic links course of charm and elegance. This natural bowl around the 10th hole provides spectators with a superb vantage point to watch the play.

at Hoylake. Formby contributed their guinea to pay for a championship trophy. This put a stamp on the personality of the club. Formby perhaps took on an air of the amateur establishment which it has never quite lost. Not only the merchants of Manchester and Liverpool but the Lancashire county set made it their club. It prospered steadily, and had the flavour of Muirfield or Royal St George's.

Willie Park, Jr and Harry Colt

In the 1890s, the course was extended to 18 holes of just under 6,000 yards, but all of them were in the same compass, packed into the area in front of the clubhouse. But early in the new century, additional land to the north and west was taken over and the course was able to march into an area of sandhills and towards the sea. In 1907 Willie Park, Jr designed 18 holes, many of them still in place after Harry Colt reviewed them in the 'Twenties. Thus Formby has been touched by two of the greatest golf architects. Park, a perfectionist and probably the first golf champion to make a professional study of course design, laid

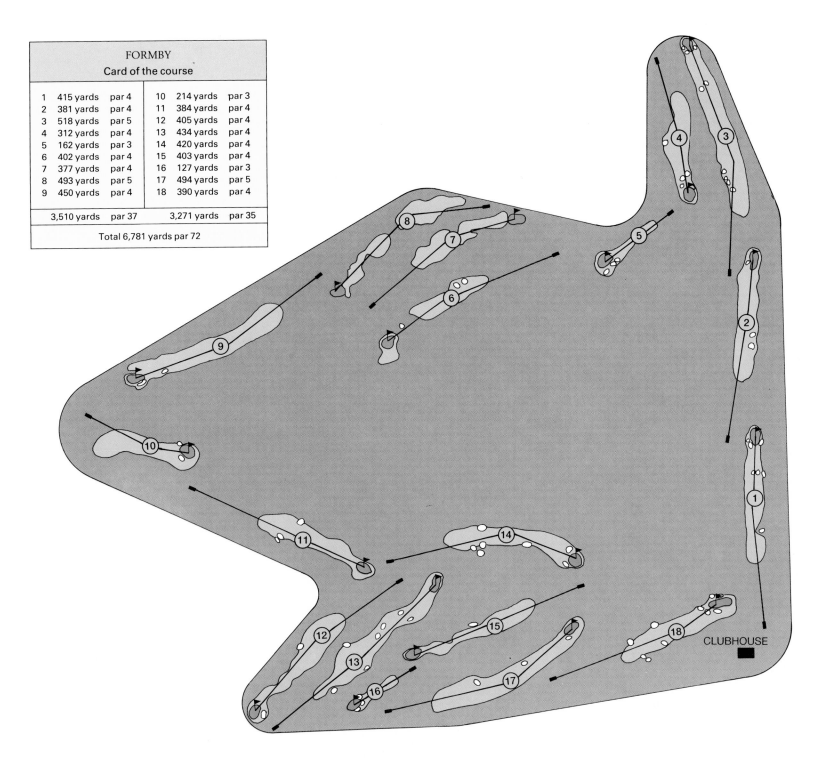

FORMBY					
Card of the course					
1	415 yards	par 4	10	214 yards	par 3
2	381 yards	par 4	11	384 yards	par 4
3	518 yards	par 5	12	405 yards	par 4
4	312 yards	par 4	13	434 yards	par 4
5	162 yards	par 3	14	420 yards	par 4
6	402 yards	par 4	15	403 yards	par 4
7	377 yards	par 4	16	127 yards	par 3
8	493 yards	par 5	17	494 yards	par 5
9	450 yards	par 4	18	390 yards	par 4
3,510 yards		par 37	3,271 yards		par 35
Total 6,781 yards par 72					

out some 70 courses in the United States, and others in Canada, Austria, Belgium and France as well as Britain.

Frank Pennink

The first three holes of the Park/Colt course at Formby run hard by the Liverpool-Southport railway line, and are reminiscent of the start at Royal Lytham. Two strong par-4s and a big 518 yards par-5 run north across fairly flat ground. The course then turns westward into a range of rising duneland garlanded with pine woods planted by the club. Like Ballybunion and Portrush, Formby has had erosion problems, but fortunately had enough spare land to allow Frank Pennink to replace a couple of holes. The last half dozen holes play every which way, giving differing wind problems and creating an extremely difficult finish.

Formby is a classic links course of charm and elegance and stillness. It does have some iron in its soul, since it can now muster 6,781 yards and a par of 72. It has offered the warmest of welcomes to amateur championships – it has staged all of them, mens' and women's, boys' and girls' – but it has been just a little indifferent to professional events.

GANTON

Glorious Ganton in North Yorkshire is nine miles from the sea, yet it has all the qualities of a typical links course. It is certainly one of the finest inland courses in Britain, and boasts a sandy sub-soil which makes it quick-draining, crisp turf, enormous banks of gorse (which have become its signature) and cavernous, links-type bunkers. The course lies snugly in the Vale of Pickering, which runs from Pickering in the west to the coast at Scarborough and in recent geological times was under sea water; this explains why, to this day, the Ganton ground staff turn up sea shells when digging new drains or bunkers.

Ganton is a beautiful golf course and, if not long at 6,720 yards, offers a keen examination for the best players, having staged Amateur Championships and a Ryder Cup match. This is hardly surprising: since it was formed in 1891, the club has been advised by Tom Sherrin, Tom Dunn, Harry Vardon, Harold Hilton, James Braid, Harry Colt, Herbert Fowler,

Harry Vardon in his prime. Six-times winner of the Open Championship, winner of the U.S. Open, he is one of the three or four most influential players in the history of golf.

Major Hutchinson, C.K. Cotton and Frank Pennink – a veritable galaxy of golfing and design talent.

In 1891 Scarborough was the premier resort in the north of England and had been a spa for more than 200 years. With the golfing explosion in England in the last quarter of the 19th century, some prominent citizens resolved that the town needed a golf course, and formed the Scarborough Golf Club. They chose a site which was part of the Ganton estate, owned by one of their number, Sir Charles Legard. It was very rough, uneven ground, covered with gorse and bushes, and had been used only for rough shooting. But it was only nine miles by road from Scarborough and only 300 yards from Ganton station on the North-Eastern railway line from York to Scarborough – an important factor in the age before motoring.

In the 1920s Dr Alistair Mackenzie was employed to redesign the greens. The result is one of his specialities: tiered

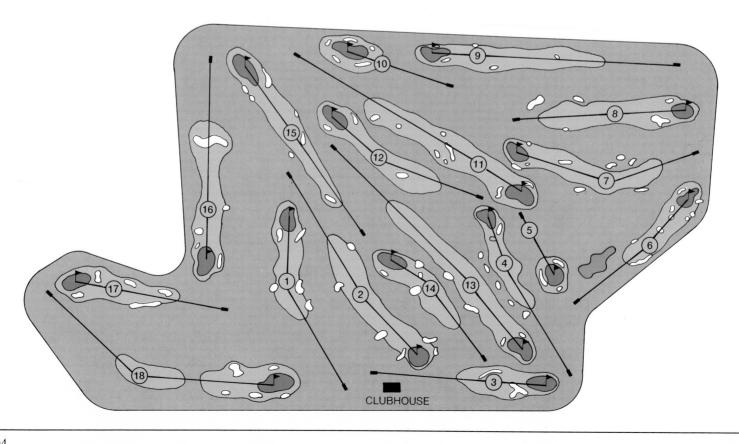

CLUBHOUSE

greens, as at the 3rd and 7th and 9th. Ken Cotton was then brought in to strengthen the course for the Ryder Cup matches of 1949 and lengthened many holes by building new tees. This was the Ryder Cup match in which Ben Hogan, the American non-playing captain, created something of a scandal by claiming that some of the British clubs were illegal, because their iron-club faces were too deeply punched.

Bernard Darwin, the venerable correspondent of *The Times* newspaper, was asked to resolve it and did so by suggesting diplomatically that there was nothing 'a little judicious filing could not put right'. This in fact was no more than a little tit-for-tat by Hogan – Henry Cotton, British captain in the previous match at Portland, Oregon, had said the same about the American clubs then.

Over the years Ganton's gorse has been allowed to grow considerably, but under control, and is now an outstanding feature of the course. Extensive planting of Scots and Corsican pine has added to the Ganton woodland, but in recent years

GANTON					
Card of the course					
1	373 yards	par 4	10	168 yards	par 3
2	418 yards	par 4	11	417 yards	par 4
3	334 yards	par 4	12	363 yards	par 4
4	406 yards	par 4	13	524 yards	par 5
5	157 yards	par 3	14	282 yards	par 4
6	449 yards	par 4	15	461 yards	par 4
7	431 yards	par 4	16	448 yards	par 4
8	414 yards	par 4	17	252 yards	par 4
9	494 yards	par 5	18	434 yards	par 4
	3,476 yards	par 36		3,349 yards	par 36
Total 6,825 yards par 72					

two elm trees, important to the play, were stricken by Dutch elm disease. One was on the right of the 282-yard 14th, a potential one-shot hole for the powerful hitter; the tree and a bunker had crucially narrowed the gap into the green. Fortunately it shows some sign of life and has been retained. The other tree, on the left of the 448-yard 16th, squeezed the line of the second shot. It had to be replaced by a flowering chestnut, 18 feet high.

The 13th hole at Ganton, a par 5 of 524 yards, demands a drive over a sierra of gorse to a none-too-wide fairway.

There are only two short holes and two par-5s on the course – neither of the latter being excessively long. Accuracy and careful driving at Ganton are more important than power – only six of the two-shot holes are more than 400 yards. Its large, bungalow-type clubhouse included, Ganton is a place of pleasure, and not of confrontation – even if you were J.H. Taylor facing the 'unknown' Harry Vardon in 1896. Vardon was professional of the club at the time. Taylor, the reigning Open Champion, wrote later: 'Little did I guess when playing him at Ganton that I was playing with a man who was to make golfing history and develop into what is in my solemn and considered judgement the finest and most finished golfer that the game has ever known'. Taylor was beaten 8 and 6.

SUNNINGDALE

When the Royal and Ancient Golf Club of St Andrews decided to award the staging of the 1987 Walker Cup match to the Sunningdale club, it was the first time that this famous match between the amateurs of Great Britain & Ireland and the United States of America had been played on an inland rather than a seaside links course. And the compliment was no more than an acknowledgement of the Sunningdale Old Course's quality, its charm and its subtleties, and of the contribution that the club and its members have made to golf, both in play and in council.

Sunningdale Old is one of the loveliest of golf courses. Only 25 miles south-west of London, it plays through heather and woodland of pine and birch and on a sandy sub-soil which gives quick drainage, encourages crisp lies in the seaside manner and allows year-round play. It is a quite splendid heathland course in which the fairways are ample, the hazards clearly seen, the greens true and the vistas stunning. And if the course, even at a modest 6,500 yards, is quite testing for all but the best tournament pros, it never quite seems so. The joy of Sunningdale is the total experience of the round, and not

the challenge of one hole more than another. The place has a certain elegance. It is altogether superior, and it knows it.

When Bobby Jones played the course in the Southern Qualifying Competition for the Open Championship of 1926, he scored what has come to be considered the perfect round of golf. His 66 had 33 shots and 33 putts. Every hole was scored in three or four. He missed only one green, the 13th, by a few feet, but chipped close for his par. In his second qualifying round, he scored 68, this time including one five and one two. He said later: 'I wish I could take this golf course home with me'. Sunningdale is that kind of place.

The end of the last century was an intriguing time for golf in the London area. Heathland was discovered to be entirely suitable for golf, and sand belts to the south and south-west of the capital quickly accommodated such fine courses as Woking in 1893 and Walton Heath in 1904. Sunningdale dates from 1901.

The golf course land was owned, and still is, by St John's College, Cambridge. It had formed part of the Benedictine nunnery of Broomhall, suppressed by Henry VIII, but John Fisher, Bishop of

SUNNINGDALE Card of the course					
1	494 yards	par 5	10	478 yards	par 5
2	484 yards	par 5	11	325 yards	par 4
3	296 yards	par 4	12	451 yards	par 4
4	161 yards	par 3	13	185 yards	par 3
5	410 yards	par 4	14	509 yards	par 5
6	415 yards	par 4	15	226 yards	par 3
7	402 yards	par 4	16	438 yards	par 4
8	172 yards	par 3	17	421 yards	par 4
9	267 yards	par 4	18	432 yards	par 4
3,101 yards	par 36		3,465 yards	par 36	
Total 6,566 yards par 72					

Rochester, was able to possess it for the College in 1524. The founding father of the golf club, T.A. Roberts had built a house in 1898 close to what is now the entrance to the club. He approached the College for a lease to allow him to build a golf course and some housing. A committee was formed of his interested friends, and Willie Park, Jr, twice Open Champion and a pioneer of golf architecture, was approached to lay out and build the course. His price was £3,800.

The ground at that time was almost entirely open, quite bare of trees, and the lovely woodlands of Sunningdale are an illustration of the hand of man improving on nature. Later, Harry Colt made some changes to the course to protect it against the longer flight of the Haskell ball. (Colt was secretary of Sunningdale for 17 years and designed the New Course, which dates from 1922.) His work now means that almost every hole treads its own pathway in some privacy, if not in complete isolation, and there is a splendid variation in the holes. No two are in any way alike.

Views over London

One of Sunningdale's most intriguing sequence of holes is 10, 11 and 12. The 10th tee is the highest point on the course, with compelling views over the forest towards London. The drive is downhill into a broad valley, with bunkers on

The view from the 5th tee, with the pond at centre-right in the fairway and beyond it the green bunkered at left and front right. All the trees in the picture are a product of Harry Colt's planting programme.

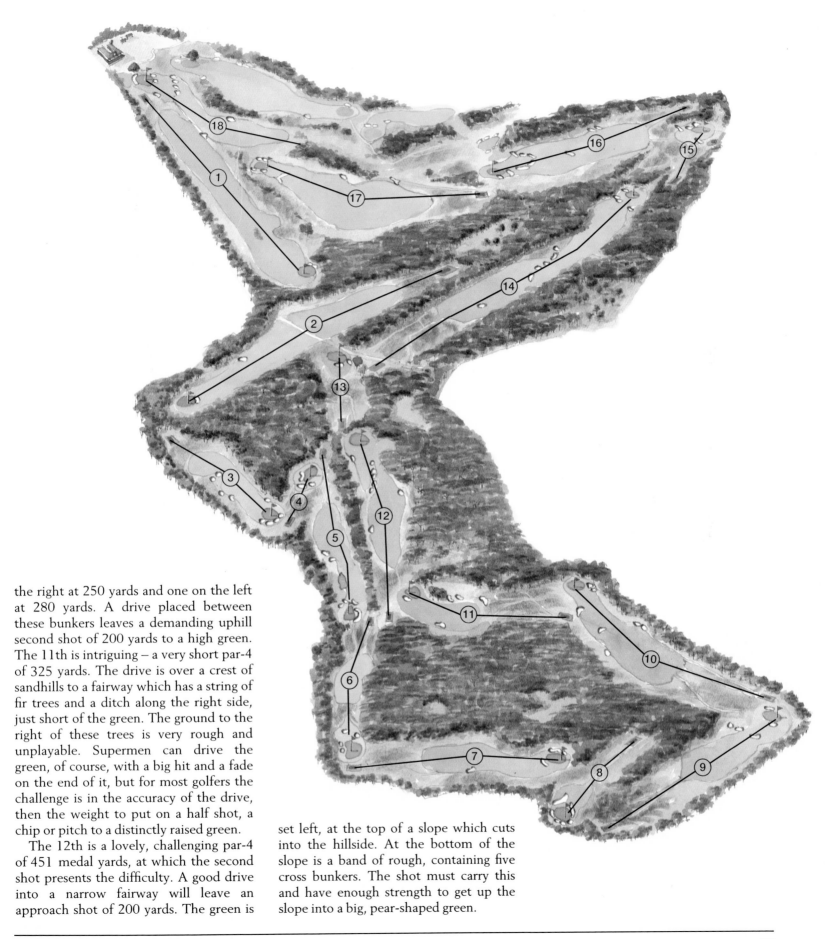

the right at 250 yards and one on the left at 280 yards. A drive placed between these bunkers leaves a demanding uphill second shot of 200 yards to a high green. The 11th is intriguing – a very short par-4 of 325 yards. The drive is over a crest of sandhills to a fairway which has a string of fir trees and a ditch along the right side, just short of the green. The ground to the right of these trees is very rough and unplayable. Supermen can drive the green, of course, with a big hit and a fade on the end of it, but for most golfers the challenge is in the accuracy of the drive, then the weight to put on a half shot, a chip or pitch to a distinctly raised green.

The 12th is a lovely, challenging par-4 of 451 medal yards, at which the second shot presents the difficulty. A good drive into a narrow fairway will leave an approach shot of 200 yards. The green is set left, at the top of a slope which cuts into the hillside. At the bottom of the slope is a band of rough, containing five cross bunkers. The shot must carry this and have enough strength to get up the slope into a big, pear-shaped green.

WALTON HEATH

Walton Heath was once common-land of the manor of Walton-on-the-Hill, owned since feudal times by lords of the manor. At the end of the 19th century it was a vast wasteland of heather and gorse. Nowadays the Walton Heath Golf Club, less than 20 miles from London, is the owner of two courses which offer the finest heathland golf to be found anywhere in the world. The golfing area of the heath is huge, some 500 acres in all, and at over 600 feet it is as high as Gleneagles. Exposed to the elements, it is a place of big skies, fine, dry, crisp turf and a wonderful feeling of spaciousness.

A man of many parts was largely responsible for the creation of the club and the courses. Cosmo Bonsor was among many things a director of the Bank of England, a Justice of the Peace and Deputy Lieutenant for Surrey, a Member of Parliament for Wimbledon from 1885 until 1900 and chairman of the South Eastern Railway Company. In this last capacity he had brought the railway to Kingswood and Tadworth, near Walton, and he was convinced that a golf course would supplement the railway in developing the area.

A second marriage for Bonsor brought William Herbert Fowler as a brother-in-law. Fowler, like Bonsor, was larger than

WALTON HEATH					
Card of the Championship course					
1	410 yards	par 4	10	341 yards	par 4
2	513 yards	par 5	11	521 yards	par 5
3	391 yards	par 4	12	462 yards	par 4
4	422 yards	par 4	13	470 yards	par 4
5	174 yards	par 3	14	465 yards	par 4
6	489 yards	par 5	15	404 yards	par 4
7	390 yards	par 4	16	475 yards	par 4
8	395 yards	par 4	17	165 yards	par 3
9	189 yards	par 3	18	432 yards	par 4
3,373 yards	par 36		3,735 yards	par 36	
Total 7,108 yards par 72					

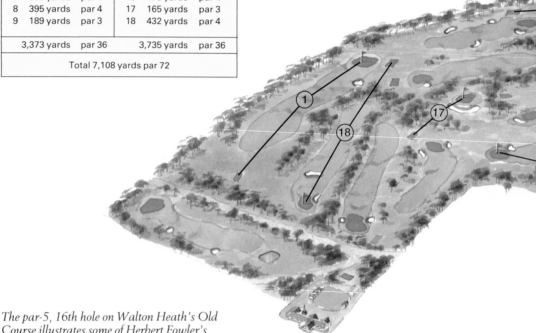

The par-5, 16th hole on Walton Heath's Old Course illustrates some of Herbert Fowler's design principles: raised green, deep greenside bunkering, the use of heather, and a reasonable width to the fairway.

life. A talented cricketer for Essex, Somerset and MCC, he took up golf only when he was 35 but quickly became scratch. As a member of the R & A and the Honourable Company, he won medals at St Andrews, St George's, Westward Ho! and Walton, and played international golf for England. He was also enchanted by St Andrews, studied the Old Course carefully, and made it very clear to Bonsor that he had ambitions as a golf-course designer. Bonsor and his eldest son Malcolm and their friends made it possible: they purchased the land, formed a company, and turned Fowler loose on the heath in August 1902.

He settled on a design, the course was seeded in August 1903 (rabbits were a problem and miles of expensive mesh fencing had to be laid), and by the spring of 1904 it was ready for play. In January of that year Fowler, who became secretary of the club, a shareholder and eventually managing director, signed a con-

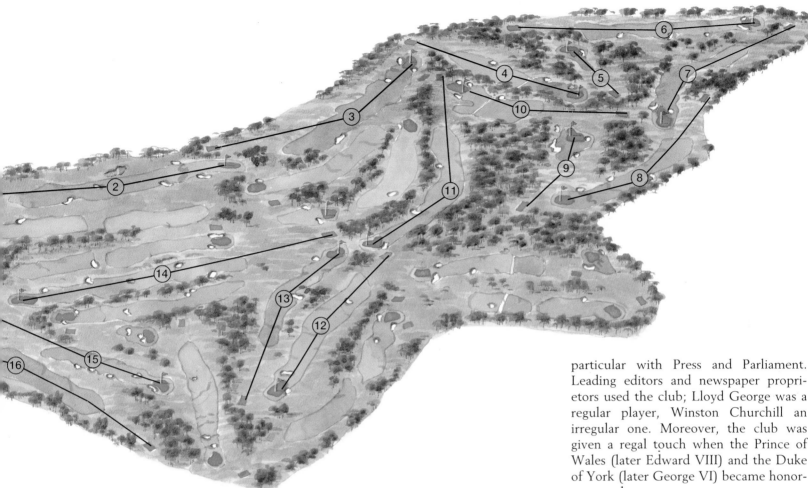

Johnny Miller ponders the destination of a drive in the 1981 Ryder Cup match. He and his partner Tom Kite (with eyeshade) halved their fourball match with Howard Clark (in white) and Sam Torrance.

tract with the great James Braid to be professional to the club. It was an association that lasted 45 years, until Braid's death in 1950 at the age of 80.

Herbert Fowler was a big, powerful man who was a powerful striker of the golf ball. He designed his courses on the grand scale, no doubt with other powerful strikers in mind. His first course at Walton ran to 6,300 yards and has been little changed, save in length, over the years. The success of Walton took him on to other projects. He worked on Saunton East and The Berkshire, and with Tom Simpson at Cruden Bay. James Braid too had an extraordinary career as a golf architect, designing dozens of courses throughout the British Isles and Ireland, travelling everywhere by train.

An additional nine-hole course was opened in 1907 and extended to 18 in 1913, by which time the club had almost 500 members. It had been an outstanding success, and quickly became associated in

particular with Press and Parliament. Leading editors and newspaper proprietors used the club; Lloyd George was a regular player, Winston Churchill an irregular one. Moreover, the club was given a regal touch when the Prince of Wales (later Edward VIII) and the Duke of York (later George VI) became honorary members.

The original course, which became the 'Old' only with the opening of the 'New', shared many characteristics with the Old at St Andrews. Fowler designed greens that would take the running approach shot. They are often raised, with ridges compromising to some extent the area in front; many have little depressions or downslopes at the sides, and feature deep greenside bunkers. But, as a principle, Fowler held that they should have reasonable entrances. He maintained the heather, the fiercest rough in the game of golf, but on the other hand did not design brutally narrow fairways – at Walton there is almost always wind, and the golfer needs room to cope with it!

Walton has had its share of the major events in golf; none more so than the Ryder Cup match of 1981, when a composite course of 'Old' and 'New' holes were played, and when the United States won by 17 to 8 with one of the strongest teams ever to play in the event.

WENTWORTH

The Wentworth Estate of 1,750 acres, 21 miles south-west of London, was one of the earliest British developments that sought to make golf the core of a major property development – as is widespread in the United States, and now the rest of the world. Wentworth House dates from 1802 and was once the home of the Duke of Wellington's sister; it now forms part of the clubhouse. The property was acquired in the 1850s by Ramón Cabrera, an exiled Spanish count, and on his death his English widow, the Countess de Morella, bought up most of the adjoining land to encompass today's acreage. In 1923 development rights and planning permissions were given. The Wentworth development was to be of large houses, each set in at least an acre of land, adjoining or very close to the golf courses.

Harry Colt of Sunningdale, only four miles away, was commissioned to design first the East Course and then the West – the 'big' course which opened in 1924; in

Nick Faldo makes the winning putt on the 18th green at Wentworth's West Course in the 1989 final of the Suntory World Match Play Championship against fellow Ryder Cup player Ian Woosnam.

addition there was a much shorter nine-hole course. Colt had the classic heathland elements with which to work: heather, pine, silver birch, a sandy, fast-draining soil and, in later years, enormous banks of rhododendron. He made the most of this, producing two lovely courses which were as testing as any golfer might imagine. The East Course, at 6,176 yards, is considered quite a few shots easier than the West. It staged the very first Curtis Cup matches in 1932. The West Course, at 6,945 yards, is an entirely different proposition. It, too, was early on the international scene: in 1925 the professionals of Great Britain and the United States played an informal match here, forerunner of the Ryder Cup matches.

Sandy subsoil, more than almost anything else, and rolling woodland give a golf architect a head start, and in the West Course, Colt created one of the finest inland courses in Britain. Significantly, his design has remained unchanged.

Colt's design demands, above all, long and accurate driving. The 13th and the 17th, quite different golf holes, illustrate this requirement. The 13th hole, playing slightly uphill at 441 yards, and turning slightly to the left, demands a drive of 250

WENTWORTH Card of the West course					
1	471 yards	par 4	10	186 yards	par 3
2	155 yards	par 3	11	376 yards	par 4
3	452 yards	par 4	12	483 yards	par 5
4	501 yards	par 5	13	441 yards	par 4
5	191 yards	par 3	14	179 yards	par 3
6	344 yards	par 4	15	466 yards	par 4
7	399 yards	par 4	16	380 yards	par 4
8	398 yards	par 4	17	571 yards	par 5
9	450 yards	par 4	18	502 yards	par 5
3,361 yards	par 35		3,584 yards	par 37	
Total 6,945 yards par 72					

yards or more to 'see round the corner' to the small green, which lies further uphill and in a hollow. And 17 is one of the great par-5s, the great driving holes, of British golf. It is a monster of 571 yards, downhill from the tee for almost 300 yards, where it turns to the left and runs uphill to a crest, then downhill to a middle-sized green. All along the left side are private gardens which are out-of-bounds. The fairway in the drive landing zone is tilted sharply from left to right, falling away towards the outside of the turn. To have any chance of reaching the green, the player must drive long, into the left centre of the fairway To get there, he simply must drive on the tightest possible line along the left, flirting with the out-of-bounds, and with draw to counter the tendency of the ball to bounce right. Time and time again, this hole has become the climax of matches in the World Match-Play Championship, that marvellous tournament which started in 1964.

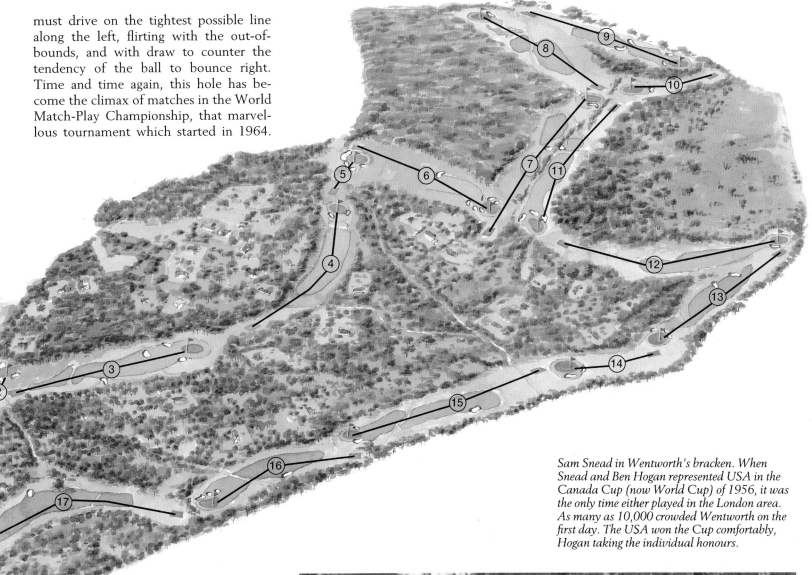

Sam Snead in Wentworth's bracken. When Snead and Ben Hogan represented USA in the Canada Cup (now World Cup) of 1956, it was the only time either played in the London area. As many as 10,000 crowded Wentworth on the first day. The USA won the Cup comfortably, Hogan taking the individual honours.

In the 1989 event, in beating Ian Woosnam at the 36th hole in a pulsating final, Nick Faldo scored a 'nominal' 64, on the second 18, including an eagle at the last. So much (or, rather, so little) for the constraints of length on today's stars when conditions are favourable.

The course staged the Ryder Cup in 1953, when the U.S. won by one slender point, and the World Cup (then the Canada Cup) of 1956, when the winning U.S. team was Sam Snead and Ben Hogan. Wentworth has also had famous professionals in George Duncan, Archie Compston, Jimmy Adams, Tom Haliburton and Bernard Gallacher. The property company that now owns Wentworth has plans for a new 18-hole course designed by Gary Player and John Jacobs.

ST ANDREWS

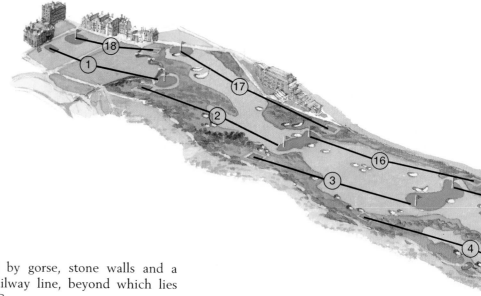

Golf has been played on the links at St Andrews since medieval times, and for better than 400 years on the turf of the present Old Course, which has 'evolved' to its present state without much interference from the hand of man. It is the most famous golf course in the world, and as such, like it or not – and many keen students of the game for one reason or the other do not care for this golf course – it must be maintained and preserved.

The course is unique. It is a links course, yet somehow it is different from all other links courses. The 1st hole runs more or less to the west. The course then turns almost at right angles and goes straight out to the 7th in a northerly direction. Holes 8, 9, 10, and 11 form a loop, and holes 12 to 17 run back more or less southwards, side by side with the outbound holes; the 18th turns to the east to form a common fairway with the first. The right side of the course on the way out is screened by banks of gorse bushes which separate the Old Course from the parallel and adjoining New Course. The right side of the course on the inward half is defined by gorse, stone walls and a disused railway line, beyond which lies the Eden Course.

The Double Greens

The course is liberally sprinkled with bunkers, some large, some small, some visible, some not, but all carefully charted. The greens are huge, in several cases one green serving one out and one in hole. And by and large the out and in fairways are shared. The course is generally flat in the sense that there is very little elevation – there are no huge sand dunes such as one would find at Birkdale or Ballybunion – but the fairways are a swelling sea of ripples and ridges, dips, swales and mounds which can turn and throw the ball in completely unexpected and incalculable directions. The bunkering and the double greens are Old Course characteristics, but the very essence of the course and its challenge is this movement in the ground. A player new to the course may well drive his ball along the perfect line to what he believes to be the required place, only to find on arrival that the ball is on a side and a down slope, and he will do well to find a proper stance for his next shot, much less hit it perfectly. To that extent, the course is unfair; or, to be strictly accurate, it can be played confidently only by those who know it well. For any apparent unfairness is counterbalanced by the other major characteristic of the Old Course: the remarkable facility its holes provide for giving the golfer alternative routes, alternative distances and alternative shots. When Bobby Jones first played the course in 1921, he was so bemused by it that he tore up his card in the middle of a round. Six years later he

Harry Vardon gets set on the first tee at St Andrews in the 1900 Open. Sandy Herd, hands behind back, is on the right, and 'Old Tom' Morris, in the big cloak, and beard, is on the left. Vardon, who had won the Open in the two preceding years, missed his hat-trick.

won the Open Championship on the Old Course and nine years later took the Amateur Championship. When in 1958 he was given the freedom of St Andrews, Jones said of the course: 'The more you study it, the more you love it, and the more you love it, the more you study it', and, to the delight of his audience, he added: 'I could take out of my life everything except my experiences at St Andrews, and I would still have a rich, full life'. It is, in short the very essence of 'strategic' design.

A St Andrews Primer
Within the variety of its strategic options a few general principles stand out. For safety, especially on the outward half, play to the left; for gorse and hidden bunkers menace the right side. If you get into a bunker, get out first time, even if it means playing backwards.

Nowhere is there an easier start to a championship course than here: a vast flat, lawn-like fairway, shared by the 1st and 18th holes. Your only peril is the possibility of a slice out-of-bounds over the fence on the right. The only hazard at this hole is the Swilcan Burn, which crosses directly in front of the green, then turns back towards the tee for 30 yards.

The 411-yard 2nd is the perfect example of the St Andrews golf hole – a telling introduction to the variety of hazards and optional routes that these holes contain. A long line of gorse marches up the right side. There is a bunker 130 yards out on the right, with two little pots backing it. On the left, between the 2nd and 17th fairways, perhaps some 250 yards out, is Cheape's Bunker. A good driving line would be slightly to the right of this. Now we face the first of St Andrews' big double greens, the second sharing with the 16th a putting surface all of 55 yards across. The flag position will govern the

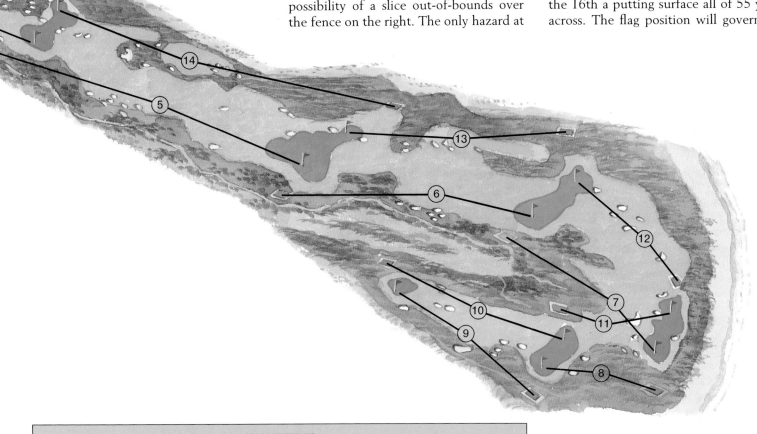

	ST ANDREWS Card of the Old course							
1	Burn	370 yards	par 4	10	Bobby Jones	342 yards	par 4
2	Dyke	411 yards	par 4	11	High (in)	172 yards	par 3
3	Cartgate (out)	371 yards	par 4	12	Heathery (in)	316 yards	par 4
4	Ginger Beer	463 yards	par 4	13	Hole o'Cross (in)	425 yards	par 4
5	Hole o'Cross (out)	564 yards	par 5	14	Long	567 yards	par 5
6	Heathery (out)	416 yards	par 4	15	Cartgate (in)	413 yards	par 4
7	High (out)	372 yards	par 4	16	Corner of the Dyke	382 yards	par 4
8	Short	178 yards	par 3	17	Road	461 yards	par 4
9	End	356 yards	par 4	18	Tom Morris	354 yards	par 4
		3,501 yards	par 36			3,432 yards	par 36
	Total 6,933 yards par 72						

playing of this hole. There is a ridge across the front of the right half of the green, the part we are concerned with.

There is also a front bunker which 'separates' the 2nd green from the 16th; and the green dips from front to centre, then rises slightly to the back, where Wig Bunker helps to give it a hollow effect.

A second shot from the centre of the fairway must find a way of coping with the ridge, the left-hand bunker and the contours of the green, while getting the ball close to the hole. The second hole is obviously better played from the right side of the fairway, which gives a much better entrance to the green. The question is: will the golfer dare to tackle that tight right-hand line on the drive, what with gorse and bunkers and broken ground and a left-to-right prevailing wind? This is the kind of dilemma which this old course will impose upon the golfer over and over again.

Perhaps the most celebrated short hole in the world, and certainly one of the most difficult, is the 11th of 172 yards, the 'High Hole In'. The green is built on a ridge above the River Eden and slopes fiercely from back to front. At the front left, is the very large, very deep Hill Bunker. At the front right, there is Strath Bunker – small, circular, deep and deadly. The flow of the ground in front of the green, even the contouring of the first part of the putting surface, gathers shots

Above: Huge, deep, one of golf's most insidious hazards, Hell Bunker on the 14th hole of the Old Course has ensnared hundreds of golfers, among them Gene Sarazen, Bobby Locke and Peter Thomson in Open Championship play.

Right: Play in the 1984 Open Championship at St Andrews showing the huge expanse of the combined 4th and 14th greens. Putts of as much as 80 feet have to be tackled on these rolling lawns.

into these bunkers. Gene Sarazen once scored six on this hole, with three shots in Hill Bunker. This is perhaps the one penal tee shot on the entire course – the only place to be on this hole is on the green, below the pin. There is almost always wind at the 11th. The green is wholly exposed and almost always lightning fast. It is well nigh impossible to stop downhill putts.

The 'Long Hole In', the 14th, at 567 yards, is fascinating in the various options it offers. A stone wall edges into the fairway from the right, then drifts back out again, marking the out-of-bounds line. The first major hazards on the hole, and a key factor in its strategy, are the Beardies in the centre of the driving line – one large and three small bunkers extending from about 160 yards to 200 yards from the medal tee. Between them and the stone wall is a rather narrow gap. Forward from the Beardies, for about 150 yards or so, stretch the Elysian Fields,

reasonably flat, uncluttered fairway, at the end of which is the huge Hell Bunker. A string of other bunkers runs up the centre and left side between the Beardies and Hell – Crescent, Kitchen and others – and on the left beyond Hell, which is 80 yards from the green, are the invisible Grave and Ginger Beer Bunkers.

On the tee, depending on wind and weather conditions, the golfer has choices to make. He can drive on either side of

Mark James calculates what is needed to face down the challenge of the Road Hole bunker at the 17th green of the Old Course at St Andrews, one of golf's most demanding shots.

the Beardies, or over them if he thinks he is capable of it. Depending on the success of his drive, he may then elect a direct line to the green, which is right over Hell – but he'll be facing a carry of some 200

yards. Or he can simply advance the ball along the Elysian Fields, staying short of Hell Bunker and take a third shot to the green. Or he can try to pass Hell on the right, but there are other bunkers and badly broken ground there. What may be his best option is to play about as far as he can to the left, onto the 5th fairway, from where he will have a fine view of, and good approach to, the green. But the 14th hole has not finished with him. There is a

architects all over the world. The hole is a very powerful par-4 of 461 yards, which doglegs to the right around the Old Course Hotel. The hotel stands on what was formerly the site of some black railway sheds, over the corner of which the golfer used to drive. Thus we have the shot across the angle and the judgement of how much or how little to cut off – a shot that has been repeated over sand, rough, rivers, lakes and the ocean, at Pebble Beach, Pine Valley and dozens of courses all over the world.

Having driven across the corner and into the fairway, the golfer faces a long second shot to a single green – the most feared in golf. It is raised on a plateau, three or four feet above the fairway. It is long from left to right, very narrow from front to back, and set diagonally to the fairway. At the front left-centre of the green is the small, steep-sided abyss called the Road Hole Bunker, biting into the green so severely that there are putting surfaces on either side of it. Players of championship class have putted into this bunker. In the 1978 Open Tommy Nakajima of Japan hit two lovely shots to the front of the green, and then putted into the bunker, took four strokes there and eventually scored 10.

Over the back of this green is a pathway, then a metal road, then a stone wall; all in bounds and all in play. Thus over the back of the green is absolutely the one place the golfer does not wish to be. As so often at St Andrews, the tactic for the second shot depends on wind and weather conditions, and the state of the competition. In the 1984 Open Championship, the Road Hole had a critical role to play. The Championship was between Tom Watson and Severiano Ballesteros, Watson playing directly behind Ballesteros in the last pairing of the event. At 17, Ballesteros hit an enormous drive right over the fairway into the left rough. From there he hit an immense shot with a six iron which reached the front edge of the green. His first putt, from long range, ran up six inches from the hole, and he had his par. When Watson came to the hole, he hit a perfect drive into the centre of the fairway but was not absolutely certain of his clubbing for the approach. He decided on the 2-iron. How odd it is:

whenever a golfer, even a great champion, is not absolutely convinced that he has the right club in his hand, the swing is affected. Watson pushed the shot slightly and the ball flew over the green, over the pathway, over the road and finished snug against the stone wall. He scuffled the ball back to the green, took two putts, and at almost the same moment Severiano Ballesteros holed a putt for a birdie on the 18th green.

Watson against the wall which became a wailing wall. With little room for a backswing, Tom Watson chips back at the 17th at St. Andrews after his second shot went over the green in the last round in 1984. He lost to Severiano Ballesteros.

These holes, these shots, this land, puts a man to the test. But the Old Course gives the thinking golfer a chance, and there is always a way to travel from point A to point B in safety. All that he needs to do is negotiate that minefield of bunkers and gorse and humps and hollows and huge greens. And the thing to do is play it, not talk about it; play it as often as possible over and over again, since every day on the Old Course seems different to the one before. Do that and you will come to agree with Bobby Jones that in all the world the Old Course is 'the most favoured meeting ground possible for an important contest'.

dip in front of the green which rises abruptly to form a bank at the front; the green then falling away, towards the back! Not surprisingly, in Open Championship play, Bobby Locke scored eight on this hole, Peter Thomson seven.

The Road Hole

The 17th hole, the Road Hole, is the most famous single hole in golf. It has features that have been used and copied by golf

MUIRFIELD

Muirfield is a patrician among golf courses, which is as it should be, since it is the home of a patrician golf club. The Honourable Company of Edinburgh Golfers, which plays its golf over the Muirfield course, came into existence in 1744 at Leith, when 'several Gentlemen of Honour skilful in the ancient and healthful exercise of Golf', petitioned the Edinburgh city council to donate a silver club for their annual competition. The council obliged, and has done so ever since – maintaining a tradition which saw them donate a fourth such club in 1980. The Honourable Company thus predates the Royal and Ancient Golf Club of St

Andrews by 10 years, and in fact is the oldest golf club in the world, with continuous records to prove that claim. It drew up golf's first set of rules – the famous 'Thirteen Rules' – and these were by and large adopted by the R & A.

The club first played on the links of Leith (Edinburgh's port on the Firth of Forth). But the public land was used by the local citizens for various purposes and occasionally by the military for drill, and by 1836 the golfers were squeezed out. They moved six miles eastward along the coast to Musselburgh and remained there for 50 years. The course was shared with the Musselburgh Golf Club (and anyone

else who cared to play on it). Initially the club used the racecourse grandstand there as their premises, but by 1868 had their own clubhouse. These early golf clubs were as much dinner clubs, and the Honourable Company's golf was match play between members.

The links at Musselburgh in turn became more and more crowded and less to the liking of the gentlemen of the Honourable Company, and another eastward move was planned for the 1890s – this time far from the clamour of the city, to Muirfield, near Gullane. The new course was opened for play in 1891 on a rainy 3rd of May, and a year later was staging

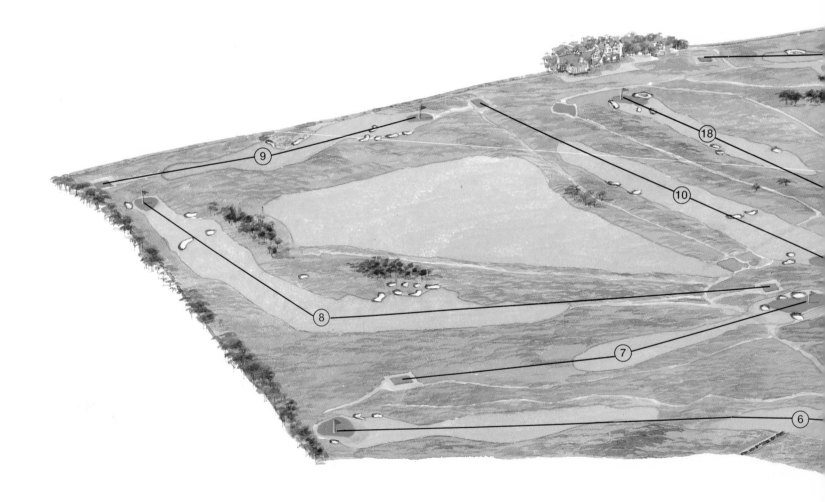

MUIRFIELD Card of the course					
1	447 yards	par 4	10	475 yards	par 4
2	351 yards	par 4	11	385 yards	par 4
3	379 yards	par 4	12	381 yards	par 4
4	180 yards	par 3	13	152 yards	par 3
5	559 yards	par 5	14	449 yards	par 4
6	469 yards	par 4	15	417 yards	par 4
7	185 yards	par 3	16	188 yards	par 3
8	444 yards	par 4	17	550 yards	par 5
9	504 yards	par 5	18	448 yards	par 4
3,518 yards	par 36		3,445 yards	par 35	
Total 6,963 yards par 71					

the Open Championship – won by an Englishman, and an amateur to boot: Harold Hilton of Hoylake (his club-mate John Ball was equal second).

Looking over the 12th green with the Forth estuary behind and beyond the hills of Fife. Arnold Palmer putts out, playing with Guy Wolstenholme, in the 1966 Open; Jack Nicklaus won the championship.

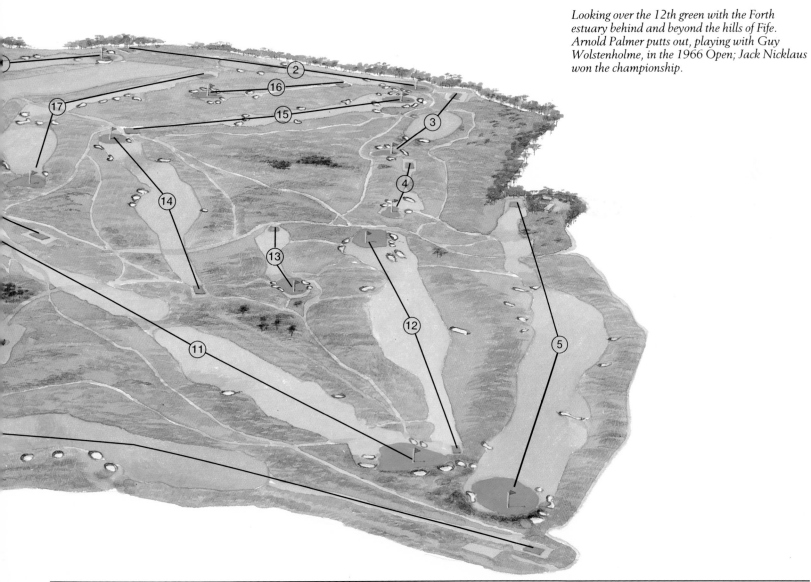

Morris, Colt and Simpson

The original course was built by hand and horse to a design by Old Tom Morris. Sixteen holes had been opened in May, two more in December of the same year, and the entire construction was completed rather casually. Not for some years did the club see any need for a greenkeeper (and to this day they see no need for a professional). Four more Open championships were held at Muirfield up to 1914 and several changes were made to the holes, but it was not until 1925, after Harry Colt, of Sunningdale fame, and Tom Simpson had been brought in that Muirfield became the magnificent course that is recognisable to us today.

One hundred yards or so down a quiet driveway off the North Berwick road, to the east of Gullane village, a majestic vista unfolds. The entire golf course can be taken in within a single compass: uninterrupted, spacious, strangely private and still, the land moving along gently, with few abrupt slopes; to the north, beyond the sand dunes, are the waters of the Forth estuary and, beyond, the hills of Fife. On its three other sides, the course is enclosed by a low stone wall. Beyond that, to the east, lies Archerfield Wood; to the west is Gullane Hill, and beyond that, on a clear day, Edinburgh and the Forth bridges are visible; to the south lies the rolling farmland of East Lothian.

The course is maintained in quite immaculate condition: the club makes sure that it is not overplayed. If there is one outstanding visual feature of Muirfield, it is the bunkering – deep, steep walls of revetted turf, as though a talented bricklayer had built them, often with surrounds that reach out and 'persuade' a ball into them. Any shot that finds a fairway bunker at Muirfield is a shot lost. It will not be possible to reach the green from any of them. Indeed the club might be offended that anyone should suggest such a possibility; after all, 'this is not Florida, old boy'.

Unlike many of the older links courses which run out to a distant point then run back again, Muirfield was one of the earliest courses in the world (with Portmarnock, 1893) to consist of two loops of nine holes – the 9th returning to the clubhouse – that run contrary to each other. Muirfield's first nine run clockwise around the outer edge of the course; its second nine run anti-clockwise inside the first nine. Only three holes, the 3rd, 4th and 5th, run in the same direction and, of these, the 4th is a short hole.

A Beautifully Balanced Course

There are no ridiculous carrys, no trees and no water hazards on the course. Muirfield's exceptional reputation is based on the fact that it is fair, honest and beautifully balanced. On the entire course there are no more than two blind shots. All its perils are open for the player to see – notably the most demanding opening and closing holes of any course on the Open Championship rota.

The 1st hole is a par-4 of 447 yards (the Honourable Company with its tradition of matchplay 'between Gentlemen', has no need of 'par' or 'bogey', neither of which appear on the club scorecard) and runs to the west along a flat and narrow fairway. There is a very large C-shaped bunker on the left side of the fairway at 200–230 yards; only part of it can be seen from the tee. The line of the drive should be just to the right of this bunker. There are twin bunkers in the left rough not quite 100 yards from the green, and a central bunker just short of the green screening off its right side. Greenside bunkers are placed right centre and left back, so that the way in to this green should preferably be from the left side of the fairway. This is a very demanding opening hole, especially into the wind.

The 18th is strikingly similar in both length (448 yards) and design. The second half of the hole runs slightly uphill. There is a big bunker on the right, 190 yards out from the medal tee. On the other side of a very narrow fairway are two bunkers at 210–250 yards. The drive, to the right of these two bunkers, is critical. Further up the fairway, in its left half, are two separate bunkers – one 40 yards short of the putting surface, the other 20 yards short. A very long green-

A time of immortality. Nick Faldo on the 72nd green of the 1987 Open Championship at Muirfield, a championship which he won with 18 relentless pars on that final soggy Sunday.

side bunker covers the left side of the green, and a comparable one, with an island of turf in it, the right side. With a strong, prevailing wind, right to left, this hole takes a good deal of playing. In 1948, on this the 72nd hole, Henry Cotton had two shots in that right bunker, scored 5, but still won the championship. In 1959, Gary Player had three putts, scored six, and still won the championship. While in 1972, Lee Trevino, leading by a stroke, was so supercharged and hit such an enormous drive that it left him an 8-iron to the green.

Glorious Par–5s

The par-5 holes at Muirfield are superb. The 5th hole (559 yards) runs west to east along the northern side of the course on the edge of dune land. It turns slightly to the right through its entire length and that side of the fairway is massively defended by bunkers and strong rough. There is a bunker placed on the left edge of the fairway 240 yards out, with a support bunker 25 yards further along, and the small green is ringed by half a dozen deep traps. The drive is quite critical here. In the 1972 Open Championship Johnny Miller hit a perfect drive of almost 300 yards into prime position in the fairway. From there, he hit a 3-wood shot which pitched short of the green, ran on and fell into the hole for an albatross!

The 9th hole, the second of Muirfield's long holes, at 504 yards, poses different but no less searching problems. The hole runs back towards the Greywalls Hotel and the spacious Muirfield clubhouse. A low, greystone wall, the boundary wall, runs straight as an arrow along the left side of the hole. About 200 yards out, a great eruption of rough streams into the fairway from the left, narrowing it down to little more than 15 yards across. On the edge of this rough, facing back towards the tee, is a very large cross bunker and about 60 yards beyond that, also on the edge of this rough, is another big bunker. On the second section of the 9th, the rough on the left vanishes and the fairway runs clear across to the wall. A ridge along the fairway leaves this left side higher than the right, and reasonably open and undefended. However, the ridge tends to throw the ball off to the right, where a

The green of the 5th hole at Muirfield, a monstrous par 5 of 559 yards which runs along the north side of the course, and a view of Muirfield's famous, carefully-revetted bunkering.

The power of the modern golfer. Johnny Miller, Open Champion on both sides of the Atlantic, almost airborne at a full drive shows how to keep the head anchored at Muirfield in 1972.

string of bunkers some 70 yards long waits to gobble the careless approach; there is also a solitary central bunker – Simpson's bunker, named after the architect who put it there – some 50 yards short of the green. Thus the whole thrust of the hole is that the drive must keep to the right, playing into the narrowest part of the fairway; the second shot must play to the left, finding the higher side of the fairway, but always under threat from the out-of-bounds wall. Peter Thomson, in the Open Championship of 1959, hooked a second shot over that wall, and Arnold Palmer, in 1966, going for a big drive, failed to find that narrow gap.

However, when conditions are right the 9th is reachable in two. In the 1972 championship, when Lee Trevino and Tony Jacklin were locked together in the last round, they each scored eagles on this hole. Jacklin drove into the left rough, between the bunkers; Trevino into the right rough. Yet they were both able to hit iron shots, they both reached the green, and they both holed their putts!

But it was the 17th hole, the 71st, the last of Muirfield's par-5s that was to settle that thrilling Championship in '72. The hole runs from west to east and therefore is usually played down the prevailing wind. It is 550 yards long and at 250 yards

doglegs to the left. There are no bunkers on the outside, the right side, of this fairway, but in the angle of the turn there is much rough, heaving ground, containing five major bunkers. Also there are fairly prominent sandhills along the left side of the hole and an unusual strip of ground extends across the entire fairway about 100 yards short of the green – perhaps 25 yards from front to back, it contain's three of Muirfield's largest and most frightening bunkers.

In the 1972 championship, Trevino drove into the first bunker on the left, knocked the ball out and up the fairway, hooked his third shot into the left rough and hit his fourth shot over the green into more rough. Jacklin, on the other hand, had hit a solid drive in the fairway, a second shot just short of the green and had chipped on. Trevino hurried to his ball, chopped it out of the rough, in resignation it seemed, and saw the ball speed into the hole for a par-5! Jacklin was so unnerved that he three-putted and lost the Championship. And the 1987 Championship also turned on that hole when Paul Azinger drove into a bunker and took 5 instead of the 4 he needed to hold off the winner, Nick Faldo. At the equivalent hole of the 1966 Open, Jack Nicklaus drove with a 3-iron and reached the green with a 5-iron!

The short holes at Muirfield are just as magnificent as the par-5s: mounded greens with fringing bunkers as deep as a man is tall, and exposed to wind and weather. And the quality of its par-4s, ranging from the 349 yards of the 2nd to the 475 yards of the 10th – one of the truly great par-4s in world golf – is just as compelling.

But perhaps the one overwhelming demand that Muirfield makes on the golfer is the tee shot. It is said that when Henry Cotton won the Open in 1948, he missed only four fairways in 72 holes. When Jack Nicklaus won in 1966, he owed his victory above all to his marvellous long-iron play in the final round.

Tom Watson, five times winner of the Open Championship, chipping at Muirfield in 1980 for his third victory. His aggregate of 271 was a record for Muirfield Opens and included a third-round 64.

ROYAL DORNOCH

Royal Dornoch is the least-known, least-played of all the great links courses. It may well be the finest natural golf course in the world; in the words of Tom Watson, five times Open Champion, it is '...at least one of the great courses of the five continents. I have played none finer, a natural masterpiece'. The village of Dornoch, of rather less than one thousand souls, lies some 60 miles north of Inverness on the east coast of Sutherland, more than 200 miles from the populous central belt of Scotland and 600 miles from London.

Records show that golf was being played there as early as 1616. Dornoch's claim to antiquity, which places it behind only St Andrews and Leith, was confirmed by the publication in 1630 of Sir Robert Gordon's *History of Sutherland*. Gordon was tutor to the house of Sutherland and had been educated at St Andrews University. He wrote: 'About this toun there are the fairest and largest links of any pairt of Scotland, fit for archery, Golfing, Ryding and all other exercise; they do surpass the fields of Montrose or St Andrews'.

Common Land

A golf club as such, however, was not formed until 1877. The two men responsible for calling a meeting and launching the Dornoch Golf Club were the local Chief Constable, Alex McHardy, a Fifer, and local man Dr Hugh Gunn, who was a St Andrews graduate, and no doubt

Roger Wethered, with his wife Joyce, the famous amateur golfer who lost the 1921 Open Championship at St Andrews in a playoff was instrumental in promoting Royal Dornoch in its early days.

learned some of his golf there. In 1883 came an event of the greatest importance for the fledgling club: John Sutherland was appointed secretary, a post he was to hold for more than 50 years. Sutherland was an estate agent and factor in the town and as such a pillar of the community – which was important to the club, since the golf course ground was owned by the town, and Sutherland was obliged to consult with the townsmen in any changes he wanted. In his early years, for example, cattle and sheep were free to roam the course, it being common land.

Sutherland was a golfing pioneer. He was a first-class player and administrator, planned several northern courses and studied greenkeeping and maintenance, with particular emphasis on the making and maintaining of greens. He added an additional nine holes to the course, and he and J. H. Taylor, who became a fairly regular summer visitor, made a number of revisions. Sutherland also wrote a weekly golf article for the London *Daily News* from 1902 for more than 20 years.

By 1903, the railway and an overnight sleeping-car service from London had

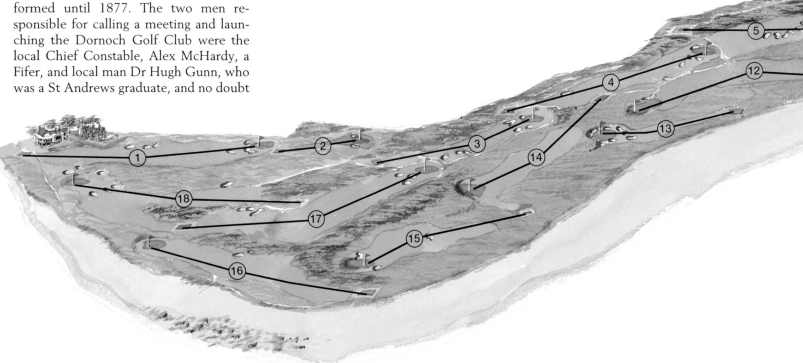

reached Dornoch, and for the next ten years the town grew and prospered as a summer resort. It would never be a Cannes, but increasingly it attracted wealthy and influential amateur golfers from the south: Roger and Joyce Wethered, Ernest Holderness and others, whose families would take a house there for the summer and who could be said to have 'learned' their golf on Dornoch's magnificent links.

Donald Ross

The year 1898 is now seen as of great significance for the future of the world game. In that year Donald James Ross emigrated to America. Ross was born in Dornoch in 1873, in a house in St Gilbert Street. He became a very good player and was apprenticed to a carpenter. But John Sutherland, noting his interest in the game, arranged for him to go to St Andrews as an 'apprentice' to Tom Morris, who had laid out Dornoch's second nine in the 1880s. Ross went there at the age of 20 but in 1895 came back to Dornoch to serve as professional and

The 17th hole at Dornoch, known as Valley. The narrow green is well guarded with three pot bunkers. The magnificent sweep of Embo Bay can be seen in the background.

greenkeeper. Then in 1898 he was persuaded by an American visitor that he could make his fortune as a teacher and course designer in the United States. There he became the most celebrated golf architect of his day. He had a hand in the design of at least 600 courses all over the country, including Pinehurst No. 2 (probably his masterpiece – see page 30), Oak Hill (page 16), Oakland Hills (page 40) and Scioto.

Ross courses were characterised by many of the features he had known at Dornoch. These were: a sense of 'naturalness', and meticulous attention to detail, particularly in the siting and contouring of greens and the siting and shaping of bunkers. Ross sought to combine beauty, subtlety and strategic alternatives in his holes. His greens were often raised, as were the Dornoch greens, with slopes running off them and seldom with bunkers biting directly into the putting surfaces – so that chipping as well as that staple of the links game, the bump-and-run with a medium iron, could be profitably employed.

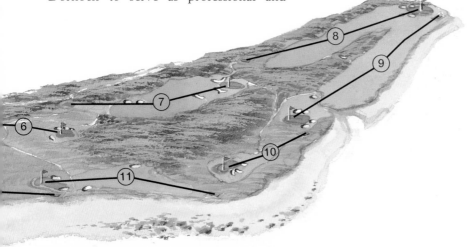

ROYAL DORNOCH							
	Card of the course						
1	First	336 yards	par 4	10	Fuaran	148 yards	par 3
2	Ord	179 yards	par 3	11	A'chlach	445 yards	par 4
3	Earl's Cross	414 yards	par 4	12	Sutherland	504 yards	par 5
4	Achinchanter	418 yards	par 4	13	Bents	168 yards	par 3
5	Hilton	361 yards	par 4	14	Foxy	448 yards	par 4
6	Whinny Brae	165 yards	par 3	15	Stulaig	322 yards	par 4
7	Pier	465 yards	par 4	16	High Hole	405 yards	par 4
8	Dunrobin	437 yards	par 4	17	Valley	406 yards	par 4
9	Craiglaith	499 yards	par 5	18	Home	457 yards	par 4
		3,274 yards	par 35			3,303 yards	par 35
		Total 6,577 yards par 70					

'Guid gear goes into sma' bulk'

In the final analysis the course of his boyhood, the magnificent course that runs along Embo Bay, was responsible for Ross's success. The first two holes do not reveal the character of Dornoch, but from the 3rd tee the course unfolds, running through gorse on a shelf above the beach holes to the eighth; then turning and running alongside the great curve of the beach all the way back, along the most perfect links ground imagineable. Among many fine holes on the back nine, the superlative 14th, a par-4 of 448 yards, ranks with any in Scotland. Virtually a double dog-leg, its fairway bears left at about 230 yards, then continues straight for some 170 yards before turning right into the green. As a two-shotter, then, the hole requires a longish drive with controlled draw off the tee, followed by an equally finely controlled fade with a medium or long iron to the green.

Donoch measures only 6,577 yards,

Left: The Royal Golf Hotel at Dornoch, by the 18th green. The gabled building with clocktower to its left is the 'new' clubhouse, opened in 1909.

Below: Another view of the 17th green with the 15th tee and green in the background. Dornoch is famous for its wild beauty and the natural feel of its links.

which is a classic confirmation of the Scottish saying that 'guid gear goes into sma' bulk'. While Dornoch is a long way from anywhere, Britain's Amateur Championship of 1985 was played there and was an outstanding success. Not surprisingly, to everyone who made the journey it was deemed well worth while and a memorable experience.

Perhaps only Turnberry can rival Dornoch in the beauty of its surroundings, for at Dornoch the vistas of sea and sand and mountain are stunning. To the north of the course are the seven miles of golden sandy beach to Littleferry and Loch Fleet. Beyond, past Dunrobin Castle (and the fine courses at Golspie and Brora) is the Ord of Caithness, and from there a breathtaking panoramic view of the immense and ancient mountains of Sutherland and Wester Ross, Tain and Tarbat-Ness, the sands of Whiteness and, on a clear day, Nairn, the Moray coast and the hills of Aberdeenshire.

All of this poses the question as to how important the surroundings may be when we pass judgement on the quality of a golf course. No doubt a subjective element in the judgement is unavoidable. Golf courses have been laid out on barren deserts, hacked out of rain forests and placed in humdrum suburbs. However, Royal Dornoch may be one of the few places in the world where the scenery is matched by the majesty of the course.

CARNOUSTIE

Stark, evil, gigantic, brutal, monstrous – these words and worse have been used to describe the championship course at Carnoustie. At 7,101 yards, it can be crushingly long. It is without a weakness. It is unrelenting. It is flat and exposed (its two or three little spinneys of trees have no bearing on the play). It is hard by the sea, but the sea is never seen. Never does it have more than two holes running in the same direction. Walter Hagen declared it to be the best course in Britain; one of the three best in the world. It is a municipally owned course, and it may be one of the wonders of the golfing world.

Golf has been played along the Angus coast for centuries, as it has on the links of the Moray Firth, and Aberdeen and Fife and East Lothian. There are parish records of 'gouff' being played on Barry Links, adjoining Carnoustie, in 1560. The Carnoustie Golf Club's date of found-ation is given variously as 1839 and 1842, but certainly at this time 10 holes were laid out by Allan Robertson of St Andrews, the first of the great early professionals. In 1857, the course was extended to 18 holes by Tom Morris; and that same year his son 'Young Tom', just 16 years old, beat all comers in a tournament there.

Carnoustie and the Open

Carnoustie and the Burnside course which it encloses are public courses and are played over by six clubs, each of which has a clubhouse adjoining the links. Thus there is nothing palatial about golf

Tom Watson chips to the 16th green in the last round of the 1975 Open. One of the most formidable par-3s in championship golf, the 248-yard 16th denied winner Watson a par in any of his rounds.

at Carnoustie; no grand and dominating clubhouse as at Troon or Muirfield or St Andrews. The game, and little else, is the thing here. But a wider world crept up on Carnoustie. In 1926 James Braid re-vamped and modernised the course to such good effect that in 1931 it staged the Open Championship for the first time, and rejoiced in the victory of a Scot, Tommy Armour, albeit a Scot who had defected to the United States!

In the 1930s a Dundee chartered accountant, James Wright, became chair-man of the Carnoustie Golf Courses Committee, administered the courses and set about improving the big course to bring it properly into the age of the steel shaft. Wright was a man of the world, with extensive land and farming interests in the United States, and he had am-bitions for the course. He produced a flexible Carnoustie which could be played

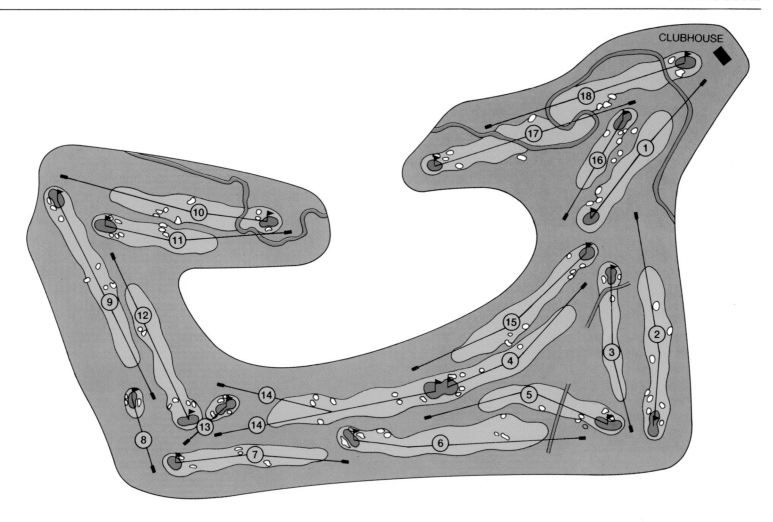

CLUBHOUSE

at various yardages. His creed: 'We do not attach much importance to length …quality, rather than pure length has been our objective'.

His altered course was ready for another Championship in 1937. It was won by Henry Cotton against a field which included the entire United States Ryder Cup team, including Densmore Shute, Byron Nelson, Sam Snead. On a final day of torrential rain, Cotton scored 71 – one of the greatest rounds of his career – and won by two shots from Reg Whitcombe.

No reference to Carnoustie and Open Championships can be made without mentioning Ben Hogan. The great American champion made a detailed study of the course and how it should be played with the small ball in practice in 1953, then applied himself quite surgically to dominating the course with rounds of 73, 71, 70 and 68. He won by four strokes. It was a performance beyond criticism, so much so that there did not seem to be one stroke more important than any other.

CARNOUSTIE					
Card of the course					
1	416 yards	par 4	10	452 yards	par 4
2	460 yards	par 4	11	358 yards	par 4
3	347 yards	par 4	12	475 yards	par 4
4	434 yards	par 4	13	168 yards	par 3
5	393 yards	par 4	14	488 yards	par 5
6	575 yards	par 5	15	461 yards	par 4
7	397 yards	par 4	16	250 yards	par 3
8	174 yards	par 3	17	455 yards	par 4
9	474 yards	par 4	18	486 yards	par 5
3,670 yards	par 36		3,593 yards	par 36	
Total 7,263 yards par 72					

But in the championship of 1968, that was certainly not the case. Gary Player produced the one critical shot. Paired with Jack Nicklaus in the last round, and battling him stroke for stroke, Player hit a 3-wood second shot on the 482 yards 14th hole over the 'Spectacle' bunkers. The ball finished three feet from the flagstick, giving the South African an eagle three and a two-shot margin with

which he won the Open Championship.

Carnoustie's finish puts the seal on the course's hostility. The 16th is a 250 yard par-3 to an elevated, undulating green surrounded by six bunkers. Into the wind, it can take a massive hit. The 17th is the Island hole, so called because the Barry Burn crosses the fairway twice in a big oxbow, at 180 yards then again at 300 yards – the entire hole stretching 455 yards. And the 18th in the reverse direction sees the same burn crossing the fairway 130 yards out from the tee, then passing across the face of the green just 20 yards short of the putting surface.

Carnoustie has made a huge contribution to the game of golf, not least in the hundreds of its citizens who have gone abroad to every corner of the golfing world as fine players and teachers of the game. A lack of local hotel and other facilities kept Carnoustie off the Open Championship rota in the 1980s. It's to be hoped this great shaggy monster of a course will soon have the chance to put the current superstars to the test.

ROYAL TROON

The Glasgow to Ayr railway, running through Troon and Prestwick, was opened in 1840. Earlier, in 1811, one of the first railways in Scotland connected Kilmarnock with Troon and helped to make the latter an important harbour on the Firth of Clyde. For the citizens of Glasgow, Paisley and Kilmarnock a beguiling stretch of the Ayrshire coast was opened up, with miles of golden sandy beaches backed by one of the longest stretches of duneland imaginable. It was ready-made for golf, and came to produce a line of magnificent links courses: Irvine, Glasgow Gailes, Western Gailes, Barassie, Troon and Prestwick. They form an almost continuous file: Troon and Prestwick, for instance, are separated only by the Pow Burn.

On Saturday, 16 March 1878 at '4 o'clock pm' in the Portland Arms Hotel, Troon, 'a Number of Gentlemen belonging to Troon and the neighbourhood, resolved to form themselves into a golf club'. The instigator of the meeting was one James Dickie of Paisley, who had a summer house on the south beach at Troon village. Dickie had arranged with the fifth Duke of Portland, who owned the land, to have the use of links lying between Craigend Burn and Gyaws Burn. Craigend Burn is now piped under the road in front of the clubhouse, while Gyaws Burn is very much part of the present course, crossing the 3rd and 15th holes. The Duke of Portland was a re-

The 'Postage Stamp', Troon's famous 8th hole, at 126 yards the shortest of all Open Championship holes in Britain. It has seen many holes in one, none more lauded than that of Gene Sarazen in 1979, 50 years after he had first played at Troon.

cluse. However, he was succeeded by a cousin who was an entirely different personality and who gave the club permission to use the land all the way out to the Pow Burn. Within a decade Troon had 18 holes of golf.

A Formidable Examination

Over the years, Willie Fernie, James Braid, Dr Alister Mackenzie, Frank Pennink and Charles Lawrie amended the course and now Troon is as frightening a Championship test as any on the roster. It is a course of long carrys, narrow, heaving fairways, very strong rough, a couple of blind shots, and greens that are almost always immaculately conditioned. If the wind blows it offers formidable examination of the finest players.

The course features the longest hole in Open championship golf – the 6th at 577

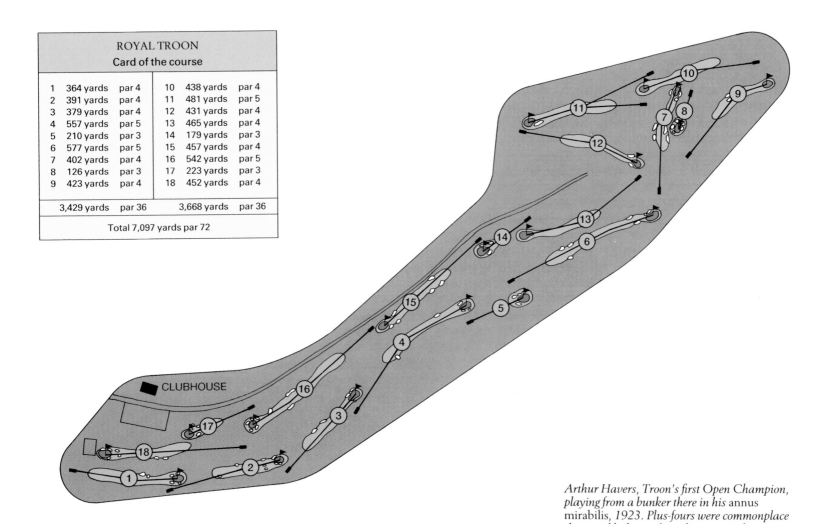

ROYAL TROON Card of the course					
1	364 yards	par 4	10	438 yards	par 4
2	391 yards	par 4	11	481 yards	par 5
3	379 yards	par 4	12	431 yards	par 4
4	557 yards	par 5	13	465 yards	par 4
5	210 yards	par 3	14	179 yards	par 3
6	577 yards	par 5	15	457 yards	par 4
7	402 yards	par 4	16	542 yards	par 5
8	126 yards	par 3	17	223 yards	par 3
9	423 yards	par 4	18	452 yards	par 4
	3,429 yards	par 36		3,668 yards	par 36
		Total 7,097 yards par 72			

Arthur Havers, Troon's first Open Champion, playing from a bunker there in his annus mirabilis, 1923. Plus-fours were commonplace then, and ladies and gentlemen wore hats.

yards – and the shortest – the 8th at 126 yards (the famous 'Postage Stamp'). The 6th hole runs to the south; and since Brian Anderson, the club's experienced senior professional, insists that Troon's prevailing wind is from the north-west and not the south-west, it may be slightly across, from right to left, on this hole. The fairway is narrow, and there is a carry of at least 150 yards to reach it. There is a bunker on the right at about 230 yards and another pair on the left at about the same distance. The drive must be just to the right of these left-hand bunkers. There is another bunker in the left rough some 80 yards short of the green, a very deep bunker on the right 30 yards short of the green, and two very deep greenside bunkers to the left.

The next five holes, 7 to 11 inclusive, plunge into and through a huge range of sandhills containing, of course, the 8th – the Postage Stamp. This green is cut into

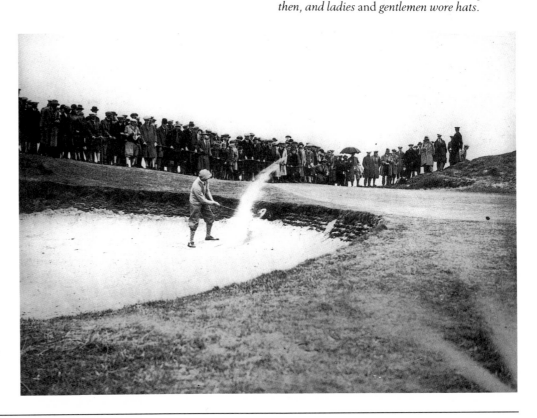

Arnold Palmer, with wife and son, practices for the 1962 Open Championship at Royal Troon. He went on to win the tournament, his second in a row (the first being at Royal Birkdale).

a sandhill on the left. There is a very large bunker covering the front of the green, with two more on either side. All are very deep, with steep faces – those on the right being also much lower than the green. The shot is down from a high tee to this very narrow green, and the only alternative it offers to being on the putting surface is to be over the green, where there is a modest area of security.

A Famous Hole-in-One

The hole is rich in history. In the 1950 Open Championship, Herman Tissies, a German amateur, scored 15 on the hole, yet took only one putt! There have been many holes-in-one, none more widely acclaimed than that of Gene Sarazen in 1973. Sarazen, in his time a winner of all golf's major championships, had played in the Troon Open of 1923, aged 22, and, caught in a gale, scored 75, 85 and failed to qualify for the championship proper. He was U.S. Open Champion at the time. Fifty years on, now aged 72, he made a

sentimental journey back to Troon for the 1973 Open. On the eve of the championship, Sir Ian Stewart, captain of the R & A, presented inscribed silver cigarette boxes to Sarazen and to Arthur Havers, the winner of that 1923 Championship. The next day Sarazen, playing honorary rounds with former champions Fred Daly (1947 at Hoylake) and Max Faulkner (1951 at Portrush), made his hole in one at the Postage Stamp. Into a slight breeze, he hit a punchy 5-iron shot which pitched short of the flag and rolled in. The next day he bunkered his tee shot at the same hole – then with his recovery shot from the sand he holed out for a two! Sarazen presented the 5-iron he had used on both days to the R & A.

Troon's finish, especially when it is into wind, is as harrowing as any in golf. The 465-yard 13th and the 457-yard 15th are very serious two-shot holes, played into wickedly uneven, narrow fairways bordered by intense rough. The carry to the fairway of the 16th, the last par-5 at 542 yards, is at least 150 yards and the Gyaws Burn crosses the fairway at 300 yards. The fairway is reasonably friendly by Troon standards and the green is rather flat, but is ringed around by five bunkers.

The 17th hole may well be the most severe par-3 in all of championship golf, and is certainly comparable to Carnoustie's 16th. The raised green falls away on all sides. Two bunkers, short and left of the green, must be carried. The prevailing wind left to right, making the three bunkers to the right very dangerous indeed. At 223 yards, this is really a par-3.5 hole. The 18th hole was stretched to 452 yards for the 1989 championship, giving a carry to the fairway of 225 yards. The green is flat, well-guarded and slopes up to a path in front of the clubhouse – the path being out-of-bounds. The hole will never see a finer shot than the second played by winner Mark Calcavecchia in the play-off in 1989 – a soaring long-iron from the right rough that finished seven feet from the flag to set up a birdie.

Mark Calcavecchia hits an inspired 5-iron shot to Troon's 18th green in the play-off to the 1989 Open. The ball finished a few feet from the hole giving the American a birdie and victory over Greg Norman and Wayne Grady.

TURNBERRY

The Ailsa Course of the Turnberry Hotel in Ayrshire, Scotland, is the course that died twice but is now enjoying its third, magnificent, incarnation. It is one of the most spectacular seaside courses in the world and rivals Pebble Beach and Cypress Point in California in being an outstanding championship course that is also stunningly beautiful.

The Turnberry Hotel, sited on a wooded slope, overlooks a fine spread of links that includes two courses, the Ailsa and the Arran; the latter is less famous but only marginally behind the Ailsa in quality. The Ailsa's run of holes from the 4th to the 11th, by the waters of the Firth of Clyde, and the landscape they inhabit, have made the course world famous.

Across the water to the north-west stands the island of Arran with its towering mountains; behind it and to the west is the long peninsula of Kintyre; to the south-west the massive volcanic outcrop of Ailsa Craig rears out of the sea; and to the east is the ripe farmland of Ayrshire. Turnberry is an enchanting place of long Scottish twilights, sea mists and blinding summer sunsets.

The Ailsa's 4th hole, aptly named 'Woe-be-Tide', is an intriguing par-3 of 167 yards. It plays from sea level across a little inlet to a green cut high into the top of a sandhill – the beginning of a long ridge which runs above the sands of Turnberry Bay and contains the valley in which holes 5, 6 and 7 run. At the 8th

green the course bursts out onto rocky cliffs and runs by the water to the 11th tee, past the famous Turnberry lighthouse.

The First Hotel/Golf Complex
The origins of Turnberry – the hotel and the golf courses – are tied, as are so many other courses, to the spread and development of the railways. The third Marquis of Ailsa was a keen golfer (in 1899 he was captain of Prestwick) and at the turn of the century he leased land at Turnberry to the Glasgow & South Western Railway Company. The Marquis commissioned Willie Fernie, professional at Troon, to design 13 holes of golf for his private course. By 1905, Fernie had designed a

TURNBERRY						
Card of the Ailsa course						
1	Ailsa Craig	350 yards	par 4	10	Dinna Fouter	452 yards	par 4
2	Mak Siccar	428 yards	par 4	11	Maidens	177 yards	par 3
3	Blaw Wearie	462 yards	par 4	12	Monument	448 yards	par 4
4	Woe-be-Tide	167 yards	par 3	13	Tickly Tap	411 yards	par 4
5	Fin' me oot	441 yards	par 4	14	Risk-an-Hope	440 yards	par 4
6	Tappie Toorie	222 yards	par 3	15	Ca Canny	209 yards	par 3
7	Roon the Ben	528 yards	par 5	16	Wee Burn	409 yards	par 4
8	Goat Fell	427 yards	par 4	17	Lang Whang	500 yards	par 5
9	Brice's Castle	455 yards	par 4	18	Ailsa Hame	431 yards	par 4
		3,480 yards	par 35			3,477 yards	par 35
		Total 6,957 yards par 70					

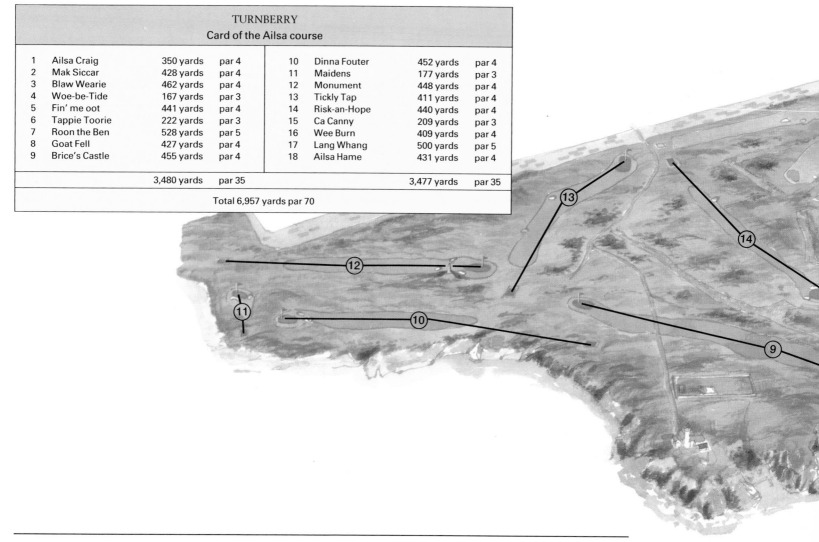

second, separate 13, and in 1907, with the hotel completed, all golfing facilities were taken over by the railway company. Willie Fernie's son Tom became the first Turnberry professional at what may have been the very first hotel-golf complex anywhere in the world.

A Triumph of Survival

The early courses offered pleasant resort golf but were badly compromised by the coming of the First World War, when the Royal Flying Corps built a training airfield on them. After that war, the Ailsa, named after the Marquis, was destined to be-

The defences around the green of the 222-yard 6th hole demand a shot of great accuracy – but the length of the hole and the prevailing wind often call for the use of a driver from the tee.

come the principal course. Major C.K. Hutchinson, who had worked with James Braid at Gleneagles, was retained to remove some blind holes and put some length into it; the course was shaping up to championship standard when the Second World War came along. This time, the Royal Air Force set up a training airfield and devastated the place with three runways with deep foundations and several inches of concrete on top, as well as buildings.

Knowledgeable folk were convinced that the Turnberry courses had gone beyond recall. But happily Frank Hole, managing director of British Transport Hotels, a British Rail subsidiary (the four

railway companies had been nationalised in 1948), did not. In a post-war campaign that lasted several years, Hole nagged the RAF and the government for the compensation he felt entitled to, and he eventually got it. Hole was an exceptional man. With the funds in place, his next triumph was to select Philip Mackenzie Ross to re-design and re-build the courses. Ross was a Musselburgh man who died in London in 1974 at the age of 83, when his credits included Royal Guernsey, Southerness, and Las Palmas in the Canary Islands; and in collaboration with the eccentric Tom Simpson, Royal Antwerp and Spa in Belgium and Deauville and Hardelot in France. With the help of Jimmy Alexander, the hotel company's superintendent of grounds and golf courses, and with Suttons of Reading as contractors, Ross created a masterpiece at Turnberry.

The courses were completed in the summer of 1951 and over the next two decades the reputation of the Ailsa was consolidated: it staged the Amateur Championship, two PGA Match Play Championships, the amateur international matches, a Walker Cup match and many professional tournaments. By 1977 it was ready to hold its first Open

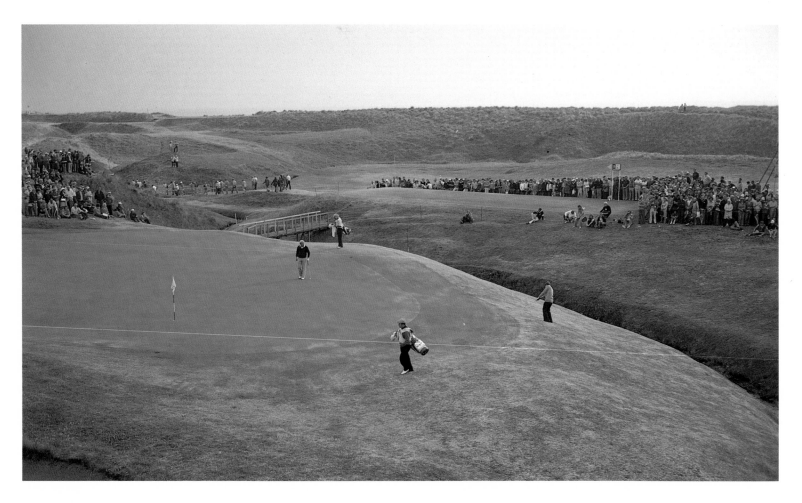

Championship, which proved to be as sensational as any Open had ever been. Jack Nicklaus and Tom Watson played three identical rounds of 68, 70 and 66. It had been a summer of drought, Turnberry's rough was meagre and playing conditions were perfect, but this was startling scoring. And paired together in the final round, they again played quite brilliantly – Nicklaus with a 66 and Watson with a 65, making Tom Open Champion for the second time. The winning total of 268, a record, was 12 under par. Only one other player, Hubert Green from the United States, was under par at 279, 11 shots behind Watson. Green quipped: 'Tom won the Open – I won the tournament the rest of us were playing'.

The Ailsa is a fine, honest, open golf course with a splendid selection of two-shot holes. One of the major drawbacks to playing well there is the distraction of its beauty. A more serious criticism is that is does not have one big, honest-to-God, under-any-conditions par-5 hole. The 7th is 528 yards at championship length, but

Top: *Turnberry's 'Wee Burn' 16th hole, at 409 yards, may be a comfortable drive and pitch for the expert, but the depth and width of Wilson's burn can be a frightening hazard for the club golfer.*

Above: *Tommy Nakajima of Japan and Greg Norman of Australia, the eventual winner, on the photographic 9th tee of Turnberry's Ailsa Course in the 1986 Open.*

Opposite: *The shot from the championship tee at the 9th, atop a 50-foot-high promontory, involves a carry of 200 yards across a rocky inlet.*

it runs approximately down the prevailing south-west wind. It calls for a drive from a tee high above the beach across broken ground and high dunes to a valley fairway running off to the left. There is a saddle in the dunes giving access to this valley. The carry is perhaps 200 yards over a perfectly positioned bunker. Watson, in his last championship round in 1977, drove over the corner, then hit a magnificent shot with his driver again, off the fairway to reach the green for his birdie. The 17th, at 500 yards, goes in quite the opposite direction. It is called 'Lang Whang', meaning a good strong crack at the ball. Into a strong prevailing wind, the best of them will need just that.

And finally, the most photographed of all Ailsa's delights is the 9th tee, perched out on a rocky promontory of cliffs, with sheer falls of 50 feet or more, and a drive that must carry a good 200 yards over an inlet in the cliffs. Rather than putting the nerves to the test with that tee shot, better to watch Turnberry's famous diving gannets.

GLENEAGLES

The King's Course at the Gleneagles Hotel is one of the best-known courses in Britain, largely because of the power of television. More tournaments and other golfing promotions have been televised from the King's than from any other course – with good reason. It is one of the most beautiful inland courses in the world. The fact that its international reputation, like that of the Augusta National course in Georgia, has been immensely enhanced by television exposure should not detract from its quality, which is of the highest order.

The King's, like the Queen's, the Prince's and the Glendevon – the other Gleneagles courses – is laid out on a wooded moorland plateau in Perthshire, a property of some 700 acres at an altitude of 600 feet. The turf is crisp, the fairways wide and smooth, the hazards in the main clearly defined and the course is immaculately groomed. There are banks of golden gorse and purple heather, stands of tall pines and the views in all directions are superb – the Ochil Hills to the east and south, with the valley of Glendevon reaching through to Fife; to the north lie the Grampians, to the west the Trossachs.

The hotel, built in the French Empire style, is the most luxurious in Scotland and has an interesting history. It was originally a railway hotel owned by the Caledonian Railway Company and was conceived by Donald Matheson, the company's general manager, just before the First World War. The truth of the matter may have been that Matheson could not tolerate the existence and success of the Turnberry Hotel, then owned by the Glasgow and South Western Railway Company, and he resolved to outdo it. Construction of Gleneagles was halted by the war, but Matheson had already engaged the great James Braid to design its courses. Braid, in collaboration with

The typically immaculate greens of the short 16th and (beyond it) the 15th. The King's course offers an enjoyable challenge to every calibre of golfer amid spectacularly beautiful scenery.

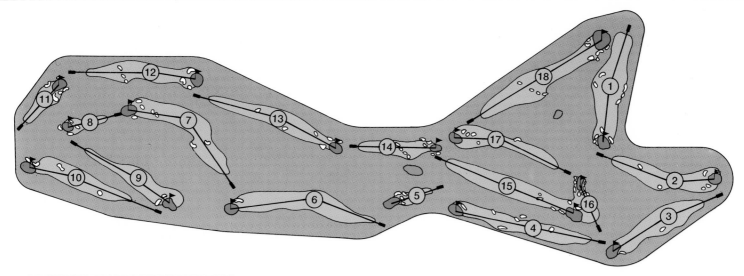

GLENEAGLES					
Card of the King's course					
1	362 yards	par 4	10	447 yards	par 4
2	405 yards	par 4	11	230 yards	par 3
3	374 yards	par 4	12	395 yards	par 4
4	466 yards	par 4	13	448 yards	par 4
5	161 yards	par 3	14	260 yards	par 4
6	476 yards	par 5	15	459 yards	par 4
7	439 yards	par 4	16	135 yards	par 3
8	158 yards	par 3	17	377 yards	par 4
9	354 yards	par 4	18	525 yards	par 5
	3,195 yards	par 35		3,276 yards	par 35
	Total 6,471 yards par 70				

Major C.K. Hutchinson, designed the King's Course and nine holes for the Queen's. A second nine was added to the Queen's, and when the hotel opened in 1924, golf was very much in place.

Braid's Moorland Masterpiece

Braid's brief for the King's Course had been: 'Make it spectacular, make it look difficult, but make it easy to get round'. That might sound like an invitation to cheat, but Braid by and large filled the client's bill. The basic feature of the site was a long ridge that ran through the entire property. The holes then follow patterns which seem to have been inflicted on the design by the ridge. Braid has a tee on the ridge, playing down into a valley. He has a green set on top of the ridge, demanding an uphill approach. On occasion, he has a blind shot over the ridge. (The blind shots may persuade some that the course is slightly old-fashioned; but the fact is that in design terms the blind shot was not frowned

upon in the first decade of this century.)

In terms of his brief, Braid certainly made it spectacular; made it look difficult. Whether or not it is easy to get round depends entirely on the talent and the wit of the golfer. There are some holes that must be difficult even for a first-class player. The 3rd hole, 374 yards, for instance, plays uphill into a valley full of heaving mounds and devious hollows. There is then that huge ridge, with a very big bunker in its face. The entire green is beyond the ridge, so that the second shot is completely blind.

The most famous hole is no doubt the 13th, 'Braid's Brawest' (it was his favourite), again with the ridge running all along the right side. A lesser ridge with a bunker in its face crosses the fairway at about 200 yards and must be carried. At 448 yards, this is a challenging two-

Philomena Garvey of Ireland in the final of the 1957 British Ladies' Championship in which she beat Mrs Valentine ('Wee Jessie' to her Scottish fans) by 4 and 3. The Gleneagles trees have grown considerably since then.

shotter. The second shot is to a plateau green above the player. It slopes from right to left, down into a dip at the front, then up towards the back. The fairway narrows as it nears the green, which is adroitly bunkered – a fine hole. The pleasures of Gleneagles are many, and go beyond the playing of the shots. Depending on the season, you may hear the call of wild geese, or grouse or pheasant or partridge or duck among the woods.

And looking to the future, there are plans for a championship course in the 1990s to be designed by Jack Nicklaus – his first major commission in Scotland.

ROYAL PORTHCAWL

Wales has much to be proud of in the range and variety of its golf courses. It boasts a good hundred of them, ranging from links to mountain courses and running the gamut of seaside, parkland, meadowland, heathland and moorland. Particularly noteworthy are Aberdovey, Ashburton, Caernarvonshire and Royal St David's – those courses that crowd along the north coast of Wales from Prestatyn to Llandudno.

The game came to Wales, as it came to England, with the great Scottish emigration of golfers and architects (often one and the same) in the last quarter of the 19th century. One of the oldest of Welsh clubs is at Tenby and dates from 1888. Clubs established in 1890 included Rhyl and Glamorganshire at Penarth, and the greatest of Welsh courses, Royal Porthcawl, dates from 1891.

Lock's Common
Early in 1891 a group of Cardiff businessmen, mainly, as you would expect, from the shipping and coal trades, resolved to start a golf club at Porthcawl, and by April of that year had arranged permission to cut nine holes for play on Lock's

Common – a dense and tangled undergrowth of gorse, whin and bracken – and the rest of the year was spent in clearing it. Early in 1892, Charles Gibson, the professional at Westward Ho!, was invited to lay out an original nine-holes course. Within three years, the club was ready for an extra nine, and before the turn of the century the original nine were abandoned and the present 18 established. These were to be revised regularly by impressive names from the ranks of golf architects – James Braid in 1910, Harry Colt in 1913, Tom Simpson and possibly Fred Hawtree between the wars, Ken Cotton in 1950 and Donald Steel in 1986.

The fruit of their labours is an out-

standing course. Royal Porthcawl has a magnificent setting on the Glamorgan coast 25 miles west of Cardiff, 14 miles east of Swansea. The property slopes towards the west and also south towards the Bristol Channel; and should probably

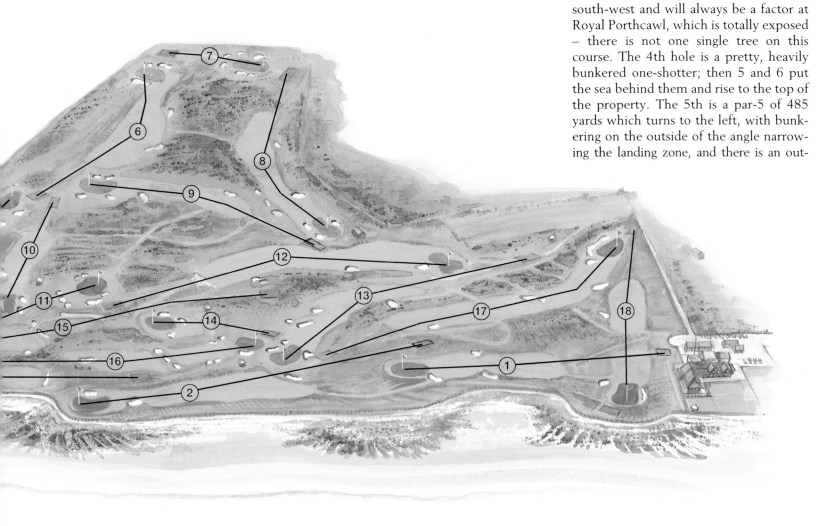

south-west and will always be a factor at Royal Porthcawl, which is totally exposed – there is not one single tree on this course. The 4th hole is a pretty, heavily bunkered one-shotter; then 5 and 6 put the sea behind them and rise to the top of the property. The 5th is a par-5 of 485 yards which turns to the left, with bunkering on the outside of the angle narrowing the landing zone, and there is an out-

be described as a seaside, rather than a links course because of the absence of dunes. However, spreading banks of gorse and broom are colourful substitutes and there is no shortage of movement in the ground. The course also provides arresting views: to the west Swansea and the Gower Peninsula; to the south, the coast of Somerset.

The Wind Factor

The first three holes are a delight, running to the west along the shore. The 1st hole, at 326 yards, is a drive (crossing the 18th fairway, by the way) into a small valley, then a pitch to a small green. The 2nd and

Royal Porthcawl's first three holes and the 18th run along the Cardigan coast looking out to the Bristol Channel. The natural humps and bumps of a linksland course are very evident here.

	ROYAL PORTHCAWL				
	\multicolumn{5}{c}{Card of the course}
1	326 yards	par 4	10	337 yards	par 4
2	447 yards	par 4	11	187 yards	par 3
3	420 yards	par 4	12	476 yards	par 5
4	197 yards	par 3	13	443 yards	par 4
5	485 yards	par 5	14	152 yards	par 3
6	394 yards	par 4	15	447 yards	par 4
7	116 yards	par 3	16	434 yards	par 4
8	490 yards	par 5	17	508 yards	par 5
9	371 yards	par 4	18	413 yards	par 4
	3,246 yards	par 36		3,397 yards	par 36
	\multicolumn{5}{c}{Total 6,643 yards par 72}

3rd holes are very fine par-4s, bunkered artfully in driving range and asking for long seconds down to greens placed closer to the shore than is comfortable for most golfers. These holes will normally have the wind against, since it prevails from the

of-bounds all the way up the left. The 6th is a par-4 of 394 yards, it too turning to the left with a bunker on the outside of the angle and out-of-bounds along the left.

The 7th is a pop of a hole, at 116 yards shorter even than Royal Troon's 'Postage Stamp' and surely the shortest hole on any championship course anywhere. In truth, it may be altogether too short, bordering on the comic. The 8th, on the other hand, is a lovely hole, turning to the left, this time with a fairway bunker on the inside of the angle, then an uphill second which must carry over cross-bunkers some 40 yards short of the green. A score of five is hard-won over its 490 yards.

Sea Views

One of the special features of Porthcawl is that there are views of the sea from almost every point on the course. This is true in spite of the fact that the remaining

holes seem to run in an almost arbitrary fashion, every which way. Nowhere is the view more striking than from the crest of the 13th fairway. The second part of the hole (a par-4 of 443 yards) falls down to the green with the sea spreading beyond. Most of the golf course can be seen from this point.

Holes 15 and 16 are powerful par-4s, at 447 and 434 yards respectively, and the 17th is a real tester. It is a double dog-leg, first to the right, then left into the green. The drive must carry a swathe of rough ground, then negotiate the turns and 508 yards of precisely bunkered fairway, running uphill to a green which is long and tightly trapped on both sides. The 18th hole plays straight downhill at 413 yards, crossing in front of the first tee and playing to a green perched perilously close to the rocky beach. This is a challenging finish to a course that measures no more than 6,643 yards, yet has never been overwhelmed by any player.

International Tournaments

The merits of Porthcawl are demonstrated by the fact that it has staged all the great events of the game with the exception of the Open Championship. It has seen five Amateur Championships, the European Amateur Team Championships of 1989 and the men's Home International-

Above: The crowd gathers by the green of Porthcawl's 485 yards, uphill par-5 5th hole, at the Amateur Championship final of 1988, when Christian Hardin of Sweden beat Ben Fouchee of South Africa in a 'foreign' final.

Right: The flavour of Porthcawl – beyond the 17th tee is the 2nd green, hard by the shore and the wide sweep of the Bristol Channel.

al Championships eight times. It has presented three Ladies's Amateur Championships, a Curtis Cup match, a Vagliano Trophy match between the ladies of Great Britain and Ireland and the Continent of Europe, the ladies' Home International matches four times, and many professional events.

The scoring of the professionals over the years is a good indication of the quality of the course and how true a test it remains. Gordon Brand, Jr scored 273, fifteen under par, in winning the 1982 Coral Classic tournament. Yet 50 years earlier, Percy Alliss had won a Penfold Tournament with 278, only five strokes adrift of Brand despite half a century of improvement in clubs and balls. And Peter Thomson, at the height of his career in 1961, had to play quite brilliantly through a stiff wind to score 284 in winning the Dunlop Masters.

ROYAL COUNTY DOWN

Royal County Down is one of the world's greatest seaside courses. It is set on a quite magnificent piece of golfing ground along the shore of Dundrum Bay, by the town of Newcastle on the east coast of Ireland, 30 miles from Belfast. It is an area of striking beauty, dominated by the mass of Slieve Donard and the Mountains of Mourne to the south of the town. The course plays through a piece of ground, in the old days known as The Warren, surely destined for nothing but a golf course. Emerald green fairways cut channels through oceans of gorse-covered dunes, ridges and swelling rises in a stunning linksland that has its own entirely distinctive character.

Royal County Down is not really comparable to any other links course. Its sand dunes don't quite tumble with the sharpness of those of Ballybunion or Lahinch. It is not as stern as Portmarnock or Portrush. Its first three holes run north-east, hard along the beach and then the course turns inland, putting the sea behind it, leaving the golfer in wondrous admiration and isolation on the most beautiful of golf courses.

The club was formed in 1889, one of the oldest in Ulster (Royal Belfast, the oldest, 1881; Royal Portrush in 1888). Newcastle was a summer resort for Belfast businessmen then, and perhaps encouraged by the success of the Belfast club and by the fact that The Warren was an obvious site for golf, a meeting was called on 23 March 1889 in 'the hall of Mr Lawrence's Dining Rooms, Newcastle. Lord Annersley presided and over 70 ladies and gentlemen were present'.

Old Tom Morris

A provisional committee meeting decided to invite 'Tom Morris of St Andrews to lay out the course at an expense not to exceed £4'. Nine holes were already in existence. Old Tom came over and played the existing holes on 16th and 17th July and left recommendations for an 18-hole course which was quickly laid out. Tees and greens would be the priority in those times – there was no sophisticated equipment in use and this was still very much in the time of the gutty ball, when 200 yards was a good hit. Golf course architecture was a simple, infant business – Horace Hutchinson, the 1887 Amateur Champion who came over to play these 18 holes, wrote ten years later: 'The laying out of a golf course is a wonderfully easy business, needing very little training'.

By 1890, the club felt able to appoint its first professional, Alex Day, and soon afterwards its first greenkeeper. One of the founder members, George Combe, contributed greatly to the evolution of the course. Captain in 1895–6, he spent many years as chairman of the greens committee and was largely responsible for changing the design to two loops of nine holes, with the ninth returning to the clubhouse area in the Muirfield fashion.

In 1898, the club was sufficiently confident and well-founded to put up 100 guineas for its first professional tournament. It attracted Harry Vardon, J.H. Taylor, Ben Sayers, Sandy Herd, Andrew

ROYAL COUNTY DOWN					
Card of the course					
1	506 yards	par 5	10	200 yards	par 3
2	424 yards	par 4	11	440 yards	par 4
3	473 yards	par 4	12	501 yards	par 5
4	217 yards	par 3	13	445 yards	par 4
5	440 yards	par 4	14	213 yards	par 3
6	396 yards	par 4	15	445 yards	par 4
7	145 yards	par 3	16	265 yards	par 4
8	427 yards	par 4	17	400 yards	par 4
9	486 yards	par 5	18	545 yards	par 5
3,514 yards	par 36		3,454 yards	par 36	
Total 6,968 yards par 72					

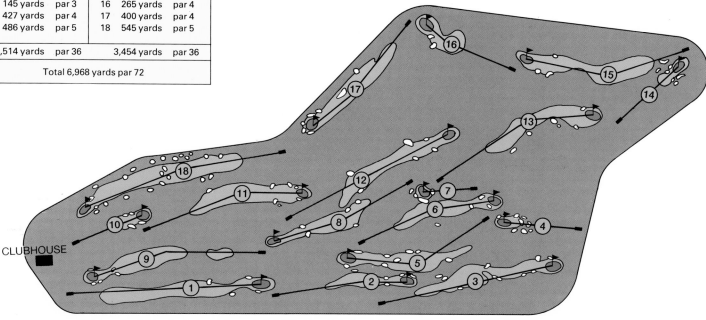

Kirkaldy and Willie Fernie. Harry Vardon beat Taylor by a staggering 12 and 11 in the final.

The Amateur Championship

In 1897 the club had opened a new clubhouse – it had previously used facilities at the nearby railway station, and early in the new century, there was an arrangement with the Belfast and County Down Railway Company to provide special trains, soon dubbed the 'Golfers' Express', leaving Belfast at 10.10am and returning from Newcastle at 5.35pm. By 1902, the course was at 5,760 yards and becoming well-known throughout Britain. And the club had such a conceit of

Three of Royal County Down's short holes are 200 yards or better. This is the 10th, running exactly 200 yards to the north away from the clubhouse, over broken ground to a green only 27 yards long.

itself that in the same year it sent a delegation to the Amateur Championship Committee – comprising representatives of the Royal and Ancient, Honourable Company, Royal St George's, Royal Liverpool and Prestwick – petitioning to have the Amateur Championship at Royal County Down. It was rejected. An indignant article in the *Northern Whig* pointed out that the local scenery 'is more to be desired than the flat lands of St

Andrews or the morass of Muirfield'. However, Royal County Down did get the Amateur Championship – 58 years later, when Michael Bonallack won his fifth championship, his third in successive years.

In 1904 Seymour Dunn, professional for a couple of years, suggested some course changes, and Harry Vardon, who was back in 1908, suggested others. The club then had good times and bad, the two World Wars being particularly difficult times, as they were for almost every golf club. By 1923, the course measured 6,451 yards, but it was not until Harry Colt had run his eye over it in 1926, and his recommended changes were put into

Above: *Royal County Down's 9th is one of the most testing holes in golf at its championship length of 486 yards, demanding a long drive, then a second shot over cross bunkers, uphill to a small, raised green.*

Left: *Rolling panorama of Royal County Down, with the formidable short 4th and its fiercely defended green in the foreground, framed in the distance by the Mourne Mountains.*

practice, that it took on its present magnificent form.

A Flawed Masterpiece
Now, at its championship length of 6,968 yards with a par of 72, it is a test for the best. The 1st hole, a par-5 of 506 yards, plays down into a long, slender valley with sandhills on either side and the five miles strand of Dundrum Bay parallel to the right. Behind lies the massive backdrop of the Mourne Mountains, and ahead, running northward, golden gorse in blossom, fierce heathery rough, restless fairways and swelling dunes. It is a magnificent place. But some have it that County Down is a flawed masterpiece, because of its blind shots.

The 'blind' holes hit the golfer so quickly that as early as the second tee he will be mumbling about the advantages of local knowledge. The drive there is blind, as it is at the 5th, over a ridge. The drive on the 6th is blind, and part of the short 7th's green is hidden from the tee. The drive at the 9th is across a mass of sandhills and the second to the 13th is blind. All told there are five tee shots at Newcastle which are shots into the unknown, and this course definitely needs to be known! But blind shots are still featured to a greater (at Prestwick) or lesser (at Royal St George's) degree in the modern game.

The par-3 holes are outstanding. The 4th is a 217 yards carry over gorse to a long green with ten (!) bunkers. The 14th at 213 yards is a very similar hole, but downhill, and has only six greenside bunkers. The 10th, at 200 yards, is played from a raised tee down to a closely trapped green. Some golfers know how to cope with such holes. In the final of the Irish Open Amateur Championship of 1933, Eric Fiddian, playing against Jack McLean, holed his tee shot at the 7th during the morning round, and repeated the feat at the 14th of the afternoon round. It was unprecedented in such a final, but McLean nevertheless, won. But, win or lose, any golfer who plays Royal County Down can only rejoice in the splendour of its scenery, in the quality of the shotmaking it requires and in the delights and damnations of its design. Royal County Down is a golf experience second to none.

ROYAL PORTRUSH

The Antrim coast road, running along the northern cliffs of Northern Ireland, is a dramatic passage, by Ballycastle Bay, White Park Bay and Benbane Head, with the boomerang shape of Rathlin Island offshore. Past the Giant's Causeway and Portballintrae it goes, and when it turns just past the ruined Dunluce Castle, there is a panorama to make the heart of any golfer skip. The entire spread of the Royal Portrush courses are laid out before him. Not ridges or mounds, but hills, minor mountains, hills of sand and wildflowers – in particular the wild dwarf rose – and sharp and sinister hollows, covering what appears to be a vast acreage.

To the west is Inishowen Head and the hills of Donegal across the mouth of Lough Foyle; to the north, over the Skerries and across the sea, lies the outline of Islay; and to the east, beyond Rathlin, there is a sight of the peninsula of Kintyre. The Dunluce Course, the championship course, may be the most severe test of all the great British championship courses. The key is driving, which might be said of every golf course in the world, but this is particularly true of Portrush. The fairways are desperately narrow. It is not so much a question of what side of the fairway to be on, it is more a question of

This is the 14th at Royal Portrush, otherwise known as 'Calamity Corner', and one of the most famous short holes in Ireland. It is 213 yards and in place of a fairway has a 50 feet deep canyon between tee and green.

being on the fairway! Almost every fairway turns one way or the other. In championship trim, Dunluce rough is fiercely tenacious. There are no trees on the course, no shelter. It is exposed to all the winds the ocean may blow. And the greens can certainly not be described as large. One peculiar feature in the Dunluce design is the paucity of bunkers, particularly at greenside. However, the greens are either protected by approaches which will run a ball off to the side, or are raised, with steep hollows on one side or the other, and with extremely narrow entrances.

The history of the club has odd similarities with those of its contemporaries, in relation to the acquiring of ground, the laying out of holes, the use of the assets

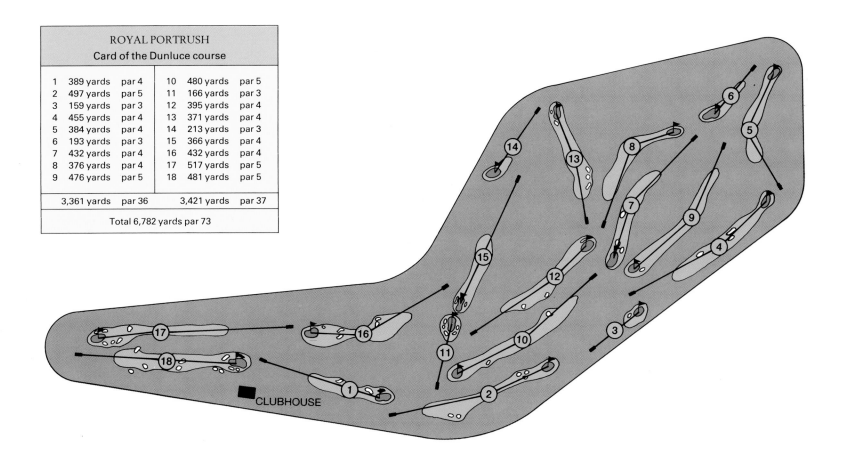

ROYAL PORTRUSH					
Card of the Dunluce course					
1	389 yards	par 4	10	480 yards	par 5
2	497 yards	par 5	11	166 yards	par 3
3	159 yards	par 3	12	395 yards	par 4
4	455 yards	par 4	13	371 yards	par 4
5	384 yards	par 4	14	213 yards	par 3
6	193 yards	par 3	15	366 yards	par 4
7	432 yards	par 4	16	432 yards	par 4
8	376 yards	par 4	17	517 yards	par 5
9	476 yards	par 5	18	481 yards	par 5
	3,361 yards	par 36		3,421 yards	par 37
		Total 6,782 yards par 73			

and goodwill of the local aristocracy, not to mention Ulster's railway system. Comparisons with Royal County Down are obvious. Royal Portrush was founded in 1888, one year before the Newcastle club. The town of Portrush at that time had a population of 1600 and was already established as a Victorian resort with a fine harbour, a railway terminus – the Northern Counties railway from Belfast – a tramway route out to the Giant's Causeway and even a direct steamer service from Glasgow and the Clyde ports ...and of course, magnificent beaches and sand dunes.

The club started as the County Club, occupying 'The Triangle', 40 acres of ground by the railway station. At one point, members of the County Club could travel first class on a day return ticket to Belfast and have a hot lunch and tea in the Northern Counties Hotel for all of ten shillings (50p). The English master at the Royal Academy in Belfast, George L. Baillie, originally from Musselburgh, resigned as honorary secretary to the Royal Belfast club, where he had helped

introduce golf to Ireland, and became honorary secretary at Portrush. As a founding father, he was very much involved with the landlord, the Earl of Antrim, in extending the course beyond The Triangle and into the natural dune land on the seaward side of the Portrush-Bushmills road. In 1889 Tom Morris, having visited County Down, came on to Portrush, played the existing course and made some suggestions for improving the design. In October that year came the first clubhouse, a hut of wood and zinc which cost £150. And by 1890, there were 18 holes in play, a new professional in Sandy Herd, 250 members and a second 18 almost completed.

The Dunluce course is built on a 'raised beach', a higher shelf of dune left by the receding sea, while the Valley course, the ladies' course, is on lower ground, in some parts below sea level. By 1909, the big course measured 6,608 yards, but not until the 'Twenties did Dunluce take on its present form. In 1923, the remarkable Harry Colt prepared new plans. These were delayed, until 1928 because of

various lease problems and thereafter by cost, but by 1933 the new courses were established, with some superb and taxing holes. The 14th, for example, at 213 yards demands a carry all the way over an evil, 50 foot deep canyon. Dubbed 'Calamity Corner', it is just that, and is one of the most famous short holes in Ireland.

The 5th hole, a dog-leg to the right, needs a careful approach to a green on the very edge of the cliff. In the winter of 1982–3, some 25 feet of cliff behind that green and the neighbouring 6th tee were eroded. The club had to take quick action and launched a fund to help meet the repair cost, estimated at £200,000. Golfers and golf clubs throughout the UK, Ireland and beyond responded, and the work was done.

The club's proudest boast remains the Open Championship of 1951, the only time it has ever been played in Ireland. It was won by the extrovert Max Faulkner, with a surprisingly restrained exhibition of shot-making and putting in highly variable weather.

PORTMARNOCK

Portmarnock is a giant among golf courses, the greatest in the Republic of Ireland. That statement will be challenged immediately by the supporters of Rosses Point, Lahinch, Ballybunion – both courses – Waterville and perhaps even Royal Dublin. And if the claim be extended to all-Ireland, what should we do with Royal County Down and Royal Portrush? But yet again, it must be remembered that we are never quite comparing like with like, and have to fall back on the old disclaimer that rubies are rubies, pearls are pearls and diamonds are diamonds. Like the other selections, Portmarnock must be classified as one of the great golf courses of the world.

The course occupies a peninsula which juts into the Irish sea some eight miles north-east of Dublin, and is arranged in two loops of nine holes through classic links terrain – without the vast sandhills of a County Down or a Ballybunion, but across rolling sandhills of crisp turf on what seems to be an isolated island.

The Wilderness
The origins of Portmarnock are poorly documented, but it appears that in 1894 George Ross and J.W. Pickeman rowed across to the peninsula and, despite the fact that the ground was something of a wilderness, they decided that it had some potential for golf. Before this the Jameson family had their own private course near the shore in the general area of the present 15th hole. John Jameson of Irish Whiskey fame was the local landlord and for many years was first president of the Portmarnock club.

The original nine holes lay more or less as the present opening nine and, within four years, they had a second nine in play and a shack for a clubhouse in place. By 1899 they had a course of 5,810 yards,

Canada Cup 1960. Sam Snead sinks the final putt watched (from left) by Kel Nagle, Arnold Palmer and Peter Thomson. The Americans won the cup by eight shots in Palmer's first ever European tournament.

their first professional tournament, and a notable winner in Harry Vardon, who had scores of 72 and 79. Vardon won the Open at Sandwich later that year. The original clubhouse burned down in 1904, and parts of the present building date from 1905, then the clubhouse was replaced. There have been other changes over the years. Fred G. Hawtree revised the original 18. His son, Fred W., designed a third nine holes in 1964, and new greens have been made at the 6th, 8th, 10th and 18th holes over the years.

In the early days, the club was reached by boat from Sutton, as Ross and Pickeman had done, and the club ferryman was a former naval man and formidable with it. It was said that once on the crossing there was a difference of opinion between himself and a clergyman not of the same faith. The clergyman did not reach Portmarnock. When the Amateur Championship was played at Portmarnock in 1949, the only time it has been played outside the U.K., Henry Longhurst, the

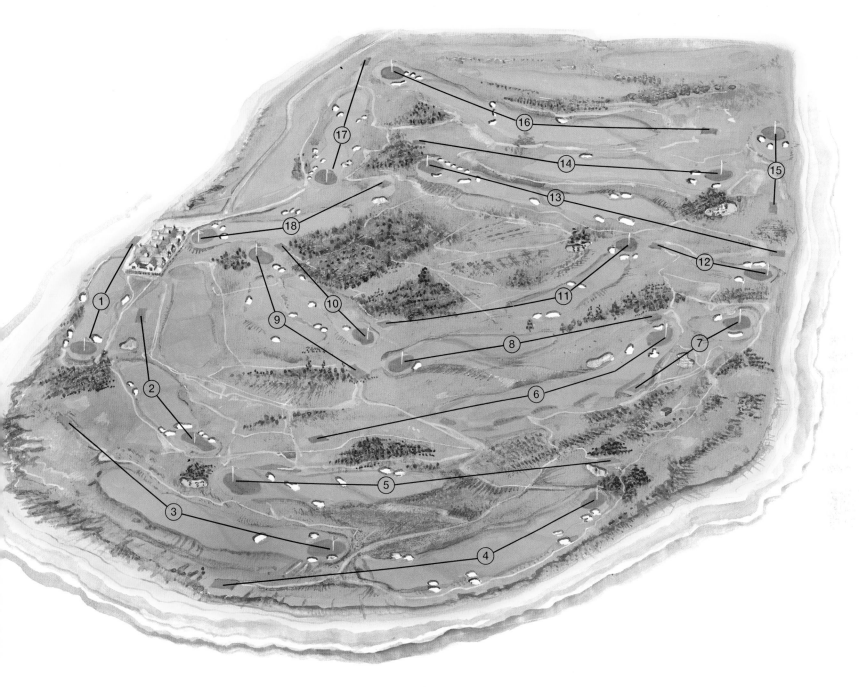

golf journalist, wrote rather pertly about having to show a passport to report the Amateur Championship, which was being played 'in a foreign country'.

An 'Easy' Opening

In championship dress, Portmarnock will play to more than 7,100 yards, with seven of its par-4 holes over 400 yards and two of its three par-5 holes at 565 yards or better. The first three holes run down to and around the very point of the peninsula and if there were easy holes at Portmar-

PORTMARNOCK					
Card of the course					
1	388 yards	par 4	10	380 yards	par 4
2	368 yards	par 4	11	445 yards	par 4
3	388 yards	par 4	12	144 yards	par 3
4	460 yards	par 4	13	565 yards	par 5
5	407 yards	par 4	14	385 yards	par 4
6	586 yards	par 5	15	192 yards	par 3
7	180 yards	par 3	16	527 yards	par 5
8	370 yards	par 4	17	466 yards	par 4
9	444 yards	par 4	18	408 yards	par 4
	3,591 yards	par 36		3,512 yards	par 36
	Total 7,103 yards par 72				

nock, it would be these opening three, giving the golfer at least some chance of getting into an early, comfortable stride. On yardage, they are all under 400 yards and therefore theoretically drive and pitch holes, but that ignores the wind, and Portmarnock is seldom without that.

The pin position at the 1st will often be behind the left front bunker. That means the drive should be in the right half of the fairway. But on that side is an area which is out of bounds! The 2nd green is two-tiered, and the 3rd hole doglegs to

the left with a ridge of rough along the left and a lateral water hazard on the right side. The 4th is where the course begins to flex its considerable muscle. The drive is over 150 yards of rough and a little ridge enters a narrow fairway which turns to the left, with pairs of bunkers carefully set up along the right side. Again, accuracy in the tee shot is essential. It must be slightly right to allow sight of the flat green with a narrow approach to it.

Harry Bradshaw, professional at the club for many years, always considered

The 17th hole is lavishly bunkered on both sides of the fairway and the right of the green. Severiano Ballesteros, seen here in the 1986 Irish Open, putts after a perfect second shot to the green.

the 5th the best hole on the course. It is straight, with a blind drive over a ridge demanding a carry of almost 200 yards to the fairway. There is a slight ridge crossing just short of the green and a bunker at the right front of it, just short of a rather small green set across the shot. The

6th is an immense hole of 586 yards, requiring, quite simply, a huge shot smashed off the tee to avoid banks of rough on the left. The second shot should get up to the region of the pond in the left rough – still some 120 yards to the front of the green. The 7th at 180 yards is a pretty and rather straightforward one shot hole, the easiest of the par-3s. The 8th hole offers a selection of Portmarnock characteristics. There is a sandhill on the right, 200 yards out, and a rough-filled hollow as the hole turns left at 250 yards.

The oval green is raised, so that the less than perfect shot is liable to run off and leave a chipping challenge. Careful driving in particular makes for scoring potential in this, the easier half of the course.

The Inward Half

Rather long carries from the tees typify the inward half, and depending on wind speed and direction these can become major problems. The 10th needs a carry of 175 yards from the very back tee, and a drive placed left to give a clear shot to

another plateaued green. The 11th is a strong dog-leg to the left. At 445 yards, it requires two solid hits to get to a closely trapped green. The 12th, the second one-shot hole, is at 144 yards deceptive – the green sloping sharply. The second par-5 at 565 yards runs straight. Two huge fairway bunkers short of the green compromise the second shot.

The 14th is one of those classic par-4 holes that you can imagine would be included in any selection of the 18 greatest something-or-other golf holes. There is a huge deep bunker in driving range on the left. There is a good deal of roll in the fairway, so the second shot may come from a downhill or uneven lie. The green is small, raised and protected by a mound and three fairly close bunkers – all in all an exceptional golf hole. The 15th is a one-shot hole of classic difficulty. Tee and green are hard by the beach, with out of bounds along the right side, the beach side, and no fairway in between. It is 185 yards of carry all the way to a high, mounded green with close-in bunkering; one right front, two left front.

Portmarnock has a strong finish, as you would expect. The 16th, a big par-5 of 527 yards, turns to the right. There is a good deal of movement in the fairway, and three solid cross bunkers at 400 yards and flanking bunkers at a green which slopes left to right. The 17th, playing due south and back towards the clubhouse,

The green of the 15th, a short hole of 'classic difficulty'. The absence of fairway calls for the most accurate assessment of the almost inevitable cross-wind.

can be a fiercely difficult hole. Pairs of bunkers police a narrow fairway. The approach shot must be long and steer its way past flanking bunkers short of the green, then three close-in on the right front guarding a green that falls away over the back. The 18th is an exciting finishing hole in any tournament. At 403 yards, it turns to the right with a dip at 250 yards and the drive must avoid three bunkers on the right. The big green is very much raised and bunkers leave the narrowest of entrance gaps for a running shot. Thus Portmarnock, in terms of its difficulty, could be described as a monster, a Carnoustie, but for its pastoral surroundings.

Monster or not, the modern tournament professional, given ideal conditions of still air and a 'soft' course, is more than a match for Portmarnock or anything the course designer can throw at him. In the 1987 Carroll's Irish Open Championship, Bernhard Langer scored 67–68–66–68 for 269, 19 under par, to win by ten strokes from the next man, Sandy Lyle. Indeed in the 1984 event, Langer won with a total of 267, two better, with 68–66–67–66 over a course that was slightly shorter.

BALLYBUNION

Ballybunion is a small seaside resort in the far south-west of Ireland, at the northern end of the county of Kerry, about 50 miles west of Limerick and 25 miles north of Tralee. It lies on the south bank of the estuary of the river Shannon, and a remote place it is. It is also the place where there is to be found, in the judgement of many serious golfing people, 'the best golf course in the world'. When Herbert Warren Wind, the much-respected American sports writer who has written extensively if not absolutely exclusively on golf, first visited the course, he wrote that Ballybunion 'revealed itself to be nothing less than the finest seaside course I have ever seen'. The much respected British golf writer, Peter Dobereiner wrote '... if sheer pleasure is

the yardstick, then Ballybunion gets my vote as the best course in the world'. And Tom Watson, the great American champion and lover of links courses, claims that 'it is a course on which many golf architects should live and play before they build golf courses'.

Duneland
Why should there be such a magnificent course in such a remote place? The inexplicable accidents of geography, history, geology and mankind have much to

The 385-yard 17th, on the Old course, shows typical Ballybunion country of high sand dunes, ridged fairways, grassed hollows and the constant presence of the cliffs and the ocean.

do with it. The Atlantic Ocean has pounded the land of the west of Ireland for aeons. The result is stark, standing, crumbling cliffs, georgeous shining beaches and vast stretches of tumbling sand dunes. At Ballybunion, the duneland above the beach is immense, rising in great ridges and peaks, leaving deep valleys and thrusting perhaps 50 feet and more above the beach — a weird and exciting landscape. Unlike dunes in other places, where the sand ridges march in ordered lines parallel with the shore, at Ballybunion they thrust and tumble and heave in all directions, giving valleys for fairways, tops for tees, and the possibility of having greens and tees on the very edge of cliffs, overlooking the strand. Made for golf it was.

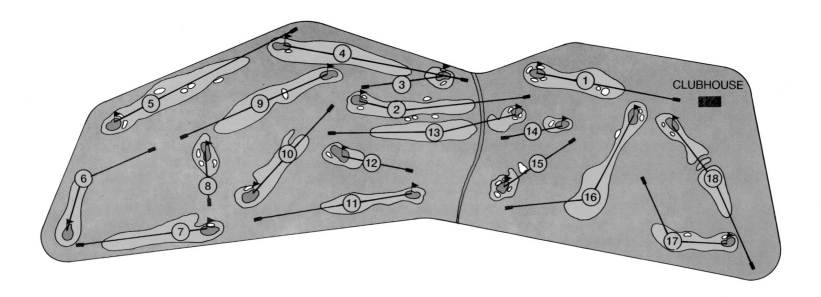

The club started in life on 4 March 1896 – the minute book has been preserved – with George Hewson of Listowel (the nearest town) as president and C. Mark Montserrat, a local estate agent, as honorary secretary. In 1897, Patrick McCarthy, manager of the Listowel and Ballybunion Railway Company, became honorary secretary. Alas, the club had not been organised on a financial footing that could keep it alive and the last entry in the club's minute book came on 13 August 1898.

James Bruen

That might well have been the end of it all but for one Colonel Bartholomew, an Indian Army man who had retired to the area. He formed the present club in 1906, with BJ Johnstone of the Bank of Ireland, Patrick Murphy of the original group, and John Macauley of Listowel, who played Rugby football for Ireland. They retained Lionel Hewson, for many years editor of *Irish Golf*, to make nine holes. The course was extended to 18 holes in 1926, by a Mr Smyth, a designer for Carter and Sons Limited, the London company famous for laying out sports ground; and in 1937 the course was chosen as the venue for the Irish Men's Close Championship. This was the championship memorable for the victory and the emergence of James Bruen, aged 17 and in many ways the greatest of all Irish golfers. He beat

BALLYBUNION					
Card of the Old course					
1	392 yards	par 4	10	359 yards	par 4
2	445 yards	par 4	11	449 yards	par 4
3	220 yards	par 3	12	192 yards	par 3
4	498 yards	par 5	13	484 yards	par 5
5	508 yards	par 5	14	131 yards	par 3
6	364 yards	par 4	15	216 yards	par 3
7	423 yards	par 4	16	490 yards	par 5
8	153 yards	par 3	17	385 yards	par 4
9	454 yards	par 4	18	379 yards	par 4
	3,457 yards	par 36		3,085 yards	par 35
	Total 6,542 yards par 71				

another famous Irish player, John Burke of Lahinch, in the final of the tournament.

In preparation for this championship, the club had asked Tom Simpson, the English architect, to review the course. When Simpson saw it, he was astonished and delighted, and did little more than move a couple of greens and plant a bunker in the middle of the fairway at what is now the 1st hole. It was dubbed, quickly and topically, 'Mrs Simpson'.

Friends of the Old Course

Ballybunion has been fortunate that everyone concerned with the existence and wellbeing of the place – from P. Murphy, who was 'employed to look after the ground at 9/- per week', to Jackie Hourigan in the late 1970s, who led a

campaign that saw 'the many friends of Ballybunion' raise £100,000 to check (successfully) erosion on the cliff face – realised the natural merits of the site, and allowed themselves to follow the land. 'The ground determines the play', the old dictum of John Lowe was never more true than at Ballybunion. The course is a mere 6,452 yards, short by modern design standards. But on such an exposed coast, the wind is always thereabouts. When the wind blows as it can, 'Anybody who breaks 70 here', in the words of Christy O'Connor, 'is playing better than he is able to play'!

The course quickly offers the golfer samples in miniature of what is to come. The very first drive, past the graveyard on the right, is downhill to a broad fairway. The hole is 392 yards. There is a huge sand mound off to the left. At 230 yards the first of a pair of bunkers closes out the left side, easing the drive over to the right, to rough and the boundary fence. The 2nd, at 445 yards, has bunkers on either side of the fairway at 210 yards and at 240 yards and the second shot must thread between two huge sand dunes. There is an upslope in front of the green, hollows behind the green, a fall off to the left and another big sand dune to the left – not bad! The 3rd, the first par-3, at 220 yards, has a large dune to the right, hollows in front of the green, bunkers right and left, and a downslope and a public road

running at the back left. At this moment, some players may feel it is time to retire to the clubhouse.

The Vintage Holes

The 4th and 5th are straightforward par-5s, but the 6th swoops out to the cliffs and starts the vintage Ballybunion holes. It is a dogleg to the left of 364 yards. Mounds and hollows mark the inside of the angle, and a mound beyond on the right might stop a really long drive on that line. The green is long, narrow, on the cliff and unprotected save for out-of-bounds on the right. But it does take us to the 7th tee! Here is an outstanding hole, at 423 yards, playing along the cliff tops. There is a mound on the left at around 200 yards. Two big ridges come in from the left further along. There is a grassy hollow just beyond them and the green, hard by the cliff, has a mound in front, hollows at the back and a bunker at the left. The 8th, 9th and 10th play away from the sea in a triangle before returning to the clifftop 11th tee. The 8th, a par-3 of 153 yards, is straight downhill. Tom Watson said of the tee shot; 'One of the most demanding shots I've ever faced'. There are huge bunkers, huge mounds crimping the front of the green, and hollows all around it.

The 11th is one of golf's most dramatic, most difficult, holes, played directly along the cliff top. There is an enormous sand

Above: The 18th at Ballybunion Old, 379 yards, displays all the elements of this famous course: the valley sharply dog-legged; the huge tumbling dunes, and in this case a big cross-bunker.

Right: The 10th, a short par-4, dog-legs left to this green perched high on the edge of the cliffs, with the Irish Sea crashing against them in the background.

dune off the fairway left, at 200 yards. At 245 yards, there are downslopes across the entire fairway. Two huge sandhills straddle the way into the green so that it is almost invisible from off-centre in the fairway, and there are fairway mounds 85 yards short of the green. Playing this hole with a strong wind from the sea hardly bears thinking about!

Holes 14 and 15 are magnificent short holes; 16, 17 and 18 quite startling in the sharpness of their dog-leg turns. The greatest problem the club golfer will have on such a course will be in ignoring his surroundings. They are so dramatic that they may frighten him, may compromise the business of just hitting the ball. The expert players do this so well – concentrating on nothing but the swing and the contact of blade on ball. The ocean, the cliffs, the dunes, the fairways, the air – all of it may be too much. Ballybunion is simply, in the words of a Duke Ellington phrase, 'beyond classification'.

LAHINCH

Old Tom Morris declared Lahinch 'as fine a natural course as it has ever been my good fortune to play over'. And Dr Alister Mackenzie thought that it might come to be regarded as 'the finest and most popular course that I, or I believe anyone else, ever constructed'. Morris and Mackenzie may have been indulging themselves a shade. Both men contributed to its evolution – Old Tom laid out the original course in 1893 and Mackenzie built new and rebuilt old holes in 1927 to put the course into its present shape and sequence.

The pretty village of Lahinch sits on Liscannon Bay on the Atlantic coast of County Clare, some 40 miles from Limerick. Its golf club dates from 1883, formed by officers of the Scottish regiment, the Black Watch, then stationed at Limerick, and of course a few interested locals. The soldier-golfers had been playing on Limerick racecourse, but were searching around for somewhere better. In the

Above: *Barometric billies: Lahinch's goats are the canniest weather prophets in these parts, making for the shelter of the clubhouse if rain threatens.*

Right: *The approach to the green of the par-4 8th is through a bottleneck between dunes some 50 yards short of the green, which is bunkered in front and to the right.*

spring of 1891 one of their officers was able to report that Lahinch, with its beach and sand dunes, was the very place. From then on, the Black Watch made Lahinch their golfing headquarters. Initially they marked out tees and green locations with, of all things, feathers.

When Old Tom Morris arrived in 1893 ('a guinea a day, and expenses, if you please'), he was greatly taken with the quality of the sand dunes and the seaward land, and virtually spurned the inland holes that existed. When he had finished he reckoned Lahinch to be one of the five best courses in the British Isles. No doubt Tom's reference was to the quality of the land as much as to his design, for Lahinch is blessed with vintage golfing ground – huge sand dunes, sheltering dells and valleys and magnificent sea views to the Cliffs of Moher and the Aran Islands.

The course is by any standards a magnificent links. Mackenzie extended the composite course which he created to

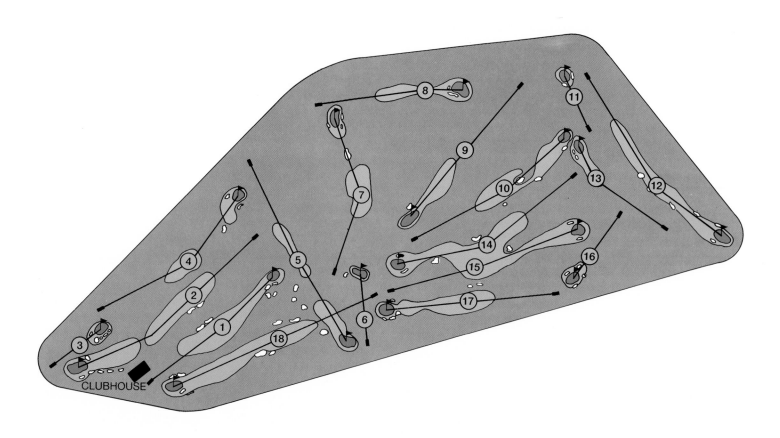

CLUBHOUSE

6,363 yards, and it can now play to just under 6,700 yards. What makes the course and the club so different is the way that it has become wholly integrated with the village. Lahinch is virtually a golf village, with the golf course the justification for its existence.

The course does get a great deal of holiday and tourist traffic, so much so that a second course of 18 holes, the 'Castle' course, designed by John Harris, became necessary and was opened in 1975.

Some holes are magnificent; others infuriating. The 2nd, for example, which plays back up towards and beyond the clubhouse, is a long 512 yards. It demands a drive into a narrow fairway, then an approach to a green which is open, but which has fairway bunkers along both sides, a high mound to the right, downward slopes at the front and to the left, and three fairly inhibiting bunkers. The third is an impish, short hole of about 150 yards with a banked-up front, but falling away at the left and back, and with a string of three bunkers set to the right.

LAHINCH					
Card of the course					
1	385 yards	par 4	10	451 yards	par 4
2	512 yards	par 5	11	138 yards	par 3
3	151 yards	par 3	12	475 yards	par 4
4	428 yards	par 4	13	273 yards	par 4
5	482 yards	par 5	14	488 yards	par 5
6	155 yards	par 3	15	462 yards	par 4
7	399 yards	par 4	16	195 yards	par 3
8	350 yards	par 4	17	437 yards	par 4
9	384 yards	par 4	18	533 yards	par 5
3,246 yards	par 36			3,452 yards	par 36
Total 6,698 yards par 72					

The best-known holes are of course the 'antiques' – the 5th, or 'Klondyke', and the 6th, the 'Dell'. They remain as Old Tom left them. The 5th is a par-5 of 482 yards, with a drive into a narrow valley with high dunes on either side. The golfer is then faced with a ridge running across the fairway so that the green is completely invisible. This demands a long, blind shot over the ridge towards a fairly flat green. The 6th is a one-shot hole of 155 yards, with the green completely hidden from the tee. A large sand ridge covers the front of the green, another crosses the back, and the green, long and narrow and imprisoned between these ridges, is laid directly across the shot. This is another hit and hope shot – the blind shot still entirely fashionable in golf in the 1890s. When Mackenzie came to re-fashion the course in 1927 he may well have been appalled at what he saw, but he was firmly warned off. The powers in the club announced that these holes were part of the tradition of Lahinch, and they were to remain untouched.

The final Irishism of Lahinch is 'See goats', the sign on the broken barometer in the clubhouse. It seems that when the weather is bad, three ancient goats who have the run of the course will come in from the most distant point to the clubhouse and huddle close to the barometer at the slightest sign of rain. The goats are such reliable forecasters, so why would anyone think of repairing the barometer?

CHANTILLY

France is the doyen of golfing nations in Europe, with more clubs and more players than any other country on the Continent. The game there has an honourable history and there is some evidence, albeit slight, of golf in the Bordeaux area as early as 1767. The first club to be established in France was at Pau in the French Pyrenees, near the Spanish border. It is said that Scottish regiments were stationed there after the Peninsular War and that the Scottish Duke of Hamilton was a prime mover in forming the club in 1856. By 1869 the club had a professional, one Joe Lloyd from the Hoylake area, who may well have been the first British professional to work abroad, and by 1879 Pau had built 18 holes of golf.

Most of the early French courses emerged at coastal resorts – namely, Biarritz in 1888, Cannes in 1891, Valescure, at St Raphael in the south, in 1896 and Dieppe in 1897. Chantilly, the finest course in France, dates from 1908 and within five years it was staging the French Open Championship, which was won by George Duncan, who became Open Champion in 1920. Over the years some impressive names have followed Duncan's: Arnaud Massy, Henry Cotton, Roberto de Vicenzo (twice), Peter Oosterhuis and Nick Faldo have all become French Open champions at Chantilly.

The course is big, some 6,713 yards with a par of 71, and features three big

The 18th green, with the clubhouse and forest beyond, during the 1988 French Open. At 525 yards, the 18th is one of the longest finishing holes in championship golf.

par-5s, four rather stern par-3s (three of them over 200 yards) and no fewer than nine par-4s of more than 400 yards. The 8th and 9th are successive long holes; the 8th straight with forest all along the left side, a barrier of bunkers crossing the fairway at a critical point short of the green, and the green itself set deep in the trees; the 9th, at 460 yards, turns to the right with formidable bunkering in the corner, and, eventually, a not unreasonable opening to the green.

Chantilly is set in one of the great forests of the Ile de France, and there is a sense of splendid separation from the outside world. Moreover, there is a good deal of movement in the ground and, in spite of its lovely woodland, a large part of the course is open. The 1st hole, for example, at 464 yards, plays over a dip and the right, and open, side of its fairway

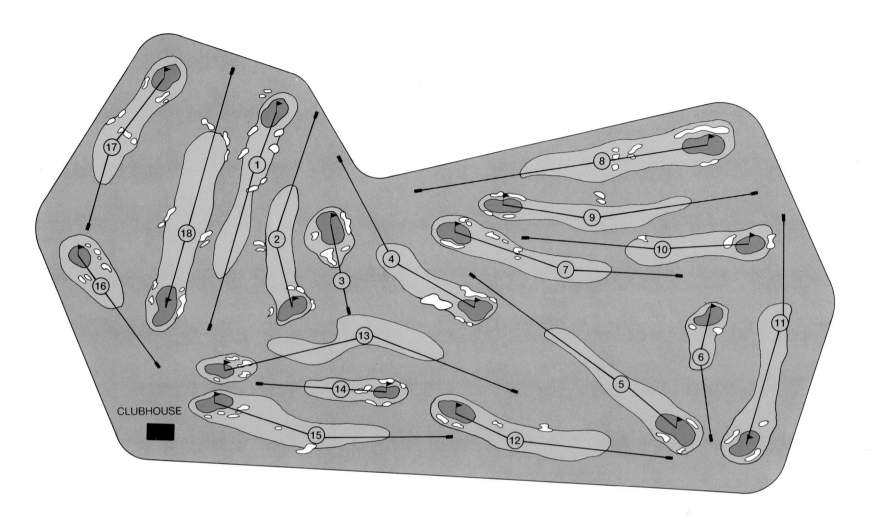

features several bunkers. The 2nd hole reverses direction and, although it turns to the left, it shares these bunkers with the first hole – there being only a narrow strip of rough between the two fairways.

On the other hand, the drive on the 4th is out of a high and narrow chute of trees – almost like the famous 18th at Augusta National. The 5th, in contrast has a completely open drive, then turns right and down a chute of trees to the green.

Chantilly's short holes are difficult, and demand very positive, precise striking. The 6th, for example, is completely screened by the forest. It is 217 yards to a green set diagonally across the shot, with bunkers front right and front left. Hole 14 is 202 yards to a green set in a little valley with two bunkers on either side; the 16th is exactly the same distance with no fewer than six bunkers scattered around it and for the majority of club members these holes demand wood shots off the tees.

Chantilly, 25 miles north of Paris, is in the heart of thoroughbred racecourse

The 14th at Chantilly, set in a tree-ringed oasis. At 202 yards it is the longest of Chantilly's par 3 holes, with a large, distracting central bunker short of the green.

	CHANTILLY	Card of the course			
1	464 yards	par 5	10	437 yards	par 4
2	327 yards	par 4	11	388 yards	par 4
3	153 yards	par 3	12	368 yards	par 4
4	359 yards	par 4	13	424 yards	par 4
5	410 yards	par 4	14	202 yards	par 3
6	217 yards	par 3	15	382 yards	par 4
7	396 yards	par 4	16	196 yards	par 3
8	576 yards	par 5	17	429 yards	par 4
9	460 yards	par 4	18	525 yards	par 5
	3,362 yards	par 36		3,361 yards	par 35
		Total 6,713 yards par 71			

country, like Olgiata (q.v.) in Rome, and it is difficult to resist calling it a thoroughbred among golf courses. Indeed, it does seem to have many of the characteristics of the courses around Ascot in England – the Berkshire, Swinley Forest, Sunningdale and Wentworth. However, despite the similarities, it undoubtedly stands on its own as one of the world's greats.

ROYAL ANTWERP

Golf in Belgium is aristocratic, of course, as it always has been on the Continent – with the exception of the resort golf that has sprung up along the coasts of Spain and Portugal. In fact, it is more than aristocratic, as Belgian golf has had the direct support of a royal family that has included active golfers for several generations. In 1906, for example, King Leopold II donated land and a country house to make possible the founding of the Royal Belgique Club at Ravenstein, near Brussels. Moreover, Leopold III was very keen and played to a high standard, while King Baudouin played his golf at the Royal Antwerp club, under the name of the Comte de Rethy, to a standard good enough to secure selection for the Belgian amateur international team.

Of Belgium's score of golf clubs, almost half of them have the 'Royal' prefix. However, no privilege is involved – when a club celebrates its 50th anniversary it qualifies automatically. Despite having no more than 5,000 golfers, this small country has some outstanding courses and the finest of these is Royal Antwerp, one of Europe's greatest courses. Founded in 1888 by six English businessmen resident in the city – then as now a huge trading post – it is the second oldest club in Europe after Pau in the French Pyrenees. Willie Park, Jr was responsible for the original 18 holes. But in 1924, Tom Simpson and Philip Mackenzie Ross, who were then in partnership, revised the 18 and added nine more.

The Royal Antwerp course is set in gorgeous woodland about 12 miles from the city. The club moved to this location after its original site – on part of an army training ground – had proved less than satisfactory. It is a beautiful piece of heathland reminiscent of Sunningdale; this means sandy subsoil, links-type turf, heather and pine and silver birch. But unlike Sunningdale, Royal Antwerp is virtually flat. However, mounding has been used here and there in the best St Andrews style.

The course plays to 7,026 yards, with a par of 73, and has several interesting

ROYAL ANTWERP Card of the course					
1	331 yards	par 4	10	416 yards	par 4
2	203 yards	par 3	11	483 yards	par 5
3	480 yards	par 5	12	183 yards	par 3
4	380 yards	par 4	13	398 yards	par 4
5	476 yards	par 5	14	477 yards	par 5
6	424 yards	par 4	15	492 yards	par 5
7	185 yards	par 3	16	146 yards	par 3
8	418 yards	par 4	17	377 yards	par 4
9	448 yards	par 4	18	394 yards	par 4
3,345 yards par 36			3,681 yards par 37		
Total 7,026 yards par 73					

design features. It has five par-5s, all of them on the short side, under 500 yards, and two of them, 14 and 15, coming in succession. Almost all the par-4s are strong holes, demanding a good range of approach iron shots, while the four par-3s become progressively shorter – from the 2nd at 203 yards, with a pair of bunkers on the left close to the line into the green, to the 16th at 146 yards, a short pop to a small green almost entirely ringed with bunkers.

However, generally there is a notice-

Willie Park, Jr, British Open champion in 1887 and 1889, was also a consumate architect of golf courses. He designed the original 18 holes at Antwerp.

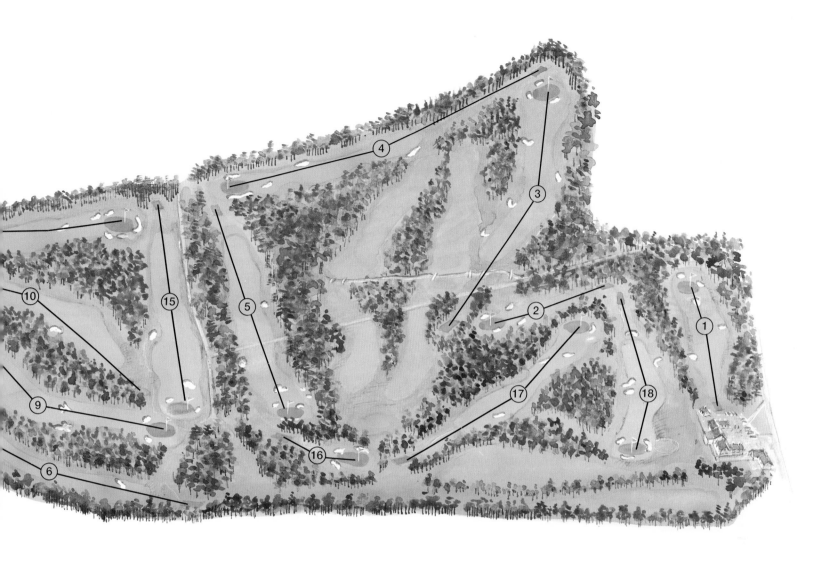

able lack of fairway bunkering at Royal Antwerp. Perhaps Simpson and Mackenzie Ross felt them to be scarcely necessary, considering the severity of the dog-legs they built into their fairways. This is a characteristic of Simpson's design work. There is one stretch, through the heart of the course from the 6th to the 14th, where each fairway breaks quite sharply, two to the right, five to the left. In this sequence there are two lovely short holes, the 7th with the ground in front of the green feeding the ball towards a bunker on the right, and the 12th, at 183 yards, protected by three bunkers, thereby putting a premium on accurate striking. Yet Royal Antwerp is not overly restricting and its woodland is neither intrusive nor claustrophobic. Altogether it is a delightful, mature, even sophisticated golf course of great charm.

Tom Simpson, in partnership with Philip Mackenzie Ross, revised the original 18 holes and added nine more. Simpson was a great believer in the dog-leg hole to which the 9th, 10th and 14th bear witness.

FALSTERBO

Falsterbo Golf Club is situated 21 miles south of Malmö, on a little finger of land prodding into the sea at Skanör, about as far south as you can go in Sweden. Just a few miles across the waters of the Öresund lies Denmark. There are three golf clubs in the area, the most famous of them being Falsterbo – a course that is almost pure links. Laid out on a flat piece of ground surrounding the old Falsterbo lighthouse, all but a few of the holes are on sandy soil, and a few (4, 5, 11 and 12) are on more marshy ground on the inland side of the course. The entire area is a nature reserve and is particularly blessed with bird life.

The course dates from 1909, when Gunnar Bauer laid out a sequence of holes which is little changed today. However, Falsterbo is not the oldest course in Sweden, a country which was slower than most in Europe – perhaps because of harsh winters and a short season – to take up the game of golf.

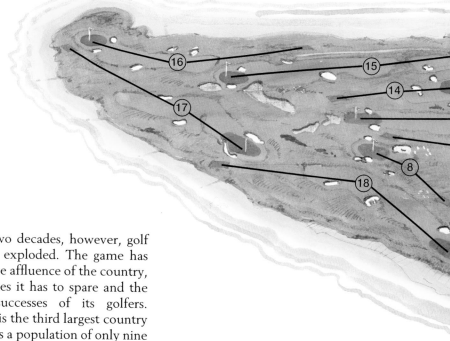

In the last two decades, however, golf in Sweden has exploded. The game has grown out of the affluence of the country, the ample spaces it has to spare and the international successes of its golfers. While Sweden is the third largest country in Europe, it has a population of only nine million. Yet the Swedish Golf Federation's coaching and support policies have brought their amateur players much international success, and several of their young professionals, notably Mats Lanner, Ove Sellberg, Magnus Persson and

FALSTERBO					
Card of the course					
1	448 yards	par 4	10	394 yards	par 4
2	175 yards	par 3	11	153 yards	par 3
3	530 yards	par 5	12	405 yards	par 4
4	427 yards	par 4	13	574 yards	par 5
5	399 yards	par 4	14	241 yards	par 3
6	186 yards	par 3	15	525 yards	par 5
7	317 yards	par 4	16	388 yards	par 4
8	191 yards	par 3	17	377 yards	par 4
9	427 yards	par 4	18	498 yards	par 5
3,100 yards	par 34		3,555 yards	par 37	
Total 6,655 yards par 71					

Anders Forsbrand, have been successful on the PGA European Tour. Major professional tournaments are now played annually in Sweden and recently the Volvo company has taken on the overall sponsorship of the European Professional Tour.

Falsterbo is almost completely exposed. There are few trees on the course, and those that are there have little influence on the play. The 1st hole requires that the golfer is ready and warmed up, for it is a

Taken from the lighthouse in the centre of the course, this picture shows the clubhouse, the 7th and 18th greens in front of it, and the open and exposed nature of the location.

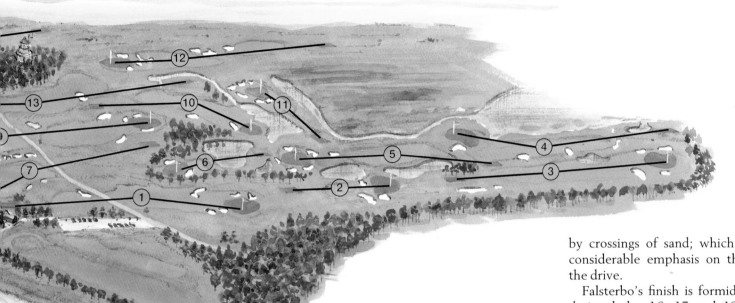

next five holes. The 11th and 12th return briefly to marshland. The 11th, at 153 yards, is a strike over the waters of an inlet all the way from tee to green, with water to the right of the green and five bunkers, no less, covering the rest of it. The 12th, at 405 yards, features two fairway 'islands' in the Pine Valley mode, separated by crossings of sand; which thus places considerable emphasis on the length of the drive.

Falsterbo's finish is formidable, and in design holes 16, 17 and 18 follow the classic oceanside layout – tee hard by the beach, fairway drifting inland then turning back, right in each case, to a green set, like the tee, hard by the beach. Each of the fairways is carefully bunkered at the angle, and each of the greens by the beach is carefully bunkered to protect the hole and distract the golfer.

stiff 448 yards, with a turn to (and an out-of-bounds) on the right, and a fairly tight entrance to the green. The 2nd is a pretty 175 yards to a small green with surrounding bunkers, but the 3rd is a long slog of 530 yards, straight out into the country. The feature here is a very large bunker placed exactly at the centre front of the green, on the premise that the shot arriving will be a high pitch – the golfer's third. For the professional player, reaching the green in two and coping with that bunker will be something of a lottery!

Holes 4 and 5 come back in the opposite direction; the 4th green being set rather close to water, the rough hereabouts being marshy reed grass. On the short 6th we are back in true heather and sand country, and stay with it for the

The 18th green and behind it the dominating feature of the course – the lighthouse. The only true linksland course in Sweden, Falsterbo is one of the finest on the Continent.

CLUB ZUR VAHR

Without being overly romantic, the Garlstedter Heide course of the Club Zur Vahr in Bremen is positively Wagnerian. Indeed, it may just be the best and most powerful course on the Continent of Europe. It stretches 7,265 yards, with a par of 74, is cut through a forest of huge pine and silver birch, and is a magnificent test of driving and longshot golf. At Garlstedt, it is not enough to drive in the fairway – the drive must be long enough to clear the angle of the many dog-legs, and it must be on the correct **side** of the fairway to allow a decent second shot. While there are few fairway bunkers, trees crowd to the very edge of the fairway and are very much an integral part of the course.

The course is part of the Club Zur Vahr, an excellent multi-sports club offering two golf courses, tennis, hockey, skeet-shooting and the like. Its origins are in a few holes played in 1895 on the racecourse at Vahr, a suburb of Bremen, the great international trading port. Foreign businessmen with local merchants teamed up to bring golf to the city, and it became part of the club in 1905. A team from Bremen had played a Berlin team in 1899 in one of the first German inter-city matches, and when Agnes Boecker von

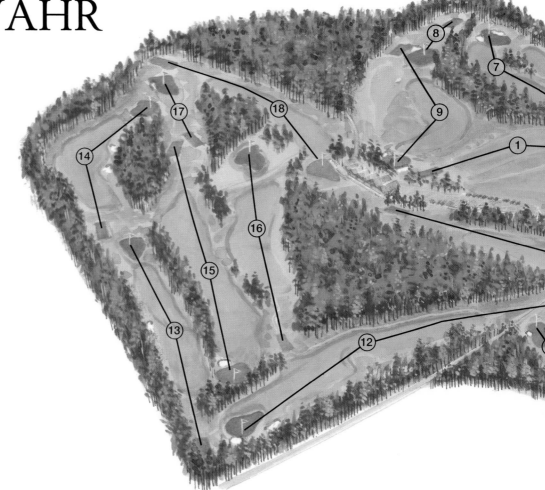

The approach to the green of the long 2nd hole, with the pond and oak tree in the middle of the fairway. Ideally, the tee shot should finish short of the stream immediately in front of the pond.

Kapff won the Danish Ladies' Championship in 1901, she became the first German golfer to hold an international title. In 1921, Dr Bernhard von Limburger won the German Amateur title at the Vahr, which still had only nine holes.

In 1945, the U.S. Army commandeered the course, but the golfers won it back in 1952 and within a few years the membership had grown so much that another course was essential. The local Weyhausen family, notably August Weyhausen who had been German Junior Champion back in 1924, found the land at Garlstedter Heide, 20 km from Bremen on the road to Bremerhaven, and Limburger, an outstanding architect and player, was put to work.

The course was officially opened in 1970, and staged its first German Open in 1971, attracting an impressive field from 23 different countries, and including Peter Thomson, Roberto de Vicenzo, Bernard Gallacher, Peter Oosterhuis, Neil Coles and many others. The cham-

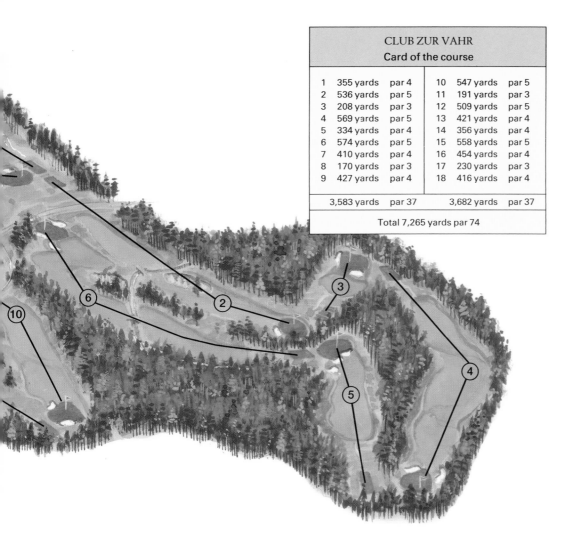

CLUB ZUR VAHR Card of the course					
1	355 yards	par 4	10	547 yards	par 5
2	536 yards	par 5	11	191 yards	par 3
3	208 yards	par 3	12	509 yards	par 5
4	569 yards	par 5	13	421 yards	par 4
5	334 yards	par 4	14	356 yards	par 4
6	574 yards	par 5	15	558 yards	par 5
7	410 yards	par 4	16	454 yards	par 4
8	170 yards	par 3	17	230 yards	par 3
9	427 yards	par 4	18	416 yards	par 4
	3,583 yards	par 37		3,682 yards	par 37
		Total 7,265 yards par 74			

fairway and a pond to the left of it. Playing boldly down the left side, to the left of the tree, will see the expert player within reach of the green in two. However, playing to the right will put him out of range. At the 6th, of 574 yards, the stream crosses the fairway again, the hole turning to the right. The player can play down the fairway in two shots, then reach the green to the right with a pitch over two bunkers covering the entrance. The alternative is to cut across the angle with his second shot, leaving a completely open line into the green. But to do that, he would have to carry over a wood!

Over the years, the sophisticated German golfers may have felt that Bremen is less accessible for championships than, say, Munich or Frankfurt. However, their Open was played there in 1975 and again in 1985. During the latter, a rainstorm flooded the course, the championship was reduced to 54 holes, the par to 66, and one kilometre was chopped off the length of the course! But all was well in the end – the winner scoring 183 – 15 under the par of the truncated course – and his name was Bernhard Langer!

West Germany's golfing superstar Bernhard Langer in action at Club Zur Vahr. He won the German Open Championship at Zur Vahr in 1985, when the tournament was reduced to 15 holes because of rain.

pionship was won by Coles with an outstanding score of 279, seventeen strokes under par, and Coles said afterwards: 'I would rate it one of the best championship courses I have played in Europe – altogether an excellent test, forcing you right to the limit all the way'. Over the four days, 6,000 spectators attended – a record at the time for a tournament in Germany.

Almost every hole on the course, save for the 1st, plays into, out of, around, across or over trees, or one single tree. Perhaps Limburger's par-5s – there are six of them – are the most fascinating of the holes; two of them almost avant-garde! The 2nd, at 536 yards, has forest hard down its left side. A stream crosses the fairway just beyond 300 yards and past that there is a tree in the middle of the

OLGIATA

With a population of around 55 million, Italy has less than 20,000 golfers, in comparison to the UK's approximately two million players. Moreover, the question arises as to just how many Italian club members actually play golf, and how many are club members for purely social reasons. In Italian society at all levels, perhaps more so than anywhere else in Europe, style is everything. Thus, and not surprisingly, the old game, with its plebian Scottish ancestry, is elevated to a patrician pastime – and the Olgiata club manifests this as much as any other.

Olgiata is set in pleasantly rolling, heavily-wooded country off the Via Cassia, 12 miles to the north of Rome. The course design and the long, low but spacious clubhouse maintain an aura of Roman elegance. The course is the work of Ken Cotton and Frank Pennink, the English designers, and an interesting pair they make. Cotton was a Cambridge graduate, a scratch golfer and secretary to various golf clubs before founding, in 1946, the golf design firm which became Cotton (CK), Pennink, Lawrie and Partners. He designed the Venice course in 1958, worked in Denmark and Singapore, and made several changes to Royal

The Spanish team of José Rivero and José-Maria Canizares flank the modest World Cup trophy after their victory over a rain-soaked Olgiata in 1984. The tournament was reduced to 54 holes.

OLGIATA Card of the course					
1	377 yards	par 4	10	396 yards	par 4
2	212 yards	par 3	11	431 yards	par 4
3	465 yards	par 4	12	427 yards	par 4
4	399 yards	par 4	13	430 yards	par 4
5	487 yards	par 5	14	170 yards	par 3
6	427 yards	par 4	15	503 yards	par 5
7	195 yards	par 3	16	202 yards	par 3
8	377 yards	par 4	17	520 yards	par 5
9	552 yards	par 5	18	427 yards	par 4
3,491 yards	par 36		3,506 yards	par 36	
Total 6,997 yards par 72					

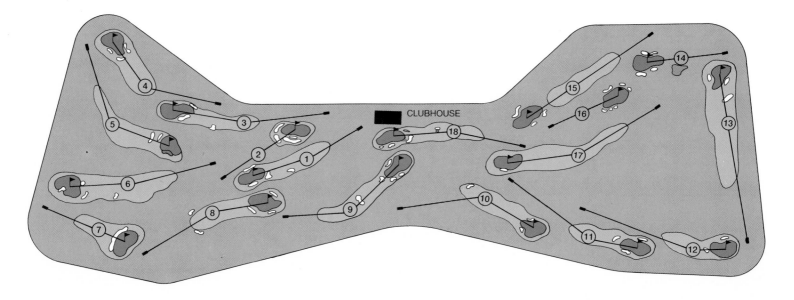

Lytham and Royal Porthcawl.

Pennink was a graduate of Oxford, won the English Amateur Championship twice and was an England international and a Walker Cup player. He had a remarkable career. For many years he concentrated on the 'overseas' commissions of the firm, working mainly outside the UK. He has a surprisingly substantial body of work to his credit and was one of the busiest international designers. One of his finest achievements, with Charles Lawrie, is the Duke's Course at Woburn, in England. He also designed both courses at Vilamoura in the Algarve, in 1969 and 1975, as well as the excellent Palmares, in 1975. And he made changes to three Royals: Liverpool (Hoylake), Lytham and St Annes and St George's.

At Olgiata Pennink and Cotton created a fine, big, mature parkland course of 6,997 yards. And within three years of its opening in 1961, the World Amateur Team championship for the Eisenhower Trophy was played there (won by Great Britain), and in 1967, the Canada Cup – which subsequently became the World Cup – was won by Al Balding and George Knudson for Canada. Balding was winner of the Individual Trophy with an aggregate of 271, 17 under par, on a course with the fire taken out of it by a good deal of rain. In 1984, Olgiata staged the World Cup again, which this time was won by Spain.

Typical of Cotton/Pennink designs are the squeezed landing zones for drives, flanked by bunkers or trees on either side of the fairway. Thus at the 4th, which turns to the right, trees standing tight on

The 16th is a longish one-shotter to a green defended by bunkers on each side. Here José-Maria Olazábal threads his tee shot between the encroaching timber in the 1989 Italian Open.

the corner push the drive to the left; and the 6th hole, at 427 yards, has a big bunker filling the left half of the fairway at the critical distance. The 8th, at 377 yards, affords the perfect example of bunkers on each side of the fairway, equidistant, squeezing it into a narrow waist. The 11th, 12th and 13th call for tee shots up to raised fairways, and the 12th green is built up and protected by a very narrow entrance. The 15th at 503 yards is one of Olgiata's few straight holes, and 17 and 18 again illustrate the Cotton/Pennink penchant for squeezing the drive with trees and/or bunkers.

Olgiata's outward and inward halves run out and back to the clubhouse, giving the course a long rectangular shape and making the golfer tackle the prevailing wind and weather from changing directions. All told, this is a splendid course that offers a tough and varied challenge in a lovely and elegant environment.

SOTOGRANDE

Sotogrande, at the western end of the Costa del Sol in Spain, and within sight of Gibraltar, was the first course in Europe to be designed by Robert Trent Jones, the outstanding architect of his time – perhaps of all time. Faced with a property of sand and scrub, wooded with cork and olive trees, which ran gently uphill away from the Mediterranean beach, Jones prompty built an 'American' golf course. That at any rate was the collective critical judgement of the hour when the course came into play in 1965.

Jones had won himself a huge reputation as a golf course architect. Born in England in 1906, he had been taken to America at the age of five, and by 1980, when he was still active, had amassed an enormous body of work – more than 400 courses in 24 countries. His courses featured very long tees, sometimes up to 80 yards, which he said gave the hole 'flexibility'. And he built huge greens, often multi-tiered, with five or six pin positions. Jones planned these pin positions into his designs as targets within the target, and one suspects he always had the great champions in mind when doing it. His

creed, expressed in one sentence, was to: 'Make it difficult for the expert to score a birdie and easy for the club player to score a bogey'. In addition, he was addicted to water hazards: thousands of cubic yards of rock and soil were excavated to make lakes, and he then used the material to make ridges and mounds. He felt that as players attacked the course, it was the architect's duty to defend it. As has been seen at Oakland Hills (q.v.), in 1951, this attitude drew the wrath of Ben Hogan, and probably many others as well.

As his fame grew, Jones' designs became more comprehensive, more expensive, and he became more and more renowned. At Sotogrande, his first problem was to grow and preserve grass in the fierce Andalusian summers. Given an ample water supply and an automatic watering system, and with sunshine and high temperatures guaranteed, Jones ex-

Sotogrande's 10th green, ringed around by five bunkers, illustrates as much as anything how expensive property developments crowd in on these courses along the Spanish coasts.

perimented and eventually decided on a strain of Bermuda grass imported from the U.S. for the fairways, while opting for 'bent' grass on the greens. Jones' success in growing grass in the local climate helped to make possible the development of the game on the Costa del Sol.

The extensive watering necessary meant that the course would 'play American' – that is, the greens would always hold the ball, and thus approach shots had to be hit firmly to the flag. The 3rd hole illustrates this clearly. It is 339 yards, a drive up towards a pair of bunkers, then a half turn left for a simple pitch. But the green is shamrock-shaped, each leaf of it covered by a bunker, thus giving a variety

SOTOGRANDE Card of the course					
1	394 yards	par 4	10	453 yards	par 4
2	527 yards	par 5	11	373 yards	par 4
3	339 yards	par 4	12	582 yards	par 5
4	235 yards	par 3	13	214 yards	par 3
5	361 yards	par 4	14	503 yards	par 5
6	517 yards	par 5	15	426 yards	par 4
7	422 yards	par 4	16	388 yards	par 4
8	199 yards	par 3	17	174 yards	par 3
9	363 yards	par 4	18	440 yards	par 4
	3,357 yards	par 36		3,553 yards	par 36
		Total 6,910 yards par 72			

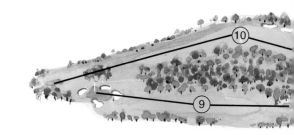

of very tight pin placements.

The first illustration of Jones' severe use of water comes at the 422-yard 7th. The second shot is slightly uphill along a narrow fairway, dog-legged left, and requiring a medium iron. The green is long and narrow, sloping from left to right down to a lake hard by its right side and supported by two right-hand bunkers. There is another bunker at the back left, under the trees, to catch a shot that is overlong. The target here is desperately tight, the margins meagre and the penalties severe.

Water is in play on at least five holes in the inward half. It is as if Jones had had visions of his work at the Augusta National! Whether he did or he didn't we will never know. But what is certain is that at Sotogrande Jones produced a beautiful and significant course.

Another illustration of Trent Jones' harsh use of water is the spectacular 7th at Sotogrande. The green, long and narrow, slopes left to right towards bunkers and lake. The hole is 422 yards, the approach shot a mid-iron.

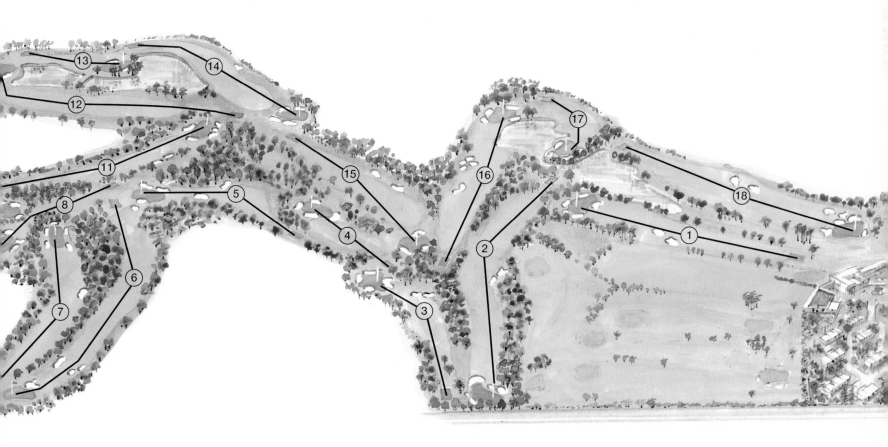

LAS BRISAS

Las Brisas follows on naturally from Sotogrande, opening as it did in 1968. Set in a valley that flows down towards Puerto Banus, a few miles from Marbella, it was a natural progression for Robert Trent Jones in Spain, and contains many of the Sotogrande/Jones features. Yet it is altogether more dramatic, more spectacular and more punishing than Sotogrande – with, for example, typical Jones' greens, which some critics have dismissed as 'unputtable'.

In the wide valley that runs out of the Sierra Blanca, with the peak of La Concha towering over the course, Jones has excavated a water course which dominates the entire golf course. It provides narrow streams, broad streams, lakes, water hazards, lateral water hazards and canals that cross directly in front of putting surfaces to snare the ball that is fractionally short. There are, needless to say, other

Jones autographs: notably, large greens with fiercely contoured slopes, huge and evil bunkering and the use of crushed marble in the bunkers, making a silvery contrast with the lush green of fairways and greens.

The clubhouse at the top of the property looks out over a descending and fairly open course; save at its lowest point, where the 12th and 13th fairways run down and the 14th and 15th run back in parallel, to form an arrowhead pointing at the sea. Here, there was deliberate planting of orange trees, olives and eucalyptus, to separate the holes and channel them into narrow fairways.

The famous 12th at Las Brisas, where architect Robert Trent Jones' penchant for the use of water is perfectly demonstrated. No matter how he tackles the hole, the golfer must twice cross a broad stream.

Jones introduces us to the water hazards at the very first hole, allowing a little spur from the main stream on the left to sneak across close to the front of the green. The 2nd hole is 425 yards, with an out-of-bounds along the right and two bunkers and some trees nipping-in the landing zone for the drive. The second shot is uphill to a positively elevated green, with five unfriendly bunkers and a very fierce slope from back to front. A downhill putt of any length is not at all certain to stay on the putting surface – vintage Jones!

The 6th requires a short pitch over a water channel and a front bunker, and there is water close to the left of the green. The 7th is the second of the four par-3 holes; the 4th and the 7th being land-locked, the two others being over water. The 8th and 12th holes are fine examples of Jones' notion of strategic

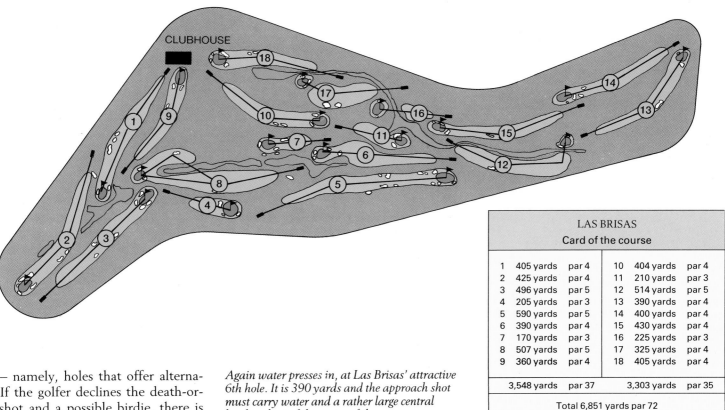

LAS BRISAS					
Card of the course					
1	405 yards	par 4	10	404 yards	par 4
2	425 yards	par 4	11	210 yards	par 3
3	496 yards	par 5	12	514 yards	par 5
4	205 yards	par 3	13	390 yards	par 4
5	590 yards	par 5	14	400 yards	par 4
6	390 yards	par 4	15	430 yards	par 4
7	170 yards	par 3	16	225 yards	par 3
8	507 yards	par 5	17	325 yards	par 4
9	360 yards	par 4	18	405 yards	par 4
3,548 yards	par 37		3,303 yards	par 35	
Total 6,851 yards par 72					

holes – namely, holes that offer alternatives. If the golfer declines the death-or-glory shot and a possible birdie, there is always a 'roundabout' route which will get him there comfortably, if at the cost of an additional stroke.

Both the 8th and 12th are par-5s. At the 8th, the drive is over a stream, which continues up the right side of a clear and ample fairway. The green is back across the water, as is a spinney of trees some way short of it. The heroic shot would be aimed over the water to the left of these trees, directly at the green. The round-about route would be over the water to the right of the trees, followed by a pitch to the putting surface. The 12th, at 514 yards, offers much the same challenge. The drive is over a stream, which this time runs along the left side, bulging into the fairway from time to time. The right side of the fairway is open, save for bunkering set to catch the over-long or faded drive. As a three-shot hole, the 12th is simple – another one along the fairway, keeping the water on the left, then a pitch across to an entirely undefended green on the other side of the water. The heroic route directly to the green, however, demands an immense shot, along and over the stream, and across a bunker by the green which Jones has placed directly on the line of flight.

Again water presses in, at Las Brisas' attractive 6th hole. It is 390 yards and the approach shot must carry water and a rather large central bunker short of the centre of the green.

The man has sometimes been considered impish to the point of being evil, and the 16th hole shows why. It is perhaps the ultimate Robert Trent Jones hole. Before it, 13, 14 and 15 are stiff, dog-legged, two-shot holes running through narrow alleyways of trees. The 16th, on the other hand, is par-3 225 yards, with the green positioned above the tee, and sloping wickedly towards the shot. Water lies at the front of the green and huge bunkers are on either side, creating difficult pin positions. This is a fearsome hole – holding the shot on the green is a major achievement – and typical of a magnificent and dramatic course that has been good enough to have held the Spanish Open and the World Cup.

VILAMOURA

When the English architect Frank Pennink was invited to design the first Vilamoura course on the Algarve in Portugal, it was to be part of a huge property and leisure development covering 4,000 acres and which, on completion, would be virtually self-contained with its own farm, airstrip, equestrian centre, marina and so on. The course was opened in 1969, at the end of a decade which had seen the opening of Faro airport and the first explosion of mass tourism on the Algarve. For the Portuguese, it was a time of much optimism. The revolution of 1974, and the years of economic instability which followed, were not foreseen. They did, however, arrive and Vilamoura stood still for a while. Now older, it boasts a second course, an impressive marina, luxury hotels and substantial and on-going property development.

Vilamoura was the third course in the Algarve, after Penina and Vale do Lobo, both designed by Henry Cotton. Pennink was given a brief to make a championship course of the quality of the better Surrey or Berkshire courses, and given a forest of umbrella pines, a few miles back from the sea, in which to do it. The plot was distinguished by a ridge – a spine – running through its centre, as though it was a transplanted King's from Gleneagles, and Pennink made the most of it, fashioning a lovely and very testing course.

Vilamoura has a par of 73 and is 6,921 yards long. The umbrella pines and cork trees are very much part of it and part of the players' interrogation. They define the margins of every fairway, encroach where necessary and, in some places, one solitary

This shot of the 9th at Vilamoura, a short par-4 of 297 yards, illustrates how the architect Pennink has squeezed the driving zone, his severe bunkering and his use of a distracting single tree on the left.

tree is positioned to affect the line of the shot. Under the trees there is no rough to speak of, nothing but beds of fallen pine needles which absorb the energy from the clubhead when recovery shots are tried. Thus, for the most part chipping out to the fairway is the most intelligent recovery shot.

Yet the trees add greatly to the pleasures of a round at Vilamoura. The umbrella pines are intrinsically lovely. They give each hole a pleasant feeling of isolation, of being divorced from care in the pleasant Portuguese sunshine. And from the top of the course there is the unexpected vista, from time to time, across the tops of this umbrella-like forest to the sea.

Pennink's greens are rather small, and although he is sparing with fairway bunkers, and certainly never uses any simply for cosmetic effect, he does tend to lavish them around the greens. This is particularly important at the par-3 holes. The

VILAMOURA Card of the course					
1	296 yards	par 4	10	176 yards	par 3
2	494 yards	par 5	11	429 yards	par 4
3	364 yards	par 4	12	536 yards	par 5
4	168 yards	par 3	13	393 yards	par 4
5	455 yards	par 4	14	504 yards	par 5
6	234 yards	par 3	15	168 yards	par 3
7	433 yards	par 4	16	570 yards	par 5
8	469 yards	par 4	17	393 yards	par 4
9	297 yards	par 4	18	542 yards	par 5
	3,210 yards	par 35		3,711 yards	par 38
	Total 6,921 yards par 73				

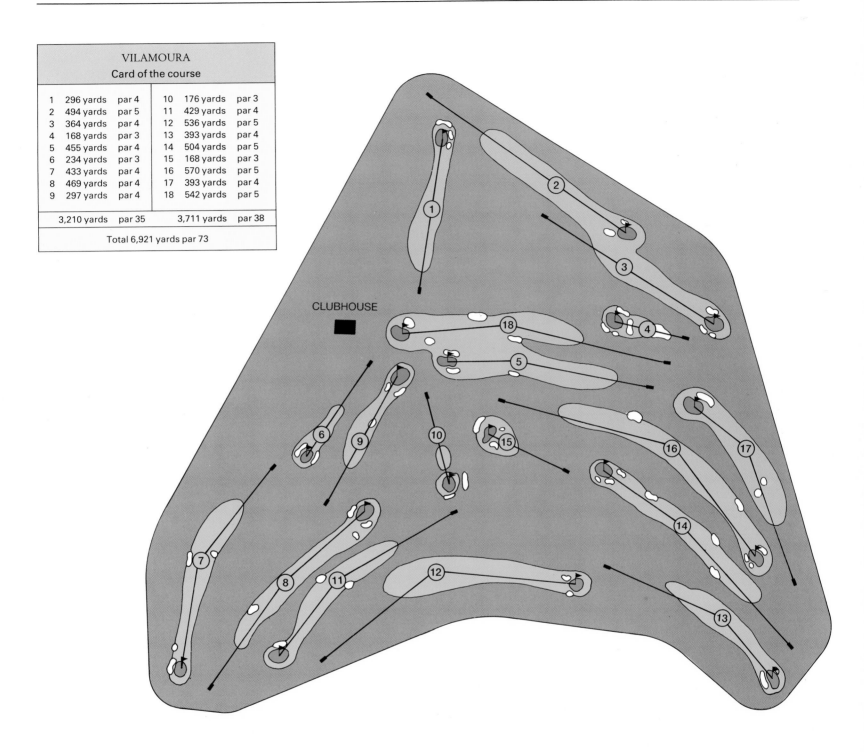

CLUBHOUSE

4th, at 168 yards, is immensely difficult for a hole of that length. The shot is over a lake, a handful of trees insinuate themselves from the right, almost cutting off the line, and the rather turtle-backed green has bunkers left and behind. The 10th at 176 yards seems unprotected, but an unseen depression – a Portuguese Valley of Sin – lies in front of the green. Anything slightly overhit here will be in the trees.

There are two very short par-4s on the outward half. The 1st, at 296 yards, is a downhill dogleg to the left, and the 9th, at 297 yards, is uphill. The temptation to go for the big drive on each of them is hard to resist, but very dangerous. Two trees in the fairway at the 9th, for example, push the drive to the left of the line. Indeed trees are used in this fashion at holes 7, 8, 9, 16 and 17. The inward half, with four par-5 holes, is very testing.

The 16th, at 570 yards, is a great hole which turns to the right from the tee with the landing area constricted by a rather big bunker on the left and trees coming out into the fairway on the right. The green, slightly downhill, is all but smothered by two of Pennink's biggest bunkers. All told, an outstanding golf hole and an outstanding golf course – but if you cannot drive the ball straight you had better stay at home!

REST OF THE WORLD

The old game, which spread from Scotland to England in the second half of the 19th century, was packed in the baggage of regiments and administrators sent abroad in the service of Empire. The Scottish regiment, The Black Watch, was largely responsible for the creation of Lahinch, the stupendous Irish links. Another Highland regiment, the Argyll and Sutherland Highlanders, with the Royal Engineers, started golf in Hong Kong. Sir James Fergusson, the Scottish governor of South Australia, brought golf to Adelaide in 1869.

Thus by the turn of the century, many clubs had been formed in South Africa, India (Royal Calcutta was the first club outside Britain, in 1829), Australia and New Zealand. They followed, by and large, the British pattern of being golf clubs only, no matter how well-appointed, rather than the ornate, all-embracing 'country club', which was favoured and developed in the U.S.

The development of golf in Japan has been phenomenal. It developed first from the long U.S. military occupation of the country following the Second World War and second, from the remarkable triumph of home professionals 'Pete' Nakamura and Kiochi Ono in the Canada (now World) Cup event of 1957. It brought golf in Japan bounding into the 20th century. Now millions of Japanese play or follow the game. Japan is a leader in the manufacture of golf clubs and balls. So precious is land in Japan that architects and constructors literally move mountains to build courses, and the game is enormously expensive.

The 18th green and fairway of one of Japan's foremost clubs, Fujioka. The Japanese attention to detail is very evident in the manicured quality of the course.

KASUMIGASEKI

The first course of the Kasumigaseki Golf Club, some 25 miles from Tokyo, was opened in 1929. It was 'reborn' in 1957, when it was the venue for probably the most significant sports event ever held in the Far East, with greater consequences even than the Tokyo Olympics of 1960, or the Seoul Olympics of 1988 – namely, the Canada Cup tournament, which was won for the first time by Japan. Ever since then, Kasumigaseki has been the most famous club in the country.

Japan's victory in the Canada Cup,

Canada Cup 1957. From right: Torakichi ('Pete') Nakamura and Koichi Ono (winners), Frank Pace, Jr (IGA President) and Dave Thomas and Dai Rees of Wales. The Japanese pair were the only players to master the course.

more recently named the World Cup, made national heroes of its players, Torakichi 'Pete' Nakamura and Koichi Ono, and sparked off a golfing boom that has continued ever since. Now there may be as many as 10 million golfers in a total population of 100 million! The Japan Golf Association has registered 1,500,000 players and 1,300 courses, but many more 'play' only at driving ranges, such is the shortage of courses because of lack of land. Sadly, only the well-to-do can afford to pay, with the average price of a club membership standing at more than

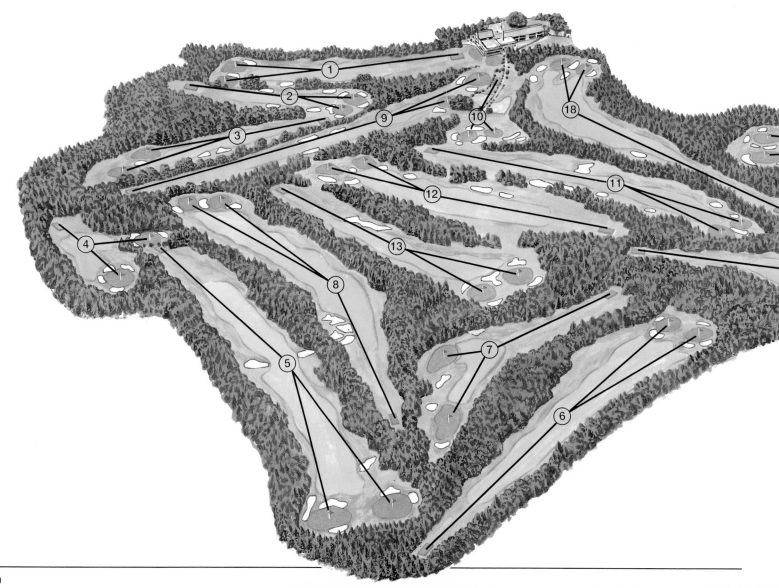

£100,000. This means that most memberships are held by corporations and are regarded as investments. Indeed, there is now a market in these memberships, with 50 traders buying and selling in Tokyo and Osaka. It is all a far cry from the economics of golf in Scotland!

Kinya Fujita's Vision

Nakamura and Ono are responsible for all of this. They conquered the world of golf – the U.S. team was Sam Snead and Jimmy Demaret, and players of the calibre of Gary Player, Roberto de Vicenzo and Dave Thomas were in the field – and they did it through their putting. Nakamura with 274 was 14 under par, Ono with 283 was five under par, and the rest, on the greens, were nowhere. And thereby hangs a tale, a tale of the two-green golf hole and the Japanese talent for lateral thinking.

The Kasumigaseki course was designed

Scotland's Eric Brown tees off at the 1st hole during the 1957 Canada Cup. Kasumigaseki's decorative trees, shrubs and flowers receive the same devoted attention as the greens and fairways.

by Kinya Fujita, of a wealthy banking family and a graduate student at the Universities of Chicago and Columbia. He spent some time in America with a silk-importing business, then back in Japan he met Hugh Alison, who was laying out the Tokyo Golf Club course in 1914. Fujita, a talented golfer, became intrigued with course design, and after the war, in 1919, travelled to Britain to study design techniques. Back again in Japan, he organised the Kasumigaseki club and laid out the course. It opened in 1929, but within a couple of years Fujita called Alison in to make a few changes. He introduced some deep bunkering –

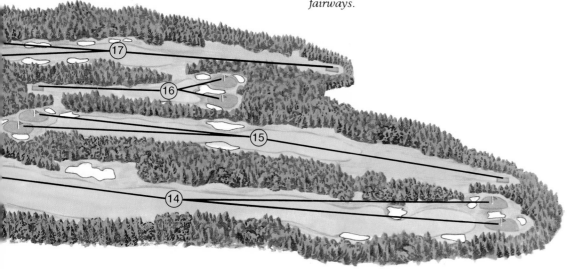

KASUMIGASEKI					
Card of the course					
1	388 yards	par 4	10	180 yards	par 3
2	374 yards	par 4	11	433 yards	par 4
3	422 yards	par 4	12	468 yards	par 4
4	158 yards	par 3	13	375 yards	par 4
5	532 yards	par 5	14	593 yards	par 5
6	372 yards	par 4	15	433 yards	par 4
7	220 yards	par 3	16	173 yards	par 3
8	474 yards	par 4	17	349 yards	par 4
9	532 yards	par 5	18	483 yards	par 5
	3,472 yards	par 36		3,487 yards	par 36
	Total 6,959 yards par 72				

which the Japanese had never seen – and to this day, they call a deep bunker an 'Arison'.

The extremes of the Japanese climate created problems on the greens. During the cold season, rye and bent grasses, such as are used in Great Britain and the northern states of America, were fine in Japan, but they could not survive the hot summers – they simply withered away. Korai grass, a stronger version of Bermuda grass, is dormant in winter, but thrives during the hot weather. Its blade is broader, tougher and sharper than its bent grass counterpart, and it is ideal for fairways. The ball sits-up on its spiky points offering a perfect lie. Run your palm over Korai grass and you feel as though it is cutting you. However, on the greens it is the devil to putt. When the pace starts to leave a putt and the line of the ball starts to break, the grain in the Korai grass will make the ball turn to such an extent that on a longer putt the ball will be rolling at right angles to its original line! Korai grain simply goes in all directions. The wily orientals had the world by the tail. Nakamura and Ono knew Korai grass backwards!

Two Greens

To solve this 'problem', the Japanese simply built two greens for each hole – one for winter use, one for summer use. The greens are invariably side by side, although sometimes one behind the other. They share the common drive, then the second shot will be slightly to the right or slightly to the left, depending on which green is in play. This has had an obvious effect on Japanese golf architecture; many holes featuring a bunker or mound to the left of the left hand green, a bunker or mound to the right of the right hand green and a bunker or mounds, or both, separating the greens, but common to both, as it were. All of this, plus the scarcity of good land and the consequent use of hilly or inferior plots, has done little for design and there has been some uninspired course construction. Japanese laws have been very protective of agricultural land, and golf course designers have often had to work with rather banal terrain.

Kasumigaseki, in contrast, was built on

Above: *The 10th has alternative tees, ponds and greens, divided by a line of trees. This is the view from the right-hand tee to a green formidably bunkered at front, back and sides.*

Left: *Kasumigaseki's huge clubhouse, behind the 9th green on the East Course. The picture also illustrates the deep 'Arison' bunker, and the well turned-out caddie, Japanese style.*

View from behind the 10th hole to the tee. This 180-yard par 3 is one of the finest in Asia.

nicely rolling farmland before these restrictions existed. It is also pleasantly wooded. A second course has been built to cope with its 2,000 members, and a ground staff of 200, many of them women, cosset the place as though it were a private garden. Benefitting from the talent the Japanese have for landscaping, the courses are immaculate.

The flowers and the flowering shrubs as well as the ponds, paths and golf courses are all carefully tended. But perhaps the most striking feature of Fujita's East Course is the size and depth and shape of the bunkers, filled with shining silver sand. Charles Hugh Alison was a very talented architect. His notion that a bunker could be deeper than a standing man – commonplace in the west – intrigued the Japanese and was copied throughout the country. Alison's creed was that if a golfer played down the straight and narrow he should not be compromised by trick hazards, and the result is that Kasumigaseki is a fair, honest, open course.

Up and Down in Two

At 6,959 yards, with a par of 72, the course takes a good deal of playing. Nakamura and Ono were not long hitters. Indeed, technically their swings left a lot to be desired. But in putting, and in the short game in general, from 100 yards in to the pin, they were outstanding. Nakamura holed four bunker shots during that 1957 Canada Cup, and *never once* failed to get up and down in two strokes from greenside bunkers. Given the nature of those bunkers, that was a truly remarkable feat. For example, the short 10th hole, at 180 yards, is really two holes in parallel; two tees, two greens, and two lakes to carry, divided by a slender line of trees and the hole in play depending on the season of the year. This is where Alison first surprised his hosts and the foreign teams competing in the Canada Cup with deep bunkering short of the green of the day. Similarly, the 14th features huge bunkers at 250 yards from the tee, huge bunkers 40 yards short of the green, and huge bunkers around both greens. They proved too much for everyone other than Nakamura and Ono, and understandably Kasumigaseki remains to this day the pride of Nippon.

FUJIOKA

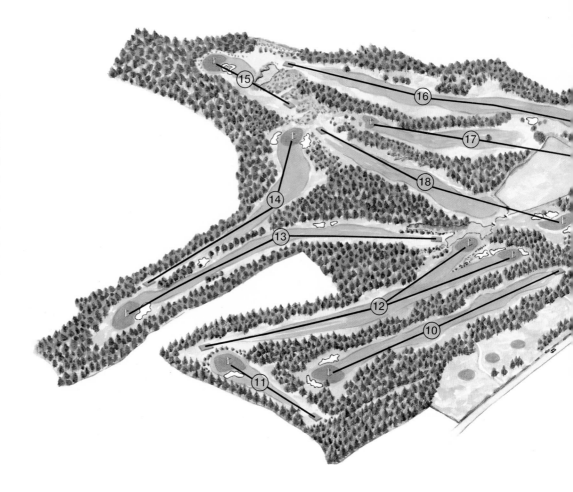

The Fujioka Country Club, near Nagoya, one of Japan's great manufacturing cities, was opened in 1971 and was a look into the future. It introduced lakes and water on a scale never before seen in Japan and it dispensed with the 'two-green' golf holes of Kasumigaseki and other older Japanese clubs. It featured a double green (shared by the 4th and 7th holes) and the fairways were laid with turf in only five months, and as many as 6,000 workers constructed the entire course, which was completed in a year.

The owner of the land, Furukawa, had the notion to build a course that would have the best of modern design, be up to the best international standards, but which would somehow dam the frenzied flood of golf in Japan, of huge clubs with huge clubhouses and huge memberships. His plan was to hold the Fujioka membership to less than 500.

The land was made up in part of pine forests and a tea plantation and there was a large natural lake. A local man, Tameshi Yamada was for some reason appointed the golf course architect. Little is known of him, or of any other work he may have done. However, to advise him, and no doubt to capitalise on the name, Peter Thomson, five times Open champion and winner of 75 professional events around the world, was hired as a consultant. Thomson brought with him, as a 'consultant to the consultant', Mike Wolveridge, an Englishman who had played for a spell on the U.S. professional tour before turning to design work with John Harris. Wolveridge had done excellent work in many countries and by 1980, when he and Thomson were in full partnership, their firm was by far the most active in the Pacific basin.

The Fujioka land had a lot of movement in it, and the design group produced many distinctive holes and distinctive features. More than 40 years on from the work at Kasumigaseki the agronomists had developed a finer strain of Korai grass good for year-round use, so that a normal one-green-per-one-hole system was adopted, save for the 12th hole.

Yamada, with encouragement from the cerebral Thomson-Wolveridge pairing, had done imaginative things with water; Japanese golf architects, unlike their gardeners, have generally been uncomfortable with the use of water. The question mark hanging over the 12th hole was: could they place the green hard by the water, as for example at the 11th hole of the Augusta National course in Georgia?

In the event, there was a compromise. They built two greens, one by the lake and one off to the right at the end of a straight fairway. There is also water at the short 2nd, where it must be carried, and to the left of the fairway at the 3rd.

Moving on, there is a lake to be carried with the drive on 13, a par-5, but at the

At the 395-yard 17th, the drive – one of the four over water at Fujioka – requires a carry of 200 yards to a point on the fairway that opens up the green to the approach shot.

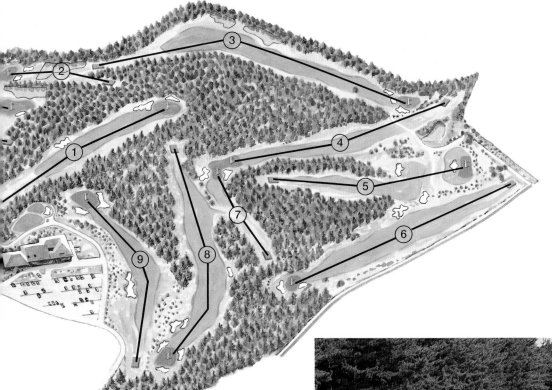

FUJIOKA Card of the course					
1	400 yards	par 4	10	400 yards	par 4
2	190 yards	par 3	11	165 yards	par 3
3	540 yards	par 5	12	440 yards	par 4
4	420 yards	par 4	13	550 yards	par 5
5	350 yards	par 4	14	370 yards	par 4
6	445 yards	par 4	15	190 yards	par 3
7	195 yards	par 3	16	605 yards	par 5
8	500 yards	par 5	17	395 yards	par 4
9	385 yards	par 4	18	430 yards	par 4
	3,425 yards	par 36		3,545 yards	par 36
	Total 6,970 yards par 72				

Fujioka's 18th is a par 4 of 430 yards which runs down a long, narrow undulating fairway, with solitary pines encroaching and a brook crossing some 50 yards short of a raised green.

short 15th the water is merely decorative. However, this hole sports a massive frontal bunker, artistically shaped, with an island of fairway in the centre, its outline copying exactly the outline of the bunker. It is as big as the green itself, and quite beautiful. This is followed by a quite monstrous par-5 16th, at 605 yards, calling for a uphill drive and a long second shot over a rise before the green, guarded by water and sand, comes into view.

Mercifully, one of the delights of Fujioka is the absence of superfluous fairway bunkering. Often a single pine tree, or the movement in the fairway itself, is just as effective. Fujioka's 17th makes the point. It is 395 yards with a carry of 200 yards on the drive across the biggest of Fujioka's lakes. This brings the player to a fairway on two levels, the line of fall being marked by a pine tree, and a split level green ahead to contend with. Positioning of the shots is all. Indeed, it is a rather sophisticated hole on a sophisticated and lovely golf course.

ROYAL CALCUTTA

Royal Calcutta is the oldest golf club in the world, outside of the British Isles. It dates from 1829, when the British Empire was still expanding, and epitomises to some extent that particularly British institution – the gentleman's club. There is some evidence that Scottish troops were involved in the creation of what was originally called the Dum-Dum Golf Club; and since Scots are inclined to the view that a golf course can be built anywhere, and that every golf club has a bar, then this was probably both a club and a golf club!

Royal Calcutta has had a chequered history. It moved from its original home at Dum-Dum, where Calcutta's international airport now functions, and after various moves settled in its present location in the southern suburbs of the teeming city of Calcutta, towards the end of last century. At first the club had 36 holes of golf, but after Indian independence in the late 1940s, the club released 18 holes of land which it could no longer afford to the Bengal government. However, it remains the doyen of India's near-100 clubs, and although Royal Calcutta has no particular authority, the other clubs accept its patriarchal position.

Calcutta's climate is classified as 'monsoon forest', which means simply that it is hot and humid. Royal Calcutta is unlikely to inflict bad bounces on the innocent or have him cry: 'It's not fair, it's not fair!' The greens will be reasonably holding, the fairways will be quite soft, and most of the time there will be not much run on

The splendid clubhouse of Royal Calcutta, home of the oldest golf club outside Britain. The flat course, moderately bunkered, is dominated by its tanks (ponds) and massive trees.

the ball. True, there is a dry season – from December to May – but the course's 7,177 yards on the par 73 championship card can look overwhelming given the lack of run.

One of Calcutta's most prominent features is the huge tees, some 70 yards long or more. The tees and greens are in fact the highest points on a flat course that is basically no more than a few feet above the level of the Hooghly river. Nevertheless, the existence of these raised tees and greens points up the single most striking feature of the Royal Calcutta course – the 'tanks'. The tanks are simply lakes or ponds which are used for the storage of water and are also part of an integrated system of channels and run-off drains which cope with the monsoon rains. The tanks dominate the course, and the soil excavated from them was used to make the raised tees and greens. They number

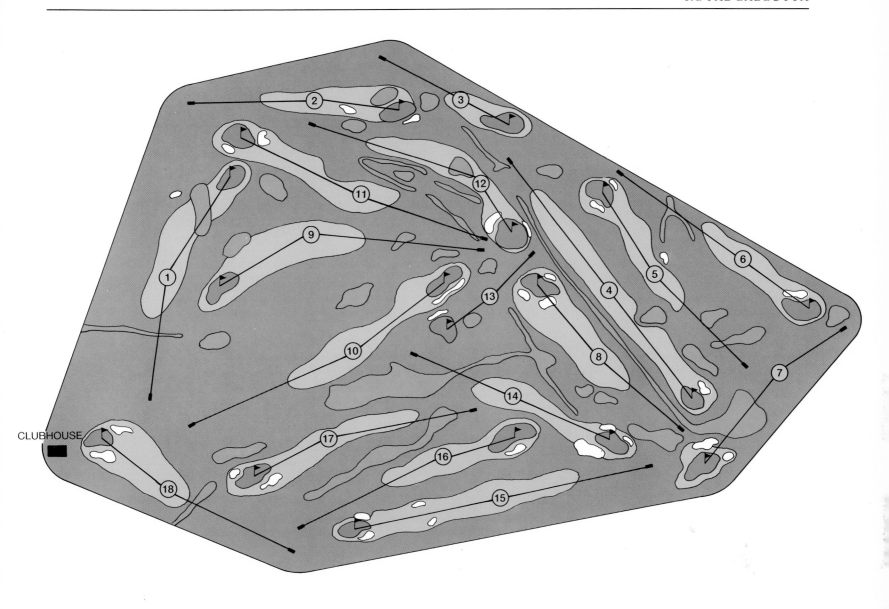

almost 30 and seem to be in play on every hole: one covers the entire fairway in front of the very first green.

Calcutta's tanks have another function in life: they also serve as swimming pools for small boys, who dive for golf balls; and their mothers often use the tanks for washing clothes, children and themselves. Such is India. The tanks take the place of many fairway bunkers, although the greenside bunkers at Royal Calcutta are very large and prettily patterned. At the 2nd hole, for example, five tanks are in the vicinity, none on the fairway, but all visible and all distracting.

However, it is the 7th hole that offers the best example of how water impinges on the strategy of play. The hole is a par-4 of 455 yards. The tee is set in a far corner of the course, behind the 6th green. The

ROYAL CALCUTTA					
Card of the course					
1	366 yards	par 4	10	448 yards	par 4
2	156 yards	par 3	11	508 yards	par 5
3	436 yards	par 4	12	359 yards	par 4
4	525 yards	par 5	13	187 yards	par 3
5	415 yards	par 4	14	431 yards	par 4
6	418 yards	par 4	15	493 yards	par 5
7	455 yards	par 4	16	364 yards	par 4
8	401 yards	par 4	17	374 yards	par 4
9	404 yards	par 4	18	437 yards	par 4
3,576 yards	par 36		3,601 yards	par 37	
Total 7,177 yards par 73					

hole turns to the left and the drive must carry over a tank in front of the tee, but should stop short of another which crosses the width of the fairway at the 250

yard mark. This tank is some 100 yards across. Finally, the green is protected by a large bunker front right and a smaller one front left. This is a challenging hole, calling for some restraint on the drive followed by a very long second shot. Perhaps the hole has a hint of the Robert Trent Jones about it – though it may be more penal than that as there are few alternative choices; certainly not on that second shot!

But perhaps Royal Calcutta's most significant feature and lasting achievement was its demonstration that grass – in this case dhoob grass, a type of Bermuda – could grow and be maintained in India; indeed in tropical and sub-tropical climates generally. That has encouraged the spread and growth of golf in dozens of countries around the world.

ROYAL HONG KONG

Golf travelled with the British Empire; with its regiments, its administrators and its businessmen. Golf came to Hong Kong in 1889, to Happy Valley on Hong Kong Island where a happy band of enthusiasts tackled an early nine holes. Their 'architect' was Captain R. E. Dumbleton of the Royal Engineers, who was not allowed to build greens or tees, or even dig the holes. The flat and open space, hard to come by on a hilly island, was shared by other sports, including polo, so, therefore, Dumbleton's 'holes' were of necessity portable granite setts – the golfer having to hole out by striking the setts with his ball.

Within a few years the club had 100 members and moved to another site on the south of the island, at Deep Water Bay, where nine holes could be squeezed out of flatland by the shore. Access was gained by sailing around the island! However, the island was soon not big enough to handle the growth in membership, and the search was on for more land to accommodate a 'proper' golf course or two. It was found at Fanling, close to the Chinese border, and what came to be known as the 'Old Course' was built in the early years of the century. Getting there meant adventurous journeys involving walking, rickshaws and

Golf is rarely played in a more beautiful setting than that of Royal Hong Kong, set against the mountains of China. The Championship course is made up of holes from the New Course, built in 1931, and the Eden, completed 40 years later.

launches. However, the railway from Kowloon to the border was opened in 1911 and by 1923, with a club membership of 800, it was time to expand the club again.

The committee proposed building a second 18 holes, which were constructed by one L. S. Greenhill and opened in 1931. It was a more spacious course than the Old, being considered an 'American'-style layout with a meadowland flavour, particularly on the inward half. Not surprisingly the expatriates persuaded themselves that the Old had more of the feel and taste of the Berkshire courses 'back home' in England!

The Japanese occupation from 1941 to 1945 saw the courses neglected and it took several years to return them to

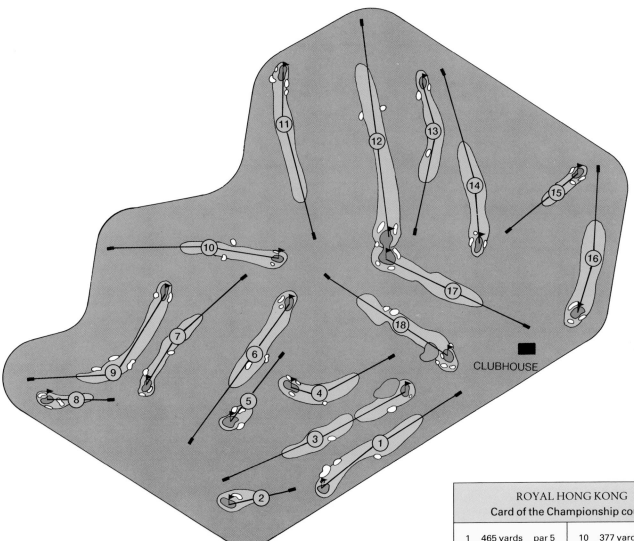

CLUBHOUSE

Card of the Championship course

1	465 yards	par 5	10	377 yards	par 4
2	155 yards	par 3	11	469 yards	par 4
3	520 yards	par 5	12	525 yards	par 5
4	295 yards	par 4	13	400 yards	par 4
5	198 yards	par 3	14	426 yards	par 4
6	425 yards	par 4	15	191 yards	par 3
7	385 yards	par 4	16	409 yards	par 4
8	192 yards	par 3	17	412 yards	par 4
9	488 yards	par 5	18	417 yards	par 4

3,123 yards	par 36	3,626 yards	par 36

Total 6,749 yards par 72

normal – until 1953, in fact. But by the early 1960s, the 36 holes of the Old and New courses could not handle the demand and the Royal Hong Kong was expanded yet again. Some adjoining land was bought from the Jockey Club next door, and to the design of John Harris and Mike Wolveridge, and under Wolveridge's supervision, a new course was built in 1963.

The new course was named the Eden, after the third course at St Andrews, and features a rather lavish use of water. On 16 of the holes water, in the shape of streams, storm channels and lakes, is on view, if not entirely in play. Fanling sits in a basin with ridges around the sides, and is a network of fairways, little knolls, stretches of rice paddies and screens of eucalyptus and casuarinas; and all around it Chinese country life goes on.

Within the picturesque setting, the Eden is the shortest of the three courses, but it is modern in design – its greens raised to allow for monsoon run-off – and full of character. The composite course, marrying holes from the Eden and the New, is used exclusively for international championship events. The Hong Kong Open, played annually in late February, attracts an international field. In 1987 the top four places went to visiting 'Brits' Ian Woosnam, Sam Torrance, David Feherty and Ronan Rafferty.

Nowadays the main concern of Royal Hong Kong and its golfers is the concern of the entire colony – namely, 1997 and the attitude of Communist China when it takes control. What will they make of the decadent, bourgeois, capitalist game of golf? They have allowed Arnold Palmer to build a course in their people's Republic, in the Canton area, with Japanese funding. So, perhaps they are beginning to realise the value of this international game – and hopefully Royal Hong Kong will continue to prosper, as will the colony it serves.

SINGAPORE ISLAND

The Singapore Island Country Club is one of the wonders of golf. It has four big courses and a membership of 7,000, at least 2,000 of whom are active golfers. It is an equatorial Pinehurst or St Andrews. That all this should happen in Singapore, one of the world's smallest nation states (224 square miles!), makes it all the more wonderful. Today's Country Club exists from an amalgamation, in 1963, of the Royal Singapore Golf Club and the Royal Island Golf Club, which in turn have their origins in the founding of the Singapore Sporting Club in 1842.

In 1891 a group of members met to form a golf club, officially started that year with nine holes in the region of the old racecourse and named, simply, the Singapore Golf Club. By 1920, John Sime, a prominent member of the club, had the idea that they should have a proper 18-hole course well away from the restrictions of the growing city. Thus in 1921, a 258 acre site in the jungle by the MacRitchie reservoir was leased to the

club for $1.00 per annum and the original Bukit Timah course was open for play in 1924, having been designed by James Braid – who disliked travelling, so never visited Singapore and designed the course by mail from topographical maps! The jungle clearance was a massive undertaking, but the course was left with a British flavour – English trees were planted.

Members who chose not to go to the Bukit (the word means 'hill') formed the Island Club, which opened in 1932. Both clubs prospered until the Japanese occupation in the 1940s, when much of the ground became farmland and the Japanese forced many members, imprisoned in Changi Gaol, into work gangs to build a road across the courses to a new Shinto shrine they were erecting. After

The well-bunkered 7th green of the Bukit course overlooks the reservoir. Beyond it, dense jungle grows to the water's edge.

the war had ended, the Singapore club, appointed Royal in 1938, reopened in 1947. The Island club took longer to recover, but by 1952 it was functioning again and had also been appointed Royal. Things went so well for the Islanders that they were able to stage the first Singapore Open in 1961.

In 1963, the two clubs merged. The Royal Singapore Golf Club and the Royal Island Golf Club became, simply the Singapore Island Country Club, and in 1968 the Island course and the Bukit course were revised by Frank Pennink. The Bukit was to be the first club in South-East Asia to stage the World Cup, which it did in 1969 – the U.S. team of Orville Moody and Lee Trevino winning the title. And in 1970, the New course, by John Harris and Pennink, was opened.

This splendid club now has four courses: the Bukit at 6,690 yards (the parent course); the Island at 6,365 yards; the New at 6,874 yards, and the Sime at 6,314 yards. The Bukit course, the most

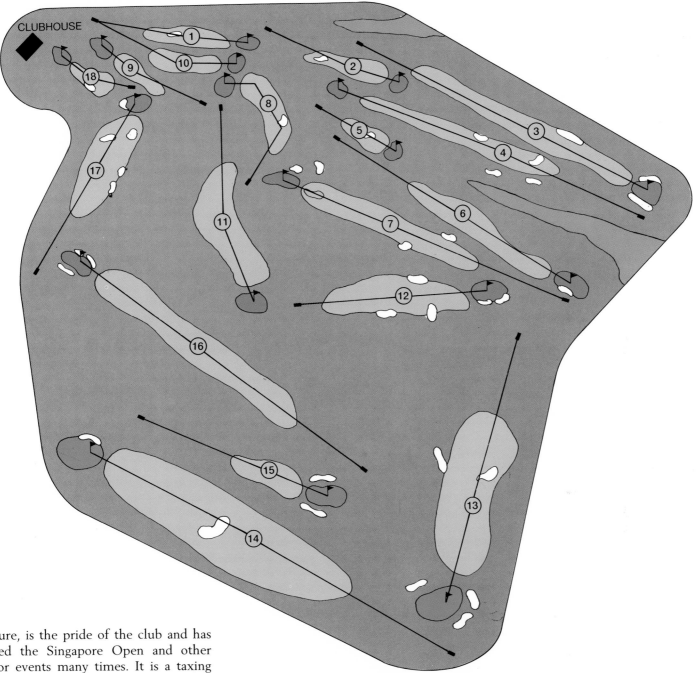

mature, is the pride of the club and has staged the Singapore Open and other major events many times. It is a taxing course in the Singapore climate, particularly from the back tees. (Singapore, so close to the equator, is hot and humid most of the year.) And Bukit has plenty of rolling, dipping fairways which demand good judgement.

Greenkeeping, too, has its challenges. Hot sun and ample water from the reservoirs mean that there is never any lack of growth – the nearby jungle is testament to that – but controlling it is the game. The greens are on a clay base and seeded, like the fairways, with a strain of Bermuda grass which gives good pos-

itive lies on the fairways but which, used on the greens as it is, can force the ball to break away from the line. Putting on Bermuda, or any of its varieties, demands a firmer stroke at the ball.

The Singapore Island club has much in common with Royal Hong Kong – large membership, four courses, more than comfortable clubhouses – all legacies of the British. But most of all, they are both marvellous refuges from the stresses and tensions of high-voltage life in these two dynamic island-states.

SINGAPORE ISLAND Card of the Bukit course			
1	407 yards par 4	10	379 yards par 4
2	205 yards par 3	11	425 yards par 4
3	408 yards par 4	12	223 yards par 3
4	537 yards par 5	13	563 yards par 5
5	175 yards par 3	14	191 yards par 3
6	448 yards par 4	15	501 yards par 5
7	449 yards par 4	16	429 yards par 4
8	366 yards par 4	17	132 yards par 3
9	364 yards par 4	18	488 yards par 5
3,359 yards par 35		3,331 yards par 36	
Total 6,690 yards par 71			

ROYAL SELANGOR

The Royal Selangor Golf Club in Kuala Lumpur, the capital of Malaysia, can boast of one 'outside agency' that makes Northern Ireland and the West of Scotland seem like drought zones. It is rain – as much as 160 inches of it in a year! It affects all the 10 million inhabitants of the country, of course, but it does create particular problems for golf greenkeepers when you consider the heat and humidity which come with it.

But such trivia never really fazed your honest golf player, and Royal Selangor has been blessed with these ever since 30 keen fellows started the club in 1893 at Petaling Hills, just outside the city. Only once in all that time has the club moved – surprising in the East when one considers the rapid growth of the cities. The move took place in 1918, when the government of the State of Selangor took over the Petaling Hills land for a building project, and in return provided a new course and clubhouse for the club. By 1921 nine holes of golf and the new clubhouse were in place. And in 1931 the 18 holes which later came to be known as the Old course, were ready for the approval of Harry Colt, the famous English architect, who made some minor changes.

The Japanese occupation of 1941–5 was a disaster for the club. There was no

The open nature of Selangor can be seen in this photograph of the 18th fairway (with the 1st fairway to the right).

ROYAL SELANGOR Card of the Old course					
1	428 yards	par 4	10	467 yards	par 4
2	405 yards	par 4	11	422 yards	par 4
3	512 yards	par 5	12	391 yards	par 4
4	164 yards	par 3	13	488 yards	par 5
5	346 yards	par 4	14	207 yards	par 3
6	463 yards	par 4	15	579 yards	par 5
7	187 yards	par 3	16	351 yards	par 4
8	388 yards	par 4	17	147 yards	par 3
9	493 yards	par 5	18	435 yards	par 4
	3,386 yards	par 36		3,487 yards	par 36
	Total 6,873 yards par 72				

damage to the clubhouse – it was used as a command headquarters by the Japanese Army – but the course was devastated. But Selangor had a remarkable man in Tom Verity, the professional appointed in 1937, who served the club for 27 years. He and the members got down to work, and within a couple of years the club was back in some kind of trim. Nowadays it

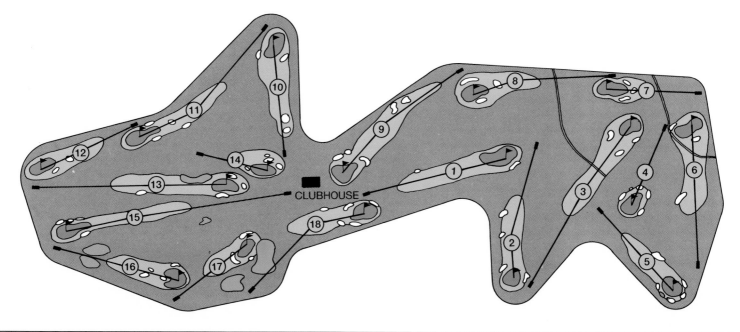

can handle hundreds of people, with its golf, Olympic pool, a dozen lawn tennis and squash courts, and comprehensive restaurant facilities.

The course is quite flat, a definite advantage in the Kuala Lumpur climate, and is also lush and beautiful. Grass here, as in all tropical and sub-tropical climates, has been both a problem and a challenge. Various types of rough grasses and Bermuda strains have been tried and tested to the point where the course now uses a finer grass, albeit a type of Bermuda. All the greens are mounded to throw off rain in the violent storms that are commonplace, and concrete-lined water channels cross several fairways. The shapes and contours of these greens call for much more chipping than is normal, since approach shots that are in the least bit

All the greens at Royal Selangor are domed to some extent to allow rainwater run-off in the monsoon. This and the subtle contours of many of the greens enforces accurate chipping.

sloppy will run off the putting surfaces.

The flatness of the course suggests that it will be easier than your average championship test. But it stretches to 6,873 yards, with a par of 72, and the very first hole shows it is no push-over. It is a flat and straight 428 yards to an open green with only one bunker along its right side. But judging distance on the second shot and holding the ball on the green is a good deal more difficult than it may look. Indeed, the start of Selangor is perhaps more challenging than the finish.

The use of water is concentrated on the

inward half, with lakes in play at 13 (where a drainage ditch crosses about 100 yards short of the green), 15, 16, 17 and 18. The 17th is a lovely short hole of 147 yards, played out of a grove of trees and over a lake, water lilies and all. And the 18th is an intriguing finishing hole. At 435 yards, it asks for a drive across a big lake, with trees on the right closing the route across the corner of the dog-leg. From the fairway, a bunker on the left has to be ignored, and a way found into a green with a rather narrow entrance and two bunkers tightening up the right hand side.

With holes such as these it is not surprising that Royal Selangor is a regular and worthy host course to the Malaysian Open Championship; it is clearly one of the finest courses in South-East Asia.

BALI HANDARA

The Bali Handara course rests 4,000 feet up a mountainside in an old volcanic crater on the island of Bali, at the eastern end of Java, the central island of Indonesia. Nine of its holes were laid out on an old dairy farm and nine were hacked out of a tropical rain forest, largely by hand. The course is a one hour drive from Bali's international airport at Denpasar – all of which takes a good deal of explaining. Golf in Indonesia until 1939 consisted of about a dozen courses, almost all of them owned by tea or rubber plantations, most of which were under British management or ownership. Probably the best-known was the Djakarta Golf Club in the capital city. But after the Second World War, the club lost half of its land to a state building project and was left with 18 holes packed into a space only sufficient for nine. However, when Indonesia's President Sukarno was ousted by General Suharto in 1967, the country had an enthusiastic golfer in power.

Not surprisingly, the game started to grow. General Ibru Suharto wanted a prestige golf course and Bali, with a future in tourism, was to be the place. Bali's highest mountain rises to 10,000 feet and Handara, at 4,000 feet, was high enough to escape the coastal heat and thus provide a reasonable environment for growing golf course grasses. The Peter Thomson-Mike Wolveridge partnership was asked to design a course and in September 1973 Guy Wolstenholme, their man, arrived. It was raining!

Wolstenholme was an Englishman who had a distinguished amateur career – English international, Walker Cup team, English Amateur Champion and so on – who turned professional and played quite successfully in the UK and Europe before moving to Australia. He played tournament golf there, but showed a keen interest in design. Thomson-Wolveridge introduced Guy Wolstenholme to the Bali Handara project, and he made a triumphant success of it.

Without machinery, but with a work force of more than 1,000 locals, Wolstenholme fashioned his greens with hand

labour, and had the fairways cleared, cleaned and sown, again all by hand. Bali has two rainy seasons – February-March and September-October – when the rain falls predictably at Handara every afternoon. A very sophisticated drainage system was installed. And Ron Fream, Thomson's American partner, brought from the U.S. a strain of Kentucky Bluegrass seed which was mixed with the local Bermuda to give a quite beautiful fairway texture.

Left: Guy Wolstenholme (seen here in the 1961 English Close Championship) oversaw the construction of the course at Bali Handara, which he had helped to design.

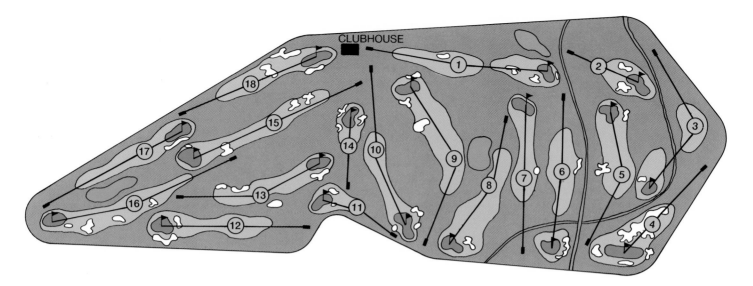

The course is a delight to the eye, as well as a testing pleasure to play – the bunkers cut out in lovely jig-saw patterns set against lush greens; small animals, deer and monkeys cross the fairways; and the whole course is dominated by a heavily wooded mountain. There is also water on the course: a large lake between the 16th and 17th fairways, another between 8 and 9, and a long, meandering stream that crosses the 3rd, 5th, 6th and the 7th. Another attractive feature of the design is the shape of the fairways – waisted here, swelling out there and vanishing in between. At the 1st hole, a par-5 of 500 yards, there is the inevitable bunker on the left to pinch the drive, but somewhere in the middle of the second shot, where a path crosses the fairway, it vanishes and is replaced by a swathe of rough. Further on there is a lovely shamrock bunker short of the green, while the latter is an hour-glass shape set across the incoming shot and severely bunkered. In short, a brilliant hole on a lovely, imaginative golf course.

BALI HANDARA					
Card of the course					
1	500 yards	par 5	10	412 yards	par 4
2	180 yards	par 3	11	180 yards	par 3
3	450 yards	par 4	12	410 yards	par 4
4	180 yards	par 3	13	410 yards	par 4
5	400 yards	par 4	14	180 yards	par 3
6	410 yards	par 4	15	540 yards	par 5
7	400 yards	par 4	16	432 yards	par 4
8	411 yards	par 4	17	442 yards	par 4
9	527 yards	par 5	18	560 yards	par 5
3,458 yards		par 36	3,566 yards		par 36
Total 7,024 yards par 72					

The view from behind the 15th green. Although downhill, the hole is a three-shotter for all except those prepared to flirt with the cunningly placed fairway bunker from the tee.

ROYAL MELBOURNE

Alister Mackenzie was born of Scottish parents in Leeds, Yorkshire in 1870. He graduated from Cambridge University with a degree in medicine and served as a surgeon in the South African War. In 1907 Harry Colt, one of the outstanding golf architects of the day, visited Mackenzie's home course, Alwoodley, in Leeds, to carry out some revisions, and stayed overnight with Mackenzie, who showed him various models of tees and greens. Impressed, Colt invited him to assist in the Alwoodley work. From that point, Mackenzie grew more and more interested in golf course design and less and less in medicine. He did return to being an army surgeon in 1914, but after the First World War, became a full-time

designer and made his first trip to the United States.

Mackenzie's philosophy was that since good health was of paramount importance to everyone, a pastime such as golf, which provided healthy exercise and clean air, could make an exceptional contribution to human health and happiness. While his motives for embracing the game were admirable, he could scarcely

have imagined that by the end of his life, in 1934, he would have been responsible for three masterpieces: Royal Melbourne West, Cypress Point and Augusta National!

The Sand Belt

When Mackenzie arrived in Melbourne in 1926, he found he was working for the club with the longest unbroken history in

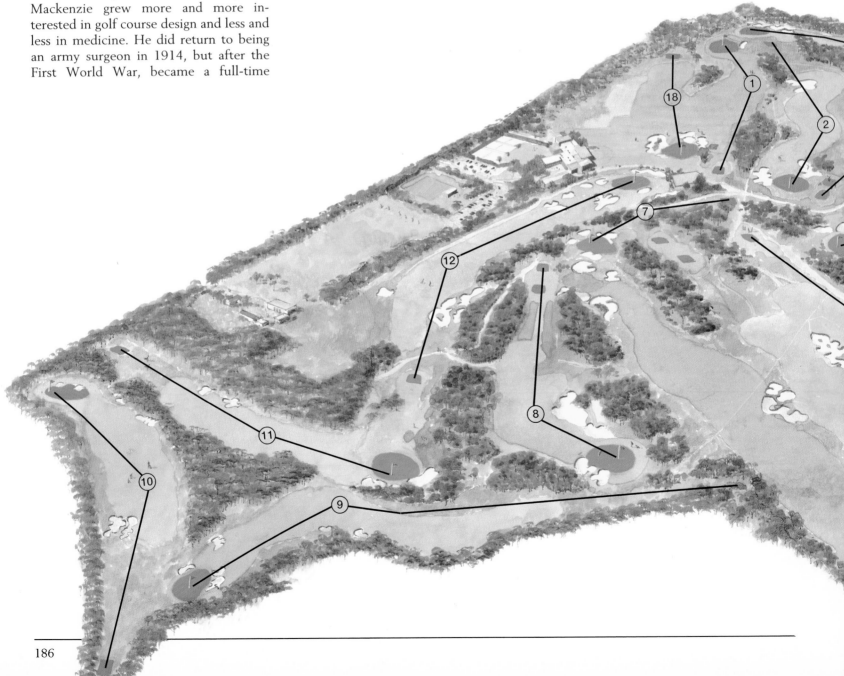

the country. The club dates from 1891 and, after a couple of moves, settled in its present location on Melbourne's 'sand belt' – which is just that, an acreage of sand dunes, heather and bracken, native oak trees and silver-sand subsoil. He could hardly wait to get to work and was lucky to have the help of Alex Russell as an assistant. A local man and a member of the club, Russell as an amateur golfer had won the Australian Open Championship in 1924 – over the existing course.

All the familiar Mackenzie – and for that matter Russell – features are in the

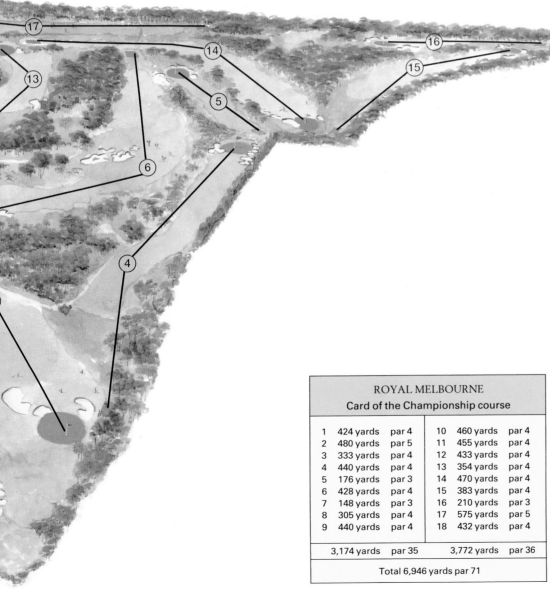

Ben Crenshaw plays from a greenside bunker at the short 7th during the 1988 World Cup. Crenshaw and Mark McCumber won the Cup for the United States, Crenshaw taking the individual prize.

course: great rashes of bunkers in the fairways, around the greens and in the angles of the turns; lightning-fast greens, several of them split-level; only one hole, the 3rd, apart from the par-3s, playing straight; and gently rising and falling ground introducing blind shots and tilted fairways.

But more than any other single factor, the Royal Melbourne greens make the course what it is: an immensely difficult par of 71 over 6,946 yards. The greens are sand-based, cut right down until they are positively sparse, severely contoured and lightning-fast. Mackenzie was already formulating what was to become almost a custodial policy with regard to the speed and contouring of greens, which reached a climax at Augusta National. In this, Mackenzie was much abetted by a greenkeeper, Claude Crockford, whose attitude to greens and putting, and golfers, was exactly that of Mackenzie and Russell.

Mackenzie's Melbourne
The 1st hole plays into a fairly wide patch of fairway, turns slightly to the left and goes up to a reasonably flat green with one bunker front right. The 2nd hole is a

	ROYAL MELBOURNE				
	Card of the Championship course				
1	424 yards	par 4	10	460 yards	par 4
2	480 yards	par 5	11	455 yards	par 4
3	333 yards	par 4	12	433 yards	par 4
4	440 yards	par 4	13	354 yards	par 4
5	176 yards	par 3	14	470 yards	par 4
6	428 yards	par 4	15	383 yards	par 4
7	148 yards	par 3	16	210 yards	par 3
8	305 yards	par 4	17	575 yards	par 5
9	440 yards	par 4	18	432 yards	par 4
	3,174 yards	par 35		3,772 yards	par 36
	Total 6,946 yards par 71				

The fearsome 6th hole at Royal Melbourne West. The right-angled dog-leg has clusters of bunkers and scrub in the angle, and the raised, subtly-controlled green is another trade mark of the architect, Alister Mackenzie.

quality par-5. It turns to the right and a huge, jigsaw-patterned fairway bunker sits on the driving line. It must be carried if the green is to be reached in regulation and up ahead there are similar sized bunkers on either side of the green.

The 3rd is a Russell hole of 333 yards. A drive downhill over a crest, then on to a green split into two levels – high on the right, falling down to a very deep bunker just off the left side. For one so short, this can be a complicated hole with a very difficult shot to the flagstick. The 5th hole has one of the most common Mackenzie characteristics at a short hole: a sharp downslope at the front of the green, so that the short ball will roll back off the putting surface and into whatever discomforts have been left there for it. This one, 176 yards, plays over a hollow, is firmly bunkered on either side and slopes rather sharply from the back down.

The 6th is a superb golf hole of 428 yards, turning to the right. In the angle is a mass of bunkering and natural scrubland tempting the player to carry the corner. The second part of the hole goes up a hill with a slightly adverse camber, to a green tucked under trees and protected by heavy side bunkering.

The 8th hole is a perfect illustration of what can be done with a short par-4. This is 305 yards. From a high tee, it crosses a valley to a plateau fairway, and turns to the left. Lining the entire inside of the turn, on a direct line to the green, is an enormous lateral bunker. You are invited to carry it, reach the green and putt for, at least, a birdie! On the direct line there are, of course, no other bunkers. On the indirect line, however, played wide of that lateral bunker, there are bunkers at the right front of the green for any incoming pitch.

Trevino Scores a Nine

The 9th, 10th, 11th and 12th holes, all in the mid-400 yard range, form the heart of the round. The 9th turns left and has a wicked green on two levels – higher at the back. The 10th demands a drive over huge fairway bunkers – the driving zone pinched between a large bunker on the right and a sandy valley on the left. The 11th goes out to a rise at around 250 yards, then turns left across a dip of 200 yards to a green completely closed off on the right. The main feature of the 13th is that the green falls off at the back – a gambit Mackenzie has used elsewhere. The 14th is one of Melbourne's most provocative holes – at 470 yards only just a par-4. The drive is played blind, over a rise which has a long ridge of bunkers on the skyline. The hole then turns quickly to the right, the fairway running downhill and tilted right to left. The second shot must carry rough in the corner, then a file of bunkers guarding the right front of the green and another big one, on the same line, on the left side.

Royal Melbourne's finish is very tough. The 16th is 210 yards, slightly uphill to a palette-shaped green. It is heavily but not closely bunkered across the front left and is played over scrubby ground. The green is quite long and the pin position might well call for two clubs more in selection. At 575 yards the 17th is a long slog – the longest on the course – with bunkers crossing the fairway at approximately 400 yards. And the 18th is a fine finishing hole of 432 yards; a dogleg left to a green that is ringed with bunkers, save at the back on the left, where it falls away. This hole has undulations typical of Royal Melbourne – a course that demands the utmost concentration, positive thinking and definitive shot-making.

The closing par-3 on Royal Melbourne's East Course, at 168 yards, is as pretty as any short hole could be. It is a simple, but not easy hole. A rather small green is surrounded by large bunkers, and is primly contoured.

ROYAL ADELAIDE

Royal Adelaide is big. It runs to just under 7,000 yards, and has a look of Muirfield about it – Muirfield with trees, that is. A sandy subsoil, marram grass in the rough, even some modest sand dunes, give it the look and feel of a links. It is a superb course, with just an occasional echo of Pine Valley as well. Such a pedigree could hardly be better, especially since the good Dr Alister Mackenzie also ran his stethoscope over it.

It has been suggested that golf came to Adelaide as early as 1869, in the person of Sir James Fergusson, new Governor of South Australia, a Scot from Edinburgh. After five years he left, and golf in Adelaide seemed to lapse, but the club was revived in 1896 and 18 holes were constructed at Glenelg, their creation helped along by one Francis Maxwell,

another expatriate Scot, who was the brother of the amateur champion, Robert Maxwell of the Honourable Company of Edinburgh Golfers.

In 1904 the club moved to its present site at Seaton – 204 acres around a railway station and a single track line which linked it to the city, half an hour away. The club also, and sensibly, appointed as its first professional a Carnoustie man named Jack Scott, who stayed with them for 20 years as an excellent teacher and clubmaker. When Alister Mackenzie looked over the course

A diagonal of no fewer than six bunkers marches across the front of Royal Adelaide's 7th green. Others at back right and back left crowd the target green, only 29 yards long on the 156-yard hole.

in 1926 he rearranged the routeing so that none of the holes played over the railway line, and of course put in some typical, and large, Mackenzie bunkering. The course has been modified here and there since, notably after visits by the Thomson-Wolveridge partnership, and there are some very fine holes.

The 1st, at 382 yards, is perhaps a shade short for an opener, but it is a modest classic of its kind. The drive is into a narrow fairway which turns to the left. On the inside of the turn are sand dunes thick with marram grass. On the outside are two bunkers on the edge of the rough and the green is slightly angled, with a very big and deep bunker covering the left side, the 'inside' line from the fairway – simple, but effective.

Adelaide has three par-3s, but five

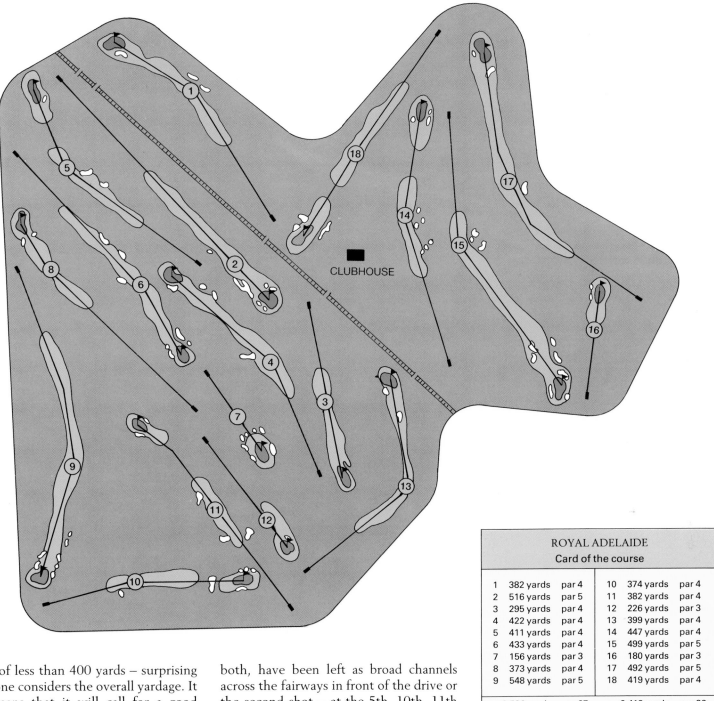

CLUBHOUSE

	ROYAL ADELAIDE				
	Card of the course				
1	382 yards	par 4	10	374 yards	par 4
2	516 yards	par 5	11	382 yards	par 4
3	295 yards	par 4	12	226 yards	par 3
4	422 yards	par 4	13	399 yards	par 4
5	411 yards	par 4	14	447 yards	par 4
6	433 yards	par 4	15	499 yards	par 5
7	156 yards	par 3	16	180 yards	par 3
8	373 yards	par 4	17	492 yards	par 5
9	548 yards	par 5	18	419 yards	par 4
	3,536 yards	par 37		3,418 yards	par 36
	Total 6,954 yards par 73				

par-4s of less than 400 yards – surprising when one considers the overall yardage. It also means that it will call for a good range of club selections – medium to long irons – on the par-4 holes. Of the shorter holes, the 3rd at 295 yards is a real challenge. The drive is blind, covering a path that leads from the tee, travelling between trees and cresting a rise. The green is undefended save for some rippling fairway short of the putting surface. For the long hitters, the drive is at the mercy of the bounce of the ball.

At several holes, swatches of Adelaide's silver sand, or rough, or a combination of both, have been left as broad channels across the fairways in front of the drive or the second shot – at the 5th, 10th, 11th and 14th. At 382 yards, the 11th is a particularly good example. The drive must skirt two large mounded bunkers on the left of the fairway while the second shot must carry a broad band of sand and rough to a green with flanking bunkers near the highest point on the course.

The 15th and 17th are outstanding par-5 holes, in the sense that trees, dunes or bunkers will push the tee shots to the outside of dogleg turns; then the classic fairway bunker short of the green will close out the long second shots seeking to get home in two, forcing them short or wide and thus necessitating a little pitch for the third shot. And finally the 18th, at 419 yards, almost straight, with no fairway bunker but ridges and humps and hollows in front of the green, makes a perfect finish to this lovely 'inland links'.

ROYAL SYDNEY

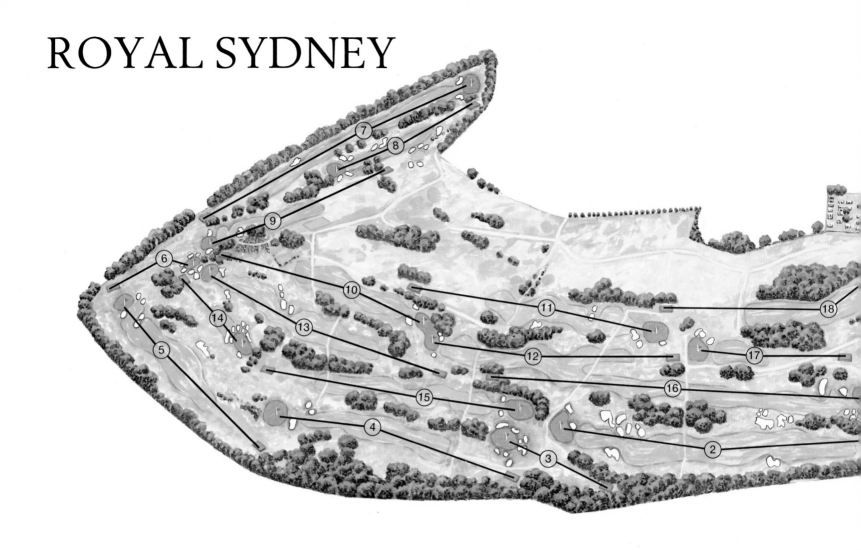

When a golf club has 5,000 members, you may be sure that it is something out of the ordinary. Royal Sydney started in 1893 as a men-only club. Now it is a golf, tennis and social club which is an intrinsic part of the fabric of the biggest Australian city, and is only a ten minute drive from the city centre. The plan of the course is not unlike that of the Old Course at St Andrews: turn right at the first green, then straight out, a loop at the end, then come straight back. However, the Old Course is only two fairways wide, where Royal Sydney is four. The original nine holes played round the outside of the present layout, but in 1896, after James Scott joined the club as its professional, the course was extended to 18 holes. A year later it acquired the Royal prefix.

Just as a links course will set its tees by the beach, so Sydney set its tees on that

ROYAL SYDNEY					
Card of the course					
1	280 yards	par 4	10	420 yards	par 4
2	547 yards	par 5	11	440 yards	par 4
3	173 yards	par 3	12	387 yards	par 4
4	426 yards	par 4	13	509 yards	par 5
5	435 yards	par 4	14	194 yards	par 3
6	154 yards	par 3	15	443 yards	par 4
7	554 yards	par 5	16	563 yards	par 5
8	302 yards	par 4	17	211 yards	par 3
9	359 yards	par 4	18	410 yards	par 4
3,230 yards		par 36	3,577 yards		par 36
Total 6,807 yards par 72					

original nine holes on the very edge of the property, the holes playing inwards and occasionally turning back so that the green was set on the perimeter and the approach shot would be slightly uphill. The second nine of the course were built

inside these holes and on sandy soil. With a sea breeze blowing most of the time, it had much of the flavour of a links.

The original design is credited to one S.J. Robbie, but in the 1920s, when Dr Alister Mackenzie spent some time in Australia, he was asked to revise the bunkering. This he did with a vengeance, digging deep, wide pits in Sydney's white sand. In combination with fierce rough, narrow fairways, small greens and strategically placed trees, and a yardage of 6,566 yards for normal play with a par of 72, Royal Sydney is no ordinary course!

The straightest hole on the course is the very first. At 280 yards it is within reach of the stronger player, although there is a tiger tee set further back beside the clubhouse. No fewer than six bunkers line the right side of the fairway, with three more around the green. The course then turns right and 2, 3, 4 and 5 run along the

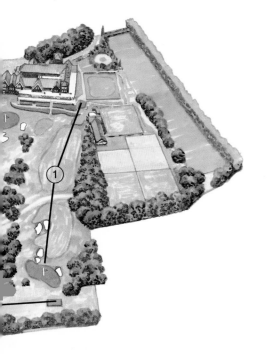

Right: *Mark Calcavecchia of the U.S. hoists the hulking Australian Open trophy in 1988, having won over the Royal Sydney course with the remarkable score of 19 under par – 269.*

rim of the property – the players driving down into valleys, then hitting up to the greens. There are bunkers galore on this stretch of very fine holes. The 6th hole, a one-shotter of 154 yards, turns towards the loop, which includes the long 7th of 554 yards, with little in the way of hazard but very narrow.

The inward half is longer by 500 yards and two strokes on the card, with two 'back-to-back' long holes at 15 (443 yards), and 16 (563 yards). The closing hole of 410 yards and a sharp dogleg to the left, makes for exciting championship finishes. The second shot is played up to a large, raised green, with bunkers short of it on both sides. Just as intriguing in its fashion is the 17th, at 211 yards. The defences are against the faded shot, three big traps being sited to the right of a fairly small green.

Royal Sydney is a fine old course that has kept abreast of the times. But, like any other course in the world, it cannot repel the onslaught of the modern professionals when conditions are right. Thus in the Australian Open of 1988, Mark Calcavecchia (Open Champion in 1989) won with 269 – 19 under par!

Below: *Greg Norman plays a short iron to the 18th in the 1988 Australian Open. He has drawn his tee shot round and beyond the dog-leg, which lies some 170 yards from the green.*

PARAPARAUMU

Peter Thomson, who ought to know, described Paraparaumu as 'the only true championship links in New Zealand or Australia'; and Bob Charles, who also ought to know, claimed that its 5th hole was 'the equal to any short hole in the world'. Yet Paraparaumu is something of a freak. Why it should be the only links course in New Zealand or Australia is a mystery, since both countries have miles and miles of beachland and dunes.

The course is situated in North Wellington, about an hour's drive from the city centre, on the west coast beneath the big Tararua range in which Mount Hector goes up to 5,000 feet, and in the shelter of Kapiti Island, which lies close offshore.

A course of sorts existed in the area for many years, but seems not to have been very successful, until one day in 1946 Douglas Whyte and Alex Russell looked down on the property from a nearby sandhill and were inspired to do something about restoring it. Whyte was a member of the Royal and Ancient of St Andrews and had played to scratch, so he had some insight into the make-up of a good golf course. Alex Russell had nothing to prove about the craft of building golf courses. He had worked very closely with the famous Dr Alister Mackenzie on the magnificent West Course of Royal Melbourne in 1926, and at Yarra Yarra in 1929. And he had designed the East Course of Royal Melbourne in 1932.

A Classic Links

By 1949 Russell's endeavours at Paraparaumu Beach were finished and the course was in play. It was quickly seen as a thing of beauty, both artful and artistic and a classic links as typical as anything in Scotland, but one to which modern design thinking had been applied. The fairways ran in general along shallow valleys, with dunes rather than huge sandhills – Birkdale-style – screening the sides. In general, there were no ferocious carrys from the tees and there was a striking absence of bunkers, both in the fairways and at greenside. Five of the par-4 holes were less than 400 yards. The par-3s were of sensible length and the whole thing ran to no more than 6,500 yards. Wherein then did Paraparaumu's greatness lie?

First and foremost it lay in the wind. During one period of ten days embracing a New Zealand Open and a match play

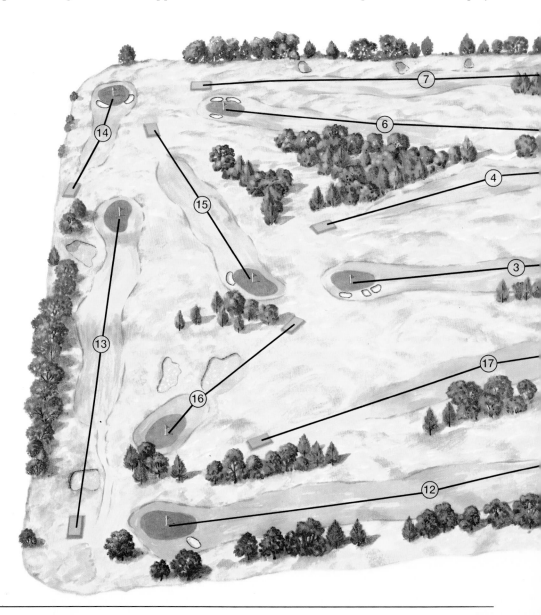

Paraparaumu's 400-yard par-4 13th hole is typical of the course. Its fairway undulates severely and it requires two precisely placed shots to obtain par.

event, the wind blew variously around 270 degrees, from north to west to south to east. And while Para does have some trees, it is as exposed as, say, Carnoustie. Secondly, it lay in the fact that Russell had used the heaving, undulating terrain to artful effect. His dogleg angles, save perhaps on the drive and pitch holes like 8 and 9, were never abrupt. Russell placed his tees so that, where he needed it, the drive would be checked by an up-slope. In other places, at the 449-yard 13th, for example, he demands that a long drive reach a plateau in the fairway from which an equally long second is needed to get to an undefended green. And Russell's greens on the whole are small. Indeed, the more closely one looks at the structure of this course, the more fascinating these holes become.

The Outward Nine

The drive at the first hole passes through a gap in low dunes to a wide expanse of fairway, moving slightly downhill and giving a clear view of the green. There is no bunker on this hole. The test here is in the putting, there being plenty of movement in the green. The 2nd hole has similarities to the 5th, at least in construction. In each case the green has been formed by chopping off and levelling the top of a dune. At 200 yards, to a long but rather narrow green which has two pot bunkers at the front left, this can be a demanding tee shot, depending on the conditions. The famous 5th hole, which Bob Charles so admires (the man has won the New Zealand Open and other events here), has a small, sitting-up green, no bunker, but slopes falling away all round,

particularly at the front. There is something of the flavour of the 5th at Gleneagles King's, or the 16th at Carnoustie, or the 17th at Troon here, although the latter two are much more critical holes.

The 6th hole, at only 309 yards long,

PARAPARAUMU					
Card of the course					
1	419 yards	par 4	10	312 yards	par 4
2	200 yards	par 3	11	427 yards	par 4
3	420 yards	par 4	12	517 yards	par 5
4	446 yards	par 4	13	449 yards	par 4
5	167 yards	par 3	14	151 yards	par 3
6	309 yards	par 4	15	379 yards	par 4
7	496 yards	par 5	16	140 yards	par 3
8	369 yards	par 4	17	440 yards	par 4
9	379 yards	par 4	18	470 yards	par 5
3,205 yards	par 35		3,285 yards	par 36	
Total 6,490 yards par 71					

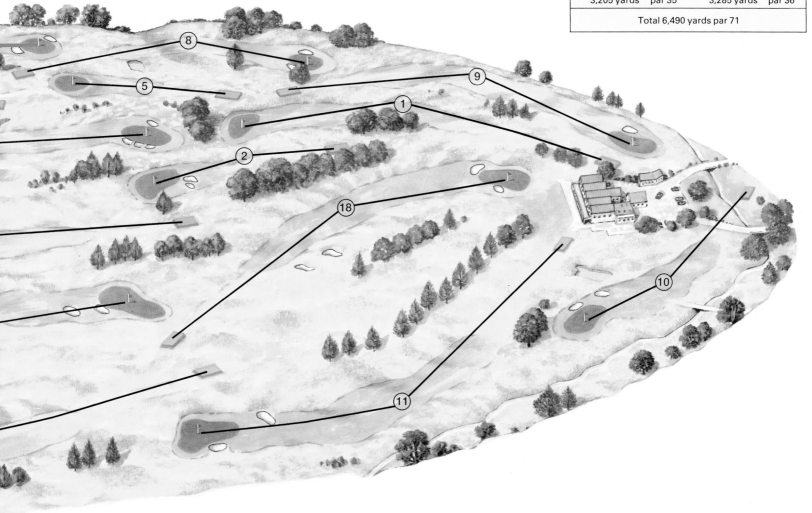

depends entirely on the bounce which the fairway gives to the tee shot. It has many humps and hollows, and again there is no fairway bunker. Indeed, it is quite astonishing that, discounting the bunker placed 25 yards or so short of the green, there are no fairway bunkers anywhere on this course! There are two bunkers in the angle of the 18th hole, some 150 to 200 yards out from the tee – but they are in the rough.

The 7th is probably the least glamorous hole on the course. The drive needs a carry over some dunes but the hole, a par-5 of 496 yards, requires little more than hard hitting. But 8 and 9 are exciting holes, short par-4s at 369 and 379 yards respectively; both turning fairly sharply to the right. On the 8th, the drive should get out a good 200 yards to climb up to a raised fairway to see a raised, small green with flanking bunkers and heavy rough around it. To 'see round the corner' at the 9th, the tee shot will have to go further, better than 200 yards, and fairly solid mounding closes the angle on the right of the fairway. The 10th is a straightaway

Above: The famous 5th hole, so admired by Bob Charles, rivals the Postage Stamp at Troon or the 11th at St Andrews. It has a small raised green, no bunkers, but slopes all the way round.

Right: Home grown talent and the greatest left-hander in the game, Bob Charles has won the New Zealand Open and many other tournaments at Paraparaumu, and holds the course record, a phenomenal 62.

drive and flick, but there is a stream and an out-of-bounds line hard along the left side. The out-of-bounds persists along the 11th and 12th as they run out along the boundary of the course.

Magical Finish
Paraparaumu's finish is superb. The 13th is a straight, strong par-4 of 449 yards. A really long – 250-yard – drive from the very back tee will catch a downslope. Short of that, the drive will stop on a level plateau giving a good look at the green, still a long shot away. The green is undefended, but small, with a dip immediately in front of it. And in the rough

on the left, in hooking territory just short of the green, is an unseen pond!

The 14th and 16th make a marvellous pair of one-shot holes of 151 and 140 yards respectively. They are short pops when there is no wind – the 14th over rough ground to a rectangular green, its entire front defended by sand; the 16th over a pond to a tilted rectangular green, its entire back defended by sand. At 15, 379 yards long, the driving line is tightened between dunes at 180 yards, forcing the ball to the outside of the turn. The approach is to a slender green, only 24 yards long, with a bunker front right, and a downslope off to the left – a very fine hole indeed.

The final holes, 17 at 440 yards and 18 at 470 yards, both turning right, demand precise driving into uneven fairways and long seconds which will be hard pressed to hit their targets. At 17, the green is 32 yards long, but is so set across the line that it becomes a target only 21 feet deep! All in all, Paraparaumu Beach is a marvellous golf course and well worth emigration to Wellington.

DURBAN COUNTRY CLUB

The existence of the Durban Country Club arises in part from the misfortunes of its predecessor, Royal Durban. Golf in South Africa started in 1882 when a Scottish regiment laid out six modest holes near Cape Town, and within a few years the Cape Golf Club, the first in South Africa, had been formed. Others quickly followed: in 1885 the Pietermaritzburg G.C.; in 1888, Bloem-

fontein; in 1889, Aliwal North; and in 1892 what was then the Durban G.C. was formed. A nine-hole course was laid on the flat, inside the racecourse, and golf in Natal was under way. However, it was soon evident that the city of Durban was in need of more golf than one club could provide; a fact that was underlined when, during the national championships of 1919, the Royal Durban club became

totally water-logged in a rainstorm; drainage at the low-lying course had always been a concern.

Thus, Laurie B. Waters, the 'father of South African golf', was asked to design a course on a piece of duneland close to the shore. A native of St Andrews, where he had been apprenticed to Old Tom Morris, Laurie had emigrated to South Africa in 1901. He introduced grass greens, won the South African Open more than once and designed Royal Johannesburg West in 1910. Helped by George Waterman, he had the Durban Country Club course in play in 1922. Two years later, it staged the first of many South African Open Championships.

The Durban course had two distinct sectors: the area near the clubhouse, which featured considerable movement in some of the fairways, making the

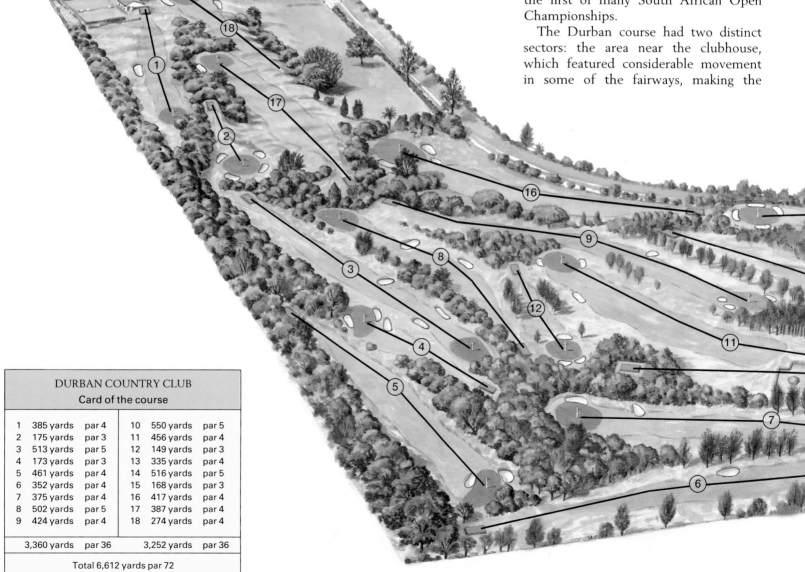

DURBAN COUNTRY CLUB					
Card of the course					
1	385 yards	par 4	10	550 yards	par 5
2	175 yards	par 3	11	456 yards	par 4
3	513 yards	par 5	12	149 yards	par 3
4	173 yards	par 3	13	335 yards	par 4
5	461 yards	par 4	14	516 yards	par 5
6	352 yards	par 4	15	168 yards	par 3
7	375 yards	par 4	16	417 yards	par 4
8	502 yards	par 5	17	387 yards	par 4
9	424 yards	par 4	18	274 yards	par 4
	3,360 yards	par 36		3,252 yards	par 36
	Total 6,612 yards par 72				

humps and hollows of the Old Course at St Andrews look positively tame; and the other area, distant from the clubhouse, and known as the flatlands.

Stafford Vere Hotchkin

Waters' course has been reviewed a couple of times, first by the splendid Stafford Vere Hotchkin in 1928. Hotchkin was born (and died) at Woodhall Spa, near Lincoln in England, and served in the 17th Lancers in the First World War, reaching the rank of Colonel before he retired from service. In 1922–3 he was a Conservative Member of Parliament and for many years served on the Lincolnshire County Council. He purchased and remodeled his famous home course at Woodhall Spa in 1920 – one of the finest inland courses in England.

Hotchkin formed a company which embraced all aspects of the golf course business, including design, construction, maintenance, equipment, seed and other materials. In the mid-Twenties he made an extended tour of South Africa, designing Maccauvlei in 1926, Humewood in Port Elizabeth in 1929, and Port Eliz-

abeth G.C. He also remodeled East London, Mowbray and Royal Port Alfred. Many South Africans thought him the best architect who had worked in the country. Bob Grimsdell, who designed the Royal Johannesburg's East Course, Swartkop in Pretoria, and other courses, revised the Durban course in 1959; but his and Hotchkin's changes left Laurie Waters' layout essentially unchanged.

The course has seen much derring-do over the years. Gary Player won the first of his many South African Open titles at Durban in 1956, and Bobby Locke and

Bob Charles have been among its South African Open Champions. The unusually short 18th hole, at 274 yards, has made for many a spectacular finish. The hole may be short, but it is not simple. The right side of the fairway falls off down a steep bank into bushes and towards the practice area. The drive must be held up on the left side of the fairway, and when conditions are right the green can be driven. The most dramatic finish to any South African Open came at this hole in 1928. Jock Brews drove the green and holed a 15 foot putt for an eagle two. He

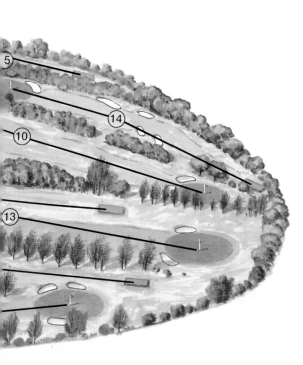

Golf in an urban setting. Durban Country Club amid the heaving escarpment of its 17th and 18th fairways within sight of downtown Durban, and squeezed between highways.

won the championship by one stroke –
from his brother, the more famous Sid.

Lunar Landscape

The course plunges straight into its lunar
landscape – this moon is green – at the
1st hole. There is an out-of-bounds along
the right side and a big deep bunker also
on the right which should be passed,
narrowly. If the drive is too far left, the
second shot, indeed any sight of the
green, may be blocked by a large dune.
The short 2nd hole is from a tee on a
ridge in a copse, across a hollow to a green
on a ridge in a copse! The 3rd hole is
from the highest point on the course, a
commanding tee that looks across a valley, then moves along a series of undulations in the fairway for the rest of its 513
yards. There is a mounded fairway bunker
on the left at driving range and others on
either side just short of the green. These
first three holes have run straight out
through the dunes, but the short 4th
turns back and plays out into the flatlands. From a high tee looking down to a
bunkered green it looks shorter than its
173 yards.

Above: *Gary Player, seen here on home territory
in a match against Arnold Palmer, won his first
South African Open championship at Durban in
1956.*

Right: *Durban's first five holes run more or less
parallel to the ocean. The 5th, seen here from
behind the green, requires two straight shots with
a driver and medium iron.*

The Wind Factor

The 5th, 6th and 7th, forming a triangle
around a wood at the end of the course,
are fair and honest holes – the first a drive
and mid-iron; the next two a drive and a
pitch, that is, in still conditions. It must be
said that Durban Country Club, close by
the sea, seldom has still conditions! Most
of the time there is some kind of wind.
The 8th hole makes a sortie back into the
'high country', a par-5 that turns left,
with a fairway bunker on the outside of
the angle, and further on featuring a very
big centre-fairway bunker to be carried
with the second shot. At 502 yards, with a
fairway rising to an oval green, this is a
big-hitting hole. The 9th hole turns back
and makes a sortie out of the 'high
country' back to the flatlands, turning
right and easing downhill to the green,
424 yards from the tee.

The 10th at 550 yards and the 11th at
456 yards are similarly orthodox; solid
hitting holes without fairway hazards and
with reasonably receptive greens. But the
12th is a rather difficult one-shotter of
149 yards. The green is on a flat-topped

dune with fall-off in all directions, a big
bunker to be carried at the front, smaller
ones back left and right and a very large
tree ominously close behind. The 13th
and 14th – flatland holes – take us round
to the seaward side of the course and after
a short pop of 168 yards at the 15th, we
are in the duneland again, and into
Durban's unusual finish.

The classic finish on a championship
course is to have a long par-4, a long
par-3, and a long par-5 in one combination or another over the final three holes.
At Durban, they are all under 400 yards.
The 17th, nevertheless, is something of a
terror. A valley falls off to the right just as
it does on 18. The fairway on the left
drops into hollows and undulations which
might well hide the green, so the drive
must be placed precisely – so high but no
higher – on the right side of the fairway.
All told it is a fascinating finish to a great
course of infinite variety.

ROYAL JOHANNESBURG

Golf came late to Johannesburg. From its simple start in the Cape in 1882, golf spread in the 1880s to Bloemfontein, Pietermaritzburg and other places, but Johannesburg, in time to become South Africa's greatest city and financial and industrial heartland, had other things, or more accurately, one other thing, on its mind – gold!

In 1890, when the first course was laid, Johannesburg was no more than a mining camp; but a mining camp with a vengeance and one that was to experience over the next few decades a boom scarcely paralleled in history.

To say that the first course was 'laid out' in 1890 is something of an exaggeration. It was virtually no more than a few cans in the ground, and with the city expanding in all directions, it was not until 1906 that the club, with the help of the industrialist Sir Abe Bailey, found a proper and reasonably secure piece of land. Laurie Waters built the original course and in 1933, when the club decided on a second course, Bob Grimsdell was commissioned to produce what has become the East, the championship course. More recently, revisions were made by the Rob Kirby-Gary Player partnership, and the course is now a modern parkland layout as spacious as anyone could imagine.

One of the first and major efforts expended on the course was the removal of the native Kikuyu grasses in favour of

Royal Johannesburg's 13th hole is one of two par-4s under 400 yards but it is lined with vast bunkers, deep enough to make the loss of a stroke inevitable.

strains less rough, and then maintaining these through Johannesburg's hot summers. Even now, with great advances in agronomy, the grasses are a good deal less fine than the fescues of Western Europe, and putting on the greens of the Transvaal is an art in itself. The grain in the grass is strong, substantially affecting the run of the ball and requiring a great deal of study. Perhaps that is why golfers from the Rand – Gary Player and above all Bobby Locke – have been such successful putters when they went abroad. They are, of necessity, experienced in the business of 'reading' the lines of putts very closely.

Royal Johannesburg's East course extends to 7,465 yards, a fearful prospect for most visitors; but the fact is that in this thin air, at 6,000 feet, the ball will fly much further (10–20 per cent further) than it does at sea level. The course moves

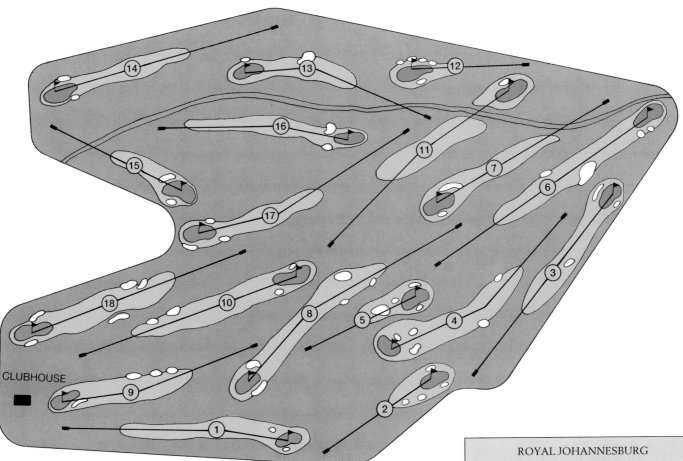

Gary Player is one of a long list of superb South African golfers who have had success worldwide. Player is a master with the sand iron and has to be at Royal Johannesburg with its massive bunkers.

along over rather gentle undulations, with little in the way of abrupt slopes, and it is nicely tree-lined, the trees often used to influence the line of the shot. On the 517-yard straight 1st hole for example, some trees edge in from the right about 100 yards short of the green. They have no serious effect on the line to the green, but the golfer is well aware of their existence.

Only two of the par-4 holes are less than 400 yards long, which is not too surprising at this altitude, and interesting holes they are too. The 13th, at 393 yards, turns to the left and calls for a drive to the left of a big right-side fairway bunker. From there, the green is but a pitch away, but a spinney edges in from the right and there is a pond at the front left. The 17th turns the other way, with the drive carrying up a rise in the fairway. The hole is 387 yards long and the pitch is critical –

the green being protected left front, left rear and right middle, with trees crowding in at the back.

All told, Royal Johannesburg East is a big and not ungenerous course that demands, above all, careful driving. And as a prime Transvaal location for the South African Open Championship, it lists the cream of South African golf among the winners: Bobby Locke, Gary Player, Bobby Cole and Harold Henning.

ROYAL JOHANNESBURG					
Card of the East course					
1	517 yards	par 5	10	513 yards	par 4
2	249 yards	par 3	11	511 yards	par 4
3	457 yards	par 4	12	203 yards	par 3
4	486 yards	par 4	13	393 yards	par 4
5	159 yards	par 3	14	435 yards	par 4
6	580 yards	par 5	15	218 yards	par 3
7	420 yards	par 4	16	490 yards	par 4
8	535 yards	par 5	17	387 yards	par 4
9	400 yards	par 4	18	512 yards	par 5
3,803 yards		par 37	3,662 yards		par 35
Total 7,465 yards par 72					

ROYAL RABAT

The game of golf has been played in Morocco after a fashion for most of this century. But its expansion into eight 18-hole courses and three nine-holers, with several other projects in hand, has been consolidated with the coming of the jet aircraft, the overcrowding of Spain and Portugal, the desire of tourists to travel further and experience different cultures, but, above all, because of the enthusiasm for the game of King Hassan II. The king, anxious to promote his tourist industry, ran the rule over the standards of all golfing facilities in Morocco, which are excellent, and which at the same time have been kept relatively inexpensive for the foreign visitor. What's more, caddies are plentiful and the courses are kept in immaculate condition.

The pride of Moroccan golf is the Red course at Royal Rabat, 10 miles from the city of that name and the nation's capital. It has a grounds staff of 500 to ensure immaculate fairways and greens; 300 days of sunshine; and, in abundance, mimosa, fuchsia, bougainvillea, orange and apricot trees, monkeys and flamingos.

Robert Trent Jones had perhaps the dream briefing for a golf course architect: a 1,000-acre forest of cork trees in which to build two and a half courses. Jones had never been one to allow a budget to come between him and his ambitions and his work here has been characterised – with his client's blessing, of course – by the movement of vast quantities of earth, either in the excavation of lakes or the building of huge mounds, or in raising the

fairways and greens; all of this as a consequence requiring even more sophisticated drainage, watering and maintenance systems.

His Red course opened at Rabat in 1971, and appropriately was king-sized at 7,329 yards in length with a par of 73. Its three short holes were each 200 yards or more. Its par-5 holes, with one exception, were massively over 500 yards each. Only two of the par-4s were less than 400 yards, and then only slightly. It seemed that Robert Trent Jones was making some kind of point.

The Moroccan Open, a PGA European Tour event, was played on the course in 1987. It was won by Howard Clark with a score of 284 against a par of 292. Only nine players were under par, and only

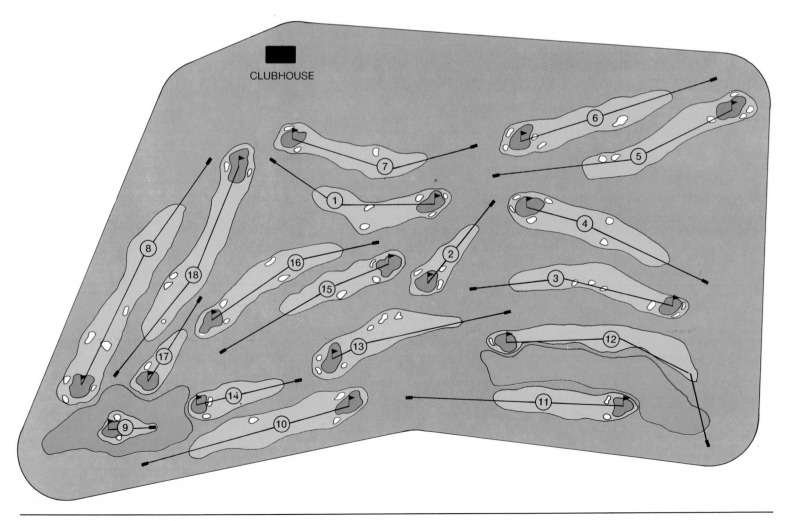

CLUBHOUSE

four players scored better than 290 – Clark, Mark James, Peter Baker and Sam Torrance. Clark scored 73, 73, 66 and 72 and, on this course, that 66 bordered on the miraculous.

Apart from sculpting the fairways and greens, Jones retained the forest to give him avenues of cork trees, laid down flamboyant bunkering, and on the far side of the course created another Jones speciality – lakes. One of them has given him the opportunity to build what many people consider a positively bizarre hole, but one which has been much copied since. His much-photographed 9th hole is an island in a lake, connected to the tee by slender wooden bridges. The hole is listed as 199 yards, but can be played from shorter tees, spotted at different positions around the lake.

Apart from the par-3 holes, almost

ROYAL RABAT					
Card of the Red course					
1	400 yards	par 4	10	481 yards	par 5
2	232 yards	par 3	11	467 yards	par 4
3	443 yards	par 4	12	526 yards	par 5
4	404 yards	par 4	13	384 yards	par 4
5	565 yards	par 5	14	206 yards	par 3
6	440 yards	par 4	15	390 yards	par 4
7	420 yards	par 4	16	424 yards	par 4
8	582 yards	par 5	17	225 yards	par 3
9	188 yards	par 3	18	552 yards	par 5
	3,674 yards	par 36		3,655 yards	par 37
	Total 7,329 yards par 73				

every hole turns or is dog-legged to a greater rather than a lesser degree. The 1st hole puts the course completely into character. It is 400 yards lined with cork trees and turns to the left. At the corner a

The climax to Royal Rabat's longest hole, the pitch to the 582 yards par-5 8th, with the tee of the 9th, the famous 'water hole', in the foreground.

huge bunker on the left forces the tee shot wide to the right. The green has a huge bunker covering the left front and side, there is a little flash trap at the back and a big bunker wide to the right.

One of the really typical Trent Jones holes is the 12th which is 526 yards long; it turns left, a lake all along the left side, and for anyone bold enough to shoot for the green with a second shot, James has allowed a spur of the lake to cover the left half of the green. And there are bunkers at the back, of course! Royal Rabat certainly is a course regal in its power, and very forbidding.

INDEX

ACKNOWLEDGEMENTS

*The Publishers wish to thank the following photographers and organisations for their
kind permission to reproduce their photographs:*

Allsport/D Cannon 1, 8-9, 33, 49, 61, 82, 83, 96, 122-3, 125, 187, 188, 189, 190, 193t, 197, 198, 199, 200, 201/Simon Bruty 120/Vandystat 152; Chris Ayley 194; Bali Handara Country Club 184-5; Paul Barton 70-1; Charles Briscoe-Knight 6, 40, 87, 106-7, 128; Club de Golf Mexico 69; Club Zur Vahr 158, 159; Colorsport 72, 73, 78-9, 85 top, 100, 104, 118, 126, 127; Jerry Cooke 77; Peter Dazeley 2, 46, 48, 54-5, 86, 91, 107, 126 bottom, 145, 146, 148 top left, 148-9; Mikael Kristersson 156, 157; Fujioka Country Club 168-9; Golf World Magazine/Robert Green 153; Matthew Harris 54 top, 62-3, 173, 174, 175; Hobbs Golf Collection 24, 132-3, 150, 151, 154, 155; Hulton Deutsch/UPI/Bettman 81, 94, 112 bottom, 121; Illustrated London News 102; The Jockey Club, Argentina 76; Marcel Joubert 199; Lagunita Country Club/Gustavo

Machado 74, 75; Bruce Longhurst/Pocket Pro 64, 65; Popperfoto 88, 101, 122, 200; Royal Calcutta Golf Club 176; Royal Dornoch Golf Club 115, 117; Royal Hong Kong Golf Club 178; Royal Montreal Golf Club 66; Phil Sheldon 4, 11, 12-3, 16, 17, 18, 21, 22, 24, 24-5, 26, 27, 28-9, 32, 33, 34, 35, 41, 43, 47, 51, 56, 90-1, 95, 98, 99, 104-5, 110-111, 112, 113, 132, 138, 160, 161, 162, 163, 164, 165, 166, 205; Singapore Island Country Club 180; Isaac Smith 136-7; South African Golf Journal/Seef Le Roux 202, 203, Bob Thomas 46 top, 92, 129, 130; Topham Picture Library 85 bottom, 109, 114, 140, 184; Tony Roberts Photography 15, 37, 38, 39; United States Golf Association 10, 14, 20, 52, 58; Stuart Windsor 182, 183; Yours In Sport, Lawrence Levy 57, 135, 137, 193.

ILLUSTRATORS

The Publishers would like to thank the following illustrators: Linda Rogers Associates/Terry McKivragan: 22-3, 26-7, 52-3, 58-9, 80-81, 84-5, 88-9, 96-7, 98-9, 100-101, 102-3, 108-9, 114-5, 124-5, 186-7; /Frank Nichols: 130-31, 140-41, 154-5, 156-7, 158-9, 162-3; /Tony Morris: 20-21, 36-7, 66-7, 74-5; Nicholas Skelton 10-11, 30-31, 44-5, 170-71, 174-5, 192-3, 194-5, 198-9.

All diagrams completed by Oxford Illustrators.